PAGE 42

ON THE ROAD

YOUR COMPLETE DESTINATION GUIDE
In-depth reviews, detailed listings and insider tips

PAGE 755

SURVIVAL GUIDE

VITAL PRACTICAL INFORMATION TO HELP YOU HAVE A SMOOTH TRIP

THIS EDITION WRITTEN AND RESEARCHED BY
Ryan Ver Berkmoes
Brett Atkinson, Celeste Brash, Stuart Butler, John Noble,
Adam Skolnick, Iain Stewart, Paul Stiles

welcome to Indonesia

Rich Diversity

The world's fourth most populace country – 245 million and counting – is a sultry kaleidoscope that runs along the equator for 5000km. It may well be the last great adventure on earth. From the western tip of Sumatra to the eastern edge of Papua, this nation defies homogenisation. It is a land of so many cultures, peoples, animals, customs, plants, features, artworks and foods that it is like 100 (or is it 200?) countries melded into one. And we're talking differences that aren't just about an accent or a preference for goat over pork; we are talking about people who are as radically different from each other as if they came from different continents. No man may be an island but here every island is a unique blend of the men, women and children who live upon it. Over time deep and rich cultures have evolved, from the mysteries of the spiritual Balinese to the utterly non-Western belief system of the Asmat people of Papua.

Beaches & Volcanoes

Venturing through the islands of Indonesia you'll see a land as diverse and unusual as those living upon it. Look at Sulawesi on a map and you'll save yourself the cost of a Rorschach test. Or view Sumatra from the air and be humbled by a legion of nearly 100 volcanoes marching off into the distance, several capable of blowing at

DENNIS WALTON/GETTY IMAGES ©

Indonesia's numbers astound: 17,000 islands (or is it 20,000?), of which 8000 are inhabited (or is it 11,000?), 300 languages spoken (or is it 400?). Yet it's all one country with myriad adventures.

(left) Gunung Agung as seen from Nusa Lembongan (p241), Bali
(below) Surfer with longboard, Java

ANDREW ROESLER/GETTY IMAGES ©

any time. Dramatic sights are the norm. There's the sublime: an orangutan lounging in a tree. The artful: a Balinese dancer executing precise moves that would make a robot seem loose-limbed. The idyllic: a deserted stretch of blinding white sand on Sumbawa set off by azure water and virescent jungle hills. The astonishing: the mobs in a cool and glitzy Jakarta mall on a Sunday. The humbling: a woman bent double with a load of firewood on Sumatra. The solemn: the quiet magnificence of Borobudur.

Great Adventure

This ever-intriguing, ever-intoxicating land holds some of the last great adventures on earth. Sitting in the open door of a train whizzing across Java, idling away time on a ferry bound for Kalimantan, hanging on to the back of a scooter on Flores or simply trekking through wilderness you're sure no one has seen before – you'll enjoy endless exploration of the infinite diversity of Indonesia's 17,000 islands.

› Indonesia

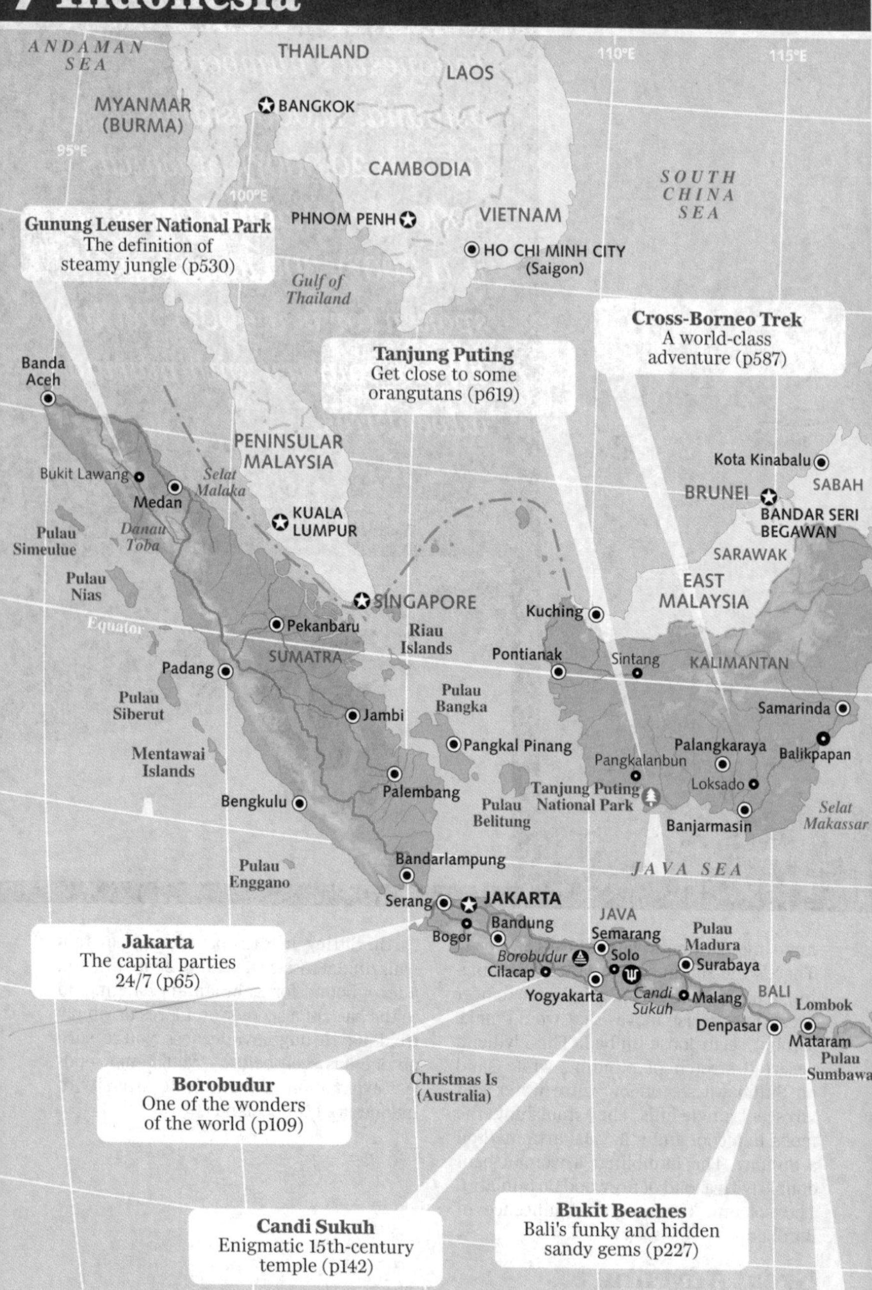

ANDAMAN SEA
THAILAND
LAOS
MYANMAR (BURMA)
BANGKOK
CAMBODIA
SOUTH CHINA SEA
Gunung Leuser National Park
The definition of steamy jungle (p530)
PHNOM PENH
VIETNAM
HO CHI MINH CITY (Saigon)
Gulf of Thailand
Cross-Borneo Trek
A world-class adventure (p587)
Tanjung Puting
Get close to some orangutans (p619)
Banda Aceh
PENINSULAR MALAYSIA
Kota Kinabalu
SABAH
Bukit Lawang
Medan
Selat Malaka
BRUNEI
BANDAR SERI BEGAWAN
KUALA LUMPUR
Pulau Simeulue
Danau Toba
SARAWAK
Pulau Nias
EAST MALAYSIA
SINGAPORE
Kuching
Equator
Pekanbaru
Riau Islands
SUMATRA
Pontianak
Sintang
KALIMANTAN
Padang
Pulau Bangka
Pulau Siberut
Jambi
Samarinda
Pangkal Pinang
Palangkaraya
Balikpapan
Mentawai Islands
Pangkalanbun
Palembang
Tanjung Puting National Park
Loksado
Bengkulu
Pulau Belitung
Banjarmasin
Selat Makassar
Bandarlampung
JAVA SEA
Pulau Enggano
Serang
JAKARTA
JAVA
Bandung
Bogor
Semarang
Pulau Madura
Jakarta
The capital parties 24/7 (p65)
Borobudur
Solo
Surabaya
Cilacap
Yogyakarta
Candi Sukuh
Malang
BALI
Lombok
Denpasar
Mataram
Pulau Sumbawa
Borobudur
One of the wonders of the world (p109)
Christmas Is (Australia)
Bukit Beaches
Bali's funky and hidden sandy gems (p227)
Candi Sukuh
Enigmatic 15th-century temple (p142)
Gili Islands
Three fun-filled idylls (p311)
INDIAN OCEAN

Tana Toraja
Wild spectacles open to visitors (p649)
Pulau Bunaken
An easy yet remote escape (p683)
Pulau Ternate
Tropical dreams that are real (p404)
Raja Ampat Islands
Stunning, remote fish-filled diving (p452)
Banda Islands
Indonesia's most beautiful archipelago? (p429)
Baliem Valley
Home to the unique Dani people (p472)
Komodo National Park
Famous lizards that look like dragons (p348)
ELEVATION
4000m
2000m
1000m
500m
0m
500 km
250 miles
MANILA
PHILIPPINES
PACIFIC OCEAN
PALAU
SULU SEA
SULAWESI SEA
Manado
Gorontalo
Kota Ternate
Pulau Halmahera
SULAWESI
MALUKU SEA
Palu
Bacan Islands
Sula Islands
SERAM SEA
Pulau Seram
Rantepao
Makale
Majene
Kendari
Watampone
Makassar
Kota Ambon
MALUKU
Banda Islands
BANDA SEA
FLORES SEA
Tanimbar Islands
Pulau Wetar
NUSA TENGGARA
Flores
Ende
DILI
EAST TIMOR
SAWU SEA
Pulau Sumba
Kupang
Pulau Timor
TIMOR SEA
Darwin
Sorong
Manokwari
Pulau Biak
Kota Biak
Sarmi
Jayapura
Fak-Fak
PAPUA
Wamena
Timika
Pulau Yos Sudarso
ARAFURA SEA
Gulf of Carpentaria
AUSTRALIA
Equator

20 TOP EXPERIENCES

Komodo National Park

1 Recently declared one of the New Seven Wonders of Nature, Indonesia's best known national park (p348) comprises several islands and some of the country's richest waters within its 1817 sq km. Expect hulking mountainous islands blanketed in savannah, laced with trails and patrolled by the world's largest lizard – the Komodo Dragon. That's the big draw here, and it's easy to spot them, but there's also big nature beneath the water's surface where kaleidoscopic bait balls draw big pelagics like sharks and mantas in numbers you just won't see anywhere else in Indonesia. Komodo Dragon, Rinca (p348)

Gili Islands

2 One of Indonesia's greatest joys is hopping on a fast boat from busy Bali and arriving on one the irresistible Gili Islands (p311). Think sugar-white sand, bathtub-warm, turquoise waters and wonderful beach bungalows just begging you to extend your stay. Not to mention the coral reefs – which haven't looked this good in years and are teeming with sharks, rays and turtles. Add in the dining and nightlife on Gili T, and you understand why long time Gili lovers call these islands Never Never Land. Gili Trawangan (p318)

1

SYLVAIN CORDIER©

2

MATTHEW WILLIAMS-ELLIS/GETTY IMAGES ©

Balinese Dance

3 Enjoying a Balinese dance (p203) performance is a highlight of a visit to Bali. The haunting sounds, elaborate costumes, careful choreography and even light-hearted comic routines add up to great entertainment. Swept up in the spectacle, you'll soon understand why Balinese culture is among the world's most developed. The music that often accompanies traditional dance is based around an ensemble known as a gamelan. The melodic, sometimes upbeat, sometimes haunting percussion is a night-time staple of life in Ubud (p246), Bali's cultural centre. Topeng mask dancer (p736)

Tana Toraja

4 Life revolves around death in this countryside of rice terraces, boat-shaped roofs and doe-eyed buffalo. Tana Torajan funeral ceremonies (p654) last days, and involve countless animal sacrifices for the upper classes. The festivities start with bet-heavy bull fights then lead into days of prayer, feasting and dances. At the end, the deceased is brought to their resting place. This could be carved into a cliff-face and fronted by their own wooden effigy, in a cave where relatives can visit the bones, or in hanging graves suspended from cave edges.

5
PETER PTSCHELINZEW/GETTY IMAGES ©

6
GERARD WALKER/GETTY IMAGES ©

7
FRANCOIS-OLIVIER DOMMERGUES/GETTY IMAGES ©

Cross-Borneo Trek

5 Welcome to the triathlon of adventure travel (p587). Start on the east coast of Borneo, the world's third-largest island, and travel hundreds of kilometres upriver into the heart of a fabled jungle. Trek through it like explorers of old, then head downriver to the west coast via a thrilling white-water canoe trip. Along the way, you'll sample everything Kalimantan has to offer, from wildlife to culture to pure adrenaline. If you can't do it all, the first stage is great by itself. Boardwalk into Sungai Wain Protected Forest, near Balikpapan (p588)

Candi Sukuh

6 There are grander temples and larger monuments scattered across Indonesia but Candi Sukuh (p142) is something else. Perched halfway up a volcano in central Java, this remarkable temple enjoys a spectacular position overlooking the Solo plain. So many of the carvings here display signs of a fertility cult that the temple has been dubbed the 'erotic' temple. Though constructed in the 15th century, stylistically the sculptures and carvings appear to hark back to a much earlier time, evoking memories of Java's animist prehistory.

Tanjung Puting National Park

7 African Queen meets National Geographic in this ever-popular national park (p619), where you can not only get up close and personal with Asia's largest ape, the orangutan, but also cruise the jungle in high style aboard your own private houseboat. The typically three-day journey takes you on a round trip up the Sungai Sekonyer to Camp Leakey, with stops at several orangutan feeding stations and plenty of impromptu wildlife spotting. Despite its creature comforts, the experience still manages to be authentic adventure travel, and is open to anyone. Orangutans

Baliem Valley

8 Trekking in Papua's Baliem Valley (p472) takes you into the world of the Dani, a mountain people whose traditional culture still stands proud despite changes wrought by Indonesian government and Christian missionaries. You'll sleep in their villages of grass-roofed huts, climb narrow jungle trails, traverse panoramic open hillsides, cross raging rivers by wobbly hanging footbridges, and be charmed by the locals' smiles. Tip for those bridges: don't look at the water, but do look where you're putting your feet! Dani man with bow and arrow

Pulau Bunaken

9 You know those gardens that seem to have hundreds of plant species artistically thriving together in small decorative plots? Now imagine that done with coral in every colour from black and white to intense purples. Next cover it all in clear water teeming with iridescent fish, some in thick schools fluttering like sprinkles of sunlight. The water around Pulau Bunaken (p684) is more beautiful than you could imagine and yet it gets better: turtles the size of armchairs, reef sharks and, if you're lucky, dolphins and dugongs that swim casually through the scene. Red giant sea fan

8

DOUG STEAKLEY/GETTY IMAGES ©

9

BORUT FURLAN/GETTY IMAGES ©

M. GEBICKI/GETTY IMAGES ©

ANUP SHAH/GETTY IMAGES ©

Banda Islands

10 Here is a rich and intoxicating cocktail of history, culture and raw natural beauty. The Banda Islands (p429) – a remote archipelago draped in jungle and spice trees, fringed with white sand, surrounded by clear blue seas and pristine reefs – kickstarted colonisation and helped shape the modern world. Fly to the capital – Bandaneira – from Ambon, stroll the wide avenues, admire late colonial relics, then charter a boat to the outer islands, where village life is warm and easy, and stress peels from your soul by the second. Becak (bicycle-rickshaw), Bandaneira (p431)

Gunung Leuser National Park

11 This vast slab of steamy tropical jungle (p530) draped across the mountains and valleys of northern Sumatra is filled with cheeping, squeaking, growling animal life. It's a naturalist's and adventure traveller's fantasy. Sitting pretty beside a chocolate coloured river, the village of Ketambe is a relaxing place to rest up for a few days. More importantly, it makes a great base camp for multi-day hiking expeditions in search of howling gibbons, lethargic orangutans and maybe even a tiger or two. White-handed gibbon

MATTHEW MICAH WRIGHT/GETTY IMAGES ©

DANITA DELIMONT/GETTY IMAGES ©

ARCO IMAGES GMBH / ALAMY ©

Bukit Beaches

12 Peering over the edge of a cliff near Bingin on Bali (p228), you'll spot yet another perfect hidden white-sand cove, cooled by mist from the awesome surf breaks directly in front. Like pearls on a string, these little cove beaches dot the west side of the Bukit Peninsula (p227) on the island's southern extreme. You can have a cheap cold beer in a bamboo hut on the sand or splash out at a luxe yet groovy hotel high on the cliffs. Padang Padang Beach (p229)

Raja Ampat Islands

13 The remote, still-being-discovered Raja Ampat Islands (p452) off Papua's northwest tip are a diver's dream. Raja Ampat is home to the greatest diversity of marine life on the planet, from giant manta rays and epaulette sharks that use their fins to 'walk' on the sea floor, to myriad multicoloured nudibranchs ('sea slugs'), fantastic pristine coral, and every size, shape and hue of fish you can imagine. The snorkelling is great too, and the above-water scenery is just as unique and sublime. Manta ray

Pulau Ternate

14 It's like something out of Polynesia: a series of perfectly formed volcanoes draped in jungle and wild spice trees, floating on azure seas. As you stand on the edge of Ternate's Bastiong Harbour (p404), look behind you to find Gunung Api Gamalama, the dominant presence on Pulau Ternate. It looms like a smouldering reminder of just how small we all are. In the foreground is a glorious channel dotted with isles perfumed with cloves and flower gardens.

Volcanoes

15 Indonesia's countless volcanoes don't get much smaller than Gunung Api (p435), a miniature Mt Fuji, which shelters the natural harbor of the Banda Islands. Topping out at a rather diminutive 666m, it erupted as recently as 1988, and can be climbed in an arduous three hours. Among the many others worth exploring are Bali's Agung (p267), Lombok's Rinjani (p327), and the infamous Krakatau (p74). Explorations can take several hours or days and guides are almost always recommended. One reward: stunning summit sunrises. Gunung Baru, inside Gunung Rinjani

Seminyak

16 South Bali's Seminyak (p218), and its neighbours Kerobokan and Canggu, may be just north of notorious Kuta, but in many respects Seminyak feels like it's almost on another island. It's flash, brash and filled with bony models and expats. Think of it as the cool kids' section of Bali. Its beach is part of a stunning swath of sand stretching to the horizon in both directions. Countless boutiques, many run by top local designers, vie for your daytime attention. At night have a fabulous meal, then hit a club.

15

WANTET/GETTY IMAGES ©

16

RHONDA GUTENBERG/GETTY IMAGES ©

Borobudur

17 The breathtaking Borobudur temple complex (p109) is a stunning and poignant epitaph to Java's Buddhist heyday in the 9th century AD and is a highlight of a visit to Indonesia. One of the most important Buddhist sites in the world and one of the finest temple complexes in Southeast Asia, the temple consists of six square bases topped by three circular ones. Nearly 1500 narrative relief panels on the terraces illustrate Buddhist teachings and tales, while 432 Buddha images sit in chambers on the terraces.

Indonesian Food

18 When you eat in Indonesia (p745), you savour the essence of the country. The abundance of rice reflects Indonesia's fertile landscape, the spices are reminiscent of a time of trade and invasion, and the fiery chilli echoes the passion of the people. Chinese, Portuguese, colonists and traders have all influenced the flavours, which include coriander, lemon grass, coconut, and palm sugar. Sate (skewered meat), nasi goreng (fried rice) and gado gado (vegetables with peanut sauce) are justly famous; regional variations are endless.

17

NIELS VAN GIJN/GETTY IMAGES ©

ANDREA PISTOLESI/GETTY IMAGES ©

GONZALO AZUMENDI/GETTY IMAGES ©

Jakarta Nightlife

19 If you have the stamina, Jakarta (p63) has the action, for this is Southeast Asia's best-kept party secret. Sure, Indonesia is a predominantly Muslim nation where traditions run deep, but in Jakarta, well, anything goes – the scene can get very underground in the north of town. The city has it all: superstylin' lounges frequented by the oh-so-beautiful crowd, low-key bars where the soundtrack is vintage 1970s funk, alt-rock music venues and electro clubs where DJs attain messiah-like status.

Harau Valley

20 Detour from dusty and bustling Bukittinggi to the sleepy Harau Valley (p553). Family homestays and rustic resorts framed by sheer cliffs and waterfalls sit beside local villages, rice paddies and lotus ponds. Challenge yourself on a rock-climbing excursion, or enjoy jungle trekking and birdwatching. If the appeal of long and bumpy Sumatran bus journeys is beginning to fade, take some time off the road with a few lazy days in simple, breezy bungalows. Minangkabau cookery classes are another relaxing option. Rice paddy

need to know

Currency
» Rupiah (Rp)

Language
» Bahasa Indonesia

When To Go

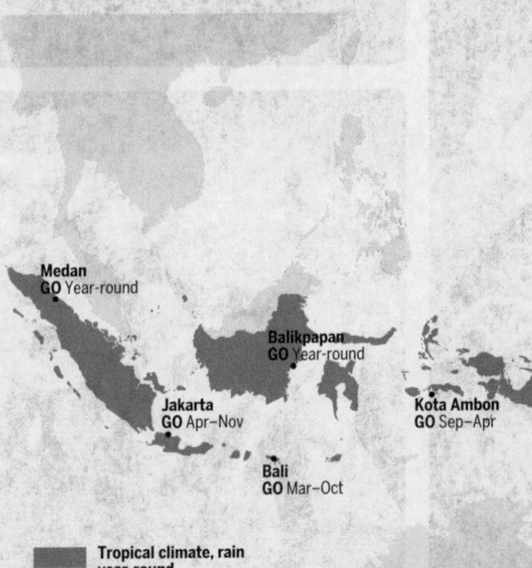

High Season
(Jul & Aug)

» Tourist numbers surge across Indonesia, from Bali to Sulawesi and beyond.

» Rates can spike by 50%.

» Dry season except in Maluku and Papua, which are rainy.

Shoulder
(May, Jun & Sep)

» Dry season outside Maluku & Papua.

» Best weather in Java, Bali and Lombok (dry, not so humid).

» You can travel more spontaneously.

Low Season
(Oct–Apr)

» Wet season in Java, Bali and Lombok.

» Dry season (best for diving) in Maluku and Papua.

» It's often easy to find deals and you can travel with little advance booking (except at Christmas and New Years).

Your Daily Budget

Budget less than 300,000Rp

» Simple rooms less than 150,000Rp

» Cheap street meals under 20,000Rp

» Travel like a local outside of major cities and tourist areas

Midrange 300,000–1.3 million Rp

» Double rooms with air-con and internet around US$30–70

» Cheap flights to shorten distances

» Guides plus meals in restaurants (where they exist)

Top end over 1.3 million Rp

» Stay at resorts, often noted boutique properties in remote places

» Use flights and cars with drivers

» Book special tours for activities like diving and visit top restaurants on Bali

Money

» ATMs available and credit cards accepted in cities and popular tourist areas such as Bali. US dollars best for exchange elsewhere.

Visas

» A 30-day visa (which can be renewed once only) sold on arrival. Apply in advance to consulates and embassies for 60-day visas.

Mobile Phones

» Cheap local SIM cards work with any unlocked GSM phone.

Transport

» Planes, some trains, boats, ferries, buses of all sizes and cars with drivers will get you across the archipelago.

Websites

» **Inside Indonesia** (www.insideindonesia.org) News and thoughtful features.

» **Indonesia Traveling** (www.indonesiatraveling.com) Info about Indonesia's parks, nature reserves and wildlife.

» **Jakarta Globe** (www.thejakartaglobe.com) Top-notch national English-language newspaper.

» **Jakarta Post** (www.thejakartapost.com) Indonesia's original English-language daily.

» **LonelyPlanet.com** (www.lonelyplanet.com/indonesia) Share knowledge and experiences with others.

Exchange Rates

Australia	A$1	10,000Rp
Canada	C$1	9700Rp
Euro zone	€1	12,400Rp
Japan	¥100	100Rp
New Zealand	NZ$1	7900Rp
UK	UK£1	15,400Rp
US	US$1	9600Rp

For current exchange rates see www.xe.com.

Important Numbers

Mobile phones are common across Indonesia; numbers usually start with 08 and don't require an area code.

Indonesia country code	☎62
International call prefix	☎001/017
International operator	☎102
Directory assistance	☎108

Arriving in Indonesia

» **Sukarno-Hatta International Airport (CGK)**
Jakarta is the primary entry point to Indonesia but most people merely change planes here before continuing on to their final destination.

» **Ngurah Rai Airport (DPS)**
Bali is the only airport with significant international service apart from Jakarta. Prepaid 24-hour taxis are available to all parts of Bali. It's 50,000Rp for Kuta, 80,000Rp to Seminyak and 200,000Rp for Ubud.

Travelling Responsibly

To visit Indonesia responsibly, try not to be invasive. Local environmental awareness is still nascent at best, but consider the following tips:

» Watch your use of water – demand often outstrips supply. Don't stay at a place with a pool, especially if the ocean is next door.

» Water bottles are convenient but they add up and are a major blight. Don't refill from the tap. Ask your hotel or eatery if you can refill from their huge containers of drinking water.

» Conserve power – using air-con strains an already overloaded system.

» Traffic is already bad, so why add another vehicle to it? Can you take a bus or bemo? Would a hike or bicycle trip be more enjoyable than a road journey to an over-visited tourist spot?

» Eat local – the food at warungs is locally sourced and usually the freshest.

if you like...

Island Hopping

With 17,000 (or more) islands to choose from, your opportunities to bounce from one idyllic little discovery to the next are endless.

Derawan Archipelago The Derawan Archipelago has several versions of tropical paradise, from popular backpacker hangouts to a massive atoll without a tourist in sight (p607)

Raja Ampat Islands These incredible islands off Papua have steep, jungle-covered hills, translucent waters, pristine beaches and weird mushroom-shaped rock islets. The waters teem with the world's greatest diversity of marine life (p452)

Karimunjawa Islands Often overlooked, these idyllic coral-fringed islets (off Java's north coast) are increasingly starting to register on travellers' itineraries thanks to better transport connections and facilities (p156)

Banyak Islands They might be a mere dot on most maps, but spend just one day on each of the Banyak Islands and and soon you'll be lost in a perfect tropical island cliche (p527)

Diving & Snorkelling

Indonesia has some of the world's best diving, from the plethora of operators and schools in Bali to remote spots that will challenge – and thrill – experts.

Komodo National Park A convergence of warm and cold currents keeps reefs nourished and attracts the big stuff. Think large schools of sharks, fleets of mantas and pods of dolphins (p349)

Pulau Weh Hover above a clown fish playing among the tentacles of an anemone and look up to see the dark shadow of a giant whale shark drift by (p523)

Derawan Archipelago For sea monsters, check out 'the channel' off Pulau Maratua, where big pelagic fish meet gawking divers. Huge schools of barracuda are common, while the lucky spot a thresher shark (p609)

Pulau Bunaken Combine a low-key, classic tropical idyl with excellent snorkelling and diving atop pristine coral reefs and critter-filled muck (p684)

Trekking

Many parts of Indonesia are still wild and remote. Treks (from part of a day to weeks) though these lands and cultures are the reason many visit the country.

Gunung Rinjani Indonesia's second-highest volcano, sacred to Balinese Hindus and Sasak Muslims, promises waterfalls, hot springs in sauna-like caves and a magical summit sunrise to those who survive her (p327)

Gunung Semeru Climbing to the frosty summit of Java's highest peak is a tough challenge. Your reward is breathtaking volcano vistas of a cone-studded horizon (p187)

Gunung Kerinci Challenge yourself on an ascent of this stunning peak in Sumatra's Kerinci Seblat National Park, and keep a careful eye out for tiger paw prints in the dense forest (p558)

Mamasa to Tana Toraja Leave the world behind as you walk past terraced rice fields and jungle to stay in villages where mattresses and toilets don't exist, but welcome is plentiful (p658)

MARK CARWARDINE/GETTY IMAGES ©

» Sumatran rhinoceros, Sumatra Rhino Sanctuary, Way Kambas National Park (p579)

Beaches

The problem isn't finding a beach, the problem is choosing one from the myriad choices.

Gili Islands Near Bali and Lombok, these three testaments to hedonism are ringed by pure white sand (p311)

Pantai Trikora Chill out in beachfront homestays along Pantai Trikora, the more rustic flipside to Pulau Bintan's luxury array of manicured resorts (p568)

Rote Known primarily for its epic surf, we love sweet Rote for its miles of empty beaches with powdery sand, sweeping bays and simple, stunning solitude (p384)

Banyak Islands With sandy dots fringed by pristine coral reefs and crowned by no more than a handful of palm trees, this chain of largely uninhabited islands offers the best beaches in Sumatra (p527)

Southwest of Yogyakarta Grab a bike or hire a car and explore this stunning coastline, a succession of gorgeous golden-sand coves divided by craggy headlands (p130)

Surfing

Surf breaks are found all across Indonesia. Each year new ones are named by surfers in search of the perfect wave.

Bali Legendary surf breaks are found across the island, depending on season. Ulu Watu is world famous (p229)

Mentawai Islands Make a waverider's pilgrimage to some of the planet's most iconic and challenging breaks – staying in a basic family losmen or an ubercomfortable private island resort (p542)

G-Land You want big? G-Land's got the power. This legendary wave, off Java's extreme south-east corner, just barrels on and on (p192)

West Sumbawa Of the many Nusa Tenggara waves that have migrated into the global surf zeitgeist, only one, Supersuck, attracts surfers from Oahu's North Shore (p338)

Nias The surfers' original paradise found: the long, hollow right of Lagundri has long been considered one of the world's best waves (p515)

Wildlife

Orangutans are the stars of a world of wildlife that includes elephants, dragons and all manner of birds.

Palangka Raya If you like espresso with your wildlife-spotting, try the luxurious *Rahai'i Pangun*. The Kahayan River will keep your camera clicking with plenty of orangutans, crocodiles and more (p626)

Meru Betiri National Park A rainforest home to exotica including rhinoceros, hornbills and the world's longest snake. Its beaches attract nesting turtles most nights of the year (p192)

Papua Birds of paradise – these birds of legendary colour and plumage, and exhibitionist mating dances – hide deep in the Papuan forests, but local guides will take you to their display spots (p470)

Way Kambas National Park Ride on elephants along meandering riverside paths, spy some of Sumatra's rarest birds and learn about efforts to save the endangered Sumatra rhino (p579)

month by month

Top Events

1. **Bali's Galungan & Kuningan**, varies
2. **Pasola**, February
3. **Idul Fitri**, July
4. **Tana Toraja Funeral Festivals**, July & August
5. **Madura Bull Races**, October

January

The first part of the month is busy in Bali as a fair bit of Australia arrives for Christmas and New Years holidays. Europeans searching for warmth arrive in large numbers.

Garebeg

Java's three most colourful festivals are held annually in Yogyakarta at the end of January and April and the beginning of November. Huge numbers of people in traditional dress march in processions with garish floats all to the tune of gamelan music.

February

It's dry season in the east. This is a good time to hit dive and snorkel sites in Maluku and Papua, where the waters will be especially clear.

Pasola

Nusa Tenggara's biggest festival (p399): vividly dressed teams of horsemen engage in mock, though sometimes bloody, battles in West Sumba. Often coincides with Nyale in Lombok (p332), a huge fishing festival celebrated by the Sasaks.

March

A good time to visit Indonesia as crowds are few and options are many. The rainy season is tailing off in Java, Bali and western Nusa Tenggara.

Java Jazz Festival

Held in early March at the Jakarta Convention Center, this huge festival (www.javajazzfestival.com) attracts acclaimed international artists (including Stevie Wonder in 2012). This is a major event on the regional cultural calendar and each year the

GALUNGAN & KUNINGAN

Galungan, which celebrates the death of a legendary tyrant called Mayadenawa, is one of Bali's major festivals. During this 10-day period, all the gods come down to earth for the festivities. Barong (mythical lion-dog creatures) prance from temple to temple and village to village, and locals rejoice with feasts and visits to families. The celebrations culminate with the Kuningan festival, when the Balinese say thanks and goodbye to the gods.

Every village in Bali will celebrate Galungan and Kuningan in grand style and visitors are welcome to join in. This is an excellent time to visit Bali. (The *wuku* calendar is used to determine festival dates, which are typically every 210 days.)

YEAR	GALUNGAN	KUNINGAN
2013	27 Mar & 23 Oct	6 Apr & 2 Nov
2014	21 May & 17 Dec	31 May & 27 Dec
2015	15 Jul	25 Jul

list of luminaries on the performance list grows.

Nyepi

Bali's major Hindu festival, Nyepi, celebrates a new year on the religious calendar. It's marked by inactivity – to convince evil spirits that Bali is un-inhabited. The night before sees community celebrations with *ogoh-ogoh*, huge papier-mâché monsters that go up in flames. Held in March or early April.

July

Although visitor numbers are high in Bali and other areas popular with tourists, July is often the coolest and driest time of the year outside Maluku and Papua.

Idul Fitri

Idul Fitri is the traditional end of Ramadan, the Muslim month of fasting, and this huge holiday sees tens of millions of people travelling to their home villages or going on holiday to places like Bali. The date is slightly earlier each year (in 2013, it's 8–9 August).

Erau Festival

Every July thousands of Dayaks from across Kalimantan attend the Erau Festival in Tenggarong, a vast intertribal party punctuated by traditional dances, ritual ceremonies and other events. It's worth making plans to attend in advance as it draws many tourists.

Tana Toraja Funeral Festivals

A Sulawesi highlight and an excellent reason to visit the island. Held during July and August, the ceremonies often shock first-time visitors. Toraja working throughout the country return home for celebrations and funeral rituals (p654).

August

Independence Day on 17 August sees a spectacle of parades and celebrations in Jakarta and across the country. You'll see school kids out practicing their marching in the prior weeks.

Bidar Races

Spectacular *bidar* (canoe) races held on South Sumatra's Sungai Musi in Palembang every 17 August and 16 June (the city's birthday). There is also a dragon-boat festival in Padang in mid-July. Up to 60 rowers power these boats.

Baliem Valley Festival

A celebration of indigenous culture in Papua's Baliem Valley (p481), with mock 'tribal fighting', full traditional regalia, dance and music. The festivities take place over two days during the second week of August.

October

A good month for travel with few crowds and many good deals. It's the start of the rainy season in Java and Bali but in recent years there has been less rain.

Ubud Writers & Readers Festival

This Ubud festival (www.ubudwritersfestival.com) brings together scores of writers and readers from around the world in a celebration of writing – especially that which touches on Bali. Its reputation is growing by the year.

Asmat Cultural Festival

Held in the Asmat Region of eastern Papua, this festival features five or six days of woodcarving exhibits, canoe races and traditional dance, song and dress at Agats in October.

Madura Bull Races

Bull racing is the major sport on Pulau Madura, the island off Java. Teams compete throughout the year to see who will go to the finals held every October in Pamekasan. These spectacular competitions feature over 100 racing bulls and legions of fervent fans (p169).

itineraries

Whether you've got 6 days or 60, these itineraries provide a starting point for a fantastic Indonesian trip. Want more inspiration? Head online to lonelyplanet.com/thorntree to chat with other travellers.

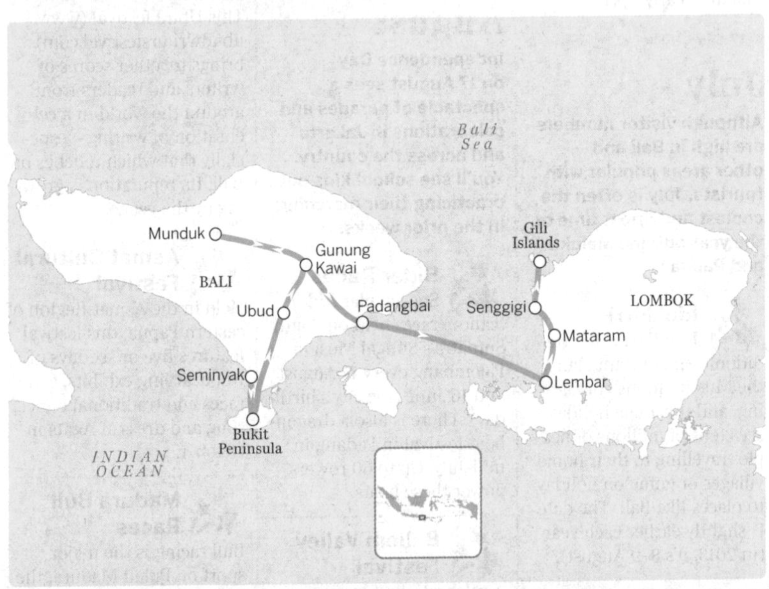

14 to 21 Days
Bali & Lombok

Start in Bali, where you can acclimatise in the resorts, clubs and shops of **Seminyak**. Dose up on sun at the beach, then go exploring the perfect little beaches and surf breaks down the **Bukit Peninsula**.

Head north to immerse yourself in the 'other' Bali – the culture, temples and rich history of **Ubud**. Visit the Unesco-nominated **Gunung Kawi**, an ancient site worthy of Indiana Jones, and the nearby craft villages. Take a cooking course or learn batik, woodcarving or silversmithing. Once you've exhausted your yen for culture, escape to the misty mountains for treks to waterfalls amid coffee plantations in and around **Munduk**.

Next on the agenda is Lombok. Take a ferry from Bali's beachy port town of **Padangbai** to **Lembar**, Lombok's launching pad. Potter through the rice fields and Hindu temples around **Mataram**, then head to **Senggigi** for indulgent resorts, fine beaches and uninterrupted R&R.

From Senggigi take a ferry to the deservedly celebrated **Gili Islands**, where seamless beaches, translucent water and vivid reefs beg for snorkel-clad swimmers. Or if you're short on time, just catch a fast boat direct to the Gilis from Bali.

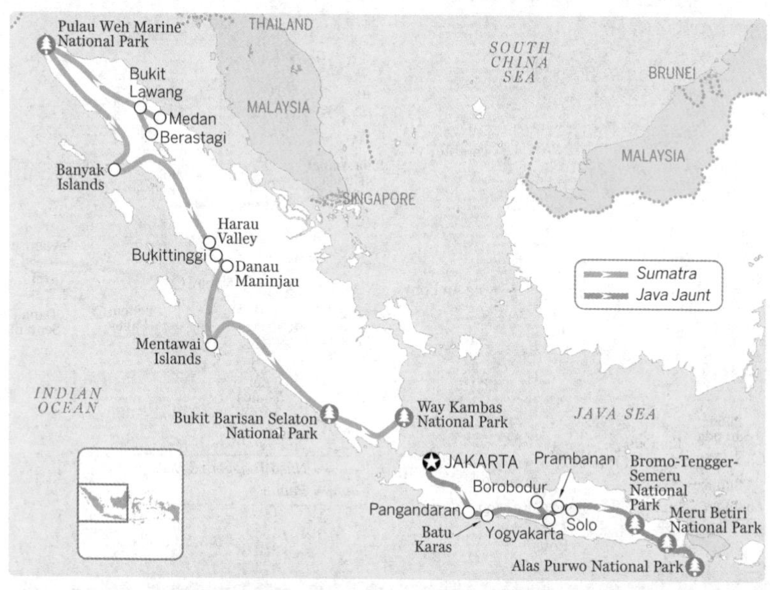

14 to 30 Days

Java Jaunt

Start your journey in **Jakarta** and wrap your senses around the dizzying smells, sounds, sights and people of Indonesia's teeming capital. Linger long enough to binge on Bintang beer and shopping, then head to **Batu Karas** for classic laid-back beach vibes or go for the resorts of nearby **Pangandaran**.

After you've worshipped the sun for a week or so, catch the train to **Yogyakarta**, Java's cultural capital. Dabble in batik, amble through the *kraton* (walled city palace) and part with your rupiah at the vibrant markets. A day trip to majestic **Borobudur** is a must. The longer you look, truly the more you'll see.

From Yogyakarta make your way to the laid-back city of **Solo**, via the enigmatic temples of **Prambanan**. Head into the clouds at awesome **Bromo-Tengger-Semeru National Park**, spending a night on the lip of Tengger crater. From here head to the southeast coast and **Meru Betiri National Park**. You just might see the amazing giant squirrel. Finally follow the coast to **Alas Purwo National Park** where there's leopards and amazing surfing at G-Land.

30 to 60 Days

Sumatra

Sumatra is quite huge and you'll have to hustle to fully appreciate it within visa constraints. Start your explorations in **Medan**, which has fab transport connections. Then get right out of town and head to **Bukit Lawang** where you can see the island's most famous residents, the orangutans. It's a short jaunt from here to **Berastagi**, a laid-back hill town set amidst volcanoes.

Travel north to the very tip of Sumatra, but don't stop, definitely don't stop. Sharks, turtles and other large sea creatures live amidst splendid coral at **Pulau Weh Marine National Park** off the coast. Head back south and travel off the west coast to **Banyak Islands**, a surfing and beach paradise. Back ashore, follow the Trans-Sumatra Highway south to **Bukittinggi**, a good base for exploring the cultures and beauty of the **Harau Valley** and **Danau Maninjau**.

There's more surf, sand and underwater joy off the coast in the **Mentawai Islands**. Finally head far south to **Bukit Barisan Selaton** and **Way Kambas National Parks**. The former has a few rhinos and tigers in lowland forests while the latter has elephants. From here it's easy to catch the Java ferry.

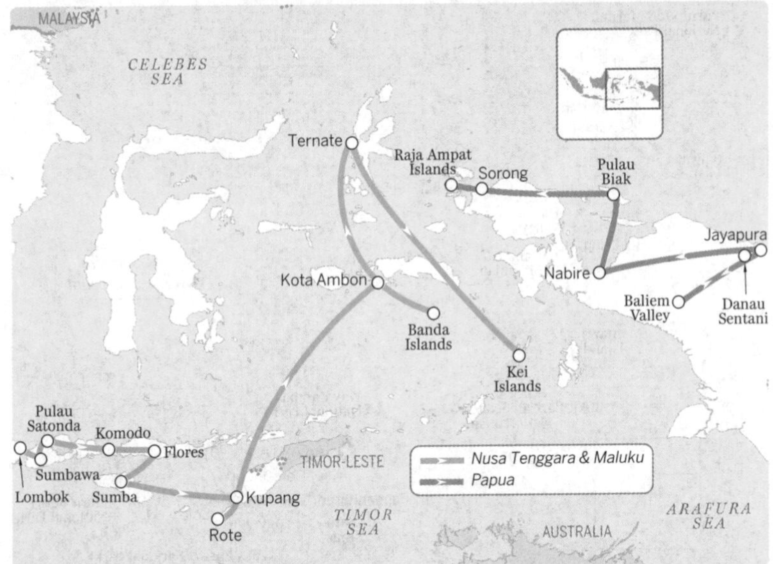

30 Days
Papua

Papua is the launching pad for this route, which can be done in 30 days with judicious use of flights. Start at the transport hub of **Jayapura**. But you'll only be there long enough to charter a boat to visit the magnificent **Danau Sentani**, a 96.5-sq-km lake with 19 islands perfect for inland island-hopping.

Back on dry land, take to the air to get to the beautiful **Baliem Valley**, rich in culture and trek-worthy mountain scenery. The valley is home to the Dani people, an ethnic group who have eschewed most modern things and live a traditional life. Enjoy mountain views from a thatched hut.

Fly to **Nabire** and spot whale sharks off the coast – you can even swim with them. Now fly up for some idle island time on **Pulau Biak**. Next it's a flight to **Sorong**, a base for trips out to the **Raja Ampat Islands** – a paradise for divers and snorkellers with Indonesia's most abundant and varied marine life. It's also good for birdwatchers and sublime tropical-island scenery.

30 to 60 Days
Nusa Tenggara & Maluku

Head east from **Lombok**. Admire the beautiful coastline along **Sumbawa** and look for hidden corners. Make your way to **Flores**, a rugged volcanic island with fishing villages, thriving culture and dramatic terrain. Stop off for some communing with dragons at **Komodo** on the way. Note that you can also do Lombok to Flores by liveaboard boat.

Now take ferries south to isolated and timeless **Sumba**, where some superb beaches are just starting to attract visitors. Ponder this at beautiful beaches around Waikabubak, such as Pantai Nihiwatu. After indulging in sun and isolation, fly to **Kupang** in West Timor. Visit villages in the surrounding areas, then jump over to **Rote** for relaxed coastal vibes.

Fly from Kupang to **Kota Ambon** on Maluku's Pulau Ambon. Pause only briefly, then take a ferry (often frustrating) or plane to the crystalline seas, multicoloured reefs and empty beaches of the historic **Banda Islands**. Make your way back to Ambon and fly to **Ternate**, which is as pretty a tropical island paradise as you'll find. Finally make the jaunt east to the **Kei Islands**, for one perfect beach after another.

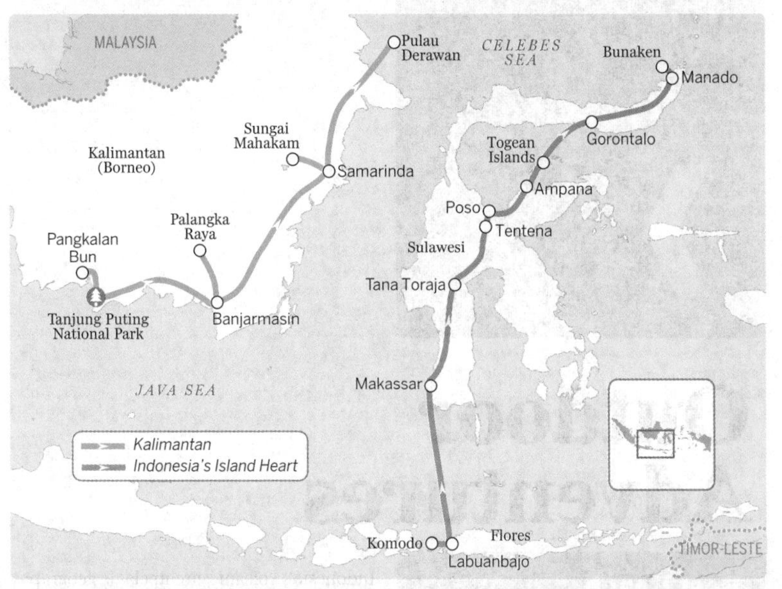

30 Days
Indonesia's Island Heart

Start on **Flores** and take a dragon-spotting hike on **Komodo**. Enjoy time in the agreeable port town of **Labuanbajo** and head off-shore for some diving. From here, fly to Makassar on Sulawesi – this may require connecting someplace.

In **Makassar**, pause amid the pandemonium for excellent seafood. But don't overdo it, as you want to be fully alive for the elaborate funeral ceremonies in **Tana Toraja**, an eight-hour bus trip from Makassar. From here, another long bus ride (13 hours) takes you to the transport hub of **Poso**. Break your journey at the tidy lakeside town of **Tentena**. A five-hour bus ride from Poso gets you to **Ampana** where you take a ferry to your reward: the amazing, beautiful and beguiling **Togean Islands**. Spend your days island- and hammock-hopping between iconic beaches.

Tearing yourself away, take a boat to **Gorontalo**, then bus it to **Manado** and take a boat to laid-back **Pulau Bunaken**, where you can finish out the time on your visa.

30 to 60 days
Kalimantan

Unassuming **Pangkalan Bun** is the entry point to this excursion – it's the launching pad for trips into glorious **Tanjung Puting National Park**, one of Indonesia's best orangutan haunts. Scan the canopy for their amber bodies from the top of a houseboat as it ambles down the beautiful Sungai Kumai.

Rejoin reality in colourful **Banjarmasin**. Dabble in Kalimantan's most beguiling city – brave a 5am call for the animated floating markets, then cruise the canals and meet the locals at dusk. Begin another classic river adventure by navigating up the Sungai Kahayan to **Palangka Raya**, a hub for yet more orangutan watching. Your boat choices range from the simple to the luxe.

From Banjarmasin, travel overland to **Samarinda** and make an expedition along **Sungai Mahakam**. Several days upstream will land you in the river's western reaches, which are peppered with semitraditional Dayak villages and preserved forests. Travel back to the coast and head north to the offshore underwater wonders of **Pulau Derawan**. This primitive teardrop-shaped island offers fabulous diving and snorkelling.

Outdoor Adventures

Best Beach

The beaches that line the bays around Lombok's Kuta are beautiful and worth a trip.

Best Diving

The Raja Ampat Islands are on many a diver's bucket list and with good reason: the wealth and variety of marine life is nothing short of astonishing.

Best Surfing

Tough competition, but Bali has to win for its huge range of breaks and vast surfing infrastructure (the after-dark partying is great as well).

Best Hiking & Trekking

The Baliem Valley draws acolytes from around the world for hikes among some of the world's most unique cultures. There are many variations possible for any level of commitment.

Best Wildlife Watching

Kalimantan's Tanjung Puting National Park is best reached on a boat along one of the iconic rivers that flow through it. Anchor and watch orangutans go about their business just metres away.

Indonesia's volcanic, archipelagic geography creates a wide range of adventure opportunities. The many seas hold superb diving, snorkelling and surfing venues. On land, the rugged peaks, dense jungles and rushing rivers are an adventurer's delight.

When to Go

There are vast variations in the weather across the huge swath of islands that is Indonesia. Generally the dry season in Java, Bali and Lombok is May to September, while Maluku and Papua have their best weather October to April. But exceptions are the rule and you'll want to research any location you plan to visit carefully if weather will play a role in your enjoyment.

Beaches

With some 17,000-plus islands, Indonesia has a lot of beaches. They range from the wildly popular beaches on South Bali to those for hardcore partiers on the Gili Islands to literally hundreds more where your footprints will be the first of the day.

Pantai is beach in Bahasa Indonesia. Note that sunscreen can be hard to find outside of major tourist areas.

Where to Go

Java

Beaches near cities in Java can be virtually overrun on weekends, but venture a little further and you'll find some great sand.

Batu Karas (p100) A simple village with two great beaches and a classic laid-back vibe.

Southwest of Yogyakarta (p130) Explore this beautiful coastline, a succession of alluring golden-sand coves divided by craggy headlands (but skip Parangritis, which is not in the same league).

Karimunjawa Islands (p156) Some 27 islands comprise this offshore marine park which gets very few tourists. It has among the finest – and least visited – beaches in Indonesia.

Papuma (p191) Amidst some so-so grey-sand beaches, this south-coast gem boasts azure waters and white sand.

Bali

Fabled for its beaches, Bali actually pales in comparison to scores of other islands in Indonesia. What the island does have is a thriving beach culture with surfing, playing, sunbathing and places to imbibe, ranging from the dead-simple to the hipster-luxe. Locals and visitors alike pause on west-facing beaches at sunset and the Balinese hold purification and other ceremonies at the shore.

Kuta Beach (p207) This is the original draw for tourists, with a golden-sand arc sweeping past Canggu to the northwest. Raw surf hits here, delighting surfers.

Bukit Peninsula (p227) The west side has famous surf spots and beaches with names such as Bingen and Balangan that feature little pockets of bright sand below limestone cliffs. The east side has reef-protected strands, such as the one at Nusa Dua.

East Bali (p264) A long series of open-water beaches begins north of reef-protected Sanur. Waves pound volcanic sand that ranges from a light grey to charcoal black. In the far east, on the Amed Coast, tiny coves of light sand front small fishing villages.

Nusa Tenggara

Nusa Tenggara is probably the region of Indonesia with the most beaches awaiting discovery – or a developer.

Gili Islands (p311) The Gilis are easily reached from Bali and Lombok, and you can snorkel right off the blinding white sands. At night Gili T is one of the country's most vibrant party scenes.

Lombok (p300) Head south for the pristine white-sand islands of Gili Asahan and the north coast of Gili Gede (p305). Kuta (p331) is an immense series of one spectacular beach or bay after another. Get there, rent a motorbike and explore.

Sumbawa (p336) In West Sumbawa the best beaches are south of Maluk (p338) in Rantung and north in Jelenga (p337). In the east, head to the Lakey area. All of Sumbawa's beaches are primarily surf beaches, but the sand stretches wide, and deep, as well.

Flores (p348) Head to the islands off Labuanbajo (p350) and you'll be in bliss, especially Pulau Sebayur and Pulau Kanawa. Pantai Merah on Komodo Island is famous for its sublime pink-sand beaches. The Seventeen Islands Marine Park (p361) off the Riung coast also has a dozen remote islands with epic and empty white-sand beaches to lounge upon.

Rote (p384) The main beach in Nemberala town is beautiful enough, but the beaches just get wider and whiter the further south you travel. Ba'a is the most beautiful of the bunch. We also enjoy the empty sugary beaches on nearby islands Pulau Do'o and Pulau Ndao.

Sumba (p387) Rarely do you see folks sunning themselves and lounging around Sumba's beautiful beaches: too many villagers descend without warning. But the well-heeled would love the five-star grace of Pantai Nihiwatu. The beach at Oro Beach House (p400) is also special and much less snooty.

Maluku

Maluku's fine beaches have barely been discovered.

Banda Islands (p429) Maluku's best beaches are all in the Bandas. Charter a boat from Bandaneira and enjoy exquisite empty beaches on Pulau Hatta, Pulau Ai, and Pulau Run. But the best of the Banda bunch is Pulau Neilaka, more a white sandbar than an island.

Kei Islands (p438) Sugary Pasir Panjang is ground zero for beach lounging. The petroglyph-swathed cliffs and mindbending scenery at Ohoidertawun are also worth consideration. Rent a bike and make the two-hour trek to the stunning, remote and drop-dead gorgeous beaches of Pantai Ohoidertutu.

Papua

Papua is not a beach destination per se but there are some fine ones here.

Raja Ampat Islands (p452) There are some divine and empty beaches here but due to the high cost of reaching the area they tend to be enjoyed mainly as a secondary activity by people who are diving and/or snorkelling.

Pulau Biak (p467) The Padaido Islands (p471) off Pulau Biak and Pulau Biak itself have some good beaches that are not too hard to reach.

Sumatra

The best beaches on this huge island are actually on tiny islands offshore, although many, such as the Mentawai Islands, are difficult and expensive to reach if you're not there for surfing.

Pulau Bintan (p566) A gem in the Riau Islands, this island has some fine beaches where you can live the tropical fantasy in a hut.

Banyak Islands (p527) Banyak means 'many' and there are many fine beaches among the 99 islands in this remote and seldom-visited chain off Aceh.

Cycling

Cycling in Indonesia is booming in popularity as petrol prices skyrocket. Lowland towns such as Yogyakarta and Solo in Java teem with bikes, and bicycles are gaining popularity in Bali. Lombok has good roads for bikes.

You can purchase a good-quality, locally manufactured mountain or road bike in most major cities. Be sure to buy a model with quick-release wheels to make it easier to squeeze the bike onto public transport if required. See p771 for more information.

Where to Go

Java

Yogyakarta is a big biking centre: pedal out to see the Prambanan temples (p132). Solo is another good place to join a bike tour.

Bali

Bike tours across the island are heavily marketed and there are scores to choose from. Some are simple downhill jaunts through rice fields while others are much more adventurous treks. You can easily rent bikes for under 20,000Rp per day.

Sumatra

Bikes can be hired in Danau Toba (p504).

Diving

With so many islands and so much coral, Indonesia presents wonderful possibilities for diving.

Where to Go

Bali

Indonesia's tourist hub has a plethora of excellent dive shops, schools and operators. The following are Bali's most spectacular diving and snorkelling locations.

Nusa Penida (p244) Serious diving that includes schools of manta rays and 2.5m sunfish. Skilled divers will enjoy the challenges, but novices and snorkellers will be in over their heads.

Pulau Menjangan (p296) Spectacular 30m wall off a small island. Good for divers of all skills and ages.

Tulamben (p278) A popular sunken WWII freighter right off the shore lures scores of divers daily.

Nusa Tenggara

A vast range of diving opportunities awaits. Major destinations have land-based dive shops. Liveaboard charters and boats offer seasonal trips. For untapped dive sites, bring your own buoyancy control devices, regulators and computers (tanks are usually accessible) and explore Rote, Sumbawa and Sumba.

Gili Islands (p317) Among the best places to get certified worldwide, with accessible reefs within a 10-minute boat ride and two dozen schools to choose from.

Lombok If you get lucky you can see schooling hammerheads at Blongas (p335), usually in mid-September.

Flores Labuanbajo (p349) is how you access the world-class sites within the Komodo National Park. In peak season, up to 50 liveaboards ply these waters. There are more than a dozen dive shops in Labuanbajo proper.

Alor Archipelago (p372) Alor has crystalline waters and arguably the most pristine reefs in Indonesia, and you'll have the sites almost all to yourself. You can base yoruself out of Kalabahi, Pulau Kepa or Pulau Pantar.

Maluku

Diving has great promise here but is mostly undeveloped.

Banda Islands (p429) There is only one solid dive operator in Bandaneira, and it's seasonal.

RODGER KLEIN/GETTY IMAGES ©

M. GEBICKI/GETTY IMAGES ©

» (above) Pink Anemonefish, Banda Islands (p429)
» (left) Beach volleyball, Legian (p209)

RESPONSIBLE DIVING

The popularity of diving puts immense pressure on many sites. Consider the following tips when diving and help preserve the ecology and beauty of Indonesia's reefs:

» Avoid touching living marine organisms with your body or dragging equipment across the reef. Never stand on corals, even if they look solid and robust.

» Be conscious of your fins. The surge from heavy fin strokes near the reef can damage delicate organisms. When treading water in shallow reef areas, take care not to kick up clouds of sand. Settling sand can easily smother delicate reef organisms.

» Practise and maintain proper buoyancy control. Major damage can be done by divers descending too fast and colliding with the reef. Make sure you are correctly weighted and that your weight belt is positioned so that you stay horizontal.

» Resist the temptation to collect corals or shells.

» Ensure that you collect all your rubbish and any litter you find as well. Plastics in particular are a serious threat to marine life.

» Resist the temptation to feed fish.

However, if you time it right, you can dive the lava flow off of Pulau Gunung Api, or the wonderful coral crusted walls off Pulau Hatta, Pulau Ai and Pulau Run.

Pulau Ambon (p424) Something of a dive mecca. There are reef dives outside the bay off the Ambon coast, but most divers come here for the excellent muck diving on the slopes within Teluk Ambon.

Papua

One of the world's most fabled dive spots is here at Raja Ampat. Bring your own equipment to ensure you get the most out of the journey.

Raja Ampat Islands (p452) Among the best in the world for the diversity and quantity of marine life. It's a remote area and quite expensive. Most divers go on liveaboard boats doing one- to two-week cruises, or stay at the handful of dive resorts.

Pulau Biak (p467) An excellent dive site that's overshadowed by Raja Ampat.

Sumatra

Diving on Mentawai is still a fledgling activity although PADI courses are now available through a handful of resorts. Pulau Weh (p523) is another small coral-ringed island growing in popularity.

Kalimantan

Choices are limited but if you want to dive the Derawan Archipelago, there are two good choices. Either you stay at the Derawan Dive Lodge (p608) on Pulau Derawan, which gives you access to other islands via some fast dive boats, or you stay at the resort islands of Nubucco or Nunukan (p609).

Sulawesi

New dive areas are opening up, but favourites like Bunaken are popular for a reason.

Pulau Bunaken (p684) Part of a large marine park, this island, which is easily reached from Manad, offers all sorts of diving. There's a fine range of places to stay and a fun, funky vibe.

Pulau Lembeh & the Lembeh Strait (p688) Muck diving at its finest, with a weird and wonderful world of bizarre critters awaiting your discovery.

Safe Diving

Before embarking on a scuba-diving or snorkelling trip, consider the following points to ensure a safe and enjoyable experience:

» Possess a current diving certification card from a recognised scuba-diving instructional agency.

» Be sure you are healthy and feel comfortable diving.

» Obtain reliable information about physical and environmental conditions at the dive site. Ask your operator or guide detailed questions.

» Dive only at sites within your realm of experience and engage the services of a certified dive instructor.

» Check your equipment thoroughly beforehand. For much of Indonesia, the equipment (if it's available) may not be in top condition. Bali is your best bet for finding reliable equipment for hire.

Snorkelling

Most dive operators will let snorkellers hitch a ride on trips, but don't expect much in the way of decent masks and fins outside of the most popular sites. Bring your own if you're picky.

Where to Go

Java

You can rent masks and fins at Baluran National Park (p195) and Karimunjawa (p156). Reefs are not always in the best condition.

Bali

Bali is ringed by good snorkelling sites that are easily reached; and some superb ones are not much more difficult to enjoy.

Pulau Menjangan (p296) A steady current takes you right along the edge of the beautiful 30m coral wall. Tours here are heavily marketed.

Tulamben (p278) A popular sunken WWII freighter is easily reached right off shore.

Nusa Tenggara

Nusa Tenggara has the best selection of snorkelling sites in the country. You can snorkel all of the Moyo and Alor dive sites and share a boat with the divers.

Gili Islands (p311) Turtle sightings are almost guaranteed from any of the many tour boats. There is a wonderful free-diving outfit as well. For many, there's bliss in the simplicity of snorkelling the beautiful waters right off the beaches.

Komodo Island (p313) The best snorkel sites are around Pulau Kanawa, Pulau Sebayur and off Pantai Merah.

Maluku

Sites around the Banda Islands (p429) can be snorkelled, though you'll need to free dive a bit to get the best views of the drop-offs. You might see turtles and sharks while snorkelling off Pulau Hatta.

Papua

Divers aren't the only ones having fun here.

Raja Ampat Islands (p454) Many superb snorkelling sites are reachable just by walking off a beach or taking a boat. Dive resorts and homestays all offer snorkelling, with gear for rent or lend.

Nabire (p471) Snorkel or swim with the whale sharks.

Sumatra

Just like diving, the best snorkelling is around the little islands offshore. Rudimentary day trips are available, but travellers are advised to bring their own snorkelling gear.

Pulau Bintan Pantai Trikora (p568) on the east coast is good for snorkelling, especially at high tide.

Pulau Weh (p523) While short on beaches, this island off the tip of Sumatra has beautiful coral gardens.

Kalimantan

Head to outer islands in Derawan Archipelago (p607), as reefs around Pulau Derawan are damaged.

Sulawesi

Sulawesi has a large number of great snorkelling sites. Equipment can be rented in many places but it's often poor quality and you're better off bringing your own.

Pulau Bunaken (p684) Great for snorkelling for many of the same reasons it is a good dive location.

Togean Islands (p672) Given the challenges in reaching these idyllic little gems, its nice that there's good underwater action once you get here.

Surfing

Indonesia lures surfers from around the globe, many with visions of empty palm-lined beaches, bamboo bungalows and perfect barrels peeling around a coral reef. The good news is that mostly the dreams come true, but just like anywhere else, Indonesia is subject to flat spells, onshore winds and crowding (particularly in Bali). A little research and preparation go a long way.

Where to Go

Java

Still being explored by surfers who find rad new breaks every year, Java's popular breaks at Cimaja, Batu Karas and Pacitan have surf schools and shops.

Alas Purwo National Park (p192) Home to the famous G-Land breaks, surf camps and tours dominate the scene in this otherwise remote hideaway. One of the world's best left-handed waves is worth all the hype.

Cimaja (p82) A popular surf spot at Pelabuhan Ratu. The fabled Ombak Tujuh break is off a pebble beach.

PAUL KENNEDY/GETTY IMAGES ©

PHOTOGRAPHY BY MANGIWAU/GETTY IMAGES ©

» (above) Surfers at Batu Karas, Java (p100)
» (left) Hiking in Keerom, Papua

Batu Karas (p100) A fast-growing and popular surf spot off the southern coast of Central Java, Batu Karas is one of several good breaks around Pangandaran.

Pacitan (p182) This town on a beautiful little horseshoe bay rewards surfers who make the trek.

Bali

It really is a surfer's paradise in Bali. Breaks are found right around the south side of the island and there's a large infrastructure of schools, board-rental places, cheap surfer dives and more that cater to the crowds. Several outfits cater to paddle-boarders.

Kuta Beach (p207) Where surfing came to Asia. This is a good place for beginners, with long, steady breaks.

Bingin (p228) A white-sand beach backed by funky accommodation makes this a natural stop.

Ulu Watu (p229) Some of the largest sets in Bali.

Medewi (p296) Famous point break with a ride right into a river mouth.

Nusa Lembongan (p242) The island is a mellow scene for surfers and nonsurfers. The breaks are right in front of the places to stay.

Nusa Tenggara

You could spend years exploring – and discovering! – places to surf in Nusa Tenggara.

Lombok (p300) South Lombok is a surf paradise. There are numerous breaks from Ekas to Gerupuk to Kuta, all of which can be accessed from the rustic tourist town of Kuta (p331). Desert Point is more of a surf camp and it's also legendary.

Sumbawa (p336) Jelenga (Scar Reef) and Maluk (p338) are among the greatest and most overlooked surf breaks in the world. Surfers regularly descend here to surf Supersuck, which offers one of the best barrels anywhere.

Rote (p384) T-Land is the legendary left (p385), but there are hollow waves in Bo'a bay (p386) too.

Sumba (p387) West Sumba has the best breaks, but it's not set up for tourists. You'll have to hire a car, drive into remote villages and paddle out on sight and feel. Nihiwatu (p398) is NT's top-dollar surf resort.

Sumatra

Arguably Indonesia's hottest surf region, new areas like Krui are attracting surfers in the know and new areas are opening up all the time.

Mentawai Islands (p542) Surfing is huge business in the Mentawais with everything from local fixers arranging speedboat transport and simple losmens to seven- to 10-day all-inclusive trips on surf boats, or in surf camps and resorts. The reason: scores of primo breaks.

Pulau Nias A low-key place for low-key surfers (p515). The one place on Sumatra where you can rent a decent board cheap. Decent schools for beginners.

Krui (p574) A largely undiscovered surf spot that has yet to attract mobs, not unlike other Sumatra

SURFING: WHAT TO PACK

A small board is usually adequate for smaller breaks, but a few extra inches on your usual board length won't go astray. For the bigger waves – 8ft and upwards – you'll need a 'gun'. For a surfer of average height and build, a board around the 7ft mark is perfect.

If you try to bring more than two or three boards into the country, you could have problems with customs officials, who might think you're going to try and sell them.

There are surf shops in major surf centres such as Bali but don't expect great boards for rent (about 50,000Rp per day).

Other recommended equipment includes the following:

- ☐ Solid luggage for airline travel
- ☐ Board-strap for carrying
- ☐ Tough shoes for walking down rocky cliffs
- ☐ Your favourite wax if you're picky
- ☐ Wetsuit or reef booties
- ☐ Wetsuit vest or other protective cover from the sun, reefs and rocks
- ☐ Surfing helmet for rugged conditions (and riding a motorbike)

SURF INFO ONLINE

Bali Waves (www.baliwaves.com) Surf reports including webcams of top spots.

Global Surfers (www.globalsurfers.com) Global online forum for surfers.

Indo Surf & Lingo (www.indosurf.com.au) Web links and general info.

SurfAid International (www.surfaidinternational.org) Surfer-run aid organisation.

Surf Travel Company (www.surftravel.com.au) Australian outfit with camps, yacht charters, destination information, surfer reviews and more.

Surf Travel Online (www.surftravelonline.com) Information on remote Indonesian locations.

WannaSurf (www.wannasurf.com) Surf reports, current conditions and a message board.

secret spots Banyaks and Simelue. Stay in simple accommodation and travel by motorbike to reach the most happening breaks up and down the coast.

White-Water Rafting

Some of the rivers tumbling down Indonesia's volcanic slopes have drawn adventure operators and thrill-seeking tourists.

Where to Go

Java

In Java, white-water rafting is well established on Sungai Citarak (p82), which churns out Class II to IV rapids. You can skip a raft altogether and go 'body rafting' in a lifejacket at Green Valley (p100) near Pangandaran.

Bali

Several Bali-based tour operators run trips down the Sungai Ayung (p251). It's suitable for rafting novices and families. Trips are heavily marketed and usually include transport from most popular areas.

Kalimantan

For all its great rivers there is surprisingly little white water in Kalimantan. There is bamboo rafting in Loksado (p632), which is really quite tame. The real charge is wild white-water canoeing on the remote Sungai Bungan (p618; best done as part of the Cross-Borneo Trek, as it is a two-day upriver journey to get there otherwise), or a longboat journey on the northern Sungai Mahakam (p598).

Sulawesi

Sulawesi's Sungai Sa'dan (p658) lures adventure junkies to tackle its 20-odd rapids (some up to Class IV). Rafting agents in Rantepao in Tana Toraja organise trips down its canyon but be prepared for haggling and be patient with details.

Hiking & Trekking

Setting off on foot for adventure and exploration in Indonesia offers limitless opportunities. From volcanic peaks with jaw-dropping dawn views to remote jungle treks, you can leave civilisation behind.

Where to Go

Java

Java has some great walks. Guides are always available at national park offices, or via guesthouses. Tents and sleeping bags can be rented at Semeru. Organised hikes can be set up in Kalibaru (to Merapi) and Malang (to Semeru).

Gunung Bromo (p184) One of three volcanic cones (one active) that emerge from an otherworldly caldera. Highly recommended and popular.

Gede Pangrango National Park (p84) Waterfalls and the nearly 3000m-high Gunung Gede, an active volcano, are the highlights.

Gunung Lawu (p142) On the border of central and east Java, this 3265m mountain is dotted with ancient Hindu temples.

Gunung Semeru (p187) It's a tough three-day trek to the top of Java's tallest peak, which is nearly always volcanically active.

Ijen Plateau (p188) Coffee plantations, misty jungle, volcanic cones and a spectacular crater lake are the allures here.

Bali

Bali is very walkable. No matter where you're staying, ask for recommendations and set off for discoveries and adventures. But Bali does not offer remote wilderness treks, even climbing its iconic volcanoes usually just involves a predawn departure from a nearby village to reach the summit by dawn.

Gunung Agung (p267) Sunrises and isolated temples on Bali's most sacred mountain.

Gunung Batur (p280) Other-worldly scenery that almost makes you forget about the hassles.

Munduk (p285) Lush, spice-scented waterfall-riven landscape high in the hills.

Sidemen Road (p266) Rice terraces, lush hills and lonely temples; comfy lodgings for walkers.

Ubud (p253) Beautiful walks between one hour and one day through rice, river-valley jungles and ancient monuments.

Nusa Tenggara

Lombok and Flores are both easily accessible and home to some top hikes.

Gunung Rinjani (p327) Indonesia's second tallest volcano is on Lombok. The standard trek is three to four days long, begins near a sacred waterfall, skirts lakes and hot springs, and culminates at sunrise on one of two peaks.

Flores (p348) Enjoy hikes to remote villages only accessible by trail, the most interesting of which is the trek to Wae Rebo in the Manggarai region (p357). You can also climb Gunung Inerie (p360) in the Bajawa area, or hike to the remote Pauleni Village (p359) near Belaragi.

Maluku

In the Banda Islands (p429) there is a three-hour, quite arduous but still self-guided trek to the top of the perfectly formed cone of Gunung Api (p435).

Papua

Trekking is the reason for many people to visit Papua.

Baliem Valley (p476) World-class trekking: great hiking in wonderful mountain scenery among friendly, traditional people. It's possible to sleep most nights in villages; some simpler routes don't require guides or porters.

Korowai Region (p484) Tough jungle trekking in an area populated by ex-headhunters who live in tree houses. You'll need a well-organised, expensive guided trip.

Sumatra

Unsurprisingly, this vast island offers a huge range of overland adventures.

Mentawai Islands (p541) There is still dense, untouched jungle here that you can penetrate by longboat on river journeys. Local guides will take you to their isolated abodes.

TREKKING: WHAT TO PACK

It's worth investigating the availability and quality of gear provided by guides before packing.

- ☐ Sleeping bag
- ☐ Tent if you are overnighting outside villages
- ☐ Torch (flashlight)
- ☐ Footwear with good grip for slippery and/or steep trails (both boots and trekking sandals)
- ☐ Mosquito net for some areas (not usually needed at 1500m-plus altitudes)
- ☐ Warm clothes for higher altitude treks: a jumper/sweater and long trousers for nights above 1500m altitude, several layers for altitudes above 2500m
- ☐ Rain gear for any time of year
- ☐ GPS-equipped mobile phone
- ☐ Map and compass
- ☐ Plenty of small-denomination banknotes (up to 20,000Rp) when trekking to remote areas and small villages

RESPONSIBLE TREKKING

To help preserve the ecology and beauty of Indonesia, consider the following tips when enjoying the land. (You may need to convince your guide to also follow these.)

Rubbish

» Carry out all your rubbish and make an effort to carry out rubbish left by others.

» Never bury your rubbish: it can take years to decompose and digging encourages erosion. Buried rubbish will likely be dug up by animals, who may be injured or poisoned by it.

» Minimise waste by taking minimal packaging and no more food than you will need. Take reusable containers or stuff sacks.

» Sanitary napkins, tampons, condoms and toilet paper should be carried out despite the inconvenience. They burn and decompose poorly.

Human-Waste Disposal

» Contamination of water sources by human faeces is a major source of pollution. Where there is no toilet, dig a small hole 15cm (6in) deep and at least 100m (320ft) from any watercourse. Cover the waste with soil and a rock.

Washing

» Don't use detergents or toothpaste in or near watercourses, even if they are biodegradable.

» For personal washing, use biodegradable soap and a water container (or even a lightweight, portable basin) at least 50m (160ft) away from any watercourse.

Berastagi (p500) A cool retreat from steamy Medan. Easy treks include volcanoes.

Bukittinggi (p545) You can meander through tiny villages or head off into the jungle for the three-day trek to Danau Maninjau (p553).

Kerinci Seblat National Park (p557) Dense rainforest, high mountains and rare animals such as rhinos are the highlights of treks through Sumatra's largest park.

Kalimantan

The jungles of Borneo remain seemingly impenetrable in vast areas and that's all the more reason for intrepid trekkers to set out.

Cross-Borneo Trek (p587) The uber-choice of Kalimantan treks is best undertaken by contacting either De'Gigant Tours (p593) in Samarinda or Kompakh (p617) in Putussibau and going from there. No one should try to organise it by themselves.

Loksado (p631) A real-life adventure park with dozens of rope and bamboo bridges across streams amidst thick jungle.

Wehea Forest (p605) Difficult to get to even by local standards, but the choice for serious eco-tourists who want virgin primary forest.

Sulawesi

The region around Tana Toraja could occupy months of trekking.

Tana Toraja (p658) Beautiful valleys and fascinating Torajan architecture and culture are highlights. Shorter treks can be done solo but there are no good maps, only spotty public transport, and it's easy to get lost. Good guides are readily available in Rantepao.

Mamasa (p664) West of Tana Toraja but with a different culture, this is where you'll be less likely to see other travellers. The 59-km trek linking Tana Toraja and Mamasa is a three-day treat.

Safe Trekking

Before embarking on a trekking trip, consider the following points to ensure a safe and enjoyable experience.

» Pay any fees and obtain any permits required by local authorities.

» Be sure you are healthy and feel comfortable walking for a sustained period.

» Obtain reliable information about physical and environmental conditions along your intended route.

» Wash cooking utensils 50m (160ft) from watercourses using a scourer instead of detergent.

Erosion

» Stick to existing tracks.

» If a track passes through a mud patch, walk through the patch so as not to increase its size.

» Avoid removing the plant life that keeps topsoils in place.

Fires & Low-Impact Cooking

» Don't depend on open fires for cooking. The cutting of wood for fires in popular trekking areas can cause rapid deforestation. Cook on a lightweight kerosene, alcohol or Shellite (white gas) stove and avoid those powered by disposable butane gas canisters.

» Fires may be acceptable below the tree line in areas that get very few visitors. If you light a fire, use an existing fireplace. Use only minimal, dead, fallen wood.

» Fully extinguish a fire after use.

Wildlife Conservation

» Do not engage in or encourage hunting. Indonesia is full of endangered critters, which need all the help they can get to survive.

» Don't buy items made from endangered species.

» Do not feed the wildlife (or leave scraps behind). It can make them dependent on handouts or seriously ill.

» Be aware of local laws, regulations and etiquette about wildlife and the environment.

» Walk only in regions and on trails/tracks within your realm of experience.

» Be aware that weather conditions and terrain vary significantly from one region, or even from one trail/track, to another. Seasonal changes and sudden weather shifts can significantly alter any trail/track. These differences influence what to wear and what equipment to carry.

» Ask before you set out about the environmental characteristics that can affect your walk and how local, experienced walkers deal with these considerations.

» Strongly consider hiring a guide. There are often good ones available in Indonesia who have invaluable local knowledge, eg trails are often poorly maintained or hard to discern.

Guides

A guide can make or break a trip. Some travellers report disappointing trips with cheap guides, but high fees alone don't guarantee satisfaction. Here are some tips for choosing one.

» Meet the guide before finalising any trip. (If you're dealing with a tour agency, insist on meeting the guide you'll travel with, not the head of the agency.)

» Quiz the guide about the itinerary. That can begin by email or telephone, also providing a sample of their ability in your language. (Be aware that guides using email may have a helper handling that correspondence.) The guide should be able to tell you which transport options are best for you and why. Listen to their ideas, and see if they listen to yours.

» The guide should inform you of local festivals and other events worth a detour or longer stay, and weather or travel conditions that may impact your plans.

» Guides usually offer package prices and should be able to roughly itemise trip costs. Be clear on what's included in the package, particularly regarding transport and food. Fixed expenses such as transport and the guide's lodging and food mean you'll get a better per-person price if you travel in a group of two or more.

» Some guides offer the option of charging you only their fee (250,000Rp to 600,000Rp per day) while you pay other expenses directly; good guides will get you the local price, or close to it.

» Find out what you'll need from the guide, such as water.

» For ambitious treks in places like Papua, you may need to hire porters to help carry your food and water, in addition to a guide.

Mountain Climbing

Indonesia has some very challenging climbs. Assaults on some of its highest peaks will require significant preparation as climbing infrastructure is sparse.

Papua

Climbing Papua's high peaks such as Carstensz Pyramid (Puncak Jaya) – the highest mountain in Indonesia and in all of Oceania – and Gunung Trikora requires hard-to-get permits and reliable, experienced local guides. Needs to be organised through specialist agencies (p449).

Sumatra

Rock climbing is popular locally and guides can be arranged in the Harau Valley (p553) and around Bukittinggi (p547). Gear is provided, but serious climbers will want to bring their own gear for more challenging and technical ascents.

Kalimantan

Mt Besar (p631) in the Meratus is accessed via a week-long hike from Loksado. Choose one of the trekking guides in Loksado or Banjarmasin.

Watching Wildlife

Indonesia's wildlife is as diverse as everything else about the archipelago. Great apes, tigers, elephants and monkeys – lots of monkeys – plus one mean lizard are just some of the more notable critters you may encounter.

Java

All the wildlife isn't in the clubs of Jakarta; the national parks have a huge range of animals and birds – and usually guides ready to lead you.

Ujung Kulon National Park (p75) Extremely rare one-horned Javan rhinoceros and panthers live amongst the Unesco-listed rainforest.

Alas Purwo National Park (p192) Various deer, peacocks and even a leopard or two may be spotted.

Baluran National Park (p195) Go on African-style excursions in 4WD vehicles to spot wild oxen and other large animals amidst natural grasslands.

Meru Betiri National Park (p192) A vast range of wildlife including leopards and the intriguing giant squirrel.

Nusa Tenggara

This vast collection of islands has one real star: Komodo National Park (p348). First and foremost is the area's namesake endemic species: the Komodo dragon. But there are slow screeching flocks of flying foxes roosting on mangrove islands in the park – and in the Seventeen Islands Marine Park (p361) near Riung – as well as barking deer, wild water buffalo and rich birdlife.

Maluku

Maluku remains a relatively untapped birder paradise. It's worth the effort and cash to access the national parks of Seram and Halmahera.

Aketajawe & Lolobata National Parks (p414) You can stalk Wallace's Standard Winged Bird of Paradise in these Eastern Halmahera reserves.

Papua

Birds of paradise and other birds – Papua is fantastic birding territory. It's hard to find other Papuan wildlife including exotic marsupials such as tree kangaroos, cuscus and sugar gliders, though some expert local guides can help.

Raja Ampat Islands (p454) Birds of paradise and many other species cause birdwatchers to flock here.

Pegunungan Arfak (p459) Thickly forested mountains hide all manner of birds.

Wasur National Park (p483) It's fairly easy to spot wallabies and deer here.

Danau Habbema (p481) Cuscus, birds of paradise and maybe tree kangaroos are found near this isolated lake.

Sumatra

Large mammals like elephants and orangutans have homes amidst the still untrodden tracts of wilderness here.

Gunung Leuser National Park (p530) Famous for orangutans but also home to monkeys, elephants and tigers.

Kerinci Seblat National Park (p557) Birds abound and in the seldom-visited Ladeh Panjang region there's even a form of bear.

Way Kambas National Park (p579) Elephant-watching and birdwatching trips can be arranged in Jakarta.

Kalimantan

Kalimantan is mostly about jungle river trips to experience wildlife such as orangutans and the myriad local cultures.

Tanjung Puting National Park (p619) The top site in Kalimantan can be reached by the Kahayan, Rungan and Sekonyer rivers. The orangutan spotting is superb but you'll also see all manner of birds and reptiles. Boating options include the luxurious *Rahai'i Pangun* (p626).

Sungai Kapuas (p617) Voyage from Pontianak to Sukadana by longboat.

Sulawesi

Tarsiers, a bizarre-looking nocturnal monkey with enormous eyes, are all the rage among Sulawesi wildlife spotters.

Tangkoko-Batuangas Dua Saudara Nature Reserve (p689) Your best bet to see tarsiers is here with a guide.

Lore Lindu National Park (p668) Tarsiers, birds of paradise, monkeys and more are found in this protected area.

regions at a glance

Indonesia's 17,000 islands are dominated by a few large ones. Sumatra, Java and Sulawesi are diverse places that have swaths of untouched lands. Kalimantan and Papua are part of even larger islands and offer plenty of opportunity for serious adventure and exploration. Java remains the heart of the country historically, culturally and economically. Nusa Tenggara and Maluku comprise hundreds of islands from ever-more-popular Lombok to the relative isolation of the Banda Islands. Although small in size, Bali figures large for visitors, drawing half of Indonesia's tourists. As always, your biggest consideration will be managing the time on your visa.

Java

Culture ✓✓
Volcanoes ✓✓✓
Temples ✓✓✓

Javanese culture fuses animist, Buddhist and Hindu influences with both mystic traditions and orthodox Islamic practices. Monuments, mosques and temples that reflect this spiritual complexity exist alongside a spectacular tropical landscape spiked with smoking volcanoes.

p44

Bali

Culture ✓✓✓
Nightlife ✓✓✓
Surfing ✓✓✓

The rich culture of Bali is matched by its myriad attractions for visitors: excellent dining and nightlife, hundreds of good places to stay, famous beaches, epic surfing, alluring shopping and a gracious welcome.

p197

Nusa Tenggara

Surfing ✓✓✓
Diving ✓✓
Culture ✓✓

Whether you're here for waves, or to dive deep underwater or into local culture, Nusa Tenggara offers gifts unmatched. From Lombok to Timor you will be tempted, blessed, satiated and leave hungry for more.

p298

Maluku

Diving ✓✓
Culture ✓✓
Beaches ✓✓

Only comparative inaccessibility keeps this stunning, spicy region from getting the visitors and notoriety it deserves. Malukan culture and natural beauty is palpable from Ternate all the way to the Kei Islands.

p401

Papua

Diving ✓✓✓
Trekking ✓✓✓
Tribal Culture ✓✓

Remote Papua is an adventurer's fantasy. From high-mountain valleys and snaking jungle rivers to translucent coastal waters teeming with life, it offers superb trekking and world-class diving among proud indigenous peoples whose traditions stand strong.

p444

Sumatra

Wildlife ✓✓
Trekking ✓✓
Surfing ✓✓✓

Sumatra is one big, steamy, jungle-draped adventure where you can go from surfing the best waves on the planet to hacking your way through dense rainforest in a search for ginger-tinged orangutans.

p485

Kalimantan

River Trekking ✓✓✓
Diving ✓✓
Wildlife ✓✓✓

Cut by countless rivers, Borneo's legendary jungle attracts the hardened trekker, the wildlife spotter and the pure adventurer alike, while the pristine underwater world of the Derawan Archipelago draws in-the-know divers.

p583

Sulawesi

Culture ✓✓✓
Diving ✓✓
Trekking ✓✓

Wind your way through this crazy-shaped island of elaborate funeral ceremonies, trails through terraced rice fields and tarsier-filled jungles to coasts of abundant corals, thriving underwater fauna and cultures that revolve around the sea.

p633

❯ **Every listing is recommended by our authors, and their favourite places are listed first**

❯ **Look out for these icons:**

 Our author's top recommendation
 A green or sustainable option
 No payment required

See the Index for a full list of destinations covered in this book.

On the Road

Java

Includes »

Best Places to Eat

- Lara Djonggrang (p62)
- Pasar Ikan, Pangandaran (p98)
- Via Via (p123)
- Ikan Bakar Cianjur (p148)
- Kiosk (p89)

Best Places to Stay

- Tugu Malang (p174)
- d'Omah (p122)
- Roemahkoe (p139)
- Kemang Icon (p61)
- Kampong Tourist (p174)

Why Go?

The heart of the nation, Java is an island of megacities, mesmerising natural beauty, and profound traditions in art, dance, spiritualism and learning.

Boasting a dazzling array of bewitching landscapes – iridescent rice paddies, smoking volcanoes, rainforest and savannah – most journeys here are defined by scenic excesses.

Java's fecund interior is one of the most fertile and heavily populated places on planet earth. Generally the cities are pretty uninspiring, though they do boast the best restaurants and art and music scenes.

Transport can be challenging at times. By road it can be slow going, particularly in the west of the island. However, the rail network is generally reliable and efficient, and flights are inexpensive.

Java is the most complex and culturally compelling island in Indonesia. Invest some time here and you've made a giant leap to understanding this utterly fascinating nation.

When to Go

Jakarta

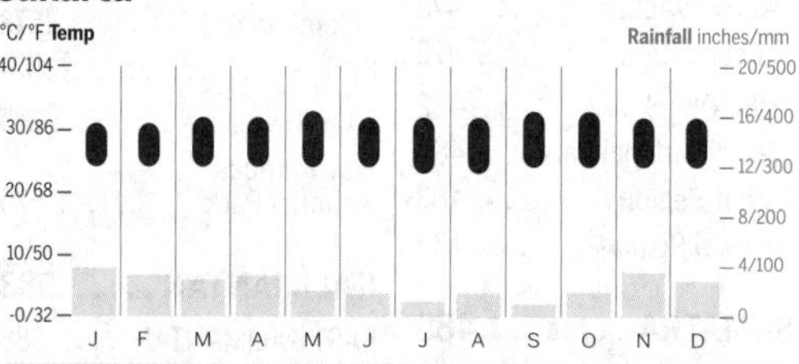

May Spectacular Waisak processions to mark the birth of Buddha in Borobudur.

Jun Perhaps the perfect month for travel, with clear skies and few crowds.

Oct The climax of the bull-racing season in Madura.

Java Highlights

1 Experiencing the ethereal beauty of **Borobudur** (p109) temple at sunrise

2 Gazing over the horizon-filling moonscape scenery at **Gunung Bromo** (p185)

3 Hiking to the crater lake of **Kawah Ijen** (p190) with strong-armed sulphur miners

4 Time travelling to Java's golden age in the cultural capital of **Yogyakarta** (p113)

5 Exploring magnificent national parks: **Ujung Kulon** (p75), **Meru Betiri** (p192), **Alas Purwo** (p193) and **Baluran** (p195)

6 Meeting the locals via a community tourism project in **Cianjur** (p85) or **Borobudur village** (p112)

7 Getting off the road and experiencing the palm-fringed **Karimunjawa Islands** (p156)

8 Surfing, or learn to surf Java's legendary waves at **Cimaja** (p82), **Batu Karas** (p100) or **G-Land** (p193)

History

Java has a history of epic proportions and a record of human habitation that extends back 1.7 million years to when 'Java Man' roamed the river banks. Waves of migrants followed, moving down through Southeast Asia.

EARLY JAVANESE KINGDOMS

Blessed with exceptional fertility from its mineral-rich volcanic soil, Java has long played host to intensive *sawah* (wet rice) agriculture.

Small principalities emerged, including the Hindu Mataram dynasty, in the 8th century, with worship centred on the god Shiva. Hinduism coexisted with Buddhism for centuries, and the massive Hindu Prambanan complex was constructed within a century of Borobudur, the world's biggest Buddhist monument.

Mataram eventually fell, perhaps at the hands of the Sumatra-based Sriwijaya kingdom. The Javanese revival began in AD 1019 under King Airlangga, a semi-legendary figure who formed the first royal link with Bali.

Early in the 13th century the legendary Ken Angrok briefly succeeded in uniting much of Central and East Java, and Javanese culture flourished brightly.

With the emergence of the much-celebrated Majapahit kingdom, ruling from Trowulan, came the first Javanese commercial kingdom. The kingdom traded with China and most of Southeast Asia, and grew to claim sovereignty over the entire Indonesian archipelago.

ISLAMIC KINGDOMS

Islamic influence grew in Java in the 15th and 16th centuries, and Muslim military incursions into East Java forced many Hindu-Buddhists eastwards to Bali. By the 17th century, the Muslim kingdoms of Mataram and Banten were the only two powers in Java left to face the arrival of the Dutch.

DUTCH PERIOD

As the Dutch set up camp in Batavia (Jakarta), Banten remained a powerful force, but civil war within the royal house led to its eventual collapse.

JAVA MAN

Charles Darwin's *On the Origin of Species* (1859) spawned a new generation of naturalists in the 19th century, and his theories sparked acrimonious debate across the world. Ernst Haeckel's *The History of Natural Creation* (1874) expounded Darwin's theory of evolution and surmised that primitive humans had evolved from a common ape-man ancestor, the famous 'missing link'.

One student of the new theories, Dutch physician Eugene Dubois, went to Java in 1889 after hearing of the uncovering of a skull at Wajak, near Tulung Agung in East Java. Dubois worked at the dig, uncovering other fossils closely related to modern humans. In 1891 at Trinil in East Java's Ngawi district, Dubois unearthed an older skullcap, along with a femur and three teeth he later classified as originating from *Pithecanthropus erectus*, a low-browed, prominent-jawed early human ancestor, dating from the Middle Pleistocene epoch. His published findings of 'Java Man' caused such a storm in Europe that Dubois buried his discovery for 30 years.

Since Dubois' findings, many older examples of *Homo erectus* (the name subsequently given to *Pithecanthropus erectus*) have been uncovered in Java. The most important and most numerous findings have been at Sangiran, where in the 1930s Ralph von Koenigswald found fossils dating back to around one million BC. In 1936, at Perning near Mojokerto, the skull of a child was discovered and was purported to be even older. Most findings have been along Sungai Bengawan Solo in Central and East Java.

Geochronologists have now dated the bones of Java's oldest *Homo erectus* specimens at 1.7 million years, but also postulate that the youngest fossils may be less than 40,000 years old. This means that *Homo erectus* existed in Java at the same time as *Homo sapiens*, who arrived on the island some 60,000 years ago, and reignites the debate about whether humankind evolved in Africa and migrated from there, or whether humans evolved on several continents concurrently. Those interested in learning more should pick up a copy of Carl Swisher, Garniss Curtis and Roger Lewin's extremely readable book *Java Man*.

The Mataram dynasty also became plagued by infighting, and following three Javanese Wars of Succession, the last in 1746, the Dutch split the kingdom, creating the royal houses of Solo and Yogyakarta.

Resistance to Dutch influence continued, erupting in the anti-Dutch Java War of 1825–30, but the colonists defeated the revolts and subsequently Javanese courts became little more than ritual establishments, overseen by a Dutch *residen* (governor).

JAVA TODAY

Java still rules the roost when it comes to political and economic life in Indonesia. It has the bulk of the country's industry, is easily its most developed island, and has over the years received the lion's share of foreign investment.

The economic crisis of the late '90s hit hard, when huge numbers of urban workers lost their jobs and rioters targeted Chinese communities. But Java bounced back relatively quickly, and enjoyed a period of comparative stability and growing prosperity in the early 21st century. Glittering shopping malls and a boom in tech-business are the most obvious signs of Java's steady (if unspectacular) modernisation.

Bali apart, Java is the most outward-looking island in Indonesia, and its literate, educated population is the most closely connected to the rest of the world. Extraneous influences matter here, and Java is the most Westernised island in the country and also the corner of the nation most influenced by radical pan-Islamic ideology. Whilst most Javanese are moderate Muslims, there's an increasingly vocal conservative population (as well as tiny numbers of fanatics prepared to cause death and destruction in the name of *jihad*). The Bali bombers all came from Java, and Java-based terrorists targeted foreign investments in Jakarta in 2003 and 2004, as well as several international hotels in 2009.

But when it comes to the ballot box, the Javanese as a whole have consistently favoured secular rather then religious political parties: in the 2009 elections Islamist parties saw their share of the vote drop slightly.

Today Java can look to the future with some optimism. Its people are increasingly prosperous and cosmopolitan (thanks to an upsurge in foreign travel). But as the island develops at pace, pressing environmental issues (including pollution and the floods that threaten Jakarta most years) are an increasing threat. Infrastructure woes – inadequate highways and a lack of investment in train and metro networks – also hamper growth.

Culture

Javanese culture is an exotic and incredibly rich mix of customs that date back to animist beliefs and Hindu times. Ancient practices are fused with endemic Muslim traditions, which retain mystical Sufi elements beneath a more obvious orthodox and conservative Islamic culture.

The Javanese cosmos is composed of different levels of belief stemming from older and more accommodating mysticism, the Hindu court culture and a very real belief in ghosts and numerous benevolent and malevolent spirits. Underneath the unifying code of Islam, magic power is concentrated in amulets and heirlooms (especially the Javanese dagger known as the kris), in parts of the human body, such as the nails and the hair, and in sacred musical instruments. The *dukun* (faith healer and herbal doctor or mystic) is still consulted when illness strikes. *Jamu* (traditional medicine) potions are widely taken to do everything from boost libido to cure asthma.

Refinement and politeness are highly regarded, and loud displays of emotion, coarseness, vulgarity and flamboyant behaviour are considered *kasar* (bad manners; coarse). *Halus* (refined) Javanese is part of the Hindu court tradition, which still exists in the heartland of Central Java. In contrast to Islam, the court tradition has a hierarchical world view, based on privilege and often guided by the gods or nature spirits.

Indirectness is a Javanese trait that stems from an unwillingness to make others feel uncomfortable. It is impolite to point out mistakes and sensitivities, or to directly criticise authority.

Java has three main ethnic groups, each speaking their own language: the Javanese of Central and East Java (where *halus* is taken very seriously); the Sundanese of West Java; and the Madurese from Pulau Madura (who have a reputation for blunt-speaking and informality). Small pockets of Hindus remain, including the Tenggerese of the Bromo area and the Badui of West Java, whose religion retains many animist beliefs. Even metropolitan Jakarta identifies its own polyglot tradition in the Betawi, the name for the original inhabitants of the city.

TOP FIVE READS

Armchair travellers and those who like to read up on background knowledge before travelling should consider picking up one or more of the following:

» Andrew Beatty's *A Shadow Falls: In the Heart of Java*. Based on sustained research in a remote Javanese village, this examines the cultural conflict between mystic Javanese traditionalists and orthodox Islam.

» *Jakarta Inside Out* by Daniel Ziv. A collection of humorous short stories tackling the vibrant underbelly of Indonesia's capital.

» *The Religion of Java* by Clifford Geertz. A classic book on Javanese religion, culture and values. It's slightly dated (it was based on research done in the 1950s) but is nonetheless fascinating reading.

» *Javanese Culture* by Koentjaraningrat. One of the most comprehensive studies of Javanese society, history, culture and beliefs. This excellent reference book covers everything from Javanese toilet training to kinship lines.

» *Raffles and the British Invasion of Java* by Tim Hannigan. An excellent, authoritative account of the brief period of British rule, and the role of Raffles, in the early 19th century.

ℹ Getting There & Around

AIR Jakarta has numerous international and domestic connections. Other useful international gateway Javanese cities are Surabaya, Solo, Bandung, Yogyakarta and Semarang. Domestic flights can be very convenient and affordable: Jakarta–Yogyakarta is a very popular route. If your time is short, it's worth booking a few internal flights to cut down on those hours on the road.

SEA Very few travellers now use Pelni passenger ships, but there are connections between Jakarta and most ports in the nation. Ferries run round the clock between Banyuwangi/Ketapang harbour in East Java and Gilimanuk in Bali and also between the Javanese port of Merak and Bakauheni in southern Sumatra.

BUS Buses connect virtually anywhere and everywhere in Java, and also run to Sumatra, Bali (and even Nusa Tenggara). Unfortunately Java's road network is woefully inadequate, so journeys tend to be very slow and tiring, particularly in the west of the island.

TRAIN Java has a fairly punctual and efficient rail service running right across the island. Overall train travel certainly beats long bus journeys, so try to take as many as you can. You can check timetables and make online bookings at www.kereta-api.co.id, though it's not very user-friendly.

Unfortunately, network capacity (many of the lines are single tracks) is very limited and demand often exceeds supply. During holiday periods trains are always booked weeks or months ahead.

JAKARTA

☎021 / POP 10.1 MILLION

One of the world's greatest megalopolises, Jakarta is a dynamic city of daunting extremes that's developing at a pace that throws up challenges and surreal juxtapositions on every street corner.

The city is certainly no oil painting, yet beneath the unappealing facade of high-rises, relentless concrete and gridlocked streets, Jakarta has many faces and plenty of surprises. Its citizens are remarkably good-natured, optimistic and positive, and compared to many of the world's capitals, crime levels are very low.

From the steamy, richly scented streets of Chinatown to North Jakarta's riotous, decadent nightlife, the city is filled with unexpected corners. Here it's possible to rub shoulders with Indonesia's future leaders, artists, thinkers and movers and shakers in a bohemian cafe or a sleek lounge bar and then go clubbing till dawn (and beyond).

Jakarta certainly isn't a primary tourist destination, but parts of the atmospheric old city (Kota) offer an interesting insight into the capital's long history. There are a handful of good museums and dozens of swanky shopping malls.

A city in the fast lane, life is lived here at a headlong pace, driven by a surging economy and an industriousness and optimism that's palpable.

History

Jakarta's earliest history centres on the port of Sunda Kelapa, in the north of the modern city. When the Portuguese arrived it was a bustling port in the last Hindu kingdom of West Java, but they were driven out in 1527 and the city was renamed Jayakarta, meaning 'victorious city'.

DUTCH RULE

At the beginning of the 17th century the Dutch and English jostled for power in the region, with the Dutch prevailing. The city was renamed Batavia and made the capital of the Dutch East Indies, as Amsterdam-style houses and canals were constructed.

By 1740 ethnic unrest lead to the massacre of 5000 Chinese, and virtually the entire community was subsequently moved to Glodok, outside the city walls. Dutch colonial rule came to an end with the Japanese occupation in 1942 and the name Jakarta was restored.

POST INDEPENDENCE

Over the next four decades, the capital struggled under the weight of an ever-increasing population of poor migrants, but by the 1990s Jakarta's economic situation had turned around. This all changed, however, with the economic collapse of 1997. The capital quickly became a political battleground and the epicentre of protests demanding Suharto's resignation.

Jakarta erupted in rioting after the deaths of student protesters, as thousands took to the streets and looted malls. The Chinese were hardest hit, with shocking tales of rape and murder emerging after the riots.

CITY TODAY

In recent years Jakarta has suffered on several fronts. Severe floods (which strike every rainy season) cause massive damage to homes and infrastructure. Terrorists have targeted Western interests, bombing US-owned hotels and the Australian embassy.

Jakarta's public transport system remains hopelessly inefficient compared with many Chinese cities, Bangkok and Kuala Lumpur. Indeed it's said to be the largest city in the world with a metro train system. There's much to be done before Jakarta becomes a modern metropolis.

Sights

KOTA

The old town of Batavia, now known as Kota, was the hub of Dutch colonial Indonesia. Today it's a faded vision of a once-grand empire, replete with crumbling historic buildings and stinky canals.

However, in the last few years, the area has begun to re-emerge from decades of neglect. Kota's core has been pedestrianised, some structures have been renovated, and, vitally, locals have started to visit the area again in numbers. There's a long, long way to go, but slowly Kota is beginning to feel like the heart of the nation again as the presence of souvenir sellers, *kaki lima* (mobile food carts) and groups of domestic tourists give the area a vote of confidence and a degree of urban bustle.

Taman Fatahillah, Kota's central cobblestone square, is still an impressive sight, surrounded by imposing colonial buildings including the former town hall.

A block west of the square is **Kali Besar**, the great canal along Sungai Ciliwung, lined with once-grand homes of the wealthy, most built in the early 18th century. Check out the red-tiled facade of **Toko Merah** (Map p53; Jl Kali Besar Barat, Red Shop), the former home of Governor General van Imhoff. At the northern end of Kali Besar is the last remaining Dutch drawbridge, the **Chicken Market Bridge**, which dates from the 17th century.

To reach Taman Fatahillah, take the busway Korridor I from Blok M or Jl Thamrin to Kota train station and walk. Trains from Gondangdia, near Jl Jaksa, also run here.

JAVA AMBASSADORS

Several excellent new community tourism initiatives have recently emerged in Java, all run by passionate and committed young Javanese eager to show travellers the best of their island. There's no better way to get to grips with the zeitgeist of the world's most populous island than sharing a day or two (and a laugh) with a local. Alongside sightseeing, other possibilities include school visits, volunteer work opportunities, cooking classes and visits to home industries such as tofu kitchens.

In Cianjur, there's a great homestay program. Borobudur's Jaker community tourism network will enlighten you about life and customs in rural Java, while in nearby Yogyakarta, Inspirasi Indonesia is a well-informed bunch of young local guides.

Jakarta

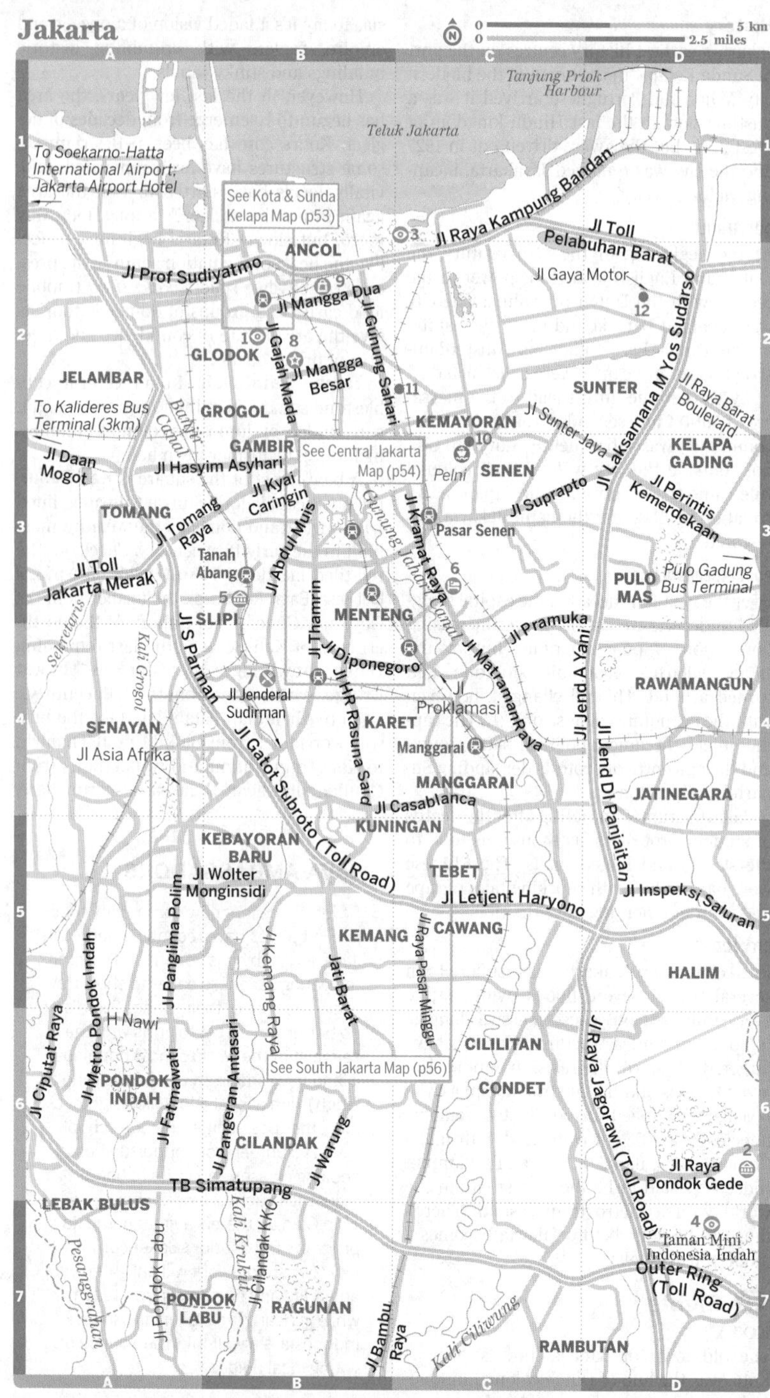

0 5 km
0 2.5 miles
Tanjung Priok Harbour
Teluk Jakarta
To Soekarno-Hatta International Airport; Jakarta Airport Hotel
See Kota & Sunda Kelapa Map (p53)
ANCOL
Jl Prof Sudiyatmo
Jl Raya Kampung Bandan
Jl Toll Pelabuhan Barat
Jl Gaya Motor
Jl Mangga Dua
Jl Gunung Sahari
Jl Gajah Mada
Jl Mangga Besar
GLODOK
JELAMBAR
GROGOL
To Kalideres Bus Terminal (3km)
Banjir Canal
Jl Daan Mogot
Jl Hasyim Asyhari
GAMBIR
See Central Jakarta Map (p54)
KEMAYORAN
Pelni
SENEN
SUNTER
Jl Sunter Jaya
Jl Laksamana M Yos Sudarso
Jl Raya Barat Boulevard
KELAPA GADING
Jl Perintis Kemerdekaan
Jl Suprapto
Pasar Senen
TOMANG
Jl Tomang Raya
Jl Kyai Caringin
Jl Abdul Muis
Gunung Jahat Canal
Jl Kramat Raya
Tanah Abang
Jl Toll Jakarta Merak
PULO MAS
Pulo Gadung Bus Terminal
SLIPI
Jl Thamrin
MENTENG
Jl Pramuka
Sekretaris
Kali Grogol
Jl S Parman
Jl Diponegoro
Jl Matraman Raya
Jl Jend A Yani
RAWAMANGUN
Jl Jenderal Sudirman
Jl HR Rasuna Said
KARET
Jl Proklamasi
Manggarai
SENAYAN
Jl Asia Afrika
Jl Gatot Subroto (Toll Road)
MANGGARAI
Jl Jend DI Panjaitan
JATINEGARA
Jl Casablanca
KUNINGAN
KEBAYORAN BARU
Jl Wolter Monginsidi
TEBET
Jl Letjent Haryono
Jl Inspeksi Saluran
Jl Panglima Polim
Jl Kemang Raya
KEMANG
Jl Raya Pasar Minggu
CAWANG
HALIM
Jl Metro Pondok Indah
Jati Barat
Jl Ciputat Raya
H Nawi
Jl Pangeran Antasari
CILILITAN
Jl Raya Jagorawi (Toll Road)
See South Jakarta Map (p56)
PONDOK INDAH
CONDET
Jl Fatmawati
CILANDAK
Jl Warung
Jl Raya Pondok Gede
TB Simatupang
LEBAK BULUS
Kali Krukut
Jl Cilandak KKO
Pesanggrahan
Taman Mini Indonesia Indah
Outer Ring (Toll Road)
Jl Pondok Labu
PONDOK LABU
RAGUNAN
Jl Bambu Raya
Kali Ciliwung
RAMBUTAN

Jakarta

Sights
Dunia Fantasi (see 3)
1 Jin de Yuan B2
2 Museum Pancasila Sakti D6
Seaworld (see 3)
3 Taman Impian Jaya Ancol C1
4 Taman Mini Indonesia Indah D7
5 Textile Museum B3

Sleeping
6 Amaris Hotel Senen C3

Eating
7 Cassius B4

Entertainment
8 Stadium B2

Shopping
9 Mangga Dua Mall B2
Pasar Pagi Mangga Dua (see 9)

Transport
Ancol Marina (see 3)
10 Merpati C3
11 Sriwijaya Air C2
12 Trac Astra D2

A taxi will cost around 35,000Rp from Jl Thamrin.

FREE **Museum Bank Indonesia** MUSEUM
(Map p53; Pintu Besar Utara III; ⌚8.30am-2.30pm Tue-Thu, to 11am Fri, 9am-4pm Sat & Sun) One of the nation's best, this museum is dedicated to the history of Indonesia from a loosely financial perspective, in a grand, expertly restored, neo-classical former bank headquarters that dates from the early 20th century. All the displays (including lots of zany audio-visuals) are slickly presented and engaging, with exhibits about the spice trade, the financial meltdown of 1997 (and subsequent riots) and a gallery dedicated to currency, with notes from virtually every country in the world.

Museum Sejarah Jakarta MUSEUM
(Map p53; Taman Fatahillah; admission 2000Rp; ⌚8am-3pm Tue-Sun) The Jakarta History Museum is housed in the old town hall of Batavia, a stately Dutch colonial structure that was once the epicentre of an empire. This bell-towered building, built in 1627, served the administration of the city and was also used by the city law courts.

Today it's a poorly presented museum of peeling plasterwork and lots of heavy, carved ebony and teak furniture from the Dutch period (plus a disparate collection of exhibits collected from across the nation). But you will find the odd exquisite piece, such as the stunning black granite sculpture of Kali, a Hindu goddess associated with death and destruction.

In the back courtyard is the huge bronze **Cannon Si Jagur**. This cannon tapers at one end into a large clenched fist, a sexual symbol in Indonesia; childless women would offer flowers and sit astride the cannon in the hope of becoming mothers.

There are long-standing plans to renovate the museum, but work had been delayed at the time of research.

Museum Wayang MUSEUM
(Map p53; ☎692 9560; Taman Fatahillah; admission 2000Rp; ⌚8am-3pm Tue-Sun) This puppet museum has one of the best collections of *wayang* puppets in Java and its dusty cabinets are full of a multitude of characters from across Indonesia, as well as China, Vietnam, India, Cambodia and Europe. The building itself dates from 1912. There are free *wayang* performances here on Sunday at 10am.

Be warned that we have received reports of a scam involving freelance guides at this museum, who pressure you into making exorbitant purchases after offering a tour of the exhibits.

Museum Bank Mandiri MUSEUM
(Map p53; Jl Pintu Besar Utara; ⌚9am-4pm Tue-Sun) In complete contrast to the polish and modernity at the Museum Bank Indonesia next door, this banking museum is all but empty, with echoing corridors and deserted tills. Nevertheless it's fascinating to explore the interior of this fine art deco structure, marvelling at the marble counters and vintage counting machines, abacuses and colossal cast-iron safes.

Balai Seni Rupa MUSEUM
(Map p53; Taman Fatahillah; admission 2000Rp; ⌚8am-2.30pm Tue-Sun) Built between 1866 and 1870, the former Palace of Justice building

is now a Fine Arts Museum. It houses contemporary paintings with works by prominent artists, including Affandi, Raden Saleh and Ida Bagus Made. Part of the building is also a ceramics museum, with Chinese ceramics and Majapahit terracottas.

Gereja Sion CHURCH
(Map p53; Jl Pangeran Jayakarta) Dating from 1695, this is the oldest remaining church in Jakarta. Also known as Gereja Portugis (Portuguese Church), it was built just outside the old city walls for slaves captured from Portuguese trading ports. The exterior of the church is very plain, but inside there are copper chandeliers, a baroque pulpit and the original organ.

SUNDA KELAPA

A kilometre north of Taman Fatahillah, the old port of **Sunda Kelapa** (admission 2000Rp) is full of magnificent Makassar schooners *(pinisi)*. The dock scene here has barely changed for centuries, with porters unloading cargo from these sailing ships by hand and trolley, though it's far less busy today. Sadly, the port itself is rundown and its waters polluted.

Museum Bahari MUSEUM
(Map p53; ☎669 3406; www.museumbahari.org; admission 2000Rp; ⊙9am-3pm Tue-Sun) Near the entrance to Sunda Kelapa, several old VOC warehouses (dating back to 1652) have been converted into the Museum Bahari. This is a good place to learn about the city's maritime history, and though the wonderful old buildings (some renovated) are echoingly empty there are some good information panels (in English and Bahasa Indonesia). Under the heavy wooden beams of the vast old storage premises are various random exhibits: a sextant (used for astronomical navigation), various traditional boats from around Indonesia, the shell of a giant clam, plenty of pickled fish and a lighthouse lamp or two. The sentry posts outside are part of the old city wall.

Watchtower HISTORIC BUILDING
(Map p53; admission 5000Rp) Just before the entrance to the museum is a watchtower, built in 1839 to sight and direct traffic to the port. There are good views over the harbour, but opening hours are haphazard – ask for the caretaker if it is closed.

Pasar Ikan MARKET
(Market; Map p53) Further along the same street from the museum is the early-morning Pasar Ikan, or fish market. It's an intense, colourful scene of busy crowds around dawn, when the day's catch is sold. Later in the day you'll find souvenir sellers here.

GLODOK

The neighbourhood of Glodok, the traditional enclave of the Chinese, is an archetypical downtown district full of bustling lanes, street markets, a shabby mall or two and some of the world's most decadent nightlife. It was also the site of the terrible riots of May and November 1998, which reduced huge swaths of the area to ash and rubble.

Most of the fun here is simply experiencing the (very) Chinese vibe of the place, eating some dumplings and browsing the myriad stalls and stores selling everything from traditional medicines to dodgy DVDs.

Jin de Yuan TEMPLE
(Dharma Bhakti Temple; Map p50; www.jindeyuan.org; Jl Kemenangan III 13) A few steps from the Petak Sembilan street market is the large Chinese Buddhist temple compound of Jin de Yuan, which dates from 1755 and is one of the most important in the city. The main structure has an unusual roof crowned by two dragons eating pearls, while the interior is richly atmospheric: dense incense and candle smoke clouding the Buddha statues, ancient bells and drums, and there's some wonderful calligraphy.

Petak Sembilan Street Market MARKET
(Map p53) Be sure to wander down the impossibly narrow Petak Sembilan street market off Jl Pancoran, lined with crooked houses with red-tiled roofs. It's a total assault on the senses, with skinned frogs and live bugs for sale next to an open sewer.

CENTRAL JAKARTA

If a centre for this sprawling city had to be chosen, then **Merdeka Square** (Lapangan Merdeka) would be it. This huge grassy expanse is home to Sukarno's monument to the nation, and is surrounded by a couple of museums and some fine colonial buildings.

Museum Nasional MUSEUM
(☎381 1551; www.museumnasional.org; Jl Merdeka Barat; adult/child 750/250Rp; ⊙8am-4.30pm Tue-Sat) On the western side of Merdeka Sq, the National Museum, built in 1862, is the best of its kind in Indonesia and is the one museum in the city that's an essential visit. A very impressive modern wing was

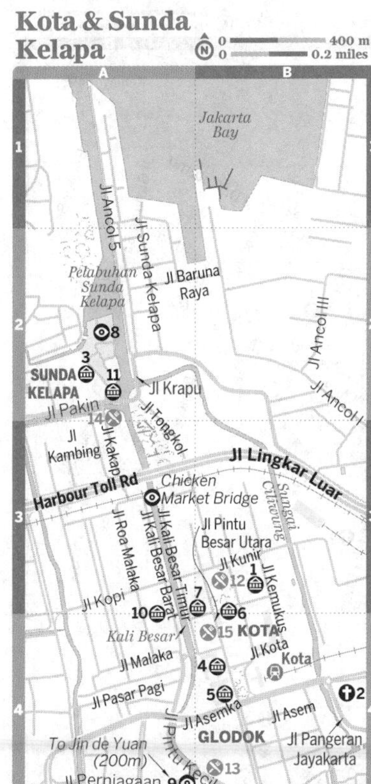

added on the north side of the neo-classical colonial structure in 2007. No photographs are allowed.

The museum has an enormous collection. Around the open courtyard is some magnificent statuary including a colossal 4.5m stone image of a Bhairawa king from Rambahan in Sumatra, who is shown trampling on human skulls. The ethnology section is superb, with Dayak puppets and wooden statues from Nias bearing beards (a sign of wisdom) plus some fascinating textiles.

Over in the spacious new wing there are four floors with sections devoted to the origin of mankind in Indonesia, including a model of the Flores 'hobbit'. There's also a superb display of gold treasures from Candi Brahu in Central Java, including some glittering necklaces, armbands and a bowl depicting scenes from the Ramayana.

The Indonesian Heritage Society (p58) organises free English tours of the National Museum, at 10:30am on Tuesdays, and on Thursdays at 10:30am and 1:30pm. Tours are also available at other times, and in French, Japanese and Korean; consult the website for the latest schedule.

Kota & Sunda Kelapa

Sights

1	Balai Seni Rupa	B3
2	Gereja Sion	B4
3	Museum Bahari	A2
4	Museum Bank Indonesia	B4
5	Museum Bank Mandiri	B4
6	Museum Sejarah Jakarta	B3
7	Museum Wayang	B3
8	Pasar Ikan	A2
9	Petak Sembilan Street Market	A4
10	Toko Merah	A4
11	Watchtower	A2

Eating

12	Café Batavia	B3
13	Santong Kuo Tieh 68	B4
14	VOC Galangan	A2
15	Warung Kota Tua	B4

Drinking

Café Batavia	(see 12)

Lapangan Banteng NEIGHBOURHOOD

(Map p54; Banteng Sq) Just east of Merdeka Sq, Lapangan Banteng has some of Jakarta's best colonial architecture.

The **Catholic cathedral** (Map p54; in Lapangan Banteng) has twin spires and was built in 1901 to replace an earlier church. Facing the cathedral is Jakarta's principal place of Muslim worship, the striking, modernist **Mesjid Istiqlal** (Map p54; Jl Veteran I), which was completed in 1978 to a design by Catholic architect Frederich Silaban. The mosque has five levels, representing the five pillars of Islam; its dome is 45m across and its minaret tops 90m. During Ramadan more than 200,000 worshippers can be accommodated here. Non-Muslim visitors are welcome. You have to sign in first and then you'll be shown around by an English-speaking guide (who will expect a tip).

To the east of Lapangan Banteng is the **Mahkamah Agung** (Supreme Court; Map p54), built in 1848, and next door is the colonial **Ministry of Finance Building** (Map p54; off Jl Dr Wahidin), formerly the Witte Huis (White House) which dates from 1809 and was the administrative centre for the Dutch.

Central Jakarta

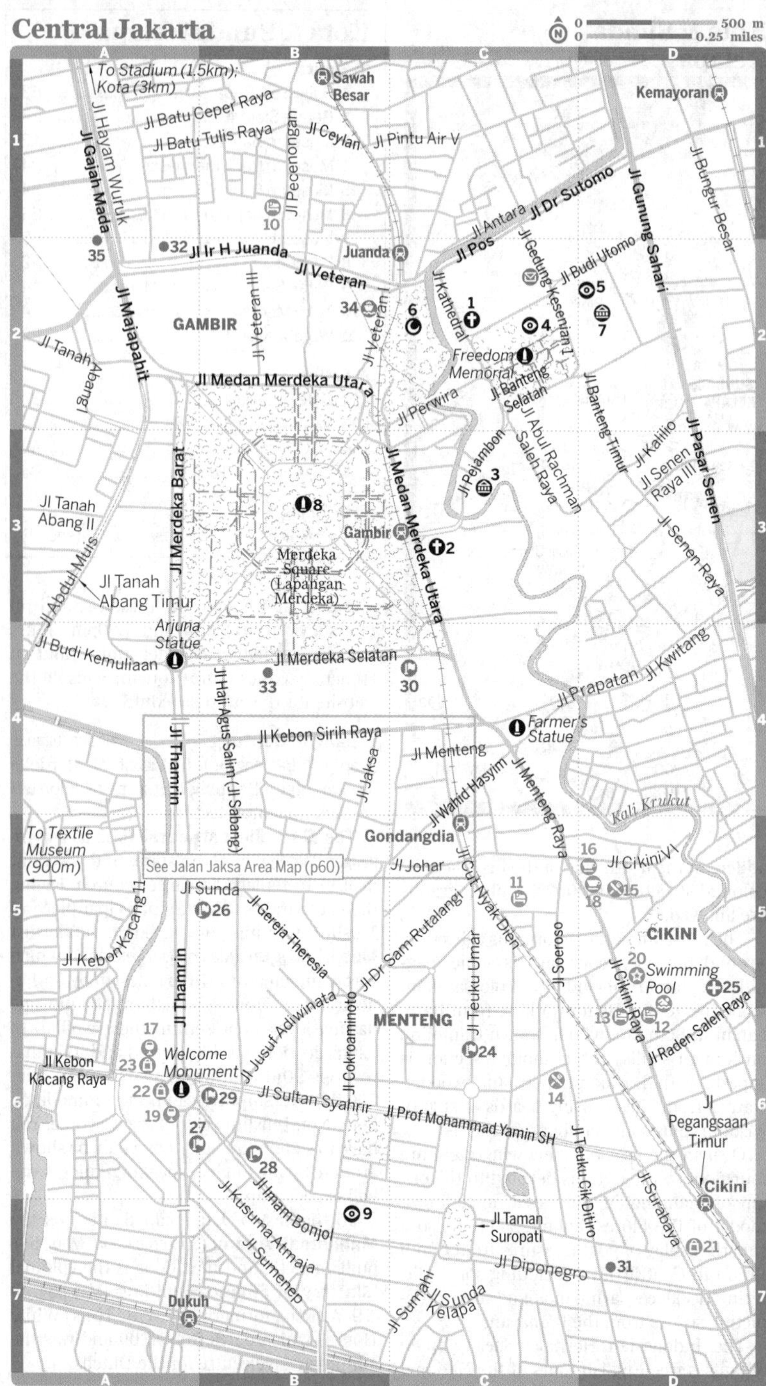

Central Jakarta

Sights

1	Catholic Cathedral	C2
2	Emanuel Church	C3
3	Gedung Pancasila	C3
4	Lapangan Banteng	C2
5	Mahkamah Agung	D2
6	Mesjid Istiqlal	C2
7	Ministry of Finance Building	D2
8	Monas	B3
9	SDN Menteng 1 School	B7

Sleeping

10	Alila Jakarta	B1
11	Gondia International Guesthouse	C5
12	Hotel Formule 1	D6
13	Six Degrees	D6

Eating

14	Lara Djonggrang	C6
15	Vietopia	D5

Drinking

16	Bakoel Koffie	D5
17	Burgundy	A6
	Cork & Screw	(see 23)
18	Dua Nyonya	D5
19	Skye	A6

Entertainment

20	Taman Ismail Marzuki	D5

Shopping

21	Flea Market	D7
22	Grand Indonesia	A6
23	Plaza Indonesia	A6

Information

	BII Bank	(see 23)
24	Brunei Darussalam Embassy	C6
25	Cikini Hospital	D5
26	French Embassy	B5
27	German Embassy	A6
28	Thai Embassy	B6
29	UK Embassy	B6
30	US Embassy	C4

Transport

31	Avis	D7
32	Batavia Air	A2
33	Garuda	B4
34	Kerta Jaya	B2
35	Lion Air	A2

To the southwest is **Gedung Pancasila** (Map p54; Jl Pejambon), which is an imposing neoclassical building built in 1830 as the Dutch army commander's residence. It later became the meeting hall of the Volksraad (People's Council), but is best known as the place where Sukarno made his famous Pancasila speech in 1945, laying the foundation for Indonesia's constitution. Just west along Jl Pejambon from Gedung Pancasila is the **Emanuel Church** (Map p54; Jl Pejambon), another classic building dating from 1893.

Monas MONUMENT
(Monumen Nasional; Map p54; Merdeka Sq; 8.30am-5pm, closed last Mon of month) Ingloriously dubbed 'Sukarno's final erection', this 132m-high National Monument, which towers over Merdeka Sq, is both Jakarta's principal landmark and the most famous architectural extravagance of the former president. Begun in 1961, Monas was not completed until 1975, when it was officially opened by Suharto. The monument is constructed from Italian marble, and is topped with a sculpted flame, gilded with 35kg of gold leaf.

Textile Museum MUSEUM
(Map p50; 392 0331; www.museumtekstiljakarta.com; Jl Aipda K.S. Tubun 2-4; admission 2000Rp; 9am-3pm Tue-Sun) Very much a worthwhile visit if you've any interest in weavings and fabrics, this museum houses a collection of around 2000 precious textiles, including hundreds of batik pieces, both antique and contemporary, lots of looms and a garden containing plants used for natural dyes. It's about 2km southwest of Merdeka Sq, and not easily reached by public transport.

SOUTHERN JAKARTA

In the southern reaches of the city reside a couple of attractions that require a day trip to fully enjoy.

Taman Mini Indonesia Indah AMUSEMENT PARK
(Map p50; 545 4545; www.tamanmini.com; Jl Raya Jagorawi; adult/child 6000/4000Rp; 8am-6pm) In the city's far southeast, Taman Mini Indonesia Indah is a 'whole country in one park'.

Covering 100-hectares, the park has full-scale traditional houses for each of Indonesia's

South Jakarta

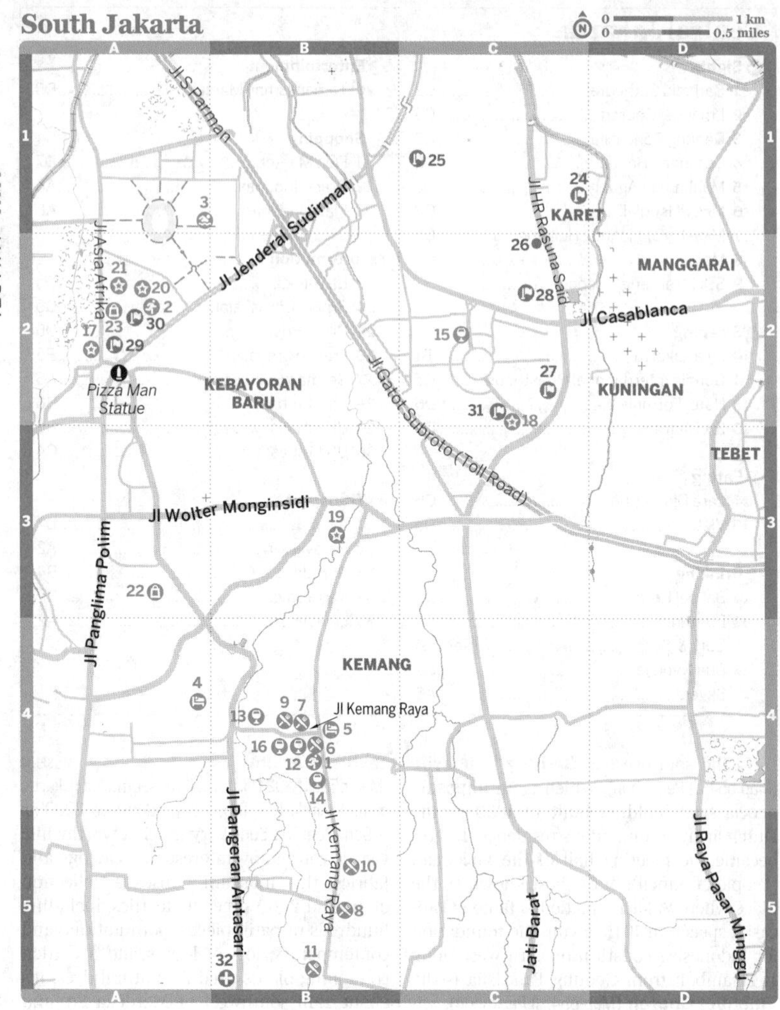

provinces, with displays of regional handicrafts and clothing, a mini-scale Borobudur, an orchid garden and a bird park. Museums, theatres and an IMAX cinema are scattered throughout the grounds, which all command additional entrance fees. Free cultural performances are staged (usually around 10am); Sunday is the big day for cultural events, but shows are also held during the week.

You can walk, drive, take a shuttle bus or use the monorail or cable car to get around the park. Taman Mini is about 18km from the city centre. To get there, take a Koridor 7 bus to the Kampung Rambutan terminal and then a T15 metro-mini to the park entrance. A taxi from central Jakarta costs about 85,000Rp.

Museum Pancasila Sakti MUSEUM
(Map p50; ☎840 0423; Jl Halim Perdana Kusumah; admission 3000Rp; ⏱8am-4.30pm) About 2km northeast of Taman Mini, this museum is a bizarre homage to anticommunism. There's dioramas depicting Communist crimes, photos of the 1960s show trials, and even bullet hole-ridden military uniforms. There's a large monument to the self-appointed 'saviours of the nation'.

South Jakarta

Activities, Courses & Tours
1 Bikram Yoga B4
2 Bikram Yoga A2
3 Bung Karno Stadium Complex A1

Sleeping
4 Dharmawangsa A4
5 Kemang Icon B4

Eating
6 Casa B4
7 D'Fest B4
Edge .... (see 5)
8 Kinara B5
9 Payon B4
10 Shy B5
11 Toscana B5

Drinking
12 Backyard Terrace B4
13 Eastern Promise B4
14 Elbow Room B4
15 Potato Head C2
16 Tree House B4

Entertainment
17 Domain A2
18 Erasmus Huis C2
19 Phoenix B3
20 Red Square A2
21 X2 .... A2

Shopping
Ak'sara .... (see 6)
22 Pasaraya A3
Perimeter Art .... (see 5)
Periplus .... (see 23)
23 Plaza Senayan A2

Information
24 Australian Embassy C1
25 Canadian Embassy C1
26 Central Immigration Office C2
27 Dutch Embassy C2
28 Malaysian Embassy C2
29 New Zealand Embassy A2
30 Papua New Guinea Embassy A2
31 Singaporean Embassy C2
32 SOS Medika Klinik B5

Activities

Fitness & Yoga

Jakarta has several public swimming pools. The best option in the centre (within walking distance of Jalan Jaksa) is the 50m **pool** (Jl Cikini Raya; admission 20,000Rp; ⏲7am-8pm) behind the Hotel Formule 1 in Cikini. There's another 50m pool over in Senayan inside the **Bung Karno stadium complex** (Map p56; Jl Jenderal Sudirman; per swim 5000Rp; ⏲7am-9pm), which also has squash, tennis and badminton courts, plus rackets for hire.

Bikram Yoga (☎719 7379; www.bikramyogajakarta.com; per session 165,000Rp) has locations in **Kemang** (Map p56; Jl Kemang Raya Selatan II) and **Senayan** (Map p56; Plaza Senayan Arcadia, Jl New Delhi Pintu I). It gets good reports for its hot yoga, Asthanga and beginners' classes.

Massage

Jakarta has massage establishments that range from ultra-luxe spas to dodgy set-ups that are simply fronts for brothels. The hygienic and affordable massage and sauna facilities at **Bersih Sehat** (Map p60; ☎390 0204; www.dayugroup.web.id; Jl Wahid Hasyim 106; 1hr massage from 120,000Rp; ⏲10am-9pm) are highly recommended.

For a really memorable experience, head to **Jamu Traditional Spa** (☎765 9691; www.jamutraditionalspa.com; Jl Cipete VIII/94B, Cipete; massage & treatments 550,000-900,000Rp; ⏲8am-9pm) in south Jakarta, which uses *jamu* (Indonesian herbs with medicinal and restorative properties) for its treatments.

Tours

Numerous travel agencies offer daily tours of Jakarta. Bookings can be made through the tourist office and major hotels.

Hidden Jakarta Tours GUIDED TOUR
(☎081 2803 5297; www.realjakarta.blogspot.com; from 500,000Rp) Want to see the other Jakarta, away from air-conditioned malls? Jakarta Hidden offers tours of the city's traditional *kampung*, the urban villages of the poor. These warts-and-all tours take you along trash-choked riverways, into cottage industry factories and allow you to take tea in residents' homes.

Gray Line GUIDED TOUR
(☎630 8105; www.grayline.com) Offers city tours (from US$40) and many other trips, including Thousand Islands (from US$140) and Bogor's botanical gardens (US$60).

OBAMA IN JAKARTA

Barack Obama moved to Jakarta in 1967 when his mother married a second husband, Lolo Soetoro, an Indonesian whom she'd met in Hawaii. Obama lived for four years in the Indonesian capital, including a period in the exclusive central suburb of Menteng, where he attended the **SDN Menteng 1** (Map p54) government-run school and studied in the Indonesian language. This school is still going strong, and there's a plaque at the front commemorating its most famous ex-pupil.

A popular child, he was nicknamed 'Barry' by his fellow students. It's been reported that he declared an ambition to become president whilst at this school. Obama lived close by on Jl Taman Amir Hamzah in a handsome terracotta-tiled Dutch villa with art deco–style windows.

When asked if he missed anything from his time in the country, Obama, who speaks Bahasa Indonesia, said he dreamt of '*bakso* (meatball soup), nasi goreng (fried rice) and rambutan (red fruit similar to lychee)'.

On his return to the city as president in 2010, he confessed 'I barely recognise it. When I first came here in 1967 everyone rode on becaks'.

Indonesian Heritage Society GUIDED TOUR
(☎572 5870; www.heritagejkt.org) The Indonesian Heritage Society organises free English tours of the National Museum at 10:30am on Tuesdays, and on Thursdays at 10:30am and 1:30pm. Tours are also available every second Saturday and last Sunday in the month at 1.30pm.

Festivals & Events

Independence Day EVENT
Indonesia's independence is celebrated on 17 August and the parades in Jakarta are the biggest in the country.

Java Jazz Festival FESTIVAL
(www.javajazzfestival.com) Held in early March at the Jakarta Convention Center in Senayan. Attracts acclaimed international artists, including Stevie Wonder in 2012.

Indonesian Dance Festival FESTIVAL
(Taman Ismail Marzuki) Features contemporary and traditional performances at the Taman Ismail Marzuki (p65) in mid-June.

Jakarta Anniversary EVENT
The 22nd of June marks the establishment of the city in 1527. Celebrated with fireworks and the Jakarta Fair.

JiFFest FESTIVAL
(Jakarta International Film Festival; www.jiffest.org) Indonesia's premier film festival.

Jalan Jaksa Street Fair FESTIVAL
Features Betawi dance, theatre and music, art and photography. Held for one week in August.

Sleeping

Backpackers be prepared: Jakarta does lack good budget places, so book ahead or consider a midrange option (which are plentiful). At the luxury end of the market, there are some excellent deals with four-star hotels available from US$70 per night.

JALAN JAKSA AREA

Jakarta's low-key backpacking hub consists of one street and a few side alleys. It feels a bit like a prehistoric Ko Sarn Rd: travellers are thin on the ground, most hotels are grungy, and the place has a slightly forgotten ambience. That said, you will find a selection of restaurants and bars here, and the location, near Jl Thamrin (for the busway), and Gambir train station is excellent.

TOP CHOICE **Hostel 35** GUESTHOUSE $
(Map p60; ☎392 0331; Jl Kebon Sirih Barat I 35; r 100,000-150,000Rp, with air-con 250,000Rp; ❄📶) Boasting charm, character and comfort, this is an excellent budget hotel, located just off the main Jaksa drag. The lobby/lounge area with rattan sofas is very inviting and decorated with fine textiles and tasteful photography. The 16 rooms are neat and attractive (all but two have private bathrooms). Your complimentary breakfast is a simple affair.

Alinda Hotel HOTEL $
(Map p60; ☎314 0373; www.alinda-hotel.com; Jl Kebon Sirih Barat VI 9; r with fan/air-con 165,000/245,000Rp; ❄@📶) Well-organised, clean and welcoming this large place definitely feels like a 'proper' hotel not a back-

packers' crash pad. The 60 or so rooms are clean and quite spacious, with a wardrobe and decent beds, and the location is quiet. There's a row of PCs for surfing, and genial owner Fauziah plans to open a cafe here too.

Max One BOUTIQUE HOTEL $$
(Map p60; ☎316 6888; www.maxonehotels.com; Jl KH Agus Salim 24; r 450,000–600,000Rp; ❄@📶) A moderately priced hip hotel, obviously designed by people with a real eye for style (check out the pop art and iMacs in the lobby). Rooms are smallish but perfectly formed, with a pleasing green-and-cream colour scheme. We love the 3pm weekend check-out time, minimart and excellent location.

Ristana Ratu Hotel HOTEL $$
(Map p60; ☎314 2464; Jl Jaksa 7-9; r 200,000-325,000Rp; ❄📶) Standards have remained quite high at this small hotel, bucking the Jaksa trend, which is set off the street. The large rooms offer style and comfort with great beds, bright duvets and soft pillows. You'll find a little cafe downstairs for your breakfast (included for the more expensive accommodation).

Cemara Hotel HOTEL $$
(Map p60; ☎390 8215; www.cemarahotel.com; Jl Cemara I; r from 440,000Rp; ❄@📶🏊) This hotel does have some local character, with a Borobudur-style stone carving in the polished lobby. Rooms are well-maintained and comfortable (but a little dated) and staff are helpful. The rooftop pool is small but has great skyline views, and there's a small spa.

Memories GUESTHOUSE $
(Map p60; ☎0878 7883 0103; Jl Jaksa 17; r with fan/air-con 90,000/200,000Rp; ❄📶) Right above one of Jaksa's most popular backpacker bar-restaurants, these small, clean, tiled rooms are ideal if you want to sink a Bintang or two and not worry about getting lost on the way home. Just don't fall down the stairs.

Bloem Steen Homestay GUESTHOUSE $
(Map p60; ☎3192 5389; Gang I 173; s/d with fan 60,000/80,000Rp, r with air-con 130,000Rp; ❄@) Age-old place with 18 no-frills rooms, all with shared bathrooms, and a pleasant front terrace for chilling with a beer or a tea. It's clean enough (shoes off at the door, folks!) and staff are reasonably welcoming.

Hotel Cipta HOTEL $$
(Map p60; ☎3193 0424; www.ciptahotel.com; Jl Wahid Hasyim 53; r 420,000Rp; ❄📶) Looking like a cross between an alpine mountain lodge and a pagoda, Cipta is no identikit chain hotel. Rooms are smallish but well presented and staff are welcoming and helpful.

Hotel Margot HOTEL $$
(Map p60; ☎391 3830; Jl Jaksa 15; r 260,000Rp; ❄@) Its reception area gives the impression that this is a half-decent hotel, but expect slightly worn rooms, all with hot water, ensuite bathrooms, TV and air-con. A little cafe out front faces the Jaksa action. Doable for a night or two.

Hotel Tator HOTEL $
(Map p60; ☎3192 3940; Jl Jaksa 37; r with fan/air-con 100,000/180,000Rp; ❄) A bare-bones option for those on a very tight budget, this

JAKARTA FOR CHILDREN

On Jakarta's bayfront, **Taman Impian Jaya Ancol** (Map p50; ☎6471 0497; www.ancol.com; basic admission incl entry to Pasar Seni 13,000Rp; ⏲24hr), the people's 'Dreamland', is a landscaped recreation complex popular with families. It features amusement rides and sporting and leisure facilities, including bowling, but gets extremely crowded on weekends.

Prime attractions include the **Pasar Seni** (Art Market), which has sidewalk cafes, a host of craft shops, cable-car rides, art exhibitions, and live jazz every Friday (at 8.30pm) and **Seaworld** (Map p50; ☎641 0080; www.seaworldindonesia.com; Mon-Fri 40,000Rp, Sat & Sun 50,000Rp; ⏲9am-6pm), with its 'sharkquarium', alligator pool and turtles.

The **Atlantis Water Adventure** water-park complex has a wave pool and a slide pool plus artificial beaches. Gondola, a new cable car system, provides great views of the bay. The huge **Dunia Fantasi** (Fantasy Land; Map p50; ☎6471 2000; Mon-Fri 60,000Rp, Sat & Sun 80,000Rp; ⏲11am-6pm Mon-Thu, 2-8pm Fri, 11am-8pm Sat & Sun) fun park includes the Halilintar twisted roller-coaster ride and Kora Kora (swinging ship).

Koridor 5 of the busway runs to Ancol. A taxi will cost around 50,000Rp from Jl Thamrin.

Jalan Jaksa Area

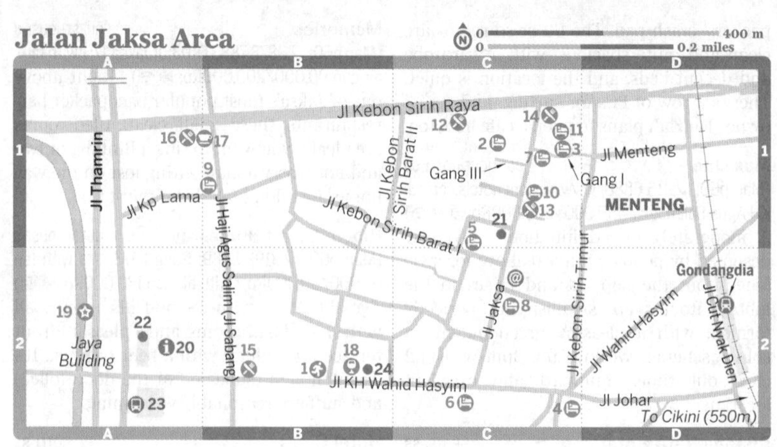

Jalan Jaksa Area

Activities, Courses & Tours
1 Bersih Sehat B2

Sleeping
2 Alinda Hotel C1
3 Bloem Steen Homestay C1
4 Cemara Hotel C2
5 Hostel 35 .... C1
6 Hotel Cipta C2
7 Hotel Margot C1
8 Hotel Tator C2
9 Max One B1
10 Memories C1
11 Ristana Ratu Hotel C1

Eating
12 Daoen Sirih C1
13 KL Village C1
14 Sate Khas Senayan C1
15 Saung Grenvil B2
16 Shanghai Blue 1920 .... A1

Drinking
17 Kopitiam Oey Sabang B1
18 Melly's B2
Memories .... (see 10)

Entertainment
19 Jaya Pub A2

Information
20 Jakarta Visitor Information Office A2
21 Robert Kencana Travel C1
22 Smailing Tours A2
Tourist Police .... (see 20)

Transport
23 Day Trans A2
24 Mandala Air B2

place has unlovely but functional and fairly clean rooms, all with bathroom.

CIKINI & MENTENG

Cikini (south) and Menteng (southeast) of Jaksa have a selection of decent midrange hotels, a guesthouse or two and some excellent restaurants and cafes.

Six Degrees HOSTEL $
(Map p54; ☎314 1657; www.jakarta-backpackers-hostel.com; Jl Cikini Raya 60 B-C; dm 120,000Rp, r 170,000-330,000Rp; ❄@📶) This new hostel, run by a helpful, friendly, informative Irish/English/Sumatran team, is proving popular with travellers. There's a relaxed, sociable atmosphere thanks to the pool table and large-screen TV and you'll find plenty of bathrooms and toilets, a guests' kitchen and roof garden. The dorms are a bit of a squeeze, but clean. Breakfast is included. It's tricky to find, but located right opposite the Formule 1 Cikini hotel.

Hotel Formule 1 HOTEL $$
(Map p54; ☎3190 8188; www.hotelformule1.com; Jl Cikini Raya 75; r/f 320,000/380,000Rp; ❄📶) A very decent, 'no frills or service' modern hotel in a good location with very affordable prices. Rooms are Spartan and a little soul-

less, but immaculately clean and have flat-screen TV and wi-fi. Downstairs there are several restaurants, a minimart and you'll find a huge pool right behind the hotel.

Amaris Hotel Senen HOTEL $$
(Map p50; ☎270 0027; www.amarishotel.com; Jl Kramat Raya 35; r from 330,000Rp; ❄📶) Located just west of the Cikini district, this modern budget hotel offers small attractive rooms with good facilities, quality mattresses and bedding, and a complimentary breakfast. The structure is very distinctive – look out for the snazzy colour scheme.

Gondia International Guesthouse GUESTHOUSE $
(Map p54; ☎390 9221; gondia@rad.net.id; Jl Gondangdia Kecil 22; r incl breakfast 210,000-270,000Rp; ❄) Looking like a youth hostel, this little guesthouse occupies a leafy garden plot on a quiet suburban street and has quite spacious tiled rooms with bathrooms.

AIRPORT

FM7 Resort Hotel HOTEL $$
(☎5591 1777; www.fm7hotel.com; Jln Raya Perancis 67; r/ste from US$87/143; ❄@📶🏊) Just 2km from the airport, this excellent modern hotel is ideal for transit passengers. The stylish rooms boast contemporary furnishings, and it has a gym, pool, sauna, and steam and massage rooms. Rates include free airport transfers.

OTHER AREAS

TOP CHOICE **Kemang Icon** BOUTIQUE HOTEL $$$
(Map p56; ☎719 7989; www.alilahotels.com/kemangicon; Jl Kemang Raya I; r from US$175; ❄@📶🏊) Terrific hip hotel with 12 simply gorgeous, suite-sized rooms, all kitted out with cutting-edge design, loaded iPods and state-of-the-art bathrooms located in the heart of the happening Kemang area. It has a rooftop lap pool, a fine restaurant, and the staff go the extra mile to help out guests.

Alila Jakarta HOTEL $$$
(Map p54; ☎231 6008; www.alilahotels.com/jakarta; Jl Pecenongan 7-17; r from US$80; ❄@📶🏊) An excellent modern hotel, in the north of the city not far from most of the sights. The attention to detail is impressive, with aromatherapy oil wafting across the stylish reception area setting a great initial impression. The outdoor pool, gym and restaurants are excellent.

Dharmawangsa LUXURY HOTEL $$$
(Map p56; ☎725 8181; www.the-dharmawangsa.com; r from US$195; ❄@📶🏊) One of *the* city addresses, this luxurious hotel exudes style and class, with huge rooms and unmatched standards of service (each guest is assigned a private butler!). The leisure facilities (including two pools, a fine spa, and squash and tennis courts) and restaurants are also outstanding.

Eating

Jakarta is a world-class eating destination. You'll find an amazing choice including oh-so refined Javanese Imperial cuisine, hit-the-spot street grub and, if you're pining for something familiar you can find Western food from gourmet French to fish 'n' chips.

Tasty street grub is everywhere, but two excellent hot spots are Jl Pecenongan (about 500m north of Monas) for *sate babi* (pork sate) and fresh seafood, and Jl Sabang (just west of Jl Jaksa) for *sate ayam* (chicken sate) with *lontong* (sticky rice) and other delicacies.

Shopping malls are also good tucker terrain, many have inexpensive food courts.

JALAN JAKSA AREA

Jl Jaksa has a crop of backpacker-geared cafes and many authentic places close by.

Daoen Sirih INDONESIAN $
(Map p60; Jl Kebon Sirih 41-43; meals 12,000-25,000Rp; ⏰11am-10pm; 🖋) A short stroll northwest of Jalan Jaksa, this large bamboo-roofed, open-sided food court has a wide selection of Indonesia cook-shacks offering Indonesian noodles, and dishes such as *nasi goreng kambing* (spicy rice with goat) and *sate madura* (skewered meat with sweet soy sauce), as well as espresso coffee. It's non-touristy and a great place to mingle with locals.

Shanghai Blue 1920 CHINESE, INDONESIAN $$$
(Map p60; ☎391 8690; www.tuguhotels.com/shblue; Jl Kebon Sirih Raya 77-79; mains 50,000-130,000Rp; ⏰12.30pm-11pm) Outstanding *masakan peranakan* (Chinese-influenced Indonesian cuisine) served in a spectacular room that's loaded with flamboyant furnishings, some rescued from an old Batavia teahouse. Standouts from the menu include drunken shrimp cooked with traditional Chinese wine and crispy tilapia fish with mango and sweet chilli sauce.

Saung Grenvil SEAFOOD $$
(Map p60; ☎392 0333; www.saung-grenvil.com; Jl Wahid Hasyim 87; meals 100,000-180,000Rp) A restaurant that's rightly renowned for its outstanding seafood, particularly crab (though there are plenty of other seafood options). First select your crab (expect to pay around 130,000Rp) and then select how you want it cooked: Padang-style and black pepper are the two signature sauces.

KL Village MALAY, INDONESIAN $
(Map p60; ☎3192 5219; Jl Jaksa 21-23; mains from 17,000Rp; ⏰7am-11pm Sun-Wed, 24hr Thu-Sat; 📶) Ever-popular Malaysian-style place that serves up inexpensive grub such as black-pepper chicken, *canai* (Malay-Indian bread) and *murtabak* (stuffed pancake). If you're suffering after a long flight (or long night), try one of the health-kick juices: 'heart and the brain' or 'sugar balance'.

Sate Khas Senayan SATE, INDONESIAN $$
(Map p60; ☎3192 6238; Jl Kebon Sirih Raya 31A; mains 25,000-50,000Rp; ⏰11.30am-10pm; 📶) Upmarket air-conditioned restaurant at the northern end of Jl Jaksa. It is renowned for its superb sate – sticked-up in chicken, beef and lamb forms – plus Indonesian favourites such as *ayam goreng kremes* (fried chicken in batter) and *gurame bakar* (grilled fish).

KOTA, SUNDA KELAPA & GLODOK

Café Batavia INTERNATIONAL $$$
(Map p53; ☎691 5531; Jl Pintu Besar Utara 14; mains 50,000Rp; 📶) This historic restaurant overlooks Taman Fatahillah square in Kota, the old Dutch quarter. Its teak floors and art deco furnishings make a richly atmospheric setting, and it's an essential stop for a drink if you're in the area, just to soak up the colonial ambience. As the menu is a little overfancy, it's best for lunch (the restaurant can also be quiet in the evening).

Warung Kota Tua INDONESIAN $
(Map p53; Jl Pintu Besar Utara 11; meals 20,000-25,000Rp; ⏰8am-8pm) On the west side of Taman Fatahillah square, this semi-renovated old warehouse (an open-sided space with exposed brick walls and artwork) is a relaxed location for a reasonably-priced meal, coffee, tea or juice. Try the *ayam bakar* (grilled chicken), *mie medan* (Sumatran noodles) or *nasi cap cai* (rice with mixed vegetables).

VOC Galangan INDONESIAN $
(Map p53; ☎667 8501; Jl Kakap I; snacks & meals from 15,000Rp; ⏰9am-5pm) This atmospheric cafe occupies the premises of a beautifully restored warehouse that dates back to 1628. Enjoy a drink or meal inside the beamed interior or out on the terrace, which overlooks a grassy courtyard containing a vintage car and horse-buggy carriage. Prices are very reasonable for dishes such as gado gado or *sup buntut* (oxtail soup).

Santong Kuo Tieh 68 CHINESE $
(Map p53; ☎692 4716; Jl Pancoran; 10 dumplings 20,000Rp; ⏰10am-9pm) You'll see cooks preparing fried and steamed Chinese pork dumplings out front of this humble but highly popular little place. The *bakso ikan isi* (fish balls) are also good.

CIKINI & MENTENG

TOP CHOICE **Lara Djonggrang** INDONESIAN $$$
(Map p54; ☎315 3252; www.tuguhotels.com/laradjonggrang; Jl Teuku Cik Ditiro 4; mains 48,000-170,000Rp; ⏰12.30pm-11pm; 📶) While many Jakartan restaurants lack atmosphere, that accusation could never be levelled at Lara Djonggrang – as you enter it's easy to think you've stumbled across some lost temple. Stunning decor combines Indonesian tribal artifacts and colossal temple statues with North African touches. Expect perfectly executed and creatively presented imperial Indonesian cuisine. There's a good wine list if you want to push the boat out and staff are well-informed and efficient.

Vietopia VIETNAMESE $$
(Map p54; ☎391 5893; Jl Cikini Raya 33; mains 35,000-60,000Rp; ⏰11.30am-10.30pm; 📶🌱) A highly enjoyable, stylish and relaxing destination for a meal, this authentic Vietnamese place offers delicious moderately priced and delicately spiced cooking, including flavoursome *pho bo* (beef broth) and other classics from Indochina.

KEMANG AREA

Kemang is a good choice for a night on the town, with some great restaurants, bars and nightlife, including many exclusive places. For inexpensive grub check out D'Fest which has 50 or so stalls.

Payon INDONESIAN $$
(Map p56; ☎719 4826; Jl Kemang Raya 17; mains 40,000-110,000Rp; ⏰11.30am-11pm) Something of a secret garden where you dine under a delightful open pagoda surrounded by greenery. Chefs prepare authentic Javanese cuisine from an open kitchen, and many

dishes are served on banana leaves, echoing the rural Indonesian flavour.

D'Fest FOOD COURT **$**

(Map p56; Jl Kemang Raya 19C; ⏲5pm-midnight) Very sociable and popular open-air food court complete with stylish sofa seating and lots of international and local food stalls. It has Middle Eastern kebab joints, lots of Japanese options, *soto* (soup) places, *roti canai* (Malay-Indian flaky flat bread), plus a beerhouse. There's often live music here on weekend nights.

Elbow Room INTERNATIONAL **$$**

(Map p56; www.elbowroomjakarta.com; Jl Kemang Raya 24A; meals 60,000-100,000Rp; ⏲11am-11pm; 📶) Highly enjoyable and atmospheric gastro pub with high ceilings and comfort grub including wraps, pasta and fish 'n' chips (the sonic burger with pork, mushrooms, onions and rocket is excellent). You'll find lots of imported beers and there's live music on weekend nights.

Edge BISTRO **$$**

(Map p56; ☎719 7989; www.theedgekemang.com; Kemang Icon, Jl Kemang Raya I; meals 100,000-180,000Rp; 📶) Gorgeous new rooftop bistro, with indoor and outside dining around an infinity pool (free for diners) and a mini-amphitheatre (used for gigs and events). The menu is short, well-chosen and affordable and includes smoked salmon salad, Spanish omelette and Indo-style comfort grub such as nasi goreng.

Casa INTERNATIONAL **$$**

(Map p56; ☎719 9289; www.casajakarta.com; Jl Kemang Raya 8B; mains 50,000-110,000Rp; 📶) A key Kemang cafe-restaurant that's home turf for the capital's creative and media professionals. Stylish seating provides easy lounging while the menu takes in Italian, Indonesian, grilled meats and gourmet sandwiches.

Shy FRENCH, INTERNATIONAL **$$$**

(Map p56; ☎719 9921; www.thepapilion.com; Jl Kemang Raya 45AA; meals from 180,000Rp; 📶) Uberhip restaurant offering cutting-edge monochrome decor and impressive French haute cuisine. It's one of the most exclusive and expensive restaurants in the city, with a hip roof bar that's ideal for an aperitif or post-dinner drink.

Kinara INDIAN **$$**

(Map p56; ☎719 2677; www.kinara.co.id; Jl Kemang Raya 78B; mains 60,000-80,000Rp; ⏲11.30am-11pm; 📶) An opulent interior of grand arches that's an impressive setting for some of the finest Indian dishes in Jakarta – sublime chicken tikka and interesting options such as fish amritsari. Tuck in with a wide choice of interesting naan breads.

Toscana ITALIAN **$$**

(Map p56; ☎718 1217; www.toscanajakarta.com; Jl Kemang Raya 120; mains 70,000-130,000Rp; ⏲5.30-11pm) Elegant Italian place renowned for its pizzas (baked in a wood-fired oven), pasta and risotto and great fish dishes (try the pan-fried grouper with potato and black olives). Also boasts a good selection of Tuscan wines.

OTHER AREAS

Cassius FRENCH **$$$**

(Map p50; ☎5794 1500; www.cassis-gourmand.com; Jl K.H. Mas Mansyur 24; mains 120,000-200,000Rp) Classic French cuisine in inviting, intimate and contemporary surrounds. Excellent meat dishes include wonderful slow-roasted pork belly and *boufe perigourdine*, and there are great seafood dishes and desserts to die for too. The set lunch menu is fine value at US$25.

Drinking

If you're expecting the capital of the world's largest Muslim country to be a pretty sober city with little in the way of drinking culture, think again. Bars are spread throughout the city, with casual places grouped around Jl Jaksa, fancy pants lounge bars in south Jakarta and many more places in between. Cafe culture has really taken off in Jakarta in the last few years. All the malls have a Starbucks (or an Indo clone) selling extortionately-priced coffee but there are some very interesting and quirky locally owned cafes emerging too.

Bars

TOP CHOICE **Potato Head** BAR

(Map p56; www.ptthead.com/Jakarta; Pacific Place Mall, Jl Sudirman 52-53; 📶) Brilliant warehouse-style bar-bistro with remarkable artistic decor (including a living green wall, lots of statement art and vintage seating) that also promotes music and cultural events (check the website). Great cocktails, great grub, great concept.

Tree House BAR

(Map p56; Jl Kemang 72; ⏲4pm-midnight Tue-Thu & Sun, to 3am Fri-Sat; 📶) A great neighbourhood bar, Tree House is an intimate, happening hangout for Kemang's cool crowd with urban art and rotating exhibitions. You'll find classic funk, soul and hip-hop on the sound system.

Melly's BAR

(Map p60; Jl Wahid Hasyim 84; 📶) A quirky little place that attracts a good mix of locals and Westerners, has cheap snacks and beer, and plenty of loungy sitting areas. It's open-sided (so it doesn't get too smoky) and there's a popular quiz here every Wednesday.

Memories BAR

(Map p60; Jl Jaksa 17; ⏲24hr) Perhaps Jaksa's principal watering hole, Memories draws fresh-in-town backpackers and seen-it-all expats in equal measure. Grab a bar stool and soak up the streetside scene over a cold Bintang. The menu includes Chinese food and good set breakfasts, and there are even a few budget rooms upstairs.

Eastern Promise PUB

(Map p56; ☎7179 0151; www.easternpromise-jakarta.com; Jl Kemang Raya 5; 📶) A classic British-style pub in the heart of Kemang, with a pool table, welcoming atmosphere and filling Western and Indian grub. Service is prompt and friendly, the beer's cold and there's live music on weekends. It's a key expat hang-out.

Skye LOUNGE

(Map p54; 56th floor, Jakarta Menara BCA Tower, Jl Thamrin I; 📶) Excuse me while I kiss the... Skye – this bar boasts an unrivalled panorama of the city from the 56th floor of a central block. Attracts an elite crowd of local actresses and models, business moguls and affluent Westerners unconcerned about the (appropriately) stratospheric prices.

Burgundy BAR

(Map p54; www.jakarta.grand.hyatt.com; Jl Thamrin, Grand Hyatt Hotel) One of Jakarta's most exclusive drinking haunts with a great view of the city. Spectacularly expensive (and fabulously moreish) cocktails, avant-garde decor and live music (jazz and mellow) nightly at 9pm.

Cork & Screw WINE BAR

(Map p54; www.corknscrew.biz; Jl Kebon Kacang Raya, Plaza Indonesia) The best option in central Jakarta for wine lovers, this stylish bar-restaurant has hundreds of bottles to choose from (though as prices start at a hefty 400,000Rp, make sure you're holding plenty of folding). Good food (modern European, Indonesian and snacks) is also served.

Backyard Terrace BAR

(Map p56; Jl Kemang I 11; ⏲5-11.30pm Mon-Fri, to 1.30am Sat-Sun) A quirky little backstreet bar (access is via a rickety metal staircase) that

A CUP OF JAVA

Java is so synonymous with coffee, one of the world's favourite drugs – sorry, *drinks* – that in some countries the term java has become a catch phrase for a cup of the hot, brown stuff.

Coffee was introduced to Indonesia by the Dutch, who initially founded plantations around Jakarta, Sukabumi and Bogor. Due to the country's excellent coffee-growing conditions, plantations began springing up across Java, and even in parts of Sulawesi and Sumatra. Early on, the prominent coffee was arabica; arabica coffees were traditionally named after the port they were exported from, hence the common worldwide terms of java and mocha (from Yemen) for coffee.

Commonly thought of as a bean, coffee is actually a fruit pit or berry. Around 2000 berries are needed to make one pound of coffee. The most expensive coffee in the world, fetching US$300 a pound, is *kopi luwak*, a fully flavoured coffee produced in Java (it is also exported from the Philippines, Vietnam and southern India). What makes *kopi luwak* – also known as civet coffee – so expensive is the process by which it gains its unusually rich flavour. The local palm civet, a catlike animal, gorges itself on coffee berries and passes the inner pit through its digestive tract unharmed. Along the way the pits are affected by the animal's stomach enzymes and come out the other end smelling of roses (or rich coffee in this case). The coffee has been appetisingly nicknamed 'cat poop' or 'monkey poo' coffee.

Today, Indonesia is the fourth-largest producer of coffee in the world. Robusta has replaced arabica as the leading coffee of choice, currently making up some 88% of the country's exports. For further reading on Indonesia's love affair with coffee pick up a copy of *A Cup of Java* by Gabriella Teggia and Mark Hanusz.

draws a student crowd with its cheap beer (a large San Miguel or Bintang is 22,000Rp) and indie tunes.

Cafes

Café Batavia BAR
(Map p53; Jl Pintu Besar Utara 14) This classy restaurant doubles as an evocative place for a cocktail, a cool Bintang or a coffee.

TOP CHOICE **Kopitiam Oey Sabang** CAFE
(Map p60; www.kopitiamoey.com; Jl Agus Salim 16A; drinks from 9000Rp;) Gorgeous little cafe, modelled on an old Chinese teahouse, complete with antique tiles and vintage prints on the walls. There's a great selection of drinks, from Vietnamese coffee to tumeric tea and snacks that reflect Indonesia's heritage, including Dutch croquettes and Padang-style *roti*.

Dua Nyonya CAFE
(Map p54; www.duanyonyacafe.com; Jl Cikini Raya 27; 11am-10pm) Primarily a cafe, Dua Nyonya is an intimate place on two levels which serves fine Indonesian coffee (from Bali, Toraja and Aceh) and traditional food including rice dishes such as *nasi bebek goreng keramat* (fried rice with duck). Classical music and art add to the ambience.

Bakoel Koffie CAFE
(Map p54; Jl Cikini Raya 25; coffees from 10,000Rp;) Occupying a fine old Dutch building, this elegant (if pricey) cafe has newspapers and magazines to browse, and offers strong coffee using beans from across the archipelago. Snacks and cakes are also served, though service can be a tad slack at times.

☆ Entertainment

Jakarta is Indonesia's most broad-minded, sophisticated and decadent city, with the nightlife to match. The club scene is dynamic, hedonistic and intense. Note that things can be a lot quieter during Ramadan.

The live music scene is also vibrant, with indie and reggae bands popular with the city's thousands of students. Many older Jakartans love their jazz and soul and traditional Javanese music.

Check the entertainment pages of Jakarta Kini magazine (www.jakartajavakini.com) for films, concerts and special events.

Cultural Performances

Museum Wayang holds *wayang kulit* and *golek* (puppet) performances on Sunday between 10am and 2pm.

Check the website of the Jakarta Arts Council (www.dkj.or.id) for event listings.

Taman Ismail Marzuki PERFORMING ARTS
(TIM; Map p54; 3193 7325; www.tamanismailmarzuki.com; Jl Cikini Raya 73) Jakarta's premier cultural centre, the Taman Ismail Marzuki, or TIM has a great selection of cinemas, theatres and exhibition spaces. Performances (such as Sundanese dance and gamelan music events) are always high quality and the complex has a couple of good casual restaurants too.

Erasmus Huis PERFORMING ARTS
(Map p56; 524 1069; www.mfa.nl/erasmushuis; Jl HR Rasuna Said Kav S-3) This cultural centre holds regular cultural events (including concerts, gigs and exhibitions).

Live Music

Jazz lovers should check out www.jakartajazz.com for event listings.

Jaya Pub LIVE MUSIC
(Map p60; 3192 5633; Jl Thamrin 12; 5pm-2am) Conventienly located in the heart of town, this pub caters to an older crowd and showcases live bluesy rock and jazz artists. Also serves food.

Phoenix LIVE MUSIC
(Map p56; 722 1188; www.phoenixjakarta.com; Jl Wijaya I 25) Formerly the Nine Muses Club, this upmarket European-style garden restaurant and lounge hosts acoustic performances on Wednesdays and Fridays, plus some jazz nights.

Clubs

Jakarta is the clubbing mecca of Southeast Asia with great venues (mostly dark 'n' sleazy in the north of the city and polished and pricey in the south), internationally renowned DJs and bombastic sound systems. If you gravitate towards the former there are underground clubs in Glodok so deep down and dirty that they make the UK's acid house scene of the 1980s seem like a teddy bear's picnic.

Entrance is typically 50,000Rp to 100,000Rp, but includes a free drink. Clubs open around 9pm, but they don't really get going until midnight; most clubs close around 5am.

TOP CHOICE **Stadium** CLUB
(Map p50; 626 3323; www.stadiumjakarta.com; Jl Hayum Waruk III FF-JJ) This hardcore club is

a Jakartan institution, drawing the world's leading DJs (such as Sasha and Derek May) and a loyal crowd of regulars with tribal house and techno. It's about as far from a commercial disco as you could imagine with an interior as dark as Hades and an eardrum-fearsome sound system – Stadium has a distinctly underground vibe. There are four levels, but the main room is where the prime dance-floor action is.

Red Square CLUB
(Map p56; www.redsquarejakarta.com; Jl New Delhi 9, Plaza Senayan Arcadia) One of the mainstays of the Jakartan night scene, and always Crammed on weekends with an up-for-it crowd in their late-twenties and thirties. Stocks an impressive vodka selection. Musically, commercial remixes of R'n'B hits and bleeping teenage techno tend to dominate.

Domain CLUB
(Map p56; Panin Tower B2 Fl, Senayan City, Jl Asia-Afrika 19) Classy, chic bar-club that draws a flirty, fashion-conscious crowd. It's quite intimate, the furnishings are inviting and modern and it hosts regular club nights with local and visiting DJs.

X2 CLUB
(Map p56; www.x2club.net; Jl Asia Afrika 8, Plaza Senayan) Huge upmarket club with a capacity to hold more than 2000. Expect a young crowd, futuristic lighting and three dance zones, though the music can be quite commercial.

Shopping

Jakarta has real retail appeal. The capital has handicrafts from across the nation, gargantuan malls stuffed with big brand and luxury labels (though prices are rarely cheaper than in the West) and lots of galleries full of interesting contemporary art and design goods.

DON'T MISS

SALE SEASON

The annual Jakarta Great Sale Festival (JGS) caters to the capital's avid mall-goers, and plenty of tourists from Malaysia. Held at many shopping centres in Jakarta during June and July, it features slashed prices, midnight sales, competitions, and social and cultural activities.

Because of the traffic in Jakarta, it is best not to try to cover too much ground. You could end up seeing a lot of exhaust fumes and no shop windows.

Arts & Handicrafts

Jl Kebon Sirih Timur, just east of Jl Jaksa, has a number of shops that sell antiques and curios.

Perimeter Art BOUTIQUE, ART GALLERY
(Map p56; www.perimeterspace.com; Jl Kemang Raya I) Leading design store stocked with desirable contemporary goodies (everything from T-shirts to sofas). Doubles as an art gallery.

Flea Market MARKET
(Map p54; Jl Surabaya) Jakarta's famous flea market is in Menteng. It has woodcarvings, furniture, textiles, jewellery, old vinyl records and many (dubious) antiques. Bargain like crazy.

Pasaraya DEPARTMENT STORE
(Map p56; www.pasaraya.co.id; Jl Iskandarsyah II/2) Opposite Blok M Mall, this department store has two huge floors that seem to go on forever and are devoted to batik and handicrafts from throughout the archipelago.

Books

Periplus BOOKS
(Map p56; ☎718 7070; Jl Asia Afrika, level 3, Plaza Senayan; ⊙9am-7pm) Excellent selection of English language magazines and books: fiction and non-fiction (including Lonely Planet guides). You'll find branches in Kemang and Plaza Indonesia too.

Ak'sara BOOKS, CLOTHING
(Map p56; www.aksara.com; Jl Kemang Raya 8B) A great range of books devoted to design, art and architecture, as well as magazines, CDs, hip homewares, stylish clothing and shoes. Full of quirky oddities such as clocks made from cutlery.

Shopping Malls

Jakarta has more shopping centres than you could spend a month of Sundays in, and the general rule is, the bigger, the better.

Plaza Indonesia MALL
(Map p54; www.plazaindonesia.com; Jl Thamrin; wi-fi) This mall is centrally located and very classy, with a wide selection of stores that includes leading Indonesian design boutiques and the likes of Cartier and Lacroix. Check out Toko Ampuh for local medicines and rem-

edies and Batik Karis for high-quality Indonesian batik. In the basement there's an excellent, inexpensive food mall.

Grand Indonesia MALL
(Map p54; www.grand-indonesia.com; Jl Thamrin) Opposite Plaza Indonesia, this luxury mall contains a tempting plethora of luxury fashion outlets, a six-storey branch of Japanese department-store giant Seibu, good local and international restaurants, and a cineplex.

Plaza Senayan MALL
(Map p56; www.plaza-senayan.com; Jl Asia Afrika;) Huge plaza with a cinema and stores including Marks & Spencer, a roster of big-bucks brands and lots of cafes.

Pasar Pagi Mangga Dua MALL
(Map p50; Jl Mangga Dua) Enormous wholesale market with some of Jakarta's cheapest clothes, accessories and shoes. Quality can be a problem, though.

Mangga Dua Mall MALL
(Map p50; Jl Mangga Dua) *The* place for electronics, DVDs and CDs (and even Russian watches) with numerous other malls in the area.

Information

Dangers & Annoyances

For such a huge city with obvious social problems, Jakarta is surprisingly safe. Violent crime is very rare and tourists are seldom targeted. You should exercise more caution after dark, particularly late at night in Glodok and Kota, however, where there are some seedy clubs and bars. Robberies by taxi drivers have been known to take place, so always opt for reputable firms, such as the citywide Bluebird group.

Jakarta's buses and trains can be hopelessly crowded, particularly during rush hours, and this is when pickpockets ply their trade.

Some foreign embassies warn against travel to Indonesia and especially Jakarta, though overall there's very little risk for travellers. That said, attacks against foreign interests have occurred and protests, although often peaceful, may still become violent with little warning.

Occasionally, bars and clubs have been smashed up by the city's self-appointed morality police, the Jakarta-based Front Pembela Islam (FPI or Islamic Defenders Front), especially during Ramadan.

Emergency

Tourist Police (Map p60; 566 000; Jln KH Wahid Hasyim) On the 2nd floor of the Jakarta Theatre.

Immigration

Central Immigration Office (Direktorat Jenderal Imigrasi; Map p56; 522 4658; www.imigrasi.go.id; Jl Rasuna Said 8 & 9) Provides information on visa extensions and renewals.

Internet Access

Free wi-fi is very common in cafes, restaurants and malls, though connection speeds are usually slow. Internet cafes are not easily found in the central area, but you'll find a few places on Jl Jaksa. Most hotels offer in-room – or at least lobby – wi-fi.

Green Net (Jl Jaksa 35; 4000Rp per hour; 24hr)

Media

Jakarta Globe (www.thejakartaglobe.com; 7500Rp) Excellent newspaper with stylish layout, quality reporting and illuminating features. The Jakarta coverage is impressive.

Jakarta Java Kini (www.jakartajavakini.com; 35,000Rp) Glossy monthly English publication that features restaurant and entertainment reviews alongside lifestyle articles; usually free in many of the bigger hotels.

Jakarta Post (www.thejakartapost.com; 7500Rp) English-language daily with news, views and cultural content.

Medical Services

Cikini Hospital (Map p54; 3899 7777, 2355 0180; http://rscikini.com; Jl Raden Saleh Raya 40) Caters to foreigners and has English-speaking staff.

SOS Medika Klinik (Map p56; 750 5980; www.sosindonesia.com; Jl Puri Sakti 10, Cipete) Offers English-speaking GP appointments, dental care, and emergency and specialist healthcare services.

Money

There are banks all over the city, and you're never far from an ATM in Jakarta.

BII Bank (Map p54; Plaza Indonesia, Jln Thamrin) In the basement level of Plaza Indonesia.

Post

Main Post Office (Jln Gedung Kesenian I; 8am-7pm Mon-Fri, to 1pm Sat) Occupying an octagonal building near Lapangan Banteng.

Tourist Information

Jakarta Visitor Information Office (Map p60; 314 2067, 316 1293; www.jakarta-tourism.go.id; Jl Wahid Hasyim 9; 9am-7pm Mon-Fri, to 4pm Sat) Inside the Jakarta Theatre building. A helpful office; the staff here can answer many queries and set you up with tours of West Java. Practical information can be lacking but it does have a good stock of leaflets and publications and a colour map. There's also a desk at the airport.

Travel Agencies

Travel agencies in the Jl Jaksa area are convenient places to start looking for international flights and long-haul bus tickets. Domestic air tickets usually cost the same from a travel agency as from the airline, but discounts are sometimes available.

Robert Kencana Travel (Map p60; ☎314 2926; Jl Jaksa 20B) The office is scruffy, but staff are used to dealing with travellers. Also runs city tours.

Smailing Tours (Map p60; ☎331 994; www.mysmailing.com; Jl Thamrin 9) The Jl Thamrin office is in the Skyline building just next to the tourist office. Also has branches across the city.

Websites

LIving in Indonesia (www.expat.or.id) Geared at longer-term visitors; boasts everything from restaurant reviews to visa information and has chat rooms.

Jakarta.go.id (www.jakarta.go.id) The Jakarta City Government Tourism Office's official site; offers plenty of listings including transport and events.

JakChat (www.jakchat.com) English-language forums where you can discuss everything from bars to politics.

Lonely Planet (www.lonelyplanet.com/indonesia/jakarta) Planning advice, author recommendations, traveller reviews and insider tips.

 Getting There & Away

Jakarta is the main international gateway to Indonesia. It's also a major centre for domestic travel, with extensive bus, train, air and boat connections.

Air

All international flights and most domestic flights operate from Sukarno-Hatta international airport. In 2012, due to capacity problems, it was announced that Halim Perdana Kusuma airport (southeast of the city) was to reopen for (a few) internal flights.

Consult www.jakartaairportonline.com for airport information and schedules.

AirAsia (☎5050 5088; www.airasia.com) Links Jakarta to Semarang, Yogyakarta and Bali.

Batavia Air (Map p54; www.batavia-air.co.id) Balikpapan to Banjarmasin and Berau; also Pontianak to Singapore.

Citilink (☎080 4108 0808; www.citilink.co.id) Flies to cities including Denpasar, Banjarmasin, Pekanbaru and Surabaya.

Garuda (Map p54; ☎080 4180 7807; www.garuda-indonesia.com; Jl Merdeka Selatan 13, Garuda Bldg) Connects Jakarta with dozens of Indonesian cities including Denpasar, Yogyakarta, Makassar and Kupang.

Lion Air (Map p54; ☎080 4177 8899; www.lionair.co.id; Jl Gajah Mada 7) Links Jakarta with cities all over the archipelago.

Mandala Air (Map p60; ☎0018 0360 1933; www.tigerairways.com) Connects Jakarta with Medan; other destinations planned.

Merpati (Map p50; ☎080 0101 2345, 654 8888; www.merpati.co.id; Jl Angkasa Blok B/15 2-3, Kemayoran) Links Jakarta with many points in the east of the nation. Some flights use Halim Perdana Kusuma airport.

Sriwijaya Air (Map p50; ☎080 4177 7777; www.sriwijayaair.co.id) Links Jakarta with many cities in Java, Sumatra, Kalimantan, Sulawesi and Papua.

Boat

Pelni shipping services operate on regular schedules to ports all over the archipelago. The **Pelni ticketing office** (☎6385 0960; www.pelni.co.id; Jl Angkasa 18) is northeast of the city centre in Kemayoran. Tickets (plus commission) can also be bought from the agent **Kerta Jaya** (Map p54; ☎021 345 1518; Jl Veteran I 27), opposite Mesjid Istiqlal.

Pelni ships all arrive at and depart from Pelabuhan Satu (dock No 1) at Tanjung Priok, 13km northeast of the city centre. Busway Koridor 12 provides a direct bus link, or a taxi from Jl Jaksa is around 85,000Rp.

Bus

Jakarta's four major bus terminals – Kalideres, Kampung Rambutan, Pulo Gadung and Lebak Bulus – are all a long way from the city centre. Take the TransJakarta busway to these terminals as the journey can take hours otherwise. Trains are generally a better alternative for travelling to/from Jakarta. Tickets (some including travel to the terminals) for the better buses can be bought from agencies.

Kalideres Serves points west of Jakarta. Buses run to Merak (25,000Rp, 2½ hours) and Labuan (36,000Rp, 3½ hours). A few buses go to Sumatra from Kalideres, but most depart from Pulo Gadung terminal. Take Busway Koridor 3 to get there.

Kampung Rambutan Mainly handles buses to points south and southwest of Jakarta such as Bogor (normal/air-con 8000/12,000Rp, 45 minutes); Cianjur (normal/air-con 23,000/26,000Rp, 2½ hours); Bandung (normal/air-con 37,000/47,000Rp, three hours); Pangandaran (68,000Rp to 85,000Rp, eight to nine hours) and Pelabuan Ratu (35,000Rp, four hours). Take Busway Koridor 7 to get there.

Pulo Gadung Buses to Bandung, Central and East Java, Sumatra, Bali and even Nusa Teng-

TRANSJAKARTA BUSWAY

TransJakarta is a network of clean, air-conditioned buses that run on busways (designated lanes that are closed to all other traffic). They are the quickest way to get around the city.

Most busways have been constructed in the centre of existing highways, and stations have been positioned at roughly 1km intervals. Access is via elevated walkways and each station has a shelter. Eleven busway lines (called *koridor*) are up and running, with a total of 15 planned.

Tickets cost 3500Rp, payable before you board, which covers you to any destination in the network (regardless of how many *koridor* you use). Buses (running 5am to 10pm) are well maintained and usually not too crowded, though you may have to wait a while for a bus with seating space during peak hours.

The busway system has been a great success, but as most middle- and upper-class Jakartans remain as addicted as ever to their cars, the city's famous traffic jams look set to continue for a good few years yet.

gara. Bandung is via the toll road (46,000Rp, three hours), Cirebon (48,000Rp, five hours) and Yogyakarta (110,000Rp to 150,000Rp, 12 hours). Sumatra is a long haul from Jakarta by bus, but destinations include Bengkulu (from 210,000Rp) and Palembang (from 240,000Rp). Take Busway 2 or 4 to get there.

Lebak Bulus Long-distance deluxe buses to Yogyakarta, Surabaya and Bali; take Koridor 8 to get here.

Minibus

Door-to-door *travel* minibuses are not a good option in Jakarta because it can take hours to pick up or drop off passengers in the traffic jams. Unless you've the patience of a saint take a train, plane or bus.

Day Trans (Map p60; ☎7063 6868; www.daytrans.co.id; Jl Thamrin; ⏰hourly 6am-8pm) Hourly minibuses to Bandung (125,000Rp) from Jl Thamrin.

Train

Jakarta's four main train stations are quite central, making trains the easiest way out of the city. The most convenient and important is Gambir station, on the eastern side of Merdeka Sq, a 15-minute walk from Jl Jaksa. Gambir handles express trains to Bogor, Bandung, Yogyakarta, Solo, Semarang and Surabaya. Pasar Senen train station is to the east and mostly has economy-class trains while Tanah Abang station has economy trains to the west.

Check timetables online at www.kereta-api.co.id, or consult the helpful staff at the station's **information office** (☎692 9194). There's a (slightly pricey) taxi booking desk inside Gambir station; the fare to Jl Jaksa is 35,000Rp.

Bogor Trains leave from Gambir and Juanda stations. Air-conditioned trains (one hour, 13,000Rp) leave roughly hourly; there are also much slower and dirtier *ekonomi* trains (two hours, 7000Rp). All trains are horribly crowded during rush hours.

Bandung There are frequent trains to Bandung along a scenic hilly track, but book in advance (especially on weekends and public holidays). Comfortable *Argo Parahyangan* services depart from Gambir train station six times daily (business 50,000Rp, executive 70,000Rp to 80,000Rp, 3¼hr) between 5.55am and 8.25pm.

Cirebon Eighteen daily trains connect Jakarta Gambir station with Cirebon. Options include the *Cirebon Express* (business/executive 65,000/105,000Rp, three hours) and several *Argo* trains (130,000Rp, three hours).

Yogyakarta and **Solo** From Gambir there are six daily exclusive-class trains (320,000Rp to 330,000Rp, 7¼ to 9 hours) to Yogyakarta, leaving between 8am and 8.45pm; four of these continue to Solo, 45 minutes further on. You'll find cheaper trains from Pasar Senen train station, including three business-class options (150,000Rp, eight to nine hours).

Surabaya There are four daily exclusive-class trains between Gambir station and Surabaya (365,000Rp, 10½ to 11 hours).

Getting Around

To/From the Airport

Jakarta's Sukarno-Hatta international airport is 35km west of the city centre. A toll road links the airport to the city and the journey takes about an hour (longer during rush hour).

Damri (☎460 3708, 550 1290; www.damri.co.id) airport buses (20,000Rp, every 15 to 30 minutes) run between 4am and 8pm between the airport and Gambir train station (near Jl Jaksa) and several other points in the city including Blok M, Tanjung Priok and Kampung Rambutan bus station. From Gambir train station to Jl Jaksa or Cikini, a taxi is around 30,000Rp, or you could walk (it's just under 1km). Damri buses also run regularly to Bogor (35,000Rp, every 15 to 30 minutes). Taxis from the airport to Jl Thamrin/ Jl Jaksa cost about 170,000Rp including tolls. Be sure to book via the official taxi desks, rather than using the unlicensed drivers outside.

Cipaganti (☎720 4616; www.cipaganti.co.id) offer direct minibus connections to Bandung (75,000Rp, hourly).

A new train line is being constructed between Manggarai station in central Jakarta and the airport; it's expected to be operational sometime in 2015.

Halim Perdana Kusuma airport is 11km south of the Cikini district and not served by pubic transport. A taxi from central Jakarta costs around 50,000Rp.

Bus

Jakarta has a good TransJakarta busway system, which has really sped up city travel in recent years. One of the most useful routes is Koridor 1 which runs north to Kota, past Monas and along Jl Sudirman.

Other buses are not very useful for visitors as they are much slower, hotter (no air-con) and crowded (pickpockets can be a problem). The tourist office can provide a map that plots the busway routes.

Car

Jakarta has branches of the major car-rental operators, including **Avis** (Map p54; ☎314 2900; www.avis.co.id; Jl Diponegoro 25), and **Trac Astra** (Map p50; ☎021 650 6565; www.trac.astra.co.id; Jl Gaya Motor 1/10). Alternatively, enquire in travel agencies, as a vehicle with driver may be the most economical option.

The big operators charge about 650,000Rp per day with a driver (550,000Rp without), while private operators are often cheaper.

A number of the 'transport' guys who hang around on Jl Jaksa can also offer good deals.

Local Transport

Bajaj (pronounced 'ba-jai') are similar to Indonesian tuk-tuks. They are not that common these days and if you hire one it's worth remembering that they are not allowed on many major thoroughfares.

Ojek are basically motorbike taxis. Drivers wait on busy street corners, they usually wear a fluorescent-coloured vest. Getting about Jakarta on two wheels is a lot quicker than in a car, though it's obviously less safe and you're directly exposed to the city's air pollution. Negotiate a price first, a short ride will be about 20,000Rp. A new city-wide *ojek* network called **Go-Jek** (☎725 1110; www.go-jek.com) has recently been introduced, using registered drivers and a call centre so you can book ahead. You can even calculate your fare online: a trip from Jl Jaksa to Kota costs 31,000Rp.

In Kota you'll find pushbike 'taxis' with an additional padded seat on the back. These contraptions are ideal for shuttling to and from Sunda Kelapa; expect to pay 4000Rp to 7000Rp for a short ride.

Taxi

Taxis are very inexpensive in Jakarta. All are metered and cost 5000Rp to 6000Rp for the first kilometre and around 300Rp for each subsequent 100m. A journey of around 6km will cost 21,000Rp, a trip right across town perhaps 60,000Rp. Tipping is expected, if not demanded. Many taxi drivers provide a good service, but Jakarta has enough rogues to give its taxis a variable reputation. Stick to reputable companies such as **Bluebird cabs** (☎794 1234; www.bluebirdgroup.com); a minimum of 20,000Rp is charged for ordered taxis. Any toll road charges and parking fees – there are lots of them – are extra and paid by the passenger.

THOUSAND ISLANDS

☎021 / POP 18,000

A string of palm-fringed islands in the Jakarta Bay, Thousand Islands (Pulau Seribu) are the perfect respite for those stuck in the capital too long. If you're travelling onward through the nation, you could easily skip them – they're expensive by Indonesian standards, and mainly geared towards weekending Jakartans. That said, they do have white-sand beaches and calm, clear seas (aside from the islands closest to the mainland which are plagued by trash).

Several have been developed into resorts with bungalows and water sports. Pulau Pramuka is the group's district centre, but most people live on Pulau Kelapa. Pulau Panjang has the only airstrip on the islands. There are actually only 130 islands, not a thousand.

You can book island trips at the **Ancol Marina** (Map p50; ☎6471 1822; Taman Impian Jaya Ancol) or via the Jakarta Visitor Information Office (p67).

ℹ Getting There & Around

The resorts have daily speedboats from Jakarta's Ancol Marina for guests and day trippers, usually leaving between 8am and 11am and returning between 2pm and 5pm, with additional services on weekends. Some are just a 20-minute ride away, but the furthest islands take around two hours to reach. Return day-trip rates to the resorts with lunch include Pulau Bidadari (395,000Rp), Pulau Sepa (690,000Rp) and Pulau Kotok (890,000Rp).

Locals will ferry you from one island to the next (but this can be pricey). Most islands are small enough to easily explore on foot and some have bikes for hire.

Pulau Bidadari

This is the closest island to Jakarta and is popular with Jakarta residents for day trips. It is one of the least interesting (and trash is a problem), but you can use it to visit other islands such as **Pulau Kahyangan**, **Pulau Kelor** (which has the ruins of an old Dutch fort), or **Pulau Onrust** (where the remains of an 18th-century shipyard can be explored). Boats can be hired for the short trip from Pulau Bidadari for 70,000Rp per hour.

The island's **resort** (☎6471 0048; www.bidadariisland.com; s/d per person incl full board from 985,000/1,605,000Rp) has 49 cottages and sports facilities.

Pulau Macan

Here, a couple of tropical dots in the ocean now host a wonderful new ecoresort, **Tiger Island Village and Eco Resort** (☎3299 5625; www.pulaumacan.com; cabins incl full board from 1,390,000Rp per person) which uses recycled rainwater, solar panels and nature-friendly products. This beachside retreat may not be cheap, but the experience and location are very special and there is good snorkelling offshore.

Pulau Sepa

Pulau Sepa is small island (on foot, it takes about 10 minutes to circumnavigate) on the outer northern reaches of the Seribu chain. It's surrounded by wide stretches of pristine white sand and has good snorkelling.

The rooms at **Pulau Sepa Resort** (☎6386 3477; full-board packages from 1,248,000Rp per person; ❄) are pretty basic, while its cottages have more character.

WEST JAVA

Many tourists only experience the lush, volcanic panoramas of West Java (Jawa Barat) through the murky window of a speeding bus or train but this dramatic, diverse region has plenty to detain the inquisitive traveller. Historically it's known as Sunda and its people and language are Sundanese.

West Java stretches from the remote islands of the Ujung Kulon National Park (last Javan home of the one-horned rhino) in the west to the sweeping beaches of Pangandaran in the east. In between, you can visit the infamous offshore volcano of Krakatau, surf in the chilled coastal resorts Cimaja and Batu Karas, get to grips with local culture in Cianjur and stroll through Bogor's lush botanical gardens.

Banten

Most visitors just head straight from Jakarta to Merak on their way to (or from) Sumatra, simply because there's not a lot in this area to attract your attention. From here it is possible to head for the west coast, though, and the historic town of Banten can be an intriguing diversion if you have time to kill.

On the coast due north of Serang, the fishing town of Banten was once a great maritime capital, where the Dutch and English first landed in Java to secure trade and struggle for economic supremacy.

Banten reached its peak during the reign of Sultan Agung (1651–83), and in 1680 he declared war on the Dutch, but conflict within the royal house ultimately led to his downfall. Agung fled Banten but finally sur-

WORTH A TRIP

PULAU DUA BIRD SANCTUARY

Off the north coast at Banten, Pulau Dua is one of Indonesia's major bird sanctuaries. The island has a large resident population – mainly herons, storks and cormorants – but the peak time is between March and July, when great numbers of migratory birds flock here for the breeding season.

It's a half-hour trip by chartered boat from the Karanghantu harbour in Banten, but you can walk across the fish ponds (via bridges) to the island. From Banten, take an *angkot* 5km east to Sawahluhur village. The trail to the island starts 100m or so before the village and then it's a hot 1km walk, weaving between the fish ponds – just keep heading for the trees on the horizon.

West Java

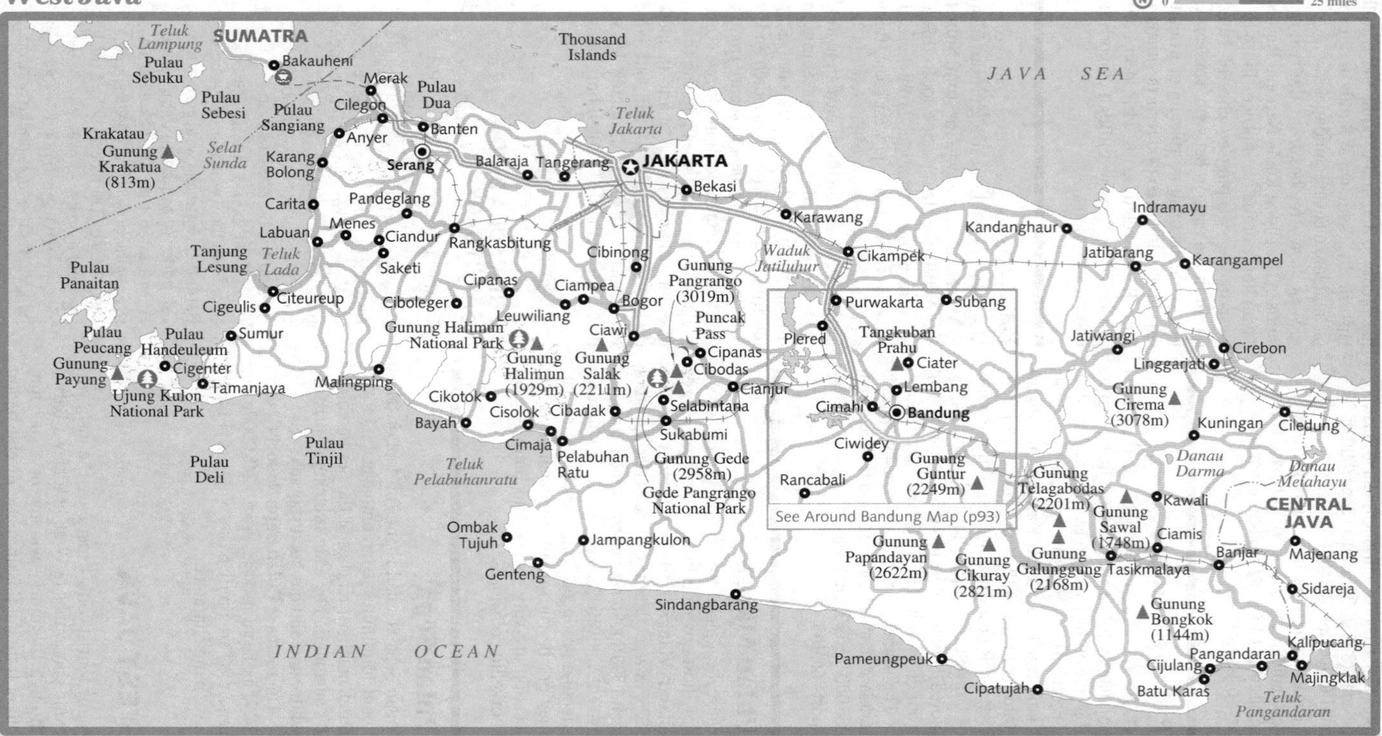
0 50 km
0 25 miles
N
SUMATRA
Teluk Lampung
Pulau Sebuku
Bakauheni
Pulau Sebesi
Krakatau
Gunung Krakatua (813m)
Selat Sunda
Pulau Sangiang
Merak
Cilegon
Pulau Dua
Banten
Anyer
Serang
Karang Bolong
Carita
Pandeglang
Labuan
Menes
Ciandur
Saketi
Rangkasbitung
Tanjung Lesung
Teluk Lada
Pulau Panaitan
Citeureup
Cigeulis
Sumur
Pulau Peucang
Pulau Handeuleum
Gunung Payung
Cigenter
Tamanjaya
Ujung Kulon National Park
Malingping
Cipanas
Ciboleger
Gunung Halimun National Park
Leuwiliang
Ciampea
Bogor
Cibinong
Thousand Islands
Teluk Jakarta
Balaraja
Tangerang
JAKARTA
Bekasi
Karawang
Waduk Jatiluhur
Cikampek
Gunung Pangrango (3019m)
Puncak Pass
Cipanas
Cibodas
Ciawi
Gunung Halimun (1929m)
Gunung Salak (2211m)
Cikotok
Cisolok
Cibadak
Bayah
Cimaja
Pelabuhan Ratu
Teluk Pelabuhanratu
Selabintana
Sukabumi
Cianjur
Gunung Gede (2958m)
Gede Pangrango National Park
Pulau Tinjil
Pulau Deli
Ombak Tujuh
Jampangkulon
Genteng
Sindangbarang
INDIAN OCEAN
JAVA SEA
Purwakarta
Subang
Plered
Tangkuban Prahu
Ciater
Lembang
Cimahi
Bandung
Ciwidey
Rancabali
Gunung Guntur (2249m)
See Around Bandung Map (p93)
Gunung Papandayan (2622m)
Gunung Cikuray (2821m)
Pameungpeuk
Cipatujah
Kandanghaur
Indramayu
Jatibarang
Karangampel
Jatiwangi
Cirebon
Linggarjati
Gunung Cirema (3078m)
Kuningan
Ciledung
Danau Darma
Danau Metahayu
Gunung Telagabodas (2201m)
Gunung Sawal (1748m)
Kawali
Ciamis
Gunung Galunggung (2168m)
Tasikmalaya
Banjar
CENTRAL JAVA
Majenang
Sidareja
Gunung Bongkok (1144m)
Kalipucang
Pangandaran
Cijulang
Majingklak
Batu Karas
Teluk Pangandaran

rendered in 1683, and his defeat marked the real beginning of Dutch territorial expansion in Java.

The chief landmark here is the 16th-century mosque **Mesjid Agung**, a good example of early Islamic architecture; its great white octagonal minaret was reputedly designed by a Chinese Muslim. Next to the mosque is an **archaeological museum** (Jl Raya Banten Lama; admission free; ⏲9am-4pm Tue-Sun), which has a modest collection of local clay artefacts, and spikes used by Banten's Debus followers. (The Debus tradition involves masochistic activities such as self-piercing, which the faithful are said to be able to perform without drawing blood).

Directly across from the mosque are the remains of early ruler Hasanuddin's fortified palace, the Surosowan, which was wrecked in the bloody civil war during the reign of Sultan Agung (and again by the Dutch in 1832).

Other points of interest around the mosque include the massive ruins of **Fort Speelwijk** to the northwest and the huge, crumbling walls and archways of the **Kaibon palace**, and nearby **tomb of Maulana Yusuf**, who died in 1580.

Getting There & Away

Take a bus from Jakarta's Kalideres bus terminal to Serang (14,000Rp, 1½ hours), 10km south of Banten, from where a minibus (3000Rp, 20 minutes) will drop you near the Mesjid Agung.

Merak

☎0254

Right on the northwestern tip of Java, 140km from Jakarta, Merak is an ugly port town, the terminus for ferries shuttling to south Sumatra. In a decade or so a new Selat Sunda bridge should connect Java and Sumatra here, but for now you'll be boarding a boat between these two great islands.

Getting There & Away

The bus terminal and train station are at the ferry dock.

Ferries to Bakauheni in Sumatra depart every 30 minutes, 24 hours a day. Foot passengers pay 11,500p, and the journey is about two hours. Fast boats (30,000Rp, 45 minutes) also make this crossing, but they don't run in heavy seas. The through-buses to Bandarlampung are the easiest option.

Very frequent buses make the run between Merak and Jakarta (22,000Rp to 30,000Rp, 2½ hours). Most go to the capital's Kalideres bus terminal, but buses also run to/from Pulo Gadung and Kampung Rambutan. Other buses run all over Java, including Bogor (42,000Rp) and Bandung (46,000Rp to 60,000Rp). For Labuan (13,000Rp), a change at Cilegon is required.

There are also infrequent trains to Jakarta, but most are economy class.

Carita

☎0253

The west-coast beaches of Java have some good swimming spots, sparkling white sands and even a little surf. They're popular with holidaying Jakartans, though few travellers make it out here.

Apart from the multiplying resorts, the area is sparsely populated. The main place of interest is Carita, for arranging tours to Krakatau, visible on the horizon from most of the resorts.

Carita is a spread-out, laidback beach resort with a slimline sandy beach and good swimming. Most hotels are aging resort-style enclaves geared at weekending Jakartan families, so prices are quite steep but there are few places aimed at budget travellers. It's a good place to set up a tour to Krakatau or Ujung Kulon National Park.

The hotel Sunset View is the best place for information.

Sights & Activities

About 2km from Carita over the rice paddies you can see the village of **Sindanglaut** (End of the Sea), which is where the giant tsunami of 1883 ended its destructive run. **Hutan Wisata Carita** is a forest reserve with walks through the hills and jungle. **Curug Gendang** waterfall is a three-hour return hike through the reserve.

Tours

Virtually everyone in town will try to peddle you a Krakatau tour. Travel agencies **Black Rhino** (☎802 818; blackrhinojava@yahoo.com), based in the the Paniisan Hotel, and **Krakatau Tour** (☎0878 7147 7780; www.krakatau-tour.com), inside the Sunset View hotel, can organise trips. Check your tour boat first as waves can be rough, and make sure it has a radio and lifejackets on board. Day trips to Krakatau start at 2,200,000Rp after bargaining. Trips to Ujung Kulon cost 7,500,000Rp for a three-day tour; overnight trips to Badui villages start at 2,000,000Rp per person.

Sleeping & Eating

Rates increase on weekends by about 20% at most places.

Sunset View HOTEL $
(☎801 075; www.augusta-ind.com; r 175,000Rp, with air-con 225,000Rp; meals around 20,000Rp; ❄☎⛱) The best option for travellers in Carita, this centrally-located hotel on the inland side of the coastal road offers large clean rooms, all with TV. The restaurant downstairs serves up Indonesian grub and a few Western dishes while the pool is more splash-about than lane-swimming. Staff are pleasant enough, but expect some tour-pushing.

Paniisan Hotel HOTEL $
(☎801 072; paniisancarita@yahoo.com; s/d with fan 100,000/120,000Rp, with air-con 150,000/200,000Rp; ❄) Next door to Sunset View, this small hotel has 16 tidy, plain, tiled rooms with front porches that are kept in decent condition by owner Maya and her family. Black Rhino tours are based here.There's a warnet (internet centre) next door.

Mutiara Carita RESORT $$
(☎801 069; www.mutiara-carita.com; r/cottages from 540,000/960,000Rp; ❄) Thatched cottages – some with beach aspects – and rooms in a large, leafy complex that has a tennis court (and, unfortunately, karaoke). The kids' facilities are excellent here. Check the website for promotional discounts.

Pondok Makan ABG INDONESIAN $
(www.pondokmakan-abg.com; Jl Raya Carita Km9; meals 14,000-26,000Rp) This traditional-style restaurant specialises in delicious chicken. Order the terrific *ayam kalasan goreng* (fried chicken with special herbs) and wash it down with a cold Bintang beer or fresh fruit juices (6000Rp). It's just behind the Hotel Rakata on the main beach road.

Getting There & Away

To get to Carita from Jakarta, take a bus to Labuan and then an *angkot* to Carita (5000Rp). On weekends allow extra time for the journey.

Labuan

☎0253 / POP 49,200

The dreary little port of Labuan is merely a jumping-off point for Carita or for Ujung Kulon National Park, but it is home to the helpful **Labuan PHKA office** (☎801 731; www.ujungkulon.org), located 2km north of town towards Carita (look out for the rhino statue).

Frequent buses depart from Kalideres bus terminal in Jakarta for Labuan (36,000Rp, 3½ hours). Regular buses also operate between Labuan and Bogor (36,000Rp, four hours). *Angkots* for Carita (5000Rp, 30 minutes) leave from the market, 100m from the Labuan bus terminal.

Gunung Krakatau

The legendary peak of Krakatau, the most famous of the world's famous volcanoes, is a name almost everyone knows – but few actually know of its location (take the film makers of *Krakatoa, East of Java*, for instance). Resting in relative peace some 50km from the West Java coast and 40km from Sumatra, the volcano is nowadays a shadow of its former self – a small group of disconnected islands centred on **Anak Krakatau** (Child of Krakatau), a volcanic mass that has been on the boil since 1928.

The highlight of any trip to Krakatau is rounding Pulau Rakata and first glimpsing the menacing peak of Krakatau's child.

Activities

Krakatau is only accessible by boat. At the time of research it was possible to land on the eastern side of Anak Krakatau and explore the lower parts of the cone, but this is very much dependent on volcanic activity. Walking to the edge of the caldera is never advisable – people have been killed by flying rocks. Always seek qualified advice before making any trip to the volcano.

After Krakatau, tours usually move on to hike and snorkel on neighbouring islands, overnight trips setting up camp on either Rakata or Verlaten islands.

Information

Labuan PHKA office (☎801 731; ⌚8am-4pm Mon-Fri) has information on the volcano; otherwise consult tour agencies in Carita about Anak Krakatau's current activity status.

Getting There & Away

Most visitors to Krakatau come from Carita. However, Krakatau officially lies in Sumatra's Lampung province, and it is slightly quicker and cheaper to reach Krakatau from the small port of Kalianda in that island.

DAY INTO NIGHT

Few volcanoes have as explosive a place in history as Krakatau, the island that blew itself apart in 1883. Turning day into night and hurling devastating tsunamis against the shores of Java and Sumatra, Krakatau quickly became vulcanology's A-list celebrity.

Few would have guessed that Krakatau would have snuffed itself out with such a devastating swan song. It had been dormant since 1680 and was regarded as little more than a familiar nautical landmark for maritime traffic passing through the narrow Selat Sunda.

But from May through to early August in 1883, passing ships reported moderate activity, and by 26 August Krakatau was raging.

At 10am on 27 August 1883, Krakatau erupted so explosively that on the island of Rodriguez, more than 4600km to the southwest, a police chief reported hearing the booming of 'heavy guns from eastward'.

With its cataclysmic eruptions, Krakatau sent up a column of ash 80km high and threw into the air nearly 20 cubic kilometres of rock. Ash fell on Singapore 840km to the north and on ships as far as 6000km away; darkness covered Selat Sunda from 10am on 27 August until dawn the next day.

Far more destructive were the great ocean waves triggered. A tsunami more than 40m high swept over the nearby shores of Java and Sumatra, and the sea wave's passage was recorded far from Krakatau, reaching Aden (on the Arabian Peninsula) in 12 hours over a distance 'travelled by a good steamer in 12 days'. Measurable wave effects were even said to have reached the English Channel. Coastal Java and Sumatra were devastated: 165 villages were destroyed and more than 36,000 people were killed.

The following day a telegram sent to Singapore from Batavia (160km east of Krakatau) reported odd details such as 'fish dizzy and caught with glee by natives', and for three years, ash clouds circled the earth, creating spectacular sunsets.

The astonishing return of life to the devastated islands has been the subject of scientific study ever since. Not a single plant was found on Krakatau a few months after the event; 100 years later – although the only fauna are snakes, insects, rats, bats and birds – it seems almost as though the vegetation was never disturbed.

Krakatau may have blown itself to smithereens, but it is currently being replaced by Anak Krakatau, which has been on the ascendant ever since its first appearance in 1930. Today 'Krakatau's child' is growing at the rate of seven metres per year, and this anger-prone volcanic kid is certainly a chip off the old block, sending out showers of glowing rocks and belching smoke and ashes.

Chartering a boat is the only way to get to Krakatau; always charter the best vessel you can afford. During the rainy season (November to March) there are strong currents and rough seas, but even during the dry season strong southeast winds can make a crossing inadvisable. Krakatau is a 90-minute ride from Carita in a fast boat when weather conditions are fine. It's a long one-day trip, but it's definitely worth the effort – *if* you can hire a safe boat.

Small fishing boats may be cheap, but being pushed around in high oceanic swells won't feel like value for money. Reliable boats with radios and life jackets start at 2,200,000Rp for a small utility boat (maximum of six people) and go up to around 3,800,000Rp for faster boats (eight to 10 people). These can be organised through Carita tour agents.

Ujung Kulon National Park

On the remote southwestern tip of Java, this Unesco World Heritage–listed **national park** (admission 59,500Rp) has remained an outpost of prime rainforest and untouched wilderness, virgin beaches and healthy coral reefs. Few people visit the park (which was Indonesia's first national park), but it is one of the most rewarding, if remote, environments in all Java.

Ujung Kulon is best known as the last refuge of the one-horned Javan rhinoceros, one of the globe's most critically endangered mammals – there are only thought to be around 40 or 50 remaining, all right here. Until recently another extremely isolated

SUNDANESE MUSIC & DANCE

Sundanese instrument makers are highly innovative and are capable of producing a sweet sound from just about anything. Of their better-known designs, the *kecapi* (a type of plucked lute) is the most idiosyncratic and is often accompanied by the *suling*, a soft-toned bamboo flute that fades in and out of the long, vibrating notes of the *kecapi*. The *angklung* is more ungainly in appearance and consists of a series of bamboo pieces of differing length and diameter, loosely suspended from a bamboo frame. When shaken, it produces an unlikely echoing sound.

Another traditional form is *gamelan degung*. This is played like Central Javanese gamelan, by a small ensemble, but with the addition of a set of small, suspended gongs *(degung)* and an accompanying *suling*. The music produced exists in the hinterland and has a sound somewhere between the soporific Central Javan and livelier Balinese styles of gamelan.

The best-known contemporary West Javan dance form, Jaipongan, is a whirlwind of fast drumming and erotic movement, interspersed with a good dose of *pencak silat* (Indonesian martial arts) and a flick of New York–style break dancing. Jaipongan is a recent mutation of a more traditional Sundanese form called Ketuktilu, in which a group of professional female dancers (sometimes prostitutes) dance for male spectators.

Other dance forms include Longser, Joker and Ogel. Longser and Joker involve the passing of a sash between two couples. Ogel is a slow and exhaustive form, featuring measured movements and a rehearsal regime that many young performers simply lack the time or patience for.

group lived in Vietnam, but the last of these was shot by poachers in 2010.

Numbers are thought to be stable, and the rhinos are breeding: in 2011 evidence of at least five babies was confirmed. However rhinos are an extremely rare sight and you are far more likely to come across banteng (wild cattle), wild pigs, otters, deer, squirrels, leaf monkeys, gibbons and big monitor lizards. Panthers also live in the forest and pythons and crocodiles in the river estuaries. Green turtles nest in some of the bays and the birdlife is excellent.

The national park also includes the nearby island of Panaitan (where Captain James Cook anchored *HMS Endeavour* in 1771) and the smaller offshore islands of Peucang and Handeuleum. Much of the peninsula is dense lowland rainforest and a mixture of scrub, grassy plains, swamps, pandanus palms and long stretches of sandy beach on the west and south coasts.

Most people visit Ujung Kulon on a tour, but it's also perfectly feasible to make your own way to Tamanjaya village and explore the park from there.

Activities

Tamanjaya village, the main gateway to the park, has budget accommodation and guides. One three-day hike across to the west coast via beaches and river crossings and on to Pulau Peucang is very popular but there are alternatives, including a route that takes in good coastal scenery and the lighthouse at Tanjung Layar, the westernmost tip of mainland Java. Or, for wildlife viewing you can set up a series of day-hikes in Tamanjaya.

Pulau Peucang is another entry point, but it can only be reached by chartered boat. There's good accommodation and a restaurant. Peucang also has beautiful white-sand beaches and coral reefs on its sheltered eastern coast (snorkelling gear is available). Hikers might be able to hitch a lift on a boat out of Peucang, but don't count on it.

There is also comfortable but simple accommodation at **Pulau Handeuleum**, which is ringed by mangroves. It has some Timor deer but doesn't have Peucang's attractions. Canoes can be hired (50,000Rp) for the short crossing to Cigenter, on the mainland opposite. You can cruise up a jungle river where you might see pythons – they're often spotted hanging on branches above the water.

Large **Pulau Panaitan** is more expensive to reach but has some fine beaches and hiking. It's a day's walk between the PHKA posts at Legon Butun and Legon Haji, or you can walk to the top of Gunung Raksa, topped by a Hindu statue of Ganesh. Panaitan is a legendary **surfing** spot, with breaks including the infamous One Palm Point, a left-hand barrel that spins over a sharp reef.

Tours

Tours can be set up in Tamanjaya itself, which works out far cheaper than using the Carita tour agencies. Basically you can either walk or boat it into the park, there are no roads. Either way you must have a guide – head to the Sunda Jaya.

Factor in food costs (around 40,000Rp per day, per person), plus your guide (100,000Rp per day) and tent rental (around 75,000Rp per trip). Bring along lightweight food, such as packaged noodles, and drinking water if you are trekking; otherwise food can be organised by tour operators or the park wardens. Supplies are available in Tamanjaya, but in Sumur and Labuan there is more choice. Boat trips are much more expensive as the boat hire costs 1,500,000Rp (for up to 10 people).

If you'd rather get organised in advance, tour agencies such as **Black Rhino** (☎802 818; blackrhinojava@yahoo.com) and Krakatau Tour (p73) in Carita offer a wide variety of trips. A three day/two night all-inclusive tour costs about 7,500,000Rp (for two people). This includes return road and boat transport, accommodation inside the national park, snorkelling, canoeing, hiking and meals.

Surf packages are also available to Panaitan; Bali-based **Surf Panaitan** (☎0361-850 0254; www.surfpanaitan.com) charges from US$900 for a seven-day trip.

Sleeping & Eating

Advance bookings are recommended for Pulau Peucang and Handeuleum, particularly at weekends; contact the Labuan PHKA office. Within the park you can camp or stay at the primitive huts for a small fee. Food and supplies are available in Tamanjaya.

Sunda Jaya Homestay GUESTHOUSE $
(☎0818 0618 1209; http://sundajaya.blogspot.co.uk; Tamanjaya; r per person 60,000Rp, meals 18,000Rp) This Tamanjaya guesthouse was orginially built by the World Wildlife Fund and has four simple, clean rooms, each with two single beds and mosquito nets. Bathrooms are shared. Good meals are offered and there's free tea and coffee. Pak Komar (the genial owner) is an expert on the national park and can organise guides and supplies.

Pulau Peucang Lodge LODGE $$
(r with fan & shared bath 165,000-440,000Rp, with air-con 715,000-825,000Rp; ❄) On Pulau Peucang there's a choice of five different accommodation options, some of them surprisingly smart given the remote location. The attractive, well-constructed air-conditioned Flora bungalows even offer home comforts such as hot-water bathrooms, reading lights and a fridge. At the cheaper eight-bed Fauna bungalow you'll find six rooms (each can sleep three), while the basic Bivek is perfect for travellers. There's a good restaurant and deer, monkeys and wild boar are often spotted around the grounds.

Pulau Handeuleum Lodge LODGE $
(r 165,000Rp) The lodge is in a coconut grove. It has been recently renovated and has six simple double rooms with fans. There's a kitchen, but you must bring your own food, as the island has no other dining options.

Wisma Wisata Alam HOMESTAY $
(☎025 380 2224; Jl Dermaga; r 50,000-65,000Rp) This Tamanjaya homestay has simple rooms, welcoming owners and good views of Krakatau.

Information

The **Labuan PHKA office** (☎804 681; www.ujungkulon.org; ⏲8am-4pm Mon-Fri) is a useful source of information, but you pay your entry fee when you enter the park at the park office in Tamanjaya or on the islands. Hikers should try to pick up a copy of the excellent, but rarely available, *Visitor's Guidebook to the Trails of Ujung Kulon National Park* (40,000Rp) from the park office.

The best time to visit Ujung Kulon is in the dry season (April to October), when the sea is generally calm and the reserve less boggy. Be aware that malaria has been reported in Ujung Kulon.

Getting There & Away

From Labuan there's one direct bus to Tamanjaya (30,000Rp, 3½ hours) daily at noon. There are also hourly *angkot*s as far as Sumur (20,000Rp, two hours) until around 4pm. From Sumur, an *ojek* to Tamanjaya is about 30,000Rp.

The road between Sumur and Tamanjaya is usually in very poor shape, particularly during rainy season.

Or you could charter a boat to get here from Carita, Labuan or Sumur. Given the long stretch of open sea, fork out for a decent one. Surf tours use their own transport.

Bogor

0251 / POP 967,400

'A romantic little village' is how Sir Stamford Raffles described Bogor when he made it his country home during the British interregnum. As an oasis of unpredictable weather – it is credited with 322 thunderstorms a year – cool, quiet Bogor was the chosen retreat of colonials escaping the stifling, crowded capital.

Today, the long arm of Jakarta reaches almost the whole way to Bogor, and while a ribbon of green still just about survives between the two, the city is already choked with the overspill of the capital's perennial traffic problems.

But while Bogor's transformation into a distant Jakartan suburb continues apace, the real oasis remains untouched. Planted in the very centre of the city, with the traffic passing idly by, Bogor's botanical gardens are truly world class.

Sights

Kebun Raya GARDENS

(Great Garden; www.bogor.indo.net.id/kri; admission 10,000Rp; 8am-5pm) At the heart of Bogor are the fabulous botanical gardens, known as the Kebun Raya, the city's green lung of around 87 hectares. Governor General Raffles first developed a garden here, but the spacious grounds of the Istana Bogor (Presidential Palace) were expanded by Dutch botanist Professor Reinwardt, with assistance from London's Kew Gardens, and officially opened in 1817. It was from these gardens that various colonial cash crops, such as tea, cassava, tobacco and cinchona, were devel-

Bogor & Kebun Raya

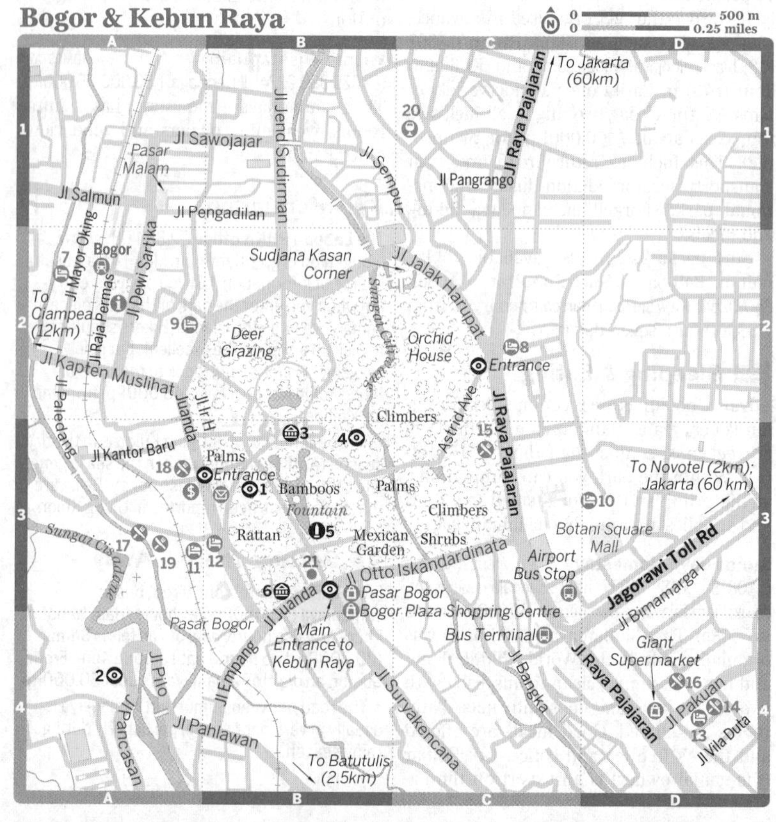

oped by Dutch botanists including Johannes Teysmann. The park is still a major centre for botanical research in Indonesia.

Allow yourself at least half a day to enjoy Kebun Raya, while keen gardeners could spend a week here and not be bored. It's tricky to pick out highlights in such a verdant wonderland – there are more than 15,000 species of trees and plants – but the gardens are said to contain 400 types of magnificent palms, including the footstool palm native to Indonesia, which tops 40m. There's a good stock of graceful pandan trees (look out for their unusual aerial roots) and some huge agave (used to make tequila) and cacti in the Mexican section. Drop by the Orchid House (admission an extra 2000Rp) and take in the lovely ponds, which have giant water lilies over a metre across, and look out for monitor lizards, exotic bird life and deer.

Near the main entrance of the gardens is a small **memorial**, erected in memory of Olivia Raffles, who died in 1814 and was buried in Batavia. There is also a **cemetery** near the palace with Dutch headstones including the tomb of DJ de Eerens, a former governor general.

Crowds flock here on Sunday, but the gardens are quiet at most other times. The southern gate is the main entrance; other gates are only open on Sunday and holidays. Don't miss wonderful Café de Daunen, the perfect spot for lunch.

Istana Bogor HISTORIC BUILDING

In the northwestern corner of the botanical gardens, the summer palace of the president was formerly the opulent official residence of the Dutch governors general from 1870 to 1942.

Today, herds of white-spotted deer roam the immaculate lawns and the building contains Sukarno's huge art collection, which largely focuses on the female figure. The palace is only open to groups (minimum 10) by prior arrangement, and children are not allowed inside. Contact the tourist office for more information.

Batutulis SHRINE

(Jl Batutulis) The Batutulis is an inscribed stone dedicated to Sri Baduga Maharaja (1482–1521), a Pajajaran king credited with great mystical power. The stone is housed in a small shrine visited by pilgrims – remove your shoes and pay a small donation before entering. Batutulis is 2.5km south of the botanical gardens. It's almost opposite the former home of Sukarno. His request to be buried here was ignored by Suharto, who wanted the former president's grave as far away from the capital as possible.

Zoological Museum MUSEUM

(admission included with Kebun Raya ticket; ⌚8am-4pm Sat-Thu, to noon Fri) This museum has a motley but interesting collection of zoological oddities, including the skeleton of a blue whale, giant stick insects, beetles as big as tennis balls and a pooch-sized Flores rat.

Gong Factory FACTORY

(☎832 4132; Jl Pancasan 17) This is one of the few remaining gongsmiths. You can see gamelan instruments smelted over a charcoal fire by hand here – it takes two weeks to

Bogor & Kebun Raya

Sights

1	Dutch Cemetery	B3
2	Gong Factory	A4
3	Istana Bogor	B3
4	Kebun Raya	B3
5	Olivia Raffles Memorial	B3
6	Zoological Museum	B3

Sleeping

7	Abu Pensione	A2
8	Amaris	C2
9	Hotel Salak	A2
10	Hotel Santika Bogor	D3
11	Pensione Firman	A3
12	Puri Bali	B3
13	Wisma Pakuan	D4

Eating

14	Bukul Bukul	D4
15	Café de Daunan	C3
16	De' Leuit	D4
17	Gumati	A3
18	Pojuk Sate Kiloan	A3
19	Salak Sunset Café	A3

Drinking

20	Sop Buah Pak Ewok	C1

Information

21	PHKA Headquarters	B3

beat a copper gong into shape. A few pricey gongs and *wayang golek* puppets are on sale.

Tours

Tours of Bogor can be arranged through the tourist office for around 150,000/250,000Rp per half-day/day. The tours take in a working-class *kampung*, and various cottage industries including a gong factory, and tofu and *krupuk* (prawn cracker) kitchens. Speak to them too about hiking trips into Halimun National Park. English-speaking guides here include **Agus** (agus_pribadi@hotmail.com) and **Wawan Hendrawan** (☎081 6195 3838). **Alwi** (☎0813 8434 3711; www.alwitours.blogspot.com) also organises excellent tours to local villages in the Bogor area and to Halimun (two-day tours €100, minimum three people).

Sleeping

Bogor does not have a great choice of budget accommodation. Prices are quite steep compared with the rest of Java.

Wisma Pakuan GUESTHOUSE $$
(☎831 9430; wismapakuanbogor@yahoo.com; Jl Pakuan 12; r with fan 225,000Rp, with air-con 270,000-355,000Rp;) This excellent, welcoming guesthouse, a short stroll from the bus terminal, has 12 spacious, well-maintained rooms with flat-screen TV and good beds. Those at the rear have views over a garden, where breakfast is served.

Amaris HOTEL $$
(☎021 270 0027; www.amarishotel.com/amaris-padjajaran; Jalan Padjajaran 25; r 360,000Rp;) Contemporary no-frills hotel where the spotless rooms all have LCD TV, wi-fi, good beds (and bedding), safes and uncluttered lines. There's a restaurant and the location opposite the Kebun Raya gardens is excellent. Book ahead.

Abu Pensione GUESTHOUSE $
(☎832 2893; Jl Mayor Oking 15; r with fan/air-con from 120,000/250,000Rp;) Set back from the road, with rooms on several levels: those around the garden are very pleasant, others facing the river at the rear are a bit dark. All are a shade overpriced but fine for a night or two, and it's secure and quiet. There's a little cafe, with cheapish grub. Expect Selfi, a guide based here, to appear at some stage and push her good (if pricey) city tours.

Puri Bali GUESTHOUSE $
(☎835 0984; Jl Paledang 50; s/d incl breakfast 100,000/120,000Rp) A solid budget choice, this little guesthouse has four spacious rooms, all with high ceilings and private bathrooms. Owner Danu offers a warm welcome and can provide a map of the city's sights and lots of local information.

Hotel Santika Bogor HOTEL $$
(☎840 0707; www.santika.com/bogor; Jl Raya Pajajaran; r from 740,000Rp; @) Sleek, stylish hotel just behind the Botani Sq mall that ticks all the right boxes in terms of minimalist design, though perhaps the effect is just a little soulless.

Hotel Salak HOTEL $$
(☎837 3111; www.hotelsalak.co.id; Jl Ir H Juanda 8; r from 710,000Rp; @) Large colonial-style hotel with a swanky marble lobby that's within walking distance of the gardens. Popular with Indonesians, so the food is good (and quite reasonably priced) in the plethora of cafes and restaurants here.

Pensione Firman GUESTHOUSE $
(☎832 3246; Jl Paledang 48; r 75,000-200,000Rp; @) For years this rambling place was a backpackers' stronghold though it's now something of a last resort due to lack of maintenance – expect very basic rooms. It's friendly enough though, and there's free tea and coffee.

Eating & Drinking

For street food check out the night market along Jl Dewi Sartika and Jl Jenderal Sudirman. Or, if it's raining, the food court inside Botani Sq shopping mall may be a better bet.

Gumati SUNDANESE, INDONESIAN $$
(☎832 4318; www.cafegumati.com; Jl Paledang 28; mains 17,000-64,000Rp; 10am-10pm;) Offers arguably the best view in town with superlative vistas over Bogor's red-tiled rooftops towards the volcanic cone of Gunung Salak. There's an extensive menu, with tapas-style snacks and traditional dishes such as *sup ikan bambu* (soup with fish and bamboo).

Café de Daunan INTERNATIONAL $$
(☎835 0023; inside Kebun Raya; meals 28,000-70,000Rp) The cafe-restaurant in the botanical gardens is a wonderfully civilised place for a bite or a drink, with sweeping views down to the water lily ponds. It's a little pricey, but the tasty Western and Indonesian

food and sublime setting make it an essential stop.

De' Leuit SUNDANESE $$
(☎839 0011; Jl Pakuan III; meals 25,000-70,000Rp;) Impressive new Sundanese restaurant with elegant premises that features open-sided seating under a soaring pyramid-shaped thatched roof. The lengthy menu includes dishes such as *nasi jambal* (rice with dried fish), delicious grilled *gurame* and lots of vegetarian choices.

Salak Sunset Café INTERNATIONAL $
(Jl Paledang 38; mains 22,000Rp) Close to a couple of popular guesthouses, this is a relaxed spot for a cool beer and has views of the city. Also serves local and Western grub.

Bukul Bukul INDONESIAN $$
(☎838 4905; Jl Pakuan 14; mains 15,000-68,000Rp; ⊙11.30am-10pm;) Modish restaurant with an eclectic menu that includes inexpensive dishes such as *sayer asem* (sweet and sour soup) and specials such as barbecued fish served on a hot plate. No alcohol is served, but there are great juices (including starfuit and avocado) or you're welcome to BYO for no charge.

Sop Buah Pak Ewok INDONESIAN
(Jl Bukittunggul 5; fruit punch 9000Rp) Highly popular for its refreshing bowls of fruit punch filled with tropical fruits of the season and served with ice. Noodles and rice dishes are also available here.

Pojuk Sate Kiloan SATE $
(Jl Juanda 42C) A no-nonsense roadside sate hotspot (look out for the goats in the window) where delicious sticks of chicken, beef (2200Rp each) and goat (39,000Rp per 1/4 kilo) are grilled to perfection. The rice dishes are so-so though.

Information

There's free wi-fi at the Botani Sq mall.

BCA Bank (Jl Ir H Juanda 28)

PHKA Headquarters (Jl Ir H Juanda 15; ⊙7am-2.30pm Mon-Thu, to 11am Fri) The official body for the administration of all of Indonesia's wildlife reserves and national parks; located next to the main garden gates.

Post Office (Jl Ir H Juanda)

Tourist Office (☎081 6195 3838; Jl Dewi Sartika 51; ⊙8am-6pm) The friendly team here can help out with most queries about the region, provide a city map, and also offer excellent, well-priced tours.

Getting There & Away

BUS Every 15 minutes or so, buses depart from Jakarta's Kampung Rambutan bus terminal (8000Rp to 12,000Rp, 45 minutes) to Bogor.

Buses depart frequently to Bandung (economy/air-con, 32,000/42,000Rp, 3½ hours), Pelabuhan Ratu (30,000Rp, three hours) and Labuan (36,000Rp, four hours). For Cianjur (22,000Rp, two hours) there are very regular white minibuses (called *colt*) from Jl Raya Pajajaran. Door-to-door *travel* minibuses go to Bandung for 60,000Rp; **Dimas Dewa** (☎653 671) has the best buses. Phone for a pick-up.

Damri buses head direct to Jakarta's Sukarno-Hatta airport (35,000Rp, two to three hours) every 20 minutes from 4am to 11pm from Jl Raya Pajajaran.

CAR The tourist board can recommend car drivers to explore the region around Bogor; rates start at 450,000Rp per day.

TRAIN Express trains (13,000Rp, one hour) connect Bogor with the capital roughly every hour, though try to avoid travelling during rush hour. Economy trains are even more frequent and they are packed with people – even some clinging to the roof.

Getting Around

Green *angkot* minibuses (2000Rp) shuttle around town, particularly between the bus terminal and train station. Angkot 03 does an anticlockwise loop of the botanical gardens on its way to Jl Kapten Muslihat, near the train station. Angkot 06 gets you to the bus terminal from the train station.

Becak are banned from the main road encircling the gardens. Taxis are extremely rare in Bogor.

Around Bogor

Sights

Batutulis Ciampea SHRINE
(Purnawarman Stone) Those in need of reminding that all great empires come to an end can head for Batutulis, where sits the large black boulder on which King Purnawarman inscribed his name and footprint around AD 450. His rather immodest inscription, in the Palawa script of South India, is uncannily reminiscent of Percy Shelley's *Ozymandias*, and reads: 'This is the footstep of King Purnawarman of Tarumanegara kingdom, the great conqueror of the world'.

The Ciampea boulder has been raised from its original place and embedded in the shallow water of Sungai Ciaruteun. The inscription on the stone is still remarkably clear after more than 1500 years.

Minibuses make the run to Batutulis from the village of Ciampea, about 12km northwest of Bogor.

Gunung Halimun National Park PARK

This national park is home to some primary rainforest, but the park has mixed usage and also includes plantations such as the Nirmala Tea Estate. The dominant feature of the park is the rich montane forest in the highland regions around Gunung Halimun (1929m), which is the highest peak.

The most-visited attractions in the park are the waterfalls near Cikidang and those near the Nirmala estate, but the big drawcard is **white-water rafting**. In Jakarta, **Pt Lintas Seram Nusantara** (☎021 835 5885; www.arusliar.co.id) organises white-water rafting on the Class II to IV (depending on season) Sungai Citarak on the southeastern edge of the park; a full-day excursion is 425,000Rp.

The usual access (you need your own transport) is through Cibadak on the Bogor–Pelabuhan Ratu road, from where you turn off to Cikadang and then on to the Nirmala Tea Estate. Rainfall in the park is between 4000mm and 6000mm per year. Most of this falls from October to May, when a visit is more or less out of the question.

Speak to the staff at the tourist board in Bogor (p80) about setting up a trip to Halimun.

Cimaja

☎0266

About 100km south of Bogor, Cimaja is an attractive, low-key surf resort with a good choice of accommodation and excellent waves on tap. There's a nice relaxed vibe to the place, and if you've been suffering in Java's teeming cities, the slow pace of life and oceanic air makes an exhilarating change. To get there you have to pass through the large, unlovely resort of Pelabuhan Ratu; Cimaja is 8km further west.

SAVE THE WAVE?

Cimaja Point is a legendary righthander that breaks over stones and is renowned for its consistency. It even barrels above seven foot. Located offshore from a riverbed, the wave depends on river water for its impressive profile. But in recent years locals have noticed that their wave has become smaller. Perhaps the reason is upriver, where heavy machinery is being used to grind up stones from Cimaja river, resulting in gravel and sand clogging the estuary and disturbing currents that create the wave.

Sights & Activities

The main beach is a pebble affair, but scenic. It's often pounded by crashing surf, and swimming can be treacherous, so take extreme care. You can stroll from the shore to the village via an idyllic patchwork of rice paddies. For a sandy beach you'll have to head west for a kilometre or so to Karang Hawu (Sunset Beach), a broad strip of dark sand with better swimming.

Cimaja is rightly renowned for its excellent **surf**. Some of the south coast's best waves include Cimaja Point, 200m from the Di Desa hotel. Indicator Point has a killer break which fires up on a high tide and big swell and Karang Hawu has a beach break that is good for beginners.

Diving, fishing, rafting and motorcycling trips can also be organised; ask in Didesa, Rumah Makan Mirasa or Café Loma. Surf lessons can be set up here for around 100,000Rp per day (excluding soft board rental); instructors hang out in Café Loma.

Sleeping & Eating

Cimaja is quiet during the week and fills up at weekends and during holidays, when prices rise by around 20% at many places.

TOP CHOICE **Cimaja Square** BUNGALOWS **$$**

(☎644 0800; http://cimajasquare.com; Jl Raya Cisolok; bungalows 150,000-300,000Rp; ❄@📶) Excellent one-stop-shop offering gorgeous, comfortable timber-and-thatch bungalows with kitchens and front decks overlooking rice fields. The bistro-style roadside restaurant offers good European and Indonesian food (set meals from 38,000Rp) and there's also a beach boutique, surf shop and internet cafe. Room rates rise on weekends by 25%.

Pondok Kencana LODGE **$$**

(☎431 465; www.ombaktujuh.net; dm/r/bungalows from 46,000/150,000/275,000Rp, meals from 35,000Rp; ❄📶) Australian-owned place that enjoys a good hilltop location at the entrance to the village. There's a wide choice of attractive accommodation, many with viewing decks and shared kitchen access. Owner Leo can usually be found in the bar-restaurant (which serves filling Western grub, including good breakfasts) mixing with his guests over a cold one.

Di Desa BUNGALOW **$$**
(☎433 288; www.desaresort.com; Jl Raya Cisolok 23; r/ste 460,000/550,000Rp; ❄📶) Beautifully built place with a choice of gorgeous modern rooms around the main house that juxtapose sculptured concrete and wood perfectly, or go for the plush stilted bungalows. There's also a restaurant, a surf shop/repair service, tower for checking wave conditions, and live reggae every Saturday night.

Sunset Plaza HOTEL **$$**
(☎0815 7202 2360, 431 125; www.sunsetplazahotel.multiply.com; Sunset Beach; r/ste 350,000/700,000Rp; ❄📶) Spacious, comfortable rooms that enjoy full-frontal ocean vistas, you pay extra for the renovated options. The bar-restaurant area is terrific, wrapping around two sides of the structure and Western meals including prime steaks and seafood are available. Prices rise on weekends and holidays.

Nurda's HOTEL **$$**
(☎431 495; www.cimajapoint.com; r 150,000-400,000Rp; ❄📶) A fine-looking timber property in a private, grassy sea-facing plot with four double rooms and a bunkhouse for sharers. There's a bar-restaurant too. It's very geared up for surfers with good info from the staff and you can actually check the waves breaking below.

Hotel Daun Daun HOTEL **$**
(☎0857 5958 1691; r incl breakfast with fan 100,000Rp, s/d with air-con 150,000/250,000Rp) On the main drag in the village this simple place has clean, freshly painted rooms, though most don't have private bathrooms. There's a TV lounge for socialising.

Café Loma INDONESIAN **$**
(Jl Raya Cisolok; meals from 12,000Rp) Very cheap little log cabin-style warung where you can score a great breakfast for 15,000Rp, fresh juice for 5000Rp or a cup of Java coffee for just 2000Rp. Most mains including *ikan mentega* (fish in butter sauce) are less than 20,000Rp. In the evening it's a low key hangout for surfers, with cold Bintang.

Rumah Makan Mirasa INDONESIAN **$**
(☎436 337; r 80,000Rp, meals 15,000-20,000Rp) A friendly little family-run eatery which offers tasty Indonesian food including *sate ikan* (fish sate) and gado gado as well as Western food including fruit salads, jaffles, omelettes and pancakes. Two simple, fairly spacious fan-cooled rooms are also available. Transport, motorbike hire and laundry can be arranged here.

Information

There are no banks in Cimaja, but you'll find several in Pelabuhan Ratu, 8km to the east, including **BCA Bank** (Jl Siliwangi) with an ATM. For internet access head to Cimaja Sq.

Getting There & Around

To reach Cimaja, you first need to get to Pelabuhan Ratu which is around four to five hours from Jakarta depending on the traffic. Regular buses (35,000Rp) run to/from the Kampung Rambutan terminal until 3pm. Buses also run throughout the day from Bogor (30,000Rp, three to four hours) to Pelabuhan Ratu.

Some buses continue on from Pelabuhan Ratu to Cimaja. These are supplemented by regular *angkot* (4000Rp, 30 minutes), which run about every 20 minutes. Some *angkot* then go on to Cisolok, past Sunset Beach.

Motorbikes can be hired for 50,000Rp per day from locals in Cimaja, and surfboard racks are available.

Around Cimaja

Sights & Activities

Pantai Karang Hawu VIEWPOINT
Pantai Karang Hawu, 4km west of Cimaja, is a towering cliff with caves, rocks and pools created by a large lava flow. According to legend, it was here where the goddess Nyai Loro Kidul leapt into the ocean to regain her lost beauty and never returned. Stairs lead up to a small *kramat* (shrine) at the top.

Cipanas HOT SPRINGS
About 3km west of Pantai Karang Hawu are the Cipanas hot springs. Boiling water sprays into the river, and you can soak downstream where the hot and cold waters mingle. It is a very scenic area, with lush forest upstream and a waterfall, though it's crowded on weekends.

Cibodas

☎0263

Southwest of Bogor the highway steadily climbs in elevation, winding through a sprawling hill resort known as the Puncak that's popular with weekending Jakartans. This traffic-choked road winds up to 1490m before descending to Cibodas, famous for its stunning gardens, the **Kebun Raya Cibodas** (☎512 233; www.bogor.indo.net.id; per person/car 6000/15,500Rp; ⊙8am-4pm). Spread over the steep lower slopes of Gunung Gede and Gunung Pangrango at an altitude of 1300m to 1440m, these lush gardens are one of the dampest places in Java. The Dutch tried to cultivate quinine here (its bark is used in malaria medication), though the East Javan climate proved more suitable.

You'll find an outstanding collection of ferns and palms, 65 species of eucalyptus, Mexican mountain pines, and glasshouses bursting with cacti and succulents. A road loops around the gardens, passing via the Japanese garden with its cherry trees, and there are also paths leading through forests of bamboo to the impressive Cismun waterfall.

There are two guesthouses and a couple of inexpensive cafes in the gardens. Visitors must pay 2000Rp to enter Cibodas village.

Sleeping & Eating

Bali Ubud Guesthouse GUESTHOUSE $
(☎512 051; r from 150,000Rp) About 4km south of the entance to the gardens this wonderful little Balinese-owned place has very attractive rooms with baconies that enjoy spectacular valley views. The restaurant here also makes the most of the views, serving good Western and Indonesian food, and cold Bintang. However they do keep caged animals here (including fighting rams).

Freddy's Homestay HOMESTAY $
(☎515 473; r without mandi incl breakfast 170,000Rp) Freddy's is *the* base in the area for birdwatchers, with books to browse and expert guides on call. Rooms here are very basic, however, and not great value. Meals are available too.

Guesthouses GUESTHOUSE $$
(☎reservations 512 233; r from 300,000Rp) Of the two guesthouses inside the gardens, Wisma Medinella is the one to book; it's a rustic stone-and-timber building which has neat little rooms with pine furniture. The more expensive Wisma Tamu is far less comfortable. Both are a 1km walk uphill from the gate. Book ahead.

Getting There & Away

The turn-off to Cibodas is on the Bogor–Bandung Hwy, a few kilometres west of Cipanas. The gardens are 5km from the main road. *Angkot* run from the roadside in Cipanas up to the gardens (3000Rp, 10 minutes).

Gede Pangrango National Park

The Cibodas gardens are right next to the main entrance to Gede Pangrango National Park, the highlight of which is the climb to the 2958m peak of the volcanically active Gunung Gede. From the top of Gede on a clear day you can see Jakarta and the south coast of Java.

Because it's close to Jakarta, this is an extremely popular mountain to climb. Numbers are restricted and during peak holiday season there may be a waiting list. At other times you can normally just rock up and trek the next day.

On arrival, register for the climb and obtain your permit (a steep 50,000Rp for foreigners) from the **PHKA office** (☎0263-512 776) just outside the entrance to the gardens. The office has an information centre and pamphlets on the park, which is noted for its alpine forest and bird life, including the rare Javan eagle. Officially, guides to the summit *have* to be hired here for 350,000Rp for a two-day round trip, though the main trail is easy to follow. Gunung Gede is closed to hikers between January and March, usually August too, and during stormy weather.

From Cibodas, the trail passes **Telaga Biru** (15 minutes), which is a blue-green lake. **Cibeureum Falls** (one hour away) lie just off the main trail. Most picnickers only go this far, though some continue on to the **hot springs**, 2½ hours from the gate. The trail continues to climb another 1½ hours to **Kandang Badak**, where a hut has been built on the saddle between the peaks of Gunung Gede and Gunung Pangrango (3019m). Take the trail to the right for a hard three-hour climb to Pangrango. Most hikers turn left for the easier, but still steep, 1½-hour climb to Gede, which has more spectacular views. The Gede Crater lies below the summit, and you can continue on to the **Suryakencana Meadow**.

The 10km hike right to the top of Gunung Gede takes at least 10 hours there and back, so you should start as early as possible and take warm clothes (night temperatures can drop to 5°C), food, water and a torch (flashlight). Most hikers leave by 2am to reach the summit in the early morning before the mists roll in.

Cianjur

☎0263 / POP 159,000

East of Cibobas it's 19km to Cianjur, a market town that's famed throughout Java for the quality of its rice; indeed the town is enveloped by shimmering green paddy fields. Cianjur has a few sights of interest in the surrounding district, but most people are here to mix with locals as part of the highly successful homestay program.

You'll find several banks on the main drag, Jl Cokroaminoto, and internet cafes are grouped together on Jl Siti Jenab.

Sights

The town (which is more an amalgamation of villages) has few attractions, but you can visit a huge **plastic recycling plant** to learn about waste management. Plastic is sent here from all over West Java to be separated by hand, then washed, chopped and dried before being sent on to plastic manufacturers.

Around 20km east of town, **Calingling** is an intriguing 'floating village' on a lake that has a substantial fish-farming community. You can hire a boat here (75,000Rp) to get across the lake to a great restaurant (meals cost around 50,000Rp for two).

There are a couple of **tea plantations** close to town that are well worth a visit; both are set in lush mountainside locations. **Gedeh tea plantation** (admission free; ⏲8am-4pm Mon-Sat), 15km northwest of town via a pot-holed road, was established by the Dutch in 1916, and most of the original machinery is still in use. Between 400,000kg and 600,000kg of black tea is produced here monthly. Alternatively **Sarongge** (⏲9am-2pm Mon-Thu & Sat) 20km north of town is a green tea plantation and processing factory; it's open by appointment only.

Cianjur also makes a good base for trips to the Cibonas gardens. If you need to cool off head to **The John** (admission 20,000Rp; ⏲9am-5pm), a leisure complex with three swimming pools that's an ideal picnic spot.

Sleeping & Eating

Most travellers stay with local families in Cianjur. After dark, **BCNY** (Jl A Rahamam Hakin 40; ⏲5-11pm) is a cool hang-out. It's an open-air food court that has live music on weekends.

Lendel Hotel HOTEL $
(☎263 268; Jl Dr Muwardi 165C; r with fan from 140,000Rp, with air-con 200,000-300,000Rp; ❄) A dependable place with a choice of spacious rooms with wardrobe and TV. The rooms are grouped around fish ponds in a garden with palm trees. Bathrooms are all cold-water *mandi* though.

Saung Bebek Cianjur SUNDANESE, INTERNATIONAL $$
(☎288 983; Jl KH Abdullah Bin Nuh 10; meals 15,000-30,000Rp) Excellent new place owned by Yayan, a Cianjur chef who lived in the Bahamas for years. The Sundanese food is superb. You can't beat the *paket nasi liwet*,

LIVE WITH THE LOCALS

The **Cianjur homestay program** (☎0821 2089 0345, 081 7085 6691; www.cianjuradventure.com) is a superb initiative set up by author Yudi Sujana (who for years lived in New Zealand) that allows travellers to experience life in a non-touristy town in Java. The team all speak fluent English, so it's a wonderful opportunity to get to understand Sundanese and Indonesian culture. School visits, sightseeing trips and hikes are offered at backpacking rates. Guests pay 175,000Rp per person per day, which includes family accommodation, three meals, laundry and local transport for trips; it's best to book ahead.

A second initiative, **Volunteer in Java** (☎0877 2003 0020, 0856 230 2486; www.volunteerinjava.com) which combines volunteering opportunities in schools with homestay living is also now up and running, operated by a group of friendly Cianjur teachers. It's cheaper at 100,000Rp per day and the rate includes accommodation and three meals.

Airport pick-ups and drop-offs can also be arranged at very moderate rates by both programs, allowing you to bypass Jakarta completely.

FLAVOURS TO SAVOUR

The Cianjur region is famous for its sweet, spicy cuisine and there are several delicious dishes unique to the area. Be sure to try the local *lontong* (sticky rice with tofu in a delicious, sweet coconut sauce); there are several warung on Jl Dewisartika that specialise in this dish. Look out for some of the best beef sate in Java, locally known as *marangi*, which is available in many places across town. Other local specialities include delicious *batagor* (crispy tofu) and *pandan wangi* rice, which is fragrantly flavoured short-grain rice that's often cooked with lemon grass and spices.

which gives you a taste of everything the region has to offer, or the duck dishes. Western food (including seafood, steaks and pasta) is also available.

Lotek LP SUNDANESE, INDONESIAN **$**
(☎264 554; Jl Aria Cikundang 76; meals 10,000Rp) A casual place that locals swear has the best gado gado (12,000Rp) in Cianjur, plus authentically sweet and sticky *sate marangi* (5000Rp per stick).

RM Batagor Ihsan SUNDANESE **$**
(☎280 737; Jl Juanda 55; meals from 8000Rp) The *batagor* (crispy tofu) here simply should not be missed. It's either eaten with *krin* (peanut sauce) or as part of a *kuah* (watery soup) with onion and garlic.

ℹ Getting There & Away

From Jakarta the easiest way to Cianjur is via a daily minibus (75,000Rp, three hours, daily at 7am). They'll pick you up from your hotel in the centre of the capital. The staff don't speak English so get one of the Cianjur homestay programs to book for you.

Otherwise, buses leave Jakarta's Kampung Rambutan every 30 minutes to Cipanas (normal/air-con 20,000/24,000Rp, two hours) and Cianjur (normal/air-con 23,000/26,000Rp, 2½ hours). At weekends (when traffic is terrible around Puncuk Pass) buses are routed via Jonggol (add an extra hour to your journey time, and 5000Rp). Buses to/from Bandung (normal/air-con 14,000/20,000Rp, two hours) run every half hour.

There are buses to Bogor from Cianjur (22,000Rp, 1½ to two hours) and the highway by Cipanas every 20 minutes.

Bandung

☎022 / POP 2.5 MILLION

After the bottle-green hills of Cibodas, the sprawling bulk of Bandung hits you like a baseball bat across the back of the head. Once the 'Paris of Java', the city is now a throng of congested, polluted streets and any romantic notions of colonial glamour have long disappeared. This is one of Indonesia's megacities (the Bandung conurbation is home to almost eight million people).

But not everything has gone to pot. Bandung attracts workers, intellectuals and students from across the archipelago, and its industries, restaurants and cafes throb with life. Today, grandiose art deco buildings, heaving market stalls, becak and multiplexes jostle for space in the city.

For travellers, the city does make a good base for daytrips to the surrounding countryside – high volcanic peaks, hot springs and tea plantations are all within easy reach.

Sights

There are some very fine Dutch art deco structures to admire on Jl Jenderal Sudirman and Jl Asia Afrika, two of the best being the **Grand Hotel Preanger** and the **Savoy Homann Hotel**, both of which have imposing facades. In the north of the city **Villa Isola** is another wonderful Dutch art deco structure.

FREE **Villa Isola** NOTABLE BUILDING
(Bumi Siliwangi; ☎201 316, 0813 2245 3101; Jl Dr. Setiabudhi 229; ⏲interior by appointment) Around 7km north of the centre Villa Isola is a landmark art deco building, a four-storey villa built by a Dutch media baron in the 1930s as a private residence. It's now the University of Education's administrative offices. This curvacious architectural masterpiece is in excellent condition; from its balconies there's a fine perspective of Bandung. It's possible to enter the building if you call ahead, but the exterior and gardens are actually more impressive than the interior.

FREE **Museum Geologi** MUSEUM
(Geological Museum; Jl Diponegoro 57; ⏲9am-3.30pm Mon-Thu, to 1.30pm Sat & Sun) About 3km north of the centre, the Museum Geologi is a good place to get to grips with all matters geological and volcanic in Indone-

sia, though there's almost no information in English. Nevertheless it's worth an hour or so poking around the lava stones, crystals and bones that include a model of *Tyrannosaurus rex* and a mammoth. From the train station you can take an angkot bound for Sadang Serang and get off at the Gedung Sate (Regional Government) complex, about 300m from the museum.

FREE **Museum Konperensi** MUSEUM
(Conference Museum; Jl Asia Afrika; 9am-3pm Mon-Fri) The Museum Konperensi inside the Gedung Merdeka (Freedom Building) is dedicated to the Asia-Africa conference of 1955, which Bandung hosted. There are a few interesting photos of Sukarno, Nehru, Ho Chi Minh, Nasser and other developing world leaders of the 1950s.

Bandung Institute of Technology UNIVERSITY
(ITB; Jl Ganeca; art gallery admission free; art gallery on request) Opened in 1920, the ITB was the first university open to Indonesians – Sukarno studied here. The institute has a reputation for political activism, and in 1998, in the lead-up to Suharto's downfall, up to 100,000 students rallied daily.

Set in spacious grounds, the complex contains some bizarre hybrid Indo-European architecture. Its fine arts school is internationally famous – do take time to drop by the **art gallery**.

To reach the ITB, take a Lembang or Dago angkot from the train station and then walk down Jl Ganeca.

Dago VIEWPOINT
In the north of Bandung, Dago Hill overlooks the entire city. The famous, but now faded, Dago Thee Huis offers views through a tangle of power lines and a forest of radio towers. The rundown complex has a cafe-restaurant, outdoor and indoor theatres and a small children's playground.

FREE **Museum Prangko** MUSEUM
(Stamp Museum; Jl Diponegoro; 9am-3pm Mon-Fri) As well as thousands of stamps from around the world, this museum has everything from postboxes to pushcarts used since colonial times.

Activities

Bersih Sehat MASSAGE
(426 0765; www.bersihsehat.com; Jl Sultan Tirtayasa 31) This is an excellent massage and treatment salon; rates are very reasonable with a one-hour body massage costing 90,000Rp.

Adu Domba RAM FIGHTS
These noisy ram-butting fights, held most Sundays between 9am and 1pm, are wildly popular in Bandung. They're a sight to behold, and at least the rams only walk away with a sore head. Consult the Tourist Information Centre for the latest program of events.

Tours

Freelance English-speaking **Enoss** (0852 2106 3788; enoss_travellers@yahoo.com) is a good-natured tour guide who runs one-day tours (350,000Rp per person) of the sights to the north and south of the city. The tours get you away from the more predicatable touristy locations. He can also set up trips to Pangandaran (around 800,000Rp) via Garut.

Sleeping

Bandung is short on good budget places. Many of the luxury hotels offer good online discounts, so shop around.

TOP CHOICE **Hotel Kenangan** HOTEL $
(421 3244; www.kenanganhotel.com; Jl Kebon Sirih 4; r incl breakfast with fan/air-con from 195,000/245,000Rp;) Towards the top end of the budget bracket, this recently renovated hotel is a great deal with modern, comfortable rooms and free wi-fi. The location, close to the Governor's Residence, is very central and quiet and staff are helpful. Prices rise a fraction on weekends.

Novotel HOTEL $$
(421 1001; www.novotel.com; Jl Cihampelas 23; r from 480,000Rp; @) A really well-run hotel where the lobby and restaurant area offer a contemporary 'wow' factor and the rooms are also stylish and excellent value. Service standards are very high, and it has a great gym and a spa, though the pool is tiny and a bit of an afterthought at the rear of the hotel.

Guesthouse Pos Cihampelas GUESTHOUSE $
(423 5213; Jl Cihampelas 12; r 90,000-250,000Rp;) This 70s-style concrete building has a plethora of different rooms – from very humble economy options with shared bathroom to air-con doubles. All are showing their age but are kept clean and the

Bandung

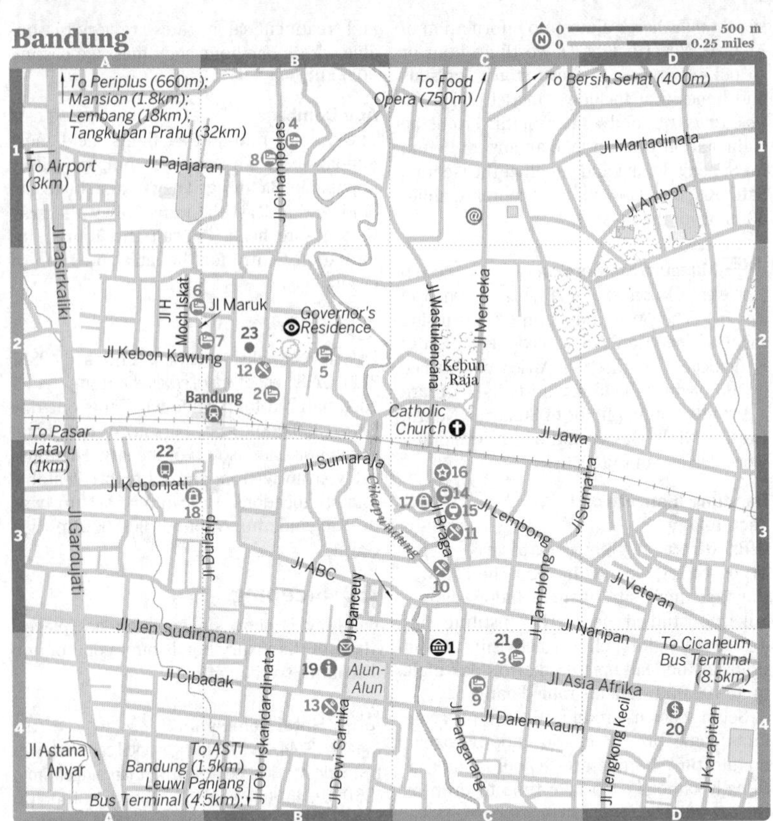

location is quiet (set back from a busy road). English is spoken and the warung (meals from 10,000Rp) here is good. Expect a price rise as the owner plans to upgrade facilities.

Arion Swiss-Belhotel HOTEL **$$**
(☎424 0000; www.swiss-belhotel.com; Jl Oto Iskandardinata 16; r from 655,000Rp; ❄@☎≋) Modern nonsmoking hotel with roomy, immaculate accommodation and excellent facilities including multichannel TV and high-speed internet. The top floor has a pool, a spa and a fitness centre.

Hotel Serena HOTEL **$$**
(☎420 4317; www.serenahotelbandung.com; Jl Maruk 4-6; r/ste incl breakfast from 368,000/468,000Rp; ❄) This pleasant modern hotel has jacked up its prices, though the smart rooms with comfortable beds are still fair value and the location is excellent. Prices rise 10% at weekends.

Savoy Homann Hotel HISTORIC HOTEL **$$**
(☎423 2244; www.savoyhomann-hotel.com; Jl Asia Afrika 112; r/ste from 660,000/840,000Rp; ❄@☎) Dating back to 1921, this wonderful-looking hotel has a superb sweeping facade, and the rooms and communal areas retain real art deco class, with period lighting and stylish detailing galore. Promo deals are available on the website.

Grand Hotel Preanger HISTORIC HOTEL **$$$**
(☎423 1631; www.preanger.aerowisata.com; Jl Asia Afrika 181; r/ste from 815,000/1,375,000Rp; ❄) Historic hotel undergoing renovation, which it needs. Retains some art deco charm, but there's an ugly modern extension. Check out the terrific English pub, though.

Hotel Patradissa GUESTHOUSE **$**
(☎420 6680; Jl H Moch Iskat 8; r 135,000-230,000Rp; ❄☎) A reasonable guesthouse with an overdose of chintz and curios, but it

Bandung

Sights

1 Museum Konperensi C4
Savoy Homann Hotel .... (see 9)

Sleeping

2 Arion Swiss-Belhotel B2
3 Grand Hotel Preanger C4
4 Guesthouse Pos Cihampelas B1
5 Hotel Kenangan B2
6 Hotel Patradissa A2
7 Hotel Serena B2
8 Novotel B1
9 Savoy Homann Hotel C4

Eating

10 Braga Huis C3
Kiosk .... (see 17)
11 Momiji C3
12 Red Tulip B2
13 Warung Nasi Ampera B4

Drinking

14 North Sea Bar C3
15 Roempoet C3

Entertainment

16 Classic Rock Café C3

Shopping

17 Braga City Walk C3
18 Pasar Baru A3

Information

19 Bandung Tourist Information Centre B4
20 Golden Megah Moneychanger D4

Transport

21 Garuda C4
22 Kramatdjati A3
23 Merpati B2
Pahala Kencana .... (see 22)

is secure and offers moderate levels of comfort. The people running it are friendly and breakfast is included. Wi-fi access is limited to the lobby area.

Eating

In the centre, Jl Braga has a strip of cafes and restaurants. Many of Bandung's most exclusive places are concentrated in the north of town. For cheap food check out the night warungs on Jl Cikapundung Barat, across from the *alun-alun*.

TOP CHOICE **Kiosk** INDONESIAN $

(Jl Braga, Braga City Walk; meals 15,000-25,000Rp; wi-fi) This great little mini-food court on the ground floor of the Braga City Walk is ideal for mixing with locals and sampling some unusual snacks from *kaki lima* (street vendor) style stalls. Try a *lotek* (Sundanese salad) or a noodle dish. Drinks include juices – try the *sirsak* (soursop) – cold beers and iced coffees.

Kampung Daun INDONESIAN, SUNDANESE $$

(278 7915; www.kampungdaun.net; Jl Sersan Bajuri Km4.7; meals 40,000-70,000Rp; 11am-11pm Sun-Fri, to midnight Sat; wi-fi) On the outer reaches of the city, with tropical forest as a backdrop, this 'culture village' is wildly popular with monied locals. You'll find dozens of little *lesehan* (low table) seating areas next to gurgling streams where you can order a Sundanese meal, try a single estate coffee, or in the evening you can catch a traditional dance performance. The whole place is litter free and very well maintained. It's about 10km from the centre of town; a taxi here is about 50,000Rp.

Momiji JAPANESE $$

(420 3786; Jl Braga 64; meals 45,000-100,000Rp; noon-10.30pm) An intimate, traditional Japanese restaurant with a relaxed, civilised ambience. Prices are surprisingly moderate given the surroundings and quality of the sushi, noodle, teriyaki and teppanyaki dishes here.

Red Tulip INTERNATIONAL $$

(420 7264; Jl Kebon Kawung II; meals 35,000-80,000Rp; 4pm-midnight) This large, centrally located restaurant is the best bet in town for Western grub, with excellent black-pepper steak, steamed tilapia and pasta. Live music rocks the joint (Mondays, Wednesdays and Fridays) and beers – including Guinness (38,000Rp) – are available. On the upper deck you get a view of the Governor's Residence.

Braga Huis INTERNATIONAL $

(Jl Braga 47; mains 16,000-32,000Rp; 11am-1am) Elegant new brasserie-style place in the thick of things that is great for a coffee (including specialty beans such as Sumatra Cintong and espresso drinks), juice, mocktail or beer.

GRIDLOCK

Various plans (and pipedreams) have been mooted to alleviate Bandung's notorious traffic congestion. First choice – a metro – is simply beyond the financial reach of the local authorities. Alternatives mooted have included a TransJakarta-style busway system, monorail and even a cable car. Of these, shelters for the busway have been built but the proposed network has stalled due to opposition from *angkot* drivers; the monorail is still at discussion stage; so it seems the cable car has the best chance of a green light. It's hoped that the latter, called the Bandung Sky Bridge, will use 55 gondolas and link Jl Pasteur with Jl Siliwangi, so Bandung will have a cable car open by 2014.

On the menu there's everything from nasi goreng to crepes (try the peach or strawberry) and steaks.

Food Opera MIDDLE EASTERN, INTERNATIONAL **$$**
(☎253 4338; Jl Juanda 72; snacks & meals from 15,000-45,000Rp; ⏰9am-10pm; 📶) Hip cafe-restaurant in an enjoyable setting with tables around an urban garden. Mainly Middle Eastern and Western food, try the *mandi* (smoked rice with lamb), Turkish pide or good old fish 'n' chips.

Bandung Supermal FOOD COURT **$**
(Jl Gatot Subroto 289; meals 10,000-45,000Rp) In the east of the city, this upmarket shopping mall has a good food court, tons of fast-food joints, cafes and a Bread Talk bakery.

Warung Nasi Ampera INDONESIAN **$**
(Jl Dewi Sartika 8; meals 14,000-20,000Rp; ⏰24hr) Cheap, clean, local place serving up Indonesian classics around the clock, such as sweet, spicy curries.

Drinking

After dark Jl Braga has a typical downtown vibe, with small bars, pool halls, karaoke lounges and live music venues. Up in north Bandung the well-heeled head to places along Jl Juanda and students to Jeans St (though there are few bars here).

North Sea Bar BAR
(Jl Braga 82; ⏰noon-1am) Locally known as the 'naughty bar' (geddit?!) the beer flows late at this pub-style expat and bar-girl hang-out. It's actually not that sleazy at all and there's a popular pool table.

Roempoet BAR
(Jl Braga 80) Intimate bar with live bands (mainly playing covers most nights) and a social vibe. Sizzling sate is also served up here.

☆ Entertainment

Cultural Performances

Bandung is the place to see Sundanese performing arts; however, performance times are haphazard – check with the Tourist Information Centre for the latest schedules.

ASTI Bandung PERFORMING ARTS
(☎731 4982; www.stsi-bdg.ac.id; Jl Buah Batu 212, Kampus STSI Bandung) In the southern part of the city about 3km from the centre, this is a school for traditional Sundanese arts – music, dancing and *pencak silat* (martial arts).

Saung Angklung PERFORMING ARTS
(☎727 1714; www.angklung-udjo.co.id; Jl Padasuka 118; adults/children under 12 75,000/50,000Rp; ⏰10.30am-5pm) Excellent *angklung* (bamboo musical instrument) performances, held daily at 3.30pm in a Sundanese cultural centre that also hosts dance events and ceremonial processions. It's around 10km northeast of the centre of town.

Live Music

Bar-come-restaurant **Roempoet** has a relaxed, informal air and live bands most evenings.

Classic Rock Café LIVE MUSIC
(☎420 7982; www.classicrockcafe.co.id; Jl Lembong I) For those about to rock – don your denim 'n' leather and head here. Showcases classic and heavy rock nights with bands playing covers, and also Indo rock nights. Live music nightly at 10pm and a modest (or no) entrance fee.

Clubs

Bandung has a vibrant clubbing scene and several venues. **Mansion** (☎8206 3554; www.mansionclubindonesia.com; Jl Sukajadi 137-139, Paris Van Java Mall) is a very popular club that draws a glam crowd with electro, house and techno DJs.

Shopping

With glitzy malls and factory outlets, shopaholics come here from as far as Malaysia in search of labels and bargains. Bandung's celebrated 'Jeans St', Jl Cihampelas is lined with cheap clothes stores, though quality is pretty iffy. Jl Cibaduyut, in southwest Bandung, is to shoes what Jl Cihampelas is to jeans. Check out Jl Braga for antiques, art and curios.

Bandung Supermal MALL
(www.bandungsupermal.com; Jl Gatot Subroto 289; 🛜) More than 200 shops including Boss and Levi's, a huge Hero supermarket, a bowling alley and cinemas.

Braga City Walk MALL
(www.bragacitywalk.net; Jl Braga; 🛜) Small upmarket shopping mall with boutiques, a food court, a cinema and supermarket.

Periplus BOOKS
(Jl Setiabudi 42-46, Setiabudi Supermarket) Excellent selection of English books, maps and magazines including some Lonely Planet guidebooks. About 5km north of the centre.

Pasar Baru MARKET
(Jl Kebonjati) Somewhat grotty central market, but good for fresh fruit.

Pasar Jatayu MARKET
(Jl Arjuna) Search this flea market for collectables hidden amidst the junk.

Information

Most of the upmarket shopping malls including the Bandung Supermal and Braga City Walk have free wi-fi. For 24-hr web access head to **Kubus** (Jl Merdeka; 24hr).

Banks are scattered across Bandung.

Adventist Hospital (203 4386; Jl Cihampelas 161) A missionary hospital with English-speaking staff.

Bandung Tourist Information Centre (420 6644; Jl Asia Afrika; 9am-5pm Mon-Sat, to 2pm Sun) Managed by the very helpful Ajid Suriana, this office is located in the foyer of the central mosque. Offers lots of free information and also tours of the Bandung region.

Golden Megah Moneychanger (Jl Asia Afrika 142) Offers decent rates for cash dollars and euros.

Main Post Office (cnr Jl Banceuy & Jl Asia Afrika)

Getting There & Away

Air

Bandung airport is fast becoming an important international and domestic transport hub; a new terminal opened in 2012 boosting capacity. It's a key hub for **AirAsia** (5050 5088; www.airasia.com), with connections to Kuala Lumpur, Penang, Singapore and domestic cities including Denpasar. **Silk Air** (424 1251; www.silkair.com) flies to Singapore; **Lion Air** (021 6379 8000; www2.lionair.co.id) to Banjarmasin, Batam, Denpasar, Medan and Surabaya; **Merpati** (426 0253; www.merpati.co.id; Jl Kebon Kawung 16) flies to Yogyakarta, Surabaya and Denpasar; **Garuda** (420 9468; Jl Asia Afrika 181, Grand Hotel Preanger) and **Sriwijaya Air** (021 6471 7999; www.sriwijayaair.co.id) to Surabaya.

Bus

Five kilometres south of the city centre, **Leuwi Panjang bus terminal** (Jl Sukarno Hatta) has buses west to places such as Cianjur (normal/air-con 14,000/20,000Rp, two hours), Bogor (32,000/42,000Rp, 3½ hours) and to Jakarta's Kampung Rambutan bus terminal (37,000Rp to 47,000Rp, three hours). Buses to Bogor take at least an hour longer on weekends because of heavy traffic.

Cicaheum bus terminal, on the eastern outskirts, serves desinations including Cirebon (normal/air-con 30,000/38,000Rp, four hours, hourly), Garut (normal/air-con 14,000/17,000Rp, two hours, every 40 minutes) and Pangandaran (normal/air-con 40,000/52,000Rp, six hours, hourly).

Cipaganti (612 6650; Jl Dr Djundjunan 143-149, Bandung Trade Center) runs minibuses every 30 minutes to many locations in Jakarta from their terminal in the Bandung Trade Center,

TRAINS FROM BANDUNG

DESTINATION	COST (RP)	DURATION (HR)	FREQUENCY
Jakarta (Gambir)	50,000-80,000	3-3¼	6 daily
Surabaya	185,000-285,000	11-12	3 daily
Yogyakarta	185,000-245,000	7¼-8	6 daily

4km northwest of the centre. **X-Trans** (☎204 2955; Jl Cihampelas 57) also offers hourly shuttle buses to central Jakarta (75,000Rp, 2½ hours) and Jakarta airport (85,000Rp, three hours). **Sari Harum** (☎639 276, 607 7065) has air-con *travel* minibuses to Pangandaran (90,000Rp, six hours) at 6am and 1pm, though try to get a local to book a pick-up for you as their staff don't speak English. **Kramatdjati** (☎423 9860; www.kramatdjatigroup.com; Jl Kebonjati 96) and **Pahala Kencana** (☎423 2911; www.pahalakencana.com; Jl Kebonjati 90) runs luxury buses to long-distance destinations, such as Yogyakarta (100,000Rp).

Getting Around

TO/FROM THE AIRPORT Bandung's Husein Sastranegara airport is 4km northwest of town; it costs around 40,000Rp to get there by taxi from the centre.

BUS, ANGKOT & TAXI Bandung is a fiendishly difficult city to negiotate on public transport, and few travellers bother as taxi rates are very reasonable. Stick to the the ever-reliable **Bluebird taxis** (☎756 1234).

Angkot run from Stasiun Hall (St Hall), on the southern side of the train station to Dago, Ledeng and other destinations, fares cost from 2000Rp to 4000Rp. City buses (called Damri) run from west to east down Jl Asia Afrika to Cicaheum bus terminal and from the train station to Leuwi Panjang bus terminal.

North Of Bandung

☎0260

Sights & Activities

Tangkuban Prahu VOLCANO

(admission 50,000Rp; ⏲information centre 7am-5pm) This volcanic crater, 30km north of Bandung, has a flat, elongated summit that resembles an upturned boat (*prahu*).

It's a huge tourist attraction and certainly a spectacular sight, but also something of a tourist trap – expect pushy vendors and big crowds. If you do decide to go, make it early in the day as by noon the mist usually starts to roll in.

It's possible to circumnavigate most of the caldera on foot but as wannabe guides can be aggressive and tourists have been robbed, there are better places for a highland walk.

Gracia Spa HOT SPRINGS

(☎724 9997; www.graciaspa.com; admission 32,000-38,000Rp; ⏲7am-11pm) Eight kilometres northeast of Tangkuban Prahu in the village of **Ciater**, Gracia Spa is a hot spring set in gorgeous grounds on the lower slopes of the volcano. Here there are three large pools, a spa and restaurant, and it's very quiet in the week.

Ciater is an attractive village surrounded by tea and clove plantations. The area has good walks, and a tea factory on the south side of Ciater can be visited.

Sari Ater Hot Spring Resort HOT SPRINGS

(☎471 700; www.sariater-hotel.com; admission 38,000Rp; ⏲24hr) This is Ciater's main attraction. Although they're quite commercialised, the pools are probably the best of all the hot springs around Bandung. Rooms (from 250,000Rp) and rustic bungalows are available here. The pools can get insanely busy on weekends.

South Of Bandung

☎022

The mountains south of Bandung offer magnificent scenery, a rolling evergreen landscape of neatly cropped tea bushes, clumps of tropical forest and misty hilltops. Beyond the town of **Ciwidey**, every second house has a strawberry patch.

It's initially a struggle to get here through the endless Bandung suburbs and traffic, even on weekdays. On weekends, when Jakartans descend en masse – well, you've been warned.

Ciwidey itself has few attractions, but does have minimarts and hotels. About 3km south of town you can drop by **Kawi Wulung** (Jl Raya Pasir Jambu), a bamboo workshop where room dividers and chairs are made by hand. Next door, **Tahu Sumedang** (Jl Raya Pasir Jambu) is a traditional tofu factory where tofu is fried in coconut oil (and is for sale).

North of Ciwidey the road winds north through hills to the turn-off to **Kawah Putih**, an undeniably beautiful turquoise crater lake that's become something of an overdeveloped tourist attraction.

It's better to push on through the stunning scenery around **Rancabali**, 42km from Bandung, which is basically one big tea estate surrounded by lush green hills. Just south of Rancabali, **Situ Patengan** is a pretty lake with tearooms and boats catering to the Sunday crowds, while 3km south of here is lovely **Kawah Rengganis** (also known as Kawah Cibuni), a pretty, isolated river fed by hot springs and surrounded by billowing steam from volcanic vents. It's yet to be discovered by the tourist hoards and is wonderful for bathing. You have to park by the road and walk for a few minutes up to the pools; villagers here ask visitors for a 4000Rp donation to visit their land.

If you want to tour a tea plantation, head for the **Malabar Tea Estate**, on the other side of Gunung Patuha, where you can tour the grounds and stay at the wonderful guesthouse, the Malabar Mess.

Sleeping & Eating

Hotel options are limited in this region, but there are a few places around Ciwidey and there's also the Malabar Mess.

Malabar Mess HISTORIC HOTEL $
(☎597 9401, bookings 022 203 8996; r weekday/weekend from 210,000/280,000Rp) It's hard to beat this idyllically situated colonial guesthouse, located at an altitude of 1500m in a working tea plantation near the town of Pengalengan. The simple, clean rooms, each with a front porch and Dutch-era furnishings make it a great place to kick back for a few days.

Saung Gawir SUNDANESE $$
(☎0812 2113 3664; www.saunggawir.com; Jl Raya Ciwidey; meals 30,000-50,000Rp, bungalows 500,000-600,000Rp) This hotel-restaurant-strawberry farm has simply startling valley views from its roadside perch in Alam Endah. Despite some tour-group action it functions best as a restaurant – pick a table and soak up the quintessentially Javanese scenery as you feast on authentic local cusine. The spacious bungalows are ageing but kept clean, and have fireplaces. And of course it would be rude not to buy some berries while you're here.

Getting There & Away

Frankly, touring this region by public transport is possible but a pain. Most travellers explore the area on a tour from Bandung.

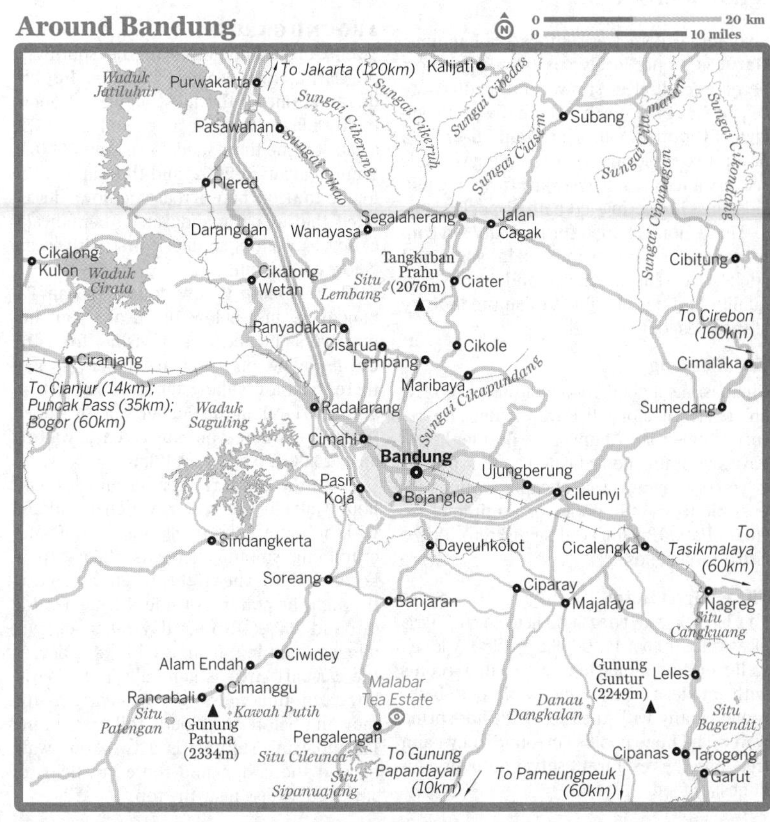

From Bandung's Leuwi Panjang terminal, very frequent buses run to Ciwidey (12,000Rp, 1¼ hours). From Ciwidey *angkot* run to Situ Patengan (7000Rp). Shared minibuses run from the highway to Kawah Putih (22,000Rp return). Buses run directly to Pengalengan (9000Rp), where *ojek* hang out at the bus terminal.

Bandung To Pangandaran

Heading southeast from Bandung, the road passes through rolling hills and stunning volcanic peaks skirting – at a safe distance – the particularly explosive **Gunung Papandayan** (2622m). This is the Bandung–Yogyakarta road as far as Banjar; the Bandung–Yogyakarta train line passes through Tasikmalaya and Banjar, but not Garut. After the choked streets of Jakarta and Bandung, these quieter back roads are a pleasure.

GARUT & CIPANAS

☎0262

Sixty-three kilometres southeast of Bandung, **Garut** is a once-lovely spa town that's now become featureless sprawl and leatherware centre. But 6km north of here the pretty village of **Cipanas** makes a tranquil base for a day or two exploring some stunning volcanic scenery and soaking away any travelling tensions in a hot spring-fed bath or pool.

The region is famed for its *dodol* – a confectionery of coconut milk, palm sugar and sticky rice. The 'Picnic' brand is the best quality, and it is possible to visit the **factory** (Jl Pasundan 102) in Garut.

Sleeping

Cipanas has a good choice of places to stay; all are strung along Jl Raya Cipanas, the resort's single road. Many of the flashier hotels have swimming pools heated by the springs; if you're staying at a cheaper option, it's possible to use the pools for a minimal fee (10,000/5000Rp for adults/children). Prices rise on weekends.

Tirtagangga Hotel HOTEL **$$**
(☎232 549; www.tirtagangga-hotel.com; Jl Raya Cipanas 130; r from 440,000Rp;) A large, well-run hotel offering good-value rooms with modern decor and generous bathrooms, many with tubs fed with hot-spring water. The huge pool is surrounded by palm trees and the restaurant serves authentic Indonesian food.

Sumber Alam RESORT **$$**
(☎238 000; www.resort-kampungsumberalam.com; r 526,000-1,350,000Rp;) This upmarket resort has attractive thatched-and-timber bungalows built around and over ponds (complete with water lillies). The pool area is great. It's very popular with Indonesian families, particularly on weekends, though note that the *azat* (call to prayer) from the nearby mosque is particuarly enthusiatic and vocal.

Hotel Nurgraha HOTEL **$$**
(☎234 829; r 100,000-400,000Rp, bungalows from 350,000Rp;) All the ageing accommodation here could use a renovation but the cheap options are decent value for a budget-priced bed. There are sunset views of the thermal pool, rice fields and coconut trees.

Getting There & Away

Garut is connected with Bandung (17,000Rp, two hours) and also Pangandaran (32,000Rp, four hours). *Angkot* connect Garut with Cipanas very regularly.

AROUND GARUT

Twenty-eight kilometres to the southwest of Garut, twin-peaked **Gunung Papandayan** is one of the most active volcanoes in West Java. Papandayan exploded in 1772, a catastrophe that killed more than 3000. It erupted again in 2002, and thousands were forced to flee when pyroclastic flows devastated the area. Papandayan is periodically closed to visitors so check first with locals before setting out.

The bubbling yellow crater (Kawah Papandayan) just below the peak is an impressive sight and clearly visible from the Garut valley on clear mornings. To get there, take a Cikajang minibus and get off at the turn-off on the outskirts of Cisurupan (6000Rp), where you can catch a waiting *ojek* (25,000Rp one way, 13km).

From the car-park area it's an easy half-hour walk to the crater, which is riddled with bubbling mud pools, steam vents and crumbling sulphur deposits. Take care – keep well to the right when ascending through the crater. Consider hiring a guide (around 250,000Rp per day, but many will allow bargaining) from the PHKA office, as the car-park area is generally full of cowboys. For fine views, go very early in the morning before the clouds roll in. Gunung Papandayan's summit is a two-hour walk beyond the crater, and there are fields of Javan edelweiss near the top.

Craters to the west of Garut that can be visited are **Kawah Darajat**, 26km away, and **Kawah Kamojang**, 23km away, the site of a geothermal plant that has defused the once spectacular geyser activity and replaced it with huge pipes.

Halfway between Garut and Tasikmalaya is **Kampung Naga**, a beautiful traditional Sundanese village of thatch-roofed timber houses nestled next to a river and surrounded by precipitous hillsides. Crowds of tourists pass through here but it's still a lovely spot. There are 360 steps up to the car park on the main highway. Freelance guides will offer to explain local customs, but they ask a hefty 50,000Rp for a tour.

Pangandaran

☎0265 / POP 9800

Situated on a narrow isthmus, with a broad stretch of sand on either side and a thickly forested national park on the nearby headland, Pangandaran is Java's premier beach resort. Walk away from the centre and the coastal scenery is reduced to its raw elements: a strip of dark sand, a vast, empty ocean and an enormous, gently curving horizon.

Most of the year Pangandaran is a quiet, tranquil place to enjoy walks along the beach or through the forest, but the town fills up on holidays (and weekends). The heavy swell that relentlessly pummels the impressive beach doesn't make for great swimming, though there are some more secluded spots along the coast. As the **surf** is consistently good, it's a great place to get out on a board, or learn how to (surfing lessons can be easily arranged).

Pangandaran was hit hard by a tsunami in 2006 (a different one from the disaster that devastated Banda Aceh in Sumatra) but the town is very much open for business again. Sadly sections of the beach are littered with plastic and flotsam and in dire need of a clean-up.

Sights & Activities

Pangandaran National Park PARK

(Taman Nasional Pangandaran; admission 7000Rp; 7am-5pm) The Pangandaran National Park, which takes up the entire southern end of Pangandaran, is a wild expanse of dense forest. Within its boundaries live porcupines, *kijang* (barking deer), hornbills, monitor lizards and monkeys (including Javan gibbons). Small bays within the park enclose pretty tree-fringed beaches. The park is divided into two sections: the recreation park and the jungle. Due to environmental degradation, the jungle is usually off limits.

Well-maintained **paths** allow the recreation park to be explored, passing small caves (including **Gua Jerang** which was used by the Japanese in the war), the remains of a Hindu temple, **Batu Kalde**, and a nice beach on the eastern side. English-speaking guides hang around both entrances and charge around 100,000Rp (per group of four) for a two-hour walk or 200,000Rp for a five-hour trip.

Pangandaran's best swimming beach, white-sand **Pasir Putih**, lies on the western side of the national park. You can swim over here from the southern end of the main resort beach if the surf is not too rough, or boats shuttle people back and forth (20,000Rp return). There's a small patch of (damaged) coral reef here.

At sunset huge **fruit bats** emerge from the forest. They fly right down the length of Pangandaran's beach but have to evade local boys who patrol with barbed-wire kites. Few are trapped this way, but every now and then a bat's wing will get caught on a kite string and the creature will be brought crashing to the ground in a fit of squeals, before being dispatched to the cooking pot.

Surfing Lessons SURFING

(per half-day incl board hire 200,000Rp) Surfing lessons are offered at the northern end of the beach. Pangandaran is a good place to learn, and local instructors have 'soft' boards ideal for beginners. The friendly staff from **Pangandaran Surf** (☎0813 2354 4583; www.pangandaransurf.com; beachside, Mungil Steak House) are all lifesavers, speak English and understand local conditions.

Tours

Popular Green Canyon and Green Valley tours (150,000Rp per person) usually combine 'home industry' visits that take in a sugar, *tahu* (tofu) or *krupuk* (prawn cracker) kitchen factory, as well as a *wayang golek* maker.

There are also tours to **Paradise Island**, an uninhabited nearby island with good beaches (including a 5km white-sand beach) and surfing. Day trips cost around 300,000Rp per person (minimum four people); for food, make an early-morning visit

Pangandaran

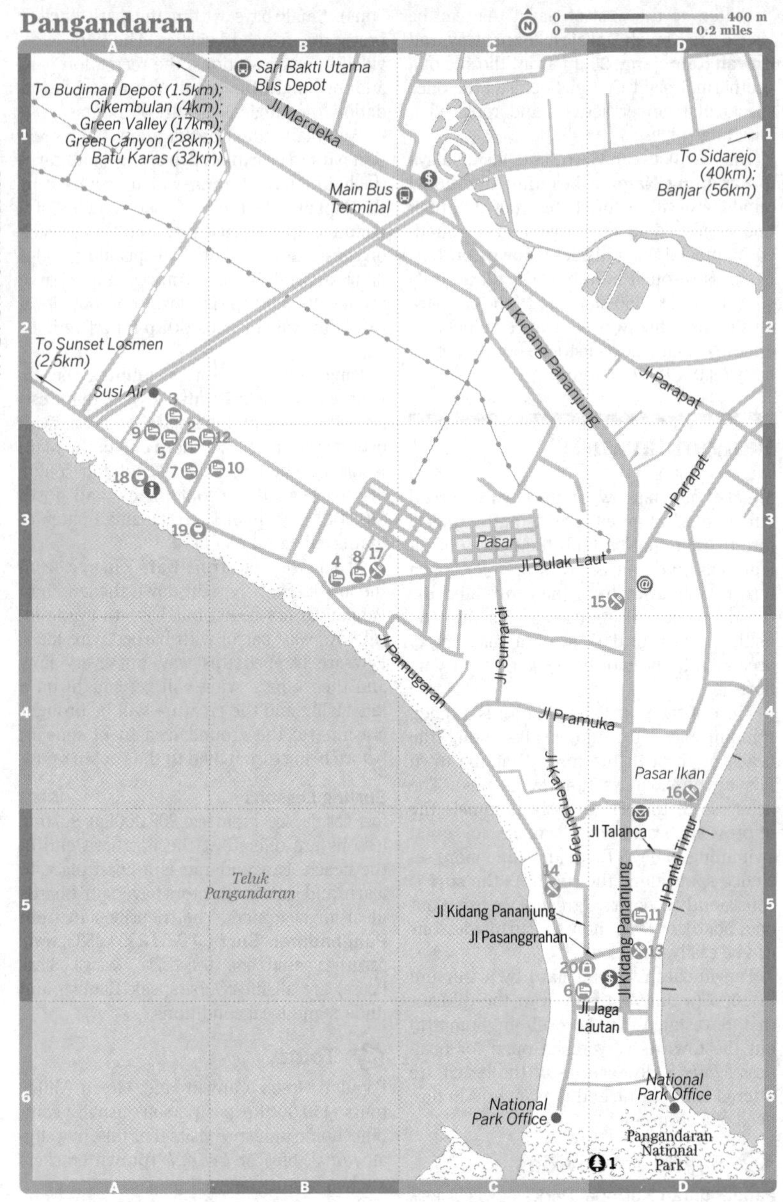

to Pangandaran's *pasar ikan* and fire up a fish barbecue when you get to the island.

Lots of tours can be organised from Tourist Information (p99) on the beach by the friendly English-speaking guides, who include **Purnama** (☎0852 9499 9906) and **Kamal** (☎0821 1869 2648). Mini Tiga Homestay also organises good trips.

Sleeping

Many places have flexible prices that are totally dependent on demand, so you've a

Pangandaran

great chance of a good deal on weekdays outside the main holiday periods. The main area for budget travellers is off the northern section of the main beach.

Pangandaran has a tightly controlled *becak* union, or mafia, depending on which side of the bike seat you're on. All hotels have to pay 15,000Rp per person in commission to the becak driver who takes you to your accommodation, so if you walk in your bargaining powers are far better primed.

Weekday prices are given; expect to pay 15% to 30% more at some places on weekends and holidays.

TOP CHOICE Mini Tiga Homestay GUESTHOUSE $
(☎639 436; katmaja95@yahoo.fr; s/d/tr incl breakfast 90,000/120,000/150,000Rp; @ wifi) A simply excellent backpackers' mecca with very reasonable rates considering the quality of the accommodation. The nine rooms are very clean, spacious and have nice decorative touches – including bamboo walls and batik wall hangings – all have en-suite bathrooms and Western toilets. From the moment you arrive you're made to feel welcome: the French owner provides free tea/coffee, wifi, DVDs to watch and even homemade yoghurt. Good tours and transport tickets are also offered.

Adam's Homestay HOTEL $$
(☎639 396; www.adamshomestay.com; Jl Pamugaran; r 250,000-550,000Rp; air-con wifi) A veritable oasis, this is a wonderfully relaxed, enjoyable place to stay with artistically presented rooms (many with balconies, beamed ceilings and outdoor bathrooms) spread around a verdant tropical garden that's just bursting with exotic plants, ponds and birdlife. There's good Western and local food available too.

Pondok Mangga GUESTHOUSE $
(☎630 754; sulastri.declercq@gmail.com; wifi) Excellent new place set just off the beach with really spacious rooms that have a gleam and a sparkle and face a pretty garden. All have en-suite cold-water bathrooms.

Rinjani Homestay GUESTHOUSE $
(☎639 757; s/d 80,000/120,000Rp; wifi) A very solid choice, this welcoming family-run place with 10 clean, tiled rooms with TV, fan, porch or balcony and private cold-water bathroom. Excellent discounts available for long-term guests.

Hotel Century HOTEL $$
(☎639 171; www.centuryhotel.co.id; Jl Bulak Laut 86; r incl breakfast 250,000-400,000Rp; air-con wifi) A few steps from the beach, this excellent modern hotel has really clean, smart rooms that show a minimalist design influence, all with TV, tea/coffee making facilities and air-con; some enjoy sea views.

Villa Angela GUESTHOUSE $
(☎639 641; Jl Pamugaran; r incl breakfast with fan/air-con 120,000/150,000Rp; air-con) Attractive guesthouse with five spacious rooms (all with TV and bathroom and a porch or balcony) in two villa-style houses. The furniture is ageing a little, but hey, it's run by a welcoming family and has a nice little garden.

Komodo Island Hotel GUESTHOUSE $
(☎630 753; komodohotel@yahoo.com; Jl Bulak Laut 105; r with fan 100,000-120,000Rp, with air-con 175,000Rp; ❄🏊) Offers a good range of well-presented rooms, all with double beds (the economy options in a separate block have bathrooms with squat toilets). There's a nice shady garden at the rear, ping pong, a kids' pool and staff offer tours of the area.

Pantai Sari HOTEL $$
(☎639 175; Jl Bulak Laut 80; r incl breakfast 300,000Rp; ❄📶) This smart-looking turquoise-and-grey hotel has good-value spacious rooms with flat-screen TVs, modern furniture and quality beds.

Sunset Losmen HOTEL $$
(☎639 462; inn_sunset@yahoo.com; beachside, 4km west of centre; r incl breakfast 220,000Rp; ❄🏊) Right on the beach road this place is owned by Purnama, a friendly local tour guide and surf instructor. The clean, spacious rooms are set around a pool at the rear of the property.

Bamboo House GUESTHOUSE $
(☎0813 2355 8555, 639 419; s/d with fan 70,000/90,000Rp, r with air-con 125,000-150,000Rp; ❄) Friendly place with 18 slightly bland but well-kept and swept concrete rooms with front porches around a parking lot. Free breakfast and tea/coffee.

Laut Biru HOTEL $$
(☎639 360; www.lautbiru.com; Jl Jaga Lautan 17-18; r 400,000Rp; ❄📶) Modernist hotel at the southern end of the main beach that has huge rooms (each with twin beds, stylish dark-wood furniture and a balcony) that tick all the right contemporary boxes.

Sunrise Beach Hotel HOTEL $$
(☎639 220; Jl Kidang Pananjung 185; r/ste incl breakfast from 580,000/860,000Rp; ❄📶🏊) This once-smart resort hotel has a great pool area and rooms (some with sea views) are spacious and comfortable enough, though the furnishings and fittings would benefit from an update. There's a restaurant and bar.

Eating

Pangandaran is famous for its excellent seafood and by far the best place to sample it is in the *pasar ikan* (fish market).

TOP CHOICE **Pasar Ikan** SEAFOOD $$
(Fish Market; Jl Raya Timor; large fish 30,000-50,000Rp) Pangandaran's terrific fish market consists of more than a dozen large open-sided restaurants just off the east beach. They all operate on exactly the same basis – select your fish or seafood from the glistening iced displays, decide which sauce (usually garlic, oyster or sweet-and-sour) you fancy and it'll arrive in minutes.

Green Garden Cafe INDONESIAN $
(Jl Kidang Pananjung 116; snacks & meals 10,000-20,000Rp; 🖉) There's not much of a garden in evidence but you must try the delicious *batagor* (crispy tofu) here, which is fried in cassava flour and served with spicy peanut sauce – it's the house specialty. Other Indonesian dishes including gado gado and *cap cai* – and great fresh juices are available.

Relax Restaurant INTERNATIONAL, INDONESIAN $
(☎630 377; Jl Bulak Laut 74; mains 16,000-35,000Rp) Dependable, slightly formal Swiss-owned restaurant with a restrained 'proper' atmosphere thanks to the starched tablecloths and attentive service. The menu covers both Western and Indonesian fare; portions are very generous. It's a great bet for breakfast with muesli, homemade yoghurt and bread available.

Christi INDONESIAN $
(Jl Pantai Barat; meals 22,000-50,000Rp; ⏲6am-late) Set just off the beach road, this clean, orderly *rumah makan*, with a large interior and bench seating outside, is a good bet for fresh fish (from 30,000Rp) and seafood, just select the sauce (options include soy sauce, butter, sweet and sour, or spicy).

Chez Mama Cilacap INDONESIAN $
(☎630 098; Jl Kidang Pananjung 187; mains 25,000-60,000Rp) Covers all bases with its menu (there are even banana pancakes) but has a good reputation for its crab, which is served up fresh and succulent.

Drinking

TOP CHOICE **Bamboo Beach Café** BAR
(Jl Pamugaran) This fine beach bar has relocated to a much better location by the waves. With surfside seats it's the perfect location for a cold Bintang, particularly at sunset, or a cocktail (a jug of *arak*, lime juice and Sprite is 80,000Rp). It also serves food (breakfasts, omelettes, chips and local grub) at fair rates and service is friendly.

Mungil Steak House BAR
(Jl Pamugaran) Much more of a beach bar than a 'steak house', Mungil boasts a great

location, with tables by the sand. Don't be put off by the bizarre sign which boasts 'king of cold drink' and 'kind of Western food', all the tucker and bevvies (including jugs of *arak*-based cocktails) are genuine, present and correct.

Shopping

Magic Mushroom Books BOOKS
(Jl Pasanggrahan) Sells Western titles from a psychedelic shack.

Information

A 3500Rp admission charge is officially levied at the gates on entering Pangandaran. There's an unofficial **Tourist Information Office** (☎0852 9499 9906; beachside) office by the waves.

Ananda Internet (Jl Kidang Pananjung; 7000Rp per hour) Not quick, but it's as good as it gets in this town.

BNI ATM (Jl Merdeka) There's a second branch on Jl Bulak Laut.

BRI Bank (Jl Kidang Pananjung) Changes cash dollars and major brands of travellers cheques.

National Park Office (Jl Pantai; ⏰7am-5pm)

National Park Office (Jl Pangandaran; ⏰7am-5pm)

Post Office (Jl Kidang Pananjung)

Getting There & Away

Pangandaran can be a frustratingly slow and complicated place to get to. The nearest train station, Sidarejo, is 41km away via a poor road. Speak to staff at the Mini Tiga Homestay or the Tourist information office about organising train tickets.

Air

Susi Air (☎639 120; www.susiair.com; Jl Merdeka 312) flies daily to Pangandaran airstrip (20km west of town) from Jakarta's Halim Perdana Kusuma airport (500,000Rp, one hour) and Bandung (375,000Rp, 40 minutes).

However, as we have received several complaints about reservations going missing it's wise to double-check all bookings.

Bus

Many *patas* buses to Jakarta and Bandung leave from the Sari Bakti Utama depot, just north of town, and Budiman bus depot, about 2km west of Pangandaran along Jl Merdeka. Other services also leave from the main terminal. Buses run to Bandung roughly every hour (40,000Rp to 52,000Rp, six hours) and to Jakarta's Kampung Rambutan terminal (68,000Rp to 85,000Rp, eight to nine hours), mainly between 7pm and 9pm. To Bandung, there are two daily **Sari Harum** (☎639 276) door-to-door *travel* minibuses (90,000Rp, six hours). To Yogyakarta, you'll find two daily **Estu Travel** (☎027 4668 4567, 0812 2284 4700) minibuses (150,000Rp, nine hours) at 7am and 4.30pm.

From the main bus terminal there are hourly buses to both Banjar (18,000Rp, two hours) and Sidareja (10,000Rp, 1½ hours) for train connections and also buses west to Cijulang (7000Rp, 40 minutes).

> WORTH A TRIP
>
> **BACKWATER BOATS**
>
> The once-popular backwater boat trip east of Pangandaran via Majingklak harbour to Cilacap is still possible but there are no scheduled connections so you'll have to charter your own *compreng* (wooden boat). The route is very scenic, passing through rich swampland. Boatmen in Majingklak will do the three-hour trip for about 350,000Rp. From Cilacap there are direct buses to Yogyakarta (52,000Rp, five hours).

Car

Travel agencies rent minibuses with drivers for about 800,000Rp per day including driver and petrol. The most popular trip is a three-day tour to Yogyakarta, usually via Wonosobo for the first night, Dieng for sunrise, then on to Borobudur. The final day is to Yogyakarta via Prambanan.

Train

The nearest stations are Sidareja and Banjar. As the overland trip by bus to Yogyakarta takes a punishing eight or nine hours, train travel makes a lot of sense. From Sidareja there are two daily trains (3½ to four hours). Agents in Pangandaran organise combined minibus to Sidareja station and economy/business/exclusive class train tickets for 150,000/250,000/350,000Rp respectively. Or you could save some rupiah by catching a local bus to Sidareja and buying a train ticket there (avoiding commission) but this risks not getting a seat reservation.

Banjar station, 65km away, is a better bet if you're heading for Jakarta.

Travel agents, hotels and the Tourist Information Office can help with travel arrangements and tickets on all routes.

Getting Around

Pangandaran's brightly painted becak start at around 6000Rp and require heavy negotiation. Bicycles can be rented for 20,000Rp per day, and motorcycles cost around 50,000Rp per day.

Around Pangandaran

The scenic coastline around Pangandaran has some terrific surf beaches, forests, lagoons, fishing villages and a recreational park or two. It's a joy to explore by motorbike, or hotels and travel agencies can set up guided trips.

WEST OF PANGANDARAN

Heading west of town you travel along a pretty but busy coastal road lined with palm trees that runs through small villages and paddy fields.

At the tiny village of **Ciokoto**, 6km along this road, there's a large *wayang golek* workshop, with high-quality puppets for sale (400,000Rp to more than 1,000,000Rp). Next up is **Karang Tirta**, a lagoon set back from the beach with *bagang* (fishing platforms). It's 16km from Pangandaran and 2km south of the highway.

Inland from Parigi, near Cigugur, **Gunung Tilu** hilltop has fine views and is included in some tour itineraries.

Activities

Green Canyon BOAT TOUR, SWIMMING

(Cujang Taneuh; per boat 75,000Rp; 7.30am-4pm Sat-Thu, 1-4pm Fri; @) The number one tour from Pangandaran is to Green Canyon (Cujang Taneuh); it's clearly signposted at several points along the highway. Many tour operators in Pangandaran run trips here for 150,000Rp and include 'countryside' excursions to make a full-day tour. To get there yourself, hire a boat from the Green Canyon river harbour on the highway, 1km before the turn-off to Batu Karas. Boats buzz up the jungle-fringed, emerald-green river to a waterfall and a beautiful canyon where there's swimming (though the current is often strong here). Boatmen work on a return-trip schedule of just 45 minutes, which only gives you about 15 minutes to swim and explore the narrowest and most beautiful part of the canyon; if you want to stay longer you'll have to pay extra.

Green Valley SWIMMING

(Sungai Citumang; entrance 10,000Rp, body rafting 25,000Rp, guide 70,000Rp; 7am-5pm) Reached by a rough inland road from the village of Cipinda (8km from Pangandaran, look out for the sign Citumang), this attraction involves an easy riverside walk from a small dam to a small but beautiful gorge, Green Valley. You can swim into the gorge and there are cliff jumps for the brave (or foolhardy). Pay extra and you've the option of 'body rafting' the river back to the entrance instead of walking, which involves floating downstream using a lifejacket for buoyancy – a surreal and delightful experience as you gaze up at the forest canopy. A guide is mandatory for body rafting.

BATU KARAS

0265 / POP 3000

The idyllic fishing village and surfing hot spot of Batu Karas, 32km west of Pangandaran, is one of the most enjoyable places to kick back in Java. It's as pretty as a picture – a tiny one-lane settlement, with two beaches that are separated by a wooded promontory.

In recent years Batu Karas's popularity has started to take off as more (very tasteful) guesthouses have opened, but the village still retains a low-key, very relaxed charm. However, an Indonesian hotel group started (and then stopped) some heavy construction work in 2012, so the situation could change.

There's good swimming, with sheltered sections that are calm enough for a dip, but many visitors are here for the breaks, and there's a lot of surf talk.

Activities

This is one of the best places in Java to learn to **surf**. The Point (offshore from Java Cove) is perfect for beginners with paddle-in access from the beach, and slow, peeling waves over a sandy bottom. Other waves include The Reef, a deep-water fun reef break, and Bulak Bender, a challenging right-hander reef break in the open ocean that's a 40-minute ride away by bike or boat.

The locally run surf co-op, just off the beach, charges 150,000Rp for a two-hour lesson including board hire. Longboards and shortboards (from 50,000Rp per day) are available from locals or the co-op.

Sleeping & Eating

TOP CHOICE **Java Cove** BOUTIQUE HOTEL $$

(708 2020; www.javacovebeachhotel.com; r with fan 400,000Rp, luxury r 690,000-1,500,000Rp, meals around 90,000Rp; @) Established by a welcoming, knowledgeable Australian couple who have spent years in Indonesia, this beautiful beachfront hotel has gorgeous contemporary-chic rooms, most with sea views, plus a couple of fan-cooled options. There's a decked garden and chillout zone with a pool, and a spa is planned. The bistro-style restaurant serves excellent Western food including healthy breakfasts, pasta and tapas, as well as mocktails and cocktails (around 60,000Rp).

Jesfa GUESTHOUSE $

(☎0813 2306 8358; weekday/weekend incl breakfast 100,000/150,000Rp) Above a little restaurant at the far end of the beach, these three rooms (all en suite) are highly attractive with exposed brick walls and lovely chunky wooden beds with thick mattresses.

Wooden House GUESTHOUSE $

(☎0813 6919 4405; woodenhouse@yahoo.com; r 150,000Rp, meals 10,000-15,000Rp) Going for the log-cabin look, these lovely rooms are kept very tidy and many access a shared balcony with sea views. Downstairs there's a good warung for local food and things like jaffles, salads and pancakes.

Bonsai Bungalows BUNGALOW $

(☎709 3199; dm 100,000Rp, r 150,000-300,000Rp, bungalows 500,000Rp; ❄) This is another good choice, with well-constructed, clean, thatched-roof accommodation – neat little wooden rooms (some with air-conditioning), family bungalows or an excellent dorm that has six beds with good-quality mattresses and fresh linen. There's a cafe at the front for a beer or coffee. Prices rise by 25% in high season.

Villa Monyet GUESTHOUSE $$

(☎0878 6135 6168; huts/bungalow incl breakfast 125,000/350,000Rp; @📶) Next to Bale Karang, this place has lovely Gili Island–style *lumbung* bungalows with mod cons including TV (but no air-con), or basic little A-frame huts, with shared bathrooms.

Kang Ayi INDONESIAN

(mains 10,000-20,000Rp) Perhaps the most popular of the three warung at the eastern end of the beach, come here for barbecued fish and good seafood, or just a tasty *nasi campur*.

Bayview Seafood SEAFOOD $$

(meals 35,000-70,000Rp) On the main junction as you enter the village this new place has bench seating, a covered terrace and fresh seafood grilled to perfection by a European/Indonesian couple.

ℹ Getting There & Away

You have to pay a toll of 5000Rp to enter the village. There's no public transport to Batu Karas but it can be reached from Pangandaran by taking a bus to Cijulang (7000Rp) and then an *ojek* for 20,000Rp.

EAST OF PANGANDARAN

The main Pangandaran–Banjar road runs east initially, passing a series of bays and beaches exposed to the full force of the Indian Ocean. The first of these, about 8km along the road, is **Karang Nini** (entrance fee 3500Rp), where there's a cluster of warung on a headland and picnic areas beneath pandan trees. The eastern section of beach here is superb, with a sweeping expanse of sand and crashing surf. Walk for 15 minutes along this beach and you'll reach a beautiful river estuary, its banks lined with tropical forest and patrolled by gliding eagles. Karang Nini is about 3km south of the highway.

Pushing eastwards you get views over **Nusa Kambangan**, the last port of call on this planet for the Bali bombers who were executed on this island prison in 2008. Around 7km from Karang Nini, there's a turn-off for the scruffy harbour of **Majingklak**, which sits on the western bank of Segara Anakan lagoon. It's possible to charter a boat to explore the lagoon for around 80,000Rp an hour after hard bargaining.

Cirebon

☎0231 / POP 298,000

The city of Cirebon on Java's north coast is a cultural melting pot, blending the scattered remains of the ancient Islamic kingdom that once had its base here with a more contemporary cocktail of Javanese, Sundanese and Chinese culture.

It's an easy-going place with venerable *kraton* (walled city palaces) and a thriving batik industry. If you've been suffering in Jakarta and Bandung, the slower pace of life and relatively light traffic will come as quite a relief. Cirebon is famous for its *tari topeng*, a type of masked dance; and *tarling*, which is music that blends guitar, *suling* and voice.

◉ Sights

Kraton Kesepuhan PALACE

(admission 4000Rp, camera 3000Rp; ⏲8am-4pm Sat-Thu, 8-11am & 1-4pm Fri) Kraton Kesepuhan is the oldest of Cirebon's *kraton*. Built in 1527, its architectural style is a curious blend of Sundanese, Javanese, Islamic, Chinese and Dutch. Although this is the home of the sultan of Kesepuhan, part of the building is open to visitors. Inside is a pavilion with walls dotted with blue-and-white Delft tiles (many depicting biblical scenes), a marble floor and a ceiling hung with glittering French chandeliers.

The *kraton* museum has an interesting, if poorly displayed, collection of *wayang*

Cirebon

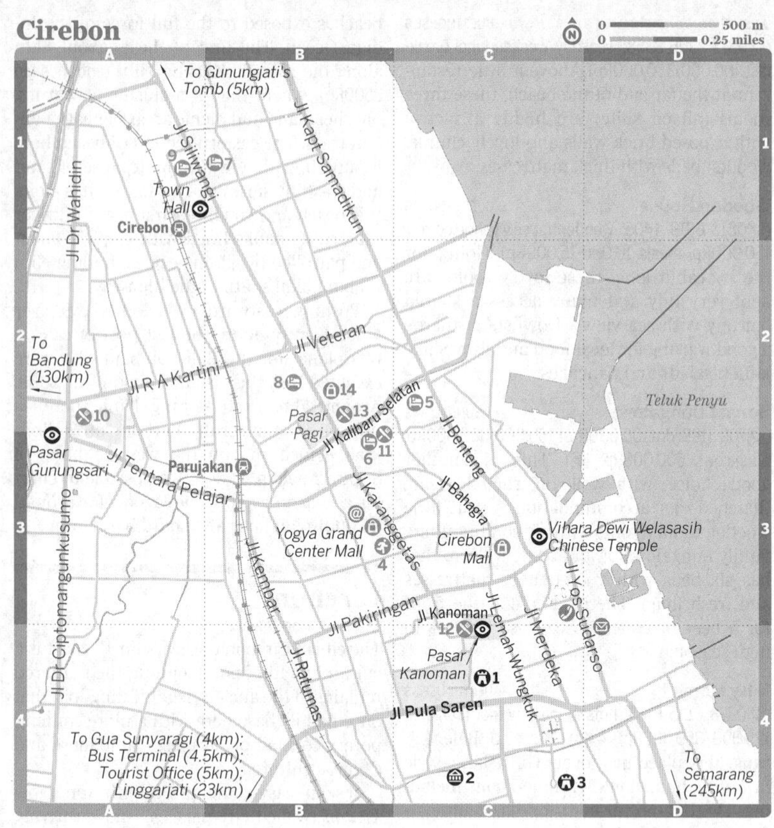

Cirebon

Sights

1 Kraton Kanoman ... C4
2 Kraton Kecirebonan ... C4
3 Kraton Kesepuhan ... C4

Activities, Courses & Tours

4 Raga Ku ... B3

Sleeping

5 Hotel Asia ... C2
6 Hotel Cahaya ... B3
7 Hotel Cordova ... B1
8 Hotel Priangan ... B2
9 Hotel Sidodadi ... A1

Eating

10 Grage Mall ... A2
11 H Moel ... B3
12 Pasar Kanoman ... C4
13 Warung Ampera ... B2

Shopping

14 Toko Sumber Jaya ... B2

puppets, kris, cannons, furniture, Portuguese armour and royal clothes. The pièce de résistance is the Kereta Singa Barong, a 16th-century gilded chariot with the trunk of an elephant (Hindu), the body and head of a dragon (Chinese-Buddhist), golden wings (Egyptian-Islamic) and the paws of a tiger. It was traditionally pulled by four white buffaloes and the suspension apparently flapped the wings and waggled the creature's tongue. It is quite possibly the wildest carriage you'll ever see.

Entry to the *kraton* includes a guided tour (payment at your discretion), which finishes in the *kraton's* museum. Here there are spice boxes, French crystal and relics from Portugal and Holland. Look out for the Javanese-Hindu Kama Sutra woodcarving.

Kraton Kanoman PALACE
(admission by donation; ⏲8am-5pm) Kraton Kanoman was constructed in 1588 but is now in very poor shape and in dire need of a full restoration. Outside the *kraton* is a red-brick, Balinese-style compound and a massive banyan tree. Further on past the white-stone lions is the *kraton*, a smaller, neglected cousin of Kraton Kesepuhan.

The museum here has some intriguing carvings (one featuring a reptile king) amidst layers of dust. It's the sultan's chariot that steals the show, however; it's a near replica of the one at Kraton Kesepuhan, but here they claim that theirs is the original.

The colourful **Pasar Kanoman** (market) just in front of the *kraton*, is at its most vibrant in the morning and is worth a visit in its own right.

Kraton Kecirebonan HISTORIC BUILDING
(admission by donation) Although it's classed as a *kraton*, this is really only a house occupied by members of the current royal family. Knock on the door and someone will be happy to show you around. Built in 1839, the house has fine colonial architecture and a small collection of swords, documents and other royal memorabilia.

Gua Sunyaragi CAVE
Approximately 4km southwest of town is this bizarre grotto of rocks, red brick and plaster, honeycombed with secret chambers, tiny doors and staircases that lead nowhere. It was originally a water palace for a sultan of Cirebon in the early 18th century.

Activities

Raga Ku MASSAGE
(☎339 1099; Jl Karanggetas 6; massages from 60,000Rp; ⏲9am-9pm) Head to Raga Ku for excellent, very reasonably priced massages and reflexology.

Sleeping

TOP CHOICE **Hotel Sidodadi** HOTEL $$
(☎202 305; www.sidodadihotel.com; Jl Siliwangi 72; r incl breakfast 275,000-400,000Rp, ste 500,000Rp; ❄📶) This new hotel's exterior (complete with flashing fairy lights) looks a bit kitsch from the street but the accommodation is high quality and great value – all rooms are modern, clean and well-equipped but book a 'superior' for extra space. Staff are friendly, and the comp breakfast buffet is a real bonus. Call for a free pick-up from the train station.

Hotel Cahaya HOTEL $
(☎206 018; Jl Kalibaru Selatan 47; r incl breakfast 95,000-150,000Rp; ❄) Nothing fancy, but the well-run Cahaya does offer clean, good-value functional rooms in a central location – shell out some extra rupiah for air-con and hot water. Your breakfast is a local fried-rice affair.

Hotel Priangan HOTEL $
(☎200 296; hpriangan@yahoo.co.id; Jl Siliwangi 108; r 90,000-260,000Rp; ❄📶) Set back from the street in a good central location, this hotel has a selection of rooms in four price categories – from basic to smart options with desks and TV. Many face a narrow garden.

Hotel Cordova HOTEL $
(☎204 677; www.hotelcordovacirebon.com; Jl Siliwangi 87; r with fan/air-con from 60,000/170,000Rp; ❄@📶) The lobby is quite fancy at the Cordova, but the rooms are more prosaic. Rooms are in five different price categories; all are old-fashioned but kept clean enough. Some have air-con.

Hotel Asia INN $
(☎204 905; Jl Kalibaru Selatan 11A; r 60,000-90,000Rp; ❄) It's looking tired, but this fine old Dutch-Indonesian inn does have character. Rooms are basic, but doable for a night and there's a courtyard setting for your breakfast.

Eating & Drinking

Cheap warungs serving seafood and snacks can be found along Jl Kalibaru Selatan, near Hotel Asia. Grage Mall (p104) has a food court, cafes and fast-food places. For ultra-fresh exotic fruit, head directly to **Pasar Kanoman** (Jl Kanoman).

Nasi Jamblang Mang Dull INDONESIAN $
(Jl Dr Cipto Mangunkusumo 4; meals 8000-22,000Rp) Highly popular, very inexpensive new place where you sit on long bench seating. You're given a teak leaf for a plate, some rice and then you help yourself to a buffet-style spread of delicious tempe, salted fish, meat, egg, curried vegetables and other Cirebon specialties.

Warung Ampera INDONESIAN, JAVANESE **$**
(☎201 205; Jl Siliwangi 247; meals from 12,000Rp) Upmarket warung serving traditional Javanese food in modern surrounds. Choose from buffet-style displays – there are always plenty of delicious fish dishes. Ampera also has wonderful fresh juices including strawberry, mango and avocado, depending on the season.

H Moel SEAFOOD **$**
(☎206 886; Jl Kalibaru Selatan 69; mains 12,000-65,000Rp) Huge place that's renowned for its fresh seafood. The menu has no prices (as you pay by the gram/kilo) but expect to pay about 30,000Rp for *ikan bakar* (grilled fish) or perhaps 70,000Rp for jumbo prawns. There's an open kitchen, so you can see the chefs at work.

Shopping

Grage Mall (Jl Tentara Pelajar) has a Matahari department store and lots of clothing and electronics shops (and a cinema and food court).

Toko Sumber Jaya SOUVENIRS
(Jl Siliwangi 211 & 229) Stocks all sorts of *oleh-oleh* (souvenirs) from Cirebon including pottery and bamboo crafts.

Information

Banks can be found all over town.

Elganet (www.elga.net.id; Ruko Grand Centre B/4; per hour 4000Rp) Internet access and gaming.

Main Post Office (Jl Yos Sudarso) Near the harbour.

Telkom (Jl Yos Sudarso) For international telephone calls.

Tourist Office (☎486 856; Jl Dharsono 5; 7am-3pm Mon-Fri) Lies 5km out of town on the bypass road, near Gua Sunyaragi. The staff are helpful here but have limited printed information.

Getting There & Away

BUS Cirebon's bus terminal is 4km southwest of the centre. Buses run between Cirebon and Jakarta (normal/air-con 42,000/56,000Rp, five hours), Bandung (normal/air-con 30,000/38,000Rp, four hours) and Semarang (normal/air-con 50,000/68,000Rp, seven hours), as well as many of Java's main cities.

ACC Kopyor 4848 (☎204 343; Jl Karanggetas 9) operates minibuses to Bandung (60,000Rp, four hours) and Semarang (80,000Rp, seven hours).

TRAIN Cirebon is serviced by frequent trains that run on both the main northern Jakarta–Semarang–Surabaya train line and the southern Jakarta–Yogyakarta–Surabaya line. The better services leave from Cirebon's main train station, just off Jl Siliwangi. For Jakarta's Gambir station, there are 18 daily trains (75,000Rp to 130,000Rp, 2¾ to three hours); to Yogyakarta there are six daily exclusive-class services (260,000Rp to 320,000Rp, 4½ to five hours).

Getting Around

Cirebon's *angkot* operate from behind the main bus terminal; a fixed 2000Rp fare is charged.

Cirebon has legions of pushy becak; you'll get harassed constantly. A ride from the train station to Pasar Pagi costs around 10,000Rp. There are also taxis, but meters are seemingly reserved for family members and royalty.

Around Cirebon

In the royal cemetery, 5km north of Cirebon, is the **tomb of Sunan Gunungjati**, who died in 1570. The most revered of Cirebon's kings, Gunungjati was also one of the nine *wali songo* (saintly men who spread Islam throughout Java), and his tomb is one of the holiest places in the country. The inner tombs are only open once a month on Kliwon Thursday of the Javanese calendar and at Idul Fitri and Maulud Nabi Muhammed. Pilgrims sit in contemplation and pray outside the doors on other days. Along from Sunan Gunungjati's tomb is the tomb of his first wife, who was Chinese – this tomb attracts Chinese worshippers.

CENTRAL JAVA

Jakarta may be the nation's capital, but the Javan identity is at its strongest here, in the island's historic heartland. As the seat of Java's first major Indianised civilisation, as well as the great Islamic sultanates centred on the *kraton* of Yogyakarta and Solo, Central Java (Jawa Tengah) remains the province in which the island's cultural pulse beats loudest.

Even though Central Java has a reputation for a short fuse when dealing with religious and political sentiments, it's a relaxed, easy-going province for tourists. Yogyakarta, at the centre of its own quasi-independent 'special region' stretching from the south coast to Gunung Merapi, and Solo, just 65km to the northeast of Yogyakarta, are

Central Java

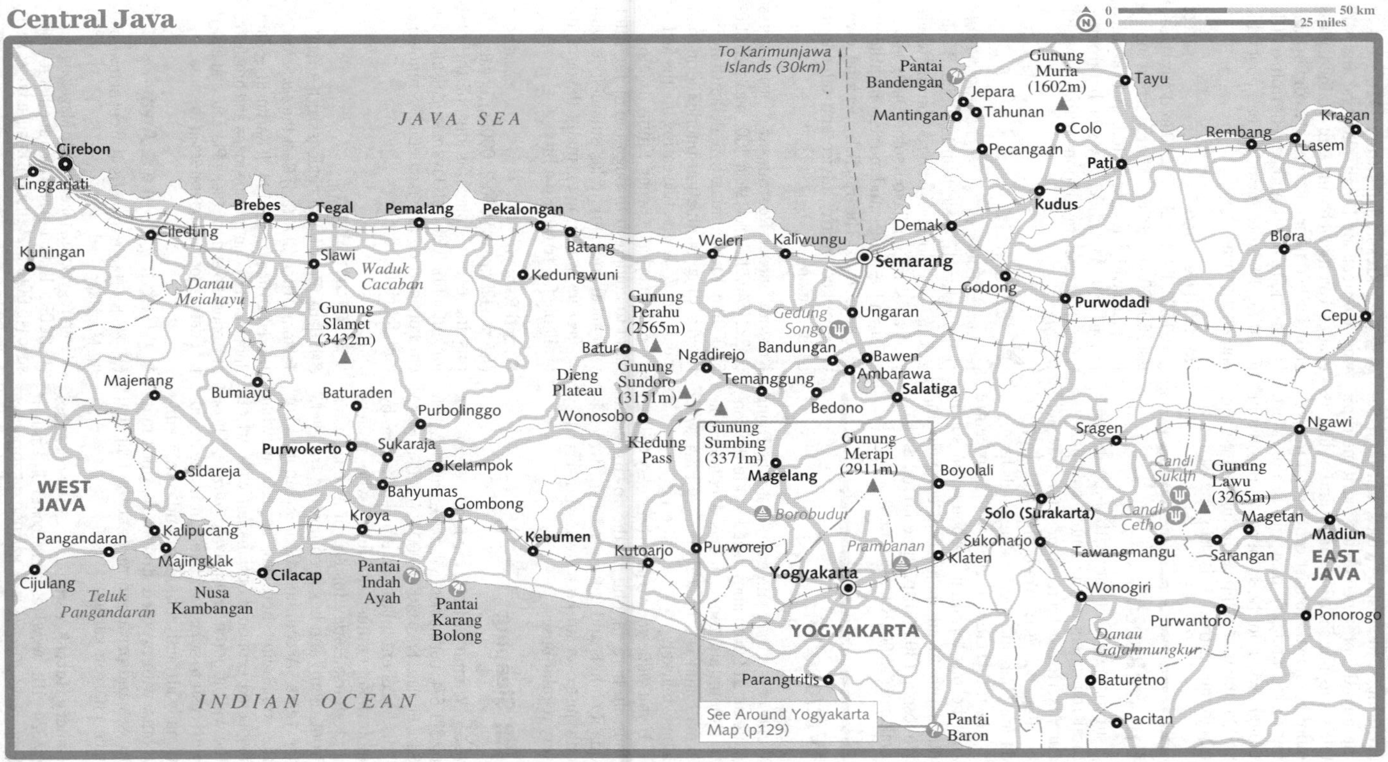

0 50 km
0 25 miles

JAVA SEA
To Karimunjawa Islands (30km)
Cirebon
Linggarjati
Kuningan
Ciledung
Brebes
Tegal
Slawi
Waduk Cacaban
Danau Meiahayu
Pemalang
Pekalongan
Batang
Kedungwuni
Gunung Slamet (3432m)
Majenang
Bumiayu
Baturaden
Purbolinggo
Purwokerto
Sukaraja
Kelampok
Bahyumas
Sidareja
WEST JAVA
Kalipucang
Pangandaran
Majingklak
Cijulang
Teluk Pangandaran
Nusa Kambangan
Cilacap
Kroya
Gombong
Pantai Indah Ayah
Pantai Karang Bolong
Kebumen
Kutoarjo
INDIAN OCEAN
Weleri
Kaliwungu
Gunung Perahu (2565m)
Batur
Dieng Plateau
Gunung Sundoro (3151m)
Wonosobo
Kledung Pass
Ngadirejo
Temanggung
Bandungan
Gedung Songo
Ungaran
Bawen
Ambarawa
Bedono
Salatiga
Semarang
Demak
Godong
Purwodadi
Gunung Sumbing (3371m)
Magelang
Gunung Merapi (2911m)
Borobudur
Prambanan
Purworejo
Yogyakarta
YOGYAKARTA
Parangtritis
See Around Yogyakarta Map (p129)
Pantai Baron
Boyolali
Klaten
Sukoharjo
Solo (Surakarta)
Sragen
Candi Sukuh
Candi Cetho
Gunung Lawu (3265m)
Tawangmangu
Sarangan
Magetan
Madiun
EAST JAVA
Ngawi
Wonogiri
Purwantoro
Danau Gajahmungkur
Baturetno
Pacitan
Ponorogo
Pantai Bandengan
Jepara
Mantingan
Tahunan
Gunung Muria (1602m)
Colo
Pecangaan
Tayu
Pati
Kudus
Rembang
Lasem
Kragan
Blora
Cepu

Java's most interesting cities. But even Semarang, the province's busy, maritime capital, has its fair share of charm and is, like its more bombastic tourist centres, an intriguing fusion of Java's past and future. Most, though, will find the stupendous Borobudur and Prambanan temples the highlight of any trip to the centre of this stunning island.

Purwokerto

A surprisingly clean city with some architectural reminders of the Dutch colonial era, Purwokerto is a crossroads for travellers heading between Wonosobo and Pangandaran. There are serviceable hotels here.

The train station is close to the city centre and the bus terminal is about 2km south. Buses run to all major centres, including Wonosobo (30,000Rp, three hours) and Yogyakarta (42,000Rp, 4½ hours).

Wonosobo

☎0286 / POP 113,000

Wonosobo is the main gateway to the Dieng Plateau. At 900m above sea level in the central mountain range, it has a comfortable climate and is a typical country town with a busy market.

If you value your comfort it's easy to base yourself here in one of the town's good-quality hotels and get up to Dieng, which is only just over an hour away and served by very regular buses.

Sleeping

TOP CHOICE **Wisma Duta Homestay** HOMESTAY $

(☎321 674; dutahomestay@yahoo.com; Jl Rumah Sakit III; r incl breakfast 60,000-320,000Rp; ❄📶) This excellent place is efficiently run by motorbike enthusiast Helly (who prefers a gleaming Harley instead of a soda in his front room) and has been hosting travellers for years. Accommodation is bipolar. For the rupiah-lite there are basic, somewhat neglected economy options, all with art on the wall, a porch and private *mandi*. Those with cash to splash will delight in the exceptionally attractive, modern and comfortable rooms, with exposed stonework, thick mattresses and private terraces at the rear that face a narrow garden.

Gallery Hotel Kresna HISTORIC HOTEL $$$

(☎324 111; www.kresnahotel.com; Jl Pasukan Ronggolawe 30; r/ste from 840,000/1,580,000Rp; ❄@📶🏊) Kresna dates from 1921, when it was a retreat for Dutch planters, and still exudes colonial charm with stained glass and polished floors. Rooms are comfortable and spacious, but would benefit from a little updating. Facilities include a bar, pool table and a large heated pool.

Hotel Sri Kencono HOTEL $$

(☎321 522; Jl A Yani 81; r 70,000Rp, d/f incl breakfast 260,000/440,000Rp) A large white motel-like place with well-presented, spacious tiled rooms with TVs and hot-water bathrooms, plus a few economy options with cold-water *mandi*.

Eating

No Limits Lounge CAFE, INDONESIAN $

(Jl Bayangkara 17; meals from 10,000Rp; 📶) Inexpensive, enjoyable cafe-restaurant where you can slurp on flavoursome Dieng coffee, savour a fresh juice and munch on authentic Javanese grub. The English-speaking owners give good travel advice and offer tours of the region.

Krishna Garden Restaurant INDONESIAN $$

(☎322 640; Jl Major Muin 100; meals 25,000-60,000Rp) Kresna makes a delightfully relaxed setting for an atmospheric Indonesian meal with *lesehan*-style eating booths facing a lovely garden. Owner Emmy is often at hand to guide you through the menu. After your meal you could relax sultan-style with a *sheesha* (water pipe), many flavours are available for 40,000Rp a hit.

Shanti Rahayu INDONESIAN $

(Jl A Yani 122; meals 9000-22,000Rp) Locals rate this inexpensive place as one of the best for authentic Central Javanese cuisine; the chicken curries are particularly renowned and delicious here.

Information

BNI Bank (Bank Negara Indonesia; Jl A Yani)

Telkom Office (Jl A Yani) Near the *alun-alun*.

Tourist Office (☎321 194; Jl Kartini III; ⌚8am-3pm Mon-Fri) Can provide maps and brochures of Wonosobo and the Dieng Plateau, and contact details for tour operators in the area.

Getting There & Away

Wonosobo's bus terminal is 4km out of town on the Magelang road.

From Yogyakarta take a bus to Magelang (13,000Rp, 1½ hours) and then another to Wonosobo (15,000Rp, 2½ hours). Regular buses also connect Borobudur and Magelang (5000Rp, 40 minutes) until about 4pm. **Rahayu Travel** (☎321 217; Jl A Yani 95) has door-to-door minibuses to Yogyakarta (40,000Rp, 3½ hours).

Hourly buses go to Semarang (36,000Rp, four hours), passing through Ambarawa (22,000Rp, 2½ hours).

Very frequent buses to Dieng (8000Rp, one hour) leave throughout the day (the last at 5pm) and continue on to Batur; you can catch them on Jl Rumah Sakit, 100m from Duta Guesthouse.

Dieng Plateau

☎0286

The spectacular lofty volcanic plateau of Dieng (Abode of the Gods) is home to some of the oldest Hindu architecture in Java. More than 400 temples, most dating from the 8th and 9th centuries, originally covered this 2000m-high plain, but they were abandoned and forgotten and only rediscovered in 1856 by the archaeologist Van Kinsbergen.

These squat, simple temples, while of great archaeological importance, can be slightly underwhelming for non-experts. Rather, Dieng's beautiful landscape is the main reason to make the long journey to this isolated region. Any number of walks across the volcanically active plateau, the marshy caldera of a collapsed volcano, are possible – to mineral lakes, steaming craters or the highest village in Java, Sembungan.

You can either stay in Dieng village, or commute up from Wonosobo, which has better facilities. The route up to Dieng is stunning, switchbacking through vertiginous hillsides of terraced vegetable fields.

The temples and the main natural sights can be seen in one day on foot. Get a very early start if you can, before the afternoon mists roll in. It's a pleasant three- or four-hour loop south from Dieng village to Telaga Warna (Coloured Lake), Candi Bima (Bima Temple), Kawah Sikidang (Sikidang Crater) and then back to Candi Gatutkaca, the Arjuna Complex and the village.

Sights

Arjuna Complex TEMPLE

(admission 20,000Rp incl Candi Gatutkaca) The five main temples that form the Arjuna Complex are clustered together on the central plain. They are Shiva temples, but like the other Dieng temples they have been named after the heroes of the *wayang* stories of the Mahabharata epic: Arjuna, Puntadewa, Srikandi, Sembadra and Semar. All have mouth-shaped doorways and strange bell-shaped windows and some locals leave offerings, burn incense and meditate here. Raised walkways link the temples (as most of this land is waterlogged), but you can see the remains of ancient underground tunnels, which once drained the marshy flatlands.

Candi Gatutkaca is a small Shiva temple (a yoni was found inside) with a square base south of the main complex.

Telaga Warna LAKE

(admission 8000Rp; ⏲8am-4.30pm) Exquisitely beautiful Telaga Warna lake, ringed by highland forest has turquoise and cobalt hues from the bubbling sulphur deposits around its shores. It's definitely on the main tourist circuit but few visitors venture beyond the initial viewing area. Follow the trail anticlockwise to the adjoining lake, **Telaga Pengilon**, and past holy **Gua Semar**, a meditation cave. Then for a lovely perspective of the lakes return to the main road via a narrow trail that leads around Telaga Pengilon and up a terraced hillside.

Museums MUSEUM

(admission incl in Arjuna Complex ticket price; ⏲8am-3pm) Just southwest of the Arjuna Complex are two small museums and a modest cafe. The site museum contains statues and sculptures including Shiva's carrier, Nandi the bull – with the body of a man and the head of a bull, it is a unique representation in Hindu iconography. There's also a headless image of Shiva himself, depicted in the lotus position, while a gargoyle sporting an erection is distinctly animist. The second museum has lots of displays about the geology of Dieng, the folklore associated with the plateau and more carved statues. All the information here is in Bahasa Indonesia only.

Candi Bima & Candi Dwarawati TEMPLES

Candi Bima is unique in Java, with *kudu* (sculpted heads) looking like spectators peering out of windows. The restored Candi Dwarawati is on the northern outskirts of the village.

Gunung Sikunir VIEWPOINT

South of Dieng village the sunrise mecca of Gunung Sikunir, 1km past Sembungan, and the shallow lake of **Telaga Cebong** are the main attractions. Views from Sikunir are spectacular, stretching across Dieng and east as far as Merapi and Merbabu volcanoes on a clear day. To reach the hill in time for sunrise, start at 4am from Dieng. It's a one-hour walk to Sembungan and another 30 minutes to the top of the hill. Most guides charge 50,000Rp to 110,000Rp per person.

Kawah Candradimuka LAKE

Nine kilometres from Dieng village is the trail to Kawah Candradimuka; it's a pleasant 1.5km walk to this crater through the fields. Another trail branches off to two lakes: **Telaga Nila** (a longer, two-hour walk away) and **Telaga Dringo**. Just a few hundred metres past the turn-off to Kawah Candradimuka is **Sumur Jalatunda**. This well is in fact a deep hole some 100m across with vertical walls plunging down to bright-green waters.

Kawah Sikidang LAKE

(admission 5000Rp) Kawah Sikidang is a volcanic crater with steaming vents and frantically bubbling mud ponds. Exercise extreme caution here – there are no guard rails to keep you from slipping off the sometimes muddy trails into the scalding-hot waters. Kawah Sibentang is a less spectacular crater nearby, and Telaga Lumut is a small lake.

Sembungan VILLAGE

South of the geothermal station, the paved road leads on to Sembungan, said to be the highest village in Java, at 2300m. Potato farming has made this large village relatively wealthy.

Kawah Sileri LAKE

Kawah Sileri, 2km off the main road and 6km from Dieng, is a smoking crater area with a hot lake.

Sleeping & Eating

Dieng's dozen or more guesthouses are notoriously poor value. Spartan conditions, semi-clean rooms and cool or luke-warm water are the norm.

Food isn't Dieng's strong point either. Hotel and restaurant, Bu Jono, is your best bet and has beer, but be prepared to wait.

While in town you must try the local herb, *purwaceng*, often served as tea or with coffee, which warms the body in cold weather and is said to act like a kind of Dieng-style coca leaf.

The village is tiny and most accommodation is on the main road.

Hotel & Restaurant Bu Jono GUESTHOUSE $

(☎642 046, 0852 2738 9949; Jl Raya, Km26; r without bathroom 80,000-100,000Rp, with bathroom 200,000Rp) This simple, friendly place has been hosting backpackers for years and has a certain ramshackle charm with basic, clean, economy rooms and better options with hot-water private bathrooms and TV. The pleasant, orderly restaurant downstairs vaguely resembles a Victorian tearoom with its tablecloths and net curtains. Good tours are offered. It's very close to the turn-off for Wonosobo.

Hotel Gunung Mas HOTEL $

(☎334 2017; d 125,000-175,000Rp, tr 200,000Rp) This solidly built hotel has a wide choice of well-scrubbed rooms, from a clean crash pad for the night to quite spacious rooms with private hot-water bathrooms. All are decent value and there's a shared upper-level balcony for *those* plateau views. However, staff on reception can be a bit gloomy and ask you to pay in advance. It's almost opposite the access road to the Arjuna Complex.

Bougenvil Homestay HOMESTAY $

(☎0813 2707 2112, 0813 2776 9399; r without/with bathroom 125,000/175,000Rp) Five clean rooms on the upper floor of a family home, which are smallish but two have a private bathroom. It has a lounge and balcony with highland views to enjoy. Located between the Wonosobo junction and Arjuna turnoff.

Dieng Plateau Homestay HOMESTAY $

(☎0813 2779 1565; Jl Raya, Km26; r 50,000Rp, meals from 12,000Rp) Expect basic rooms with concrete floors, a stick or two of furniture and rough blankets. That said, Titu, a worker here, is a very amusing and hospitable guy (ask him to do one of his 'dancing cleaning' routines!) who runs good tours (sunrise trips are 60,000Rp). There's a restaurant downstairs for local and Western grub. It's by the Wonosobo junction.

Information

The BRI Bank, near Hotel Gunung Mas, changes US dollars.

Getting There & Away

Dieng is 26km from Wonosobo (8000Rp, one hour), which is the usual access point. It's possible to reach Dieng from Yogyakarta in one day (including a stop at Borobudur) by public bus, provided you leave early enough to make the connection; the route is Yogyakarta–Borubudur–Magelang–Wonosobo–Dieng.

Travel agents including **Great Tour** (☎027 458 3221; www.greattoursjogja.com) in Yogyakarta offer day-trips for 175,000Rp that include sunset at Borobudur, but you'll spend a lot of your time on a bus and (unless you're fortunate) generally end up seeing Dieng clouded in mist.

Borobudur

☎0293

Like Angkor Wat in Cambodia and Bagan in Myanmar, Java's Borobudur makes the rest of Southeast Asia's spectacular sites seem almost incidental. Looming out of a patchwork of bottle-green paddies and swaying palms, this colossal Buddhist monument has survived Gunung Merapi's eruptions, terrorist bombs and the 2006 earthquake to remain as enigmatic and as beautiful as it must have been 1200 years ago.

It's well worth planning to spend a few days in the Borobudur region, which is a supremely beautiful landscape of impossibly green rice fields and traditional rice-growing *kampung*, all overlooked by soaring volcanic peaks. Locals call it the garden of Java.

This region is establishing itself as Indonesia's most important centre for Buddhism, and there are now three monasteries in the surrounding district. Visitors are welcome and you can even join the monks at prayer time for chanting.

History

Rulers of the Sailendra dynasty built Borobudur some time between AD 750 and AD 850. Little else is known about Borobudur's early history, but the Sailendras must have recruited a huge workforce, as some 60,000 cubic metres of stone had to be hewn, transported and carved during its construction. The name Borobudur is possibly derived from the Sanskrit words 'Vihara Buddha Uhr', which mean 'Buddhist Monastery on the Hill'.

With the decline of Buddhism and the shift of power to East Java, Borobudur was abandoned soon after completion and for centuries lay forgotten. It was only in 1815, when Sir Thomas Stamford Raffles governed Java, that the site was cleared and the sheer magnitude of the builders' imagination and technical skill was revealed. Early in the 20th century the Dutch began to tackle the restoration of Borobudur, but over the years the supporting hill had become waterlogged and the whole immense stone mass started to subside. A mammoth US$25-million Unesco-sponsored restoration project was undertaken between 1973 and 1983 to stabilise and restore the monument. This involved taking most of it apart stone by stone, adding new concrete foundations, inserting PVC and a lead drainage system, and then putting the whole shebang back together again.

In 1991 Borobudur was declared a World Heritage Site.

Sights

Borobudur Temple TEMPLE

(adults/students with ID US$20/10, sunrise 280,000Rp, guided 90-min tour for 1-5 people

UNDER ATTACK

In its 1200 years, Borobudur has repeatedly suffered attack from forces of nature and at the hands of humans.

During its period of abandonment, which lasted for as much as a millennia, earthquakes and volcanic eruptions destablised the monument further and the Javanese jungle reclaimed the site as giant roots penetrated the monument and prised apart stone blocks.

After rediscovery its fame grew and in 1896 King Chulalongkorn of Siam visited and removed dozens of sculptures and relief panels; some are now on display in the National Museum in Bangkok.

On 21 January 1985, bombs planted by opponents of Suharto exploded on the upper layers of the monument. Nine small stupas were damaged, but were later fully restored.

Periodically, the highly active Merapi volcano has also damaged the site – in 2010 eruptions covered the monument with a thick layer of dust and 55,000 stone blocks had to be removed so the blocked drainage system could be cleared.

Right now it's the sheer pressure of numbers which is most worrying. On holidays up to 90,000 people ascend the temple, and despite (deafening) warnings from PA systems, some idiots still clamber over the statues and deface the reliefs.

Many locals feel that a system to manage numbers must be introduced, with guides escorting groups around the monument.

MAKE THE MOST OF BOROBUDUR

Borobudur is Indonesia's most popular tourist attraction; it's crowded and noisy, at all times, especially on weekends.

The golden rule is to arrive as early as you can, ideally be at the gate just before the site opens at 6am, or fork out extra for sunrise entry (4.30am). This way you'll arrive at the least crowded, coolest and most photogenic time of day. Most of the tour groups and school parties don't get in till 7.30am or later.

Hawkers both outside and inside the archaeological park can be very pushy but are sometimes put off if you tell them in Bahasa Indonesia that you are a resident of Yogyakarta (*saya tinggal di Yogyakarta*).

Most visitors are groups from distant corners of Java. Many have never seen foreigners in the flesh before so expect plenty of requests for photos.

An mp3 player and some inspirational music helps cut out the noise of the crowds. There's a small hill with some shade 100m or so directly south of the temple, where you can escape the hoards and contemplate the monument in peace.

Visitors who stay locally in Borobudur village hotels qualify for a 20,000Rp discount (ask for a voucher), another worthwhile reason to stay in the region for a few days and escape urban Java.

70,000Rp; ⏲6am-5.15pm) Borobudur is built from two million stone blocks in the form of a massive symmetrical stupa, literally wrapped around a small hill. Standing on a 118m by 118m base, its six square terraces are topped by three circular ones, with four stairways leading up through carved gateways to the top. The paintwork is long gone, but it's thought that the grey stone of Borobudur was once coloured to catch the sun.

Viewed from the air, the structure resembles a colossal three-dimensional tantric mandala (symbolic circular figure). It has been suggested, in fact, that the people of the Buddhist community that once supported Borobudur were early Vajrayana or Tantric Buddhists who used it as a walk-through mandala.

The monument was conceived as a Buddhist vision of the cosmos in stone, starting in the everyday world and spiralling up to nirvana, the Buddhist heaven. At the base of the monument is a series of reliefs representing a world dominated by passion and desire, where the good are rewarded by reincarnation as a higher form of life, while the evil are punished by a lowlier reincarnation. These carvings and their carnal scenes are covered by stone to hide them from view, but they are partly visible on the southern side.

Starting at the main eastern gateway, go clockwise (as one should around all Buddhist monuments) around the galleries of the stupa. Although Borobudur is impressive for its sheer bulk, the delicate sculptural work when viewed up close is exquisite. The pilgrim's walk is about 5km long and takes you along narrow corridors past nearly 1460 richly decorated narrative panels and 1212 decorative panels in which the sculptors have carved a virtual textbook of Buddhist doctrines as well as many aspects of Javanese life 1000 years ago – a continual procession of ships and elephants, musicians and dancing girls, warriors and kings.

On the third level there's a lengthy panel sequence about a dream of Queen Maya, which involved a vision of white elephants with six tusks. Monks and courtiers interpret this as a premonition that her son would become a Buddha, and the sequence continues until the birth of Prince Siddhartha and his journey to become a Buddha. Many other panels are related to Buddhist concepts of cause and effect or karma.

Some 432 serene-faced Buddha images stare out from open chambers above the galleries, while 72 more Buddha images sit only partly visible in latticed stupas on the top three terraces – one is considered the lucky Buddha. The top platform is circular, signifying never-ending nirvana.

Admission to the temple includes entrance to **Karmawibhangga archaeological museum**, which is just east of the monument and contains 4000 original stones and carvings from Borobudur and some interesting photographs.

Samudraraksa Museum MUSEUM
(inside Borobudur site; admission incl with Borobudur ticket) This museum is dedicated to the importance of the ocean and sea trade in Indonesia, and houses an 18m wooden outrigger, a replica of a boat depicted on one of Borobudur's panels. This boat was sailed to Madagascar and on to Ghana in West Africa in 2003, a voyage that retraced ancient Javanese trading links – the original spice trade – with the continent more than a thousand years ago.

Mendut Temple & Monastery TEMPLE, MONASTERY
(admission 3300Rp; ⏲8am-4pm) This exquisite temple, around 3.5km east of Borobudur, may look insignificant compared with its mighty neighbour, but it houses the most outstanding statue in its original setting of any temple in Java. The magnificent 3m-high figure of Buddha is flanked by Bodhisattvas: Lokesvara on the left and Vairapana on the right. The Buddha is also notable for his posture: he sits Western-style with both feet on the ground.

The statues are particularly evocative at night, when spotlit against the evening sky, and the inner chamber appears charged with an almost supernatural energy. Guards here will allow visitors to enter Mendut after dark if accompanied with a local guide (speak to Jaker).

Next to the temple is the Mendut Buddhist Monastery. You can join the monks here for prayers at around 6pm every day, and meditation courses are often held in December.

Candi Pawon TEMPLE
(admission 3300Rp; ⏲8am-4pm) Around 1.5km east of Borobudur, this small solitary temple is similar in design and decoration to the Mendut temple. It is not a stupa but resembles a Central Javanese temple, with its broad base, central body and pyramidal roof. Elaborately carved relief panels adorn its sides. Pot-bellied dwarfs pouring riches over the entrance to this temple suggest that it was dedicated to Kuvera, the Buddhist god of fortune.

Tours

Jaker (☎029 378 8845; jackpriyana@yahoo.com.sg) is a group of guides and local activists based in the small settlement of Borobudur that surrounds the world's largest Buddhist monument. All Jaker members were born in the area, can provide expert local knowledge and speak fluent English. Backpacking rates are charged for trips to Selogriyo (towering rice terraces and a small Hindu temple), Tuksongo (a centre of glass-noodle production), tofu and pottery villages, a large batik workshop and to Setumbu hill for sunrise over the Borobudur monument.

Kelaidoscope of Java (p118) is another excellent tour agency that operates fascinating tours of the Borobudur region.

Festivals & Events

Waisak FESTIVAL
The Buddha's birth, his enlightenment and his reaching of nirvana are all celebrated on the full-moon day of Waisak. A great procession of saffron-robed monks travels from Mendut to Pawon then Borobudur, where candles are lit and flowers strewn about as offerings, followed by praying and chanting. This holiest of Buddhist events attracts thousands of pilgrims, and usually falls in May.

Festival of Borobudur FESTIVAL
Around June, the Festival of Borobudur kicks off with a *Ramayana*-style dance, and goes on to feature folk-dancing competitions, handicrafts, white-water rafting and other activities.

Sleeping

There's a reasonable selection of hotels around Borobudur, though good budget places are limited. Visitors who stay in locally owned hotels get discounted entry to the monument; ask for your voucher.

Kelaidoscope of Java (p118) also offers the possibility of experiencing life in Kamal, a traditional village high up in the hills with stunning views of Borobudur temple. Accommodation is in a comfortable Javanese wooden house with private bathroom.

TOP CHOICE **Lotus II** GUESTHOUSE $
(☎788 845; jackpriyana@yahoo.com.sg; Jl Balaputradewa 54; r incl breakfast 200,000Rp; ❄@🛜) This very popular, friendly place is owned by one of the founders of Jaker, so there's great local information and everyone speaks good English. Staff could not be more helpful, and are always around for a chat. Most of the artistically styled rooms here are exceptionally large, with mosquito nets draped from high ceilings and lovely comfy beds, plus huge bathrooms (with tubs). The long rear balcony, overlooking rice fields, is perfect for

WORTH A TRIP

VILLAGES AROUND BOROBUDUR

Away from the temples, the region around Borobudur is supremely beautiful – a verdant, incredibly fertile and classically Javanese landscape of villages and rice fields. Borubudur itself sits in a large bowl-shaped valley ringed by mountains and volcanoes that the locals call *mahagelan* – the giant bracelet.

Around 3km southwest of the monument, the small village of **Karang** is prime tofu-making terrain. There are several kitchens in the village, each producing around 50kg of *tahu* daily using traditional methods, cooking with coconut oil over a wood fire. The next settlement of **Nglipoh** is a ceramics centre, where locals say claypots have been made for more than 1000 years; everyone in the village is involved in production in some way. Today mostly *ibu* (cooking vessels) are made, though glazed ashtrays and other pots are for sale too. The potters are very friendly and will let you try your hand on their wheels (just expect a giggle or two).

At **Candirejo**, 3km from Borobudur, locals have set up a **homestay program** (☎789 675; incl 3 meals 200,000Rp) that allows you to experience life in a Javanese village. Trekking, rafting (125,000Rp) and tours (60,000Rp) of local home industries including palm sugar and *krupuk* kitchens are also offered.

your breakfast or an afternoon tea or beer. Book well ahead.

Homestay Rajasa GUESTHOUSE $
(☎788 276; ariswara_sutomo@yahoo.com; Jl Badrawati II; r incl breakfast with fan & cold water/air-con & hot water 160,000/350,000Rp, meals 20,000-25,000Rp; ❄) A deservedly popular, welcoming guesthouse with rooms that face rice fields (through railings) about 1.5km south of the bus terminal. The fan-cooled rooms are the best value, as you pay a lot more for air-conditioning and slightly smarter furniture. Meals are well-priced here.

Rumah Boedi HOTEL $$
(☎559 498; www.rumahboedi.com; r 550,000-700,000Rp, ste 900,000Rp; ❄📶) In a very peaceful location about 3km east of the monument, this new place offers gorgeous contemporary rooms (all feel very private) dotted around extensive, shady grounds. There's a (pricey) cafe-restaurant too.

Amanjiwo LUXURY HOTEL $$$
(☎788 333; www.amanresorts.com; ste from US$1028; ❄@📶🏊) Perched on a hillside 4km south of Borobudur, with panoramic views towards the stupa, this grand hotel has it all. The incredibly commodious suites, many with private pools, are some of the finest in Indonesia (David Beckham was a guest in 2007). Facilities include two tennis courts, a 40m pool and a spa.

Manohara Hotel HOTEL $$
(☎788 131; www.manoharaborobudur.com; r incl breakfast from 745,000Rp; ❄📶) The Monohara enjoys an unrivalled location in the grounds of the monument, with a cafe-restaurant that has views across to the main temple. Though the rooms are smallish for the price and slightly dated they are comfortable and kept clean. This hotel's real trump card is that unlimited entry (and a discounted sunrise rate) to Borobudur is included, so if there are two of you it's a good deal.

Saraswati HOTEL $$$
(☎788 843; www.saraswatiborobudur.com; Jl Balaputradewa 10; r US$120-174, ste from US$210; ❄@📶🏊) The grand, chintzy lobby is a bit over the top but the rooms set to the rear of the property are elegant, spacious and boast all mod cons. There's a delightful, shady pool area but expect an early wake-up call from the nearby mosque.

Lotus Guesthouse GUESTHOUSE $
(☎788 281; Jl Medang Kamulan II; r incl breakfast 70,000-220,000Rp, meals 12,000Rp) Bare, basic rooms scattered over a rambling building but a very hospitable local family and the authentic local food here is very cheap and tasty.

Plataran LUXURY HOTEL $$$
(☎788 888; www.plataranborobudur.com; 4km west of monument; r/villas from US$167/300; ❄📶) Landmark new hotel that enjoys billion-rupiah views of the monument from a blissfully tranquil hilltop location. There's a swanky colonial-style restaurant and lovely spa but the 15 faux-traditional timber villas are overpriced, so try to negotiate a discount.

Eating

For inexpensive local grub head to the Lotus Guesthouse (try the *soto*) or you'll find warung outside the monument entrance.

Saung Makan Bu Empat SEAFOOD $$
(☎0293 914 0085; Jl Borobudor, Nyrajek; meals 45,000-70,000Rp) Around 5km east of Borobudur village on the road to Yogyakarta, this large traditional bamboo-and-timber restaurant is set around rice fields and gurgling streams. It's renowned for its fish and shrimp dishes. No alcohol is served but you'll find lots of delicious fresh fruit juices (10,000Rp).

Patio INTERNATIONAL $$$
(☎788 888; www.plataranborobudur.com; 4km west of monument; meals from 160,000Rp) For a really special setting this colonial-style hotel restaurant is hard to match – eat in the formal dining room or out on the terrace with views of Borobudur. Local mains are 60,000Rp to 100,000Rp while Western dishes (try the rack of lamb) can cost up to 300,000Rp. There's a long wine list.

Information

For tourist information contact the **information office** (☎788 266; www.borobudurpark.com; ⏰6am-5.30pm; 🚌from Yogyakarta's Giwangan bus terminal) just beyond the temple's entrance, or speak to the Jaker guys who really know the area intimately. A **BNI Bank ATM** (Jl Medang Kamulan) is near the temple's entrance. Head to **Intaneto** (Jl Badrawati 5; per hr 4000Rp) just south of the bus station for internet connections.

Getting There & Away

From Yogyakarta buses leave Jombor terminal (15,000Rp, every 30 minutes, 1¼ hours) to Borobudur – the last bus to/from Borobudur is at 4.30pm.

From Borobudur terminal buses go regularly to Magelang (5000Rp) until 4pm. In Borobudur, becak cost 5000Rp to 7000Rp anywhere in the village. Bicycles (20,000Rp) and motorbikes (50,000Rp) can be hired from hotels. Tours of Borobudur are easily arranged in Yogyakarta.

Yogyakarta

☎0274 / POP 396,000

If Jakarta is Java's financial and industrial powerhouse, Yogyakarta is its soul. Yogyakarta (pronounced 'Jogjakarta' and called Yogya for short), is where the Javanese language is at its purest, Java's arts at their brightest and its traditions at their most visible.

Fiercely independent and protective of its customs, Yogya is now the site of an uneasy truce between the old ways of life and the onslaught of modernity. Still headed by its sultan, whose *kraton* remains the hub of traditional life, contemporary Yogya is nevertheless a huge urban centre (the Yogya conurbation is 1.6 million) of cybercafes, malls and traffic jams, as it is a stronghold of batik, gamelan and ritual.

Yogya remains Java's premier tourist city, with countless hotels, restaurants and attractions. It's also an ideal base for exploring nearby attractions, including Indonesia's most important archaeological sites, Borobudur and Prambanan.

History

Yogyakarta owes its establishment to Prince Mangkubumi, who in 1755 returned to the former seat of Mataram and built the *kraton* of Yogyakarta. He took the title of sultan and created the most powerful Javanese state since the 17th century.

Yogya has always been a symbol of resistance to colonial rule; it was the heart of Diponegoro's Java War (1825–30) and became the capital of the republic from 1946 until independence in 1949.

When the Dutch occupied Yogya in 1948, the patriotic sultan locked himself in the *kraton* and let rebels use the palace as their headquarters. The Dutch did not dare move against the sultan for fear of arousing the anger of millions of Javanese who looked upon him almost as a god. As a result of the sultan's support of the rebels, Yogya was granted the status of a special region when independence finally came.

Sights

Most of Yogya's sights are in a small central area of the city centred on the *kraton* complex, and just to the north. But away from here and out in the eastern and southern suburbs are other attractions.

THE KRATON & AROUND

The historic *kraton* area harbours most of Yogya's most important buildings and tourist attractions and is eminently walkable.

Kraton PALACE
(Map p114; ☎373 321; admission 12,500Rp, camera 1000Rp, guided tour by donation; ⏰8am-1.30pm Sat-Thu, to noon Fri) The cultural and political

Yogyakarta

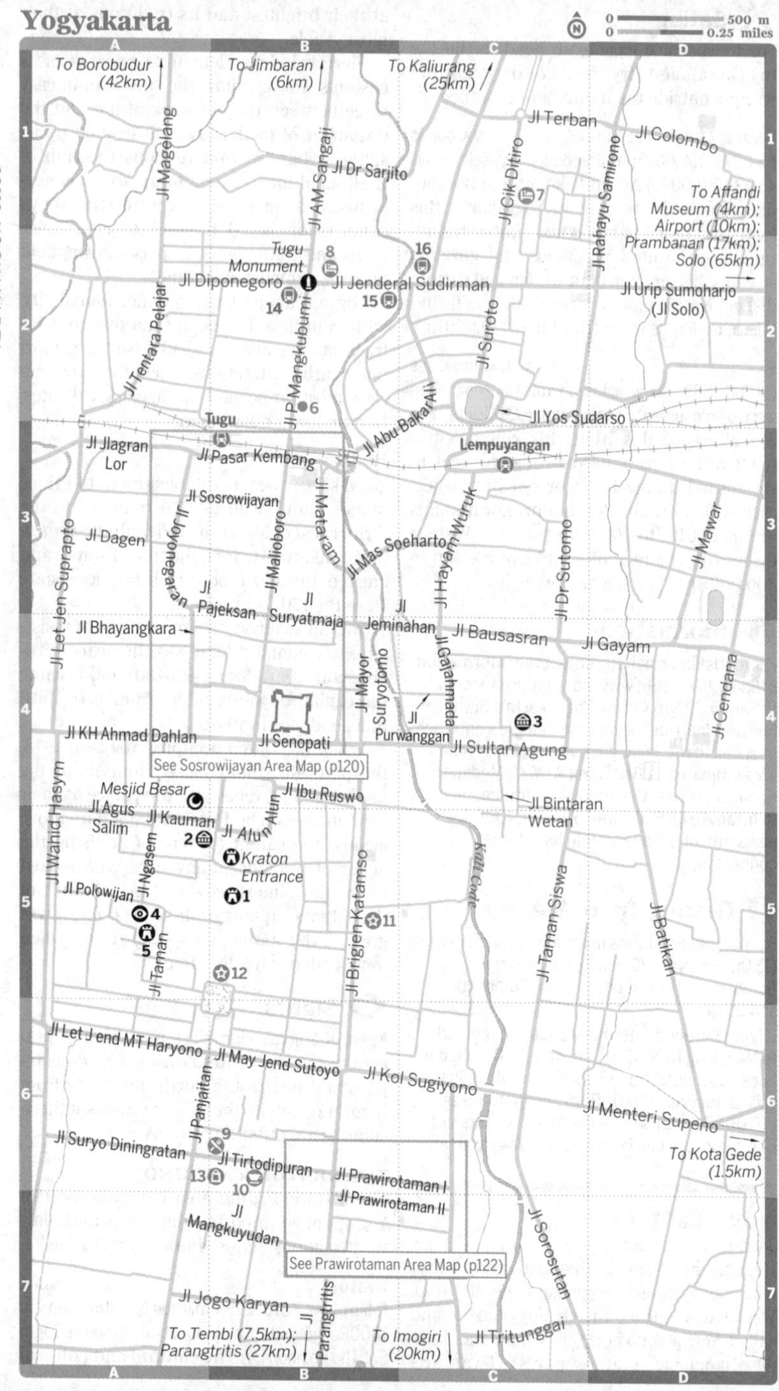

0 500 m
0 0.25 miles
To Borobudur (42km)
To Jimbaran (6km)
To Kaliurang (25km)
Jl Terban
Jl Colombo
Jl Magelang
Jl AM Sangaji
Jl Dr Sarjito
Jl Cik Ditiro
7
Jl Rahayu Samirono
To Affandi Museum (4km); Airport (10km); Prambanan (17km); Solo (65km)
Tugu Monument
8
16
Jl Diponegoro
Jl Jenderal Sudirman
Jl Urip Sumoharjo (Jl Solo)
14
15
Jl Tentara Pelajar
Jl P Mangkubumi
6
Jl Suroto
Jl Abu Bakar Ali
Jl Yos Sudarso
Tugu
Lempuyangan
Jl Jlagran Lor
Jl Pasar Kembang
Jl Sosrowijayan
Jl Let Jen Suprapto
Jl Dagen
Jl Joyonegaran
Jl Malioboro
Jl Mataram
Jl Mas Soeharto
Jl Hayam Wuruk
Jl Dr Sutomo
Jl Mawar
Jl Pajeksan
Jl Suryatmaja
Jl Jeminahan
Jl Bhayangkara
Jl Bausasran
Jl Gayam
Jl Mayor Suryotomo
Jl Gajahmada
Jl Purwanggan
3
Jl Cendana
Jl KH Ahmad Dahlan
Jl Senopati
Jl Sultan Agung
See Sosrowijayan Area Map (p120)
Mesjid Besar
Jl Ibu Ruswo
Jl Wahid Hasym
Jl Agus Salim
Jl Kauman
Jl Alun Alun
Jl Bintaran Wetan
2
Kraton Entrance
Kali Code
Jl Polowijan
Jl Ngasem
1
4
5
Jl Taman
11
Jl Brigjen Katamso
Jl Taman Siswa
Jl Batikan
12
Jl Let Jend MT Haryono
Jl May Jend Sutoyo
Jl Kol Sugiyono
Jl Menteri Supeno
Jl Panjaitan
9
Jl Suryo Diningratan
Jl Tirtodipuran
To Kota Gede (1.5km)
13
10
Jl Prawirotaman I
Jl Prawirotaman II
Jl Mangkuyudan
Jl Sorosutan
See Prawirotaman Area Map (p122)
Jl Jogo Karyan
Jl Parangtritis
To Tembi (7.5km); Parangtritis (27km)
To Imogiri (20km)
Jl Tritunggai

Yogyakarta

Sights
1 Kraton ... B5
2 Museum Kareta Kraton ... A5
3 Pakualaman Kraton ... C4
4 Pasar Ngasem ... A5
5 Taman Sari ... A5

Activities, Courses & Tours
6 Bima Tour & Travel ... B2

Sleeping
7 Indraloka Home Stay ... C1
8 Phoenix Hotel Yogyakarta ... B2

Eating
9 Kedai Kebun ... B6

Drinking
10 Lecker ... B6

Entertainment
11 Purawisata ... B5
12 Sasono Hinggil ... B5

Shopping
13 Batik Plentong ... B6
Batik Winotosastro ... (see 13)

Transport
Niki Vita Tour & Travel ... (see 14)
14 Rahayu ... B2
15 Rajawali Putra ... B2
16 Terban Bus Terminal for Kaliurang ... C2

heart of this fascinating city is the huge palace of the sultans of Yogya, or *kraton*.

Effectively a walled city, this unique compound is home to around 25,000 people, and has its own market, shops, batik and silver cottage industries, schools, and mosques. Around 1000 of its residents are employed by the sultan.

Disappointingly, the treasures here are poorly displayed and not well labelled – don't expect much information to put the palace, its buildings and contents in context.

The innermost group of buildings, where the current sultan still resides, was built between 1755 and 1756. European-style touches to the interior were added much later, in the 1920s. Structurally this is one of the finest examples of Javanese palace architecture, providing a series of luxurious halls and spacious courtyards and pavilions. An appreciation of history runs deep in Yogya, and the palace is attended by very dignified elderly retainers who wear traditional Javanese dress.

The centre of the *kraton* is the reception hall, the **Bangsal Kencana** (Golden Pavilion), with its marble floor, intricately decorated roof, Dutch-style stained glass windows and great columns of carved teak.

A large part of the *kraton* is used as a museum and holds an extensive collection, including gifts from European monarchs, gilt copies of the sacred *pusaka* (heirlooms of the royal family) and gamelan instruments. One of the most interesting rooms contains the royal family tree, old photographs of grand mass weddings and portraits of the former sultans of Yogya.

A modern memorial building within the *kraton* is dedicated to the beloved Sultan Hamengkubuwono IX, with photographs and personal effects.

Other points of interest within the *kraton* include the male and female entrances, indicated by giant-sized 'he' and 'she' dragons (although the dragons look very similar).

Outside the *kraton*, in the centre of the northern square, there are two sacred *waringin* (banyan trees), where, in the days of feudal Java, white-robed petitioners would patiently sit hoping to catch the eye of the king. In the *alun-alun kidul* (southern square), two similar **banyan trees** are said to bring great fortune if you can walk between them without mishap blindfolded; on Friday and Saturday nights you can see the youth of Yogya attempting the feat to a chorus of laughter from friends.

There are **performances** (10am to noon) in the *kraton's* inner pavilion that are included in your entrance ticket. There's gamelan on Monday, Tuesday and Thursday, *wayang golek* on Wednesday, Javanese singing and poems on Friday, *wayang kulit* on Saturday and classical dance on Sunday.

The *kraton*'s entrance is on the northwestern side. It's closed on national holidays and for special *kraton* ceremonies.

Be careful as there are scams practised by batik sellers who hang around here (p127).

Taman Sari PALACE
(Map p114; Jl Taman; admission 7000Rp; 8am-3.30pm) Just southwest of the *kraton* is this complex, which once served as a splendid

YOGYA IN...

Two Days

Start your day with a visit to the **Kraton** and a traditional performance of gamelan, *wayang* or dance, then spend the afternoon exploring the *kampung* surrounding the sultan's palace and nearby **Taman Sari**. In the evening explore the narrow streets of the traditional Sosrowijayan area and its myriad restaurants.

Your second day could start with a wander down Jl Malioboro scouting for batik bargains, and a meander through Yogya's main market, **Pasar Beringharjo**. A becak ride to **Kota Gede** to seek out silver could be finished off with a trip to **Prawirotaman** or neighbouring Jl Tirtodipuran for dinner.

Four Days

After exploring the city of Yogya it's time to get out and see wonders within striking distance of the city. Rise early and catch the sunrise at the incomparable Buddhist temple of **Borobudur**, before exploring the verdant countryside and fascinating villages around the monument, ideally with a community guide from Jaker.

On day four, move on to the Prambanan, the Hindu masterpiece on the other side of the city; it's fun to make a whole day of it by cycling there via some of the minor outlying temples.

pleasure park of palaces, pools and waterways for the sultan and his entourage. It's said that the sultan had the Portuguese architect of this elaborate retreat, built between 1758 and 1765, executed in order to keep his hidden pleasure rooms secret.

The complex, which is also known by its old Dutch name *waterkasteel* (water castle), was damaged first by Diponegoro's Java War, and an earthquake in 1865 helped finish the job. While much of what you see today lies in ruins, the bathing pools have been restored.

Sono-Budoyo Museum MUSEUM

(Map p120; ☎376 775; admission 5000Rp; ⏲8am-1.30pm Tue-Thu, to 11.15am Fri, to noon Sat & Sun) This is the pick of Yogya's museums, even if it is dusty and dimly lit, with a first-class collection of Javanese art, including *wayang kulit* puppets, *topeng* (masks), kris and batik. It also has a courtyard packed with Hindu statuary and artefacts from further afield, including superb Balinese carvings. *Wayang kulit* performances are held here.

Pasar Beringharjo MARKET

(Map p120; Jl A Yani; ⏲8am-4.30pm) Yogya's main market, 800m north of the *kraton*, is a lively and fascinating place. The front section has a wide range of batik – mostly inexpensive *batik cap* (stamped batik) – while the 2nd floor is dedicated to cheap clothes and shoes. Most interesting of all, though, is the old section towards the back. Crammed with warungs and stalls selling a huge variety of fruit and vegetables, this is still very much a traditional market. The range of *rempah rempah* (spices) on the 1st floor is quite something.

Museum Kareta Kraton MUSEUM

(Map p114; admission 7500Rp; ⏲8am-1.30pm Sat-Thu, to noon Fri) Near the *kraton* entrance, Museum Kareta Kraton has exhibits of the opulent chariots of the sultans, although the bug-eyed horse statues are almost more interesting than the main event.

Pakualaman Kraton MUSEUM

(Map p114; Jl Sultan Agung; ⏲9.30am-1.30pm Tue, Thu & Sun) This small museum includes a *pendopo* that can hold a full gamelan orchestra, and a curious colonial house. Outside opening times you can explore the grounds.

EASTERN YOGYAKARTA

The east of the city has several more interesting sights, including the silver village of Kota Gede and a couple of museums.

Kota Gede NEIGHBOURHOOD

(sacred tomb admission 1000Rp; ⏲sacred tomb around 9am-noon Sun, Mon & Thu, around 1-3pm Fri) Kota Gede has been famed as the hub of Yogya's silver industry since the 1930s. But this quiet old town, which is now a suburb of Yogyakarta, was the first capital of the Mataram kingdom, founded by Panembahan

Senopati in 1582. Senopati is buried in the small graveyard of an old mosque located to the south of the town's central market. You can visit the **sacred tomb**, but be sure to wear conservative dress when visiting. On days when the tomb is closed there is not much to see here.

Jl Kemasan, the main street leading into town from the north, is lined with busy silver workshops. Most of the shops have similar stock, including hand-beaten bowls, boxes, fine filigree and modern jewellery.

Kota Gede is about 5km southeast of Jl Malioboro. Catch bus 3A or 3B, take a becak (about 16,000Rp), or cycle there; it's flat most of the way.

Affandi Museum MUSEUM

(☎562 593; www.affandi.org; Jl Laksda Adisucipto 167; admission incl 1 soft drink 20,000Rp, camera 10,000Rp; ⏲9am-4pm except holidays) One of Indonesia's most celebrated artists, Affandi lived and worked in a wonderfully quirky riverside house-come-studio, about 6km east of the town centre. Today his former home is the Affandi Museum, which has an extensive collection of his paintings, including some astonishing self-portraits and personal items. Check out his car, a real boy racer's dream: a lime-green and yellow customised 1967 Galant car with an oversized rear spoiler.

There's a great little cafe here, and Affandi's artistic touch even extends to the *mushullah* (prayer room), which occupies a converted horse carriage, painted in technicolour tones – it looks like a psychedelic gypsy cart. Catch bus 1A to reach this museum from Jl Malioboro.

OTHER AREAS

Pasar Ngasem MARKET

(Map p114; Ring Rd Selatan; ⏲8am-4pm) Yogya's bird market has song birds and pigeons (for training, not eating), but occasionally ravens (which are used in black magic), owls and raptors are also sold.

If you poke around you'll also come across reptiles including snakes, lizards, iguanas and probably various endagered species are also for sale.

It's 5km south of the city centre.

Museum Sasana Wiratama MUSEUM

(Monumen Diponegoro; admission by donation; ⏲8am-noon Tue-Sun) In the northwest of the city, this museum honours the Indonesian hero Prince Diponegoro, who was leader of the bloody but futile rebellion of 1825–30 against the Dutch. A motley collection of the prince's belongings and other exhibits are kept in the small museum at his former Yogya residence.

Tembi MUSEUM

(☎368 000; www.tembi.net; admission by donation; ⏲8am-8pm) Down in the deep south of the city, Tembi is a Javanese cultural centre in a lovely position surrounded by rice paddies. The fine old wooden houses here contain an outstanding collection of kris, a few *wayang* puppets, batik and basketry and some historic photographs of Yogya. There's a highly recommended restaurant and accommodation too. To get to Tembi, jump aboard any bus bound for Parangtritis beach from Jl Parangtritis and get off at kilometre 8.4 on the highway; Tembi is 400m east of here along a side road.

Activities

Two good places for yoga are Via Via (p123) in the south of the city and Sangam (p124) in the north of town. Both offer holistic and hatha sessions for 40,000Rp most days of the week.

Courses

Yogya offers a variety of courses, with everything from cooking demonstrations to Bahasa Indonesia classes.

Via Via COURSE

(Map p122; ☎386 557; www.viaviajogja.com; Jl Prawirotaman I 30) Well-structured language, cooking, batik and silver jewellery-making courses for 80,000Rp to 170,000Rp, depending on the numbers.

Alam Bahasa Indonesia LANGUAGE COURSE

(☎589 631; www.alambahasa.com; Kompleks Kolombo III, Jl Cendrawasih; US$9.50 per hour) One-on-one and small group Bahasa Indonesia language study from a professional school. Discounts for students.

Tours

Tour agents on Jl Prawirotaman and in the Sosrowijayan area offer a host of tour options at similar prices. Typical day tours and per-person rates (excluding entrance fees) are Borobudur (80,000Rp), Dieng (175,000Rp), Gedung Songo and Ambarawa (200,000Rp), Prambanan 70,000Rp, Prambanan and Parangtritis 180,000Rp, and Solo and Candi Sukuh 250,000Rp.

Longer tours, such as to Gunung Bromo and on to Bali (from 400,000Rp for two days and one night) and Bromo/Ijen (800,000Rp for three days and two nights) are also offered. Tours depend on the number of people (a minimum of four is often necessary).

Operators also arrange cars with driver, with rates starting at 350,000Rp per day.

Via Via Tours TOUR
(Map p122; www.viaviajogja.com; Jl Prawirotaman I 30) This cafe-restaurant offers 14 tours, including some really creative options. There are numerous bike and motorbike tours, including a backroad trip to Prambanan (115,000Rp), city walks and Merapi hikes, rafting, and a *jamu* (herbal medicine) and massage tour (200,000Rp) that takes in a visit to a specialist market. Tours to the Solo region, and to East Java are also offered.

Kaleidoscope of Java TOUR
(Map p122; ☎0812 2711 7439; www.kaleidoscopeofjavatour.com; Gang Sartono 823, Rumah Eyang) Fascinating tours of the Borobudur region, curated by Atik, who was born in Borobudur village. The day trip (305,000Rp) from Yogya involves sunrise from Menoreh hill; visits to Borobudur, Pawon and Mendut temples and a monastery, cottage industries and Javanese dance practices; and all meals.

Jogja Trans TOUR
(☎081 6426 0124, 439 8495; www.jogjatrans.com; Gang 04/09, Madurejo, Prambanan) A highly professional agency that can provide cars (around 400,000Rp per day) with reliable drivers and also arrange bespoke tours throughout Java.

Great Tours TOUR
(Map p120; ☎583 221; www.greattoursjogja.com; Jl Sosrowijayan 29) Good all-rounder for tours to places in Central Java and beyond, including Bromo and Ijen. Also sells bus and minibus tickets.

Inspirasi Indonesia GUIDE
(☎085 6285 9193, 781 9925; www.inspirasiindonesiaholidays.com; Gesik RT 03 Kalipucang, Kasongan) Previously known as Rumah Guides, these enthusiastic young locals offer off-the-beaten-path tours to Borobudur that include small villages in the area and cottage industries. They can set up tours around Yogya too.

Bima Tour & Travel TOUR
(Map p114; ☎510 156; www.bimatourjogja.blogspot.co.uk; Jl Pangeran Mangkubumi 68) Daily tour packages from Yogya to Borobudur and Prambanan. It also has good rates for trips to Bromo.

Festivals & Events

Gerebeg FESTIVAL
The three Gerebeg festivals – held each year at the end of January and April and the beginning of November – are Java's most colourful and grand processions. In traditional court dress, palace guards and retainers, not to mention large floats of decorated mountains of rice, all make their way to the mosque, west of the *kraton*, to the sound of prayer and gamelan music. Contact the Tourist Information Centre for exact schedules.

Arts Festival FESTIVAL
This annual festival, held in late June and July, features a wide range of shows and exhibitions. Most events are held at the Benteng Vredeburg.

Sleeping

Yogya has Java's best range of guesthouses and hotels, many offering excellent value for money. During the high season – July, August and around Christmas and New Year – you should book ahead.

SOSROWIJAYAN AREA

This area is very popular with backpackers as most of Yogya's cheap hotels are in the *gang* (alleys) of this traditional neighbourhood. It's just south of the train station.

TOP CHOICE **Andrea Hotel** GUESTHOUSE $
(Map p120; ☎563 502; www.andreahoteljogja.wordpress.com; Sosrowijayan I/140 Gang II; r incl breakfast 125,000-250,000Rp; ❄📶) Excellent new guesthouse owned by an informative, helpful Swiss guy and his Indonesian wife that has immaculately clean, if smallish, rooms with good quality beds, fresh linen and compact, well-designed bathrooms. There's a slim street terrace where you can watch the Sosrowijayan world go by with a drink or snack.

Bladok Losmen & Restaurant HOTEL $
(Map p120; ☎560 452; www.bladok.web.id; Jl Sosrowijayan 76; r 90,000Rp, with balcony/air-con from 140,000/260,000Rp; ❄📶🏊) A dependable, well-run place that looks vaguely like an Austrian mountain chalet. Bladok's rooms won't disappoint with lovely chunky wooden beds and furniture, high cleanliness standards and crisp, fresh linen; some have

balconies. The (small) pool is a real bonus and the cafe-restaurant serves European food and homemade bread.

Losmen Setia Kawan GUESTHOUSE **$**
(Map p120; ☎560 966; www.bedhots.com; r with fan 125,000-150,000Rp, with air-con 150,000-370,000Rp; ❄@) Inviting, well-run place that occupies a fine artistically decorated house. There are nice touches evident everywhere, with classic Vespa scooters in the lobby, a lounge area with TV/DVDs, computers for internet access and a good information board. Rooms are smallish but very attractive, though the swirling, hippyish murals could be a bit much after a heavy night.

Dewi Homestay HOMESTAY **$**
(Map p120; ☎516 014; dewihomestay@hotmail.com; r 90,000-150,000Rp) An attractive long-running place that has character with a leafy, shady garden and spacious, charming rooms – many have four-poster beds draped with mosquito nets.

Losmen Lucy GUESTHOUSE **$**
(Map p120; ☎513 429; r with fan/air-con 100,000/150,000Rp; ❄) One of the best losmen in the area, this place is run by a house-proud lady and has 12 tidy, very clean rooms with good beds; all have en-suite *mandi*. Bikes are available for 25,000Rp per day.

105 Homestay GUESTHOUSE **$**
(Map p120; ☎582 896; homestay_105@yahoo.co.id; r with fan 100,000-125,000Rp, with air-con 150,000Rp; ❄) A lobby complete with Gaudiesque tiles and a welcoming owner sets a nice introduction at this guesthouse, which has no less than seven classes of tidy, neat rooms. It's in the heart of Sosrowijayan's souk-like backstreets.

1001 Malam HOTEL **$$**
(Map p120; www.1001malamhotel.com; Sosrowijayan Wetan Gt I/57; d/ste 569,000/902,000Rp; ❄📶) A veritable palace in the backstreets, 1001 Malam ("1001 nights") is a beautifully-built Moroccan-style structure complete with hand-carved wooden doorways and a lovely Moorish courtyard. It's certainly an inspirational setting, though arguably a bit overpriced given the comfortable but unexceptional rooms and lack of a pool.

Tiffa Losmen GUESTHOUSE **$**
(Map p120; ☎027 451 2841; tiffaartshop@yahoo.com; s/d incl breakfast 80,000/120,000Rp) A tidy little losmen owned by a hospitable family, with four smallish rooms, each with private *mandi* above an art shop. There's a communal balcony where you can tuck into your free breakfast and slurp tea or coffee.

Gloria Amanda HOTEL **$$**
(Map p120; ☎565 286; www.gloriaamanda-hotel.com; Jl Sosrowijayan 195; r with fan 175,000Rp, with air-con from 325,000Rp; ❄📶🏊) Set off the street, this efficient modern hotel has 35 neat, if plain, rooms with good beds and TVs. The tiny pool is covered.

Rejeki Homestay HOMESTAY **$**
(Map p120; ☎516 084; r 95,000Rp) It's a bit cramped, but these 11 little doubles and twins each have a stick or two of furniture, ceiling fan and private cold-water *mandi*.

PRAWIROTAMAN AREA

This area is definitely more upmarket than Sosrowijayan and has a few cheap places mixing it with lots of midrange choices. Plenty of hotels have a pool and the choice of restaurants is excellent.

Eclipse Hotel BOUTIQUE HOTEL **$$**
(Map p122; ☎380 976; www.eclipsehtl.com; Prawirotaman I 35; r incl breakfast 525,000-650,000Rp; ❄📶🏊) The attention to detail at this modern, minimalist-style hotel is impressive, with high quality furnishings, luxury bedding, modish bathrooms and an attractive pool that's big enough for laps (though the shady area is not good for sunbathing). Some of the cheaper rooms suffer a little from traffic noise. Breakfast is quite a feast.

Via Via GUESTHOUSE **$**
(Map p122; www.viaviajogja.com; r incl breakfast 150,000-200,000Rp; ❄📶) Part of the expanding Via Via empire, this fine new guesthouse enjoys a quiet side street location not far from the mothership cafe-restaurant and has seven cute, stylish rooms with high celings, good-quality beds and semi-open bathrooms. There's a garden at the rear for socialising.

Prambanan Guesthouse HOTEL **$$**
(Map p122; ☎376 167; www.prambanangh.be; Jl Prawirotaman I 14; r with fan & cold shower 160,000-210,000Rp, r with air-con & hot shower 240,000-320,000Rp; ❄📶🏊) A peaceful place with a small pool and attractive gardens, this little guesthouse enjoys a prime location. Cheaper rooms are quite plain, but the better options are very comfortable and have *ikat*-style textiles draped on good-quality beds.

Sosrowijayan Area

Sosrowijayan Area

Delta Homestay GUESTHOUSE $
(Map p122; ☎327 051; www.dutagardenhotel.com; Jl Prawirotaman II 597A; s/d 95,000/120,000Rp, with mandi 160,000/170,000Rp, with air-con 185,000/195,000Rp; ❄📶🏊) A great little hideaway with a selection of small but perfectly formed rooms built from natural materials, each with a little porch, grouped around a pool. It's very peaceful here, staff are welcoming and breakfast is included.

Dusun Jogja Village Inn HOTEL $$$
(Map p122; ☎373 031; www.jvidusun.co.id; Jl Menukan 5; r incl breakfast 910,000-1,430,000Rp; ❄📶🏊) This fine hotel has a lovely Javanese feel thanks to its design and decor and maintains high standards. Most of the luxurious rooms have ample balconies overlooking the stunning tropical garden and huge pool. It's a 10-minute walk from the restaurant action of Prawirotaman.

Kampoeng Djawa Hotel GUESTHOUSE $
(Map p122; ☎378 318; www.kampoengdjawahotel.com; Jl Prawirotaman I 40; r incl breakfast 100,000-215,000Rp; ❄📶) Occupying a long, thin house, this place really has some local character. The rooms (in five price categories) have artistic touches including exposed brick walls, mosaic tiling and pebble-walled bathrooms. There's a peaceful little rear garden for your complimentary tea or coffee (available all day) and afternoon snack. Staff are eager to help here.

Rumah Eyang GUESTHOUSE $
(Map p122; ☎0812 2711 7439; www.rumaheyangjogja.com; Jl Parangtritis, Gang Sartono 823; r incl breakfast from 150,000Rp, with air-con 200,000Rp; ❄@) A stylish suburban house that's been converted into a guesthouse. Rooms are simple and comfortable, but the real benefit here is that Atik, the lovely Javanese writer-owner is a font of knowledge about the region and offers great tours.

Hotel Winotosatro HOTEL $$
(Map p122; ☎387 110; Jl Parangtritis 92A; r incl breakfast 253,000-374,000Rp; ❄🏊) This large hotel in a peaceful location is divided into two sections with spacious, if slightly dated, rooms that all have air-con, TV and wooden furniture. The wonderful oval pool here must be 40m across.

CITY CENTRE

TOP CHOICE **Phoenix Hotel Yogyakarta** HISTORIC HOTEL $$
(Map p114; ☎566 617; Jl Jenderal Sudirman 9-11; r incl breakfast from 650,000Rp; ❄@📶🏊) Right in the heart of the city, this historic hotel is easily the best in its class and is a Yogya landmark. Dating back to 1918, it's been sensitively converted to incorporate modern facilities. Rooms are gorgeous; it's worth paying a little extra for those with balconies overlooking the pool area. There's a spa, great cafe and the buffet breakfast spread is a sight for hungry bellies.

Prawirotaman Area

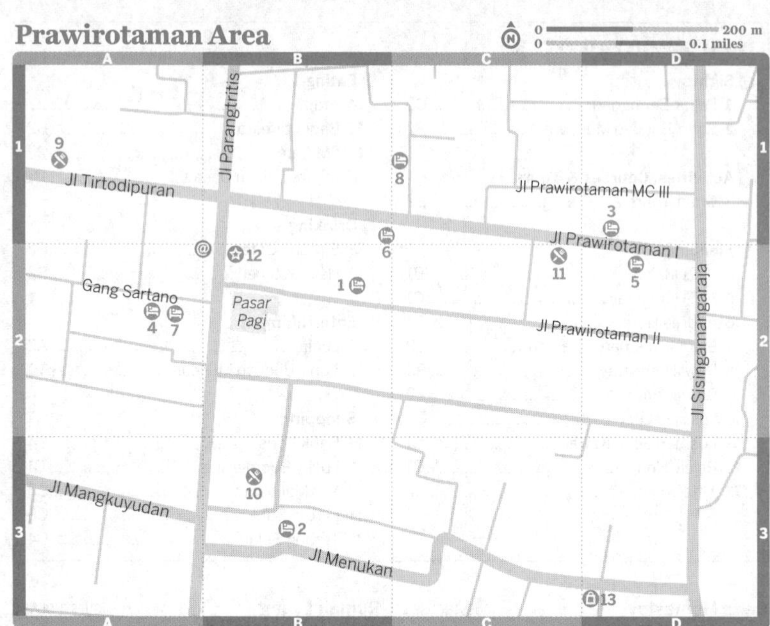

Prawirotaman Area

Activities, Courses & Tours
Kaleidoscope of Java ..... (see 7)
Via Via ..... (see 11)
Via Via Tours ..... (see 11)

Sleeping
1 Delta Homestay B2
2 Dusun Jogja Village Inn B3
3 Eclipse Hotel D1
4 Hotel Winotosatro A2
5 Kampoeng Djawa Hotel D2
6 Prambanan Guesthouse B1
7 Rumah Eyang A2
8 Via Via C1

Eating
9 K Meals A1
10 Milas B3
11 Via Via C2

Entertainment
12 Rastabar B2

Shopping
13 Lana Gallery D3

Indraloka Home Stay HOMESTAY **$$**
(Map p114; ☎564 341; manunggal@yogya.wasantara.net.id; Jl Cik Ditiro 18; r incl breakfast 280,000-450,000Rp; ❄☎) In a striking 1930s mansion this homestay is the ideal alternative to the anonymous hotel experience with with bags of period charm, antique furniture and art. Some of the cheaper rooms are quite poky. It's north of Jl Sudirman.

OUTSKIRTS

TOP CHOICE **d'Omah** LUXURY HOTEL **$$$**
(☎368 050; www.yogyakartaaccommodation.com; Jalan Parangtritis KM8.5, Tembi; r US$84-94; ❄@☎≈) An incredibly tasteful place, built in traditional Javanese style with 19 gorgeous rooms, grouped in four compounds (each has a pool). It's a delight to explore the grounds, replete with art and sculpture and fringed by rice fields (illuminated by flickering torchlight at night). Minor quibbles are the proximity of the highway (so there's some traffic noise) and the overamplified speakers of the nearby mosque. About 8km south of the centre.

Villa Hanis BOUTIQUE HOTEL **$$$**
(r from US$129; ❄@☎) Highly atmpospheric luxury B&B, owned by a Belgium/Indonesian couple, with rooms in a traditional

Javanese house made from teak. It's in a rural location, about 7km north of the centre, surrounded by rice fields and with views of the Merapi volcano. The adjoining deli-restaurant is exceptional.

Tembi BUNGALOW $$
(☎368 000; www.tembi.net; Jl Parangtritis, Km8.4; bungalows 425,000-697,500Rp, family bungalows 999,000Rp; ❄📶) This cultural centre has seven commodious wooden bungalows, built in traditional Javanese style, with four-poster beds and wonderful open-air, pebble-floored bathrooms. Rates include three meals in the fine restaurant. The location is semi-rural, with paddy fields all around, but as it's 8km south of central Yogya it's best to have your own transport.

Eating

Yogya is a great place to eat out with authentic street food and local places in the centre and Western-geared places concentrated in the Prawirotaman and adjacent Jl Tirtodipuran area to the south.

SOSROWIJAYAN AREA

There are loads of inexpensive noshing options in this area including a row of good warung on Jl Pasar Kembang, beside the train line.

Bedhot Resto INTERNATIONAL $
(Map p120; Gang II; mains 14,000-28,000Rp; 📶✎) Bedhot means 'creative' in old Javanese and this place is one of the more stylish eateries in Sosrowijayan. There's tasty Indonesian and Western food, good juices and internet access upstairs.

Atap INDONESIAN, INTERNATIONAL $
(Map p120; Jl Sosrowijayan GT I/113; meals 16,000-30,000Rp; ⏲5.30-10pm) Quirky, boho restaurant with tables made from car tyres and a great little outdoor terrace. The menu is strong on grilled meat, with daily specials including spicy Balinese chicken and Cajun-style barbecued beef.

Mi Casa es Tu Casa SPANISH, INDONESIAN $
(Map p120; www.micasaestucasa.mye.name; Sosrowijayan Wetan GT I/141; meals 15,000-40,000Rp; 📶) OK, the name is a cliché, but as this stylish place is Basque owned it's worth a try if you're in need of a *paella* (100,000Rp for two, order well ahead) or other Spanish food. You won't have to wait long for the Indo grub however, and if you want to try snake – this is the place.

FM Café INTERNATIONAL $
(Map p120; Jl Sosrowijayan 14; mains around 20,000Rp; 📶) FM Café has a great courtyard setting and an eclectic menu ranging from nasi goreng to pizza. Happy hour lasts from 1pm to 8pm; bands perform here on Friday nights.

PRAWIROTAMAN AREA

TOP CHOICE **Via Via** INTERNATIONAL, INDONESIAN $
(Map p122; ☎386 557; www.viaviajogja.com; Jl Prawirotaman I 30; mains 18,000-42,000Rp; 📶) Setting the bar high for both Western and Indonesian food, this hip cafe-restaurant has a fresh, inventive menu and always some tempting daily specials and great breakfasts. The decor mixes exposed concrete and bamboo screens, and there's a great outdoor terrace and art exhibitions. Also hosts daily yoga sessions and offers lots of tours and courses.

Kedai Kebun INDONESIAN $
(Map p114; www.kedaikebun.com; Jl Tirtodipuran III; meals 20,000-40,000Rp; 📶✎) Bohemian cafe-gallery that's a key hangout for Yogya's artistic community. On the menu there's lots of Indonesian food and snacks, and always a dish of the day for 15,000Rp (10,000Rp for students); vegans and vegetarians are well catered for here. The venue hosts regular events including art exhibitions and DJ events.

K Meals FRENCH, PIZZA $$$
(Map p122; ☎829 0097; www.kmealsrestaurant.com; Jl Tirtodipuran 67; meals US$15-30) Excellent French restaurant where the menu features classics such as country pâté, imported tenderloin with pepper sauce, duck confit and lots of pizza options from a wood-fired oven. Round it off with a crème brûlée or mango crumble.

Milas INDONESIAN $
(Map p122; ☎742 3399; Jl Prawirotaman IV 127; meals from 24,000Rp; ✎) A great retreat from the streets, this secret garden restaurant is a part of a project centre for street youth. Offers tasty vegetarian cooking including healthy snacks, sandwiches, salads and organic coffee.

OTHER AREAS

Tembi INDONESIAN $
(☎368 000; www.tembi.net; Jl Parangtritis, Km8.4; meals 12,000-30,000Rp; 📶) In a bucolic rural setting, with paddy fields around an open-sided dining room this restaurant in the

STREET GRUB

In the evening street-food vendors line the northern end of Jl Malioboro; here you can try Yogya's famous *ayam goreng* (deep-fried chicken soaked in coconut milk) and dishes such as *sambal welut* (spicy eel) and *nasi langgi* (coconut rice with tempe). Many students head here in the evening to snack on *oseng oseng*, which is a kind of mini *nasi campur* (rice with a bit of everything) and only costs 3000Rp or so a hit. It's a lot of fun with impromptu *lesehan* seating mats spread on the ground and young Indonesians strumming their guitars into the wee small hours. Look out for Yoyga's famous *gudeg*, a jackfruit curry served with chicken, egg and rice, which is served from stalls all over town, particularly around markets.

Tembi cultural centre specialises in traditional Javanese dishes. Prices are very modest given the surroundings and experience. You can also get a good Western or Indonesian breakfast here.

Jimbaran SEAFOOD **$$**
(☎745 2882; Jl Damai; meals 40,000-70,000Rp; ⊙noon-10pm) Overlooking rice fields, this enjoyable place specialises in seafood. Everything is priced by the ounce; feast on steamed crab, lobster, clams, jumbo prawns and grilled fish and wash it down with a cold Bintang. Jimbaran is about 7km north of Yogya.

Warung Sido Semi INDONESIAN **$**
(Jl Canteng, Kota Gede; meals 10,000Rp; ⊙9am-6pm Wed-Mon) Historic Kota Gede warung festooned with old portraits and antiques where you can turn back the decades while you slurp an ice tea or *bakso* (meatball soup). There are myriad ice-based desserts available, *es buah* is a mix of tropical fruits, while *kacang ijo* is green bean flavour. It's extremely cheap.

Sangam House INDIAN **$$**
(☎562 132; Jl Pandega Siwi 14; mains 40,000-65,000Rp; 🛜✎) Atmospheric Indian restaurant with a selection of dining rooms decorated with ethnic art and tables around a garden. Choose from pretty authentic classics including kormas, rogan josh or samosas and the veggie selection is sound. Sangam is a little tricky to find; it's down a lane just south of the ring road in north Yogya, about 5km from the centre. There's also yoga (40,000Rp a session) here.

Omar Duwur Restaurant INDONESIAN, INTERNATIONAL **$$$**
(☎374 952; www.omahdhuwur.net; Jl Mondorakan 252; mains 40,000-150,000Rp; 🛜) Out in Kota Gede, this is one of Yogya's best restaurants, with a lavish setting in a 150-year-old colonial mansion, or eat outside on a wonderful garden terrace if the rain gods permit. Offers a wide selection of Western (try the Australian tenderloin steak) and Eastern dishes (seafood fried rice is well executed).

Drinking

Cool cafes are opening across Yoyga, particularly in the Prawirotaman area. If you want to sip a few beers, both Jl Sosrowijayan and Jl Parangritis (in the Prawirotaman area) both have a crop of bars; many with live music.

Hell's Kitchen CAFE, BAR
(Map p120; Jl Sosrowijayan; meals 30,000-40,000Rp; ⊙noon-1am) Open-sided bar-cafe with quirky decor that's a great bet for a beer, as the street-terrace tables offer the best people-watching perch in Sosrowijayan. Also hosts live bands (everything from punk to acoustic) in the evenings and has filling Western (salads, sandwiches and pasta) and Indo grub.

Lecker CAFE, EUROPEAN
(Map p114; www.lecker.kopiresto.com; Jl Tirtodipuran 38; coffee from 15,000Rp, meals 30,000-60,000Rp; 🛜) Large modern cafe that offers a great opportunity to sample your way around the Indonesian coffee archipelago – luwak, Lombok ginger coffee, Bali, Toraja, Medan and Flores are some of the beans available. Meals including *kwetiaw* (Chinese noodles) and salmon steak with pappardelle are also available.

Bintang Café BAR
(Map p120; Jl Sosrowijayan 54; mains from 16,000Rp; 🛜) This (un)imaginatively named bar in Sosrowijayan has live music (reggae, blues and rock 'n' roll) between Wednesday and Saturday nights. The food is bog-standard travellers' fare.

☆ Entertainment

Yogya is one of the epicentres of traditional Javanese performing arts. Dance, *wayang* or gamelan is performed every morning at the *kraton*; check with the tourist office for current listings and any special events (such as the spectacular Ramayana ballet held at Prambanan in the dry season).

Wayang Kulit

Leather-puppet performances can be seen at several places around Yogya every night of the week.

Sasono Hinggil PUPPETRY
(Map p114; South Main Sq) Most of the centres offer shortened versions for tourists, but here in the *alun-alun selatan* of the *kraton*, marathon all-night performances are held every second Saturday from 9pm to 5am (20,000Rp). Bring a pillow.

Sono-Budoyo Museum PUPPETRY
(Map p120; ☎376 775; admission 5000Rp; ⏲Mon-Sat) Popular two-hour performances nightly from 8pm to 10pm (20,000Rp); the first half-hour involves the reading of the story in Javanese, so most travellers skip this and arrive later.

Dance

Most performances are based on the Ramayana or at least billed as 'Ramayana ballet' because of the famed performances at Prambanan.

Purawisata TRADITIONAL DANCE
(Map p114; ☎375 705; Jl Brigjen Katamso) This amusement park stages Ramayana performances daily at 8pm (tickets 160,000Rp). You can dine here and watch the show.

Live Music

Jl Sosrowijayan is something of a live-music mecca with casual venues that include the bars Hell's Kitchen (p124), Bintang Café (p124) and Lucifer. Down south, check out the bars on Jl Parangritis, including **Rastabar** (Map p122; ☎371 587; Jl Parangritis 95).

Lucifer LIVE MUSIC
(Map p120; Jl Sosrowijayan) An intimate bar and one of the city's key live-music venues. There are bands every night, with everything from jazz to classic rock.

Nightclubs

Hugo's CLUB
(☎484 208; Jl Adisucipto, Sheraton Mustika Resort & Spa) Upmarket club popular with Yogya's rich crowd and beautiful people. Live bands alternate with house DJs playing R'n'B and house.

Boshe CLUB
(☎624 041; www.boshevvipclub.com/jogja; Jl Magelang, Km6.5) Boasts a large central dance floor, a pumping sound system and draws a young studenty crowd with electronic DJs, (unfortunately alternated with cheesy dance troupes). There's always a drink promo.

 Shopping

Yogya is a shopper's paradise for crafts and antiques.

Jl Malioboro is one great long throbbing bazaar of souvenir shops and stalls selling cheap clothes, leatherwork, batik bags, *topeng* masks and *wayang golek* puppets. Look in some of the fixed-price shops on Jl Malioboro or nearby streets to get an idea of prices; **Mirota Batik** (Map p120; ☎588 524; Jl A Yani 9) is an excellent place to start looking; when you're done shopping here try the traditional Javanese food on the roof terrace.

In the south of the city, Jl Prawirotaman and Jl Tirtodipuran (west of Jl Prawirotaman) have a selection of upmarket galleries, art shops and expensive batik factories. You'll find furniture, antiques, and a variety of crafts and curios from Java and further afield.

For regular shopping in the heart of town head to **Mal Malioboro** (Map p120; Jl Malioboro). **Ambarukmo Plaza** (Jl Laksda Adisucipto), 5km west of the centre is more up-

BATIK BUYING

If there's one Indonesian word that you'll remember from your trip to Yogya it's batik, which translates to something of a blessing and a curse. Batik is both one of Yogya's biggest draws (it's one of the city's purist art forms) and worst blights (due to the hard sell and scams directed at tourists).

Plenty of tourists get suckered into buying overpriced batik. Perhaps the best strategy is to see as much stuff as you can first before opening the purse strings – window shop and start looking in the cheapest places, including the markets and mass-production galleries around Taman Sari. Small batik paintings start at around 50,000Rp (although the asking price may be 500,000Rp). You can then graduate to the upmarket galleries.

market with boutiques, a good food court, cinema and supermarket; take bus 1B from the main post office.

Batik

Most of the batik workshops and several large showrooms are along Jl Tirtodipuran, south of the *kraton*. Many, such as **Batik Plentong** (Map p114; Jl Tirtodipuran 48) and **Batik Winotosastro** (Map p114; Jl Tirtodipuran 54), give free guided tours of the batik process. These places cater to tour groups, so prices are very high – view the process here and shop elsewhere.

Batik is cheapest in the markets, especially Pasar Beringharjo, but quality is questionable. Jl Malioboro and Jl A Yani have good fixed-price places.

Batik Keris CLOTHING
(Map p120; www.batikkeris.co.id; Jl A Yani 71) Excellent-quality batik at fixed prices. Best for traditional styles – men's shirts start at about 200,000Rp.

Terang Bulan CLOTHING
(Map p120; Jl A Yani 108) Good fixed-price place for batik.

Antiques, Curios & Furniture

Although a few antiques can be found in the shops and markets, be aware that dealers spend an inordinate amount of time ageing puppets, masks and all manner of other goods in the pursuit of antiquity.

Jl Tirtodipuran and Jl Prawirotaman have stores selling artefacts and furniture from all over Indonesia. Prices are generally high – bargain furiously.

Bookstores

Gramedia (☎433 1141; Jl Laksda Adisucipto, Ambarukmo Plaza), 5km west of the centre, stocks a few new English-language titles. **Lucky Boomerang** (Map p120; ☎895 006; Gang I 67) has used guidebooks and fiction, Periplus maps and books, plus souvenirs.

Silver

The village of Kota Gede specialises in silverwork, but it can be found all over town. Fine filigree work is a Yogya speciality. Kota Gede has some very attractive jewellery, boxes, bowls, cutlery and miniatures, and there are dozens of smaller silver shops on Jl Kemesan and Jl Mondorakan, where you can get some good buys if you bargain.

You can get a guided tour of the process, with no obligation to buy, at the large factories.

HS JEWELLERY
(www.hssilver.com; Jl Mondorakan I) Ask for a substantial discount off the marked prices.

MD JEWELLERY
(☎375 063; Jl Pesegah KG 8/44) Rings, bracelets, earrings and more. Down a small alley off the street; try for discounts.

Tom's Silver JEWELLERY
(☎525 416; Jl Ngeski Gondo 60) An extensive (and expensive) selection and some superb large pieces.

Art

Lana Gallery ART GALLERY
(Map p122; ☎0878 3998 0340; rlhwildan@yahoo.com; Jl Menukan; ⏰Tue-Sun) A great range of contemporary art from new and emerging artists, many graduates of Yogya's Fine Arts school. Run by Wildan, one of the friendliest Indonesians you'll ever meet.

Information

The website www.yogyes.com is an excellent portal to the city and central Java.

Dangers & Annoyances

Hassles from smooth-talking batik salesmen are a constant issue for every traveller in town. The tourist board get hosts of complaints about these sharks, who may strike up conversations pretending to be guides. Inevitably you'll end up at a gallery where you'll get the hard sell and they'll rake in a big commission if you buy. A time-honoured scam is to pressure you to visit a 'fine-art student exhibition' or a 'government store' – there are no official shops or galleries in the city.

Some of these dodgy batik salesmen hang around the *kraton*, where they tell you that the *kraton* is closed or there are no performances, but they might offer to show you to the 'sultan's batik workshop' (which is actually just a very expensive commission-paying showroom).

Be aware too that due to a schism in the ruling family there are actually two separate entrances, and ticket offices, at the *kraton*. One entrance (with a 5000Rp charge) only allows you to view a small area, which contains some dioramas and horse carriages; it may be signposted 'Pagelaran'. Official-looking guys with IDs will try to shepherd you in here before inviting you to look at some of the 'sultan's batik'. This is *not* the main entrance to the *kraton*, which has a big clock by its ticket window (and an entrance fee of 12,500Rp).

Becak drivers are very pushy in Yogya; those offering 'special rates' of 1000Rp for one hour are also trying to get you into a batik gallery.

BROMO BY BUS

Minibus trips to Gunung Bromo (and on to Bali) are very popular with travellers. However few enjoy the experience, as the route involves a long, slow overland journey in cramped conditions. Ten-hour journeys can take up to 13, and the air-conditioned bus promised turns out to be a rusty tin can on wheels. The most comfortable way to Bromo is to take a train (or even fly) to Surabaya and then another train or bus on to Probolinggo.

If you do decide to do the trip by minibus (from 120,000Rp, 11 to 13 hours) note that many operators often terminate short of Cemoro Lawang, and drop you off at a (poor) hostel on the way up the volcano (which is sure to be paying a commission).

Travellers also have regularly reported mysterious 'breakdowns' on the Bromo route, which cut into travelling time and mean that you don't reach Cemoro Lawang. Others have experienced problems with onward connections to Bali. Purchase your ticket from a reliable agent – try Great Tours (p118) – and check up-to-date information with other travellers and on Lonely Planet's Thorn Tree internet forum.

Internet Access

Internet cafes can be found all over town. **11 Net** (Jl Parangtritis; per hr 5000Rp) is equipped with modern terminals and Skype facilities.

Medical Services

Ludira Husada Tama Hospital (620 333; Jl Wiratama 4; 24hr)

Money

There are numerous banks (and a few money changers) in the tourist areas.

BNI Bank (Jl Trikora I) Opposite the main post office.

Mulia (Jl Malioboro 60, Inna Garuda Hotel) Has the best moneychanging rates in Yogya, and changes euros, pounds, Australian, Canadian and US dollars, and Swiss francs.

Post

Main Post Office (Jl Senopati)

Tourist Information

Tourist Information Office (562 000; Jl Malioboro 16; 8am-8pm Mon-Thu, to 7pm Fri & Sat; @) A well-organised office with helpful staff, free maps and good transport information. Produces a number of publications (including a calendar of events). Also has counters at the airport and on the eastern side of the Tugu train station.

Travel Agencies

Great Tours (p118) is good for sunrise tours, bus and minibus tickets, and tours to places including Bromo and Ijen.

 Getting There & Away

Air

Yogyakarta has international connections to Singapore and Kuala Lumpur, plus many domestic links. Departure taxes for domestic/international flights are 35,000/110,000Rp.

Solo airport, 60km away, also has international and domestic flights.

AirAsia (5050 5088; www.airasia.com) Flies to Singapore, Kuala Lumpur, Jakarta and Denpasar.

Batavia Air (080 4122 2888; www.batavia-air.com) Connections to Balikpapan, Batam, Jakarta, Medan, Pontianak and Surabaya.

Garuda (551 515; Inna Garuda Hotel, Jl Malioboro 60) Links Yogya with Balikpapan, Denpasar and Jakarta.

Indonesia Air Transport (021 8087 0668; www.indonesia-air.com) To Pangkalanbun and Pontianak.

Lion Air (555 028; Jl Mayor Suryotomo 31, Melia Purosani Hotel) Flies to Balikpapan, Banjarmasin, Denpasar, Makassar, Jakarta and Surabaya.

Sriwijaya Air (www.sriwijayaair.co.id) To Balikpapan, Jakarta and Surabaya.

Wings Air (021 6379 8000; www2.lionair.co.id) To Bandung and Surabaya.

Bus

Yogya's main bus terminal, Giwangan, is 5km southeast of the city centre; bus 3B connects it with Tugu train station and Jl Malioboro. Buses run from Giwangan to points all over Java, and also to Bali. For really long trips make sure you take a luxury bus. It's cheaper to buy tickets at the bus terminal, but it's less hassle to simply check fares and departures with the ticket agents along Jl Mangkubumi, Jl Sosrowijayan or Jl Prawirotaman. These agents can also arrange pick-up from your hotel.

To go to Prambanan (7000Rp) take a 1A city bus from Jl Malioboro. Buses to/from Borobudur use the Jombor terminal, to get there take a

TRANSPORT FROM YOGYAKARTA

Bus

DESTINATION	COST (RP)	DURATION (HR)	FREQUENCY
Bandung	normal/air-con 80,000/100,000	10	3 daily
Borobudur	normal 15,000Rp	1½	every 30 min
Denpasar	air-con 235,000Rp	19	3 daily
Jakarta	normal/air-con 110,000/150,000	12	10-12 daily between 3pm and 5pm

Train

DESTINATION	COST (RP)	DURATION (HR)	FREQUENCY
Bandung	150,000-245,000	7-8¾	6 daily
Sidareja (for Pangandaran)	120,000-185,000	3½-4	2 daily
Jakarta	320,000-330,000	7-9	6 daily
Malang	160,000-350,000	7	3 daily
Solo	12,000-35,000	1	14 daily

Transjogya bus 3A from Jl Malioboro to Jl Ahmad Dahlan and change to a 2B for Jombor.

Minibus

Door-to-door *travel* minibuses run to all major cities from Yogya. Sosrowijayan and Prawirotaman agents sell tickets. Prices are very similar to air-conditioned buses. Journeys of more than four hours can be cramped – trains and buses offer more comfort. It's much faster to get to Solo by train.

You can also buy direct from the minibus companies, which include **Cip Ganti** (☎6500 0000; www.cipaganti.co.id; Jl Magelang Km4), **Rajawali Putra** (Map p114; ☎583 535; Jl Jenderal Sudirman 42), **Rahayu** (Map p114; ☎561 322; Jl Diponegoro 9A) and **Niki Vita Tour & Travel** (Map p114; ☎561 884; Jl Diponegoro 25). Destinations served include Semarang (50,000Rp, four hours), Surabaya (85,000Rp) and Malang (90,000Rp). For Pangandaran (100,000Rp, eight hours), **Estu Travel** (☎668 4567; Jl Gampingan) has minibuses daily at 8am and 6.30pm.

Train

Centrally located, Yogya's Tugu train station handles all business- and executive-class trains. Economy-class trains also depart from and arrive at Lempuyangan station, 1km to the east.

Getting Around

TO/FROM THE AIRPORT Yogya's Adi Sucipto airport, 10km east of the centre, is very well connected to the city by public transport. Bus 1A (3000Rp) runs there from Jl Malioboro. *Pramek* trains stop at Maguwo station, which is right by the airport as well. Taxis from the airport to the city centre cost about 55,000Rp.

BECAK Yogyakarta has an oversupply of becak (cycle rickshaws); most are very pushy. It can be a fun way to get around, though watch out for drivers who offer cheap hourly rates unless you want to do the rounds of all the batik galleries that offer commission. A short trip is about 6000Rp, from Jl Prawirotaman to Jl Malioboro costs around 12,000Rp.

BICYCLE Bikes cost about 15,000Rp a day from hotels, or try the shops at the southern end of Gang I in Sosrowijayan. Always lock your bike.

BUS Yogya's reliable bus system, TransJogja consists of modern air-conditioned buses running from 6am to 10pm on six routes around the city to as far away as Prambanan. Tickets cost 3000Rp per journey, or 27,000Rp for a carnet of 10. TransJogja buses only stop at the designated bus shelters. Bus 1A is a very useful service, running from Jl Malioboro past the airport to Prambanan. TransJogja route maps are available at the Tourist Information Centre.

CAR & MOTORCYCLE Travel agencies on Jl Sosrowijayan and Jl Prawirotaman rent out cars with drivers for trips in the Yogya region for 350,000 to 500,000Rp per day including petrol. Few drivers speak English, but it can still be an excellent way to explore the area. One reliable company is **Jogya Trans** (☎081 6426 0124; Gang 04/09, Prambanan). Motorcycles cost around 50,000Rp a day.

TAXI Taxis are cheap, and have meters, costing 10,000 to 20,000Rp for short trips. From Prawirotaman to the airport is 55,000Rp. Call **ASA Taxi** (☎545 545).

Imogiri

A royal graveyard perched on a hilltop 20km south of Yogyakarta, Imogiri was first built by Sultan Agung in 1645 to serve as his own mausoleum. Since then it has become something of an A-list cemetery for royalty. There are three major courtyards – the central one contains the tombs of Sultan Agung and succeeding Mataram kings; the other two are dedicated to the sultans of Solo and Yogyakarta.

Pilgrims from across central Java flock to the **tomb of Sultan Agung** (admission 1000Rp; ⏲10am-1pm Sun-Mon, 1.30-4pm Fri). You're welcome to join them but you must don full Javanese court dress, which can be hired for a small fee.

It's an impressive site, reached by a daunting flight of 345 steps. From the top of the stairway, a walkway circles the whole complex and leads to the summit, with a superb view over Yogyakarta to Gunung Merapi.

To get to Imogiri (7000Rp, 40 minutes), take an *angkot* to Panggang and ask the conductor to let you off at the *makam* (graves).

Angkots and buses from Yogyakarta (4000Rp) stop at the car park, from where it is about 500m to the base of the hill and the start of the steps. Note that the only compulsory entry charge is payable when you sign the visitors' book, inside the main compound.

Kasongan

Yogyakarta's prime pottery centre is Kasongan, where dozens of workshops produce pots and some superb figurines, giant dragons and peacocks. Kasongan pottery is generally sold painted or unpainted – very little glazing work is done.

Catch a Bantul-bound bus and get off on the main road at the entrance to the village, 6.5km south of Yogyakarta. It is then about a 1km walk to the centre of the village and most of the pottery workshops.

Gunung Merapi

Few of Southeast Asia's volcanoes are as evocative, or as destructive, as Gunung Merapi (Fire Mountain). Towering 2930m over Yogyakarta, Borobudur and Prambanan, this immense Fujiesque peak is a threatening, disturbingly close presence for thousands. Merapi has erupted dozens of times over the past century; the massive 2010 eruption killed 353 and forced the evacuation of 360,000 more.

This is offically Indonesia's most active volcano – quite an accolade in a nation with 127 active cones. Some observers have theorised that it was responsible for the mysterious evacuation of Borobudur and the collapse of the old Mataram kingdom during the 11th century.

Merapi is revered and feared in equal measure. Every year, offerings from Yogya's *kraton* are made to appease the mountain's foul temper. Eruptions, however, have not put a stop to people living on the mountain. With a population density of 700 people per sq km, Merapi supports hundreds of small communities.

The hill resort of Kaliurang, 25km north of Yogyakarta, is the main access point for views of Merapi. Yogyakarta travel agencies sell night trips for views of the lava flows – there are several good viewpoints – but you can also do this yourself. Take a bus for Kaliurang (8000Rp, one hour) from the Giwangan terminal, get off at the Kaliurang Hill Resort, then catch one of the waiting *ojek*

Around Yogyakarta

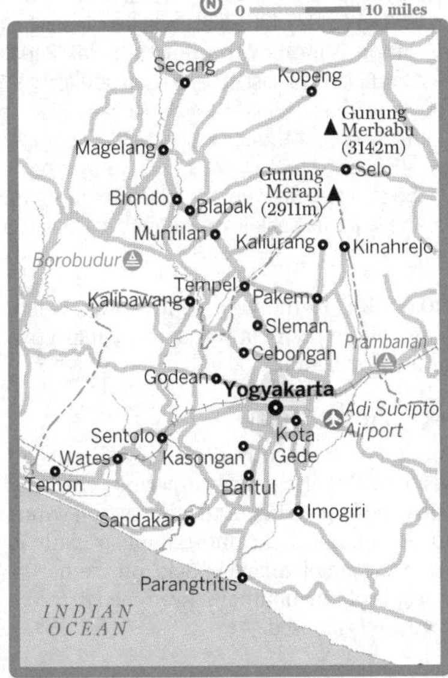

WORTH A TRIP

BEACHES SOUTHWEST OF YOYGAKARTA

Southwest of Yogyakarta, the coastline consists of a stunning series of sandy cove beaches divided by volcanic stone headlands and pounded by the full force of the Indian Ocean. It's an isolated corner of Java, with few facilities but with the coming of electricity (pylons were being installed in mid-2012) expect things to gradually change in the next few years.

The scenery is sublime, and exploring the coastal road as it winds through rolling hills, past fields of peanuts and cassava, and taking turn-offs down dirt roads to empty, exposed bays makes a wonderful excursion from Yogyakarta. However, as the sea is oceanic by nature, swimming is only really possible in selected, sheltered spots. Also, you'll need your own wheels as there's no public transport. As ever in Java, try to avoid weekends when local tourism peaks.

It's 65km from Yogya to **Indrayanti Beach** (also known as Pulang Syawal), a lovely sandy cove with a steep profile and framed by giant boulders at one end. The tiny ocean-facing **Indrayanti** (☎0878 3962 5215; huts incl breakfast 350,000Rp, meals 25,000-50,000Rp) huts here are well overpriced but seafood at the restaurant is excellent. It's a serene scene, with no trash, but daytrippers crowd the place on weekends.

Heading west it's a short hop to horseshoe-shaped **Sundak Barat** with some sheltered swimming and then on to **Krakal**, which has a few scruffy warung near the main car park. If you nip over to the east side of Krakal bay there's a great stretch of deserted sand and you can grab a meal at the good, sea-facing **Rumah Makan Pantai Asmara** (meals 20,000-40,000Rp).

Around 5km west of Indrayanti, **Drini** forms a pretty double crescent of beaches, separated by a large offshore islet that you can cross to via a walkway. Next up is Sepanjang, a long slim exposed beach and then **Kukup**, the most touristy beach on this stretch, with an excess of souvenir stalls and warung. Still, you might want to try the *peyek* (seaweed crackers) for sale, and it does have three accommodation options, the best of which is **Penginapan Kukup Indah** (☎0878 3966 5441; r 75,000-200,000Rp; ❄).

Just a kilometre to the west, **Baron** is a very touristy cove beach that you can give a miss. To head back to Yogyakarta, it's best to push on to **Parangritis**. This is a sprawling, unattractive resort geared at daytripping city dwellers, with gray sand and dozens of places to stay. However, it does have a trash problem. For a cheap bed head to **Losmen Widya** (☎027 436 7165; r with fan/air-con from 60,000/125,000Rp). Or, for a better one, the clifftop **Queen of the South hotel** (Puri Ratu Kidul; ☎367 196; www.queen-of-the-south.com; r incl breakfast 450,000-550,000Rp; ❄), 2km east of the centre, is in a class of its own, where you can gaze over the ocean rollers from an inspirational perch. Rooms are ageing but spacious and the restaurant is impressive.

Buses from Yogyakarta's Giwangan bus terminal, which pass down Jl Parangtritis at the end of Jl Prawirotaman, leave throughout the day for the one-hour journey (9000Rp). The last bus back from Parangtritis leaves at around 6pm.

(10,000Rp) to the viewpoint of Kalu Aden, from where there's a wonderful perspective of the lava action.

Activities

Merapi is frequently declared off-limits to visitors. But if conditions permit, climbing the cone is possible in the dry season (April to September). The most popular path is from the small village of Selo, on the northern side of the mountain. Even then *extreme caution* is advised.

During quiet periods, a 1am start from Selo is necessary to reach the summit for dawn (a three- to four-hour trip). It is a tough, demanding walk, but usually manageable by anyone with a reasonable level of fitness.

The trail passes a rocky, chilly campsite at 2500m (known as Pasar Bubrah) that some tours use as a last staging post. Depending on the state of the volcano's activity it may not be possible to continue further (in July 2012 this was the permitted limit). If conditions are favourable, the final ascent is very tough, past billowing vents and through loose volcanic scree and sand which will consume all your remaining strength.

From the summit, on clear days, you'll be rewarded with amazing views deep into the 500m-wide crater from the crater rim, which is often enveloped by choking sulphurous gas. Be *ultra cautious* on the crater rim due to freezing winds and the instablity of the terrain.

Treks from Selo are not always well organised. Guides should warn against climbing if it looks dangerous. While they don't want to endanger lives, they may be prepared to take risks in order to be paid. Even during quieter periods, Merapi can suddenly explode into action.

It has not been possible to climb the peak from Kaliurang since 1994 due to volcanic activity. However there is still excellent hiking around the lower reaches of Merapi, with superb views of lava flows. Christian Awuy, owner of Vogels Hostel, has organised climbs for years and is an an excellent reference point. Six-hour sunrise hikes (US$15, minimum two people) from his hostel usually start at 4am and include a licensed guide equipped with two-way radios and food.

For up-to-date Merapi information and hiking accounts, consult www.gunungbagging.com

Kaliurang

☎0274

Kaliurang, 25km north of Yogyakarta, is the nearest hill resort to the city. At 900m, it has a cool, refreshing climate. During the rainy season, Kaliurang often sits in a thick blanket of cloud, but on clear days the views of Merapi are magical.

Sights

Ullen Sentalu MUSEUM

(☎895 161; www.ullensentalu.com; admission 50,000Rp; ⏰8.30am-4pm Tue-Fri, to 5pm Sat & Sun) The Ullen Sentalu museum is a surprise find on the slopes of Merapi. This large complex has a principal structure that resembles a Bavarian baron's mansion, and extensive gardens; most of the rich collection of Javanese fine art, including oil paintings and sculpture, is housed in connecting underground chambers. There are wonderful artefacts to admire (including some priceless batik), but perhaps a little too much royal family glorification during the hour-or-so tour (English guides are available). Be sure to have a drink or meal in the fine, if pricey, restaurant here.

Forest Park FOREST

(Hutan Wisata Kaliurang; admission 20,000Rp; ⏰8am-5pm) There is an excellent forest park on the slopes of the mountain. Maps at the park entrance show areas you are allowed to explore. Heed them and don't venture further; in a sudden eruption, lava can flow down the mountain at 300km/h. Normally you can take a 15-minute walk to the Promojiwo viewpoint for vistas of Merapi. This takes you past forest incinerated in the 2010 eruption. A trail then leads on to Tlogo Muncar waterfall, which is just a trickle in the dry season, and then back to the entrance.

Vogels Hostel arranges **mountain walks** to see the lava flows. The six-hour return trek starts at 4am and climbs 1400m up the mountain to see the glowing lava at its best (US$15 per person, minimum two people). Overnight camping trips, village tours and birdwatching walks can also be arranged.

Merapi Museum MUSEUM

(Jl Kaliurang Km25.7; admission 3000Rp; ⏰9am-3.30pm Tue-Sun) This impressive new museum is located in a striking white angular structure that resembles a volcano. You'll find exhibits dedicated to Merapi (including a scale model that demonstrates previous eruptions) and lots of information about other volcanoes around the world, as well as an earthquake simulation room.

Sleeping & Eating

Kaliurang is a sprawling hill resort with dozens of places to sleep.

Vogels Hostel HOSTEL $

(☎895 208; vogelsinternational@yahoo.co.id; Jl Astamulya 76; dm 25,000Rp, tw without bathroom 60,000Rp, bungalows with bathroom & hot water 125,000-200,000Rp, meals 15,000-25,000Rp; @) Vogels is a travellers' institution. The structure itself is a faded villa constructed in 1926, and accommodation is pretty archaic too, with ageing furnishings. However it's undoubtedly the best address for hikers. The owner, Christian Awuy, is an authority on Merapi and its many moods, can organise good guides and tours, and the whole place is stuffed with maps and information.

Fuji Villa HOTEL **$$**
(☎820 8777; www.fujivilla.com; Jl Pelajar 8, Kaliurang; r 250,000-300,000Rp, ste 330,000Rp; ❄📶) Japanese-style villa hotel in a leafy garden that caters to all budgets with elegant rooms and suites that have four-poster beds and LCD TV/DVD. There is also a super-clean dorm for the backpackers. There are mountain bikes for guests, and a free shuttle-bus service to central Yogya. Prices rise at weekends; book ahead for a 25% discount.

Penginapan Kalegan GUESTHOUSE **$**
(☎447 8471; 4km south of forest park; r with cold/hot water 50,000/80,000Rp, f 150,000Rp, meals 12,000Rp; ❄) An excellent value, two-storey, modern hotel with very clean, tiled rooms, many with TV and hot water, and some very cheap but decent options at the rear of the compound. The welcoming family here speak almost no English but promise that their daughter is learning!

Restaurant Joyo INDONESIAN **$**
(Jl Astamulya 63; mains 10,000Rp) Half-shop, half-restaurant, Jojo has tasty Chinese and Indonesian food and some eclectic traditional artefacts for sale. It's over the road from Vogels.

ℹ Getting There & Away

Angkot from Yogyakarta's Terban station to Kaliurang cost 8000Rp; the last leaves at 4.30pm. A taxi from Malioboro will cost around 100,000Rp.

Selo

On the northern slopes of Gunung Merapi, 50km west of Solo, the village of Selo has a few homestays where guides (150,000Rp return) can be arranged for the Merapi climb (p131). Contact the local **guide association** (☎0878 3632 5955).

From Selo, it is a very steep, four-hour trek to the volcano's summit, and around 2½ hours for the descent. At the top the sulphurous fumes can be overpowering – take great care.

Selo can be reached from Solo: take a bus to Magelang, stopping at Selo (16,000Rp, two hours) on the way. From Yogyakarta take a Magelang bus to Blabak (9000Rp, one hour) and an *angkot* or bus to Selo (6000Rp). A taxi from Yogya is around 250,000Rp one way.

Prambanan

☎0274

The spectacular temples of Prambanan, 17km northeast of Yogyakarta, are the best remaining examples of Java's extended period of Hindu culture. Indeed, the wealth of sculptural detail on the great Shiva temple here is the nation's most outstanding example of Hindu art.

All the temples in the Prambanan area were built between the 8th and 10th centuries AD, when Java was ruled by the Buddhist Sailendras in the south and the Hindu Sanjayas of Old Mataram in the north. Possibly by the second half of the 9th century, these two dynasties were united by the marriage of Rakai Pikatan of Hindu Mataram and the Buddhist Sailendra princess Pramodhavardhani. This may explain why a number of temples, including those of the Prambanan temple complex and the smaller Plaosan group, reveal Shivaite and Buddhist elements in architecture and sculpture.

Following this creative burst over a period of two centuries, the Prambanan Plain was abandoned when the Hindu-Javanese kings moved to East Java. In the middle of the 16th century there is said to have been a great earthquake that toppled many of the temples. Their destruction was accelerated by treasure hunters and locals searching for building materials. Most temples have now been restored to some extent, and, like Borobudur, Prambanan made the Unesco World Heritage list in 1991.

Prambanan suffered extensive damage in the 2006 earthquake. Though the temples survived, hundreds of stone blocks collapsed to the ground or were cracked (479 in the Shiva temple alone). Today the main structures have been restored, though there remains a lot of work to be done, so expect some areas to be fenced off.

◉ Sights

Prambanan Temples TEMPLE
The huge Prambanan complex was erected in the middle of the 9th century – around 50 years later than Borobudur – but little is known about its early history. It's thought

that it was built by Rakai Pikatan to commemorate the return of a Hindu dynasty to sole power in Java.

Prambanan was in ruins for years, and while efforts were made in 1885 to clear the site, it was not until 1937 that reconstruction was first attempted. Of the original group, the outer compound contains the remains of 244 temples. Eight minor and eight main temples stand in the highest central courtyard.

Candi Shiva Mahadeva, dedicated to Shiva, is not only the largest of the temples but also the finest.

The main spire soars 47m and the temple is lavishly carved. The 'medallions' that decorate its base have a characteristic Prambanan motif – small lions in niches flanked by *kalpatura* (trees of heaven) and a menagerie of stylised half-human and half-bird *kinnara* (heavenly beings). The vibrant scenes carved onto the inner wall of the gallery encircling the temple are from the Ramayana – they tell how Lord Rama's wife, Sita, is abducted and how Hanuman the monkey god and Sugriwa the white-monkey general eventually find and release her.

The following descriptions apply to the temple's interior, which has not been accessible since the earthquake of 2006. The main chamber at the top of the eastern stairway has a four-armed statue of Shiva the Destroyer and is notable for the fact that this mightiest of Hindu gods stands on a huge lotus pedestal, a symbol of Buddhism. In the southern cell is the pot-bellied and bearded Agastya, an incarnation of Shiva as divine teacher; in the western cell is a superb image of the elephant-headed Ganesha, Shiva's son. In the northern cell, Durga, Shiva's consort, can be seen killing the demon buffalo. Some people believe that the Durga image is actually an image of the Slender Virgin, who, legend has it, was turned to stone by a man she refused to marry. She is still an object of pilgrimage and her name is often used for the temple group.

Candi Vishnu touches 33m and sits just north of Candi Shiva Mahadeva. It's still possible to get up front and personal with this magnificent temple. Its impressive reliefs tell the story of Lord Krishna, a hero of the Mahabharata epic, and you can ascend its stone staircase to the inner chamber and see a four-armed image of Vishnu the Preserver.

Candi Brahma is Candi Vishnu's twin temple. It is south of Candi Shiva Mahadeva and carved with the final scenes of the Ramayana. It has a spectacular 'monster mouth' doorway. If you're able to gain access to its inner chamber it contains a four-headed statue of Brahma, the god of creation.

Candi Sewu, the 'Thousand Temples', dating from around AD 850, originally consisted of a large central Buddhist temple surrounded by four rings of 240 smaller 'guard' temples. Outside the compound stood four sanctuaries at the points of the compass, of which Candi Bubrah is the most southern one. The renovated main temple has finely carved niches around its inner gallery – these niches once held bronze statues.

Plaosan Temples TEMPLE

This northeastern group of temples is 3km from the Prambanan complex. It can be reached on foot by taking the road north from the main gate, going past Candi Sewu and then walking east for about 1km.

Built around the same time as the Prambanan temple group, the Plaosan temples also combine both Hindu and Buddhist religious symbols and carvings. Plaosan Lor (Plaosan North) comprises two restored, identical main temples, surrounded by some 126 small shrines and solid stupas, most of which are now just a jumble of stone.

Two giant *dwarapala* (temple guardian statues) stand at the front of each main temple. The main temples, notable for their unusual three-part design, are two-storey, three-room structures, with an imitation storey above and a tiered roof of stupas rising to a single, larger one in the centre. Inside each room are impressive stone Bodhisattvas on either side of an empty lotus pedestal, and intricately carved *kala* (dragon) heads above the many windows.

Plaosan Kidul (Plaosan South) has more stupas and the remnants of a temple, but little renovation work has been done.

Southern Group TEMPLE

Kraton Ratu Boko (Palace of King Boko) is a partly-ruined Hindu palace complex dating from the 9th century. Perched on top of a hill overlooking Prambanan, it is believed to have been the central court of the mighty Mataram dynasty. Renovations, while only partially successful, have included new stonework. You can see the large gateway, walls, the platform of the main *pendopo*, Candi Pembakaran (Royal Crematorium) and a series of bathing places on different levels leading down to the nearby village. The view from this site to the Prambanan Plain is magnificent, especially at sunset, and worth the walk.

To reach Ratu Boko, travel 1.5km south on the road from Prambanan village to just southwest of where the river crosses the road. Near the 'Yogya 18km' signpost a steep rocky path leads up to the main site. Altogether it is about a one-hour walk. The site can be reached by car or motorcycle via a much longer route that goes around the back of the mountain.

The remains of the Buddhist temple, Candi Sajiwan, are not far from the village of Sajiwan, about 1.5km southeast of Prambanan village. Around the temple's base are carvings from the Jataka (episodes from the Buddha's various lives).

Western Group TEMPLE

There are three temples in this group between Yogyakarta and Prambanan; two are close to Kalasan village on the main Yogyakarta road. Kalasan and Prambanan villages are 3km apart, so it is probably easiest to take an *angkot* or bus to cover this stretch.

Candi Kalasan stands 50m off the main road near Kalasan village and is one of the oldest Buddhist temples on the Prambanan Plain. A Sanskrit inscription of AD 778 refers to a temple dedicated to the female Bodhisattva, Tara. It has been partially restored and has some fine detailed carvings on its southern side, where a huge, ornate *kala* head glowers over the doorway. At one time it was completely covered in coloured, shining stucco, and traces of the hard, stonelike 'diamond plaster' that provided a base for paintwork can still be seen. The inner chamber of Kalasan once sheltered a huge bronze image of Buddha or Tara.

Candi Sari is about 200m north from Candi Kalasan, in the middle of coconut and banana groves. This temple has the three-part design of the larger Plaosan temple but is probably slightly older. Some experts believe that its 2nd floor may have served as a dormitory for the Buddhist priests who took care of Candi Kalasan. The sculptured reliefs around the exterior are similar to those of Kalasan but are in much better condition.

Candi Sambisari is an isolated temple about 2.5km north of the main road, reached via a country lane. Sambisari is a Shiva temple and possibly the latest temple at Prambanan to be erected by the Mataram dynasty. It was discovered by a farmer in 1966. Excavated from under ancient layers of protective volcanic ash and dust, it lies almost 6m below the surface of the surrounding fields and is remarkable for its perfectly preserved state. The inner sanctum of the temple is dominated by a large lingam and yoni (stylised penis and vagina), typical of Shiva temples.

☆ Entertainment

Ramayana Ballet TRADITIONAL DANCE

(☎496 408; www.borobudurpark.com) Held at the outdoor theatre just west of the main temple complex, the famous Ramayana Ballet is Java's most spectacular dance-drama. The story of Rama and Shinta unfolds over four successive nights, twice or three times each month from May to October (the dry season), leading up to the full moon. With the magnificent floodlit Candi Shiva Mahadeva as a backdrop, nearly 200 dancers and gamelan musicians take part in a spectacle of monkey armies, giants on stilts, clashing battles and acrobatics.

Performances last from 7.30pm to 9.30pm. Tickets are sold in Yogyakarta through the tourist information office and travel agencies at the same price that you'll pay at the theatre box office (but they usually offer packages that include return transport from your hotel for 50,000Rp extra). Tickets cost from 50,000Rp to 150,000Rp, or 300,000Rp for VIP seats (padded chairs up the front). All seats are on stone benches except the VIP.

Alternatively, the *Ramayana Ballet Full Story* is a good two-hour performance (condensing the epic into one night), and alternates with the four-part episodic performances. It's held at the Trimurti Covered Theatre from November to April. Performances start at 7.30pm every Tuesday, Thursday and Saturday.

ℹ Information

The Prambanan temples (p132) are usually visited from Yogyakarta (17km away), but they can also be visited from Solo (50km away). The main temple complex lies on the Yogyakarta–Solo highway. A 'minitrain' (5000Rp) from the museum loops to Candi Sewu. The admission price includes camera fees and admission to the museum. Guides charge 75,000Rp for a one-hour tour for one to 20 people.

Most of the other (seldom-visited) outlying temples are within a 5km radius of Prambanan village. You'll need at least half a day to see them on foot, or they can be explored by bicycle or motorcycle if you ride to Prambanan. The best time to visit Prambanan is in the early morning or late in the day, when it's quiet, though you can never have Prambanan to yourself – expect plenty of attention from visiting school groups and requests for photos.

Getting There & Away

Bicycle & Motorcycle

You can visit all the temples by bicycle from Yogyakarta. The most pleasant route, though it's a longer ride, is to take Jl Senopati out past the zoo to the eastern ring road, where you turn left. Follow this right up to Jl Solo, turn right and then left at Jl Babarsari. Go past the Sahid Garden Hotel and follow the road anticlockwise around the school to the Selokan Mataram. This canal runs parallel to the Solo road, about 1.5km to the north, for around 6km to Kalasan, about 2km before Prambanan.

To view the western temples you really need to come back via the Solo road. The turn-off north to Candi Sambisari from the Solo road crosses the canal before leading another 1km to the temple. You can visit the temple, backtrack to the canal path and continue back to Yogyakarta.

If you are coming by motorcycle, you can combine the visit with a trip to Kaliurang. From Kaliurang, instead of going back to the main Yogyakarta–Solo road, take the 'Solo Alternatif' route signposted in the village of Pakem, about halfway between Yogyakarta and Kaliurang. From there the road passes through some beautiful countryside, before tipping you onto the main highway just before Prambanan's main entrance.

Bus

From Yogyakarta, take TransYogya bus 1A (3000Rp, 40 minutes) from Jl Malioboro. From Solo, buses take 1½ hours and cost 15,000Rp.

Solo (Surakarta)

☎0271 / POP 508,000

Arguably the epicentre of Javanese identity and tradition, Solo is one of the least Westernised cities in the island. An eternal rival to Yogyakarta, this conservative city often plays second fiddle to its more conspicuous neighbour. But with backstreet *kampung* and elegant *kraton*, traditional markets and gleaming malls, Solo has more than enough to warrant at least an overnight visit. And as there are some fascinating temples close by, it also makes a great base for forays into the lush hills of Central Java.

In many ways, Solo is also Java writ small, incorporating its vices and virtues and embodying much of its heritage. On the downside, the island's notoriously fickle temper tends to flare in Solo first – the city has been the backdrop for some of the worst riots in Java's recent history. On the upside, the city's long and distinguished past as a seat of the great Mataram empire means that it competes with Yogyakarta as the hub of Javanese culture.

Solo attracts many students and scholars to its academies of music and dance. The city is an excellent place to see traditional performing arts, and traditional crafts – especially batik – are also well represented.

History

Following the sacking of the Mataram court at Kartosuro in 1742, the *susuhunan*, Pakubuwono II, decided to look for a more auspicious site. A location near the river Solo was chosen, and his imposing palace completed by 1745.

Pakubuwono II died after only four years in the city, and his heir, Pakubuwono III, managed to lose half of his kingdom to the court of Yogyakarta. Pakubuwono X (1893–1938), however, had more luck. He revived the prestige of the court through the promotion of culture and gave no time to fighting rival royals.

Following WWII, the royal court fumbled opportunities to play a positive role in the revolution, and lost out badly to Yogyakarta, which became the seat of the independent government. The palaces of the city soon became mere symbols of ancient Javanese feudalism and aristocracy.

With the overthrow of Suharto, Solo erupted following the riots in Jakarta in May 1998. For two days rioters went on a rampage, systematically looting and burning every shopping centre and department store and targeting Chinese-owned businesses.

Today things have settled down again, and sleek new shopping malls and hotels have risen from the ashes of the old. But Solo retains a reputation as a hotbed of radicalism, and its *madrassahs* (Islamic schools) have maintained links to extremist groups such as Jemaah Islamiah.

Sights & Activities

Kraton Surakarta PALACE, MUSEUM

(Kraton Kasunanan; ☎656 432; admission 15,000Rp, guide 25,000Rp; ⌚9am-2pm Sat-Thu) Once the hub of an empire, today the Kraton Surakarta is a faded memorial of a bygone era. It's worth a visit, but much of the *kraton* was

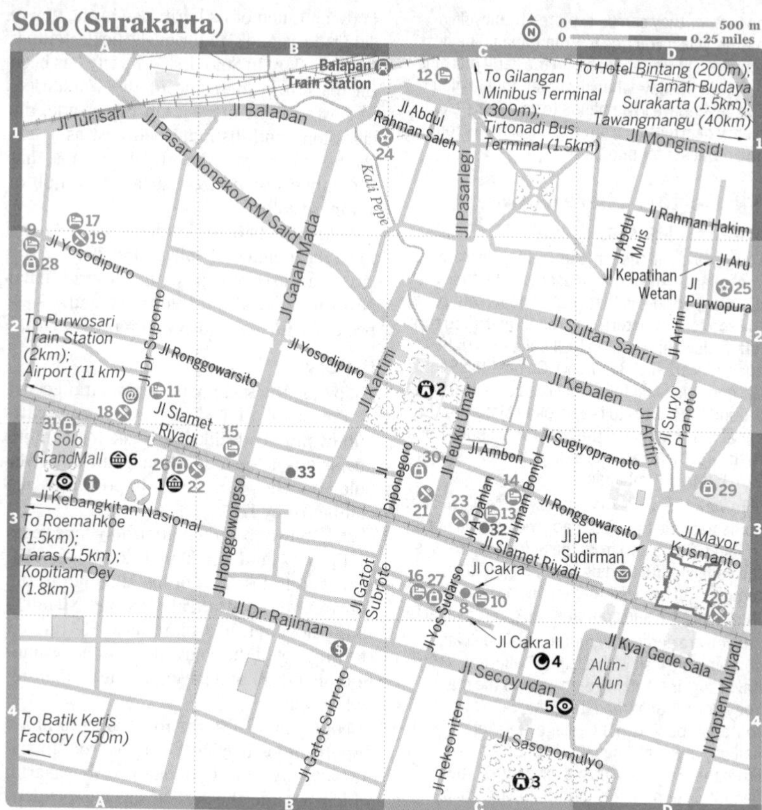

destroyed by fire in 1985. Many of the inner buildings were rebuilt, but today the allure of this once-majestic palace has largely vanished and its structures left bare and unloved.

The poor condition of today's *kraton* belies its illustrious history. In 1745 Pakubuwono II moved from Kartosuro to Solo in a procession that transplanted everything belonging to the king, including the royal banyan trees and the sacred Nyai **Setomo cannon** (the twin of Si Jagur in old Jakarta), which now sits in the northern palace pavilion here.

The main sight for visitors is the **Sasono Sewoko museum**. Its exhibits include a array of silver and bronze Hindu-Javanese figures, weapons, antiques and other royal heirlooms, plus the mother of all horse-carriage collections. Labelling is poor or nonexistent and termites, woodworm and rot are serious issues.

A carved doorway leads to an inner courtyard, but most of the *kraton* is off-limits and it's still the residence of the *susuhunan* (sultan or king).

One edifice that has survived is the distinctive tower known as **Panggung Songgo Buwono**. It was built in 1782 and looks like a cross between a Dutch clocktower and a lighthouse. Its upper storey is a meditation sanctum where the *susuhunan* is said to commune with Nyai Loro Kidul (the Goddess of the South Seas).

Dance practices are held here on Sundays at 1pm.

Istana Mangkunegaran PALACE, MUSEUM
(admission 18,000Rp; ⏲8.30am-2pm) Dating back to 1757, the Istana Mangkunegaran is in better condition than the *kraton* and is the home of the second house of Solo. It was founded after a bitter struggle against Pakubuwono II, launched by his nephew. Members of the aristocratic family still live at the back of the palace.

Solo (Surakarta)

Sights
1 Danar Hadi ... A3
2 Istana Mangkunegaran ... C2
3 Kraton Surakarta ... C4
4 Mesjid Agung ... C4
5 Pasar Klewer ... C4
6 Radya Pustaka Museum ... A3
7 Sriwedari Amusement Park ... A3

Activities, Courses & Tours
8 Miki Tours ... C3

Sleeping
9 Solo Paragon ... A2
10 Cakra Homestay ... C3
11 De Solo ... A2
12 Fave Hotel Adi Sucipto ... C1
13 Istana Griya ... C3
14 Istana Griya 2 ... C3
15 Novotel Solo ... B3
16 Paradiso Guesthouse ... C3
17 Rumah Turi ... A1

Eating
18 Adem Ayem ... A2
19 Bizztro Saraswati ... A2
20 Galabo ... D3
21 Nasi Liwet Wongso Lemu ... C3
22 O Solo Mio ... B3
23 Warung Baru ... C3

Entertainment
24 RRI Auditorium ... B1
25 SMKI ... D2
Sriwedari Theatre ... (see 7)

Shopping
26 Batik Danar Hadi ... A3
27 Batik Keris Shop ... C3
28 Paragon Mall ... A2
29 Pasar Gede ... D3
Pasar Klewer ... (see 5)
30 Pasar Triwindu ... C3
31 Solo Grand Mall ... A3

Transport
32 AA Trans ... C3
33 Garuda ... B3
Silk Air ... (see 15)

The centre of the palace compound is the *pendopo*, a pavilion built in a mix of Javanese and European architectural styles, and one of the largest in the country. Its high, rounded ceiling was painted in 1937 and is intricately decorated with a central flame surrounded by figures of the Javanese zodiac, each painted in its own mystical colour. In Javanese philosophy yellow guards against sleepiness, blue against disease, black against hunger, green against desire, white against lust, rose against fear, red against evil and purple against wicked thoughts.

Behind here is the *dalem* (residence), which forms the delightful **palace museum**. Most exhibits are from the personal collection of Mangkunegara VII. On display are gold-plated dresses for royal dances, a superb mask collection, jewellery and a few oddities, including huge Buddhist rings and gold genital covers. A **guide** is mandatory (and worthwhile) for the museum. Most guides are very informative and speak English (a tip of 25,000Rp is appreciated).

At the pavilion, there's gamelan music, singing and dance-practice sessions on Wednesday, from 10am until noon.

Danar Hadi MUSEUM

(☎722 042; www.houseofdanarhadi.com; Jl Slamet Riyadi 261; admission 25,000Rp; ⏰9am-4pm, showroom to 9pm) Danar Hadi is one's of the world's best batik museums, with a terrific collection of antique and royal textiles from Java, China and beyond. It occupies a stunning whitewashed colonial building. Entry includes an excellent guided tour (around 1½ hours, in English), which explains the history of the many pieces (10,000 in the collection), though no photos are allowed. There's a workshop where you can watch craftswomen at work creating new masterpieces. There's an upmarket storeroom and souvenir shop too.

Radya Pustaka Museum MUSEUM

(Jl Slamet Riyadi; admission 5000Rp; ⏰8.30am-2.30pm Tue-Sun) A small museum with good displays of gamelan instruments, jewelled kris, puppets and *wayang beber* (scrolls that depict *wayang* stories).

Mesjid Agung MOSQUE

On the western side of the *alun-alun*, Mesjid Agung, featuring classical Javanese architecture, is the largest and most sacred mosque in Solo.

Sriwedari Amusement Park AMUSEMENT PARK
(admission 3000Rp; ⏲5-10pm Mon-Fri, to 11pm Sat, 9am-10pm Sun) Solo's Sriwedari Amusement Park has fair rides and sideshow stalls. Nightly *wayang orang* performances (and other cultural shows) are held here.

Jaladara Steam Train TRAIN
(☎0856 4200 3322; www.solosteamloco.com; ticket 150,000Rp; ⏲9am-11.30am) Trundling through the heart of the city, the Jaladara steam train (built in Germany in 1896) is a fun morning excursion in carriages that have Victorian-style wood fittings. The trip (with English-speaking guide) starts at Purwosari train station (3km west of the centre), and stops at places including Kampung Batik Kauman (for a visit to a batik worshop) before terminating at Sangkrah train station. Tickets can be bought at hotels including the Novotel.

Courses

Batik Mahkotalaweyan (☎712 276; www.batikmahkotalaweyan.com; Sayangan Kulon 9, Kampung Laweyan; 2-hr course 30,000Rp) offers batik-making courses ranging from a two-hour taster session to intensive programs lasting several days. The tourist office also has a list of places offering courses.

Tours

For some reason tours quoted from Solo can be very pricey, so consider renting a car and a driver and doing it yourself for much less. AA Trans (p142) is a good option.

Guesthouses and freelance guides offer city, regional and bike tours. **Ajib Bond** (☎0818 0447 8488; ajib_efata@yahoo.com) offers good city tours (400,000Rp, minimum two people). His bike trip (175,000Rp) to Mojolaban village via various cottage industries and the Bengawan Solo river is recommended.

Travel agent **Miki Tours** (☎729 292; www.tiket24jam.com; Jl Yos Sudarso 17) offers tours to the countryside around Solo, including Candi Sukuh (475,000Rp, minimum two people).

Festivals & Events

Kirab Pusaka CULTURAL
(Heirloom Procession) Since 1633, these colourful processions have been held on the first day of the Javanese month of Suro (between March and May). They start at Istana Mangkunegaran in the early evening and continue late into the night.

Sekaten RELIGIOUS
This festival marks the Prophet Muhammed's birthday, and is held between May and July. It comprises two ceremonies with a week in between, culminating with a fair erected in the *alun-alun* and the sharing of a rice mountain.

Solo Batik Carnival CULTURAL
Annual carnival in late June with processions, fashion shows and performances in the R.Maladi stadium.

TRADITION & DISASTER

Solo is a deeply superstitious city and many of its citizens are acutely observant of Javanese and Islamic ritual. So when the *kraton* (palace) ignited in flames on 1 January 1985, many locals saw it as a consequence of the incumbent sultan Pakubuwono XII's lack of observance of tradition. For years he'd been lax with his ceremonial duties, and his alleged womanising was the talk of the town. The sultan had also taken to living the high life in Jakarta rather than presiding over court life in Solo.

Firefighters responding quickly to the blaze found their engines could not fit through the main gateway (which was thought to be sacred), and initially refused to smash through it. Around 60% of the palace subsequently burned to the ground.

To appease deeply felt Javanese customs, a purification ceremony was performed. The head of a tiger, snake, buffalo and deer were buried, and tons of ashes were returned to the coast to quell the wrath of Nyai Loro Kidul, the Queen of the Southern Sea, whose influence over the tragic events was seen to be pivotal by many.

However General Benny Murdani, who investigated the fire, was eager to counter locally held superstitions in his judgement, "reporters will *not* reach their own conclusions. The reason for the fire was an electrical short circuit".

When Pakubuwono XII died in 2004, he left 37 children from six wives and mistresses, but no clear heir.

Sleeping

Solo has a few good budget hotels. Almost all offer travel information, tours, bus bookings, bicycles for rent, breakfast, and free tea/coffee. The midrange choice is excellent, though Solo isn't loaded with truly top-end hotels.

TOP CHOICE **Roemahkoe** HISTORIC HOTEL $$
(☎714 024; www.roemahkoe.info; Jl Dr Rajiman 501; r/ste incl breakfast from 650,000/750,000Rp; ❄📶) This remarkable art-deco hotel is simply dripping in history and loaded with atmosphere. Most of the 14 rooms boast wood-panelling and stained-glass windows plus all the modern facilities you'd expect. Set at the rear is a wonderful restaurant and the whole place is efficiently managed by Noer, a Solo native, who lived in the UK for years. Noer can arrange tours of the traditional *kampung batik* (batik village) directly behind the hotel.

Rumah Turi BOUTIQUE HOTEL $$
(www.rumahturi.com; Jl Srigading II 12, Turisari; r incl breakfast US$67-77, ste US$97; ❄📶) Breaking new ground in Java, this fine new eco-sensitive hotel has chic accommodation grouped around a lovely garden. Most of the material used for the construction of the place has been recycled, rainwater is reused and it's solar powered. There's also a great open-sided cafe-restaurnant with excellent Javanese food. A free ride from the airport or train station is offered.

Fave Hotel Adi Sucipto HOTEL $$
(☎719 222; www.favehotels.com; Jl Adisucipto 60; r from 275,000Rp; ❄@📶) This new no-frills budget hotel adopts a hip design with a striking lobby and inviting, if small, rooms with good linen, modish fixtures and satellite TV. The location is about 2km north of the centre, right next to Balapan train station. Book online for the best rates.

Lorin LUXURY HOTEL $$$
(☎724 500; www.lorinhotel.com; Jl Adisucipto 47; r/ste from US$90/300; ❄@📶≋) About 5km north of the centre, this hotel's trump card is its absolutely stunning tropical garden, complete with towering palms, dramatic statues and a vast pool. Rooms are comfortable and spacious and the gym is excellent. Book by the web for promo rates as low as US$60.

Novotel Solo HOTEL $$
(☎724 555; www.accor.com; Jl Slamet Riyadi 272; r from 438,000Rp; ❄@📶≋) In the heart of the city, with most attractions withing walking distance, the Novotel has an enviable central location. Rooms are spacious and modern, staff are professional and helpful, and you'll find two pools, a spa and a fitness centre.

Istana Griya GUESTHOUSE $
(☎632 667; www.istanagriya.tripod.com; Jl Ahmad Dahlan 22; r with fan/air-con from 110,000/160,000Rp; ❄📶) Istana Griya is popular with backpackers thanks to its sociable atmosphere and clean if unexciting rooms (many don't have outside windows). Staff are knowledgeable and friendly enough, but their tours are overpriced.

De Solo HOTEL $$
(☎714 887; www.de-soloboutiquehotel.com; Jl Dr Sutomo 8; r/ste incl breakfast from 410,000/1,100,000Rp; ❄📶) An expanding modern hotel (boutique is pushing it) with a selection of uncluttered but smallish rooms in a quiet, convenient location. There's an attractive little garden cafe and a reasonably priced spa (massages from 100,000Rp per hour).

Istana Griya 2 GUESTHOUSE $
(☎661 118; Jl Imam Bonjol 35; r incl breakfast 220,000Rp; ❄📶) In a good central location, this renovated place is a sister hotel to the original around the corner. It is more upmarket, with large modern, inviting rooms and hot-water showers. Staff are eager to help out.

Solo Paragon LUXURY HOTEL $$
(☎765 5888; www.soloparagonhotel.com; Jl Dr Sutomo; r/ste from 390,000/700,000Rp; ❄📶≋) This 25-storey tower hotel opened in 2012 on the west side of the centre, right above the vast Paragon mall. The rooms are decked out with contemporary flourishes including bold prints, and it has a pool and a fitness room.

Cakra Homestay HOMESTAY $
(☎634 743; Jl Cakra II 15; r incl breakfast without mandi 100,000-125,000Rp, with mandi 150,000Rp, with air-con 175,000Rp; ❄≋) This atmospheric place scores highly for those interested in Javanese culture (and the welcoming staff are keen to promote it). There's an amazing gamelan room with free performances on Monday, Tuesday, Thursday and Sunday evenings. It also has a gorgeous pool area. However the plain rooms are a little disappointing and could be cleaner.

Hotel Bintang HOTEL $
(☎648 737; www.hotelasiasolo.com/bintang; Jl Ir Sutami 104; r 192,000-450,000Rp; ❄📶) The

location, 2km northeast of the centre, is a bit inconvenient, but the standard-class rooms here are fair value, with air-con and TV; the deluxe and superior rooms less so. There's a cafe-restaurant.

Paradiso Guesthouse GUESTHOUSE $
(☎652 960; Kemlayan Kidul I; r 60,000-120,000Rp) This guesthouse – in an historic residence with ornate lighting and mirrors – would be a mighty fine place if they only spent a rupiah or two on maintenance. Rooms are unloved but at least they are cheap.

Eating & Drinking

Solo has a superb street-food tradition and a great traffic-free area called **Galabo** (Jl Slamet Riyadi; ⏰5-11pm), a kind of open-air food court with dozens of stalls where you can sample some. Local specialities such as *nasi gudeg* (unripe jackfruit served with rice, chicken and spices), *nasi liwet* (rice cooked in coconut milk and eaten with a host of side dishes) or the beef noodle soup *timlo solo* can be found here.

There is no bar scene in Solo but you will find the odd good cafe.

Kopitiam Oey CAFE $
(www.kopitiamoey.com; Jl Perintis Kemerdekaan 35; snacks 10,000-25,000Rp, coffee from 9000Rp; ⏰9am-midnight; 📶) In a lovely old colonial-era villa, this cafe is well worth seeking out if you're in need of a snack and coffee during a hot day of sightseeing. Relax in the art deco-style seating or in the rear garden while you sip your iced cappuccino or Vietnam coffee and munch on some French toast. It's about 2km southwest of the centre.

Laras JAVANESE, INTERNATIONAL $$
(☎714 024; www.roemahkoe.com; Roemahkoe hotel, Dr Rajiman 501; meals 60,000-120,000Rp; @📶) A wonderfully classy hotel-restaurant where you can savour the unique surrounds of this historic building, which was once a batik factory. It's particularly evocative at night when candlelit, and on Saturdays when a gamelan orchestra plays. Specials include the Dutch-style *kroket* (croquettes with cheese), and *bakmie godog juragan* (noodle broth with chicken, egg and vegetables).

Nasi Liwet Wongso Lemu JAVANESE $
(Jl Teuku Umar; meals 12,000-18,000Rp; ⏰5pm-1am) Solo street dining at its best, this evening-only stall run by an *ibu* in traditional batik specialises in *nasi liwet*: coconut-flavoured rice served on a banana leaf topped with shredded chicken, egg, turmeric-cooked tofu and special seasonings. *Enak* (delicious)!

O Solo Mio ITALIAN $$
(☎727 264; Jl Slamet Riyadi 253; mains 40,000-60,000Rp) Authentic-to-the-last-olive Italian that's as close as you'll get to a taste of the Roman homeland in Central Java; it has a wood-fired pizza oven and delicious pasta.

Bizztro Saraswati INTERNATIONAL, CAFE $$
(☎717 100; Jl Yosodipuro 122; meals 40,000-120,000Rp; ⏰2-10pm; 📶) Classy European-owned place with an open-air lounge area and dining room. Excellent for Western food including lamb chops with mash (80,000Rp), steaks or salmon. Or just drop by for a coffee (the espresso is perfect) or herbal tea.

Adem Ayem INDONESIAN $
(☎716 992; Jl Slamet Riyadi 342; meals around 17,000Rp) Huge canteen-like place with swirling fans and photos of ye olde Surakarta. Grab one of the plastic-fantastic chairs and order the chicken – fried, or served up *gudeg*-style – which is what everyone's here for.

Warung Baru INTERNATIONAL $
(☎656 369; Jl Ahmad Dahlan 23; mains from 10,000Rp; 🖉) Old school backpackers' hangout, the Baru bakes great bread and caters quite well to vegetarians but the rest of the enormous menu is a bit forgettable. Still, the friendly owners arrange tours and batik classes.

Entertainment

Solo is an excellent place to see traditional Javanese performing arts; Istana Mangkunegaran and Kraton Surakarta both have traditional Javanese dance practice.

At the back of Sriwedari Amusement Park, **Sriwedari Theatre** (admission 3000Rp; ⏰performances 8-10pm Tue-Sat) has a long-running *wayang orang* (masked dance-drama); you can come and go as you please.

Contact the tourist office for the latest schedules for all events.

RRI Auditorium PERFORMING ARTS
(☎641 178; Jl Abdul Rahman Saleh 51) RRI holds an eclectic program of cultural performances, including *wayang orang* and *ketoprak* (folk theatre). There's a free *wayang orang* event on the second Tuesday of each month at 8pm.

SMKI PERFORMING ARTS
(☎632 225; Jl Kepatihan Wetan) The high school for the performing arts has dance practice from 8am to noon Monday to Thursday and Saturday, and 8am to 11am Friday. There's also an impressive cultural performance on the 25th of every month here.

Taman Budaya Surakarta PERFORMING ARTS
(TBS; ☎635 414; Jl Ir Sutami 57) This cultural centre hosts all-night *wayang kulit* performances; private dance lessons are also available.

Shopping

Solo is one of Indonesia's main textile centres, producing not only its own unique, traditional batik but every kind of fabric.

For everyday shopping, check out the markets, or the malls, including **Solo Grand Mall** (Jl Slamet Riyadi) and **Paragon Mall** (www.solo-paragon.com; Jl Dr Sutomo; 📶).

Batik

Solo has two urban batik villages, narrow streets full of family-run workshops that are a delight to explore. **Kampung Batik Kauman** is just south of Jl Slamet Riyadi, around Jl Cakra in one of the main backpackers' districts. **Kampung Batik Laweyan** (www.kampoenglaweyan.com) is centred in the lanes south of the Roemahkoe hotel (which was once a batik workshop). Residents in both areas are normally very welcoming to visitors, and eager to sell a piece or two. The **Pasar Klewer** (Jl Secoyudan; ⏲8am-6pm) also has dozens of batik stalls.

There are also some well-established manufacturers with showrooms displaying their range of sophisticated work.

Batik Keris Factory CLOTHING
(☎714 400; Jl Batik Keris; ⏲8am-5pm Mon-Sat) This factory, in Kampung Batik Laweyan, allows you to see the batik process up close. Its **shop** (Jl Yos Sudarso 62) has icy air-con and two full floors of fixed-price batik bags, skirts and shirts.

Batik Danar Hadi CLOTHING
(www.houseofdanarhadi.com; Jl Slamet Riyadi 261) Danar Hadi is an important Solonese manufacturer and has a good store at its museum-come-showroom.

Curios

Kris and other souvenirs can be purchased from street vendors found at the eastern side of the *alun-alun* near Kraton Surakarta. The gem sellers have a mind-boggling array of semi-precious stones. Jl Dr Rajiman (Secoyudan), which runs along the southern edge of the *alun-alun*, is the goldsmith street.

Solo has a good flea market, Pasar Triwindu (p141).

Markets

Pasar Triwindu MARKET
(Windujenar Market; Jl Diponegoro; ⏲9am-4pm) Pasar Triwindu, Solo's flea market is the place to search for antiques including *wayang* puppets, old batik and ceramics as well as clocks, vinyl records, coins and vintage cameras.

Pasar Gede MARKET
(Jl Urip Sumoharjo; ⏲8am-6pm) This is the city's largest general market, selling all manner of produce, particularly fruit and vegetables.

Pasar Klewer MARKET
(Jl Secoyudan) Has hundreds of stalls selling fabrics.

Information

BCA Bank (cnr Jl Dr Rajiman & Jl Gatot Subroto) Has currency-exchange facilities.

Main post office (Jl Jenderal Sudirman)

Internet Cafe Garden (Jl Dr Supomo; per hour 5000Rp; ⏲24hr)

Tourist office (☎711 435; Jl Slamet Riyadi 275; ⏲8am-4pm Mon-Sat) Staff are well-informed here and have maps, brochures and reliable information on cultural events. They also peddle (slightly pricey) tours.

Getting There & Away

AIR Solo's Adi Sumarmo airport only has one international connection, **Silk Air** (☎724 604/5; www.silkair.com; Jl Slamet Riyadi 272, Novotel Hotel), which flies to/from Singapore. Domestic services include very regular flights to Jakarta with **Garuda** (☎737 500; www.garuda-indonesia.com; Hotel Riyadi Palace, Jl Slamet Riyadi 335) and **Sriwijaya Air** (☎021 2927 9777; www.sriwijayaair-online.com) and connections to Balikpapan, Banjarmasin, Berau, Pangkalan Bun, Ketapang and Pontianak with **Trigana** (☎021 860 4867; www.trigana-air.com).

BUS The Tirtonadi bus terminal is 3km from the centre of the city. Only economy buses leave from here to destinations such as Prambanan (14,000Rp, 1½ hours), Yogyakarta (16,000Rp, two hours) and Semarang (28,000Rp, 3¼ hours), plus Surabaya and Malang. Near the bus terminal, the Gilingan minibus terminal has express air-con *travel* minibuses to Yogyakarta (25,000Rp), Semarang (45,000Rp), Surabaya

TRAINS FROM SOLO

DESTINATION	COST (RP)	DURATION (HR)	FREQUENCY
Jakarta	320,000-365,000	8¼-9	4 daily
Surabaya	135,000–285,000	3½-4	6 daily

and Malang (both 80,000Rp). **Citra** (☎713 684), based at Gilingan, runs *travel* minibuses to most main cities; call for a pick-up.

TRAIN Solo is located on the main Jakarta–Yogyakarta–Surabaya train line and most trains stop at **Balapan** (☎714 039), the principal train station. Jebres train station, in the northeast of Solo, has a few very slow economy-class services to Surabaya and Jakarta.

Getting Around

Air-conditioned Batik Solo Trans buses connect Adi Sumarmo airport, 10km northwest of the centre with Jl Slamet Riyadi. A taxi costs around 60,000Rp; **Kosti Solo taxis** (☎856 300) are reliable. Becak cost about 8000Rp from the train station or bus terminal into the centre. Homestays can arrange bike hire for around 15,000Rp or a motorcycle for around 60,000Rp per day.

Solo is an inexpensive place to set up car hire. Avoid homestays and hotels and book directly with **AA Trans** (☎632 811; Hotel Keprabon, Jl Ahmad Dahlan 8). You'll pay 325,000Rp for a 12-hour hire period in the city region in a modern air-con car, with driver, excluding petrol; 400,000Rp for trips outside Solo. This company is sometimes reluctant to offer pick-ups from your hotel (many of whom have their own car-hire deals); so you may have to head to their office to meet your driver.

Sangiran

Sangiran is a very important archaeological excavation site (so important it gained World Heritage status in 1996), where some of the best examples of fossilised skulls of prehistoric 'Java Man' *(Pithecanthropus erectus)* were unearthed by a Dutch professor in 1936.

The town's main (if not only) attraction is its small **museum** (admission 7500Rp; ⏲8am-4pm Tue-Sun), with a few skulls (one of *Homo erectus*), various pig and hippopotamus teeth, and fossil exhibits, including huge mammoth bones and tusks. Guides will also offer to take you to the area where shells and other fossils have been found in the crumbling slopes of the hill.

Take a Purwodadi-bound bus from Solo's bus terminal and ask to be dropped off at the Sangiran turn-off (4000Rp), 15km from Solo. It's then 4km to the museum (around 10,000Rp by *ojek*).

Gunung Lawu

Towering Gunung Lawu (3265m), lying on the border of Central and East Java, is one of the holiest mountains in Java. Mysterious Hindu temples dot its slopes and each year thousands of pilgrims seeking spiritual enlightenment climb its peak.

Although popular history has it that when Majapahit fell to Islam, the Hindu elite all fled east to Bali, Javanese lore relates that Brawijaya V, the last king of Majapahit, went west. Brawijaya's son, Raden Patah, was the leader of Demak and led the conquering forces of Islam against Majapahit, but rather than fight his own son, Brawijaya retreated to Gunung Lawu to seek spiritual enlightenment. There he achieved nirvana as Sunan Lawu, and today pilgrims come to the mountain to seek his spiritual guidance or to achieve magic powers.

The unique temples on the mountain – which are some of the last Hindu temples built in Java before the region converted to Islam – show the influence of the later *wayang* style of East Java, though they incorporate elements of fertility worship. The most famous temple is Candi Sukuh; Candi Cetho is another large complex that still attracts Hindu worshippers.

Sights

Candi Sukuh TEMPLE

(admission 12,000Rp; ⏲7am-4.30pm) In a magnificent position on the slopes of Gunung Lawu, 900m above the Solo plain, Candi Sukuh is one of Java's most enigmatic and striking temples. It's not a large site, but it has a large, truncated pyramid of rough-hewn stone, and there are some fascinating reliefs and statues. It's clear that a fertility cult was practised here: several explicit carvings have led it to be dubbed the 'erotic' temple. It's a quiet, isolated place with a strange, potent atmosphere.

Built in the 15th century during the declining years of the Majapahit kingdom, Candi Sukuh seems to have nothing whatsoever to do with other Javanese Hindu and Buddhist temples. The origins of its builders and strange sculptural style (with crude, squat and distorted figures carved in the *wayang* style found in East Java) remain a mystery and it seems to mark a reappearance of the pre-Hindu animism that existed 1500 years before.

At the gateway before the temple are a large stone lingam and yoni. Flowers are still often scattered here, and locals believe these symbols were used to determine whether a wife had been faithful, or a wife-to-be was still a virgin. The woman had to wear a sarong and jump across the lingam – if the sarong fell off, her infidelity was proven. Other interesting cult objects include a monument depicting Bima, the Mahabharata warrior hero, with Narada, the messenger of the gods, both in a stylised womb. Another monument depicts Bima passing through the womb at his birth. In the top courtyard three enormous flat-backed turtles stand like sacrificial altars. A 2m lingam once topped the pyramid, but it was removed by Sir Stamford Raffles in 1815 and now resides in the National Museum in Jakarta.

If you're driving here note that there are almost no signposts to help direct you to the site and you have to pay a small fee to pass through the *kampung* of Kemuning.

Virtually all travellers get here on a tour from Solo or Yogyakarta. Public transport is very tricky: take a bus bound for Tawangmangu from Solo as far as Karangpandan (7000Rp), then a Kemuning minibus (3000Rp) to the turn-off to Candi Sukuh; from here it's a steep 2km walk uphill to the site or a 10,000Rp *ojek* ride. For around 40,000Rp, *ojeks* will take you to both Sukuh and Cetho.

Candi Cetho TEMPLE

(Ceto; admission 10,000Rp; ⏲7am-4.30pm) Even higher up the slopes, Candi Cetho sits on the southern face of Gunung Lawu at around 1400m. Thought to date from around 1350, this *candi* closely resembles a Balinese temple in appearance, though it combines elements of Shivaism and fertility worship. It's a larger temple than Sukuh and is spread over terraces rising up the misty hillside. There's little carving here, but the stonework is well constructed and close-fitting. The entrance is marked by temple guardians and you'll find a striking platform with a turtle head and a large lingam on the upper terrace.

WORTH A TRIP

SUHARTO'S MAUSOLEUM

In a commanding hilltop location, 34km southeast of Solo, ex-President Suharto's mausoleum, **Astana Giribangun** (admission by donation; ⏲8am-5pm) is a curious sight. Suharto planned this monument to himself well in advance of his death, securing the land and appointing an architect back in 1998. The resulting building is curiously low-key and lacking the gaudy excesses favoured by many ex-dictators – an unadorned mosque-like structure built on traditional Javanese *pendopo* lines.

Tombs of various less-favoured relatives are dotted around the edges of the building, while the inner sanctum, separated by carved wooden screens, contains five marble sarcophagi: Suharto himself, his mother, father, wife and one sister. Oddly enough, the whole place is eerily peaceful, and few visitors pay their respects these days – in stark contrast to the scenes in 2008 when tens of thousands lined the route of his funeral cortège from Solo airport. The Suharto cult of personality certainly has waned over the years.

While you're here you can stroll up to the burial place of Solo's royal Mangkunegara family, whose monuments pale by comparison. It's just 300m away on a neighbouring forested hilltop.

There's a cafe and a souvenir stall where you can purchase kitsch keyrings and the like. There is no public transport to the monument. Tour guides in Solo will include Giribangun on trips to Candi Sukuh and Candi Cetho. By road, head east of Solo to Karangpandan, and it's 7km south of the highway near the village of Mangadeg.

Perhaps most interestingly, this temple is still the focus of active worship, and Balinese (and Javanese) Hindus visit Candi Cetho to pray and give offerings. Indeed, the villagers who live just below the temple form one of Java's last remaining Hindu populations.

There are several homestays in the village, with simple rooms available for 75,000Rp per night. Cetho is usually included in the temple tours from Solo and Yogyakarta. By road, it's 9km past the Sukuh turn-off.

Sleeping

Sukuh Cottage HOTEL **$$**
(☎0271 702 4587; www.sukuh-cottage.com; r/f/villa incl breakfst 265,000/485,000/1,200,000Rp; 📶) Just before Sukuh temple – and enjoying the same exquisite views – this rural hotel has attractive rooms and villas built from natural materials dotted around a sublime grassy plot studded with mature trees. There's an elevated viewing platform and restaurant.

Tawangmangu

☎0271

Tawangmangu, a large hill resort on the western side of Gunung Lawu, is a popular weekend retreat for Solonese. It's a pleasant enough, if sprawling, place to escape the city heat and do a hike or two in the hills.

Sights

Grojogan Sewu WATERFALL
(admission 3500Rp; ⏲6am-6pm) About 2km from town, Grojogan Sewu, a 100m-high waterfall, is a favourite playground for monkeys. It is reached by a long flight of steps down a hillside, but you probably won't want to have a dip in the chilly (dirty) swimming pool. From the bottom of the waterfall a trail leads to a good track to Candi Sukuh, a 2½-hour walk away (some Solo guides offer treks). This path is steep in parts but is also negotiable by motorbike. *Ojek* hang out at the beginning of the trail on weekends.

Sleeping & Eating

There are plenty of losmen on Jl Grojogan Sewu, a quieter street running between the waterfall and Jl Raya Lawu.

For cheaper eats, the road near the waterfall is inundated with warungs.

Hotel Bintang HOTEL **$**
(☎696 269; www.bintangtw.hotelasiasolo.com; Jl Raya Lawu; r from 220,000Rp; ❄📶) Modern hotel on the main drag with three floors of sleek, contemporary rooms, all with dark-wood furniture, LCD TV and stylish lighting. Not much English is spoken but staff try to be helpful. There's a minimart, a cafe-restaurant (and unfortunately karaoke on weekends).

TOP CHOICE **Warung Grio** JAVANESE **$$**
(☎700 7413; meals around 50,000Rp) An outstanding riverside warung, part of an outdoor activity centre, that offers absolutely delicious traditional Javanese dishes cooked on log fires. You eat under wooden shelters overlooking a fast-flowing stream. The food takes time to prepare, so expect to wait a while or call ahead. It's 2km west of Tawangmangu, on the road back to Solo.

Getting There & Away

Buses travel to Solo (12,000Rp) regularly. Minibuses (2000Rp) loop through town from the bus terminal up the main road, across to the waterfall and back.

WORTH A TRIP

CLIMBING GUNUNG LAWU

The village of Cemoro Sewu, 10km east of Tawangmangu, is the starting point for the hike to the summit of Gunung Lawu. Thousands of pilgrims flock to the summit on 1 Suro, the start of the Javanese new year, but mystics and holidaying students make the night climb throughout the year, especially on Saturday night. Most start around 8pm, reaching the peak at around 2am for meditation.

For the best chance of witnessing a clear sunrise, start by 10.30pm at the latest. It is a long, steady six-hour hike, but one of the easiest mountains in Java to tackle. While the stony path has handrails in places, it is still best to bring a torch. Alternatively, guides can make a night climb easier and lead you to the various pilgrimage sites along the way. Guides in Cemoro Sewu cost around 120,000Rp. Sign in at the PHKA post before starting the climb (admission to walk 2000Rp).

NORTH COAST

Central Java's north coast features little on the itineraries of most travellers, but this steamy strip of land is not without its charm.

For starters, the towns dotting the north coast are steeped in history. For many centuries the coast was the centre for trade with merchants from Arabia, India and China, who brought with them both goods and cultural values. In the 15th and 16th centuries the area was a springboard for Islam into Java, and the tombs of most of the country's great saints all lie along this coast.

Craft traditions are also impressive. Pekalongan is celebrated for its batik, while Jepara is a major centre for wooden furniture. If the sweet smell of *kretek* (clove cigarettes) is to your liking, then a trip to Kudus may appeal.

Central Java's capital, Semarang, is located here, and while it won't hold your interest for too long, it is a gateway to the splendid (and often forgotten) Karimunjawa Islands.

Semarang

☎024 / POP 1.4 MILLION

The bustling, north-coast port of Semarang is a schizophrenic city, embodying the polarity of modern Java. On one side, this old Dutch administrative centre is still deeply traditional, with a fantastically atmospheric, if decrepit, port district full of rambling colonial architecture and a vibrant Chinese quarter. On the other side, the commercial area around Simpang Lima (Five Ways), with its malls, clogged freeways and business hotels, is emblematic of Java's sudden and dramatic shift into the 21st century.

It may well be the provincial capital of Central Java, but Semarang lacks the pull of Solo and Yogyakarta. It does, however, have some appealing corners and good connections (including international flights) so you may well pass through.

Sights

Old City NEIGHBOURHOOD

(Outstadt) Semarang's richly atmospheric old city, often referred to as the Outstadt, its Dutch name, is well worth investigating. Sadly, most of the area's tremendous stock of colonial buildings are in an advanced state of decay, seemingly unloved and left to rot by the city authorities.

At the heart of this old port quarter, is the elegant church **Gereja Blenduk** (Jl Jenderal Suprapto), built in 1753, which has a huge cupola, a spectacular baroque-style organ and an unusual wooden pulpit. Knock on the door and the caretaker will let you in. Towards the river from the church there are dozens of crumbling old Dutch warehouses, municipal buildings and townhouses with shuttered windows, flaking plaster and peeling paint. Be sure to drop by the **Semarang Gallery** (☎024 355 2099; www.galerisemarang.com; Jl Taman Srigunting 5-6), dedicated to Indonesian contemporary art – it promotes young talented artists and is located in an evocative old warehouse.

The old city is very prone to flooding; if you visit during the rainy season it may not even be possible to explore some of the back streets.

Back towards the centre of the city, Pasar Johar is one of Semarang's main markets. Facing the market is Semarang's **Mesjid Besar** (Grand Mosque; Jl Pemuda).

Chinatown NEIGHBOURHOOD

(S of Jl Jenderal Suprapto) Semarang's Chinatown is atmospheric and worth investigating (particularly around the riverside Gang Lombok), rich with pagodas, Chinese pharmacists, fortune tellers and food stalls. Chinese characters are rarely on show (the Chinese language was long discriminated against by law) but Semarang is Indonesia's most Chinese city and the depth of culture evident here is compelling.

The focus of the entire community is the classically Chinese **Tay Kak Sie temple** (Gang Lombok), dating back to 1746, with its huge drums and incense-clouded interior. This temple looks over the Sungai Semarang river, where there's a model of one of legendary Chinese explorer Admiral Cheng Ho's ships (he visited Java several times). Next to the temple is Pujasera Tay Yak Sie, a Chinese food court and also a community hall used for martial arts. Sadly the river is grossly polluted these days and its odor is not easy on the nostrils.

Lawang Sewu HISTORIC BUILDING

(Jl Permuda; admission 10,000Rp; ⌚7am-9pm) Semarang's most famous landmark Lawang Sewu ('Thousand Doors') is actually two colossal colonial buildings that were once one of the headquarters of the Indonesian railways, during the Dutch era. Some renovation has recently been completed but most

Central Semarang

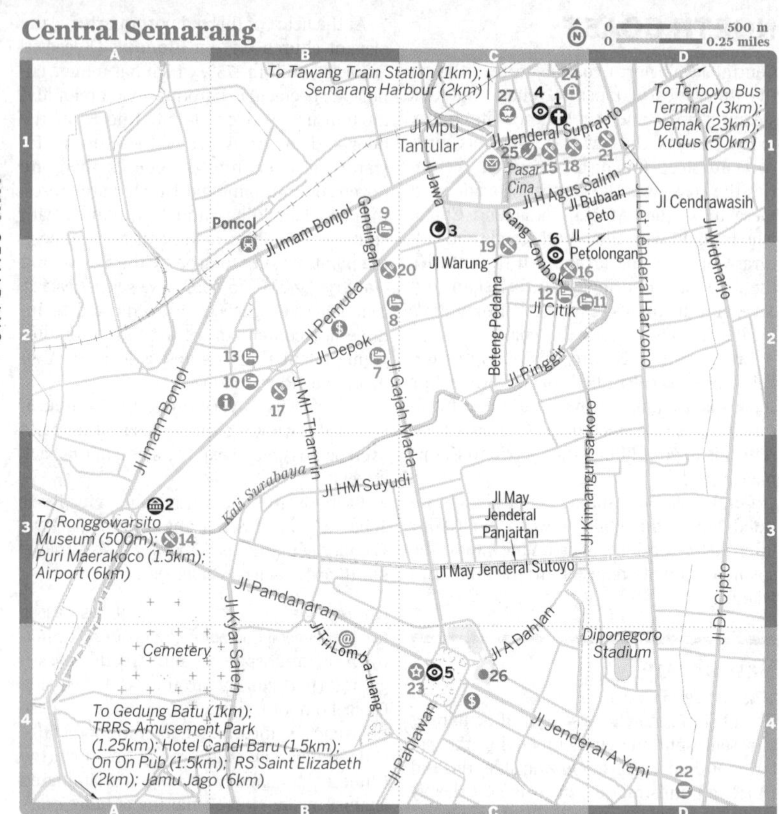

of the main L-shaped structure remains closed to visitors. Nevertheless, you can wander the empty corridors of the other huge building, where clerks and engineers once worked, and admire the features (including some magnificent stained glass and marble staircases). There are also displays about the ongoing restoration process.

The building is regarded as a haunted house by locals, for during WWII, the Japanese occupied the building and used the dungeons for interrogation. You can tour the flooded basement on a guided tour (not always available in English). You can see where many lost their lives and hear the gruesome tales of the atrocities that were committed here; a deeply moving experience, particularly at night.

Gedung Batu TEMPLE
(Sam Po Kong Temple; admission free to worshippers, viewing compound 10,000Rp, temples 30,000Rp; ⏲24hr) This huge Chinese temple complex stands 5km southwest of the centre of the city. It was built in honour of Admiral Cheng Ho, the famous Muslim eunuch of the Ming dynasty, who led a Chinese fleet on seven expeditions to Java and other parts of Southeast and West Asia in the early 15th century. Cheng Ho has since become a saint known as Sam Po Kong. He first arrived in Java in 1405 and is believed to have helped spread Islam.

Gedung Batu has three main temple buildings, and many smaller structures. Most are classically Indo-Chinese, with soaring pagoda-style roofs, massive drums and plenty of Chinese lanterns and dragons. But Sam Po Kong temple is quite different: it has an inner chamber in the form of a cave flanked by two great dragons, hence the temple's popular name, *gedung batu* (stone building). Inside the cave is a gilded statue of Sam Po Kong, surrounded by fairy lights.

Central Semarang

Sights
1 Gereja Blenduk C1
2 Lawang Sewu A3
3 Mesjid Besar C1
4 Old City C1
5 Simpang Lima C4
6 Tay Kak Sie Temple C2

Sleeping
7 Gumaya Tower Hotel B2
8 Hotel Quirin B2
9 Hotel Surya B1
10 Novotel Semarang B2
11 Roemah Pantes C2
12 Tjiang Residence C2
13 Whiz Hotel B2

Eating
14 Holiday Restaurant A3
15 Ikan Bakar Cianjur C1
16 Lumpia Gang Lombok C2
17 Paragon Mall B2
18 Sate & Gule Kabing C1
19 Semawis Night Market C2
20 Toko Oen B2
21 Toko Wingko Babad D1

Drinking
22 Blue Lotus Coffee House D4

Entertainment
23 E Plaza C4

Shopping
24 Semarang Gallery C1

Information
25 Telkom C1

Transport
26 Garuda C4
27 Pelni C1

Note that women are not allowed to enter the temples if they are menstruating, but can visit the complex.

To get to Gedung Batu, take the Damri bus 2 from Jl Pemuda to Karang Ayu (a suburb west of central Semarang), and then an *angkot* to the temple. It takes about half an hour from central Semarang.

Ronggowarsito Museum MUSEUM
(www.museumronggowarsito.org; Jl Abdulrachman; admission 4000Rp; ⏲8am-2pm Tue-Sun) Ronggowarsito Museum is a large provincial museum with antiquities, crafts including batik and *wayang* puppets, and assorted fossils and curios collected from all over the state. One of the most interesting exhibits is a recycled stone panel from the Mantingan mosque – one side shows Islamic motifs, while the reverse shows the original Hindu-Buddhist scene. Javanese dance displays are held here on Friday morning. It's approximately 2km before the airport.

Semarang Harbour HARBOUR
Semarang harbour is worth a look to see *pinisi* and other traditional ocean-going vessels that dock at Tambak Lorok wharves.

Sleeping

Semarang lacks decent, really cheap hotels. Backpackers be prepared to fork out more here. Midrange accommodation is good value however.

TOP CHOICE **Tjiang Residence** GUESTHOUSE $
(☎354 0330; www.tjiangresidence.com; Jl Gang Pinggir 24; d incl breakfast 150,000Rp; ❄📶) In the heart of Chintown, this fine new hotel makes a superb budget base just a short stroll from the Tay Kak Sie temple. The gleaming scarlet door, Chinese calligraphy and oriental design of the hotel's frontage sets a dramatic tone, and staff could not be more welcoming and helpful. All 24 rooms are immaculately clean and great value, with spring mattresses and soft linen, LCD TVs, reading lights and tea-making facilties, though they are small and all (but one) lack windows.

Novotel Semarang HOTEL $$
(☎356 3000; www.novotel.com; Jl Pemuda 123; r from 438,000Rp; ❄@📶🏊) Enjoys a good location between the old city and Simpang Lima and its facilities are first class, with an outdoor pool, a state-of-the-art gym and a spa with moderate prices. Rooms are contemporary, spacious and comfortable, many with city vistas. There are two cafe-restaurants and the breakfast buffet is excellent.

Hotel Surya HOTEL $$
(☎356 2000; www.suryahotel.net; Jl Imam Bonjol 28; r 266,000-310,000Rp, ste 370,000Rp; ❄📶)

WORTH A TRIP

JAMU (HERBAL MEDICINES)

Semarang is known for its *jamu* and has two large manufacturers; both have museums and offer tours. **Jamu Nyonya Meneer** (☎658 3088; www.nyonyameneer.com; Jl Raya Kaligawe, Km4; ⊙museum 10am-3.30pm Sun-Fri) is near the bus terminal, while **Jamu Jago** (☎747 2762; www.jago.co.id; Jl Setia Budi 273) is 6km south of the city on the Ambarawa road.

Represents a pretty good deal, though the neat, functional and spotless modern rooms (some with very soft matresses) are not nearly as smart as the hip lobby would indicate. There's a lift (elevator) and a cafe-restaurant.

Whiz Hotel HOTEL **$$**
(☎356 6999; www.whizhotels.com/semarang; Jl Kapten Piere Tendean 9; s/d 245,000/325,000Rp; ❄@🛜) Sharp-looking green-and-white no-frills hotel with competitive rates for its good quality, inviting, though slightly cramped rooms. Fine if you're after a moderately priced place to kip, but don't expect much in the way of service. Breakfast is very basic.

Gumaya Tower Hotel LUXURY HOTEL **$$$**
(☎355 1999; www.gumayatowerhotel.com; Jl Gajah Mada 59-61; r from 770,000Rp; ❄@🛜🏊) Towering over the city this luxury edifice has understated, well-designed rooms, all with large LCD TVs, fast wi-fi and gorgeous bathrooms with tubs. There's an infinity pool, and panoramic city views from the top-deck Sky Line bar. Popular with business travellers.

Hotel Quirin HOTEL **$$**
(☎354 7063; www.quirinhotel.com; Jl Gajah Mada 44-52; r 285,000-400,000Rp, f 530,000Rp; ❄🛜) A motel-style place that benefited from a minimalist overhaul a few years back. Rooms are modern, comfortable and in good condition. There's a sleek lobby, a cafe-restaurant and room service.

Roemah Pantes HOTEL **$**
(☎358 0628; Jl Kalikuping 18; tw/tr incl breakfast 200,000/225,000Rp) In a hard-to-find lane close to Gang Lombok in the heart of Chinatown, this small hotel has seven fairly spacious, clean, tiled rooms with duvets and hot-water bathrooms. No English is spoken.

Hotel Candi Baru HOTEL **$**
(☎831 5272; Jl Rinjani 21; r incl breakfast 85,000-260,000Rp, VIP 320,000Rp; ❄🛜) In a magnificent, though faded, hillside mansion (with the occasional ghost) Candi Baru certainly doesn't lack grandeur or atmosphere. Rooms, from economy to near-palatial, are simply enormous, the best with renovated bathrooms. It's about 4km south of the centre and also home to the On On pub.

Eating & Drinking

Semarang has a large Chinese population, and this is a good place to sample traditional dishes. If you're here on a weekend head straight to the **Semawis night market** (⊙5-11pm Fri-Sun) on Jl Warung for fine Chinese-style noodles, tofu and *babi sate* (pork sate). There's always a sociable atmosphere here, with a bit of low-key karaoke crooning and fortune telling going on.

Simpang Lima is another good bet in the evenings with dozens of *kaki lima* (food carts) set up around the huge square, serving up snacks and offering traditional *lesahan* dining (on straw mats).

The spanking new **Paragon Mall** (www.paragonsemarang.com; Jl Permuda) has Indonesian and Asian restaurants, cafes, and also a large supermarket in the basement for supplies. Plaza Simpang Lima also has an extensive food court on the 4th floor.

TOP CHOICE **Ikan Bakar Cianjur** INDONESIAN **$$**
(☎356 2333; www.ibcgroup.co.id; Jl Jenderal Suprapto 19; meals 25,000-80,000Rp) In a glorious, senstively restored building (Semarang's former courthouse), this restaurant has art-deco chandeliers, antique tiles, soaring ceilings and real colonial character. There's a good choice of snacks and meals – *gurame* fish (from 48,000Rp) is a house speciality – as well as cold beer, coffee and juices. It's right opposite the Gereja Blenduk.

Lumpia Gang Lombok CHINESE **$**
(Gang Lombok II; meals 10,000Rp; ⊙8am-4.30pm) Riverside warung, next to the Tay Kak Sie temple, where you can feast on delicious prawn *lumpia* (spring rolls) that are served with pickled cucumber, lettuce and shredded vegetables. It's a tiny place where you chow down rubbing elbows with other diners.

Holiday Restaurant CHINESE **$$**
(☎841 3371; Jl Pandanaran 6; meals 40,000-100,000Rp; 📝) This new smart two-storey restaurant gets the local Chinese population's

vote as the best place to eat in town, and with super-fresh seafood, excellent chicken and duck, and good snacks (try the shrimp toast) it's not hard to see why. Book ahead.

Toko Wingko Babad BAKERY $
(☎354 2064; Jl Cendrawasih 14; cakes 2400-3200Rp) A simply brilliant, anacronistic bakery and store where you can roll back the years and sample the delicious *wingko* – wonderful coconut cakes, which are plain, or flavoured with banana or durian, and served warm.

Blue Lotus Coffee House CAFE
(Jl Ahmad Yani 197; snacks & meals from 10,000-25000Rp; ⏲9am-9pm Tue-Sun; 📶) Modish cafe-restaurant that serves the best coffee in town, including *kopi luwak* and cappuccinos. Also good for a bite to eat with sandwiches and full meals (try the chicken cordon bleu with mash). The house cheesecake is fabulously creamy.

Toko Oen INTERNATIONAL $
(☎354 1683; www.tokooen.com/en; Jl Pemuda 52; mains from 20,000Rp) For the quintessential colonial experience this venerable old place is worth a visit. It's well past its heyday, but prices are actually quite affordable and it's not hard to imagine the scene back in 1936 when Oen opened. It sells snacks, Chinese and Indonesian food, a few Western dishes, cold beer, coffee and (dry) biscuits and cakes, but people travel for miles to taste the famous tutti frutti ice cream.

Sate & Gule Kabing SATE $
(☎024 354 9692; Jl Jenderal Suprapto 29; meals 30,000Rp; ⏲11.30am-10pm) Almost opposite the Gereja Blenduk church, this modest restaurant serves up goat meat and nothing else. Order a mixed sate and you'll get six skewers of grilled cuts including liver, served with pepper, slices of red onion and coconut-flavoured sauce. *Gule* is goat meat soup.

On On Pub PUB
(☎831 3968; Jl Rinjani 21) Classic expat hangout in the hilly south of town, this pub sells ice-cold draught Bintang ('towers' for sharing are available for 190,000Rp) as well as Western grub – try the German mixed grill (30,000Rp). There's a pool table and a darts board.

☆ Entertainment

E Plaza CLUB, CINEMA
(www.eplaza.co.id; Jl Ruko Gajahmada Lantai II 29; club entrance 50,000Rp) Semarang can be lacking when it comes to nightlife but this complex, right by the Simpang Lima, is highly popular and contains an upmarket club, three-screen cinema and lounge bar. It draws a young energetic crowd and is a good bet for a night out.

TBRS Amusement Park AMUSEMENT PARK
(☎831 1220; Jl Sriwijaya 29, Tegalwareng) For more traditional entertainment, this amusement park holds *wayang orang* performances every Saturday from 7pm to midnight, and *wayang kulit* most Thursdays. Check the latest schedule at the tourist office.

ℹ Information

ABN Amro (Jl Jenderal A Yani) Bank just off Simpang Lima.

Asanet (Jl Tlogo Bayan; per hour 4000Rp) Neighbourhood internet cafe.

BCA Bank (Jl Pemuda 90-92) Changes most currencies.

Central Java Tourist Office (☎351 5451; www.central-java-tourism.com; Jl Pemuda 147; ⏲8am-3pm Mon-Fri) The Central Java Tourist Office is certainly worth dropping by with good booklets and information devoted to the city and entire Central Java region. Transport and hotel information about the Karimunjaya Islands is reliable.

Main post office (Jl Pemuda) On a busy intersection near the Chinese market.

RS Saint Elizabeth (☎831 0076; www.rs-elisabeth.com; Jl Kawi) The best hospital in town. It's in the Candi Baru district.

Telkom (Jl Jenderal Suprapto 7)

ℹ Getting There & Away

AIR Semarang airport (which should boast a modern terminal by 2015) is a busy little airport with two international and many domestic connections. **AirAsia** (☎5050 5088; www.airasia.com) flies to Kuala Lumpur and Jakarta. **Batavia Air** (☎762 5171; www.batavia-air.co.id) flies to Singapore and Jakarta. **Garuda** (☎845 4737; www.garuda-indonesia.com; Jl Ahmad Dahlan, Hotel Horison) links Semarang with Jakarta. **Lion Air** (☎080 477 8899; www.lionair.co.id) connects Semarang with Jakarta. **Kal Star** (☎021 2934 3456; www.kalstaronline.com) flies to Ketapang, Pangkalanbun, Sampit and Pontianak. **Merpati** (☎080 4162 1621; www.merpati.co.id) flies to Bandung and Sampit. **Sriwijaya Air** (☎021 640 5566; www.sriwijayaair-online.com) flies to Banjarmasin, Jakarta and Surabaya, and **Wings Air** (☎080 477 8899; www2.lionair.co.id) flies to Denpasar and Surabaya.

Departure tax for domestic/international flights is 30,000/100,000Rp.

TRANSPORT FROM SEMARANG

Bus

DESTINATION	COST (RP; ECONOMY/AIR-CON)	DURATION (HR)
Cirebon	50,000/68,000	7
Jepara	18,000/25,000	2½
Kudus	10,000/13,000	1¼
Pekalongan	22,000/31,000	3
Wonosobo	30,000/38,000	4
Yogyakarta	31,000/40,000	4

Train

DESTINATION	COST (RP)	DURATION (HR)	FREQUENCY
Cirebon	125,000-295,000	3-4¾	8 daily
Jakarta	260,000-310,000	6	5 daily
Pekalongan	35,000-85,000	1¼	8 daily

BOAT For ferry information, the **Pelni office** (☎354 0381, 354 6722; www.pelni.co.id; Jl Mpu Tantular 25; ⏲ticketing 8am-2pm Mon-Thu, to noon Fri-Sat) has timetables you can consult after its ticket sales windows shut (around 5pm). There are economy/1st class boats to the following Kalimantan ports about every three or four days: Kumai (148,000/561,000Rp), Sampit (167,000/638,000Rp) and Pontianak (218,000/844,000Rp). Pelni ships also sail to Makassar (from 309,000/1,212,000Rp).

BUS Semarang's Terboyo bus terminal is 4km east of town, just off the road to Kudus. Air-con minibuses also travel to destinations across the island, including Pekalongan (40,000Rp), Wonosobo (45,000Rp), Solo (42,000Rp), Yogyakarta (50,000Rp) and Surabaya (100,000Rp). Agents for luxury buses and air-conditioned minibuses include **Cipa Ganti** (☎024 9128 8588; www.cipaganti.co.id; Jl Sultan Agung 92), **Rahayu** (☎024 354 3935; Jl Let Jenderal Haryono 9) and **Nusantara Indah** (☎355 3984; Jl Let Jenderal Haryono 9B).

TRAIN Semarang lies on the main north coast Jakarta–Cirebon–Surabaya train route. **Tawang** (☎354 4544) is Semarang's main station for all exclusive- and business-class services. Economy-class trains depart from Semarang's Poncol train station.

Getting Around

TO/FROM THE AIRPORT Ahmad Yani airport is 6km west of the centre. A taxi into town costs 40,000Rp (there's an official desk at arrivals), and around 30,000Rp when returning to the airport using the taxi meter.

PUBLIC TRANSPORT City buses charge a fixed 3000Rp fare and terminate at the Terboyo bus terminal. Buses 1, 2 and 3 run south along Jl Pemuda to Candi Baru. Short becak rides cost around 5000Rp, a ride of more than 3km around 10,000Rp. Semarang has plenty of metered taxis, call **Bluebird** (☎760 1234) or **Kosti taxis** (☎761 3333).

Ambarawa

☎0298 / POP 89,000

Ambarawa, 28km south of Semarang, was once the site of a Japanese internment camp where up to 15,000 Europeans were held during WWII. Today it's a market town that's of interest to trainspotters as the site of the **Ambarawa Train Station Museum** (Museum Kereta Api Ambarawa; admission 5000Rp; ⏲8am-4pm), located in the premises of the old Koening Willem I station, which opened in 1873. Today's museum has exhibits of rail memorabilia, old Morse code telegraph equipment and 21 steam locomotives built between 1891 and 1928.

Though the line has closed, groups of (up to 100) passengers can charter a train for the 18km round trip from Ambarawa to Bedono for 2,700,000Rp. Book through the **Ambarawa train station** (☎591 035) as far in advance as you can. Between June and August, Dutch tourists charter a train several days a week, so it may be worth showing up and seeing if you can hitch a ride.

The museum is a couple of kilometres outside town, just off the road to Magelang. Ambarawa has hotels, but nearby Bandungan is a nicer place to stay.

Nestled in a 22-hectare coffee plantation at an altitude of 900m, the **Mesa Stila Resort** (☎596 333; www.mesahotelsandresorts.com/mesastila; Pingit; villas from US$420; ❄), formerly the Losari Coffee Plantation, is one of Indonesia's most special (and expensive) hotels. The location, ringed by volcanoes, is sublime and commodious villas make the most of the stunning views. All sorts of themed spa packages are offered: from 'de-stress and indulgence' to 'escapism' that make the most of the outstanding spa and fitness facilities. There's an organic garden that provides for the resort's two restaurants, or you can sample the plantation's organic tea and coffee in the historic Club House. It's near Pingit village, some 12km southwest of Ambarawa. From Ambarawa, it's best to take a taxi (40,000Rp) to the resort.

Ambarawa can be reached by bus from Semarang (9000Rp, one hour), and Yogyakarta (32,000Rp, three hours) via Magelang.

Bandungan

☎0298

Bandungan is a pleasant hill resort at 980m, but the main attractions are the nearby Gedung Songo temples and train museum at Ambarawa. Try to avoid weekends when Semarang folk flood here to escape the north coast heat.

There are several hotels. **Hotel Azaya** (☎711 445; www.azayabandungan.com; r from 320,000Rp; ❄📶) has attractive, recently renovated rooms that are light and airy. You'll enjoy the fine views from its hilltop perch, plus there's a colonial-style restaurant and tennis court. In town, **Hotel Parahita** (☎711 017; r 80,000Rp) has basic rooms and a friendly owner (who speaks no English).

Buses run directly from Semarang to Bandungan (12,000Rp). If you are coming from the south, get off at Ambarawa and take an *angkot* to Bandungan (2000Rp).

Sights

Gedung Songo Temples TEMPLE
(admission 5000Rp; ⏲7am-5pm) These nine (Gedung Songo means 'nine buildings' in Javanese) small Hindu temples are scattered along the tops of the foothills around Gunung Ungaran. The temples are not huge, but the setting is magnificent. The 1000m perch gives one of the most spectacular views in Java – south across shimmering Danau Rawa Pening to Gunung Merbabu and, behind it, smouldering Gunung Merapi; and west to Gunung Sumbing and Gunung Sundoro. Arrive early in the morning for the best views.

WORTH A TRIP

PEKALONGAN

Less than 100km west of Semarang, the sleepy, steamy coastal city of Pekalongan is known as Kota Batik (Batik City) throughout Indonesia. The one outstanding sight is the **Batik Museum** (Jl Majapahit 7A; admission free; ⏲9am-1pm Mon-Sat). It houses one of the world's most important collections, including many antique pieces, in a stately art-deco structure, the former old city hall. Here you can check out Pekalongan's unique batik style, which is less formal, more colourful and more innovative in design than those in Central Java, with apparent influences from China, Arabia and Europe.

The lanes along Jl Blimbing in the north of the city form the city's venerable Chinese quarter, with pagodas and old terraced houses. To the east, Jl Patiunus and the streets leading off it make up the Arab quarter, another good area for batik. Not far to the south is the town's main batik market, **Pasar Banjarsari**.

You'll find budget hotels opposite the train station on Jl Gajah Mada, including **Hotel Damai** (☎422 768; Jl Gajah Mada 7; r with fan/air-con 65,000/170,000Rp; ❄). For more creature comforts head to **Hotel Dafam Pekalongan** (☎028 5441 1555; www.dafamhotels.com; Jl Urip Sumoharjo 53; r 320,000-490,000Rp; ❄📶).

Pekalongan is located on the main Jakarta–Surabaya highway and train route. The bus terminal, 4km southeast of town, has frequent buses to Semarang (normal/air-con 21,000/30,000Rp, three hours) and Cirebon (36,000/46,000Rp, four hours). Train tickets can be hard to find on the busy nothern coastal route, so book ahead.

Built in the 8th century AD and devoted to Shiva and Vishnu, five of the temples are in good condition after major restoration in the 1980s; however, most of the carvings were lost. A hill path goes past three temple groupings – the temples at the third grouping are the most impressive. Halfway up, the trail leads down to a ravine and hot sulphur springs, and then up again to the final temple and its expansive views. The 3km loop can be walked in an hour, but allow longer to savour the atmosphere. Horses can also be hired.

The temples are about 5km from Bandungan. Take a Sumawono bus (2000Rp) to the turn-off to the temples. Buses also run from Semarang (10,000Rp) and Ambarawa (4000Rp). The final 3km uphill to Gedung Songo (3000Rp) can be tackled either by foot or *ojek* (10,000Rp).

Demak

Demak, 25km east of Semarang, was the springboard from which Islam made its leap into Java. As the capital of the island's first Islamic state, it was from here that the Hindu Majapahit kingdom was conquered and much of Java's interior was converted.

The town's economic heyday has now passed and even the sea has retreated several kilometres, leaving this former port landlocked. But the role this small town once played has not been forgotten.

Buses from either Semarang or Kudus (both 7000Rp) can drop you right outside the great mosque.

Sights

Mesjid Agung MOSQUE

Demak's venerable Mesjid Agung is one of the archipelago's foremost Muslim pilgrimage sites.

Constructed in 1466, this is Java's oldest mosque, built with a triple-tiered roof. Legend has it that it was built from wood by the *wali songo* (nine holy men) in a single night. Four main pillars in the central hall were originally made by four of the Muslim saints, and one pillar, erected by Sunan Kalijaga, is said to be made from scraps of timber magically fused together. In the grounds there's a rickety-looking minaret that looks more like an electricity pylon.

Today the history of the mosque is outlined in the small **museum** (admission by donation; ⌚irregular, in theory 8am-5pm) to the side. Some of the original woodwork, including magnificent carved doors, is on display.

The tombs of Demak's rulers are next to the mosque; the tomb of Raden Trenggono (leader of Demak's greatest military campaigns), attracts the most pilgrims.

Mesjid Agung is on the main road in the centre of town, beside the huge grassy *alun-alun*.

Kudus

☎0291 / POP 92,000

Kudus takes its name from the word *al-Quds* – the Arabic name for Jerusalem. Founded by the Muslim saint Sunan Kudus, it's an important pilgrimage site. Like much of Java, Kudus retains links with its Hindu past and the slaughter of cows is still forbidden here.

The town is moderately attractive, with an elongated main street that contains a huge tobacco factory. This is where the first clove cigarettes were produced, and today Kudus is still a stronghold of *kretek* production – there are said to be 25 factories in the town. Sukun, a manufacturer outside the town, still produces *rokok klobot* (clove tobacco rolled in corn leaves).

Sights & Activities

Old Town NEIGHBOURHOOD

West of the river, **Kauman**, the oldest part of town, has narrow streets and is slightly reminiscent of a *kasbah* in the Middle East, with traders selling religious souvenirs, dates, prayer beads and caps.

Here you'll find the **Mesjid Al-Manar** (also known as Al-Aqsa and Menera); constructed in 1549 by Sunan Kudus and famous for its red-brick *menara* (minaret). This minaret may have originally been the watchtower of the Hindu temple the mosque is said to be built on – its curiously squat form and flared sides certainly have more in common with Balinese than with Islamic architecture. Inside the main temple Muslim worshippers pray before a Hindu-style brick gateway, a fascinating juxtaposition of Javanese religious heritage.

From the courtyards behind the mosque, a palm-lined path leads to the imposing **Tomb of Sunan Kudus**, shrouded with a curtain of lace. The narrow doorway, draped with heavy gold-embroidered curtains, leads through to an inner chamber and the grave.

Kretek Museum MUSEUM

(Jl Museum Kretek Jati Kulon; donations accepted; ⌚7.30am-4pm; ❄) This museum has some interesting exhibits of the history of *kretek* production, including some fascinating old photographs and machinery. Almost all explanations are in Bahasa Indonesia but there's a guide here who speaks good English. Next door, Rumah Adat is a traditional wooden Kudus house exhibiting the fabulous carving work the town is noted for.

Djarum Kretek Factory FACTORY

(Jl A Yani) Djarum, which started in 1951, is the main employer and third-biggest *kretek* manufacturer in Indonesia. Ninety-minute tours of its modern factory are available between 8am and 11am.

Swimming SWIMMING

Kudus is a hot town. If you want to cool off Omah Mode (p154) has a lovely pool area (25,000Rp, open 6am to 8pm) and there's a large water boom (15,000Rp) just behind the Kretek Museum with slides and a channel that's ideal for kids. There's also a pool at the Hotel Notasari Permai (p154; 12,500Rp to non-residents).

Sleeping & Eating

Kudus has several good inexpensive hotels, all are on or just off the main drag Jl Ahmed Yani.

You have to try *soto kudus* (a rich chicken soup), which the town is famous for. It's usually served up bright yellow (from turmeric) with lots of garlic, and the chicken is sometimes shredded. *Jenang kudus* is a sweet that's made of glutinous rice, brown sugar and coconut.

The best place for inexpensive food and local specialities is **Taman Bojana**, a food-stall complex on the main roundabout in the centre of town.

Wisma Karima GUESTHOUSE $

(☎431 712; Jl Museum Kretek Jati Kulon III; r incl breakfast with fan 55,000-90,000Rp, with air-con 130,000Rp; ❄) Just off the highway on the south side of town, this guesthouse is orderly and good value. It's run by a welcoming family and has nine rooms, some quite spacious, but all a little old-fashioned.

Hotel Kenari Asri HOTEL $$

(☎446 200; www.hotelkenari-central.com; Jl Kenari II; r incl breakfast 250,000-350,000Rp, ste

KRETEK CIGARETTES

If Java has a smell, it is the sweet, spicy scent of the clove-flavoured *kretek*. The *kretek* has only been around since the early 20th century, but today the addiction is nationwide and accounts for 90% of the cigarette market, while sales of *rokok putih* (cigarettes without cloves) are languishing. So high is the consumption of cloves used in the *kretek* industry that Indonesia, traditionally a supplier of cloves in world markets, has become a substantial net importer from other world centres.

The invention of the *kretek* is attributed to a Kudus man, Jamahri, who claimed the cigarettes relieved his asthma. Later another local, Nitisemitol, who had a gift for business, started selling the cigarettes commercially. He mixed tobacco with crushed cloves rolled in *rokok klobot* (corn leaves); this was the prototype for his Bal Tiga brand, which he began selling in 1906.

Kudus became the centre for the *kretek* industry and at one stage the town had more than 200 factories, though today fewer than 50 cottage industries and a few large factories remain. Rationalisation in the industry has seen *kretek* production dominated by big producers, such as Sampoerna in Surabaya, Gudang Garam in Kediri, and Djarum in Kudus.

Although filtered *kretek* are produced by modern machinery – Djarum churns out up to 140 million a day – nonfiltered *kretek* are still rolled by hand on simple wooden rolling machines. The best rollers can turn out around 4000 cigarettes in a day.

As to the claim that *kretek* are good for smoker's cough, cloves are a natural anaesthetic and so do have a numbing effect on the throat. Any other claims to aiding health stop there – the tar and nicotine levels in the raw, slowly cured tobaccos are so high that some countries have banned or restricted their import.

Filtered *kretek* now dominate the market. There are 'mild' versions on offer, but for the *kretek* purist, the conical, crackling, nonfiltered *kretek* has no substitute – Sampoerna's Dji Sam Soe ('234') brand is regarded as the Rolls Royce of *kretek*. To see Sampoerna rollers in action visit the factory in Surabaya.

600,000Rp; ❄📶) Down a little lane off the main drag, this gaudy hotel looks like a fancy wedding cake, rising up in levels from the road. Its rooms, all recently renovated, are in excellent condition, with new mattresses, wi-fi, LCD TV and modern furniture.

Hotel Notasari Permai HOTEL **$**
(☎437 245; Jl Kepodang 12; r incl breakfast with fan 100,000Rp, with air-con 200,000-300,000Rp; ❄📶🏊) An ageing hotel with plain rooms; however the 18m pool at the rear certainly is a bonus if you're feeling the heat.

Omah Mode FOOD COURT **$**
(Jl A Yani 38; pool admission 20,000Rp; ⏲8am-8pm) A surprise find in downtown Kudus, this lovely colonial building (dating from 1836) is fun to explore with lots of stalls selling fashionable clothes and a delightful swimming pool at the rear. You'll also find food stations here offering everything from Thai food to traditional Kudus fare.

Rumah Makan Lembur Kuring INDONESIAN **$**
(Jl Agil Kusumadya 35; mains 12,000-30,000Rp) A large, pleasant restaurant complete with water features where you can tuck into tasty Sundanese and Javanese food under a shady pagoda.

Information

The **BII Bank** (Jl Dr Lukmonohadi) has an ATM, and there are several more beside the Taman Bojana food complex (which also has public toilets).

Getting There & Away

Kudus is on the main Semarang–Surabaya road. The bus terminal is around 4km south of town. City minibuses run from behind the bus terminal to the town centre (2000Rp), or you can take a becak. Buses go from Kudus to Demak (5000Rp, 50 minutes) and Semarang (15,000Rp, 1½ hours), while minibuses go to Colo (6000Rp). Buses to Jepara (10,000Rp, 1¼ hours) leave from the Jetak subterminal, 4km west of town (2000Rp by minibus).

Jepara

☎0291 / POP 55,000

Famed as the best woodcarving centre in Java, Jepara's booming furniture business has brought it all the trappings of prosperity. As you enter town you'll pass dozens of furniture showrooms offering contemporary, 'distressed' and 'antique' designs. Even the fields here are full of wood carvings and half-finished wardrobes rather than rice and vegetables.

The town's broad avenues, relaxed atmosphere and nearby beaches make it a tranquil spot to take a break from the road. The area is home to quite a few expats and visited by buyers from all over the world so it's more cosmopolitan than many Indonesian towns.

Jepara is also a jumping-off point for the Karimunjaya Islands.

Sights

Museum RA Kartini MUSEUM
(admission 2000Rp; ⏲8am-2pm) On the north side of the *alun-alun* this museum is dedicated to one of Indonesia's most celebrated women (see boxed text, above). One room is devoted to Kartini and contains portraits of her (and her family) plus memorabilia, including letters. Other rooms contain assorted archaeological findings, including a *yoni* and *lingga*, and local art and artefacts, such as fine woodcarvings and ceramics. There's also the 16m skeleton of a whale.

It is sometimes possible to visit Kartini's old rooms – if you contact the tourist office first – which are now local government offices on the eastern side of the *alun-alun*.

Benteng VOC FORTRESS
Heading north from the museum, cross the river and veer left up the hill to the old Dutch Benteng VOC. Over the last 50 years the fort's stonework has been pillaged, but the site has good views across town to the Java Sea. The cemetery nearby has some Dutch graves.

Pantai Kartini BEACH
The most popular, though touristy, beach is Pantai Kartini, 3km west of town – locals often call it Pemandian. From there you can rent a boat (around 90,000Rp return) to nearby Pulau Panjang, which has excellent white-sand beaches.

Sleeping

Ocean View Residence HOTEL, APARTMENTS **$$**
(☎429 9022; www.oceanview-residence.com; r/apartment 650,000/750,000Rp; ❄📶) Down a narrow lane that zigzags through rice fields, this beachside resort is a development of modernist units – beautifully finished rooms and spacious apartments with all mod cons – that match natural materials and modish furniture well. It's a pity that the beach in front is scruffy. The complex has a cafe-restaurant.

AN INDO ICON

Raden Ajeng Kartini, a writer, feminist and progressive thinker, was born in 1879, the daughter of the *bupati* (regent) of Jepara. She grew up in the *bupati*'s residence, on the eastern side of the *alun-alun*, excelled at school and learnt to speak fluent Dutch by the age of 12. It was in this residence that Kartini spent her *pingit* ('confinement' in Javanese), when girls from 12 to 16 are kept in virtual imprisonment and forbidden to venture outside the family home. She later used her education to campaign for women's rights and against colonialism, before dying at the age of 24 just after the birth of her first child. A national holiday is held on 21 April, known as 'Kartini Day', in recognition of her work.

Hotel Elim HOTEL **$**
(☎591 406; Jl Dr Soetomo 13-15; r with fan/air-con from 80,000/165,000Rp; ❄) Representing a pretty good deal, this place has a selection of slightly old-fashioned rooms which are nevertheless kept clean and in decent condition. Manager Thomas is helpful and can assist with transport, and there's a pleasant outdoor restaurant.

Kalingga Star HOTEL **$**
(☎591 054; Jl Dr Soetomo 16; r incl breakfast 165,000-375,000Rp; ❄📶) The piped muzak and brown uniforms set a neglected tone at this large, ageing hotel which has a huge range of tiled rooms in different price categories; most are spacious but a bit soulless. The economy rooms are OK for a night and have air-conditioning.

Eating

Yam-Yam INTERNATIONAL **$$**
(☎598 755; Jl Pantai Karang Kebagusan, Km5; meals from 50,000Rp) A stylish beachside restaurant with a pool and excellent Thai, Indonesian and Western food, including great pizza. Service is sharp and friendly, there's a well-stocked bar and also live music here some nights.

Pondok Rasa JAVANESE **$**
(☎591 025; Jl Pahlawan II; mains 15,000-65,000Rp; ✎) Inland, just across the river from the *alun-alun*, Rasa is a traditional Javanese restaurant with a pleasant garden setting and tasty Indonesian food served *lesahan* style. There's lots of choice for vegetarians, or try the *gurame* (from 45,000Rp).

Shopping

Intricately carved *jati* (teak) and mahogany furniture and relief panels are on display at shops and factories all around Jepara. However, the main carpentry centre is the village of **Tahunan**, 4km south of Jepara on the road to Kudus, where it's wall-to-wall furniture.

Brightly coloured, Sumba-style ikat weavings, using traditional motifs, are woven and sold in the village of **Torso**, situated 14km south of Jepara and 2km off the main road. Other original designs are also produced here. Unusual for the area, men predominantly do the weaving.

Pecangaan, 18km south of Jepara, produces rings, bracelets and other jewellery from *monel* (a stainless-steel alloy).

Information

The **tourist office** (☎591 493; www.gojepara.com; Jl AR Hakim 51; ⏰8am-4pm Mon-Thu, 7-11am Fri), in the western part of town, has very helpful staff and runs a particularly informative website.

Getting There & Around

Frequent buses make the trip from Jepara to Kudus (10,000Rp, 1¼ hours) and Semarang (18,000Rp to 25,000Rp, 2½ hours). A few buses also go to Surabaya, but Kudus has more connections.

Becak are cheap and the best way to get around. From the terminal, about 1km west of the town centre, 5000Rp to 8000Rp will get you to anywhere in town, including the Kartini harbour for boats to Karimunjawa.

Around Jepara

Sights

Mantingan MOSQUE
The mosque and tomb of Ratu Kali Nyamat, the great warrior-queen, are in Mantingan village, 4km south of Jepara. Kali Nyamat twice laid siege to Portugal's Melaka stronghold in the latter part of the 16th century.

The mosque, dating back to 1549, was restored some years ago and the tomb lies to the side of it. It's noted for its Hindu-style embellishments and medallions.

Mantingan is easily reached from Jepara. *Angkudes* (minibuses) from the bus terminal can drop you outside the mosque for 2000Rp.

Pantai Bandengan BEACH

Jepara has some fine white-sand beaches. Pantai Bandengan (aka Tirta Samudra), 7km northeast of town, is one of the best beaches on the north coast – an arc of gently shelving white sand. The main public section can get littered, but just a short walk away the sand is clean, the water clear and the swimming safe. It's beautiful at sunset. To get there from Jepara, take a bemo (2000Rp) from Jl Pattimura. On weekdays you may have to charter a whole bemo (around 35,000Rp).

Karimunjawa Islands

0297 / POP 9000

The dazzling offshore archipelago of Karimunjawa, a marine national park, consists of 27 coral-fringed islands that lie about 90km north of Jepara. The white-sand beaches are sublime, swimming is wonderful and the pace of life as relaxed as a destination defined by coconut palms and turquoise seas should be.

Holidaying Indonesians account for most of the visitors here, though Western travellers are starting to be seduced by the islands too.

The main island, **Pulau Karimunjawa**, is home to most of the archipelago's facilities, and the majority of the islanders, most of whom are Javanese, though there are also some Bugis and Madurese. Fishing, tourism and seaweed cultivation are the main livelihoods. This is also the site of the islands' only real town, Karimunjawa, and, despite widespread mangroves, a couple of good beaches. An airstrip is located on adjacent **Pulau Kemujan**.

The archipelago is divided into zones to protect the rich ecosystem. Zone One is completely out of bounds to all except national park rangers, with other areas set aside for sustainable tourism.

Access has improved recently, although during the rainy season boats don't always run.

Sights & Activities

Pulau Karimunjawa is a delight to explore by bike. Most of the shoreline is fringed by mangroves. The best two stretches of sandy beach are **Pantai Tanjung Gelam** (5000Rp entrance), 7km north of the main village, which also has some good snorkelling; and the lovely **private beach** at the Nirvana Laut hotel (12,500Rp entrance).

If you can find one of the park rangers, organise a hike up Pulau Karimunjawa's 600m peak, **Gunung Gendero**. In the far north of the island there's a network of walkways and platforms that allow you to explore the extensive mangroves that fringe Pulau Karimunjawa and neighbouring Pulau Kemujan.

Boat trips to other islands are an excellent day out; to charter a boat costs around 350,000Rp per day, or hotel owners can often hook you up with tour groups to save costs. The uninhabited islands of Menjangan Besar and Menjangan Kecil both have sweeping white sands and decent snorkelling, and are within easy reach of Karimunjawa town.

Further out, Pulau Menyawakan is the site of Karimunjawa's only major resort. Pulau Nyamuk, Pulau Parang, Pulau Bengkoang and Pulau Genting are all home to small, traditional communities. The reefs around many of these islands offer quite decent **snorkelling**. Diving can be arranged through the Kura Kura Resort.

As a marine park, many parts of Karimunjawa – including Pulau Burung and Pulau Geleang, home to nesting sea eagles – are officially off-limits (though this protected status is not always strictly enforced).

The islands can experience violent weather between December and February; during this time, flights and boat trips can be badly disrupted.

Sleeping & Eating

The main village of Karimunjawa has a handful of simple homestays. There's very little to choose between, most of them have prices set at 70,000 to 100,000Rp per person a night for a fan-cooled room and shared bathroom. The tourist office in Semarang can help out with names and contact numbers.

Book all accommodation well in advance, particularly if you're staying over on a Saturday night or during peak holiday times. Many hotels offer package deals that include transport from Jepara or Semarang.

TOP CHOICE Hotel Escape HOTEL $$

(☎0813 2574 8481; www.escapekarimun.com; r/ste 200,000/305,000Rp, meals from 25,000Rp; ❄📶) A well-constructed two-storey hotel that offers the best value on the island, with 12 attractive, well-maintained, air-conditioned rooms (book one on the upper level for the best sea views). Manager Pak Wono is a welcoming soul eager to help his guests – he can arrange motorbike and boat rentals. Good Indonesian and Western food is available in the restaurant. It's a five-minute walk to the right of the main dock.

Nirvana Laut HOTEL $$

(☎024 9131 5015; www.karimun-jawa.com; 2km north of dock; r 650,000-750,000, ste from 1,300,000Rp; ❄@📶) Right on a white-sand beach with good snorkelling, this small resort has lovely rooms (two with en-suite bathroom) in an attractive house with a kitchen that's ideal for small groups. Additionally, the luxurious suites here have panoramic sea views and teak floors. There's a great decked restaurant area and plenty of fresh seafood available. Hiking and fishing trips can be arranged.

Kura Kura Resort RESORT $$$

(☎Semarang 024 7663 2510; www.kurakuraresort.com; Pulau Menyawakan; cottage/pool villa incl 2 meals from US$305/430; ❄📶🏊) Luxury tropical island escape situated on its own private island, with gorgeous sea-view cottages and wonderful villas with private pools. There's about 800m of fine, white sand, a restaurant (the menu includes lots of Italian dishes) and water-sports facilities (but note that the dive school here is *not* PADI affiliated). Most guests arrive by plane (US$210 each way from Semarang); supplements can be charged if planes are not full. Kura Kura closes in the rainy season (November to March).

Wisma Apung HOMESTAY $

(☎0813 2511 0999, 312 185; wismaapung@yahoo.co.id; r per person incl breakfast with fan/air-con 100,000/140,000Rp, meals from 20,000Rp; ❄📶) Apung is the only floating homestay on the island. It's an all-wooden building where you could waste (or invest) a week or two, escaping the world with some good books, gazing out over the ocean. Meals here (including lots of fresh seafood; sometimes lobster) are delicious and served in generous portions. There's even a shark pool, where you can observe reef sharks at play. It's offshore from the village, connected by wooden walkways.

Puri Karimun HOMESTAY $

(☎0853 2506 7341; r with fan 125,000Rp) A new village homestay with modern, neat, well-presented rooms with en-suite bathrooms. There's a sociable vibe – you can chat to other guests around a pretty garden and help yourself to complimentary tea and coffee.

Karimunjawa Inn HOTEL $

(☎312 253; www.karimunjawainn.com; r incl breakfast with fan/air-con 131,000/191,000Rp, ste 281,000-382,000Rp; ❄📶) This hotel, just up from the dock, offers a choice of accommodation, from simple fan-cooled tiled rooms to suites with air-conditioning and sea views; all are functional rather than exceptional, but fair value. It's popular with Indonesian tour groups on weekends. There's an open-air restaurant with good seafood, Chinese dishes and fresh juices.

Wisma Wisata GUESTHOUSE $

(☎312 118; r 75,000Rp) On the *alun-alun*, Wisata is a decent choice for a budget bed. It has beer, clean rooms and a good spot near the harbour.

Cafe Amore INTERNATIONAL $

(just outside village, on rd to main dock; meals 20,000-50,000Rp; @📶) Refined coastal *joglo*-style cafe-restaurant with a nice garden and great sea views from the rear. Offers the best (and only) international grub in the village area, including sandwiches, pasta and grilled meats. It also has good coffee and cold beer. Doubles as an internet cafe.

Ibu Ester INDONESIAN $

(alun-alun; mains around 17,000Rp) Right on the *alun-alun*, this is the most popular warung in town, and offers lots of seafood and Indonesian dishes.

ℹ Information

The small **tourist information booth** (☎312 253, 085 325 0673; by the dock) at the harbour is usually open to greet boats. Alex, who works here, is extremely helpful and knowledgeable about the islands. Semarang tourist office can also help out with practicalities.

Karimunjawa has a post office, and there's internet access and wi-fi at Cafe Amore. There's a BRI ATM in the village but it's often not working so bring enough cash to last you. Electricity is very spotty; many places use generators at night.

Getting There & Away

It's expensive but possible to reach Karimunjawa by air. Kura Kura Resort charters planes from Semarang airport; these cost US$210 each way, but you then have to factor in a hefty charge for a boat transfer. Flights only operate between April and October.

Karimunjawa's boat connections are improving every year, and there are links from both Semarang and Jepara. Check all schedules with the Semarang tourist office; it can also book tickets and make reservations.

From Jepara's Kartini harbour, the new *Express Bahari* boat (executive class/VIP 60,000/80,000Rp, two hours) sails to Karimunjawa on Mondays and Tuesdays at 10.30pm, Fridays at 2pm and Saturdays at 10.30am, returning on Mondays at 1pm, Tuesdays at 10.30am, Saturdays at 8am and Sundays at 2pm.

The much slower *Muria* (economy/VIP 30,500/85,000Rp, six to seven hours) sails from Jepara on Monday, Wednesday and Saturday at 8am, returning at the same time on Tuesday, Thursday and Sunday.

The *Kartini I* sails from both Semarang and Jepara. It leaves Semarang at 9am on Mondays and Saturdays, returning on Wednesdays and Sundays at 1pm (business/executive class 135,000/150,000Rp, four hours). From Jepara, the *Kartini I* sails on Wednesdays at 8am and returns to Jepara on Tuesdays at 9am (business/executive class 70,000/85,000Rp, four hours).

Getting Around

From Pulau Karimunjawa it costs around 350,000Rp to charter a wooden boat for a day trip to the outer islands or 60,000Rp for the short hop to Pulau Menjangan Besar and Kecil. There are very infrequent *angkot* operating on the islands and *ojek* will do short trips for 10,000Rp. Hiring a moped (60,000Rp per day) is a superb way to get around the main island's 22km of roads. Local guide **Supri** (☎0878 3370 2229) can organise a boat to rent and leads tours to good snorkelling spots around the islands.

EAST JAVA

The least densely populated of Java's provinces, East Java (Jawa Timur) is a wild, rolling region with dizzying peaks, smoking volcanoes and unspoilt panoramas. While the regional capital Surabaya has all the accoutrements of a booming Indonesian city, including freeways, multiplexes and a trademark traffic problem, there are far more attractive bases. Malang is a civilised city with a temperate climate ringed by some fascinating Hindu temples, while Blitar has more temples and a historic site or two to explore.

For most visitors, East Java is all about the raw, rugged appeal of its volcano-studded scenery and awesome landscapes. Nowhere is more synonymous with this than the sublime Bromo-Tengger Massif, incorporating the volcanic peaks of Gunung Bromo (2392m) and Gunung Semeru (3676m) – Java's highest mountain. The Bromo area and its puffing giants is an undisputed highlight, but the Ijen Plateau ranks very close, with a stunning crater lake, good hiking and fewer travellers.

Baluran National Park is the most accessible of Java's wildlife reserves, but the southern route through East Java is the most scenic and has two great national parks – Meru Betiri, where there is a protected beach where turtles nest, and Alas Purwo, which is hallowed among surfers for its gigantic reef breaks. Just off the coast near Surabaya is the island of Madura, a place where traditions are particularly strong and famous bull races, known as *kerapan sapi*, are staged between August and October.

Surabaya

☎031 / POP 2.4 MILLION

Your initial impressions are not going to be great. A big, polluted, congested, business-driven city, Surabaya is not well set up for visitors. Just crossing the eight-lane highways that rampage through the centre is a challenge in itself. Attractions are slim on the ground, and against the calm of rural East Java, it is pandemonium writ large.

And yet if you've the patience to explore, Surabaya has quixotic little corners of interest. Its historic Arab quarter is fascinating: a labyrinthine warren of lanes leading to a historic mosque that's a place of pilgrimage. Surabaya also has one of Indonesia's biggest Chinatowns and a roster of impressive, though disintegrating, Dutch buildings.

For most foreign visitors, the city is merely a place to change planes, trains or buses. For locals, however, Surabaya is closely linked to the birth of the Indonesian nation, as it was here that the battle for independence began. To them, Surabaya is Kota Pahlawan (City of Heroes), and statues commemorating independence are scattered all over the city.

East Java

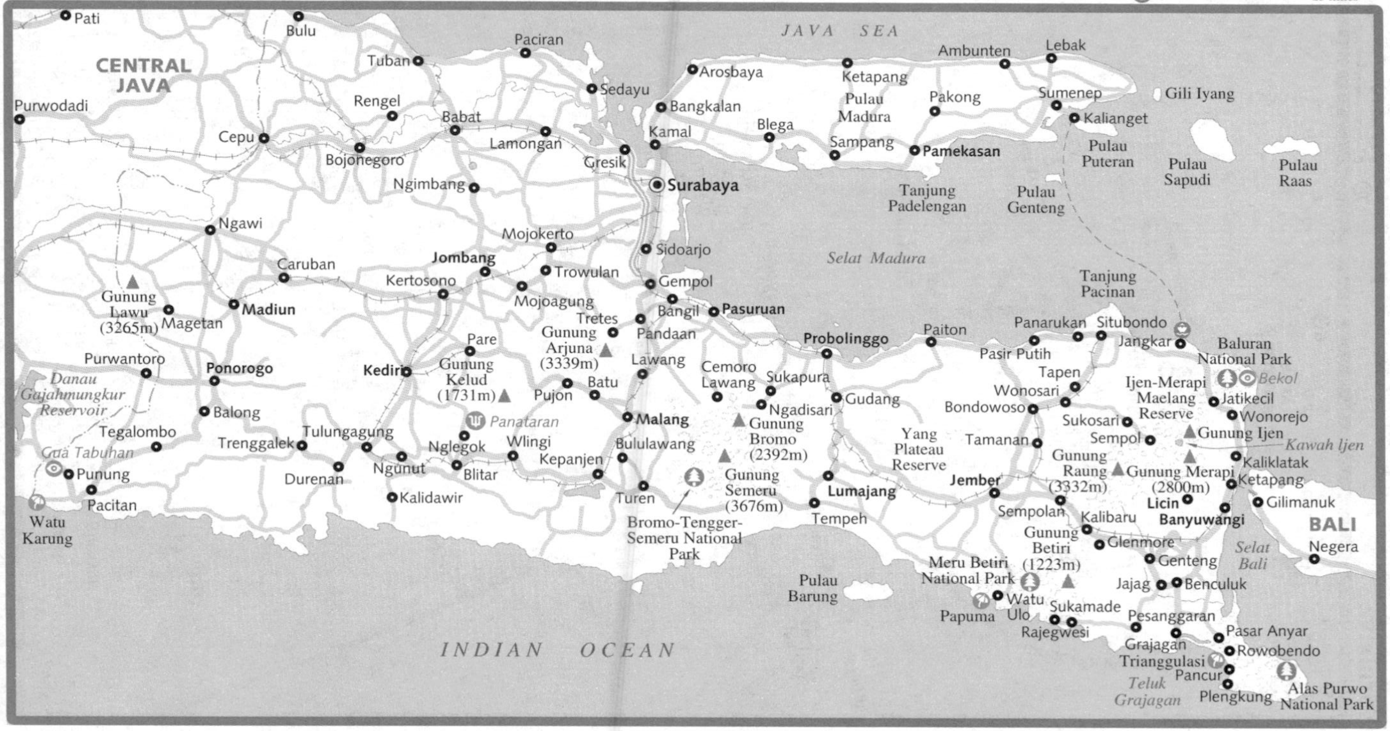

0 50 km
0 25 miles

JAVA SEA
INDIAN OCEAN
CENTRAL JAVA
BALI
Selat Madura
Selat Bali
Teluk Grajagan

Pati
Purwodadi
Bulu
Cepu
Tuban
Rengel
Bojonegoro
Babat
Paciran
Lamongan
Sedayu
Gresik
Ngimbang
Surabaya
Arosbaya
Bangkalan
Kamal
Blega
Ketapang
Pulau Madura
Sampang
Pamekasan
Pakong
Ambunten
Lebak
Sumenep
Kalianget
Gili Iyang
Pulau Puteran
Pulau Sapudi
Pulau Raas
Tanjung Padelengan
Pulau Genteng
Tanjung Pacinan
Ngawi
Caruban
Gunung Lawu (3265m)
Magetan
Madiun
Purwantoro
Ponorogo
Danau Gajahmungkur Reservoir
Balong
Tegalombo
Gua Tabuhan
Punung
Pacitan
Watu Karung
Trenggalek
Tulungagung
Durenan
Ngunut
Kalidawir
Kediri
Kertosono
Jombang
Mojokerto
Trowulan
Mojoagung
Pare
Gunung Kelud (1731m)
Panataran
Nglegok
Blitar
Wlingi
Kepanjen
Pujon
Batu
Gunung Arjuna (3339m)
Tretes
Pandaan
Sidoarjo
Gempol
Bangil
Pasuruan
Lawang
Malang
Bululawang
Turen
Cemoro Lawang
Sukapura
Ngadisari
Gunung Bromo (2392m)
Gunung Semeru (3676m)
Bromo-Tengger-Semeru National Park
Probolinggo
Gudang
Lumajang
Tempeh
Pulau Barung
Yang Plateau Reserve
Paiton
Pasir Putih
Panarukan
Situbondo
Jangkar
Tapen
Wonosari
Bondowoso
Tamanan
Jember
Sempolan
Sukosari
Sempol
Gunung Raung (3332m)
Gunung Merapi (2800m)
Licin
Ijen-Merapi Maelang Reserve
Gunung Ijen
Kawah Ijen
Baluran National Park
Bekol
Jatikecil
Wonorejo
Kaliklatak
Ketapang
Gilimanuk
Banyuwangi
Negera
Kalibaru
Gunung Betiri (1223m)
Glenmore
Genteng
Jajag
Benculuk
Meru Betiri National Park
Watu Ulo
Papuma
Sukamade
Rajegwesi
Pesanggaran
Grajagan
Pasar Anyar
Rowobendo
Trianggulasi
Pancur
Plengkung
Alas Purwo National Park

Surabaya

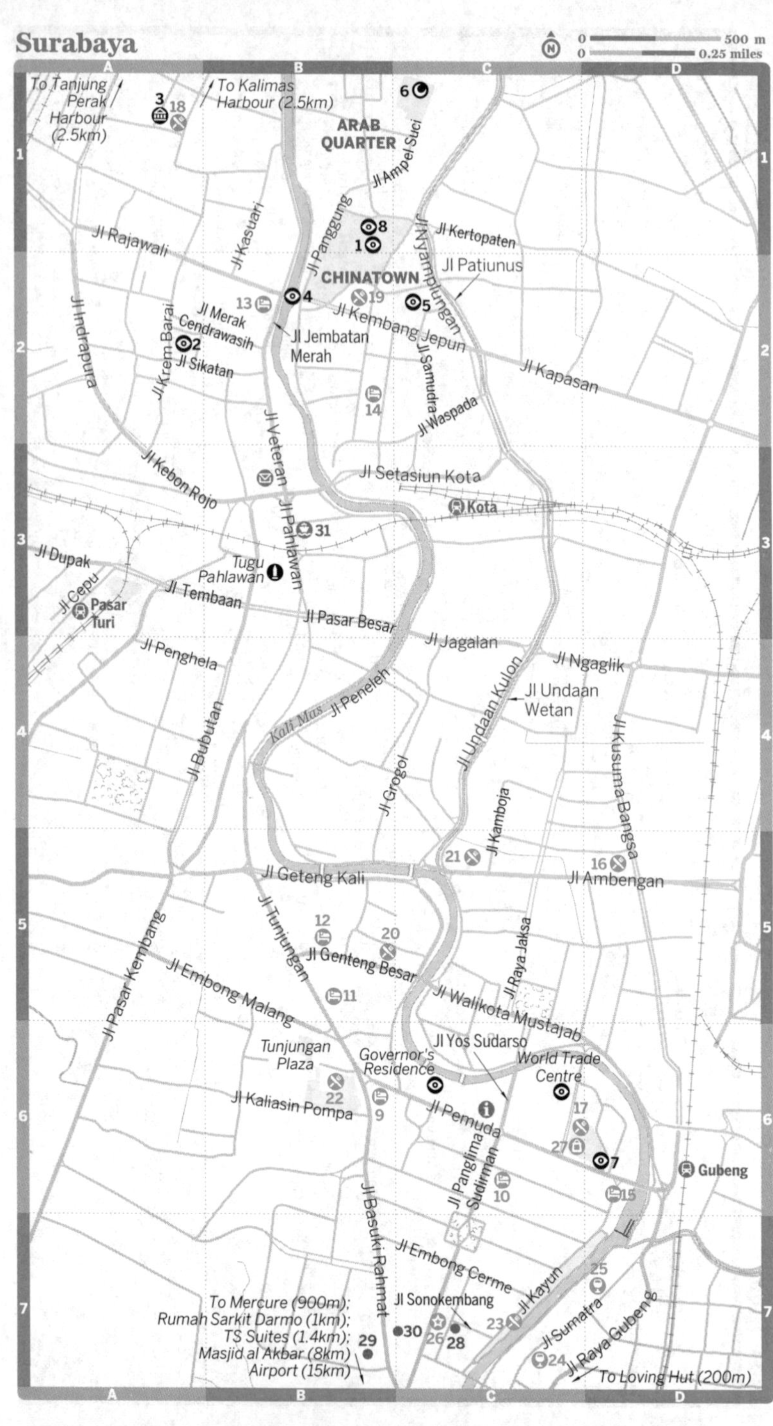

To Tanjung Perak Harbour (2.5km)
To Kalimas Harbour (2.5km)
ARAB QUARTER
Jl Ampel Suci
Jl Rajawali
Jl Kasuari
Jl Panggung
Jl Kertopaten
Jl Nyamplungan
Jl Patiunus
CHINATOWN
Jl Kembang Jepun
Jl Merak
Cendrawasih
Jl Jembatan Merah
Jl Indrapura
Jl Krem Barai
Jl Sikatan
Jl Samudra
Jl Waspada
Jl Kapasan
Jl Veteran
Jl Kebon Rojo
Jl Setasiun Kota
Kota
Jl Pahlawan
Jl Dupak
Tugu Pahlawan
Jl Cepu
Pasar Turi
Jl Tembaan
Jl Pasar Besar
Jl Jagalan
Jl Penghela
Jl Ngaglik
Jl Undaan Wetan
Jl Peneleh
Kali Mas
Jl Undaan Kulon
Jl Kusuma Bangsa
Jl Bubutan
Jl Grogol
Jl Kamboja
Jl Geteng Kali
Jl Ambengan
Jl Tunjungan
Jl Genteng Besar
Jl Pasar Kembang
Jl Embong Malang
Jl Raya Jaksa
Jl Walikota Mustajab
Jl Yos Sudarso
Tunjungan Plaza
Governor's Residence
World Trade Centre
Jl Kaliasin Pompa
Jl Pemuda
Jl Panglima Sudirman
Gubeng
Jl Basuki Rahmat
Jl Embong Cerme
Jl Kayun
Jl Sonokembang
To Mercure (900m); Rumah Sarkit Darmo (1km); TS Suites (1.4km); Masjid al Akbar (8km) Airport (15km)
Jl Sumatra
Jl Raya Gubeng
To Loving Hut (200m)

Surabaya

Sights

1	Chinatown	B1
2	Gedung PTP XXII	A2
3	House of Sampoerna	A1
4	Jembatan Merah	B2
5	Kong Co Kong Tik Cun Ong Temple	C2
6	Mesjid Ampel	C1
7	Monumen Kapal Selam	D6
8	Pasar Pabean	B1

Sleeping

9	Citihub	B6
10	Hotel Kenongo	C6
11	Hotel Majapahit Surabaya	B5
12	Hotel Paviljoen	B5
13	Ibis Rajawali	B2
14	Orchid Guesthouse	B2
15	Sparkling Backpacker Hotel	D6

Eating

16	Ahisma	D5
17	Food Stalls	C6
18	House of Sampoerna Café	A1
19	Kya Kya	B2
	Long's Seafood	(see 9)
20	Pasar Genteng	B5
21	Soto Ambengan Pak Sadi Asli	C5
22	Tunjungan Plaza	B6
23	Warungs	C7

Drinking

24	Colors	C7
25	Lava Lounge	D7

Entertainment

26	Elbow Cafe	C7
	Tunjungan 21	(see 22)

Shopping

27	Plaza Surabaya	C6

Information

28	Haryono Tours & Travel	C7

Transport

29	Cathay Pacific	B7
	Garuda	(see 29)
30	Globe	C7
31	Pelni	B3

Sights

OLD CITY

Even though much of Surabaya's historical centre is literally falling to pieces, the old city easily wins the 'Most Attractive Neighbourhood' prize. With crumbling Dutch architecture, a souk-like Arab quarter and strong Chinese influences, it's also by far the most atmospheric and idiosyncratic area of Surabaya to explore.

From the old city you can head north to the Kalimas harbour, where brightly painted *pinisi* (Makassar or Bugis schooners) from Sulawesi and Kalimantan unload their wares.

Arab Quarter NEIGHBOURHOOD

(Ampel) Surabaya's Arab Quarter – usually called Ampel or Kampung Arab – has the atmosphere and appearance of a Middle Eastern *medina*. It is a warren of narrow lanes with stalls selling prayer beads, *peci* (black Muslim felt hats) and other religious paraphernalia, alongside perfumes, dates and a plastic camel or two. All alleys lead to the **Mesjid Ampel** (Jl Ampel Suci), the most sacred mosque in Surabaya. It was here that Sunan Ampel (one of the *wali songo* who brought Islam to Java) was buried in 1481. The mosque itself is a huge space, the vast expanse of its marble floor divided by dozens of wooden pillars, but there's very little in the way of ornamentation. Behind the mosque pilgrims chant and present rose-petal offerings at Sunan Ampel's grave.

You have to access the mosque on foot. The most direct route is to take the lane that leads west from Jl Ampel Suci – a crowd of becak marks the entrance.

FREE **House of Sampoerna** MUSEUM

(☎353 9000; www.houseofsampoerna.com; Jl Taman Sampoerna; ⏰9am-10pm) Undoubtedly the city's best-presented attraction, the House of Sampoerna is the home of one of Indonesia's most famous *kretek* cigarette manufacturers (though it's now owned by US-giant Philip Morris). Whatever you think about the tobacco industry, this factory and museum makes a fascinating place to visit.

The building itself is a wonderful 19th-century Dutch structure, originally an orphanage but later converted into a theatre (indeed Charlie Chaplin once dropped by). The former lobby is now the museum and is something of a shrine to the Sampoerna empire. It has exhibits on the use of cloves and the history of *kretek* in Indonesia, alongside uniforms and drums of the Sampoerna marching band and other quirky company curios. There's also an incredible collection of cigarette lighters, holders and cases, mainly from Europe.

Upstairs there's a bird's-eye perspective of the factory's shop floor, where hundreds of women hand roll, trim and pack the Dji Sam Soe brand (banned from most countries as the tar content is so strong). The fastest rollers here churn out 4000 cigarettes a day, their fingers a blur of motion. Because air-conditioning can affect the tobacco (and fans would blow it around) it's a steamy, humid workplace.

You'll be accompanied by a highly informative, English-speaking guide; the complete tour lasts between 30 minutes and an hour depending on your interest. Note that the museum is open late, but the factory section closes around 3pm.

After your visit, be sure to have a drink in the excellent neighbouring cafe-restaurant and consider a trip on the company's intriguing sightseeing bus tour, the Surabaya Heritage Track (p164).

Chinatown NEIGHBOURHOOD

(E of Jembatan Merah) Directly south of the Arab Quarter is Surabaya's Chinatown, with hundreds of small businesses and warehouses. Its historic buildings are crumbling and the streets are crowded and none-too-clean, but it's loaded with atmosphere. Becak and hand-pulled carts are still the best way to transport goods through the narrow streets. **Pasar Pabean** is a sprawling, darkly-lit market where you can buy everything from Madurese chickens to Chinese crockery.

Further east near the canal, the highly evocative **Kong Co Kong Tik Cun Ong temple** (Jl Dukuh) is primarily Buddhist, but has a variety of Confucian and Taoist altars – if you can see them through the plumes of incense smoke.

Jembatan Merah BRIDGE

Originally the old city was divided along ethnic lines, with Europeans on the west side of the Kali Mas river and Chinese, Arabs and Javanese on the east bank. Jembatan Merah is a famous bridge that connected the two halves of the city; it also saw fierce fighting during Indonesia's battle for independence.

Jl Jembatan Merah, running parallel to the canal, is a grungy replica of Amsterdam, but worthy (though rundown) examples of **Dutch architecture** can be seen here. Another impressive structure is the Indo-European–style **Gedung PTP XXII** government office building on Jl Merak Cendrawasih.

ELSEWHERE

Masjid al Akbar MOSQUE

(Jl Masjid Al Akbar Timur I) Perhaps the most impressive modern mosque in Indonesia, you'll probably get a glimpse of Masjid al Akbar's magnificent array of bulbous turquoise-tiled domes as you exit the city. Staff are happy to show visitors around and will accompany you up the elevator to the top of the free-standing ottoman-style minaret, which offers spectacular views.

Take any bus heading for the main bus terminal, ask for the mosque and you'll be dropped off on Jl Ahmad Yani, a kilometre from the building. From here you can walk through quiet residential streets or take a becak. A taxi from central Surabaya is around 50,000Rp.

Monumen Kapal Selam SUBMARINE

(Jl Pemuda; admission 5000Rp; ⏲9am-9pm) In keeping with Indonesia's fascination with all things military, Surabaya's foremost stretch of renovated water-side real estate centres on the hulk of the *Pasopati*, a Russian submarine commissioned into the Indonesian navy in 1962. You can poke around the interior, peek through the periscope and even climb into the torpedo tubes. It's in a small landscaped **park** and there are a couple of cafes popular with young smoochers.

Sleeping

Surabaya has a real dearth of good budget places: standards are low, and poor-value rooms and disinterested staff tend to be the norm. This is another place in Java where you should consider blowing your budget and treating yourself. If you're struggling to find a bed, the tourist board is well informed and is able to assist backpackers.

Midrange accommodation options have improved greatly in recent years due to fierce competition. There are some excellent deals available in the luxury hotel sector, with rooms starting at US$50 for four-star hotels.

TOP CHOICE **Hotel Majapahit Surabaya** HISTORIC HOTEL **$$$**

(☎545 4333; www.hotel-majapahit.com; Jl Tunjungan 65; r from US$137; ❄@☜≋) A memorable place to stay, this landmark colonial hotel simply exudes class and heritage. It's all very tasteful indeed, with colonnaded courtyards, fountains, verdant greenery and a gorgeous pool area (though as it's located on a busy road there is some background traffic noise). Rooms, some with private terraces overlooking the gardens, are beautifully presented and boast all modern facilities. Staff are extremely helpful and well trained, and the Sarkies Chinese restaurant is one of the best in the city.

Citihub HOTEL $$
(☎535 7066, 502 9292; www.citihubhotels.com; Jl Gub Suryo IJ; r 235,000-335,000Rp; ❄@📶) Right in the heart of the city, almost opposite the Tunjungan Plaza mall, this bright, inviting budget hotel is a superb place to stay if you value your home comforts and don't mind compact living quarters. All rooms have luxury bedding, hip decor, a large LCD TV and wi-fi. There's a minimart downstairs and a huge internet cafe to the rear. You have to leave a cash deposit of 200,000Rp, and rent towels (5000Rp). Three other Citihub hotels are under construction in Surabaya; check the website for details.

Mercure HOTEL $$
(☎562 3000; www.mercuresurabaya.com; Jl Raya Darmo 68-78; r from 532,000Rp; ❄@📶🏊) An excellent choice, this large hotel has first-class facilities, above all its idyllic palm-fringed pool area. There's also a decent gym and a reasonably priced spa. Rooms are modern, spacious and good value but the cheaper options lack wow factor. Staff are efficient and helpful.

Ibis Rajawali HOTEL $$
(☎353 9994; www.ibishotel.com; Jl Rajawali 9-11; r from 375,000Rp; ❄@📶) Rajawali is a fine choice if you're looking to stay in the north of town. The entire place, from the reception to the rooms, is modern and business-like, and there's a small gym and a spa. Some upper-floor rooms have views of the Suramadu Bridge.

Hotel Sulawesi Kertajaya HOTEL $$
(☎503 9555; Jl Kertajaya IV Raya II; r incl breakfast 250,000Rp; ❄📶) A new hotel down a quiet lane in a residential area with accommodation grouped around a courtyard/parking lot. Rooms are nothing fancy but they're tiled and well-swept, and have flat-screen TV, pine furniture and en-suite bathrooms with hot water. There's a little restaurant here; wi-fi access is in the lobby area only.

Hotel Kenongo HOTEL $
(☎531 0009; www.hotelkenongo.com; Jl Embong Kenongo 12; r 225,000-240,000Rp; ❄📶) Offering good comfort levels for the price, this hotel has clean, light, airy rooms, all with air-con, TV, phone and a hot-water shower or bath tub. The location is a bonus, on a quiet street off Jl Pemuda, with malls and monuments a short walk away. There's a 24-hour restaurant.

TS Suites BUSINESS HOTEL $$$
(☎563 1222; www.tssuites.com; Jl Hayam Wuruk 6, Surabaya Town Sq; r from US$90; ❄@) These hip, spacious suites are located above Surabaya Town Square, one of the city's most popular malls, so you won't have to walk far to access dozens of restaurants, cafes and a large cinema complex.

Orchid Guesthouse GUESTHOUSE $
(☎355 0211; orchidguesthousesby@yahoo.com; Jl Bongkaran 49; d incl breakfast 135,000Rp; ❄) Offers clean rooms, all with air-con, spring mattresses and TV, and there's a cafe. However the design of the place – all rooms face a corridor with no outside windows – means that they are not well ventilated; the location is also pretty dead at night. That said, it's one of the better backpacker options in town.

Hotel Paviljoen HOTEL $
(☎534 3449; Jl Genteng Besar 94; r with fan/air-con from 110,000/165,000Rp; ❄) A real respite from Surabaya's manic streets, this venerable, but slightly shabby, colonial villa still has a twinkle of charm and grandeur. Rooms are basic and Spartan with a capital 'S' but there are some lovely touches including Mediterranean-style shuttered windows. The location could not be better.

Sparkling Backpacker Hotel HOSTEL $
(☎532 1388; www.sparklingbackpacker.com; Jl Kayoon 2A; r incl breakfast 105,000-155,000Rp, VIP 250,000Rp; ❄📶) 'Sparkling' is far too optimistic, but this hostel-style place has some positives. The location in the heart of the city is excellent, within a short walk of malls, restaurants and the river. Unfortunately, cleanliness could be better and the layout is not great; many rooms lack a bathroom and the only one is located on the ground floor. Staff can be pretty vacant too.

Eating

You won't be left hungry in Surabaya – the city has a huge array of eating options. Local dishes include *rawon*, a thick, black beef soup that tastes better than it sounds.

DON'T MISS

ALL ABOARD!

Exploring north Surabaya from a sightseeing bus is a lot of fun, and also free. The House of Sampoerna (p161) has a Surabaya Heritage Track, a tram-style bus that leaves the factory three times daily (Tuesday to Sunday) to take in the sights of Chinatown and the Arab quarters, plus visit cottage industries (such as a noodle factory). The route changes from time to time; check the website for details. It's essential to book your place ahead, particularly on weekends.

For cheap eats, **Pasar Genteng** (Jl Genteng Besar; mains 8000Rp; ⏲9am-9pm) has good night warungs. Late-night munchies can also be had at the offshoot of Jl Pemuda, opposite the **Plaza Surabaya**, which buzzes with **food-stall** activity around the clock, or the strip of **warungs** with their backs to the river along Jl Kayun.

Sadly the once-throbbing Chinese night market **Kya Kya** (Jl Kembang Jepun; ⏲6-11pm) in the old city is now far less popular, though there are still a few food stalls here.

For an air-conditioned setting, **Tunjungan Plaza** (Jl Tunjungan) has a colossal selection of squeaky-clean Asian, Western restaurants and cafes; the food court is on the 5th floor.

TOP CHOICE **House of Sampoerna Café** INTERNATIONAL, INDONESIAN **$$**
(☎353 9000; Jl Taman Sampoerna; meals 30,000-82,000Rp; 📶) This cafe is adjacent to the House of Sampoerna museum and occupies a gorgeous colonial structure complete with stained-glass windows and classy seating – a memorable spot for a meal. The menu is divided into east and west, with classic Indonesian-style nasi goreng and Singapore *laksa*, along with New Zealand steaks and fish 'n' chips. There are great desserts, espresso coffee and a full bar, including cocktails and cognac.

Casa Fontana ITALIAN **$$**
(☎567 7679; www.casafontanaresto.com; Jl Imam Bonjol 119; meals 50,000-120,000Rp) The best Italian in town, serving up grilled meats, seafood, pasta and pizza in intimate surrounds, with candlelit gingham tablecloths at night. It's run by a welcoming Italian and local team who look after their guests well. Casa Fontana is particularly renowned for its desserts, with home-made gelato (the moka is great) and frozen yoghurt (try the blueberry), tiramisu and more. Order a bottle of prosecco and you're set.

Long's Seafood SEAFOOD **$$**
(Jl Gub Suryo 1J; meals 35,000-60,000Rp) An intriguing new seafood concept, with a fast-food–style set-up downstairs where you choose your fish (*gurame* is 6000Rp per ounce) or seafood (prawns are 17,000Rp) from a terrific selection in the tanks and freezers, it's weighed, then cooked to order in the style of your choice. The dining room is upstairs.

Ahisma VEGETARIAN **$**
(☎535 0466; Jl Kusuma Bangsa 80; meals 35,000-50,000Rp; ⏲noon-10pm; 🌶) Elegant upmarket vegetarian restaurant owned by a welcoming Indo-Chinese family with delicious rice dishes (try *nasi hainan*), salads and soups, including Tom Yang (minus the seafood). No MSG is used.

Soto Ambengan Pak Sadi Asli INDONESIAN **$**
(☎532 3998; Jl Ambengan 3A; mains 20,000Rp) This is the original location of a chain with several branches across Surabaya. Everyone is here for the delicious *soto ayam* (chicken soup), which is served with herbs, turmeric, plenty of peanuts and an egg or two if you want.

Loving Hut VEGETARIAN **$**
(Jl Sumbawa 37; meals 25,000-40,000Rp; ❄🌶) Large modern, air-conditioned vegetarian restaurant with extensive menu including 'fancy nut' sate (20,000Rp), mango fried rice, salads, soups, lots of noodle dishes and excellent fresh juices.

Drinking

There are very few bars in Surabaya and the city does not really have much of a drinking culture, though expats ensure the beers keep flowing at a few key places.

Lava Lounge LOUNGE
(Big Box complex, Jl Sumatra 40) The coolest hangout in town, this bar-restaurant has sofas and tables set round an open courtyard. It's part of the Big Box complex that includes a fashion boutique or two. It's the perfect spot on sultry evenings for a relaxing drink, with live jazz and DJs playing lounge music

on weekends. Food is also served; try a pepper burger (30,000Rp) if you want a bite.

Colors BAR
(☎503 0562; www.colorspub.com; Jl Sumatra 81) Very popular with expats, this large upmarket pub-club has live music and a DJ every night. There's a full bar and drinks are expensive. It doesn't really get going until after 9pm.

☆ Entertainment

Cinema complexes are found all around the city.

Tunjungan 21 CINEMA
(Jl Tunjungan, Tunjungan Plaza) One of the best in town, this large cinema complex shows recent Hollywood releases in English and has good sound quality.

Elbow Cafe LIVE MUSIC
(Jl Sono Kembang 4) Lively bar that hosts live bands most nights of the week (alternative rock and metal, punk and blues) and draws a studenty crowd. There's cheap beer and grub.

Shopping

Periplus BOOKS
(☎593 7360; Jl Dharmahusada 37, Galaxy Mall) Has a great selection of English-language titles and magazines. There are also two branches inside the departures lounge at the airport.

Information

Jl Pemuda has plenty of banks, as does Tunjungan Plaza.

Malls, including Tunjungan Plaza, have wi-fi. There's a huge internet cafe at Citihub (p163) hotel with more than 100 terminals for internet access (5000Rp per hour), Skype and wi-fi; it also has a non-smoking section.

East Java Regional Tourist Office (☎853 1822; Jl Wisata Menanggal; ⏱7am-2pm Mon-Fri) About 3km south of the centre; has a few brochures on the province.

Main post office (Jl Kebon Rojo) Inconveniently located 4km north of the city centre.

Rumah Sakit Darmo (☎567 6253; www.rsdarmo.co.id; Jl Raya Darmo 90) Hospital with English- and Dutch-speaking doctors.

Tourist information centre (☎534 0444; www.sparklingsurabaya.com; Jl Pemuda; ⏱8am-8pm) Has helpful English-speaking staff, and can offer plenty of leaflets, a map of the city and also a file with good details about backpacker accommodation.

Getting There & Away

Air

Surabaya Juanda airport is Indonesia's third busiest and is used by more than 20 airlines. There are international connections to cities in Asia and numerous domestic flights.

For a reliable travel agency head to **Haryono Tours & Travel** (☎503 4000; www.haryonotours.com; Jl Sulawesi 27-29; ⏱8am-5pm Mon-Fri, to 1pm Sat)

AirAsia (☎021 2927 0999; www.airasia.com) Flies to Bangkok and the Malaysian cities of Johor Bahru, Kuala Lumpur and Penang. Domesitc routes include Bandung, Denpasar and Medan.

Batavia Air (☎080 4122 2888; www.batavia-air.co.id) Operates flights to Ambon, Balikpapan, Banjarmasin, Batam, Denpasar, Jakarta, Kupang, Makassar, Mataram, Palangkaraya, Pontianak and Yogyakarta.

Cathay Pacific (☎080 4188 8888; www.cathaypacific.com; Jl Basuki Rachmat 124-128, Hyatt Regency) Flies daily to/from Hong Kong.

Citilink (☎080 4108 0808; www.citilink.co.id) Flies to Balikpapan, Banjarmasin, Denpasar, Jakarta and Makassar.

Garuda (☎546 8505; www.garuda-indonesia.com; Jl Basuki Rahmat 106-128) Connections to Balikpapan, Bandung, Denpasar, Jakarta and Makassar.

Lion Air (☎503 6111; www.lionair.co.id; Jl Sulawesi 75) Flights to Ambon, Balikpapan, Bandung, Banjarmasin, Batam, Denpasar, Jakarta, Kendari, Kupang, Makassar, Manado, Palangkaraya, Tarakan and Yogyakarta.

Merpati (☎568 8111; www.merpati.co.id; Jl Darmo 109-111) Offers routes to Bandung, Banyuwangi, Denpasar, Jakarta, Kupang and Makassar.

Sriwijaya Air (☎021 2927 9777; www.sriwijayaair.co.id) Flies to Balikpapan, Bandung, Banjarmasin, Denpasar, Jakarta, Kupang, Makassar, Mataram, Manado, Semarang and Yogyakarta.

Wings Air (☎021 6379 8000; www.lionair.co.id) To/from Denpasar, Praya (Lombok), Semarang and Yogyakarta.

Boat

Surabaya is an important port and a major transport hub for ships to the other islands. Boats depart from Tanjung Perak harbour; bus P1 from outside Tunjungan Plaza heads here. Pelni ships sail to Makassar in Sulawesi roughly twice a week (economy/1st class from 217,000/838,000Rp), Pontianak in Kalimantan (262,000/1,019,000Rp) about every 10 days and Jakarta (171,000/729,000Rp) weekly.

TRANSPORT FROM SURABAYA

Bus

DESTINATION	COST (RP; ECONOMY/AIR-CON)	DURATION (HR)
Banyuwangi	42,000/60,000	7
Kudus	57,000/70,000	8
Malang	15,000/20,000	2-3
Probolinggo	16,000/23,000	2½
Semarang	60,000/90,000	9
Solo	57,000/73,000	7½
Sumenep	30,000/42,000	4½

Train

DESTINATION	COST (RP)	DURATION (HR)	FREQUENCY
Banyuwangi	115,000	7	2 daily
Probolinggo	60,000	2	2 daily
Semarang	145,000310,000	4	5 daily
Solo	135,000-285,000	3½-4	6 daily
Yogyakarta	125,000-260,000	5	4 daily

Head to the **Pelni ticket office** (☎352 1044; www.pelni.co.id; Jl Pahlawan 112) for more information.

Bus

Surabaya's main bus terminal, called Purabaya (or Bungurasih), is 10km south of the city centre. It's reasonably well organised and computer monitors display bus departure times, however watch out for pickpockets. Crowded Damri city buses run between the bus terminal and the Jl Tunjungan/Jl Pemuda intersection in the city centre. A metered taxi costs around 65,000Rp.

Buses from Purabaya head to points all over Java, Madura and Bali. Most buses on long-distance routes, such as to Solo, Yogyakarta, Bandung and Denpasar, are night buses that leave in the late afternoon or evening. Bookings can be made at Purabaya bus terminal, or travel agencies in the city centre sell tickets with a mark-up. The most convenient bus agents are those on Jl Basuki Rahmat.

All buses heading south of Surabaya on the toll road get caught up in heavy traffic around the Gembol junction – this is because of the snarl-up around the mud volcano. During rush hour this can add an hour to your journey.

Minibus

Door-to-door *travel* minibuses are not normally a good way of travelling from Surabaya. The city is so big that you can spend two hours just collecting passengers from their hotels and homes before you even get started. Destinations and sample fares include Malang (35,000Rp), Solo (80,000Rp), Yogyakarta (85,000Rp) and Semarang (95,000Rp). **Cipa Ganti** (☎031 546 0302; www.cipaganti.co.id) is a recommended company, or you can try the agencies along Jl Basuki Rahmat.

Train

From Jakarta, trains taking the fast northern route via Semarang arrive at the **Pasar Turi train station** (☎534 5014) southwest of Kota train station. Trains taking the southern route via Yogyakarta, and trains from Banyuwangi, arrive at **Gubeng train station** (☎503 3115) and most carry on through to Kota. Gubeng train station is much more central and sells tickets for all trains. Most Jakarta-bound trains leave from Pasar Turi. There are only very infrequent, and very slow economy-class trains to Malang.

ℹ Getting Around

TO/FROM THE AIRPORT Taxis from Juanda airport (17km) operate on a coupon system and cost around 110,000Rp to/from the city centre including toll road fees. There are also regular Damri buses (15,000Rp) from the airport to Purabaya bus terminal, and then on to the city centre.

BUS Surabaya has an extensive city bus network, with normal buses (2000Rp) and *patas* buses (3000Rp per journey). Watch out for pickpockets, as buses can be very crowded. One of the most useful services is the *patas* P1 bus, which runs from Purabaya bus terminal into the city along Jl Basuki Rahmat. In the reverse direction, catch it on Jl Tunjungan.

TAXI Surabaya has air-conditioned metered taxis. Flag fall is 4000 to 5000Rp; reckon on around 20,000Rp for a trip of around 4km. **Bluebird taxis** (☎372 1234) are the most reliable and can be called in advance. To hire a car with a driver, try **Globe** (☎031 548 1111; www.globerentacar.com; Jl Basuki Rahmat 147); rates start at 400,000Rp per day plus petrol.

Trowulan

Trowulan was once the capital of the largest Hindu empire in Indonesian history. Founded by Singosari prince Wijaya in 1294, it reached the height of its power under Hayam Wuruk (1350–89), who was guided by his powerful prime minister, Gajah Mada. During this time Majapahit received tribute from most of the regions encompassing present-day Indonesia and even parts of the Malay Peninsula.

Its wealth was based on its control of the spice trade and the fertile rice-growing plains of Java. The religion was a hybrid of Hinduism – with worship of the deities Shiva, Vishnu and Brahma – and Buddhism, but Islam was tolerated, and Koranic burial inscriptions found on the site suggest that Javanese Muslims resided within the royal court. The empire came to a catastrophic end in 1478 when the city fell to the north-coast power of Demak, forcing the Majapahit elite to flee to Bali and opening Java up to the Muslim conquest.

Sir Thomas Stamford Raffles, the great British explorer and governor general of Java, rediscovered Trowulan in 1815, and though it was choked in forest, described the ruins as 'this pride of Java'.

The remains of the court are scattered over a large area around the village of Trowulan, 12km from Mojokerto. The Majapahit temples were mainly built from red-clay bricks that quickly crumbled. Many have been rebuilt and are relatively simple compared to the glories of structures such as Borobudur, but they do give a good idea of what was once a great city. As the temples are spread over a such a large area, it's best to either hire a becak or come in a car.

One kilometre from the main Surabaya-Solo road, the impressive **Trowulan Museum** (admission 3000Rp; ⏰7am-3.30pm Tue-Sun) houses superb examples of Majapahit sculpture and pottery from East Java. Pride of place is held by the splendid statue of Kediri's King Airlangga as Vishnu astride a huge Garuda, taken from Belahan. It should be your first port of call for an understanding of Trowulan and Majapahit history, and it includes descriptions of the other ancient ruins in East Java.

Some of the most interesting ruins include the gateway of **Bajang Ratu**, with its strikingly sculpted *kala* heads; the **Tikus Temple** (Queen's Bath – used for ritual bathing and cleansing); and the 13.7m-high **Wringinlawang Gate**. The **Pendopo Agung** is an open-air pavilion built by the Indonesian army. Two kilometres south of the pavilion, the **Troloyo cemetery** is the site of some of the oldest Muslim graves found in Java, the earliest dating from AD 1376.

Trowulan is refreshingly hawker-free, though as there's a distinct lack of information on site you may want to hire a freelance guide (there's often one waiting at the museum). Expect to pay around 70,000Rp for a half-day guide.

ℹ Getting There & Away

Trowulan can be visited as a day trip from Surabaya, 60km to the northeast. From Surabaya's Purabaya bus terminal, take a Jombang bus (9000Rp, 1½ hours), which can drop you at the turn-off to the museum; a becak tour of the sites will cost around 30,000Rp for a half-day excursion after bargaining.

Pulau Madura

POP 3.6 MILLION

The flat, rugged and deeply traditional island of Madura may now be connected to Java by Indonesia's longest bridge, but the character of the people and scenery are a world apart. This is an island famous for its colourful bull races, *kerapan sapi*, and its virility drink, *jamu madura*.

Traditional culture is strong, the sarong and *peci* are the norm and people are deeply Islamic – virtually all children attend *pesantren* (religious schools). Madurese have a reputation throughout the nation for their quick tempers and brusqueness. While the Madurese can be disconcertingly blunt at times, they can also be extremely hospitable.

Madura's southern side is lined with shallow beaches and cultivated low-

land, while the northern coast alternates between rocky cliffs and great rolling sand-dune beaches, the best of which is at Lombang. At the extreme east is a tidal marsh and vast tracts of salt around Kalianget. The interior is riddled with limestone slopes, and is either rocky or sandy, so agriculture is limited. The spectacular annual bull races are a huge draw, but otherwise Sumenep is the only town that attracts a trickle of tourists.

History

In 1624 the island was conquered by Sultan Agung of Mataram and its government united under one Madurese princely line, the Cakraningrats. Until the middle of the 18th century the Cakraningrat family fiercely opposed Central Javanese rule and harassed Mataram, often conquering large parts of the kingdom.

By the beginning of the 1700s, however, the Dutch had secured control of the eastern half of Madura. The Cakraningrats then agreed to help the Dutch put down the 1740 rebellion in Central Java, but in the end they fared little better than their Javanese counterparts and ceded full sovereignty to the Dutch in 1743.

Under the Dutch, Madura was initially important as a major source of colonial troops, but later it became the main supplier of salt to the archipelago.

Overpopulation and poverty in Madura during the 1960s and 1970s lead to a policy of *transmigrasi* as millions of Madurese were resettled across the nation. Today the diaspora is one of Indonesia's largest, and you'll find communities of (often staunchly traditional) Madurese in Kalimantan, Papua and Sumatra.

Getting There & Away

Buses go directly from Surabaya's Purabaya bus terminal via Bangkalan and Pamekasan through to Sumenep (normal/*patas* 30,000/40,000Rp, four hours) roughly every hour. Buses also run to Sumenep (passing through Surabaya) from Banyuwangi (via Probolinggo), Malang, Semarang and Jakarta.

From East Java there's a daily **ferry** (☎032 866 3054) from Jangkar harbour (near Asembagus) to Kalianget (50,000Rp, five to six hours) in Madura. The ferry departs Jangkar at 1pm and from Kalianget at 8am. Schedules change regularly (contact the Sumenep tourist information office to check times). Buses run from Situbondo to Jangkar. To get to Kalianget take minibus 'O' (3000Rp, 20 minutes) from Sumenep.

Getting Around

From Bangkalan, buses run along the main highway to Pamekasan (21,000Rp, 2½ hours) and Sumenep (27,000Rp, four hours). Minibuses also travel along the northern route to Arosbaya, Tanjung Bumi, Pasongsongan and Ambunten.

Madura's roads are almost all paved and in excellent condition, with relatively little traffic. As the island is mostly flat, Madura is a good cycling destination, although it does get very hot.

SOUTH COAST

The first port of call for most visitors is **Kamal**, a scruffy place of little interest. Many head directly to **Bangkalan**, the next town north of Kamal, to watch the bull races. If you've time to kill before a race, **Museum Cakraningrat** (⌚8am-2pm Mon-Sat) will entertain you for an hour or so with displays on Madurese history and culture. For a day trip you could do worse than head to the beach at **Sambilangan**, 7km south of town, where there's a lonely 90m lighthouse that gazes out over the Madura strait.

Sampang, 61km from Bangkalan, also stages bull races and is the centre of the regency of the same name. Further east is the important town of **Pamekasan**, the island's capital. Bull races are held in and around Pamekasan every Sunday from the end of July until early October; during October each year it throbs with the festivities of the **Kerapan Sapi Grand Final**. About 35km east of Pamekasan, before Bluto, is **Karduluk**, a woodcarving centre.

SUMENEP

☎0328 / POP 101,000

Compared with the rest of Madura, Sumenep, in the far east of the island, is a sleepy, refined town, with a Mediterranean air and quiet, lazy streets. By mid-afternoon the whole town seems to settle into a slow, collective siesta. With dozens of crumbling villas and a fine *kraton* and mosque, it is easily Madura's most interesting town.

Sights

Kraton PALACE

(⏰7am-5pm) Occupied by the present *bupati* of Sumenep, the grand *kraton* and its **Taman Sari** (Pleasure Garden; admission 2000Rp; ⏰7am-5pm) date back to 1750. The bathing pools once used by the royal women are still here, though they're no longer in use. Part of the *kraton* building is a small museum with an interesting collection of royal possessions, including Madurese furniture, stone sculptures and *binggel* (heavy silver anklets worn by Madurese women). The complex can only be visited on a guided tour arranged at the royal carriage-house museum.

Royal Carriage-House Museum MUSEUM

(admission 2000Rp included in Taman Sari entry, traditional dance or gamelan practice admission free; ⏰7am-5pm, traditional dance or gamelan practice 10am-1pm) Opposite the *kraton*, the royal carriage-house museum contains the throne of Queen Tirtonegoro and a Chinese-style bed, which is reputedly 300 years old. On the first Sunday of the month, **traditional dance or gamelan practice** is held at the *kraton*.

A BULL RACE AT PACE

In Madurese folklore, the tradition of *kerapan sapi* began long ago when plough teams raced each other across the arid fields. This pastime was encouraged by Panembahan Sumolo, an early king of Sumenep. Today, with stud-bull breeding big business on Madura, *kerapan sapi* are an incentive for the Madurese to produce good stock. Only bulls of a high standard can be entered for important races – the Madurese keep their young bulls in superb condition, dosing them with an assortment of medicinal herbs, honey, beer and raw eggs.

Traditional races are held in bull-racing stadiums all over Madura. Practice trials are held throughout the year, but the main season starts in late August and September, when contests are held at district and regency levels. The finest bulls fight it out for the big prize in October at the grand final in Pamekasan, the island's capital.

This is the biggest and most colourful festival and as many as 100 bulls wearing richly decorated halters, ribbons and flowers, are paraded through town to a loud fanfare. For each race, two pairs of bulls are matched. They are stripped of their finery and have their 'jockeys' perched behind on wooden sleds. Gamelan music is played to excite the bulls and then, after being fed a generous tot of *arak* (palm wine), they're released and charge flat out down the track – often plunging straight into the crowd. The race is over in a flash – the best time recorded so far is nine seconds over 100m, faster than Usain Bolt. After the elimination heats the victors get to spend the rest of the year as studs.

Pamekasan is the main centre for bull racing, but Bangkalan, Sampang, Sumenep and some of the surrounding villages also host races. The East Java calendar of events, available from tourist offices in Surabaya, has a general schedule for the main races, but if you are on Madura over a weekend during the main season, you can be guaranteed that races or practices will be held somewhere on the island.

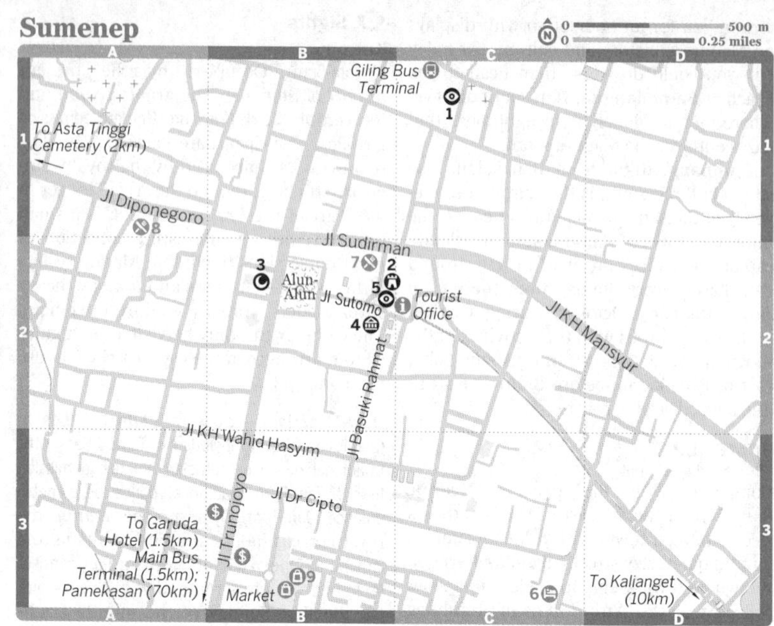

Sumenep

Sights

1 Giling Stadium C1
2 Kraton B2
3 Mesjid Jamik B2
4 Royal Carriage-House Museum B2
5 Taman Sari B2

Sleeping

6 Hotel C-1 .... C3

Eating

7 Rumah Makan 17 Agustus B2
8 Rumah Makan Kartini A1

Entertainment

Bull Races .... (see 1)

Shopping

9 Rachma Batik B3

Asta Tinggi Cemetery CEMETERY
The tombs of the royal family are at the Asta Tinggi Cemetery, which looks out over the town from a peaceful hilltop 2km northwest of the centre. The main royal tombs are decorated with carved and painted panels; two depict dragons said to represent the colonial invasion of Sumenep.

Mesjid Jamik MOSQUE
Sumenep's 18th-century Mesjid Jamik is notable for its three-tiered Meru-style roof, Chinese porcelain tiles and ceramics.

Festivals & Events

The **Festival of Sumenep** is usually celebrated biannually on 31 October and marks the founding of the town, with a program of cultural performances.

Sleeping & Eating

There are plenty of good, inexpensive eateries. Be sure to order the local speciality *sate kambing* (goat sate), which is often served with raw shallots and rice cakes. *Soto madura*, a spicy soup with nuts, lemongrass and beef is another speciality. Good places to try these dishes include **Rumah Makan Kartini** (☎662 431; Jl Diponegoro 83; mains around 9000Rp) and **Rumah Makan 17 Agustus** (☎662 255; Jl Sudirman 34; meals from 10,000Rp).

Hotel C-1 HOTEL $
(☎674 368; www.hotelc1.net; Jl Sultan Abdurrahman; r 125,000-400,000Rp; ❄📶) The newest, smartest place in town, this modern hotel has a good selection of rooms that combine contemporary and traditional design

influences, including hand-carved wooden furnitue and banana-yellow bathrooms. Cleanliness standards are good, mattresses are springy and the linen is fresh. It's about 2km southeast of the centre.

Garuda Hotel HOTEL $
(☎662 424; Jl Trunojoyo 280; r 65,000-210,000Rp, ste from 225,000Rp; ❄) Set back from the road, and very handy for the bus terminal, this hotel is a good deal with a wide range of accommodation, from no-frills economy digs with fans to large rooms with air-con and en-suite bathrooms.

☆ Entertainment

Bull Races BULL RACING
Sumenep is a centre for champion bull breeding, and on most Saturday mornings bull races can be seen at the **Giling stadium**.

Shopping

The main business in town is antiques and batik, and many homes seem to have something for sale. In the market, **Rachma Batik** has good-quality gear and fair prices.

ℹ Information

Sumenep's **tourist office** (☎081 7933 0648, 667 148; kurniadi@consultant.com; Jl Sutomo 5; ⏲7am-3.30pm Mon-Fri) is run by the very enthusiastic and knowledgeable Adi Wijaya, who can help out with most matters relating to both Sumenep and the island. He also acts as a guide. Sumenep has several internet places. **BCA** and **BNI banks** are on Jl Trunojoyo; both change cash. There's free wi-fi around the *alun-alun*.

ℹ Getting There & Away

Sumenep's main bus terminal is on the southern side of town, a 7000Rp becak ride from the centre. Buses leave roughly hourly until 4pm for Surabaya's Purabaya bus terminal (normal/*patas* 30,000/40,000Rp, four hours) and big cities across Java, including Malang. Bus agents along Jl Trunojoyo sell tickets. The Giling bus terminal for *angkots* heading north is right near the stadium, a short walk or becak ride from the centre. From Giling, minibuses go to Lombang, Slopeng, Ambunten and other north-coast destinations.

AROUND SUMENEP

From Sumenep, the road to **Kalianget**, 10km southeast, passes many fine villas. About halfway between the two towns are the ruins of a Dutch fort dating from 1785, and a cemetery.

The Kalianget region is a centre for salt production – you'll see great mounds of the white powder piled up for export if you pass by in the dry season. Daily boats sail from here for Jangkar in East Java and to other islands in the Sumenep district.

You can go **snorkelling** at Pulau Talango, just offshore.

WORTH A TRIP

NORTH COAST

Fishing villages and their brightly painted *perahu* (boats) dot the north coast. The coast is lined with beaches, but few are particularly wonderful.

Near Arosbaya, 27km north of Kamal, the tombs of the Cakraningrat royalty are at **Air Mata** (Tears) cemetery, superbly situated on the edge of a small ravine. The ornately carved headstone of Ratu Ibu, consort of Cakraningrat I, is the most impressive.

The village of **Tanjung Bumi** is situated on the northwest coast of Madura, about 60km from Kamal. Although primarily a fishing village, it is also a manufacturing centre for traditional Madurese batik and *perahu*.

Pasongsongan is a fishing settlement on the beach, where it may be possible to stay with villagers. Further east, **Ambunten** is the largest settlement on the north coast and has a bustling market. Just over the bridge, you can walk along the picturesque river, which is lined with *perahu* (boats), and through the fishing village to the beach. East of Ambunten, **Slopeng** has a wide beach with sand dunes and coconut palms. The water is usually calm enough for swimming, but it is not always clean. Men fish the shallower water with large cantilevered hand nets. Slopeng is also known for its *topeng* (wooden mask) making.

The stunning white sands of **Pantai Lombang**, 30km northeast of Sumenep, form the best beach in Madura; there's no development here to spoil the idyllic scene. Locals harvest tree saplings for the bonsai market and sell coconuts to visitors.

Malang

☎0341 / POP 771,000

With leafy, colonial-era boulevards and a breezy climate, Malang moves at a far more leisurely pace than the regional capital, Surabaya. It's a cultured city with several important universities, home to a large student population. The central area is not too large and quite walkable.

Established by the Dutch in the closing decades of the 18th century, Malang earned its first fortunes from coffee, which flourished on the surrounding hillsides. Today, the city's colonial grandeur is quickly disappearing behind the homogenous facades of more modern developments, but there's still much to admire for now.

And with a number of Hindu temples and sights outside the city, Malang makes an ideal base to explore this intriguing corner of East Java.

Sights

Hotel Tugu Malang MUSEUM

(www.tuguhotels.com/malang; Jl Tugu III; wi-fi) Malang's most impressive museum isn't actually a museum at all but a hotel – the five-star Hotel Tugu Malang. This hotel acts as a showcase for its culturally obsessed owners and their astonishing collection of art, sculpture and treasures here, including 10th-century ceramics, ancient *wayang*, antique teak furniture, glassware and even the complete facade of a Chinese temple. The portrait of a lady in the mirror is one of Java's most famous paintings. Visitors are welcome to browse the collection, which is spread throughout the hotel premises (though you might consider it polite to buy a drink while you're here).

Jl Besar Ijen NEIGHBOURHOOD

Malang has some wonderful colonial architecture. Just northwest of the centre, Jl Besar Ijen is Malang's millionaires' row, a boulevard lined with elegant whitewashed mansions from the Dutch era. Many have been substantially renovated, but there's still much to admire. In late May, the entire area is closed to traffic and becomes the setting for the city's huge Malang Kembali festival.

Balai Kota NOTABLE BUILDING

(Town Hall; Jl Tugu) Close to the city centre, the Balai Kota is an immense Dutch administrative building, built in a hybrid of Dutch and Indonesian architectural styles with a tiered central roof that resembles a Javanese mosque.

Pasar Senggol MARKET

(⏲7am-5pm) This bird market is fascinating to explore: you'll see ravens in cages (their blood is used in black-magic ceremonies) and maybe a snake or two.

Pasar Bunga MARKET

(⏲7am-5pm) The flower market, Pasar Bunga, has a pleasant aspect around a river valley and it is the place to stroll in the morning.

Candi Badut TEMPLE

On the northwestern outskirts of town, Candi Badut is a small Shivaite temple dating from the 8th century.

Activities

If you're looking for a great, inexpensive massage (which also supports the local community) head to **Nuansa Fajar** (☎324 531; Jl Kahuripan 11A; massage per hour 20,000Rp, hotel visit per hour 30,000Rp; ⏲5.30am-10pm), a training centre that employs blind masseurs. Shiatsu, reflexology and traditional Javanese massages are offered.

Tours

Malang is a good place to set up a tour to Bromo; these are usually on the route via Tumpang. Costs very much depend on numbers and transport but two/three/four people can expect to pay 650,000/550,000/450,000Rp per person for a sunrise tour in a 4WD (they usually leave at 1.30am). Options to continue the trip on to Ijen and then Ketapang harbour (for Bali) are also popular, costing around 1,350,000/1,050,000/950,000Rp respectively. Some tour agents also include Baluran National Park (p194) in an itinerary.

Trips to southern beaches and temples around Malang are also possible. If you want to create your own itinerary, a day's car hire (with driver) starts at around 550,000Rp.

Helios Tours TOUR

(☎362 741; www.heliostour.net; Jl Pattimura 37) A well-organised operator with an incredible number of tour options, from standard day-trips to Bromo to hard-core trekking expeditions to Gunung Semeru. Staff are switched-on and deal with lots of travellers.

Sunrise Holiday TOUR

(☎359 070; www.sunriseholiday.com; Jl Majapahit 1K) Well-informed agency that runs a lot of

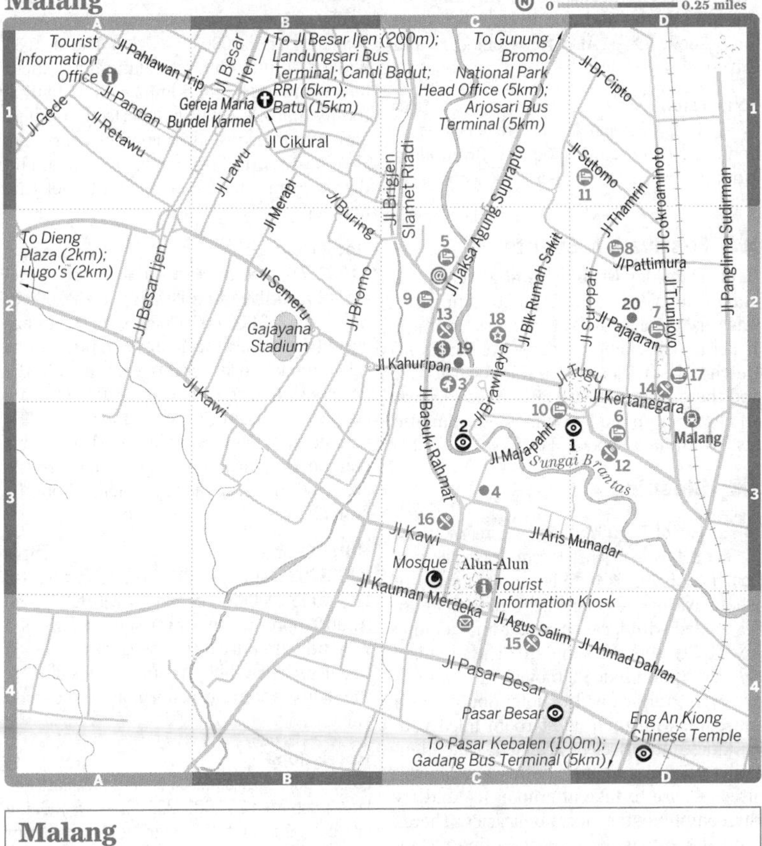

Malang

Sights

1	Balai Kota	D3
	Hotel Tugu Malang	(see 10)
	Pasar Bunga	(see 2)
2	Pasar Senggol	C3

Activities, Courses & Tours

	Helios Tours	(see 8)
	Jona's Homestay	(see 11)
3	Nuansa Fajar	C2
4	Sunrise Holiday	C3

Sleeping

5	Citihub	C2
6	Hotel Aloha	D3
7	Hotel Emma	D2
8	Hotel Helios	D2
9	Hotel Trio Indah II	C2
10	Hotel Tugu Malang	C3
11	Jona's Homestay	D1
	Kampong Tourist	(see 8)

Eating

12	Rumah Makan Inggil	D3
13	Agung	C2
14	Kertanegara	D2
	Melati	(see 10)
15	Night Food Market	C4
16	Toko Oen	C3

Drinking

17	MLG Coffee Shop	D2

Entertainment

18	Taman Rekreasi Senaputra	C2

Information

19	Haryono Tours	C2
20	Wijaya Travel	D2

tours in East Java. Has Dutch- and English-speaking guides and can arrange transport for bespoke trips. Also rents out cars and drivers.

Jona's Homestay TOUR
(☎324 678; Jl Sutomo 4) The owners of this homestay can organise tours to Bromo and around Malang, they also rent scooters to guests.

Festivals & Events

Held in late May, **Malang Kembali** celebrates *ludruk*, an old-time music hall tradition that was very popular in Java in the last century. Jl Besar Ijen, home to many wonderful old Dutch villas, is closed to traffic for five days and there's street theatre, live music, shows, and actors in period costumes. You can also taste traditional food and drinks.

Sleeping

TOP CHOICE **Hotel Tugu Malang** LUXURY HOTEL $$$
(☎363 891; www.tuguhotels.com; Jl Tugu III; r/ste from US$105/195; ❄@📶) For a real flavour of what Java has to offer, this remarkable hotel, loaded with local character and genuine hospitality, sets the standard. The premises are very grand indeed, though the contents are even grander, as the hotel doubles as a museum, with room after room filled with antiques and priceless artefacts. The attention to detail and little extras are impressive: be sure to take afternoon tea and try the complimentary local delicacies. There's a great spa, wine bar and two fine restaurants. Rooms enjoy classy furnishings and teak floors; for a real blowout book one of the suites that has hosted presidents and princes.

TOP CHOICE **Kampong Tourist** HOSTEL $
(☎351 801; www.kampongtourist.com; Hotel Helios, Jl Patimura 37; dm 50,000Rp, r 125,000-150,000Rp; 📶) The owners of this superb new backpacking place have fashioned an excellent hostel on the rooftop of Hotel Helios. Most of the buildings have been beautifully constructed from bamboo and timber. The vision is impressive, with top-quality mattresses in the dorm (though it does have a *lot* of beds), lovely gazebo-style private rooms, a great shower block and guests' kitchen. You can tour the town and then socialise in the bar-cafe, with commanding city views, cold beer and snacks.

Citihub HOTEL $$
(☎369 385; www.citihubhotels.com; Jl Jaksa Agung Suprapto 11; r 250,000Rp; ❄@📶) The deluxe-budget Citihub chain's Malang hotel sticks to a winning formula: immaculate, inviting rooms that are small but perfectly formed, with all mod cons and a contemporary feel. The location on busy Suprato is good, and there's a minimart and huge internet cafe here too.

Hotel Helios HOTEL $$
(☎362 741; www.hotelhelios-malang.com; Jl Patimura 37; r incl breakfast with fan 95,000-180,000Rp, with air-con 250,000-400,000Rp; ❄📶) Helios has steadily upgraded the quality and prices of its accommodation in recent years. Behind the flash reception you'll find a selection of clean, comfortable rooms, most with flat-screen TV and modern bathrooms grouped around a rear garden (and cafe). The economy options are tiny and very Spartan. Helios Tours is based here.

Hotel Emma HOTEL $
(☎363 198; Jl Trunojoyo 21; r incl breakfast with fan 125,000-150,000Rp, with air-con 240,000Rp; ❄) Almost opposite the train station, this is a very tidy, friendly little hotel. Cleanliness is taken seriously here, rooms are spacious – the deluxe rooms are enormous – and good value.

Hotel Aloha HOTEL $$
(☎326 950; Jl Gajah Mada I; r incl breakfast with fan/air-con from 205,000/285,000Rp; ❄) Being critical, this hotel's beige interior colour scheme is a touch bland but the leafy green location in an attractive street is definitely a plus. Tiled, clean rooms are set around a covered courtyard.

Jona's Homestay HOMESTAY $
(☎324 678; Jl Sutomo 4; r with shared mandi from 65,000Rp, with air-con 175,000-300,000Rp; ❄📶) This long-running homestay in a huge old Dutch villa is run by a sweet family who look after guests well and offer tours. The location is convenient and quiet but the ageing rooms could do with a little more TLC: those at the rear are very basic; some of the air-con options are simply huge.

Hotel Trio Indah II HOTEL $$
(☎359 083; www.hoteltrio2.com; Jl Brigjen Slamet Riadi 1-3; r 260,000-440,000Rp; ❄@📶) This hotel's great arched frontage resembles a Victorian railway terminal. It has 37 clean,

if unexceptional, rooms, all with TV and air-con. There's room service and a cafe.

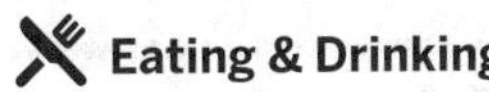

Eating & Drinking

For cheap eats head for Jl Agus Salim, which comes alive at night to the sights and smells of Malang's **night food market**. Local specialities *nasi rawon* (beef soup served with fried onion and rice) and *bakso malang* (meatball soup served with noodles and grilled fish) are always worth a try.

Melati INDONESIAN, WESTERN **$$**
(☎363 891; www.tuguhotels.com; Jl Tugu III; most mains 40,000-120,000Rp; 📶) The Tugu hotel's poolside restaurant is a romantic, atmospheric setting for a meal, with a relaxed air and attentive staff to guide you through the delicious Indonesian and Chinese Peranakan food. Western dishes, including pasta and grilled meats, are also excellent. Melati also makes a great place to hit for a power breakfast or brunch.

Rumah Makan Inggil INDONESIAN **$**
(Jl Gajah Mada 4; meals 25,000-45,000Rp; 📶) On a leafy street near the Balai Kita roundabout, this quirky restaurant is festooned with old photographs of Malang and a motley collection of curios (gramaphones, typewriters, maps, cameras, indeed anything vaguely old). The Indonesian food is good, with tasty fish and meat (try the *ayam bakar*, or grilled chicken), though service can be a bit spotty.

MLG Coffee Shop CAFE
(Jl Trunojoyo 10E; coffee 9000-20,000Rp) Just up from the station this small cafe is run by locals passionate about their robusta and arabica – there are beans from Thailand, Brazil and Colombia to taste here. Sip an espresso or treat yourself to a *kopi luwak*. You'll also find lots of teas and a few snacks, including brownies.

Agung INDONESIAN **$**
(☎357 061; Jl Basuki Rahmat 80; meals 12,000-18,000Rp) A kind of modern warung, this stylish little place has very tasty, inexpensive local food including *martabak* (meat, egg and vegetable pancake-like dish), rice and fish dishes, plus great juices.

Kertanegara INDONESIAN **$$**
(☎704 4141; www.kertanegararesto.com; Jl Kertanegara I; most mains 33,000-55,000Rp; ⏲noon-11pm) Occupying a large corner plot, this upmarket place has a great garden terrace and serves flavoursome European, Indonesian and Chinese food with quite a good choice for vegetarians and lots of seafood – try the milkfish.

Toko Oen INTERNATIONAL **$**
(☎364 052; Jl Basuki Rahmat 5; mains 22,000-60,000Rp) Boasting an imposing art deco frontage that dates from 1930, Toko Oen is a throwback to ye olde days, with rattan furniture, waiters in starched whites and Sinatra on the stereo. In truth it's looking a tad tired, and the Indonesian and Western food (taking in steaks and stir fries) could be better. So you could just down a big Bintang (24,000Rp) or a coffee.

☆ Entertainment

Taman Rekreasi Senaputra PERFORMING ARTS
(Jl Brawijaya; admission 7000Rp, children aged 1-13 6000Rp) Malang's cultural and recreational park has a swimming pool and children's playground and some quirky events. *Kuda lumping* (horse trance) dances (7000Rp) are performed every Sunday morning at 10am. The dancers ride rattan 'horses' then fall into a trance, writhing around on the ground with their eyes bulging. Still in a trance-like state they perform assorted masochistic acts without any apparent harm, such as eating glass. The bizarre spectacle will not be to everyone's taste.

On a more sober tip, *wayang kulit* shows are reguarly held here (usually on the fourth Sunday of the month), the tourist board has the latest schedule.

RRI PERFORMING ARTS
(☎387 500; Jl Candi Panggung) About 5km northwest of the city, this place has *wayang kulit* from 9pm on the first Saturday of the month.

ℹ Information

Malang has plenty of banks; most are congregated along Jl Basuki Rahmat, including **BCA**.

Citihub Internet (Jl Jaksa Agung Suprapto 11; per hour 5000Rp; ⏲24hr)

Gunung Bromo National Park Head Office (☎490 885; tn-bromo@malang.wasantara.net.id; Jl Raden Intan 6; ⏲8am-3pm Mon-Thu, to 11am Fri) For Bromo info.

Main post office (Jl Kauman Merdeka) Opposite the *alun-alun*.

Tourist information kiosk (In the alun-alun) This small kiosk is staffed by students.

Tourist information office (☎558 919; Jl Gede 6; ⏲8am-4pm Mon-Fri) Helpful, but 3km northwest of the *alun-alun*.

Getting There & Away

BUS & ANGKOT Malang has three bus terminals. Arjosari, 5km north of town, is the main one with regular buses to Surabaya, Probolinggo and Banyuwangi. Long-distance buses to Solo, Yogyakarta, Denpasar and even Jakarta mostly leave in the early evening. Minibuses (called *angkot* or *mikrolet* locally) run from Arjosari to nearby villages such as Singosari and Tumpang. Gadang bus terminal is 5km south of the city centre, and has buses along the southern routes to destinations such as Blitar (14,000Rp, two hours). Landungsari bus terminal, 5km northwest of the city, has buses to destinations west of the city, such as Batu (4000Rp, 40 minutes). You can also book bus tickets at **Haryono Tours** (☎034 1367 5000; www.haryonotours.com; Jl Kahuripan 22) and at guesthouses for a commission.

MINIBUS Plenty of door-to-door *travel* companies operate from Malang, and hotels and travel agencies can book them. Helios Tours (p172) and **Wijaya Travel** (☎327 072) are two reliable agencies. Minibuses travel to Solo (90,000Rp), Yogyakarta (110,000Rp) and Probolinggo (40,000Rp). Minibuses to Surabaya (40,000Rp) will drop you off at hotels in Surabaya (thus saving the long haul from Surabaya's bus terminal) but be warned that this can add up to a couple of hours to your trip.

TAXI For a reliable taxi company, use **Citra** (☎490 555).

TRAIN **Malang train station** (☎362 208) is centrally located but not well connected to the main network. There are three daily trains to Yogyakarta (160,000Rp to 350,000Rp, seven hours) via Solo. Surabaya is only served by very slow and crowded economy trains.

Getting Around

Mikrolet run all over town. Most buzz between the bus terminals via the town centre. These are marked A–G (Arjosari to Gadung and return), A–L (Arjosari to Landungsari) or G–L (Gadang to Landungsari). Trips cost 2000Rp to 3000Rp.

Around Malang

SINGOSARI TEMPLES

The Singosari temples lie in a ring around Malang and are mostly funerary temples dedicated to the kings of the Singosari dynasty (AD 1222–92), the precursors of the Majapahit kingdom.

Tumpang is also home to the **Mangun Dhama Arts Centre** (☎034 178 7907), which has Javanese dance classes and performances, plus some gamelan, *wayang* and woodcarving courses. *Wayang kulit* and dance shows can be staged if pre-arranged, and books, dance DVDs, masks, puppets and batik are usually for sale.

If coming from Singosari, go to Blimbing where the road to Tumpang branches off the highway, and then catch a minibus. In Tumpang, the temple is only a short stroll from the main road.

Sights

FREE **Candi Singosari** TEMPLE

(⏲7am-5pm) Situated right in the village of Singosari, 12km north of Malang, this temple stands 500m off the main Malang–Surabaya road. This temple – one of the last monuments erected to the Singosari dynasty – was built in 1304 in honour of King Kertanegara, the fifth and last Singosari king, who died in 1292 in a palace uprising. The main structure of the temple was completed, but for some reason the sculptors never finished their task. Only the top part has any ornamentation and the *kala* heads have been left strangely stark. Of the statues that once inhabited the temple's cham-

BUSES FROM MALANG

DESTINATION	COST (RP)	DURATION (HR)	FREQUENCY
Banyuwangi	55,000	7	daily at 7am and 1pm
Denpasar	110,000-150,000	12	4 daily 5am-7pm
Jember	32,000	4½	every 1½hr
Lovina (Bali)	150,000	12	5pm daily
Probolinggo	14,000-22,000	2½	hourly 5am-5pm
Solo	75,000	10	2 daily
Surabaya	15,000-20,000	2½-3	every 20 min
Yogyakarta	95,000	11	2 daily

Around Malang

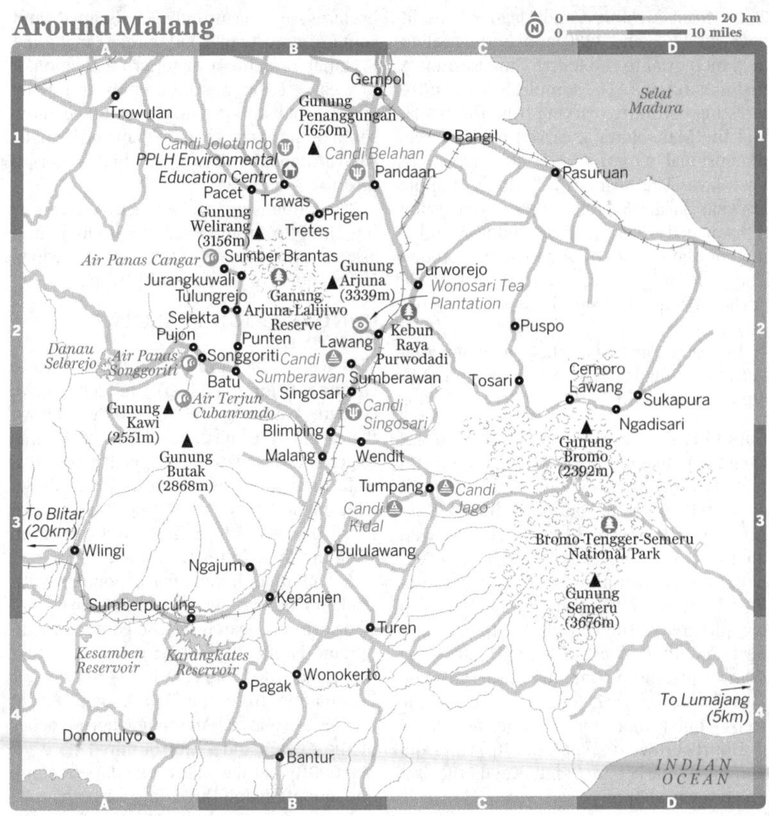

bers, only the statue of Agastya (the Shivaite teacher who, legend has it, walked across the water to Java) remains. Statues of Durga and Ganesha that were in the temple are now exhibited in the National Museum in Jakarta. Locals visit this temple to meditate and leave offerings of flower petals.

About 200m beyond the temple are two enormous figures of *dwarapala* (guardians against evil spirits) wearing clusters of skulls and twisted serpents.

To reach Singosari, take a green *angkot* (4000Rp) from Malang's Arjosari bus terminal and get off at the Singosari market on the highway.

FREE Candi Sumberawan TEMPLE

(⏲7am-5pm) This small, squat Buddhist stupa lies in the foothills of Gunung Arjuna, about 5km northwest of Singosari. Originating from a later period than the Singosari temples, it was built to commemorate the visit of Hayam Wuruk, the great Majapahit king, who visited the area in 1359.

Take an *angkot* (3000Rp) from Singosari *pasar* on the highway to Desa Sumberawan, walk 500m down the road to the canal, then follow the canal rice paddies for 1km to the temple. This delightful walk is the highlight of the visit.

Young men use the canal for washing themselves, so don't be surprised to see a naked body or two en route to the stupa. In Javanese culture it's polite to avert your eyes – the boys will duck down into the water in fits of giggles as you pass by.

Sumberawan village is a shoemaking centre where wooden soles are shaped by hand for export to Bali; prospective purchasers can drop by the Echarispen's family home at Jl Candirawan 17.

Candi Jago TEMPLE

(Jajaghu; admission 5000Rp; ⏲7am-5pm) Along a small road near the market in Tumpang,

22km from Malang, Candi Jago was built between 1268 and 1280 and is thought to be a memorial to the fourth Singosari king, Vishnuvardhana. The temple has some interesting decorative carving from the Jataka and the Mahabharata, carved in the three-dimensional, *wayang kulit*–style typical of East Java. This primarily Buddhist temple also has Javanese-Hindu statues, including a six-armed, death-dealing goddess and a lingam, the symbol of Shiva's male potency. There are two photocopied leaflets available at the entrance. Consult these to learn more about its history.

To reach Candi Jago take a white *angkot* from Malang's Arjosari bus terminal to Tumpang (4000Rp).

Candi Kidal TEMPLE
(admission 5000Rp; 24hr) This graceful temple, 7km south of Candi Jago, was built around 1260 as the burial shrine of King Anusapati (the second Singosari king, who died in 1248). It's now 12m high but originally topped 17m and is a fine example of East Javanese architecture. Its slender form has pictures of the Garuda (mythical man-bird) on three sides, plus bold, glowering *kala* heads and medallions of the *haruna*. Two *kala makara* (dragons) guard the steps – one is male and the other female.

Hourly brown *angkot* (3000Rp) run from Tumpang market to Candi Kidal; the last one returns at 4pm.

WONOSARI TEA PLANTATION

About 30km north of Malang, the **Wonosari Tea Plantation** (Kebun Teh Agro Wonosari; 034 142 6032; www.agro-ptpn12.com; weekday/weekend 8000/15,000Rp) has sweeping views and a temperate climate; the setting is glorious. This agrotourism venture and leisure park offers everything from tea-plantation tours (40,000Rp), a minitrain and zip lines to tennis and a swimming pool. You can arrange a guide here (around 175,000Rp for the day) to hike to the top of Gunung Arjuna. You can also purchase tea grown on the estate and good accommodation is available (rooms 180,000Rp to 1,400,000Rp). From Malang, catch a bus or *mikrolet* to the town of Lawang (7000Rp) and then an *ojek* (12,000Rp).

PURWODADI

The **Kebun Raya Purwodadi** (admission 4000Rp, tours 7500Rp; 7am-4pm) are expansive dry-climate botanical gardens. The 85 hectares are beautifully landscaped and contain more than 3000 species, including 80 kinds of palm, a huge fern collection, a Mexican section, myriad orchids and many varieties of bamboo. The garden office to the south of the entrance has a map and leaflets. **Air Terjun Cobanbaung** is a high waterfall next to the gardens.

The gardens are easily reached; take any bus (7000Rp) from Malang to Surabaya and ask to be dropped off at the entrance, which is 3km north of the town of Lawang,

GUNUNG ARJUNA-LALIJIWO RESERVE

This reserve includes the dormant volcano **Gunung Arjuna** (3339m), the semi-active **Gunung Welirang** (3156m) and the Lalijiwo Plateau on the northern slopes of Arjuna. Experienced and well-equipped hikers can walk from the resort town of Tretes to Selekta in two days, but you need a guide to go all the way. Alternatively, you can climb Welirang from Tretes or Lawang.

A well-used hiking path, popular with students on weekends and holidays, and also with soul-searchers who come to meditate on the mountain, begins in Tretes near the Kakak Bodo Recreation Reserve. Get information from the **PHKA post** (081 2178 8956; Jl Wilis 523) in the northern reaches of the town. Guides can be hired here for 300,000Rp per day; allow two days to climb one mountain and three days for both.

It's a hard, five-hour, 17km walk to the very basic huts used by the Gunung Welirang sulphur collectors. Hikers usually stay overnight here in order to reach the summit before the clouds roll in around mid-morning. Bring your own camping gear, food and drinking water (or hire it all at the PHKA post for around 140,000Rp per day), and be prepared for freezing conditions. From the huts it's a 4km climb to the summit. Allow at least six hours in total for the ascent, and 4½ hours for the descent.

The trail passes Lalijiwo Plateau, a superb alpine meadow, from where a trail leads to Gunung Arjuna, the more demanding peak. From Arjuna, a trail leads down the southern side to Junggo, near Selekta and Batu. It's a five-hour descent from Arjuna this way; a guide is essential.

Getting There & Away

To get to the start of the hike, take a bus to Pandaan (10,000Rp) from Malang or Surabaya and then a minibus to Tretes (7000Rp).

GUNUNG PENANGGUNGAN

The remains of no fewer than 81 temples are scattered over the slopes of Gunung Penanggungan (1650m). This sacred Hindu mountain is said to be the peak of Mt Mahameru, which according to legend broke off and landed at its present site when Mt Mahameru was transported from India to Indonesia.

Historically this was a very important pilgrimage site for Hindus and a few Javanese mystics, meditators and Hindus still visit the mountain today. Pilgrims make their way to the top of the mountain and stop to bathe in the holy springs adorned with Hindu statuary. The two main bathing places are **Candi Jolotundo** and **Candi Belahan**, the best examples of remaining Hindu art. Both are difficult to reach.

In a stunning setting on the evergreen western slopes of Penanggungan, **PPLH Environmental Education Centre** (☎032 1722 1045; dm/bungalows 25,000/275,000Rp) is a supremely relaxing and interesting place. It's mainly set up to teach groups about the merits of organic agriculture, composting and garbage management. Expert guides can be hired for hikes (140,000Rp per day) and they'll gladly explain about plants used for herbal medicines. There's an organic restaurant and good, rustic accommodation is available in pretty bungalows with outdoor bathrooms, or in more basic dorms. School groups pass through from time to time, disturbing the tranquility somewhat, but most of the time it's very peaceful. To get there, take a Trawas-bound minibus (6000Rp) from Pandaan and an *ojek* (10,000Rp) from Trawas.

BATU

☎0341 / POP 79,000

Batu, 15km northwest of Malang, is a large hill resort on the lower reaches of Gunung Arjuna, surrounded by volcanic peaks. It's a popular weekend destination for locals, but makes a relaxed base during the week, if you want to avoid staying in Malang.

There are several banks.

Sights & Activities

Songgoriti HOT SPRINGS

(admission 8000Rp; ⏲7.30am-5pm) Songgoriti, 3km west of Batu, has well-known hot springs and a small, ancient Hindu temple in the grounds of the Hotel Air Panas Songgoriti. Nearby, Pasar Wisata is a tourist market selling mostly apples, bonsai plants, and volcanic stone mortars and pestles. The waterfall **Air Terjun Cubanrondo** (admission 10,000Rp; ⏲7.30am-5pm) is 5km southwest of Songgoriti.

Sumber Brantas HOT SPRINGS

Higher up the mountain, the small village of Sumber Brantas, far above Selekta, is at the source of Sungai Brantas. From here you can walk 2km to **Air Panas Cangar** (admission 5000Rp; ⏲7.30am-5pm), hot springs high in the mountains surrounded by forest and mist.

Selekta SWIMMING

(admission 12,500Rp; ⏲7.30am-5pm) Selekta, a small resort 5km further up the mountain from Batu and 1km off the main road, is home to the **Pemandian Selekta**, a large swimming pool with a superb setting in landscaped gardens.

Sleeping & Eating

Accommodation is available in Batu, Songgoriti and all along the road to Selekta. Songgoriti and Selekta are small, quiet resorts; Batu has the best facilities but is more built-up. Add around 25% to prices for weekend rates.

Batu's Jl Panglima Sudirman is lined with restaurants and warung.

Kampung Lumbung LODGE $$

(☎540 6941; www.grahabunga.com; r/cottage from 520,000/1,250,000Rp;) Wonderful ecohotel where the complex resembles a traditional village and all the buildings make good use of recycled wood and solar power. Staff go the extra mile to look after guests and there's a coffee shop and excellent local food in the restaurant. The natural environment really is sublime here; the climate is refreshing and the air is deliciously fresh. It's a kilometre south of central Batu.

Mutiara Baru HOTEL $

(☎511 259; Jl Panglima Sudirman 89; r 125,000-450,000Rp;) The more pricey rooms here are pleasant, light and airy, and face the garden and pool. Cheaper options are basic but clean and you have to request hot water from reception.

Hotel Kartika Wijaya HISTORIC HOTEL $$

(☎592 600; www.kartikawijaya.com; Jl Panglima Sudirman 127; r incl breakfast from 525,000Rp;) A very imposing colonial residence in sweeping lawned grounds dotted with palms and tennis courts. The carpeted rooms are spacious and comfortable, though not that grand.

Pantara Cafe JAVANESE $

(Jl Panglima Sudirman 123; meals 15,000-22,000Rp) On the main drag in Batu, the Pantara serves up delicious Javanese food in atmospheric surrounds.

Getting There & Away

From Malang's Landungsari bus terminal take a Kediri bus or a *mikrolet* to Batu (4000Rp, 40 minutes). *Mikrolet* connect Batu's bus terminal with the centre via Panglima Sudirman.

From the bus terminal, *mikrolet* run to Selekta (3000Rp, 20 minutes) and Sumber Brantas (6000Rp, 45 minutes). *Mikrolet* turn off to Sumber Brantas at Jurangkuwali village. For Air Panas Cangar, walk 2km straight ahead from Jurangkuwali.

You'll find plenty of *ojek* around Batu to get you to all of these destinations.

SOUTH-COAST BEACHES

The coast south of Malang has some good beaches, but facilities are limited. **Sendangbiru** is a picturesque fishing village separated by a narrow channel from **Pulau Sempu**. This island nature reserve has a couple of lakes, **Telaga Lele** and **Telaga Sat**, both ringed by jungle. Boats can be hired (around 150,000Rp return) to get you to Sempu. Take your own provisions.

A few kilometres before Sendangbiru, a rough track to the left leads 3km to **Tambakrejo**, a small fishing village with a sweeping sandy bay, which (despite the surf) is generally safe for swimming.

Balekambang is best known for its picturesque Hindu temple on the small island of Pulau Ismoyo, connected by a footbridge to the beach. Balekambang is one of the most popular beaches and is crowded on weekends. There are basic guesthouses in the village.

Getting There & Away

Minibuses from Malang's Gadang bus terminal travel to Sendangbiru (16,000Rp, two hours), past the turn-off to Tambakrejo. For Balekambang, buses run direct from Malang for 15,000Rp.

Blitar

☎0342 / POP 132,000

A low-key provincial city, Blitar makes a good base for visiting Panataran temple and the spectacular active volcano of Gunung Kelud. It's also of interest as the site of former president Sukarno's home and memorial.

Sights

Makam Bung Karno MONUMENT

(admission by donation; ⊙7am-5pm) At Sentul, 2km north of the town centre, former president Sukarno's grave is marked by an elaborate monument of concrete, columns and murals of the man's achievements. Sukarno (or Bung Karno) is widely regarded as the father of the Indonesian nation, although he was only reinstated as a national hero in 1978.

Despite family requests that he be buried at his home in Bogor, Sukarno was buried in an unmarked grave next to his mother in Blitar. His father's grave was also moved from Jakarta to here. It was only in 1978 that the lavish million-dollar monument was built and the grave site was opened to visitors. There's also a small museum devoted to the man, which has hundreds of historic photographs of Sukarno with heads of state including John F Kennedy and Ho Chi Minh.

The monument has an undeniable poignancy, and thousands of Indonesian pilgrims come here each year to pay their respects. Sadly, as you leave, things descend abruptly into tacky consumerism as you're directed through a seemingly never-ending maze of souvenir stalls.

A becak from Blitar town centre is around 8000Rp. Panataran-bound *angkudes* (yellow minibuses; 2000Rp) pass by; ask for the *makam* (grave).

Museum Sukarno MUSEUM

(Jl Sultan Agung 59; admission by donation; ⊙7am-5pm) For a more personal look into the life of Sukarno, head for the Museum Sukarno, located in the house where he lived as a boy. Photos, revolutionary posters and memorabilia (including a Bung Karno clock) line the front room, and you can see the great man's bedroom and check out his old Mercedes in the garage. The museum is about 1.5km from the centre of town.

Pasar Legi MARKET

Blitar's large Pasar Legi, next to the bus terminal, is also worth a wander.

Sleeping & Eating

TOP CHOICE **Hotel Tugu Blitar** HISTORIC HOTEL $$

(☎801 766; www.tuguhotels.com; Jl Merdeka 173; r 160,000-375,000Rp, ste from 650,000Rp; ❄📶) A rare find in East Java, this hotel is a bastion of refinement. There's a real sense of history throughout the main structure, a

Dutch colonial building from the 1850s. Be sure to ask staff to let you see the Sukarno room (he was a frequent visitor here) where you can sit at his old desk. The rooms in the principal part of the hotel are incredibly atmospheric, with high ceilings and grand teak beds; those in the modern extension at the rear are neat and functional. Service is warm and professional, and staff are full of tips about the city and region.

Hotel Sri Rejeki HOTEL **$**
(☎801 718; Jl TGP 13; r without/with mandi from 45,000/70,000Rp, with air-con & breakfast from 100,000Rp; ❄) The welcoming Sri Rejeki is well set up for budget travellers with a central location and plenty of clean, functional rooms. Some rooms have TV and Western toilets, but none have hot water.

Waroeng Tugu Blitar JAVANESE **$**
(www.tuguhotels.com/blitar; Jl Merdeka 173; tea & snacks 20,000Rp; ⏲4-6pm) After a hot day's sightseeing, drop by this fine hotel's *'waroeng'* for a Javanese-style afternoon tea of delicious traditional snacks and cakes, local coffee and tea. It's served between 4pm and 6pm daily by a kindly, elderly gent. Be sure to tour the hotel while you're here.

RM Retno JAVANESE **$**
(☎802 158; Jl Ir Sukarno 37A; meals 12,000-16,000Rp) For authentic East Javanese food try the lunch buffet at this bustling *rumah makan* (restaurant), where there's a great selection of meat, fish and vegetable options. It's about 300m from Sukarno's grave.

Information

There are several banks in town including **BCA Bank** (Jl Merdeka). **Warnet Mitra** (Jl Lawu 71; per hr 3000Rp) has internet access and is behind the main street; you can also Skype here.

Getting There & Away

Regular buses run from Blitar to Malang (16,000Rp, 2½ hours) and Surabaya (40,000Rp, 4½ to five hours), as well as Solo (52,000Rp, six hours). The bus terminal is 4km south of town along Jl Veteran (2000Rp by *angkot* from the centre). *Angkudes* run from the western end of Jl Merdeka to Panataran temple for 3000Rp, passing close to Makam Bung Karno; you'll have to walk the last 300m or so.

Blitar has a few useful train connections, with three daily services heading to both Solo (175,000Rp to 270,000Rp, 4½ hours) and Yogyakarta (175,000Rp to 230,000Rp, five to 5½ hours).

Hiring a car and driver makes a lot of sense to see the sights; the Hotel Tugu Blitar can organise this for 450,000Rp per day. Or hire an *ojek* for much less at around 80,000Rp.

Panataran

The **Hindu temples** (admission by donation; ⏲7am-5pm) at Panataran (locally called 'Penataran') are the largest intact Majapahit temples, and the finest examples of East Javanese architecture and sculpture. Construction began in 1197, during the Singosari dynasty, with building work continuing for another 250 years. Most of the important surviving structures date from the great years of the Majapahit kingdom during the 14th century.

Around the base of the first-level platform, the comic-strip carvings tell the story of a test between the fat, meat-eating Bubukshah and the thin, vegetarian Gagang Aking.

Further on is the small Dated Temple, so called because of the date '1291' (AD 1369) carved over the entrance. On the next level are colossal serpents snaking endlessly around the Naga Temple, which once housed valuable sacred objects.

At the rear stands the Mother Temple, its lowest panels depicting stories from the Ramayana. Behind is a small royal *mandi* with a frieze depicting lizards, bulls and dragons around its walls.

Three hundred metres beyond the turn-off to the temples, the **Museum Panataran** (admission by donation; ⏲8am-2pm Tue-Thu, Sat & Sun, to 11am Fri) has an impressive collection of statuary from the complex, but labelling is poor.

Panataran is 16km from Blitar (4000Rp by bus), and 3km north of the village of Nglegok.

Gunung Kelud

Around 30km directly north of Panataran, Gunung Kelud (1731m) is one of Java's most active, accessible and rewarding volcanoes to visit, with a plunging crater, steaming vents and a small crater lake. Kelud is in a near-permanent state of growl – an eruption in 1919 killed 5000 people and one in 2007 sent smoke 2.5km into the air and created a 250m-high cone within the caldera.

To get to the crater itself you have to walk through a 200m tunnel, built under the Japanese occupation. A torch (flashlight) isn't necessary but will reveal many bats. To get the best perspective of Kelud you need to hike a steep path up the side of the crater.

Entrance to Gunung Kelud is controlled at a **gateway** (admission 15,000Rp; ⊙6.30am-4pm Mon-Fri, 6am-5pm Sat & Sun) 10km before the summit because of the active nature of the beast.

There's no public transport to Kelud. The easiest way here is to hire a car or *ojek* from Blitar. After bargaining, the latter will do a half-day return trip via Panataran for around 80,000Rp.

Pacitan

☎0357

A long way from anywhere, the small south-coast town of Pacitan lies on a horseshoe bay ringed by rocky cliffs. It's a beach resort with a good choice of accommodation and fresh seafood restaurants. Few foreigners make it here; if you visit during the week you've a good chance of bagging a virtually deserted beach cove to yourself, if you have some wheels. There are also some excellent **surf spots** dotted along this spectacular shoreline.

Pantai Ria Teleng, 4km or so from town, has golden sand and good surfing conditions for beginners as the waves break over a sandy bottom. Surf and bodyboards can be hired here, and there are lifeguards. Swimming is possible when the seas are calm – the safest area is towards the fishing boats at the southwestern end of the bay, where there's also a pool.

Pacitan has several banks and a couple of internet cafes.

Sleeping & Eating

TOP CHOICE **Harry's Oceanhouse** GUESTHOUSE $

(☎0878 9514 5533; beachside; r/bungalows from 70,000/80,000Rp; ❄📶) Just off the beach, this place is the best bet in town for budget travellers. It has lovely, well-constructed bungalows with pagoda-style roofs and outdoor bathrooms, plus comfortable rooms (including en suite options) and a guest's kitchen. The helpful management offer local knowledge (for free) and rent out mopeds (with racks) and surfboards for very little (30,000Rp per day).

Happy Bay Beach Bungalows BUNGALOW $

(☎881 474; r/bungalows 70,000/90,000Rp) On the beach, this place has good fan-cooled rooms and bungalows with semi-open-air bathrooms. Bicycles and motorbikes can be rented and it's next to a good seafood restaurant.

Srikandi HOTEL $

(☎881 252; Jl A Yani 67; r with fan/air-con from 140,000/200,000Rp, meals 15,000-35,000Rp; ❄) Srikandi overlooks rice paddies on the western edge of the town. Its restaurant serves up tasty local food: try the *nasi pecel* or grilled fish at around 30,000Rp.

Getting There & Around

Buses run to Pacitan from Solo (40,000Rp, 4½ hours) and also from Ponorogo (16,000Rp, 2½ hours) via a scenic road. From Ponorogo, direct buses go to Blitar (26,000Rp, three hours).

Direct *travel* minibuses (40,000Rp, three hours) connect Yogyakarta with Pacitan, call **Aneka Jaya** (☎304 4560) or **Purwo Widodo** (☎027 445 1690).

There's very little public transport around Pacitan. Motorbikes (with surfboard racks) can be rented from Pacitan guesthouses (from 30,000Rp to 50,000Rp per day).

Around Pacitan

About 13km southwest of Pacitan via a rough hilly road, stunning **Watu Karung** is a blissful cove beach with an arc of fine white sand and turquoise water offshore. This is one of Java's best surf beaches, with rights and lefts and occasional barrels. There's a village behind the bay but no surf gear for hire.

At Punung village, on the Solo road 30km northwest of Pacitan, is the turn-off to some magnificent limestone caves. **Goa Putri** is 2km from the highway and the much more impressive **Gua Gong**, 8km away, is the largest and most spectacular cave system in the area.

The more famous **Gua Tabuhan** (Musical Cave) is 4km north on the highway beyond Punung, and then another 4km from there. This huge limestone cavern was a refuge for prehistoric humans 50,000 years ago. Pay the resident musicians here and they'll strike up an impressive 'orchestral' performance by striking rocks against stalactites, each in perfect pitch, and echoing pure gamelan melodies. You must hire a guide and lamp.

This is also agate country, and hawkers sell reasonably priced polished stones and rings.

Probolinggo

☎0335 / POP 187,000

For most travellers, Probolinggo is a bustling, featureless transit point on the route to Gunung Bromo. You probably won't want to hang around here long, but the innovative tourist information people might try to change your mind – they have a few ideas to try to get you to stick around.

Dangers & Annoyances

Probolinggo's bus terminal has a poor reputation with travellers. It's by no means dangerous, just not very honest and has more than its fair share of ticket touts eager to make a buck.

The main scam involves overcharging for bus tickets. Some reputable-looking ticket agents ask for double or more the standard price. You can check departure times and prices on the monitor in the waiting area, or head to Toto Travel (p183). Unless it's a holiday (when you might want to book ahead) often the best thing to do is find the bus you need and pay the fare on board.

Also, when travelling to Probolinggo, make it clear to the ticket collector you want to be dropped off at the Bayuangga bus terminal; we've received letters from travellers complaining of being left at random travel agents and charged exorbitant fares for bus tickets.

Thieves are common on the buses in East Java, especially on buses departing from Probolinggo.

Sleeping & Eating

Sinar Harapan HOTEL $
(☎701 0335; Jl Bengawan Solo 100; r 75,000-125,000Rp; ❄📶) This new hotel has a contemporary feel and high comfort standards. Its three classes of rooms represent excellent value. They rent out motorbikes here for 60,000Rp per day.

Hotel Paramita HOTEL $
(☎421 535; Jl Siaman 7; r incl breakfast 95,000-265,000Rp; ❄) Just off the town's main drag, this place's doesn't look appealing from the street but prevail and you'll find decent rooms around a peaceful garden.

Sumber Hidup CHINESE, INDONESIAN $
(Jl Dr Mosh Saleh II; mains 14,000-30,000Rp; ⏲11.30am-10pm) Large restaurant on the main strip that serves good Chinese food and Indonesian dishes. Doubles as an ice-cream parlour.

WORTH A TRIP

SWIM WITH STARFISH

Each year between January and March an annual migration causes quite a stir in Probolinggo. Twenty or more whale sharks, some measuring up to eight metres, gather in the shallow seas off Pantai Benter, 8km east of the town. Boats take camera-toting local tourists on trips to see these marine giants, the world's largest fish – a harmless plankton feeder. In Javanese they're known as *geger lintang* ('stars on the back'), a reference to the star-like spots these sharks can be identified by. Boats only charge 5000Rp or so per passenger. As the sea is usually very murky, snorkelling is not that rewarding.

Information

The efficient **Tourist Information Centre** (☎432 420; www.dispobpar-kotaprobolinggo.com; Jl Suroyo; ⏲8am-3.30pm) by the train station is trying hard to change people's perceptions of Probolinggo. Staff, including Pandu and Kholid, can organise city tours. They can also hook you up with local schools that are looking for English speakers to help students; you only need to spare an hour or two of your time.

The main post office and most of the banks are also on Jl Suroyo, which leads off the main drag Jl Panglima Sudirman.

Getting There & Away

BUS Probolinggo's Bayuangga bus terminal is located about 5km from town on the road to Gunung Bromo. There are TV monitors here with bus departure information. Buses to Banyuwangi, Bondowoso and Surabaya are very frequent; most transport to Denpasar is between 7pm and 11pm. If you do want to make an advance reservation head to **Toto Travel** (☎443 8267; Bayuangga bus terminal) where the owners speak good English.

Angkot run to/from the main street and the train station for 3000Rp.

MINIBUS Gunung Bromo minibuses leave from a stop just outside Probolinggo's Bayuangga bus terminal, heading for Cemoro Lawang (15,000Rp, two hours) via Ngadisari (12,000Rp, 1½ hours) until around 4pm. Overcharging tourists is very common on this route.

BUSES FROM PROBOLINGGO

DESTINATION	COST(RP; ECONOMY/AIR-CON)	DURATION (HR)
Banyuwangi	36,000/46,000	5
Bondowoso	10,000/15,000	2½
Denpasar	70,000/25,000	11
Jember	16,000/23,000	2½
Malang	14,000/22,000	2½
Surabaya	16,000/24,000	2½-3
Yogyakarta	66,000/100,000	10-11

Late-afternoon buses charge more to Cemoro Lawang when fewer passengers travel beyond Ngadisari. Make sure your bus goes all the way to Cemoro Lawang when you board.

TRAIN About 2km north of town, the train station is 6km from the bus terminal. Probolinggo is on the Surabaya–Banyuwangi line. There are two daily exclusive- and business-class trains to Surabaya, both called *Mutiara Timur*, leaving at 2.39am and a more reasonable 12.51pm (40,000Rp to 60,000Rp, two hours). Trains travelling east to Banyuwangi leave at 11.14am and 11.46pm (60,000Rp to 85,000Rp, five hours).

Angkot D (4000Rp) connects the train station with the bus terminal.

TAXI Taxis and freelance car drivers meet trains, and wait for business at the bus station. A trip up to Cemoro Lawang costs around 200,000Rp after bargaining; more if it's late in the day.

Gunung Bromo & Bromo-Tengger-Semeru National Park

☎0335

A lunarlike landscape of epic proportions and surreal beauty, the volcanic Bromo region is one of Indonesia's most breathtaking sights.

Rising from the guts of the ancient Tengger caldera, Gunung Bromo (2392m) is one of three volcanoes to have emerged from a vast crater, stretching 10km across. Flanked by the peaks of Kursi (2581m) and Batok (2440m), the smouldering cone of Bromo stands in a sea of ashen, volcanic sand, surrounded by the towering cliffs of the crater's edge. Just to the south, Gunung Semeru (3676m), Java's highest peak and one of its most active volcanoes, throws its shadow – and occasionally its ash – over the whole scene.

The vast majority of independent travellers get to Bromo via the town of Probolinggo and stay in Cemoro Lawang where facilities are good. There are other options in villages on the road up from Probolinggo.

Other approaches via Wonokitri and Ngadas are also possible but due to irregular public transport and poor road conditions they're only occasionally used by small tour groups.

GUNUNG BROMO

Gunung Bromo really is something else. It's not the mountain itself, but the sheer majesty of the experience: the immense size of the entire Tengger crater, the supernatural beauty of the scenery and the dramatic highland light really are what dreams are made of.

Virtually all tours are planned to enable you to experience the mountain at sunrise. This is when the great crater is at its ethereal best and colours are most impressive. But visibility is usually good throughout the day in the dry season, even though the slopes below Cemoro Lawang may be covered in mist. Later in the day you'll also avoid the dawn crowds – things get especially busy during holiday periods. In the wet season it's often bright and clear at dawn but quickly clouds over.

If you want to just hike to Bromo from Cemoro Lawang, it's a 3km (40 minute) walk down the crater wall and across the eerie Laotian Pasir (Sea of Sand) to the slopes of Bromo. White stone markers are easy to follow during the day but can be more elusive in the dark. Make sure you climb the right cone; Bromo has a stone staircase. Some hikers, disoriented in the dark, have attempted to climb neighbouring Batok.

After ascending the 253 steps you'll come face to face with the steaming, sulphurous guts of the volcano. There are sweeping views back across the Laotian Pasir to the lip of the crater and over to Batok and the Hindu temple (this only opens on auspicious days in the pilgrim calendar) at its base.

Mercifully there's little of the tacky commercialism (bar the odd souvenir seller) that besmirches many Indonesian beauty spots. The local Tengger people may press you into accepting a horse ride across the crater bed but there's no really serious hassle. It's still easy to connect spiritually with this sacred peak if you wander around the lip of the Bromo cone, away from the main viewing point.

History

Unsurprisingly, the eerie landscape of Bromo and its neighbouring volcanoes has spawned countless myths and legends. It is said that the Tengger crater was originally dug out with just half a coconut shell by an ogre smitten with love for a princess.

But Bromo is of particular religious significance to the Hindu Tengger people who still populate the massif. They first fled here to escape the wave of Islam that broke over the Majapahit kindgom in the 16th century. The Tengger believe that Bromo once fell within the realm of the childless King Joko Seger and Queen Roro Anteng, who asked the god of the volcano for assistance in producing an heir. The god obliged, giving them 25 children, but demanded that the youngest, a handsome boy named Dian Kusuma, be sacrificed to the flames in return. When the queen later refused to fulfil her promise, the young Dian sacrificed himself to save the kingdom from retribution.

Activities

The classic Bromo **tour** peddled by all hotels and guides in Cemoro Lawang (and other villages) involves a pick-up around 3.30am and a 4WD drive up to the neighbouring peak of Gunung Penanjakan (2770m). This viewpoint offers the best vistas (and photographs) of the entire Bromo landscape, with Gunung Semeru puffing away on the horizon. After sunrise, 4WDs head back down the steep lip of the crater and then over the Laotian Pasir (Sea of Sand) to the base of Bromo. It's usually easy to hook up with others for this tour to share costs; prices seem to be fixed at 275,000Rp per car load.

Alternatively, it's a two-hour **hike** to Gunung Penanjakan from Cemoro Lawang. Trekkers can also take an interesting walk across the Laotian Pasir to the village of Ngadas (8km), below the southern rim of the Tengger crater. From here, motorbikes and 4WDs descend to Tumpang, which is connected by regular buses to Malang.

Festivals & Events

The wrath of Bromo is appeased during the annual **Kasada festival**, when Tenggerese Hindus come to Bromo to make peace with the mountain, and pray for health and good harvests. During this time, local daredevils descend into the crater and attempt to catch offerings in nets (money, food and even live chickens) thrown down by others above. It's a risky business and is as dangerous as it sounds – every few years someone slips and the volcano claims a victim. The park's PHKA offices can tell you when Kasada occurs.

In June, the Java Banana hotel hosts a jazz festival, **Gunung Jazz** (www.jazzgunung.com) with performances from international and domestic artists held in the open air in the hotel grounds.

Sleeping & Eating

CEMORO LAWANG

On the lip of the Tengger crater overlooking Bromo, Cemoro Lawang is a tiny charming highland village in a spectacular location. Its relaxed atmosphere and cool climate will come as quite a relief if you've been clocking up the kilometres in Java.

STAY SAFE

Bromo is a highly active volcano and during eruptive periods (roughly every five to 10 years) access can be forbidden. A 2km exclusion zone was declared around the peak between January and April 2011 due to the risk of explosions, falling projectiles and lava flows.

During this period tourists could still view the volcano from the lip of the crater at Cemoro Lawang and Gunung Penanjakan, but if eruptions recommence expect access to be limited again. Consult Lonely Planet's Thorn Tree (www.lonelyplanet.com/thorntree) and Gunung Bagging (www.gunungbagging.com) for the latest situation.

TIPS FOR VISITING BROMO

» Bromo's popularity means that during high season (July, August, Indonesian holidays and the Christmas period) and weekends the main two viewpoints can get very crowded between sunrise and the early morning. Organised tours all follow the same schedule, so consider visiting Gunung Penanjakan and the Bromo crater at other times of day.

» Walking from Cemoro Lawang to the Bromo crater only takes around 40 minutes. Walking enables you to really take in the scenery and get your boots dusty in the grey volcanic sands of the Laotian Pasir.

» At any time of year it's cold in the early morning and temperatures can drop to single figures or near-freezing. Guesthouses rent out jackets for around 25,000Rp.

» The lip of the crater in Cemaro Lawang (between the Cemara Indah hotel and Lava View Lodge) has lots of viewing spots where you can savour Bromo's superb scenery away from the crowds.

» If you're unlucky and cloudy weather curtails your views of Bromo, drop by the gallery at the Java Banana hotel to see what you've missed. And then stay another day and hope that the skies clear.

Unfortunately two hotels (both Lavas) have a near-duopoly here and charge prices that are heavily inflated from the norm in Indonesia. Annoyingly, both operate a triple-level pricing scheme, ramping up their rates from low (5 January to end-April) to high (May to mid-September) and up again in peak season (mid-September to 4 January). Rates increase further (by around 20%) on selected weekends, some days in August and over Christmas and New Year. Rates quoted here are for high season.

Cafe Lava Hostel HOTEL $

(☎541 020; r without bathroom from 178,500Rp, with bathroom & breakfast from 396,000Rp) With a sociable vibe thanks to its streetside cafe and attractive layout (rooms are scattered down the side of a valley) this is first choice for most travellers, despite the steep prices. Economy rooms are very small but neat, and have access to a shared veranda and clean communual bathrooms (fitted with all-important hot showers). More expensive rooms are highly attractive; all have little porches with great views and furniture. The restaurant serves up reasonable Indonesian and Western grub and cold Bintang; though the breakfast buffet is not so great.

Lava View Lodge HOTEL $$

(☎541 009; www.globaladventureindonesia.com; r/bungalows from 634,000/713,000Rp; 📶) This is a well-run hotel located 500m along a side road on the eastern side of the village. As it's almost on the lip of the crater, you can virtually stumble out your door to magnificent Bromo views. Due to the lack of competition it's seriously overpriced, but at least the wooden rooms and bungalows are comfortable enough (if dated) and staff are very friendly and helpful. There's a huge restaurant here with the usual mix of Indonesian and Western food, but beware the bad cover songs masquerading as live music some nights.

Cemara Indah Hotel HOTEL $$

(☎541 019; www.hotelcemaraindah.com; r 350,000-800,000Rp) Enjoys a great position on the edge of the crater, but rooms are very average and overpriced. You can do a lot better than eat in the restaurant here. Watch out for the staff trying to push tours and rent jackets. Doable for a night if all else is full.

Toko Warung Edi INDONESIAN $

(meals 10,000-20,000Rp) In the centre of the village, this clean shop-come-warung offers flavoursome, moderately priced food such as *nasi pecel* (rice with steamed veggies and peanut sauce), *semur* (Javanese beef soup), omelettes and pancakes.

NGADISARI & WONOTORO

TOP CHOICE **Java Banana** HOTEL $$$

(☎033 554 1193; www.java-banana.com; r incl breakfast 750,000-2,250,000Rp, ste/lodge from 3,630,000/4,000,000Rp, meals from 40,000Rp; 📶) A kind of ultra-modern mountain lodge, this excellent place has expanded its operations in recent years. It now has a huge selection of stylish rooms (largely built from wood) that are of a very high standard, though many are quite compact. There are also two huge lodges for large groups. You'll love the elevated cafe-restaurant which has sweeping views over villages and vegetable fields. The whole place is enhanced by the oversized prints of Indonesia, taken by the incredibly talented photographer-owner.

Yoschi's Guesthouse GUESTHOUSE **$**
(☎033 554 1018; yoschi.bromo@gmail.net; r without/with shower 134,000/422,000Rp, cottages from 534,000Rp; @📶) This rustic place has lots of character, with little bungalows and small rooms dotted around a large, leafy garden compound (and more upmarket rooms under construction). However many lack hot water and cleanliness standards could be better. There's a huge restaurant that serves up pricey Western and Indonesian food (subject to a stiff 20% service charge). It's 4km below Bromo and tours can be arranged. Room prices rise by around 25% in high season (July to September, Christmas and New Year).

Information

An entrance fee of 24,500Rp is charged to enter the Gunung Bromo & Bromo-Tengger-Semeru National Park. Information is available from the **PHKA post** (☎541 038; ⌚8am-3pm Tue-Sun) in Cemoro Lawang and also at the **PHKA post** (☎034 357 1048; ⌚8am-3pm Tue-Sun) on the southern outskirts of Wonokitri. Both extend their opening hours during busy periods. The park's official office is located in Malang. There's a BNI ATM close to the crater lip in Cemoro Lawang.

Getting There & Away

Probolinggo is the main gateway to Bromo. Hotels in the Bromo area can book long-distance bus tickets from Probolinggo to Yogyakarta (120,000Rp to 140,000Rp) and Denpasar (115,000Rp to 150,000Rp). Many people arrive on tours from Yogyakarta (from 110,000Rp, 11 to 13 hours) which involves a punishing overland journey, usually in a cramped minibus (p127). Alternatively, if you don't mind changing transport, the most comfortable (and fastest) way to cover this route is Yogyakarta to Surabaya by train, then a train or bus to Probolinggo and a minibus up to Cemoro Lawang.

Tours to Bromo are also easily organised in Malang, where you can arrange 4WD hire in hotels and travel agencies.

GUNUNG SEMERU

Part of the huge Tengger Massif, the classic cone of Gunung Semeru is the highest peak in Java, at 3676m. Also known as Mahameru (Great Mountain), it is looked on by Hindus as the most sacred mountain of all and the father of Gunung Agung on Bali.

Semeru is one of Java's most active peaks and has been in a near-constant state of eruption since 1818 – it exploded as recently as March 2009. At the time of research the mountain was open to hikers, but periodically, officials will warn against attempting the summit due to volcanic acitivity.

Trekking tours from Malang usually take two (or sometimes three) days to get to the summit and back. Helios Tours (p172) in Malang charges 2,750,000Rp per person (for a group of four) for a three-day, two-night hike including all supplies, meals and an English-speaking guide.

To hike the peak independently take an *angkot* (6000Rp, 45 minutes) from Malang's Arjosari bus station to Tumpang. Here you can charter an *ojek*/4WD (70,000/450,000Rp) to Ranu Pani village, the start of the trek. There are several **homestays** (all around 70,000Rp per person) in Ranu Pani (2109m). Good ones include Pak Tasrip and Pak Tumari, both of which serve meals and can organise guides (150,000Rp

SEMERU ESSENTIALS

» Semeru is a highly active volcano and its status changes rapidly – check with the national park office in Malang, locally in Ranu Pani village and also online at www.gunungbagging.com.

» Because several hikers have died of heart attacks climbing Semeru, officially you're supposed to have a health certificate to confirm that you should be able to make it there and back. These are best obtained in Malang in advance.

» Nights on the mountain are bitterly cold (often near-freezing) and inexperienced climbers have died of exposure. Make sure you have adequate gear and clothing.

» The best time of year to make the climb is May to October when you have a decent chance of clear skies and dry weather.

per day), tents and sleeping bags (which are essential).

Hikers *must* register with the **PHKA post** (Tumpang Office 034 178 7972), which is towards the lake in Ranu Pani. They will have the latest information about conditions – you may not be able to access the summit and may only make it as far as the Arcopodo campsite. They also might ask you to produce a health certificate. Expect to pay a small fee for a climbing permit and entrance for the national park (24,500Rp), as well as a camera permit (50,000Rp).

Rangers will direct you to the trailhead for Semeru. The route is lined with markers for some distance and passes three shelters, so it's difficult to get lost. You'll pass pretty Ranu Kumbolo crater lake (2400m), 13km or 3½ hours from Ranu Pani. The trail then crosses savannah before climbing to Kalimati (three hours), at the foot of the mountain. From Kalimati it is a steep hour-or-so climb to Arcopodo, where there is a flattish campsite.

From Arcopodo, it is a short, steep climb to the start of the volcanic sands, and then a tough three-hour climb through loose scree to the peak. Semeru explodes every half hour and the gases and belching lava make the mountain dangerous – stay well away from vents. On a clear day, there are breathtaking views of Java's north and south coasts, as well as vistas of Bali. To see the sunrise, it is necessary to start at about 1.30am for the summit.

Bondowoso

0332 / POP 73,000

Bondowoso, suspended between the highlands of Tengger and Ijen, is one of the cleanest towns in Java. It is the home of some of the island's best *tape*, a tasty, sweet-and-sour snack made from boiled vegetable roots. It's merely a transit point for nearby attractions such as Ijen, but does have banks and internet facilities. Tours to Ijen can be organised here.

Tape can be found on Jl PB Sudirman, where dozens of shops sell it by the basket (15,000Rp). The '321' brand is reportedly the best.

There are many (cramped) minibuses to Ijen (20,000Rp), all leaving before noon for the 2½-hour trip. Other destinations from Bondowoso include Jember (6000Rp, 45 minutes), Probolinggo (15,000Rp, two hours) and Surabaya (normal/air-con 32,000/45,0000Rp, five hours).

Sleeping

Palm Hotel HOTEL **$$**
(421 201; www.palm-hotel.net; Jl A Yani 32; r incl breakfast with fan & mandi 132,000Rp, with air-con 275,000-550,000Rp;) Just south of the huge, grassy *alun-alun*, this good-value hotel's huge, heat-busting pool makes it a great escape from Java's punishing humidity. Take your pick from simple fan-only options with cold water *mandi* or smart, spacious air-conditioned rooms that show a minimalist design influence. The restaurant is good. Transport to Ijen can be arranged (4WD costs 600,000Rp).

Hotel Anugerah HOMESTAY **$**
(421 870; Jl Sutoyo 12; r 100,000Rp, with air-con 150,000-200,000Rp, meals around 14,000Rp;) More of a homestay than a hotel, this is a secure, friendly family-run place with a wide selection of clean, though not very inviting rooms – prepare yourself for some truly garish colour schemes. The English-speaking folks here offer inexpensive meals and trips to Ijen (180,000/600,000Rp return by *ojek*/4WD) can be arranged.

Hotel Baru HOTEL **$**
(421 474; Jl Kartini 26; r incl breakfast 80,000Rp;) Around 100m north of the *alun-alun*, this place has a selection of rooms in different price categories; the cheapest options are best value, with private *mandi* and a few pieces of furniture.

Ijen Plateau

The fabled Ijen Plateau is a vast volcanic region dominated by the three cones of Ijen (2368m), Merapi (2800m) and Raung (3332m). A beautiful forested alpine area, these thinly populated highlands harbour coffee plantations and a few isolated settlements – Gunung Ijen is Javanese for 'Lonely Mountain'. Access roads to the plateau are poor and perhaps because of this visitor numbers are low (but steadily increasing).

Virtually everyone that does come is here for the hike up to the spectacular crater lake of Kawah Ijen. But with sweeping vistas and a temperate climate, the plateau makes a great base for a few days up in the clouds and away from the crowds.

A HEAVY LOAD

The Ijen volcano produces a lot of sulphur, historically known as brimstone. Around 300 collectors (all men) work here, getting up at around 3am to hike up the crater and hack out the yellow stuff by hand. Their only protection against the cone's noxious fumes are cotton scarfs, which they tie around their noses. These DIY miners then spend the next six-or-so hours scurrying back down the volcano with 60kg to 80kg loads on their backs.

It's incredibly tough work that pays very little (around 700Rp per kilo), and yet the physical exercise keeps the collectors incredibly fit. Few report health problems despite breathing great lungfuls of sulphurous fumes virtually every day of their lives. The sulphur collected is used for cosmetics and medicine, and is added to fertiliser and insecticides.

Sights

Java's finest coffee, both arabica and robusta varieties, is produced in the Ijen Plateau area, as well as cacao, cloves and rubber. It's possible to visit coffee plantations, including **Kebun Balawan** (admission free); visits will usually include a wander through coffee groves and an impromptu tour of the plantation's factory. This plantation has thermal pools and a gushing thermal waterfall (2000Rp) set amongst lush jungle.

Activities

The magnificent turquoise sulphur lake of **Kawah Ijen** lies at 2148m above sea level and is surrounded by the volcano's sheer crater walls. At the edge of the lake, sulphurous smoke billows from the volcano's vent and the lake bubbles when activity increases. Ijen's last major eruption was in 1936, though due to an increased threat access was closed in late 2011, and again in March 2012 for a few weeks.

Ijen is a major sulphur-gathering centre and you'll pass the collectors as you hike up the trail. Most now ask for a fee for photographs, though a cigarette will usually be accepted as payment.

The ideal time to make the Kawah Ijen hike is in the dry season between April and October. However, while the path is steep, it's usually not too slippy, so the hike is certainly worth a try in the rainy season if you have a clear day. Make it for sunrise if you can.

The starting point for the trek to the crater is the **PHKA post** (7am-5pm) at Pos Paltuding, which can be reached from Bondowoso or Banyuwangi. Sign in and pay your 15,000Rp entry fee here. The steep 3km path up to the observation post (where there's a teahouse) takes just over an hour; keep an eye out for gibbons. From the post it's a further 30-minute walk to the lip of the wind-blasted crater and its stunning views.

From the crater rim, an extremely steep, gravelly path leads down to the sulphur deposits and the steaming lake. The walk down takes around 30 minutes; the path is slippery in parts and the sulphur fumes towards the bottom can be overwhelming. Expect burning lungs and streaming eyes if you do make it to the bottom. Take great care – a French tourist fell and died here some years ago.

Back at the lip of the crater, turn left for the climb to the highest point (2368m) and magnificent views, or keep walking anticlockwise for even more expansive vistas of the lake. On the other side of the lake, opposite the vent, the trail disappears into crumbling volcanic rock and deep ravines.

Sleeping

This is a remote mountain region and with little competition, the budget accommodation is pretty sketchy. The two guesthouses are run by coffee estates, whose owners clearly prioritise beans over beds. Few staff speak any English and email bookings may or may not be answered. So prepare yourself accordingly!

Sempol village has a couple of warungs. Pos Paltuding has a small shop for provisions and a cafe serving little more than noodles.

Arabika GUESTHOUSE $

(081 1350 5881, 082 8330 1347; arabica.homestay@gmail.com; r incl breakfast from 140,000-280,000Rp) This dated, usually chilly, mountain lodge is managed by the Kebun Kalisat coffee plantation, which is a short walk away. Sadly it's not in great shape these days, and cleanliness could be better – the more you pay the cleaner the room seems to get –

but all rooms have hot water and a bathtub in which to enjoy it. Staff are friendly, but can find it difficult to cope during busy periods. Meals are served, and there's ping pong. It's at Sempol, 13km before Pos Paltuding on the Bondowoso side.

Kartimore GUESTHOUSE **$**
(☎0813 5799 9800, 0813 3619 9110; catimor_n12@yahoo.com; r 145,000-290,000Rp;) This place boasts an excellent location in the Kebun Balawan coffee plantation, close to hot springs. Unfortunately there has been little or no maintenance for some time and the whole place is pretty creaky (especially inside the original wooden Dutch lodge, which dates back to 1894). There's a separate block of cheap, reasonably clean, if featureless, rooms in a long row. Be sure to indulge yourself in the spring-fed hot tub, or brave the chilly swimming pool. Smiley staff do their best here considering the remote location, and the meals are quite good. An *ojek* from Sempol is around 22,000Rp.

Ijen Resort LUXURY HOTEL **$$$**
(☎033 3773 3338; www.ijendiscovery.com; Dusun Randuagung; r/ste from US$230/329;) This top-end resort is the only luxury lodge in the Ijen region and has magnificent views over rice terraces and the foothills of the volcano. Rooms have some style, with stone or timber floors, open-air bathrooms and attractive furnishings, but are overpriced. There's an expensive restaurant that serves local and Western food, and tours and transport can be fixed. The resort is about 25 minutes above Banyuwangi on the road up to Ijen.

Pos Paltuding HUT **$**
(r 135,000Rp) The PHKA post at the start of the Kawah Ijen hike has a bare, chilly cottage with very basic rooms. There's no hot water and blankets are not provided.

Getting There & Away

It is possible to travel nearly all the way to Kawah Ijen by public transport, but most visitors charter transport. Both access roads are badly potholed and slow going.

FROM BONDOWOSO From Wonosari, 8km from Bondowoso towards Situbondo, a rough, potholed road runs via Sukosari and Sempol to Pos Paltuding. It's normally just passable in a high-clearance vehicle, but sometimes a 4WD is necessary. Sign in at the coffee-plantation checkpoints (around 4000Rp) on the way. Hotels in Bondowoso can arrange day tours to Ijen for around 600,000Rp.

By public transport, several *angkot* run from Bondowoso to Sempol (20,000Rp, 2½ hours), most in the late morning, but there's a final one at 3pm. If passengers want to continue on to Pos Paltuding drivers will sometimes do so, though foreigners are regularly overcharged on this route. Otherwise *ojek* in Sempol charge around 30,000Rp one-way. At Pos Paltuding, there are usually a few drivers to take you back.

FROM BANYUWANGI At the time of research, the steep Banyuwangi–Ijen road was in worse condition than the Bondowoso route and only passable by 4WD or a motorbike. There's no public transport all the way from Banyuwangi to Pos Paltuding, which is a sparsely-populated region.

Jeep-style cars (550,000Rp per vehicle) can be arranged through the Banyuwangi tourist office. Chartering an *ojek* from Banyuwangi to Ijen is possible for around 180,000Rp (including a wait of four hours). *Ojek* drivers hang around the ferry terminal in Ketapang and Banyuwangi bus station, or ask at your guesthouse.

Heading back down the mountain, *ojek* charge around 75,000Rp for a one-way ride to Banyuwangi from Pos Paltuding, maybe 90,000Rp from the guesthouses.

Jember

☎0331 / POP 327,000

Jember is a large city and service centre for the surrounding coffee, cacao, rubber, cotton and tobacco plantations. It's a relatively clean city, with a futuristic mosque (it looks like a flying saucer) by its *alun-alun*, but there's no reason to linger here. If you plan to go to Meru Betiri, you could drop by the **Meru Betiri National Park Office** (☎335 535; www.merubetiri.com; Jl Sriwidjaya 53; ⊙8am-3pm Sun-Fri), which has accommodation details and background information on the park.

Jember has an excess of transport terminals. The main one, Tawung Alun (or Terminal Jember), 6km west of town, has buses to Banyuwangi (23,000Rp, three hours) and Kalibaru (8000Rp, one hour), and economy buses to Denpasar, Solo and Yogyakarta. *Angkot* run from here to Terminal Arjesa, which serves Bondowoso (7000Rp, 45 minutes). There are also subterminals to the east (for Banyuwangi) and south (for Watu Ulo).

Jember is also located on the Surabaya–Banyuwangi train line; the station is in the town centre.

Watu Ulo & Papuma

0331

Watu Ulo is popular on weekends, but like most of the beaches on Java's south coast, it has grey sand, and crashing surf makes swimming dangerous. The real surprise lies just west around the headland from Watu Ulo at **Papuma** – a lovely beach with white sand, turquoise waters, several warung and relatively sheltered swimming.

To reach Watu Ulo, head to the Ajung subterminal in Jember and then take an *angkot* (confusingly also known as 'taxis' in these parts) to Ambulu (7000Rp, one hour). From Ambulu, *ojek* drivers go to Watu Ulo (15,000Rp, 20 minutes) or on to Papuma via a steep headland.

On Pantai Papuma, **Tanjung Papuma** (033 133 6841; www.tanjungpapuma.com; tents from 25,000Rp, r 150,000-300,000Rp, cottages 450,000Rp;) is a kind of outdoor pursuits centre geared at Indonesian school groups. It offers lots of organised activities such as snorkelling and trekking. Its well-maintained bungalows can be rented by all and there's a shady campsite.

Kalibaru

0333 / POP 4000

The picturesque road from Jember to Banyuwangi winds around the foothills of Gunung Raung, through rainforest, and up to the small hill town of Kalibaru (428m).

The village itself is not much to look at, but it has a benign climate and a remarkable array of excellent midrange accommodation. It's a good base for visiting the nearby plantations around Glenmore, to the east, or the smaller, more easily visited plots of coffee and cloves to the north of Kalibaru train station.

The area has many plantations, but **Kebun Kandeng Lembu** (admission 25,000Rp; 9am-noon Mon-Thu & Sat, 8.30am-noon Fri), 5km south of Glenmore, is one of the most scenic. Guides can be hired (80,000Rp) for group tours to see rubber tapping and processing, as well as cacao and coffee plantations.

Tours

Margo Utomo Resort (p191) offers several tours. English-speaking guides will show you around the estate (90-minute tour, 50,000Rp per person), which is totally organic and has a butterfly park, peppercorn, cinnamon and nutmeg trees, and vanilla and cacao plants. Jeep trips to surrounding villages are on offer, and take in a waterfall and cacao factory. Excursions to Pantai Sukamade (Turtle Beach) and Alas Purwo are also possible.

Sleeping & Eating

There are warung in town for cheap eats. Restaurants can be found at some of the accommodation in the area.

Margo Utomo Resort HOTEL **$$**
(897 700; www.margoutomo.com; Jl Lapangan 10; r incl breakfast 425,000Rp;) This classy former plantation enjoys a resplendent garden, bursting with shrubs and flowers (all neatly labelled). Its cottages are a little pricey considering their simplicity, but they are tasteful and have charm; and all have ceiling fans. Follow the path and you'll find a wonderful 20m pool at the rear of the grounds. There is also a restaurant. It's very popular with Dutch tour groups from June to August when prices rise and you should book well ahead.

Margo Utomo Hill View Cottages BUNGALOW **$$**
(897 420; www.margoutomo.com; Jl Putri Gunung III; r 425,000Rp;) A smaller, quieter operation than its sister hotel, this place has cottages scattered around a lovely garden plot that extends down to a forested riverbank. The pool area is stunning, surrounded by tropical greenery. Each cottage has a little veranda and high ceilings, and no TV. It's 3km east of town and there is a restaurant on site.

Kalibaru Cottages BUNGALOW **$$**
(897 333; www.kalibarucottages.com; r incl breakfast 370,000-580,000Rp;) A large, well-run resort boasting expansive, manicured grounds with a T-shaped pool that's fringed by palm trees. Faux-traditional cottages are very spacious, though the restaurant is a bit pricey. It's 4km west of town on the Jember road.

Getting There & Away

Buses running between Jember (8000Rp, one hour) and Banyuwangi (15,000Rp, two hours) can drop you near the hotels. The train station is in the village centre; Kalibaru is on the main Banyuwangi–Jember–Probolinggo–Surabaya train line.

Meru Betiri National Park

The Meru Betiri National Park, covering 580 sq km between Jember and Banyuwangi districts, is an area of magnificent coastal rainforest and abundant wildlife, making it one of Java's finest parks. It's famous as one of the last refuges of the Java tiger, now almost certainly extinct. Meru Betiri is very difficult to access (often impossible in the rainy season), which keeps the number of visitors to a trickle.

The future of the park is under threat on several fronts. Illegal loggers, farmers and hunters encroach on its territory. Mining companies are also eyeing up the park after significant gold deposits were found here.

Sights & Activities

The park's major attraction is the protected turtle beach at **Sukamade**, one of Indonesia's most important turtle-spawning grounds, where several species of turtle come ashore to lay their eggs. You've a good chance of seeing a turtle here, green turtles and olive ridleys are most common. Giant leatherbacks used to be seen between December and February, but sightings are very rare these days. Mess Pantai arranges night turtle-watching trips (100,000Rp per person) and gathers eggs which are hatched inland so that wild pigs do not dig them up.

Wildlife, found mostly in the mountain forests, includes leopards, wild boars, monkeys, banteng, black giant squirrels, civets, reticulated pythons (the world's longest snake) and Javanese eagles. You're sure to see a lot of monkeys, monitor lizards and hornbills – maybe even the rhinoceros hornbill, which emits a bark-like honk.

Trails are limited in the park and a guide (70,000Rp) is usually necessary. There are good coastal walks but sadly there's quite a bit of trash around, on the beach and inland.

Rajegwesi, at the entrance to the park, is on a large bay with a sweeping beach and a fishing village. Past the park entrance the road climbs, giving expansive views over spectacular **Teluk Hijau** (Green Bay), with its cliffs and white-sand beach. A trail leads 1km from the road down to Teluk Hijau, or it is about a one-hour walk east from Mess Pantai.

Sleeping

There are guesthouses on the Sukamade plantation and in Rajegwesi but these are some distance from the beach.

Mess Pantai BUNGALOW $
(☎033 133 5535; r without/with bathroom 100,000/200,000Rp) Set in the forest about 700m behind Pantai Sukamade, Mess Pantai is a basic but wonderfully located place to stay in the park, with simple, comfortable cottages. Instant noodles are usually all the food available (around 8000Rp) so it's best to stock up in Sarongan and bring your own food – staff will prepare it for you. There's very limited electricity and no mobile-phone coverage, but there is bottled water for sale.

Information

The park is very wet for much of the year as the coastal mountains trap the rain. Visit in the dry season from April to October – the road into the park fords a river, which easily floods. Even in the dry season you may have to wade across the river and walk into the park.

The park's office in Jember (p190) has plenty of information; entrance to the park costs 20,000Rp.

Getting There & Away

Meru Betiri can be a tough place to reach, even by 4WD. Roads are rough and you have to ford rivers in some places. The most direct way to Sukamade from Banyuwangi or Jember is to first take a bus to Jajag, then a minibus to Pesanggaran (8000Rp, one hour), where you'll probably have to change and get in another to Sarongan (10,000Rp, around one hour), a small town with warung and stores where you can stock up on supplies. Watch out for the Sarongan transport mafia who will try to get you to charter a 4WD. *Ojeks* to Sukamade (around 100,000Rp) can be arranged here, but generally only in the dry season; during the wet season the rivers are impassable. Otherwise, you'll have to get a truck ('taxi' in these parts), as they don't run to a fixed schedule. This should cost 25,000Rp, though foreigners are routinely overcharged. The truck has no problem with swollen rivers unless there is severe flooding.

Readers have told us they've made it all the way to Sukamade on motorcycle, in the dry season; however a dirt bike is preferable.

Alas Purwo National Park

Occupying the whole of the remote Blambangan Peninsula on the southeastern tip of Java, Alas Purwo has fine beaches, good opportunities for wildlife-spotting, and savannah, mangrove and lowland monsoon forests. Apart from daytrippers and surfers, the park gets few visitors. Facilities are limited.

Alas Purwo means First Forest in Javanese – according to legend, this is where the earth first emerged from the ocean. Many soul-searchers and mystics flock here during the month of Suro, which marks the Javanese New Year. These pilgrims meditate in caves and pray to Nyai Loro Kidul. Pura Giri Selokah, a Hindu temple in the park, also attracts many pilgrims, especially during Pagerwesi, the Hindu new year.

The huge surf at Plengkung, on the isolated southeastern tip of the peninsula, forms one of the best left-handed waves in the world, breaking over a shallow reef in a perfect tube. Surfers have dubbed it G-Land. It's best between April and September.

Sights & Activities

This limestone peninsula is relatively flat and the rolling hills reach a peak of only 322m. Alas Purwo has plenty of lowland coastal forest but few trails to explore it – vast expanses of the eastern park are untrammelled, even by park staff.

You can use Trianggulasi as a base for some interesting short walks. The white-sand beach here is beautiful, but swimming is usually dangerous.

Sadengan WILDLIFE RESERVE

Sadengan grazing ground has the largest herd of wild banteng in Java, and *kijang* (deer) and peacocks are seen here from the viewing tower. This beautiful meadow, backed by forest, is a 2km walk from Trianggulasi.

Alas Purwo also has a small population of *ajag* (Asiatic wild dogs), jungle fowl, leaf monkeys, *muntjac* deer, sambar deer and even leopards. The park guards can arrange interesting, although often fruitless, night leopard-spotting expeditions for around 100,000Rp.

Ngagelan BEACH

Park guards can arrange a motorbike trip to the turtle hatchery at Ngagelan, or you can walk. It's 6km from Rowobendo along a rough road, or a 7km walk along the beach at low tide from Trianggulasi.

Gua Istana & Gua Padepokan CAVE

From Pancur, a trail heads 2km inland through some good forest to Gua Istana, a small cave, and another 2km further on to Gua Padepokan.

Plengkung BEACH

From Pancur, it's a 10km walk (two hours) around Teluk Grajagan to the fine beach at Plengkung, one of Asia's premier surfing spots, and home to several surf camps.

Tours

There are three surf camps at Plengkung. The surfing packages usually include transfers – most commonly from Bali – accommodation and meals.

Bobby's Camp SURFING

(bookings in Bali 036 175 5588; www.grajagan.com;) Right opposite the waves, this attractive camp has three standards of bungalow in shady grounds with a restaurant and bar. It has beach volleyball, ping pong, pool tables, and boat and fishing trips can be arranged. This camp is organised in Kuta, Bali, and offers three-night packages (from US$400), including land transfers (a 10-hour trip), grog and grub. Speed-boat transfers from Bali can also be arranged.

G-Land Joyo's Surf Camp SURFING

(bookings in Bali 036 176 3166; www.g-land.com;) Joyo's has steadily upped its game over the years. It has good-quality thatched wooden bungalows with a fan or air-conditioning, a large-screen TV for sports, pool tables, internet access and table tennis. There's free yoga and the crew who run the place are a blast. Packages start at US$350 for three nights, plus $100 for a return boat transfer. Joyo's is open November to March only.

Sleeping & Eating

From Trianggulasi, the nearest warung (meals 10,000Rp) is at Pancur, where there are also simple rooms (60,000Rp per person).

Pesanggrahan HUTS $

(0333 428 675; r per person 60,000Rp) Close to the beach at Trianggulasi, this PHKA establishment has elevated bungalows with spartan rooms. Though primitive, this is a lovely, relaxing spot and many who come for a day or two end up staying longer. If it's full you can usally bed down on a *bale* (open-sided shelter) on the lovely beach here.

There's usually no food, so bring supplies with you (rangers will heat up grub for a small charge). The PHKA office at Pasar Anyar sells basic provisions.

Information

The usual park entry is by road, via the village of Pasar Anyar, which has a **large national park office** (☎0333 410 857) and interpretive centre. Call in here to check on accommodation; alternatively, check with the head office in Banyuwangi. The actual gateway to the park is 10km south along a bad road at Rowobendo where you need to pay your admission fee (20,000Rp). From here it's 2.5km to Trianggulasi.

Getting There & Away

Alas Purwo is a pain to get to by public transport. The best way here is to hire a motorbike or car in Banyuwangi; the access roads are poor but usually doable.

By bus, you need to get to Brawijaya bus terminal in Banyuwangi from where there are buses to Kalipahit (12,000Rp, 1½ hours). Then take an *ojek* for around 60,000Rp to the park office in Pasar Anyar to check on accommodation, and then on to the park. The 12km road from Pasar Anyar to Trianggulasi is badly potholed but is flat and negotiable by car.

Banyuwangi

☎0333 / POP 115,000

The end of the line, Java's land's end is a pleasant-enough town, but there's no reason to hang around.

Confusingly, the ferry terminus for Bali, bus terminal and train station are all some 8km north of town in the port of Ketapang, though all transport uses 'Banyuwangi' as a destination.

Sights

Kongco Tan Hu Cin Jin Chinese Temple TEMPLE
(Jl Ikam Gurani 54) One of the few sights in Banyuwangi is the Kongco Tan Hu Cin Jin Chinese temple; built in 1784, it's well worth a peek.

Blambangan Museum MUSEUM
(Jl A Yani; ⏲7.30am-4pm Mon-Thu, to 11am Fri) At the tourist office, this small museum is devoted to culture from the area with batik and traditional costumes, ceramics and curios.

Sleeping & Eating

For cheap eats, there are warungs on the corner of Jl MT Haryono and Jl Wahid Haysim.

TOP CHOICE **Hotel Ketapang Indah** HOTEL $$
(☎422 280; www.ketapangindahhotel.com; Jl Gatot Subroto; r 385,000-730,000Rp; ❄📶🏊) This lovely hotel makes a blissfully peaceful place to stay. Its huge, well-kept rooms and traditional-style cottages are dotted around a simply magnificent garden, shaded with coconut palms and extending down to the sea. The 18m pool is big enough for laps, and the restaurant is decent (though watch out for cheesy bands in the evening). It's 2km south of the ferry terminal.

Hotel Baru HOTEL $
(☎421 369; Jl MT Haryono 82-84; r with fan & mandi 50,000Rp, with air-con & shower 100,000Rp; ❄) On a quiet backstreet near the *alun-alun*, this welcoming place has friendly staff, very cheap rooms and a cafe-restaurant.

Information

Alas Purwo National Park Head Office (☎428 675; Jl A Yani 108; ⏲7.30am-3pm Mon-Thu, to 11am Fri) Two kilometres south of the town centre.

Baluran National Park Head Office (☎424 119; Jl Agus Salim 132; ⏲7am-3.30pm Mon-Thu, to 11am Fri) Four kilometres southwest of the centre.

Banyuwangi Tourist Office (☎424 172; Jl Ahmad Yani 78; ⏲7am-4pm Mon-Thu, to 11am Fri) Staff are helpful at this office. Mr Aekanu (☎081 5590 5197; aekanu@plasa.com), who works here, speaks Dutch and some English, and can organise tours.

Getting There & Away

AIR Banyuwangi's tiny Blimbingsari airport is 9km south of the centre. Merpati (p768) connects the city with Surabaya daily from 291,000Rp. There's no public transport to the airport; a taxi will cost around 35,000Rp.

BOAT Ferries depart around the clock for Gilimanuk in Bali (every 45 minutes, one hour). The ferry costs 8000Rp for passengers and 18,000Rp for a motorcycle. Through-buses between Bali and Java include the fare in the bus ticket. Pelni ships no longer call at Banyuwangi.

BUS Banyuwangi has two bus terminals. The Sri Tanjung terminal is 3km north of Ketapang ferry terminal, 11km from the centre. Buses from here head along the north coast road to Baluran (8000Rp, one hour), Probolinggo (normal/*patas* 36,000/46,000Rp, five hours) and Surabaya (42,000/60,000Rp, seven hours). Buses also go right through to Yogyakarta (*patas* 120,000Rp, 15 hours) and Denpasar (from 55,000Rp, five hours including the ferry trip). Brawijaya terminal (also known as Karang Ente), 4km south of town, covers buses along the southern highway to Kalibaru (15,000Rp, two hours) and Jember (23,000Rp, three hours).

TRAIN The main Banyuwangi train station is just a few hundred metres north of the ferry terminal. The express *Mutiara Timur* leaves at 8am and 9.45pm for Probolinggo (business/executive 60,000/85,000Rp, five hours) and Surabaya (75,000/105,000Rp, seven hours).

Baluran National Park

Baluran National Park harbours an amazingly diverse range of ecosystems in a 250-sq-km chunk of northeastern Java. Extensive grasslands cover parts of the park, providing rich grazing for Javanese wild oxen (banteng), *kijang* and water buffaloes – you've a good chance of seeing a wide range of wildlife here. The savannah-like terrain is reminiscent of East Africa.

Located just off the main north-coast highway, Baluaran is one of Java's most accessible national parks. Independent travellers will love the forest trails, cheap accommodation and fine sandy beach. Or you can sign up for all kinds of tours: safari trips, hikes up the Baluran crater, or visiting local villages to learn about home industries.

Sights & Activities

Baluran is rich in wildlife and supports important populations of around 500 Timor deer and 200 banteng, plus sambar deer, *muntjac* deer, two species of monkey, and wild boars. Visit in July and August and you might see male Timor deer rutting for breeding rights.

The park is home to leopards, but there have only been two recent sightings. Bird life is excellent, with green peafowl, red and green jungle fowl, hornbills, white-bellied woodpeckers and bee-eaters all quite easy to see.

Pantai Bama BEACH

Fringed by mangroves, the lovely cove beach of Bama is 4km north of Bekol. You could easily spend a few days snorkelling the coral reef offshore, swimming, sunbathing and exploring the mangroves (walkways have been constructed) where monitor lizards and wild boars are sometimes spotted. It's a popular weekend retreat for local families, but usually peaceful at other times. Canoes (30,000Rp) and snorkelling gear (40,000Rp) can be hired. Watch out for the cheeky long-tailed macaques here, who have been known to pinch food.

Bekol HIKING

From the PHKA office on the highway it's 14km down a flat gravel track to Bekol. The friendly rangers here look after a couple of lodges and can act as guides (100,000Rp per half-day). You don't need a guide to hike along a well-maintained trail to Pantai Bama (1½ hours), an idyllic walk which follows a riverbank where deer are common.

On the hill above the guesthouses at Bekol there is a viewing tower that provides a panoramic view over a 300-hectare clearing. Banteng and deer can be seen here, and wild dogs can sometimes be seen hunting, usually in the early morning.

Sleeping

Bookings can be made in advance through the Baluran National Park head office (p194) in Banyuwangi. Most visitors tend to day-trip, so accommodation is often available, but it pays to book, especially in the peak June-to-August holiday period.

At Bekol **Pesanggrahan** (☎033 346 1936; per person 35,000-50,000Rp) has basic rooms in either concrete or wooden houses and simple bungalows to one side. The accommodation is very basic but in fair shape, though you should bring your own mosquito net if you have one. You'll find a kitchen for guests or you can buy packet noodles and drinks.

Pantai Bama is a preferable location as you're right on the beach and it's quite well set up for visitors. There is accommodation available in concrete bungalows and an excellent little warung for cheap meals (around 12,000Rp) and drinks. The rooms (single/double costs 100,000/150,000Rp) are functional but the location is amazing. There's also a more comfortable wooden house (300,000Rp) that has a private bathroom.

Rosa's Ecolodge GUESTHOUSE **$$**

(☎033 845 3005; www.rosasecolodge.com; Ds Sidomulyo RT 03/03; r incl breakfast 350,000Rp; ❄@) This guesthouse is run by Rene and Rosa, good hosts who are passionate and informative about the Baluran. The accommodation is overpriced, however the spacious rooms are well-presented with private bathrooms and front porches. Buffet-style meals of tasty Javanese food are served here. Rosa's is geared towards guests booking its quite pricey Baluran tours, so priority is given to tour-bookers during busy times. It's on the northern edge of the park in the village of Sumberwaru.

Information

You'll find the **PHKA office** (☎033 346 1936, 033 346 1650; ⏲8am-4pm) on the coastal highway in the village of Wonorejo, on the main coast road between Surabaya and Banyuwangi. Guides can be booked for around 200,000Rp per day. The park's head office is in Banyuwangi. Entrance costs 20,000Rp and an extra 6000Rp is charged for a car.

Baluran can be visited at any time of the year, but the dry season (June to November) is usually the best time because the animals congregate near the waterholes at Bekol and Bama.

Getting There & Away

A regular stream of Surabaya–Banyuwangi buses all pass right by the almost-hidden park entrance. From Banyuwangi it's a 40-minute journey (6000Rp). Coming from the west, Baluran is four hours from Probolinggo. PHKA rangers at the entrance can arrange an *ojek* (around 35,000Rp) to take you the next 12km to Bekol; the road is in pretty good shape and should be passable by most cars; a 4WD is not necessary.

Bali

POP 3.5 MILLION

Includes »

Best Places to Eat

» Sardine (p224)
» Warung Teges (p257)
» Biku (p224)
» Cak Asm (p240)
» Sopa (p256)

Best Places to Stay

» Hotel Tugu Bali (p226)
» Oberoi (p219)
» Matahari Cottages (p254)
» Temple Lodge (p228)
» Alila Villas Ulu Watu (p231)

Why Go?

Impossibly green rice terraces, pulse-pounding surf, enchanting Hindu temple ceremonies, mesmerising dance performances, ribbons of beaches, a truly charming people: there are as many images of Bali as there are flowers on the ubiquitous frangipani trees.

This small island looms large for any visit to Indonesia. No place is more visitor-friendly. Hotels range from surfer dives to sybaritic retreats in the lush mountains. You can dine on local foods bursting with flavours fresh from the markets or let a world-class chef take you on a culinary journey around the globe. From a cold Bintang (beer) at sunset to an epic night clubbing, your social whirl is limited only by your fortitude.

And small obviously doesn't mean homogeneous. Manic Kuta segues into glitzy Seminyak. The artistic swirl of Ubud is a counterpoint to misty treks amid the volcanoes. Mellow beach towns such as Bingin, Amed and Pemuteran are found right round the coast.

When to Go

Denpasar

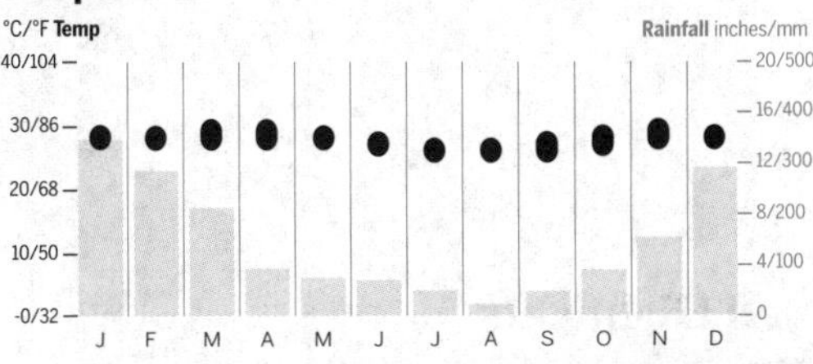

Jul & Aug High season is Bali's busiest and buzziest time. Book ahead for rooms.

May, Jun & Sep Often the best weather: slightly cooler and drier; less crowded.

Jan–Apr, Oct & Nov Low season makes spontaneous travel easy. Note the Nyepi holiday.

Bali Highlights

1 Shopping by day and hitting the hotspots by night in **Seminyak** (p218) and **Kerobokan** (p223)

2 Discovering the beautiful string of hidden beaches in and around **Bingin** (p228), where the surfing is also fab

3 Revelling in Bali's elaborate cultural life in **Ubud** (p246), where you can enjoy your choice of the island's iconic dance and gamelan performances nightly

4 Gazing in awe at the rice terraces leading to the mystical temple **Pura Luhur Batukau** (p286)

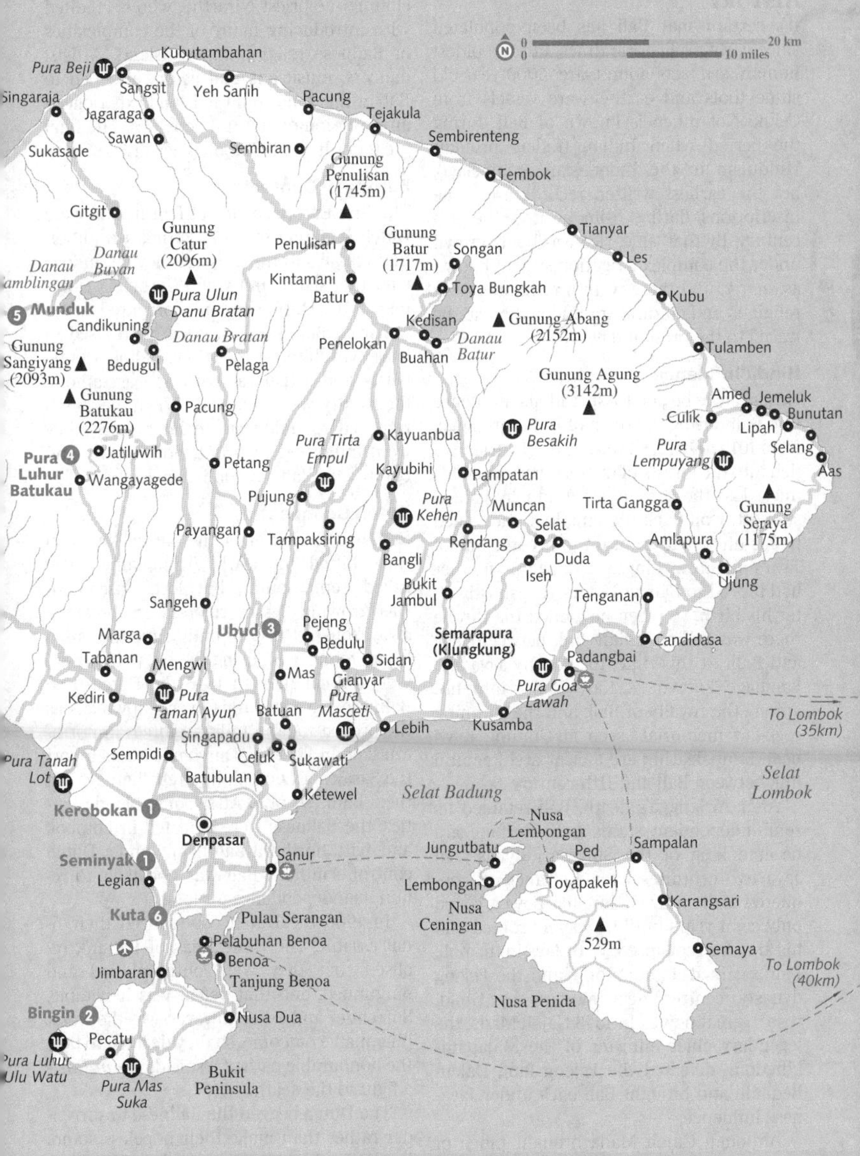

5 Feeling the mist of waterfalls while trekking the lush region around **Munduk** (p285)

6 Plunging into the hedonistic nightlife of **Kuta** (p207)

7 Thrilling to the easily accessed underwater beauty of **Pulau Menjangan** (p296)

HISTORY

It's certain that Bali has been populated since early prehistoric times, but the oldest human artefacts found are 3000-year-old stone tools and earthenware vessels from Cekik. Not much is known of Bali during the period when Indian traders brought Hinduism to the Indonesian archipelago, but the earliest written records are stone inscriptions dating from around the 9th century. By that time, rice was being grown under the complex irrigation system known as *subak,* and there were precursors of the religious and cultural traditions that can be traced to the present day.

Hindu Influence

Hindu Java began to spread its influence into Bali during the reign of King Airlangga, from 1019 to 1042. At the age of 16, Airlangga fled into the forests of western Java when his uncle lost the throne. He gradually gained support, won back the kingdom once ruled by his uncle and went on to become one of Java's greatest kings. Airlangga's mother had moved to Bali and remarried shortly after his birth, so when he gained the throne there was an immediate link between Java and Bali. At this time, the courtly Javanese language known as Kawi came into use among the royalty of Bali, and the stunning rock-cut memorials seen at Gunung Kawi near Tampaksiring are a clear architectural link between Bali and 11th-century Java.

After Airlangga's death, Bali retained its semi-independent status until Kertanegara became king of the Singasari dynasty in Java two centuries later. Kertanegara conquered Bali in 1284, but his power lasted only eight years until he was murdered and his kingdom collapsed. With Java in turmoil, Bali regained its autonomy and the Pejeng dynasty, centred near modern-day Ubud, rose to great power. In 1343 Gajah Mada, the legendary chief minister of the Majapahit kingdom, defeated the Pejeng king Dalem Bedaulu and brought Bali back under Javanese influence.

Although Gajah Mada brought much of the Indonesian archipelago under Majapahit control, Bali was the furthest extent of its power. Here the 'capital' moved to Gelgel, near modern-day Semarapura (once known as Klungkung), around the late 14th century, and for the next two centuries this was the base for the 'king of Bali', the Dewa Agung.

As the Majapahit kingdom fell apart, many of its intelligentsia moved to Bali, including the priest Nirartha, who is credited with introducing many of the complexities of Balinese religion to the island. Artists, dancers, musicians and actors also fled to Bali at this time, and the island experienced an explosion of cultural activities. The final great exodus to Bali took place in 1478.

European Contact

The first Europeans to set foot in Bali were Dutch seafarers in 1597. Setting a tradition that prevails to the present, they fell in love with the island, and when Cornelius Houtman – the ship's captain – prepared to set sail from Bali, some of his crew refused to leave with him. At that time, Balinese prosperity and artistic activity, at least among the royalty, were at a peak. When the Dutch returned to Indonesia in later years, they were interested in profit, not culture, and barely gave Bali a second glance.

Dutch Conquest

In 1710 the capital of the Gelgel kingdom was shifted to nearby Klungkung (now called Semarapura), but local discontent was growing, lesser rulers were breaking away from Gelgel domination and the Dutch began to move in, using the old policy of divide and conquer. In 1846 the Dutch used Balinese salvage claims over shipwrecks as the pretext to land military forces in northern Bali. In 1894 the Dutch chose to support the Sasaks of Lombok in a rebellion against their Balinese raja. After some bloody battles, the Balinese were defeated in Lombok and, with northern Bali firmly under Dutch control, southern Bali was not likely to retain its independence for long.

In 1906 the Dutch commenced their final assault. The three rajas of Badung realised that they were outnumbered and outgunned, and that defeat was inevitable. Surrender and exile, however, was the worst imaginable outcome, so they decided to take the honourable path of a suicidal *puputan* – a fight to the death.

The Dutch begged the Balinese to surrender rather than make their hopeless stand, but their pleas went unheard and wave after wave of the Balinese nobility marched forward to their deaths. In all, nearly 4000 Balinese died in the *puputan.*

The kingdoms of Karangasem and Gianyar had already capitulated to the Dutch and were allowed to retain some powers, but other kingdoms were defeated and the rulers exiled. Finally, the raja of Klungkung followed the lead of Badung and once more the Dutch faced a *puputan*. With this last obstacle disposed of, all of Bali was now under Dutch control and became part of the Dutch East Indies. Dutch rule over Bali was short-lived, however, as Indonesia fell to the Japanese in WWII.

Independence

On 17 August 1945, just after WWII ended, the Indonesian leader Sukarno proclaimed the nation's independence, but it took four years to convince the Dutch that they were not going to get their colony back. In a virtual repeat of the *puputan* nearly half a century earlier, a Balinese resistance group was wiped out in the Battle of Marga on 20 November 1946; Bali's airport, Ngurah Rai, is named after its leader. It was not until 1949 that the Dutch finally recognised Indonesia's independence.

Modern Bali

The tourism boom, which started in the early 1970s, has brought many changes, and has helped pay for improvements in roads, telecommunications, education and health. Though tourism has had some marked adverse environmental and social effects, Bali's unique culture has proved to be remarkably resilient.

Bali, like most places, has also been affected by global politics. In October 2002 two simultaneous bomb explosions in Kuta – targeting an area frequented by tourists – injured or killed more than 500 people. Tourism (meaning the economy) was devastated. In recent years however, Bali has been on a roll. Tourism has soared and over three million people visit annually; development – and traffic – is everywhere. With concerns about trash, pollution, congestion and more, people are asking: 'Can we be too popular?'

CULTURE

Bali's culture strips the cliché from the word unique. The version of Hinduism practiced with great fervour is found no place else in the world and has inspired fervent artistic expressions that charms visitors.

The population in Bali is almost all Indonesian; over 90% are of Balinese Hindu descent and could be described as ethnic Balinese. The remaining residents are mostly from other parts of the country, particularly Java.

The traditional Balinese society is intensely communal; the organisation of villages, the cultivation of farmlands and even the creative arts are communal efforts. A person belongs to their family, clan, caste and to the village as a whole.

Although tourism has brought much economic wealth to the island and there is a burgeoning middle class, Bali's traditional rice-growing culture remains revered even as whole swaths of land are sold for development. In 2012 Unesco recognised the island's rice-growing traditions, including the communal *subak* water distribution system.

Balinese society is held together by collective responsibility. If a woman enters a temple while menstruating, for instance, it is a kind of irreverence, an insult to the gods, and their displeasure falls not just on the transgressor but on the whole community. This collective responsibility produces considerable pressure on the individual to conform to *adat* – the traditional values and customs that form core Balinese values.

Religion

You can't get away from religion in Bali – there are temples in every village, shrines in every field and offerings made at every corner.

The Balinese are nominally Hindus, but Balinese Hinduism is half a world away from that of India. When the Majapahits evacuated to Bali they took with them their religion and its rituals, as well as their art, literature, music and culture. The Balinese already had strong religious beliefs and an active cultural life, and the new influences were simply overlaid on existing practices –

BALI WEBSITES

Useful online resources:

Bali Advertiser (www.baliadvertiser.biz) Bali's expat newspaper and website has voluminous ads (including many for long-term rentals), comprehensive information and idiosyncratic columnists.

The Beat (www.beatmag.com) Extensive entertainment and cultural listings.

Bali Discovery (www.balidiscovery.com) Good compendium of Bali news.

Lonely Planet (www.lonelyplanet.com/bali) Planning advice, author recommendations, traveller reviews and insider tips.

TOP FIVE TEMPLES

Pura Luhur Ulu Watu (p229) On the Bukit Peninsula, with a spectacular cliff-top location, this is one of Bali's nine directional temples.

Pura Tirta Empul (p261) At Tampaksaring, renowned for its beauty and nearby springs and bathing pools.

Pura Luhur Batukau (p286) On the slopes of Gunung Batukau, with its cool, misty atmosphere.

Pura Taman Ayun (p293) Northwest of Denpasar, it was recognised by Unesco in 2012 for its vital spiritual role in Bali's traditional rice-growing culture.

Pura Maduwe Karang Near Kubutambahan in north Bali, this is an elaborate seaside temple with some surprising carvings, including depictions of Bali's first bike.

hence the peculiar Balinese interpretation of Hinduism.

The Balinese believe spirits are everywhere, an indication that animism is the basis of much of their religion. Good spirits dwell in the mountains and bring prosperity to the people, while giants and demons lurk beneath the sea, and bad spirits haunt the woods and desolate beaches. The people live between these two opposites and their rituals strive to maintain this middle ground. Offerings are carefully put out every morning to pay homage to the good spirits and nonchalantly placed on the ground to placate the bad ones.

TEMPLES

The word for temple is *pura*, which is a Sanskrit word meaning 'a space surrounded by a wall'. As in so much of Balinese religion, the temples, though nominally Hindu, owe much to the pre-Majapahit era. Their *kaja*, *kelod* or *kangin* (alignment towards the mountains, the sea or the sunrise) is in deference to spirits that are more animist than Hindu.

Almost every village has at least three temples. The most important is the *pura puseh* (temple of origin), which is dedicated to the village founders and is at the *kaja* end of the village. In the middle of the village is the *pura desa* for the spirits that protect the village community in its day-to-day life. At the *kelod* end of the village is the *pura dalem* (temple of the dead). The graveyard is also here and the temple will often include representations of Durga, the terrible incarnation of Shiva's wife.

Families worship their ancestors in family temples, clans in clan temples and the whole village in the *pura puseh*. Certain temples in Bali are of such importance that they are deemed to be owned by the whole island rather than by individual villages. Overall Bali has more than 10,000 temples and shrines in all shapes and sizes.

The simple shrines or thrones you see, for example, in rice fields or next to sacred old trees are not real temples, as they are not walled. You'll find these shrines in all sorts of places, often overlooking intersections or dangerous curves in the road to protect road users.

For much of the year Balinese temples are deserted, but on holy days it's believed that the deities and ancestral spirits descend from heaven to visit their devotees, and the temples come alive with days of frenetic activity and nights of drama and dance. Temple festivals come at least once every Balinese year (210 days). Because most villages have at least three temples, you're assured of at least five or six annual festivals in every village. The full-moon periods, around the end of September to the beginning of October, or early to mid-April, are often times of important festivals.

Galungan-Kuningan is a 10-day festival when *lots* of activity takes place at family and community temples all over the island.

ARTS

The Balinese have no words for 'art' and 'artist' because, traditionally, art has never been regarded as something to be treasured for its own sake. Prior to the tourism boom, art was just part of everyday life and what was produced went into temples, palaces or festivals. Although respected, the painter or carver was not considered a member of some special elite, the artist's work was not signed and there were no galleries or craft shops.

It's a different story today, with thousands of art outlets tucked into every possible crevice. Although much Balinese art is churned out quickly as cheap souvenirs, buried beneath the reproductions of reproductions there's still much beautiful work to be found.

Even the simplest activities are carried out with care, precision and artistic flair. Just glance at those little offering trays thrown down on the ground for the demons every morning – each one a throwaway work of art. Look at the temple offerings, the artistically stacked pyramids of fruit or other beautifully decorated foods. Look for *penjor*, long decorated bamboo poles, at doorways during festivals.

Most visitors to the island discover the greatest concentration of the arts in and around Ubud.

Balinese Painting

The art form most influenced both by Western ideas and tourist demand is painting. Traditional painting was very limited in style and subject matter, and was used primarily for temple decoration. The arrival of Western artists after WWI introduced new subject matter and materials with which artists could work.

Traditional Balinese paintings were narratives with mythological themes, illustrating stories from Hindu epics and literature. Paintings were executed in the *wayang* style – the flat two- dimensional style that imitates the *wayang kulit* (shadow puppets), with the figures invariably shown in three-quarter view. The colours that artists could use were strictly limited to a set list (red, blue, brown, yellow and light ochre for flesh).

Bali's painting traditions remain vibrant and rich today. Ubud is the place to ponder the best paintings in museums and galleries.

Dance

Many visitors are seduced by the haunting and melodic charms of a dance performance in Ubud, a quintessential Bali experience.

Music, dance and drama are closely related in Bali. In fact, dance and drama are synonymous, though some 'dances' are more drama and less dance, and others more dance and less drama.

Balinese dance tends to be precise, shifting and jerky, like the accompanying gamelan music, which has abrupt shifts of tempo and dramatic changes between silence and crashing noise. There's virtually no physical contact in Balinese dancing – each dancer moves independently, but every movement of wrist, hand and finger is important. Even facial expressions are carefully choreographed to convey the character of the dance.

Dances are a regular part of almost every temple festival, and Bali has no shortage of these. There are also dances virtually every night at tourist centres, although the most authentic are found in and around Ubud.

KECAK

One of the best-known dances of Bali is the Kecak. It is unusual because it does not have a gamelan (traditional orchestra) accompaniment. Instead, the background is provided by a chanting 'choir' of men who provide the 'chak-a-chak-a-chak' noise that distinguishes the dance.

The Kecak tells the tale of the Ramayana, the quest of Prince Rama to rescue his wife Sita after she had been kidnapped by Rawana, the King of Lanka. Rama is accompanied to Lanka by Sugriwa, the king of the monkeys, with his monkey army. Throughout the Kecak dance, the circle of men, all barechested and wearing checked cloth around their waists, provide a nonstop accompaniment, rising to a crescendo as they play the monkey army and fight it out with Rawana and his cronies.

BARONG & RANGDA

The Barong Keket is half shaggy dog, half lion – and is played by two men in much the same way as a pantomime horse. Its opponent is the Rangda (witch).

The Barong represents good and protects the village from the Rangda, but is

TOP BALI READS

» *Bali Daze - Freefall Off the Tourist Trail* Cat Wheeler's accounts of daily life in Ubud ring more true than other recent books.

» *Secrets of Bali: Fresh Light on the Morning of the World* One of the most readable books about Bali, its people, its traditions and more. Authors Jonathan Copeland and Ni Wayan Murni have a winner.

» *Eat, Pray, Love* Hate it or love it, this bestseller lures believers to Bali every year, hoping to capture something in Elizabeth Gilbert's prose.

also a mischievous creature. It flounces into the temple courtyard, snaps its jaws at the gamelan, dances around and enjoys the acclaim of its supporters – a group of men with kris (traditional daggers). Then the Rangda makes her appearance, with long tongue lolling, pendulous breasts wobbling, human entrails draped around her neck, fangs protruding from her mouth and sabre-like fingernails clawing the air.

The two duel with their magical powers, and the Barong's supporters draw their kris and rush in to attack the witch. The Rangda puts them in a trance and the men try to stab themselves, but the Barong also has great magical powers and casts a spell that stops the kris from harming the men. This is the most dramatic part of the dance: as the gamelan rings crazily the men rush back and forth, waving their kris around, all but foaming at the mouth, sometimes even rolling on the ground in a desperate attempt to stab themselves. Finally, the Rangda retires defeated: good has won again.

LEGONG

This is the most graceful of Balinese dances and, to connoisseurs of Balinese dancing, the one of most interest.

There are various forms of the Legong but the Legong Kraton (Legong of the Palace) is the one most often performed. A performance involves just three dancers – the two Legongs and their 'attendant' known as the Condong. The Legongs are identically dressed in tightly bound gold brocade. So tightly are they encased that it's something of a mystery how they manage to move with such agility and speed. Their faces are elaborately made up, their eyebrows plucked and repainted, and their hair decorated with frangipanis.

The dance relates how a king takes a maiden, Rangkesari, captive. When Rangkesari's brother comes to release her, he begs the king to let her free rather than go to war. The king refuses and, on his way to the battle, meets a bird bringing ill omens. He ignores the bird and continues on to meet Rangkesari's brother, who kills him. The dance, however, relates only the lead-up to the battle and ends with the bird's appearance. When the king leaves the stage he is going to the battle that will end in his death.

Gamelan

As in Sumatra and Java, Balinese music is based around the gamelan orchestra. The whole gamelan orchestra is known as a *gong* – an old fashioned *gong gede* or a more modern *gong kebyar*. It's easy to hear gamelan music in Bali, not only is it a core part of ceremonies but groups practise regularly.

BALI'S NEW TOLL ROAD

Due for completion before 2014, Bali's new toll road is meant to avoid the worst of the traffic in and around Kuta. Some 12km in length, it runs from the bypass near Denpasar over the mangroves to a point near Nusa Dua with a branch to the airport.

The toll will be 10,000Rp; how much time will be saved compared to the current clogged roads is hard to quantify. The road's northern end is at the turn to Benoa off the bypass, already one of the most congested spots in the south.

Getting There & Away

AIR

Bali is the second most common entry point to Indonesia. The only airport in Bali, Ngurah Rai International Airport (DPS), is just south of Kuta; however, it is sometimes referred to internationally as Denpasar (which is 15km north) or, on some internet flight booking sites, as Bali. The airport should have a vast new terminal replacing the overcrowded old one by 2014.

Bali is also a hub for flights across the archipelago. Some airlines flying to and from Bali:

AirAsia (☎0361-760 116; www.airasia.com; ticket office outside international terminal) Serves Jakarta as well as Bangkok, Kuala Lumpur and Singapore, plus Darwin and Perth in Australia.

Cathay Pacific Airways (www.cathaypacific.com) Serves Hong Kong.

China Airlines (www.china-airlines.com) Serves Taipei.

Eva Air (www.evaair.com) Serves Taipei.

Garuda Indonesia (www.garuda-indonesia.com) Serves Australia (Darwin, Melbourne, Perth and Sydney), Japan, Korea and Singapore direct, plus cities across Indonesia.

KLM (www.klm.com) Serves Amsterdam via Singapore.

Korean Air (www.koreanair.com) Serves Seoul.

Lion Air (www.lionair.co.id) Serves cities across Indonesia and Singapore.

Malaysia Airlines (www.mas.com.my) Serves Kuala Lumpur.

Qantas Airways (www.qantas.com.au) Serves Australia (Brisbane, Darwin, Melbourne, Perth and Sydney).

Qatar Airways (www.qatarairways.com) Serves Doha via Singapore.

Singapore Airlines (www.singaporeair.com) Several Singapore flights daily.

Thai Airways International (www.thaiair.com) Serves Bangkok.

Virgin Australia (www.virginaustralia.com) Serves Australia.

BUS

Bali's **long-distance bus terminal** (Mengwi) has moved 12km northwest of Denpasar to a large new terminal near Mengwi, just off the main road to west Bali. It even has an airport-style 'control tower', possibly to guide in the buses arriving from Java.

You can get bemos (minibuses) from here to Denpasar's Batubulan terminal (20,000Rp) and on to Padangbai (50,000Rp) for the Lombok ferry.

Taxis from here to Kerobokan cost 100,000Rp; Kuta is 120,000Rp.

Many buses from numerous companies travel daily between Bali and major cities in Java (via ferry); most travel overnight. Fares vary between operators and depend on what sort of comfort you want – it's worth paying extra for a decent seat and air-con.

SEA

Ferries operate between Gilimanuk in western Bali and Ketapang (Java).

This island is accessible by regular public ferry from Padangbai. Fast boats for tourists serve the Gili Islands and Lombok.

Services to other islands in Indonesia are often in flux, although **Pelni** (www.pelni.co.id), the national shipping line, is reasonably reliable. It schedules large boats on long-distance runs throughout Indonesia.

For Bali, Pelni ships stop at the harbour in Benoa as part of their regular loops throughout Indonesia. Schedules and fares are found on the website. You can enquire and book at the **Pelni ticket office** (☎0361-763 963, 021-7918 0606; www.pelni.co.id; Jl Raya Kuta 299; ⏰8am-noon & 1-4pm Mon-Fri, 8am-1pm Sat) in Tuban.

TRAIN

Bali doesn't have trains but the state railway company does have an **office** (☎227 131; Jl Diponegoro 150/B4; ⏰8.30am-6.30pm) in Denpasar. From here buses leave for eastern Java where they link with trains at Banyuwangi for Surabaya, Yogyakarta and Jakarta among others. Fares and times are comparable to the bus but the air-conditioned trains are more comfortable, even in economy class.

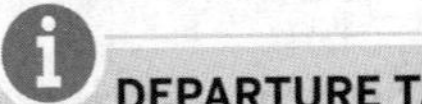

DEPARTURE TAX

The departure tax from Bali is 50,000Rp for domestic flights and 150,000Rp for international ones. Have exact cash ready.

Getting Around

The best way to get around Bali is with your own transport, whether you drive, hire a driver or ride a bike. This gives you the flexibility to explore at will and allows you to reach many places that are otherwise inaccessible.

Public transport is cheap but can result in very long journeys if you're not sticking to a major route. In addition, some places are just impossible to reach.

There are also tourist shuttle buses, which combine economy with convenience.

TO/FROM THE AIRPORT

From the official counter at the airport arrivals area, there are supposedly fixed-price taxis. However, efforts may be made to charge you the high end of the range, and if you say you don't have a room booking, there will be pressure to go to a commission-paying hotel. Costs depend on drop-off point.

DESTINATION	COST (RP)
Denpasar	70,000-90,000
Jimbaran	75,000-95,000
Kuta Beach	45,000-50,000
Legian	55,000-65,000
Nusa Dua	95,000-105,000
Sanur	95,000
Seminyak	70,000-80,000
Ubud	195,000-225,000

If you have a surfboard, you'll be charged at least 35,000Rp extra, depending on its size. Ignore any touts that aren't part of the official scheme. Many hotels will offer to pick you up at the airport, however there's no need to use this service if it costs more than the above rates.

Any taxi will take you to the airport at a metered rate that should be less than the taxis *from* the airport.

BEMO

The bemo was once the dominant form of public transport in Bali. But widespread motorbike ownership (which can be cheaper than daily bemo use) has caused the system to wither. On Lombok, however, bemos are still important.

PERAMA TOURIST SHUTTLES

Consider the following advantages and disadvantages when deciding whether to book your Perama tourist shuttle ticket (one day in advance is a good idea).

Advantages

» Fares are reasonable (eg Kuta to Lovina is 100,000Rp)

» Buses have air-con

» You'll meet other travellers

Disadvantages

» Perama stops are often outside the centre, requiring another shuttle/taxi

» Buses may not provide a direct service – stopping, say, at Ubud between Kuta and Padangbai

» Like bemos, the service has ossified, resolutely sticking to the routes it ran years ago and not recognising popular new destinations such as Bingen or Seminyak

» Three or more people can hire a car and driver for less

A bemo is normally a minibus or van with a row of low seats down each side. They usually hold about 12 people in very cramped conditions.

Riding bemo can be part of your Bali adventure or a major nightmare, depending on your outlook at the time. You can certainly expect journeys to be lengthy and you'll find that getting to many places is both time-consuming and inconvenient. It's uncommon to see visitors on bemos in Bali.

BICYCLE

More and more people are touring the island by *sepeda* (motorcycle). Many visitors are using bikes around the towns and for day trips in Bali and on Lombok. Cycling tours are popular.

Ask at your accommodation about renting a bike; hotels often have their own. Prices are about 15,000Rp to 35,000Rp per day.

BOAT

Boats of various sizes serve Nusa Lembongan and Nusa Penida from Sanur and Padangbai.

BUS

In what may become Bali's modern public transport system, a new company, **Trans-Sarbagita** (fare 3500Rp), is operating routes with the kind of large air-con buses you find in major cities the world over. At the time of research it had two routes (with more planned): one along the bypass linking Sanur to Nusa Dua and the other running from Denpasar to Jimbaran. The highly visible roadside bus stops have maps. The routes converge at a stop just east of Kuta in the large parking lot south of the Istana Kuta Galleria shopping centre. Fares are a cheap 3500Rp.

CAR & MOTORCYCLE

The most popular rental vehicle is a small jeep – they're compact and are well suited to exploring back roads. Automatic transmissions are unheard of.

Hire and travel agencies in tourist centres rent vehicles quite cheaply. A small jeep costs a negotiable 200,000Rp per day to hire, with unlimited kilometres and very limited insurance. Extra days often cost much less than the first day.

There's no reason to book hire cars in advance or with a tour package; doing so will almost certainly cost more than arranging it locally. Any place you stay can set you up with a car, as can the ever-present touts in the street.

Motorbikes are easily hired. Ask at your accommodation or look for the inevitable offers on the street. The engines are modest (a fuel-stingy 125cc is typical), so your chances of going fast are nil. They'll cost you 30,000Rp to 50,000Rp a day, less by the week. This should include minimal insurance for the motorcycle (probably with a US$100 excess), but not for any other person or property. Many have racks for surfboards.

Think carefully before hiring a motorbike. It is dangerous and every year visitors go home with lasting damage – this is no place to learn to ride. Helmet use is mandatory.

TAXI

Metered taxis are common in south Bali and Denpasar (but not Ubud). They are essential for getting around Kuta and Seminyak, where you can easily flag one down. Elsewhere, they're often a lot less hassle than haggling with drivers offering 'transport!'.

The usual rate for a taxi is 5000Rp flag fall and 4000Rp per kilometre, but the rate is higher in the evening. If you phone for a taxi, the minimum charge is 10,000Rp. Avoid any driver who claims to have meter problems or won't use the meter.

By far the most reputable taxi company is **Bluebird Taxi** (701 111), which uses blue vehicles with a light on the roof bearing a stylised bluebird. Watch out for myriad fakes – there are many. Look for 'Blue Bird' over the windscreen and the phone number. Drivers speak reasonable English and use the meter at all times.

After Bluebird Taxi, standards decline. Some other companies are acceptable, although you may have a hassle getting the driver to use the meter after dark. Others may claim that their meter is 'broken' or nonexistent, and negotiated fees can be way over the odds.

TOURIST SHUTTLE BUS

Perama (0361-751 170; www.peramatour.com) has a near monopoly on this service in Bali (although you may see small-time competitors advertising in Kuta). It has offices or agents in Kuta, Sanur, Ubud, Lovina, Padangbai and Candidasa and at least one bus a day links these tourist centres. Services to Kintamani and along the east coast from Lovina to/from Candidasa via Amed are by demand. Perama also has a very limited service around Senggigi on Lombok.

SOUTH BALI

For many people South Bali *is* Bali; for many others it is anything but. Chaotic Kuta and upscale Seminyak throb around the clock. In the south, the Bukit Peninsula is home to some of the island's best hidden beaches, while in the east Sanur follows the subdued beat of its reef-protected surf. Denpasar is a fascinating excursion into Balinese culture.

Kuta & Legian

0361

Loud, frenetic and brash are just some of the adjectives commonly used to describe Kuta and Legian, the centre of mass tourism in Bali. Only a couple of decades ago, local hotels tacked their signs up to palm trees. Amid the wall-to-wall cacophony today, such an image seems as foreign as the thought that the area was once rice fields. Worse, parts are just plain ugly, like the unsightly strips that wend their way inland from the beach.

Although this is often the first place many visitors hit in Bali, the region is not for everyone. Kuta has narrow lanes jammed with cheap cafes, surf shops, incessant motorbikes and an uncountable number of T-shirt vendors. However, newly opened flashy shopping malls and chain hotels suggest a more mainstream future.

Kuta has Bali's most raucous clubs, and you can still find a simple room for 150,000Rp in

SURFING IN BALI

It really is a surfer's paradise in Bali. Breaks are found right around the south side of the island and there's a large infrastructure of schools, board-hire places, cheap surfer dives, and more that cater to the crowds.

Here are five famous spots you won't want to miss:

Kuta Beach (p209) Where surfing came to Asia. This is a good place for beginners, with long, steady breaks.

Echo Beach (p227) Northwest of Kerobokan, there is a good surfer scene here with cafes, board rental and more.

Ulu Watu (p229) Some of the largest – and most famous – sets in Bali.

Medewi (p296) Famous point break with a ride right into a river mouth.

Nusa Lembongan (p241) The island is a mellow scene for surfers and nonsurfers. The breaks are right in front of the places to stay.

Stalls on the side streets hire out surfboards (for a negotiable 30,000Rp per day) and boogie boards, repair dings and sell new and used boards.

Pro Surf School (www.prosurfschool.com; Jl Pantai Kuta; lessons from €45) is right across from the classic stretch of Kuta Beach. Facilities here include a swimming pool and semiprivate lesson areas. **Rip Curl School of Surf** (735 858; www.ripcurlschoolofsurf.com; Jl Arjana; lessons from 650,000Rp) run by the high-profile, local surf-wear conglomerate. The school offers classes for beginners and experts alike. Located right on ever-popular Double Six Beach.

South Bali

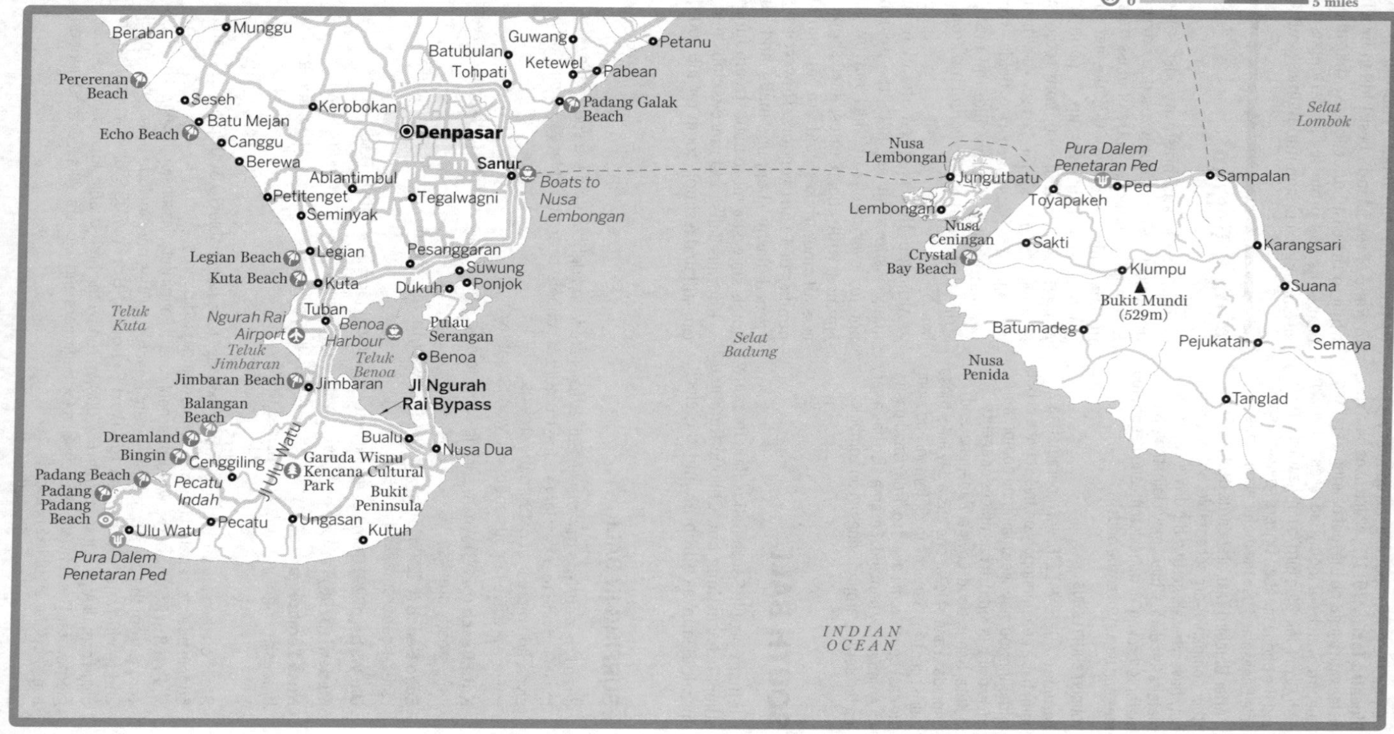
0 10 km
0 5 miles
N
Beraban
Munggu
Pererenan Beach
Seseh
Batu Mejan
Echo Beach
Canggu
Berewa
Kerobokan
Denpasar
Batubulan
Tohpati
Guwang
Ketewel
Petanu
Pabean
Padang Galak Beach
Sanur
Boats to Nusa Lembongan
Abiantimbul
Petitenget
Tegalwagni
Seminyak
Legian Beach
Legian
Kuta Beach
Kuta
Pesanggaran
Suwung
Ponjok
Dukuh
Teluk Kuta
Ngurah Rai Airport
Tuban
Benoa Harbour
Pulau Serangan
Teluk Jimbaran
Teluk Benoa
Benoa
Jimbaran Beach
Jimbaran
Jl Ngurah Rai Bypass
Balangan Beach
Dreamland
Bingin
Cenggiling
Jl Ulu Watu
Garuda Wisnu Kencana Cultural Park
Bualu
Nusa Dua
Padang Beach
Padang Padang Beach
Pecatu Indah
Bukit Peninsula
Ulu Watu
Pecatu
Ungasan
Kutuh
Pura Dalem Penetaran Ped
Selat Badung
INDIAN OCEAN
Nusa Lembongan
Jungutbatu
Lembongan
Nusa Ceningan
Crystal Bay Beach
Pura Dalem Penetaran Ped
Toyapakeh
Ped
Sampalan
Selat Lombok
Sakti
Karangsari
Klumpu
Bukit Mundi (529m)
Suana
Batumadeg
Pejukatan
Semaya
Nusa Penida
Tanglad

dozens of hotels. Legian appeals to a slightly older crowd (wags say it's where fans of Kuta go after they're married). It is equally commercial and has a long row of family-friendly hotels close to the beach. Tuban differs little in feel from Kuta and Legian, but does have a higher percentage of visitors on package holidays.

As for the waves, they break on the beach that put Kuta on the map. The strand of sand stretching for kilometres from Tuban north to Kuta, Legian and beyond to Seminyak and Echo Beach is always a scene of surfing, playing, massaging, chilling, imbibing and more.

Navigating the region will drive you to a cold one even earlier than you had planned. Busy Jl Legian runs roughly parallel to the beach from Kuta north into Seminyak.

Sights

The real sight here is, of course, the **beach.** You can immerse yourself in local life without even getting wet. A pleasant walkway runs south from where Jl Pantai Kuta meets the beach. Stretching almost to the airport, it has fine views of the ocean and the efforts to preserve some of Tuban's nearly vanished beach.

From Legian the beach becomes less crowded as you go north until very popular **Double Six Beach** (Jl Arjuna), which is alive with pick-up games of football and volleyball all day long. It's a fine place to meet locals.

Reflecting the international scope of the 2002 bombings is the **memorial wall** (Jl Legian; ⏲24hr), where people from many countries pay their respects. Listing the names of the 202 known victims, including 88 Australians and 35 Indonesians, it is starting to look just a touch faded. Across the street, a parking lot is all that is left of the **Sari Club site**.

Activities

From the Kuta region you can easily go surfing, sailing, diving, fishing or rafting anywhere in southern Bali, and be back for the start of the evening happy hour.

Spas have proliferated, especially in hotels, and offers are numerous. Check out a few before choosing.

Jamu Spa SPA
(☎752 520; www.jamutraditionalspa.com; Jl Pantai Kuta, Alam Kul Kul; massage from 550,000Rp; ⏲9am-9pm) In serene surrounds at a resort hotel, you can enjoy indoor massage rooms that open onto a pretty garden courtyard. If you've ever wanted to be part of a fruit cocktail, here's your chance – treatments involve tropical nuts, coconuts, papayas and more, often in fragrant baths.

Garbugar MASSAGE
(☎769 121; Istana Kuta Galleria, Blok OG 09; massage from 100,000Rp; ⏲10am-8pm) Blind masseurs here are experts in sensing exactly where your kinks are located. It's no-frills all the way but hard to beat for a deeply relaxing experience.

Waterbom Park AMUSEMENT PARK
(☎755 676; www.waterbom.com; Jl Kartika Plaza; adult/child US$31/19; ⏲9am-6pm) Just south of Kuta, this watery amusement park covers 3.5 hectares of landscaped tropical gardens. It has assorted water slides, swimming pools and play areas, a supervised park for children under five years old, and a 'lazy river' ride. Other indulgences include the 'pleasure pool', a food court and bar, and a spa.

Sleeping

Kuta, Legian and Tuban have hundreds of places for you to stay. The top-end hotels are along the beachfront, midrange places are mostly on the bigger roads between Jl Legian and the beach, and the cheapest losmen (basic, often family-run, accommodation) are generally along the smaller lanes in between.

Note that large hotels are now cropping up in areas far from the beach. Once you get east of Jl Legian and its northern extension Jl Seminyak, the beach will be at best a slog. Get east of Jl Sunset and you'll be needing a scarce cab to get to the mostly interesting areas of the Kuta–Seminyak conurbation. East of Jl Ngurah Rai Bypass you'll be on the wrong side of a traffic-choked road unsafe to cross as a pedestrian and with nothing nearby worth a walk.

KUTA FOR CHILDREN

Except for the traffic, the Kuta area is a pretty good place for kids. With supervision – and sunscreen! – they can cavort on the beach for hours. Almost all the hotels and resorts have pools.

There are great rafting trips in Bali's hills and it is worth checking out the popular Bali Safari and Marine Park (p264).

Kuta, Legian & Seminyak

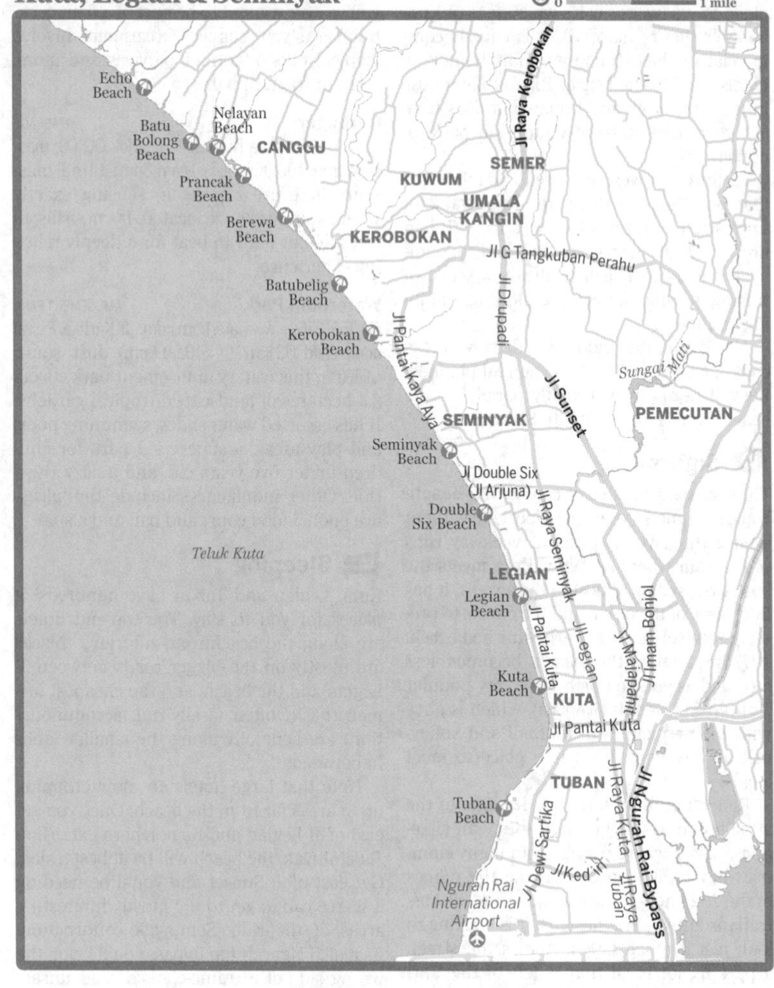

Beachfront hotels in Kuta actually front busy Jl Pantai Kuta, while most of Legian's top hotels (and some more modest ones) front a fine swath of beach and a road closed to traffic – in effect, a long promenade.

KUTA

Wandering the *gangs* (alleys) and lanes looking for a cheap room is a rite of passage for many. Small and family-run options are still numerous even as chains crowd in. Some of the hotels along Jl Legian are of the type that assume men booking a single actually aspire to a double.

TOP CHOICE Un's Hotel HOTEL **$$**
(☎757 409; www.unshotel.com; Jl Benesari; r US$35-80; ❄📶🏊) A hidden entrance sets the tone for the secluded feel of Un's. It's a two-storey place with bougainvillea spilling over the pool-facing balconies. The 30 spacious rooms in a pair of blocks (the southern one is quieter) feature antiques, comfy cane loungers and open-air bathrooms. Cheaper rooms are fan only.

Poppies Cottages HOTEL **$$**
(☎751 059; www.poppiesbali.com; Poppies Gang I; r US$95-120; ❄@📶🏊) This Kuta institution

has a lush, green setting for its 20 thatch-roofed cottages with outdoor sunken baths. Bed choices include kings and twins. The pool is surrounded by stone sculptures and water fountains in a garden that almost makes you forget you are in the heart of Kuta.

Kuta Puri Bungalows HOTEL **$$**
(☎751 903; www.kutapuri.com; Poppies Gang I; r US$60-130; ❄📶🏊) The 47 bungalow-style rooms here are well maintained and nestled in verdant tropical grounds. The pool has a shallow kids' area. Enjoy the splish-splash of a fountain. Some rooms are fan only.

Bali Bungalo HOTEL **$$**
(☎755 109; www.bali-bungalo.com; off Jl Pantai Kuta; r 500,000-600,000Rp; ❄📶🏊) Large rooms close to the beach yet away from irritations are a big part of the appeal of this older, 44-room hotel. It's well maintained and there are statues of prancing horses to inspire horseplay in the pool. Rooms are in two-storey buildings and have patios/porches; not all have wi-fi.

Suji Bungalow HOTEL **$**
(☎765 804; www.sujibglw.com; off Poppies Gang I; r US$38-50; ❄@📶🏊) This cheery place offers a choice of 47 bungalows and rooms in two-storey blocks set in a spacious, quiet garden around a pool (which has a slide into the kiddie area). The verandas and terraces are good for relaxing. Not all rooms have wi-fi.

Berlian Inn HOTEL **$**
(☎751 501; off Poppies Gang I; r 120,000-250,000Rp; ❄) A stylish cut above other budget places, the 24 rooms in two-storey buildings here are pleasingly quiet and have ikat (woven cloth) bedspreads and an unusual open-air bathroom design. Pricier rooms have air-con and hot water.

Mimpi Bungalows HOTEL **$**
(☎751 848; kumimpi@yahoo.com.sg; r 200,000-500,000Rp; ❄📶🏊) The cheapest of the 10 bungalow-style rooms here are the best value (and are fan-only). Private gardens boast orchids and shade, and the pool is a good size. Mimpi's owner, Made Supatra, is a tireless promoter of Kuta. There are many more choices nearby.

LEGIAN

There is a building boom going on along Legian's beach. Wander off the main roads for some quiet gems.

Bali Mandira Hotel HOTEL **$$$**
(☎751 381; www.balimandira.com; Jl Pantai Kuta; r US$140-250; ❄📶🏊) Gardens filled with bird-of-paradise flowers set the tone at this 191-room, full-service resort. Cottages have modern interiors, and the bathrooms are partly open-air. A dramatic pool at the peak of a stone ziggurat (which houses a spa) offers sweeping ocean views, as does the cafe.

Sari Beach Inn HOTEL **$$**
(☎751 635; www.saribeachinn.com; off Jl Padma Utara; r US$70-100; ❄📶) Follow your ears down a long *gang* to the roar of the surf at this good-value beachside hotel that defines mellow. The 21 rooms have patios and the best have big soaking tubs. Grassy grounds boast many little statues and water features.

Island HOTEL **$$**
(☎762 722; www.theislandhotelbali.com; Gang Abdi; dm US$25, r 550,000-700,000Rp; ❄@📶🏊) A real find, literally. Hidden in the attractive maze of tiny lanes west of Jl Legian, this hotel lies at the confluence of *gang* 19, 21 and Abdi. In a rarity for Bali, it has a very deluxe dorm room with eight beds. Regular rooms are stylish and surround a nice pool.

Hotel Kumala Pantai HOTEL **$$**
(☎755 500; www.kumalapantai.com; Jl Werkudara; r 700,000-1,000,000Rp; ❄@📶) One of the better deals in Legian. The 108 rooms are large, with marble bathrooms featuring separate shower and tub. The three-storey blocks are set in very lush grounds across from popular Double Six Beach. Wi-fi charges can be high.

Blue Ocean HOTEL **$**
(☎730 289; off Jl Pantai Arjuna; 200,000-400,000Rp; ❄) Almost on the beach, the Blue Ocean is a clean and basic place with hot water and pleasant outdoor bathrooms. Many of the 24 rooms have kitchens and there's action nearby day and night.

Eating

There's a profusion of places to eat around Kuta and Legian. Tourist cafes, with their cheap menus of Indonesian standards, sandwiches and pizza, are ubiquitous. Look closely and you'll find genuine Balinese warungs (food stalls) tucked in amid it all.

If you're looking for the laid-back scene of a classic travellers' cafe, wander the *gang* and look for the crowds. For quick snacks and 4am beers, Circle K convenience stores are everywhere and are open 24 hours.

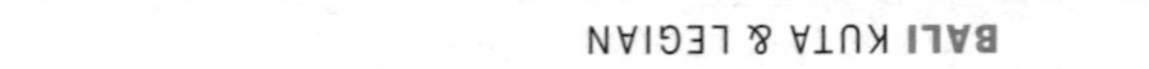

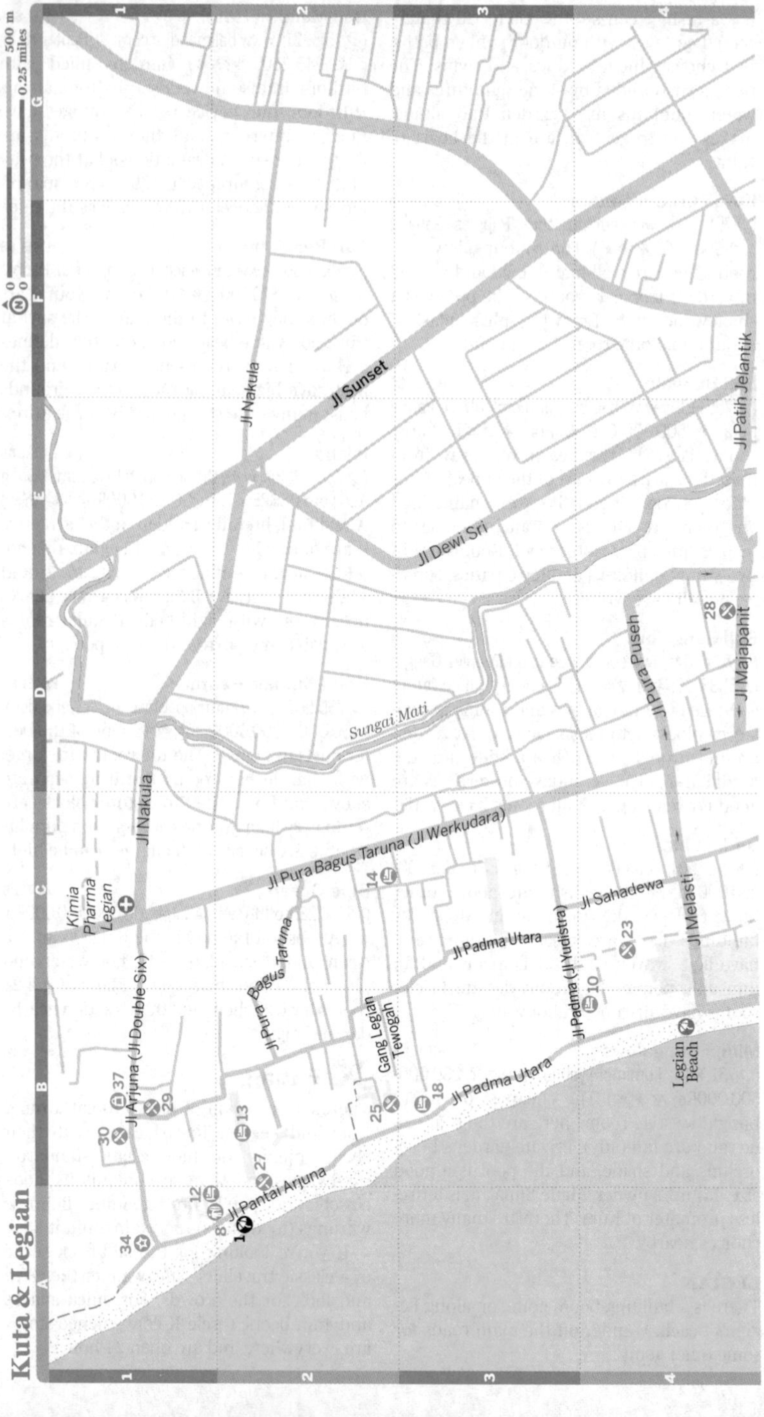

Kuta & Legian

0 — 500 m
0 — 0.25 miles

Kimia Pharma Legian
Jl Arjuna (Jl Double Six)
Jl Nakula
Jl Pantai Arjuna
Jl Pura Bagus Taruna
Jl Pura Bagus Taruna (Jl Werkudara)
Gang Legian Tewogah
Sungai Mati
Jl Sunset
Jl Dewi Sri
Jl Padma Utara
Jl Padma (Jl Yudistra)
Jl Sahadewa
Jl Pura Puseh
Legian Beach
Jl Melasti
Jl Majapahit
Jl Patih Jelantik
1 8 10 12 13 14 18 23 25 27 28 29 30 34 37

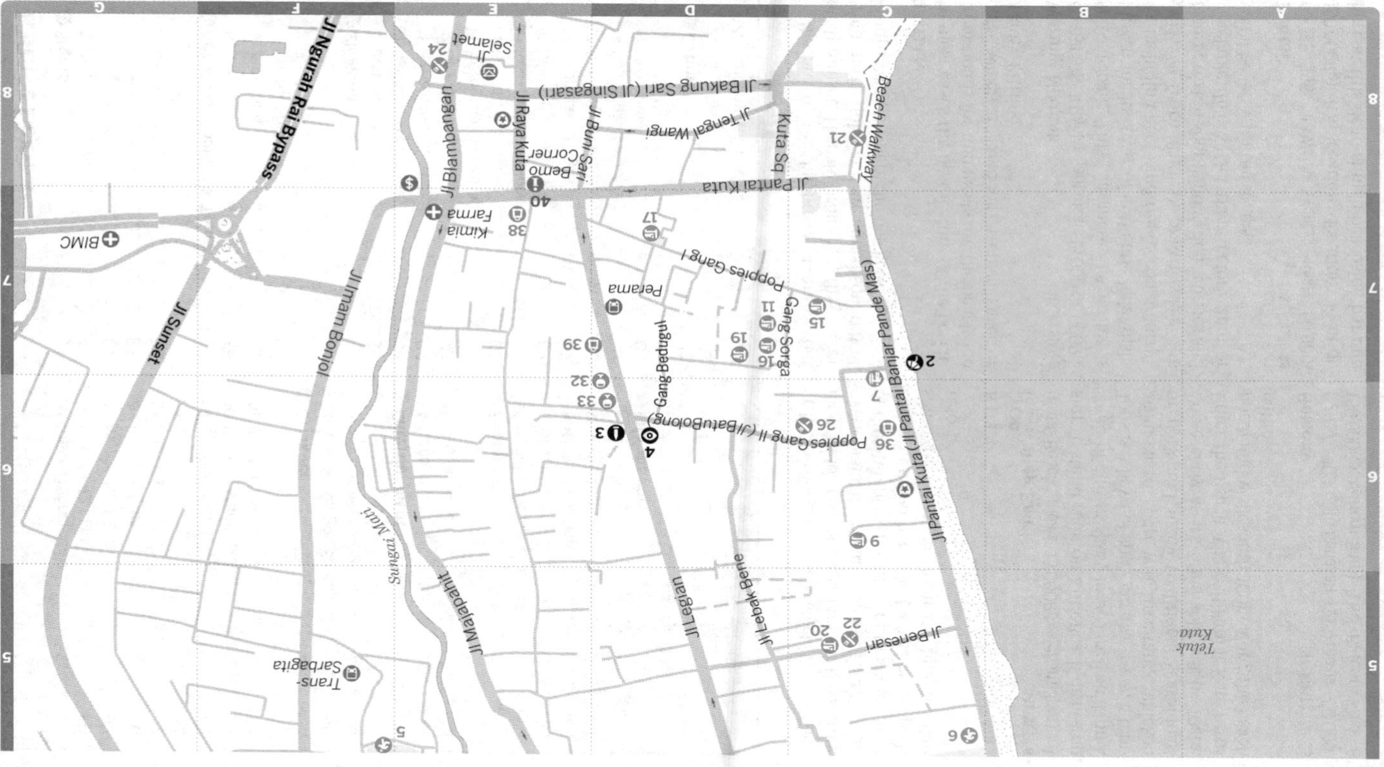
Jl Sunset
Jl Ngurah Rai Bypass
BIMC
Jl Imam Bonjol
Trans-Sarbagita
Sungai Mati
Jl Majapahit
Jl Blambangan
Kimia Farma
Jl Selamet
Jl Raya Kuta
Bemo Corner
Jl Buni Sari
Jl Bakung Sari (Jl Singasari)
Jl Tengal Wangi
Kuta Sq
Jl Pantai Kuta
Beach Walkway
Jl Legian
Gang Bedugul
Perama
Poppies Gang I
Poppies Gang II (Jl Batu Bolong)
Gang Sorga
Jl Lebak Bene
Jl Benesari
Jl Pantai Kuta (Jl Pantai Banjar Pande Mas)
Teluk Kuta
A
B
C
D
E
F
G
5
6
7
8

Kuta & Legian

Sights

1 Double Six Beach ... A2
2 Kuta Beach ... C7
3 Memorial Wall ... D6
4 Site of Sari Club ... D6

Activities, Courses & Tours

5 Garbugar ... F5
6 Jamu Spa ... C5
7 Pro Surf School ... C7
8 Rip Curl School of Surf ... A1

Sleeping

9 Bali Bungalo ... C6
10 Bali Mandira Hotel ... B4
11 Berlian Inn ... D7
12 Blue Ocean ... A1
13 Hotel Kumala Pantai ... B2
14 Island ... C2
15 Kuta Puri Bungalows ... C7
16 Mimpi Bungalows ... D7
17 Poppies Cottages ... D7
18 Sari Beach Inn ... B3
19 Suji Bungalow ... D7
20 Un's Hotel ... C5

Eating

21 Ajeg Bali ... C8
22 Balcony ... C5
23 Indo-National ... C4
24 Kuta Night Market ... E8
25 Mozarella ... B2
26 Rainbow Cafe ... C6
27 Seaside ... B2
28 Take ... D4
29 Warung Asia ... B1
30 Warung Murah ... B1
31 Warung Nikmat ... E8

Drinking

32 Apache Reggae Bar ... D6
33 Sky Garden Lounge ... D6

Entertainment

34 Cocoon ... A1
35 DeeJay Cafe ... D8

Shopping

36 Beachwalk ... C6
37 Busana Agung ... B1
38 Kerta Bookshop ... E7
39 Surfer Girl ... D7

Information

40 Hanafi ... E8

Beware of the big-box restaurants out on Jl Sunset. Heavily promoted, they suffer from traffic noise and are aimed squarely at groups who go where the bus goes.

TUBAN

In most cases the best feature of the beachfront hotels for nonguests are the beachside cafes, which are good for a tropical snack or a sunset drink.

Warung Nikmat INDONESIAN **$**
(☎764 678; Jl Banjar Sari; meals 15,000-25,000Rp; ⏲10am-3pm) This Javanese favourite is known for its array of authentic halal dishes, including beef *rendang* (coconut curry), *perkedel* (corn fritters), prawn cakes, *sop buntut* (oxtail soup) and various curries and vegetable dishes. Get there before 2pm or you'll be left with the scraps.

Pantai SEAFOOD **$$**
(☎753 196; Jl Wana Segara; meals 50,000-150,000Rp) It's location, location, location here at this dead-simple beachside bar and grill. The food is purely stock tourist (seafood, Indo classics, pasta etc) but the setting overlooking the ocean is idyllic. There's none of the pretence (or prices) of the hotel cafes common down here. Follow the beach path south past the big Ramada Bintang Bali resort.

KUTA

TOP CHOICE **Ajeg Bali** BALINESE **$**
(Kuta Beach; meals 15,000Rp; ⏲8am-3pm) A simple stand right on Kuta Beach dishes up some of the freshest local fare you'll find. Tops is a bowl of spicy *garang asem*, a tamarind-based soup with free-range chicken or pork and many traditional seasonings. Come early as it's often sold out by 10am. Enter the beach where Jl Pantai Kuta turns north and walk south 100m along the beach path.

Balcony INTERNATIONAL **$$**
(☎757 409; Jl Benesari 16; meals 50,000-150,000Rp; ⏲from 5am) The Balcony has a

breezy tropical design and sits above the din of Jl Benesari below. Get ready for the day with a long breakfast menu. At night it's sort of upscale surfer: pasta, grilled meats and a few Indo classics. It's all nicely done and the perfect place for an impromptu date night.

Rainbow Cafe INTERNATIONAL $

(☎765 730; Poppies Gang II; meals from 50,000Rp) Join generations of Kuta denizens quaffing the afternoon away. The vibe at this deeply shaded spot has changed little since people said things like 'I grok that, man'. Many current customers are the offspring of backpackers who met at adjoining tables.

Take JAPANESE $$

(☎759 745; Jl Patih Jelantik; meals 70,000-300,000Rp) Flee Bali for a relaxed version of Tokyo just by ducking under the traditional fabric shield over the doorway here. Hyper-fresh sushi, sashimi and more are prepared under the fanatical eyes of a team of chefs behind a long counter. Dine at low tables or hang out in a booth.

Kuta Night Market INDONESIAN $

(Jl Blambangan; meals 15,000-25,000Rp; ⏲6pm-midnight) This enclave of stalls and plastic chairs bustles with locals and tourism workers chowing down on hot-off-the-wok treats, grilled goods and other fresh foods.

LEGIAN

TOP CHOICE Mozarella ITALIAN, SEAFOOD $$

(www.mozzarella-resto.com; Maharta Bali Hotel, Jl Padma Utara; meals from 60,000Rp) The best of the beachfront restaurants on Legian's car-free strip, Mozarella serves Italian fare more complex and authentic than that of its south Bali competition. Fresh fish also features; service is rather polished and there are various open-air areas for star-highlighted dining, plus a more sheltered dining room.

Warung Murah INDONESIAN $

(Jl Arjuna; meals from 30,000Rp) Lunch goes swimmingly at this authentic warung specialising in seafood. An array of grilled fish awaits; if you prefer fowl over fin, the *sate ayam* (chicken sate) is succulent *and* a bargain. Hugely popular at lunch; try to arrive right before noon.

Indo-National WESTERN, SEAFOOD $$

(Jl Padma 17; meals from 50,000Rp) This popular restaurant is a home away from home for legions of happy fans. Grab a cold one with the rest of the crew at the bar while you take in the sweeping view of Legian's action, such as deciding which hair-plaiting style you like best. Then order the heaped-up grilled seafood platter.

Warung Asia ASIAN, CAFE $

(off Jl Arjuna & Jl Pura Bagus Taruna; meals from 30,000Rp; 📶) Look down a little *gang* for this gem: traditional Thai and Indonesian dishes served in a stylish open-air cafe, an authentic Italian espresso machine and lots of newspapers to peruse.

Seaside INTERNATIONAL $$

(☎737 140; Jl Double Six; meals 60,000-180,000Rp) The curving sweep of seating at this sleek place provides beach views for one and all. Upstairs, there's a vast patio with oodles of tables for counting stars after the sun goes down. Seafood and meat dishes come with a touch of style.

Discovery Mall FOOD COURT $

(Jl Kartika Plaza; ❄) This mall is home to many places to eat, including a top-floor food court (meals 15,000Rp to 30,000Rp) with scores of vendors selling cheap, fresh Asian food. You can eat outside on a terrace overlooking Kuta Beach. Elsewhere the mall has several chain cafes and bakeries.

Drinking & Entertainment

Around 6pm every day, sunset on the beach is the big attraction, perhaps while enjoying a drink at a cafe with a sea view or with a beer vendor on the beach. Later on, the legendary nightlife action heats up. Many ragers spend their early evening at one of the hipster joints in Seminyak before working their way south to oblivion.

TOP CHOICE Sky Garden Lounge BAR, CLUB

(www.61legian.com; Jl Legian 61; ⏲24hr) This multilevel palace of flash flirts with height restrictions from its rooftop bar where all of Kuta twinkles around you. Look for top DJs, a ground-level cafe and paparazzi-wannabes. Munchers can enjoy a long menu of bar snacks and meals, which most people pair with shots. Roam from floor to floor of this vertical playpen, where everybody seems to end up at some point.

Apache Reggae Bar BAR

(Jl Legian 146; ⏲11pm-4am) One of the rowdier spots in Kuta, Apache jams in locals and visitors, many of whom are on the make. The music is loud, but that pounding you feel the next day is from the *arak* (palm wine) served in huge plastic jugs. Stumbling between here and other bars is a Kuta tradition.

DeeJay Cafe CLUB

(☎758 880; Jl Kartika Plaza 8X, Kuta Station Hotel; ⊙midnight-9am) The choice for closing out the night (or starting out the day). House DJs play tribal, underground, progressive, trance, electro and more. Beware of posers who set their alarms for 5am and arrive all fresh.

Cocoon CLUB

(www.cocoon-beach.com; Jl Arjuna; ⊙from 10am-late) A huge pool with a view of Double Six Beach anchors this sort of high-concept club (alcohol-branded singlets not allowed!) which has parties and events around the clock. Beds, loungers and VIP areas surround the pool; at night some of Bali's best DJs spin theme nights.

Shopping

Kuta has many cheap tawdry shops, as well as huge, flashy surf-gear emporiums, including popular local megabrands Surfer Girl and Quicksilver. As you head north along Jl Legian, the quality of the shops improves and you start finding cute little boutiques, especially past Jl Melasti. Continue into Seminyak for absolutely fabulous shopping.

Large malls are also making inroads. In Tuban, the Discovery Mall is popular but has been literally massively overshadowed by the flash new Beachwalk complex on Jl Pantai Kuta. In need of new energy, Kuta Sq stumbles along.

Bali's top-selling souvenir for those left at home are penis-shaped bottle-openers in a range of colours and sizes. Bargain hard to avoid paying a stiff price.

Surfer Girl SURF WEAR

(Jl Legian 138) A local legend, the winsome logo says it all about this vast store for girls of all ages. Clothes, gear, bikinis and plenty of other stuff in every shade of bubblegum ever made.

Beachwalk MALL

(www.beachwalkbali.com; Jl Pantai Kuta; ⊙10am-midnight) This vast open-air mall and condo development across from Kuta Beach is filled with international chains: from Gap to Starbuck's. Cooling mists pour from the ceilings and water features course through the generic retail glitz. Other developments planned nearby will vastly overshadow quaint and tawdry Poppies Gang II and continue Kuta's transformation into a glitzy international beach resort.

Joger SOUVENIRS

(Jl Raya Kuta; ⊙11am-6pm) Look for the mobs of Indonesian tourists in front of this huge T-shirt shop east of Tuban. The sign out front says *'Pabrik kata-kata',* which means 'factory of words'. The T-shirts are nationally iconic and bear sayings in Bahasa Indonesia that are wry, funny or simply arch.

Busana Agung TEXTILES

(☎733 442; Jl Arjuna) Here you'll find stacks of vibrant batiks and other fabrics that scream 'sew me!'. One of several fabric emporiums on Jl Arjuna.

Kerta Bookshop BOOKS

(☎758 047; Jl Pantai Kuta 6B) A book exchange with a better-than-average selection; many break the Patterson–Brown–Cornwell mould.

Information

Dangers & Annoyances

The streets and *gang* are usually safe but there are annoyances. Scooter-borne prostitutes (who hassle single men late at night) cruise after dark. Walking along you may hear 'massage' followed by 'young girl' and the ubiquitous 'transport'

FOLLOW THE PARTY

Bali's trendiest clubs cluster in about a 300m radius of the top-rated Sky Garden Lounge (p215). The distinction between drinking and clubbing is blurry at best, with one morphing into another as the night wears on (or the morning comes up). Most bars are free to enter, and often have special drink promotions and 'happy hours' that run at various intervals until after midnight. Savvy partiers follow the specials from venue to venue and enjoy a massively discounted night out (club owners count on the drink specials to lure in punters who then can't be bothered to leave). Look for cut-price drinks coupon fliers.

Bali club ambience ranges from the laid-back vibe of the surfer dives to high-concept nightclubs with long drink menus and hordes of prowling servers. Prostitutes have proliferated at some Kuta clubs.

followed by 'blow'. But your biggest irritation will likely be the sclerotic traffic.

Other things to watch out for include the following:

Alcohol poisoning There are ongoing reports of injuries and deaths among tourists and locals due to *arak* (the local booze, traditionally distilled from palm or cane sugar) being adulterated with methanol, a poisonous form of alcohol. Avoid free cocktails and any offers of *arak*.

Hawkers Street selling is common, especially on hassle street, Jl Legian, where selling and begging can be aggressive.

Surf The surf can be dangerous, with a strong current on some tides, especially up north in Legian. Lifeguards patrol swimming areas of the beaches at Kuta and Legian, indicated by red-and-yellow flags. If they say the water is too rough or unsafe to swim in, they mean it. Red flags with skull and crossbones mean no swimming allowed.

Theft Visitors lose things from unlocked (and some locked) hotel rooms and from the beach. Going into the water and leaving valuables on the beach is simply asking for trouble. Snatch thefts by crooks on motorbikes are more common. Valuable items can be left at your hotel reception.

Water pollution The sea around Kuta is commonly contaminated by run-off from both built-up areas and surrounding farmland, especially after heavy rain. Swim far away from streams, including the often foul and smelly one at Double Six Beach.

Emergency

Police Station (☎751 598; Jl Raya Kuta; ⊙24hr) Next to the Tourist Information Centre.

Tourist Police Post (☎784 5988; Jl Pantai Kuta; ⊙24hr) This is a branch of the main police station in Denpasar. Situated right across from the beach, the officers have a gig that is sort of like a Balinese *Baywatch*.

Internet Access

There are scores of places to connect to the internet. Most have slow connections and charge about 300Rp a minute.

Medical Services

BIMC (☎0361-761 263; www.bimcbali.com; Jl Ngurah Rai 100X; ⊙24hr) On the bypass road just east of Kuta near the Bali Galleria. It's a modern Australian-run clinic that can do tests, hotel visits and arrange medical evacuation. Visits can cost US$100 or more.

Kimia Pharma Kuta (☎755 622; Jl Pantai Kuta; ⊙24hr) This local chain of pharmacies also has branches in **Tuban** (☎757 483; Jl Raya Kuta 15; ⊙24hr) and **Legian** (Jl Legian; ⊙24hr). It's well stocked and carries hard-to-find items, eg that antidote for irksome roosters in the morning: earplugs.

Money

ATMs abound and can be found everywhere, including in the ubiquitous Circle K and Mini Mart convenience stores.

Numerous 'authorised' moneychangers are efficient, open long hours and may offer good exchange rates. Be cautious, though, where the rates are markedly better than the norm. Extra fees may apply or they may be adeptly short-changing their customers.

Central Kuta Money Exchange (☎762 970; Jl Raya Kuta) Trustworthy; deals in myriad currencies.

Post

Postal agencies that can send but not receive mail are common.

Main Post Office (Jl Selamet; ⊙7am-2pm Mon-Thu, 7-11am Fri, 7am-1pm Sat) On a little road east of Jl Raya Kuta, this small and efficient post office has an easy, sort-it-yourself poste restante service. It's well practised in shipping large packages.

Getting There & Away

Bemo

Dark-blue public bemo (minibuses) regularly travel between Kuta and the Tegal terminal in Denpasar – the fare should be 8000Rp. The route goes from a bemo stop onto Jl Raya Kuta near Jl Pantai Kuta, looping past the beach and then on Jl Melasti and back past Bemo Corner for the trip back to Denpasar.

Tourist Shuttle Bus

Perama (☎751 551; www.peramatour.com; Jl Legian 39; ⊙7am-10pm) is the main shuttle-bus operation in town, and may do hotel pick-ups and drop-offs for an extra 10,000Rp (confirm this with the staff when making arrangements). It usually has at least one bus a day to its destinations.

DESTINATION	COST (RP)	DURATION
Candidasa	60,000	3½hr
Lovina	100,000	4½hr
Padangbai	60,000	3hr
Sanur	25,000	30min
Ubud	50,000	1½hr

Getting Around

The hardest part about getting around south Bali is the traffic. Besides using taxis, you can hire a motorbike, often with a surfboard rack, or a bike – just ask staff where you're staying. One of the nicest ways to get around the area is by foot along the beach.

Seminyak

Seminyak is flash, brash, phoney and filled with bony models. It's also the centre of life for hordes of the island's expats, many of whom own boutiques or design clothes, surf, or seem to do nothing at all. It may be immediately north of Kuta and Legian, but in many respects Seminyak feels almost as if it's on another island.

It's also a very dynamic place, home to dozens of restaurants and clubs and a wealth of creative shops and galleries. World-class hotels line the beach – and what a beach it is, as deep and sandy as Kuta's but less crowded.

Seminyak seamlessly merges with Kerobokan, which is immediately north – in fact the exact border between the two is as fuzzy as most other geographic details in Bali. Note that, despite the hype, not every beachfront hotel here is world-class or charges world-class prices. All those restaurants and clubs combine to give travellers the greatest choice of style and budget in Bali.

Sights

Pura Petitenget TEMPLE

(Jl Pantai Kaya Aya) This large complex, the scene of many ceremonies, is an important temple in a string of sea temples that stretches from Pura Luhur Ulu Watu on the Bukit Peninsula, north to Pura Tanah Lot in western Bali. The temple honours the visit of a 16th-century priest and is a fascinating place to ponder the intricacies of Balinese offerings.

DON'T MISS

SEMINYAK BEACH SUNSETS

At the beach end of Jl Abimanyu in Seminyak you have a choice: turn right for trendy beach clubs, or turn left for a much more frolicsome experience. You'll discover mock-Moorish affairs with oodles of huge pillows for lounging, and all manner of simple bars lining the path along the sand. It's all more flash than the local guys selling beers from coolers in Legian but just as much fun. Often there's live music as the light fades.

Activities

Beaches

Seminyak continues the long sweep of Kuta Beach. A good stretch is found near Pura Petitenget. It is usually uncrowded and has plenty of parking (2000Rp). It is often the scene of both religious ceremonies and surfing.

Another good stretch of beach runs south from the end of Jl Abimanyu to Jl Arjuna in Legian. The vendors here are mellow and a sunset lounger and ice-cold Bintang (an Indonesian beer) cost about 15,000Rp. A walkway makes wandering this stretch a breeze and you can choose from various beach bars. Come here for sunsets.

Because of the limited road access, the beaches in Seminyak tend to be less crowded than further south in Kuta. This also means that they're less patrolled and the water conditions are less monitored. The odds of encountering dangerous rip tides and other hazards are ever-present, especially as you head north.

Spas

Seminyak's spas are among the best in Bali and offer a huge range of treatments, therapies and pleasures.

TOP CHOICE **Jari Menari** SPA

(☎736 740; Jl Raya Seminyak 47; sessions from 300,000Rp; ⏲10am-9pm) Jari Menari is true to its name, which means 'dancing fingers': your body will be one happy dance floor. The all-male staff use massage techniques that emphasise rhythm. Many say this is the best place for a massage in Bali, a claim backed up by numerous awards.

Bodyworks SPA

(☎733 317; www.bodyworksbali.com; Jl Kayu Jati 2; massage from 222,000Rp; ⏲9am-10pm) Get waxed, get your hair done, get the kinks rubbed out of your joints – all this and more is on the menu at this uber-popular spa in the heart of Seminyak. The rooms are airy and everything is stress-free casual.

Sleeping

Seminyak has a wide range of places to stay, from world-class resorts such as the Oberoi to more humble hotels hidden away on backstreets. This is also the start of villa-land, which runs north from here through the vanishing rice fields.

TOP CHOICE **Oberoi** HOTEL **$$$**
(☎730 361; www.oberoihotels.com; Jl Laksmana; r from US$260, villas from US$500;) One of the world's top hotels, the beautifully understated Oberoi has been a refined Balinese-style beachside retreat since 1971. All accommodation has its own veranda and, as you move up the food chain, additional features include villas, ocean views and private walled pools. From the cafe, overlooking the almost exclusive sweep of beach, to the numerous luxuries, this is a place to spoil yourself.

Casa Artista GUESTHOUSE **$$$**
(☎736 749; www.casaartistabali.com; Jl Sari Dewi; r from US$150;) You'll literally dance for joy at this cultured guesthouse where the owner, a professional tango dancer, offers lessons. Ten compact rooms in an elegant two-storey house surround a pool. Go for a 2nd-floor room and relax amid flamboyant bling.

Raja Gardens GUESTHOUSE **$$**
(☎730 494; jdw@eksadata.com; Jl Abimanyu; r 500,000-700,000Rp;) Enjoy spacious, grassy grounds in this quiet inn almost on the beach. The nine rooms are fairly bare-bones but there are open-air bathrooms and plenty of potted plants. The basic rate gets you a fan; more money buys air-con and a fridge.

Sarinande Beach Inn HOTEL **$$**
(☎730 383; www.sarinandehotel.com; Jl Sarinande 15; r 450,000-600,000Rp;) Excellent value. The 26 rooms are in older two-storey blocks around a small pool; the decor is older but everything is well maintained. Amenities include fridges, satellite TV and a cafe. The beach is three minutes by foot.

Ned's Hide-Away GUESTHOUSE **$**
(☎731 270; nedshide@dps.centrim.net.id; Gang Bima 3; r from 120,000Rp;) There are 18 good-value basic rooms behind Bintang Supermarket. A new expansion includes some extra-cheap rooms.

Inada Losmen GUESTHOUSE **$**
(☎732 269; putuinada@hotmail.com; Gang Bima 9; r from 150,000Rp) Buried in a *gang* behind Bintang Supermarket, this budget champ is a short walk from clubs, the beach and other Seminyak joys. The 12 rooms are small and somewhat dark.

Eating

Jl Laksmana is the focus of Seminyak eating but there are great choices for every budget virtually everywhere. Note that some restaurants morph into clubs as the night wears on. Conversely, some bars and clubs also have good food.

TOP CHOICE **Mama San** FUSION **$$**
(☎730 436; www.mamasanbali.com; Jl Raya Kerobokan 135; meals 60,000-120,000Rp) All the action is on the 2nd floor of this buzzy warehouse-sized restaurant right on the edge of Seminyak and Sunset roads. A long cocktail list provides liquid balm for the mojito set and has lots of tropical-flavoured pours. The menu emphasises small dishes from across Southeast Asia.

TOP CHOICE **Ultimo** ITALIAN **$$**
(www.balinesia.co.id; Jl Laksmana 104; meals 60,000-220,000Rp) It's simple to count your way to dining joy at this vast and always popular restaurant in a part of Seminyak as thick with eateries as a good risotto. Choose a table overlooking the street action, out the back in one of the gardens, or inside. Ponder the surprisingly authentic menu and then let the army of servers take charge.

Warung Taman Bambu BALINESE **$**
(Jl Plawa 10; meals from 20,000Rp;) You'll be diverted from reaching the pretty back garden by the array of lovely food out the front. This classic warung may look simple from the street but the comfy tables are – like the many fresh and spicy dishes on offer – a cut above the norm. There's a small stand for *babi guling* (roasted suckling pig) right next door.

Sate Bali INDONESIAN **$$**
(Jl Laksmana; meals from 90,000Rp; ⏲11am-10pm) Ignoring the strip-mall location, enjoy traditional Balinese dishes at this small cafe run by chef Nyoman Sudiyasa (who also has a cooking school here). The multicourse *rijsttafel* (selection of Indonesian dishes) is a symphony of tastes, including the addictive *babi kecap* (pork in a sweet soy sauce) and *tum bebek* (minced duck in banana leaf).

Warung Mimpi INDONESIAN **$**
(☎732 738; Jl Abimanyu; meals from 40,000Rp) A sweet little open-air shopfront warung in the midst of cacophonous nightlife. A dear

Seminyak

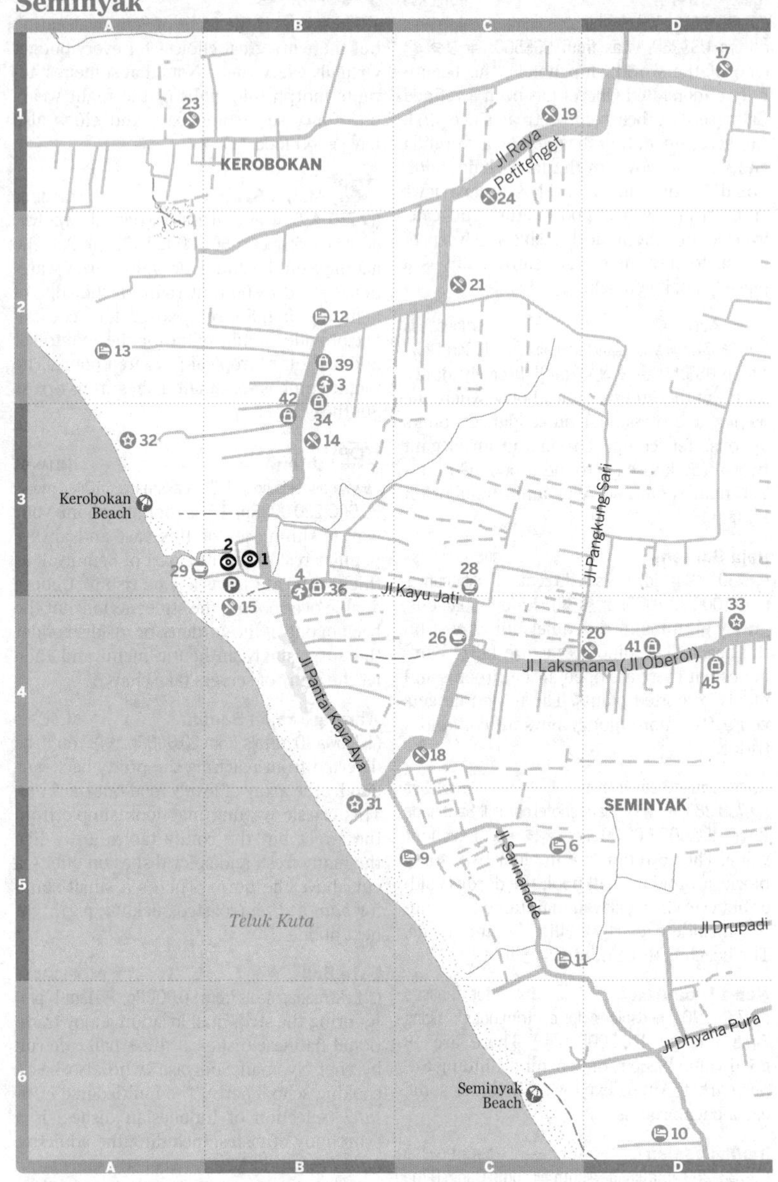

husband-and-wife team cook Indo classics simply and well. It's all fresh and tasty.

La Lucciola FUSION **$$$**
(☎730 838; Jl Pantai Kaya Aya; meals from 120,000Rp) A sleek beachside restaurant with good views from the 2nd-floor tables across a lovely lawn and sand to the surf. The bar is big with sunset-watchers, although most then move on to dinner. The menu is a creative melange of international fare with an Italian flair.

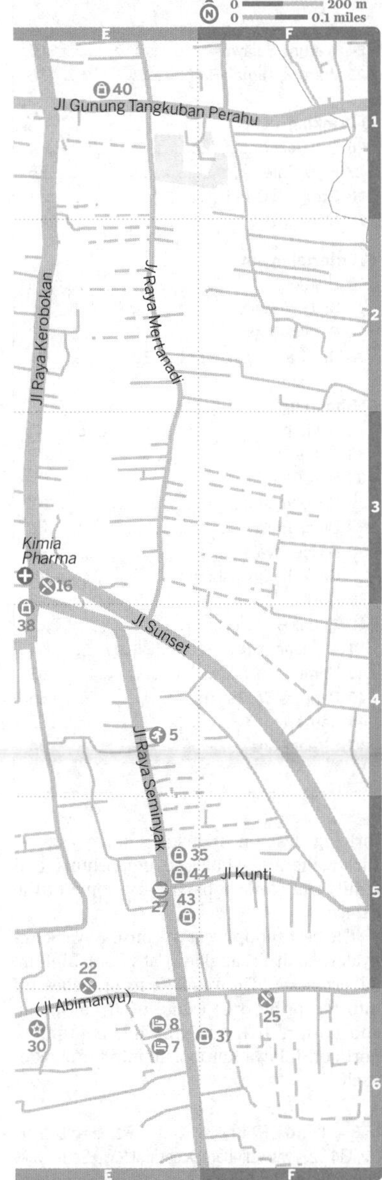

Drinking

Seminyak has developed a full-on cafe culture. The idle masses can while away hours with a coffee on terraces or overlooking the beach.

TOP CHOICE Buzz Cafe CAFE
(Jl Raya Seminyak 99; wi-fi) The name is eponymous at this busy cafe located behind some rare Seminyak trees right where Jl Kunti T-bones Jl Seminyak. The open front lets you wave in fellow glitterati as they saunter past. The fresh drink of choice is the Green Hornet – a combo of lemon, lime and mint. The food is fresh and simple.

Grocer & Grind CAFE
(081 735 4104; Jl Kayu Jati 3X; mains 20,000-60,000Rp; wi-fi) Keep your vistas limited and you might think you're at just another sleek Sydney cafe, but look around and you're unmistakably in Bali, albeit one of the trendiest bits. Classic sandwiches, salads and big breakfasts issue forth from the open kitchen (although many are here just for the coffee). Eat in the open-air or choose air-con tables in the deli area.

Bali Bakery CAFE
(Jl Laksmana; wi-fi) The best features of the fashionable Seminyak Sq open-air mall in the heart of Seminyak are this bakery's shady tables and long menu of excellent coffees, baked goods, salads, sandwiches and other fine fare. A good place to linger before heading back out to shop.

Mano CAFE
(Petitenget Beach) Tucked away behind Pura Petitenget, this basic beachside cafe overlooks a lovely and uncrowded swath of sand in otherwise busy Seminyak. Escape the crowds and fake glam elsewhere for a cold one here; the sunset is just as spectacular.

Entertainment

Like your vision at 2am, the division between restaurant, bar and club blurs in Seminyak. Although it lacks any real hardcore clubs where you can greet the dawn (or vice versa), stalwarts can head south to the rough edges of Kuta and Legian in the wee hours.

Numerous bars popular with gay and straight crowds line Jl Abimanyu.

Bali Jo LIVE MUSIC
(Jl Abimanyu; 8pm-3am) Simply fun – albeit with falsies. Drag queens rock the house, crowds line the street and the entire neighbourhood is blasted with songs amped to 11pm nightly. Surprisingly intimate, it's a good place to lounge about for a few.

Seminyak

Sights
- 1 Pura Masceti ... B3
- 2 Pura Petitenget ... B3

Activities, Courses & Tours
- 3 Amo Beauty Spa ... B2
- 4 Bodyworks ... B3
- 5 Jari Menari ... E4

Sleeping
- 6 Casa Artista ... C5
- 7 Inada Losmen ... E6
- 8 Ned's Hide-Away ... E6
- 9 Oberoi ... C5
- 10 Raja Gardens ... D6
- 11 Sarinande Beach Inn ... C5
- 12 Taman Ayu Cottage ... B2
- 13 W Retreat & Spa Bali – Seminyak ... A2

Eating
- 14 Biku ... B3
- 15 La Lucciola ... B4
- 16 Mama San ... E3
- 17 Sardine ... D1
- 18 Sate Bali ... C4
- 19 Tulip ... C1
- 20 Ultimo ... D4
- 21 Warung Kolega ... C2
- 22 Warung Mimpi ... E5
- 23 Warung Sobat ... A1
- 24 Warung Sulawesi ... C1
- 25 Warung Taman Bambu ... F6

Drinking
- 26 Bali Bakery ... C4
- 27 Buzz Cafe ... E5
- 28 Grocer & Grind ... C3
- 29 Mano ... A3

Entertainment
- 30 Bali Jo ... E6
- 31 Ku De Ta ... B5
- 32 Potato Head ... A3
- 33 Red Carpet Champagne Bar ... D4

Shopping
- Ashitaba ... (see 44)
- 34 Bathe ... B2
- 35 Blue Glue ... E5
- 36 Coco Rose ... B3
- 37 Dinda Rella ... F6
- 38 Divine Diva ... E4
- Ganesha Bookshop ... (see 14)
- 39 Horn ... B2
- 40 JJ Bali Button ... E1
- 41 Lily Jean ... D4
- 42 Namu ... B3
- 43 Periplus Bookshop ... E5
- 44 Samsara ... E5
- 45 Street Dogs ... D4

Red Carpet Champagne Bar BAR
(Jl Laksmana 42) This over-the-top glam bar on Seminyak's couture strip is the closest most will come to posing for paparazzi. Waltz the red carpet and toss back a few namesake flutes while contemplating a raw oyster and displays of frilly frocks. It's open to the street so you can observe the rabble.

Ku De Ta CLUB
(Jl Laksmana; 7am-1am) Ku De Ta teems with Bali's beautiful people (including those whose status is purely aspirational). Scenesters perfect their 'bored' look over drinks during the day, gazing at the fine stretch of surf right out the back. Sunset brings out crowds, who snatch a cigar at the bar or dine on eclectic fare at tables. The music throbs with increasing intensity through the night.

Shopping

Seminyak shops could occupy days of your holiday. Designer boutiques (Bali has a thriving fashion industry), funky stores, slick galleries, wholesale emporiums and family-run workshops are just some of the choices.

The best shopping starts on Jl Raya Seminyak (aka Jl Basangkasa) at about Bintang Supermarket. The retail strip branches off into the prime real estate of Jl Laksmana and upstart Jl Kayu Jati while continuing north on Jl Raya Kerobokan into Kerobokan itself.

TOP CHOICE **Dinda Rella** WOMEN'S CLOTHING
(734 228; www.dindarella.com; Jl Raya Seminyak) Upscale frocks for women are designed and made in Bali by this much-honoured brand. The place to get that sexy little cocktail dress. There's another location on Jl Laksmana.

TOP CHOICE **Ashitaba** HANDICRAFTS
(Jl Raya Seminyak 6) Tenganan, the Aga village of east Bali, produces the intricate and

beautiful rattan items sold here. Containers, bowls, purses and more (from US$5) display the very fine weaving.

Blue Glue WOMEN'S CLOTHING
(Jl Raya Kerobokan) How best to show off your form on the see-and-be-seen stretches of Bali beach, especially in uber-hip Seminyak? Try one of these trendy Bali-designed bathing suits at this flash new boutique.

Street Dogs ACCESSORIES
(Jl Laksmana 60) Bracelets made with shells and resin as well as recycled brass demand immediate wearing.

Lily Jean WOMEN'S CLOTHING
(Jl Laksmana) Saucy knickers underpin sexy women's clothing that both dares and flirts; most is Bali-made. This popular shop has flash digs in fashion's ground zero.

Samsara CLOTHING
(Jl Raya Seminyak) True Balinese-made textiles are increasingly rare as production moves to Java and other places with cheaper labour. But the local family behind this tidy shop still source hand-painted batik for a range of exquisite casualwear.

Divine Diva WOMEN'S CLOTHING
(Jl Laksmana 1A) It's like a Dove soap commercial for real women in this shop, filled with Bali-made breezy styles for larger figures. One customer told us: 'It's the essence of agelessness.'

Coco Rose CLOTHING
(Jl Kayu Jati) On an up-and-coming strip of shops, this boutique has ultra-casual resortwear; think the sorts of sundresses you yank on over your bikini so you can go parading through the lobby.

Periplus Bookshop BOOKS
(Seminyak Sq) A large outlet of the island-wide chain of lavishly fitted bookshops. Besides enough design books to have you fitting out even your garage with 'Bali Style', there are bestsellers, magazines and newspapers.

Information

Seminyak and the areas to the north are more hassle-free than Kuta but its worth noting the warnings for surf safety and water pollution.

Kimia Pharma (☎916 6509; Jl Raya Kerobokan 140; ⏲24hr) At a major crossroads, this pharmacy, part of Bali's best chain of pharmacies, has a full range of prescription medications.

Getting There & Around

Metered taxis are easily hailed. A trip from the airport in an official airport taxi costs about 80,000Rp, to the airport about half that. You can beat the traffic, save the ozone and have a good stroll by walking south down the beach; Legian is only about 15 minutes away.

Kerobokan

Continuing seamlessly north from Seminyak, Kerobokan combines some of Bali's best restaurants, lavish lifestyles and still more beach. Hotels are upstaged by villas, which sprout from the ground like a bad rash. At times the mix of commerce and rice fields can be jarring.

Sights & Activities

Unless you are eating, drinking, shopping or sleeping, there is little reason to visit Kerobokan, with one exception: **Batubelig Beach**, which continues the long curve of sand from Kuta.

Amo Beauty Spa SPA
(☎275 3337; www.amospa.com; 100 Jl Petitenget; massage from 180,000Rp; ⏲9am-9pm) With some of Asia's top models lounging about, it feels as if you've stepped into the studios of *Vogue*. Besides massages, services range from hair care to pedicures and unisex waxing.

Umalas Stables HORSE RIDING
(☎731 402; www.balionhorse.com; Jl Lestari 9X; beach rides from US$72) Pick your pony in this elegant compound set among the paddies. It has a stable of 30 horses and ponies, and offers 30-minute rice-field tours and two- and three-hour beach rides (a trip highlight for many tourists).

Sleeping

Kerobokan is villa country, with walled developments simmering away amid rice fields. See p757 for considerations in renting a villa.

Taman Ayu Cottage HOTEL $$
(☎730 111; www.tamanayucottage.com; Jl Petitenget; r US$50-100; ❄@☜≋) In a fast-growing part of Kerobokan sits this great-value hotel. The cottage in the name here is a bit of a misnomer, as most of the rooms are in two-storey blocks around a pool shaded by mature trees. Everything is a bit frayed around the edges, but all is forgotten when

one of the hotel's pet rabbits romps over to say hello.

W Retreat & Spa Bali – Seminyak RESORT **$$$**
(☎473 8106; www.starwoodhotels.com; Jl Petitenget; r from US$300; ❄@📶) The big flash on Kerobokan's beach is this huge new resort under the guise of the trendy W brand. The usual too-cute-for-comfort vibe is at work (how 'bout an 'Extreme Wow Suite'?) but the location on a wild stretch of sand and the views are hard to quibble with. Amble down the long entrance lane and have a gander, noting that this is the best way to the beach in the vincinity.

Eating

Kerobokan boasts some of Bali's best restaurants, whether top end or budget.

TOP CHOICE **Biku** FUSION **$$**
(☎857 0888; www.bikubali.com; Jl Petitenget; meals 40,000-120,000Rp) Housed in an old shop that used to sell antiques, Biku retains the timeless vibe of its predecessor. The menu combines Indonesian, other Asian and Western influences; book for lunch or dinner. Dishes, from the exquisite breakfasts and the elegant local choices to Bali's best burger, are artful and delicious. There's a long list of teas and myriad refreshing cocktails. Many swoon at the sight of the cake table.

TOP CHOICE **Sardine** SEAFOOD **$$$**
(☎738 202; www.sardinebali.com; Jl Petitenget 21; meals US$20-50) Seafood fresh from the famous Jimbaran market is the star at this elegant yet intimate, casual yet stylish restaurant in a beautiful bamboo pavilion that is ably presided over by Pascal and Pika Chevillot. Open-air tables overlook a private rice field that is patrolled by Sardine's own flock of ducks. The inventive bar is a must and open to 1am. The menu changes to reflect what's fresh. Booking is vital.

TOP CHOICE **Warung Sobat** SEAFOOD **$**
(☎738 922; Jl Batubelig 11; meals 50,000-150,000Rp) Set in a sort of bungalow-style brick courtyard, this old-fashioned restaurant (with bargain prices) excels at fresh Balinese seafood with an Italian accent (lots of garlic!). First-time visitors feel as if they've made a discovery and, if you have the sensational lobster platter (a bargain at 350,000Rp for two; order in advance), you will too. Book.

Warung Sulawesi INDONESIAN **$**
(Jl Petitenget; meals from 25,000Rp; ⏰10am-6pm) Although seemingly upscale, Kerobokan is blessed with many a fine place for a local meal. Find a table in this quiet family compound and enjoy fresh Balinese and Indonesian food served in classic warung style. Choose a rice, then pick from a captivating array of dishes that are always at their peak at noon. The green beans are yum!

Warung Kolega INDONESIAN **$**
(Jl Petitenget; meals 25,000Rp; ⏰11am-3pm) A Javanese halal classic. Choose your rice (we prefer the fragrant yellow), then pick from a delectable array that includes tempeh in sweet chilli sauce, *sambal terung* (spicy eggplant), *ikan sambal* (spicy grilled fish) and other daily specials. Most of the labels are in English.

Naughty Nuri's INDONESIAN **$$**
(Jl Batubelig 41; meals from 50,000Rp) This large Kerobokan cafe avoids the over-hype of the Ubud original by delivering solid fare and the trademark kickass martinis. As you'd expect, ribs are grilling on open coals up front but whereas the main location often runs short of tables, this commodious outpost nearly always has room for you to enjoy a cold Bintang or something more fun.

☆ Entertainment

Some of Kerobokan's trendier restaurants such as Sardine and **Tulip** (☎785 8585; www.tulipbali.com; Jl Petitenget 69; meals 60,000-200,000Rp) have stylish bar areas that stay open late.

TOP CHOICE **Potato Head** CLUB
(Jl Petitenget; 📶) Kerobokan's popular beach club is south Bali's grooviest. Wander up off the sand or follow a long drive off the main road and you'll discover a truly captivating creation on a grand scale. The clever design is striking and you'll find much to amuse you, from an enticing pool to a cafe and a swanky restaurant.

Shopping

Look for boutiques interspersed with the trendy restaurants on Jl Petitenget. Jl Raya Kerobokan, extending north from Seminyak, has interesting shops primarily selling decorator items and housewares.

TOP CHOICE **JJ Bali Button** ARTS & CRAFTS

(Jl Gunung Tangkuban Perahu) Zillions of beads and buttons made from shells, plastic, metal and more are displayed in what at first looks like a candy store. Elaborately carved wooden buttons are 700Rp. Kids may have to be bribed to leave.

Bathe BEAUTY, HOMEWARES

(Jl Petitenget 100X) Double-down on your villa's romance with the handmade candles and bath salts at this shop that evokes the feel of a 19th-century French dispensary. You can't help but smile at the tub filled with rubber ducks.

Namu CLOTHING

(Jl Petitenget) Designer Paola Zancanaro creates comfy and casual resortwear for men and women that doesn't take a holiday from style. The fabrics are lusciously tactile; many are hand-painted silk.

Horn VINTAGE

(Jl Petitenget) Vintage clothing for all ages is curated with a kooky sensibility in this large and engaging shop. The classic silks are irresistible and the accessories fun.

Ganesha Bookshop BOOKS

(Jl Petitenget) In a corner of the fabulous Biku restaurant, this tiny branch of Bali's best bookstore up in Ubud has all manner of local and literary treats.

Getting There & Around

Taxis from the airport will cost at least 100,000Rp. In either direction at rush hour the trip may verge on an hour. Note also that Jl Raya Kerobokan can come to a fume-filled stop for extended periods.

The plethora of villas can stymie even the savviest of cab drivers so it's helpful to have some sort of map or directions when you first arrive and for forays out and about during your stay. Taxis can be hailed along the main roads.

Although the beach may seem tanalisingly close, few roads or *gang* actually reach the sand from the east.

North of Kerobokan

Growth is marching north and west along the coast, much of it anchored by the endless swath of beach, which, despite rampant development, remains fairly uncrowded. Kerobokan morphs into Canggu, while neighbouring Echo Beach is a big construction site. Cloistered villas lure the well-heeled who whisk past stooped rice farmers in air-con comfort. Traffic may be the ultimate commoner's revenge: road building is a decade or two behind settlement.

CANGGU

More a state of mind than a place, Canggu is the catch-all name given to the villa-filled swath of land between Kerobokan and Echo Beach. It is getting ever-more trendy cafes, restaurants and places to stay. It includes many beaches such as Berewa and Batu Bolong (and which are referred to by some generically as 'Canggu Beach').

DON'T MISS

BEACHES: KEROBOKAN TO ECHO BEACH

The 4km of sand curving between Kerobokan's Batubelig Beach and Echo Beach has several uncrowded beaches that can be reached by road or on foot from either direction.

Berewa Beach A greyish beach, secluded among rice fields and villas, about 2km up the sand from Seminyak. There are a couple of surfer cafes by the pounding sea.

Prancak Beach Marked by the large temple complex of Pura Dalem Prancak. There is usually at least one vendor at this quiet beach.

Nelayan Beach A collection of fishing boats and huts marks this very mellow stretch of sand that fronts villa-land just inland.

Batu Bolong Beach The beach *(pantai)* at Batu Bolong boasts the large Pura Batumejan complex with a striking pagodalike temple. There are surfboard rentals (100,000Rp per day), impromptu lessons and some groovy cafes. About 200m further on there's a slightly upscale beach vendor with comfy loungers for rent and drinks.

Echo Beach & Canggu

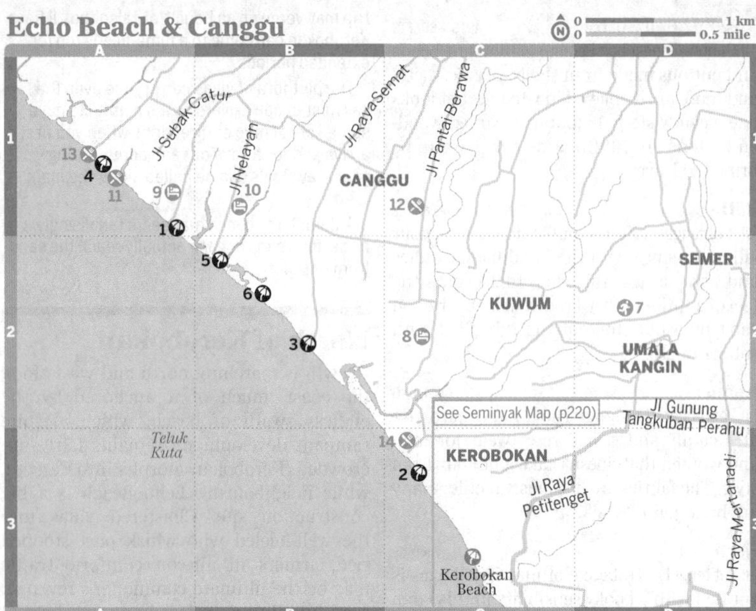

Echo Beach & Canggu

Sights

Activities, Courses & Tours

Sleeping

Eating

Sleeping & Eating

TOP CHOICE **Hotel Tugu Bali** HOTEL $$$

(☎731 701; www.tuguhotels.com; Jl Pantai Batu Bolong; r US$200-500; ❄@☜) Right at Batu Bolong Beach, this is an exquisite hotel surrounded by rice fields and beach. It blurs the boundaries between a museum and a gallery, especially the Walter Spies and Le Mayeur Pavilions, where memorabilia from the artists' lives decorates the rooms. The stunning collection of antiques and artwork begins in the lobby and extends throughout the hotel. There's a spa and customised dining options. Even by day, candles twinkle amid the flowing fabrics in the breezy public areas. The cooking classes (from US$100) are quite luxe.

Desa Seni HOTEL $$$

(☎844 6392; www.desaseni.com; Jl Kayu Putih 13; r US$150-400; ❄@☜) One person described this place as like a hippie Four Seasons, and that's not far from the truth. Desa Seni bills itself as a 'village resort' and what a village it is. Ten classic wooden homes up to 220 years old have been brought to the site from across Indonesia and turned into luxurious quarters. Guests enjoy a menu of organic and healthy cuisine plus popular yoga courses.

Villa Serenity GUESTHOUSE $

(www.balivillaserenity.com; Jl Nelayan; r 150,000-500,000Rp; ❄☜) Funky in the best way, this is an oasis among the walled villas. Rooms range from shared-bathroom singles to quite nice doubles with air-con and bathrooms. The grounds are appealingly eccentric; the beach a five-minute walk away. There is a cafe, a huge DVD library, yoga, and you can rent surfboards, bikes, cars and more.

TOP CHOICE **Green Ginger** ASIAN $

(Jl Pantai Berawa; meals from 30,000Rp;) Art, a profusion of flowering plants and eccentric bits of furniture mark this cool little boho cafe on a fast-changing strip in Canggu. The menu has fresh and tasty vegetarian dishes from across Asia.

Getting There & Around

You can reach the Canggu area by road from the south by taking Jl Batubelig west in Kerobokan almost to the beach and then veering north along a curvaceous road. It's much longer to go up and around via the traffic-clogged Tanah Lot road.

Getting to the Canggu area can cost 70,000Rp or more by **taxi** from Kuta or Seminyak. Don't expect to find taxis cruising, but any business can call you one.

ECHO BEACH

One of Bali's most popular surf breaks, Echo Beach has reached critical mass in popularity and is quite the scene with tourists, expats and locals, who come down to wet their feet at the often spectacular sunsets.

The burgeoning number of cafes includes **Mandira Cafe** (Jl Pura Batu Mejan; meals 25,000-50,000Rp;), which has a timeless menu of jaffles, banana pancakes, club sandwiches and smoothies.

Slicker yet, the **Beach House** (Jl Pura Batu Mejan; dishes 30,000-100,000Rp;) faces the waves and draws stylish loungers for upscale cafe fare. On Sunday nights it offers a hugely popular outdoor barbecue.

A local taxi cooperative has taxis waiting to shuttle you back to Seminyak and the south for about 70,000Rp.

Bukit Peninsula

0361

Hot and arid, the southern peninsula is known as Bukit (meaning 'hill' in Bahasa Indonesia). It's popular with visitors, from the cloistered climes of Nusa Dua to the sybaritic retreats along the south coast.

The booming west coast with its string-of-pearls beaches is a real hotspot. Accommodation sits precariously on the sand at Balangan Beach while the cliffs are dotted with idiosyncratic lodges at Bingin and elsewhere. New places sprout daily and most have views of the turbulent waters here, which have world-famous surf breaks all the way south to the important temple of Ulu Watu (p229).

JIMBARAN

Just south of Kuta and the airport, Teluk Jimbaran (Jimbaran Bay) is an alluring crescent of white sand beach and blue sea, fronted by a long string of seafood warungs and ending at the southern end in a bushy headland, home to the Four Seasons Jimbaran Bay.

Sights & Activities

TOP CHOICE **Fish Market** MARKET

(Jimbaran Beach; 6am-3pm) A popular morning stop on Bukit Peninsula ambles is this smelly, lively and frenetic fish market – just watch where you step. Brightly painted boats bob along the shore while huge cases of everything from small sardines to fearsome langoustines are hawked. The action is fast and furious.

Jimbaran Beach BEACH

One of Bali's very best beaches, Jimbaran's 4km-long arc of sand fronts its namesake bay. The sand is mostly very clean and there is no shortage of places to get a snack, a drink, a seafood dinner or rent a sun lounger. The bay keeps the surf mellower than at Kuta, although you can still get breaks that are fun for body surfing.

Morning Market MARKET

(Jl Ulu Watu; 6am-noon) This is one of the best markets in Bali for a visit because: a) it's compact so you can see a lot without wandering forever; b) local chefs swear by the quality of the fruit and vegetables (ever seen a cabbage that big?); and c) they're used to tourists tromping about.

Eating

Jimbaran's seafood warungs are the destination of tourists across the south. The open-sided affairs are right on the beach and perfect for enjoying sea breezes and sunsets.

The usual deal is to select your seafood fresh from iced displays or tanks, and to pay according to weight. Expect to pay around 40,000Rp per 100g for live lobster, 15,000Rp to 25,000Rp for prawns, and 9000Rp for fish, squid and clams. Prices are open to negotiation and the accuracy of the scales is a joke among locals. Agree to a price before ordering. Some places simplify things with fixed menu prices.

The best kitchens marinate the fish in garlic and lime, then douse it with chilli and oil while grilling over coconut husks.

The longest row of warungs is at the **northern seafood warungs**, south of the fish market. This is the area you will be taken to by a taxi if you don't specify otherwise.

The **middle seafood warungs** are in a compact group just south of Jl Pantai Jimbaran and Jl Pemelisan Agung. These are the simplest affairs, with old-fashioned thatched roofs and wide-open sides.

The **southern seafood warungs** (Muaya group) are a compact collection at the very south end of the beach. There's a parking area off Jl Bukit Permai.

Getting There & Away

Plenty of taxis wait around the beachfront warungs in the evening to take diners home (about 60,000Rp to Kuta). Some of the seafood warungs provide free transport if you call first.

BALANGAN BEACH

Balangan Beach is a real find. A long, low strand at the base of the cliffs is covered with palm trees and fronted by a ribbon of near-white sand, picturesquely dotted with white sun umbrellas. Surfer bars, cafes in shacks and even slightly more permanent guesthouses precariously line the shore where buffed tourist bods soak up rays amid local sanitation. Think of it as a bit of the Wild West not far from Bali's glitz.

At the northern end of the beach is a small temple, **Pura Dalem Balangan**. Bamboo beach shacks line the southern end, visitors laze away with one eye cast on the action at the fast left surf break here.

Sleeping & Eating

Flower Bud Bungalows GUESTHOUSE $$
(0828 367 2772; www.flowerbudbalangan.com; r 350,000-600,000Rp;) On the knoll. Eight bamboo bungalows are set on spacious grounds near a classic kidney-shaped pool. There's a certain Crusoe-esque motif, and fans and sprightly pillows are among the 'luxuries'.

Point GUESTHOUSE $
(0857 3951 8317; r 200,000-300,000Rp) Built on actual rocks on the beach using cement blocks, the Point sits slightly apart from its bamboo-stilted neighbours. The five rooms have fans and windows; a couple look out to the surf, some 10m distant. The porch cafe is shady.

Nasa Café CAFE $
(meals from 30,000Rp) Inside the shady bamboo bar built on stilts above the sand, the wraparound view through the drooping thatched roofis a vibrant azure ribbon of crashing surf. Simple Indo meals set the tone; the bare-bones rooms (about 100,000Rp) off the bar are little more than a mattress on the floor. It's one of about a dozen similar choices.

Getting There & Away

Balangan Beach is 6.2km off the main Ulu Watu road via Cenggiling. Turn west at the crossroads at Nirmala Supermarket.

Taxis from the Kuta area cost at least 50,000Rp per hour for the round trip and waiting time.

BINGIN

An ever-evolving scene, Bingin comprises several funky lodgings scattered across cliffs and on the strip of **white sand beach** below. A rough 1km road turns off the paved main road (look for the thicket of accommodation signs).

The scenery here is simply superb, with sylvan cliffs dropping down to a row of surfer cafes and the foaming edge of the azure sea. The beach is a five-minute walk down a fairly steep path.

Sleeping

More than two dozen places to stay are scattered along and near the cliffs. All have at least simple cafes, although for nightlife – like the rest of this coast – you'll be heading north to Kuta.

TOP CHOICE **Temple Lodge** BOUTIQUE HOTEL $$
(0857 3901 1572; www.thetemplelodge.com; r US$60-230;) Funky and artsy just begin to describe this beautiful collection of huts and cottages made from thatch, driftwood and other natural materials. Sitting on a jutting shelf on the cliffs above the surf breaks, it has superb views from the infinity pool and some of the seven units. At night you can arrange for suitably exquisite meals.

Mick's Place GUESTHOUSE $$
(0812 391 3337; www.micksplacebali.com; r from US$100, villas from US$300;) The turquoise water in the postage-stamp infinity pool matches the turquoise sea below. Something of a hippie-chic playground,

this highly personable place with six artful round huts is set in lush grounds. Candles provide the flickering ambiance at night, by day there's the 180° view. Don't expect luxe amenities, this is all about roughing it in style.

Bingin Garden GUESTHOUSE $
(☎0816 472 2002; tommybarrell76@yahoo.com; r from 250,000Rp) Six basic rooms in bungalows are set around tidy grounds back from the cliffs and 300m north of the toll gate. Each unit sleeps two and has cold water and a fan.

PADANG PADANG

Small in size but nearing perfection, **Padang Padang Beach** is a cute little cove near Jl Melasti, where a small river flows into the sea. Parking is easy and it is a short walk through a temple and down a well-paved trail.

If you are feeling adventurous, you can beat the crowds here and enjoy a much longer stretch of deserted white sand that begins on the west side of the river. Ask locals how to get there.

Sleeping & Eating

Pink Coco Bali HOTEL $$
(☎824 3366; www.pinkcocobali.com; Jl Melasti; r US$60-150;) One of the pools at this romantic hotel is suitably pink (tiled). The 21 rooms have terraces and balconies plus artistic touches. There is a lush Mexican motif throughout. Surfers are catered to and you can rent bikes and other gear.

Thomas Homestay GUESTHOUSE $
(☎0813 3803 4354; r from 200,000Rp) Enjoy stunning views up and down this spectacular coast. Seven very simple rooms lie at the end of a very rough 400m track off the main road. You can take a long walk down steps to the mostly deserted swath of Padang Padang Beach west of the river.

Getting There & Away

A metered taxi from Kuta will cost about 150,000Rp and take an hour, depending on traffic.

ULU WATU & AROUND

Ulu Watu has become the generic name for the southwestern tip of the Bukit Peninsula. It includes the much-revered temple and the fabled namesake surf breaks.

About 2km north of the temple there is a dramatic cliff which has steps that lead to the legendary Ulu Watu surf breaks. All manner of cafes and surf shops spill down the nearly sheer face to the water below. Views are stellar and it is quite the scene.

BEATING ULU WATU

Observe where other surfers paddle out and follow them. If you are in doubt, ask someone. It is better to have some knowledge than none at all. When the swell is bigger you will be swept to your right from the cave. Don't panic: it is an easy matter to paddle around the white water from down along the cliff. Coming back in you have to aim for the cave. When the swell is bigger, come from the southern side of the cave as the current runs to the north. If you miss the cave, paddle out again and repeat the procedure.

Sights & Activities

TOP CHOICE **Pura Luhur Ulu Watu** TEMPLE
(admission incl sarong & sash rental 20,000Rp; ⏲8am-7pm) This important temple is perched precipitously on the southwestern tip of the peninsula, atop sheer cliffs that drop straight into the ceaseless surf. You enter through an unusual arched gateway flanked by statues of Ganesha. Inside, the walls of coral bricks are covered with intricate carvings of Bali's mythological pantheon. Only Hindu worshippers can enter the small inner temple that is built onto the jutting tip of land. However, the views of the endless swells of the Indian Ocean from the cliffs are almost spiritual. To escape crowds, walk around the clifftop to the left (south) of the temple. Watch out for kleptomaniac monkeys.

An enchanting and popular **Kecak dance** (Pura Luhur Ulu Watu; admission 80,000Rp; ⏲sunset) is held in the temple grounds at sunset.

Surf Breaks SURFING
Ulu Watu (Ulu's) is a storied surf spot – the stuff of dreams and nightmares. Its legend is matched closely by nearby **Pantai Suluban**. Since the early 1970s these breaks have drawn surfers from around the world. The left breaks seem to go on forever. It's easy to rent surfboards, get ding repairs etc.

Sleeping & Eating

The cliffs above the main Ulu Watu breaks are lined with cafes and bars. There are also

Ulu Watu & Around

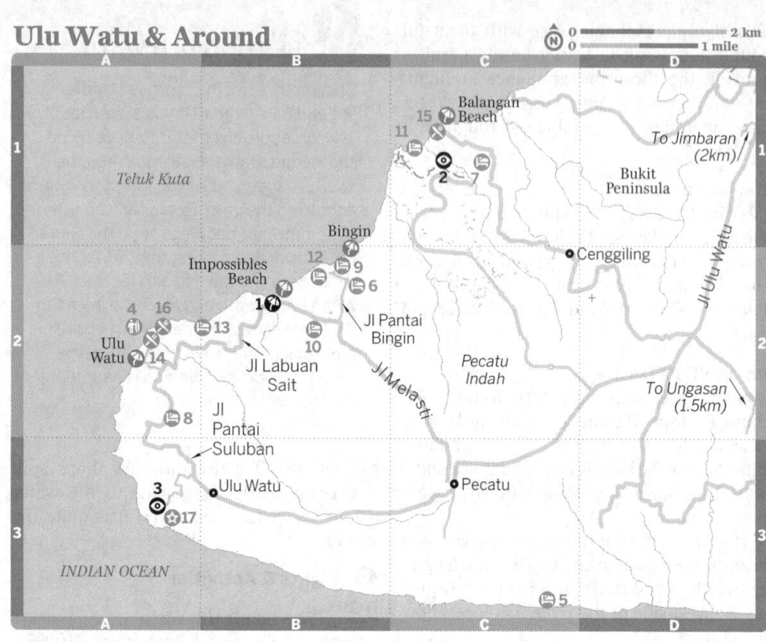

Ulu Watu & Around

Sights

1 Padang Padang Beach B2
2 Pura Dalem Balangan C1
3 Pura Luhur Ulu Watu A3

Activities, Courses & Tours

4 Ulu Watu A2

Sleeping

5 Alila Villas Ulu Watu C3
6 Bingin Garden B2
7 Flower Bud Bungalows C1
8 Gong A2
9 Mick's Place B2
10 Pink Coco Bali B2
11 Point C1
12 Temple Lodge B2
13 Thomas Homestay B2

Eating

14 Delpi Rock Lounge A2
15 Nasa Café C1
16 Single Fin A2

Entertainment

17 Kecak Dance A3

plenty of cheap and midrange places to stay: in fact, your best bet is to wander around and check out a few.

Gong GUESTHOUSE $
(☎769 976; thegongacc@yahoo.com; Jl Pantai Suluban; r from 200,000Rp; @≋) Few stay away long from the Gong. Twelve tidy rooms with good ventilation and hot water face a small compound with a lovely pool; some have distant ocean views. It is about 1km south of the Ulu Watu cliffside cafes.

TOP CHOICE **Delpi Rock Lounge** CAFE $
(meals from 50,000Rp) At one branch of the Delpi empire on the cliffs above the surf breaks, you can nab a sunbed on a platform atop a rock nearly surrounded by surf. Further up the cliff there is a cafe which has three simple rooms for rent.

Single Fin CAFE $
(meals from 50,000Rp) Right near the east parking area above the Ulu Watu surf break and cliffs, this is a top spot for those who don't want to clamber down the steep concrete steps to the cafes close to the ac-

tion. The views are panoramic and you can choose from a classic beach menu of sandwiches, seafood and Indo fare. The cocktail list reflects the splash of style at the bar.

Getting There & Away

The best way to see the Ulu Watu region is with your own wheels.

Coming to the Ulu Watu cliffside cafes from the east on Jl Melasti you will first encounter a gated parking area (car/motorcycle 5000/3000Rp), which is right at the cliffs. Continuing over a bridge, there is an a side road that leads to another parking area (car/motorcycle 2000/1000Rp), which is a pretty 200m walk north to the cliffside cafes.

A taxi ride out here from Kuta will cost at least 160,000Rp which makes getting a car and driver for the day a better bet, given the flexibility you'll have to explore.

UNGASAN & AROUND

If Ulu Watu is all about celebrating the surfer vibe, Ungasan is all about celebrating yourself. From crossroads near this otherwise nondescript village, roads radiate to the south coast where some of Bali's most exclusive ocean-side resorts can be found. With the infinite turquoise waters of the Indian Ocean rolling hypnotically in the distance, it's hard not to think you've reached the end of the world, albeit a very comfortable one.

Bali's southernmost **beach** can be found at the end of a 3km-long road from Ungasan village. Newish concrete steps lead down the 200m cliff to a sweet crescent of sand on the pounding ocean. Bring a picnic and a good book to enjoy the atmosphere.

Sleeping

TOP CHOICE Alila Villas Ulu Watu RESORT $$$
(848 2166; www.alilahotels.com; r from US$685;) Visually stunning, this vast new destination resort has the full seal of eco-approval from Green Globe (something others in the area might emulate...). Designed in an artful contemporary style that is at once light and airy while still conveying a sense of wealth, the 85-unit Alila offers gracious service in a setting where the blue of the ocean contrasts with the green of the surrounding (hotel-tended) rice fields. It's 2km off the main Ulu Watu road, about 1km south of Pecatu Indah.

NUSA DUA

Nusa Dua translates literally as 'Two Islands' – the islands are actually small raised headlands, each with a little temple. Nusa Dua is better known as Bali's gated beach enclave – a gilded ghetto of enormous resorts. The drawback is the isolation from any sense of Balinese community life; in many ways, you could be at any international tropical beach resort the world over.

Nusa Dua is very spread out. You enter the enclave through one of the big gateways, and inside there are expansive lawns, manicured gardens and sweeping driveways leading to the lobbies of large hotels.

Sights & Activities

TOP CHOICE Pasifika Museum MUSEUM
(774559; Bali Collection Shopping Centre, Block P; admission 70,000Rp; 10am-6pm) When groups from the nearby resorts aren't around, you'll probably have this large museum to yourself. Several centuries of art from cultures around the Pacific Ocean are displayed (the tikis are cool). The influential wave of European artists who thrived in Bali in the early 20th century is well represented. Look for works by Arie Smit, Adrien Jean Le Mayeur de Merpes and Theo Meier.

Beach Promenade WALKING
One of the nicest features of Nusa Dua is the 5km-long beach promenade that stretches the length of the resort and continues north along much of the beach in Tanjung Benoa. Not only is it a good stroll at any time but it also makes it easy to sample the pleasures of the other beachside resorts. The **beach** along the walk is clean; offshore reefs mean that surf sounds are almost nil. It's a good place for day-tripping families.

Sleeping

Nusa Dua's resorts are mostly on the beach (a few line the golf course) and are primarily affiliated with international chains. Prowl the internet looking for deals.

St Regis Bali Resort RESORT $$$
(847 8111; www.starwoodhotels.com; ste from US$600;) This lavish Nusa Dua resort leaves most of the others in the sand. Every conceivable luxury is provided, from the electronics to the furnishings and the marble to a personal butler. Pools abound and units are huge. The golf course and the beach adjoin.

Getting There & Around

The fixed taxi fare from the airport is 85,000Rp; a metered taxi to the airport will be less. Taxis to/from Seminyak average 70,000Rp.

A free shuttle bus connects Nusa Dua and Tanjung Benoa resort hotels with the Bali Collection shopping centre about every hour. Better: walk the delightful beach promenade.

TANJUNG BENOA

The peninsula of Tanjung Benoa extends about 4km north from Nusa Dua to Benoa village. It's flat and lined with family-friendly resort hotels, most of midrange calibre. By day the waters buzz with the roar of dozens of motorised water-sports craft. Group tours arrive by the busload for a day's excitement straddling a banana boat, among other thrills.

Sights

The village of **Benoa** is a fascinating little fishing settlement that makes for a good stroll. Amble the narrow lanes of the peninsula's tip for a multicultural feast. Within 100m of each other are a brightly coloured **Chinese Buddhist temple**, a domed **mosque** and a **Hindu temple** with a nicely carved triple entrance. Enjoy views of the busy channel to the port.

Activities

Water-sports centres along Jl Pratama offer daytime diving, cruises, windsurfing and waterskiing. Each morning convoys of buses arrive from all over south Bali bringing day trippers, and by 10am parasailers float over the water.

All feature unctuous salespeople whose job it is to sell the banana boat ride of your dreams while you sit glassy eyed in a thatched-roof sales centre and cafe. Check equipment and credentials before you sign up, as a few tourists have died in accidents.

Among the established water-sports operators is **Benoa Marine Recreation** (0361-77 1757; Jl Pratama). As if by magic, all operators have similar (negotiable) prices.

Water sports include the very popular parasailing (per round US$20) and jet skiing (per 15 minutes US$25). You'll need at least two people for banana-boat rides (per 15 minutes US$20), or glass-bottomed boat trips (60-minute tour US$50).

Courses

Bumbu Bali Cooking School COOKING
(774502; www.balifoods.com; Jl Pratama; course US$90; 6am-3pm) Heinz Von Holzen runs this much-lauded cooking school at his restaurant that strives to get to the roots of Balinese cooking. It starts with a 6am visit to Jimbaran's fish and morning markets, continues in the large kitchen and finishes with lunch.

Sleeping & Eating

Tanjung Benoa's east shore is lined with midrange low-key resorts aimed at groups. They are family-friendly, offer kids' programs and enjoy repeat business by holidaymakers. There's also a couple of simple guesthouses. The nightlife of Kuta and Seminyak is a hike.

Pondok Agung GUESTHOUSE $
(771 143; roland@eksadata.com; Jl Pratama; r 250,000-500,000Rp;) The nine airy rooms (most with bathtubs) in a large, house-like building are spotless. Higher-priced rooms come with small kitchens. The gardens are fairly large and attractive.

Princess Benoa Beach Resort HOTEL $$
(771 604; www.princessbenoaresort.com; Jl Pratama 101; r US$85-120; @) Newly constructed on the site of a resort of the same name, the 61-room Princess is across the street from the beach, which means you're that much further away from the howl of the jet skis. The grounds are spacious as is the 25m pool. The service is classically Balinese, relaxed yet caring.

TOP CHOICE **Bumbu Bali** BALINESE $$
(774 502; www.balifoods.com; Jl Pratama; mains from 90,000Rp, set menus from 225,000Rp; noon-9pm) Long-time resident and cookbook author Heinz von Holzen, his wife Puji and enthusiastic staff serve exquisitely flavoured dishes at this superb restaurant. Many diners opt for one of several lavish set menus. The *rijstaffel* shows the range of cooking in the kitchen from sates served on their own little coconut-husk grill to the tender *be celeng base manis* (pork in sweet soy sauce), with a dozen more courses in between. Book.

Getting There & Around

Taxis from the airport cost 120,000Rp. A free shuttle connects many beach resorts in Tanjung Benoa and Nusa Dua, or stroll along the beach promenade.

Sanur

0361

Sanur is a genteel alternative to Kuta. The white-sand beach is sheltered by a reef. The resulting low-key surf contributes to Sanur's nickname 'Snore', although this is also attributable to the area's status as a haven for expat retirees. Some parents prefer the beach at Sanur because its calmness makes it a good place for small children to play.

Sanur stretches for about 5km along an east-facing coastline, with the lush and green landscaped grounds of resorts fronting right onto the sandy beach. West of the beachfront hotels is the busy main drag, Jl Danau Tamblingan, with hotel entrances and oodles of tourist shops, restaurants and cafes.

Sights

Sanur's **beachfront walk** (Promenade) delights locals and visitors alike. Over 4km long, it follows the sand south as it curves to the west. Lots of cafes with tables in the sand will give you plenty of reason to pause and enjoy the views of Nusa Penida. Offshore you'll see gnarled fishermen in woven bamboo hats standing in the shallows, rod-fishing.

TOP CHOICE Museum Le Mayeur MUSEUM
(☎286 201; adult/child 10,000/5000Rp; ⏲7.30am-3.30pm) Le Mayeur de Merpes (1880–1958) arrived in Bali in 1932. Three years later he met and married the beautiful Legong dancer Ni Polok when she was just 15. They lived in this compound, which houses the museum, when Sanur was still a quiet fishing village.

Despite problems with security (some Le Mayeur paintings have sold for US$150,000) and conservation, almost 90 Le Mayeur paintings are displayed inside the museum in a naturalistic Balinese interior of woven fibres. Some early works are impressionist paintings from his travels in Africa, India, the Mediterranean and the South Pacific. Paintings from his early period in Bali are romantic depictions of daily life and beautiful Balinese women – often Ni Polok.

Activities

Jamu Traditional Spa SPA
(☎286 595; www.jamutraditionalspa.com; Jl Danau Tamblingan 41; massage from 550,000Rp) The beautifully carved teak and stone entry sets the mood at this gracious spa, which offers a range of face and body treatments including a popular earth and flower body mask and a Kemiri nut scrub. Can't you just feel the 'ahhhhhhhh'?

Crystal Divers DIVING
(☎286 737; www.crystal-divers.com; Jl Danau Tamblingan 168; intro dives from US$60) This slick diving operation has its own hotel and a large diving pool right outside the office. Recommended for beginners, the shop offers a long list of courses, including PADI open-water for US$450.

Surya Water Sports WATER SPORTS
(☎287 956; Jl Duyung 10; ⏲9am-5pm) One of several water sports operations along the beach, Surya is the largest. You can go parasailing (US$20 per ride), snorkelling by boat (US$35, two hours), windsurfing (US$30, one hour) or rent a kayak and paddle the smooth waters (US$5 per hour).

Sleeping

Usually the best places to stay are right on the beach; however, beware of properties that have been coasting for decades. Modest budgets will find comfort on the nonbeach side of Jl Danau Tamblingan. Don't stay anywhere near the noisy, noxious bypass.

TOP CHOICE Hotel La Taverna HOTEL $$$
(☎288 497; www.latavernahotel.com; Jl Danau Tamblingan 29; r US$100-200, ste from US$250; ❄@📶) One of Sanur's first hotels, La Taverna has been thoughtfully updated while retaining its artful, simple charms. The pretty grounds and paths linking buildings hum with a creative energy that infuses the 36 vintage bungalow-style units with an understated luxury. It all seems timeless yet with just a hint of sly youth. Art and antiques abound; views beckon.

TOP CHOICE Flashbacks GUESTHOUSE $
(☎281 682; www.flashbacks-chb.com; Jl Danau Tamblingan 110; r with fan/air-con from 250,000/410,000Rp; ❄📶) This welcoming retreat has nine rooms that vary greatly in size. The better ones are bungalows or suites while more modest rooms share bathrooms and have cold water. The lovely design takes a lot of cues from traditional Balinese style. Porch Cafe is out front.

Tandjung Sari HOTEL $$$
(☎288 441; www.tandjungsari.com; Jl Danau Tamblingan 29; bungalows from US$180; ❄@📶🏊) The mature trees along the shaded driveway set the gracious tone at this Sanur veteran, which was one of the first Balinese boutique hotels. Like a good tree, it has flourished since its start in 1967 and continues to be lauded for its stylish design. The 26 traditional-style bungalows are superbly decorated with crafts and antiques. At night, lights in the trees

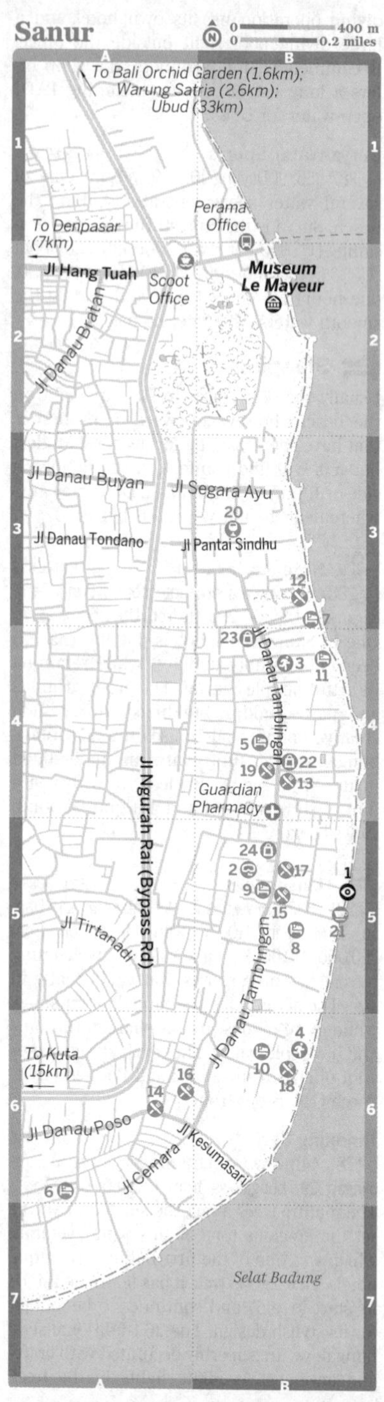

Sanur

Top Sights

Museum Le Mayeur B2

Sights

1 Beachfront Walk B5

Activities, Courses & Tours

2 Crystal Divers B5
3 Jamu Traditional Spa B4
4 Surya Water Sports B6

Sleeping

5 Flashbacks B4
6 Gardenia A6
7 Hotel La Taverna B3
8 Hotel Peneeda View B5
9 Hotel Rita B5
10 Hotel Segara Agung B6
11 Tandjung Sari B4

Eating

12 Bonsai Cafe B3
13 Café Smorgås B4
14 Denata Minang A6
15 Manik Organik B5
16 Massimo A6
17 Organic Market B5
Porch Cafe .... (see 5)
18 Sanur Bay B6
19 Three Monkeys Cafe B4

Drinking

20 Kalimantan B3
21 Warung Pantai Indah B5

Shopping

22 A-Krea B4
23 Ganesha Bookshop B4
24 Hardy's Supermarket B5

above the pool are magical. The gracious staff are a delight. Balinese dance classes are taught by one of Bali's best dancers.

Hotel Peneeda View HOTEL $$
(☎288 425; www.peneedaview.com; Jl Danau Tamblingan 89; r 850,000-1,600,000Rp; ❄@) One basic, small beachfront hotel among the many Sanur seems to grow like seaweed, the Peneeda (which is *not* phonetically accurate for Penida) is a good choice for sun, sand and room service at an affordable price. The scope of recent room updates is as narrow as the beach frontage. There's free wi-fi in common areas.

Gardenia GUESTHOUSE $$
(☎286 301; www.gardeniaguesthousebali.com; Jl Mertasari 2; r US$50-60; ❄📶≋) Like its many-petalled namesake, the Gardenia has many facets. The seven rooms are visions in white and sit well back from the road. Nice verandas face a small pool in a pretty courtyard. Up front there is a good cafe.

Hotel Segara Agung HOTEL $
(☎288 446; www.segaraagung.com; Jl Duyung 43; r US$40-60; ❄@📶≋) Down a quiet, sandy lane lined with villas, this hotel is only a three-minute walk from the beach. The 18 rooms are clean though Spartan; the cheapest have fans and cold water only. The big swimming pool is secluded.

Hotel Rita HOTEL $
(☎287 969; ritabali2@yahoo.co.id; Jl Danau Tamblingan 152; r 300,000-350,000Rp; ❄) Lovely Rita is tailor-made for those who want a basic room in a nice garden. You've nothing to fear from meter maids at this secluded compound well off busy Jl Danau Tamblingan. The beach is a 10-minute walk east.

Eating

Dine on the beach in a traditional open-air pavilion or in a genial bar – the choice is yours in Sanur. Although there are plenty of uninspired choices on Jl Danau Tamblingan, there are also some gems. Many of the places listed under Entertainment also do food.

For groceries and personal items, there's a large **Hardy's Supermarket** (☎285 806; Jl Danau Tamblingan 136). On Sundays, there's an **organic market** (Jl Danau Tamblingan; ⏲10am-2pm Sun) in the Gudang Keramik car park.

BEACH

The beach path offers restaurants, warungs and bars where you can catch a meal, a drink or a sea breeze. There are usually places near the end of each road that leads to the beach.

Bonsai Cafe PIZZA, SEAFOOD $
(Jl Danau Tamblingan 27; meals 40,000-90,000Rp; 📶) Although the menu is all beachside standards (and good ones), the real reason to seek this place out is for the proof that the name is not notional: there are hundreds of bonsai trees, from tiny to small.

Sanur Bay SEAFOOD $$
(☎288 153; Jl Duyung; meals 60,000-160,000Rp) You can hear the surf and see the moonlight reflecting on the water at this classic beachside seafood grill, set on the sand amid palm trees and fishing boats.

JALAN DANAU TAMBLINGAN

TOP CHOICE **Manik Organik** ORGANIC $
(www.manikorganikbali.com; Jl Danau Tamblingan 85; meals from 50,000Rp; 🖉) Actual trees shade the serene terrace at this creative and healthful cafe. Vegetarians are well cared for but there are also meaty dishes made with free-range chicken and the like. Smoothies include the fortifying 'immune tonic' and there is a range of house-brand products on offer.

Café Smorgås CAFE $$
(☎289 361; Jl Danau Tamblingan; meals 50,000-150,000Rp; 📶🖉) Set back from traffic, this popular place has nice wicker chairs on a large terrace outside and cool air-con inside. The menu has a healthy bent of fresh Western fare from breakfasts to sandwiches to soups and salads.

Three Monkeys Cafe CAFE $$
(Jl Danau Tamblingan; meals 60,000-150,000Rp; 📶) This branch of the splendid Ubud original is no mere knock-off: spread over two floors, there's cool jazz playing in the background and live performances some nights. Set well back from the road, you can enjoy Sanur's best coffee drinks on sofas or chairs. The menu mixes healthy Western fare with pan-Asian creations.

Porch Cafe CAFE $
(☎281 682; Jl Danau Tamblingan; meals from 40,000Rp; 📶) Fronting Flashbacks, a charmer of a small hotel, this cafe is housed in a traditional wooden building replete with the namesake porch. Snuggle up to a table out the front or shut it all out in the air-con inside. The menu is a tasty mix of comfort food such as burgers and freshly baked goods. Popular for breakfast; there's a long list of fresh juices.

Massimo ITALIAN $$
(☎288 942; Jl Danau Tamblingan 206; meals 80,000-200,000Rp) The interior is like an open-air Milan cafe, the outside like a Balinese garden – a combo that goes together like spaghetti and meatballs. Pasta, pizza and more are prepared with authentic Italian flair. No time for a meal? Nab some gelato from the counter up front.

SOUTH SANUR

Denata Minang INDONESIAN $

(Jl Danau Poso; meals from 15,000Rp) One of the better Padang-style warung, it's located just west of Cafe Billiard, the rollicking expat bar. Like its brethren, it has fab *ayam* (chicken) in myriad spicy forms – only better.

Drinking

Many of Sanur's drinking establishments cater to retired expats and are, thankfully for them, air-conditioned. This is not a place where things go late. Note that many places to eat are good for drinks and vice versa.

TOP CHOICE **Warung Pantai Indah** CAFE

(Beachfront Walk) Sit on benches in the sand under a tin roof at this uberauthentic old Sanur beach cafe. Just north of the Hotel Peneeda View and near some of Sanur's most expensive private beach villas, this outpost of good cheer has cheap beer and regular specials on fresh-grilled seafood (100,000Rp). The views and owners are delightful.

Kalimantan BAR

(☎289 291; Jl Pantai Sindhu 11) Aka Borneo Bob's, this veteran boozer is one of many casual joints on this street. Enjoy cheap drinks under the palms in the large, casual garden or squint at live American football on the satellite TV. The Mexican food features homegrown chilli peppers.

Shopping

Sanur is no Seminyak in the shopping department, although a few well-known shops have branches here. You can kill an afternoon browsing the length of Jl Danau Tamblingan.

A-Krea CLOTHES

(Jl Danau Tamblingan 51) A range of items designed and made in Bali are available in this attractive store that takes the colours of the island and gives them a minimalist flair. Clothes, accessories, housewares and more are all handmade.

Ganesha Bookshop BOOKSHOP

(Jl Danau Tamblingan 42) Bali's best bookshop for serious readers has a new shop in the heart of Sanur. Besides excellent choices in new and used fiction, Ganesha has superb selections on local culture and history. There's also a special reading area for kids.

Information

There are numerous ATMs and banks along Jl Danau Tamblingan.

Guardian Pharmacy (☎284 343; Jl Danau Tamblingan 134) The chain pharmacy has a doctor on call.

Getting There & Away

Bemo

The public bemo stops are at the southern end of Sanur on Jl Mertasari, and just outside the main entrance to the Inna Grand Bali Beach Hotel on Jl Hang Tuah. You can hail a bemo anywhere along Jl Danau Tamblingan and Jl Danau Poso – although drivers will first try to hail you. Green bemos go along Jl Hang Tuah to the Kereneng terminal in Denpasar (7000Rp).

Boat

Public boats and the Perama (p236) boat to Nusa Lembongan leave from the beach at the end of Jl Hang Tuah. The fast boat, **Scoot** (☎285 522; Jl Hang Tuah), has an office in Sanur; fast boats depart from a nearby portion of beach. None of these services uses a dock – be prepared to wade to the boat.

Tourist Shuttle Bus

The **Perama office** (☎285 592; Jl Hang Tuah 39; ⏰7am-10pm) is at Warung Pojok at the northern end of town. It runs shuttles to the following destinations, most only once daily:

DESTINATION	COST (RP)	DURATION
Candidasa	60,000	2¾hr
Kuta	25,000	15min
Lovina	125,000	4hr
Padangbai	60,000	2½hr
Ubud	40,000	1hr

Getting Around

Official taxis cost about 100,000Rp from the airport. Bemos go up and down Jl Danau Tamblingan and Jl Danau Poso for 4000Rp. Metered taxis can be flagged down in the street, or call **Bluebird Taxi** (☎701 111).

Benoa Harbour

Bali's main port is at the entrance of Teluk Benoa (Benoa Bay), the wide but shallow body east of the airport runway. Benoa Harbour is on the northern side of the bay – a square of docks and port buildings on reclaimed land, linked to mainland Bali by a 2km causeway. It's referred to as Benoa Port or Benoa Harbour to distinguish it from Benoa village, on the south side of the bay.

Benoa Harbour is the port for some tourist boats to Nusa Lembongan and the Gilis as well as for Pelni ships to other parts of Indonesia; however, its shallow depth prevents cruise ships from calling.

Denpasar

0361 / POP 800,000

Denpasar might not be a tropical paradise, but it's as much a part of 'the real Bali' as the rice paddies and clifftop temples. This is the hub of the island for almost 800,000 locals and here you will find their shopping malls and parks. Most enticing, however, is the growing range of fabulous restaurants and cafes aimed at the burgeoning middle class. You'll also want to sample Denpasar's markets, its excellent museum and its purely modern Balinese vibe. Most visitors stay in the tourist towns of the south and visit Denpasar as a day trip (if traffic is kind you can get here in 15 minutes from Sanur and 30 minutes from Seminyak).

In contrast to the rest of Denpasar, the Renon area, southeast of the town centre, is laid out on a grand scale, with wide streets, large car parks and huge tracts of landscaped space. You'll find the government offices here, many of which are impressive structures displaying an ersatz Balinese style.

Sights

TOP CHOICE Museum Negeri Propinsi Bali MUSEUM

(222 680; adult/child 10,000/5000Rp; 8am-12.30pm Fri, to 4pm Sat-Thu) Think of this as the British Museum or the Smithsonian of Balinese culture. It's all here although, unlike those world-class institutions, you have to work at sorting it out.

The museum comprises several buildings and pavilions, including many examples of Balinese architecture. The main building, to the back as you enter, has a collection of prehistoric pieces downstairs, including stone sarcophagi and stone and bronze implements. Upstairs are examples of traditional artefacts, including items still in everyday use. Look for the intricate wood-and-cane carrying cases for transporting fighting cocks, and tiny carrying cases for fighting crickets.

The **northern pavilion**, in the style of a Tabanan palace, houses dance costumes and masks, including a sinister Rangda (widow-witch), a healthy-looking Barong (mythical lion-dog creature) and a towering Barong Landung (tall Barong) figure.

The **central pavilion**, with its spacious veranda, is like the palace pavilions of the Karangasem kingdom (based in Amlapura), where rajahs held audiences. The exhibits are related to Balinese religion, and include ceremonial objects, calendars and priests' clothing.

The **southern pavilion** (Gedung Buleleng) has a varied collection of textiles, including *endek* (a Balinese method of weaving with pre-dyed threads), double ikat, *songket* (silver- and gold-threaded cloth, hand-woven using a floating weft technique) and *prada* (the application of gold leaf or gold or silver thread in traditional Balinese clothes).

Ignore 'guides' who offer little except a chance to part with US$5 or US$10.

Pura Jagatnatha TEMPLE

(Jl Surapati) Next to the museum, the state temple, built in 1953, is dedicated to the supreme god, Sanghyang Widi. Part of its significance is its statement of monotheism. Although the Balinese recognise many gods, the belief in one supreme god (who can have many manifestations) brings Balinese Hinduism into conformity with the first principle of Pancasila – the 'Belief in One God'.

Two major festivals are held here every month, during the full moon and new moon, and feature *wayang kulit* (shadow-puppet plays).

Bajra Sandhi Monument MONUMENT

(264 517; Jl Raya Puputan; adult/child 10,000/5000Rp; 8.30am-5pm) Inside this vaguely Borobudur-like structure, which dominates a large park in Renon, are dioramas tracing Bali's history. Taking the name as a cue (it means: Monument to the Struggle of the People of Bali), you'll understand the jingoistic soap-opera quality of the dolls and their mayhem.

Festivals & Events

The annual **Bali Arts Festival** (www.baliartsfestival.com) is based at the Taman Wedhi Budaya arts centre in Denpasar, and lasts for about one month from mid-June to mid-July. It's a great time to visit Bali and the festival is an easy way to see an enormous variety of traditional dance, music and crafts from all over the island. Tickets are usually available

Denpasar

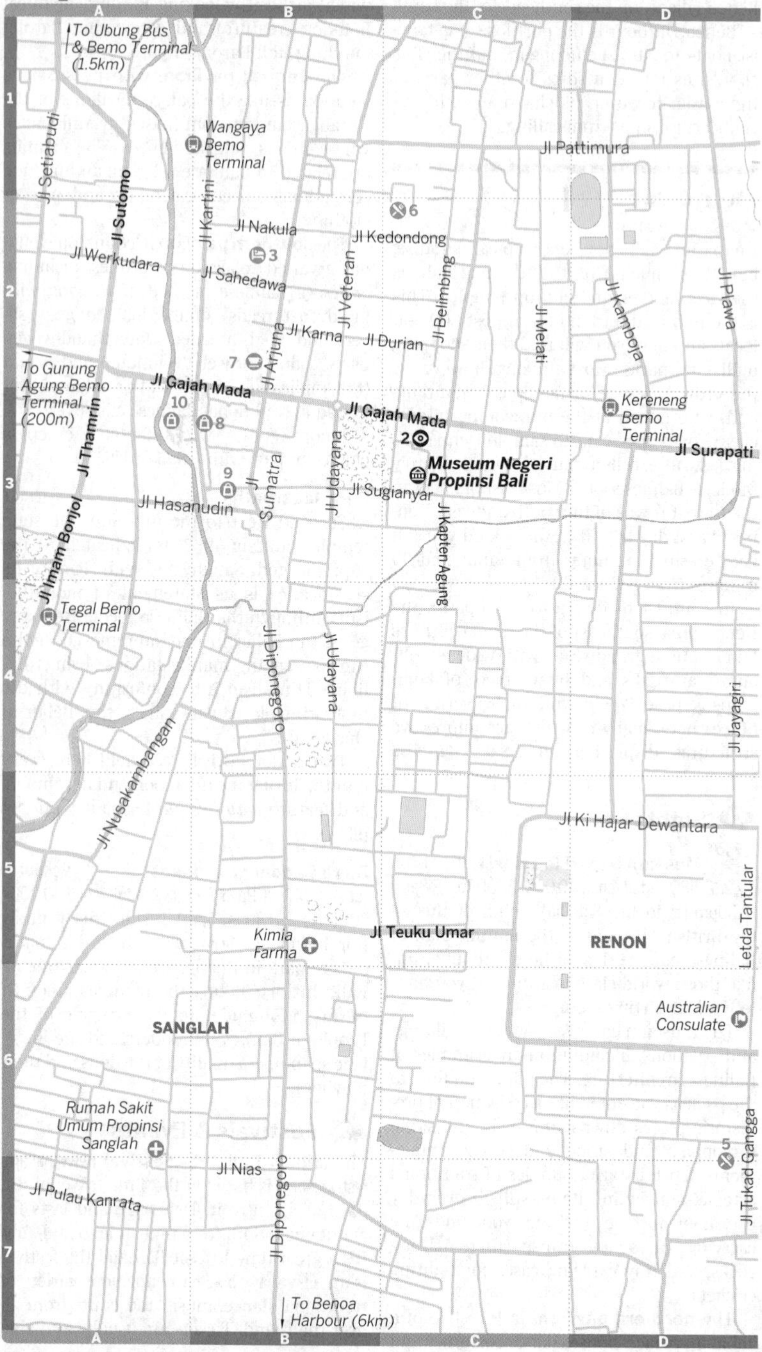

A B C D

1 2 3 4 5 6 7

To Ubung Bus & Bemo Terminal (1.5km)

Wangaya Bemo Terminal

Jl Pattimura

Jl Setiabudi

Jl Sutomo

Jl Kartini

Jl Nakula

6

Jl Kedondong

3

Jl Werkudara

Jl Sahedawa

Jl Veteran

Jl Belimbing

Jl Melati

Jl Kamboja

Jl Plawa

Jl Karna

Jl Durian

Jl Arjuna

7

To Gunung Agung Bemo Terminal (200m)

Jl Gajah Mada

10

8

Jl Gajah Mada

Kereneng Bemo Terminal

2

Jl Surapati

Jl Thamrin

Museum Negeri Propinsi Bali

9

Jl Sumatra

Jl Udayana

Jl Sugianyar

Jl Hasanudin

Jl Kapten Agung

Jl Imam Bonjol

Tegal Bemo Terminal

Jl Diponegoro

Jl Udayana

Jl Jayagiri

Jl Nusakambangan

Jl Ki Hajar Dewantara

Letda Tantular

Jl Teuku Umar

Kimia Farma

RENON

Australian Consulate

SANGLAH

Rumah Sakit Umum Propinsi Sanglah

5

Jl Nias

Jl Tukad Gangga

Jl Pulau Kanrata

Jl Diponegoro

To Benoa Harbour (6km)

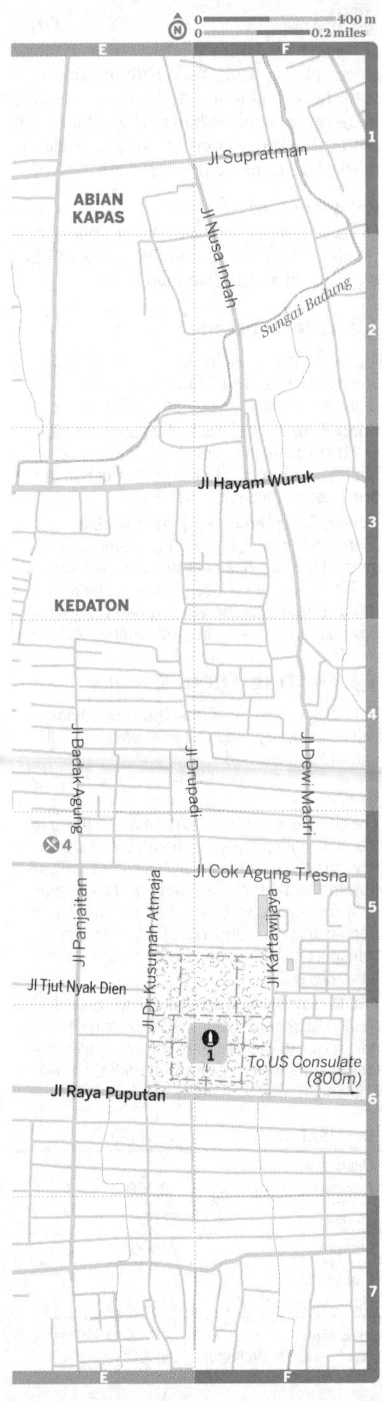

Denpasar

right before performances and schedules are widely available.

Sleeping

Denpasar has dozens of hotels aimed at business travellers; it's hard to think of a compelling reason to stay here as the myriad choices in Sanur, Seminyak and Kerobokan are close by.

TOP CHOICE Nakula Familiar Inn GUESTHOUSE $
(226 446; www.nakulafamiliarinn.com; Jl Nakula 4; r 130,000-200,000Rp;) The eight rooms at this sprightly urban family compound, which has been a traveller's favourite since before Seminyak existed, are clean (some with air-con and cold-water showers only) and have small balconies. The traffic noise isn't too bad and there is a nice courtyard and cafe in the middle. Tegal–Kereneng bemos go along Jl Nakula.

Eating & Drinking

Denpasar has the island's best range of Indonesian and Balinese food. Savvy locals and expats each have their own favourite warungs and restaurants.

TOP CHOICE Warung Satria INDONESIAN $
(Jl Kedondong; dishes 8000-15,000Rp; 11am-3pm) This is a long-running warung on a quiet street; try the wonderful seafood sate

served with a shallot sambal. Otherwise, choose from the immaculate displays of what's fresh, but don't wait too long after lunch or it will all be gone. There is a **second location** (Jl WR Supratman) near the junction where the main road to Ubud branches off from the bypass, east of the centre of Denpasar.

TOP CHOICE Cak Asm BALINESE $
(Jl Tukad Gangga; meals from 25,000Rp) Join the government workers and students from the nearby university for superb dishes cooked to order in the bustling kitchen. Order the *cumi cumi* (calamari) with *telor asin* sauce (a heavenly mixture of eggs and garlic). The resulting buttery, crispy goodness could well be the best dish you have while you're in Bali. Fruity ice drinks are a cooling treat. An English-language menu makes ordering a breeze.

Ayam Goreng Kalasan INDONESIAN $
(Jl Cok Agung Tresna 6; meals from 25,000Rp) The name here says it all: fried chicken *(ayam goreng)* named for a Javanese temple (Kalasan) in a region renowned for its fiery, crispy chicken. The version here falls off the bone on the way to the table; the meat is redolent with lemongrass from a long marinade prior to the plunge into boiling oil. There are several other excellent little warungs in this strip.

Bhineka Jaya Cafe COFFEE
(☎224 016; Jl Gajah Mada 80; coffee 4000Rp; ⏲9am-4pm) Home to Bali's Coffee Co, this storefront sells locally grown beans and makes a mean espresso, which you can enjoy at the two tiny tables while watching the bustle of Denpasar's old main drag.

Shopping

Denpasar's main market is vast and a good reason to visit.

TOP CHOICE Pasar Badung MARKET
(Jl Gajah Mada) Bali's largest food market is busy in the morning and evening (although dull and sleepy from 2pm to 4pm); it's a great place to browse and bargain. You'll find produce and food from all over the island, as well as easy-to-assemble temple offerings that are popular with working women. Get lost here – as it won't be permanent – and revel in the range of fruits and spices on offer. Ignore the services of 'guides'.

Anis TEXTILES
(Jl Sulawesi 27) Jammed into a string of fabric stores just east of Pasar Badung, this narrow shop stands out for its huge selection of genuine Balinese batik. The colours and patterns are bewildering, while the clearly marked, reasonable prices are not.

Kampung Arab MARKET
(Jl Hasanudin & Jl Sulawesi) Has jewellery and precious-metal stores run by scores of Middle Eastern and Indian merchants.

Information

All major Indonesian banks have offices in Denpasar, and most have ATMs. Several are on Jl Gajah Mada, near the corner of Jl Arjuna.

Kimia Farma (☎227 811; Jl Diponegoro 125; ⏲24hr) The main outlet of the island-wide pharmacy chain has the largest selection of prescription medications in Bali.

Rumah Sakit Umum Propinsi Sanglah (Sanglah Hospital; ☎227 911; ⏲24hr) The city's general hospital has English-speaking staff and an ER. It's the best hospital on the island and has a special wing for well-insured foreigners, Paviliun Amerta Wing International (☎257 499).

Getting There & Away

Denpasar is *the* hub of road transport in Bali – you'll find buses and minibuses bound for all corners of the island.

Bemo

The city has several bemo terminals – if you're travelling independently around Bali you'll often have to go via Denpasar, and transfer from one terminal to another. Each terminal has regular bemo connections to the other terminals in Denpasar for 7000Rp. Note that as personal transport has flourished, Bali's bemo network has suffered.

FROM UBUNG Well north of the town, on the road to Gilimanuk, Ubung is the terminal for northern and western Bali. This used to be the long-distance bus terminal but that has moved 12km northwest to Mengwi.

DESTINATION	COST (RP)
Gilimanuk (for the ferry to Java)	30,000
Mengwi	12,000
Munduk	27,000
Pancasari (for Danau Bratan)	22,000
Singaraja (via Pupuan or Bedugul)	35,000

FROM BATUBULAN Located a very inconvenient 6km northeast of Denpasar on a road to Ubud, this **terminal** is for destinations in eastern and central Bali. This is where you get minibuses to the new long-distance bus terminal in Mengwi (20,000Rp, one hour).

DESTINATION	COST (RP)
Gianyar	15,000
Padangbai (for the Lombok ferry)	18,000
Sanur	7000
Semarapura	23,000
Singaraja (via Kintamani)	35,000
Ubud	13,000

FROM TEGAL On the western side of town on Jl Iman Bonjol, Tegal is the terminal for Kuta and the Bukit Peninsula.

DESTINATION	COST (RP)
Airport	15,000
Jimbaran	17,000
Kuta	13,000
Ulu Watu	22,000

FROM GUNUNG AGUNG This terminal, at the northwestern corner of town (look for orange bemo), is on Jl Gunung Agung, and has bemos to Kerobokan and Canggu (10,000Rp).

FROM KERENENG East of the town centre, Kereneng has bemo service to Sanur (7000Rp).

FROM WANGAYA Near the centre of town, this small terminal is the departure point for bemo services to northern Denpasar and the outlying Ubung bus terminal (8000Rp).

Getting Around

BEMO Bemos take various circuitous routes from and between Denpasar's many bus and bemo terminals. They line up for various destinations at each terminal, or you can try to hail them from anywhere along the main roads – look for the destination sign above the driver's window. The Tegal–Nusa Dua bemo is handy for Renon; and the Kereneng–Ubung bemo travels along Jl Gajah Mada, past the museum.

TAXI As in South Bali, taxis prowl the streets of Denpasar looking for fares. The cabs of **Bluebird** (☎701 111) are the most reliable choice.

NUSA LEMBONGAN & ISLANDS

Look towards the open ocean southeast of Bali and the hazy bulk of Nusa Penida dominates the view. But for many visitors the real focus is Nusa Lembongan, which lurks in the shadow of its vastly larger neighbour. Here there's great surfing, quiet white beaches and the kind of funky vibe travellers cherish. This is a popular destination and justly so – it's an easy way to escape the hubbub of South Bali.

Nusa Penida is seldom visited, which means that its dramatic vistas and unchanged village life are yours to explore. Tiny Nusa Ceningan huddles between the larger islands. It makes an interesting quick jaunt from Lembongan.

This has been a poor region for many years. Income from tourists is supplemented by seaweed cultivation, which you'll see growing in the waters off Jungutbatu and smell drying on land. Extracts are used as food additives in products such as ice cream.

Nusa Lembongan

☎0366

This is the Bali many imagine but never find: simple rooms on the beach, cheap beers with incredible sunsets, days spent surfing and diving, and nights spent riffling through a favourite book or hanging with new friends.

Nusa Lembongan grows in popularity each year but even as rooms for travellers proliferate it remains a mellow place. The 7000 locals welcome the money brought by visitors and time is marked by the crow of a rooster and the fall of a coconut.

Sights

Jungutbatu VILLAGE

The **beach** here, a lovely arc of white sand with clear blue water, has superb views across to Gunung Agung in eastern Bali. The village itself is pleasant, with quiet lanes, no cars and a couple of temples, including **Pura Segara** and its enormous banyan tree.

Mushroom Bay Beach BEACH

This gorgeous little bay, unofficially named for the mushroom corals offshore, has a perfect crescent of white-sand beach. During the day, the tranquillity may be disturbed by banana-boat rides or parasailing. In the morning and the evening, it's delightful.

The most pleasant way to get here from Jungutbatu is to walk along the **trail** that starts from the southern end of the main beach and follows the coastline for a kilometre or so past a couple of little beaches. Veer inland after the last, **Pantai Selegimpak**.

Nusa Lembongan

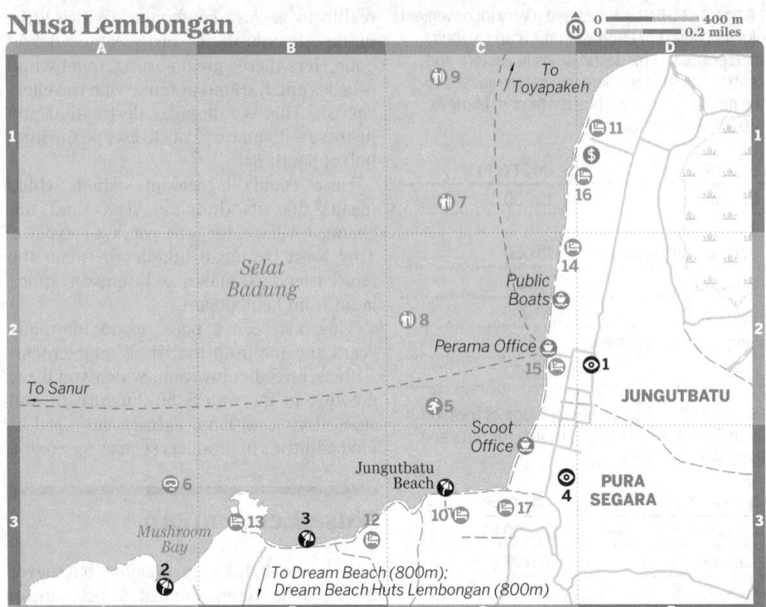

Nusa Lembongan

Sights

1 Jungutbatu ... D2
2 Mushroom Bay Beach ... A3
3 Pantai Selegimpak ... B3
4 Pura Segara ... C3

Activities, Courses & Tours

5 Bounty Cruise ... C2
6 Bounty Pontoons ... A3
7 Lacerations ... C1
8 Playground ... C2
9 Shipwreck ... C1
World Diving ... (see 15)

Sleeping

10 Batu Karang ... C3
11 Indiana Kenanga ... D1
12 Morin Lembongan ... B3
13 Mushroom Beach Bungalows ... B3
14 Nusa Indah Bungalows ... C2
15 Pondok Baruna ... C2
16 Two Thousand Cafe & Bungalows ... D1
17 Ware-Ware ... C3

Dream Beach BEACH

Down a track, on the southwestern side of the island, this 150m-deep pocket of white sand has pounding surf and pretty azure waters. It's a good escape although daytrippers can crowd in.

A new low-key resort, **Dream Beach Huts Lembongan** (☎0812 3983 772; www.dreambeachlembongan.com; Dream Beach; r from US$75;), has a pool that you can use for 50,000Rp plus an okay cafe.

Activities

Most places will rent bicycles for 30,000Rp per day, surfboards for 50,000Rp and motorbikes for 30,000Rp per hour.

Surfing

Surfing here is best in the dry season (April to September), when the winds come from the southeast. It's definitely not for beginners, and can be dangerous even for experts. There are three main breaks on the reef, all aptly named. From north to south are **Shipwreck**, **Lacerations** and **Playground**. Depending on where you are staying, you can paddle directly out to whichever of the three is closest; for others it's better to hire a boat. Prices are negotiable – from about 30,000Rp to 50,000Rp for a one-way trip. You tell the owner when to return. A fourth break – **Racecourses** – sometimes emerges south of Shipwreck.

You can easily rent surfboards and paddleboards.

Diving

World Diving DIVING

(☎081 2390 0686; www.world-diving.com) This outfit, based at Pondok Baruna on Jungutbatu Beach, is well regarded and offers a complete range of courses, including five-day PADI open-water courses for US$375, and dive trips – from US$27 to US$40 per dive – to sites around all three islands.

Snorkelling

You'll find good snorkelling just off the Mushroom Bay and **Bounty pontoons** off Jungutbatu Beach, as well as in areas off the north coast of the island. Charter a boat from 150,000Rp per hour, depending on demand, distance and the number of passengers.

A trip to the challenging waters of Nusa Penida costs 400,000Rp for three hours; to the nearby mangroves costs about 300,000Rp. Snorkelling gear can be rented for about 30,000Rp per day. World Diving allows snorkellers to join dive trips and charges 230,000Rp for a four-hour trip.

Cruises

A number of boats offer day trips to Nusa Lembongan from Benoa Harbour in South Bali. Trips include hotel transfer from South Bali, basic water sports, snorkelling, banana-boat rides, island tours and a buffet lunch. These day trips can make for a long day.

Bounty Cruise ADVENTURE TRIP

(☎726 666; www.balibountycruises.com; adult/child US$95/47.50) Boats dock at a garish yellow offshore pontoon with water slides and other amusements.

Sleeping & Eating

With notable exceptions, rooms and amenities become increasingly posh as you head south and west along the water to Mushroom Bay. Almost every property has a cafe serving (unless noted) basic Indonesian and Western dishes for about 30,000Rp.

JUNGUTBATU

Many lodgings in Jungutbatu have shed the surfer shack cliché and are moving upmarket. But you can still find cheapies with cold water and fans.

Indiana Kenanga HOTEL $$$

(www.indiana-kenanga-villas.com; r US$110-460; ❄🛜🏊) Wow! Jungutbatu will never be the same. Six stylish rooms and two posh villas shelter near a pool behind the beach at Lembongan's most-glossy-magazine-ready digs. The French designer-owner has decorated the place with purple armchairs and other whimsical touches. The restaurant has an all-day menu of seafood, sandwiches and various surprises cooked up by the French chef. People have been known to swoon over the chocolate fondant.

Pondok Baruna GUESTHOUSE $$

(☎0812 394 0992; www.pondokbaruna.com; r 250,000-700,000Rp; ❄@🛜🏊) Associated with World Diving), this place offers four very simple rooms with terraces facing the ocean. They are an excellent budget option. Six plusher rooms with air-con surround a dive pool off the beach. Eight more 'Frangipani' rooms have been added back in the palm trees around a large pool. Staff, led by the manager, Putu, are charmers.

Two Thousand Cafe & Bungalows GUESTHOUSE $

(☎0812 381 2775; r 200,000-500,000Rp; ❄🛜) Grassy grounds surround 28 rooms in two-storey blocks; some have hot water and air-con. There's a fun cafe-bar right on the sand, with various sunset drink specials.

Nusa Indah Bungalows GUESTHOUSE $$

(☎081 139 8553; www.lembongansurferbeachcafe.com; r 300,000-500,000Rp; ❄🛜) Solid cottages on a sizeable beachfront and a popular cafe make this a good choice. Fan-only rooms are a good budget option on the beach. The beach loungers have a fine position.

HILLSIDE

The steep hillside just south of Jungutbatu offers great views and an ever-increasing number of more luxurious rooms.

Batu Karang HOTEL $$$

(☎24880; www.batukaranglembongan.com; r from US$230; ❄@🛜🏊) This upmarket resort has a large infinity pool perched on a terraced hillside with 23 luxury units. Some are villa-style and have multiple rooms and private plunge pools. All have open-air bathrooms and wooden terraces with sweeping views.

Ware-Ware GUESTHOUSE $

(☎0812 397 0572; www.warewaresurfbungalows.com; r 400,000-700,000Rp; ❄🛜) The units at this hillside place are a mix of traditional square and groovy circular numbers with thatched roofs. The large rooms (some fan only) have rattan couches and big bathrooms.

DIVING THE ISLANDS

There are great diving possibilities around the islands, from shallow and sheltered reefs, mainly on the northern side of Lembongan and Penida, to very demanding drift dives in the channel between Penida and the other two islands. Vigilant locals have protected their waters from dynamite bombing by renegade fishing boats, so the reefs are relatively intact. And a side benefit of seaweed farming is that locals no longer rely so much on fishing. The islands were also designated a marine conservation district in 2012.

If you arrange a dive trip from Padangbai or South Bali, stick with the most reputable operators, as conditions here can be tricky and local knowledge is essential.

Diving accidents regularly happen and people die diving in the waters around the islands every year.

Using one of the recommended operators on Nusa Lembongan puts you close to the action from the start. A particular attraction are the large marine animals, including turtles, sharks and manta rays. The large (3m fin-to-fin) and unusual *mola mola* (sunfish) is sometimes seen around the islands between mid-July and October, while manta rays are often seen south of Nusa Penida.

The best dive sites include **Blue Corner** and **Jackfish Point** off Nusa Lembongan and **Ceningan Point** at the tip of that island. The channel between Ceningan and Penida is renowned for drift diving, but it is essential you have a good operator who can judge fast-changing currents and other conditions. Upswells can bring cold water from the open ocean to sites such as **Ceningan Wall**. This is one of the world's deepest natural channels and attracts all manner and sizes of fish.

Sites close to Nusa Penida include **Crystal Bay**, **SD**, **Pura Ped**, **Manta Point** and **Batu Aba**. Of these, Crystal Bay, SD and Pura Ped are suitable for novice divers and are good for snorkelling. Note that the open waters around Penida are challenging, even for experienced divers.

The cafe scores with a spectacular, breezy location on a cliffside wooden deck. It does well with seafood.

Morin Lembongan GUESTHOUSE **$**
(☎0812 385 8396; wayman40@hotmail.com; r US$30-60; @) More lushly planted than many of the hillside places, Morin has woodsy rooms with views over the water from the verandas. This is a good choice if you want to feel close yet removed from Jungutbatu.

MUSHROOM BAY

It's your own treasure island. This shallow bay has a nice beach, plenty of overhanging trees and some of the nicest lodging on Lembongan. Get here from Jungutbatu by road (15,000Rp) or boat (50,000Rp).

Mushroom Beach Bungalows GUESTHOUSE **$$**
(☎24515; www.mushroom-lembongan.com; r US$70-125; ❄) Perched on a tiny knoll at the eastern end of Mushroom Bay, this family-run place has a great variety of rooms, some with fan only. There are good-sized bathtubs and a popular cliffside cafe for viewing sunsets. Packages including direct trasnsport from Sanur are available.

ℹ Information

It's vital that you bring sufficient cash in rupiah for your stay, as there is only one ATM (and it was not operating at time of research).

If the name **Money Changer** (⏰8am-9pm) conjures images of the usurers being chased from the temple, you'd be right. Cash advances here on credit cards incur an 8% service charge.

Wi-fi is now common.

ℹ Getting There & Away

Getting to/from Nusa Lembongan offers numerous choices. In descending order of speed are the fast boats like Scoot, the Perama boat and the public boats. Note: anyone with money for a speedboat is getting into the fast-boat act; be wary of fly-by-night operators with fly-by-night safety. Boats anchor offshore, so be prepared to get your feet wet.

Public boats to Nusa Lembongan leave from the northern end of Sanur beach at 8am (60,000Rp, 1¾ to two hours). This is the boat used for supplies, so you may have to share space with a chicken.

Perama tourist boat leaves Sanur at 10.30am (return 180,000Rp, 1¾ hours). The **Lembongan office** (www.peramatour.com; Jungutbatu Beach) is near the Mandara Beach Bungalows. It also has boats to Lombok and the Gilis.

Scoot (www.scootcruise.com), located on the waterfront, runs speedboats (return adult/child 550,000/270,000Rp, 30 to 40 minutes) that fly over and through the waves. There are several returns daily; check schedules when you book. It also has Gili services.

Nusa Penida boats take locals between Jungutbatu and Toyapakeh (one hour) between 5.30am and 6am for 30,000Rp. Otherwise, charter a boat for 150,000Rp one way.

Getting Around

The island is fairly small and you can easily walk to most places. There are no cars (although pick-up trucks are proliferating); bicycles (25,000Rp per day) and small motorbikes (50,000Rp per hour) are widely available for hire. One-way rides on motorbikes or trucks cost 20,000Rp and up.

Nusa Ceningan

There is a narrow suspension bridge crossing the lagoon between Nusa Lembongan and Nusa Ceningan, which makes it quite easy to explore the network of tracks on foot or by bicycle – not that there is much to see. The lagoon is filled with frames for seaweed farming and there's also a fishing village and several small agricultural plots. The island is quite hilly and, if you're up for it, you'll get glimpses of great scenery as you wander or cycle around the rough tracks.

This is one of the places you can visit with **JED** (Village Ecotourism Network; ☎0361-366 9951; www.jed.or.id; per person US$130), the Village Ecotourism Network.

Nusa Penida

☎0366

Largely overlooked by tourists, Nusa Penida awaits discovery. It's an untrammelled place that answers the question: what would Bali be like if tourists never came?

Nusa Penida was once used as a place of banishment for criminals and other undesirables from the kingdom of Klungkung. It's thought to be home to demons. Life is simple; you'll still see topless older women carrying huge loads on their heads. There are not a lot of formal activities or sights; rather, you go to Nusa Penida to explore and relax.

Nusa Penida can make for an adventurous day trip from Nusa Lembongan. Services are limited to small shops in the main towns. Bring cash and anything else you'll need.

Getting There & Away

The strait between Nusa Penida and southern Bali is deep and subject to heavy swells – if there is a strong tide, boats often have to wait. You may also have to wait a while for the public boat to fill up with passengers. Boats to/from Kusamba are not recommended.

FROM SANUR Speedboats leave from the same part of the beach as the public boats to Nusa Lembongan. **Maruti Express** (☎0852 6861 7972; www.balimarutiexpress.com; return adult/child 480,000Rp/280,000Rp) is the main operator.

FROM PADANGBAI Off the beach just east of the car park in Padangbai, you'll find the twin-engine fibre-glass boats that run across the strait to Buyuk, 1km west of Sampalan on Nusa Penida (50,000Rp, 45 minutes, four daily). The boats run between 7am and noon. A large and modern car ferry operates daily (16,000Rp, two hours) from Kusamba.

FROM NUSA LEMBONGAN Boats run between Toyapakeh and Jungutbatu (30,000Rp, one hour) between 5.30am and 6am. Enjoy the mangrove views on the way. Otherwise, charter a boat for 150,000Rp.

WORTH A TRIP

AROUND NUSA PENIDA

A trip around the island, following the north and east coasts and crossing the hilly interior, can be completed in a few hours by motorcycle.

At **Batukandik**, a rough road and 1.5km track leads to a spectacular **waterfall** *(air terjun)* that crashes onto a small beach. Get a guide (20,000Rp) in **Tanglad**.

The important temple of **Pura Dalem Penetaran Ped** is near the beach at **Ped**, a few kilometres east of Toyapakeh. It houses a shrine for the demon Jero Gede Macaling. The temple structure is sprawling and you will see many people making offerings for safe sea voyages. The island's best food is nearby at **Warung Wayan** (Ped; meals from 15,000Rp). Enjoy Gunung Agung views across the water while sipping a coconut drink. From here, the road follows the lush coast back to Sampalan.

Getting Around

To see the island you should charter your own bemo or private vehicle with driver for about 60,000Rp to 100,000Rp.

SAMPALAN

Sampalan, the main town on thinly populated Penida, is quiet and pleasant, with a market, schools and shops strung out along the curving coast road. The **market area**, where the bemos congregate, is in the middle of town.

Made's Homestay (☎0852 3764 3649; r from 150,000Rp) has four small, clean rooms in a pleasant garden. Breakfast is included. A small side road between the market and the harbour leads here.

TOYAPAKEH

If you come by boat from Lembongan, you'll probably be dropped at the beach at Toyapakeh, a pretty town with lots of shady trees. The **beach** has clean white sand and clear blue water. Step up from the beach and you're at the road head, where bemos can take you to Ped or Sampalan (7000Rp).

South of Toyapakeh, a 10km road through the village of Sakti leads to idyllic **Crystal Bay Beach**, which fronts the popular dive spot. The sand here is the whitest around Bali and you'll likely have it to yourself.

UBUD

☎0361

Ubud is culture, yes. It's also home to good restaurants, cafes and streets of shops, many selling goods from the region's artisans. Every street and lane seems to have a place exhibiting artwork for sale (galleries vary enormously in the choice and quality of items offered). There's somewhere to stay for every budget and, no matter what the price, you can enjoy lodgings that reflect the local zeitgeist: artful, creative and serene.

Ubud's popularity continues to grow. Tour buses with day trippers can choke the main streets and cause traffic chaos. Being named the top city in Asia by *Conde Nast Traveler* only added to the hoopla from bestselling *Eat, Pray, Love*. Fortunately Ubud adapts, and a stroll away from the intersection of Jl Raya Ubud and Monkey Forest Rd can quickly restore sanity. There's nothing like a walk through the verdant rice fields to make all right with the world.

Spend a few days in Ubud to appreciate it properly. It's one of those places where days can become weeks and weeks become months, as the noticeable expat community demonstrates.

Sights

TOP CHOICE **Museum Puri Lukisan** MUSEUM

(Museum of Fine Arts; Map p250; ☎975 136; www.museumpurilukisan.com; off Jl Raya Ubud; adult/child 20,000Rp/free; ⏰9am-5pm) The Museum of Fine Arts displays fine examples of all schools of Balinese art. Just look at the lush composition of *Balinese Market* by Anak Agung Gde Sobrat to see the vibrancy of local painting.

It was in Ubud that the modern Balinese art movement started, when artists first began to abandon purely religious themes and court subjects for scenes of everyday life. Rudolf Bonnet was part of the Pita Maha artists' cooperative, and together with Cokorda Gede Agung Sukawati (a prince of Ubud's royal family) and Walter Spies they helped to establish a permanent collection.

The museum's collection is well curated and labelled in English. The museum has a good bookshop and a cafe. The lush, garden-like grounds alone are worth a visit.

Ubud Palace PALACE

(Map p250; cnr Jl Raya Ubud & Jl Suweta) This palace in the heart of town shares space with **Puri Saren Agung** (Map p250; cnr Jl Raya Ubud & Jl Suweta). The compound has many ornate corners and was mostly built after the 1917 earthquake. The local royal family still lives here and you can wander around most of the large compound exploring the many traditional and not excessively ornate buildings. If you really like it, you can stay the night (p254). Take time to appreciate the stone carvings, many by noted local artists such as I Gusti Nyoman Lempad. Just to the north, **Pura Marajan Agung** (Map p250; Jl Suweta) has one of the finest gates you'll find and is the private temple for the royal family.

Pura Desa Ubud TEMPLE

(Map p250; Jl Raya Ubud) Pura Desa Ubud is the main temple for the Ubud community. It is often closed.

Pura Taman Saraswati TEMPLE

(Map p250; Jl Raya Ubud) Just a bit west of Pura Desa Ubud is the very picturesque Pura Taman Saraswati. Waters from the temple at the rear of the site feed the pond in the front which overflows with pretty lotus blossoms. There are carvings that honour Dewi Saraswati, the goddess of wisdom and the arts, who has clearly given her blessing to Ubud. There are weekly dance performances by night; by day, painters set up easels.

Neka Art Museum GALLERY

(Map p248; ☎975 074; www.museumneka.com; Jl Raya Sanggingan; adult/child 50,000Rp/free; ⏲9am-5pm Mon-Sat, noon-5pm Sun) Quite distinct from Neka Gallery, the Neka Art Museum is the creation of Suteja Neka, a private collector and dealer in Balinese art. It has an excellent and diverse collection and is a good place to learn about the development of painting in Bali.

You can get an overview of the myriad local painting styles in the **Balinese Painting Hall**. Look for the *wayang* works.

The **Arie Smit Pavilion** features Smit's works on the upper level, and examples of the Young Artist school, which he inspired, on the lower level. Look for the Bruegel-like *The Wedding Ceremony* by I Nyoman Tjarka.

The temporary exhibition hall has changing displays, while the **Photography Archive Centre** features black-and-white photography of Bali in the early 1930s and 1940s. Also look for the large collection of ceremonial kris (daggers).

Agung Rai Museum of Art GALLERY

(ARMA; Map p250; ☎976 659; www.armamuseum.com; Jl Raya Pengosekan; admission 50,000Rp; ⏲9am-6pm daily, Balinese dancing 3-5pm Mon-Fri, 10.30am-noon Sun) Founded by Agung Rai as a museum, gallery and cultural centre, the impressive Arma is housed in several traditional buildings set in gardens with water coursing through channels.

The only place in Bali to see haunting works by the influential German artist Walter Spies, it also features work by 19th-century Javanese artist Raden Saleh and exhibits classical Kamasan paintings, Batuan-style work from the 1930s and '40s, and works by Lempad, Affandi, Sadali, Hofker, Bonnet and Le Mayeur. The collection is well labelled in English.

Museum Rudana GALLERY

(Map p248; ☎975 779; www.museumrudana.com; admission 50,000Rp; ⏲9am-5pm) This imposing museum is the creation of local politician and art-lover Nyoman Rudana and his wife Ni Wayan Olasthini. The three floors contain over 400 traditional paintings, including a calendar dated to the 1840s, some Lempad drawings and more modern pieces. The museum is beside the Rudana Gallery, which has a large selection of paintings for sale.

Blanco Renaissance Museum ART MUSEUM

(Map p248; ☎975 502; www.blancomuseum.com; Jl Raya Campuan; admission 50,000Rp; ⏲9am-5pm) The picture of Antonio Blanco mugging with Michael Jackson says it all. His namesake Blanco Renaissance Museum captures the artist's theatrical spirit. Blanco came to Bali from Spain via the Philippines. He specialised in erotic art, illustrated poetry and playing the role of an eccentric artist à la Dali. He died in Bali in 1999, and his flamboyant home is now this museum. More prosaically: enjoy the waterfall on the way in and good views over the river.

Neka Gallery GALLERY

(Map p250; ☎975 034; Jl Raya Ubud; ⏲9am-5pm) Operated by Suteja Neka, the low-key Neka Gallery is a separate entity from the Neka Art Museum. It has an extensive selection from all the schools of Balinese art, as well as works by European residents such as the renowned Arie Smit.

Rio Helmi Gallery GALLERY

(Map p250; ☎972 304; www.riohelmi.com; Jl Suweta 5; ⏲10am-8pm) Noted photographer and Ubud resident Rio Helmi has a small gallery where you can see examples of journalistic and artistic work. Photos change often and offer beautiful insight into Helmi's travels worldwide and across Bali. His passionate pleas for the preservation of Bali in the face of massive change have appeared on the Huffington Post (www.huffingtonpost.com) and elsewhere.

Adi's Gallery GALLERY

(Map p250; ☎977 104; www.adi-s-gallery.com; Jl Bisma 102; ⏲10am-5pm) Many of the better local artists display their works here. Adi's hosts occasional special events such as live music and many popular special exhibits. The gallery is a project of German artist Adi Bachmann.

Sacred Monkey Forest Sanctuary WILDLIFE RESERVE

(Mandala Wisata Wanara Wana; Map p250; ☎971 304; Monkey Forest Rd; adult/child 20,000/10,000Rp; ⏲8.30am-6pm) This cool

Ubud Area

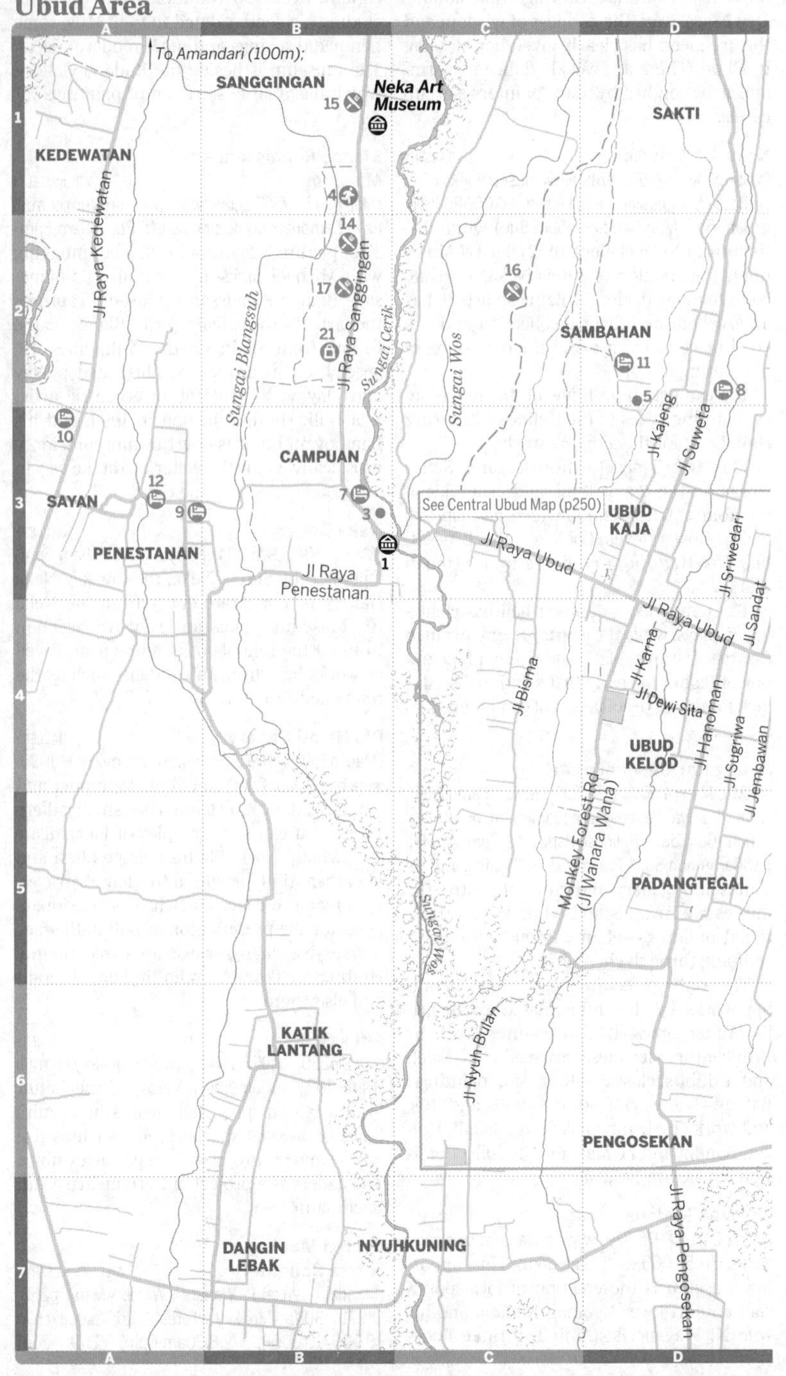
To Amandari (100m);
SANGGINGAN
Neka Art Museum
15
KEDEWATAN
Jl Raya Kedewatan
4
14
17
21
Jl Raya Sanggingan
Sungai Blangsuh
Sungai Cerik
Sungai Wos
16
SAKTI
SAMBAHAN
11
5
8
Jl Kajeng
Jl Suweta
10
CAMPUAN
SAYAN
12
9
7
3
1
See Central Ubud Map (p250)
UBUD KAJA
PENESTANAN
Jl Raya Penestanan
Jl Raya Ubud
Jl Sriwedari
Jl Sandat
Jl Karna
Jl Dewi Sita
Jl Bisma
Jl Hanoman
Jl Sugriwa
Jl Jembawan
UBUD KELOD
Monkey Forest Rd (Jl Wanara Wana)
PADANGTEGAL
Sungai Wos
Jl Nyuh Bulan
KATIK LANTANG
PENGOSEKAN
Jl Raya Pengosekan
DANGIN LEBAK
NYUHKUNING
A
B
C
D
1
2
3
4
5
6
7

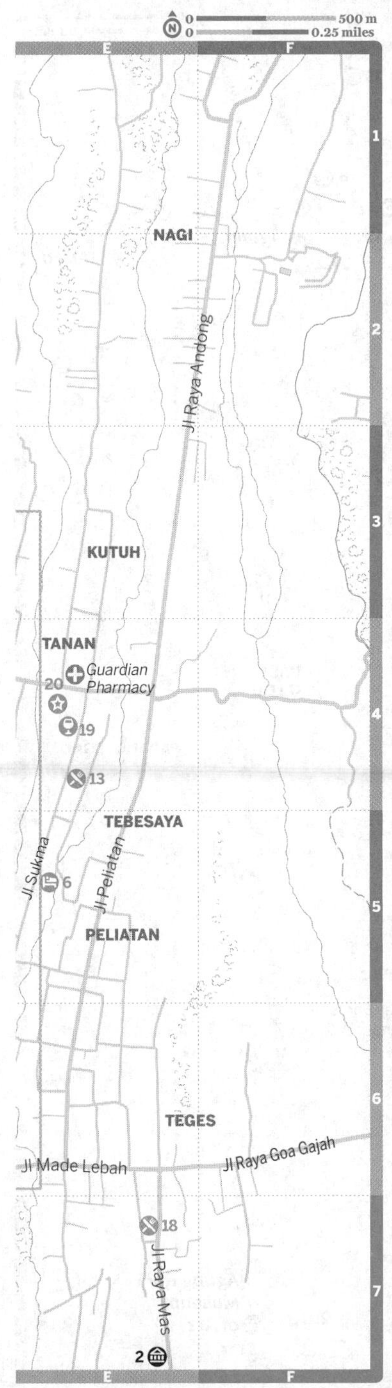

Ubud Area

Top Sights

Neka Art Museum.......B1

Sights

1 Blanco Renaissance Museum.......B3
2 Museum Rudana.......E7

Activities, Courses & Tours

3 Bali Bird Walks.......B3
4 Bali Botanica Day Spa.......B1
5 Threads of Life Indonesian Textile Arts Center.......D2
Ubud Sari Health Resort.......(see 11)

Sleeping

6 Family Guest House.......E5
7 Hotel Tjampuhan.......B3
8 Ketut's Place.......D2
9 Santra Putra.......A3
10 Sayan Terrace.......A3
11 Ubud Sari Health Resort.......D2
12 Villa Nirvana.......A3

Eating

13 Mama's Warung.......E4
14 Mozaic.......B2
15 Naughty Nuri's.......B1
16 Warung Bodag Maliah.......C2
17 Warung Pulau Kelapa.......B2
18 Warung Teges.......E7

Drinking

19 Jazz Café.......E4

Entertainment

20 Oka Kartini.......E4

Shopping

21 Bintang Supermarket.......B2

and dense swath of jungle, officially called Mandala Wisata Wanara Wana, houses three holy temples. The sanctuary is inhabited by a band of grey-haired and greedy long-tailed Balinese macaques who are nothing like the innocent-looking doe-eyed monkeys on the brochures. They are ever vigilant for passing tourists who just might have peanuts and ripe bananas available for a quick hand-out. Don't hand food directly to these creatures.

The interesting **Pura Dalem Agung** (Map p250) is in the forest and has a real Indiana Jones feel to it. Look for the Rangda figures devouring children at the entrance to the inner temple.

Central Ubud

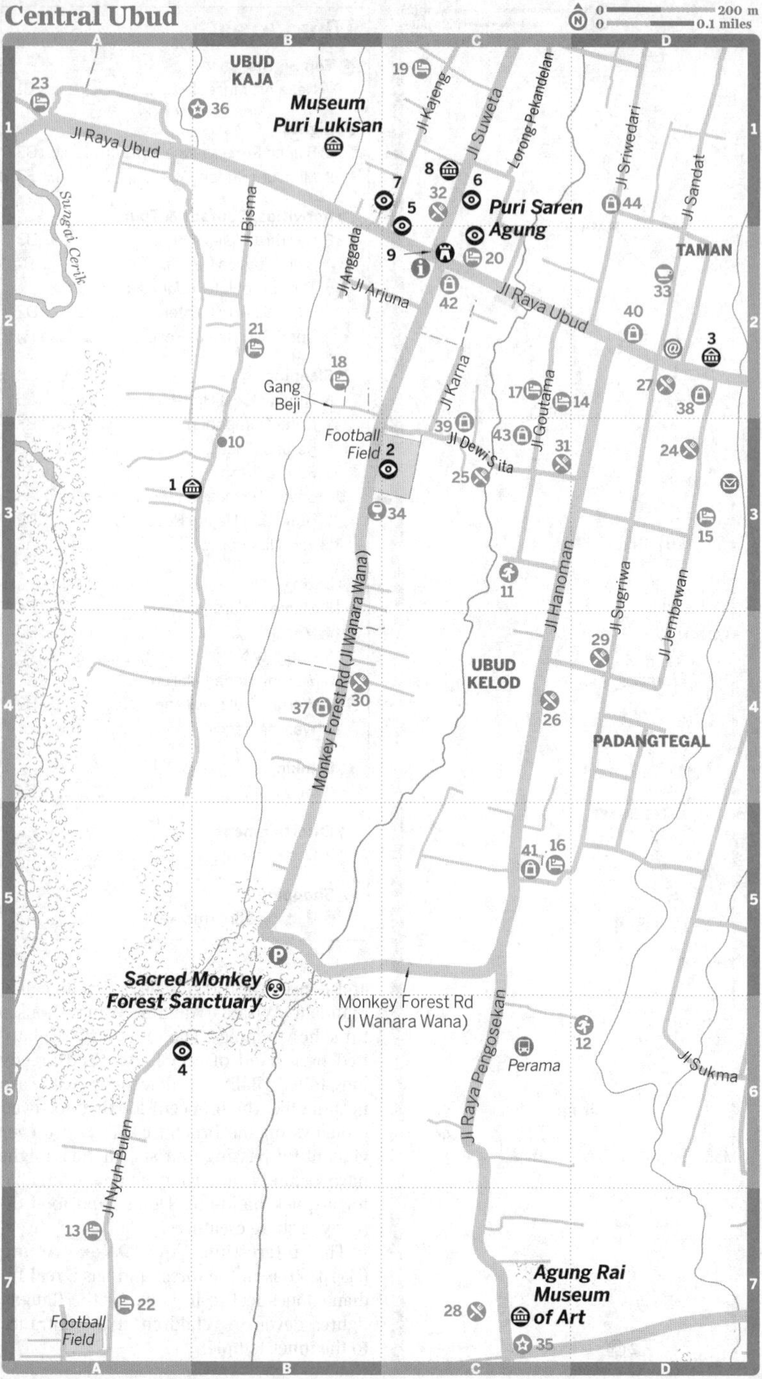

0 200 m
0 0.1 miles

UBUD KAJA
Museum Puri Lukisan
Puri Saren Agung
Jl Raya Ubud
Sungai Cerik
Jl Bisma
Jl Kajeng
Jl Suweta
Lorong Pekandelan
Jl Sriwedari
Jl Sandat
TAMAN
Jl Anggada
Jl Arjuna
Gang Beji
Football Field
Jl Karna
Jl Goutama
Jl Dewi Sita
Monkey Forest Rd (Jl Wanara Wana)
Jl Hanoman
Jl Sugriwa
Jl Jembawan
UBUD KELOD
PADANGTEGAL
Sacred Monkey Forest Sanctuary
Monkey Forest Rd (Jl Wanara Wana)
Jl Raya Pengosekan
Perama
Jl Sukma
Jl Nyuh Bulan
Football Field
Agung Rai Museum of Art

Central Ubud

Top Sights

- Agung Rai Museum of Art C7
- Museum Puri Lukisan B1
- Puri Saren Agung C2
- Sacred Monkey Forest Sanctuary B5

Sights

- 1 Adi's Gallery B3
- 2 Football Field C3
- 3 Neka Gallery D2
- 4 Pura Dalem Agung A6
- 5 Pura Desa Ubud C2
- 6 Pura Marajan Agung C1
- 7 Pura Taman Saraswati C1
- 8 Rio Helmi Gallery C1
- 9 Ubud Palace C2

Activities, Courses & Tours

- Arma .... (see 35)
- 10 Casa Luna Cooking School B3
- Nirvana Batik Course .... (see 17)
- 11 Taksu Spa C3
- 12 Yoga Barn D6

Sleeping

- 13 Alam Indah A7
- 14 Donald Homestay C2
- 15 Matahari Cottages D3
- 16 Ni Nyoman Warini Bungalows C5
- 17 Nirvana Pension & Gallery C2
- 18 Oka Wati Hotel B2
- 19 Padma Accommodation C1
- 20 Puri Saren Agung C2
- 21 Sama's Cottages B2
- 22 Swasti Cottage A7
- 23 Warwick Ibah Luxury Villas & Spa A1

Eating

- 24 Bali Buddha D3
- 25 Juice Ja Cafe C3
- 26 Kebun C4
- 27 Kué D2
- 28 Pizza Bagus C7
- 29 Sopa D4
- 30 Three Monkeys B4
- 31 Toro Sushi Café C3
- 32 Warung Ibu Oka C1

Drinking

- 33 Chillout Lounge D2
- 34 Lebong Cafe B3

Entertainment

- 35 Arma Open Stage C7
- 36 Pura Dalem Ubud B1
- Pura Taman Saraswati .... (see 7)
- Ubud Palace .... (see 9)

Shopping

- 37 Ashitaba B4
- 38 Ganesha Bookshop D2
- 39 Kou C3
- 40 Moari D2
- 41 Namaste C5
- 42 Pasar Seni C2
- 43 Sarasari C3
- 44 Smile Shop D1

Activities

Ubud brims with **salons and spas** where you can heal, pamper, rejuvenate or otherwise focus on your personal needs, physical and mental. Visiting a spa is at the top of many a traveller's itinerary and the business of spas, yoga and other treatments grows each year. Expect the latest trends from any of many practitioners (the bulletin board outside Bali Buddha is bewildering).

The nearby Sungai Ayung is the most popular river in Bali for **white-water rafting**.

TOP CHOICE **Bali Botanica Day Spa** SPA

(Map p248; ☎976 739; www.balibotanica.com; Jl Raya Sanggingan; massage from 150,000Rp; ⏲9am-8pm) Set beautifully on a lush hillside past little fields of rice and ducks, this spa offers a range of treatments including Ayurvedic ones. Like a good pesto, the herbal massage is popular. Will provide transport.

Yoga Barn YOGA

(Map p250; ☎070 992; www.balispirit.com; off Jl Raya Pengosekan; classes from 110,000Rp; ⏲7am-8pm) Listen for the serenity leeching out from these trees back near a river valley. The name exactly describes what you'll find – although this barn never needs shovelling. A huge range of classes in yoga and life-affirming offshoots are held through the week.

Ubud Sari Health Resort SPA

(Map p248; ☎974 393; www.ubudsari.com; Jl Kajeng; 1hr massage from US$15; ⏲8am-8pm) A spa

BIG CHANGES IN UBUD

As its popularity has grown, Ubud has become traffic-clogged and tourist-choked in a way that reminds both locals and visitors of – horrors! – Kuta. And day-trippers from that very place, having endured 90 minutes or more of traffic, wonder why they bothered coming.

In an effort to alleviate the traffic, deal with parked cars and give the wandering masses somewhere to dawdle, the local government announced some big plans in 2012:

» **Pasar Seni** (Art Market; Map p250; Jl Raya Ubud), the large market that has stood at the corner of Jl Raya Ubud and Monkey Forest Rd for generations, has been demolished. Long the main shopping venue for locals, in recent years it has become little more than a mass-market outlet for low-end souvenirs. The new version will have far fewer shops, supposedly higher-quality merchandise, and will face onto a large open plaza where people can rest and simply hang out.

» A three-level underground parking garage is planned for the land under the iconic **Football Field** (Map p250) in the centre of Ubud. Other parking lots will be built on the periphery, with shuttles bringing visitors into the centre.

» The central part of the main drag, Jl Raya Ubud, will be closed off to through traffic and a new bypass road built to the north of the palace.

and hotel in one, this is a serious place with extensive organic treatments bearing such names as 'total tissue cleansing'. Besides a long list of daytime spa and salon services, there are packages that include stays at the hotel. Many treatments focus on cleaning out your colon.

Taksu Spa SPA
(Map p250; ☎971 490; www.taksuspa.com; Jl Goutama; massage from 65,000Rp; ⏰9am-10pm; 📶) Somewhat hidden yet still in the heart of Ubud, Taksu has a long and rather lavish menu of treatments as well as a strong focus on yoga. There are private rooms for couples massages, a healthy cafe and a range of classes.

Bali Adventure Tours RAFTING
(☎0361-721 480; www.baliadventuretours.com; rafting trips adult/child from $79/52) Fun and exciting trips down the beautiful river valley.

Courses

Ubud is a very pleasant place to spend a few weeks developing your artistic skills, or learning about Balinese culture. Most places ask that you register in advance.

TOP CHOICE **Arma** CULTURAL
(Map p250; ☎976 659; www.armamuseum.com; Jl Raya Pengosekan; ⏰9am-6pm) A cultural powerhouse offering classes in painting, woodcarving and batik. Other courses include Balinese history, Hinduism and architecture. Classes cost US$25 to US$55.

TOP CHOICE **Casa Luna Cooking School** COOKING COURSE
(Map p250; ☎973 282; www.casalunabali.com; Jl Bisma, Honeymoon Guesthouse; classes from 300,000Rp) There are regular cooking courses at Honeymoon Guesthouse and/or Casa Luna. Half-day courses cover ingredients, cooking techniques and the cultural background of the Balinese kitchen (not all visit the market). Tours are also offered including a good one to the Gianyar night market.

Nirvana Batik Course TEXTILE
(Map p250; ☎975 415; www.nirvanaku.com; Jl Goutama 10, Nirvana Pension & Gallery; ⏰classes 10am-2pm Mon-Sat) Nyoman Suradnya teaches the highly regarded batik courses. Classes cost about US$45 to US$50 per day depending on duration (one to five days).

Threads of Life Indonesian Textile Arts Center TEXTILE
(Map p248; ☎972 187; www.threadsoflife.com; Jl Kajeng 24) Textile appreciation courses in the gallery and educational studio last from one to eight days. Some classes involve extensive travel around Bali and should be considered graduate level.

Tours

Day tours around Ubud are popular, especially ones that involve activities or themed programs.

Bali Herbal Walk WALKING TOUR
(☎975 051; www.utamaspicebali.com; walks US$18; ⏰8.30am Mon-Thu) Three-hour walks through

lush Bali landscape; medicinal and cooking herbs and plants are identified and explained in their natural environment. Includes herbal drinks. The couple behind the walks also run **Utama Spice** (www.utamaspicebali.com), which makes natural home and spa products.

Banyan Tree Cycling Tours CYCLING
(☎0813 3879 8516, 805 1620; www.banyantreebiketours.com; tours from 450,000Rp) Enjoy day-long tours of remote villages in the hills above Ubud. It's locally owned by Bagi; the tours (from 450,000Rp) emphasise interaction with villagers. Very popular.

Bali Bird Walks BIRDWATCHING
(Map p248; ☎975 009; www.balibirdwalk.com; tour US$37; ⌚9am-12.30pm Tue, Fri, Sat & Sun) Started by Victor Mason, this tour is ideal for keen birders. On a gentle morning's walk (from the former Beggar's Bush Bar) you may see up to 30 of the 100-odd local species.

Festivals & Events

One of the best places to see the many religious and cultural events celebrated in Bali each year is the Ubud area. The tourist office is unmatched for its comprehensive information on events each week.

Bali Spirit Festival (www.balispiritfestival.com) is a popular yoga, dance and music festival from the people behind the Yoga Barn. There are over 100 workshops and concerts plus a market and more. It's usually held in early April.

The **Ubud Writers & Readers Festival** (www.ubudwritersfestival.com) brings together scores of writers and readers from around the world in a celebration of writing – especially writing that touches on Bali. It is usually held in October.

Sleeping

Ubud has the best and most appealing range of places to stay in Bali, including fabled resorts, artful guesthouses and charming, simple homestays. Choices can be bewildering, so give some thought to where you want to stay.

Generally, Ubud offers good value for money at any price level. Simple accommodation within a family home compound is a cultural experience and costs around US$20. Ubud enjoys cool mountain air at night, so air-con isn't necessary, and with your windows open you'll hear the symphony of sounds from the rice fields and river valleys.

CENTRAL UBUD

There are many good-value homestays here. Hotels at all price ranges can be found on the streets north of Jl Raya Ubud, along Monkey Forest Rd, Jl Goutama (our favourite) and Jl Bisma.

TOP CHOICE **Oka Wati Hotel** HOTEL **$$**
(Map p250; ☎973 386; www.okawatihotel.com; off Monkey Forest Rd; r US$55-95; ❄📶) Oki Wati, the lovely owner, grew up near the Ubud Palace. The 19 rooms have large verandas where the delightful staff will deliver your choice of breakfast (do not miss the homemade yoghurt). The decor features vintage details such as four-poster beds; some rooms have views of a small rice field and river valley. Follow narrow footpaths to get here.

WALKS AROUND UBUD

There are lots of awe-inspiring walks to surrounding villages or through the rice paddies.

It's good to start walks at daybreak, before it gets too hot. In the walk below, distances are approximate and are measured with the Ubud Palace as the start and end point.

This 8.5km Campuan Ridge walk passes over the lush river valley of Sungai Wos, offering views of Gunung Agung and glimpses of small village communities and rice fields.

The walk leaves Jl Raya Campuan at the Warwick Ibah Luxury Villas (p255). Enter the hotel driveway and take the path to the left, where a walkway crosses the river to **Pura Gunung Lebah**. From there follow the concrete path north, climbing up onto the ridge between the two rivers.

Continuing north along the Campuan ridge, the road improves as it passes through rice paddies and the small village of **Bangkiang Sidem**. On the outskirts of the village, an unsigned road heads west, which winds down to Sungai Cerik (the west branch of Sungai Wos), then climbs steeply up to **Payogan**. From here you can walk south to the main road and on to the centre of Ubud.

TOP CHOICE **Sama's Cottages** GUESTHOUSE $$
(Map p250; ☎973 481; www.samascottagesubud.com; Jl Bisma; r 330,000-650,000Rp;) This lovely little hideaway is terraced down a hill. The 10 bungalow-style rooms have lashings of Balinese style layered on absolute simplicity. The oval pool feels like a jungle oasis. Ask for low-season discounts.

Nirvana Pension & Gallery GUESTHOUSE $
(Map p250; ☎975 415; www.nirvanaku.com; Jl Goutama 10; r 250,000-450,000Rp;) There are *alang-alang* (woven thatch) roofs, a plethora of paintings, ornate doorways and six rooms with modern bathrooms in a shady, secluded locale next to a large family temple. Batik courses are also held.

Padma Accommodation GUESTHOUSE $
(Map p250; ☎977 247; aswatama@hotmail.com; Jl Kajeng 13; r 200,000-250,000Rp) There are five very private bungalows in a tropical garden here (three are newish). Rooms are decorated with local crafts and the modern outdoor bathrooms have hot water. Nyoman Sudiarsa, a painter and family member, has a studio here and often shares his knowledge with guests.

Puri Saren Agung GUESTHOUSE $$
(Map p250; ☎975 057; Jl Suweta 1; r from US$65;) Part of the Ubud royal family's historic palace. Rooms are tucked behind the courtyard where the dance performances are held. Accommodation is in traditional Balinese pavilions, with big verandas, four-poster beds, antique furnishings and hot water. Give a royal wave to wandering tourists from your patio.

Donald Homestay HOMESTAY $
(Map p250; ☎977 156; Jl Goutama; r 200,000-250,000Rp;) The four rooms – some with hot water – are in a nice back corner of the family compound. As in many family-compound places, the chickens running around here have a date with a bamboo skewer.

PADANGTEGAL & TEBESAYA

East of central Ubud, but still conveniently located, Padangtegal has several budget lodgings along Jl Hanoman. A little further east, the quiet village of Tebesaya comprises little more than its main street, Jl Sukma, which runs between two streams. Cute homestays can be found down small footpaths.

TOP CHOICE **Matahari Cottages** GUESTHOUSE $$
(Map p250; ☎975 459; www.matahariubud.com; Jl Jembawan; r US$50-90;) This delightful place has six flamboyant, themed rooms, including the 'Batavia Princess' and the 'Indian Pasha'. The library is a vision out of a 1920s fantasy. It also boasts a self-proclaimed 'jungle jacuzzi', an upscale way to replicate the old Bali traidtion of river-bathing. There's a multicourse breakfast and high tea elaborately served on silver. And in a nod to the modern day, the hotel recycles.

Ni Nyoman Warini Bungalows HOMESTAY $
(Map p250; ☎978 364; Jl Hanoman; r 120,000-150,000Rp;) There's a whole pod of simple family compounds with rooms for rent back on a little footpath off Jl Hanoman. It's quiet, and without even trying you'll find yourself enjoying the rhythms of family life. The four rooms here have hot water and traditional bamboo furniture.

Family Guest House HOMESTAY $$
(Map p248; ☎974 054; familyhouse@telkom.net; Jl Sukma; r 250,000-600,000Rp;) There's a bit of bustle from the busy family at this charming homestay. Healthy breakfasts featuring brown bread from Café Wayan are served. The rooms have all had upgrades and most have air-con and spiffy new decor. Some also include bathtubs; and rooms at the top have a balcony with a valley view.

SAMBAHAN & SAKTI

Going north from Jl Raya Ubud, you are soon in rolling terraces of rice fields. Tucked away here you'll find interesting and often luxurious hotels, yet a beautiful walk will get you to the centre in well under an hour.

Ketut's Place GUESTHOUSE $$
(Map p248; ☎975 304; www.ketutsplace.com; Jl Suweta 40; r US$35-75; @) The nine rooms here range from basic with fans to deluxe versions with air-con and bathtub. All have artful accents and enjoy a dramatic pool shimmering down the hillside and river-valley views. On some nights, an impressive Balinese feast is served by Ketut, a local luminary.

Ubud Sari Health Resort GUESTHOUSE $$
(Map p248; ☎974 393; www.ubudsari.com; Jl Kajeng; r with fan/air-con US$60/75;) The name for the rooms at this noted health spa says it all: Zen Village. The plants in the gardens are labelled for their medicinal qualities and the cafe serves organic, vegetarian fare. Guests can use the health facilities, including the sauna and whirlpool.

NYUHKUNING

A very popular area just south of the Monkey Forest, Nyuhkuning has some creative guesthouses and hotels, yet is not a long walk to the centre.

TOP CHOICE Swasti Cottage GUESTHOUSE $$
(Map p250; ☎974 079; www.baliswasti.com; Jl Nyuh Bulan; r 500,000-950,000Rp; @🛜) One of Ubud's most inventive and appealing places to stay is just five minutes' walk from the south entrance to the Monkey Forest. Run by an egaging French-Balinese couple, this guesthouse and bungalow compound has large manicured grounds that feature a bounteous organic garden (produce is used in the excellent cafe). Some rooms are in simple two-storey blocks; others are in vintage traditional houses brought here from across Bali.

Alam Indah HOTEL $$
(Map p250; ☎974 629; www.alamindahbali.com; Jl Nyuh Bulan; r US$60-140; ❄🛜🏊) Just south of the Monkey Forest, this isolated and spacious resort has 10 rooms that are beautifully finished in natural materials to traditional designs. The Wos Valley views are entrancing, especially from the multilevel pool area. The walk in at night follows a driveway lined with tea candles.

CAMPUAN & SANGGINGAN

The long sloping road that takes its names from these two communities has a number of posh properties on its east side that overlook a lush river valley.

TOP CHOICE Warwick Ibah Luxury Villas & Spa HOTEL $$$
(Map p250; ☎974 466; www.warwickibah.com; off Jl Raya Campuan; ste US$200-300, villas US$400-600; ❄@🛜🏊) Overlooking the rushing waters and rice-clad hills of the Wos Valley, the Ibah offers refined luxury in 15 spacious, stylish individual suites and villas that combine ancient and modern details. Each could be a feature in an interior design magazine. The swimming pool is set into the hillside amid gardens and lavish stone carvings.

Hotel Tjampuhan HOTEL $$
(Map p248; ☎975 368; www.tjampuhan-bali.com; Jl Raya Campuan; r US$105-215; ❄@🛜) This venerable place overlooks the confluence of Sungai Wos and Campuan. The influential German artist Walter Spies lived here in the 1930s, and his former home, which sleeps four people (US$240), is now part of the hotel. Bungalow-style units spill down the hill and enjoy mesmerising valley views.

PENESTANAN

Just west of the Campuan bridge, steep Jl Raya Penestanan branches off to the left and climbs up and around to Penestanan, a large plateau of rice fields and lodgings. Simple rooms and bungalows in the rice fields are pitched at those seeking low-priced, longer-term lodgings. You can also get here via a steep climb up a set of concrete stairs off Jl Raya Campuan; but the reward – sweeping views and little coursing streams between the fields – is worth it.

TOP CHOICE Santra Putra GUESTHOUSE $
(Map p248; ☎977 810; karjabali@yahoo.com; off Jl Raya Campuan; r US$25-35; 🛜) Run by internationally exhibited abstract artist I Wayan Karja (whose studio-gallery is also on site), this place has nine big, open, airy rooms with hot water. Enjoy paddy-field views from all vantage points. Painting and drawing classes are offered by the artist.

Villa Nirvana BOUTIQUE HOTEL $$$
(Map p248; ☎979 419; www.villanirvanabali.com; Penestanan; r US$145-290; ❄🛜) You may find nirvana just for reaching Villa Nirvana: access is either along a 150m path through a small river valley from the west or along a rice field path that begins at the top of steep steps from the east. Obviously the compound – designed by local architect Awan Sukhro Edhi – is a retreat from daily life and you might just take up yoga on the spot.

SAYAN & AYUNG VALLEY

Two kilometres west of Ubud, the fast-flowing Sungai Ayung has carved out a deep valley, its sides sculpted into terraced paddy fields or draped in thick rainforest. Overlooking this verdant valley are some of Bali's best hotels.

TOP CHOICE Sayan Terrace HOTEL $$
(Map p248; ☎974 384; www.sayanterraceresort.com; Jl Raya Sayan; r from US$130, villas from US$250; ❄@🛜) Gaze into the Sayan Valley from this venerable hotel and you'll understand why this was the site of Colin McPhee's *A House in Bali*. Stay here while your neighbours – distant neighbours it should be said – are housed in luxury resorts paying far more. Here the 11 rooms and villas are

simply decorated but are large and have *that* view. Rates include afternoon tea.

Amandari HOTEL $$$
(☎975 333; www.amanresorts.com; ste from US$850;) In Kedewatan village, the storied Amandari does everything with charm and grace – sort of like a classical Balinese dancer. The superb views over the jungle and down to the river – the 30m green-tiled swimming pool seems to drop right over the edge – are just some of the inducements. The 30 private pavilions may prove inescapable.

Eating

Ubud's cafes and restaurants are some of the best in Bali. Local and expat chefs produce a bounty of authentic Balinese dishes, as well as inventive Asian and other international cuisines. Note: Ubud's nightlife fades fast after the last note of gamelan music; don't wait past 9pm to eat or you won't.

Good **organic farmers markets** are held each week, 9am to 1pm on Saturdays at **Pizza Bagus** (Map p250; ☎978 520; www.pizzabagus.com; Jl Raya Pengosekan; meals 40,000-100,000Rp;) and 9.30am to 2pm on Wednesdays at the Agung Rai Museum of Art (p247). Bali Buddha (p256) is another good source. And in keeping with the local ethos, organic produce is a feature on many menus.

Bintang Supermarket (Map p248; Bintang Centre, Jl Raya Campuan) is well located and has a large range of food and other essentials. The traditional **produce market** is a multi-level carnival of tropical foods and worth exploring behind the construction of the new market.

CENTRAL UBUD

TOP CHOICE **Three Monkeys** FUSION $$
(Map p250; Monkey Forest Rd; meals from 80,000Rp) Have a passionfruit-crush cocktail and settle back amid the rice field's frog symphony. Add the glow of tiki torches for a magical effect. By day there are sandwiches, salads and gelato. At night there's a fusion menu of Asian classics (the prawn rolls are a must), pasta and steaks.

Kué CAFE $
(Map p250; ☎976 7040; Jl Raya Ubud; meals 30,000-80,000Rp;) A top-end organic bakery and chocolate shop with a couple of stools downstairs; climb the side stairs for a lovely cafe that sits above the road chaos. Good baked items as well as sandwiches, organic wraps and Indo mains make it a great casual stop.

Bali Buddha CAFE $
(Map p250; Jl Jembawan 1; meals from 30,000Rp;) This breezy upper-floor place offers a full range of vegetarian *jamu* (health tonics), salads, tofu curries, savoury crepes, pizzas and gelato. It has a comfy lounging area and is candlelit at night. On the ground floor a market sells organic fruit and vegetables, wondrous blueberry muffins, breads and cookies. The bulletin board is packed with idiosyncratic Ubud notices.

Juice Ja Cafe CAFE $
(Map p250; ☎971 056; Jl Dewi Sita; snacks from 20,000Rp) Glass of spirulina? Dash of wheat grass with your papaya juice? Organic fruits and vegetables go into the food at this funky bakery-cafe. Little brochures explain the provenance of items such as the organic cashew nuts. Enjoy the patio.

Toro Sushi Café JAPANESE $
(Map p250; Jl Dewi Sita; meals from 35,000Rp) A few stray Japanese lanterns hang over the completely open front of this California-roll-sized sushi joint. But if the decor is a bit lax that's because all the effort is being expended on preparing some of Bali's best sushi. Look for daily specials.

Warung Ibu Oka BALINESE $
(Map p250; Jl Suweta; meals 30,000Rp-50,000Rp; 11am-4pm) Opposite Ubud Palace, you'll see lunchtime crowds waiting for one thing: the Balinese-style roast suckling pig (*babi guling*). Line up and find a place under the shelter for one of the most authentic meals you'll have in Ubud. Order a *spesial* to get the best cut. Get there early to avoid the day-tripping bus tours.

PADANGTEGAL & TEBESAYA

TOP CHOICE **Sopa** VEGETARIAN $
(Map p250; Jl Sugriwa 36; meals 30,000-60,000Rp;) Open air and oh so groovy, this popular place captures the Ubud vibe with creative and (more importantly) tasty vegetarian fare with a Balinese twist. Look for specials of the day on display; the ever-changing *nasi campur* (rice with a choice of side dishes) is a treat.

Kebun MEDITERRANEAN $$
(Map p250; ☎780 3801; www.kebunbistro.com; 44 Jl Hanoman; mains from 60,000Rp) Napa meets Ubud at this cute little bistro and it's a good

WORTH A TRIP

WALKING FOR ORGANIC TREATS

Looking for a fun walk of an hour or so? In a beautiful location on a plateau overlooking rice terraces and river valleys, a small cafe – **Warung Bodag Maliah** (Map p248; ☎780 1839; meals from 30,000Rp; ⏰11am-4pm) is in the middle of a big organic farm belonging to the locally popular Sari Organic brand.

Yes, the food's healthy, but more importantly, given that half the fun is getting here, the drinks are cool and refreshing. Look for a little track off Jl Raya Ubud that goes past Abangan Bungalows, then follow the signs along footpaths for another 800m.

Once you are walking through the lush rice fields, you can keep heading north as long as your interest or endurance lasts. Look for little offshoot trails to either side that lead to small rivers.

match. A long wine list (with specials) can be paired with French- and Italian-accented dishes large and small. There are daily specials including pastas and risottos. Dine inside or out on the appealing terrace.

Mama's Warung INDONESIAN $
(Map p248; Jl Sukma; dishes 10,000-20,000Rp) A real budget find among the bargain homestays of Tebesaya. Mama herself cooks up Indo classics that are spicy and redolent with garlic (the avocado salad, yum!). The freshly made peanut sauce for the sate is silky smooth.

TEGES

Jl Raya Mas which runs due south to the namesake village from Peliatan has one excellent choice for Balinese food.

TOP CHOICE **Warung Teges** BALINESE $
(Map p248; Jl Cok Rai Pudak; meals from 20,000Rp) The *nasi campur* is better here than almost anywhere else around Ubud. They get just about everything right, from the pork sausage to the chicken, the *babi guling* and even the tempeh.

CAMPUAN & SANGGINGAN

TOP CHOICE **Mozaic** FUSION $$$
(Map p248; ☎975 768; www.mozaic-bali.com; Jl Raya Sanggingan; menus from 1,250,000Rp; ⏰6-10pm Tue-Sun) Chef Chris Salans oversees this much-lauded top-end restaurant. Fine French fusion cuisine features on a constantly changing seasonal menu that takes its influences from tropical Asia. Dine in an elegant garden or ornate pavilion. Choose from four tasting menus, one of which is simply a surprise. The preparation and service are world class.

Warung Pulau Kelapa INDONESIAN $
(Map p248; Jl Raya Sanggingan; dishes 15,000Rp-30,000Rp) A popular place along the road from Campuan to Sanggingan, Kelapa has stylish takes on local classics. The surrounds are stylish as well: plenty of whitewash and antiques. Terrace tables across the wide expanse of grass are best.

Naughty Nuri's BARBECUE $$
(Map p248; ☎977 547; Jl Raya Sanggingan; meals from 80,000Rp) This legendary expat hangout packs 'em in for grilled steaks, ribs and burgers, even if all the chewing needed gets in the way of chatting. Thursday night grilled-tuna specials are ridiculously popular, making something of a party scene. Potent martinis are the real draw.

Drinking

No one comes to Ubud for wild nightlife. A few bars get lively around sunset and later in the night, but the venues often close by 11pm.

TOP CHOICE **Chillout Lounge** CAFE
(Map p250; Jl Sandat) The name says it all: chill out. Loungers spaced around a large lawn are sheltered from the street thanks to shrubs and a wall. The open-air dining area has long tables with benches. It's the perfect venue for meeting up and planning your night; linger and you can doze under the stars. Best of all the proceeds go to support the Sacred Childhoods Foundation (www.sacredchildhoods.org), a nonprofit that supports programs to help impoverished Indonesian children.

Jazz Café BAR
(Map p248; Jl Sukma 2; ⏰5pm-midnight) Ubud's most popular nightspot (and that's not faint

praise even though competition might be lacking), Jazz Café offers a relaxed atmosphere in a charming garden that features coconut palms and ferns. The menu offers a range of good Asian fusion food and you can listen to live music from Tuesday to Saturday after 7.30pm. The cocktail list is long.

Lebong Cafe BAR
(Map p250; Monkey Forest Rd) Get up, stand up, stand up for your…reggae. This nightlife hub stays open at least until midnight, with live reggae and rock most nights. A few other places good for drinks are nearby.

☆ Entertainment

Few travel experiences can be more magical than experiencing a Balinese dance performance, especially in Ubud. Cultural entertainment keeps people returning and sets Bali apart from other tropical destinations.

In a week in Ubud, you can see Kecak, Legong and Barong dances, *wayang kulit* puppets, gamelan orchestras and more.

Venues will usually host a variety of performances by various troupes through the week and aren't tied to a particular group. Nearby towns, such as Batuan, Mawang and Kutuh, also offer dance performances.

Ubud Tourist Information has performance information and sells tickets (usually 80,000Rp). For performances outside Ubud, transport is often included in the price. Tickets are also sold at many hotels, at the venues and by street vendors who hang around outside Ubud Palace – all charge the same price. To learn more about the most popular forms of dance, see p203.

You can also find shadow-puppet shows – although these are greatly attenuated from traditional performances, which often last the entire night. Regular performances are held at **Oka Kartini** (Map p248; ☎975 193; Jl Raya Ubud; tickets 50,000Rp), which has bungalows and a gallery.

Ubud Palace TRADITIONAL DANCE
(Map p250; Jl Raya Ubud) Performances are held here almost nightly against a beautiful backdrop in the palace compound, with the carvings highlighted by torches. You'll see lots of locals peeking over walls and around corners to see the shows.

Pura Dalem Ubud TRADITIONAL DANCE
(Map p250; Jl Raya Ubud) At the west end of Jl Raya Ubud, this open-air venue has a flamelit carved-stone backdrop and in many ways is the most evocative place to see a dance performance. Watch for the Semara Ratih troupe.

Pura Taman Saraswati TRADITIONAL DANCE
(Ubud Water Palace; Map p250; Jl Raya Ubud) The beauty of the setting may distract you from the dancers, although at night you can't see the lily pads and lotus flowers that are such an attraction by day.

Arma Open Stage TRADITIONAL DANCE
(Map p250; ☎976 659; Jl Raya Pengosekan) Has among the best troupes.

DANCE TROUPES: GOOD & BAD

All dance groups on Ubud's stages are not created equal. You've got true artists with international reputations and then you've got some who really shouldn't quit their day jobs. If you're a Balinese dance novice, you shouldn't worry too much about this; just pick a venue and go.

But after a few performances, you'll start to appreciate the differences in talent, and that's part of the enjoyment. Clue: if the costumes are dirty, the orchestra seems particularly uninterested and you find yourself watching a dancer and saying 'I could do that', then the group is B-level.

Some excellent troupes who regularly perform in Ubud:

Semara Ratih High-energy, creative Legong interpretations.

Gunung Sari Legong dance; one of Bali's oldest and most respected troupes.

Semara Madya Kekac dance; especially good for the hypnotic monkey chants. A mystical experience for some.

Sekaa Gong Wanita Mekar Sari An all-woman Legong troupe from Peliatan.

Tirta Sari Legong dance.

Sadha Budaya Barong dance.

Shopping

Ubud has myriad art shops, boutiques and galleries. Many offer clever and unique items made in and around the area. Ubud is the ideal base for exploring the enormous number of craft galleries, studios and workshops in villages north and south.

You can spend days in and around Ubud shopping. Jl Raya Ubud, Monkey Forest Rd, Jl Hanoman and Jl Dewi Sita should be your starting points.

The large market, Pasar Seni, which once dominated the intersection of Jl Raya Ubud and Monkey Forest Rd, has vanished under a cloud of construction.

TOP CHOICE Sarasari HANDICRAFTS
(Map p250; Jl Goutama) Wakjaka, a master of Balinese dream mask carving, works his magic in this tiny shop almost daily. Stop by, watch him work and learn about Bali's complex and rich traditions around masks.

Ganesha Bookshop BOOKS
(Map p250; www.ganeshabooksbali.com; Jl Raya Ubud) Ubud's best bookshop has an amazing amount of stock jammed into a small space; there's an excellent selection of titles on Indonesian studies, travel, arts, music, fiction (including used titles) and maps. Good staff recommendations.

Kou BEAUTY
(Map p250; Jl Dewi Sita) Luxurious locally handmade organic soaps perfume your nose as you enter. Put one in your undies drawer and smell fine for weeks. The range is unlike that found in chain stores selling luxe soap.

Ashitaba HOMEWARES
(Map p250; ☎464 922; Monkey Forest Rd) Tenganan, the Aga village of East Bali, produces the intricate and beautiful rattan items sold here (and in Seminyak). Containers, bowls, purses and more (from 50,000Rp) display the fine and intricate weaving.

Moari MUSICAL INSTRUMENTS
(Map p250; ☎977 367; Jl Raya Ubud) New and restored Balinese musical instruments are sold here. Splurge on a cute little bamboo flute for US$3.

Namaste NEW AGE
(Map p250; Jl Hanoman 64) Just the place to buy a crystal to get your spiritual house in order, Namaste is a gem of a little store with a top range of New Age supplies. Incense, yoga mats, moody instrumental music – it's all here.

Information

Along the main roads you'll find most services you need, including lots of ATMs.

@Highway (☎972 107; Jl Raya Ubud; per hr 30,000Rp; ⊙24hr; ❄📶) Full-service and very fast internet access.

Guardian Pharmacy (Jl Raya Ubud) An outlet of the large international chain.

Main Post Office (Jl Jembawan; ⊙8am-5pm) Has a sort-it-yourself poste restante system. Address poste restante mail to Kantor Pos, Ubud 80571, Bali, Indonesia.

Ubud Tourist Information (Yaysan Bina Wisata; ☎973 285; Jl Raya Ubud; ⊙8am-8pm) The one really useful tourist office in Bali. It has a good range of information and a noticeboard listing current happenings and activities. The staff can answer most regional questions and have up-to-date information on ceremonies and traditional dances held in the area; dance tickets are sold here.

Getting There & Away

Bemo

Ubud is on two bemo routes. Bemos travel from Gianyar to Ubud (10,000Rp) and larger brown bemos from Batubulan terminal in Denpasar to Ubud (13,000Rp), and then head to Kintamani via Payangan. Ubud doesn't have a bemo terminal; there are bemo stops on Jl Suweta near the market in the centre of town.

Tourist Shuttle Bus

Perama (☎973 316; Jl Hanoman; ⊙9am-9pm) is the major tourist-shuttle operator, but its terminal is inconveniently located in Padangtegal; to get to your final destination in Ubud will cost another 10,000Rp.

DESTINATION	COST (RP)	DURATION (HR)
Candidasa	50,000	1¾
Kuta	50,000	1¼
Lovina	125,000	3
Padangbai	50,000	1¼
Sanur	40,000	1

Getting Around

TO/FROM THE AIRPORT Official taxis from the airport to Ubud cost 210,000Rp. A car with driver *to* the airport will cost about the same.

BEMO Bemos don't directly link Ubud with nearby villages; you'll have to catch one going to Denpasar, Gianyar, Pujung or Kintamani and get off where you need to. The fare for a ride within the Ubud area shouldn't be more than 7000Rp.

BICYCLE Shops renting bikes have their cycles on display along the main roads; your accommodation can always arrange bike hire.

CAR & MOTORCYCLE With numerous nearby attractions, many of which are difficult to reach by bemo, hiring a vehicle is sensible. Ask at your accommodation.

TAXI There are no metered taxis based in Ubud – those that honk their horns at you have usually just dropped off passengers from southern Bali and are hoping for a fare back. Instead, you'll probably use one of the ubiquitous drivers with private vehicles hanging around on the streets hectoring passers-by (the better drivers politely hold up signs that say 'transport').

Most of the drivers are very fair; a few – often from out of the area – not so much. If you find a driver you like, get his or her number to call for rides during your stay. From central Ubud to, say, Sanggingan should cost about 40,000Rp, which is rather steep, actually. A ride from the palace to the end of Jl Hanoman should cost about 20,000Rp.

It's easy to get a ride on the back of a motorbike; rates are half those of cars.

AROUND UBUD

0361

The region east and north of Ubud has many of the most ancient monuments and relics in Bali. Some of them predate the Majapahit era and raise as yet unanswered questions about Bali's history. Others are more recent, and in other instances newer structures have been built on and around the ancient remains.

Bedulu

Bedulu was once the capital of a great kingdom. The legendary Dalem Bedaulu ruled the Pejeng dynasty from here, and was the last Balinese king to withstand the onslaught of the powerful Majapahits from Java. He was eventually defeated by Gajah Mada in 1343. The capital shifted several times after this, to Gelgel and then later to Semarapura (Klungkung).

Sights

Goa Gajah CAVE

(Elephant Cave; adult/child 10,000/5000Rp, parking 2000Rp; 8am-6pm) There were never any elephants in Bali (until tourist attractions changed that); Goa Gajah probably takes its name from the nearby Sungai Petanu, which at one time was known as Elephant River, or perhaps because the face over the cave entrance might resemble an elephant.

The cave (dating to the 11th century and rediscovered by Dutch archaeologists in 1923) is carved into a rock face and you enter through the cavernous mouth of a demon. Inside the T-shaped cave you can see fragmentary remains of the lingam, the phallic symbol of the Hindu god Shiva, and its female counterpart, the yoni, plus a statue of Shiva's son, the elephant-headed god Ganesha. In the courtyard in front of the cave are two square bathing pools with water trickling into them from waterspouts held by six female figures.

Some 2km southeast of Ubud on the road to Bedulu, a large car park with clamorous souvenir shops indicates that you've reached this popular attraction. Try to get here before 10am, when the big tourist buses begin lumbering in like, well, elephants.

Yeh Pulu HISTORIC SITE

(adult/child 10,000/5000Rp) A man having his hand munched by a boar is one of the scenes on the 25m-long carved cliff face known as Yeh Pulu, believed to be a hermitage from the late 14th century. Apart from the figure of Ganesha, the elephant-headed son of Shiva, most of the scenes deal with everyday life, although the position and movement of the figures suggests that it could be read from left to right as a story. One theory is that they are events from the life of Krishna, the Hindu god.

You can walk between here and Goa Gajah, following small paths through the paddy fields, but you might need to pay a local to guide you. By car or bicycle, look for the signs to 'Relief Yeh Pulu' or 'Villa Yeh Pulu', east of Goa Gajah.

Even if your interest in carved Hindu art is minor, this site is quite lovely and rarely will you have much company. From the entrance, it's a 300m lush, tropical walk to Yeh Pulu.

Getting There & Away

About 3km east of Teges, the road from Ubud reaches a junction where you can turn south to Gianyar or north to Pejeng, Tampaksiring and Penelokan. Any Ubud–Gianyar bemo will drop you off at the Bedulu junction, from where you can walk. Coming by bicycle is a good option.

Tampaksiring

Tampaksiring is a small village about 18km northeast of Ubud with a large and important temple and the most impressive ancient site in Bali, Gunung Kawi. It sits in the lush Pakerisan Valley.

Sights

TOP CHOICE **Gunung Kawi** MONUMENT

(adult/child 10,000/5000Rp, sarong 3000Rp, parking 2000Rp; 7am-5pm) On the northern outskirts of town, a sign points east off the main road to Gunung Kawi and its ancient monuments. From the end of the access road, a steep stone stairway leads down to the river, at one point cutting through an embankment of solid rock. There, in the bottom of this lush green river valley, is one of Bali's oldest and largest ancient monuments.

Gunung Kawi consists of 10 rock-cut *candi* (shrines) – memorials cut out of the rock face in imitation of actual statues. They stand in awe-inspiring 8m-high sheltered niches cut into the sheer cliff face. A solitary *candi* stands about 1km further down the valley to the south; this is reached by a trek through the rice paddies on the western side of the rushing river. Be prepared for long climbs up and down – it is over 270 steps, although these are broken up into sections and at times the views as you walk through ancient terraced rice fields are as fine as any in Bali.

Each *candi* is believed to be a memorial to a member of the 11th-century Balinese royalty, but little is known for certain. Legends relate that the whole group of memorials was carved out of the rock face in one hard-working night by the mighty fingernails of Kebo Iwa.

As you wander between monuments, temples, offerings, streams and fountains, you can't help but feel a certain ancient majesty here.

Tirta Empul MONUMENT

(adult/child 10,000/5000Rp, parking 2000Rp; 8am-6pm) A well-signposted fork in the road north of Tampaksiring leads to the popular holy springs at Tirta Empul, discovered in AD 962 and believed to have magical powers. The springs bubble up into a large, crystal-clear pool within the temple and gush out through waterspouts into a bathing pool – they're the main source of Sungai Pakerisan (Pakerisan River), the river that rushes by Gunung Kawi only 1km or so away. Next to the springs, Pura Tirta Empul is one of Bali's most important temples.

Come in the early morning or late afternoon to avoid the tourist buses. You can also use the clean, segregated and free public baths here.

Getting There & Away

Tampaksiring is an easy day trip from Ubud, or a stop between Ubud and Danau Batur. Tirta Empul and Gunung Kawi are easy to find along the Penelokan to Ubud road, and are only about 1.5km apart.

North of Ubud

Abused and abandoned logging elephants from Sumatra have been given refuge in Bali at the **Elephant Safari Park** (721 480; www.baliadventuretours.com; tour incl transport adult/child US$66/44; 8am-6pm). Located in the

DON'T MISS

BALI'S CHOCOLATE FACTORY

You might think Swiss or Belgian when you think chocolate but soon you could be thinking Bali. **Big Tree Farms** (846 3327; www.bigtreefarms.com; Sibang), a local producer of quality foodstuffs that has made a big splash internationally, has built a chocolate factory about 10km southwest of Ubud in the village of Sibang.

And this not just any factory, rather it is a huge and architecturally stunning creation made sustainably from bamboo – an ethos that extends to the company's very philosophy. The chocolate made here comes from cocoa beans grown by over 13,000 farmers across Indonesia.

Just seeing one of the world's largest bamboo structures is an attraction in itself – toss in fabulous chocolate and you've got a great tour.

Reaching the factory is easy as Sibang is on one of the roads linking Ubud to south Bali.

cool, wet highlands of **Taro** (14km north of Ubud), the park is home to almost 30 elephants. Besides seeing a full complement of exhibits about elephants, you can ride an elephant for an extra fee. The park has received praise for its conservation efforts; however, be careful that you don't end up at one of the rogue parks, designed to divert the unwary to unsanctioned displays of elephants.

The usual road from Ubud to Batur is through Tampaksiring, but there are other lesser roads up the gentle mountain slope. One of the most attractive goes north from Peliatan, past Petulu and its birds, and through the rice terraces between Tegallalang and Ceking, to bring you out on the crater rim between Penelokan and Batur. It's a sealed road all the way and you also pass through **Sebatu**, which has all manner of artisans tucked away in tiny villages.

The one off-note will be **Pujung**, where the rice terraces are beautiful but have attracted a strip of ugly tourist traps overlooking them.

South of Ubud

The road between South Bali and Ubud is lined with places making and selling handicrafts. Many visitors shop along the route as they head to Ubud, sometimes by the busload, but much of the craftwork is actually done in small workshops and family compounds on quiet back roads.

For serious shopping and real flexibility in exploring these villages, it's worth hiring or chartering your own transport, so you can explore the back roads and carry your purchases without any hassles. Note that your driver may receive a commission from any place you spend your money – this can add 20% to 30% or more to the cost of purchases. Also, drivers might try to steer you to workshops or artisans that they favour rather than those of most interest to you.

The following places are presented in the order you'll encounter them on the way to Ubud from the south.

BALI BIRD PARK & RIMBA REPTILE PARK

More than 1000 birds from 250 species flit about this **bird park** (☎299 352; www.bali-bird-park.com; bird & reptile parks adult/child US$25/12.50; ⏲9am-5.30pm), including rare *cendrawasih* (birds of paradise) from West Papua and the all-but-vanished Bali starlings. Many of these birds are housed in special walk-through aviaries; in one of them you follow a walk at tree-level, or what some with feathers might say is bird-level. The 2 hectares of landscaped gardens feature a fine collection of tropical plants.

Next door, **Rimba Reptile** (☎299 344) has about 20 species of creatures from Indonesia and Africa, as well as turtles, crocodiles, a python and a solitary Komodo dragon. The parks are popular with kids; allow at least two hours.

SUKAWATI

Sukawati is a centre for the manufacture of wind chimes, temple umbrellas and masks. It has a busy **craft market** in an obvious, two-storey building on the main road – bemos stop right outside. Every type of quality craftwork and touristy trinket is on sale, at cheap prices for those who bargain hard. Across the road is the colourful morning produce market, with the old royal palace behind; it's worth a stop.

Wayang kulit and *topeng* (masks) are also made in the backstreets of Sukawati and in **Puaya**, about 1km northwest of the main road.

MAS

Mas means 'gold', but **woodcarving**, particularly mask carving, is the craft practised here. The road through Mas is lined with craft shops for the tour-busloads, but there are plenty of smaller carving operations in the back lanes. Historically, carving was limited to temple decorations, dance masks and musical instruments, but in the 1930s carvers began to depict people and animals. Today it's hard to resist the oodles of winsome creatures produced here.

Setia Darma House of Masks and Puppets (☎977 404; Jl Tegal Bingin; admission by donation; ⏲8am-4pm) is both the newest and one of the best museums in the Ubud area. Over 4600 ceremonial masks and puppets from Indonesia and across Asia are beautifully displayed in a series of renovated historic buildings. The museum is about 2km northeast of the main Mas crossroads.

North of the Mas, the galleries become ever-more glitzy as you near Ubud.

EAST BALI

The eastern side of Bali is dominated by the mighty Gunung Agung, the 'navel of the world' and Bali's 'mother mountain'. The

East Bali

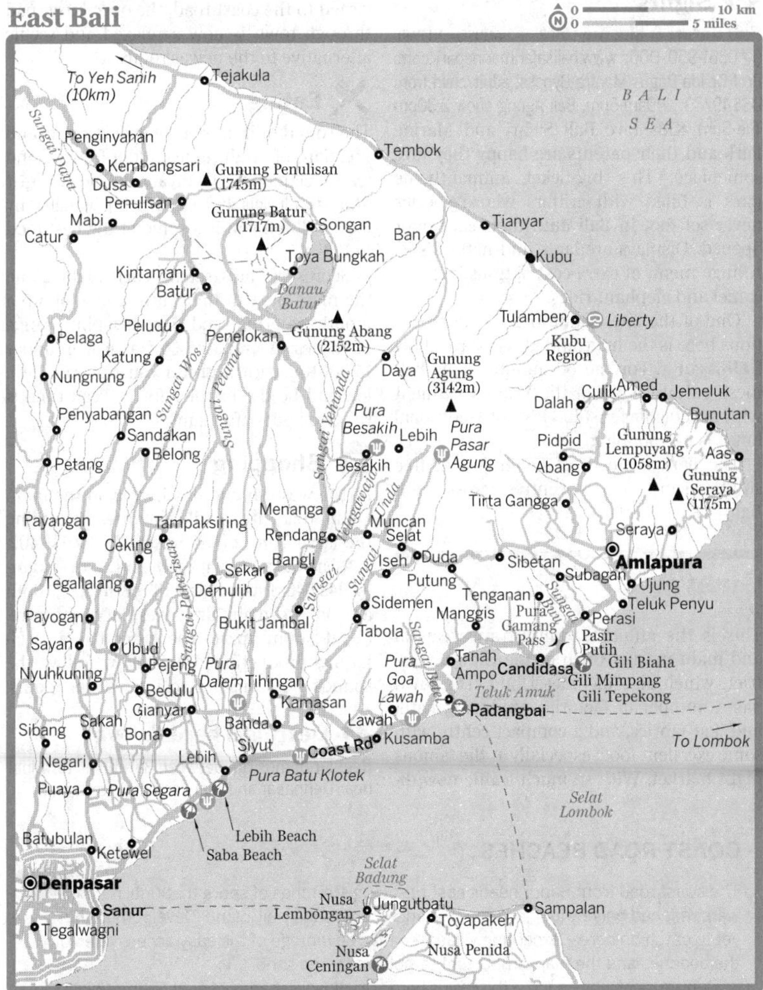

slopes of this and the other peaks at this end of the island hold some of the most verdant rice fields and tropical vistas you can imagine. It's a good place to have your own transport, as you can simply 'get lost' wandering side roads and revel in the exquisite scenery.

The coast is dotted with beaches, many rough, rugged and untrammelled. Add in some ancient cultural sites and the popular areas of Sideman, Padangbai and Amed, and you have an area that will lure you from the South Bali–Ubud juggernaut.

Coast Road To Kusamba

Bali's coast road, running from just north of Sanur east to a junction past **Kusamba**, is a great way to reach scores of uncrowded beaches. The road (formally the Prof Dr Ida Bagus Mantra Bypass – named for a popular 1980s Balinese governor who did much to promote culture) has brought Padangbai, Candidasa, and other points to the east, closer to south Bali by one or two hours. Much of the region is now an easy day trip, depending on traffic.

Sights

Bali Safari & Marine Park AMUSEMENT PARK

(☎0361-950 000; www.balisafarimarinepark.com; Prof Dr Ida Bagus Mantra Bypass; adult/child from US$49/39; ⏰9am-5pm, Bali Agung show 2.30pm Tue-Sun) Kids love Bali Safari and Marine Park and their parents are happy they love someplace. This big-ticket animal-theme park is filled with critters whose species never set foot in Bali until their cage door opened. Displays are large and naturalistic. A huge menu of extra-cost options includes camel and elephant rides.

One of the latest additions to the attractions here is the huge and glossy stage show **Bali Agung**. For the 60-minute show, Balinese culture is given the Vegas treatment with spectacular results. It's not traditional but it is eye-popping.

The park is north of Lebih Beach; free shuttles run to tourist centres across south Bali.

Gianyar

☎0361

This is the affluent administrative capital and main market town of the Gianyar district, which also includes Ubud. The town has a number of factories producing batik and ikat fabrics, and a compact centre with some excellent food, especially at the famous night market. With so much traffic now diverted to the coast road, the once-busy road through town is now a relaxed and scenic alternative to the newer route.

Eating

The sound of hundreds of cooking pots and the glare of bright lights add a frenetic and festive clamour to Gianyar's delicious **Night Market** (Jl Ngurah Rai; ⏰5-11pm), which any local will tell you has some of the best food in Bali.

Scores of stalls set up each night along the main drag in the centre and cook up a mouth-watering and jaw-dropping range of dishes. Average cost of a dish is under 15,000Rp; with a group you can sample a lot, and be the happier for it. Peak time is the two hours after sunset.

Shopping

At the western end of Gianyar on the main Ubud road are textile factories, including the large **Tenun Ikat Setia Cili** (☎943 409; Jl Astina Utara; ⏰9am-5pm) and **Cap Togog** (☎943 046; Jl Astina Utara 11; ⏰8am-5pm). Both are on the main drag west of the centre, about 500m apart. The latter has a fascinating production area below, follow the sounds of dozens of clacking wooden looms.

Getting There & Away

Regular bemos run between Batubulan terminal near Denpasar and Gianyar's main terminal

COAST ROAD BEACHES

The coast road from Sanur heads east past long stretches of shore that until recently were reached only by long and narrow lanes from roads well inland. Development has yet to catch on here – excepting villas – so take advantage of the easy access to enjoy the beaches and the many important temples near the sand.

Don't expect white sand – the grains here are volcanic shades of grey. Swimming in the often pounding surf is dangerous. You'll need your own transport to reach these beaches. Except where noted, services are few, so bring your own drinking water and towels.

These beaches, from west to east, are recommended:

Saba Beach Has a small temple, covered shelters, a shady parking area and a short, junglelike drive from the coast road; it's about 12km east of Sanur.

Pura Masceti Beach About 15km east of Sanur with a few drink vendors. Pura Masceti is one of Bali's nine directional temples. It is right on the beach and is both architecturally significant and enlivened with gaudy statuary.

Lebih Has sand composed of mica that sparkles with a billion points of light. There are a couple of cafes. The large Sungai Pakerisan, which starts near Tampaksiring, reaches the sea near here. The impressive Pura Segara looks across the strait to Nusa Penida.

Pura Klotek Beach Has very fine black sand. The quiet at Pura Batu Klotek belies its great significance. Sacred statues are brought here from Pura Besakih for ritual cleansing.

(15,000Rp), which is behind the main market. Bemos to and from Ubud (10,000Rp) use the bemo stop across the road from the main market.

A driver from Ubud will charge 100,000Rp for a night-market excursion.

Bangli

☎0366

Halfway up the slope to Penelokan, Bangli – once the capital of a kingdom – has an interesting temple and cultural centre, though if there's no ceremony or festival happening, it's pretty quiet.

Sights

Pura Kehen TEMPLE

(adult/child 10,000/5000Rp; ⏰9am-5pm) The state temple of the Bangli kingdom, Pura Kehen, one of the finest temples in eastern Bali, is a miniature version of Pura Besakih. It is terraced up the hillside, with a flight of steps leading to the beautifully decorated entrance. The first courtyard has a huge banyan tree with a *kulkul* (alarm drum made from a hollow tree-trunk) entwined in its branches. Chinese porcelain plates were set into the walls as decoration, but most of the originals have been damaged or lost. The inner courtyard has an 11-roof *meru* (shrine), and there are other shrines with thrones for the Hindu trinity – Brahma, Shiva and Vishnu. The carvings are particularly intricate. See if you can count all 43 altars.

Pura Dalem Penunggekan TEMPLE

The exterior wall of this fascinating temple of the dead features vivid relief carvings of wrongdoers getting their just desserts in the afterlife. One panel addresses the lurid fate of adulterers (men, in particular, may find the viewing uncomfortable). Other panels portray sinners as monkeys, while another is a good representation of evildoers begging to be spared the fires of hell. It's to the south of the centre.

Semarapura (Klungkung)

☎0366

A tidy regional capital, Semarapura should be on your itinerary for its fascinating Kertha Gosa complex, a relic of Bali from the time before the Dutch. Once the centre of Bali's most important kingdom, Semarapura is still commonly called by its old name, Klungkung.

It's a good place to stroll and get a feel for modern Balinese life. The markets are large, the shops many and the streets are almost pleasant now that the coast road has diverted a lot of the traffic away.

Sights

Semara Pura Complex LANDMARK

(adult/child 12,000/6000Rp, parking 1000Rp; ⏰7am-6pm) When the Dewa Agung dynasty moved here in 1710, a new palace, the Semara Pura, was established. Most of the original palace and grounds were destroyed during Dutch attacks in 1908, and the **Pemedal Agung**, the gateway on the southern side of the square, is all that remains of the palace itself – the carved wooden doors are beautiful.

Kertha Gosa

The **Hall of Justice** was effectively the supreme court of the Klungkung kingdom, where disputes and cases that could not be settled at the village level were brought. This open-sided pavilion is a superb example of Klungkung architecture, and its ceiling is covered with fine paintings in the Klungkung style. The paintings, done on asbestos sheeting, were installed in the 1940s, replacing cloth paintings that had deteriorated.

Bale Kambang

The ceiling of the beautiful **Floating Pavilion** is painted in Klungkung style. As in the Kertha Gosa, the different rows of paintings deal with different subjects. The first row is based on the astrological calendar; the second on the folk tale of Pan and Men Brayut and their 18 children; and the upper rows on the adventures of the hero Sutasona.

Museum Semarajaya

This recently renovated **museum** has an interesting collection of archaeological and other pieces. There are exhibits of *songket* weaving, salt-making, palm toddy and palm-sugar extraction, and a display about the 1908 *puputan*, along with some interesting old photos.

Market MARKET

(Jl Diponegoro) Semarapura's sprawling market is one of the best in East Bali. It's a vibrant hub of commerce and a meeting place for people of the region. You can easily spend an hour wandering about the warren of stalls as well as shops on nearby streets. It has some excellent food stalls.

Getting There & Away

The best way to visit Semarapura is with your own transport and as part of a circuit taking in other sites up the mountains and along the coast.

Bemos from Denpasar (Batubulan terminal) pass through Semarapura (13,000Rp) on the way to points further east. They can be hailed from near the Puputan Monument.

Sidemen Road

☎0366

Winding through one of Bali's most beautiful river valleys, the Sidemen road offers marvellous paddy-field scenery, a delightful rural character and extraordinary views of Gunung Agung (when the clouds permit). The region is becoming more popular every year as a verdant escape, where a walk in any direction is a communion with nature.

There are many **walks** through the rice fields and streams in the multihued green valley. One involves a spectacular 2½-hour climb up to **Pura Bukit Tageh**, a small temple with big views. No matter where you stay, you'll be able to arrange guides for in-depth trekking (about 50,000Rp per hour), or just set out on your own exploration.

Sleeping

Views throughout the area are sweeping, from terraced green hills to Gunung Agung. Most inns have cafes; it can get cool and misty at night.

Near the centre of Sidemen, a small road heads west for 500m to a fork and a signpost with the names of many places to stay.

TOP CHOICE **Samanvaya** INN $$
(☎082 147 103 884; www.samanvaya-bali.com; r US$70-100;) Just opened in 2012, this attractive inn has sweeping views over the rice fields all the way south to the ocean. The owners, an energetic couple from the UK. are dedicated to promoting the Sideman area, especially its culture. The individual units have thatched roofs and deep, wooden terraces. The infinity pool is a dream and the cafe has a long list of Asian and Western dishes.

Pondok Wisata Lihat Sawah GUESTHOUSE $
(☎530 0516; www.lihatsawah.com; r 300,000-1,000,000Rp) Take the right fork in the road to this guesthouse with lavish gardens. All 12 rooms have views of the valley and mountain (all have hot water – nice after a morning hike – and the best have lovely wooden verandas); there are also three private bungalows. Water courses through the surrounding rice fields. A cafe offering Thai and Indo menu items shares the views (dishes 13,000Rp to 30,000Rp). It's worth stopping here just for their useful map of the area.

Darmada GUESTHOUSE $$
(☎0853 3803 2100; www.darmadabali.com; r from 500,000Rp;) Beautifully set in a small river valley on spacious, lush grounds, this new guesthouse has four stylish rooms set in two villas. There is a large pool amidst the palms lined with tiles in gentle shades of green. Rooms are mostly done in shades of white and have hammocks on the patio near the babbling waters. The small cafe has food made with vegetables grown on the grounds.

Pura Besakih

Perched nearly 1000m up the side of Gunung Agung is Bali's most important temple, **Pura Besakih** (admission per person 10,000Rp plus per vehicle 5000Rp). In fact, it is an extensive complex of 23 separate-but-related temples, with the largest and most important being Pura Penataran Agung. Unfortunately, many people find it a deeply disappointing experience due to the avarice of numerous local characters (see p267).

Sights

The largest and most important temple is **Pura Penataran Agung**. It is built on six levels, terraced up the slope, and the entrance is approached from below by ascending a flight of steps. This entrance is an imposing *candi bentar* (split gateway); beyond it, the even more impressive *kori agung* is the gateway to the second courtyard. Note that tourists are not allowed inside this temple.

The other Besakih temples – all with individual significance and often closed to visitors – are markedly less scenic. Just as each village in Bali has a *pura puseh* (temple of origin), *pura desa* (village temple) and *pura dalem* (temple of the dead), Pura Besakih has three temples that fulfil these roles for Bali as a whole – Pura Basukian, Pura Penataran Agung and Pura Dalem Puri, respectively.

When it's mist-free, the view down to the coast is sublime.

AN UNHOLY EXPERIENCE

So intrusive are the scams and irritations faced by visitors to Besakih that many wish they had skipped the complex altogether. What follows are some of the ploys you should be aware of before a visit.

Near the main parking area at the bottom of the hill is a building where guides hang around looking for visitors. Guides here are likely to tell you emphatically that you need their services and quote a ridiculously high price of US$25 for a short visit. You don't: you can always walk among the temples, and no 'guide' can get you into a closed temple.

Other 'guides' may foist their services on you throughout your visit. There have been reports of people agreeing to a guide's services only to be hit with a huge fee at the end.

Once inside the complex, you might receive offers to 'come pray with me'. Visitors who seize on this chance to get into a forbidden temple can face demands of 100,000Rp or more.

Information

The temple's main entrance is 2km south of the complex on the road from Menanga and the south.

About 200m past the ticket office, there is a fork in the road with a sign indicating Besakih to the right and Kintamani to the left. Go left, because going to the right puts you in the main parking area at the bottom of a hill some 300m from the complex. Going past the road to Kintamani, where there is another ticket office, puts you in the north parking area only 20m from the complex, and away from scammers at the main entrance.

Getting There & Away

The best way to visit is with your own transport, which allows you to explore the many gorgeous drives in the area.

Rendang to Amlapura Road

A scenic road goes around the southern slopes of Gunung Agung from **Rendang** to near **Amlapura**. It runs through some superb countryside, descending more or less gradually as it goes further east.

Starting in the west, Rendang is an attractive town that is easily reached either by bemo from Semarapura or via a particularly pretty minor road from Bangli. Siutated about 4km along a winding road is the old-fashioned village of **Muncan** with its quaint shingle roofs.

The road then passes through some of the most attractive rice country in Bali before reaching **Selat**, where you turn north to get to Pura Pasar Agung, a starting point for climbing Gunung Agung.

Further on is **Duda**, where the scenic Sidemen road branches southwest to Semarapura.

Continuing east, **Sibetan** is famous for growing *salak,* the delicious fruit with a curious 'snakeskin' covering, which you can buy between December and April. *Salak* are the spiky low palm trees you'll see, and the fruit grows in clusters at the base of the trunks. This is one of the villages you can visit with **JED** (Village Ecotourism Network; ☎0361-366 9951; www.jed.or.id; tours from US$75).

Gunung Agung

Bali's highest and most revered mountain, Gunung Agung is an imposing peak seen from most of South and East Bali, although it's often obscured by cloud and mist. Many references give its height as 3142m, but some say it lost its top in the 1963 eruption and opinion varies as to the real height. The summit is an oval crater, about 700m across, with its highest point on the western edge above Besakih.

Activities

It's possible to **climb** Agung from various directions. The two shortest and most popular routes are from Pura Besakih, on the southwest side of the mountain, and from Pura Pasar Agung, on the southern slopes.

Guides

Trips with guides on either of the routes up Gunung Agung generally include breakfast and other meals as well as a place to stay, but be sure to confirm all details in advance. Guides are also able to arrange transport.

Most of the places to stay in the region, including those at Selat, along the Sidemen road and Tirta Gangga, will recommend guides for

CLIMBING GUNUNG AGUNG

» Use a guide.

» Respect your guide's pauses at shrines for prayers on the sacred mountain.

» Get to the top before 8am – the clouds that often obscure the view of Agung also obscure the view from Agung.

» Take a strong torch (flashlight), extra batteries, plenty of water (2L per person), snack food, waterproof clothing and a warm jumper (sweater).

» The descent is especially hard on your feet, so wear strong shoes or boots and have manicured toes.

» Climb during the dry season (April to September); July to September are the most reliable months. At other times the paths can be slippery and dangerous and the views are clouded over (especially true in January and February).

» Climbing Gunung Agung is not permitted when major religious events are being held at Pura Besakih, which generally includes most of April.

Gunung Agung climbs. Expect to pay a negotiable 450,000Rp to 1,000,000Rp for one or two people for your climb.

The following guides are recommended:

Gung Bawa Trekking GUIDE
(☎0812 387 8168; www.gungbawatrekking.com) Experienced and reliable.

Ketut Uriada GUIDE
(☎0812 364 6426; ketut.uriada@gmal.com) This knowledgeable guide can arrange transport for an extra fee (look for his small sign on the road east of Muncan).

Wayan Tegteg GUIDE
(☎0813 3852 5677; tegtegwayan@yahoo.co.id) Wins reader plaudits.

From Pura Pasar Agung

This route involves the least walking, because **Pura Pasar Agung** (Agung Market Temple) is high on the southern slopes of the mountain (around 1500m) and can be reached by a good road north from Selat. From the temple you can climb to the top in three or four hours, but be aware it is still very demanding, as one reader wrote: 'it's a relentless up, up, up, followed by down, down, down'.

Start climbing from the temple at around 3am. There are numerous slippery trails through the pine forest but after an hour or so you'll climb above the treeline. Then you're climbing on solidified lava, which can be loose and broken in places, but a good guide will keep you on solid ground. At the top (2900m), you can gawk into the crater, watch the sun rise over Lombok and see the shadow of Agung in the morning haze over southern Bali, but you can't make your way to the very highest point and you won't be able to see central Bali.

Allow at least six hours total for this trek.

From Pura Besakih

This climb is much tougher than the already demanding southern approach and is only for the very physically fit. For the best chance of a clear view before the clouds close in, you should start at midnight. Allow at least six hours for the climb, and four to six hours for the descent. The starting point is Pura Pengubengan, northeast of the main temple complex; attempting this without a guide would be folly.

Kusamba to Padangbai

A small road at the east end of the new coast road from Sanur goes south to **Kusamba**, a fishing and salt-making village, where you'll see lines of colourful fishing *perahu* (boats) lined up on the beach. Fishing is normally done at night and the 'eyes' on the front of the boats help navigation through the darkness. The thatched roofs of salt-making huts can be seen along the beach.

Sights

Pura Goa Lawah CAVE
(Bat Cave Temple; adult/child 10,000/5000Rp, car park 2000Rp; ⏰8am-6pm) Three kilometres east of Kusamba is Pura Goa Lawah, one of nine directional temples in Bali. The cave in the cliff face is packed, crammed and jammed full of bats, and the complex is equally overcrowded with tour groups, foreign

and local. You might exclaim 'Holy bat guano, Batman!' when you get a whiff of the odours emanating from the cave. Superficially, the temple is small and unimpressive, but it is very old and of great significance to the Balinese.

Legend says the cave leads all the way to Pura Besakih, some 19km away, but it's unlikely that you'd want to try this route. The bats provide sustenance for the legendary giant snake, the deity Naga Basuki, which is also believed to live in the cave.

Padangbai

☎0363

There's a real backpacker vibe about this funky little beach town that sits on a small bay and has a nice little curve of beach. It is also the port for the public ferry and fast boats connecting Bali with Lombok and the Gilis.

Padangbai is on the upswing. It has a whole compact seaside travellers scene with cheap places to stay and some funky and fun cafes. The pace is slow but, should ambition strike, there's good snorkelling and diving, some easy walks and a couple of great beaches.

Sights

Padangbai is interesting for a stroll. At the west end of town near the post office there's a small **mosque** and a temple, **Pura Desa**. Towards the middle of town are two more temples, **Pura Dalem** (Gang Segara II) and **Pura Segara**, and the **central market** (Jl Silayukti), which is home to numerous vendors and cafes.

Blue Lagoon Beach BEACH

On a headland at the northeast corner of the bay, a path uphill leads to three temples. On the other side is the small, light-sand Blue Lagoon Beach.

Activities

Diving

There is good diving on the coral reefs around Padangbai, but the water can be a bit cold and visibility is not always ideal. The most popular local dives are **Blue Lagoon** and **Teluk Jepun**, both in Teluk Amuk, the bay just east of Padangbai. There's a good range of soft and hard corals and varied marine life, including sharks, turtles and wrasse, and a 40m wall at Blue Lagoon.

Many local outfits offer diving trips in the area, including to Gili Tepekong and Gili Biaha, and on to Tulamben and Nusa Penida. All dive prices are competitive, costing from US$55 for dives in the area to US$110 for trips out to Nusa Penida.

Geko Dive DIVING

(☎41516; www.gekodive.com; Jl Silayukti) The longest-established operator; has a nice cafe across from the beach.

Water Worx DIVING

(☎41220; www.waterworxbali.com; Jl Silayukti) Another good dive operator.

Snorkelling

One of the best and most accessible walk-in snorkel sites is off Blue Lagoon Beach (p269). Note that it is subject to strong currents when the tide is out. Other sites, such as **Teluk Jepun** (Jepun Bay), can be reached by local boat (or check with the dive operators to see if they have any room on their dive boats). Snorkel sets cost about 30,000Rp per day.

Local *jukung* (small sampans) offer snorkelling trips (bring your own gear) around Padangbai (50,000Rp per person per hour) and as far away as Nusa Lembongan (400,000Rp for two passengers).

Sleeping

Accommodation in Padangbai – like the town itself – is pretty laid-back. Prices are fairly cheap and it's pleasant enough; there's no need to hurry off on a boat if you want to hang out on the beach and in cafes with other travellers.

The tiny village area has some family-run guesthouses. Slightly more substantial hotels are in a row by the narrow beach.

Bloo Lagoon Village HOTEL $$$

(☎41211; www.bloolagoon.com; r from US$140; ❄@☜) Perched above Blue Lagoon Beach, the 25 cottages and villas here are all designed in traditional thatched style and the compound is dedicated to sustainable practices. Units come with one, two or three bedrooms and are well thought out and stylish.

Topi Inn GUESTHOUSE $

(☎41424; www.topiinn.com; Jl Silayukti; r from 120,000Rp; @☜) Sitting at the east end of the strip in a serene location, Topi has five pleasant rooms, some of which share bathrooms. The cafe is excellent for breakfast.

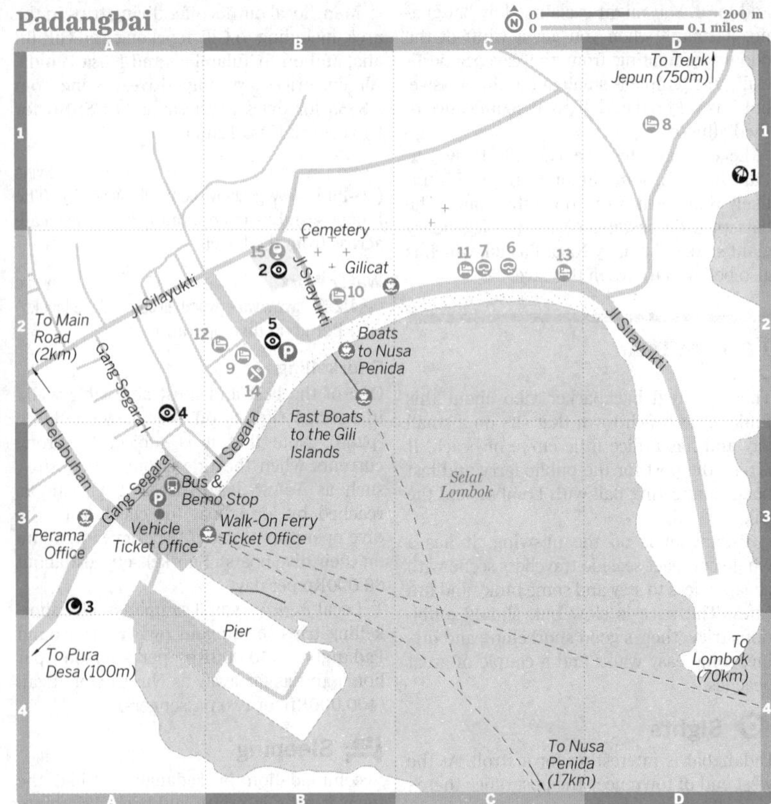

Padangbai Beach Resort HOTEL $$
(☎41417; www.padang-bai-beach-resort.com; Jl Silayukti; r US$55-85; ❄📶🏊) The bungalows are attractive, with open-air bathrooms, in a classic Balinese garden setting that has a large pool across from the beach. All 24 rooms have air-con and the ones in front have pleasant beach views.

Pondok Wisata Parta GUESTHOUSE $
(☎41475, 0817 975 2668; off Gang Segara III; r 1500,000-350,000Rp; ❄📶) The pick of the nine rooms in this hidden and snoozy spot is the 'honeymoon room', which has a harbour view and good breezes. The most expensive rooms have air-con, a common terrace and views.

Kembar Inn GUESTHOUSE $
(☎41364; kembarinn@hotmail.com; near Gang Segara III; r 100,000-250,000Rp; ❄📶) There are 11 rooms with hot water (some with fans) at this inn, linked by a steep and narrow staircase. The best awaits at the top and has a private terrace with views.

Eating & Drinking

Beach fare and backpacker staples are what's on offer in Padangbai – lots of fresh seafood, Indonesian classics, pizza and, yes, banana pancakes.

Babylon Bar (Jl Silayukti) and **Kinky Reggae Bar** (Jl Silayukti) are tiny adjoining bars in the market area back off the beach. They have a few chairs, tables and pillows scattered about and are perfect places to while away the evening with new friends.

TOP CHOICE **Topi Inn** CAFE $
(☎41424; Jl Silayukti; mains 20,000-40,000Rp) Juices, shakes and good coffees are served throughout the day. Breakfasts are big, and whatever is landed by the fishing boats outside the front door during the day is grilled by night. The seats right out on the

Padangbai

Sights

1 Blue Lagoon Beach D1
2 Market B2
3 Mosque A3
4 Pura Dalem A2
5 Pura Segara B2

Activities, Courses & Tours

6 Geko Dive C2
7 Water Worx C2

Sleeping

8 Bloo Lagoon Village D1
9 Kembar Inn B2
10 Made's Homestay B2
11 Padangbai Beach Resort C2
12 Pondok Wisata Parta B2
13 Topi Inn C2

Eating

14 Depot Segara B2
Topi Inn .... (see 13)

Drinking

15 Babylon Bar B2
Kinky Reggae Bar .... (see 15)

sandy road are conducive to permanent hanging out.

Depot Segara SEAFOOD $
(☎41443; Jl Segara; dishes 10,000-30,000Rp) Fresh seafood such as barracuda, marlin and snapper is prepared in a variety of ways at this slightly stylish cafe. Enjoy harbour views from the elevated terrace. In a town where casual is the byword, this is the slightly more upmarket option.

Information

The small commercial strip has ATMs.

Getting There & Away

Bemo

Padangbai is 2km south of the main Semarapura–Amlapura road. Bemos leave from the car park in front of the port; orange bemos go east through Candidasa to Amlapura (10,000Rp); blue or white bemos go to Semarapura (10,000Rp).

Boat

Public ferries (child/adult/motorbike/car 23,000/36,000/101,000/659,000Rp, five hours) travel nonstop between Padangbai and Lembar on Lombok. Passenger tickets are sold near the pier. Boats supposedly run 24 hours and leave about every 90 minutes, but the service can be unreliable – boats have caught on fire and run aground.

Perama (☎41419; Café Dona, Jl Pelabuhan; ⏲7am-8pm) runs boats to Senggigi and the Gilis.

Gilicat (☎0361-271 680; www.gilicat.com) serves Gili Trawangan with fast boats. Its local agent is at **Made's Homestay** (☎41 441; madespadangbai@hotmail.com; Jl Silayukti). Several other fast boat services also operate from Padangbai and there are often fare wars.

Be sure to consider important safety information (p772).

Bus

To connect with Denpasar, catch a bemo out to the main road and hail a bus to the Batubulan terminal (18,000Rp).

Tourist Shuttle Bus

Perama (p271) has a stop here for its services around the east coast.

DESTINATION	COST (RP)	DURATION
Candidasa	25,000	30min
Kuta	60,000	3hr
Lovina	150,000	5hr
Sanur	60,000	2¼hr
Ubud	50,000	1¼hr

Padangbai To Candidasa

It's worth prowling some of the beachside lanes off the main road for little places to stay. It's 11km along the main road from the Padangbai turn-off to the resort town of Candidasa, and there are bemos or buses every few minutes. Between the two towns is an attractive stretch of coast, which has some tourist development, and a large oil-storage depot in Teluk Amuk.

MENDIRA

Coming from the west, there are hotels and losmen (basic accommodation) well off the main road at Mendira, before you reach Candidasa. Although the beach has all but vanished and unsightly sea walls have been constructed, this area is a good choice for a quiet getaway if you have your own transport. Think views, breezes and a good book.

Sleeping & Eating

All of the following are on small tracks between the main road and the water; none are far from Candidasa.

They are reached via narrow roads from a single turn off the main road, 1km west of Candidasa. Look for a large sign listing places to stay.

TOP CHOICE **Amarta Beach Inn Bungalows** INN $
(☎41230; amartabeachcottages@yahoo.com; r 250,000-400,000Rp, villa from 600,000Rp; ❄@☜) In a panoramic and private seaside setting, the 10 rooms here are right on the water and are good value. The more expensive ones have interesting open-air bathrooms; villas are even more private. At low tide there is a tiny beach; at other times you can sit and enjoy the views out to Nusas Lembongan and Penida.

The **cafe** (meals from 30,000Rp) is a top choice for lunch whether you are staying here or not.

Anom Beach Inn HOTEL $$
(☎419 024; www.anom-beach.com; r US$40-60; ❄) This older resort from a simpler time has 24 rooms in a variety of configurations. The cheapest have fan only – not a problem given the constant offshore breezes. The best are bungalow-style. Many customers have been coming for years and couldn't imagine staying anyplace else.

Tenganan

Tenganan is occupied by the Bali Aga people, descendants of the original Balinese people who inhabited Bali prior to the Majapahit arrival. The village is surrounded by a wall, and basically consists of two rows of identical houses stretching up the gentle slope of the hill.

Tenganan retains strong and distinct craft traditions that include basket weaving, *lontar* (traditional books written on dried palm leaves) and textile weaving.

A magical cloth known as *kamben gringsing* is woven here – a person wearing it is said to be protected against black magic. Traditionally this is made using the 'double ikat' technique, in which both the warp and weft threads are 'resist dyed' before being woven. It's very time-consuming, and the exquisite pieces for sale are quite expensive (from 600,000Rp).

As you enter the village (10,000Rp donation), you'll likely be greeted by a guide who will take you on a tour – and generally lead you back to his family compound to look at textiles and *lontar* strips. Unlike Besakih, however, here there's no pressure to buy anything, although a tip for your guide will be appreciated (20,000Rp).

This is one of the villages you can visit with **JED** (Village Ecotourism Network; ☎0361-366 9951; www.jed.or.id; tours from US$75).

Getting There & Away

Tenganan is 3.2km up a side road just west of Candidasa. At the turn-off where bemos stop, motorcycle riders offer *ojek* (motorcycle that carries pillion passengers) rides to the village for about 10,000Rp. A nice option is to take an *ojek* up to Tenganan, and enjoy a shady downhill walk back to the main road, which has a Bali rarity: wide footpaths.

Candidasa

☎0363

Candidasa is slouching into idle age, no longer the tourism darling it once was. The main drawback is the lack of a beach, which, except for the far eastern stretch, has eroded away as fast as hotels were built. Most of the coastline has breakwaters, so you can't even walk along it. The main drag is noisy and doesn't get sea breezes.

However the relaxed ambience and sweeping views from the seaside hotels do appeal to a more mature crowd of visitors. Candidasa is a good base from which to explore the interior of East Bali and the east coast's diving and snorkelling sites.

Activities

Diving and snorkelling are popular activities in Candidasa. **Gili Tepekong**, which has a series of coral heads at the top of a sheer drop-off, is perhaps the best dive site. It offers the chance to see lots of fish, including some larger marine life.

A recommended dive operator is **Dive Lite** (☎41 660; www.divelite.com; Jl Raya Candidasa; dives from US$50), which dives the local area plus the rest of the island. An intro dive is US$90; snorkelling trips are US$30.

Hotels and shops along the main road rent snorkel sets for about 30,000Rp per day. For the best snorkelling, take a boat to offshore sites or to Gili Mimpang (a one-hour boat trip should cost about 100,000Rp for up to three people).

Candidasa

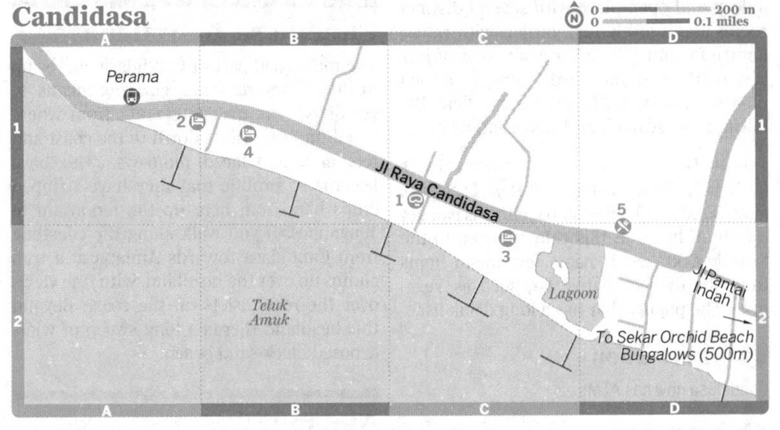

Sleeping

Candidasa's noisy main drag is well supplied with seaside accommodation. The small roads branching off Forest Rd east of the lagoon lead to several places hidden among the banana trees and palms. It's quiet and you can hear chickens. You might also consider staying west of town; many places are close.

Hotel Ida's GUESTHOUSE $
(☎41096; jsidas1@aol.com; Jl Raya Candidasa; bungalows 170,000-300,000Rp) Set in a dense seaside grove of coconut trees so perfectly realised that it looks like a set for *South Pacific*, Ida's has five thatched bungalows with open-air bathrooms. Rustic balcony furniture, including a daybed, gets you to thinking just what you'd choose for *Desert Island Discs* – for yet more tropical cliché.

Ashyana Candidasa HOTEL $$
(☎41538; www.ashyanacandidasa.com; Jl Raya Candidasa; r US$50-80) The staff here are so sharply trained they almost salute – but manage to smile instead. This well-managed waterside hotel has 12 older but immaculate bungalow-style units plus a spa. Most are far enough from the road to escape noise. The waterfront cafe Le-Zat has standard Indonesian fare and fabulous views.

Seaside Cottages GUESTHOUSE $
(☎41629; www.balibeachfront-cottages.com; Jl Raya Candidasa; cottages 150,000-470,000Rp) The 15 rooms here are scattered in cottages and span the gamut from cold-water basic to restful units with air-con and tropical bathrooms. The seafront has loungers right along the breakwater. The Temple Café is a mellow place.

Sekar Orchid Beach Bungalows GUESTHOUSE $
(☎41086; www.sekarorchid.com; Jl Pantai Indah 26; r US$30-40) The grounds here live up to the name, with orchids and bromeliads growing in profusion. The six large rooms are good value, with nice views from the 2nd floor. The site feels isolated but is only a short walk from the centre, and there's a small beach.

Candidasa

Activities, Courses & Tours
1 Dive Lite C1

Sleeping
2 Ashyana Candidasa A1
3 Hotel Ida's C2
4 Seaside Cottages B1

Eating
Temple Café ..... (see 4)
5 Vincent's D2

Eating & Drinking

The cafes and restaurants along Jl Raya Candidasa are mostly simple and family-run, but you should beware of traffic noise, although it abates after dark. Ashyana Candidasa (p273) has a good waterfront cafe.

TOP CHOICE **Vincent's** INTERNATIONAL $$
(☎41368; www.vincentsbali.com; Jl Raya Candidasa; meals 60,000-150,000Rp) Candi's best is

a deep and open place with several distinct rooms and a lovely rear garden with rattan lounge furniture. The bar is an oasis of jazz (live on the first and third Thursday of each month). The menu combines excellent Balinese, fresh seafood and European dishes.

Temple Café INTERNATIONAL $
(☎41 629; Seaside Cottages, Jl Raya Candidasa; meals 30,000-70,000Rp) Global citizens can get a taste of home at this cafe attached to the Seaside Cottages. It has a few menu items from the owner's native Oz, such as Vegemite. The popular bar has a long drink list.

Information

Candidasa now has ATMs.

Getting There & Away

Candidasa is on the main road between Amlapura and South Bali, but there's no terminal, so hail bemos (buses probably won't stop). You'll need to change in either Padangbai or Semarapura. You can charter a ride to Amed in the far east for about 150,000Rp, and Kuta and the airport for 250,000Rp. Ask at your accommodation about vehicle and bicycle hire. **Perama** (☎41114; Jl Raya Candidasa; ⏲7am-7pm) is at the western end of the strip.

DESTINATION	COST (RP)	DURATION
Kuta	60,000	3½hr
Lovina	150,000	5¼hr
Padangbai	25,000	30min
Sanur	60,000	2¾hr
Ubud	50,000	1¾hr

Candidasa To Amlapura

The main road east of Candidasa curves up to **Pura Gamang Pass** (*gamang* means 'to get dizzy' – an overstatement), from where you'll find fine views down to the coast and lots of greedy-faced monkeys (who have become so prolific that they have stripped crops bare from here up the mountain to Tenganan). If you walk along the coastline from Candidasa towards Amlapura, a trail climbs up over the headland, with fine views over the rocky islets off the coast. Beyond this headland there's a long sweep of wide, exposed black-sand beach.

Amlapura

☎0363

Amlapura is the capital of Karangasem district, and the main town and transport junction in eastern Bali. The smallest of Bali's district capitals, it's a multicultural place with Chinese shophouses, several mosques and confusing one-way streets (which are the tidiest in Bali). It's worth a stop to see the royal palaces but a lack of options means you'll want to spend the night elsewhere, such as Tirta Gangga.

Sights

Amlapura's palaces, on Jl Teuk Umar, are stolid reminders of Karangasem's period as a kingdom at its most important when supported by Dutch colonial power in the late 19th and early 20th centuries.

WORTH A TRIP

PASIR PUTIH

No longer a secret, Pasir Putih (aka Dream Beach) is an idyllic white-sand beach whose name indeed means 'White Sand'. When we first visited in 2004, it was empty, save for a long row of fishing boats at one end. Just a few years later, it is sort of an ongoing lab in seaside economic development.

A dozen thatched beach **warungs** and **cafes** have appeared. You can get *nasi goreng* (fried rice) or grilled fish. Bintang is of course on ice and sunloungers await bikini-clad bottoms. The beach itself is truly lovely: a long crescent of white sand backed by coconut trees. At one end, cliffs provide shade. The surf is often mellow; you can rent **snorkelling** gear to explore the waters.

The one thing saving Pasir Putih from being swamped is the difficult access. Look for crude signs saying either 'Virgin Beach Club' or 'Jl Pasir Putih' near the village of Perasi. Turn off the main road (5.6km east of Candidasa) and follow a pretty paved track for about 1.5km to a temple where locals will collect a fee (per person 2500Rp). You can park here and walk the gentle hill down or drive a further 600m directly to the beach on a road that barely qualifies as such.

Puri Agung Karangasem PALACE
(Jl Teuku Umar; admission 10,000Rp; ⏲8am-5pm) Outside the Puri Agung Karangasem, there is an impressive three-tiered entry gate and beautiful sculpted panels. After you pass through the entry courtyard, a left turn takes you to the main building, known as the Maskerdam (Amsterdam), because it was the Karangasem kingdom's acquiescence to Dutch rule that allowed it to hang on long after the demise of the other Balinese kingdoms. Inside you can see several rooms, including the royal bedroom and a living room with furniture that was a gift from the Dutch royal family.

Puri Gede PALACE
(Jl Teuku Umar; donation requested; ⏲8am-6pm) Still used by the royal family, this modest palace is surrounded by long walls and the palace grounds feature many brick buildings dating from the Dutch colonial period. Look for 19th-century stone carving and woodcarvings.

Getting There & Away

Amlapura is a major transport hub. Buses and bemos regularly ply the main road to Denpasar's Batubulan terminal (25,000Rp; roughly three hours) via Candidasa, Padangbai and Gianyar. Plenty of minibuses also go around the north coast to Singaraja (about 20,000Rp) via Tirta Gangga, Amed and Tulamben.

Tirta Gangga

☎0363

Tirta Gangga (Water of the Ganges) is the site of a holy temple, some great water features and some of the best views of rice fields and the sea beyond in East Bali. High on a ridge, it is a relaxing place to stop for an hour, or longer – to allow for some treks in the surrounding terraced countryside, which ripples with coursing water.

Sights

Amlapura's water-loving rajah, after completing his lost masterpiece at Ujung, had another go at building the water palace of his dreams. He succeeded at **Taman Tirta Gangga** (adult/child 10,000/5000Rp, parking 2000Rp; ⏲site 24hr, ticket office 6am-6pm), which has a stunning crescent of rice-terrace-lined hills for a backdrop.

Originally built in 1948, the water palace was damaged in the 1963 eruption of Gunung Agung and again during the political events that rocked Indonesia two years later. Today it is an aquatic fantasy with several swimming pools and ornamental ponds filled with huge koi and lotus blossoms, which serve as a fascinating reminder of the old days of the Balinese rajahs. 'Pool A' is good for **swimming** and is in the top part of the complex. 'Pool B' is pondlike. Look for the 11-tiered fountain and plop down under the huge old banyans.

Activities

Hiking in the surrounding hills is recommended. The rice terraces around Tirta Gangga are some of the most beautiful in Bali. Back roads and walking paths take you to many picturesque traditional villages. Or you can ascend the side of Gunung Agung. Guides are a good idea. Ask at any of the accommodation we've listed, especially Homestay Rijasa (p276) where the owner I Ketut Sarjana is an experienced guide. Another local guide who comes with good marks is **Komang Gede Sutama** (☎0813 3877 0893).

Among the possible treks is a six-hour loop to Tenganan village, plus shorter ones across the local hills, which include visits to remote temples and all the stunning vistas you can handle. Rates average about 50,000Rp per hour for one or two people.

TOP CHOICE **Bung Bung Adventure Biking** CYCLING
(☎21873, 0813 3840 2132; bungbungbikeadventure@gmail.com; Tirta Gangga; tours 250,000-300,000Rp) Ride downhill through the simply gorgeous rice fields, terraces and river valleys around Tirta Gangga with this locally owned tour company. Itineraries last from two to four hours and include use of a mountain bike and helmet, plus water. The office is close to Homestay Rijasa, across from the Tirta Gangga entrance. Book in advance.

Sleeping & Eating

You can overnight in luxury in old royal quarters overlooking the water palace or lodge in humble surrounds in anticipation of an early morning trek. Many places to stay have cafes that offer mains for under 20,000Rp and there's a cluster by the sedate fruit vendors near the shady parking area.

Tirta Ayu Hotel HOTEL $$
(☎22503; www.hoteltirtagangga.com; villas US$125-175; ❄🛜≋) Right in the palace compound, this has four pleasant villas that are clean and have basic, modern decor in the limited palette of creams and coffees. Flop about like a fish in the hotel's private pool or use the vast palace facilities. The restaurant is a tad upscale (mains from 50,000Rp) and serves creative takes on local classics which you enjoy overlooking the palace.

Homestay Rijasa GUESTHOUSE $
(☎21873, 0813 5300 5080; r 150,000-250,000Rp) With elaborately planted grounds, this well-run, nine-room guesthouse is a recommended choice opposite the water palace entrance. Better rooms have hot water, good for the large soaking tubs. The owner, I Ketut Sarjana, is an experienced trekking guide.

Good Karma HOMESTAY $
(☎22445; goodkarma.tirtagangga@gmail.com; r 200,000-250,000Rp; 🛜) A classic homestay, Good Karma has four very clean and simple bungalows and a good vibe derived from the surrounding pastoral rice field. The good cafe's gazebos look towards the parking lot; often you'll see the winsome Nyoman playing bamboo flute music out front.

Getting There & Away

Bemos and minibuses making the east-coast haul between Amlapura and Singaraja stop at Tirta Gangga, right outside the water palace or any hotel further north. The fare to Amlapura should be 5000Rp.

Amed & The Far East Coast

☎0363

Stretching from Amed to Bali's far eastern tip, this once-remote stretch of semi-arid coast draws visitors to a succession of small, scalloped, grey-sand beaches, a relaxed atmosphere and excellent diving and snorkelling.

The coast here is often called simply 'Amed' but this is a misnomer, as the coast is a series of seaside *dusun* (small villages) that start with the actual Amed in the north and then run southeast to the Aas end. If you're looking to get away from crowds, this is the place to come and try some yoga. Everything is spread out, so you never feel like you're in the middle of anything much except maybe one of the small fishing villages.

Traditionally this area has been quite poor, with thin soils, low rainfall and very limited infrastructure. Villages rely on fishing, and colourful *jukung* line up on every available piece of beach. Inland, the steep hillsides are generally too dry for rice – corn, peanuts and vegetables are the main crops.

Activities

Diving & Snorkelling

Snorkelling is excellent at several places along the coast. **Jemeluk** is a protected area where you can admire live coral and plentiful fish within 100m of the beach. There's a wreck of a Japanese fishing boat near **Aas**, offshore from Eka Purnama bungalows, and coral gardens and colourful marine life at **Selang**. Almost every hotel rents snorkelling equipment for about 30,000Rp per day.

Scuba diving is good and the *Liberty* wreck at Tulamben is only a 20-minute drive away. Dive operators have similar prices for a long list of offerings (eg local dives from about US$75, open-water dive course about US$375).

Eco-Dive DIVING
(☎23482; www.ecodivebali.com; Jemeluk Beach; 🛜) Full-service shop with simple, free accommodation for clients. Has led the way on environmental issues.

Euro Dive DIVING
(☎23605; www.eurodivebali.com; Lipah) Has a large facility and offers packages with hotels.

Trekking

Quite a few trails go inland from the coast, up the slopes of **Gunung Seraya** (1175m) and to some little-visited villages. The countryside is sparsely vegetated and most trails are well defined, so you won't need a guide for shorter walks – if you get lost, just follow a ridge-top back down to the coast road. Allow a good three hours to get to the top of Seraya, starting from the rocky ridge just east of Jemeluk Bay, near Prem Liong Art Bungalows. To reach the top for sunrise, you'll need to start in the dark, so a guide is a good idea – ask at your hotel.

Sleeping

The entire area is very spread out, so take this into consideration when choosing accommodation. You will also need to choose between staying in the little beachside villages or on the sunny and dry headlands between the inlets. The former puts you right on the sand and offers a small amount of community life while the latter gives you broad, sweeping vistas and isolation.

Accommodation can be found in every price category; almost every place has a restaurant or cafe. Those with noteworthy dining are indicated in the Eating listings.

EAST OF AMED VILLAGE

TOP CHOICE Hotel Uyah Amed HOTEL $$
(☎23462; www.hoteluyah.com; r €40-50; ❄📶) This cute place features four-poster beds set in stylish, conical interiors bathed in light. From all 27 rooms (some with air-con) you can see the saltworks on the beach. The hotel makes the most of this by offering fascinating and free salt-making demonstrations. The tasty Cafe Garam is appropriately named for salt.

JEMELUK

Pondok Kebun Wayan GUESTHOUSE $
(☎23473; www.amedcafe.com; Jemeluk; r €20-50; ❄) This Amed empire features a range of 30 bungalow-style rooms mostly on a hillside across from the beach. The most expensive rooms have views, terraces and amenities such as air-con while the cheapest have cold water and showers. The eponymous Amed Cafe has a good grilled-seafood menu.

Aiona Garden of Health GUESTHOUSE $$
(☎0813 3816 1730; www.aionabali.com; Banutan Beach; r from €30) This characterful place has enough signs outside to qualify as a genuine roadside attraction. The simple bungalows are shaded by mango trees and the natural food may be the healthiest of your trip. You can partake of organic potions and lotions, classes in yoga, meditation, tarot reading etc. If you don't get a natural high, your inner peace might improve with the high-fibre diet, or try the fermented tea – pow! A small **shell museum** (Aiona Garden of Health, Banutan Beach; ⏲2-4pm) boasts that no bivalves died in its creation.

BUNUTAN

These places are on a sun-drenched, arid stretch of highland.

TOP CHOICE Onlyou Villas VILLA $$
(☎23595; www.onlyou-bali.com; Bunutan; villas €50-90; ❄) You could go nuts trying to find the missing 'y' in the name of this hillside villa complex. Happily it is such a good deal that you'll say 'y not!'. Villas are large and have many amenities such as DVD players, multiple beds, luxurious teak furniture and an array of genial pets. Among the services are 'beddye bye candy and cocktails'.

Wawa-Wewe II HOTEL $$
(☎23506, 23522; www.bali-wawawewe.com; Bunutan; r 400,000-700,000Rp; ❄📶🏊) From the headlands, this restful place has 10 bungalow-style rooms on lush grounds that shamble down to the water's edge. The natural-stone infinity pool is shaped like a Buddha and is near the water, as are two rooms with delectable ocean views.

LIPAH

This village is just large enough for you to go wandering – briefly.

Hidden Paradise Cottages HOTEL $$
(☎23514; www.hiddenparadise-bali.com; Lipah; r US$50-100; ❄📶🏊) The 16 simply decorated bungalow-style rooms at this older beachside resort are set on manicured grounds and have large patios and open-air bathrooms. The pool is the classic kidney shape in a natural garden setting. Several dive packages are available.

DECODING AMED

The entire 10km stretch of far east coast is often called 'Amed' by both tourists and marketing-minded locals. Most development at first was around three bays with fishing villages: **Jemeluk**, which has cafes and a few shops; **Bunutan**, with both a beach and headlands; and **Lipah**, which has warungs, shops and a few services. Development has marched onwards through tiny **Lehan**, **Selang**, **Bayuning** and **Aas**, each a minor oasis at the base of the dry, brown hills. To appreciate the narrow band of the coast, stop at the viewpoint at Jemeluk, where you can see fishing boats lined up like a riot of multi-hued sardines on the beach.

Besides the main road via Tirta Gangga, you can also approach the Amed area from Aas in the south using a curving, scenic road from Amlapura.

LEHAN

TOP CHOICE Life in Amed INN $$
(☎23 152, 0813 3850 1555; www.lifebali.com; Lehan; r US$65-110, villas US$100-170;) Life here is posh. The six bungalow-style units are in a slightly cramped compound around a sinuous pool; two villas are directly on the beach. Bathrooms are open-air works of art, created from beach stones. The cafe concentrates on seafood and showy local dishes (meals 50,000Rp to 120,000Rp). This is a fave with expats living in Bali.

AAS

The last community of any size on the road from Amed, Aas is very quiet.

TOP CHOICE Meditasi GUESTHOUSE $
(☎082 8372 2738; http://meditasi.8m.com; Aas; r 300,000-500,000Rp) Get off the grid and take respite from the pressures of life at this chilled-out and charming hideaway. Meditation and yoga help you relax, and the eight rooms are close to good swimming and snorkelling. Open-air baths allow you to count the colours of the bougainvillea and frangipani that grow in profusion.

Eating & Drinking

Most places to stay have cafes. The following are worth seeking out.

Cafe Garam INDONESIAN $
(☎23462; Hotel Uyah Amed, east of Amed; meals 20,000-50,000Rp) There's a relaxed feel here, with pool tables and Balinese food plus the lyrical and haunting melodies of live *genjek* (traditional form of Balinese music with percussion instruments) music at 8pm on Wednesday and Saturday. *Garam* means salt and the cafe honours the local salt-making industry. Try the *salada ayam*, an addictive mix of cabbage, grilled chicken, shallots and tiny peppers.

Smiling Buddha Restaurant ORGANIC $
(☎082 8372 2738; Meditasi, Aas; meals from 30,000Rp;) Newly built, the restaurant and highly recommended guesthouse has excellent organic fare, much sourced from its own garden. Balinese and Western dishes are excellent and there are good views out to sea. They even manage some full moon fun on the appropriate nights.

Wawa-Wewe I BAR
(☎23506; meals from 30,000Rp;) Spend the evening here and, if you try the local *arak* made with palm fronds, you won't know your wawas from your wewes. This is the coast's most raucous bar – which by local standards means that sometimes it gets sorta loud. Local bands jam on many nights. You can also eat and sleep here (simple air-con rooms).

Information

You might be charged a tourist tax. Enforcement of a 5000Rp per-person fee at a tollbooth on the outskirts of Amed is sporadic. When collected, the funds go, in part, to developing the infrastructure at the beaches.

There are moneychangers in Lipah but the closest ATMs and banks are in Amlapura. Many places don't take credit cards. Wi-fi is becoming common as the phone lines are extended south.

Getting There & Around

Most people drive here via the main highway from Amlapura and Culik. The spectacular road going all the way around the twin peaks from Aas to Ujung makes a good circle.

You can arrange for a driver and car to/from south Bali and the airport for about 400,000Rp.

Public transport is difficult. Minibuses and bemos between Singaraja and Amlapura pass through Culik, the turn-off for the coast. Infrequent bemos go from Culik to Amed (3.5km), and some continue to Seraya until 1pm. Fares average 8000Rp.

You can also charter transport from Culik for a negotiable 50,000Rp (by *ojek* is less than half). Specify which hotel you wish to go to – agree on 'Amed' and you could come up short in Amed village.

Amed Sea Express (☎0819 3617 6914, 80 852; www.gili-sea-express.com; per person 600,000Rp) makes crossings to Gili Trawangan on an 80-person speedboat in under an hour. This makes many interesting itineraries possible.

Tulamben

☎0363

The big attraction here sank over 70 years ago. The WWII wreck of the US cargo ship *Liberty* is among the best and most popular dive sites in Bali and this has given rise to an entire town based on scuba diving. Other great dive sites are nearby and even snorkellers can easily swim out and enjoy the wreck and the coral.

But if you don't plan to explore the briny waves, don't expect to hang out on the beach either. The shore is made up of rather beautiful, large washed stones, the kind that cost a fortune at a DIY store.

For non-aquatic delights, check out the **morning market** in Tulamben village, 1.5km north of the dive site.

Activities

Diving and **snorkelling** are the reason Tulamben exists.

The shipwreck **Liberty** is about 50m directly offshore from Puri Madha Bungalows (where you can park); look for the schools of black snorkels. Swim straight out and you'll see the stern rearing up from the depths, heavily encrusted with coral and swarming with dozens of species of colourful fish – and with scuba divers most of the day. The ship is more than 100m long, but the hull is broken into sections and it's easy for divers to get inside.

Many divers commute to Tulamben from Candidasa or Lovina, and in busy times it can get quite crowded between 11am and 4pm, with up to 50 divers at a time around the wreck. Stay the night in Tulamben or in nearby Amed and get an early start.

Most hotels have their own diving centre, and some will give a discount on accommodation if you dive with their centre. Expect to pay from US$40/70 for one/two dives at Tulamben, and a little more for a night dive or dives around Amed. Snorkelling gear is rented everywhere for 30,000Rp.

Note that there is now a privately run parking area behind Tauch Terminal. There are gear-rental stands, vendors, guides and more here, ready to get your attention. There are also pay-showers and toilets. You can still park for free by Puri Madha Beach Bungalows.

Tauch Terminal DIVING
(☎774 504, 22911; www.tauch-terminal.com) Among the many dive operators, Tauch Terminal is one of the longest-established operators in Bali. A four-day PADI open-water certificate course costs from €350.

Sleeping & Eating

At high tide, none of the places situated on the water have much rocky beach at all, but the waves are dramatic.

TOP CHOICE **Puri Madha Beach Bungalows** HOTEL $
(☎22921; r 200,000-500,000Rp; ❄📶🏊) Restyled bungalow-style units are directly opposite the wreck on shore. The best of the 15 rooms have air-con and hot water. The spacious grounds feel like a public park and there is a swish new pool area overlooking the ocean. You can't beat getting out of bed and paddling right out to a famous shipwreck.

Tauch Terminal Resort HOTEL $$
(☎0361 774 504, 22 911; www.tauch-terminal.com; r €65-95; ❄📶🏊) Down a side road, this sprawling waterfront hotel has 27 rooms in several categories. Many of the rooms are recently built and all are comfortable in a modern, motel-style way. Expect amenities such as satellite TV and fridges. Of the two waterfront pools, one is reserved for swimming only. The cafe serves a fine breakfast.

Deep Blue Studio GUESTHOUSE $
(☎22919; www.subaqua.cz; r US$25-50) Owned by Czechs, this dive operation has 10 rooms in two-storey buildings on the hill side of the road. Rooms have fans and balconies. Offers a variety of packages with the affiliated dive shop.

Getting There & Away

Plenty of buses and bemos travel between Amlapura and Singaraja and will stop anywhere along the Tulamben road, but they're infrequent after 2pm. Expect to pay 12,000Rp to either town.

Perama (p274) offers charter tourist-bus services from Candidasa; the cost is 125,000Rp each for a minimum of two people. This is similar to the cost of hiring a car and driver.

If you are driving to Lovina for the night, be sure to leave by about 3pm, so you will still have a little daylight when you get there. There's a petrol station just south of town.

If you are just going to snorkel the wreck and are day-tripping with a driver, don't let them park at a dive shop away from the wreck where you'll get a sales pitch.

CENTRAL MOUNTAINS

Most of Bali's mountains are volcanoes; some are dormant, but some are definitely active. The mountains divide the gentle sweep of fertile land to the south from the narrow, more arid strip to the north. Northwest of Gunung Agung is the stark and spectacular caldera that contains the volcanic cone of Gunung Batur (1717m), the waters of Danau Batur and numerous smaller craters. In central Bali, around Bedugul, is another complex of volcanic craters and lakes, with much lusher vegetation.

It's all a big change from the coastal areas. Temperatures fall and you may need something warmer than shorts! There are two main routes through the mountains to the north coast (via Gunung Batur and via Bedugul), which allow you to make a circuit. There are treks to do, clear lake waters to enjoy and a few other natural and sacred sites of note, especially the mysterious temple Pura Luhur Batukau, the nearby Unesco-recognised ancient rice terraces in and around Jatiluwih, and stupendous hiking around the old colonial village of Munduk.

Gunung Batur

☎0366

Most day visitors come on organised tours and stop at the crater rim at Penelokan for views and lunch; most overnight visitors stay in the villages around the lake. The views both from above and from lake level are truly wonderful – if you hit the area on a clear day.

Activities

The setting for Gunung Batur is otherworldly: it's like a giant dish, with the bottom half covered with water and a set of volcanic cones growing in the middle. Visit the area on a clear day and you'll understand what all the fuss is about. Soaring up in the centre of the huge outer crater is the cone of Gunung Batur (1717m), formed by a 1917 eruption. A cluster of smaller cones lies beside, created variously by eruptions in 1926, 1963, 1974 and 1994.

But is it worthwhile to go through the hassle and the expense of making the climb? You'll get some amazing photos and come close to volcanic action not easily seen anywhere. But the flipside is that it's costly, you have to deal with various characters and at some point you may just say, 'I could have enjoyed all this from the carpark viewpoint in Penelokan'.

Even reputable and highly competent adventure tour operators from elsewhere in Bali cannot take their customers up Gunung Batur without paying the HPPGB (Mt Batur Tour Guides Association) and using one of their guides, so these tours are relatively expensive.

Pretty much all the accommodation in the area can help you put a trek together. They can recommend hassle-free alternatives to Batur, such as the outer rim of the crater, or trips to other mountains such as Gunung Agung.

HPPGB HIKING GUIDES

(Mt Batur Tour Guides Association; ☎52362; ⊙3am-noon) The HPPGB has a monopoly on guided climbs up Gunung Batur. It requires that all trekking agencies that operate on the mountain hire at least one of its guides for trips up the mountain. In addition, the cartel has developed a reputation for tough tactics in requiring climbers to use its guides and during negotiations for its services.

That said, many people use the services of HPPGB guides without incident, and some of the guides win plaudits from visitors for their ideas in customising trips. To circumvent some of the hassles, be absolutely clear in your agreement with the HPPGB about the terms you're agreeing to, such as whether fees are per person or per group and include breakfast, and exactly where you will go. If you deal with one of the trekking agencies, an HPPGB guide will still accompany you on the trip but all arrangements will be done through the agency.

HPPGB rates and times are posted at its office. The Batur Sunrise trek goes from 4am to 8am, the Gunung Batur Main Crater trek from 4am to 10am.

Equipment

If you're climbing before sunrise, take a torch (flashlight) or be absolutely sure that your guide provides you with one. You'll need good strong footwear, a hat, a jumper (sweater) and drinking water.

Routes

Most travellers use one of two trails that start near Toya Bungkah. The shorter one is straight up (three to four hours return), while a longer trek (five to six hours return) links the summit climb with the other craters. Climbers have reported that they have easily made this journey without a HPPGB guide, although it shouldn't be tried while it's dark. The major obstacle is actually avoiding any hassle from the guides themselves. There are a few separate paths at first, but they all rejoin sooner or later and after about 30 minutes you'll be on a ridge with quite a well-defined track. It gets pretty steep towards the top and it can be hard walking over the loose volcanic sand – climbing up three steps and sliding back two. Allow about two hours to get to the top.

Gunung Batur Area

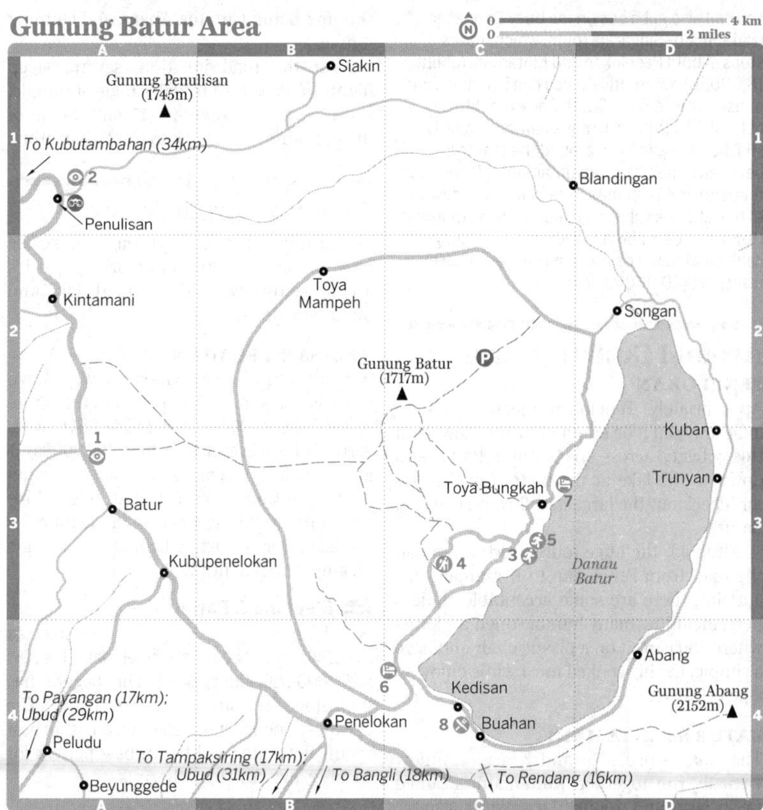

There's also a third track, which enables you to use private transport to within about 45 minutes' walk of the top. From Toya Bungkah, take the road northeast towards Songan and take the left fork after about 3.5km at Serongga, just before Songan. Follow this inner-rim road for another 1.7km to a well-signposted track on the left, which climbs another 1km or so to a car park. From here, the walking track is easy to follow to the top.

Information

Gunung Batur has developed a well-deserved reputation as a money-grubbing place where visitors (mainly around Penelokan) are hassled by touts and wannabe mountain guides (mainly around the lake area). Of course, the guides themselves can be a problem too. Don't leave valuables in your car, especially at any car park at the start of a volcano trail. Don't even leave a helmet with a motorcycle.

Gunung Batur Area

Sights

1 Pura Batur A3
2 Pura Puncak Penulisan A1

Activities, Courses & Tours

3 Batur Natural Hot Spring C3
C.Bali .... (see 6)
4 HPPGB C3
5 Toya Devasya C3

Sleeping

6 Hotel Segara C4
7 Under the Volcano III C3

Eating

8 Kedisan Floating Hotel C4

Getting There & Around

From Batubulan terminal in Denpasar, bemos make regular trips to Kintamani (18,000Rp).

You can also get a bus on the busy Denpasar (Batabulan)–Singaraja route, which makes stops in both Penelokan and Kintamani (about 18,000Rp). Alternatively, you can just hire a car or use a driver. From South Bali expect to pay at least 450,000Rp. Orange bemos regularly shuttle back and forth around the crater rim, between Penelokan and Kintamani (8000Rp for tourists). Public bemos from Penelokan down to the lakeside villages go mostly in the morning (tourist price is about 6000Rp to Toya Bungkah). Later in the day, you may have to charter transport (40,000Rp or more).

Around Gunung Batur

PENELOKAN

Appropriately, Penelokan means 'place to look' and you'll be stunned by the view from this village, across to Gunung Batur and down to the lake at the bottom of the crater (check out the large lava flow on Gunung Batur).

Although the huge tourist restaurants on the road from Penelokan to Kintamani disappoint, there are some acceptable choices here, including many humble open-air joints where you can sit on a plastic chair and have a simple, freshly cooked meal while enjoying a priceless view.

BATUR & KINTAMANI

The villages of **Batur** and **Kintamani** now virtually run together. Kintamani is famed for its large and colourful **market** (Kintamani; ⏲6am-3pm), which is held every three days. The town is like a string bean: long, with pods of development. Activity starts early, and by 11am everything's packed up. If you don't want to go on a trek, the sunrise view from the road here is good.

Spiritually, Gunung Batur is the second most important mountain in Bali (only Gunung Agung outranks it), so the temple, **Pura Batur** (admission 6000Rp, sarong & sash rental 3000Rp), is of considerable importance. It's a great stop for the architectural spectacle. Within the complex is a Taoist shrine.

PENULISAN

The road gradually climbs along the crater rim beyond Kintamani, and is often shrouded in clouds, mist or rain. Penulisan is where the road bends sharply and heads down towards the north coast and the remote scenic drive to Bedugul. A **viewpoint** about 400m south from here offers an amazing panorama over three mountains: Gunung Batur, Gunung Abang and Gunung Agung.

Near the road junction, several steep flights of steps lead to Bali's highest temple, **Pura Puncak Penulisan** (1745m). Some of the sculptures date back to the 11th century.

Around Danau Batur

The farming villages down on the lakeside grow onions and other aromatic crops. It's a crisp setting with often superb lake and mountain views.

KEDISAN & BUAHAN

A hairpin-bend road winds its way down from Penelokan to **Kedisan** on the shore of the lake. **C.Bali** (☎0813 5342 0541; www.c-bali.com; Hotel Segara; tours from 400,000Rp) is an excellent tour company (operated by an Australian-Dutch couple) that offers bike tours around the craters and canoe tours on the lake. Prices start at US$40 and include pick-up across South Bali.

Sleeping & Eating

Hotel Segara GUESTHOUSE $
(☎51136; www.batur-segarahotel.com; Kedisan; r 200,000-500,000Rp; @ wi-fi) The Segara has bungalows set around a courtyard. The cheapest rooms have cold water, the best rooms hot water and bathtubs – perfect for soaking away the hypothermia.

TOP CHOICE **Kedisan Floating Hotel** CAFE $$
(☎0813 3775 5411; Kedisan; r US$30-100, meals from 35,000Rp) So nothing floats here – except maybe your rubber duck from home in the soaking tubs – but this hotel on the shores of the lake is popular for its daily lunches. On weekends tourists vie with daytrippers from Denpasar for tables out on the piers over the lake. The Balinese food, which features fresh lake fish, is excellent. You can also stay: the best rooms are cottages at the water's edge.

TOYA BUNGKAH

The main tourist centre for the area is Toya Bungkah, which is scruffy but has a cute charm and a serene lakeside setting.

Beside the lake, **Toya Devasya** (☎51 204; admission 150,000Rp; ⏲8am-8pm) is built around a hot spring. The huge hot pool is 38°C while the comparatively brisk lake-fed pool is 20°C.

Unless noted, hotels only have cold water, which can be a boon for waking up for a sunset climb. Most have restaurants, some of which serve *ikan mujair*, a delicious small lake fish, which is barbecued to a crisp with onion, garlic and bamboo shoots.

Activities

Hot springs bubble in a couple of spots, and have long been used for bathing pools.

Batur Natural Hot Spring HOT SPRINGS
(0813 3832 5552; admission from 120,000Rp; 8am-6pm) Walk down a cinder path and you'll reach this low-key complex of three pools on the edge of the lake. Different pools have different temps, so you can simmer yourself successively. The overall feel of the hot springs rather nicely matches the slightly shabby feel of the entire region. Lockers and towels are included with admission, and the simple cafe has good views.

Sleeping

Under the Volcano III GUESTHOUSE $
(0813 3860 0081; r 200,000Rp) With a lovely, quiet lakeside location opposite chilli plots, this inn has six clean and pretty rooms; go for room 1 right on the water. There are two other nearby inns in the Volcano empire, all run by the same lovely family.

Danau Bratan

0368

Approaching from the south, you gradually leave the rice terraces behind and ascend into the cool, often misty mountain country around Danau Bratan. The name **Bedugul** is sometimes used to refer to the whole lakeside area, but strictly speaking, Bedugul is just the first place you reach at the top of the hill when coming up from South Bali. Candikuning is the main village in the area, and has an important and picturesque temple. Marvellous Munduk anchors a region with fine trekking to waterfalls and cloud-cloaked forests.

The choice of accommodation near the lake is limited, as much of the area is geared towards domestic, rather than foreign, tourists. Many new inns aimed at international visitors are opening around Munduk.

Wherever you go, you are likely to see the tasty local strawberries on offer. Note that it is often misty and can get chilly up here.

CANDIKUNING

Dotting the western side of the lake, Candikuning is a haven for plant lovers. Its **market** (Candikuning; parking 2000Rp) is touristy, but among the eager vendors of tat you'll find locals shopping for fruit, veg, herbs, spices and potted plants.

Sights & Activities

TOP CHOICE **Bali Botanical Gardens** GARDENS
(21273; www.balibotanicgarden.org; Kebun Raya Eka Karya Bali; admission walking/driving 7000/12,000Rp, car parking 6000Rp; 7am-6pm) This garden is a showplace. Established in 1959 as a branch of the national botanical gardens at Bogor, near Jakarta, it covers more than 154 hectares on the lower slopes of Gunung Pohen and boasts an extensive collection of trees and flowers. Some plants are labelled with their botanical names, and there's a helpful booklet of self-guided walks (20,000Rp). The gorgeous orchid area is often locked to foil flower filchers; you can ask for it to be unlocked.

Pura Ulun Danu Bratan TEMPLE
(adult/child 15,000/10,000Rp, parking 5000Rp; tickets 7am-5pm, site 24hr) This very important Hindu-Buddhist temple was founded in the 17th century. It is dedicated to Dewi Danu, the goddess of the waters, and is actually built on small islands, which means it is completely surrounded by the lake. Pilgrimages and ceremonies are held here to ensure that there is a supply of water for farmers all over Bali.

The tableau includes classical Hindu thatch-roofed *meru* reflected in the water and silhouetted against the often cloudy mountain backdrop.

At the temple gardens, you can hire a four-passenger speedboat with driver (150,000Rp per 30 minutes), a five-person rowboat with rower (100,000Rp per 30 minutes), or a two-person pedal boat (35,000Rp per 30 minutes).

There's a bit of a sideshow atmosphere, however. Animals in small cages and opportunities to caress a snake or hold a huge bat amuse the punters.

Bali Treetop Adventure Park OUTDOORS
(0361-852 0680; www.balitreetop.com; Kebun Raya Eka Karya Bali, Bali Botanical Gardens; adult/child US$21/14; 7am-6pm) Within the botanical gardens, you can cavort like a bird or a squirrel at the Bali Treetop Adventure Park. Winches, ropes, nets and more let you explore the forest well above the ground.

Sleeping & Eating

The Candikuning area can make a good place for a break in exploring the highlands.

Danau Bratan Area

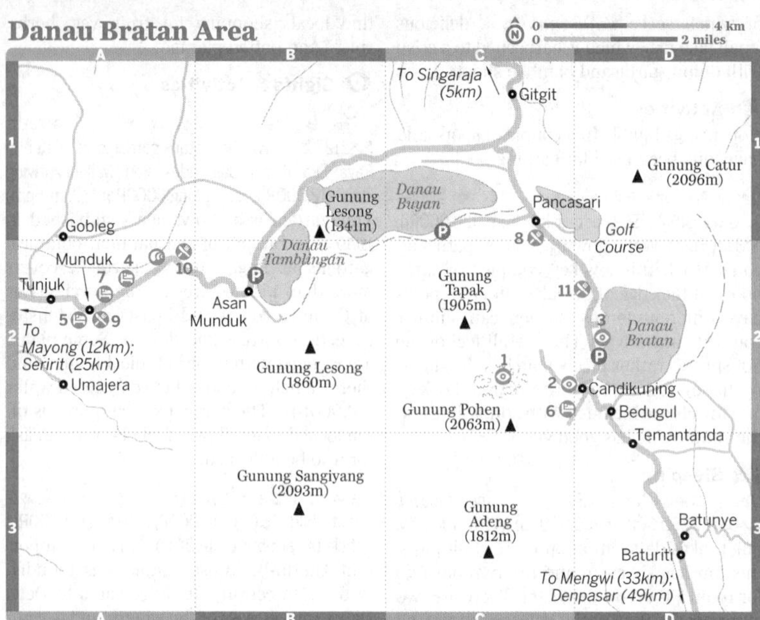

Danau Bratan Area

Sights

1 Bali Botanical Gardens........C2
2 Candikuning Market........C2
3 Pura Ulun Danu Bratan........D2

Activities, Courses & Tours

Bali Treetop Adventure Park...... (see 1)

Sleeping

4 Manah Liang Cottages........A2
5 Meme Surung........A2
6 Pondok Wisata Dahlia Indah........C2
7 Puri Lumbung Cottages........A2

Eating

8 Cafe Teras Lempuna........C1
9 Don Biyu........A2
10 Ngiring Ngewedang........A2
11 Strawberry Stop........D2

From simple market snacks to meals featuring the region's fresh strawberries, you'll have much to choose from.

Pondok Wisata Dahlia Indah GUESTHOUSE $
(☎21233; Jl Kebun Raya Bedugul; r 100,000-200,000Rp) In the village along a lane near the road to the botanical gardens, this is a decent budget option whose 17 comfortable, clean rooms have hot-water showers set in a garden of mountain flowers.

Strawberry Stop CAFE $
(☎21060; snacks from 10,000Rp; ⌚8am-7pm) Locally grown strawberries star in milkshakes, juices, pancakes and other treats. You can also get full meals. Bananas are used when berries are out of season, which might drive you to drink the self-proclaimed 'dry' – ha! – strawberry wine (100,000Rp).

Cafe Teras Lempuna INTERNATIONAL $
(☎0362-29312; meals 25,000-60,000Rp; ❄) North of the temple, this indoor/outdoor cafe is stylish and modern. The menu ranges from burgers to Japanese, and the coffee, tea and juices refresh no matter what the temperature. When it's sunny, enjoy the inviting covered patio; when it's cool, put on the heat with the hot chilli soup.

Getting There & Away

Danau Bratan is beside the main north–south road, so it's easy to reach from South Bali or Lovina. Although the main terminal is in Pancasari, most minibuses and bemos will stop along the road in Bedugul and Candikuning. There are frequent connections from Denpasar's Ubung terminal (20,000Rp) and Singaraja's Sukasada terminal (20,000Rp). For Gunung

Batur, you have to connect through Singaraja or hire transport.

MUNDUK & AROUND

0362

The simple village of Munduk is one of Bali's most appealing mountain retreats. It has a cool, misty ambience set among lush hillsides covered with jungle, rice, fruit trees and pretty much anything else that grows on the island. Waterfalls tumble off precipices by the dozen. There are hikes and treks galore and a number of really nice places to stay, from old Dutch summer homes to retreats where you can plunge full-on into local culture.

When the Dutch took control of north Bali in the 1890s, they experimented with commercial crops, establishing plantations for coffee, vanilla, cloves and cocoa. Quite a few Dutch colonial buildings are still intact along the road in Munduk and further west. Look for shrines nestled in the crooks of hills.

Sights & Activities

Heading to Munduk from Pancasari, the main road climbs steeply up the rim of the old volcanic crater. It's worth stopping to enjoy the **views** back over the valley and lakes. Turning right (east) at the top will take you on a scenic descent to Singaraja. Taking a sharp left turn (west), you follow a ridge-top road to Munduk with Danau Buyan on one side and views far down to the sea on the other. Consider a stop at **Ngiring Ngewedang** (0828 365 146; snacks 15,000-40,000Rp; 10am-5pm), a coffeehouse 5km east of Munduk that grows its own coffee on the surrounding slopes.

About 2km east of Munduk look for signs indicating parking for a 15m **waterfall** near the road. This is the most accessible of many in the immediate area.

Almost everything in the Munduk area is at an elevation of at least 1000m. Numerous trails are suitable for **treks** of two hours or much longer to coffee plantations, rice paddies, waterfalls, villages, or around both Danau Tamblingan and Danau Buyan. You will be able to arrange a guide through your lodgings.

Sleeping & Eating

The hikes around Munduk draw many visitors and consequently there are many places for them to stay. Enjoy simple old Dutch houses in the village or more naturalistic places in the countryside. Most have cafes, usually serving good local fare. There are a couple of cute warungs in the village and a few stores with very basic supplies (including bug spray).

TOP CHOICE **Puri Lumbung Cottages** GUESTHOUSE $$
(0812 383 6891, 0812 387 3986; www.purilumbung.com; cottages US$80-160; @) Founded by Nyoman Bagiarta to develop sustainable tourism, this lovely hotel has 33 bright two-storey cottages and rooms set among rice fields. Enjoy intoxicating views (units 3, 8, 10, 11, 14A and 14B have the best) down to the coast from the upstairs balconies. Dozens of trekking options and courses, including dance and cooking, are offered. The hotel's restaurant, **Warung Kopi Bali**, is excellent. The hotel is on the right-hand side of the road coming from Bedugul, 700m before Munduk.

Manah Liang Cottages INN $$
(700 5211; www.manahliang.com; r US$55-135;) About 800m east of Munduk, this country inn (whose name means 'feeling good') has traditional cottages overlooking the lush local terrain. The open-air bathrooms (with tubs) are as refreshing as the porches are relaxing. A short trail leads to a small waterfall. There are cooking classes and guided walks.

Meme Surung GUESTHOUSE $
(700 5378; www.memesurung.com; r US$35-45;) Two atmospheric old Dutch houses adjoin each other in the village and the compound has a total of 10 rooms. The decor is traditional and simple, which is just as well, as the view from the long wooden veranda is both the focus and the joy here. The cafe is good.

Don Biyu CAFE $
(www.donbiyu.com; mains 20,000Rp;) You know Munduk has arrived as a destination when it gets its first travellers' cafe. Catch up on your blog, enjoy good coffee, zone out to the sublime views and choose from a mix of Western and Asian fare. It's all served in mellow open-air pavilions.

Getting There & Away

Bemos leave Ubung terminal in Denpasar for Munduk (22,000Rp) frequently. Morning bemos from Candikuning also stop in Munduk (13,000Rp). If you're driving to the north coast, a decent road west of Munduk goes through a number of picturesque villages to Mayong (where you can head south to west Bali). The road then goes down to the sea at Seririt in north Bali.

Gunung Batukau Area

Often overlooked (probably a good thing, given what the vendor hordes have done to Gunung Agung), Gunung Batukau is Bali's second-highest mountain (2276m), the third most spiritully significant of Bali's three major mountains and the holy peak of the island's western end. Enjoy a magical visit to one of the island's holiest and most evocative temples, Pura Luhur Batukau, and revel in the ancient rice-terrace greenery around Jatiluwih.

Sights

TOP CHOICE Pura Luhur Batukau TEMPLE

(donation 10,000Rp) On the slopes of Gunung Batukau, Pura Luhur Batukau was the state temple when Tabanan was an independent kingdom. It has a seven-roofed *meru* dedicated to Maha Dewa, the mountain's guardian spirit, as well as shrines for Bratan, Buyan and Tamblingan lakes. The main *meru* in the inner courtyard have little doors shielding small ceremonial items. This is certainly the most spiritual temple you can easily visit in Bali.

The temple is surrounded by forest and the atmosphere is cool and misty; the chants of priests are backed by birds singing. Facing the temple, take a short walk around to the left to see a small white-water stream where the air resonates with tumbling water. Note the unusual fertility shrine.

There's a general lack of touts and other characters here – including hordes of tourists. A sign indicates that 'mad ladies/gentlemen' are not allowed to visit. Look sane. Respect traditions and act appropriately while visiting temples. Sarongs can be borrowed. Get here early for the best chance of seeing the dark and foreboding slopes of the volcano.

Jatiluwih Rice Fields VIEWPOINT

(per person 10,000Rp, plus 5000Rp per car) At Jatiluwih, which means 'Truly Marvellous', you will be rewarded with vistas of centuries-old rice terraces that exhaust your ability to describe green. The locals will also be rewarded with your 'green', as there's a road toll for visitors.

The terraces are included in Unesco's recognition of Bali's rice-growing traditions. You'll understand why just by viewing the panorama from the narrow, twisting 18km road, but get out for a **rice-field walk**. Follow the water as it runs through channels and bamboo pipes from one plot to the next.

Along the drive you'll pass cafes with tables overlooking the terraces, including the simple and tasty **Ada Babi Guleng** (lunch 35,000Rp; ⏲10am-4pm).

Getting There & Away

The only realistic way to explore the Gunung Batukau area is with your own transport.

NORTH BALI

Although one-sixth of the island's population lives in North Bali, this vast region, centred on Singaraja and the Buleleng regency, is overlooked by many visitors who stay trapped in the South Bali–Ubud axis. And that's ironic because the north was once the gateway to Bali, with Dutch steamers bringing the island's first visitors to the port in Singaraja.

Today, tourism in the north is focused on Lovina, the mellow beach town with cheap hotels and even cheaper sunset beer specials. To the west, Pemuteran charms all who discover the crescent of appealing resorts around a cute little bay. Diving is big here and all along the north coast.

Getting to North Bali for once lives up to the cliché: it's half the fun. Routes follow the thinly populated coastlines east and west, or you can go up and over the central mountains by any number of routes, marvelling at crater lakes and maybe stopping for a misty trek on the way.

Singaraja

☎0362 / POP 120,000

Singaraja (which means 'Lion King') is Bali's second-largest city and the capital of Buleleng Regency, which covers much of the north. With its tree-lined streets, surviving Dutch colonial buildings and charmingly sleepy waterfront area north of Jl Erlangga, it's worth exploring for a couple of hours. Most people stay in nearby Lovina.

Singaraja was the centre of Dutch power in Bali and remained the administrative centre for the Lesser Sunda Islands (Bali through to Timor) until 1953. Today it is a major educational and cultural centre.

North Bali

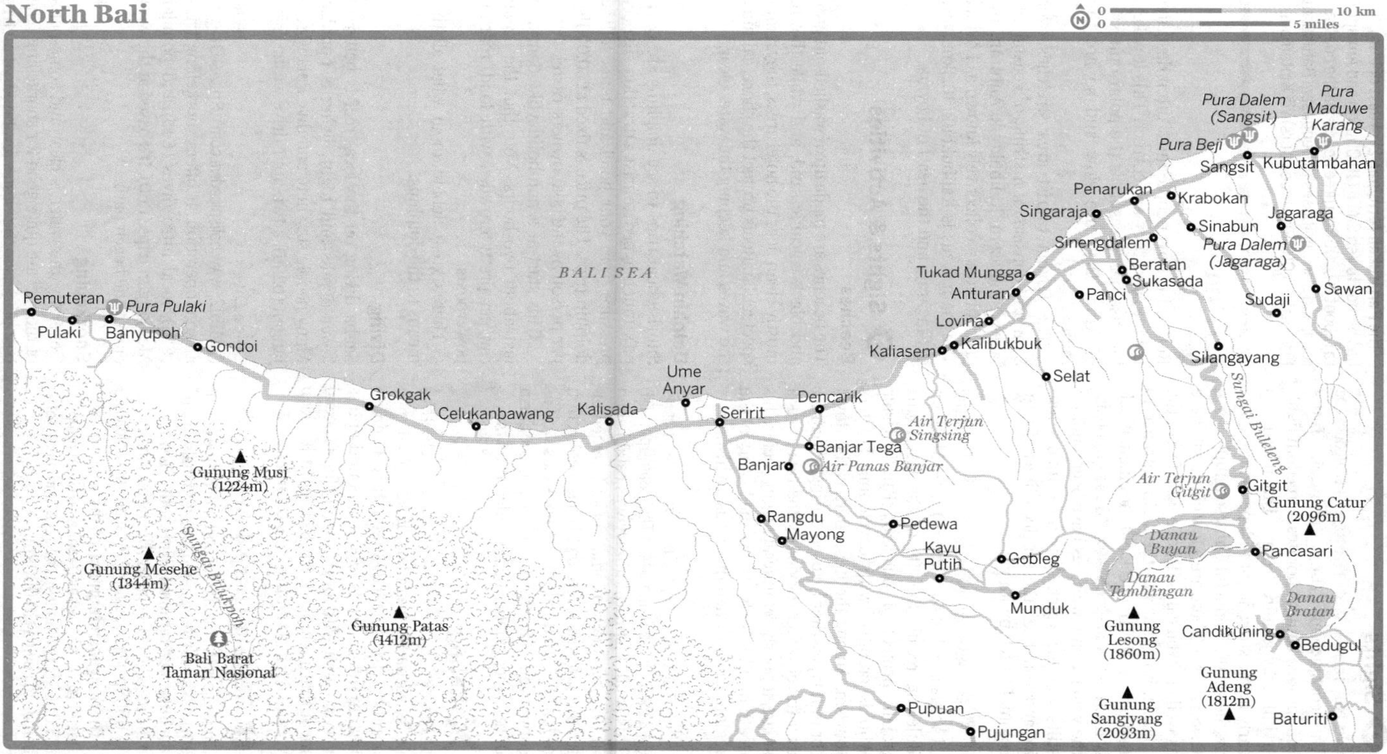

0 10 km
0 5 miles

BALI SEA
Pemuteran
Pura Pulaki
Pulaki
Banyupoh
Gondoi
Grokgak
Celukanbawang
Kalisada
Ume Anyar
Seririt
Dencarik
Kaliasem
Kalibukbuk
Lovina
Anturan
Tukad Mungga
Panci
Singaraja
Penarukan
Sinengdalem
Beratan
Sukasada
Krabokan
Sinabun
Pura Dalem (Jagaraga)
Jagaraga
Pura Beji
Pura Dalem (Sangsit)
Sangsit
Kubutambahan
Pura Maduwe Karang
Sawan
Sudaji
Silangayang
Selat
Sungai Buleleng
Air Terjun Singsing
Banjar Tega
Banjar
Air Panas Banjar
Rangdu
Mayong
Pedewa
Kayu Putih
Gobleg
Munduk
Air Terjun Gitgit
Gitgit
Gunung Catur (2096m)
Danau Buyan
Danau Tamblingan
Pancasari
Danau Bratan
Candikuning
Bedugul
Gunung Lesong (1860m)
Gunung Adeng (1812m)
Gunung Sangiyang (2093m)
Baturiti
Pupuan
Pujungan
Gunung Musi (1224m)
Gunung Mesehe (1344m)
Sungai Bilukpoh
Bali Barat Taman Nasional
Gunung Patas (1412m)

Sights

Old Harbour & Waterfront NEIGHBOURHOOD

The conspicuous **Yudha Mandala Tama monument** commemorates a freedom fighter killed by gunfire from a Dutch warship early in the struggle for independence. Close by, there's the colourful Chinese temple, **Ling Gwan Kiong**. There are a few old canals here as well and you can still get a little feel of the colonial port that was the main entrance to Bali before WWII; check out the cinematically decrepit **old Dutch warehouses** opposite the water. Some warungs have been built on stilts over the water. Walk up Jl Imam Bonjol and you'll see the art deco lines of late-colonial Dutch buildings.

FREE **Museum Buleleng** MUSEUM

(Jl Veteran; 9am-4pm Mon-Fri) The Museum Buleleng recalls the life of the last Radja (rajah; prince) of Buleleng, Pandji Tisna, who is credited with developing Lovina's tourism. Among the items here is the Royal (brand) typewriter he used during his career as a travel writer (obviously the rajah was a smart, if poorly remunerated, guy) before his death in 1978. It also traces the history of the region back to when there was no history.

FREE **Gedong Kirtya Library** LIBRARY

(22645; 8am-4pm Mon-Thu, 8am-1pm Fri) This small historical library was established in 1928 by Dutch colonialists and named after the Sanskrit for 'to try'. It has a collection of *lontar* (dried palm-leaf) books, as well as some even older written works in the form of inscribed copper plates called *prasasti*.

Eating

Manalagi BALINESE $

(Jl Sahadewa 8A; meals from 15,000Rp) Down a pretty, tree-shaded street, this Balinese restaurant sits in its own compound and is very popular with locals looking for a special meal that includes fresh fish. With its deep verandas, the building feels colonial.

Getting There & Away

Singaraja is the main transport hub for the northern coast, with three bemo/bus terminals. From the **Sukasada terminal**, 3km south of town, minibuses go to Denpasar (Ubung terminal, 35,000Rp) via Bedugul/Pancasari sporadically.

The **Banyuasri terminal**, on the western side of town, has buses heading to Gilimanuk (25,000Rp, two hours) and Java, and plenty of bemos to Lovina (10,000Rp).

The **Penarukan terminal**, 2km east of town, has bemos to Yeh Sanih (10,000Rp) and Amlapura (about 20,000Rp, three hours) via the coastal road; and also minibuses to Denpasar (Batubulan terminal, 35,000Rp, three hours) via Kintamani.

Lovina

0362

Relaxed is how people most often describe Lovina, and they are correct. This low-key, low-rise beach resort is the polar opposite of Kuta. Days are slow and so are the nights.

The Lovina tourist area stretches over 8km and consists of a string of coastal villages – Kaliasem, Kalibukbuk, Anturan, Tukad Mungga – collectively known as Lovina. The main focus is Kalibukbuk, 10.5km west of Singaraja and the heart of Lovina.

Sights & Activities

Beaches

The beaches are made up of washed-out grey and black volcanic sand, and while they're mostly clean near the hotel areas, they're not spectacular. Reefs protect the shore, calming the waves and keeping the water clear.

Dolphin Watching

Sunrise boat trips to see dolphins are Lovina's much-hyped tourist attraction. Expect pressure from your hotel and touts selling dolphin trips. The price is fixed at 50,000Rp per person by the boat-owners' cartel.

Trips start at a non-holidaylike 6am and last about two hours. Note that the ocean can get pretty crowded with loud, roaring powerboats.

There's great debate about what all this means to the dolphins.

Diving

Scuba diving on the local reef is better at lower depths and night diving is popular. Many people stay here and dive Pulau Menjangan (p296), a two-hour drive west.

Spice Dive DIVING

(41512; www.balispicedive.com) Spice Dive is a large operation. It offers snorkelling trips (€25), local intro dives (€45) and popular Menjangan trips (€60). It's based at the west end of the beach path.

Snorkelling

Generally, the water is clear and some parts of the reef are quite good for snorkelling. The best place is to the west, a few hundred metres

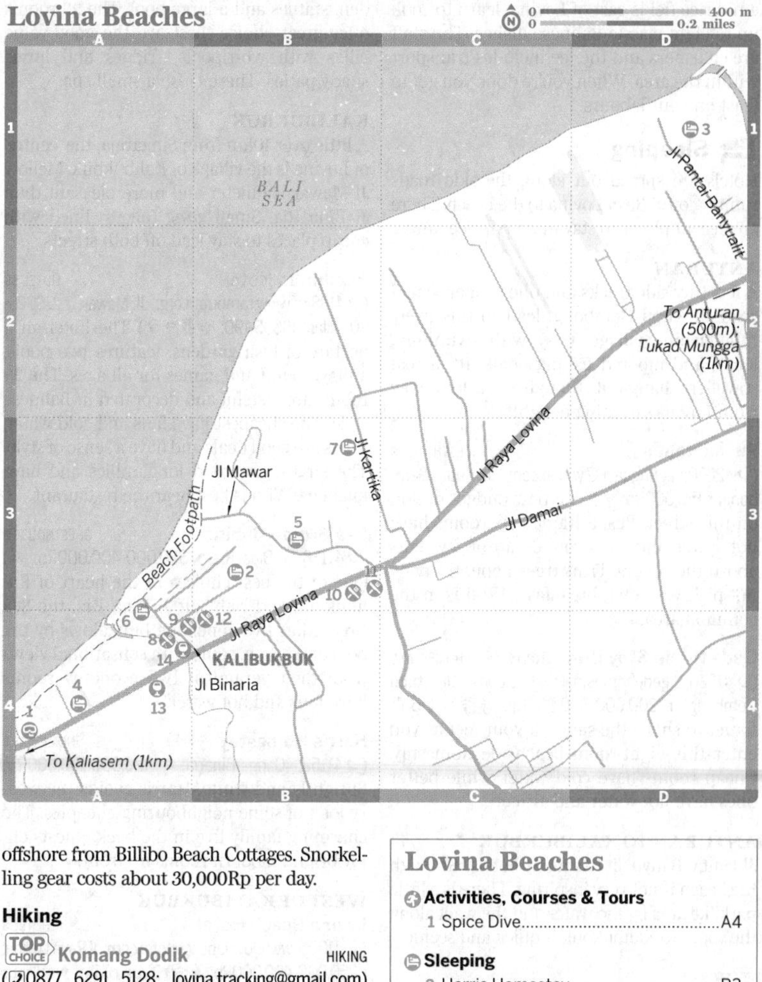

Lovina Beaches

offshore from Billibo Beach Cottages. Snorkelling gear costs about 30,000Rp per day.

Hiking

TOP CHOICE **Komang Dodik** HIKING
(☎0877 6291 5128; lovina.tracking@gmail.com) Komang Dodik leads highly recommended hikes in the hills along the north coast. Trips start at 250,000Rp per person and can last from three to seven hours. The highlight of most is a series of waterfalls, over 20m high, in a jungle grotto. Routes can include coffee and vanilla plantations.

Courses

Warung Bambu Pemaron COOKING COURSE
(☎31455; www.warung-bambu.mahanara.com; Pemaron; 1/2 persons 500,000/660,000Rp; ⏲8am-1pm) Start with a trip to Singaraja's large food market and then, in a breezy setting

Lovina Beaches

Activities, Courses & Tours
1 Spice Dive A4

Sleeping
2 Harris Homestay B3
3 Hotel Banyualit D1
4 Lovina Beach Hotel A4
5 Rambutan Hotel B3
6 Sea Breeze Cabins A4
7 Villa Taman Ganesha B3

Eating
8 Akar A4
9 Jasmine Kitchen A4
10 Khi Khi Restaurant B3
11 Night Market B3
12 Seyu B4

Drinking
13 Kantin 21 .... A4
14 Poco Lounge A4

amid rice fields east of Lovina, learn to cook up to eight classic Balinese dishes. The staff are charmers and the fee includes transport within the area. When you're done you get to feast on your labours.

Sleeping

Hotels are spread out along the side roads running off Jl Raya Lovina to the beach. There are decent places to stay in every price range.

ANTURAN

A few tiny side tracks and one proper sealed road, Jl Kubu Gembong, lead to this lively little fishing village, busy with swimming locals and moored fishing boats. It's a real travellers' hang-out, though it's a long way from Lovina's evening delights.

Puspa Rama GUESTHOUSE $
(☎42070; agungdayu@yahoo.com; Jl Kubu Gembong; r 150,000Rp;) The best budget option on this street, Puspa Rama's six rooms have hot water and the grounds are a few cuts above the others. Fruit trees abound – why not pick your own breakfast? Wi-fi is in the common area.

Gede Home Stay Bungalows HOMESTAY $
(☎41526; gedehomestay@yahoo.com; Jl Kubu Gembong; r 200,000-300,000Rp;) Don't forget to shake the sand off your feet as you enter this eight-room beachside homestay. Cheap rooms have cold water while better ones have hot water and air-con.

ANTURAN TO KALIBUKBUK

Jl Pantai Banyualit has many hotels, although the beach is not very inspiring. There is a little parklike area by the water and the walk along the shore to Kalibukbuk is quick and scenic.

TOP CHOICE **Villa Taman Ganesha** GUESTHOUSE $$
(☎41272; www.taman-ganesha-lovina.com; Jl Kartika 45; r €30-60;) Down a quiet lane lined with Balinese family compounds is this lovely guesthouse. The grounds are lush and fragrant with frangipani plants from around the world that have been collected by the owner, a landscape architect from Germany. There's a large pool. The four units are very private and have all the comforts of home. The beach is 400m away and it's a 10-minute walk along the sand to Kalibukbuk.

Hotel Banyualit HOTEL $$
(☎41789; www.banyualit.com; Jl Pantai Banyualit; r from 650,000Rp;) About 100m back from the beach, the Banyualit has a lush garden, statues and a large pool. The 23 rooms offer great choice; best are the good-value villas with whirlpools, fridges and large, shady patios. There's also a small spa.

KALIBUKBUK

A little over 10km from Singaraja, the 'centre' of Lovina is the village of Kalibukbuk. Mellow Jl Mawar is quieter and more pleasant than Jl Bina Ria. Small *gang* (alleys) lined with cheap places to stay lead off both streets.

Rambutan Hotel HOTEL $$
(☎41388; www.rambutan.org; Jl Mawar; r US$25-80, villas US$95-190; @) The hotel, in a hectare of lush gardens, features two pools, a playground and games for all ages. The 28 rooms are tasteful and decorated in Balinese style. The cheapest have fans and cold water. Villas are good deals and have a sense of style. The largest are good for families and have kitchens. Wi-fi is best near the restaurant.

Sea Breeze Cabins GUESTHOUSE $
(☎41138; Jl Bina Ria; r 350,000-400,000Rp;) One of the best choices in the heart of Kalibukbuk and right off Jl Bina Ria, the Sea Breeze has five appealing bungalows by the pool and beach, some with sensational views from their verandas. Two economy rooms have fans and hot water.

Harris Homestay HOMESTAY $
(☎41152; Gang Binaria; r 120,000-150,000Rp) Sprightly and white, Harris avoids the weary look of some neighbouring cheapies. The charming family live in the back; guests enjoy bright, modern rooms up front.

WEST OF KALIBUKBUK

Lovina Beach Hotel HOTEL $
(☎41005; www.lovinabeachhotel.com; Jl Raya Lovina; r 250,000-400,000Rp;) This older, well-run beach hotel hasn't changed in years and neither have its prices. The 24 rooms, in a two-storey block, are clean if a bit frayed. Bungalows feature carving and Balinese details, the ones on the beach are a bargain. The grounds feel like a park.

Eating

Just about every hotel has a cafe or restaurant. Close to the centre of Lovina you can find several places that go beyond the usual travellers' fare. Beachside places are good just for drinks if you're planning to do some hopping.

A small **night market** (Jl Raya Lovina; meals from 15,000Rp; 5-11pm) is a good choice for fresh and cheap local food.

ANTURAN

Warung Rasta SEAFOOD $

(meals 15,000-50,000Rp) Right on a strip of beach, a growing number of tables, chairs and picnic benches mix with fishing boats. The menu not surprisingly leans towards simply grilled fresh seafood; given the name, the endless loop of music shouldn't surprise either. It's run by dudes who have clearly realised that lounging around here all day beats fishing.

KALIBUKBUK

TOP CHOICE **Jasmine Kitchen** THAI $$

(☎41565; Gang Binaria; meals 40,000-100,000Rp) The Thai fare at this elegant two-level restaurant lives up to the promise of the trays of chillis drying out front: it's excellent. The menu is long and authentic and the staff gracious. While soft jazz plays, try the home-made ice cream for dessert. You can refill water bottles here for 2000Rp.

TOP CHOICE **Seyu** JAPANESE $$

(www.seyulovina.com; Jl Binaria; dishes from 40,000Rp;) A great addition to Lovina, this truly authentic Japanese place has a skilled sushi chef and a solid list of fresh nigiri and sashimi choices. The dining room is suitably spare and uncomplicated.

Akar VEGETARIAN $

(☎0817 972 4717; Jl Binaria; meals 30,000-50,000Rp;) The many shades of green at this cute-as-a-baby-frog cafe aren't just for show. They reflect the earth-friendly ethics of the owners. Refill your water containers here and then enjoy organic smoothies and fresh and tasty noodle dishes that include Asian sesame, beetroot and cheese lasagne and chilli garlic spaghetti. A tiny back porch overlooks the river.

Khi Khi Restaurant CHINESE $

(☎41548; meals 10,000-100,000Rp) Well off Jl Raya Lovina and behind the night market, this barn of a place specialises in Chinese food and grilled seafood, including lobster. It's always popular in a rub-elbows-with-your-neighbour kind of way.

Drinking & Entertainment

Lovina's modest social scene centres on Kalibukbuk.

Kantin 21 BAR

(☎0812 460 7791; Jl Raya Lovina; ⊙11am-1am) Funky open-air place where you can watch traffic by day and groove to acoustic guitar or garage-band rock by night. There's a long drinks list (jugs of Long Island iced tea for 80,000Rp), fresh juices and a few local snacks. The old VW bus out front completes the groovy tableau.

Poco Lounge BAR

(☎41535; Jl Binaria; ⊙11am-1am) Movies are shown at various times, and cover bands perform at this popular bar-cafe. Classic travellers' fare (dishes 12,000Rp to 25,000Rp) is served at tables open to street life in front and the river in back.

Information

Kalibukbuk has internet places and ATMs.

Getting There & Away

Bus & Bemo

To reach Lovina from South Bali by public transport, you'll need to change in Singaraja. Regular blue bemos go from Singaraja's Banyuasri terminal to Kalibukbuk (about 10,000Rp) – you can flag them down anywhere on the main road.

If you're coming by long-distance bus from the west you can ask to be dropped off anywhere along the main road.

Tourist Shuttle Bus

Perama buses stop at its office, in front of **Hotel Perama** (☎41 161) on Jl Raya Lovina in Anturan. Passengers are then ferried to other points on the Lovina strip (10,000Rp).

DESTINATION	COST (RP)	DURATION (HR)
Candidasa	150,000	5½
Kuta	100,000	4
Padangbai	150,000	4¾
Sanur	100,000	3¾
Ubud	100,000	2¾

Getting Around

The Lovina strip is *very* spread out, but you can easily travel back and forth on bemo (5000Rp).

West Of Lovina

The main road west of Lovina passes temples, farms and towns while it follows the thinly developed coast. You'll notice a lot of vineyards, where the grapes work overtime producing the sugar that's used in Bali's very sweet local vintages.

DON'T MISS

WATERFALLS

About 5km west of Lovina, a sign points to **Air Terjun Singsing** (Daybreak Waterfall). About 1km from the main road, there is a warung on the left and a car park on the right. Walk past the warung and along the path for about 200m to the lower falls. The waterfall is not huge, but the pool underneath is ideal for swimming. The water isn't crystal clear, but it's cooler than the sea and very refreshing.

The area is thick with tropical forest and makes a nice day trip from Lovina. The falls are more spectacular in the wet season (October to March); they can be just a trickle at other times.

Pemuteran

☎0362

This oasis in the far northwest corner of Bali has a number of artful resorts set on a little dogbone-shaped bay that's alive with local life, such as kids playing soccer until dark. Pemuteran is the place to come for a real beach getaway. Most people dive or snorkel the underwater wonders at nearby Pulau Menjangan while here.

Sights & Activities

Strolling the **beach** is popular, especially at sunset, as you'd expect.

The extensive coral reefs are about 3km offshore. Coral that's closer in is being restored as part of a unique project involving electrical stimulation of coral growth, which has won international plaudits.

Diving and **snorkelling** are universally popular. Local dives cost from US$60; snorkelling gear rents from 40,000Rp.

Pemuteran is well placed for diving and snorkelling beautiful Pulau Menjangan (p296). A dock for boats out to the island is just 7km west of town, so you have only a short ride before you're on a boat for the relaxing and pretty 45-minute journey to Menjangan. The dive shops and all the local hotels run snorkelling trips that cost US$35 to US$50, and dive trips from US$90.

Easy Divers DIVING

(☎94736; www.easy-divers.eu) The founder, Dusan Repic, has befriended many a diver new to Bali and this shop is well recommended. It is on the main road near the Taman Sari Bali Cottages and Pondok Sari hotel.

TOP CHOICE **Reef Seen** DIVING

(☎93001; www.reefseen.com) Right on the beach in a large compound, Reef Seen is active in local preservation efforts. It is a PADI dive centre and has a full complement of classes. It also offers sunset and sunrise cruises aboard glass-bottomed boats (per person from 250,000Rp), and pony rides on the beach for kids (from 200,000Rp for 30 minutes).

Sleeping & Eating

Pemuteran has one of the nicest selections of beachside hotels in Bali. Many have a sense of style and all are low-key and relaxed, with easy access to the beach. There are small warungs along the main drag, otherwise all the hotels have good midrange restaurants. You can wander between them along the beach debating which one to choose.

TOP CHOICE **Taman Sari Bali Cottages** HOTEL $$

(☎93264; www.balitamansari.com; bungalows US$50-200; ❄@📶) Thirty-one rooms are set in gorgeous bungalows that feature intricate carvings and traditional artwork inside and out. The open-air bathrooms inspire extended ablutions. Most rooms are under US$100 – those over are quite palatial. It's located on a long stretch of quiet beach on the bay, and part of the reef restoration project.

TOP CHOICE **Taman Selini Beach Bungalows** BOUTIQUE HOTEL $$

(☎94746; www.tamanselini.com; r US$100-250; ❄📶) The 11 bungalows recall an older, refined Bali, from the quaint thatched roofs down to the antique carved doors and detailed stonework. Rooms, which open onto a large garden running to the beach, have four-poster beds and large outdoor bathrooms. The outdoor daybeds can be addictive. It's immediately east of Pondok Sari, on the beach and right off the main road.

Pondok Sari HOTEL $$

(☎94 738; www.pondoksari.com; r €40-170; ❄🏊) There are 36 rooms here set in densely planted gardens that assure privacy. The pool is down by the beach; the cafe has sweet water views through the trees (and serves breakfast until 3pm!). Traditional Balinese details abound; bathrooms are open-air and a calling card for the stone-carvers. Deluxe units have elaborate stone tubs among other details. The resort is just off the main road.

Rare Angon Homestay HOMESTAY $
(☎94747, 081 2467 9462; www.pemuterandive.com; r 250,000-500,000Rp; ❄) Good basic rooms in a homestay located on the south side of the main road. K&K Dive Centre is here.

Getting There & Away

Pemuteran is served by any of the buses and bemo on the Gilimanuk–Lovina run. Labuhan Lalang and Bali Barat National Park are 12km west. It's a three- to four-hour drive from South Bali, either over the hills or around the west coast.

WEST BALI

Some of Bali's most sacred sites are in the west, from the ever-thronged Pura Tanah Lot to the Unesco-recognised Pura Taman Ayun. In between you can cruise along beside coursing streams on rural roads with bamboo arching overhead and fruit piling up below.

But the real star of the underachieving west is Bali Barat (West Bali) National Park, the only protected place of its kind on the island. Few who dive or snorkel the rich and pristine waters around Pulau Menjangan (p296) forget the experience. Others go for the challenge and trek through the savannah flats, mangroves and hillside jungles. Amid it all you'll find isolated resorts and hideaway inns in places such as Balian Beach or Mengwi.

Tanah Lot

☎0361

One of the most popular day trips from South Bali, **Pura Tanah Lot** (adult/child 30,000/15,000Rp, parking 5000Rp) is the most visited and photographed temple in Bali. It's an obligatory stop, especially at sunset, and it is very commercialised. It has all the authenticity of a stage set – even the tower of rock that the temple sits upon is an artful reconstruction (the entire structure was crumbling). Over one-third of the rock you see is artificial.

For the Balinese, Pura Tanah Lot is one of the most important and venerated sea temples. Like Pura Luhur Ulu Watu, at the tip of the southern Bukit Peninsula, it is closely associated with the Majapahit priest, Nirartha.

Tanah Lot, however, is a well-organised tourist trap. To reach the temple, a walkway runs through a sort of sideshow alley with dozens of souvenir shops down to the sea. To ease the task of making purchases, there is an ATM.

To visit the temple you should pick the correct time – everybody shows up for sunset and the mobs obliterate any spiritual feel the place has. If you visit before noon, crowds are few and the vendors are all but asleep.

Getting There & Away

Coming from South Bali with your own transport, take the coastal road west from Kerobokan, north of Seminyak, and follow the signs or the traffic. It can take well over an hour in the afternoon before sunset.

DON'T MISS

PURA TAMAN AYUN

The huge royal water temple of **Pura Taman Ayun** (adult/child 15,000/7500Rp; ⏰8am-6pm), surrounded by a wide, elegant moat, was the main temple of the Mengwi kingdom, which survived until 1891, when it was conquered by the neighbouring kingdoms of Tabanan and Badung. The large, spacious temple was built in 1634 and extensively renovated in 1937. It's a spacious place to wander around and you can get away from speed-obsessed group-tour mobs ('Back on the bus, pilgrims!'). The first courtyard is a large, open, grassy expanse and the inner courtyard has a multitude of *meru* (multi-tiered shrines). Lotus-blossoms fill the pools; the temple forms part of the subak system of sites recognised by Unesco in 2012.

Pura Taman Ayun is a stop-off on many organised tourist tours and an easy stop on a drive to/from Bedugal and the Jatiluwih rice fields.

West Bali

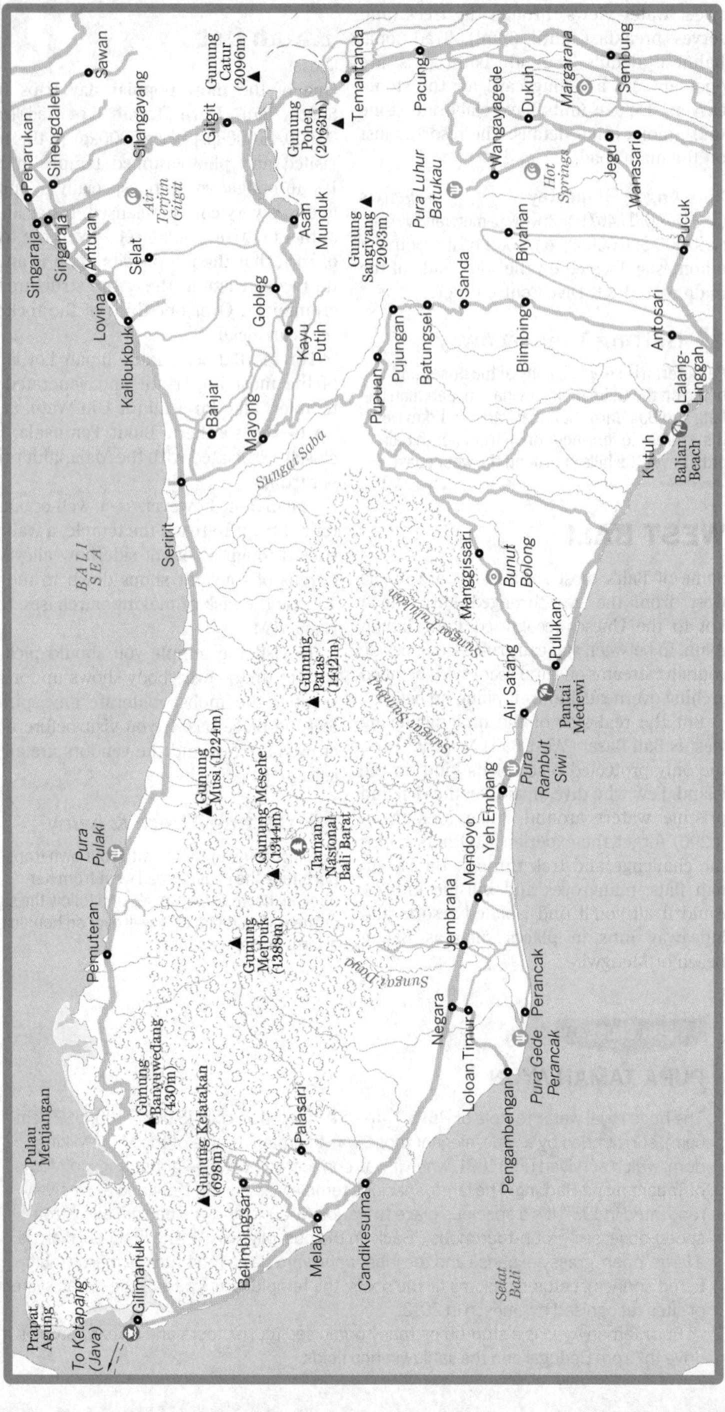

0 10 km
0 5 miles
Prapat Agung
Pulau Menjangan
To Ketapang (Java)
Gilimanuk
Pemuteran
Pura Pulaki
BALI SEA
Singaraja
Penarukan
Singaraja
Sinengdalem
Lovina
Anturan
Sawan
Kalibukbuk
Selat
Air Terjun Gitgit
Silangayang
Seririt
Gunung Banyuwedang (430m)
Gunung Kelatakan (698m)
Belimbingsari
Gunung Musi (1224m)
Gunung Merbuk (1388m)
Gunung Mesehe (1344m)
Taman Nasional Bali Barat
Gunung Patas (1412m)
Palasari
Melaya
Candikesuma
Banjar
Mayong
Sungai Saba
Gobleg
Kayu Putih
Asan Munduk
Gitgit
Gunung Catur (2096m)
Gunung Pohen (2063m)
Temantanda
Gunung Sangiyang (2093m)
Pupuan
Pujungan
Batungsei
Pura Luhur Batukau
Pacung
Sanda
Wangayagede
Dukuh
Biyahan
Blimbing
Hot Springs
Margarana
Jegu
Wanasari
Sembung
Antosari
Pucuk
Kutuh
Balian Beach
Lalang-Linggah
Sungai Daya
Sungai Sumbul
Sungai Pulukan
Negara
Jembrana
Mendoyo
Loloan Timur
Yeh Embang
Manggissari
Selat Bali
Pengambengan
Pura Gede Perancak
Perancak
Pura Rambut Siwi
Air Satang
Bunut Bolong
Pantai Medewi
Pulukan

Tabanan

☎0361

Tabanan, like most regional capitals in Bali, is a large, well-organised place. The verdant surrounding rice fields are emblamatic of the Bali's rice-growing traditions and are part of its Unesco recognition.

Playing a critical role in rural Bali life, the *subak* is a village association that deals with water, water rights and irrigation. With water passing through many, many scores of rice fields before it drains away for good, there is always the chance that growers near the source would be water-rich while those at the bottom would be selling carved wooden critters at Tanah Lot. Regulating a system that apportions a fair share to everyone is a model of mutual cooperation and an insight into the Balinese character. (One of the strategies used is to put the last person on the water channel in control.)

This complex and vital social system was recognised by Unesco in 2012 and added to the World Heritage list. Specific sites singled out include much of the rice-growing region around Tabanan, Pura Taman Ayun and the Jatiluwih rice terraces.

Learn more about Bali's rice-growing traditions at the **Mandala Mathika Subak** (Subak Museum; Jl Raya Kediri; adult/child 15,000/7500Rp; ⏲7am-4.30pm), a simple museum just east of Tabanan.

The road to Pura Luhur Batukau and the beautiful rice terraces of Jatiluwih heads north from the centre of town.

Balian Beach

☎0361

One of Bali's new hotspots, Balian Beach has the slight pioneer charm of a place that's still on the brink of discovery. A rolling area of dunes and knolls overlooks the pounding surf here which attracts ever-more people for the **surfing**. You can easily rent a surfboard on the beach.

A critical mass of villas and beach accommodation has appeared and you can wander between cafes and join other travellers for a beer, sunset and talk of surf. Nonsurfers will simply enjoy the wild waves and good cafes.

Black-sand Balian Beach is right at the mouth of the wide Sungai Balian (Balian River). It is 800m south of the town of **Lalang-Linggah**, which is on the main road 10km west of Antosari.

Sleeping & Eating

All of the accommodation listed below is fairly close together, near the beach. Warungs and simple cafes mean a bottle of Bintang is never more than a minute's walk away.

TOP CHOICE **Pondok Pitaya** GUESTHOUSE $

(☎0819 9984 9054; www.baliansurf.com; r 200,000-800,000Rp; 📶) A lodge as memorable as its spray-scented location right on wave-tossed Balian Beach, the complex combines vintage Indonesian buildings (including a 1950 Javanese house and an 1860 Balinese alligator hunter's shack) with more modest accommodation. Room choices are like the surf: variable. Couples have a choice of rather lavish king-bed rooms, and a tribe can occupy a vast house that sleeps eight in one room. The cafe has surfer fare.

Pondok Pisces GUESTHOUSE $$

(☎780 1735, 0813 3879 7722; www.pondokpiscesbali.com; r 520,000-1,000,000Rp; 📶) You can certainly hear the sea at this tropical fantasy of thatched cottages and flower-filled gardens. Of the 10 rooms, those on the upper floor have large terraces with surf views. In-house **Tom's Garden Cafe** has grilled seafood and surf views. Down by the river and slightly upstream, there are three large villas and bungalows in **Balian Riverside Sanctuary**, lushly set in a teak forest.

Surya Homestay GUESTHOUSE $

(☎0813 3868 5643; wayan.suratni@gmail.com; r 100,00-150,000Rp) There are five rooms here in new bungalow-style units at this sweet little family-run place that is about 200m along the lane to Gajah Mina. It's spotless and rooms have cold water and fans. Ask about long-term rates.

Jembrana Coast

About 34km west of Tabanan you cross into Bali's most sparsely populated district, Jembrana. The main road follows the south coast most of the way to Negara. There's some beautiful scenery but little tourist development along the way, with the exception of the surf action at Medewi.

MEDEWI

Along the main road, a large sign points down the paved road (200m) to the surfing mecca of Pantai Medewi. The beach is a stretch of huge, smooth grey rocks interspersed among round black pebbles. It's a placid place where cattle graze by the beach. Medewi is noted not for its beach but for its *long* left-hand wave – there is little else here.

Sleeping & Eating

You'll find accommodation along the main lane to the surf break and down other lanes about 2km east. For a casual meal, some of the finest fare is freshly stir-fried and served up at a cart right by the beach/rocks.

Hotel CSB GUESTHOUSE $

(☎0813 3866 7288; r 150,000-300,000Rp; ❄) Some 900m east of the Medewi surf break at Pulukan, look for signs along the main road. Venture 300m down a track and you'll find a great family-run guesthouse. The best of these simply furnished rooms have air-con, hot water and balconies with views that put anything in South Bali to shame. The coast and churning surf curve to the east, backed by jade-green rice fields and rows of palm trees. It's rather idyllic.

Medewi Beach Cottages HOTEL $$

(☎0361-852 8521; www.medewibeachcottages.com; r from 750,000Rp; ❄≋) A large pool anchors modern, comfortable rooms (with satellite TV) scattered about nice gardens right down by the surf break. The one off-note: security measures obstruct what should be a good view.

Gilimanuk

☎0365

Gilimanuk is the terminus for ferries that shuttle back and forth across the narrow strait to Java.

Most travellers to or from Java can get an onward ferry or bus straight away, and won't need to stop here.

Getting There & Away

Frequent buses battle traffic along the main road between Gilimanuk's huge bus depot and Denpasar's Ubung terminal (30,000Rp, two to three hours), or along the north-coast road to Singaraja (25,000Rp). Long-distance busses to/from Java use the new bus terminal near Mengwi.

Car ferries to and from Ketapang on Java (30 minutes) run around the clock.

Bali Barat National Park

☎0365

Call it nature's symphony. Most visitors to Bali's only national park, Bali Barat (West Bali) National Park, are struck by the mellifluous sounds from myriad birds. It's a place where you can hike through forests, enjoy the island's best diving at Pulau Menjangan and explore coastal mangroves.

DON'T MISS

DIVING PULAU MENJANGAN

Bali's best-known dive area, Pulau Menjangan has a dozen superb dive sites. The diving is excellent – iconic tropical fish, soft corals, great visibility (usually), caves and a spectacular drop-off. One of the few complaints we've ever heard came from a reader who said that while snorkelling she kept getting water in her mouth because she was 'smiling so much'.

Of the dozen or so recognsied sites here, most are close to shore and suitable for snorkellers or diving novices. Some decent snorkelling spots are not far from the jetty – ask the boatman where to go. Venture a bit out, however, and the depths turn inky black as the shallows drop off in dramatic cliffs, a magnet for experienced divers looking for wall dives. The **Anker Wreck**, a mysterious sunken ship, challenges even experts.

The closest and most convenient dive operators are found at Pemuteran, where the hotels also arrange diving and snorkelling trips. Independent snorkellers can arrange for a boat (three-hour trip for two, 350,000Rp) from the tiny dock at Labuhan Lalang just across the turquoise water from Menjangan. Warungs here rent snorkelling gear (a pricey 50,000Rp for four hours; negotiate). There is a park divers fee of 75,000Rp and a snorkellers fee of 60,000Rp.

The park covers over 70,000 hectares of the western tip of Bali as well as almost 7000 hectares of coral reef and coastal waters.

Sights & Activities

By land, by boat or by water, the park awaits exploration. Most of the natural vegetation in the park is not tropical rainforest, which requires rain year-round, but coastal savannah, with deciduous trees that become bare in the dry season. The southern slopes receive more regular rainfall, and hence have more tropical vegetation, while the coastal lowlands have extensive mangroves.

Boat Trips

The best way to explore the mangroves of Teluk Gilimanuk or the west side of Prapat Agung is by chartering a boat (maximum of five people) for about 250,000Rp per boat per hour, including guide and entrance fees. You can arrange this at either of the park offices. This is the ideal way to see birdlife, including kingfishers, Javanese herons and plenty of others.

Trekking

All trekkers must be accompanied by an authorised guide. It's best to arrive the day before you want to trek, and make enquiries at the park offices in Cekik or Labuhan Lalang.

The set rates for guides in the park depend on the size of the group and the length of the trek – with one or two people it's 350,000Rp for one or two hours, with rates steadily increasing from there. Early morning, say 6am, is the best time to start – it's cooler and you're more likely to see some wildlife. The following are two of the more popular treks.

From a trail west of Labuhan Lalang, hike around the mangroves at **Teluk Terima**. Then partially follow Sungai Terima into the hills and walk back down to the road along the steps at Makam Jayaprana. You might see grey macaques, deer and black monkeys (allow two to three hours).

From Sumber Kelompok, go up **Gunung Kelatakan** (698m), then down to the main road near Kelatakan village (six to seven hours). You may be able to get permission from park headquarters to stay overnight in the forest – if you don't have a tent, your guide can make a shelter from branches and leaves, which will be an adventure in itself. Clear streams abound in the dense woods.

Information

The **park headquarters** (☎61060; ⏰7am-5pm) at Cekik displays a topographic model of the park area, and has a little information about plants and wildlife. The Labuhan Lalang **visitors centre** (⏰7.30am-5pm) is in a hut located on the northern coast, where boats leave for Pulau Menjangan.

Getting There & Away

The national park is too far for a comfortable day trip from Ubud or South Bali, though many dive operators do it. Better to stay in Pemuteran.

Nusa Tenggara

POP 8.3 MILLION

Includes »

Best Places to Eat

» Restaurant Laryss (p367)

» Blu da Mare (p324)

» Cantik Homestay (p373)

» Rumah Makan Murah Muriah (p362)

» Best Places to Stay

» Malole Surf House (p385)

» La Petite Kepa (p372)

» Amanwana (p341)

» Oro Beach Houses & Restaurant (p400)

Why Go?

If you've ever been into white sand, azure bays, frothing hot springs and hidden traditional villages, Nusa Tenggara is your wonderland. Here's an arc of islands that is lush and jungle-green in the north, more arid savannah in the south and in-between has some of the world's best diving, limitless surf breaks, and Technicolor volcanic lakes. It's a land of pink-sand beaches, schooling sharks and rays, and swaggering dragons. You'll also find a cultural diversity that is unmatched in Indonesia. Animist rituals and tribal traditions still thrive alongside the countless minarets, temples, convents and chapels, and though Bahasa Indonesia is a unifying tongue, each main island has at least one native language, which is often subdivided into dialects. Whether your wish is to drop into the easy, tourist-ready life of a carless Gili, or you crave something, somewhere less comfortable, more challenging and a shade deeper, you're exactly where you're supposed to be.

When To Go

Mataram

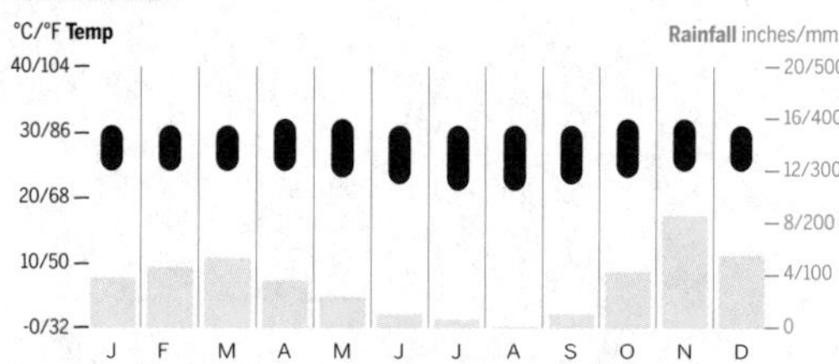

Apr–Sep Divers descend during the dry season when visibility clarifies throughout the province.

May & Oct These months often see epic waves and thin crowds in Rote and Sumbawa.

Oct–Mar Sumba's Pasola festival, in February, is reason enough to brave Nusa Tenggara in the wet.

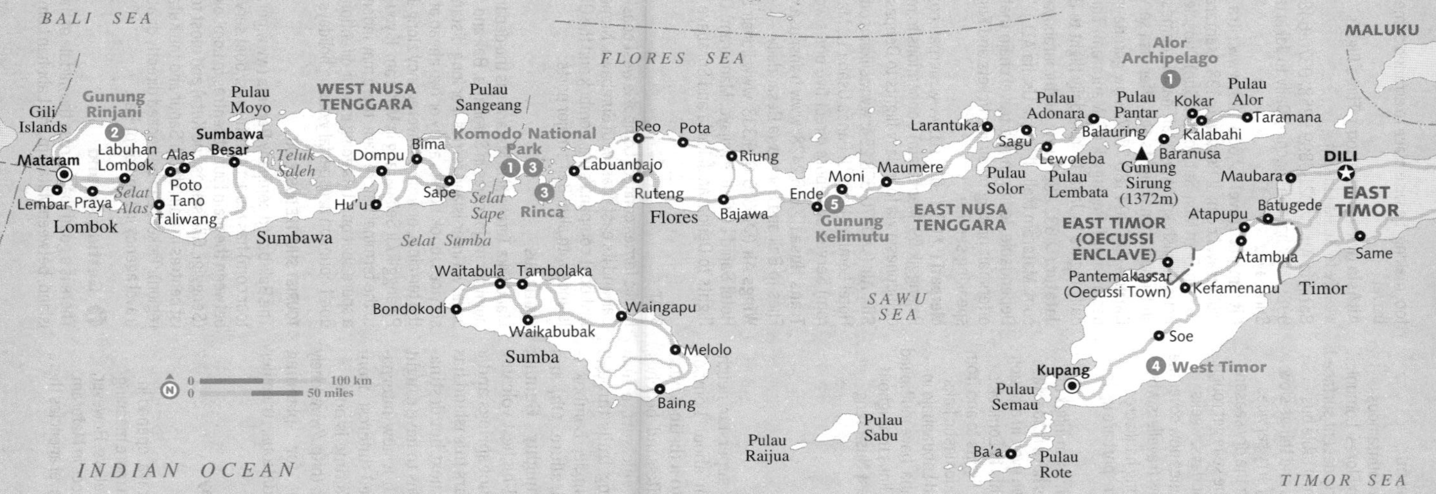

Nusa Tenggara Highlights

1. Snorkelling or diving in coral reefs teeming with marine life around the **Komodo National Park** (p348) and the **Alor archipelago** (p371)
2. Trekking up the lush slopes of **Gunung Rinjani** (p327), the sacred volcano that dominates northern Lombok
3. Coming face-to-face with the mother of all lizards in **Komodo** or **Rinca** (p346)
4. Exploring the remote villages of **West Timor** (p374), characterised by their beehive-shaped clan houses, and experiencing the island's unique tribal culture, markets and textiles
5. Gazing at the lunar-like landscape atop **Gunung Kelimutu** (p365), with its three astonishing crater lakes

Getting There & Around

Overland travel is arduous in mountainous Nusa Tenggara, particularly in Flores. Lombok, Sumbawa and Timor have fairly decent surfaced main roads and relatively comfortable bus services. Get off the highways and things slow down considerably, however. Ferry services are frequent and consistent in the dry season, but in the wet season, when the seas get rough, your ship may be cancelled for days, weeks even. Fortunately, several airlines now cover the main inter-island routes, as few travellers who have endured the punishing long haul across Nusa Tenggara by surface transport are up for a repeat.

Don't be scared off, however, as an influx of fast boats and air connections have made Nusa Tenggara more accessible than ever. In addition to increased international flights to Lombok's new airport, including regular flights to and from Singapore and Kuala Lumpur, domestic links to Maumere, Bajawa, Ende and Labuanbajo in Flores, and Tambolaka in Sumba, have multiplied to augment the typical sound links throughout Indonesia to/from Kupang, East Nusa Tenggara's main hub.

LOMBOK

Long overshadowed by its superstar neighbour, there's a steady hum about Lombok that's beginning to turn into a distinct buzz. Blessed with exquisite white-sand beaches, the gorgeous Gili Islands, epic surf, a lush forested interior, and hiking trails through tobacco, rice fields and jungle, Lombok is fully loaded with tropical allure. Oh, and you'll probably notice mighty Gunung Rinjani, Indonesia's second-highest volcano, its summit complete with hot springs and a dazzling crater lake. For years this island has been touted as Indonesia's next hot destination. Finally the reality seems to have caught up with the hype, and with a new international airport and renewed interest from around the globe, Lombok's time is now.

Head to **Lonely Planet** (http://www.lonelyplanet.com/indonesia/lombok) for planning advice, author recommendations, traveller reviews and insider tips.

Getting There & Away

AIR

Lombok's new airport, near Praya, opened in 2011, rendering Mataram even more meaningless to most international travellers. However, major airlines retain ticket offices in Mataram, and there are two excellent travel agencies there too, making it a wise place to arrange domestic travel.

AirAsia (www.airasia.com) Three flights weekly to Kuala Lumpur.

Batavia Air (☎021-3899 9888, 0370-648 998; www.batavia-air.com) Daily to Jakarta via Surabaya.

Citramulia Travel (☎633 469; www.citramuliatravel.com; Jl Pejanggik 198, Mantaram; ⏰8am-8pm Mon-Sat, to 7pm Sun) Conscientious English-speaking staff handle domestic and international flights and offer visa services.

Garuda (☎0804 180 7807; www.garuda-indonesia.com; Jl Pejanggik 42, Mantaram) Three daily flights to Jakarta, one daily flight to Bali.

Jatatur (☎632 888; www.jatatursurabaya.com; Mataram Mall, Jl Panca Usaha A11,) Dependable, long-running travel chain that offers fair pricing on airline tickets and English-speaking service.

Merpati (☎0370-621 111; www.merpati.co.id; Jl Pejanggik 69, Mantaram) Connections to most of Indonesia via four daily flights to Denpasar.

Silk Air (☎0370-628 254; www.silkair.com; Hotel Lombok Raya, Jl Panca Usaha 11, Mantaram) Serves Singapore direct five times weekly.

Trans Nusa (☎616 2428; www.transnusa.co.id) Flies to Bali and Sumbawa Besar daily.

Wings Air (☎0370-629 333; www.lionair.co.id; Hotel Sahid Legi, Jl Sriwijaya, Mantaram) Daily flights to Denpasar, Jakarta and Surabaya.

BOAT

Public ferries connect Lombok's west coast with Bali and its east coast with Sumbawa. Numerous fast boat companies link Lombok and the Gili Islands with all of Bali's major ports.

PUBLIC BUS

Mandalika Terminal in Mataram is the departure point for major cities in Sumbawa, Bali and Java, via inter-island ferries. For long-distance services, book tickets a day or two ahead at the terminal, or from a travel agency along Jl Pejanggik/Jl Selaparang in Mataram. If you get to the terminal before 8am, there may indeed be a spare seat on a bus going in your direction, but don't count on it, especially during holidays.

TOURIST SHUTTLE BUS/BOAT

The Bali-based company **Perama** (www.peramatour.com) has tourist shuttle bus/boat services between the main tourist centres in Lombok (Senggigi, Gili Islands and Kuta) and most tourist centres in Bali (Ubud, Sanur and the Kuta region). Tickets can be booked directly or at any travel agency in Lombok or Bali.

Getting Around

There is a good road across the middle of the island, between Mataram and Labuhan Lombok.

Though narrow, the Mataram–Praya–Kuta and Mataram–Senggigi–Anyar routes are also decent sealed roads. Public transport is generally restricted to the main routes; away from these, you need to hire a car or motorbike, or charter a bemo, *cidomo* (horse-drawn cart) or *ojek* (motorcycle taxi). During the wet season, remote roads are often flooded or washed away, particularly around the foothills of Gunung Rinjani.

BUS & BEMO

Mandalika Terminal, is in Bertais, 6km southeast of central Mataram; other regional terminals are in Praya, Anyar and Pancor (near Selong). You may have to go via one or more of these terminals to get from one part of Lombok to another. Fixed fares should be displayed. Public transport becomes scarce in the late afternoon and normally ceases after dark. Chartering a bemo can be convenient and reasonably cheap – about 250,000Rp per bemo per day (including petrol), depending on distance and road conditions, although some bemos are restricted to specific routes or regions.

CAR & MOTORCYCLE

Senggigi is the best place to organise car or motorcycle rental. Arrangements can be made in Mataram and other places, but rates are much higher. Hotels and travel agencies offer the most competitive rates; 'official' car-rental companies often have a wider range of vehicles but tend to be more expensive. SUVs are best for Lombok's roads. Suzuki Jimmys cost from 150,000Rp per day, and Toyota Kijangs cost about 350,000Rp, excluding petrol. Discounts are offered for longer periods. Hiring a car with a driver is a very sensible and popular option as you won't be liable for any damage – expect to pay between 400,000Rp and 550,000Rp per day, depending on the season. Motorbikes can be rented for around 60,000Rp per day. Motorcycles run for 75,000Rp per day in Senggigi. Indonesian law dictates that you should carry an International Driving Licence if you plan on operating a motor vehicle. Your rental agency won't request it, but police may ask for one at checkpoints, and will issue a fine (to be paid immediately) if you don't have one. Check your insurance arrangements carefully. Some agencies do not offer any

Lombok

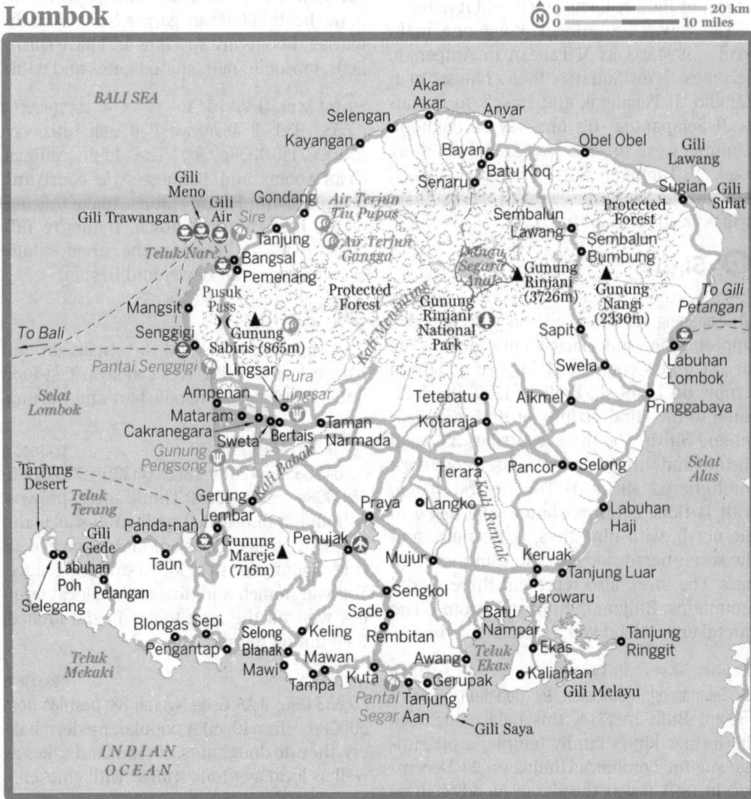

coverage at all, and others offer only basic coverage. Even insured Balinese vehicles are often not covered in Lombok. It is best to proceed to Lombok and arrange a rental in Senggigi.

Mataram

0370 / POP 403,000

Lombok's capital is a blending sprawl of several (once separate) towns with fuzzy borders: Ampenan (the port); Mataram (the administrative centre); Cakranegara (the business centre, often called simply 'Cakra') and Bertais, where you'll find the bus terminal. Stretching for 12km from east to west, it's home to nearly half a million people. There aren't many tourist attractions, Senggigi is close by, and the airport has moved too, so unless you're booking plane tickets, or need a hospital, there isn't any reason to visit, much less stay the night. Yet Mataram's broad tree-lined avenues buzz with bemos, thrum with motorbike traffic and are teeming with classic markets. If you're hungry for a blast of Indo realism, you'll find it here.

The towns are spread along one main road – it starts as Jl Pabean in Ampenan, becomes Jl Yos Sudarso, then changes to Jl Langko, Jl Pejanggik and travels to Bertais as Jl Selaparang. It's one-way throughout, running west to east. A parallel one-way road, Jl Tumpang Sari–Jl Panca Usaha–Jl Pancawarga–Jl Caturwarga–Jl Pendidikan, brings traffic back to the coast.

Sights

Pura Meru TEMPLE

(Jl Selaparang; admission by donation; 8am-5pm) Opposite the water palace, Pura Meru is the largest and second most important Hindu temple on Lombok. Built in 1720, it's dedicated to the Hindu trinity of Brahma, Vishnu and Shiva. The inner court has 33 small shrines and three thatched, teak-wood *meru* (multi-tiered shrines). The central *meru*, with 11 tiers, is Shiva's house; the *meru* to the north, with nine tiers, is Vishnu's; and the seven-tiered *meru* to the south is Brahma's. The *meru* also represent three sacred mountains, Rinjani, Agung and Bromo. The caretaker will lend you a sash and sarong.

Mayura Water Palace TEMPLE

(Jl Selaparang; admission by donation; 7am-7.30pm) Built in 1744, this palace includes the former king's family temple, a pilgrimage site for Lombok's Hindus on 24 December. In 1894 it was the site of bloody battles between the Dutch and Balinese. Unfortunately, it has become a neglected public park with a polluted artificial lake.

Sleeping

Most folks nest among Cakranegara's quiet streets off Jl Pejanggik/Jl Selaparang, east of Mataram Mall.

Lombok Plaza BOUTIQUE HOTEL $$

(629 718; www.lombokplazahotel.com; Jl Pejanggik 8; r 450,000-785,000Rp;) Mataram's newest and shiniest hotel has welcome flash and class. Rooms are sizeable with stylish wood desks and end tables, wall-mounted LG flat-screen TVs, high ceilings, a breakfast buffet and 20m lap pool on the second floor mezzanine. The Chinese restaurant serves excellent *dim sum* and a wonderful *soto ayam* (Indonesian chicken noodle soup) at reasonable prices.

Ratu Guesthouse HOMESTAY $

(0852 8100 8284, 0819 1590 4275; Jl AA Gede Ngurah 45; s/d 60,000/80,000Rp;) Great value in the heart of Cakranegara, a block from the market. Rooms are spacious and have spring beds, mosquito nets, shared baths and wi-fi.

Hotel Melati Viktor 1 GUESTHOUSE $

(633 830; Jl Abimanyu 1; d with fan/air-con 100,000/150,000Rp;) The high ceilings, clean rooms and Balinese-style courtyard, complete with Hindu statues, make this one of the best values in town. If they're full, head to **Viktor II** across the street, where everything is a bit newer and fresher.

Eating

The Mataram Mall (and the streets around it) are loaded with Western-style fast-food outlets, Indonesian noodle bars and warung.

TOP CHOICE **Ikan Bakar 99** SEAFOOD $

(643 335, 664 2819; Jl Subak III 10; mains 20,000-55,000Rp; 11am-10pm) Think: squid, prawns, fish and crab brushed with chilli sauce and perfectly grilled or fried, and drenched in spicy Padang or sticky sweet-and-sour sauce. You will munch and dine among local families who fill the long tables in the arched, tiled dining room.

Mi Rasa BAKERY $

(633 096; Jl AA Gede Ngurah 88; pastries from 5000Rp; 6am-10pm) A popular, modern bakery, they do doughnuts, cookies and cakes as well as local *wontons* stuffed with chicken.

Mataram

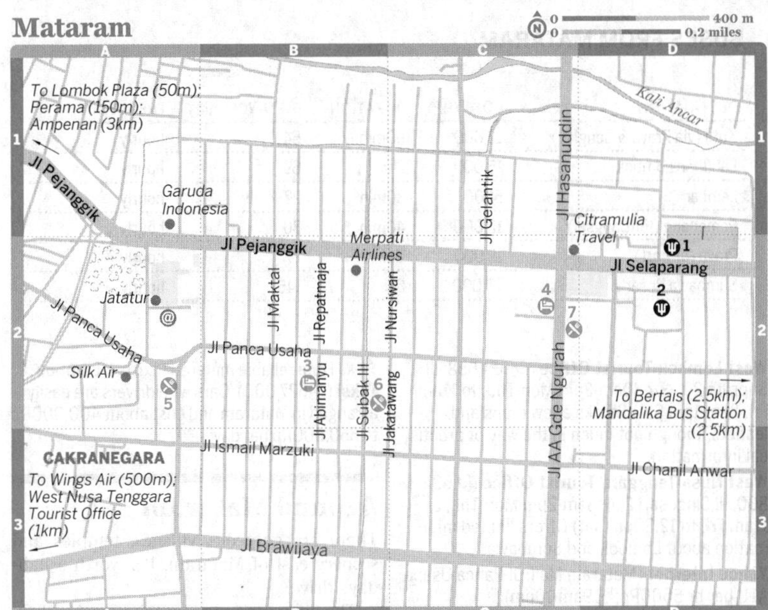

Bakmi Raos NOODLES $
(Jl Panca Usaha; dishes 9000-20,000Rp) An authentic yet modern Indonesian noodle-and-soup joint behind the mall that attracts a steady stream of Mataram's hip, young and beautiful.

Shopping

For handicrafts try the many stores on Jl Raya Senggigi, the road heading north from Ampenan towards Senggigi. Jl Usaha is the pre-eminent upscale shopping street sprinkled with cute boutiques.

TOP CHOICE **Pasar Mandalika** MARKET
(⏲7am-5pm) A great place to get localised after you've overdosed on the *bule* circuit. There are no tourists at this market near the Mandalika bus terminal, but they've got everything else: fruit and veggies, fish (fresh and dried), baskets full of colourful, aromatic spices and grains, freshly butchered beef, palm sugar, pungent bricks of shrimp paste and cheaper handicrafts than you will find anywhere else in West Lombok.

Information

You'll find plenty of banks with ATMs scattered along Cakra's main drag. Moneychangers in Mataram Mall and on Jl Pejanggik often provide the best rates for cash.

Kantor Imigrasi (☎632 520; Jl Udayana 2; ⏲8am-4pm Mon- Fri)

Police Station (☎631 225; Jl Langko) In an emergency, dial ☎110.

Post Office (Jl Langko; ⏲8am-4.30pm Mon-Thu, 8-11am Fri, 8am-1pm Sat)

Rumah Sakit Harapan Keluarga (☎670 000, 617 7000; www.harapankeluarga.co.id/rshk; Jl Ahmad Yani 9) The newest and best private hospital in Nusa Tenggara is just east of downtown Mataram and has English-speaking doctors and modern facilities. At research time there was talk of adding a decompression chamber.

BUSES FROM MATARAM

DESTINATION	COST (RP)	DURATION	DISTANCE (KM)	FREQUENCY
Kuta (via Praya & Sengkol)	13,000	90min	54	hourly
Labuhan Lombok	15,000	2hr	69	hourly
Lembar	5000	30min	22	hourly
Pemenang (for Bangsal)	12,000	40min	30	hourly
Praya (airport)	15,000	1hr	27	hourly
Sumbawa Besar	70,000	6hr	145	hourly

West Lombok Tourist Office (☎621 658; Jl Suprato 20; ⏱7.30am-2pm Mon-Thu, to 11am Fri, 8am-1pm Sat) Stocks a few maps and leaflets, though not much in the way of practical information.

West Nusa Tenggara Tourist Office (☎634 800; Jl Singosari 2; ⏱8am-2pm Mon-Thu, to 11am Fri, to 12.30pm Sat) Offers limited information about Lombok and Sumbawa.

Yahoo Internet (Mataram Mall, Jl Panca Usaha A11; per hr 5000Rp; ⏱9am-10pm)

Getting There & Away

BUS & BEMO The sprawling Mandalika bus station in Bertais is the main bus and bemo (minibus) terminal for the entire island, and also for long-distance buses to Sumbawa, Bali and Java. It's a chaotic, badly organised place, so be sure to keep a level head to avoid the 'help' of the commission-happy touts. Long-distance buses leave from behind the main terminal building, while bemo and smaller buses leave hourly from one of two car parks on either side.

Kebon Roek bemo terminal in Ampenan has bemo to Bertais (2500Rp) and Senggigi (4000Rp).

TOURIST SHUTTLE BUS **Perama** (☎635 928; www.peramatour.com; Jl Pejanggik 66) operates shuttle buses to popular destinations in Lombok (including Bangsal, Senggigi and Kuta) and Bali.

Getting Around

TO/FROM AIRPORT Mataram's Selaparang Airport has been phased out, and a new airport near Praya is up and running. By taxi (100,000Rp) it is only about 30 minutes from Mataram. Buses leave from the Mandalika Terminal for the airport (15,000Rp) on the hour.

BEMO Mataram is *very* spread out. Yellow bemo shuttle between Kebon Roek bemo terminal in Ampenan and Mandalika terminal in Bertais (10km away), along the two main thoroughfares. Outside the Pasar Cakranegara there is a handy bemo stop for services to Bertais, Ampenan, Sweta and Lembar. Fares cost 2000Rp to 3000Rp.

TAXI For a reliable metered taxi, call **Lombok Taksi** (☎627 000). Cars with drivers are easily arranged in Mataram and cost about 400,000Rp to 550,000Rp per day.

Around Mataram

There are gorgeous villages, temples and scenery east of Mataram. It's worth a half-day's drive.

The holiest temple compound in Lombok, **Pura Lingsar** (admission by donation; ⏱7am-6pm), was built in 1714 by King Anak Agung Ngurah, and is nestled beautifully in the lush rice fields. It's multidenominational, with a temple for Balinese Hindus (Pura Gaduh) and one for followers of Lombok's mystical take on Islam, the Wektu Telu religion.

Pura Gaduh has four shrines: one orientated to Gunung Rinjani (seat of the gods on Lombok), one to Gunung Agung (seat of the gods in Bali) and a double shrine representing the union between the two islands.

The **Wektu Telu temple** is noted for its enclosed pond devoted to Lord Vishnu, and the holy eels, which can be enticed from their lair with hard-boiled eggs (available at stalls outside). It's considered good luck to feed them. You will be expected to rent a sash and/or sarong (or bring your own) to enter the temple.

Pura Lingsar is 9km northeast of Mandalika. Take a bemo from the terminal to Narmada, and another to Lingsar. Ask to be dropped off near the entrance to the temple complex.

Lembar

☎0370

Lembar is Lombok's main port for ferries, tankers and Pelni liners coming in from Bali and beyond. Though the ferry port itself is scruffy, the setting – think azure inlets ringed by soaring green hills – is stunning. However, there's no reason to linger, with good transport connections to Mataram and Senggigi. If you need cash, stop by the BNI bank, 100m from the harbour's entrance.

Bemo shuttle regularly between Lembar and the Mandalika terminal in Cakra (15,000Rp). From there switch to an Ampenan-bound bemo (3000Rp), where you can get another to Senggigi (2500Rp). There are also regular shuttles (per person 45,000Rp) connecting Senggigi and Lembar. A taxi from Mataram is 70,000Rp.

Ferries run hourly, day and night, to Bali (child/adult/motorbike/car 23,000/36,000/101,000/659,000Rp, five hours).

Southwestern Peninsula

☎0370

The sweeping coastline that stretches west of Lembar is blessed with boutique sleeps on deserted beaches and tranquil offshore islands set in azure waters. Pearl Beach (p306), Dive Zone's new resort on Gili Asahan, and Cocotino's (p306) offer diving, which is fun if not spectacular. And whether you are a diver or not, you can waste weeks here among the pearl farms, salty old mosques, friendly locals and relatively pristine islands – three of which have accommodation. Our favorites are **Gili Gede**, and the wonderful **Gili Asahan**, where soothing winds gust, birds flutter and gather in the grass just before sunset, muted calls to prayer rumble, stars and moonbeams bathe the night in sweet tenderness, and silence is deep and nourishing.

The only blot on the landscape is the goldrush town of **Sekotong**. The hills above Sekotong are rich in the precious metal, and up to 6000 locals mined illegally here in huge open-cast pits (using mercury) until a crackdown in December 2009. Unofficial and not-so-clandestine mining still continues despite government opposition and environmental damage. You'll see some of these crude goldmines riddle the rugged hills as you follow the narrow (but paved) coastal road, along the contours of the peninsula, skirting white-sand beaches on your way to Tanjung Desert (Desert Point) one of Asia's legendary surf breaks.

HAZARD PAY *ADAM SKOLNICK*

So this actually happened. Took a wrong turn on the way to Tanjung Desert (Desert Point) for a spot of research. Ended up on a virgin beach, but the wrong virgin beach. A happy accident, say. It looked like ideal kite surf country. The kinda place our readers might dig. You know, wide turquoise striped bay, sugar white sand, thumping waves, heavy metal wind. Made some notes. Place was called Pantai Mukaki (Mukaki Beach) according to the local we met, a reasonably friendly guy. Or was he?

Fixer's face changed and he became anxious to get into the car. I was on the beach taking snapshots. He whistled, I hustled over, and was still jotting notes as we rolled down the road. Then, suddenly, the car was surrounded by an onrushing mob. Fifty villagers with crude yet presumably sharp bamboo spears and glinting sickles. They mistook me, a career renter, for the swindling investor who hath bilked them. Point is, apparently said land was in dispute. And, well, wouldn't be a bad place for a resort, but you know, bad idea jeans.

'Better you go, we kill you,' said the Mouthpiece. A woman. 'We kill you! More people coming!' She barked ominously. They searched the car, painfully slowly and suspiciously for the local landbroker we'd never met and they were sure we knew.

Nobody move nobody get hurt.

Mouthpiece glanced at my dog-eared research copy of Lonely Planet on the seat beside me and realised that I was indeed just a tourist. Or was I? Mouthpiece let us off with a warning of certain death by dismemberment upon return. Ya, 'bu, don't wait up.

The moral of our tale: ever since the Suharto days, large developers or holding companies (usually based in Jakarta) have attempted to purchase and develop East Indonesian paradise, often by making shady deals with people unfamiliar with the true financial value of their ancestral land. When deals go bad, and some do, tensions flare on the ground. South Lombok (including and especially the Kuta region) has been ground zero for this kind of activity for years, and there are similar land sovereignty issues on Gili Trawangan as well. Although it is incredibly rare to get caught in the middle of the fight.

Sleeping & Eating

There are a few hotels and resorts sprinkled along the Southwest coast, though the best beaches and lodgings are on the sweet offshore islands. You'll eat where you sleep.

MAINLAND

Less a working community, and more an informal surf camp, only one of the three sleeping options on Tanjung Desert even have a phone. When the swell comes, it's first-come, first-surf. If these spots are all booked up – and it does happen, you'll have to nest in nearby **Labuhan Poh** where there are a handful of decent choices. **Grower Warung** (Tanjung Desert; mains 25,000-45,000Rp) offers simple, basic meals on the cheap.

Bola Bola Paradis INN $
(☎0817 578 7355; www.bolabolaparadis.com; Jl Raya Palangan Sekotong, Pelangan; r 300,000-465,000Rp; ❄) Just west of Pelangan, this nice inn has super clean octagonal bungalows on grassy palm-shaded grounds that bleed into the sand, and comfortable air-con rooms with tiled floors and private patios in the main lodge building. It also has an aromatic kitchen recommended for spicy Indonesian food.

Cocotino's RESORT $$$
(☎0819 0797 2401; www.cocotinos-sekotong.com; Jl Raya Palangan Sekotong, Tanjung Empat; r/villas from 1,300,000/2,700,000Rp; ❄@📶) The mainland newcomer, this resort has an oceanfront location, private beach and high-quality bungalows (some with lovely outdoor bathrooms), though not all have sea views. There's a professional dive shop and a full spa here too. Walk-in for significant discounts.

Desert Point Bungalow BUNGALOW $
(Tanjung Desert; r 250,000Rp) There are seven clean woven bamboo and thatched bungalows with bamboo beds, hammocks on the porch and private baths attached. They even have one attractive, three-sided shelter stilted above the beach.

Desert Point Lodge LODGE $
(☎0878 610 4439; Tanjung Desert; d 250,000Rp) Thatched, fan-cooled bungalows with tiled outdoor baths, four-poster beds and private wooden decks set on a lawn in a blooming garden.

Hendra Surf Camp LODGE $
(Tanjung Desert; r 80,000Rp) Simply a wooden house where you can crash on a mattress on the floor of a cell-like room with thin walls. Simple meals get rave reviews.

ISLANDS

TOP CHOICE **Pearl Beach** BUNGALOW $$
(☎0813 3954 4998, 0819 0724 7696; www.divezone-lombok.com; Gili Asahan; cottages/bungalows incl breakfast 370,000/570,000Rp; 📶) A brand new resort on a private island with a wonderful sweep of white sand leading to a turquoise sea. The cottages are simple, bamboo affairs with tasteful outdoor baths and a hammock on the porch. The bungalows, however, are quite chic, with polished yellow concrete floors, soaring ceilings, queen beds, gauzy mosquito netting, sliding glass doors, a river rock garden and plumeria trees in the outdoor bath, and a fabulous day bed swing on the wood porch. It's owned by the folks behind Dive Zone, mainland Lombok's best dive shop. So, yes, there is diving. Electricity from 6pm to 6am only.

Madak Belo BUNGALOW $
(☎0878 6471 2981, 0818 0554 9637; www.madak-belo.com; Gili Gede; r/bungalows 125,000/250,000Rp) Here's a sensational French hippie-chic paradise with three rooms upstairs in the main wooden-and-bamboo lodge. They share a bath with wash basins crusted with shells and a magnificent bamboo lounge area strung with hammocks, and blessed with a perfect white-sand, turquoise-sea view. It also has two spacious private bungalows with queen beds and private baths. Meals are delicious. Electricity only runs for about eight hours each day.

Via Vacare BUNGALOW $
(☎0819 1590 4275; www.viavacare.com; Gili Gede; bungalows/ r including meals 750,000/250,000Rp) A secret yoga retreat with four spacious, simple and stylish octagonal bungalows. Backpacker digs are a comfy mattress on the floor and a mosquito net in a large open-sided longhouse. There's no beach to speak of, but you can go swimming at high tide. There's an open-air yoga pagoda, and fine home-cooked meals. Management will arrange free shuttle to the island from nearby Tebowong.

Getting There & Away

Bemo run between Lembar and Pelangan (5000rp, 1½ hours) via Tembowong and Sekotong every 30 minutes until 5pm. West of Pelangan, transport is less regular, but the route is still served by infrequent bemo until Selegang.

Taxi boats (per person 10,000Rp) shuttle between Tembowong (on the mainland) to Gili Gede. You'll see them bobbing in the sea near the Pertamina station. Chartered boats also connect Tembowong with Gili Asahan (300,000Rp return). Pearl Beach (p306) will organise your transport to Gili Asahan from the mainland if you book in advance.

Senggigi

☎0370

Lombok's original tourist town rambles along a series of sweeping bays and wide beaches dappled in coconut palms. Blood-red views of Bali's Gunung Agung are revealed at sunset when locals congregate on the cliffs and watch yet another day turn to night. As darkness descends, the bright lanterns of the local fishing fleet glint like fallen stars against the black sea.

The tacky main strip could look more appealing, the influx of bar girls is an issue, and the resident beach hawkers can be persistent. Still, tourist numbers are relatively modest here, except in high season, and you'll find some excellent-value hotels and restaurants.

The Senggigi area spans 10km of coastal road; the upscale neighbourhood of Mangsit is 3km north of central Senggigi.

Sights

Pura Batu Bolong HINDU

(admission by donation; 7am-7pm) It's not the grandest, but Pura Batu Bolong is Lombok's sweetest Hindu temple, and particularly lovely at sunset. Join an ever-welcoming Balinese community as they leave offerings at the 14 altars and pagodas that tumble down a rocky volcanic outcropping into the foaming sea about 2km south of central Senggigi. The rock underneath the temple has a natural hole, hence the name (*batu bolong* literally means 'rock with hole').

Activities

Snorkelling, Diving & Surfing

There's reasonable snorkelling off the point in Senggigi and in front of Windy Cottages, 3km north of the town. You can rent snorkelling gear (25,000Rp per day) from several spots on the beach. Diving trips from Senggigi usually visit the Gili Islands.

Blue Coral Diving DIVING

(☎693 441; www.bluecoraldive.com; Jl Raya Senggigi; two tanks 700,000Rp, Open Water Certificate 3,600,000Rp) Senggigi's newest and biggest dive shop.

Blue Marlin DIVING

(☎693 719; www.bluemarlindive.com; Holiday Resort Lombok, Jl Raya Senggigi; per dive 400,000Rp) The Senggigi shingle of Gili T's original.

Dream Divers DIVING

(☎693 738, 692 047; www.dreamdivers.com; Jl Raya Senggigi; per dive 400,000Rp) The Senggigi depot of the Gili original.

Adventure Lombok SURFING

(☎665 0238; www.adventurelombok.com; Pasar Seni; short-/longboards per day 100,000/200,000Rp, surf lessons US$40, bike rental per day 50,000Rp) Rents surfboards and offers surf lessons that include a helmet and transport to and from the break. Also organises Rinjani treks without the hard sell.

Hiking

Rinjani Trekking Club ADVENTURE TOUR

(☎693 202; rtc.senggigi@gmail.com; Jl Raya Senggigi Km 8; trips incl transport from 1,750,000Rp) Pushy yet well-informed about routes and trail conditions on Gunung Rinjani, with a wide choice of guided hikes.

Sleeping

Senggigi's accommodation is very spread out. But even if you're located a few kilometres away (say, in Mangsit) you're not isolated as many restaurants offer free rides to diners and taxis are inexpensive. Heavy discounts of up to 50% are common in midrange and top-end places outside the July to August peak season.

SENGGIGI

TOP CHOICE **Beach Club** BUNGALOW $$

(☎0818 0520 8807, 693 637; www.thebeachclublombok.com; Jl Raya Senggigi; r with fan US$24, bungalows US$70;) There are few three-star bamboo bungalow properties in Indo as comfy and homey as this boutique gem. All are crafted from wood and bamboo, and outfitted with flat-screen TVs, DVD, queen beds and wired with wi-fi. The outdoor baths are leafy and tasteful, and they all surround a pool shaded by lush foliage within earshot of the rolling sea, just steps away. It also has two less expensive rooms, if you're on a budget. The restaurant-bar serves Aussie comfort food and draws a crowd.

Senggigi

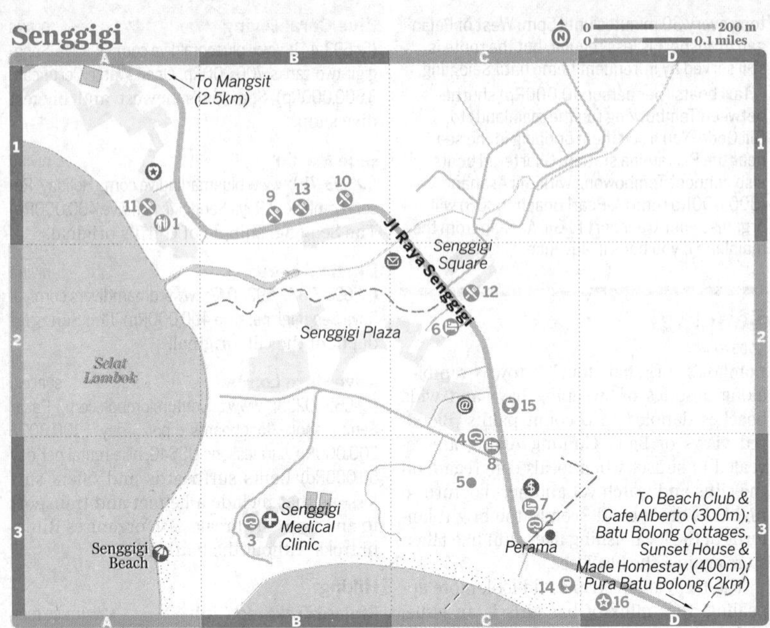

Senggigi

Activities, Courses & Tours
1 Adventure Lombok A1
2 Blue Coral Diving C3
3 Blue Marlin B3
4 Dream Divers C3
5 Rinjani Trekking Club C3

Sleeping
6 Central Inn C2
7 Sendok Guesthouse C3
8 Wira C3

Eating
9 Asmara B1
10 Kayu Manis B1
11 Office A1
12 Square C2
13 Warung Cicak B1

Drinking
14 Hotel Lina C3
15 Papaya Café C2

Entertainment
16 Paragon D3

Shopping
Asmara Collection .... (see 9)

Wira GUESTHOUSE $
(692 153; www.thewira.com; Jl Raya Senggigi Km 8; d 200,000-300,000Rp;) This boutique losmen is a nice new addition to the Senggigi strip. It has simple, tasteful, sizeable rooms with bamboo furnishings, flat-screen TVs, DVD player, and private porches out back. Cheaper fan rooms can be musty.

Sendok Guesthouse INN $
(www.sendokbali.com; Jl Raya Senggigi; r 200,000-380,000Rp;) A kitschy new inn with kitted-out guestrooms behind a friendly pub. Rooms pair lovely Javanese antiques with garrish tile, but they have high ceilings, flat-screen TVs, rain showerheads, wi-fi and security boxes. All are bright and airy with their own private front porch. Superior rooms have hot water.

Sunset House HOTEL $$
(667 7196, 692 020; www.sunsethouse-lombok.com; Jl Raya Senggigi 66; r 450,000Rp;) Now with 20 rooms, including six in the new

wing and all with the same tasteful, well-equipped simplicity on this quiet stretch of shoreline near the Batu Bolong temple. Rooms on the upper-floors have sweeping ocean views towards Bali.

Batu Bolong Cottages HOTEL $$
(☎693 198, 693 065; Jl Raya Senggigi; d inland 350,000Rp, beachside 500,000-600,000Rp;) Bamboo is the operative term at this charming bungalow-style hotel set on both sides of the road south of the centre. Beach-front rooms have quaint touches like carved doors, and there's a lovely pool area off the beach.

Made Homestay HOMESTAY $
(☎0819 1704 1332; Jl Raya Senggigi; r with fan 100,000-150,000Rp, with air-con 170,000-200,000Rp;) A terrific new cheapie. Tiled rooms have big bamboo beds, a private front porch and free wi-fi. The air-con rooms cost a bit more, but remain tremendous value into the high season. Cold water showers only.

Central Inn HOTEL $
(☎692 006; Jl Raya Senggigi; d 250,000Rp;) A brand-new block hotel set in centre of town. Rooms have high ceilings and crown mouldings, bowl sinks, hot water, wi-fi, fresh tiles, and a bamboo seating area with views of the surrounding hills.

Chandi BOUTIQUE RESORT $$$
(☎692 198; www.the-chandi.com; Batu Balong; r from US$150;) Another of Senggigi's new mod offerings, this one is about 1km south of the Batu Balong temple. Each room has an outdoor living room and stylish modern interior with high ceilings, flat-screen TV and groovy outdoor baths. The ample ocean-front perch is pretty damn sweet.

Bale Kampung Homestay GUESTHOUSE $
(☎0818 0360 0001, 660 0001; r with fan 100,000-150,000Rp, r with air-con 200,000Rp;) Set 300m south of Pura Batu Bolong, this thatched brick compound is rather cramped, but there's a range of good value new rooms, the most expensive of which have hot water and air-con. It's a little out of the way, but it offers free transport to and from Senggigi town.

MANGSIT

TOP CHOICE **Qunci Villas** RESORT $$$
(☎693 800; www.quncivillas.com; Jl Raya Mangsit, Mangsit; r from US$115, plus 21% tax;) A spectacular, lovingly imagined property that comes close to a 5-star experience at a fraction of the price. Everything from the food to the jaw-dropping pool area to the spa, and especially the sea views (160m of beachfront), are magical. Despite ourselves, we even loved the traditional dance performances put on poolside at dinner time. It would be hard to find an equivalent hotel on Bali's coast and it's impossible to find one elsewhere on Lombok. This hotel is a destination in itself.

Jeeva Klui RESORT $$$
(☎693 035; www.jeevaklui.com; Jl Raya Klui Beach; r ocean view/beachfront US$197/263, pool villas US$362;) This place has a shimmering infinity pool and a lovely, almost private, beach sheltered by rocky outcrop. Rooms are stylishly thatched with bamboo columns and private porches. Villas are 5-star luxe. A fine choice if you've got the dosh.

Windy Beach COTTAGE $$
(☎693 191; www.windybeach.com; Jl Raya Mangsit; cottages 500,000-550,000Rp;) Deservedly popular and on a fine sandy beach. Attractive traditional-style thatched cottages (with bamboo walls and mosquito nets) are scattered around a wonderful garden, and there's a bar-restaurant and decent snorkelling offshore.

Eating

Senggigi's dining scene ranges from fine dining to simple warung. Many places offer free transport for evening diners – phone for a ride.

TOP CHOICE **Warung Cicak** NOODLES $
(Jl Raya Senggigi; mains 12,000-17,000Rp; ⏲3-10pm) Everybody loves an Asian noodle joint, and these upstart, roadside gourmets use only homemade noodles in their chicken, beef, mushroom or shrimp stir-frys and soups. Served in a cute, open air warung sheltered by a tasteful tiered tin roof.

Square INTERNATIONAL $$
(☎693 688; Senggigi Square; mains 40,000-150,000Rp;) Destination restaurant with beautifully crafted seating, and a menu that features Western and Indonesian fusion such as wok-fried king prawns with Worcestershire sauce. The atmosphere is perhaps a little too formal, though the cooking is certainly very accomplished. Steaks get rave reviews from longtime expats.

Coco Beach INDONESIAN $
(☎0817 578 0055; Pantai Kerandangan; mains from 25,000Rp; ⏰noon-10pm; ☎) About 2km north of central Senggigi, this wonderful beachside restaurant features a healthy menu that includes lots of salads and choices for vegetarians (and uses organic produce wherever possible). The *nasi goreng* is famous among Senggigi expats. It has a full bar, blends authentic *jamu* tonics and offers tastefully secluded seating.

Office THAI, INTERNATIONAL $
(☎693 162; Jl Raya Senggigi, Pasar Seni; mains 25,000-65,000Rp; ⏰9am-10pm) This art market pub offers the typical Indonesian and Western choices along with the pool tables, ball games and bar flies. But it also has a popular Thai menu thanks to the Bangkok-born manager. Think: authentic *prik king*, *pad Thai*, *phat plaa meuk yat sai* (fried baby squid stuffed with chicken and mushrooms), *som tam* (papaya salad) and a tasty Thai grilled beef salad.

Kayu Manis INTERNATIONAL $
(☎693 561; Jl Raya Senggigi; mains 25,000-35,000Rp) This exciting new restaurant has a casual vibe (think polished-wood bench seating) and an East-meets-West menu that reflects the life of chef-patron Berri, an Indonesian who lived in Australia for years. Dishes such as beer-battered calamari and snapper fillet topped with green veggies are superb.

Asmara INTERNATIONAL $$
(☎693 619; www.asmara-group.com; Jl Raya Senggigi; mains 18,000-75,000Rp) An ideal family choice, this place spans the culinary globe from tuna Carpaccio to Wiener schnitzel to Lombok's own *sate pusut* (minced-meat or fish sate). It also has a playground and kids menu.

Cafe Alberto ITALIAN $$
(☎693 039; www.cafealbertolombok.com; Jl Raya Senggigi; mains from 45,000Rp; ⏰8am-midnight) A long-standing and well-loved beachside Italian kitchen. It does three types of ravioli, and six flavours of spaghetti, tagliatelle and penne, but is known for its pizza. Free transport to and from your hotel is offered.

Warung Manega SEAFOOD $$
(Jl Raya Senggigi; meals 75,000-250,000Rp; ⏰11am-11pm) If you fled Bali before experiencing the Jimbaran fish grills, you can make up for it here. Choose from a fresh daily catch of barracuda, squid, snapper, grouper, lobster, tuna and prawns – all of which are grilled over smouldering coconut husks and served on candlelit tables in the sand.

Drinking & Entertainment

Not long ago, Senggigi's bar scene was pretty vanilla. Enter the bar girls. Like something out of a Pattaya fever-dream, cinderblock malls were, um, erected on vacant lots and filled with 'karaoke' joints and massage parlors. One of these bar girl complexes is literally on the doorstep of the local mosque. If that sort of irony isn't your thing, find one of the restaurants or bars that feature live bands playing rock and pop covers, or hunker down over a cocktail by the pool at Qunci (p309). It hosts an inviting Happy Hour.

Hotel Lina BAR
(☎693 237; Jl Raya Senggigi) Lina's seafront deck is a great spot for a sundowner. Happy hour starts at 4pm and ends an hour after dusk.

Papaya Café BAR
(☎693 136; Jl Raya Senggigi) The decor is slick, with exposed stonewalls, rattan furniture and evocative Asmat art from Papua. There's a nice selection of liquor, and there's a tight house band.

Paragon CLUB
(☎693 750; Jl Raya Senggigi Km 12; ⏰noon-2am; ☎) Part cafe, part nightclub, part karaoke bar, Paragon has a nice perch on the beach, but that thumping music isn't always so magical. It does draw a crowd though, as well as the occasional live act from Jakarta. Look for the cheap louvered facade.

Shopping

Asmara Collection HANDICRAFTS
(☎693 619; Jl Raya Senggigi; ⏰8am-11pm) A cut above the rest, this store has well-selected tribal art, including wonderful carvings and textiles from Sumba and Flores.

Information

BCA (Jl Raya Senggigi) Bank with ATM.
Millennium Internet (☎693 860; Jl Raya Senggigi; per hour 24,000Rp; ⏰24hr)
Police Station (☎110)
Post Office (Jl Raya Senggigi; ⏰8am-6pm)
Senggigi Medical Clinic (☎693 856; Jl Raya Senggigi; ⏰8am-7pm) At the Senggigi Beach Hotel.
Tourist Police (☎632 733)

Getting There & Away

BOAT **Perama** (☎693 007; www.peramatour.com; Jl Raya Senggigi) operates daily fast boats to Padangbai in Bali (400,000Rp, two to three hours) at 1.30pm and shuttles to the Gili Islands (200,000Rp, 75 minutes) at 10am.

BUS, BEMO & TAXI Regular bemo travel between Senggigi and Ampenan's Kebon Roek terminal (2500Rp). Wave them down on the main drag. There are also two tourist shuttles running daily between Senggigi and Lembar (45,000Rp) and between Senggigi and the airport in Praya (25,000Rp). Ask your hotel about the latest departure times.

A taxi to Lembar is 70,000Rp. Taxis to the airport in Praya cost a standard 150,000Rp. Strangely, there's no public bemo service north to Bangsal harbour. Charter one for 75,000Rp.

Getting Around

The central area is easy to negotiate on foot. If you're staying further away, remember that many restaurants offer a free lift for diners. Motorbikes are readily available for hire in Senggigi, starting from 60,000Rp per day. Car hire is available at a handful of places on the main drag, with rates starting at 150,000Rp for an ageing Suzuki Jimny to around 350,000Rp for a newish Kijang. Car rental per day with driver costs 400,000Rp to 550,000Rp.

Gili Islands

☎0370

Picture three miniscule desert islands, fringed by white-sand beaches and coconut palms, sitting in a turquoise sea. These islets have exploded in popularity, and are booming like nowhere else in Indonesia – speedboats zip visitors direct from Bali and a new hip hotel opens every month. It's not hard to understand the Gilis' unique appeal, for a serenity endures (no motorbikes or dogs!) and a green consciousness is growing. Most development is incredibly tasteful and there are few concrete eyesores.

Each island has its own special character. Trawangan is by far the most cosmopolitan: its bar and party scene vibrant, its accommodation and restaurants close to definitive tropical chic. Gili Air has the strongest local character, the best beaches, and lovely views from Rinjani. Meno is simply tranquillity. But all have one thing in common: they are incredibly hard to leave.

Find more reviews and recommendations at **Lonely Planet** (http://www.lonelyplanet.com/indonesia/nusa-tenggara/gili-islands).

Dangers & Annoyances

There are seldom police on any of the Gilis (though this is changing). Report thefts to the island *kepala desa* (village head) immediately, who will deal with the issue; staff at the dive schools will direct you to him. On Gili Trawangan, contact **Satgas**, the community organisation that runs island affairs, via your hotel or dive centre. Satgas are usually able to resolve problems and track down stolen property. Although it's rare, some foreign women have experienced sexual harassment and even assault while on the Gilis – it's best to walk home in pairs to the quieter parts of the islands.

As tranquil as these seas do appear, currents are extremely heavy in the channels between the islands. Do not try to swim between Gili Islands unless you fancy a 24-hour swim to Lombok.

Gili Islands

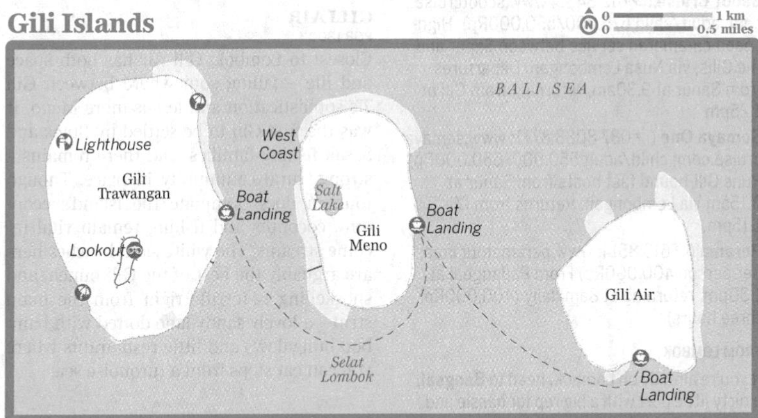

The drug trade remains endemic to Trawangan. Weed and mushrooms are the mainstays, but these days crystal meth is also on the menu. And it does get annoying after about the 100th cold call.

Getting There & Away

FROM BALI

Several fast boats offer swift connections (about two hours) between Bali and Gili Trawangan. They leave from several departure points in Bali, most dock at Teluk Nare on Lombok before continuing onto Air and Trawangan (you'll have to disembark for Meno). Two helpful websites, **Gili Bookings** (www.gilibookings.com) and **Gili Fastboat** (www.gili-fastboat.com), present a range of fast boat operations. Gili Bookings is the most discerning, vetting companies for safety and reliability. Be warned that the sea between Bali and Lombok can get very rough (particularly during rainy season). Book ahead in July and August.

Gili Getaway (☎Bali reservations 0813 3707 4147, Gili reservations 0878 6432 2515; www.giligetaway.com; child/adult 490,000/660,000Rp) From Serangan at 9am, returning at 11.30am. We enjoy their impeccable service and race car seating.

Kuda Hitam Express (☎0363-23482; www.kudahitamexpress.com; child/adult 450,000/650,000Rp) Departs from Amed at 9am daily. Returning from Trawangan at 10.15am

Blue Water Express (☎614 4460; www.bluewater-express.com; child/adult US$55/67) From Serangan, Bali direct at 8am and 10am. Returning at 11am and 1.30pm.

Gili Cat (☎0361-271 680; www.gilicat.com; child/adult 475,000/660,000Rp) Departs daily from Padangbai at 9.15 am, returning from Trawangan at 11.20am

Scoot Cruise (☎612 3433; www.scootcruise.com; adult/child 675,000/550,000Rp) High-speed catamaran service between Sanur and the Gilis, via Nusa Lembongan. Departures from Sanur at 9.30am, returning from Gili at 1.25pm

Semaya One (☎087 8088 8771; www.semayacruise.com; child/adult 550,000/650,000Rp) Runs Gili-bound fast boats from Sanur at 9.15am via Lembongan. Returns from Gili T at 1.15pm.

Perama (☎613 8514; www.peramatour.com; per person 400,000Rp) From Padangbai at 1.30pm, returning at 8am daily (400,000Rp, three hours).

FROM LOMBOK

If you're already on Lombok, head to **Bangsal,** a dirty little port with a big rep for hassle and public boats on the cheap. Boats leave for all three Gili islands (10,000Rp) from 7am. They typically wait until full (26 passengers) before departure. The last boat is at 4.30pm. Keep an eye on your gear. From Mataram, catch a bus or bemo to Pemenang, from where it's about 1km to Bangsal.

From Senggigi there's a daily Perama (p311) shuttle bus–boat connection at 10am (200,000Rp), but all things considered, we'd rather deal with Bangsal – the Perama boat is uncomfortable and not a great value for money.

Finally, there are various chartered **speedboat** options available to and from Gili Trawangan. The Beach House (p324) and Juku (p324) both have dependable services to mainland Lombok (350,000Rp for two people). Or hop on a Dream Divers (p319; 4pm, 50,000Rp) or Gili Divers (p319; 5pm, 50,000Rp) crew boat, both of which accept passengers aboard daily Lombok crossings.

Getting Around

There's no motorised transport on the Gilis. In fact, the only motorbike in Trawangan is on the Bio-rock reef, 5m deep in front of Cafe Gili.

BOAT There's a twice-daily island-hopping boat service that loops between all three islands (20,000Rp to 23,000Rp), so you can hit the ATM on Trawangan if you're based on Meno, or snorkel another island's reefs for the day. Check the latest timetable at the islands' docks. You can always charter boats between the islands (220,000Rp to 250,000Rp).

CIDOMO The Gilis are flat and easy enough to get around by foot or bicycle. A torch (flashlight) is useful at night. You can buy one at local shops for around 25,000Rp. Hiring a *cidomo* (horse-drawn cart) for a clip-clop around an island is a great way to explore; a short trip costs between 40,000Rp and 50,000Rp. You'll pay 150,000Rp or more for a two-hour jaunt.

GILI AIR

POP 1800

Closest to Lombok, Gili Air has both space and life – falling somewhere between Gili T's sophistication and less-is-more Meno. It was the first Gili to be settled by Bugis and Sasak fishing families, and there remains a strong, rural community in place. Though tourism does dominate the island's economy, coconuts and fishing remain vital income streams. The white-sand beaches here are arguably the best of the Gili bunch, and snorkelling is terrific right from the main strip – a lovely sandy lane dotted with bamboo bungalows and little restaurants where you can eat steps from a turquoise sea.

Activities

SNORKELLING & DIVING

Scuba diving is excellent throughout the Gilis, and no matter where you stay, you'll dive the same sites. A dive is around 370,000Rp at most operators.

The entire east coast has an offshore reef teeming with colourful fish; there's a dropoff about 100m to 200m out. Snorkelling gear can be hired from Wiwin Café (p315) from 25,000Rp a day.

Watch out for currents. Never try and swim between the islands.

Blue Marlin Dive Centre DIVING
(☎634 387; www.bluemarlindive.com)

Dream Divers DIVING
(☎634 547; www.dreamdivers.com) An off-shoot of the Gili T original.

Gili Air

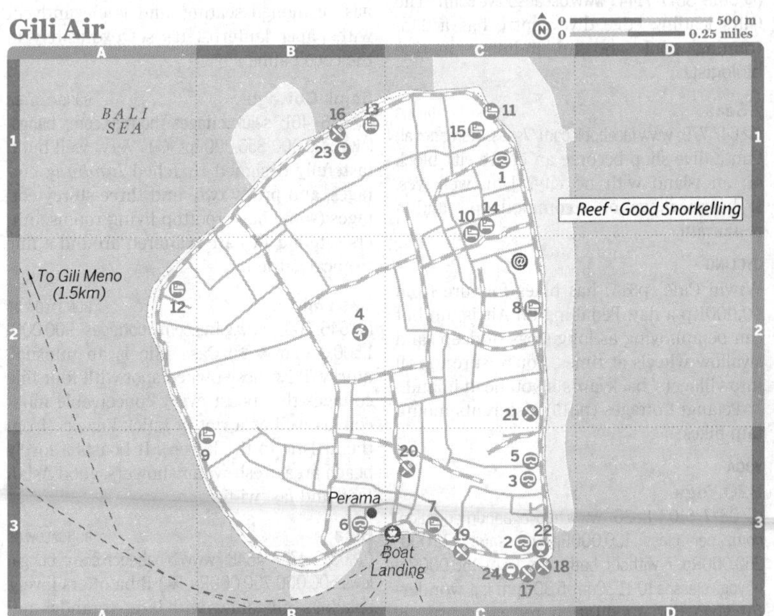

Gili Air

Activities, Courses & Tours

7 Seas .... (see 7)
1 Blue Marlin Dive Centre C1
2 Dream Divers C3
3 Gili Air Divers C3
4 H2O Yoga B2
5 Manta Dive C3
6 Oceans 5 .... B3

Sleeping

7 7 Seas C3
8 Biba C2
9 Casa Mio B3
10 Damai C1
11 Gusung Indah C1
12 Kai's Beachouse A2
13 Pelangi Cottages B1
14 Sejuk Cottages C1
15 Youpy Bungalows C1

Eating

Biba .... (see 8)
16 Harmony Café B1
17 Paradiso 2 .... C3
18 Scallywags C3
19 Tami's Neverland C3
20 Warung Gili C3
21 Wiwin Café C2

Drinking

22 Chill Out Bar C3
23 Mirage B1
24 Zipp Bar C3

Gili Air Divers DIVING
(☎0878 6536 7551; www.giliairdivers.com) This new French-Indo owned dive shop is long on charm and skill.

Manta Dive DIVING
(☎0813 3778 9047; www.manta-dive.com) A long-running dive operation with excellent lodging available.

Oceans 5 DIVING
(☎0813 3877 7144; www.oceans5dive.com) The Gili's leading edge dive centre has a 25m training pool, and an in-house marine biologist.

7 Seas DIVING
(☎647 779; www.facebook.com/7seas.international) Can a dive shop become an entire city block on an island with no city? Um, well, yes. It has a range of accommodation and a restaurant.

CYCLING

Wiwin Café (p315) has bikes for hire from 40,000Rp a day. Pedalling on Air is fun but can be annoying as long slogs of deep sand swallow wheels at times. You're sure to roll into villagers' backyards if you head inland.

Pelangi Cottages (p315) also rents mountain bikes.

YOGA

H2O Yoga YOGA
(☎0877 6103 8836; www.h2oyogaandmeditation.com; per class 100,000Rp, massage 125,000-250,000Rp, r without bathroom from 150,000Rp; ⏲yoga classes 10-11.30am, 5.30-7pm), a wonderful yoga and meditation retreat centre, is brand new to Air and set back 500m from the beach on a well-signed path into the village. Top quality classes are held in a lovely circular *beruga*. There's massage available, and a few bungalows, with more on the way.

Sleeping

Gili Air's 40 or so places to stay are mainly located on the east coast. Steep discounts from listed prices are available off-peak.

TOP CHOICE **Kai's Beachouse** HOUSE $$
(☎0813 3776 4350, 0819 1723 2536; www.kaisbeachhouse.com; d 700,000-1,500,000Rp; ❄📶🏊) Air's newest and best. There are just three rooms here, two in the main house and another in a Javanese *gladak* (middle-class home) out back. All the rooms have sponge-painted walls, four-poster beds, outdoor baths, and tasteful rattan light fixtures. The downstairs great room is cushy and groovy with a flat-screen TV, and a massive kitchen. Lounges surround a tiny plunge pool, with a virginal beach just out front. It's around the corner from the harbour with Meno views.

Damai GUESTHOUSE $$
(☎0878 6142 0416; www.facebook.com/pages/damai-homestay-gili-air; d 500,000-600,000Rp; @) It's worth finding this funky, thatched enclave. Rooms are basic yet tasteful and open onto a garden. The cosy dining patio has cushioned seating, and is elegantly lit with paper lanterns. It's set exquisitely in the coco palms.

Sejuk Cottages BUNGALOW $$
(☎636 461; sejukcottages@hotmail.com; bungalows 500,000-850,000Rp; ❄) Very well-built, tastefully designed thatched *lumbung* cottages, and pretty two- and three-storey cottages (some have rooftop living rooms, others satellite TV) are scattered around a fine tropical garden.

Casa Mio BUNGALOW $$
(☎646 160; www.giliair.com; cottages 900,000-1,500,000Rp; ❄📶) Casa Mio is an unusual, quirky, Taiwanese-owned spot with four fine cottages that boast every conceivable mod-con, as well as a riot of knick-knacks (from the artistic to the kitsch). It boasts a lovely beach area, fresh-water showers, good Asian food and fast wi-fi.

Biba BUNGALOW $$
(☎0819 1727 4648; www.bibabeach.com; bungalows 500,000-700,000Rp; ❄) Biba offers lovely, spacious bungalows with large verandas and zany, grotto-like bathrooms that have walls inlaid with shells and coral. The gorgeous garden has little chill-out zones. It's also home to a splendid Italian restaurant (p315).

7 Seas HOSTEL $
(☎647 779; www.facebook.com/7seas.international; hostel per person 70,000Rp; 📶) Yes, they do have a range of rather splashy, spacious bungalows, but we like them for their bamboo loft-like hostel rooms.

Gusung Indah BUNGALOW $
(☎0878 6434 2852; bungalows fan/air-con 300,000/600,000Rp; ❄) Choose among *lumbung*-style bungalows and concrete rooms at this well-looked after property. Some bungalows are covered in pebbles, others are dark wood constructions, and all have thatched roofs and outdoor baths. The best have air-con and hot water.

Pelangi Cottages BUNGALOW $
(☎0819 3316 8648; r 400,000Rp; ❄) Set out on the north end, with a sweet slab of white sand out front, it has spacious but basic concrete and wood bungalows with friendly management. It also rents quality mountain bikes to all comers.

Youpy Bungalows BUNGALOW $$
(☎0819 1706 8153; d 600,000Rp; ❄) Among the driftwood decorated beach cafes strung along the coast north of Blue Marlin, Youpy has some of the best quality bungalows. Bathrooms have colourful sand walls, the beds are big, and the ceilings high.

Eating

Most places on Gili Air are locally owned and offer an unbeatable setting for a meal, with tables right over the water facing Lombok's Gunung Rinjani. But some tasty new spots have begun to raise the bar.

TOP CHOICE **Scallywags** INTERNATIONAL $$
(☎645 301; www.scallywagsresort.com; mains 46,000-95,000Rp; 📶) Set on Gili Air's softest and widest beach, and more a groovy hippie-chic beach club than a mere restaurant, you can make any number of excuses to spend the day here (and many do). There's the elegant decor, upscale comfort food (we love the tuna sashimi drizzled with olive oil and sprinkled with rock salt), homemade gelato, superb cocktails and free wi-fi. But best all is the alluring beach dotted with lounges.

TOP CHOICE **Biba** ITALIAN $
(☎0819 1727 4648; www.bibabeach.com; mains 25,000-70,000Rp; ⏰11.30am-10pm) Book a table on the sand for a memorable, romantic setting. Biba serves the best wood-oven pizza and foccacia on the islands. It also does authentic ravioli, gnocchi and tagliatelle. The pizza oven fires up at 7pm nightly.

Wiwin Café INDONESIAN $
(dishes 25,000-60,000Rp; ⏰7am-10pm) A great choice for grilled fish in one of five homemade sauces. Service is attentive and there's a nice bar area.

Harmony Café INDONESIAN $$
(dishes 15,000-100,000Rp; ⏰4-9pm) This is the island's classiest dinner spot. It's set on a bamboo pier, with pink tablecloths, ample pillows to lean into and exquisite sunset views. Come for a sundowner at happy hour (cocktails 25,000Rp) or for a full grilled-fish dinner (50,000Rp to 100,000Rp).

Paradiso 2 INDONESIAN $
(mains 25,000-60,000Rp) On a fabulous stretch of sand, this place has beachside bamboo lounges and serves Indonesian food.

Tami's Neverland CAFE $
(meals from 35,000Rp; ⏰7am-1am) A large bamboo in-holding in the midst of 7 Seas domination, this place serves hearty Western and Indo grub at fair prices.

Warung Gili INDONESIAN $
(mains 15,000-30,000Rp; ⏰7am-10pm) One of a few Indo greasy spoons in the village. This one has a palapa roof, bamboo tables and all the Indo nibbles.

Drinking

On full and dark moons the island can rock, but usually Gili Air is as mellow as Meno.

TOP CHOICE **Mirage** BAR
(drinks 40,000-55,000Rp) Set on a sublime stretch of beach with technicolour sunsets nightly and live bands on Fridays. There is no better place for a sundowner.

Zipp Bar BAR
This large bar has tables dotted around a great beach and an excellent booze selection (try the fresh-fruit cocktails). It hosts a beach party every full moon.

Chill Out Bar BEACH BAR
(⏰until 2am) Popular with both visitors and locals, it has a good selection of spirits and cocktails.

Information

The island's lone **ATM** is on the 7 Seas strip, and it accepts foreign cards. Dive centres typically charge at least 8% for cash advances on credit cards. There's a **clinic** in the village for medical services and a small **Perama** (☎637 816) office next to the Gili Indah Hotel.

Ozzy Internet & Wartel Hendra (☎622 179; internet per hr 24,000Rp, international calls per min 13,000Rp; ⏰8am-9pm) A mini-mart, a warnet, a wartel and money exchange all in one place.

GILI MENO

POP 300

Gili Meno is the smallest of the three islands and the perfect setting for your Robinson Crusoe fantasy. Even in high season Meno feels delightfully tranquil. Most accommodation is strung out along the east coast, near the widest and most picturesque beach. Inland you'll find scattered homesteads, coconut plantations and a briney lake.

Sights

Turtle Sanctuary TURTLE HATCHERY
(www.gilimenoturtles.com) Meno's turtle sanctuary consists of an assortment of little pools and bathtubs on the beach, bubbling with filters and teeming with baby turtles, where they're nurtured for eight months before being released. The impact of the hatchery on the turtle populations has been considerable. A simple snorkel and you're all but guaranteed a sighting. Donations are encouraged.

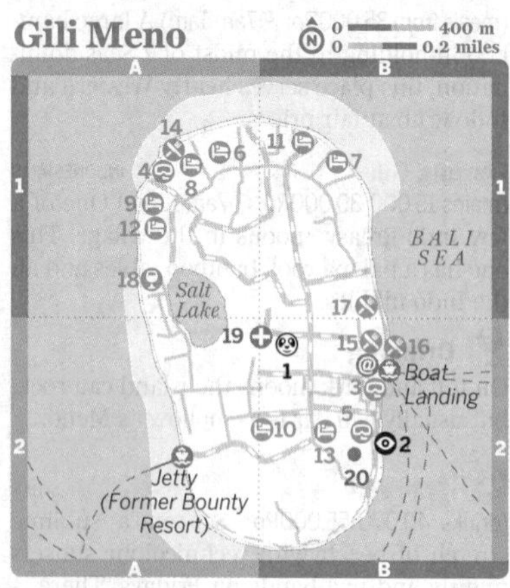

Gili Meno

Sights
1 Taman Burung B2
2 Turtle Sanctuary B2

Activities, Courses & Tours
3 Blue Marlin Dive Centre B2
4 Divine Divers A1
5 Gili Meno Divers B2

Sleeping
6 Adeng Adeng A1
7 Ana Bungalow B1
8 Balenta Bungalows A1
9 Maha Maya A1
10 Rawa Indah B2
11 Shacks 58 & 59 .... B1
12 Sunset Gecko A1
13 Tao Kombo B2

Eating
14 Balenta Café A1
15 Jali Café B2
16 Rust Warung B2
17 Ya Ya Warung B1

Drinking
18 Diana Café A1
Jungle Bar .... (see 13)

Information
19 Medical Clinic B2
20 Perama B2

Taman Burung WILDLIFE RESERVE
(☎614 2321, 0361 289 032; admission 50,000Rp; ⊙9am-5pm) Taman Burung is home to over 200 exotic birds from Asia and Australia, and some Indonesian wildlife. It also has a range of rooms from backpacker dorms (per person 30,000Rp) to more comfortable private digs (150,000Rp to 450,000Rp).

Activities

It takes around two hours to circumnavigate Meno on foot. The best beach is the blonde beauty that unfurls, south of the main harbour, just before the signed turn-off to Tao Kombo.

Snorkelling is good off the northeast coast near Amber House; on the west coast near Good Heart; and around the former jetty of the (abandoned) Bounty Resort. Gear is widely available from 25,000Rp per day.

Gili Meno Divers DIVING
(☎0878 6409 5490; www.giliairdivers.com) French- and Indonesian-owned; our favourite dive shop on Meno.

Divine Divers DIVING
(☎0852 4057 0777; www.divinedivers.com) A new dive shop on the far coast. It also has a restaurant-bar on a sweet slice of beach.

Blue Marlin Dive Centre DIVING
(☎613 9980; www.bluemarlindive.com) The Meno shingle of the Trawangan original. There are rooms here too.

Sleeping

Meno has a limited selection of rustic bungalows and it's essential to reserve well ahead in the high season. Prices quoted are high-season rates – reductions of up to 50% are possible the rest of the year. Taman Burung (p316) has backpacker beds on the cheap.

TOP CHOICE **Adeng Adeng** BUNGALOW $$
(☎0818 0534 1019; www.adeng-adeng.com; bamboo house d 350,000Rp, standard/superior 500,000/650,000Rp) An understated elegant resort set back in the trees from a fine stretch of sand. The simple wooden bungalows have all the creature comforts and styl-

ish outdoor terrazzo baths, and the rambling property is sprinkled with artisanal accents. It also manages a two-room bamboo house on the beach for budgeteers.

Shacks 58 & 59 VILLA $$
(☎0813 5357 7045; www.shack58.com; villas €45-70 plus 21% tax; ❄) Tropical slumming as high art. Consider two magnificent one-room villas featuring natural materials, antique furniture and local textiles. Each 'shack' has a lovely private beach gazebo, ideal as a shady retreat from the heat, complete with daybed. Shack 58 is right on the beach, 59 is 150m inland. Online reservations only.

Maha Maya BOUTIQUE HOTEL $$$
(☎088 8715 5828, 637 616; www.mahamaya.co; d from US$150; 📶) A white-washed mod pearl with four-star service and plans for 20 rooms. At research just two were complete. Each had natural jogja stone floors, a rough-cut marble patio, white-washed wood furnishings, and free bottled water. Oh, and the kitchen is fabulous.

Ana Bungalow BUNGALOW $
(☎0819 1595 5234; d 250,000-350,000Rp) Sweet peaked-roof, fan-cooled bungalows with picture windows, and pebbled floors in outdoor baths. There's also an incredibly cute used book shop on the beach next to the four lovely dining *berugas* lit with paper lanterns.

Rawa Indah BUNGALOW $
(☎0817 578 6820; bungalows 150,000-350,000Rp) Six spacious A-frame bungalows, simple but super clean, dangling with seashell wind chimes in a garden setting in the village. Bottled water is free.

Tao Kombo BUNGALOW $
(☎0812 372 2174; www.tao-kombo.com; d 200,000-300,000Rp; 📶) An innovatively designed place with two open-sided backpackers' huts that have bamboo screens for privacy, plus

UNDERWATER GILIS

The Gili Islands are a superb dive destination as the marine life is plentiful and varied. Turtles and black- and white-tip reef sharks are common, and the macro life (small stuff) is excellent, with sea horses, pipefish and lots of crustaceans. Around the full moon, large schools of bumphead parrotfish appear to feast on coral spawn; at other times of the year manta rays cruise past dive sites.

Though years of bomb fishing and an El Niño–induced bleaching damaged corals above 18m, the reefs are now well into a profound recovery and haven't looked this great in years. The Gilis also have their share of virgin coral.

Safety standards are reasonably high, but with the proliferation of new dive schools, 14 operators have formed the Gili Islands Dive Association (GIDA) who come together for monthly meetings on conservation and dive impact issues, and all mind a written list of safety and ecological standards. They also have a price agreement. Each dive costs 370,000Rp for the first five dives, with a 10% discount until your tenth dive and a 15% discount thereafter. A PADI or SSI open-water course costs 3,700,000Rp, Advanced is 2,950,000Rp, Divemaster training starts at 8,350,000Rp. Nitrox, Tri-mix and rebreather courses are also available in Trawangan.

Some of the best dive sites include:

Deep Halik A canyon-like site ideally suited to drift diving. Black- and white-tip sharks are often seen at 28m to 30m.

Deep Turbo At around 30m, this site is ideally suited to nitrox diving. It has impressive sea fans and leopard sharks hidden in the crevasses.

Hidden Reef It was never bombed and has vibrant, pristine soft coral and table coral formations.

Japanese Wreck For experienced divers only (it lies at 45m), this shipwreck of a Japanese patrol boat (c WWII) is another site ideal for tech divers.

Shark Point Perhaps the most exhilarating Gili dive: reef sharks and turtles are very regularly encountered, as well as schools of bumphead parrotfish and mantas.

Sunset (Manta Point) Some impressive table coral; sharks and large pelagics are frequently encountered.

eight *lumbung* cottages with thatched roofs, stone floors and outdoor bathrooms. It's home to the **Jungle Bar** (Tao Kombo), 200m inland from the main strip.

Balenta Bungalows BUNGALOW $$
(☎0819 3674 5046; s/d 350,000/500,000Rp; ❄) The half dozen tin-roof bungalows aren't the most striking from the outside but are among the newest and best maintained on Meno. All have private outdoor baths, patios with bamboo furnishings, queen beds, fresh-water showers, and the attached cafe specialises in vegetarian dishes.

Paul's Last Resort BUNGALOW $
(☎0878 6569 2272; r 150,000Rp) Choose from five woven, open-sided bamboo shacks on the beach, crafted with care. They have electricity and share a toilet and shower. Yes, visitors from the insect kingdom are common, and you may get inundated with Gili T's thumping bass, but if you bed down here you will be privvy to an unparalleled starry night show and superb Rinjani views when the clouds clear.

Sunset Gecko BUNGALOW $
(☎0813 5356 6774; www.thesunsetgecko.com; r 80,000-500,000Rp; 📶) Sometimes romantically rickety is just plain rickety, and while we still love this groovy collection of bamboo and wooden houses, it is falling apart in places. However, the third-floor room in the massive African-themed jungle house out back is marvellous and sleeps up to four people.

Eating & Drinking

Virtually all Meno's restaurants have sea views, which is just as well as service can be slow everywhere. Wood-fired pizza ovens are oddly de rigueur on Meno. Looking for a splurge? Try the Thai-inspired elegance of Adeng Adeng (p316). Owned by Swedes, it does a few homeland dishes (mains 25,000Rp to 70,000Rp), has tasty Thai eats, and you may cap the night with a fine cognac, whiskey and cigar from the rather well-stocked bar. It accepts credit cards.

Rust Warung SEAFOOD $
(☎642 324; mains 15,000-75,000Rp) The only 'proper' restaurant on Meno, and the most visible cog of the 'Rust' empire. Renowned for its grilled fish (with garlic or sweet-and-sour sauce), it also serves pizza and the only espresso on the island.

Jali Café INDONESIAN $
(☎613 9800; dishes 10,000-20,000Rp) Friendly owners serve up tasty Indonesian, Sasak and curry dishes. At night they grill fresh fish and strum guitars by the fire.

Balenta Café INDONESIAN $
(mains from 20,000Rp) A wonderful location for a meal, Balenta has low tables sunk in the sand with turquoise water a metre away. It scores for omelettes, Sasak and Indonesian food like *kelak kuning* (snapper in yellow spice), and staff fire up a seafood barbecue most nights too.

Ya Ya Warung INDONESIAN $
(dishes 10,000-20,000Rp) Ramshackle warung on the beach that serves up Indonesian faves, curries, pancakes and pasta.

Diana Café BAR
(drinks 12,000-30,000Rp; ⏲8am-9pm) If by any remote chance you find the pace of life on Meno too busy, head to this amazing little tiki bar par excellence. Diana couldn't be simpler: a wobbly-looking bamboo-and-thatch bar, a few tables on the sand, a hammock or two, reggae on the stereo and a chill-out zone that makes the most of the zillion-rupiah views.

Information

There are a couple of minimarkets and a wartel near the boat landing; this is also where you can get access to **internet** (per hour 30,000Rp). **Perama** (☎632 824; www.peramatour.com) is based at Kontiki Meno bungalows. A resident nurse attends the **medical clinic** (⏲8am-6pm) near the bird park. Doctors are on call in Mataram.

GILI TRAWANGAN

POP 1500

Well, the secret is definitely out. Long an obscure speck in the big blue, Gili Trawangan has become a paradise of global repute, ranking alongside Bali and Borobudur as one of Indonesia's essential destinations.

Settled just 50 years ago (by Bugis fishermen from Sulawesi), travellers arrived in the 1980s, seduced by the white-sand beaches and coral reefs. By the 1990s Trawangan had mutated into a kind of tropical Ibiza, a stoney idyll where you could rave away from the eyes of the Indonesian police. And then the island began to grow up – resident Western hedonists morphed into entrepreneurs and diving became more important to the island economy than partying.

Today, Trawangan's main drag boasts a glittering roster of lounge bars, hip hotels, cosmopolitan restaurants, and dive schools. And yet behind this glitzy facade, a bohemian character endures, with rickety warung and reggae joints surviving between the cocktail tables. But even as massive 200-plus room hotels begin to colonise the wild and ragged west coast, you can head just inland to a village laced with sandy lanes roamed by free-range roosters, kibbitzing ibus and wild-haired island kids playing hopscotch. Here the call of the muezzin, not happy hour, defines the time of day.

Activities

DIVING

Trawangan is a dive mecca, with 22 professional scuba schools and one of Asia's only free-diving schools. Below is a partial list of GIDA-associated dive schools (p317). All have accommodation at a high standard unless otherwise noted.

Big Bubble DIVING
(☎612 5020; www.bigbubblediving.com) The original engine behind the Gili Eco Trust, and a long-running dive school.

Blue Marlin Dive Centre DIVING
(☎613 2424, 0813 3993 0190; www.bluemarlindive.com) Gili T's original dive shop, and one of the best tech diving schools in the world.

Dream Divers DIVING
(☎613 4496; www.dreamdivers.com) One of the longest-tenured shops.

FREE DIVING THE GILIS

Free diving is an advanced breath-hold technique that allows you to explore much deeper depths than snorkelling (to 30m and beyond!). Trawangan's professional school, **Freedive Gili** (☎614 0503, 0871 5718 7170; www.freedivegili.com; beginner/advanced course 2,150,000/3,150,000Rp) – owned by Michael Board, a UK-record holding free diver, who has touched 90m on a single breath – offers two-day beginner and three-day advanced courses that include theory sessions, breathing techniques and depth-training. After a two-day course many students are able to get down to 20m on a single puff.

CULTURAL RESPECT

The Gili Islands may be a huge tourism destination but they are culturally very different from Bali. Virtually all locals are Muslim and visitors should dress appropriately away from the beach or hotel pool. It's not at all acceptable to wander the lanes of the village in a bikini, and nude or topless bathing anywhere is a no-no. So is naked yoga, by the way. And, yes, that *has* happened. During the month of Ramadan many locals fast during daylight hours and there are no parties on Gili Trawangan.

Gili Divers DIVING
(☎0821 4789 0017; www.gilidivers.com; liveaboard per person incl gear rental 14,300,000Rp) A gorgeous new dive centre with terrific value rooms. It's most noteworthy for its week-long liveaboard to Komodo National Park.

Lutwala Dive DIVING
(☎689 3609; www.lutwala.com) A Nitrox and 5-star PADI centre owned by the women's world record holder for deepest open-circuit dive (190m). It no longer offers accommodation.

Manta Dive DIVING
(☎614 3649; www.manta-dive.com) The biggest, and one of the best, dive schools on the island. They also seem to have the most fun.

Trawangan Dive DIVING
(☎614 9220, 0813 3770 2332; www.trawangandive.com) A top, long-running dive shop with a fun pool-party vibe.

SNORKELLING

There's fun snorkelling off the beach north of the jetty. The coral isn't in the best shape here, but there are tons of fish. The reef is healthier off the northwestern coast, but you may have to scramble over coral to access it at low tide. If the current is quick, you'll have fun flying above the reef, but will have to walk back to your starting point.

Snorkelling gear can be hired from around 25,000Rp per day from shops near the jetty.

SURFING

Trawangan has a fast right reef break that can be surfed year-round, though it is temperamental and at times swells overhead.

Gili Trawangan

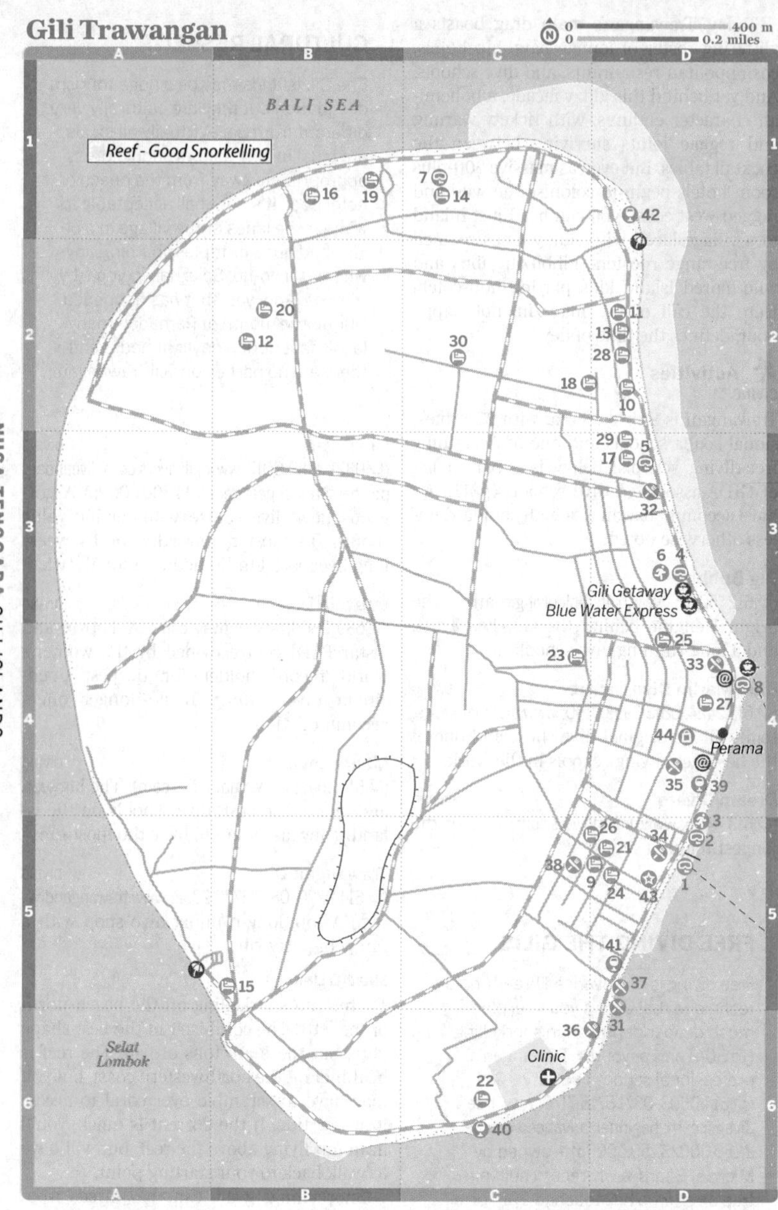

Surf Bar (p325) rents boards on the beach opposite the break.

WALKING & CYCLING

Trawangan is fun to explore on foot or by bike. You can walk around the whole island in a couple of hours – if you finish at the hill on the southwestern corner (which has the remains of an old Japanese WWII gun placement), you'll have terrific sunset views of Bali's Gunung Agung.

Bikes are the preferred mode of transport and are easily hired from 60,000Rp per day.

Gili Trawangan

Activities, Courses & Tours

1 Big Bubble ... D5
Blue Marlin Dive Centre ... (see 39)
2 Dream Divers ... D5
3 Exqisit Spa ... D5
4 Freedive Gili ... D3
5 Gili Divers ... D3
6 Gili Yoga ... D3
7 Lutwala Dive ... C1
8 Manta Dive ... D4
Trawangan Dive ... (see 29)

Sleeping

9 Alexyane Paradise ... D5
10 Balé Sampan ... D2
11 Blu da Mare ... D2
12 Coconut Garden ... B2
13 Danima ... D2
14 Eden Cottages ... C1
15 Exile ... B5
16 Gili Eco Villas ... B1
17 Gili Hostel ... D3
18 Gili Joglo ... C2
19 Karma Kayak ... B1
20 Kelapa Villas ... B2
21 Koi Gili ... D5
22 Kokomo ... C6
23 Lumbung Cottages 2 ... C4
24 Oceane Paradise ... D5
25 Pondok Gili Gecko ... D4
26 Rumah Hantu ... D5
27 Sama Sama Bungalows ... D4
28 Tanah Qita ... D2
29 Trawangan Dive ... D3
30 Woodstock ... C2

Eating

31 Beach House ... D5
Blu da Mare ... (see 11)
32 Cafe Gili ... D3
33 Juku ... D4
Karma Kayak ... (see 19)
Kokomo ... (see 22)
34 Pesona ... D5
35 Rumah Makan Kikinovi ... D4
36 Scallywags ... D6
37 Trattoria ... D5
38 Warung Indonesia ... C5

Drinking

39 Blue Marlin ... D4
40 Surf Bar ... C6
41 Tir na Nog ... D5
42 Top End Bar ... D1

Entertainment

43 Rudy's Pub ... D5

Shopping

44 Vintage ... D4

Your hotel can arrange rental or you can find a bike shop on the main drag.

YOGA & WELLNESS

Gili Yoga YOGA

(☎0878 6579 4884; www.giliyoga.com; per person 100,000Rp; ⊙5.30pm daily, 7.30-9am Mon, Wed & Fri) A superb new yoga centre that runs daily Vinyasa classes.

Exqisit Spa SPA

(☎612 9405; www.exqisit.com; treatments 30/60 min from 80,000/150,000Rp; ⊙10am-10pm) A new day spa on the waterfront with curtained off treatment rooms. It does Tibetan hot stone massage (180,000Rp), shiatsu, and a hangover recovery massage too. Talk about knowing the marketplace.

Sleeping

Gili T has 5000 rooms and over 100 places to stay, ranging from thatched huts to sleek, air-conditioned villas with private pools. Yet, at peak season the entire island is often booked. It's wise to reserve your room well ahead. Virtually all dive schools offer really good midrange accommodation, which may come with price breaks on diving packages. The cheapest digs are in the village, where the mosque is everyone's alarm clock. You'll pay more for a beachside address. Head to the north or west coasts to escape the crowds.

All budget and most midrange places have brackish tap water. Pure water is available in some upmarket bungalows. Quoted high-season rates drop up to 50% off-peak.

VILLAGE

TOP CHOICE **Woodstock** BUNGALOW $

(☎081 2396 7744; www.woodstockgili.com; d with fan 350,000Rp, with air-con 450,000-700,000Rp; ❄📶🏊) The hippest spot on Trawangan. Commune with the spirit of the Dead, Baez and Hendrix in 11 super clean rooms with tribal accents, private porches and outdoor baths, surrounding a fabulous pool area.

Gili Hostel HOSTEL $
(☎0812 3984 4157; www.gilihostel.com; per person 100,000Rp; ❄📶) The island's only dedicated hostel, an all co-ed dorm complex with a shaggy Torajan-styled roof, is brand new. Rooms sleep seven, have concrete floors, high ceilings and a sleeping loft. There's a rooftop bar with bean bags, sun lounges, and hammocks with views of the treetops and the hills, as well as DVD stations to screen your own films.

Alexyane Paradise BUNGALOW $
(☎0878 6599 9645; r with fan/air-con 350,000/500,000Rp; ❄) Great quality dark wood cottages with high ceilings, bamboo beds, and lovely light-flooded outdoor baths sprouting with foliage.

Oceane Paradise COTTAGE $
(☎0812 3779 3533; s/d 200,000/250,000Rp) A terrific new compound of five wooden cottages with stylish outdoor bathrooms.

Lumbung Cottages 2 BUNGALOW $
(☎0819 3679 6353; www.lumbungcottage.com; bungalows from 400,000Rp; ❄📶🏊) New *lumbung*-style cottages set deep in the village, tucked up against the hillside, surrounding a black bottom pool.

Rumah Hantu GUESTHOUSE $
(☎0819 1710 2444; d 150,000-250,000Rp) A well-tended if simple collection of woven bamboo rooms with high ceilings and fresh paint in a rootsy garden plot.

Koi Gili GUESTHOUSE $
(☎0819 5995 760; s/d 250,000/350,000Rp; ❄) The young and hip gravitate to this groovy guesthouse with a daybed in the garden and a mod colour scheme on the facade.

Pondok Gili Gecko GUESTHOUSE $
(☎0818 0573 2814; r 250,000-350,000Rp) An inviting guesthouse with a charming gecko motif. Rooms have ceiling fans and private tiled patios overlooking the garden.

Gili Joglo VILLA $$$
(☎0813 5678 4741; www.gilijoglo.com; villas from €120) Two fabulous villas. One is crafted out of an antique *joglo* (traditional Javanese house) with polished concrete floors, two bedrooms and a massive indoor-outdoor great room. Though slightly smaller, we prefer the one built from two 1950s *gladaks* (middle-class home). Rooms come with butler service.

MAIN STRIP

Kokomo LUXURY VILLAS $$$
(☎613 4920; www.kokomogilit.com; villas from 1,400,000Rp; ❄📶🏊) Offering beautifully finished and lavishly equipped modern accommodation, these mini-villas are set in a small complex at the (quiet) southern end of the main strip. All have private pools, contemporary decor and lovely indoor-outdoor living quarters.

Sama Sama Bungalows BUNGALOW $
(☎612 1106; r with fan 150,000, with air-con 400,000-500,000Rp; ❄) We like the six new, fan-cooled backpacker rooms with high beamed ceilings, modern baths and a great price.

BEACHSIDE

Blu da Mare BUNGALOW $$
(☎0858 8866 2490; www.bludamare.it; d 500,000-850,000Rp; ❄) Most notable for its exquisite kitchen, you can bed down in one of four lovely, antique *joglos* from 1920s Java, with gorgeous old wood floors, queen beds, and fresh water showers in a sunken bath.

Balé Sampan BOUTIQUE HOTEL $$
(☎0812 3702 4048; www.balesampanbungalows.com; r garden/pool 820,000/880,000Rp; ❄📶🏊) Fine modern-edge rooms served with stone baths, a freshwater pool, plush duvet covers and a proper English breakfast. Rooms have all been recently refreshed right down to new mattresses.

Trawangan Dive HOSTEL $
(☎614 9220, 0813 3770 2332; www.trawangandive.com; dm per person 50,000Rp, bungalows 800,000Rp; ❄📶) Most notable for the 12 backpacker dorms that sleep two on the cheap. Book the whole room for 100,000Rp

Tanah Qita BUNGALOW $
(☎613 9159; martinkoch-berlin@hotmail.de; bungalows with fan/air-con 200,000/600,000Rp; ❄) Another excellent set-up. Tanah Qita ('Homeland') has four large, immaculate *lumbung* (with four-poster beds) and smaller fan-cooled versions. The garden is a bucolic delight.

NORTH, SOUTH & WEST COASTS

TOP CHOICE **Karma Kayak** INN $$
(☎0818 0559 3710; www.karmakayak.com; bungalows from 550,000Rp; ❄📶) Simplicity is the key at this wonderful retreat where everything seems to exist in harmony with the tranquil location. All the fine rooms adopt a

less-is-more uncluttered design, with soothing natural colours, large windows and generous balconies or verandas. The beachside cafe is first-class.

Eden Cottages COTTAGE $$

(0819 1799 6151; www.edencottages.com; cottage 550,000Rp;) Six clean, thatched concrete bungalows wrapped around a pool, fringed by a garden, and shaded by a coconut grove. Rooms have tasteful rattan furnishings, stone baths, TV-DVD and freshwater showers.

Coconut Garden BUNGALOW $$

(0821 4781 8912; www.coconutgardenresort.com; s/d 550,000/600,000Rp;) A simple spot with just four bright and airy glass-box Javanese *joglos* with tiled roofs connected to outdoor terrazzo baths. Expect plush linens, queen beds and a rolling lawn dotted with coco palms. It's on its own in the quiet middle of the island and can be hard to find. Call ahead.

Exile BUNGALOW $

(0819 0707 7475; d 350,000-500,000Rp; @) One of our favourite newcomers is an uber-groovy compound of woven bamboo bungalows, with a sweet beach bar and bamboo lounges on the sand. Indonesian owned, they're only 15 to 20 minutes to the main strip on foot, or an easy bike ride.

Danima HOTEL $$

(0878 6087 2506; www.giliresortsdanima.com; d 900,000-950,000Rp;) An intimate four-room boutique property. Nests are blessed with floating beds, vaulted ceilings, tasteful lighting, rattan deck seating and rain showers. There is a romantic pool and beach area too.

Gili Eco Villas VILLA $$$

(0361 847 6419; www.giliecovillas.com; villas US$297 plus 21% tax;) Classy villas made from recycled teak salvaged from old Javanese colonials are set back from the beach on Trawangan's idyllic north coast. Comfort and style are combined with solid green principles (water is recycled, there's an organic vegetable garden, and solar and wind energy provide most of the power). Low season walk-in rates plummet to 1,000,000Rp.

Kelapa Villas VILLA $$$

(613 2424; www.kelapavillas.com; villas US$195-620, plus 21% tax;) Luxury development in an inland location with a selection of 22 commodious villas, all with private pools, that offer style and space in abundance. There's a tennis court and gym in the complex, and five beachfront villas on the way.

Eating

In the evenings, several places on the main strip display and grill delicious fresh seafood, and there's a marvellous Pasar Malam

GREEN GILI

Though Gili T looks like paradise, there's been severe pressure on the island (intensive development and rubbish) and offshore reefs (fishermen using cyanide and dynamite to harvest fish) for years. More recently Trawangan's once wide white-sand beaches have eroded. In some places they've been swallowed whole, but several initiatives started by the **Gili Eco Trust** (www.facebook.com/giliecotrust) have tried to reclaim the reef and stem the rising tide. **Biorock**, a coral regeneration project, has been staggeringly successful in mitigating beach erosion and nurturing marine life. Loose pieces of living coral (perhaps damaged by an anchor or a clumsy diving fin) are gathered and transplanted onto frames in the sea. Electrodes supplied with low-voltage currents cause electrolytic reactions, accelerating coral growth and ultimately creating an artificial reef. There are now 42 Biorock installations around the Gilis. You'll see them as you snorkel or dive; their shapes look quite startling in the water – flowers, an airplane, turtle, star, manta and even a heart – covered in fledgling coral and sponges.

In 2009 the Gili Eco Trust tackled rubbish. An education program implemented in schools has raised awareness, and in May 2010 over 1000 recycling bins were introduced to the Gilis. Plastic bags are the main culprit, so strong re-useable bags (you can purchase them for 20,000Rp) have been introduced and it's hoped a complete ban will be agreed on in the future. Straws are evil too. About 2000 of them are picked up on Trawangan beaches monthly. If you want to get involved you can join the island clean-up (first Friday of every month) and collect land or sea garbage; kids are very welcome to help out.

(night market) at Pasar Seni (art market) with more than a dozen stalls and carts serving everything from Javanese-style pick-and-mix *nasi campur* to grilled chicken thighs and grilled fish, to noodle soup, *bakso* and sate. Meals hover around 25,000Rp. At write-up there was talk about moving it onto the village soccer field.

TOP CHOICE Blu da Mare ITALIAN $$
(☎0858 8866 2490; www.bludamare.it; mains 60,000-110,000Rp; ⏰12.30-3pm & 6.30-10pm Sat-Thu) An authentic and intimate (few tables, limited seatings available) Italian-owned trattoria where the lady of the house bakes the bread, makes her own pasta and grills meat, fish and seafood to perfection. Speaking of seafood, her hubbie and co-owner (who, oh by the way, used to race yachts) spears fresh catch daily, which is carved into melt in your mouth carpaccio. Don't leave without enjoying the chocolate salami for desert. If only there was wine.

Rumah Makan Kikinovi INDONESIAN $
(meals from 15,000Rp) Run by a formidable *ibu* (mother), this is Indonesian pick-and-mix cuisine at its tastiest. Dishes usually come out fresh at 11.30am, just before the divemaster lunch crush.

Kokomo INTERNATIONAL $$
(☎613 4920; www.kokomogilit.com; mains 60,000-160,000Rp; ❄📶) Kokomo is the only genuine fine-dining restaurant in town, using hyper-fresh local seafood and select imported meats. Lots of fresh salads, wonderful steaks and pasta, but for the ultimate treat opt for a seafood or sashimi (with Atlantic salmon and yellowfin tuna) platter. Service can be painfully slow, but you'll leave happy.

Trattoria ITALIAN $$
(www.trattoriaasia.com; mains 55,000-152,000Rp; 📶) The Gili shingle of the Bali original. The Italian chef crafts homemade pastas, excellent pizzas and mains like grilled tuna with basil emulsion, and beef tenderloin sliced on a bed of fresh rocket and parmesan. All served on a dining deck over the marina.

Pesona INDIAN $$
(☎660 7233; www.pesonaresort.com; mains 59,000-80,000Rp; ⏰7am-11pm; ❄✍) The refined bungalows and lovely pool area are nice, but we love the Indian kitchen, with an abundance of vegetarian options along with a menu of tandoori chicken and fish, and six flavours of naan. Once sated, lay back on the cushions and fire up a *sheesha* (90,000Rp).

Scallywags INTERNATIONAL $$
(☎614 5301; www.scallywagsresort.com; meals 40,000Rp-100,000Rp; 📶) Scallywags is an Aussie-owned restaurant that offers casual, yet elegant decor, polished glassware, switched-on service, free wi-fi and superb cocktails. The dinner menu features tasty seafood – fresh lobster, tuna steaks, snapper and swordfish – and a great salad bar.

Warung Indonesia INDONESIAN $
(dishes from 15,000-20,000Rp; ⏰8am-9pm; 📶) Tucked away at the rear of the village, it scores high marks for its tasty pick-and-mix bar, as well as a menu of Indo staples like oxtail soup, *soto ayam* and *ikan goreng*. The lofted thatched dining room is lit with vintage lanterns, and is wired.

Beach House INTERNATIONAL $$
(☎642 352; mains 45,000-150,000Rp) This is a hugely popular place with a seafront terrace that's best for fresh fish (or grilled meats) and its comprehensive salad-bar selection.

Karma Kayak TAPAS $
(☎0818 0559 3710; tapas from 15,000Rp) Terrific tapas are served on a blissfully tranquil beach location. Wash it down with a jug of sangría. It's magical at sunset here, with volcanoes filling the pink horizon.

Juku SEAFOOD $
(mains 25,000-45,000Rp) Long known as the most affordable fish grill on the island, Juku ventures into international territory but if you stick to Indonesian seafood dishes, like fiery sambal tuna, you'll be fine.

Cafe Gili INTERNATIONAL $
(www.facebook.com/cafegilitrawangan; mains 35,000-58,000Rp; ⏰8am-10pm; 📶) Think: cushioned beachside seating, candlelight and a bit too much Jack Johnson (an island-wide sin). The kitchen spills from a shabby chic white-washed dining room and rambles across the street to the shore. The menu meanders from eggs Florentine and breakfast baguettes, to deli sandwiches and salads, to decent pasta, quesadillas and seafood dishes.

🍷 Drinking & Entertainment

Trawangan's rotating parties are no secret. They fire up at around 11pm and go on until 4am as imported DJs from Bali and beyond mix techno, trance and house music (except during Ramadan when the action is completely curtailed out of respect for local culture). The party schedule shifts between Blue Marlin (Monday), Tir na Nog (Wednesday) and Rudy's (Friday). But with this many cool beach bars, every night is a good time.

TOP CHOICE Tir na Nog PUB
(613 9463; 7am-2am Thu-Tue, to 4am Wed;) Known simply as 'The Irish', this barn-like place has a sports-bar interior with big-screen TVs ideal for international football matches, and tasty pub grub. Its shoreside bar is the busiest meeting spot in the island. Jovial mayhem reigns on Wednesday nights.

Blue Marlin BAR
Of all the party bars, this upper-level venue has the largest dance floor and the meanest sound system – it pumps out trance and tribal sounds on Monday.

Top End Bar BAR
(10am-midnight) If you wish to chill on a luscious white beach, one with bamboo lounges, and reggae music pumping from the tiki bar, or if you desire a 'ticket to the moon', then you'll come here, to Trawangan's best beach bar.

Surf Bar BAR
(8am-late) Opposite the break and just south of the Villa Ombak, this tiki bar has a sweet slab of beach, a rack of boards for rent, a pumping stereo and a young crowd. It does full and dark moon parties.

Rudy's Pub BAR
Rudy's hosts arguably the best party on the island, with a good mix of locals and visitors and legendary drinks specials. The huge dance floor at the rear is verging on meat-market terrain on party nights.

Shopping

Once the domain of cheap knick-knack stalls and not much else, a trickle of refinement has arrived.

TOP CHOICE Vintage VINTAGE
(www.vintagedelivery.com; 9am-9pm) The best boutique on Gili T is tucked in the back of Pasar Seni, and it's a treasure trove of vintage fashion sourced internationally and displayed with grace. Browse chunky earrings, superb leather hand and shoulder bags, baby doll dresses, and John Lennon shades. A round of applause please for the stylish lady from Sweden.

Information

Boats dock on the island's eastern shore, which is also home to most of Trawangan's accommodation, restaurants and facilities. The best stretch of beach is on the stunning northwest corner. Stay here, and you'll have a longer trek to the action.

EMERGENCY There's a health **clinic** (9am-5pm) just south of Hotel Vila Ombak. For security issues contact **Satgas**, a community organisation, via your hotel or dive school.

INTERNET & TELEPHONE Wi-fi has proliferated on Trawangan. Most midrange hotels have connections as do several restaurants and bars including Scallywags, Tir na Nog, and Cafe Gili. **Creative Internet** (per hour 18,000Rp; 8am-midnight; @) and **Fahri Internet** (per hour 24,000Rp; 8am-11pm) offer speedy connections on the strip.

MONEY There are seven **ATMs** on the main strip and four on the west side of the island. Stores and hotels change cash and travellers cheques, but rates are poor. Cash advances on credit/debit cards involve a commission of up to 10%.

TRAVEL AGENCIES Perama (613 8514; www.peramatour.com) Fast-boat tickets to Bali, and connections to all locations on Lombok by shuttle boat and bus. Komodo crossings can also be arranged here.

North & Central Lombok

0370

Lush and fertile, Lombok's scenic interior is stitched together with rice terraces, undulating tobacco fields, fruit and nut orchards, swatches of monkey forest, and it's capped by sacred Gunung Rinjani, which haemorrhages springs, rivers and waterfalls. Entwined in all this big nature are traditional Sasak settlements. Public transport is not frequent or consistent enough to rely on, but with wheels you can explore it all, and if you're here in August, you can attend the annual Sasak stick-fighting tournament.

Getting There & Away

Bangsal is a hassle and public transport north from here is infrequent. Several minibuses a day go from Mandalika terminal in Bertais (Mataram) to Bayan, but you'll have to get connections in Pemenang and/or Anyar, which can be difficult to navigate. Simplify things with your own wheels.

SIRE

Fast becoming Lombok's most upmarket enclave, the jutting Sire (or Sira) peninsula is blessed with gorgeous, broad white-sand beaches and good snorkelling offshore.

Opulent resorts and one gem of a midranger are now established here, alongside a couple of fishing villages and some amazing private villas.

Sleeping

TOP CHOICE **Rinjani Beach Eco Resort** BOUTIQUE HOTEL $$
(☎0878 6450 9148, 0813 3993 0773; www.lombok-adventure.com; Karang Atas; bungalows 350,000-900,000Rp;) A midrange gem in an exclusive zip code where the sun rises over Rinjani and sets over Agung. A young French-Scandinavian family offer five jumbo bamboo bungalows, each with its own color scheme and theme, a queen bed, upcycled wood floors, and a sofa that can be converted into a twin. There are hammocks on private porches, a pool on the black-sand beach, a dive shop and restaurant, and sea kayaks and mountain bikes for guests. It's got beauty, grace and warmth. And there are cheaper, smaller bungalows for backpackers too.

Tugu Lombok RESORT $$$
(☎620 111; www.tuguhotels.com; bungalows US$220, villas from US$270, plus 21% tax;) An astonishing fantasy of a hotel that's like no other on Lombok. This bigger than life amalgamation of luxury accommodation, off-beat design and spiritual Indonesian heritage sits on a wonderful white-sand beach. Room decor reflects Indonesian tradition, the exquisite spa is modelled on Java's Borobudur temple and the main restaurant is like a rice barn on steroids. Service is spot on. Drop by for a meal or drink if you can't afford to stay.

Oberoi Lombok RESORT $$$
(☎638 444; www.oberoihotels.com; r from US$260, villas from US$425, plus 21% tax;) For sheer get-away-from-it-all bliss the Oberoi simply excels. The hotel's core is a triple-level pool which leads the eye to a lovely private beach. Indonesian rajah-style luxury is the look: sunken marble bathtubs, teak floors, antique entertainment armoires and oriental rugs. Service is flawless, facilities are superb.

GONDANG & AROUND

Just northeast of Gondang village, a 6km trail heads inland to **Air Terjun Tiu Pupas**, a 30m waterfall that's only worth seeing in the wet season. Trails continue from here to other wet-season waterfalls including **Air Terjun Gangga**, the most beautiful of all. A local guide will turn up at the trailhead to lead you there.

BAYAN

Wektu Telu, Lombok's animist-tinted form of Islam, was born in humble thatched mosques nestled in these Rinjani foothills. The best example is **Masjid Kuno Bayan Beleq**, next to the village of Baleq. Its low-slung roof, dirt floors and bamboo walls reportedly date from 1634, making this mosque the oldest on Lombok. Inside is a huge old drum which served as the call to prayer before PA systems.

SENARU & BATU KOQ

These scenic villages merge into one along a steep road with sweeping Rinjani and sea views. Most visitors here are volcano-bound but beautiful walking trails and spectacular waterfalls beckon to all.

Sights & Activities

Air Terjun Sindang Gila (5000Rp) is a spectacular set of falls 20 minutes' walk from Senaru via a lovely forest and hillside trail. The hearty and the foolish make for the creek, edge close and then get pounded by the hard foaming cascade that explodes over volcanic stone 40m above. A further 50 minutes or so uphill is **Air Terjun Tiu Kelep**, another waterfall with a swimming hole. The track is steep and guides are compulsory (60,000Rp).

In the traditional Sasak village of **Dusun Senaru**, at the top of the road, locals will invite you to chew betel nut (or tobacco) and show you around (for a donation). A guided **rice-terrace and waterfalls walk** (per person 150,000Rp), which takes in Sindang Gila, rice paddies and an old bamboo mosque, and the **Senaru Panorama Walk** (per person 150,000Rp), which incorporates stunning views, and insights into local traditions can be arranged at Transit Cafe (p327).

Sleeping & Eating

Most of the dozen or so places here are simple mountain lodges, and since the climate's cooler, you won't need fans. All are dotted along the road from Bayan to Senaru and listed in order from the top of the road down.

Gunung Baru Senaru COTTAGE $
(☎0819 0741 1211; d 80,000Rp) A small family run property with five simple, tiled cottages with Western toilets and *mandi* in a blooming garden.

Pondok Senaru & Restaurant LODGE $
(☎622 868, 0818 0362 4129; r 250,000-600,000Rp) A class act, this place has lovely little cottages with terracotta-tiled roofs, and well-equipped superior rooms with TV, four-poster beds and hot water. The restaurant, with tables perched on the edge of a rice-terraced valley, has a sublime setting.

Horizon LODGE $
(☎0817 576 0936; www.horizonsenaru.com; d 300,000Rp) Decent value contemporary rooms (in one, you can gaze over the Senaru valley from your bed), pebble-floored bathrooms and high standards of cleanliness. It's also home to a small restaurant.

Sinar Rinjani LODGE $
(☎081 854 0673; d with cold/hot water 100,000/150,000Rp) Rooms are huge with rain showers, crown mouldings and king-sized beds, and the rooftop restaurant has outstanding views.

Transit Cafe INDONESIAN $
(☎0818 0365 2874; www.rudytrekker.com; Jl Raya Pariwisata; mains 20,000-40,000Rp;) Part cafe, part Rinjani launch pad, Transit serves pastas, sandwiches and assorted Indo classics along with wi-fi. Offers waterfall and panorama hikes, and Rinjani trekking packages.

Information

Rinjani Trek Centre (RTC; ☎0878 6432 3094, 0817 5724 863; www.info2lombok.com), at the top of the hill, is the local guiding and mountain authority. Even if you arrange a trip elsewhere, all Senaru-based Rinjani trips are packaged with their guides and approval.

Getting There & Away

From Mandalika terminal in Bertais (Mataram), catch a bus to Anyar (25,000Rp to 30,000Rp, 2½ hours). Bemo no longer run from Anyar for Senaru, so you'll have to charter an *ojek* (per person 15,000Rp to 20,000Rp).

THE SEMBALUN VALLEY

☎0376

High on the eastern side of Gunung Rinjani is the beautiful Sembalun Valley, a rich farming region where the golden foothills turn vivid green in the wet season. When the high clouds part, Rinjani goes full frontal from all angles. The valley has two main settlements, Sembalun Lawang and Sembalun Bumbung, tranquil bread baskets primarily concerned with growing cabbage, potatoes, strawberries and, above all, garlic – though trekking tourism brings in a little income too. This is the best access point for an attempt on Rinjani's summit.

Activities

The national-park rangers who staff the **Rinjani Information Centre** (RIC; ☎0878 6334 4119; 6am-6pm) in the centre of town speak decent English and are well informed. They can hook you up with guides for day treks such as the four-hour **village walk** (minimum 2 people, per person 150,000Rp) and the two-day **wildflower walk** (per person incl guide, porters, meals & camping gear 550,000Rp) through blooming savannah. But most are here to summit Rinjani.

Sleeping & Eating

The Rinjani Information Centre now offers six simple and tiled guest rooms (r 200,000Rp) with double beds, cable TV, private baths and tiny decks behind their office.

Lembah Rinjani LODGE $
(☎0852 3954 3279, 0818 0365 2511; d 300,000-400,000Rp) The property has been spruced up and is in great shape. Basic but clean tiled rooms have queen beds, wood funishings, private porches and breathtaking mountain and sunrise views.

Maria Guesthouse GUESTHOUSE $
(☎0852 3956 1340; r 250,000Rp) A new place with large tin-roofed bungalows at the rear of a family compound. Digs are bright with garrish tiled floors and some can smell musty, but the family vibe is fun and the garden location sweet.

Getting There & Away

From Mandalika bus terminal (Mataram), take a bus to Aikmel (20,000Rp) and change for a bemo to Sembalun Lawang (15,000Rp).

There's no public transport between Sembalun Lawang and Senaru, so you'll have to charter an *ojek*, for around 150,000Rp.

Gunung Rinjani

Lording over the northern half of Lombok, 3726m Gunung Rinjani is Indonesia's second-tallest volcano. It's an astonishing peak, and sacred to Hindus and Sasaks who make pilgrimages to the summit and lake to leave offerings for the gods. To the Balinese, Rinjani is one of three sacred mountains, along with Bali's Agung and Java's Bromo. Sasaks ascend throughout the year around the full moon. The mountain also has climatic significance. Its peak attracts a steady stream

Gunung Rinjani

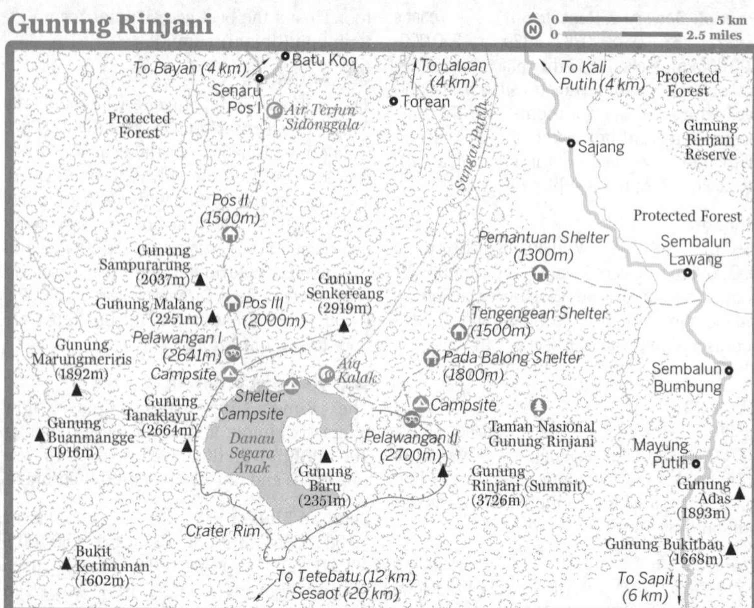

of swirling rain clouds, while its ash bring fertility to the island's rice fields and tobacco crops, feeding a tapestry of paddies, fields, and cashew and mango orchards.

Inside the immense caldera, sitting 600m below the rim, is a stunning, 6km-wide, cobalt-blue crescent lake, **Danau Segara Anak** (Child of the Sea). The Balinese ceremonially toss gold and jewellery into the lake, before they slog towards the sacred summit. The mountain's newest cone, the minor peak of Gunung Baru, only emerged a couple of hundred years ago. Its scarred, smouldering profile rising above the lake as an ominous reminder of the apocalyptic power of nature.

Activities

Organised Treks

The best and least expensive way to organise a trip is to head to either the Rinjani Trek Centre (p327) in Senaru or the Rinjani Information Centre (p327) in Sembalun Lawang. The centres use a rotation system so that all local guides get a slice of the trekking purse. And though guides are always eager for a gig, they are laid-back and easy to work with.

Whether you book through your losmen, or directly at the RTC or RIC, the same trek packages are offered, but in Senaru the prices often vary depending on demand and level of luxury. Trekking packages to the summit including food, equipment, guide, porters, park fee and transport start from US$185. An overnight trek to the crater rim costs US$135.

Two Senaru outfitters stand out. **John's Adventures** (☎0817 578 8018; www.rinjani-master.com; per person 3-day, 2-night from 1,750,000Rp) has been leading Rinjani climbs since 1982. He has toilet tents, offers four meals a day, provides thick sleeping mats and offers itineraries that begin in either Senaru or Sembalun Lawang. Transit Cafe (p327) is another conscientious outfitter based in Senaru. It has a variety of itineraries, though most prefer the three-day, two-night package starting from Sembalun.

Guides & Porters

Hiking independently is prohibited, and hiring guides and porters independently in Senaru is now discouraged as the RTC sells trekking packages only. If you did manage to bring all of your own gear from home, packed enough provisions for you and your support team, and wish to create your own itinerary on the mountain, you can book your own guide and porters at the RIC in

Sembalun. Guides charge 150,000Rp per day and porters 125,000Rp per day. Guides are knowledgeable and informative, but won't carry anything for you, so take at least one porter.

Entrance Fee & Equipment

Entrance to Taman Nasional Gunung Rinjani (Gunung Rinjani National Park) is a hefty 150,000Rp – you register and pay at the RTC in Senaru or the RIC in Sembalun Lawang before your trek. Sleeping bags and tents are essential and can be hired at either RTC or RIC. Decent footwear, warm clothing, wet-weather gear, cooking equipment and a torch (flashlight) are important (all, except your boots, can be hired if necessary). Expect to pay upwards of 100,000Rp a head per day for all your gear. Muscle balm (to ease aching legs) and a swimming costume (for the lake and hot springs) could also be packed. Poaching firewood at high altitude is an environmental no-no, so take a stove. And bring home your rubbish, including toilet tissue. Sadly several Rinjani camps are litter strewn.

Food & Supplies

Trek organisers at RTC and RIC arrange food supplies if you sign on to a package tour. If you bring your own, buy most of your supplies in the Mataram markets, where it's cheaper and there's more choice. Bring a lighter, and pack and drink more water than seems reasonable. Dehydration can spur altitude sickness.

Tetebatu

☎0376

Laced with Rinjani spring-fed streams and blessed with rich volcanic soil, Tetebatu is a Sasak bread basket. The surrounding countryside is quilted with tobacco and rice fields, fruit orchards and cow pastures that fade into remnant monkey forest gushing with waterfalls. Tetebatu's sweet climate is ideal for long country walks (at 400m it's high enough to mute that hot, sticky coastal mercury). Dark nights come saturated with sound courtesy of a frog orchestra accompanied by countless gurgling brooks. Even insomniacs snore here.

The town is spread out, with facilities on roads north and east (nicknamed 'waterfall road') of the central *ojek* stop. Internet has yet to colonise tiny Tetebatu. The closest connection is in Kotaraja, 5km away.

Sights & Activities

Taman Wisata Tetebatu FOREST

A shady 4km track leads from the main road, just north of the mosque, into Taman Wisata Tetebatu (Monkey Forest) with black monkeys and two waterfalls. Both waterfalls are accessible by private transport or a spectacular two-hour walk (one way) through rice fields from Tetebatu. If walking, hire a guide (125,000Rp), easily arranged through your hotel.

Air Terjun Jukut WATERFALL

(admission 20,000Rp) Locals still believe that water from Air Terjun Jukut will increase hair growth. So if baldness frightens you, wade over and let the frigid cascade rain down on your man-scalp. It's a 2km walk from the car park at the end of the road north from town.

Sleeping & Eating

TOP CHOICE **Tetebatu Mountain Resort** LODGE $

(☎0819 1771 6440, 081 2372 4040; d/tr 400,000/500,000Rp) These two-storey, two-bedroom Sasak bungalows are the best digs in town and are perfect for travelling buddies. The top floor balcony has magical rice field views.

Cendrawasih Cottages COTTAGE $

(☎0878 6418 7063; r 175,000Rp) Sweet little *lumbung*-style brick cottages with bamboo beds and private porches nestled in the rice fields. You'll sit on floor cushions in the stunning stilted restaurant, which offers Sasak, Indonesian or Western grub and 360-degree paddy views. It's about 500m east of the intersection. Low season discounts are common.

Hakiki Inn BUNGALOW $

(☎0819 1836 0477; bungalow 150,000-250,000Rp) Another collection of sweet if slightly worn Sasak bungalows in a blooming garden at the edge of the rice fields. The largest of the bunch sleep three. You'll find it perched over the family rice plot about 600m from the intersection.

Pondok Tetebatu LODGE $

(☎0818 0576 7153, 632 572; d 100,000-150,000Rp) About 500m north of the intersection, these detached, ranch-style rooms set around a flower garden are basic and reasonably clean, but the staff are fantastic. The restaurant, which specialises in Sasak cooking, is a

CLIMBING GUNUNG RINJANI

The most popular way to climb Gunung Rinjani is the four-day trek that starts at Senaru and finishes at Sembalun Lawang. Other possibilities include a summit attempt from Sembalun (which can be done as a gruelling two-day return hike). You might like starting from Sembalun as it's brighter and sunnier and sits higher on the slope, which means you don't have as much altitude to gain. No matter which way you walk, a guide is mandatory, and it's usually forbidden to climb Rinjani during the wet season (November to March), due to the threat of landslides.

Day One: Senaru Pos I to Pos III (Five to Six Hours)

Just beyond the Rinjani Trek Centre, where you pay your park fee, the trail climbs steadily through scrubby farmland to the signed entrance of Gunung Rinjani National Park. About 2½ hours of steady climbing brings you to Pos II (1500m), where there's a shelter. Water can be found 100m down the slope from the trail, but it should be treated or boiled. Another 1½ hours' ascent brings you to Pos III (2000m), the best place to camp. Water is 100m to the right of the collapsed shelters.

Day Two: Pos III to Danau Segara Anak & Aiq Kalak (Four Hours)

From Pos III, it takes about 1½ hours to reach the rim, Pelawangan I (2641m). Set off very early for the stunning sunrise. It's possible to camp at Pelawangan I, but level sites are limited, there's no water and it can be blustery.

It takes about two more hours to descend to Danau Segara Anak and around to Aiq Kalak (hot springs). The first hour is a very steep descent and involves boulder-hopping. From the bottom of the crater wall it's an easy 30-minute walk across undulating terrain around the lake's edge, where you'll find the nicest sites. Yet, most prefer to rest and recuperate near the hot springs. Fresh water can be gathered from a spring near Aiq Kalak. The climb back up the rim is taxing – allow at least three hours and start early to make it back to Senaru in one day. Allow five hours from the rim down to Senaru. Or complete the Rinjani trek by continuing to Sembalun Lawang.

good bet, and guided walks through farming villages to the falls are offered.

Getting There & Around

Public transport to Tetebatu is infrequent. All cross-island buses pass Pomotong (15,000Rp from Mandalika terminal) on the main east–west highway. Get off here and you can hop an *ojek* (15,000Rp) to Tetebatu.

Private cars (with drivers) can be arranged at Pondok Tetebatu (p329) to all Lombok destinations (300,000Rp to 600,000Rp) including the airport (350,000Rp); bicycles (per day 50,000Rp) and motorbikes (per day 50,000Rp) can be rented here too.

South Lombok

☎0370

Beaches just don't get much better: the water is warm, striped turquoise and curls into barrels, and the sand is silky and snow white, framed by massive headlands and sheer cliffs that recall Bali's Bukit Peninsula 30 years ago. Village life is still vibrant, as well, with unique festivals, jubilant drum corps, and an economy based on seaweed and tobacco harvests. The south is noticeably drier than the rest of Lombok and more sparsely populated, with limited roads and public transport. But, with Lombok's state-of-the-art international airport now operating, flights have already increased and change will surely come. Soon.

PRAYA

POP 37,000

Sprawling Praya is the main town in the south, with tree-lined streets and the odd crumbling Dutch colonial relic. But the real (and only) reason you're here is to fly in or out of Lombok's new airport, which is around 5km south of the centre. The bemo terminal is on the northwest side of town.

Although it looks far on the map, a massive four lane bypass shrinks the distance between the airport and Mataram, which is less than 45 minutes away. Taxi rates to

Day Three: Aiq Kalak to Pelawangan II (Three to Four Hours)

The trail starts beside the last shelter at the hot springs and heads away from the lake for about 100m before veering right. It then traverses the northern slope of the crater, and it's an easy one-hour walk along the grassy slopes before you hit a steep, unforgiving rise; from the lake it takes about three hours to reach the crater rim (2639m). A sign points the way back to Danau Segara Anak. Water can be found down the slope near the sign. The trail forks here; go straight to Lawang or continue along the rim to the campsite of Pelawangan II (2700m). It's only about 15 minutes futher to the campsite, located on a bare ridge strewn with rubbish.

Day Four: Pelawangan II to Rinjani Summit (Five to Six Hours Return)

Gunung Rinjani stretches in an arc above the campsite at Pelawangan II and looks deceptively close. Start the climb at 3am in order to reach the summit for sunrise and before the clouds roll in. It takes about 45 minutes to clamber up a steep, slippery and indistinct trail to the ridge that leads to Rinjani. Once on the ridge, that peak you see ahead isn't the finish line. After an hour, the real summit of Rinjani looms. The trail gets steeper and steeper, and with just 350m to go before the summit, your footing deteriorates into loose scree – it's easiest to scramble on all fours. This section can take about an hour, and the views from the top are magnificent.

It's possible to reach Sembalun Lawang the same day. After a two-hour descent to camp, it's a long and hot three-hour walk back to the village. From the campsite, head back along the ridge-crest trail. A couple of hundred metres past the turn-off to Danau Segara Anak there is a signposted right turn leading down a subsidiary ridge to Pada Balong and Sembalun Lawang. At the bottom of the ridge (where you'll find Pada Balong shelter; 1800m) the trail levels out and crosses undulating grassland. After about an hour you will hit the Tengengean shelter (1500m); it's then another 30 minutes to Pemantuan shelter (1300m). Early in the season, long grass obscures the trail until about 30 minutes beyond Pemantuan. The trail crosses many bridges; at the final bridge, just before it climbs uphill to a lone tree, the trail seems to fork; take the right fork and climb the rise. From here, the trail follows the flank of Rinjani before swinging around to Lawang. As always, a guide is essential.

and from Mataram (100,000Rp, 45 minutes), Kuta (60,000Rp, 25 minutes), Senggigi (150,000Rp, one hour), Bangsal (200,000Rp, 90 minutes), where you can access the Gili Islands, and to the Labuhan Lombok ferry port (230,000Rp, two hours) have been standardised. There's also a Senggigi-bound shuttle (25,000Rp), but it doesn't leave the terminal until it's full.

REMBITAN & SADE

The area from Sengkol down to Kuta is known for traditional villages full of towering *lumbung* and *bale tani*, homes made from bamboo, cow and buffalo dung, and mud. Regular bemo cover this route. Sade's **Sasak Village** has been extensively renovated and has some fascinating *bale tani*. Further south, **Rembitan** boasts an authentic cluster of houses and *lumbung*, and the 100-year-old **Masjid Kuno**, an ancient thatched-roof mosque that is a pilgrimage destination for Lombok's Muslims. Both villages are worth a look but you must hire a guide (around 30,000Rp).

KUTA

Imagine a crescent bay – turquoise in the shallows and deep blue further out. It licks a huge, white-sand beach, wide as a football pitch and framed by headlands. It's deserted, save for a few fishermen, seaweed farmers and their children. Now imagine a coastline of nearly a dozen such bays, all backed by a rugged range of coastal hills spotted with lush patches of banana trees and tobacco fields, and you'll have a vague idea of Kuta's majesty.

Southern Lombok's incredible coastline of giant bite-shaped bays is startling, its beauty immediate, undeniable and arresting. Yet this region has historically been the island's poorest, its sun-blasted soil parched and unproductive. These days those hills are also pocked with illegal gold mines, which you'll see and hear grinding away as you head west to the surf beaches. Kuta proper consists of no more than a few hundred houses, a likeable but scruffy around-the-edges place with a ramshackle market area, and a seafront lined with simple seafood shacks and barefoot bars (and some very persistent, if sweet, child hawkers). Its original attractions were the limitless world-class breaks within a short ride of town. And while a vast Dubai-backed scheme has been called off, other resort developers have purchased huge swaths of coastline. For now everyone seems to be sitting on their land, but with the new airport a 30-minute drive away, the town's real estate agents – who are already spearheading increasing villa development – are betting on change real soon.

Dangers & Annoyances

If you decide to rent a bicycle or motorbike, take care who you deal with – arrangements are informal and no rental contracts are exchanged. We have received occasional reports of visitors having motorbikes stolen, and then having to pay substantial sums of money as compensation to the owner (who may or may not have arranged the 'theft' himself). Renting a motorbike from your guesthouse is safest.

As you drive up the coastal road west and east of Kuta, watch your back – especially after dark. There have been reports of knifepoint muggings in the area.

Activities

SURFING

Waves break on the reefs, including lefts and rights, in Teluk Kuta (Kuta Bay), as well as on the reefs east of Tanjung Aan. If you're after a reef break, get local boatmen to tow you out for around 100,000Rp. About 7km east of Kuta, Gerupak also has good surf shops and no fewer than five breaks. West of Kuta, gorgeous Mawi offers consistent world-class surf.

Kimen Surf SURFING
(☎655 064; www.kuta-lombok.net; board rental per day 50,000Rp, lessons per person 360,000Rp) Swell forecasts, tips, guided surf trips, board rental, repairs and lessons.

Gloro SURFING
(☎0818 0576 5690; board per day 50,000Rp, lessons for one/two people 300,000/500,000Rp; ⏱10am-6pm) A solid, rootsy shop. It's on the road to Kuta Indah.

DIVING

Scuba Froggy (☎0819 0795 2965, 0878 6426 5958; www.scubafroggy.com; per dive 375,000Rp; ⏱9am-7pm) is the only dive shop in town. It runs local trips to 12 sites, most above 18m and one site as deep as 26m. From June to November it also runs trips to the spectacular ocean pinnacles in Blongas Bay (two dives 1,000,000Rp), famous for schooling hammerheads and mobula rays. Currents and conditions can be very challenging in Blongas.

NYALE FISHING FESTIVAL

On the 19th day of the 10th month in the Sasak calendar – generally February or March – hundreds of Sasaks gather on the beach at Kuta, Lombok. When night falls, fires are built and teens compete in a Sasak poetry slam, where they spit rhyming couplets called *pantun* back and forth. At dawn the next day, the first of millions of *nyale* (worm-like fish who appear here annually) are caught, then teenage girls and boys take to the sea separately in decorated boats – and chase one another spurring riots of laughter. The *nyale* are eaten raw or grilled, and, like laughter, are considered to be an aphrodisiac. A good catch is a sign of a coming bumper crop of rice.

Sleeping

Prices are often halved outside the July to August high season.

TOP CHOICE **Yuli's Homestay** HOMESTAY $
(☎0819 1710 0983; www.yulishomestay.com; r 350,000Rp; ❄📶🏊) A wonderful new place, the eight rooms are immaculate, extremely spacious and nicely furnished with huge beds and wardrobes. It has big front terraces, but cold-water bathrooms. There's a guests' kitchen and a huge garden and pool to enjoy. Head north from the intersection and make your first left onto a narrow gang. It's the third driveway on the left.

Hey Hey Homestay HOMESTAY $
(☎0818 0522 8822; r 100,000Rp) An outstanding homestay with clean, spacious rooms and sea views from private patios. If you get lucky, score the bamboo room on the top floor where the view is epic. Take the dirt road south from the intersection.

Novotel Lombok RESORT $$$
(☎615 3333; www.novotel.com; r from US$94, villas from US$244, plus 21% tax;) This appealing, Sasak-themed four-star resort spills onto a superb beach 3km east of the junction. Rooms have high sloping roofs and modern interiors. There are two pools, a wonderful spa, good restaurants, a swanky bar and a plethora of activities on offer including catamaran sailing, fishing and scuba diving.

Kuta Baru HOMESTAY $
(☎081 854 8357; Jl Pariswata Kuta; r 125,000Rp;) One of Kuta's two best homestays. There's a cute patio strung with the obligatory hammock, daily coffee service, free wi-fi, sparkling tile and an all-around good vibe. It's 110m east of the intersection.

GR Homestay GUESTHOUSE $
(☎0819 0727 9797; s/d 160,000/180,000Rp;) A solid new Balinese-owned spot with 10 simple tiled rooms with crown mouldings, pastel paint jobs, and rain showerheads in otherwise simple baths. There's a nice pool out front. Just south of the intersection.

Lamancha Homestay HOMESTAY $
(☎0819 3313 0156, 615 5186; s 80,000-100,000Rp, d 100,000-150,000Rp) A super charming homestay offering somewhat frayed bamboo rooms with concrete floors, and charming new fan-cooled rooms draped with colourful tapestries and canopied beds. Rooms are very clean and management is endearing. Set back off the main road to the beach.

Sekar Kuning INN $
(☎654 856; Jl Pariwisata; r 150,000-180,000Rp;) A charming beach-road inn east of town. Tiled rooms have ceiling fans, high ceilings, pastel paint jobs and bamboo furniture on the patio. Top-floor rooms have ocean views and are more expensive.

Surfers Inn INN $
(☎655 582; www.lombok-surfersinn.com; r 180,000-400,000Rp;) A very smart, stylish and orderly place with five classes of modern rooms, each with huge windows and large beds, and some with sofas. Book ahead as it's very popular.

Mimpi Manis B&B $
(☎0818 369 950; www.mimpimanis.com; r 120,000-220,000Rp;) An inviting English-Balinese–owned bed and breakfast with two spotless rooms in a two-storey house, both with en suite shower and TV/DVD player. It's 2km inland from the beach, but the owners offer a free drop-off service and can arrange bike and motorbike rental.

Seger Reef Homestay INN $
(☎655 528; Jl Pariwisata; r 130,000-150,000Rp) Seven bright, spotless, family-owned bungalows across the street from the beach. Newest rooms are kitted out with wardrobes, and bizzarro headboards.

Eating & Drinking

Kuta's dining scene has improved with growth, but at most local joints the Indo nosh, or fresh seafood, are always the wisest orders.

TOP CHOICE **Astari** VEGETARIAN $
(dishes 18,000-30,000Rp; ⊙8am-6pm Tue-Sun;) Perched on a mountaintop 2km west of town on the road to Mawan, this breezy, Moroccan-themed vegetarian lounge-restaurant has spectacular vistas of pristine bays and rocky peninsulas that take turns spilling further out to sea. And its delicious, health-conscious menu lives up to the setting. The blackboard always has a daily dish and drink of the day, but the mainstays are the focaccia sandwiches, salads and superb shakes. You will not eat and run.

Warung Bule SEAFOOD $$
(☎0819 1799 6256; mains 37,000-135,000Rp; ⊙8am-10pm) A recent revelation on the Kuta dining scene, founded by the long-time executive chef at the Novotel who delivers tropical seafood tastes at an affordable price. We like the tempura starter and his Tahitian take on ceviche. The grilled mahi is good, and so is his lobster *tom yam* soup. He has other creative concoctions like a Sasak chicken wrap, and an angel hair pasta with chili crab. You'll find something tasty.

Warung Jawa 1 INDONESIAN $
(Jl ke Mawan; meals 10,000Rp; ⊙11am-10pm) On the Mawan road about 120m east of the intersection, this little bamboo shack has a cheap and mean *nasi campur*. Munch and watch buffalo graze with an ocean backdrop.

Solah Cafe CAFE $
(mains 22,000-46,000Rp, yoga 50,000Rp; ⊙9am-10pm, yoga at 8am;) A lovely new addition to the beach strip, it serves up an array of Western and Indonesian breakfasts in the morning (try the *bubur*, a rice porridge with palm sugar). At lunch and dinner the menu diverges into Niçoise salads, a pumpkin and coconut-milk soup, four flavours of spaghetti

and an array of Indonesian and Sasak flavours, including a dynamite coconut-milk curry that is served vegetarian or with chicken or seafood. It also offers daily yoga at 8am and a lovely swatch of beach outfitted with bamboo lounges facing Kuta Bay.

Dwiki's PIZZERIA **$$**
(☎0859 3503 4489; mains 35,000-65,000Rp; ⊙8am-11pm; 📶🌱) The choice spot for wood-fired thin-crust pizza in tiki bar environs. And they deliver!

The Spot INTERNATIONAL **$$**
(☎702 2100; www.thespotbungalows.com; Jl Pariwisata Kuta 1; mains 30,000-60,000Rp; ⊙7am-10pm; 📶) The collection of nine bamboo bungalows set around a grassy plot is worth checking into but the restaurant is the real find. It does fish and chips, burgers, and a couple of Thai curries. All are served in a tasteful dining room with wi-fi. The bar is popular at happy hour and for football matches of international import.

Shore Beach Bar BAR
(Jl Pariwisata; ⊙10am-late, live band on Sat night) Owned by Kimen, Kuta's original surf entrepreneur, the open dance-hall interior has been recently renovated, the sound system is fantastic, there's breezy patio seating, cushy red booths, an expansive bar, a projection screen and a new beachside annex. If you're in town on a Saturday night, you'll probably wind up here.

Information

Virtually everything in Kuta is on a single road that parallels the beach, and intersects the road from Praya. The market fires up on Sunday and Wednesday.

Lombok International Medical Service (☎655 155; ⊙4-9pm) Doctor and pharmacy.

Perama (☎654 846; Jl Pariwisata) Shuttle buses all over Lombok.

Dehril Cell (internet per hour 10,000Rp; ⊙8am-9pm) Has speedy internet access with a hotspot for laptop and smartphone addicts. It rents bicycles too.

Getting There & Away

Kuta is tricky to reach by public transport – from Mataram you'll have to go via Praya (5000Rp), then to Sengkol (3000Rp) and finally to Kuta (2000Rp), usually changing buses at all these places. Perama (p334) run shuttle buses to/from Mataram (110,000Rp, two hours), Senggigi (120,000Rp, 2½ hours), the Gilis (180,000Rp, 3½ hours), and Senaru 260,000Rp. Several agents around town can book a seat on an airport shuttle (50,000Rp to 65,000Rp) or arrange a private car (80,000Rp to 100,000Rp) to pick you up from your hotel.

Getting Around

Irregular bemo go east of Kuta to Awang and Tanjung Aan (5000Rp), and west to Selong Blanak (10,000Rp), or can be chartered to nearby beaches. Guesthouses rent motorbikes for about 50,000Rp per day. *Ojek* congregate around the main junction as you enter Kuta.

EAST OF KUTA

Decent roads traverse the coast to the east and west, passing a seemingly endless series of beautiful bays punctuated by headlands. **Pantai Segar** is about 2km east around the first headland. The enormous rock of **Batu Kotak**, 2km further on, divides two glorious white-sand beaches. Continuing east, **Tanjung Aan** is an idyllic turquoise, horseshoe bay with five powder-white-sand beaches. It's also the best swimming beach on this end of Kuta. The road continues another 2km to **Gerupak**, the fishing village where local souls earn their keep from fishing, seaweed harvesting and farmed lobster exports. Oh, and guiding and ferrying surfers to the five exceptional surf breaks in its huge bay.

There are a couple of hotels and warung popular with surfers. **Edo Homestay** (☎0818 0371 0521; r 120,000Rp) has clean, simple rooms with colourful drapes and double beds. It has a decent restaurant and a surf shop too (boards per day 50,000Rp), and staying here gets you to the break quicker than those who commute from Kuta. **Spear Villa** (☎0818 0371 0521; www.s-pear.com; r 300,000Rp; ❄) is the nicest spot in town. Wonderfully remote **Bumbangku** (☎620 833, 0852 3717 6168; www.bumbangkulombok.com; r bamboo/superior 400,000/650,000Rp; ❄) is set across the bay on its own private beach. It costs 100,000Rp to hire a boat to/from the breaks in Gerupuk.

Unfortunately even Gerupuk can get crowded, so consider moving further on to **Ekas**, where there are more breaks and soaring cliffs that recall a deserted Uluwatu. You can get a boat to Ekas (per person 150,000Rp, private charter 1,000,000Rp) from the fishing village of Awang, accessed by a side road that branches off from the eastbound coastal road just before Tanjung Aan. Boats only leave when full.

WEST OF KUTA

West of Kuta is another series of beaches that all have sick surf when conditions are right. The road is potholed and very steep in places, detours inland and skirts tobacco, sweet potato and rice fields in between turnoffs to the sand. The first left after Astari leads to **Mawan** (parking costs 3000/5000Rp for a motorbike/car), a serene cove with a majestic old shade tree, a wide stretch of white sand that extends into the deep sea, and views of offshore islands. It's a terrific swimming beach when the undertow isn't too treacherous.

The very next left – although it's quite a bit further down the road – leads through a gate (admission 5000Rp), down a horribly rutted track to **Mawi** (parking 5000Rp), 16km from Kuta. Although the white-sand beach is relatively thin, it's still a stunning scene, with several additional beaches scattered around the bay. Surfers descend for the legendary barrels that roll in liberally. Sadly, thefts have been reported here.

Further west from Mawi, and just when you think you've seen the most beautiful beaches Kuta has to offer, you reach **Selong Blanak**. Park and cross the rickety pedestrian bridge to a wide, sugar-white beach with water streaked a thousand shades of blue, ideal for swimming. **Sempiak Villas** (☎0852 5321 3172; www.sempiakvillas.com; Solong Blanak; d 1,500,000Rp; ❄≋) offers villas built into the hillside above the beach that sleep up to four guests and share an infinity pool. At sea level, the wonderful **Laut Biru Cafe** (Solong Blanak; mains 24,000-54,000Rp, plus 20% tax and service) is open to all comers.

From **Pengantap** the road climbs across a headland then descends to another superb bay; follow this around for about 1km, then look out for the turn-off west to **Blongas**, which is a very steep, rough and winding road with breathtaking scenery that leads to the village's secluded namesake bay. The **Lodge at Blongas Bay** (☎645 974; www.thelodge-lombok.com; bungalows 850,000-950,000Rp) offers spacious wooden bungalows with tiled roofs in a coconut grove. **Dive Zone** (☎0813 3954 4998; www.divezone-lombok.com; 2/3 dives 950,000/1,250,000Rp), once based in Kuta, moved here to better access the famed dive site, **Magnet**, a pinnacle that is at its best in mid-September when you may see schooling mobula rays in addition to the hammerheads, which school from June to November. It's not an easy dive, so you must be experienced and prepared for heavy current.

East Lombok

☎0376

All that most travellers see of the east coast is Labuhan Lombok, the port for ferries to Sumbawa. But the real highlight is the remote southeastern peninsula. If you've ever wondered what Bali's Bukit looked like before all the villages, villas and surf rats, here's your chance.

LABUHAN LOMBOK

Labuhan Lombok (or Labuhan Kayangan) is the Sumbawa-bound ferry port. The town centre, 3km west of the ferry terminal, is a scruffy place with great views of Gunung

A BLOODY MESS

Every day between one and three fishing boats, crewed by five men each, sail in and out of Tanjung Luar, a long-running fish market in southeast Lombok. On new moon nights, crews pull 40 sharks per day, and if more than one boat comes into port around then, as many as 100 sharks and mantas will get finned and gilled. Once in market, the meat is sold locally, but the shark fins and manta gills are auctioned to just four buyers who ship their bounty to Hong Kong via their exporter in Surabaya.

Each buyer represents the same Surabaya exporter and does about 1 billion rupiah in annual business or US$100,000. Multiply that by four and you have US$400,000 worth of shark fins moving through this backwater port each year. After speaking at length with two of the buyers in Tanjung Luar, we learned that this same exporter has similar shark finning operations in Ambon, Sorong (gateway to the Raja Ampats) and in Bau Bau. The buyers confessed that few sharks remain in the sea around Lombok. In the 1990s, fishermen didn't have to go far to hunt their take. These days they travel all the way to the Sumba strait between Australia and Indonesia, an important shark migration channel. Obviously, if things continue this way the future does not bode well for Indonesia's sharks – or for these fishermen.

Rinjani. Very regular buses and bemo buzz between Mandalika terminal in Mataram and Labuhan Lombok (also known as Labuhan Kayangan or Tanjung Kayangan); the journey takes two hours (20,000Rp). Some buses will only drop you off at the port entrance road – catch another bemo to the ferry terminal. Don't walk – it's too far.

Ferries run every 45 minutes, 24 hours a day, between Labuhan Lombok and Poto Tano (22,000Rp, 1½ hours). You can also bring your hired car (352,000Rp) or motorcycle (85,000Rp). If you wish to access the epic West Sumbawa surf breaks and you're not travelling by car or motorbike, book the passenger-only fast ferry (100,000Rp, 90 minutes) to Benete Harbour in Maluk. Boats depart Lombok at 10am and 4.30pm daily, and at 1pm on Sunday. Returning at 7.30am and 2pm daily, with an additional 11.30am boat on Sunday

SOUTH OF LABUHAN LOMBOK

Selong, the capital of the East Lombok administrative district, has some dusty Dutch colonial buildings. The transport junction for the region is just to the west of Selong at **Pancor**, where you can catch bemo to most points south. Tanjung Luar is one of Lombok's main fishing ports. From here, the road swings west to **Keruak**, where wooden boats are built. Just west of Keruak, a hard-to-follow road leads south to Jerowaru and the spectacular southeastern peninsula.

A sealed road (though there is no signage and it's easy to get lost) branches west beyond Jerowaru to **Ekas**, where you'll find a huge bay framed by stunning sheer cliffs on both sides. There are two sensational surf breaks (Inside and Outside) best accessed from the aptly named, Kiwi-owned **Heaven on the Planet** (☎812 3797 4846, 081 2375 1103; www.heavenontheplanet.co.nz; per person all-inclusive AU$150). Chalets, huts and villas (some with three bedrooms and marble flooring) are scattered along the cliff's edge, from where you'll have mind-blowing bird's-eye views of the sea and swell lines. Heaven is primarily a surf resort (you can even surf at night here thanks to ocean spotlights), but kite surfing, scuba diving (fun dives and courses) and snorkelling are also possible.

A second resort, **Ocean Heaven** (☎0812 3797 4846; www.oceanheaven.co.nz; r all-inclusive per person AU$170), with chalets right on Ekas beach, is under the same ownership. Both resorts have tasty food, a full bar and friendly staff, and guests receive free airport or ferry transfers and massages (every second day). Rates also include free shuttle to and from the Outside break. The road to Heaven is rough and rocky(!); if you're already in Kuta it's easiest to head to Awang and charter a boat from there rather than looping overland.

SUMBAWA

Beautifully contorted and sprawling into the sea, Sumbawa is all volcanic ridges, terraced rice fields, jungled peninsulas and sheltered bays. The southwest coast is essentially a layered series of headlands and wide, silky white beaches with incredible surf. The southeast is no slouch. It's also a bit more accessible, which explains why Lakey Peak has become Sumbawa's premier year-round surf magnet. Massive, climbable Gunung Tambora (2850m), a mountain that exploded so large it forever influenced the climate and topography of the island, looms in the north.

Though well connected to Bali and Lombok, Sumbawa is a very different sort of place. It's far less developed, much poorer, extremely conservative, and split between two distinct peoples. Those who speak Sumbawanese probably reached the west of the island from Lombok. Bimanese speakers dominate the Tambora Peninsula and the east. Although Sumbawa is an overwhelmingly Islamic island, in remote parts underground *adat* (traditional laws and regulations) still thrive. During festivals you may come across traditional Sumbawan fighting, a sort of bare-fisted boxing called *berempah*. Dynamic horse and water-buffalo races, best glimpsed in Bima each August, are held before the rice is planted.

Transport connections off the cross-island road are infrequent and uncomfortable, and most overland travellers don't even get off the bus in Sumbawa as they float and roll from Lombok to Flores. For now, it's the domain of surfers, miners and mullahs.

Dangers & Annoyances

Most Sumbawans are friendly and hospitable, but you may encounter some tension or even civil unrest. Weeks before our arrival in 2012, there were rumblings of a new gold mine in the mountains above Hu'u. Protests swelled into riots in Sape, where three people allegedly died and 20 were injured at the hands of police, and in Bima where the *bupati's* (governor) office was torched by

Sumbawa

protesters. The mine was still under speculation when we visited, with choppers regularly transporting large boulders, excavated from the mining site, to inspect for value, and farmers watching and fretting about the long term impact on their fields and water supply.

Getting Around

Sumbawa's main highway is in great condition and runs from Taliwang (near the west coast) through Sumbawa Besar, Dompu and Bima to Sape (on the east coast). Fleets of long-distance buses, most of them air-conditioned, link all the towns on this road as far as Bima.

Car hire is possible through hotels in Sumbawa Besar or Bima, but prices are higher than in Bali or Lombok at about 600,000Rp to 800,000Rp per day, including a driver. Plan on paying for your driver's meals and lodging as well. Motorbikes are a far cheaper option at 50,000Rp to 75,000Rp a day.

West Sumbawa

0372

West Sumbawa is drop-dead gorgeous. Beaches are wide, sugar-white, framed with domed headlands and backed by rolling jungled hills. Bays are enormous and dynamic. They can be tranquil one hour and fold into overhead barrels the next. Sumbawa Besar is a humble Muslim town with a friendly population and a damn fine morning market. Pulau Moyo, a lush jewel off the northern shore, has special diving and snorkelling, but it's difficult to access unless, of course, you're rolling with your black Amex.

POTO TANO

Poto Tano, the main port for ferries to/from Lombok, is a ramshackle harbour, fringed by stilt-fishing villages with tremendous views of Gunung Rinjani. Pretty place, but there's no need to sleep here.

Ferries run every 45 minutes, 24 hours a day, between Labuhan Lombok and Poto Tano (22,000Rp, 1½ hours). You can also bring your hired car (352,000Rp) or motorcycle (85,000Rp). Through buses from Mataram to Sumbawa Besar or Bima include the ferry fare.

Buses meet the ferry and go to Taliwang (15,000Rp, one hour) and Sumbawa Besar (25,000Rp, two hours), though some demand the entire Mataram–Sumbawa Besar fare (70,000Rp).

TALIWANG & AROUND

It may be the regional capital and transport hub, but **Taliwang** is just a small, conservative village, 30km south of Poto Tano. There's a BRI Bank with ATM on the main road, a few internet cafes, plenty of Padang-food warungs, and no reason to hang around.

Buses go from Taliwang to Poto Tano (15,000Rp) almost hourly, where you can hop on a bus to Mataram or Sumbawa Besar. Hourly bemo head to Maluk (20,000Rp, two hours).

From Taliwang, bemos and trucks also run 11km south to **Jereweh**, your gateway to the remarkable beach and enormous horseshoe bay at **Jelenga**, a humble country village with rice fields, goat farms and a world class 'left' break known as Scar Reef.

Scar Reef Villa (0813 3774 2679; www.scarreefvilla.com; r with/without view 700,000/

600,000Rp) is a shiny, modern crash pad for surfers. Its four rooms, which sleep up to four, have soaring ceilings, wood furnishings, air-con, and a common beachside porch and lounge area with satellite TV and PlayStation. Two of them have ocean views. **Jelenga Mulia** (☎0813 5369 1920; bungalows 150,000-200,000Rp) is another solid option. The cute, simple beach huts are clean and have private outdoor baths. Jelenga is 6km southwest of Jereweh, and you'll need private transport to get here.

MALUK, RANTUNG & SEKONGKANG

As you continue south, the beaches and bays try to outdo one another. Your first stop is the working-class commercial district of **Maluk**, 30km south of Taliwang. Yes, the town is ugly, but the beach is superb. The sand is a blend of white and gold, and the bay is buffered by two headlands. There's good swimming in the shallows, and when the swell hits, the reef further outside sculpts perfect barrels.

One of the world's largest copper mines, about 30km inland of Maluk, has driven a wave of development and attracted international and domestic staff from the US, Australia and Java to the area. The Newmont Mining Corporation employs about 8000 workers, and had a huge impact on Maluk when it first opened, but most of the expat restaurant and bar traffic has now shifted to **Townside**, a private company enclave complete with health club, golf courses and the best hospital in Sumbawa. You need a personal invitation to breach the gates, but you can arrange one with a week's notice. Some spill-over still trickles into Maluk, along with a pinch of the nearly US$1.6 billion in annual mining proceeds. There's a BNI bank with ATM on Jl Raya Maluk, adjacent to the Trophy Hotel. Just north, **Warnet BW** (Jl Raya Maluk 7; per hour 5000Rp; ⊙9am-1am; @) offers broadband access. The fun beachside marketplace is packed with warungs selling everything from *soto ayam* (chicken soup) to cappuccinos, juices and *ikan bakar* (grilled fish).

Directly south of Maluk, within walking distance of the beach (though it is a long walk) is **Supersuck**, consistently rated as the best 'left' in the world. Surfers descend regularly from Hawaii's North Shore to surf here, which should tell you something, and many lifelong surfers have proclaimed it the finest barrel of their lives. It really pumps in the dry season (May to October).

About 15km further south, the spread-out settlement of **Sekongkang** includes three superb beaches with another handful of surf breaks. It also has the best range of accommodation and a gorgeous all-natural vibe. **Pantai Rantung**, 2km downhill from Sekongkang Atas, spills onto a secluded and majestic bay framed by 100m-high headlands. The water is crystal-clear and waves roll in year-round at **Yo Yo's**, a right break at the north end of the bay. **Hook**, which breaks at the edge of the northern bluff, is also a terrific right. **Supershit**, breaks straight in front of the Rantung Beach Hotel, and is a consistent year-round beginner's break, but gets heavy and delivers a long left when the swell comes in. The next bay down is where you'll find **Tropical**, another phenomenal beach (named for the resort) and home to great left and right breaks that beginners would enjoy.

As you head north again toward Maluk, hang a right at the new government building in Sekongkang, down a degrading dirt road, through a stream, and under a bridge until it dead ends. Park, cross the river to your left, then follow the trail up for 20 minutes and you'll discover a hidden **waterfall** home to dozens of dragonflies. Better get wet!

North of Rantung is **Pantai Lawar**, a tree-shaded stretch of white sand on a turquoise lagoon sheltered by volcanic bluffs draped in jungle. When the surf is flat, come here to swim, snorkel or spearfish.

Sleeping & Eating

The following hotels are listed in geographical order from north to south.

Maluk Resort HOTEL $$
(☎635 424; Jl Pasir Putih, Maluk; standard/deluxe 200,000/275,000Rp; ❄≋) One block west of the main road and steps from the sand is this decent collection of garden rooms surrounding a small pool. Most have a private terrace, upstairs deluxe rooms are slightly larger, have bathtubs and a better view.

TOP CHOICE **Santai** GUESTHOUSE $
(☎0878 6393 5758; Senkongkang; r with shared/private bath 80,000/150,000Rp; @) The choice budget spot in the area offers a collection of spacious, well-tended tiled rooms. Those with private bath have sensational sea views from the front porch and all have amazing views from the thatched restaurant where there's a pool table, ping pong and internet (not wi-fi). Beware the electric fence (a live-

stock thing). Book ahead. When that swell hits they're full for weeks.

Rantung Restaurant & Cottages BUNGALOW $$
(☎0878 6469 7663; Rantung; cottages 650,000Rp, dishes 30,000-70,000Rp; ❄) The expat and Indonesian mining crowd has enjoyed more than a few sundowners at this fantastic beach location. The food always delivers (we love the cassava chips and goat *rending*), and the spacious, stylish cottages are the best beachfront option in the region with high ceilings, queen beds, wooden wardrobes, and hot water. They open onto leafy private decks with sea views.

Yo Yo's RESORT $$
(☎0819 3592 1777, 0819 3591 7888; Yoyoshotel@yahoo.co.id; Rantung; dorm/standard/deluxe 150,000/400,000/600,000Rp; ❄@📶) A gregarious Rantung surf nest owned by three Aussies who work at Newmont. Deluxe rooms are quite large and well appointed with wood furnishings, though ceilings are low. Standard rooms are smaller, and a bit worn, but still good value. The 'surf camp' is a clean, hostel-like bunk house with bright, air-conditioned rooms (two beds each), and a frequently soggy shared bath. All rooms share a common tile porch with bamboo or wood furniture, and then there's the bar. A fabulous indoor-outdoor affair, it attracts a motley expat stew – SAS types who served in Rhodesia, or grizzled Hawaii-born surfers who may flaunt a once-severed pinky. It's the kind of joint Hunter Thompson might enjoy. We certainly did.

Depot Balikpapan SEAFOOD $
(Pantai Wisata, Maluk; meals 20,000-50,000Rp) Its fish-grill aroma stands out among the other stalls in Maluk's thatched beach dining complex. Fish plates come with a snarling, spicy *sambal* (chilli sauce).

Lesehan Bu Diah INDONESIAN $$
(Jl Raya, Maluk; meals 10,000-80,000Rp; ⏰11am-10pm) Sit cross-legged on the floor of wooden pagodas and dine on fresh seafood and Chinese Indo faves overlooking an artificial pond in a leafy garden. Located on Maluk's far south end, it gets a nice local dinner crowd.

ℹ Getting There & Around

Bemos travel between Taliwang and Maluk (20,000Rp, two hours) almost hourly from 7am to 6pm. Three daily buses leave Terminal Maluk, north of town across from the entrance to the Newmont mine (look for the big gates and massive parking area), for Sumbawa Besar (30,000Rp, four hours).

From Benete Harbour, Newmont's port, a fast ferry (100,000Rp, 90 minutes) to Kayangan Lombok (adjacent to Labuhan Lombok) leaves at 7:30am and 2pm daily, with an additional 11:30am boat on Sunday, but this is not a vehicle ferry. The same boat departs Lombok at 10am and 4:30pm daily, and at 1pm on Sunday.

Chartered Kijangs to or from Sumbawa Besar (800,000Rp) are possible, if pricey. Contact Yun at Rantung Restaurant & Cottages to make arrangements.

If you're based in Senkongkang, you'll need a motorbike, and any of the hotels can arrange one for you for 50,000Rp per day.

Sumbawa Besar

☎0371 / POP 55,000

Sumbawa Besar, often shortened to 'Sumbawa', is the principal market town of the island's west. It's leafy, devoutly Muslim (that legion of nearby karaoke bars notwithstanding), and runs on the bushels of beans, rice and corn cultivated on the outskirts. It's also quite friendly and easy to navigate, but there's not much to see here aside from the old palace, and a lively morning market. Trips to Pulau Moyo and to nearby villages are worthwhile but take time and money, which is why most travellers simply consider this town a respite on the trans-Sumbawa highway.

Traffic runs in a high-speed Jl Hasanuddin–Jl Diponegoro loop. The best sleeping and eating options are clustered along Jl Hasanuddin.

👁 Sights

Dalam Loka PALACE
(Sultan's Palace; Jl Dalam Loka 1; admission by donation; ⏰8am-noon & 1-5pm Mon-Fri, 8-11am & 1.30-5pm Sat & Sun) Originally built over 200 years ago for Sultan Mohammad Jalaluddin III, the remains of the Dalam Loka, a once-imposing structure that covers an entire city block, had deteriorated until near dereliction by the 1980s, which is why Japanese archaeologists, with blessings from the Indonesian government, dismantled it to the frame and restored its antique reverence. Inside are old photos of the royal family, antique parasols and carriages.

Pasar Syketeng MARKET
Rise early and hit the steamy, exotic Pasar Syketeng. Beginning at 7am, its dank alleyways come alive as young and old descend to barter and haggle for every conceivable item from grandma panties to live chickens. The fish market is interesting and the spicy aroma of chilli and turmeric competes with recently slaughtered beef for your olfactory attention. Locals are always happy to laugh and chat if you produce even a modicum of Bahasa.

Sleeping

Hotels congregate on Jl Hasanuddin. The nearby mosque provides free wake-up calls.

TOP CHOICE **Garuda Hotel** HOTEL $
(☎21780; Jl Garuda 78; standard/superior/VIP 165,000/250,000/330,000Rp; ❄) Conveniently located across the street and to the left as you emerge from the airport, rooms are spacious with high ceilings, cheery bathroom tiles, a garish two-tone paint job, and a nice private terrace out front. VIP rooms are larger, quieter and have hot water.

Hotel Suci HOTEL $
(☎21589; Jl Hasanuddin 57; r with fan/air-con 100,000/200,000Rp; ❄) Right next to the mosque, there's a range of rooms here, but the best are on the top floor of the new building with high ceilings, air-con and new tiles. The economy rooms aren't great.

Hotel Pantai Kencana BUNGALOW $$
(☎0813 3981 4555; Jl Raya Tano Km 11; bungalows 300,000Rp; ❄) A bit out of town, with an underwhelming entry. Still, the wooden bungalows outfitted with air-con, TV and minibar are in decent shape and set on a peaceful beach with a village feel.

Eating

Warung Kita 2 INDONESIAN $
(☎23065; Jl Setiabudi 13) A bright, delicious pick 'n' mix diner with trays of broiled chicken, tasty fried shrimp, and curried green beans.

Aneka Rasa Jaya CHINESE $$
(☎21291, 23670; Jl Hasanuddin 16; dishes 21,000-65,000Rp; ⏰10am-3pm & 6-10pm) Clean and popular, this Chinese seafood house plates tender fish fillets, shrimp, squid, crab and scallops in oyster, Szechuan, and sweet-and-sour sauce. The *soto kepiting* (crab soup) is particularly popular.

Information

There are ATMs at **Bank Mega** (Jl Diponegoro 55; ⏰8am-2.30pm Mon-Fri, 8am-noon Sat) and **BNI** (Jl Kartini 10; ⏰8am-2.30pm Mon-Fri, 8am-noon Sat), which also offers limited currency exchange.

Bala.net (Jl Sudirman; per hour 3000Rp; ⏰24hr) A dusty shop with two terminals, it's the only reliable place to digi-surf.

Kantor Imigrasi (Immigration Office; Jl Garuda 131) Extend your tourist visa relatively painlessly.

Klinik Lawang Gali (☎270 5993; Jl Sudirman 18-20) New-ish hospital with ambulance services.

Main post office (Jl Garuda)

Perlindungan Hutan dan Konservasi Alam (PHKA; ☎23941; ⏰8am-3pm Mon-Fri) The local office of the national-park service has information about Pulau Moyo. It's about 4km southwest of town in the village of Nijang; take a bemo from the roundabout on Jl Garuda.

Telkom (Jl Yos Sudarso; ⏰24hr) Still the cheapest place to make international calls.

Tourist Office (☎23714; Jl Bungur 1; ⏰7am-2pm Mon-Thu, to 11am Fri, to 1pm Sat) Just off Jl Garuda, 100m south of the main post office on the edge of town. Expect nothing more than a few brochures.

Getting There & Away

AIR At research time **Transnusa** (☎7162 6161; Jl Garuda 41) was Sumbawa Besar's only active

BUSES FROM SUMBAWA BESAR

DESTINATION	TYPE	COST (RP)	DURATION (HR)	FREQUENCY
Bima	bus	60,000-90,000	7-8	7 daily, departing 2-3pm
Poto Tano	bus	25,000	3	hourly, 8am-midnight
Mataram	bus	70,000 (incl ferry ticket)	6	8am, 10am & 9pm daily
Mataram	minibus	100,000 (incl ferry ticket)	5½	5 daily

carrier, with daily flights to Lombok (274,000Rp, 40 minutes, departing 2.05pm). On Sundays that same flight connects on to Denpasar. The office is at the airport. Departure tax is 11,000Rp.

BUS Sumbawa Besar's main long-distance bus station is **Terminal Sumur Payung**, 5.5km northwest of town on the highway. You can also book tickets at **Tiara Mas** (☎21241; Jl Yos Sudarso). **Panca Sari Tours & Travel** (☎21513; Jl Diponegoro 49; ⊙departing at 5:30am, 10:30am, 1:30pm, 5pm, 9pm) books the slightly faster 11-seat minibuses to Mataram.

Getting Around

There are no taxis awaiting your arrival, but it's easy to walk into town from the airport, just turn to your right as you exit the terminal. The walk is less than 1km. Alternatively, take a yellow bemo (2000Rp) or an *ojek* (3000Rp). Bemo and *benhur* cost 2000Rp for trips anywhere around town. The local **Seketeng bemo terminal** (Jl Setiabudi) is in front of the *pasar* (market). A Kijang, or similar-style SUV is 600,000Rp per day with a driver.

Around Sumbawa Besar

You'll need private transport to navigate the outskirts effectively. Some of the best ikat and *songket* sarongs are made by members of a women's weaving *klompok* (collective) in the conservative mountain village of **Poto**, 12km east of Sumbawa Besar and 2km from the small town of Moyo. Traditional designs include the *prahu* (outrigger boat). You'll hear the clack of their looms from the street and are welcome to duck into their humble huts. The most intricate pieces take up to 45 days to produce.

If you're doing the trans-Sumbawa disco with your own wheels, stop for lunch at **Warung Santong** (Pantai Santong; meals 30,000-50,000Rp; ⊙24hr), a tasty fish shack teetering on the rocky shore at the island's midway point. Dine on fresh catch, grilled or fried, in the 'dining room', or on one of three stilted pagodas at the water's edge.

PULAU MOYO

A gently arcing crescent of jungled volcanic rock, Moyo – all 36,000 hectares of it – floats atop the gorgeous azure seas north of Sumbawa Besar. The same size as Singapore, it has almost no commercial development and is peopled by just five small villages. The majority of the island, and its rich reefs, form a nature reserve laced with hiking and biking trails, dripping with waterfalls and offering some of the best diving west of Komodo. Loggerhead and green turtles hatch on the beaches, long-tail macaques patrol the canopy, and wild pigs, barking deer and a diverse bird population all call Moyo home.

Unfortunately, accommodation is limited to just one expensive (like 'if you have to ask, you can't afford it' expensive) resort, but it is possible to visit Moyo on a day trip.

Head to **Pantai Goa** (don't let the name fool you) 8km west of the city centre (10,000Rp by *ojek*) and charter a speedboat (1,500,000Rp, two hours, up to four passengers). Or hop on a public bemo (9000Rp, one hour) to Air Bari, 20km northeast of Sumbawa Besar, and charter a boat (1,000,000Rp, one hour) from there. There are four bemo a day to Air Bari. They leave from the turn-off at the far end of Jl Sudirman.

The boats will take you to snorkelling spots **Air Manis**, and **Tanjung Pasir** (the better of the two). Good reefs with a plunging wall can be found all around the island if you are prepared to charter your boat for a bit longer. Just northeast of Pulau Moyo is small **Pulau Satonda**, which also has good beaches and tremendous snorkelling. It's three hours by boat from Air Bari.

There are only two ways to dive at Pulau Moyo. You can join a Bali- or Lombok-based, Komodo-bound liveaboard or check in to the luscious Amanwana, the swankiest dive camp on the planet. There are worse fates.

The seas around Moyo get turbulent from December to March. If boat operators are hesitant to launch, they have good reason.

Sleeping

Amanwana Resort RESORT **$$$**
(☎22233; www.amanresorts.com; all-inclusive jungle tents US$850, ocean tents US$950, plus 21% tax; ❄@📶) On Moyo's western side, Amanwana is the ultimate island hideaway. This is where the rich and famous go 'camping', albeit in lavish permanent tents with antique wood furnishings, king-sized beds, two sofas and, of course, air-con. But nature still rules here. The resort is built around diving, hiking and mountain biking, they sponsor turtle hatcheries, deer breeding and reef-protection projects. There's a full-service spa and a dive school where courses and dive trips are private. They even have their own liveaboard which they charter for private seven-day cruises into Komodo National Park and further on to the Bandas in Maluku and Papua's Raja Ampat archipelago. Guests arrive by private seaplane from Bali (US$400 return) or are shuttled

over from mainland Sumbawa on an Aman cruiser.

East Sumbawa

0373

Twisted into a shape all its own, and linguistically and culturally distinct from the west, the eastern half of Sumbawa sees the most visitors thanks to accessible year-round surf near Hu'u village. Adventurous souls may also want to tackle majestic Gunung Tambora, a mountain that changed the world.

GUNUNG TAMBORA

Looming over central Sumbawa is the 2850m volcano, Gunung Tambora. Its peak was obliterated during the epic eruption in April 1815, which buried residents alive, killed tens of thousands, affected weather everywhere (the following year was known as 'the year without a summer' as the sun was muted worldwide) and forever altered the region's geography. Tambora, not deforestation, is the reason that the oldest trees on Moyo are under 200 years old. In 2004, University of Rhode Island and Indonesian vulcanologists unearthed bronze bowls and ceramic pots from a Pompeii-like village, which indicate that the region once had strong trading links with Vietnam and Cambodia.

But you're here to bag the peak. From the summit you'll have spectacular views of the 6km-wide caldera, which contains a two-coloured lake, and endless ocean vistas that stretch as far as Gunung Rinjani (Lombok). The base for ascents is the village of **Pancasila** near the town of **Calabai** on the western slope, which is five hours by a very crowded bus from Dompu (35,000Rp), two hours by wooden boat (250,000Rp plus petrol), or two hours by speedboat from Air Bairi, 20km northeast of Sumbawa Besar (1,000,000Rp). From Calabai take a *benhur* (15,000Rp) or *ojek* (25,000Rp) to Pancasila, where guides and porters (100,000Rp each per day) can be arranged. Due to trail conditions, it can only be climbed in the dry season (June to October). The hike takes about two days.

HU'U & PANTAI LAKEY

Sights & Activities

Pantai Lakey, a gentle crescent of golden sand 3km south of Hu'u, is where Sumbawa's tourist pulse beats, thanks to seven world-class surf breaks that curl and crash in one massive bay. **Lakey Peak** and **Lakey Pipe** are the best-known waves and are within paddle distance of the various hotels and bungalow properties. You'll need to rent a motorbike or hire an *ojek* to get to **Nungas**, **Cobblestone**, and **Nangadoro**. **Periscope** is 150m from the sand at the far north end of the bay near **Maci Point**, another good spot. Most surfers share the cost of a boat (700,000Rp, maximum five people) to get there and back. Waves can be very good (and very big) year-round, but the most consistent swell arrives between June and August. From August to October the wind gusts, which turns Pantai Lakey into Indonesia's best kite-surfing destination – regarded as one of the 10 best in the world. Kites are banned from Lakey Peak, but they descend on Lakey Pipe and Nungas when it's pumping.

Inexperienced surfers should take good care. Waves break over a shallow reef, and serious accidents do happen. Jimmy Anwar runs the local lifeguard station, which he founded.

Hu'u is a small, poor, but very friendly fishing village, 3km north of Lakey. It's suffused with the scent of drying fish and blessed with breathtaking pink sunsets. When the swell gets really big, there's a beach break here, as well.

Sleeping & Eating

There are plenty of decent-value digs strung along Pantai Lakey. Most have their own restaurants. Prices fluctuate depending on the season. Options are listed in the order you reach them from Dompu:

TOP CHOICE **Hotel Aman Gati** RESORT $$

(0821 4473 4511, 623 031; www.lakeypeakamangati.com; Jl Raya Hu'u; s/d 315,000/415,000Rp, deluxe r US$55;) The most professional operation on the beach, this Balinese-run, three-star spot, has new, attractive and modern rooms perfectly oriented to the break. However, rooms in the old building have higher ceilings and bigger beds, and you should check out the cottages too. All come with wood furnishings, (almost) hot water, DVD players, international cable TV and air-con.

Blue Lagoon BUNGALOW $

(0813 3982 3018; r 170,000-250,000Rp;) A vast complex of well looked after tiled rooms with private patios that stretches from the beach to the cell tower. All are spacious, have high ceilings and crown mouldings, but some are in better shape than others. Garishly tiled newer rooms are near the back. Most expensive rooms have air-con, hot water and satellite TV. The restaurant and bar draws a crowd.

Alamanda Bungalows BUNGALOW **$**
(☎623 519; Jl Raya Hu'u; s/d 80,000/100,000Rp) The cheapest joint on the block is also one of the most charming. Crash on a bamboo bed in a stand-alone hexagonal *casita* that is quite spacious and brushed with two-tone paint jobs. All have tiled roofs and are sprinkled through a palm garden.

Puma Bungalows BUNGALOW **$**
(r with fan 70,000-110,000Rp, with air-con 110,000-160,000Rp; ❄) Expect colourful concrete bungalows with tiled roofs, shady front porches and leafy grounds with fabulous views. This is our favorite cheapie on the beach.

Nungas Surf House HOUSE **$$**
(www.lakeypeaksurf.com; small house 290,000Rp, big house 450,000-790,000Rp) Bertrand Fleury, a world-class kite surfer and Lakey pioneer hosts a revolving door of kite pros from July to November for the wind season. But when he's gone he rents his two excellent wood houses that sleep up to five, with full kitchen, private decks, outdoor baths, and set right on the Nungas break. You can rent by the night or the month. Price depends upon the number of people in your group.

Nasi Nina INDOENSIAN **$**
(nasi campur 15,000Rp; ⌚9am-9pm) Starving for super cheap eats? Lakey lovers swear by the *nasi campur* (rice with a choice of side dishes) from this cart at the main intersection off the beach. Grab yours and head to the top floor of the concrete lookout tower for a cheap and tasty picnic with a view.

Lakey Beach Inn INTERNATIONAL **$$**
(mains 27,000-50,000Rp; 🛜) The beach's best kitchen serves up tasty homestyle fish dinners, pizza, and Indo specials like *mie goreng* (fried noodles) or gado gado (dish with vegetables and peanut sauce). Grind as you screen daily surf exploits shot by shoreside cinematographers. The wi-fi doesn't always work.

Information

Most hotels will change US and Australian dollars at poor rates; bring ample rupiah. There's a wartel at Balumba and an expensive but decent internet cafe at **Aman Gati** (per hour 35,000Rp; ⌚8am-noon, 1-5.30pm & 6.30am-10pm) that broadcasts a public wi-fi signal which you can tap into on a pay-as-you-go basis.

Getting There & Away

From Dompu there are two daily (slow) buses as far as Hu'u (20,000Rp, 1½ hours), where you can hire an *ojek* (10,000Rp) to Pantai Lakey.

Try doing this with a surfboard and you'll see why so many people take a taxi from Bima airport (around 600,000Rp, four people). Leaving Hu'u, there's one early morning bus, but any of the hotels can arrange a taxi to Bima. *Ojeks* to Dompu cost 150,000Rp.

The *ojek* cartel is omnipresent in Lakey, but to minimise the haggle, they've issued a new fixed price list for round-trip *ojek* transport to the surf breaks: Periscope (50,000Rp), Nungas (25,000Rp), Cobblestone (50,000Rp), Nunga D'oro (60,000Rp) and Kite Surf (70,000Rp).

BIMA

☎0374 / POP 120,000

East Sumbawa's largest metropolitan centre is a conservative Islamic place with one mediocre sight – the former sultan's palace, and it's nobody's favourite getaway. The streets can be traffic choked, the architecture charmless and crumbling, and doing business here can feel like the hard sell Olympics. Still, if you keep your cool and get a room in one of Bima's inviting new sleeps, you may find charm in the chaotic intensity of it all. Or, like most, you may flee to the waves at Lakey Peak or Labuanbajo and the Komodo National Park immediately.

Sights

Museum Asi Mbojo MUSEUM
(Jl Sultan Ibrahim; tourist admission 5000Rp; ⌚8am-5pm Mon-Sat) The Sultan's Palace, former home of Bima's rulers, is now a grab-bag of dusty curios, including a royal crown, battle flags and weapons.

Masjid Bima PALACE
The new palace, Masjid Bima, also looks pretty damn royal, with a gushing fountain and five towers.

Activities

Horse racing is held four times a year, in May, July, August and December at the Desa Panda horse stadium, 14km from town on the airport road. There's a large grandstand, a gaggle of warungs and plenty of cheering as horses thunder around a dusty track. Action peaks on 17 August as independence fever kicks in.

TRANSPORT FROM BIMA

Air

DESTINATION	COMPANY	DURATION (HR)	FREQUENCY
Denpasar	Merpati, Transnusa, Travel Lancar Jaya for Lion Air	1¼	daily
Makassar	Merpati	1½	4 weekly

Bus

DESTINATION	COST (RP)	DURATION (HR)	FREQUENCY
Dompu	15,000	2	almost hourly, 6am-5pm
Mataram	120,000-180,000	11-14	9.30am, 7pm
Sape	20,000	2	almost hourly, 6am-5pm
Sumbawa Besar	80,000	7	9.30am, 7pm

Sleeping

TOP CHOICE Marina Hotel HOTEL **$$**
(☎42072; Jl Sultan Kaharuddin 41; r from 328,000Rp; ❄📶) Bima lodging has a new top dog. Rooms here are bright and airy with flat-screen TVs, glassed-in showers, plush bed linens and air-con. All get plenty of light though some have more windows than others. There are beautiful views from the common lounge.

Bima Mantika INN **$$**
(☎646 736; www.bimamantika.com; Jl Noor Latif; r with fan 130,000-220,000Rp, with air-com 320,000-380,000Rp; ❄📶) Owned by a Flemish-Indonesian couple, this new seven room inn offers a range of rooms, the best of which have satellite TV, hot water and air-con. It's set in a quiet neighborhood not far from Bima's city center, and they can help arrange transport anywhere in Sumbawa.

Hotel Lila Graha HOTEL **$**
(☎42740; Jl Lombok 20; r 110,000-330,000Rp; ❄📶) One of two four-storey, block-long hotels, each with a wide range of rooms. Ground floor suite rooms are newest and nicest, but you can get into a room with TV, hot water and air-con for as low as 150,000Rp.

Eating

Dine cheaply at the *pasar malam*, which sets up along the walking streets within the Old Palace compound. There's fish and chicken sate, *mie goreng* and *nasi goreng* (fried rice), *bakso* (meatball soup) and gado gado aplenty.

TOP CHOICE Rumah Makan Sabur Sabur SEAFOOD **$**
(☎646 236; Jl Salahudin, Bandara; meals 20,000Rp; ⏰7am-6pm) The long wooden tables are always crowded with locals who come to munch *bandeng goreng* (a flash-fried freshwater fish). Like herring, you can eat it whole, bones and all. It's best combined with their fiery crushed-tomato *sambal*, torn leaves of lemon basil and a bit of rice.

Rumah Makan Arena Raya PADANG **$**
(☎44960; Jl Hasanudin; meals 20,000-30,000Rp; ⏰7am-10pm) The cleanest and most popular Padang food depot in town. Pick and mix from an array of curried, baked and fried fish and chicken dishes, or get adventurous and select a strange looking 'cut' of beef. Be warned, it gets quite spicy here.

Restaurant Lila Graha INDONESIAN **$**
(Jl Sumbawa; mains 15,000-25,000Rp) Attached to the hotel of the same name, this clean and friendly joint serves up Chinese and Indonesian reliables, with a few Western dishes thrown in.

Information

BNI Bank (Jl Sultan Hasanuddin; ⏰8am-2pm Mon-Fri) Has an ATM and changes foreign currency.

Dinas Pariwisata (☎44331; Jl Soekarno Hatta; ⏰7am-3pm Mon-Fri, 7am-noon Sat) This tourist office in Raba's Kantor Bupati, 2km from Bima, is staffed by friendly English speakers.

Doro Parewa Makmur (☎42926; Jl Sumbawa 16; hours vary) Organises trips to Komodo and Rinca from Sape.

Travel Lancar Jaya (☎43737; Jl Sultan Hasanuddin 11) Bima's Lion Air agent.

Warnet Cabang Malake (Jl Soekarno Hatta; per hour 3000Rp; ⏲8am-midnight)

Getting There & Away

AIR Bima is served by **Merpati** (☎42857; Jl Soekarno Hatta 58), **Transnusa** (☎647 251; Jl Sulawesi 26) and Travel Lancar Jaya.

Departure tax from Bima is 20,000Rp. There's a new passport check, set up to tally international tourist entries into Bima. Bring at least a copy of your passport.

BOAT *Awu* travels twice monthly from Bima to Waingapu, Ende and Kupang, and back to Benoa in Bali. *Tilongkabila* sails to Labuanbajo and Sulawesi, and returns via Lembar and Benoa every two weeks. Travel agencies in town can organise tickets, since the **Pelni office** (☎42625; Jl Kesatria 2) is at Bima port.

BUS Buses heading west leave from the Bima bus terminal, a 10-minute walk south along Jl Sultan Kaharuddin from the centre of town, though you can buy a ticket in advance from bus company offices on Jl Sultan Kaharuddin. Buses for Sape depart the Kumbe terminal in Raba (a 2000Rp bemo ride away). If you leave at 6am sharp, you'll make it to Sape for the 8am ferry to Flores. Or sleep a little later and charter a car (250,000Rp, 1½ hours).

Getting Around

The airport sits amid salt flats 17km from the centre. You can walk out to the main road and catch a passing bus. Alternatively, taxis meet arrivals, charging 80,000Rp to Bima or 600,000Rp to Hu'u and Lakey Peak. A bemo around town costs 2000Rp per person; *benhur* are 5000Rp. As there are no official rental agencies, try hiring a motorbike through your hotel or one of the travel agencies; expect to pay around 75,000Rp per day.

SAPE

☎0374

It's got a tumbledown port-town vibe, perfumed with the conspicuous scent of drying cuttlefish. The outskirts are quilted in rice fields backed by jungled hills, and the streets are busy with *benhur* and bustling with early morning commerce. There's decent food and doable lodging here too, so if you are catching a morning ferry, consider this an alternative to Bima.

There's a **PHKA Komodo Information Office** (⏲8am-2pm Mon-Sat) 500m inland from the port with a few brochures and maps.

Sape's best lodging option is **Losmen Mutiara** (☎71337; Jl Pelabuhan Sape; r economy/standard/deluxe 50,000/120,000/200,000Rp; ❄), right next to the port gates. Rooms are reasonably clean. The smiling ladies of **Rumah Makan Citra Minang** (Jl Pelabuhan Sape; meals 30,000Rp) bring Padang's finest and spiciest dishes to life. The cracked concrete floor and water-stained walls betray the quality and flavour of the food.

Getting There & Around

BOAT Regular breakdowns and big water disrupt ferry services – always double-check the latest schedules in Bima and Sape. Or you can call **Cabang Sape** (☎71075; Jl Yos Sudarso, Pelabuhan Penye Berangan Sape).

BUS Express buses with service to Lombok and Bali meet arriving ferries. Buses leave every hour for Bima (20,000Rp, two hours), where you can catch local buses to Sumbawa destinations. Taxi drivers will no doubt claim buses have stopped running and you must charter their vehicle to Bima – all lies!

KOMODO & RINCA ISLANDS

Nestled between Sumbawa and Flores, the islands of Komodo and Rinca, their jagged hills carpeted with savannah and fringed with mangroves, are home to the legendary Komodo dragon. The world's largest lizard, known locally as *ora*, it can reach over 3m in length and weigh up to 100kg. It hunts alone and feeds on animals as large as deer and buffalo, both of which are found here. The males also try to eat the females' eggs, inevitably sparking a vicious battle of the sexes.

These isolated islands are surrounded by some of the most tempestuous waters in Indonesia. The convergence of warm and cold currents breeds nutritious thermal

FERRIES FROM SAPE

DESTINATION	COST (RP)	DURATION (HR)	FREQUENCY
Labuanbajo	35,000	7	8am daily
Waikelo (Sumba)	50,000	8	10pm Mon & Wed

climes, rip tides and whirlpools that attract large schools of pelagics, from dolphins and sharks to manta rays and blue whales. The coral here is mostly pristine (p354). Add it all up and you have some of the best diving in the world, which is why nearly 50 liveaboards ply these waters between April and September when the crossing is smooth and the diving at its finest.

There are numerous hiking trails, but it's not permitted to explore without an armed guide, a forked staff his only weapon, as dragons have very occasionally attacked (and killed) humans. Two villagers have died in the last 20 years, and in June 2012 a ranger was once again attacked on Rinca in his office. He survived. Dragons are generally a docile bunch, but they can snap your leg as fast as they'll cut a goat's throat. Respect the beasts.

Komodo

Spectacular Komodo, its steep hillsides jade in the short wet season, frazzled by the sun and winds to a deep rusty red for most of the year, is the largest island in the national park. A succession of eastern peninsulas spread out like so many fingers, fringed in pink sand, thanks to the abundance of red coral offshore. The main camp of **Loh Liang** and the PHKA office, where you can organise treks, is on the east coast. There are also rumblings of a new privately owned resort being built on the island, which would be a first.

The fishing village of **Kampung Komodo** is an hour-long walk south of Loh Liang. It's a friendly stilted Bugis village that's full of goats, chickens and children. The inhabitants are said to be descendants of convicts exiled to the island in the 19th century by one of the sultans in Sumbawa.

Activities

Dragon Spotting

You're likely to see dragons if you do the standard stroll to **Banu Nggulung**, a dry river-bed about a half-hour walk from Loh Liang. When you do encounter one, it's wise to keep a safe distance and move slowly and calmly. A telephoto lens is handy but not essential. It is also possible to spot dragons foraging for food and fresh water on some of the other walks, but it's never guaranteed.

Hiking

Most visitors stay one night at Komodo and only do the short hike to Banu Nggulung – bad decision. The longer you hike, the more spectacular the scenery.

Walks from Loh Liang include the climb to the 538m-high **Gunung Ara** (200,000Rp,

Komodo & Rinca Islands

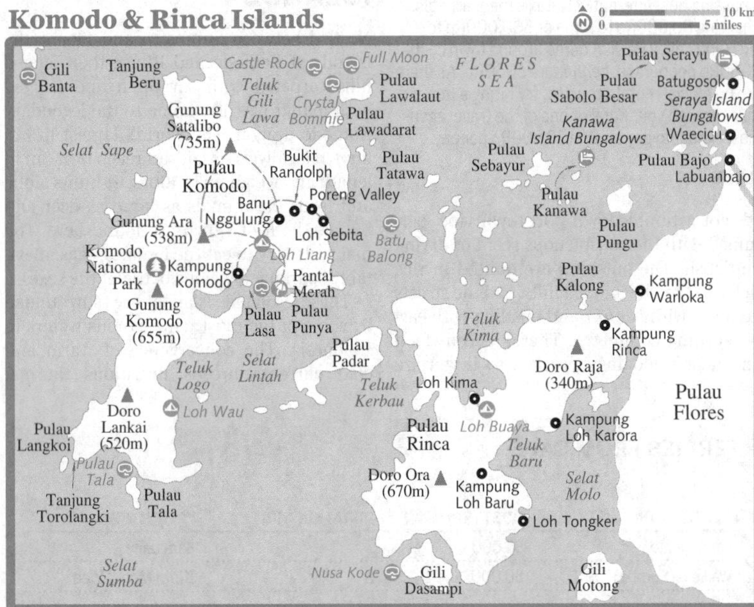

KOMODO DRAGONS

There were rumours of these awesome creatures long before their existence was confirmed in the West. Fishers and pearl divers working in the area had brought back tales of ferocious lizards with enormous claws, fearsome teeth and forked yellow tongues. One theory holds that the Chinese dragon is based on the Komodo lizard. The first Dutch expedition to the island was in 1910; two of the dragons were shot and their skins taken to Java, resulting in the first published description.

The Komodo dragon is actually a monitor lizard. All monitors have some things in common: the head is tapered, the ear openings are visible, the neck is long and slender, the eyes have eyelids and round pupils, and the jaws are powerful. But the dragons also have massive bodies, powerful legs (each with five-clawed toes) and long, thick tails (which function as rudders underwater, but can also be used for grasping or as a potent weapon).

They are dangerous if driven into a corner and will attack even a much larger opponent. Komodo dragons often rise up on their hind legs just before attacking, and the tail can deliver well-aimed blows that will knock down a weaker adversary. Their best weapons are their sharp teeth and dagger-sharp claws, which can inflict severe wounds.

Ora can expand their jaws considerably, enabling them to swallow prey as large as a goat. To tackle even bigger prey, they ambush their victim, bite it and wait for the potent bacteria their mouths contain to take effect – waiting and lurking for up to two weeks for a buffalo to die – before dining. Mature dragons are also cannibalistic, and small *ora* live the first five years of their lives up in trees for safety, not moving to ground level until they are 1m in length.

Of all the monitors, the *ora* lay the largest eggs – around 90mm long and weighing around 200g. The female lays 15 to 30 eggs at a time then protects them for three months from predators – including male dragons. The incubation period is nine months.

Why they exist only on and around Komodo is a mystery, as is why males outnumber females by a ratio of 3.4 to one. Around 1250 *ora* live on Komodo, perhaps 1100 on Rinca and a small number (around 50) on the west coast of Flores. Today the *ora* are a protected species.

9km, five hours return). The chances of seeing a dragon are slim, but there are expansive views from the top. **Poreng Valley** (150,000Rp, 5.5km, four to five hours return) is another potential dragon haunt, and has a more out-in-the-wild feeling than Banu Nggulung. The trail continues over **Bukit Randolph**, a memorial to the 79-year-old Randolph Von Reding who disappeared on Komodo in 1974, to **Loh Sebita** (150,000Rp, 9km, four hours). This is the best hike. It's challenging, the sea views are spectacular, you'll likely see a dragon or two, and you can organise your boat to pick you up in Loh Sebita, so you don't have to retrace your steps. There's also plenty of other wildlife, such as buffalo, deer, wild boar and Komodo's rich bird life, including the fabled megapodes.

Snorkelling & Diving

Almost everybody who visits the park hires a boat in Labuanbajo. Boats always offer snorkelling (gear included) as part of the itinerary. Most folks snorkel around the small island of **Pulau Lasa** near Kampung Komodo, and just off the pink sands of **Pantai Merah** (Red Beach), which is just an hour's walk from Loh Liang.

Of course, diving is the thing here. Given the conditions – up and down currents, and chilly temperatures – and the effort involved in diving these amazing sites, it is not recommended for the inexperienced diver. But if you're seasoned (with 50 or more dives), stay calm and mind your dive guide, you will have a tremendous experience.

Getting There & Away

Ferries travelling between Sape and Labuanbajo haven't been stopping at Komodo for several years now, so the only way here is by some sort of charter. One way to arrive is on a boat tour between Lombok and Flores – these stop at Komodo for a night or two. Labuanbajo is the best jumping-off point for Komodo and Rinca. It *is* possible to charter boats from Sape in Sumbawa to Komodo, but be extremely cautious, as many boats here are barely seaworthy. Two-day Ko-

VISITING KOMODO NATIONAL PARK

Declared one of the New Seven Wonders (www.n7w.com) of nature, this **national park** (www.komodonationalpark.org), established in 1980, encompasses Komodo, Rinca, several neighbouring islands, and the rich marine ecosystem within its 1817 sq km.

A three-day visitor permit includes your park entrance fee (50,000Rp) and the conservation fee (20,000Rp), collected on arrival by rangers. Camera (50,000Rp), video camera (150,000Rp), snorkelling (60,000Rp) and diving (75,000Rp) taxes apply, as well. All fees are good for three days.

A short, guided dragon-spotting trek is included with your entrance fee. For a longer, hour-long trek on Rinca you'll pay an additional 50,000Rp. On Komodo, where the hiking is superb, you can pay from 50,000Rp to 250,000Rp for guided treks that range from flat 3km strolls to steep 10km hikes over peaks and into deep valleys. Arrange your trek upon registration in Komodo. All guides speak some English and are very knowledgeable about the islands' flora and fauna.

modo trips from Labuanbajo cost 1,100,000Rp (two people) for a mattress but no cabin, and up to 2,500,000Rp for a better outfitted boat with a private cabin. Price includes landings on Rinca and Komodo, meals and snorkelling gear, but not park entry, which you'll pay at the ranger station.

Rinca

Rinca is slightly smaller than Komodo, close to Labuanbajo and easily done in a day trip. Boats arrive at the sheltered dock of Loh Kima, from where it's a five-minute walk through the mangroves, home to long-tail macaques and wild water buffalo, to the PHKA station camp at **Loh Buaya**. Pay your fee here, and keep the entrance ticket if you're heading to Komodo. Two types of guided walks are offered. An hour's loop trail is included with your admission, or you could pay an extra 50,000Rp for a two-hour hike. As temperatures will inevitably be furnace-hot, most people opt for an hour's walk close to camp.

There are supposedly no set dragon-feeding places on Rinca, but there are often a half-dozen massive beasts near the camp kitchen at Loh Buaya, so you do the math. As a result, finding dragons in the bush is not so easy, but the guides know spots where Komodo dragons sun themselves, and they'll show you dragon nests (the females dig huge burrows to lay their eggs). Wildlife is much more abundant than on Komodo; in addition to the monkeys and buffalo you may find Timor deer, horses or even wild boar. Bird life includes spangled drongos, fish eagles, megapodes and orange-footed scrub fowl.

Sleeping & Eating

Komodo's **PHKA camp** (per person per night 400,000Rp) accommodation is merely an overpriced version of a basic Indo hotel, complete with musty interior. Most folks opt to sleep on the decks of their chartered boats – a lot more palatable, with less mosquitoes if a bit cramped. The camps has a restaurant with a limited menu of *nasi/mie goreng*, fish and other simple meals.

Getting There & Away

Chartering a boat to Rinca costs about 750,000Rp return from Labuanbajo. Boats usually leave at about 8am for the two-hour journey to the island and then return via snorkelling spots. You can book through your hotel, Labuanbajo agents or the captains themselves, which will allow you check that the vessel has a radio and life jackets.

FLORES

Flores used to get by on Bali's overflow alone, and thanks to easy transport links, the vast majority of that trickle of travellers landed in the once sleepy west coast port town of Labuanbajo, used it as a spring board to the epic Komodo National Park, and fled. But that trickle has become a river, and the island named 'flowers' by 16th-century Portuguese colonists, who were astonished by the island's lush, fragrant forests, has become Indonesia's 'Next Big Thing'.

It makes sense. After all, Flores is the kind of gorgeous that grabs hold of you tightly. Here are empty white sand beaches and bay islands, excellent diving and snorkelling and a skyline of perfectly shaped volcanoes.

The 670km serpentine, pot-holed, but steadily improving trans-Flores highway skirts knife-edge ridges that sheer into spectacular river canyons, brushes by dozens of traditional villages, leads to multi-hued volcanic lakes, and connects the east and west coasts. For years this tropical jewel box remained a travellers secret, its gems accessible only to those willing to venture off the beaten track. But thanks to steadily improving transport connections, a maturing tourism industry that has brought increasing comfort and better facilities into remote towns, and enthusiastic word of mouth from fellow travellers, Flores is blooming.

Culture

The island's 1.8 million people are divided into five main linguistic and cultural groups. From west to east, these are the Manggarai (main town Ruteng), the Ngada (Bajawa), the closely related Ende and Lio peoples (Ende), the Sikkanese (Maumere) and the Lamaholot (Larantuka). In remote areas, especially those accessible only by trail, some older people don't speak a word of Bahasa Indonesia, and their parents grew up in purely animist societies.

Around 85% of the people are Catholic, but in rural areas Christianity is welded onto *adat*. Animist rituals are still used for births, marriages and deaths and to mark important points in the agricultural calendar. Even educated, English-speaking Florinese participate in the odd chicken, pig or buffalo sacrifice to the ancestors when rice is planted.

Muslims congregate in fishing villages and coastal towns such as Ende (where they make up half the population) and Labuanbajo.

ℹ Getting Around

The 'trans-Flores highway' twists and tumbles 670km from Labuanbajo to Larantuka, at the eastern end of the island. It's sealed, but often rutted and narrow. Buses are invariably small, cramped and overcrowded, but the stunning scenery certainly helps compensate. For those with more money than time, car rental is available in Labuanbajo or Maumere, both have regular air connections to Kupang and Denpasar. The trans-island rate is 550,000Rp to 600,000Rp per day, including driver and petrol. This is becoming a very popular option for small groups, as you can stop for photo-ops where you like, and take in remote attractions. Be warned that Labuanbajo to Bajawa is considered a two-day

DIVING & SNORKELLING AROUND KOMODO & LABUANBAJO

Komodo National Park has some of the most exhilarating scuba diving in Indonesia. It's a region swept by strong currents and cold upswellings, created by the convergence of the warmer Flores Sea and the cooler Selat Sumba (Sumba Strait) – conditions that create rich plankton soup and an astonishing diversity of marine life. Mantas and whales are drawn here to feed on the plankton during their migration from the Indian Ocean to the South China Sea. Dolphins are also common in the waters between Komodo and Flores.

Among the several dozen dive sites mapped in the park are **Batu Bolong**, a split pinnacle with pristine coral and a relatively light current, and **Crystal Bommie** (aka Crystal Rock), with electric soft corals, turtles and schooling pelagics. We saw 19 reef and grey sharks in one dive. The currents are strong here and at **Castle Rock** (aka Tako Toko Toko), a tremendous sunrise dive site where, with a little luck, you'll dive with dolphins or see magnificent pinwheels of tropical fish. **Makassar Reef** is a shallow drift dive over moonscape rubble where massive manta rays school and clean themselves on the rocks. If you've never seen mantas before, dive here. It's (almost) guaranteed.

When it comes to Komodo outfitters, there are several choices. You could sign up for day trips with the Labuanbajo dive shops, which is the cheapest way to go (800,000Rp for two dives). They operate year-round, but it's a long haul (up to three hours) to and from the sites. Wicked Diving (p351) offers three- and six-day liveaboard itineraries with three dives per day. Most Labuanbajo dive shops, including Divine Diving (p351) and **CN Dive** (☎41159, 0813 3928 5913), offer cheaper dive safaris, and the upstart **Komodo Resort Diving Club** (☎42095; www.komodoresort.com; all-inclusive per person €130), based on Pulau Sebayur, is another unique choice that offers exceptional value and standard of service for multi-day divers. Current Junkies (p352) is an undercover value play, considering they only take four guests at a time. These guys seek big currents at the best sites and are recommended for experienced divers only.

Flores

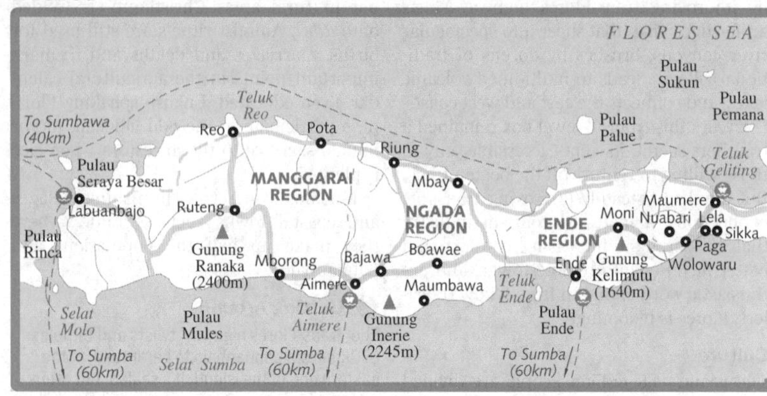

drive by most transport fixers. Motorcycling across the island is fantastic with the combination of roads and scenery, but it's only for experienced bikers, due to tough conditions and numerous blind bends.

Labuanbajo

☎0385

Tucked into Flores' west coast and blessed with surrealist sunsets, Labuanbajo is a romantically ramshackle little harbour town, that isn't so little anymore. According to state reports, Labuanbajo is the fastest growing regency in Indonesia. Within the last three years, the harbour has doubled in size while the population has exploded. More than ever, international visitors bound for the spectacular Komodo National Park, check into a growing number of homey guesthouses etched into the rugged hills – or one of the new tower hotels down the coast. Meanwhile, hundreds of young Florinese stream in for steady work, which lends a lively boomtown bustle. Sure, Labuanbajo's chief attractions remain offshore, but two stalwart Italian kitchens have raised the bar on a growing dining and nightlife scene in this charming town that is hard to leave.

With such rapid growth comes increasing concerns about expanding development and its environmental impact. Causes for concern include the dumping of raw sewage into the bay and rumours of alleged corruption. Tower hotels continue to open on a once lonely coast, and the recent arrival of a splashy Euro beach club lead some to believe there is an even bigger boom waiting down the line. While more business in Flores is doubtless a boon to the people, many are left to question what impact this development will have on the Komodo ecosystem as a whole.

 Activities

Excursions to nearby islands make great day trips, offering the chance to snorkel or lounge on a deserted beach. Most hotels will offer to set you up with a boat to the uninhabited island of your choice, or you can bargain at the docks. Charters to **Pulau Bidadari**, where there's lovely coral and crystalline water, cost around 250,000Rp to 350,000Rp. You can snooze on **Pantai Waecicu** and snorkel around the tiny offshore islet of **Kukusan Kecil**. **Pulau Seraya** and **Pulau Kanawa** are both gorgeous and have basic beach-hut accommodation with free transport. Boats leave from the shoreline at the northern end of the main street.

Diving & Snorkelling

With dive sites around the islands near Labuanbajo and the proximity of Komodo National Park, there are some excellent scuba opportunities here. We're talking about some of the best sites on earth, which explains the recent explosion of dive shops. There are 12 dedicated dive shops, not including the in-house shops at the big beach resorts, and more than 40 liveaboards in the area, many of which operate seasonally.

Local dive operators share uniform prices. The price is around 800,000Rp for two dives around Rinca, plus a 200,000Rp surcharge to stop and see the dragons. Some offer Open Water certification and dive master programs. And you'll need to have

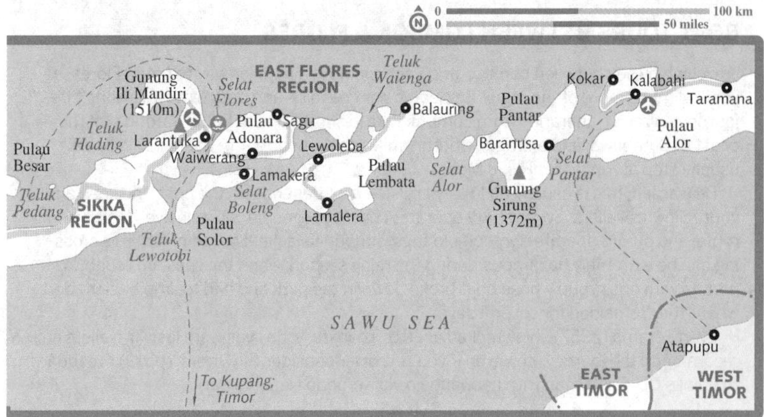

Advanced Open Water to hit the best sites. Custom dive safaris to the northern Komodo sites are also available. Itineraries hover around 1,500,000Rp to 3,000,000Rp per person with a two- to four-person minimum depending on the dive shop. Wicked Diving offers three- and six-day liveaboards departing twice weekly. Dive offices are strung along or just off the seafront road.

It's best to chat with all the dive schools first, and survey their equipment and boats before you make a decision. There have been reports of broken dive gauges, which can be critical when dealing with Komodo's currents. Bring your own computer.

Dive operators will rent snorkelling gear, as will some hotels. July and August is peak season. In March, April and September crowds thin and the diving is magical.

Divine Diving DIVING

(☎41948; www.divinediving.info; Jl Soekarno Pelabuhan 1; safari per person 4,200,000Rp) The 18m boat (the town's second biggest) makes for a suprisingly comfortable passage to North Komodo dive sites. The dive guides know the sites well, you'll enter during slack tide whenever possible and the food and service are wonderful. Occasionally the day-trip boat goes out on safari, which makes for an affordable liveaboard. You'll make nine dives in three days and two nights.

Wicked Diving DIVING

(☎42124; www.wickeddiving.com/komodo; Jl Soekarno-Hatta; 3-day/6-day liveaboards US$620/1150) A relative newbie offering popular three- and six-day liveaboards on a classic Bugis schooner. At research time they only ran day trips outside the national park boundaries. If you want to hit the best sites with Wicked, you must liveaboard.

Bajo Dive Club DIVING

(☎41503; www.komododiver.com; Jl Soekarno-Hatta) A popular, long-running choice with the biggest day-trip boat in town. That means comfort on the long haul to the national park sites. It also offers dive safaris.

Blue Marlin DIVING

(www.bluemarlindivekomodo.com; Jl Soekarno-Hatta) The Gili Islands' original dive shop has hung its hat in Labuanbajo. Long before the recent boom, it was running liveaboards between the Gilis and Labuanbajo, and has *boucoup* experience in the Komodos. They are also expert tech divers. Its custom, fiberglass 15m boat will allow for three dives per day instead of two on the standard day trip, which leaves at 8am and returns at 5.30pm. The bayfront compound boasts three guest rooms, a swimming pool and what promises to be Labuanbajo's best scuba retailer.

CNDive DIVING

(☎41159; per person per day from US$120) Condo Subagyo, the proprietor of CNDive, is the area's original Indonesian dive operator and a former Komodo National Park ranger with over 10,000 dives. He offers two and three-day trips with three dives per day. He doesn't do day trips.

Reefseekers DIVING

(☎41443; www.reefseekers.net; Jl Soekarno-Hatta) One of the three longest tenured dive shops in town. If you want a special dive vacation,

BOAT TOURS BETWEEN LOMBOK & FLORES

Travelling by sea between Lombok and Labuanbajo is a popular way to get to Flores, as you'll glimpse more of the region's spectacular coastline and dodge painfully long bus journeys. Typical itineraries from Lombok take in snorkelling at Pulau Satonda off the coast of Sumbawa, and a dragon-spotting hike on Komodo. From Labuanbajo boats usually stop at Rinca and Pulau Moyo.

Be warned, this is usually no luxury cruise – a lot depends on the boat, the crew and your fellow travellers. Some shifty operators have reneged on 'all-inclusive' deals en route, and others operate decrepit old tugs without lifejackets or radio. And this crossing can be extremely hazardous during the rainy season, when the seas are rough. We met up with one group whose boat broke down in the park and had to limp back to port where they remained for several days.

Even Perama (p357) shipwrecked in 2011. Thankfully, no lives were lost. Travellers still recommend the journey, however. If you're a diver consider Gili Divers' (p319) liveaboard that links Gili Trawangan with Labuanbajo via Komodo National Park.

consider their new luxurious offshore dive resort, on Angel Island (p355).

Current Junkies DIVING
(www.currentjunkies.com; per person 10,000Rp, equipment rental 1,000,000Rp, national park fees 400,000Rp) One of the newest and most interesting liveaboards in the area, Current Junkies does not shy away from ripping current. They dive into them, because the current brings pelagics. Trips are six days and five nights and include 14 dives, but do not include national park fees. They only accept four divers per trip, and no beginners. Online bookings only.

Climbing & Canyoning

Climbing up the rain-forested slopes of **Gunung Mbeliling** (1239m) has become a popular attraction in West Flores. The two-day trip (per person 850,000Rp) includes eight hours of hiking, sunrise at the summit and a stop-off at the Cunca Rami Air Terjun, where you can bathe in fresh swimming holes, on the way down. The **Reo Ecotourism Association** (☎0812 3659 2612; www.floreskomodo.com; depending upon group size, per person 400,000-600,000Rp) organises the treks. Reo is just an hour's drive from Labuanbajo.

If you like canyoning, you'll enjoy the **Cunca Wulang Cascades**, where local guides lead you down natural rock waterslides, off 7m rock jumps and into swimming holes beneath a series of waterfalls. Trips generally last half a day and cost about 200,000Rp per person.

Massage

There are only two choices. You can head to **Yayasan Ayo Mandiri** (☎41318; www.yam-flores.com; Jl Puncak Waringin; 70 min/100min 70,000/100,000Rp; ⏲9am-12:30pm, 3-8pm Mon-Sat) and enjoy a massage at the hands of a gifted, sightless therapist. A home for the blind, it offers top quality treatments including acupressure, hot stone and reflexology. The local dive pros swear by it. Or you can hit **Flores Spa** (☎0857 3958 0888; www.floresspa.com; Jl Soekarno-Hatta; treatments 60,000-200,000Rp; ⏲10am-8pm Mon-Sat, 1-8pm Sun), a storefront spa with recommended treatments like the jasmine body scrub, reflexology or full body massage.

Tours

Manumadi Tours & Travel ADVENTURE TOUR
(☎41533; www.manumadi.com; Jl Soekarno-Hatta; Wae Rebo trek per person 3,800,000Rp) It has the most interesting, creative and challenging trekking itineraries in all of Flores, and operates trips out of Ruteng and Bajawa, as well. Consider the three-day, two-night trek to Wae Rebo village in manggarai country. Staff speak great English.

Sleeping

There are plenty of aged, stilted, harbor-oriented cheap sleeps of varying cleanliness and value to consider. Hotel rates include breakfast.

CENTRAL AREA

TOP CHOICE **Green Hill Hotel** HOTEL $$
(☎41289; Jl Soekarno Hatta; per person 400,000Rp; ❄📶) Spacious, spotless and lovingly tended rooms with soaring beamed ceilings, stained-glass accents, hot water, queen beds, satellite tv and a lovely common patio overlooking the harbor. It's one of

the best values in town and comes with not just free breakfast, but a free 4.30am wake-up call from not one, not two, but three mosques. Hey, there's always fine print.

Bagus Bagus GUESTHOUSE $
(☎0812 386 0084; stefankomodo@gmail.com; d 200,000Rp) Accessed from the walkway that leads to and from Paradise Bar, you will find these spacious, tiled rooms with wooden beds, mosquito nets, woven-bamboo and beamed ceilings, open-air baths and exquisite sunset views from the common porch. It can get loud on party nights (Wednesdays and Saturdays), otherwise it's perfect.

Labuanbajo

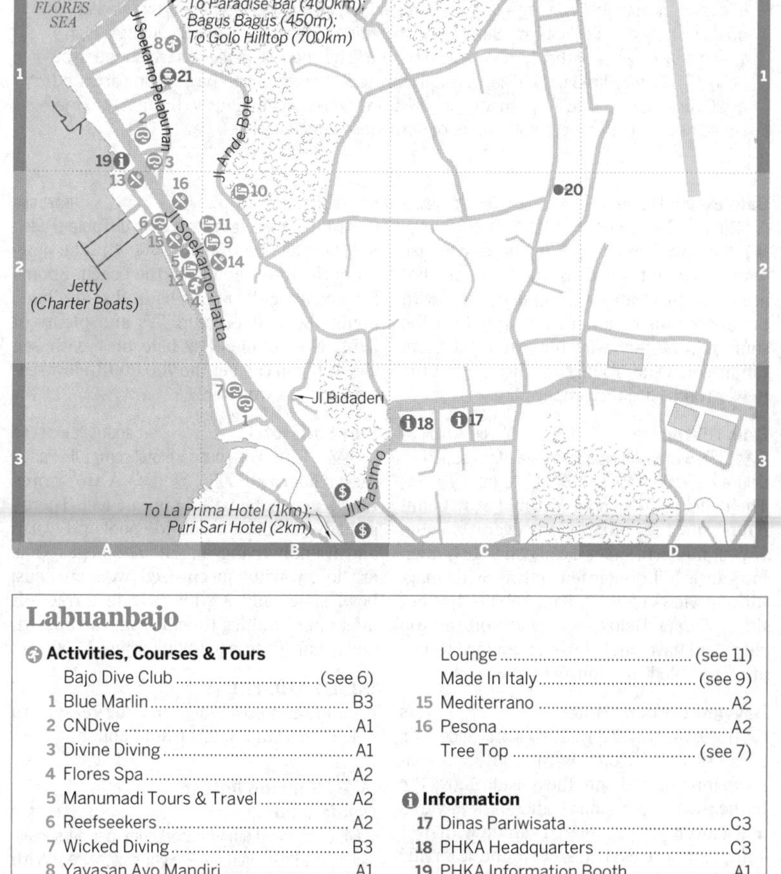

Labuanbajo

Activities, Courses & Tours
- Bajo Dive Club ......(see 6)
- 1 Blue Marlin B3
- 2 CNDive A1
- 3 Divine Diving A1
- 4 Flores Spa A2
- 5 Manumadi Tours & Travel A2
- 6 Reefseekers A2
- 7 Wicked Diving B3
- 8 Yayasan Ayo Mandiri A1

Sleeping
- 9 Bajo Beach Hotel B2
- 10 Bayview Gardens Hotel B2
- 11 Green Hill Hotel B2
- 12 Kanawa Island Bungalows A2

Eating
- 13 Aneka Baru A2
- 14 Bajo Bakery B2
- Lounge ...... (see 11)
- Made In Italy ...... (see 9)
- 15 Mediterrano A2
- 16 Pesona A2
- Tree Top ...... (see 7)

Information
- 17 Dinas Pariwisata C3
- 18 PHKA Headquarters C3
- 19 PHKA Information Booth A1
- Varanus Travel ...... (see 12)

Transport
- 20 Merpati C2
- 21 Pelni A1
- Transnusa ...... (see 12)

DIVING INTO THE FUTURE

Tension between dive shops and PHKA park administration peaked recently when several dynamite fishing incidents were discovered within the Komodo National Park's borders. According to sources and international media, fishermen dropped a bomb on three of the area's best dive sites: Tanjung Besar, Castle Rock and Crystal Rock.

In response, videographers from local dive shops posted footage of the damage on YouTube. Word got back to PHKA superiors and since then park staff have been more active in enforcing anchorage rules and running down illegal fishermen.

In 2012 local marine police tracked three gangs with compressors on their boat – a sign of dynamite fishing. One of the boats was registered locally in Labuanbajo, two similar boats launched out of Sape on Sumbawa. According to the marine police, during a high speed chase of one of the Sumbawa vessels, the fishermen allegedly started shooting at police. The police fired back, killed a fisherman, took possession of the boat and arrested all 20 men aboard. The event made the newswire, and drew attention to the fact that there would now be increased enforcement of Komodo's national park status.

Bajo Beach Hotel GUESTHOUSE **$**
(☎41008; Jl Soekarno Hatta; r 120,000-275,000Rp; ❄) A damn fine cheapie in the city centre with basic but spacious tiled rooms that are quite clean and well tended, each with private seating area out front. You'll get the same room either way, but pay a bit more for air-con. Older rooms are cheaper but the newer rooms are the proper play.

Golo Hilltop BUNGALOW **$$**
(☎41337; www.golohilltop.com; standard/superior/deluxe 250,000/400,000/450,000Rp; ❄📶🏊) The delicious new pool just makes Labuanbajo's most popular nest even sweeter. Expect modern, super clean concrete bungalows in a hilltop garden setting with magnificent views of Teluk Labuanbajo (but not the harbour). Deluxe rooms are on the top ridge and have safety boxes. Standard rooms are fan-cooled. You must reserve ahead.

Bayview Gardens Hotel INN **$$**
(☎41549; www.bayview-gardens.com; Jl Ande Bole; s/d 350,000/450,000Rp; ❄📶) A lovely seven-room inn notched onto the hillside above the harbor with epic sunset and harbor views and a lovely gray-water–fed garden with over 450 plant species. It has wi-fi and a terrific breakfast served in your room which isn't fancy but is sweet with an outdoor living room, separate indoor bedroom and huge bath. It books up. Reserve in advance.

BY THE BEACH

This is where Labuanbajo's newest hotels are rising. The massive Jayakarta Hotel opened its 200-room resort in 2011, signaling the coming dawn of mass tourism to Labuanbajo.

La Prima Hotel HOTEL **$$$**
(☎41700; www.hotellaprima.com; Jl Pantai Pedeh 8; d 1,000,000-2,500,000Rp ; ❄@📶) The newest of the tower hotels on the beach. Rooms have ceramic-tile floors, bathtubs, minibars, double beds, flat-screen TVs and plenty of light. Not to mention balconies with sea views. If you can get the 700,000Rp low season deal, it's worth it.

Puri Sari Hotel BOUTIQUE HOTEL **$$**
(☎244 3710; www.purisarihotel.com; Jl Pantai Pede; d from 550,000Rp; ❄📶🏊) A two-storey ranch-style hotel with boutique feel. There's a shady garden, a beachside pool and warm and friendly management. The new rooms are lovely with queen-sized wooden beds, bowl sinks, and a wide private terrace. It offers free shuttles to and from the airport, and a daily shuttle to town for just 25,000Rp.

ISLAND HOTELS

It's an hour's boat ride – free for guests – to reach the island hotels from Labuanbajo.

TOP CHOICE **Komodo Resort Diving Club** RESORT **$$$**
(☎42095; www.komodoresort.com; per person all-inclusive €130, minimum 2-night stay; ❄📶) With 14 *lumbung*-style bungalows spread along the white sand beach on Pulau Sebayur, this is our favorite island resort. Bungalows have wood floors, queen beds, plush linens, 24-hour electricity, tented marble bathrooms with hot water, and a satellite wi-fi connection. The Indonesian chef makes lunch, an Italian chef bakes the bread and crafts dinners from herbs and vegetables grown on the property. Price includes three meals and

two dives per day in the national park, as well as boat trips to both Komodo and Rinca islands. It offers walk-in discounts, making this place superb value for spontaneous diving couples.

Angel Island Resort RESORT **$$$**
(☎41443; www.angelisleflores.com; per person from €120, minimum 2-night stay) Think: 10 luxurious villas scattered on a private 15-hectare island with sheer rock faces on either end, and a stunning white sand beach in between. Price includes meals, accommodation and transfers to and from the airport. It does not include diving, though they offer day trips into the national park. Book through Reefseekers (p351) in Labuanbajo.

Seraya Island Bungalows BUNGALOW **$**
(☎41258; www.serayaisland.com; s/d with fan & mosquito net 160,000/200,000Rp) Get-away-from-it-all bliss exists on Pulau Serayu. Bunk in simple bamboo bungalows with *mandis* set on a white-sand beach, with offshore snorkelling and a rugged hilltop where you can wonder at spectacular sunsets for days on end. No frills, just deeply relaxing.

Kanawa Island Bungalows BUNGALOW **$$**
(☎0858 5704 3197; www.kanawaislandandresort.com; office Jl Yos Sudarso; bungalows s/d 300,000/360,000Rp) There's no denying this beach hideaway its loveliness. There's an elegant strip of white sand, a turquoise lagoon with magnificent snorkelling, endless island views and a long crooked jetty that is the tropical romantic ideal. However, accommodation is rather basic, meals cost from 25,000Rp to 40,000Rp, and electricity only runs from 6pm to 11pm. Plus, you'll have to pay the usual 800,000Rp fee for two dives. So it's not the best value. Contact the Kanawa office for a lift.

Eating & Drinking

Once a fairly dull palate, two dueling Italian restaurants have raised the culinary standard in town. And while there's no real bar scene here, Paradise Bar, set up a steep hill on the north side of town, does attract a regular sunset and weekend crowd.

Made In Italy ITALIAN **$$**
(☎41366; www.miirestaurants.com; Jl Soekarno Hatta; mains 55,000-78,000Rp, cruise per person 1,500,000Rp; ⏰11am-11pm; 📶) A fun and stylish indoor-outdoor dining room known the island over for having Flores' best pizza and pasta. You'll dig the rattan lighting, custom wood furnishings, ceiling fans, home-baked bread and fabulous pizza. It also does lovely risotto, *carpaccio* and an incredible looking seafood soup. Skip the salads, but do sniff one of the five grappas! Oh, and ask about the fine dining dinner cruise aboard the new all wood schooner. For 1,500,000Rp you get a cocktail, a glass of wine, four courses and a full wine list. Cruises depart 4pm and return at 11pm.

Mediterrano ITALIAN **$$**
(☎42218; www.mediterraneoinn.com; Jl Soekarno Hatta; dishes 38,000-96,000Rp; ⏰7am-midnight; 📶) While we enjoy the pastas, pizzas, and the excellent barracuda *carpaccio*, we absolutely adore the groovy interior, which rambles beneath white-washed rafters dangling with woven rattan lanterns. Grab an upcycled wooden table or sink into a beanbag, surf the wi-fi, read or play board games for as long as you wish. The Italian owners have just opened Labuanbajo's first Euro-style beach club (p356), as well.

Aneka Baru NOODLES **$**
(☎41365; Jl Soekarno-Hatta; mains 10,000-25,000Rp; ⏰9am-10pm) A hole-in-the-wall warung beloved by local dive pros for the house special – crispy noodles smothered with veggies, chicken and egg. A vegetarian version is available.

Bajo Bakery BAKERY **$**
(Jl Soekarno Hatta; mains 20,000-40,000Rp, sweets 9000Rp; ⏰7am-7pm) They don't try to do too much, and that works just fine. Expect only good fresh breads, seductive banana muffins, tasty breakfasts, a few sandwiches and a quiche of the day.

Tree Top INDONESIAN **$$**
(Jl Soekarno Hatta; mains 28,000-100,000Rp; ⏰9am-11pm; 📶) This fun, triple-decker art cafe offers a pub vibe and billiards table downstairs, and harbor and island views from the split-level upstairs dining rooms where it serves tasty spicy Indonesian seafood and forgettable takes on Western classics. Go Indo or dine elsewhere.

Lounge INTERNATIONAL **$$**
(☎41962; Jl Soekarno-Hatta; mains 35,000-65,000Rp; 📶) Come here for holy comfort food. Think: burgers that demand two hands. Knife and fork calzones bigger than your face, fish and chips, paninis and salads. Staff mix *arak* cocktails from a bar stocked with premium liquids. There's a flat-screen TV for ball games of international import,

and *shisha* pipes. Not to mention cushy built-in lounges (hence the name). Dinner music is of the drum 'n' bass variety, so there is that.

Pesona INDONESIAN $
(☎41950; Jl Soekarno Hatta; meals 26,000Rp) Cute, ramshackle wooden restaurant perched above the harbour, specialising in fresh seafood. Try the whole snapper steamed or grilled. Meals include salad and fries or rice.

Paradise Bar PUB
(mains 22,000-45,000Rp; ⏲11am-2am) Set on a hilltop, Paradise satisfies all the requirements of a definitive tropical watering hole. There's ample deck space, a mesmerising sea view, a natural wood bar serving ice-cold beer, and live music. An acoustic collective takes the stage every night from 8pm to 10pm, but Saturday night brings the electrified two-band spectacular that ends in a massive jam into the wee hours. The grub is good here too. On Wednesday nights it has a fresh fish barbecue.

Atlantis BEACH CLUB
(☎42218; www.mediterraneoinn.com; ⏲11am-11pm Mon-Thu, to 2am Fri-Sun; 📶) Labuanbajo's first beach club has received mixed reviews. It's light years fancier and more polished than any other Labuanbajo watering hole, and it provides free shuttle services to and from Mediterraneo in town. It's a nice place to lounge and sip cocktails but even during high season they had a hard time filling the place on Friday and Saturday nights as drinks are expensive and it is a bit far from town. The free shuttle runs from 7pm to 2am daily.

Information

INTERNET ACCESS & TELEPHONE The Telkom office, 1km west of town, offers the best long-distance rates. Centrally located **Varanus Travel** (☎41709; Jl Soekarno Hatta; per hour 8000Rp; ⏲internet 8am-midnight, travel agency 8am-noon & 1-5pm) has one of the strongest connections in town.

MONEY The **BNI** (Jl Soekarno-Hatta; ⏲8am-4.30pm Mon-Fri) ATM accepts Visa/Plus cards. **BRI's** (Jl Soekarno-Hatta; ⏲8am-3.30pm Mon-Fri) accepts MasterCard/Cirrus only. Both should change US dollars.

TOURIST INFORMATION **Dinas Pariwisata** (☎41170; ⏲7am-2pm Mon-Thu & Sat, to 11am Fri) is about 1km out of town on the road to the airport, but you'll source much more essential tips in the dive shops. **PHKA** administers the Komodo National Park; its headquarters on Jl Kasimo has no tourist info. Staff at the **PHKA information booth** (☎41005; tnkomodo@indosat.net.id; Jl Soekarno-Hatta; ⏲8am-2.30pm Mon-Thu, to 11am Fri) do provide practical information for Komodo and Rinca islands. They'll also issue your ticket and collect fees.

Getting There & Away

AIR At the time of this writing, work crews had finally broken ground on a new 'international' terminal, which was slated to be complete in six months. The runway still won't accomodate jets of a certain (read: normal) size, so that's the next project. Air routes in Nusa Tenggara Timor tend to fluctuate from year to year, so it is best to inquire locally for updated information. **Merpati** (☎41177) and **Transnusa** (☎41800, 41955; Jl Soekarno-Hatta) have offices in Labuanbajo, and you can book flights with Sky and Wings Air through Varanus Travel (p356). Departure tax from Labuanbajo is 11,000Rp.

TRANSPORT FROM LABUANBAJO

Air

DESTINATION	COMPANY	FREQUENCY
Denpassar	Merpati, Transnusa, Sky, Wings Air	daily
Ende	Transnusa	2 weekly
Kupang	Merpati	2 weekly

Bus

DESTINATION	TYPE	COST (RP)	DURATION (HR)	FREQUENCY
Bajawa	bus	80,000	10	6am daily
Bajawa	minibus	120,000	10	varies
Ruteng	bus	50,000	4	every 2hr, 6am-6pm

BOAT The ASDP ferry from Labuanbajo to Sape (40,000Rp, eight to nine hours) is scheduled to leave at 8am and 4pm daily, but is prone to cancellation when seas are rough. Tickets for Sape can be purchased at the harbour master's office (in front of the pier) one hour before the vessel's departure. The **Pelni agent** (☎41106) is easy to miss, tucked away in a side street in the northeast of town. The *Tilongkabila* heads to Makassar and the east coast of Sulawesi; or to Bima, Lembar and Benoa twice monthly. Many travellers choose to take a boat trip, like Perama's popular cruise, between Flores and Lombok, stopping at Komodo and Sumbawa along the way for snorkelling and exploration. The local Perama boat contact is **PT Diana Perama Matteru** (☎42016, 42015; www.peramatour.com; Jl Soekarno Hatta; deck/cabin berth 1,300,000/1,800,000Rp).

BUS With no bus terminal in Labuanbajo, most people book their tickets through a hotel or agency, which makes them more expensive than buying directly from the bus company. If you get an advance ticket, the bus will pick you up from your hotel. All buses run via Ruteng, so no matter where you're headed just take the first available east-bound bus. **Gunung Harta** (☎42068) runs a minibus service to Bajawa (120,000Rp), Ende (180,000Rp), Moni (250,000Rp) and Maumere (300,000Rp) without making endless loops searching for passengers prior to departure.

Getting Around

The airfield is 1.5km from the town. Hotel reps and dive shops will meet flights and offer free lifts. A private taxi to town costs a fixed flat rate of 50,000Rp. Once you're in town you can walk to most places, or hop aboard an *ojek* (day/night 3000/5000Rp to 10,000Rp) or into a bemo (2000Rp); they do continual loops following the one-way traffic. After dark, however, the bemos cease running, *ojeks* are hard to find, and you may be forced to hoof it. Speak to transport wrangler **Jak Terming** (☎0852 3896 4782; jakflores@gmail.com) about renting a Kijang (550,000Rp per day, max three people, including driver and fuel) for trips across Flores. Our favorite driver is **Andy Rona** (☎0813 3798 0855; andyrona7@gmail.com; per day 600,000Rp): he speaks excellent English, is trustworthy and highly recommended. Motorbike rental is possible through most hotels.

Manggarai Country

To compare gradations of beauty on Flores is as futile as it is fun. And if you do get into such a debate, know that if you've explored Manggarai's dense and lush rainforests, studded with towering stands of bamboo and elegant tree ferns, and climbed her steep mountains to isolated traditional villages accessible only by trail, you may have the trump card.

Getting There & Away

AIR Transnusa flies to and from Kupang four times a week from Ruteng. Merpati makes the hop five times weekly.

BUS The bus terminal for eastern destinations is located 3.5km and a 2000Rp bemo ride out of Ruteng. Local buses heading west still run from the central bus/bemo terminal near the police station. Buses heading to Bajawa (50,000Rp, five hours) and on to Ende (90,000Rp, nine hours) depart beginning at 7am until the last bus at around 11am. Buses to Labuanbajo leave at 7am, 1pm and 3pm (50,000Rp, four hours).

RUTENG

The somewhat charmless market city of Ruteng is the area's base of operations. Although local attractions are thin on the ground, don't miss the lively, sprawling **pasar** (Jl Kartini), a vital lifeline for villagers in the surrounding hills. The best sleep is actually on convent grounds at **Kongregasi Santa Maria Berdukacita** (☎22834; Jl A Yani 45; standard d 130,000-180,000Rp, VIP r 200,000-260,000Rp), where the rooms are huge and spotless, service is excellent, smoking is prohibited, and there is a 9pm curfew. If you crave late nights, **Rima Hotel** (☎22196; Jl A Yani 14; economy s/d 125,000/150,000Rp, standard s/d 175,000/200,000Rp) is another solid budget option. It also rents motorbikes. When hunger strikes, find **Rumah Makan Simpang Andalas** (Jl Bhayankari 1; meals 25,000-40,000; ⏰7am-10pm), a decent, clean, and locally popular pick and mix warung across from **Telkom** (Jl Kartini; ⏰24hr), where you can make cheap international calls. **Z-Net** (☎21347; Jl Adi Sucipto 8; per hr 5000Rp; ⏰9am-6pm) has the best internet connection. **BNI Bank** (Jl Kartini; ⏰8am-3.30pm Mon-Sat) changes cash, and has a Visa/Plus ATM.

LIANG BUA

The limestone cave of Liang Bua, where the remains of the Flores 'hobbit' were famously found in 2003 (p358), is about 14km north of Ruteng, down a very rough dirt track that is often impassable after periods of heavy rain. Archaeologists believe that the lip along the entrance permitted sediments to build up steadily as water flowed through the cave over millennia, sealing the remains of the humans and animals that lived and died

THE FLORES 'HOBBIT'

The Manggarai have long told folk tales of *ebo gogo* – hairy little people with flat foreheads who once roamed the jungle. Nobody paid them much attention until September 2003, when archaeologists made a stunning find.

Excavating the limestone cave at Liang Bua, they unearthed a skeleton the size of a three-year-old child but with the worn-down teeth and bone structure of an adult. Six more remains appeared to confirm that the team had unearthed a new species of human, *Homo floresiensis*, which reached around 1m in height and was nicknamed the 'hobbit'.

Lab tests brought another surprise. The hominid with the nutcracker jaw and gangly, chimplike arms lived until 12,000 years ago, practically yesterday in evolutionary terms, when a cataclysmic volcanic eruption is thought to have wiped out the little people and devastated the island of Flores.

But not all scientists are convinced about the origins of the Flores find. The prevailing school of thought argues that the Flores hominids are descendants of *Homo erectus*, a species that fled Africa around two million years ago and spread throughout Asia. Until recently it was thought that the arrival of *Homo sapiens* in Asia led to the demise of *Homo erectus* around 50,000 years ago. Flores humans could indicate that the species survived in isolated places.

Rival anthropologists suggest that the Flores find could represent *Homo sapiens* (who were known to be travelling between Australia and New Guinea 35,000 years ago) that suffered from microcephaly – a neurological disorder causing stunted head growth, and often dwarfism, that runs in families.

But the momentum still seems to be with the original theory, given that in 2005 a second large jawbone was found, of similar dimensions to the first discovery. And with tools very similar to those found in Liang Bua reportedly unearthed in Timor, and possibly in Sulawesi, more little people could yet emerge from the evolutionary backwoods.

here. There is not much to see, although some sticks mark the place where the little folk were found. Local guides, whose service is included in your 30,000Rp entry fee, will meet you at the cave's entrance and explain why Liang Bua is considered sacred. To get here take an *ojek* (75,000Rp) from Ruteng.

WAE REBO

Wae Rebo is the best of Manggarai's traditional villages. If you are willing to take the time and hike 10km through the jungled steeps, you can overnight in the thatched conical homes of the indigenous Wae Rebo people. The splendid but challenging hike takes four hours and winds past waterfalls and swimming holes, as well as spectacular views of the Savu Sea. Once you arrive in the village you will also be treated to indigenous music and dance, and a demonstration of local weaving practices, then bed down in a *Mbaru Tembong* (traditional home). Labuanbajo-based **Manumadi Tour & Travel** (www.manumadi.com; per person 3,800,000Rp) offers a splendid three-day, two-night trip from either Labuanbajo or Ruteng, which includes a stop at seldom visited Pela village, 27km from Ruteng, and a three-hour drive to Denge, where you'll overnight at the basic **Wejang Asi Guest House** (r 200,000Rp) before starting out early the next day for Wae Rebo. The next morning, you can retrace your steps or choose to hike another six hours over a pass. Either way Manumadi's vehicle will meet and drive you on to Labuanbajo.

Bajawa

☎0384

Framed by forested volcanoes and blessed with a pleasant climate, Bajawa, a laid-back hill town at 1100m, is a great base from which to explore dozens of traditional villages that are home to the local Ngada people. Bajawa is the Ngada's de facto trading post, and you'll mingle with them as you stroll these quiet streets edged by blooming gardens. Gunung Inerie (2245m), a perfectly conical volcano looms to the south where you'll also find some hot springs. The recently emerged volcano, Wawo Muda, with its Kelimutu-esque lakes, is another favourite among the trans-Flores set.

Sleeping

Thanks to a growth spurt in Bajawa tourism, local accomodation has been happily spruced up. All prices include breakfast.

TOP CHOICE Hotel Happy Happy GUESTHOUSE $$
(☎421 763, 0853 3370 4455; www.hotelhappyhappy.com; Jl Sudirman; s/d 250,000/300,000Rp;) The newest addition to Bajawa is a simple yet classy guesthouse with six immaculate tiled rooms, brushed with lavender walls, dressed with high quality linen – a scarcity in Bajawa. There's a groovy sitting area on the patio, lovely wooden windows, wi-fi and breakfast. It's across the river and past the soccer field from the main downtown area.

Edelweis HOTEL $
(☎21345; Jl Ahmad Yani 76; standard s/d 150,000/175,000Rp, superior s/d 250,000/300,000Rp; @) Bajawa's venerable choice offers a range of rooms including cheaper tiled jobs in the main building, older but still quaint garden rooms, and sparkling new ones with hot water and flat-screen TVs. New rooms are smaller than the cheapies. If you grab a garden room without hot water, staff will heat up a bucket upon request.

Villa Silverin LODGE $$
(☎0852 5345 3298, 222 3865; www.villasilverinhotel.com; Jl Bajawa; r 300,000Rp) A sweet hillside lodge set just outside town on the road to Ende, with beckoning verandas and jaw-dropping valley views. VIP rooms are bright and clean with queen beds and hot water.

Hotel Bintang Wisata HOTEL $$
(☎21744; Jl Palapa 4; standard/VIP r 175,000/320,000Rp) Very nice and clean basic tiled rooms with two-tone paint jobs are set in an arc around the parking lot. Upstairs VIP rooms have terraces, hot water and lovely views of that, um, cell tower? Rooms with hot water and no TV are discounted to 270,000Rp.

Eating

Dito's INDONESIAN $
(☎21162; Jl Ahmad Yani; mains 20,000-50,000Rp) Twinkling with Christmas lights, Dito's does a brisk business serving pork and chicken sate and fresh tuna bakar, which is sourced from nearby Aimere and grilled to perfection.The tamarillo juice is *delish*.

Lucas INDONESIAN $
(☎21340; Ahmad Yani 6; mains 18,000-35,000Rp) Set in a cute cabin, done up with lanterns and chequered tablecloths, it serves fine pork sate and other local faves, including a fearsome yet quaffable *arak*.

Camellia INDONESIAN $
(☎21458; Jl Ahmad Yani 74; mains 20,000-35,000Rp) The dining room is too bright, but the food works. There are Western dishes, but try the chicken sate (17,000Rp). It comes with a unique sweet, smoky pepper sauce.

Information

BNI Bank (Jl Pierre Tendean; 8am-3pm Mon-Fri, to 12.30pm Sat) Has an ATM and exchanges dollars.

Tourist office (☎21554; Jl Soekarno Hatta; 8.30am-3pm Mon-Fri, to 1pm Sat)

Warnet 31 (Jl Ahmad Yani 12; per hour 5000Rp; 8am-10pm) Internet cafe set on the main tourist drag. Has a decent, not swift, connection

Getting There & Away

Transnusa and Merpati fly to Kupang several times a week. An ASDP ferry departs on Wednesays at 1pm for Kupang (65,000Rp to 197,000 Rp) and on Wednesdays at 7pm for Waingapu (60,000Rp to 105,000Rp).

There are buses and bemos to various destinations. Buses don't necessarily leave on time,

WORTH A TRIP

BELARAGI

Most visitors to the Bajawa area rely on Kijangs (or Kijang-like vehicles) to whisk them between traditional villages. But it's much more fulfilling to trek through the rainforest to villages like Belaragi, accessible only by trail. Your trek will begin in **Pauleni Village**, approximately 45km (90 minutes) from Bajawa by car. From there it's a steep 90-minute hike to the village itself. Here are more than a dozen traditional homes and welcoming villagers. It can be done in a day trip, but you'll be tired by now, so you may as well stay the night. The *Kepala Kampung* (village head) offers a bed and meals for 250,000Rp per person. You can't find it on your own, but most Bajawa area guides can arrange the trip.

BUSES FROM BAJAWA

DESTINATION	TYPE	COST (RP)	FREQUENCY
Aimere	bemo	15,000	11am daily
Bena	truck	5000-15,000	frequent
Ende	bus	40,000	11am daily
Labuanbajo	bus	100,000	11am daily
Langa	truck	5000-15,000	frequent
Riung	bus	20,000	noon & 2pm daily
Ruteng	bus	50,000	frequent 8-11am
Soa	truck	500-15,000	frequent

only when the bus is almost full. Kijangs, or travel cars also leave throughout the day for Ruteng (60,000Rp), departing from the bemo **terminal** (Jl Basoeki Rahmat).

 Getting Around

Yellow bemos (2000Rp) cruise town, but it is easy to walk almost everywhere except to the bus terminals. *Treks* (trucks) serve remote routes, most leaving traditional villages in the morning and returning in the afternoon. Motorbikes cost 75,000Rp a day. A private Kijang (with driver) is 600,000Rp. Most hotels can arrange rental. The airport is 25km from Bajawa and about 6km outside Soa.

Around Bajawa

Bajawa's big draw is the chance to explore traditional villages in the gorgeous countryside. Their fascinating architecture features carved poles supporting a conical thatched roof. It is certainly possible to visit the area alone, but you'll learn a lot more about the culture and customs (like the caste system) with a guide. Some organise meals in their home villages, others will suggest treks to seldom visited villages accessible only by trail. Guides linger around hotels and can arrange day trips from 250,000Rp per person with transport, village entry fees and lunch.

GUNUNG INERIE

One of the gorgeous volcanoes looming above Bajawa, Gunung Inerie (2245m), 19km from town, beckons all would-be climbers. Or does she taunt them? The journey is not easy, but than this spectacularly jagged cone is worth sweating and suffering for. You can do it as a 10-hour roundtrip but it's also possible to camp by the lake. You'll need a guide and remember to bring extra water even if your guide says he has that covered. You'll require more hydration than any local guide can possibly imagine. Did we mention it was a difficult trail?

BENA

Resting on Inerie's flank, Bena is one of the most traditional Ngada villages. It's home to nine clans, and its fabulous stone monuments are the region's best. Houses with high thatched roofs line up in two rows on a ridge, the space between them filled with fine *ngadhu, bhaga* (smeared with sacrificial blood) and megalithic tomblike structures. Most houses have male or female figurines on their roofs, and doorways are decorated with buffalo horns and jawbones – a sign of the family's prosperity.

Bena is the most visited village, and weavings and souvenir stalls line the front of houses. Although the village is crowded when tour groups arrive during high season and all villagers are now officially Catholic and attend a local missionary school, traditional beliefs and customs endure. Sacrifices are held three times each year, and village elders still talk about a rigidly enforced caste system that prevented 'mixed' relationships, with those defying the *adat* facing possible death.

Bena is 12km from Langa down a degraded road. There's one daily market truck from Bena to Bajawa (15,000Rp) at 6am, returning from Bajawa at 1pm. All visitors are asked to make a donation to the village.

LUBA

Tucked into the jungle like a beautiful secret, the traditional village of Luba is just a short hop from Bena and much more intimate. Just four clans live here in a baker's dozen homes. You'll see four *ngadhu* and *bhaga* in the common courtyard, and within the local population are a few artists whose houses are decorated with depictions of horses, buffalo and snakes which translate as symbols of power, status and protection. Photography is welcomed by most, and if you visit, leave a donation. The Bajawa–Bena bemo can drop you here, but it's easier to charter an *ojek* from Bajawa (around 50,000Rp).

WAWO MUDA

Wawo Muda (1753m) is the latest volcano to emerge in Flores, exploding in 2001 and leaving behind a mini-Kelimutu, complete with several small crater lakes coloured a burnt orange. Pine trees charred by the eruption stand in isolated patches, and there are spectacular views of Gunung Inerie.

The volcano is best visited in the wet season from November to March, if the trails are not too muddy. The lakes usually evaporate in the dry. To get there take one of the regular bemos from Bajawa (8000Rp, 50 minutes) or an *ojek* to the village of Ngoranale, near Menge, and walk an hour up an easy-to-follow trail. Some *ojek* drivers may offer to take you the whole way up, as the path is doable on a motorbike.

DON'T MISS

AIR PANAS SOA

In this cool, lush and palpably volcanic region, it's no surprise that the Bajawa area has a few hot springs on offer. The best of the bunch is **Air Panas Soa** (per person 5000Rp; ⏲6:30am-6pm), situated just east of town on the rough road to Riung. Clean and fresh, there are two pools here. One is a scintilating 45-degrees, and the other a more pedestrian 35 to 40 degrees. You'll find it in the Soa district, surrounded by coconut trees. It can get busy with locals on weekends, but mid-week you may have the pools to yourself.

Riung

Riung is a wonderful little town, lush and isolated, stitched with rice fields, stilted with fisherman shacks, framed with coconut palms and buzzing with only 13 hours of daily electricity. Coming from Ende you'll drive along a parched and arid coastline that skirts a spectacularly blasted volcano before a sudden burst of foliage swallows the road as it winds into town. The effect makes Riung feel like an island unto itself, part of some whole other time and place. Locals are even more warm and ever smiling than elsewhere in Indonesia (and that's saying something). The guesthouses are homey, the quiet streets are made for walking, and the waterfront a gateway to a marine park. Only its relative inaccessibility (read: horrifying roads) keep it from profound development.

Sights & Activities

The main Riung attraction is the **Seventeen Islands Marine Park**. There are actually 21 islands, all uninhabited, but government authorities decided on the number as a convenient tie-in with Indonesia's Independence Day (17 August). Guides will appear at your hotel offering to organise boat trips to the islands. **Al Itchan** (☎0813 8759 0964) is one of Riung's most experienced and dependable. A day trip

THE NGADA

Over 60,000 Ngada people inhabit the upland Bajawa plateau and the slopes around Gunung Inerie and most practice a fusion of animism and Christianity. They worship Gae Dewa, a god who unites Dewa Zeta (the heavens) and Nitu Sale (the earth).

The most evident symbols of continuing Ngada tradition are pairs of *ngadhu* and *bhaga*. The *ngadhu* is a parasol-like structure about 3m high, consisting of a carved wooden pole and thatched 'roof', and the *bhaga* is a miniature thatched-roof house.

The *ngadhu* is 'male' and the *bhaga* is 'female'. Each pair is associated with a particular family group within a village. Some were built over 100 years ago to commemorate ancestors killed in long-past battles.

Agricultural fertility rites continue (sometimes involving gory buffalo sacrifices), as well as ceremonies marking birth, marriage, death and house building – always a communal event. The major annual festival is the six-day Reba ceremony at Bena, held in late December or early January. Villagers wear specially made all-black ikat, sacrifice buffalo and sing and dance through the night.

costs 500,000Rp (for up to six), including boat charter, but not including park admission (per person 15,000Rp). There are other guides (150,000Rp to 200,000Rp) in town and you can certainly charter a boat (300,000Rp) from the harbour on your own if you have your own snorkel gear and don't care for an escort or catering. However, the captains don't snorkel and aren't familiar with all 20 snorkelling sites. Guides also give you the versatility to easily change the itinerary on the fly. Plus, the local Riung guys are quite fun and the meals they prepare are sensational. Basically, if you are trying to save 200,000Rp, do it elsewhere.

Three or four islands are usually included in the boat trip, and the first is almost always **Pulau Ontoloe**, a mangrove isle where a massive colony of flying foxes (these huge fruit bats blacken the sky around Riung at sunset) roost and mewl. A few resident Komodo dragons live here as well. **Pulau Rutong** is popular for its lovely wide white-sand beach. **Pulau Temba** is another slender slice of white sand tucked against a rugged hillside. Picturesque and wild it tends to avoid the crowds. **Pulau Tiga** is likewise not to be missed. The sea is a glassy turquoise, the hard corals off the east coast nourish schools of tropical fish, and the long sweep of white sand is perfect for barefoot strolls. The best snorkelling we experienced was at an offshore site called **Laingjawa**. Mingling among the hard corals were schools of bump heads, some colourful cuttlefish, an occasional black tip and at least two resident turtles.

While snorkelling has always been the draw to Riung's signature marine park, be aware that this coral was impacted by the El Nino bleaching that hammered the Gili Islands in 2002. While visibility is quite good – frequently at least 10m to 15m, don't expect colorful corals. Still, the number and variety of fish here is special, and the standard island tour remains a dynamite day out.

Sleeping & Eating

Pondok SVD GUESTHOUSE $
(☎0813 3934 1572; www.pondoksvdriung.com; s/d with fan 150,000/200,000Rp, s/d with air-con 250,000/300,000Rp; ❄) Here are 21 super clean rooms with desks, reading lights and Western toilets, set down a gravel road from the main drag. Management is warm and relaxed, however, it is right next door to the town generator, which runs all night.

Nirwana BUNGALOW $
(☎0813 3852 8529; bungalows 150,000Rp) Six fun detached hippie shacks with thatched roofs, private patios, and outdoor baths all fan-cooled and set in a garden surrounded by coco palms. It's a quiet and romantic. It doesn't serve meals, but the groovy owner offers guided trips to the islands, and if you join him, you'll eat like royalty.

TOP CHOICE **Rumah Makan Murah Muriah** INDONESIAN $$
(☎0813 3717 2918; mains 25,000-45,000Rp; ⏲7am-10pm) Widely regarded as the best kitchen in Riung, the house specialty is the *sop ikan asam pedas*, Nusa Tenggara Timor's endemic spicy and sour tamarind fish soup. This one is as good as it gets, and they also do grilled fish, fried squid and veggies, chicken sate, fried noodles and much more.

Cafe Del Mar CAFE $$
(☎0813 8759 0964; mains 30,000-50,000Rp; ⏲7am-10pm) The hippest warung in Riung, this tiki bar strung with shell strands and Christmas lights rumbles with rock and roll, and grills a fresh catch over smouldering coconut husks. The electricity may only last 12 hours but the beer here is cold all day and night. It's owned by the area's top guide, Al Itchan (p361).

Information

The PHKA office on the main drag has information about the Riung area. Before going to the islands you must sign in and pay 15,000Rp per person at a separate booth by the dock. Your captain or guide should pay the 20,000Rp anchorage fee for your boat. There's a new ATM at the BRI branch, but it's not compatible with most foreign cards and there's no official currency exchange facilities in Riung. Come with ample rupiah.

Getting There & Away

Charter a private car from Riung to Bajawa (500,000Rp), and stop at hot springs along the way. And if you can't bear the trans-Flores highway for another second, consider a boat from Riung all the way to Labuanbajo (1,800,000Rp, 10 hours). It's a seldom used option, and a bit pricey, but you'll enjoy a coastline most visitors never see and stop in virgin coves, catch fish, and snorkel along the way. Just bring headphones or earplugs. Those outboard motors are loud!

Ende

☎0381 / POP 94,000

The saving grace of this muggy, crowded transport hub is its spectacular setting. The

BUSES & KIJANGS FROM RIUNG

DESTINATION	TYPE	COST (RP)	DURATION (HR)	FREQUENCY
Bajawa	bus	20,000	3	6am daily
Bajawa	kijang	500,000	2½	charter
Ende	bus	40,000	4	6am daily
Ende	kijang	75,000	3½	7am daily

eye-catching cones of Gunung Meja (661m) and Gunung Iya (637m) loom over the city and the nearby black-sand and cobblestone coastline. The views get better just northeast of Ende as the road to Kelimutu rises along a ridge opposite misty peaks overlooking a roaring river and gushing with ribbons of waterfalls in the wet season. Throw in the jade rice terraces and you have some of Flores' most jaw-dropping scenery. Which may be why Sukarno was exiled here in the 1930s, when he reinvented himself as a playwright…kind of.

Sights

Waterfront Market MARKET
(Jl Pasar) Meander through the aromatic waterfront market with the requisite fruit pyramids and an astonishing fish section. The adjacent **ikat market** (cnr Jl Pabean & Jl Pasar) sells hand-woven tapestries from across Flores and Sumba.

Musium Bung Karno MUSEUM
(Jl Perwira; admission by donation; 7am-noon Mon-Sat) History buffs can visit Sukarno's house of exile. Most of the original period furnishings remain. This is where the beloved revolutionary penned the *Frankenstein* knock-off, *Doctor Satan*.

Sleeping

At long last there some decent bedrooms in this sprawling market town.

TOP CHOICE **Grand Wisata** HOTEL $$
(22984; Jl Kelimutu 32; standard/superior/deluxe 500,000/600,000/700,000Rp;) The newest and flashest hotel in town, and easily the most professional. Be warned, some rooms can be dark and cramped, and the price category doesn't necessarily correlate with room size, so have a look around. Rooms on the second floor have views of the 15m lap pool with the epic Gunung Meja looming beyond. It's walking distance to the airport.

Guesthouse Alhidayah GUESTHOUSE $
(23707; Jl Yos Sudarso ; r with fan 100,000Rp, air-con 150,000-250,000Rp;) Relatively new, this spot offers sparkling but otherwise basic tiled rooms with high ceilings and a private porch area. Priciest rooms have air-con and hot water, and are solid value. The location isn't ideal, but it's still the best budget choice in Ende.

Hotel Mentari HOTEL $$
(21802; Jl Pahlawan 19; standard/superior/VIP r 250,000/300,000/350,000Rp;) Well-run and popular with young business travellers, rooms are clean, with high ceilings, some have garden views and catch a bit of breeze. The priciest have Indovision.

Hotel Safari HOTEL $
(21997; Jl Ahmad Yani 65; s/d with fan 75,000/100,000Rp, with air-con 200,000/250,000Rp;) Sporting a fresh paint job, rooms aren't fabulous but are large, bright and reasonably clean.

Eating

TOP CHOICE **Roda Baru** PADANG $
(24135; Jl Kelimutu; meals from 35,000Rp; 9am-midnight) You can trust the cleanliness and care of this spotless pick and mix Padang diner. The fish, chicken and shrimp are all fried or grilled and sauced five ways, the beef *rendang* is locally beloved, and the ample veggie matter and tasty sambal make this easily Ende's best kitchen.

Rumah Makan Tiana INDONESIAN $
(Jl Pahlawan 31; meals 20,000-35,000Rp) A fun hole-in-the-wall with terrific Indonesian soul food, including a gingery *soto ayam* (chicken soup), a chilli-fired *rendang*, and *ayam sate* (chicken sate) drenched in ginger sauce.

Rumah Makan Istana Bambu SEAFOOD $
(21921; Jl Kemakmuran 30A; mains 15,000-35,000Rp) Here's a classic, funkified Chinese fish house. The cast includes a sweet mouthy

Ende

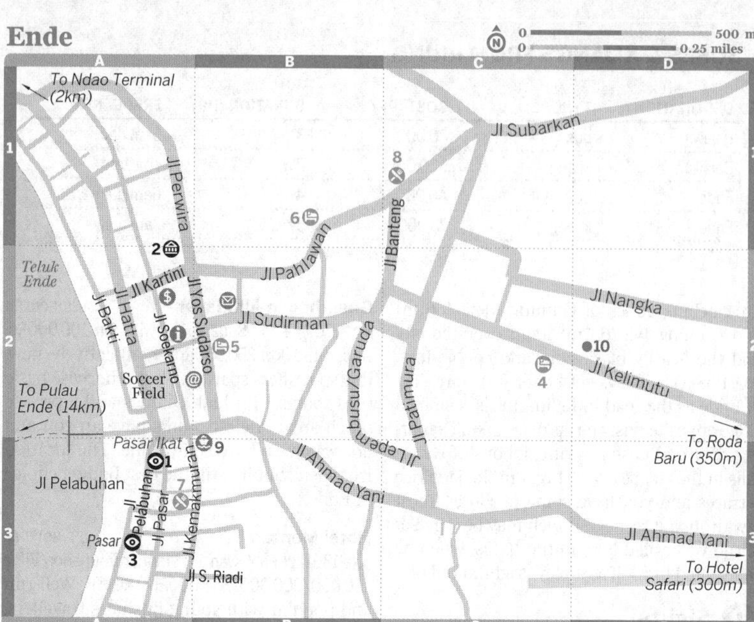

matriarch, her dour smirking sisterhood, fresh fish, squid, shrimp and lobster, and a spicy *sambal* (which they bottle and sell).

Information

Bank Danamon (Jl Soekarno; ⌚8am-3.30pm Mon-Fri, to noon Sat) Has an ATM and offers larger credit-card withdrawals.

BNI Bank (Jl Gatot Subroto) Out near the airport. Also has an ATM.

Main post office (Jl Gajah Mada) Out in the northeastern part of town.

Sub-post office (Jl Yos Sudarso) Sells stamps; opposite Hotel Dwi Putri.

Tourism office (☎21303; Jl Soekarno 4) The enthusiastic staff here dispense up-to-date transport information.

Zyma Internet (☎24697; Jl Yos Sudarso 3; per hr 3000Rp; ⌚11am-10pm) Offers a good connection in the cathedral's shadow.

Getting There & Away

Air and ferry schedules in East Nusa Tenggara are historically fluid, and it's best to confirm all times and carriers on the ground prior to planning your trip. Wings Air flies to Denpasar three times weekly. There are daily flights to Kupang with Wings Air, **Transnusa** (☎24333, 0852 3925 8392; Jl Kelimutu 37) and **Merpati** (☎21355; Jl Nangka).

Pelni's *Awu* stops in Ende every two weeks. It sails west to Waingapu, Benoa and Surabaya, then east to Kupang and Sabu. Visit the helpful **Pelni office** (☎21043; Jl Kathedral 2; ⌚8am-noon & 2-4pm Mon-Sat). There's an **ASDP** ferry to Kupang at 10am on Mondays (54,000Rp to 158,000Rp, 19 hours) and Waingapu at 10am on Saturdays (42,000Rp to 105,000Rp, 13 hours).

East-bound buses leave from the Wolowana terminal, 5km from town. Buses heading west leave from the Ndao terminal, 2km north of town on the beach road.

Getting Around

The airport is on the east end of the town centre. Taxis to most hotels cost around 50,000Rp. Bemos run frequently to just about everywhere (even Pelabuhan Ipi) for a flat rate of 2000Rp.

Kelimutu

There aren't many better ways to wake up than to sip ginger coffee as the sun crests Kelimutu's western rim, filtering mist into the sky and revealing three deep, volcanic lakes – nicknamed the tri-coloured lakes because for years each one was a different striking shade. **Kelimutu National Park** (☎23405; Jl El Tari 16; per car/ojek 6000/3000Rp, per person 20,000Rp, camera/handycam 50,000/150,000Rp; ⏰4am-sunset) remains a Nusa Tenggara must. It is spectacular even though at research time there were two turquoise lakes – one with flecks of rust, while the third was dark green, but from the right angle looked like black glass. The colours are so dense that the lakes seem the thickness of paint. It's thought that dissolving minerals (a process that can accelerate in the rainy season) account for the chameleonic colour scheme – although one of the turquoise lakes never changes, the others fluctuate to countless shades of yellow, orange, red and brown. The summit's moonscape gives Kelimutu an ethereal atmosphere, especially when clouds billow across the craters and sunlight shafts burn luminescent pinpoints to the water's surface.

Kelimutu is sacred to local people, and legend has it that the souls of the dead migrate here: young people's souls go to the warmth of Tiwu Nuwa Muri Koo Fai (Turquoise Lake), old people's to the cold of Tiwu Ata Polo (Brown Lake) and those of the wicked to Tiwi Ata Mbupu (Black Lake).

Ever since locals led early Dutch settlers here, sightseers have made the sunrise trek. Today there's a sealed road up to the lakes from Moni, 13.5km away at the base of the mountain. Visit in the rainy season or in the afternoon and you will probably have Kelimutu to yourself, but pray for a sunny day – the turquoise lakes reach full brilliance in the sunlight.

There's a staircase up to the highest lookout, Inspiration Point, from where all three lakes are visible. It's not advisable to scramble around the craters' loose scree. The footing's so bad and the drop so steep, a few careless hikers have perished here.

Getting There & Away

Moni is the usual base for visiting Kelimutu. It's normally best to view the lakes in the early morning after the predawn mist rises, and before clouds drift in. There are no longer any public bemos, so you'll have to charter an *ojek* (one way/return 40,000/70,000Rp) or bemo (one way/return 175,000/250,000Rp, maximum four people). Actual prices may depend on your negotiating skills. There's a PHKA post halfway up, where you'll pay the 20,000Rp admission, plus 3000Rp for your *ojek* or 6000Rp for your car or bemo. Then there's the new 50,000Rp surcharge if you're toting a camera and 150,000Rp for a video camera. From the car park it's a nice 20-minute walk up through the pines to Inspiration Point. Some prefer to hire transport to the top and stroll down the mountain, through the village, past rice fields and along cascading streams all the way to Moni. The walk takes about 2½ hours and isn't too taxing. A *jalan potong* (short cut) leaves the road back to Moni 1km south of the PHKA gate and goes through Manukako village, then meanders back to the main road 750m uphill from Moni. A second short cut diverges from the trail and goes through Tomo, Mboti, Topo Mboti, Kolorongo

BUSES FROM ENDE

DESTINATION	COST (RP)	DURATION (HR)	FREQUENCY
Bajawa	50,000	5	7am & 11am daily
Labuanbajo	150,000	15	7am daily
Larantuka	70,000	9	7am daily
Maumere	50,000	5	regularly, 7am-4pm
Maumere (Kijang)	62,500	4½	regularly, 7am-4pm
Moni	25,000	2	hourly, 6am-2pm
Riung	40,000	4	1pm daily
Ruteng	120,000	9	7.30am daily

and Koposili villages, skirts a waterfall and returns to Moni without rejoining the highway.

Moni

Moni is a picturesque village sprinkled with upcountry rice fields, ringed by soaring volcanic peaks and blessed with distant sea views. It's a slow-paced, easy-going, cool breeze of a town that serves as a gateway to Kelimutu. On clear, dark moon nights, you'll walk the silent streets beneath a black dome universe. The turn-off to Kelimutu is 2km west of town. The Monday market, held on the soccer pitch, is a major local draw and a good place to snare local ikat.

Activities

Apart from the trek to/from Kelimutu, there are several other walks from Moni. About 750m along the Ende road from the centre of Moni, paths lead down to a 10m **air terjun** (waterfall), with a swimming hole and **air panas** (hot springs) near the falls. The trail branches to the left of Rainbow Cafe. There are more gorgeous hot springs in the middle of the rice fields at **Kolorongo** (3.5km from Moni) on the way to Kelimutu. Or walk south past the church to **Potu** and **Woloara** (about 2.5km from Moni).

Sleeping

Aside from the new ecolodge, Moni accommodation is virtually all in the budget to low midrange category and sprinkled along the highway (the town's only road). Guesthouses may book up in the June to August high season, so it makes sense to reserve ahead.

TOP CHOICE Kelimutu Ecolodge LODGE $$$
(☎0361 747 4205, 0813 5399 9311; www.ecolodgesindonesia.com; r/bungalows US$90/100; ❄) The sweetest spot in Moni is on the east end of town by the riverside where you'll find five thatched bungalows and five lodge rooms, all with pebbled tiles, hot water, solar power and outdoor sitting areas. The bungalows have outdoor baths, too. Great views of Kelimutu and surrounding rice fields bling from all angles, and they organise a variety of treks here.

Bintang Lodge GUESTHOUSE $$
(☎0812 3761 6940, 0852 3790 6259; www.bintang-lodge.com; Jl Trans Flores km 54; r 150-350,000Rp; ❄) Easily the best of the old guesthouse standbys, its two floors of new rooms are the cleanest and largest in the town centre. It also has hot water, which is nice on chilly mornings and evenings. The older bungalows have been open for years, and are a touch smaller but have a cute homey feel. Ownership is conscientious, and it draws a fun young crowd.

Christin Lodge GUESTHOUSE $
(☎0812 4659 4236; Jl Trans Flores; d without/with hot water 200,000/300,00Rp) A solid new addition. Rooms aren't fabulous, but they're new with fresh tiles, queen beds and hot water in the one superior room.

Watugana Bungalows LOSMEN $
(Jl Trans Flores; r 150,000-200,000Rp) You have two choices at this friendly budget haunt. Downstairs rooms are older and kept reasonably clean though they are dark and the bathrooms a bit moist. The new rooms upstairs are a steal. Fresh, new and bright.

Hidayah GUESTHOUSE $$
(☎0853 3901 1310; briandanros@gmail.com; Jl Trans Flores; d 200,000-300,000Rp) Four huge rooms with outstanding mountain and valley views from the common porch. The temperamental owner is a great source of trekking information, and organises car trips to west and east Flores.

Eating

Rainbow Café INDONESIAN $
(mains 15,000-25,000Rp) This little yellow bamboo cafe up the hill from Hidayah looks creative at first glance (its *nasi campur* is called 'hot gossip'), but the food is more of Moni's typical cheap and forgettable Indo and Western mains.

Chenty Restaurant & Café INDONESIAN/MONI $
(dishes 12,000-40,000Rp) Long-running, popular place with a nice porch overlooking the rice fields. The special here is the Moni cake (25,000Rp), a vegetable and mashed potato pie topped with cheese.

Hidayah Cafe CAFE $
(☎0853 3901 1310; briandanros@gmail.com; mains 15,000-40,000Rp; ⏲7am-10pm) The funky indoor-outdoor cafe, attached to the guesthouse of the same name, serves basics like nasi goreng, *ayam bakar*, and a take on the Moni cake called the Hidayah cake. Staff are lively and the owner is a terrific source of local trekking and transport information.

Getting There & Away

It's always best to travel in the morning, when buses are often half-empty. Afternoon buses are

BUSES & KIJANGS FROM MONI

DESTINATION	TYPE	COST (RP)	DURATION (HR)	FREQUENCY
Ende	bus	25,000	2	regularly, 7am-4pm
Ende	kijang	25,000	1½	regularly, 7am-9pm
Maumere	bus	40,000	4	regularly, 9am-6pm
Maumere	kijang	60,000-80,000	3½	regularly, 8am-9pm

usually overcrowded. Don't book through your homestay – hail the bus as it passes through town. Bintang Lodge (p366) rents motorbikes (per day 75,000Rp)

Around Moni

DETUSOKO

Wedged into the misty peaks above an emerald valley blanketed with rice fields is the friendly village of Detusoko. Located halfway between Ende and Moni, and just a 45-minute drive to Kelimutu, it's a great alternative to bunking in Moni. You can sleep at **Wisma Santo Fransiskus** (☎0812 4673 2839; d 125,000-175,000Rp), a convent with a dozen tidy guestrooms with private patios and mosquito nets. The cheaper rooms have better views, but shared baths. Breakfast is included and dinner is 50,000Rp. The best part? The place is managed by a mother superior beaming with loving kindness. She alone is worth seeking out.

PAGA

One of our favorite slices of Flores is the rice farming and fishing hamlet of Paga, halfway between Moni and Maumere. Its wide rushing river kissing the shore is a treat, so is the lovely beach and placid bay. But you're here to lunch at the fabulous **Restaurant Laryss** (☎0852 5334 2802; www.floresgids.com; Jl Raya Maumere-Ende; meals 40,000-75,000Rp, guided trips couples/groups 250,000/350,000Rp, with transport 750,000Rp), a tumbledown, beachfront fish joint, that is easily the best restaurant in Flores. Owner Agustinus Naban speaks German and English. Sometimes he has snapper, generally it's tuna, plucked fresh that morning, rubbed generously with turmeric and ginger, squeezed with lime and roasted on an open flame flavored with coconut shells. It will be served with red rice and a buttery sambal that is hot but not scalding and full flavored. Or get the soul-stirring *ikan kuah assam* (tamarind fish soup), an oily, savory, spicy broth swimming with a chunk of steamed fish.

If you fall in love with Agustinus after such a magnificent feast, and why wouldn't you, hire him as your guide, and he'll show you megalithic stone graves and amazing ocean views from the nearby village of **Nuabari**. You can barely see his restaurant from the road east of town and buses won't stop here, so you'll need private transport. Drivers know it well.

Maumere

☎0382 / POP 53,000

Blessed with a long, languid coastline backed by layered hills, Maumere, is one of the main gateways to Flores, and remains well connected with Bali and Timor, so you'll probably wind up here for a night. Yet despite recent, mostly effective, efforts to pave the crumbling streets and control its once overwhelming litter problem, this is not exactly a charming urban destination. Thankfully, you don't have to stay in the city. Snag one of the sweet beach bungalows on the coast.

Sleeping

There's one good budget choice in Maumere, and some terrific beach spots west of the city, and along the road to Larantuka in Waiara and Waiterang.

Hotel Sylvia HOTEL **$$**
(☎21829; Jl Gajah Mada 88; r from 300,000Rp; ❄📶) Yes, you could say it looks a bit too shabby, as new as this hotel is, and point out that the 'hot water' baths are luke warm at best, but rooms are spacious with wood floors, breakfast is a decent buffet, service is solid and there's wi-fi in the lobby.

Gardena Hotel HOTEL **$**
(☎22644; Jl Patirangga 28; r with fan/air-con 100,000/150,000Rp; ❄) Still the favoured budget choice among backpackers. There's

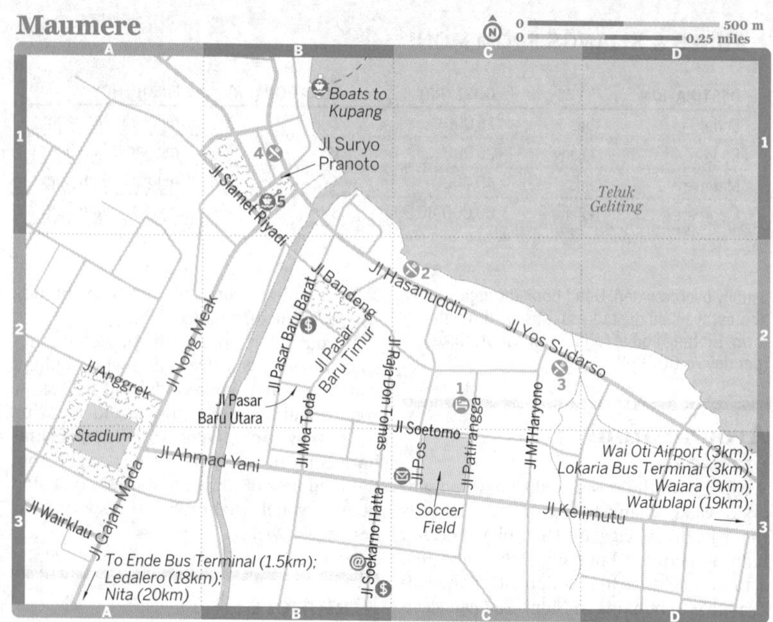

Maumere

Sleeping

Eating

Transport

a nice common space, but the basic tiled rooms – while they do come with breakfast and private *mandis* – are showing their age and were never that fabulous.

Gading Beach Hotel BUNGALOW $$
(☎0813 3910 1242; Jl Raya Don Siripe; r with fan 150,000Rp, bungalows with fan/air-con 200,000/250,000Rp; ❄) A three-year-old beach property, right on the sea, 8.5km west of town. This one is a collection of groovy rooms with high ceilings and artsy motifs on the walls, and even more charming bamboo bungalows with the same imaginative paint jobs. The barefoot bamboo restaurant has an upstairs terrace that catches the rare sea breeze. It's just a 5000Rp bemo ride into Maumere.

Wailiti Hotel BUNGALOW $$
(☎23416; Jl Raya Don Silva; bungalows 300,000-350,000Rp; ❄≋) Warm welcoming management will lead you to wooden bungalows with tin roofs set around a lovely pool area or along a black-sand beach with views of off-shore islands. Bungalows are spacious, clean and well kept with private porch and flat-screen TVs. It even has an in-house dive operation (two dives, 775,000Rp). It's 6.5km west of Maumere.

Eating

Maumere is known for its seafood.

Rumah Makan Jakarta SEAFOOD $
(☎0812 379 5559; meals 25,000-45,000Rp) Though it has been evicted from its harbour perch, this place remains popular for fresh fish, perfectly prepared and served almost instantly with a sensational roasted chilli *sambal* that will make you sweat.

Restaurant Gazebo SEAFOOD $$
(☎22212; Jl Yos Sudarso 73; meals 50,000-80,000Rp; ⏲9am-10pm Mon-Sat, 5-10pm Sun) A reasonably priced fish house. The spicy, *kuah asam* soup is delicious and the *ikan bakar* is nice too. Or perhaps it'll be the lobster tonight?

Golden Fish Restaurant SEAFOOD $$
(☎21667; Jl Hasanuddin; meals 50,000-150,000Rp) Walk through the open kitchen and peruse the day's live catch – including crab and lobster – on your way to the breezy second-storey dining room with a harbour view.

Information

Bank Danamon (Jl Pasar Baru Barat) Has an ATM.

BNI Bank (Jl Soekarno Hatta) Has the best exchange rates in town, an ATM, and a branch opposite the market in Geliting, on the way to Waiterang.

Flobamora Net (Jl Soekarno Hatta; per hour 5000Rp; 24 hr) Has a speedy internet connection.

Post office (Jl Pos) Next to the soccer field.

Getting There & Away

There are two bus terminals. Buses and Kijang heading east to Larantuka leave from the Lokaria (or Timur) terminal, 3km east of town. The Ende (or Barat) terminal, 1.5km southwest of town, is the place for westbound departures. Departure times are rarely precise – be prepared to wait around until there are sufficient passengers

There's a weekly **Pelni** (☎21013; Jl Suryo Pranoto) ferry for Kupang (15 to 18 hours).

Getting Around

TO/FROM THE AIRPORT Maumere's Wai Oti Airport is 3km from town, 800m off the Maumere–Larantuka road. A taxi to/from town is a non-negotiable, flat rate of 50,000Rp, 75,000Rp from the Wairara area or 125,000Rp from the beach hotels in Waiterang. It's a 1km walk out of the airport to the Maumere–Larantuka road where you can hop an *ojek* (10,000Rp) or bemo (2000Rp) into and around town.

CAR & MOTORCYCLE Car rental is 500,000Rp to 750,000Rp per day, including driver and fuel. Those organising road trips to Moni and further west should agree on an itinerary and a schedule of staggered payments before departure. PT Floressa Wisata and the Gardena Hotel (p367) can organise rental cars. Gardena staff can arrange motorbike (75,000Rp per day) rental.

Around Maumere

SIKKA & LELA

The highway descends through coconut and banana groves to the south coast weaving and fishing village of **Lela**, 22km from Maumere. Villagers live in bamboo huts sprinkled on a rocky black-sand beach. Around 4km further is the charming seaside village of **Sikka**, one of Flores' first Portuguese settlements. Its kings dominated the Maumere region until the 20th century. You'll be swarmed by ikat-*wallahs* as soon as you enter town, but they're a charming bunch. Buy one piece and all of them will smile. For a 20,000Rp to 50,000Rp donation you can watch them work the looms. But the big draw is Sikka's gorgeous, narrow Catholic **cathedral**, which dates from 1899. The open windows in the arched, beamed

TRANSPORT FROM MAUMERE

Air

DESTINATION	COMPANY	DURATION (HR)	FREQUENCY
Denpasar	Batavia Air, Wings Air	2	3 weekly
Kupang	Transnusa, Wings Air, Batavia Air, Merpati	1.5	daily
Makassar	Merpati	2	4 weekly

Bus & Kijang

DESTINATION	TYPE	COST (RP)	DURATION (HR)	FREQUENCY
Ende	bus	50,000	5	7am & 3pm daily
Ende	kijang	75,000	4½	7.30am daily
Larantuka	bus	40,000	4	7.30am & 3pm daily
Larantuka	kijang	60,000-75,000	3	7.30am daily
Moni	bus	30,000	3	7am & 3pm daily

eaves allow the sound of crashing waves to echo through the sanctuary.

The road to Sikka leaves the Ende road 20km from Maumere. Regular bemos (5000Rp) run from Maumere to Sikka.

WAIARA

Waiara is the departure point for the Maumere 'sea gardens', once regarded as one of Asia's finest dive destinations. The 1992 earthquake and tidal wave destroyed the reefs around Pulau Pemana and Pulau Besar, but they've recovered.

Just off the Larantuka road, 9km east of Maumere, in Waiara, you'll find the **Sea World Club** (Pondok Dunia Laut; ☎242 5089; www.sea-world-club.com; s/d cottages US$40/45, bungalows US$65/70; ❄). It's not just a suburban Maumere beach resort, it's an Indo-German Christian collaborative started to provide local jobs and build tourism. The simple, thatched cottages have wood floors and fresh paint, and the more modern and comfortable, air-conditioned bungalows have ikat bedspreads and hot water on a quiet black-sand beach with views of Pulau Besar. The restaurant is decent, and it has a dive shop (US$70 for two dives including gear).

To get here, catch any Talibura- or Larantuka-bound bus from Maumere to Waiara (3000Rp). Sea World Club is signposted from the highway.

AHUWAIR, WODONG & WAITERANG

The greater Maumere area does not get any more tranquil or beautiful than the narrow, palm-dappled beaches of **Ahuwair**, **Wodong** and **Waiterang**, 26km to 29km east of Maumere. There are two simple bungalow operations here and a shockingly inexpensive and classy barefoot resort with a scuba school.

There are many dive and snorkelling sites with lots of marine life around Pulau Babi and Pulau Pangabaton, a sunken Japanese WWII ship, and colourful microlife in the 'muck' (shallow mudflats). **Happy Dive** (☎0812 466 9667), based at Ankermi cottages, charges €55 for two dives, including gear and boat transfers. In November whale-watching trips are also offered, although you'll probably see migrating sperm whales spout from the beach.

Wodong, the main village in the area, is on the Maumere–Larantuka road. Take any Talibura, Nangahale or Larantuka bemo or bus from the Lokaria terminal in Maumere (3000Rp). A bemo from Wodong to Waiterang costs another 1000Rp. A taxi or chartered bemo from Maumere is around 50,000Rp. Buses and shared taxis to Larantuka pass by throughout the day.

Sleeping

All of the following places are signposted from the highway and are located down trails 10m to 500m from the road; they are listed in the order you approach them from Maumere. Rates include breakfast.

Sunset Cottages BUNGALOW $
(☎0821 4768 7254, 0812 4602 3954; www.sunsetcottagesflores.com; Maumere–Larantuka Rd Km 25; d with/without private bathroom 150,000/95,000Rp) Nestled on a secluded black-sand beach, with views of offshore islands, shaded by swaying coco palms, the seven thatched, coconut-wood and bamboo bungalows have Western toilets and *mandis,* with decks overlooking the sea. Snorkel gear is available for hire, and it offers overnight camping trips to the islands' deserted beaches. Order ahead for fresh fish.

TOP CHOICE **Lena House** BUNGALOW $
(☎0813 3940 7733; s/d 85,000/95,000Rp) Chill out in one of three clean bamboo bungalows, operated by a sweet family and set on a spectacular stretch of beach, with jungled mountains painted against the eastern horizon. Owners arrange snorkelling trips, but you may be just as happy to let your mind drift as you watch local fishermen ply the glassy bay in their dugouts. If you'd like a bit more privacy, you can opt to stay at **Lena 2**, an easy 10-minute walk down the beach. It's tidier and more secluded. It's convenient to stay here if you're diving with Happy Dive.

Ankermi BUNGALOW $$
(☎0812 466 9667; www.ankermihappydive.com; s/d 242,000/284,000Rp) These cute, tiled thatched bungalows have private porches with stunning sea views. The dive shop is the best in the Maumere area, they grow their own organic rice and vegetables on site, and meals are fresh and delicious. We suggest pumpkin soup and fish sate.

Larantuka

☎0383

A bustling little port of rusted tin roofs at the easternmost end of Flores, Larantuka rests against the base of **Gunung Ili Mandiri** (1510m), separated by a narrow strait from Pulau Solor and Pulau Adonara. It has a fun vibe at dusk, when street markets sell fresh fruit and fish, but most visitors stay just one night on their way to Kupang or Alor. Easter is a particularly good time to be in town, when there are huge processions of penitents and cross-bearers.

Sleeping & Eating

These three guesthouses are all set up in a row on the west end of town within walking distance of the Adonara pier and the night market.

TOP CHOICE Hotel Rulies GUESTHOUSE $
(☎21195; Jl Yos Sudarso 40; s/d/tr 75,000/120,000/150,000Rp) This funky spot near the harbour and across the street from the sea has clean rooms with concrete floors, saggy beds and private *mandis*. Management is warm and friendly, English-speaking and on top of current transport schedules.

Hotel Lesthari GUESTHOUSE $
(☎0852 5303 1152, 232 5517; Jl Yos Sudarso; r 200,000Rp; ❄) Newly done up rooms, some with double beds dressed in funky sheets, are air-conditioned, have private patios and are within walking distance to the pier.

Hotel Tresna GUESTHOUSE $
(☎21072; Jl Yos Sudarso 8; s/d 100,000/150,000Rp, with air-con 150,000/200,000Rp; ❄) Decent ceramic-tiled rooms with high ceilings, set around a garden courtyard.

Rumah Makan Nirwana INDONESIAN $
(Jl Yos Sudarso; meals 20,000-30,000Rp; ⏰7am-9pm) Still the one and only edible kitchen in town. Don't expect miracles, though the *soto ayam* (chicken soup) is tasty and the house *sambal*, scintillating.

Information

Most hotels, the ferry pier, shipping offices and the main bus terminal are in the southern part of town. Further northeast is the Muslim quarter, the post office, **Telkom Warnet** (per hour 7000Rp; ⏰24hr), which has solid internet access, and airport. **BNI bank** (Jl Fernandez 93) and **BRI bank** (Jl Udayana) both have branches with ATMs but neither exchanges currency.

Getting There & Away

Transnusa (☎232 5386, 0852 3910 9100) flys to Kupang three times a week. **Pelni** (☎21155; Jl Diponegoro) runs twice monthly ships to Kupang and weekly ferries to Kalabahi (Alor). There are also smaller wooden ferries to Kupang (71,000Rp to 128,000Rp, 15 hours) on Mondays and Fridays, and Kalabahi (75,000Rp, 24 hours) on Saturdays and Sundays. Flight and ferry schedules can shift and cancellations happen.

The main bus terminal is 5km west of town. Buses (40,000Rp, five hours) and Kijangs (60,000Rp to 75,000Rp, four hours) to Maumere run frequenty between 7am and 5pm.

Getting Around

Bemos (3000Rp) run up and down Jl Niaga and Jl Pasar, and to outlying villages. *Ojeks* also run to the pier and bus terminal for about 5000Rp.

ALOR ARCHIPELAGO

The final link of the island chain that stretches east of Java is wild, volcanic and drop-dead gorgeous. There are crumbling red-clay roads, jagged peaks, white-sand beaches and crystal-clear bays that have some remarkable diving – with plenty of pelagics and sheer walls draped in vast eye-popping coral gardens. The cultural diversity here is simply staggering. In this tiny archipelago alone there are over 100 tribes who, by some accounts, speak eight languages and 52 dialects. The terrain and lack of roads isolated the 185,000 inhabitants from one another and the outside world for centuries. Although the Dutch installed local rajas along the coastal regions after 1908, they had little influence over the interior, where people were still taking heads into the 1950s, and indigenous animist traditions endure. Though a network of new roads now covers the island, boats are still a common form of transport. The few visitors who land here tend to linger on nearby Pulau Kepa or dive these waters from liveaboards. But if you take the time to explore the tribal interior, you will meet some of the most upbeat, charming people on earth; folks who are always psyched to share their culture – and their home-cured tobacco – with visitors. And if you want to spend the night, all you have to do is ask.

Kalabahi

☎0386 / POP 59,000

Kalabahi is the chief town on Alor, located at the end of a spectacular 15km-long, palm-fringed bay on the west coast. Yet the town's main drag is a long, hot concrete sprawl that doesn't so much as hint at the sea. Thanks to the punishing heat, the streets only come to life in the morning, and again an hour before sundown, when the city park is a jumble of volleyball and basketball games.

ALOR OFFSHORE

The top destination in the entire Alor archipelago is **La Petite Kepa** (☎SMS only 0813 3910 2403; www.la-petite-kepa.com; bungalows incl meals per person 150,000-350,000Rp). This French-owned solar powered dive resort, the only nest on **Pulau Kepa**, offers 10 bungalows, three of which are replicas of traditional Alor homes and have shared baths. The others are more standard thatched woven bamboo *casitas* with attached outdoor baths, one of which is big enough for a whole family. All have sea and island views. The delicious meals, crafted from fresh ingredients (their *sambal* could launch a thousand ships), are eaten family style. There are two beaches on Kepa, including an exquisite sliver of white sand on the west side with spectacular sunset views and good snorkelling offshore. The owners offer two dives per day (€27 to €33 per dive, including equipment), with price breaks at six dives or more. Snorkelling equipment is available for 50,000Rp per day, and snorkellers can join the dive boat for 100,000Rp per day. In July and August it only reserves one bungalow for non-divers, as that's their busiest season. Phone service is hit and miss on Kepa, so to book your room send them an SMS a few days prior to your desired arrival.

Alor's dive operators regularly visit upwards of 30 dive sites, sprinkled throughout the archipelago. There are wall dives, slopes, caves, pinnacles and really good muck diving in the Alor bay. What makes Alor special isn't the huge number of pelagics, but rather the completely unspoiled reefs with intact hard and vibrant soft corals. The water is absolutely crystal clear. Dive sites are never crowded, and pelagic disclaimer aside you may well see a thresher shark, a pod of dolphins or even migrating sperm whales wander past. Just know, there is frequently unpredictable current and the water can be cold (as low as 22C), which is what keeps the coral well-nourished and spectacular. It's best to have 30 dives under your belt before venturing into these waters.

All divers must pay a marine park fee of 35,000Rp per day to fund the management of a 400,000-hectare marine park. At research time the WWF was trying to influence the government to develop a park management plan but so far it hasn't happened.

Sandwiched between Pantar and Alor is **Pulau Pura**, which has some of Alor's best dive sites. **Pulau Ternate**, not to be confused with the Maluku version, also has some magnificent dive and snorkel sites. (Who are we kidding, it's all magical here). **Uma Pura** is an interesting weaving village on Ternate, with a rather prominent wooden church. To get there charter a boat from Alor Besar or Alor Kecil (150,000Rp).

Sights

Museum Seribu Moko MUSEUM
(Jl Diponegoro; per person 10,000Rp; 7am-2pm Mon-Fri) Named for its collection of 1000 *moko* (bronze drums), this humble museum located just west of the market usually stays locked. But the office staff will open it so you can audit the drum collection (1000 is an ambitious figure) and the fine ikat, and assorted artefacts.

Activities

Scuba diving in Alor is exceptional. La Petite Kepa offers two dives for €60, including gear. Other scuba schools offering dives around the island include **Alor Dive** (☎222 2663, 0813 3964 8148; www.alor-dive.com; Jl Gatot Subroto 33) in Kalabahi, and Alor Divers (p373) on Pulau Pantar.

Sleeping

The most popular place to stay around Alor is La Petite Kepa (p372) on Pulau Kepa, near Alor Kecil.

Cantik Homestay HOMESTAY $
(☎21030, 0813 3229 9336; Jl Dahlia 12; r 150,000Rp; ❄) Set in a family home tucked into a residential neighbourhood are six simple, tiled, air-conditioned rooms. The owner rents motorbikes, and the home cooking here is sensational. Room rates include breakfast.

Hotel Pelangi Indah HOTEL $
(☎21251; Jl Diponegoro 34; s/d with fan 65,000/130,000Rp, with air-con 125,000/220,000Rp, VIP 185,000/275,000Rp; ❄) Set on the main drag, the reasonably well-tended rooms flank a flower garden, and the VIP rooms have new air-con units and spring-mattresses.

Standard air-con rooms are the same size and still good value.

Hotel Nur Fitra GUESTHOUSE $
(☎0813 5387 1891; Pasar Kadelang; d 200,000Rp; ❄) Tucked into the estuary, well off the road, spacious, octagonal VIP bungalows are a touch frayed, but they do have beamed ceilings, private decks with bamboo furnishings and mangrove views. The restaurant is decent, though service is slow. If you plan on diving with Alor Dive (p372), it will book your room here.

Eating

A half-dozen warungs set up near the harbour on **Pantai Reclamasi** (⏱7-11pm) and turn out tasty sate, *soto ayam, nasi goreng* and tremendous fresh grilled fish. It's also the closest thing to nightlife in Kalabahi.

TOP CHOICE **Restaurant Mama** INDONESIAN $$
(☎0813 5382 3280, 222 2845; mains 22,000-65,000Rp; ⏱10am-10pm) A brand new and very welcome addition, here's a wood and bamboo dining room perched over the bay on stilts, 50m west of the big waterfront market. It does all the seafood delights including two kinds of grilled fish, four flavours of fried fish and shrimp, as well as a locally lauded slow-cooked goat (order one day in advance). But the house special is an *ikan kuah asam mama*, an addictive local fish soup with a fiery, tamarind inflected broth. Be warned, karaoke will happen. It... can't... be... stopped.

TOP CHOICE **Cantik Homestay** SEAFOOD $
(☎0813 3229 9336; Jl Dahlia 12; meals per person 20,000-25,000Rp) The lady of the house at Cantik Homestay also does a ridiculously good *ikan kuah asam*, fries a whole fish to crispy moist perfection and makes a stunning veggie dish out of papaya flower. It may lack the location, choice and atmosphere of elsewhere, but you will not eat better for this price anywhere else in Nusa Tenggara. There's no menu and you won't need one.

Information

There are no currency exchange options on Alor, although there is a Visa/Plus ATM at the gleaming new **BNI Bank** (Jl Sutomo; ⏱8am-4pm Mon-Fri). There's a **Telkom office** (Jl Soetomo; ⏱24hr) about 2km north of town, and a **warnet** (Jl Martadinata Kampung Raya; per hr 5000Rp; ⏱24hr) next to the mosque near the harbour.

Getting There & Away

Merpati (www.merpati.co.id) and **Transnusa** (☎21039; Jl Sudirman 100) make the one-hour flight to Kupang. The **airport**, one of the most disorganised in the country, is 9km from Kalabahi, and offers one of the most dramatic approaches we've ever experienced. Line up early for check-in to avoid the hellish bottle neck. Departure tax is 10,000Rp.

Ferries leave from the **ferry terminal** 1km southwest of the town centre, a 10-minute walk or 2000Rp bemo ride.

Pelni (☎21195) ships leave from the main pier in the centre of town (the Pelni office is opposite the pier).There are weekly boats to Kupang (13 hours) and Larantuka (18 hours).

Getting Around

Transport around town is by red bemo (2000Rp). It's possible to rent a motorbike through Pak Chris at Cantik Homestay for 60,000Rp to 70,000Rp per day. He's also a dependable driver (per day 500,000Rp) who

WORTH A TRIP

PANTAR

The second-largest island of the Alor group is way off the beaten track. A daily ferry from Kalabahi docks at **Baranusa**, the island's sleepy main town, with a straggle of coconut palms, a **homestay**, and a couple of general stores. Smouldering Gunung Sirung (1372m) draws a few hearty climbers each year. From Baranusa take a truck to Kakamauta and walk for three hours to Sirung's crater. Bring water from Baranusa and stay with the *kepala desa* (50,000Rp) in **Kakamauta**.

Pantar is also home to the area's newest and most upscale dive resort. **Alor Divers** (☎0813 1780 4133; www.alor-divers.com; week-long dive packages from €890), built and operated by a French-Slovenian couple on the island's eastern shore, caters exclusively to divers and their plus-ones. Guests stay a minimum of six nights, in smart, thatched bungalows, and dive at least twice daily. Orcas, sperm and pilot whales migrate off the west coast in June and December.

FERRIES FROM KALABAHI

DESTINATION	COST (RP)	DURATION	FREQUENCY
Baranusa	35,000	2	8am daily
Kupang	70,000	18	Sun
Larantuka	75,000	24	Sun, Thu

speaks iffy English. *Ojeks* are easily hired for 100,000Rp per day.

Around Kalabahi

Takpala is a stunning traditional village etched into a hillside about 13km east of Kalabahi. There are several *lopo* (traditional high-roofed houses), held together with lashings scattered beneath mango trees, papaya and banana groves. The villagers are charming, and will be more than happy to teach you how to use a traditional bow and arrow, or roll you one of their home-cured cigarettes, which go well with a pinch of betel. To get here take a Mabu bus (3000Rp) from the terminal at Kalabahi market. Walk about 1km uphill on a sealed road from where the bus drops you off.

You can also do a fascinating village tour of Alor's bird's head. From Kalabahi head to **Mombang**, up through the clove trees and coffee plots of **Kopidil** to **Tulta**, and then down to the stunning sweep of white sand and coconut palms that is **Batu Putih**. It's backed by granite bluffs and cornfields, and cradles a turquoise and emerald lagoon 10km north of Mali. You'll either need to hire a motorbike (60,000Rp to 70,000Rp) or charter an *ojek* (100,000Rp per day) for this. Bring plenty of water, a boxed lunch, *sirih pinang* (betel nut), smokes, a few essential food items, and the best Bahasa Indonesia you've got to share with your new friends.

For hikers or motorbikers who like rugged back country, consider a longer, two or three days hiking along the verdant, mountainous spine of Central Alor. One route connects **Mainang** with **Kelaisi** and on to **Apui**. Another loop begins in **Ateng**, stops in **Melang** and ends in **Lakwati**. These are all very poor, pure traditional villages. The roads and trails are very bad and they are not easy trips. You'll be sleeping in basic village accomodation (per person 50,000Rp), and meals will be extremely basic too. Be prepared. Not all villages have latrines, and you'll need to bring extra food and water! The trip will be easier if you hire **Pak Marlon** (☎0853 3896 1214), an English- and German-speaking guide.

Nearby, the fishing village of **Alor Besar** is where you'll find **Al Quaran Tua**, a 12th-century Koran integral to the seeding of Islam in the Alor archipelago. Take care if you choose to handle the handmade parchment. It's held at the town mosque, **Masjid Jami Babussholah**, and is open to tourists by donation from sunrise to sundown.

There are also nice white-sand beaches in both Alor Besar and nearby **Alor Kecil,** with excellent snorkelling. The best is at **Sebanjar**, 3km north of Alor Kecil. The water here is wonderfully cool, with a gorgeous soft-coral garden offshore. Alor Kecil is also the jumping-off point for beautiful Pulau Kepa.

Buses and blue bemos to Alor Kecil (3000Rp, 30 minutes) and Alor Besar leave from the Kalabahi Pasar Inpres. You can also charter a bemo (50,000Rp) or a taxi from the airport (100,000Rp to 150,000Rp). If you're heading to Kepa, stop by the pier and the resort will ferry you across for free.

WEST TIMOR

With rugged countryside, empty beaches and scores of traditional villages, West Timor is an undiscovered gem. Deep within its mountainous, lontar palm–studded interior, animist traditions persist alongside tribal dialects, and ikat-clad, betel nut–chewing chiefs govern beehive-hut villages. Hit one of the many weekly markets in tribal country and you'll get a feel for rural Timor life, while eavesdropping on several of some 14 languages spoken on the island. In West Timor even Bahasa Indonesia is often a foreign tongue. Except in Kupang, its coastal capital and East Nusa Tenggara's top metropolis, which buzzes to a frenetic Indonesian beat.

History

The Tetum of central Timor are one of the largest ethnic groups on the island, and boast the dominant indigenous language. Before Portuguese and Dutch colonisation, they were fragmented into dozens of small states led by various chiefs. Conflict was common, and head-hunting a popular pastime.

The first Europeans in Timor were the Portuguese, who prized its endemic *cendana* (sandalwood) trees. In the mid-17th century the Dutch landed in Kupang, beginning a prolonged battle for control of the sandalwood trade, which the Dutch eventually won. The two colonial powers divvied up the island in a series of treaties signed between 1859 and 1913. Portugal was awarded the eastern half plus the enclave of Oecussi, the island's first settlement.

Neither European power penetrated far into the interior until the 1920s, and the island's political structure was left largely intact. The colonisers spread Christianity and ruled through the native aristocracy, but some locals claim Europeans corrupted Timor's royal bloodlines by aligning with imported, and eventually triumphant, Rotenese kingdoms. When Indonesia won independence in 1949 the Dutch left West Timor, but the Portuguese still held East Timor, setting the stage for the tragedy that continued until the East's independence in 2002.

During August 1999, in a UN-sponsored referendum, the people of East Timor voted in favour of independence. Violence erupted when pro-Jakarta militias, backed by the Indonesian military, destroyed buildings and infrastructure in East Timor, leaving up to 1000 dead before peacekeepers intervened. In West Timor, the militias were responsible for the lynching of three UN workers in Atambua in 2000, making West Timor an international pariah.

By 2006, relations had stabilised and transport links by road and air were thriving. Today, West Timor is among Indonesia's safest secrets.

Kupang

☎0380 / POP 340,000

Kupang is the capital of Nusa Tenggara Timur (NTT) and despite the city's scruffy waterfront, its sprawling gnarl of deafening traffic, and complete lack of endearing cultural or architectural elements, this is a place you can get used to. Chalk it up to Kupang's easy-to-navigate but still vaguely chaotic public transport system; the romantic, ramshackle Lavalon bar with its incredible oceanfront perch; and its funky, bass-heavy bemo fleet which

West Timor

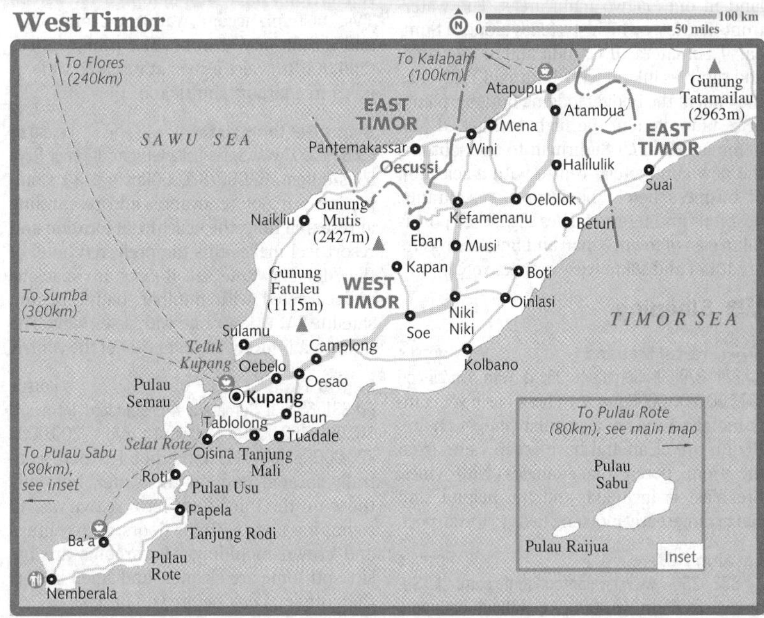

EAST TIMOR VISA RUN

Hitting Dili in East Timor is one way to renew your Indonesian visa from Nusa Tenggara. If you decide to go, be aware that East Timor is considerably more expensive than Indonesia and the return trip normally takes more than a week by the time you've got to Dili, hung around for your visa and returned to West Timor.

Apply for your visa to East Timor at the Timor Leste Consulate in Kupang with a valid passport, a photocopy and passport photos. It costs US$30 and takes three working days to process. Next, book a Dili-bound minibus from Kupang, which will take you to the border and an onward bus for the 2½ hour trip to Dili.

The next morning, head to the Indonesian consulate for your new tourist visa (US$35). The consulate is near the Pertamina office on the western outskirts of Dili. Travellers have been issued with 60-day visas here upon request. Visas take five working days to issue, though some persuasive visitors have received theirs in three. Enjoy Dili's delights then run the route in reverse.

Direct minibuses (10 to 11 hours) to Dili are operated by **Timor Tour & Travel** (☎881543; 185,000Rp), **Paradise** (☎0813 3944 7183, 830 414; standard/executive 175,000/200,000Rp) and **Livau** (☎821892; 185,000Rp). Call for a hotel pick-up.

ferries Kupang's young, diverse student population. Kupang is a university town, after all. It's also a regional transport hub, so you will do some Kupang time. Just don't be surprised if between trips to the interior, Alor or Rote, you discover that you actually dig it. England's Captain Bligh had a similar epiphany when he spent 47 days here after that emasculating mutiny on the *Bounty* incident in 1789.

Kupang sprawls and you'll need to take bemos or *ojeks* to get around. You will likely land in one of two main areas. The waterfront district – which stretches along Jl Sumba, Jl Sumatera, Jl Garuda and Jl Siliwangi, and rambles inland with Jl Ahmad Yani – has the bulk of the budget lodging options, plenty of restaurants and the night market. Jl Mohammad Hatta/Jl Sudirman to the south, is the new commercial centre with a selection of business hotels, bookstores, restaurants, hospitals and internet cafes. El Tari airport is 15km east of town; Tenau and Bolok harbours are 10km and 13km west, respectively.

Sleeping

TOP CHOICE Hotel Maliana MOTEL $

(☎821 879; Jl Sumatera 35; d with fan/air-con 130,000/200,000Rp; ❄📶) These basic yet comfy motel rooms are a popular budget choice. Rooms are clean and have ocean views from the front porch that dangles with vines. Breakfast is included, and the helpful staff can arrange early morning taxis to the airport.

Lavalon B&B HOSTEL $

(☎832 236; www.lavalontouristinfo.com; Jl Sumatera 8; dorm 40,000Rp, r without bathroom 55,000Rp) The best value in town with clean, ceramic-tiled rooms and Western-style bathrooms. Guests can use the kitchen. Run by the much-loved, living NTT encyclopedia, Edwin Lerrick.

Hotel T-More HOTEL $$

(☎881 555; Jl Piet A Tallo; s/d 625,000/750,000Rp; ❄📶) Timor's newest hotel, and the closest to the airport, is arguably the best hotel in Kupang. Rooms sprawl around an interior atrium, offer wall-mounted flat-screen TVs, tasteful accent wallpaper, mini bar, and a built-in wardrobe. The promo prices (299,000Rp) were a steal at research time. It has a free airport shuttle too.

Swiss Bel Inn Kristal RESORT $$

(☎825 100; www.swiss-belhotel.com; Jl Timor Raya 59; s/d from 762,000/871,000Rp; ❄📶🏊) Completing a major renovation and rebranding at research time, the beachfront location and resort feel makes this the preferred hotel of the Alor and Rote set. Rooms are spacious and carpeted with minibar, bathtubs, and satellite TV. Ask for one with a sea view. The pool area is lovely. It's 2km east of the centre.

Pantai Timor HOTEL $

(☎831 651; Jl Sumatera 44; standard from s/d 140,000/160,000Rp, deluxe s/d 200,000/220,000Rp; ❄) This large hotel is both centrally located and on the water, but only those on the third floor have sea views. All rooms are huge with tile floors, high ceilings and crown mouldings. Bathrooms are basic, and some are cleaner (and smell better) than others. Look before you nest!

Eating & Drinking

Kupang was never considered a particularly exciting town, and until the lamp-lit **pasar malam** (Jl Garuda; dishes from 10,000Rp; ⏱6-10pm) was launched, there was nothing much to do at all. These days, however, Jl Garuda is closed to motorised traffic after sun down when it's the domain of streetside grill, and wok chefs prepare inexpensive fish (choose yours from the cooler), chicken and vegetable dishes. As inviting as it is, however, know that some travellers have reported food poisoning after eating here.

TOP CHOICE **Rumah Makan Palembang** CHINESE **$$**
(☎0821 4796 6011; Jl Mohammad Hatta 2; dishes 17,500-85,000Rp; ⏱10am-2:30pm & 6-11pm) This is first-rate Chinese Indonesian food, and among the best restaurants in NTT. Get the *ikan bakar rica rica* (grilled fish with chilli sauce). Its sauce is a sweet, smoky wonder. The squid and shrimp are fresh daily, the veggies are perfectly cooked, and do not sleep on that beautiful cucumber *sambal*. If you like spicy pickle, you'll be thrilled.

Rumah Makan Wahyu Putra Solo PADANG **$**
(☎821 552; Jl Gunung Mutis 31; meals 10,000-25,000Rp; ☑) Kupang's best pick-and-mix warung offers beef, chicken, fish, potatoes and greens, deep- and stir-fried, stewed in coconut sauce, and chilli-rubbed and roasted. Vegetarians will find something tasty here.

Kupang

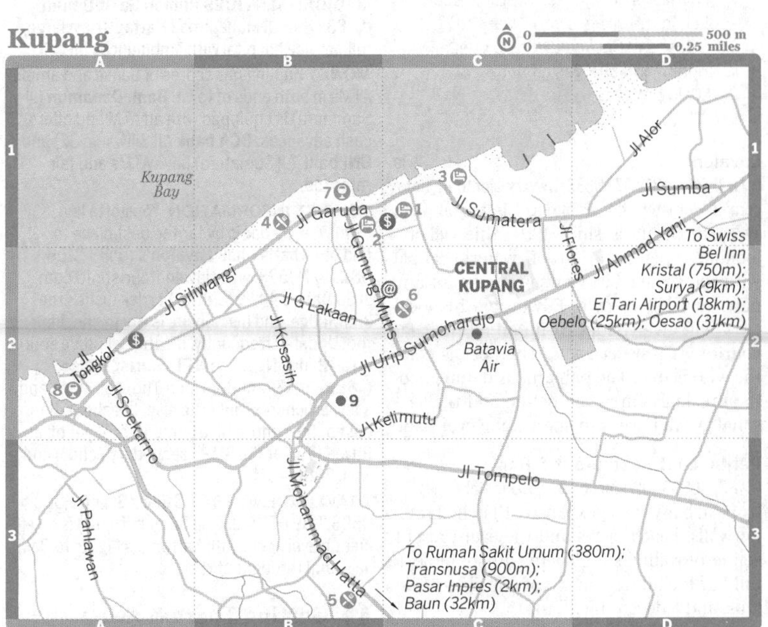

Kupang

Sleeping

1 Hotel Maliana ... C1
2 Lavalon B&B ... B1
3 Pantai Timor ... C1

Eating

4 Pasar Malam ... B1
5 Rumah Makan Palembang ... B3
6 Rumah Makan Wahyu Putra Solo ... C2

Drinking

7 Lavalon ... B1
8 Pantai Laut Restaurant & Bar ... A2

Information

Lavalon ... (see 7)
9 PT Stindo Star ... B2

EXPLORING TIMOR

Kupang is a gateway to West Timor's fascinating and welcoming traditional villages. Bahasa Indonesia – let alone English – is often not spoken, so a local guide is advisable. **Oney Meda** (☎0813 3940 4204) is a highly recommended English-speaking guide with 15 years of experience who organises anthropological tours and treks throughout West Timor and Alor. His guiding services run from 300,000Rp to 600,000Rp per day depending on the itinerary.

Eben Oematan (☎0852 3795 8136) has 25 years of experience and is also a rock-solid choice. He's from Kapan, which means he speaks several dialects spoken in the villages you'll want to visit. Based in Soe, he picks up guests in Kupang and charges a flat rate of 300,000 per day.

Lavalon PUB
(☎832 256, 0812 377 0533; www.lavalontouristinfo.com; Jl Sumatera 44; ⌚8am-as late as you want; @📶) In business since 1994, this rickety-looking, open-air, tin-roof watering hole with spectacular sea views is a must for any new traveller in town. Edwin and his local crew will give you an earful on all their favourite NTT sweet spots. The beer is cold, the wi-fi is free. The pub grub is damn good, the breakfasts are even better, and the seasonal guava juice is the best we've ever had.

Pantai Laut Restaurant & Bar BAR
(☎802 0999; Jl Tongkol 3; ⌚10am-late; 📶) A tropical bar with an expansive thatched roof, no walls, beach views and the ever-present sound of rolling surf. There's a pool table, a full bar including a menu of day-glow cocktails, and a decent menu too.

Shopping

Kupang's main shopping mall is the **Flobamora** (Jl Lamamentik), 3km southeast of town. Take bemo 6 from the roundabout at Jl Beringin.

The main market is the rambling **Pasar Inpres** (⌚7am-4pm) off Jl Soeharto in the south of the city. To get there, take bemo 1 or 2 and follow the crowd.

Sandalwood oil is something of a local specialty. You can buy oils of varying quality at the shops in the old town, off Jl Garuda. The purest oils are upwards of 300,000Rp for a small vial.

Ina Ndao TEXTILES
(☎821 178; Jl Kebun Raya II; ⌚8am-7pm Mon-Sat) It's worth seeking out this neighbourhood ikat shop. Textile lovers should be pleased with the wares sourced from across NTT. They offer naturally and chemically dyed varieties, and demonstrate the weaving process upon request.

Information

INTERNET ACCESS & TELEPHONE Lavalon is a wi-fi hub for thirsty laptop luggers. **Ratunet** (Jl Gunung Mutis 31, 2nd floor; per hour 4,000Rp; ⌚24hr) is the best choice if you're looking for an air-conditioned warnet.

MEDICAL SERVICES **Rumah Sakit Umum** (☎832 892; Jl Mohammad Hatta 19) is a large, full-service hospital with ambulances on call.

MONEY Kupang has scores of banks and ample ATMs in both ends of town. **Bank Danamon** (Jl Sumatera) is equipped with an ATM and offers cash advances. **BCA bank** (Jl Siliwangi 37) and **BNI bank** (Jl Sumatera) have ATMs and fair rates too.

TOURIST INFORMATION You gotta love a town where a bar is by far the best place to find out what's what. **Lavalon's** (☎832 256, 0812 377 0533; www.lavalontouristinfo.com; Jl Sumatera 44; 📶) Edwin Lerrick dishes the knowledge, and his website is worth checking too. Updated freqeuntly, it's the definitive source on all things NTT. The **NTT Tourist Office** (☎21540; ⌚7am-3pm Mon-Thu) has maps and a few brochures, but little else. It's about 4km east of the centre; take bemo 10 or 7, get off at Jl Raya El Tari at the SMP5 secondary school and walk 200m east.

TRAVEL AGENCIES **PT Stindo Star** (☎809 0583, 809 0584; Jl Urip Sumohardjo 2) is an efficient travel agency that arranges flights to Bali, Java and throughout NTT.

Getting There & Away

Kupang is the most important hub for air travel in Nusa Tenggara. Frequent flights to Surabaya and Denpasar offer easy connections to Jakarta. Departure tax is 20,000Rp for domestic flights and 70,000Rp for non-existent international flights. The Pelni office is near the waterfront.

Getting Around

To/From the Airport

Kupang's El Tari Airport is 15km east of the town centre. Taxis from the airport to town cost a fixed 60,000Rp. For public transport, turn left out of the terminal and walk 1km to the junction with the main highway, from where bemos to town cost 3000Rp. Going to the airport, take the Penfui bemo to the junction and walk.

Bemo

A ride in one of Kupang's unique bass-thumping hip-hop bemos (2000Rp) is one of the city's essential experiences. Windscreens are festooned with either girlie silhouettes, Jesus of Nazareth, his mum, or English football stars. The low-rider paint job is of the *Fast & Furious* technicolour variety, while banks of subwoofers will have your ass involuntarily shaking to the drivers' C-list hip-hop soundtrack. They stop running by 9pm.

Kupang is too spread out to walk. The bemo hub is the Kota Kupang terminal. Useful bemo routes:

1 & 2 Kuanino–Oepura; passing many popular hotels.

5 Oebobo–Airnona–Bakunase; passing the main post office.

6 Goes to the Flobamora shopping mall and the post office.

10 Kelapa Lima–Walikota; from terminal to the tourist office, Oebobo bus terminal and East Nusa Tenggara Museum.

TRANSPORT FROM KUPANG

Air

DESTINATION	COMPANY	DURATION (HR)	FREQUENCY
Bajawa	Merpati, Transnusa	1¼	6 days weekly
Denpasar	Merpati, Garuda	2	2 daily
Jakarta	Merpati	4	daily
Kalabahi	Merpati, Transnusa	1	daily
Labuanbajo	Merpati	1½	2 weekly
Larantuka	Transnusa	1¼	3 weekly
Makassar	Merpati, Transnusa	2½	5 weekly
Maumere	Merpati, Transnusa, Wings Air	1	daily
Ruteng	Merpati, Transnusa	1½	6 days weekly
Surabaya	Batavia Air, Wings Air	2½	daily
Tambolaka	Merpati, Transnusa	1½	6 days weekly
Waingapu	Merpati, Batavia Air, Aiastar	1	6 days weekly

Bus

DESTINATION	COST (RP)	DURATION (HR)	FREQUENCY
Kefamenanu	45,000	5½	7am, 9am, noon, 5pm
Niki Niki	35,000	3½	hourly, 5am-6pm
Soe	25,000	3	hourly, 5am-6pm

Boat

DESTINATION	TYPE	COST (RP)	DURATION (HR)	FREQUENCY
Kalabahi	ferry	79,000-149,000	17	Tue & Sat
Larantuka	ferry	71,000-128,000	15	Sun & Thu
Larantuka	Pelni	varies	varies	weekly
Maumere	Pelni	varies	varies	2 monthly
Rote	ferry	50,000	5	9am daily
Rote	Bahari Express	120,000-165,000	2	9am daily
Waingapu	ferry	73,000-230,000	13	Mon & Fri

OJEK WARNING

Sexual assault against women by their *ojek* drivers has become an issue in Kupang. Don't hail an *ojek* randomly. Ask hotel staff to recommend someone.

Several bemos use names instead of numbers. *Tenau* and *Belok Harbour* bemos run to the docks. The *Penfui* bemo links to the airport.

Car & Motorcycle

It's possible to rent a car with a driver from 400,000Rp to 750,000Rp per day, depending upon the destination. Motorcycles cost around 60,000Rp per day. You can arrange one at your hotel or ask Edwin at Lavalon (p378).

Around Kupang

OENESU

Hidden in this sleepy farming village just off the Kupang–Tablolong road is an impressive three-stage, turquoise-tinted waterfall (admission 2000Rp). There's a nice swimming hole beneath the last cascade. Locals love it, which explains the profound rubbish issue. The turn-off is 13km from Kupang near Tapa village, serviced by regular bemos from Tabun. From the main road it's a 2.5km walk to the falls. Take the road to Sumlili; after the Immanuel church turn and walk 800m along a rough road.

OEBELO & OESAO

Oebelo, a small salt-mining town 22km from Kupang on the Soe road, is notable for a terrific Rotenese musical-instrument workshop, **Sasandu** (0813 3913 7007, 0852 3948 7808), run by Pak Pah and his family. Traditional 20-stringed harps, aka *sasando* (featured on the 5000Rp note), are made and played in all sizes. Pak may treat you to a haunting instrumental number, or a perversion of *Yellow Submarine*.

Oesao is another 6km down the road and has a war memorial dedicated to the 2/40th Australian Infantry Battalion. It also happens to have one marvellous sweets shop. **Cucur Sitepu Oesao** (4am-10pm), located just east of the main market serves a variety of traditional Timorese cakes. Our favorites were the pancakes stuffed with cream and the sublime flying saucer–shaped discs of fried dough stuffed with candied rice. Your driver will know the place. Stock up for the road.

Soe

0388 / POP 31,000

About 110km from Kupang, the cool, leafy market town of Soe (800m) makes a decent base to explore West Timor's interior, which comes dotted with ubiquitous *ume kebubu* (beehive-shaped hut) villages that are home to local Dawan people. With no windows and only a 1m-high doorway, *ume kebubu* are cramped and smoky. Government authorities have deemed them a health hazard and are in the process of replacing them with cold concrete boxes, which the Dawan have deemed a health hazard. They've built new *ume kebubu* behind the approved houses, and live there.

Sleeping

Hotel Bahagia II HOTEL $$
(21095; Jl Gajah Mada 55; standard/VIP/deluxe 185,000/265,000/290,000Rp, cottages 300,000-725,000; @) Soe's best choice with a range of spacious, tiled rooms, queen and double beds (with wooden headboards), and a few cottages that make sense for families. All rooms are fan-cooled, but you won't need air-con here anyway.

Hotel Jati Asih HOTEL $
(22407; Jl Tien Soeharto; economy/standard/VIP 150,000/190,000/225,000Rp) The newest hotel in town doesn't look all that new. Rooms are massive, fan-cooled and have windows facing an inner courtyard. They're reasonably clean with wooden beds and VIP rooms have hot water. You'll see it on the left as you roll into Soe.

Hotel Gajah Mada HOTEL $$
(21197; Jl Gajah Mada; standard/VIP r 250,000/400,000Rp) Well situated above the valley and, as it happens, the town's utility (you'll hear that generator hum all night). Rooms are huge, comfortable and clean with queen beds, crown mouldings, TV and hot water. There are nice mountain views from the second-storey terrace.

Eating

Bundo Kanduang PADANG $
(0813 3947 0896; Jl Gajah Mada; meals 25,000-35,000Rp) If you've been waiting to find a fresh spot to try Padang food, this is it. There are devilled eggs with chilli, fried and cur-

ried fish, *rendang*, stewed veggies, and potato cakes. Almost everything is spicy and it all rocks. It's 1.5km west of Soe centre.

Rumah Makan Favorite INDONESIAN $
(☎21031; Jl Diponegoro 38; dishes 10,000-25,000Rp) The hippest spot in Soe. You'll dig the 1970s paint job, tablecloths and silk flowers. The menu is all chicken and shrimp dishes made to order, and the fresh ginger muffins are lovely.

Shopping

If you're interested in antiques and handicrafts, do not miss **Timor Art Shop** (☎21419; Jl Bill Nope 17; ⊙by appointment) where you'll find Timor's best selection of masks, sculpture and carvings at unbelievable prices. There's no sign, so call owner Alfred Maku before coming over. He speaks excellent English.

Information

The **tourist information centre** (☎21149; Jl Diponegoro) has good detail on the surrounding area and is the best place to arrange guides. Both **BNI** (Jl Diponegoro) and **BRI** (Jl Hatta) banks have ATMs, but exchange rates are poor. At research time there was no working warnet in Soe.

Getting There & Away

The Haumeni bus terminal is 4km west of town (2000Rp by bemo). Regular buses go from Soe to Kupang (25,000Rp, three hours), Kefamenanu (15,000Rp, 2½ hours) and Oinlasi (20,000Rp, two hours), while bemos cover Niki Niki (5000Rp) and Kapan (5000Rp).

Around Soe

OINLASI

Regular buses from Soe (20,000Rp, two hours) make the 51km trip along a twisted, rutted mountain road to Oinlasi. The painful drive is worth it, especially on Tuesdays, when a traditional market spreads for blocks along a ridge overlooking two valleys. Villagers from the surrounding hills, many of whom wear traditional ikat, descend to barter, buy and sell weavings, carvings, masks and elaborately carved betel-nut containers, along with fruit, livestock, local sweets and some of the worst popular music ever recorded. The market starts early in the morning and continues until 2pm, but is at its best before 10am.

If you want to immerse yourself in Timor life or troll the surrounding villages for handicrafts, stay the night 1.5km from Oinlasi at **Sungar Budaya** (r incl 3 meals 100,000Rp), a simple homestay in Desa Anin, with just two clean rooms with concrete floors.

BOTI

Hidden out of sight on an isolated mountain ridge 12km from Oinlasi, and accessible only by a degrading mountain road that's often impassable without a 4WD, is the traditional, almost orthodox, village of Boti, where the charismatic *kepala suku* (chief), often referred to as the last king in West Timor, has vowed to maintain the strict laws of *adat*. He's also the only king we've ever heard of who works the fields side by side with his people.

The Boti people have maintained their own language, lived off their own land (they grow bananas, corn, papaya, rice, pumpkin, coconuts and a cash crop of peanuts) their own way (they live by a nine-day week and always rest on that 9th day), and have steadfastly refused government assistance of any kind. Their autonomy was given an early assist when the Dutch colonial powers never found Boti. Neither did the head hunters before them, which allowed them to live peacefully in an isolated corner of Timor, unmolested, for centuries.

Villagers wear shirts, ikat sarongs and shawls made only from locally grown and hand-spun cotton thread coloured with natural dyes. Men are encouraged to marry outside the village and bring their new wife back into the fold. After marriage the men must let their hair grow long. Similiar to Rastas, their hair is viewed as their connection to nature. Their head is like the mountain, they say, and their hair, like the trees. Cutting their hair-trees is considered a bad omen and carries a fine, payable to the... well, to the king.

Women, on the other hand, are forever shunned if they marry outside the village, and children are only allowed to attend primary school. High school is forbidden, as it is considered by elders to be the key to unhappiness, which may sound familiar. The Boti people also use their own brand of plant-based medicine to treat illness, infection and disease. Boti's 316 villagers (70 families) still follow ancient animist rituals, though another 700 neighbouring families who live in Boti's geographical sphere of influence have adopted Protestantism and attend public schools.

They have been hosting guests since 1981, but see less than 300 visitors per year. Make sure you're one of them. This place is magical. On arrival you will be led to the raja's house, where, in keeping with tradition, you will offer betel nut to the chief as a gift. It's possible to stay in the leafy, cool, charming village, in your own lovely lontar guesthouse, and sleep on soft beds swathed with local ikat. All meals are provided for 100,000Rp per person, and for another 100,000Rp the wives and mothers will play their early days gamelan and sing a haunting tune. The king will strum his indigenous ukelele and young women will twirl in the village courtyard before the young men demonstrate their war dance. Day-trippers are expected to contribute a donation, as well (25,000Rp should work).

The Boti king requests that you do not visit independently; bring a guide from Soe conversant with local *adat*. But you won't need mosquito repellent. Somehow there are no mosquitoes here.

Getting There & Away

The newer Niki Niki road was blocked by a landslide and has been impassable since 2010. Instead, you'll have to come through Oinlasi, on a road passable only by motorcycles or 4WD vehicles. Make sure to bring water from Soe. You can hire a 4WD in Soe for 750,000Rp or hop an *ojek* from Niki Niki for 50,000Rp. From Kupang, a car to Boti – including an overnight – costs 1,500,000Rp.

NONE

About 18km east of Soe is Kefa's last head-hunting village and one of the area's best attractions. A trail begins 1km from where the bemo will drop you off on the main road. Stroll past corn and bean fields and hop over a stream and you'll reach scattered *ume bubu* (traditional beehive huts), home to 52 families that have lived here for nine generations. Parents still bury their baby's placenta in the centre of their hut, and the village is protected by a native rock fort, which abuts a sheer cliff. At the cliff's edge you'll find a 200-year-old banyan tree and a totem pole where shamans once met with warriors before they left on head-hunting expeditions. The wise ones consulted chicken eggs and their wooden staff before predicting if the warriors would prevail. Villagers are warm and welcoming, and break out their looms at the village *lopo* (meeting place) for weaving demonstrations upon request. It is so peaceful here that it's hard to believe they were taking heads just two generations ago.

Kefamenanu

☎0388 / POP 33,000

A former Portuguese stronghold, Kefamenanu was just another quiet hill town as recently as 2007, but with a manganese boom in full effect, commerce has arrived along with new construction and a fair bit of clear-cutting in the leafy outskirts. It remains devoutly Catholic and has a couple of impressive colonial churches. There's a decent choice of rooms in town, though with a mining boom comes a certain variety of night commerce, and all hotels provide shelter for such transactions. Still, it is the jumping-off point to Temkessi, one of West Timor's 'can't miss' villages. Known locally as Kefa, it lies at the heart of an important weaving region. Prepare to haggle with the ikat cartel.

Sleeping & Eating

TOP CHOICE Hotel Litani HOTEL $$
(☎233 258; Jl Pasar Baru; economy 100,000-150,000Rp, standard/VIP 250,000/350,000Rp; ❄)

THE MIDWIFE

Living in her dark, smoky beehive hut in the head-hunting village of None is a humble silver-haired woman, with *sirih-* (betel nut) stained lips, a generous smile and a gift. Helena Talam is a midwife, and for more than three decades she's delivered all the village children and hundreds, maybe thousands of others whose mothers come from kilometres away to see 'the one with blessed fingers'. As she tends the cook fire in the centre of her hut, the smoke snaking into the roof's storage cavity preserving bushels of rice and corn, she says 'I never studied as a nurse, what I have is a blessing from God.' She shares her wisdom with other Timorese midwives freely. 'They listen because I have never had a fatality. I just want to make mothers' lives easier and safer before, during and after delivery.' And while the government has built her a modern home that seems a good deal cleaner, she isn't moving. 'I prefer to stay here', she says.

Rooms at this brand new option are large, tiled affairs with high ceilings, crown mouldings and pastel paint jobs. VIP rooms have TV and air-con. All are super clean and have *mandis* rather than showers. Economy rooms are slightly smaller and have shared baths. Unsigned from the main drag (Jl El Tari), you'll find it down a gravel road that accesses the Pasar Baru (new market).

Hotel Ariesta HOTEL **$$**
(☎31007; Jl Basuki Rahman 29; economy/standard/superior/suites 100,000/150,000/225,000/300,000Rp; ❄) Set on a leafy backstreet, this long-time budget joint is still rocking with a newer annex behind the weathered original. Older rooms are sizeable but scruffy with scuffed walls and saggy beds. The new all-suite annex boasts firm beds, fresh paint, plenty of light, hot-water showers, air-con, TV and a private porch out front.

Hotel Livero HOTEL **$$**
(☎233 2222; Jl El Tari; standard/deluxe/business 250,000/300,000/350,000Rp; ❄) The airy lobby has grace, and the rooms are decent with wooden bed-frames, and flat-screen TVs. A few standard rooms have private terraces in the tree tops, but some have no windows at all, or have been tainted by nicotine. Sniff before you commit.

Litani INDONESIAN **$**
(Jl El Tari; dishes 15,000-45,000Rp) If you're over Padang food, dine in these breezy bamboo environs, and munch fresh fish, prawns and squid – grilled or fried – dive into a noodle or rice dish or opt for the rather tasty baked chicken.

Rumah Makan Kota Sari INDONESIAN **$**
(☎31872; Jl El Tari; mains 30,000-35,000Rp; ⊙8am-10pm) A humble, Chinese Indonesian diner where you can buy trophies, silk flowers, lunch or all of the above. Seriously, it gets good marks for its beef, fish, squid and shrimp dishes, wok fried eight different ways.

ℹ Information

Kefa stretches in all directions from the old market, *pasar lama*, which is around 2.5km north of the bus terminal. Use the Visa-compatible ATM at the gleaming new **Danamon Bank** (Jl Kartini).
Dinas Pariwisata (☎21520; Jl Sudirman), the tourist office, opposite the field north of the highway, can help locate a guide.

ℹ Getting There & Around

The new bus terminal is in Kefamenanu's center, 50m from the Jl El Tari market, which blooms most days. From here there are regular buses to Kupang (45,000Rp, 5½ hours), Soe (15,000Rp, 2½ hours) and Atambua (15,000Rp, two hours), on the East Timor border, from 6am until about 4pm. Hotel Ariesta rents motorbikes for 60,000Rp per day. Rental cars in Kefa run 550,000Rp per day with driver.

Around Kefamenanu

OELOLOK

Oelolok, a weaving village 26km from Kefa by bus and a further 3km by bemo, is home to **Istana Rajah Taolin**, a massive beehive hut with a huge outdoor patio and carved beams dangling with corn from decades of harvests. Royals have lived here for five generations, and its current residents are more than happy to share the myths and legends of their culture and kingdom. Ask about the power of the 'sword with seven lines'.

TEMKESSI & AROUND

Accessible through a keyhole between jutting limestone cliffs, 50km northeast of Kefa, is one of West Timor's most isolated and best-preserved villages. The raja's house overlooks the village. That's your first stop, where you'll offer gifts of betel nut, make a donation and pay your respects. After that you can shoot pictures of the low-slung beehive huts built into the bedrock and connected by red clay paths that ramble to the edge of a precipice. If you drop something, don't pick it up. Let local villagers do it, lest you bring bad vibes into your life. Oh, and about that vertical rock on the left. At least once every seven years, young warriors climb its face, *sans* rope, with a red goat strapped to their back. They slaughter the animal on top and can't come down until they roast and eat it in full. This Natamamausa ritual is performed to give thanks for a good harvest or to stop or start the rain. Very little Bahasa Indonesia is spoken here, so a guide is essential.

Regular buses run from Kefa to Manufui, about 8km from Temkessi. On market day in Manufui (Saturday), trucks or buses should run through to Temkessi. Otherwise, charter an *ojek* in Manufui or hike over limestone ridges with Oecussi sea views.

Maubesi is home to the Kefa regency's best textile market. You'll find it 19km from Kefa on the road to Temkessi. Market day is Thursday, when goods are spread beneath

THE STORY OF SEVEN

Ethnic Timorese are known as the 'people of the sunrise' and trace their ancestry back to seven sisters who came down to earth from the sun for a bath. A lustful man watched as they bathed, and hid the most beautiful sister's robes. Naked and ashamed, she was left behind, and eventually became mother of the Timorese people.

The number seven permeates Timor. Their sacred swords have seven lines, special rituals are carried out every seven years, and seven also symbolises completion of the human life cycle; from birth, through childhood and adulthood, to marriage and the cultivation of wisdom, and finally death and the merging of the soul back into the universe.

riverside shade trees. Sometimes cockfights break out. **Maubesi Art Shop** (☎0852 8508 5867) has a terrific selection of local ikat, antique masks, statues, and carved beams, reliefs and doors from old Timorese homes. Prices are quite low. Look for the plain yellow-and-black 'Textile' sign. It can also organise traditional war dances (1,000,000Rp) with advance notice.

ROTE

A slender, rain-starved limestone jewel with powdery white-sand beaches and epic surf, Rote floats just southwest of West Timor, but has an identity all of its own. From a tourism perspective it's all about the surf, which can be gentle enough for beginners and sick enough for experts. Stunning Pantai Nemberala is home to the world-renowned T-Land break, and there are dozens of hidden white-sand beaches, aquamarine lagoons, and seldom-surfed waves on the beaches south and north of Nembrala. To find them you'll roll through thatched traditional villages, over natural limestone bridges and through an undulating savannah that turns from green in the November to March 'wet season' to gold in the 'dry season' which also happens to be when the offshore winds fold swells into barrels. The whole experience lends a nostalgic *Endless Summer* feeling. And don't overlook the tiny offshore islands where you can find gorgeous ikat, more silky white sand and turquoise bays, and, of course, more surf.

Historically, the simple local economy revolved around the majestic and nutritious lontar palm. Then in the late 17th century, after a bloody campaign, Rote became the source of slaves and supplies for the Dutch. But the Rotenese also took advantage of the Dutch presence, adopted Christianity and, with Dutch support, established a school system that eventually turned them into NTT's best-educated islanders. This allowed them to influence the much larger island of Timor both politically and economically for generations.

ℹ Getting There & Away

The swiftest and most comfortable way to land on Rote is via the Baharai Express (executive/VIP 120,000/165,000Rp, two hours), a fast ferry that departs from Kupang at 9am daily, docks at Ba'a and returns at 11am. Book your ticket in advance and arrive at the dock by 8:30am as the boat sometimes leaves slightly early. There is now a formal departure tax (10,000Rp) payable at the Kupang harbour as well as a surfboard tax (per board 20,000Rp) payable in Ba'a. Be warned, this service is sometimes cancelled due to rough seas.

There's no longer a daily flight to Rote, but when the fast boat is cancelled, **Transnusa** (☎in Kupang 0380-822 555) operates a flight between Rote and Kupang (300,000Rp to 500,000Rp, 20 minutes). There's also a slow ferry (50,000Rp, five hours) that docks at Pantai Baru, north of Ba'a, and leaves for Kupang between 9am and 10.30am daily, returning at around 3pm.

ℹ Getting Around

Local touts will try to convince you that to get to Nemberala from the fast boat port in Ba'a you'll have to charter a bemo (250,000Rp to 350,000Rp, two hours), or hire an *ojek* (100,000Rp to 200,000Rp). But just outside the harbour gates you can easily flag down a public bemo (with/without surf board 25,000/50,000Rp). Of course, the most comfortable option is to book a car charter through Anugrah (p386; 350,000Rp to 500,000Rp, max four people). Once you're in Nemberala, hire a motorbike (70,000Rp per day) through your hotel or guesthouse, and explore.

Ba'a

Ba'a, Rote's commercial centre, is a sleepy port town that snakes south along the island's west coast among banyan trees, banana and coconut groves. The fast ferry and flights land here. Some houses have curious boat-shaped thatched roofs, but the town doesn't offer enough of a reason to linger, although the coast from the ferry port at Pantai Baru to Ba'a is sparsely populated and has some superb beaches. There is a **BRI bank** (Jl Pabean) with an ATM on the main drag, but it won't accept Visa. Bring plenty of rupiah from Kupang, as exchanging cash is difficult here.

Nemberala

A surfers' secret for years, word has leaked out about Nemberala, a chilled-out fishing village on an exquisite white-sand beach sheltered by a reef that helps form the legendary 'left', **T-Land**. This wave gets big, especially between June and August, but it's not heavy, so the fear factor isn't ridiculous. Like other once undiscovered waves in east Indo, the line-up gets busy in the high season, thanks to an influx of expats and vacation home owners who have bought up large swatches of beachfront in the area. Their new and mostly tasteful villas sprouting like so many lontar palms. If you rent a motorbike and drive the spectacularly rutted coastal road north or south, you'll notice that you're within reach of a half-dozen other desolate beaches and a few superb uncharted surf breaks. Beginners take note, just north of the Nemberala fishing-boat harbour is a terrific novice break called **Squealers**.

Sleeping & Eating

The surf and tourist season peaks between June and September. Accommodation range and value are solid, but there aren't a lot of rooms. Book ahead. While all but one of the lodges and guesthouses are all-inclusive, a few local warungs have popped up in recent months, so you do have (limited) options if you've soured on *makan* homestay.

TOP CHOICE **Malole Surf House** LODGE $$$
(☎0813 5317 7264, 0813 3776 7412; www.rotesurfhouse.com; per person incl 3 meals US$125-180; ❄@☎) One of our favorite hotels in all of Indonesia was built by surf legend Felipe Pomar and it's run by his business partners Diego Arrarte and Maria Pineiro. It's a surf lodge that blends comfort, cuisine and style better than anywhere else in Rote. The four rooms are set in a large wooden house and guesthouse with accent lighting, day beds, ikat bedspreads, limitless laundry and bottled water, and security boxes. Diego, the longest-tenured expat in Nemberala, will make sure you get to the right waves at the right time via the house boat. Maria, the chef, presides over a sublime international seafood kitchen, carves fresh sashimi, bakes fresh bread, and blends spectacular soups and curries. Mountain bikes, fishing trips and island excursions are also on offer. They have a satellite wi-fi feed and a level of comfort and elegance that feels effortless (it isn't) and belies its extremely remote location. Closed during the wet season.

Lualemba Bungalows BUNGALOW $$
(☎0813 3914 7465, 0812 3947 8823; www.facebook.com/lualemba.rote; s/d incl meals 300,000Rp/550,000Rp) A highly recommended new spot, set 300m inland from Jenet's Cafe and just a three minute walk to Nemberala Beach. Digs are set in attractive, thatched lontar bungalows with stone foundations and private verandas strung with hammocks. Rates include boat rides to the surf break and neighbouring islands, three meals and use of mountain bikes. Tremendous value.

Ti Rosa BUNGALOW $
(☎0821 4633 7016; per person incl meals 150,000Rp) Run by sweet Ibu Martine, this

LONTAR PALM

Rote remains dependent on the drought-resistant lontar palm. The palm is extremely versatile; its tough yet flexible leaves are woven to make sacks and bags, hats and sandals, roofs and dividing walls. Lontar wood is fashioned into furniture and floorboards. But what nourishes the islanders is the milky, frothy *nirah* (sap) tapped from the *tankai* (orange-stemmed inflorescences) that grow from the crown of the lontar. Drunk straight from the tree, the *nirah* is refreshing, nutritious and energising. If left to ferment for hours, it becomes *laru* (palm wine), which is hawked around the lanes of Rote. With a further distillation, the juice is distilled into a gin-like *sopi* – the power behind many a wild Rote night.

fine collection of lime-green, concrete, tiled bungalows are super clean and the cheapest beach option available. Budget surfers love it so much, some book rooms for the whole season. Turn right at the first intersection in town, and head north along the dirt road for 500m.

Anugrah BUNGALOW $$
(☎0852 3916 2645; s/d incl meals from 300,000/450,000Rp) It's a touch overpriced, but the cute, compact, lontar-palm bungalows with patios and *mandis,* right on the beach opposite T-Land, are well situated and popular, though some have torn linens. Even better are the larger, new bungalows (s/d 450,000/500,000Rp) with pressed linens, wooden table and chairs out front, and outdoor baths. The restaurant, which is decked out with ikat tablecloths, serves *ikan bakar* (grilled fish), fried squid and other basics. Reserve ahead during surf season.

Nemberala Beach Resort RESORT $$$
(☎0813 3773 1851; www.nemberalabeachresort.com; s/d surfers from US$275/380, non-surfers US$235/340; ❄☒) Right on the ocean, this relaxed four-star, all-inclusive spot has spacious slate-and-timber bungalows with ceiling fans, outdoor baths and freshwater showers. There's a swimming pool, volleyball court and pool table, and a terrific beach bar where sundowners can easily phase into late night cocktails. The food has received mixed reviews of late, but it does have a speedboat to whisk you out to nearby surf breaks, and it offers excursions to limestone caves and tidal lagoons. Fishing trips for dog-toothed tuna and mackerel can also be arranged. It's closed during the wet season.

Jenet's Place CAFE $
(☎0812 3947 8823; mains 20,000-40,000Rp) This cute patio joint, just north of the soccer field, is decked out with tablecloths, silk flowers and offers a simple menu (think pastas, *nasi goreng*, burgers and recommended fish and chips). And icy Bintang, of course.

Rumah Makan Tessa Lifu INDONESIAN $
(mains 20,000-40,000Rp; ⊙closed Sun) Tasty and cheap local eats served out of the owner/chef's family house next to the soccer pitch.

Around Nemberala

You really must explore this lonely limestone coast by motorbike in order to absorb its majesty. If you prefer a heavier, hollow wave, your first stop should be 3km north to **Suckie Mama's**. About 8km south of Nemberala, **Bo'a** has a spectacular white-sand beach and consistent off-season surf. And set on a notch in the headland that bisects this absurdly wide and almost unjustly beautiful bay, is Rote's best new addition. **Bo'a Hill** (☎0813 3935 1165; www.surfrote.com; per person incl meals 600,000Rp), owned by Axel – a charming Bali expat brat gone rogue – is a three-hecatre ecofarm with just one idyllic, spacious three sided bungalow. In addition to a canopied bed, there is a terrazzo bath and a spectacular perch with 180-degree ocean views. Axel grows fruit and herbs, pigs and ducks, collects honey and has plans for two more houses, outfitted with full kitchens, set to open in 2013. He'll also point out the best surf breaks and get you hooked into ideal fishing spots.

From Bo'a continue south over the dry rocky road, look out for monkeys, and after you traverse the natural limestone bridge, negotiate the descent and reach **Oeseli** village; then make a right on the dirt road which leads to another superb beach with some good waves, and a huge natural tidal lagoon that shelters local fishing boats and floods limestone bat caves. There's an ideal kite surf launch here too.

The southernmost island in Indonesia, **Pulau Ndana** can be reached by local fishing boat from Nemberala. It's currently a military camp, but for years it was uninhabited. Legend has it that the entire population was murdered in a 17th-century revenge act, staining the island's small lake with the victims' blood. Ndana has wild deer and a wide variety of birds. Its beaches are prime turtle-nesting territory, and the snorkelling here is superb.

Boni is about 15km from Nemberala, near the northern coast, and is one of the last villages on Rote where traditional religion is still followed. Market day is Thursday. To get here, rent a motorcycle in Nemberala.

Pulau Do'o is a flat spit of pale golden sand with terrific though finicky surf. You can see it from Pantai Nemberala. Further on is the stunning **Pulau Ndao**, which has more powdery white-sand beaches, limestone bluffs, and a tidy, charming ikat-weaving, lontar-tapping, fishing village that is home to nearly 600 people who speak their own indigenous dialect, Bahasa Ndao. There are some fantastic swimming beaches up the west and east coast, and good though inconsistent surf off the southern point. Ndao is 10km west of Nemberala. To get here you'll have to charter a boat (800,000Rp to 1,000,000Rp, maximum five people). You could easily do both islands in one trip.

SUMBA

Sumba is a dynamic mystery. With its rugged undulating savannah and low limestone hills knitted together with more maize and cassava than rice, physically it looks nothing like Indonesia's volcanic islands to the north. Sprinkled throughout the countryside are hilltop villages with thatched clan houses clustered around megalithic tombs, where villagers claim to be Protestant but still pay homage to their indigenous *marapu* with bloody sacrificial rites. Throw in outstanding hand-spun, naturally dyed ikat, and the annual **Pasola festival** – where bareback horsemen ritualise old tribal conflicts as they battle one another with hand-carved spears – and it's easy to see that Sumba runs deep. One of the poorest islands in Indonesia, an influx of welcome government investment has brought recent improvements in infrastructure – best seen in Tambolaka, the island's newest city. And change has trickled down to traditional villages, as well. Thatched roofs are becoming tin, tombs are now made from concrete, traditional dress is increasingly rare, and remote villagers expect larger donations from visitors. Some traditions persist, however. Sumba's extensive grasslands make it one of Indonesia's leading horse-breeding islands. Horses still serve as a mode of transport in more rugged regions, they remain a symbol of wealth and status, and can still win a bride.

History

According to local legend, a great ladder once connected heaven and earth. Down it clambered the original earthlings to Sumba, where they settled at Tanjung Sasar, on the northern tip of the island.

Though 14th-century Javanese chronicles place Sumba under Majapahit control, Sumbanese history is more a saga of internal wars over land and trading rights between small kingdoms. Despite their mutual hostility, they often depended on each other economically. The inland regions produced horses, timber, betel nut, rice, fruit and dyewoods, while coastal people concentrated on ikat production and trade with other islands.

The Dutch initially paid little attention to Sumba because it lacked commercial possibilities. But in the early 20th century they finally decided to bring Sumba under their control and invaded the island. In 1913 a civilian administration was set up, but Sumbanese nobility continued to reign as the Dutch ruled through them. When the Indonesian republic ceased to recognise the native rulers' authority, many of them became government officials. These long-time ruling clans continued to exert hegemony by monopolising local government appointments.

It all came to a head during the 1998 Waikabubak riots. Initially sparked by demonstrations against such nepotism, and Suharto-era corruption in general, the bad political blood developed into a full-scale tribal conflict perpetrated by a horseback posse of at least 3000 men. Armed with machetes, they rode through town killing at least 26 people.

These days, the island is benefitting from recent improvements to infrastructure – Tambolaka (formerly called Waitabula) is on the verge of becoming a boom town, and better air links to Denpasar and Kupang point to a more connected future.

Culture

IKAT

Sumbanese ikat is the most dramatic and arguably best executed in Indonesia. Natural dyes are still preferred by weavers who sell their wares to serious collectors in Bali and beyond. The earthy orange-red colour comes from *kombu* tree bark, indigo-blue and yellow tones are derived from *loba* leaves. Some motifs are historical: a record of tribal wars and precolonial village life. Others depict animals and mythical creatures, such as *marapu*.

Traditionally, ikat cloth was only worn ceremonially. Less than 90 years ago, only members of Sumba's highest clans and their personal attendants could make or wear it. Dutch conquest broke the Sumbanese royal ikat monopoly and opened up an external market, which increased production. In the late 19th century ikat was collected by Dutch ethnographers and museums, and by the 1920s visitors were already noting the introduction of nontraditional designs, such as lions from the Dutch coat of arms.

Sumba

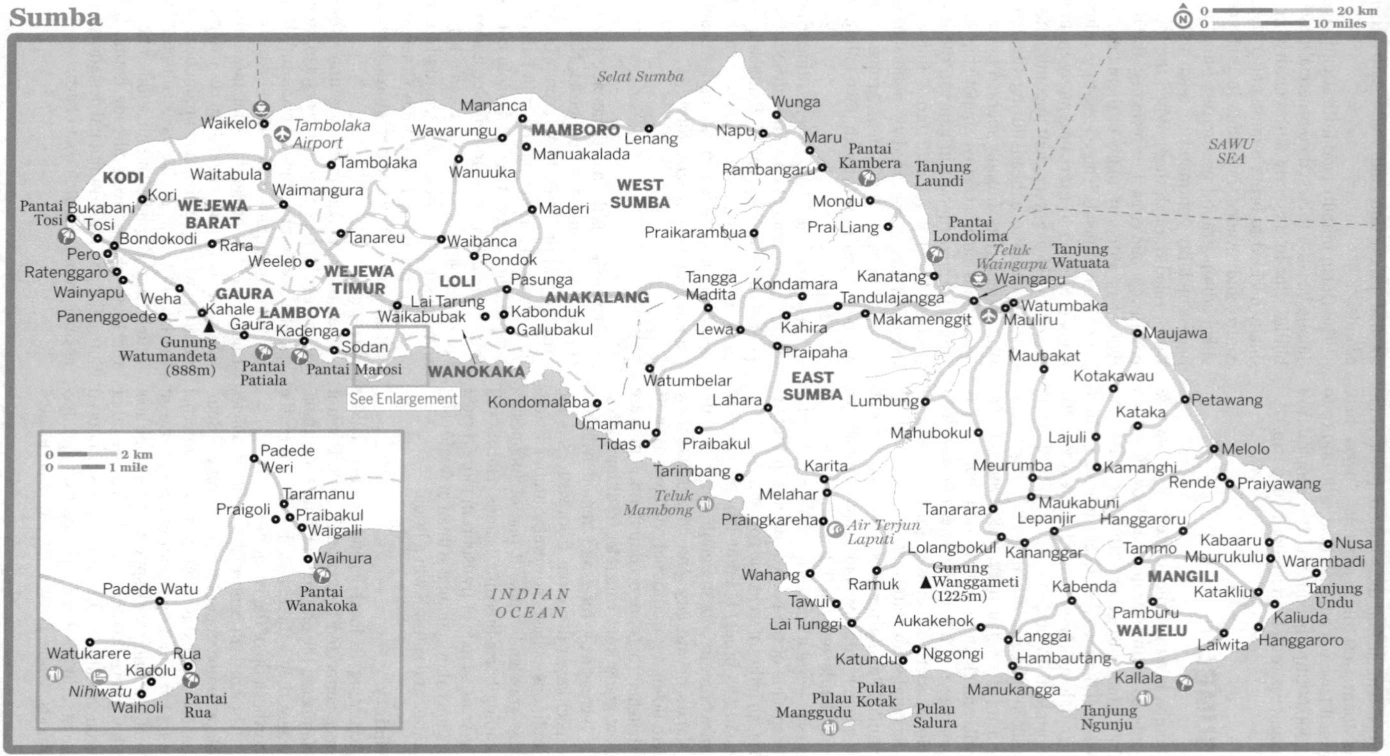

0 20 km
0 10 miles
Selat Sumba
SAWU SEA
INDIAN OCEAN
KODI
WEJEWA BARAT
WEJEWA TIMUR
GAURA
LAMBOYA
LOLI
WANOKAKA
ANAKALANG
MAMBORO
WEST SUMBA
EAST SUMBA
MANGILI
WAIJELU
Waikelo
Tambolaka Airport
Tambolaka
Waitabula
Waimangura
Kori
Pantai Bukabani
Tosi
Bondokodi
Rara
Pero
Ratenggaro
Wainyapu
Weha
Paneggoede
Kahale
Gaura
Gunung Watumandeta (888m)
Pantai Patiala
Kadenga
Sodan
Pantai Marosi
See Enlargement
Weeleo
Tanareu
Mananca
Wawarungu
Wanuuka
Manuakalada
Maderi
Waibanca
Pondok
Lai Tarung
Waikabubak
Pasunga
Kabonduk
Gallubakul
Lenang
Napu
Wunga
Maru
Rambangaru
Pantai Kambera
Tanjung Laundi
Mondu
Prai Liang
Praikarambua
Tangga Madita
Kondamara
Kanatang
Pantai Londolima
Teluk Waingapu
Tanjung Watuata
Waingapu
Watumbaka
Mauliru
Tandulajangga
Makamenggit
Kahira
Lewa
Praipaha
Watumbelar
Lahara
Kondomalaba
Umamanu
Tidas
Praibakul
Tarimbang
Teluk Mambong
Karita
Melahar
Praingkareha
Air Terjun Laputi
Lumbung
Mahubokul
Maubakat
Maujawa
Kotakawau
Petawang
Kataka
Lajuli
Melolo
Meurumba
Kamanghi
Rende
Praiyawang
Maukabuni
Tanarara
Lepanjir
Hanggaroru
Lolangbokul
Kananggar
Gunung Wanggameti (1225m)
Wahang
Ramuk
Tawui
Lai Tunggi
Aukakehok
Katundu
Nggongi
Langgai
Hambautang
Manukangga
Pulau Manggudu
Pulau Kotak
Pulau Salura
Kabenda
Tammo
Kabaaru
Mburukulu
Nusa
Warambadi
Tanjung Undu
Katakliu
Kaliuda
Pamburu
Laiwita
Hanggaroro
Kallala
Tanjung Ngunju
0 2 km
0 1 mile
Padede Weri
Taramanu
Praigoli
Praibakul
Waigalli
Waihura
Pantai Wanakoka
Padede Watu
Watukarere
Rua
Kadolu
Nihiwatu
Waiholi
Pantai Rua

VILLAGES

A traditional Sumba village usually consists of two parallel rows of houses facing each other, with a square between. In the middle of the square is a stone with another flat stone on top of it, upon which offerings are made to the village's protective *marapu*. These spirit stones, or *kateda*, can be found in the fields around the village and are used for offerings to the agricultural *marapu* when planting or harvesting.

The village square also contains the stone-slab tombs of important ancestors, once finely carved, but nowadays virtually always made of cement and occasionally covered in garish bathroom tile. In former times the heads of slain enemies would be hung on a dead tree in the village square while ceremonies and feasts took place. These skull trees, called *andung*, can still be seen in some villages and are a popular motif on Sumbanese ikat.

A traditional Sumbanese dwelling is a large rectangular structure raised on stilts, held together with lashings and dowels rather than nails, it houses an extended family. The thatched (or nowadays often corrugated tin) roof slopes gently upwards from all four sides before abruptly rising to a peak.

Rituals accompanying the building of a house include an offering, made at the time of planting the first pillar, to find out if the *marapu* agree with the location. One method is to cut open a chicken and examine its liver. Many houses are seasonally decked out with buffalo horns or pigs' jaws from past sacrifices.

RELIGION

The basis of traditional Sumbanese religion is *marapu*, a collective term for all Sumba's spiritual forces, including gods, spirits and ancestors. At death the deceased join the invisible world, from where they can influence the world of the living. *Marapu mameti* is the collective name for all dead people. The living can appeal to them for help, especially their own relatives, though the dead can be harmful if irritated. The *marapu maluri* are the original people placed on earth by god; their power is concentrated in certain places or objects, which are kept safe in the family's thatched loft.

DEATH CEREMONIES

On the day of burial, buffalo or pigs are sacrificed while ornaments and a *sirih* (betel nut) bag are buried with the body. The living must bury their dead as richly as possible to avoid being reprimanded by the *marapu mameti* and to ensure the dead can enter the invisible world.

Funerals may be delayed for up to 10 years (the body of the deceased is sometimes also stored in the loft of the family's house or given a temporary burial) until enough wealth has been accumulated for a full ceremonial funeral, and a massive stone- or concrete-slab tomb.

When the Indonesian republic was founded, the government introduced a slaughter tax in an attempt to stop the liquidation of valuable livestock. This reduced the number of animals killed and stemmed hunger among the poor, but it didn't alter basic attitudes. The Sumbanese believe you *can*, and should, take the animal with you.

VISITING VILLAGES

Many Sumbanese villagers are now accustomed to tourists. If you're interested in their weavings or other artefacts, the villagers put you down as a potential trader. If all you want to do is chat and look around, and simply turn up with a camera and start putting it in their faces, they're likely to be confused or offended. On the other hand, though you may assume that you're the one on an anthropological jones, the local people – especially the children – will likely be just as interested in you as you are in them. Often the tables turn, and it is you that just might feel under the microscope.

On Sumba, offering *sirih pinang* (betel nut) is the traditional way of greeting guests or hosts. You can buy it at most markets in Sumba, and it's a terrific and respectful ice breaker. Offer your gifts to the *kepala desa* and to other village elders.

Many villages keep a visitors' book, which villagers will produce for you to sign, and you should donate about 20,000Rp per person. Hiring a guide to the isolated villages is a big help and offers some protection from getting into the wrong situation. No matter where you go, taking the time to chat with the villagers helps them see you more as a guest than a customer or visiting alien.

Waingapu

☎0387 / POP 55,000

Waingapu is a leafy, laid-back town that is plenty walkable and makes a decent base to explore the surrounding villages. It became an administrative centre after the Dutch military 'pacified' the island in 1906 and

Waingapu

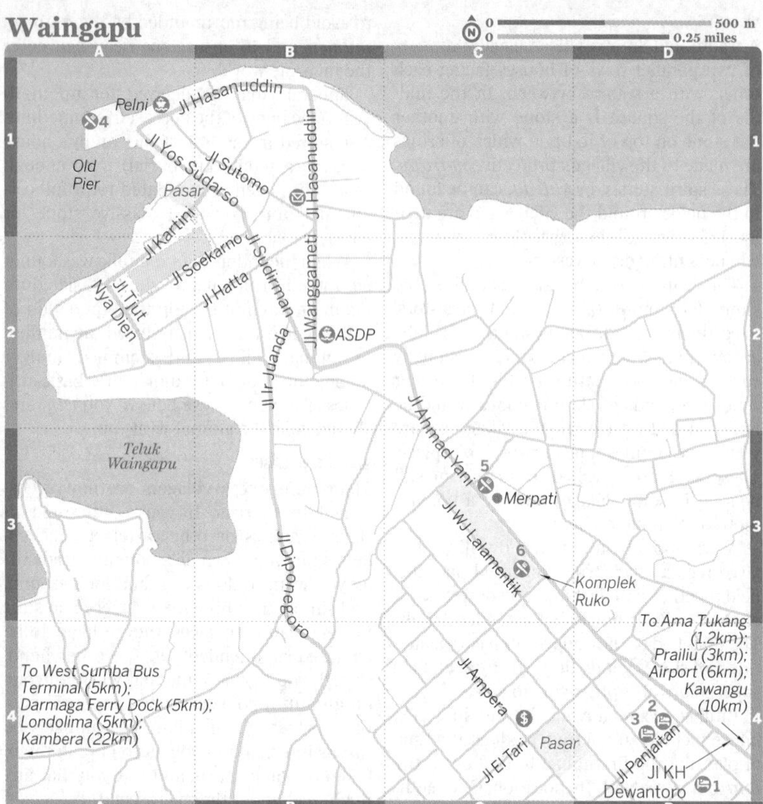

Waingapu

Sleeping

1	Hotel Kaliuda	D4
2	Hotel Merlin	D4
3	Hotel Sandle Wood	D4

Eating

	Merlin Restaurant	(see 2)
4	Warung Enjoy Aja	A1
5	Warung Kedau Etnik	C3
6	Yenny's Bakery	C3

has long been Sumba's main trading post for textiles, prized Sumbanese horses, dyewoods and lumber. The town has a groovy harbourfront dining scene, a few ikat shops and workshops. Traders with bundles of textiles and carvings hang around hotels or walk the streets touting for rupiah.

Sleeping

Breakfast and free airport transfer (if you call in advance) are usually included in accommodation rates.

Hotel Merlin HOTEL $
(☎61300; Jl Panjaitan 25; standard/VIP 132,000/154,000Rp; ❄📶) This long-standing travellers' favourite has a decent assortment of rooms over three floors, with Flores views from the rooftop restaurant. Rooms are large, with wood furnishings, fresh paint and room service, but they vary in quality. For instance, the top-floor fan rooms are nicer and cleaner than the VIP rooms on the 1st floor.

Hotel Sandle Wood HOTEL $
(☎61887; Jl Panjaitan 23; r with fan 99,000-143,000Rp, s/d with air-con 187,000/209,000Rp; ❄) Decent-value rooms set around a bright courtyard on a quiet street. The cheapest

have shared baths. VIP rooms come with air-con. Management can hook you up with cars (with drivers) and motorbikes.

Hotel Kaliuda HOTEL $
(☎61264; Jl Lalamentik 3; r 125,000-200,000Rp) This reasonably clean, quiet motel has just six basic rooms with fans at a decent value. It also has a small antique collection.

Eating

Good restaurants are thin on the ground in Waingapu. The best dinner option is the **pasar malam** at the old wharf, where three permanent warungs and half a dozen gas-lit carts set up to grill, fry and sauté seafood on the cheap. It's especially nice when the moon glows. Another collection of **night warungs** blooms across from **Komplek Ruko**. They offer *mie ayam*, gado gado and *soto ayam*.

TOP CHOICE **Warung Enjoy Aja** SEAFOOD $
(Pelabuhan; mains 15,000-40,000Rp; ⏲6-10pm) Part of the harbour night market, this is the last *warung* before the pier on the eastside. The fish and squid are expertly grilled and served with three types of sambal and a sea salt garnish.

Warung Kedau Etnik INDONESIAN $
(Jl Ahmad Yani 67; mains 15,000-50,000Rp; ⏲11am-10pm) A cute bamboo warung, with classy glass sandbox tables and the usual Indo flavors. This is as stylish as Waingapu gets.

Yenny's Bakery BAKERY $
(☎62449; Komplek Ruko; pastries 2000-12,000Rp) Got a sweet tooth? Peruse the shelves of doughnuts, cakes, pastries and breads at this friendly bakery. They'll pack a box for the road.

Merlin Restaurant INDONESIAN $
(☎61300; Jl Panjaitan 25; mains 10,000-35,000Rp; 📶) Hotel Merlin's rooftop dining room is actually one of the best choices in town. The menu is typical Chinese Indonesian, and the views are superb. Try the chicken with mustard greens.

Shopping

Waingapu has a few 'art shops' selling Sumbanese ikat and artefacts. Vendors also descend on hotels – some will squat patiently

TRANSPORT FROM WAINGAPU

Air

DESTINATION	COMPANY	DURATION (HR)	FREQUENCY
Denpasar	Batavia Air	2	3 weekly
Kupang	Merpati, Batavia Air, Aviastar	1	6 days weekly

Boat

DESTINATION	COMPANY	COST (RP)	DURATION (HR)	FREQUENCY
Aimere (Flores)	ASDP	65,000-105,000	10	8am Wed
Ende (Flores)	ASDP	36,000-105,000	7	4pm Sun
Ende (Flores)	Pelni	varies	6	twice monthly

Bus & Truck

DESTINATION	TYPE	COST (RP)	DURATION (HR)	FREQUENCY
Baing	bus	30,000	4	7am, 8am, 11am, 1pm
Melolo & Rende	bus	15,000	1½	frequent until 5pm
Puru Kambera	bus	10,000	1	3 daily
Tarimbang	truck	35,000	5	daily
Waikabubak	bus	30,000-50,000	5	7am, 8am, noon, 3pm

all day. Prices are fair, and there's far more choice here than in the countryside.

Ama Tukang IKAT

(☎62414; Jl Hawan Waruk 53) Do not miss this ikat workshop, even if you've overdosed on weaving. You'll see the whole process from motif design to colouring to weaving, and the collection – featuring *marapu,* village scenes, horsemen and buffalo, is arguably the best in all of Indonesia. To get there, head south of the bridge on the southern side of Waingapu and turn left onto Jl Hawan Waruk. It's on the left.

Information

BNI bank's (Jl Ampera) ATM accepts Visa/Plus cards and it usually has the best exchange rates. The **post office** (Jl Hasanuddin; ⏲8am-4pm Mon-Fri) is close to the harbour. **Warnet Hamu Eti** (Jl Panjaitan 92; per hour 6000Rp; ⏲24hr) has the most consistent connection and plenty of terminals.

Getting There & Away

TX Waingapu (☎61534; www.txtravel.com; Jl Beringin 12) books tickets on all Batavia Air and Aviastar flights, and there's a **Merpati** (☎61323; Jl Soekarno 4) office in town. **Pelni** (☎61665; www.pelni.co.id; Jl Hasanuddin) ships leave from the newer Darmaga dock to the west of town. Ferry schedules are subject to change. Check the latest timetable at the **ASDP** (☎61533; Jl Wanggameti 3) office. The terminal for eastbound buses is in the southern part of town, close to the market. The new West Sumba terminal is about 5km west of town.

Getting Around

The airport is 6km south on the Melolo road. A taxi into town costs a standard 50,000Rp, but most hotels offer a free pick-up and drop-off service for guests. It's 3000Rp for a bemo ride to any destination around town, and 5000Rp to the western bus terminal.

Sumba has some of the highest car-hire rates in Nusa Tenggara. Even after bargaining, 600,000Rp is a good price per day, including driver and petrol. The Sandle Wood and Merlin hotels can help sort you out. Virtually any hotel worker can arrange a motorbike (from 75,000Rp per day).

Around Waingapu

Londolima, a sliver of sand about 7km northwest of town, is a favourite local swimming spot on weekends and holidays. The bay is turquoise and glassy; the beach isn't so magical. Bemos from Terminal Kota (the local name for the West Sumba bus terminal) pass by regularly. Continue along this road and you'll reach an even better beach, **Puru Kambera**, where you can stay the night at the new **Villa Cemara** (☎081 138 0335, 0812 246 54448; standard r 600,000-800,000Rp, deluxe r 1,900,000Rp; ❄📶) resort in tasteful wood cottages on the beach, with pebbled baths, mosquito net, air-con and a fussy wi-fi signal. It's also close to the traditional **Prai Liang** and **Prai Natang** villages, which are just 15 minutes from the resort. Three daily buses (10,000Rp) go to/from Waingapu.

Three kilometres southeast of Waingapu, **Prailiu** is an ikat-weaving centre that's worth a quick look. Alongside traditional thatched houses are some concrete tombs bearing carvings of crocodiles and turtles, as well as empty graves that will be filled when the deceased's family can afford the funeral. Visitors are asked for a cash donation. Bemos to Prailiu run from Waingapu's main bus and bemo terminal. Continuing southeast, it's a further 7km to **Kawangu**, which has two massive stone-slab tombs in the pasture, 300m off the road to Melolo.

East Sumba

Southeast of Waingapu, nestled in dry undulating savannah interspersed with cashew orchards, are several traditional villages, some with striking ancestral tombs. This area produces some of Sumba's best ikat. Most villages are quite used to tourists – you'll have to pay to visit, and be prepared for plenty of attention from handicraft vendors.

PRAIYAWANG & RENDE

Nestled in a shallow valley between grassy hills, **Praiyawang** is a traditional compound of Sumbanese houses and is the ceremonial focus of the more modern village of **Rende**, located 7km south of Melolo. It has an imposing line-up of nine big stone-slab tombs. The largest is that of a former chief. Shaped like a buffalo, it consists of four stone pillars 2m high, supporting a monstrous slab about 5m long, 2.5m wide and 1m thick. Two stone tablets stand atop the main slab, carved with figures. A massive Sumbanese house with concrete pillars faces the tombs, along with a number of older *rumah adat.*

Several buses go from Waingapu to Rende (15,000Rp), starting at about 7am. The last bus back to Waingapu leaves at 3pm.

KALLALA

Kallala, 126km from Waingapu and 2km down a dirt road from the nearby village of **Baing**, has emerged as the surf capital of East Sumba. It's an absolutely stunning stretch of white-sand beach that arcs toward the coastal mountains, which tumble down to form East Sumba's southernmost point. Waves break 500m offshore.

If you plan on spending the night, you'll bunk at the once-renowned **Mr David's** (☎0813 3787 3589; all-inclusive bungalows 300,000Rp). Mr David (as he is referred to throughout East Sumba) has lived in Sumba for over 30 years, but the resort has seen (much!) better days. Bungalows have warped wooden floors, weathered mattresses and no furnishings. But the open dining room has some definite remote surf-camp appeal. Old boards decorate the rafters and there's a stack of sticks for rent too. Plus, Mrs David (the lovely Yohanna) whips up outstanding meals in short order. You will also have the wave to yourself, so dedicated surf rats won't mind it here at all, though they might whine about the price.

Four buses a day go to Baing (30,000Rp, four hours), leaving Waingapu between 7am and 8am, and then again at around 11am and 1pm. The road is sealed all the way but is bumpy past Melolo. A dirt track with many branches runs from Baing to Kallala. Buses will drop you off at the beach if you ask the driver.

South-Central Sumba

This part of the island is gorgeous, but difficult to access. Although there are daily buses from Waingapu to Tarimbang and trucks to Praingkareha, getting around may require a 4WD or motorcycle and, often, some hiking.

If you're looking for more deserted waves, check out **Tarimbang**, a life-altering crescent of white sand framed by a massive limestone bluff 88km southwest of Waingapu. The beach thumps with terrific surf, there's some nearby snorkelling, and rustic accommodation at **Marthen's Homestay** and the *kepala desa*'s six-room place. Both charge about 100,000Rp per person including meals. Daily trucks to Tarimbang leave Waingapu in the morning (35,000Rp, five hours).

Waikabubak

☎0387 / POP 20,000

A dusty, country market town, home to both thatched clan houses and rows of concrete stores, administrative buildings and tin-roof homes sprouting satellite dishes, Waikabubak makes Waingapu feel like a metropolis. It's a welcoming place, surrounded by thick stands of mohagony, and at about 600m above sea level, it's a little cooler than the east and a good base for exploring the traditional villages of West Sumba. The big market is on Saturday.

Sights

Within the town are some friendly and quite traditional *kampung* (villages) with stone-slab tombs and thatched houses. You don't need a guide here. Locals will love to show off their spacious homes lashed with old ironwood columns and beams. Charming children will mug for the camera. Old folks will offer betel nut. Bring gifts, offer a donation (5000Rp to 25,000Rp), or buy a handicraft or two and the villagers will beam with gratitude and pride.

Kampung Tambelar, just off Jl Sudirman, has very impressive tombs, but the most interesting *kampung* are on the western edge of town. It's only a short stroll from most hotels to **Prai Klembung** and then up the slippery slope that juts from the center of town to **Tarung**, **Waitabar**, and **Belakilu**, three villages that bleed into one.

In November, Kampung Tarung, reached by a concrete path off Jl Manda Elu, is the scene of an important month-long ritual, the **Wula Podhu**. This is an austere period when even weeping for the dead is prohibited. Rites consist mainly of offerings to the spirits (the day before the ritual ends, hundreds of chickens are sacrificed), and people sing and dance for the entire final day. Tanjung is home to five tribes, each with their own small, thatched shrine where only the local priest is allowed to pray and commune with the *marapu*.

Other interesting *kampung* occupying ridge or hilltop positions outside town include **Praiijing**, with traditional huts set around some cool primitive stone tombs and surrounded by coconut palm and bamboo groves. **Bondomarotto**, **Kampung Prairami** and **Kampung Primkateti** are also beautifully located on adjacent hilltops. You can take a bemo to the turn-off for Praiijing (2000Rp).

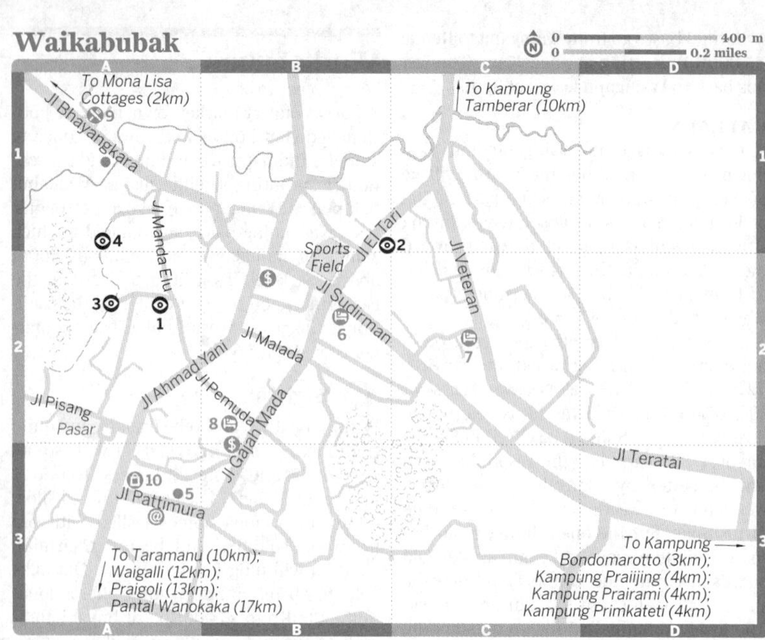

Waikabubak

Sights

1 Kampung Prai Klembung....A2
2 Kampung Tambelar....B1
3 Kampung Tarung....A2
4 Kampung Waitabar....A1

Activities, Courses & Tours

5 Sumba Adventure....A3

Sleeping

6 Hotel Aloha....B2
7 Hotel Artha....C2
8 Hotel Manandang....B2

Eating

9 Rumah Makan Gloria....A1

Shopping

10 A Hamid Algadi Art Shop....A3

Tours

Yuliana Ledatara GUIDE

(☎0852 3918 1410; Kampung Tarung; per day 300,000Rp (max four people), horse tours per person 50,000-100,000Rp) A wonderful local English- and French-speaking guide who lives in Tarung, Waikabubak's hilltop traditional village. She can organise tours of traditional villages throughout West Sumba where she sniffs out funerals and sacrifices, or horse tours through rice fields, and can arrange village homestays. She's one of Indonesia's very few women guides, and she's a good one.

Sumba Adventure TOUR OPERATOR

(☎21727, 0813 3710 7845; sumbaadventure@yahoo.com; Jl Pemuda; guiding services per day 250,000Rp, per day with car and driver 850,000Rp) Experienced professional guide Philip Renggi is one of the best in West Sumba. He and his team of guides lead trips into seldom-explored villages north of Waikabubak, including his native Manukalada village and Wawarungu, where there are several sacred *marapu* houses that only shaman can enter. He has offices in Waikabubak and Tambolaka.

Sleeping

TOP CHOICE **Mona Lisa Cottages** BUNGALOW $$

(☎21364; www.monalisacottages-sumba.com; Jl Adhyaska 30; standard s/d 120,000/180,000Rp, cottages s 240,000-600,000Rp, d 300,000-

720,000Rp; ❄@) You'll find the best night's sleep 2km northwest of town, across from the rice fields. It has recently expanded to include attractive, fan-cooled budget rooms, and a few higher-end cottages as well. The cottages all have peaked tin roofs, each has a private patio with bamboo furnishings, spring beds, minifridge, and some have air-con and TV. The deluxe cottage (single/double 600,000/720,000Rp) has a king-sized bed, DVD player and a bathtub.

Hotel Manandang HOTEL **$$**
(☎21197; Jl Pemuda 4; 2nd-/1st-class/VIP 235,000/285,000/345,000Rp; ❄) Tidy, good-value rooms clustered around a back garden, and management works hard to keep it that way. First-class rooms have air-con and satellite TV, while the very decent 2nd-class rooms offer fans and private baths. Both have cold water. The largest and newest rooms are the VIP varietal set in the rear of the property. Expect new tiles, high ceilings with crown mouldings, satellite TV and hot water.

Hotel Artha GUESTHOUSE **$$**
(☎21112; Jl Veteran 11; standard s/d from 120,000/150,000Rp, VIP s/d from 225,000/300,000Rp) Spacious rooms horseshoe the garden, and though some are a bit dark and walls can be scuffed, the tiled floors and bathrooms are super clean. VIP rooms even have fresh bathroom tiles. Good value.

Karanu Hotel GUESTHOUSE **$**
(☎21645; Jl Sudirman 43; r 80,000-200,000Rp) A bright garden hotel east of the downtown swirl and within view of nearby rice fields. Rooms are clean, with new tiles and crisp sheets, though the mattresses are a bit tired and the *mandis* blotched with wet spots. There's no air-con, but it does have a fading 'Last Supper' rug tacked to the lobby wall.

Hotel Aloha GUESTHOUSE **$$**
(☎21245; Jl Sudirman 26; r with fan 125,000Rp, r with TV and air-con 275,000-300,000Rp; ❄) Bright, cleanish, basic fan rooms with soft mattresses and Indo toilets, and six overpriced air-con rooms, all set around a plot of grass and a fledgling garden. It is also the town's Aviastar agent.

Eating

TOP CHOICE **Rumah Makan Gloria** INDONESIAN **$**
(☎21140; Jl Bhayangkara 46; dishes 10,000-30,000Rp) Cute and cheerful, with chequered tablecloths, silk flowers and colourful handwritten menus offering an array of Indonesian classics. Consider just three. The *soto ayam* (chicken soup) is uber-turmericy, truly excellent, and massive; maybe the best we've ever had. It likewise does a wonderful take on that NTT tamarind classic, *ikan kuah assam* (tamarind fish soup), and if you special order it, there is *ayam kafir*, a Sumba-style fire-roasted chicken, salted and served with a sublime, super spicy *sambal*. It's off the menu, but they will do it for you.

Rumah Makan Fanny INDONESIAN **$**
(☎21389; Jl Bhayangkara 55; mains 15,000-40,000Rp; ⏰8am-9pm) A Waikabubak staple, it's favoured for flavourful but crazy spicy *ikan kuah asam* (tamarind fish soup, 40,000Rp) – one is enough to feed two. It also has assorted Chinese Indo seafood dishes and a house special fried chicken.

Shopping

Traders gather at hotels with ikat from East Sumba, locally made bone, wood, horn and stone carvings, and jewellery. **Tarung** is known for beaded jewellery, which you can easily find on a walk through the village.

A Hamid Algadi Art Shop HANDICRAFTS
(☎21170; Jl Ahmad Yani 99; ⏰9am-6pm Mon-Sat) Fantastic stone carvings in the front yard, wooden antiques and some cool old stone grinders and bronze jewellery indoors. Not to mention its all-natural ikat. Your Sumbanese treasure hunt starts here.

Information

BNI Bank (Jl Ahmad Yani; ⏰8am-3.30pm Mon-Fri) Has an ATM and offers fair exchange rates.

BRI Bank (Jl Gajah Mada) The ATM only accepts Cirrus cards.

Telkom (per hr 5000Rp; ⏰24hr) Has the only internet connection in town and it's a good one.

Tourist office (☎21240; Jl Teratai 1; ⏰8am-3pm Mon-Sat) The staff here are well informed about forthcoming funerals and cultural events. It's on the outskirts of town.

Getting Around

Tambolaka, 42km northwest of Waikabubak, is the closest airport. A bus to the Waitabula (an older town being swallowed by Tambolaka) terminal and a bemo or *ojek* from there is the cheapest ride, but most people get a taxi or charter a bemo (around 150,000Rp) from Waikabubak. Bemos, trucks and minibuses service most other towns and villages in West Sumba. Generally, it's best to leave early in the day,

BUSES & BEMOS FROM WAIKABUBAK

DESTINATION	TYPE	COST (RP)	DURATION	FREQUENCY
Ankalang	bemo	5000	30 min	frequent
Lemboya	bus	10,000	2 hr	3 daily, first bus 8am
Memboro	bus	10,000	2 hr	daily
Tambolaka	bus	10,000-15,000	1 hr	frequent until 6pm
Waingapu	bus	30,000-50,000	5 hr	8am, 1pm

when they tend to fill up and depart quickest. Waikabubak is the place to rent a motorbike for exploring West Sumba. Expect to pay 75,000Rp a day. For car rental (around 650,000Rp with a driver), contact Hotel Manandang (p395) or Sumba Adventure (p394).

West Sumba

☎0387

If you're hungry for traditional Sumba culture, you'll head west into the golden rice fields that crawl up blue mountains, carved by rivers and sprouting with bamboo and coconut palms. *Kampung* of high-roofed houses are still clustered on their hilltops (a place of defence in times past), surrounding the large stone tombs of their ancestors. Rituals and ceremonies for events like house building and marriage often involve animal sacrifices and can take place at any time. Even though *kampung* seem accustomed to visiting foreigners, gifts of betel nut help warm the waters with the older crowd and are a sign of respect.

Give yourself a few days around West Sumba. Once you have learned some basic manners as a guest arriving in a village – hopefully armed with some Bahasa Indonesia – it's possible to do it without a guide, though it always helps to have one.

Getting Around

If you have limited time and want to explore remote villages and the wild coast without having to worry about transport schedules or language barriers, call Phillip, the owner of the island's best tour operator, **Sumba Adventure** (☎0813 3710 7845, 21727; www.sumbarentcar.com; chartered SUV per day 600,000Rp, guide per day 250,000Rp). His team of drivers (most of whom speak English) have good cars, are trustworthy and know Sumba well. The price is good for up to four people, perfect for two couples travelling together. He's based in Tambolaka but can arrange island-wide itineraries.

ANAKALANG VILLAGES

Set in a fertile valley carpeted in rice fields, the Anakalang district (east of Waikabubak) has some exceptional stone megaliths that are worth seeing. Historically the seat of power (though geographically it is in the island's centre), Anakalang royals ruled West Sumba for centuries, and during colonisation only royal children were educated, so when government bureaucracies took hold the royals still ruled thanks to wealth and educational access bias. Eventually educational access evened out, and the government diversified.

Right beside the main road to Waingapu, 22km east of Waikabubak, **Kampung Pasunga** boasts one of Sumba's most impressive tombs. The grave of particular interest consists of an upright stone slab carved with images of a chief and his wife with their hands on their hips. This monument dates from 1926 and took six months to carve; 150 buffalo were sacrificed for the funeral ceremony. It is visible from the road. Pasunga's *kepala desa,* whose house has racks of buffalo horns, is friendly if you share some *sirih* or cigs with him. He will ask you to sign the visitors' book and leave a donation.

At **Gallubakul**, 2.5km down the road from the modernising village of **Kabonduk**, tombs are largely crafted from concrete and cheesy tile, but it's also home to Sumba's heaviest tomb, weighing in at 70 tonnes. It is said that 6000 workers took three years to chisel the Umbu Sawola tomb out of a hillside and drag it 3km to town. The tomb is a single piece of carved stone, about 5m long, 4m wide and nearly 1m thick. At its eastern end is a separate upright slab with carvings of the raja and queen who are buried here, as well as buffalo and cockerel motifs. The raja's son lives right by the tomb with his wife and can tell its story. He'll also ask you to sign in and make a donation.

Regular minibuses run between Waikabubak and Anakalang (fewer after 1pm). Buses to Waingapu can drop you off on the highway.

NORTH OF WAIKABUBAK

Head north from Ankalang villages along the mostly paved road and you will traverse mountains sprouting with bamboo, palms and wild fruit trees, over a pass and down into a river valley home to a number of rarely visited *kampung*. **Memboro**, set right on the river, is one of the largest, and it used to be a huddle of field houses – places the farmers slept during the planting and harvest seasons – but lately it's grown into a somewhat modern place where people live full time because of its wide blue river and abundant water supply. **Manuakalada**, is a traditional thatched village nearby, but most of the residents have abandoned it in favour of Memboro.

Waiwarungu, accessible by faint wheel tracks from Memboro, is a proper traditional village. One that is very remote and quite poor, with 15 thatched houses, one *marapu* house and nearly three dozen slab tombs, all within view of the sea. Pigs rut under the houses, puppies and children run and play everywhere. Still, it's hard, unforgiving country, especially in the parched dry season. There was a time not too long ago when visiting *bule* sent locals into a mild panic, so few foreigners had ever arrived.

There's at least one daily bus from Waikabubak to Memboro (10,000Rp, one hour), but to get to Waiwarungu you'll need wheels and a guide.

SOUTH OF WAIKABUBAK

The Wanokaka district south of Waikabubak has stunning mountain and coastal scenery and several very traditional *kampung*. It's a gorgeous drive from Waikabubak, taking a sealed but narrow road that splits at Padede Weri junction 6km from town. This is where golden, white-headed eagles soar over mountains, which tumble to the azure sea. Turn left at the junction, and the road passes through the riverside settlement of **Taramanu**, 4km further on. About 2km further downhill you'll meet a rugged earth track that leads to **Waigalli**, a huddle of about 25 thatched peak roof houses around a fabulous stone grave site on a promontory above the sea. You'll see slabs blanketed with corn kernels drying in the sun, women weaving or children pounding rice in the old timber grinder, and a marvellous view of the rice fields in the valley below. A few families have traded the thatched roof for tin. You'll be asked to make a donation (20,000Rp per person will suffice) and sign the guest book.

You'll find the nearly 200-year-old Watu Kajiwa tomb in the deeply traditional and isolated if sprawling village of **Praigoli**, notched in the dusty leafy hills above Sumba's southwest coast. From here it's just a short drive further on to lovely **Pantai Wanakoka**, where there's a crescent of sand, craggy palm dotted cliffs and massive bluffs to the south, a bay bobbing with fishing boats, and a beachfront Pasola site. In the rocky coves west of the beach, the water becomes clearer and rolls into decent, if inconsistent, surf. But the wind is consistent, which makes for interesting kite surf possibilities. Most of the action gathers around the concrete public fishermen house where you can buy their catch in the morning and watch them mend their nets in late afternoon. Nearby is the traditional village of **Wangli**, with views of rice fields, a river, the sea and coastal mountains, and another stone tomb with a 2.5m-tall fleur-de-lis.

Rua, the next in a series of luscious south Sumba beaches, is 5km southwest of the Padede Weri junction. It's yet another tumbledown rustic fishing village with a failed jetty bisecting its wide bay. At one time the Bima ferry docked here but a big storm trashed the jetty and the new dock was situated in Waikelo. Expect more lovely pale golden sand, turquoise water, and great waves when the swell hits between June and September. There looks to be a point break in the south and stiff onshore wind in the afternoon. There's only one very basic lodging option.

Heading west again, the road passes through the village of **Lemboya**, with its gorgeous rice fields scalloped into the inland side of the rugged coastal mountains and boasting one of Sumba's greatest Pasola fields. Set on a rolling grassland it's big and wide and attracts thousands of people in February. From here there's yet another turn-off south to the idyllic white sands of **Pantai Marosi**, 32km from Waikabubak. Set on a ridge above the coast, is the sweet Sumba Nautil (p398) resort. Stay or dine here, and the owner can point out the secluded, powdery white **Pantai Etreat**, and the glassy seas of **Pantai Tarikaha**, from his stunning dining room, and take you to **Magic Mountain**, a coral-draped underwater volcano that is Sumba's best dive site. Just before Sumba Nautil, the road forks. If you take the right fork you'll reach *kampung* **Litikaha** where there is now a graded gravel road to **Tokahale**, **Kahale**, and **Malisu**, three hilltop villages with spectacular panoramas. It's a 15-minute drive to the villages, or you can walk it in about 40 minutes each way.

The world-class surf spot known as *Occy's Left*, featured in the film *The Green Iguana,* is on **Pantai Nihiwatu**, east of Morosi on another absolutely stunning stretch of sand buffered by a limestone headland. Unfortunately, only Nihiwatu's paying guests have the right to walk this beach, and surfers who try to ride its legendary waves are reportedly chased off by resort security. Thankfully, there are a few more 'lefts' and 'rights' scattered within a 30-minute boat ride from both Marosi and Nihiwatu.

Sleeping & Eating

Ama Homestay HOMESTAY **$**

(0821 4716 2012; Rua; per person incl all meals 150,000Rp) Just five simple, tiled rooms in a sweet guesthouse made from cinder blocks and woven bamboo. Rooms are just big enough for a double bed and mosquito net, and stay cool thanks to louvered windows which funnel the sea breeze. Sheltered by trees and lots of potted plants, and graced with the power of a century old stone *marapu*, there is a deeply good vibe here. The drawbacks: electricity is cut at midnight, and all rooms share just one *mandi*.

Sumba Nautil RESORT **$$$**

(0813 3747 1670, 21806; www.sumbanautilresort.com; cottages US$136, r without/ with bathroom 450,000/650,000Rp, two dives US$100;) One of the best situated resorts in all of Nusa Tenggara, it sits on the rugged coastal hills with panoramic views of Pantai Marosi and the magnificent bluffs that roll north in a series of jutting headlands. Stay in a plush brick cottage which have ceiling fans, hot water, minibar, day beds and outrageous sea views, or grab a more affordable villa room. The menu (dishes US$3 to US$9) is French with North African flair, just like the owner, who makes his own pastas, breads, ice creams and chocolate. Meals are served in a marvellous open-air dining room. It has trail maps for hikers, a courtesy car to shuttle you to the beaches and surf breaks, and a somewhat spare dive shop. Village visits can be organised. Rates include breakfast. Diving must be arranged well in advance.

Nihiwatu Resort RESORT **$$$**

(www.nihiwatu.com; bungalows & villas from US$420-1500, plus 21% tax;) Hefty price tag notwithstanding, you can certainly understand the draw of this place. There's a virgin beach crashing with head high (or higher) surf that folds into turquoise barrels on the rugged, beautiful, tribal, raw west coast of Sumba. The American hotel owner has restricted access to the beach itself, allowing only guests, tour groups and a few locals, which isn't magnanimous. But if you can afford it, grab one of seven luxurious air-con bungalows or three villas, all of which face the ocean and are fully equipped with modern amenities. Plenty of activities – fishing, surfing, diving, horse riding and mountain biking – are offered for additional costs. The minimum stay is five nights.

Getting There & Away

Two daily buses run southeast to Waigalli from Waikabubak. Lemboya district buses cover the southwest towns and run through Padede Watu to Kabukarudi and Walakaka. Four buses a day run between Wanokaka and Waikabubak, stopping in Praigoli village. By far the best way to visit the area is by car or motorbike. Most roads are sealed and traffic is light. The hills south of Waikabubak are a taxing yet exhilarating ride for cyclists.

PERO & AROUND

Pero is a small Muslim fishing village, with a natural harbour inlet sheltered by a sand bar and mangroves. The village does tend to waft with the scent of drying squid, but the all-natural beach just north of town has blonde sand, a palm and scrubby grass backdrop and a sneaky good left-hand break just offshore, as well as ideal side shore wind for kite surfers. From here you won't hit land again until Africa. The long-running **Homestay Stori** (per person incl all meals 150,000Rp) is run by a hospitable family, has a handful of rooms in a rather frayed concrete home with peeling linoleum floors and shared slimy *mandis* in the backyard. But, hey, it's the only surf crash pad in the area and it's dirt cheap. It's on the main drag in town, on the right side of the street as you head toward the sea. To visit traditional *kampung,* go north or south along the coastline.

Take the paved road from **Bondokodi**, or go off-road for about 3km along **Pantai Radukapal** – a sliver of white sand along a pasture, and you'll come to the *kampung* of **Ratenggaro**, framed by a low rock wall. Although they had a fire in February 2012, and were rebuilding with government support when we visited, it is still a remarkable place and our favourite village in Sumba. There are eight houses supported by intricately carved columns, one for each cardinal point. The tall, peaked roof homes are situated on a grassy lawn on a bluff above the mouth of **Sungai Rateboya** (Crocodile River) with an absolutely breathtaking view along the coconut-palm–fringed shoreline. You can easily pass hours watching the waves of **Miller's Point** (a famous surf break) pound the rocks, with the high roofs of **Wainyapu**, a collection of 12 *kampung* and more than 40 homes, peeking out above the trees across the river. On the near side of the river mouth – where the mocha river meets the turquoise sea – unusual stone tombs occupy a small headland. Visitors are asked to contribute a donation (20,000Rp will suffice). The villagers here are full of life, and after a few minutes you'll realise that you're not here to check them out, or to inspect another exotic culture. Rather you are here to be inspected yourself. Don't worry, it's fun. To get to Wainyapu, you'll have to wade across the river at low tide.

On the way to Ratenggaro, look out for the thinner, high-peaked roofs of **Kampung Paranobaroro** through the trees, about 1km inland. The best of which have enormous timber columns intricately carved and cured by an almost perpetually smoldering cookfire in the centre of the raised bamboo platform. Stone statues decorate the public space. During the day only women and children are in the village. Women are often weaving and happy to chat. During ceremonial time you may see pig jaws and buffalo horns displayed on the front porch.

From Waikabubak there are direct buses to Tambolaka and frequent bemos and trucks from there to Pero.

TAMBOLAKA & AROUND

☎0387

Located 42km west of Waikabubak, this once sleepy market town has become West Sumba's main transport hub – it's booming and it's got a whole new name, at least in tourism brochures and other government literature. We've followed suit, even if many locals of a certain age still refer to it as Waitabula. While it's still in its early stages of growth, Tambolaka, home to our absolute favourite sleep in Sumba (set on a slice of pristine beach), is easily accessible from Bali, and is the gateway to the island's sensational western half – where the surf rocks,

PASOLA: LET THE BATTLES BEGIN

A riotous tournament between two teams of spear-wielding, ikat-clad horsemen, the Pasola has to be one of the most extravagant (and bloodiest) harvest festivals in Asia. Held annually in February and March, it takes the form of a ritual battle – not so much a quarrel between opposing forces as a need for human blood to run to keep the spirits happy and bring a good harvest. The riders gallop at each other, hurling their *holas* (spears) at rival riders (it's not permitted to use a spear as a lance). Despite the blunt spears, there will be blood, and sometimes deaths still do occur. Accidentally, of course.

Pasola takes place in four areas, its exact timing determined by the arrival on nearby coasts of a certain type of sea worm called *nyale*. Two days before the main events, brutal boxing matches called *pajura* are held, the combatants' fists bound in razor-sharp local grasses.

Before the Pasola can begin, priests in full ceremonial dress must first wade into the ocean to examine the worms at dawn; they're usually found on the eighth or ninth day after a full moon. Fighting begins on the beach, and continues further inland later that same day. Opposing 'armies' are drawn from coastal and inland villages.

In February, Pasola is celebrated in the Kodi area (centred on Kampung Tosi) and the Lemboya area (Kampung Sodan); in March it's in the Wanokaka area (Kampung Waigalli) and the remote Gaura area, west of Lamboya (Kampung Ubu Olehka). Call hotels in Waingapu or Waikabubak to find out the approximate dates before travelling to Sumba, or log onto www.lavalontouristinfo.com and call Edwin Lerrick at Lavalon (p378) in Kupang. He always knows the score in NTT.

and the villages are as pure and raw as the land. Yes, it makes a damn fine base.

Tambolaka's big market day is Saturday.

Sights

Lembaga Studi & Pelestarian Budaya Sumba MUSEUM
(☎0813 3936 2164; museum by donation, r 300,000Rp; ⌚8am-6pm Mon-Sat) Just 3km outside of town, Lembaga Studi & Pelestarian Budaya Sumba is a Catholic-run NGO with a working plantation and a surprisingly good cultural museum. It was developed by introspective priests who noticed how frequently Sumbanese break clean from their old culture and develop negative associations with the *marapu* and other totems once they are baptised. In addition to displays of old photographs, money and pottery, there are collections of gongs and drums and some cool statues all laid out rather tastefully. There is a small *penginapan* (guesthouse) here too, with two simple rooms in a thatched brick house with private porch. It's not fabulous but certainly a quiet, leafy option.

Sleeping & Eating

TOP CHOICE **Oro Beach Houses & Restaurant** BUNGALOW $$
(☎0813 5378 9946, 0813 3911 0068; www.oro-beachbungalows.com; r 450,000Rp, bungalows 500,000Rp) Our favourite place in all of Sumba, replete with low-lying bluffs, lilac dawns, smoldering sunsets and starry night skies, is but a 15-minute, mostly-rutted dirt road drive from Tambolaka airport. Think: three wild beachfront acres owned by a special family (she used to run an NGO, he's an architect with a disaster relief background), where you can nest in a circular thatched bungalow blessed with a canopied driftwood bed and outdoor bath. They offer excellent seafood meals, mountain biking and snorkelling just off their stunning, virtually private, 100m long beach.

Hotel Sinar Tambolaka HOTEL $$
(☎253 4088; Jl Tambolaka; standard 125,000Rp, VIP 300,000-350,000Rp, mains 15,000-30,000Rp; ⌚9am-10pm; ❄📶) Set on a sunken plateau below Jl Tambolaka and perched on the edge of a green valley is Tambolaka town's newest, freshest sleep. Standard rooms are cramped, fan-cooled and have twin beds, but VIP rooms have security boxes, LG flat-screen TVs, high ceilings with crown mouldings, and wood furnishings. They're very clean and excellent value. It also has a restaurant recommended by locals, and it has lovely views.

Penginapan Melati INN $
(☎0813 5396 6066, 24055; Jl Waitabula; r with fan/air-con 125,000/200,000Rp; ❄) In the midst of a front yard renovation that will be complete before your visit, rooms are simple but immaculate with fresh paint and tile throughout. It even has rain shower heads in the *mandi*. Of the 16 rooms, only two have air-con.

Resto Dewata WARUNG $
(☎081 2393 12777; Jl Waitabula; mains 15,000-30,000Rp) A Balinese-owned warung with a limited menu that includes a tasty Bakso as well as fried fish and chicken with rice. It's basic but, according to local expats, consistently good.

Information

BNI Bank (Jl El Tari; ⌚8am-5pm Mon-Thu, 7.30am-4pm Fri) Has an ATM and changes US$100 bills.

Warnet Made Josel Yoliyo (Jl El Tari; per hour 6000Rp; ⌚8:30am-10pm) Offers a decent internet connection downtown.

Getting There & Away

AIR Tambolaka's new airport terminal was nearing completion at research time, which meant bags were unloaded in the shiny, almost completed new terminal (baggage claim wasn't ready yet), and wires dangled from exposed rafters. Nevertheless, flights had already increased in frequency making Sumba more accessible than ever. At research time Lion/Wings Air and **Merpati** (☎21051; Jl Bhayangkara 20) were each flying to Denpasar three times weekly. Merpati also flew five times weekly to Kupang. **Aviastar** offered four weekly Bali flights. Departure tax is 10,000Rp.

BOAT Waikelo, a small and predominantly Muslim town north of Waitabula has a small picturesque harbour that is the main port for West Sumba and offers ferry service to Sape (Sumbawa) twice a week. It departs from Sape for Waikelo on Monday and Friday at around 10pm and returns to Sape (50,000Rp, eight hours) at 5pm on Tuesday and Saturday.

BUS Buses leave throughout the day for Waikabubak (10,000Rp, one hour) from the centre of town.

Maluku

POP 2.1 MILLION

Includes »

Best Places to Eat

» Floridas (p407)
» Mutiara Guesthouse (p433)
» Delfika (p434)
» Savana Cottages (p439)
» Rumah Makan Nifia (p419)

Best Places to Stay

» Mutiara Guesthouse (p433)
» CDS Bungalow (p437)
» Bela International Hotel (p406)

Why Go?

Welcome to the original Spice Islands. Back in the 16th century when nutmeg, cloves and mace were global commodities that grew nowhere else, money really did 'grow on trees'. It was the search for Maluku's valuable spices that kick-started European colonisation and, thanks to a series of wrong turns and one auspicious land swap, shaped the modern world. Today, spices have minimal economic clout and Maluku (formerly called the Moluccas) has dropped out of global consciousness. What remains is a scattering of idyllic islands where the complex web of cultures envelops visitors with an effusive welcome and an almost Polynesian charm. While transport can prove infuriatingly inconvenient, with flexibility and patience you can explore pristine reefs, stroll empty stretches of powdery white sand, book idyllic over-water bungalows, scale 16th-century fort walls, snap endless photos of perfectly formed volcanoes, and revel in a tropical discovery that seems almost too good to be true.

When to Go

Ambon

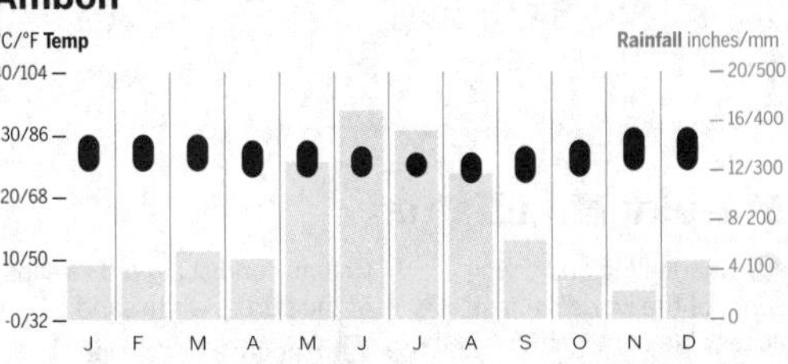

Nov–Mar The dry season is the best time to visit, with consistently spectacular diving.

Apr–May, Sep–Oct The shoulder seasons are a good time for the Banda and Kei Islands.

Jun–Aug Monsoons prevail, upsetting transport schedules and shuttering dive shops.

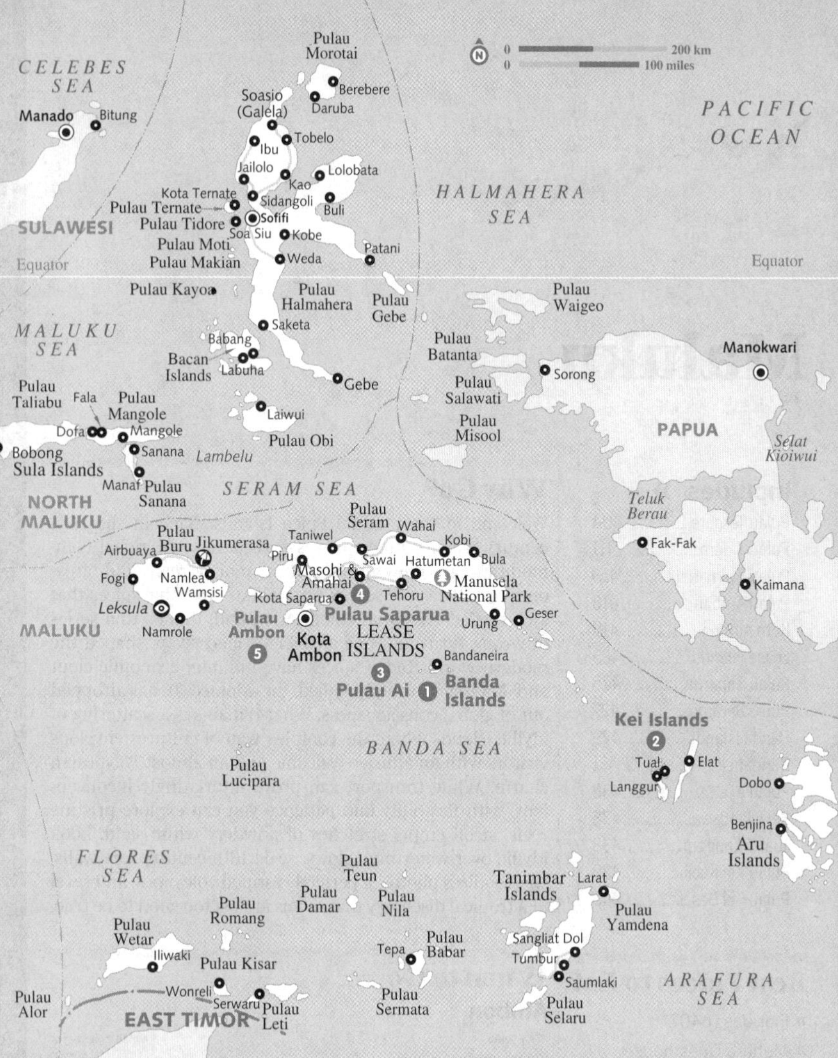

Maluku Highlights

1. Snorkelling and diving some of the world's finest accessible coral gardens in the historically fascinating **Banda Islands** (p429)

2. Unwinding at **Ohoidertawun** (p439) or **Pasir Panjang** (p441) in the Kei Islands, two stunning yet virtually undiscovered sweeps of the purest white sand

3. Finding a beachside homestay and indulging in your own village retreat on **Pulau Ai** (p436)

4. Staying at one of the offbeat getaways on **Pulau Saparua** (p425) before mainstream tourism discovers the island's white-sand beaches, friendly villages and extensive diving potential

5. Plunging into the muck with **Maluku Divers** (p424), Pulau Ambon's finest dive operator and most appealing resort

Getting There & Away

AIR Ambon and Ternate are the region's air hubs. Both have several daily connections to Jakarta, mostly via Makassar, Manado (Sulawesi) or Surabaya. There are several connections from Ambon to Papua.

SEA Five Pelni liners visit Ambon on biweekly cycles from Bau Bau (southeast Sulawesi, 12 hours), Makassar (31 to 36 hours), Surabaya (60 to 68 hours) and/or Jakarta (Tanjung Priok; four days). *Ciremai* handily continues east via the Banda and Kei Islands, as does the infinitely slower and overloaded *Kelimutu*, which is reportedly infested with roaches. These ships, along with the *Dorolonda*, continue on to various ports in Papua. The *Lambelu* instead swings north via Buru and Ternate to terminate in Bitung (northern Sulawesi). *Sinabung* stops in Ternate between Bitung and Sorong.

Getting Around

AIR Trigana operates numerous regional flights. NBA flies three times weekly to Banda Islands from Ambon and once weekly to Seram on little prop-planes. Bad weather, low passenger loads and engine trouble make cancellations quite frequent. Wings connects Ambon with the Kei Islands daily. Express Air flies between Ternate and Halmahera.

BOAT Pelni services within North Maluku are patchy and notoriously changeable, but you can count on the routes that connect Ambon with the Banda Islands and onward to the Kei Islands. Some medium-range hops are served by uncomfortable ASDP ferries or by wooden boats known as *kapal motor*. Perintis cargo boats are bigger but not at all designed with passengers in mind. You might choose to hop on one of these from the Banda Islands, but if you do, bring waterproof clothes. Speedboats link nearby islands and roadless villages. Locals use very specific terms for boat types: if there isn't a *spid* (covered multi-engine speedboat) to your destination, there might still be a *Johnson* (outboard-powered longboat) or a *ketinting/lape-lape* (smaller, short-hop motorised outrigger canoe). Regular speedboats connect short and midrange destinations (eg Tertnate–Tidore, Ternate–Halmahera, Ambon–Lease Islands, Ambon–Seram). The longer rides are only available in the dry season and are best early in the morning when seas are calmest. Chartering is widely available and most convenient in the Banda Islands.

ROAD TRANSPORT In mountainous Maluku, the few asphalted roads are often potholed and narrow, while many areas have only mud tracks or no roads at all. On most islands, shorter routes are operated by bemo (minibus), known locally as *mobil*. On Halmahera and Seram, pricey shared Kijangs (fancy seven-seat Toyotas) are more common than long-distance buses. Renting an *ojek* (motorcycle taxi) is a pleasant, inexpensive way to travel if the rain holds off.

NORTH MALUKU

Although dwarfed by sprawling Pulau Halmahera, North Maluku's historically and politically most significant islands are the pyramidal volcanic cones of Ternate and Tidore. Both of these were ancient Islamic sultanates that were once the world's only sources of cloves. Nowadays cloves may seem trivial additions to mulled wine or *kretek* cigarettes, but in the Middle Ages they were enormously valuable as food preservatives and were considered cures for everything from toothache to halitosis to, ahem, sexual dysfunction. Funded by the spice trade, Ternate's and Tidore's sultans became the most powerful rulers in the medieval Indies, but wasted much of their wealth fighting each other.

In 1511 the first Portuguese settlers arrived in Ternate. Tidore responded by inviting in the Spaniards. Both islands found their hospitality rapidly exhausted as the Europeans tried to corner the spice market and preach Christianity. Ternate's Muslim population, already offended by the Europeans' imported pigs and heavy-handed 'justice', rebelled in 1570 when Ternate's Sultan Hairun (Khairun) was executed and his head exhibited on a pike. The besieged Portuguese held until 1575 when the new Ternatean sultan took it over as his palace. Five years later he entertained the English pirate-adventurer Francis Drake. After an amicable meeting, Drake astounded his host by his almost total disinterest in buying cloves. In fact, Drake's ship *Golden Hind* was already so full of stolen Spanish-American gold that he simply couldn't carry anything more.

The Spaniards, and later the Dutch, made themselves equally unpopular. In a history that's as fascinating as it is complicated and Machiavellian, they played Ternate off against Tidore and also confronted one another for control of an elusive clove monopoly. The Dutch prevailed eventually, though the sultanates continued almost uninterrupted for most of the period and remain well-respected institutions to this day.

Today Ternate remains the main hub of North Maluku (Malut), though in 2007 Sofifi on Halmahera was named the province's official capital, and by research time in 2012, many government offices had finally relocated there. Few islands in North Maluku have any real history of tourism, so visits beyond Ternate will often prove to be something of an adventure.

Pulau Ternate

0921

The dramatic volcanic cone of Gunung Api Gamalama (1721m) dominates Pulau Ternate. Settlements are sprinkled around its lower coastal slopes with villages on the east coast coalescing into North Maluku's biggest town, Kota Ternate. The city makes a useful transport gateway for the region and has fishing harbours filled with colourful boats and a few remnant stilt-house neighbourhoods. And the neighbouring volcanic islands look particularly photogenic when viewed from one of the hillside hotel and restaurant terraces.

KOTA TERNATE

POP 172,000

Ternate is gorgeous, swathed in jungle and wild clove trees. However, when you first land there, in the shadow of spectacular Gunung Api Gamalama and with several

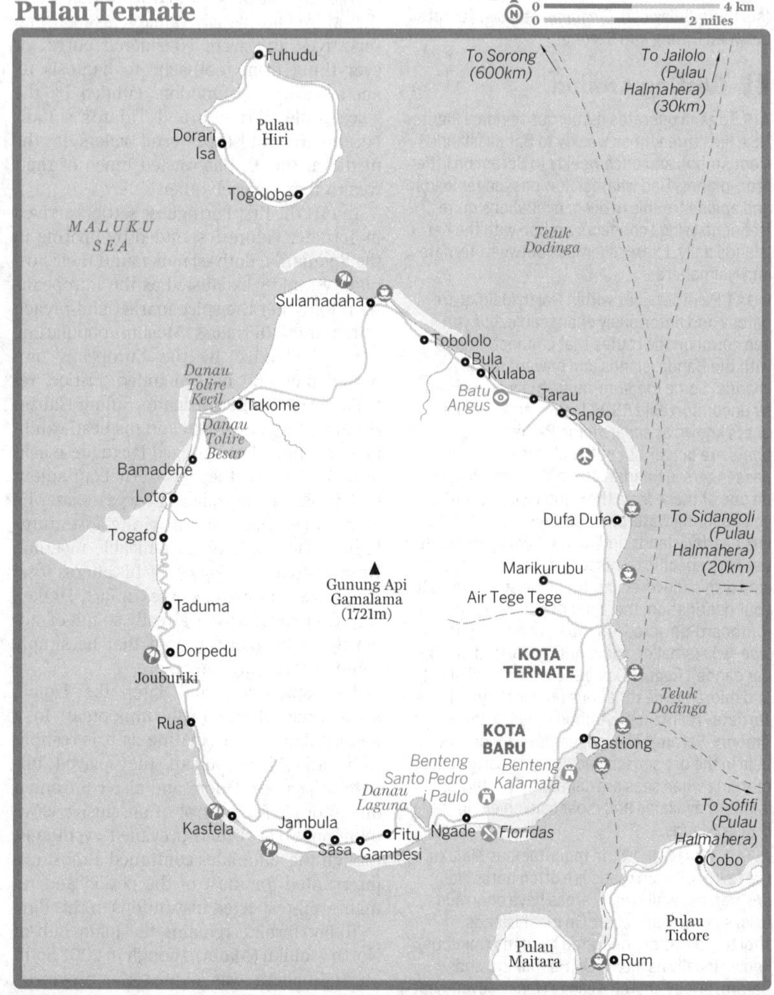

more volcanic islands dotting the deep blue channel beyond, you may be shocked to find it such a frenetic place. Here's a growing, growling and increasingly middle-class city that tends to lure business travellers from throughout Indonesia. And that principal business appears to be government. Still, it's a worthy stopover if you care to wander rebuilt 16th-century forts, sample strangely textured yet interesting flavours, or visit those nearby isles.

Sights

Kota Ternate's three fortresses were rebuilt by the Dutch between 1606 and 1610. By the 1990s only decrepit ruins remained. Since then, the empty, remnant shells have been over-renovated.

Keraton MUSEUM

(Istana Kesultan; Map p406; ☎312 1166; admission by donation; ⊙9am-5pm Mon-Fri, to 3pm Sat, to 1pm Sun; festival 6-13 April) Built in 1834 and restored in semicolonial style, the Sultan's Palace is still a family home. The palace contains a museum section with a small but interesting collection of historic weaponry and memorabilia from the reigns of past sultans, whose lineage dates back to 1257. You need a special invitation from the sultan to see the famous *mahkota* (royal crown). Topped with cassowary feathers, it supposedly has magical powers such as growing 'hair', which needs periodic cutting. Some claim it can even stop Gamalama from erupting. The *mahkota* is only worn at coronations and during the Legu Gam ceremonies, Ternate's main **festival**. Legu Gam culminates on the sultan's birthday and involves a variety of traditional musicians, dancers and performers. On the 27th evening of Ramadan, Laila tul Qadr celebrations see the sultan's procession arrive to a mass of flaming torches at the **Royal Mosque** (Map p406; Jl Sultan Babullah), which has impressive heavy interior timber work.

The Keraton is sometimes closed, even during normal hours of operation. At the time of research, a separate building was being built for the museum. It was scheduled to open in 2013, but by the look of things, that may have been ambitious.

Benteng Oranye FORTRESS

(Map p408) The biggest and most central, but least complete, of Kota Ternate's three fortresses is the 1606 Benteng Oranye (originally Fort Malayo), once headquarters of the Dutch VOC operation and later the residence of Ternate's Dutch governors. Today you can wander some sections of cannon-topped bastion accessed through a restored gateway arch.

Benteng Tolukko FORTRESS

(Map p406; 20,000Rp donation appropriate) The smallest and cutest of the town forts, little Benteng Tolukko was the first Portuguese stronghold on Ternate (1512). It has beautifully manicured floral gardens and attractive sea views; stroll among the turrets for a sweeping panorama. If it's locked, knock on the door of the family home next door. They will have the key.

Benteng Kalamata FORTRESS

(Map p406) The 1540 Benteng Kalamata has an unusual waterside location 1km southwest of Bastiong, with waves lapping its angular walls. There are great views across to Ternate's old foe, Tidore.

Majolica Ulama Indonesia MOSQUE

(Masjid Al Munawwah; Map p408) This truly grand, if modern, mosque is worthy of a sultanate, with its eye-catching dome covered in stylised Arabic calligraphy (the repeating name of Allah). It is so vast that it overshoots its new land-reclamation site with outer minarets thrusting directly from the sea. Of course, one has already buckled thanks to a sinister storm surge and shoddy construction.

Sleeping

You'll value accommodation with a powerful air conditioner, given Ternate's oppressive heat and humidity.

Accommodation under 150,000Rp is plentiful around Ahmad Yani Port but conditions are often abysmal. Although there are a few exceptions, even the nicest cheapies often have damp patches, a slimy *mandi* (a large water tank from which water is ladled over the body) and a hint of dysfunction.

TOP CHOICE **Bukit Pelangi Hotel** HOTEL $$

(☎312 2180; Jl Jati Selatan 338; standard/deluxe/executive d 200,000/275,000/325,000Rp; ❄@☎) It has rooms in both an older building and a much newer, brighter building on the same property. In the newer building you'll find fresh tiles, wood furnishings, TVs and new air-con units. Those facing the seaside open onto a common terrace with gorgeous harbour and Tidore views.

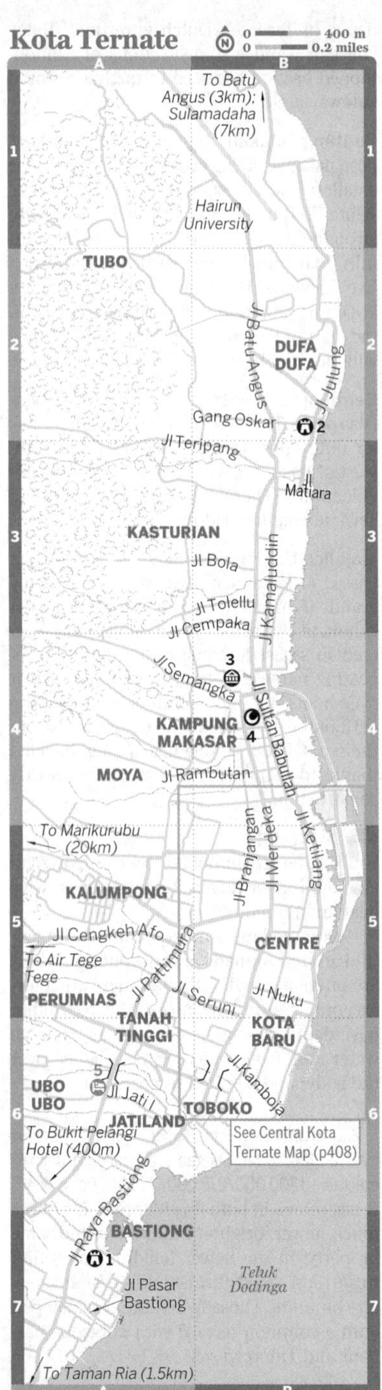

Kota Ternate

Sights

Sleeping

TOP CHOICE **Bela International Hotel** HOTEL **$$$**
(☎312 1800; www.belainternationalhotel.com; Jl Jati Raya 500; deluxe/executive 1,000,000/1,250,000Rp; ❄📶) Far and away Ternate's most luxurious option, and easily the finest hotel in Maluku, the Bela International has 195 immaculate, gently fashionable rooms in coffee-and-cream colours, all with balconies and massive sea or volcano views. Even the cheapest one is spacious and equipped to international standards. Executive rooms have a bathtub and free wi-fi.

Villa Ma'rasai INN **$$**
(☎0821 3733 7395, 0813 9288 9475; www.vilamarasai.com; Kampung Gambesi; r without/with terrace 330,000/350,000Rp; ❄) Lovingly imagined by a former tour guide and fluent English speaker, this sweet boutique is 7km from the city centre and next to the university in Gambesi village. It is set high on the Gamalama slopes and nestled among clove trees, with stunning sea and Tidore views from every room. The exterior is colourfully dressed in yellows and oranges, the interior decorated with ikat (woven cloth) and other handicrafts. The immaculate rooms are spacious with hardwood floors, ample windows, high wooden ceilings, and two-tone paint jobs. Our three nitpicky complaints: low water pressure, no hot water, and no wi-fi. Otherwise this spot is a tremendous choice. Meals are fabulous and the owner arranges hikes into the jungle behind the villa (600,000Rp per person, including lunch box).

Hotel Archie HOTEL **$$**
(Map p408; ☎311 0555; Jl Nuku 6; standard/superior 275,000/295,000Rp; ❄) Vastly better than most equivalently priced competitors, Archie has English-speaking staff and rooms with dated charm, along with hot water, fancy crown mouldings, satellite TV, toilet paper, and minibar. However, some rooms can smell like a cigar box. Rooms in **Archie 2**

(Map p408; ☎312 1197; Jl Nuku 100; d 295,000Rp) across the road are a bit more sterile, but still comfy with curious theatrical columns in front of the bathtubs.

Seqavia Guesthouse GUESTHOUSE $
(Map p408; ☎311 1147; Jl Kampung Kodok; r 120,000Rp; ❄) Decent-value rooms with pastel walls, crown mouldings, new air-con units and a quaint neighbourhood location. It's reasonably clean, if not spotless.

Tiara Inn GUESTHOUSE $
(Map p408; ☎311 1017; Jl Salim Fabanyo; s/d 176,000/205,000Rp; ❄) Bright, basic, tiled rooms with a desk, clean bathroom, new air-con units and warm management. Rooms are freshly painted and free of must or moisture. It's simply one of the best choices in the area at this price.

Taman Ria HOTEL $
(☎322 2124; d 165,000Rp; ❄) After breaching the seemingly eroding gateway you'll enter a pleasantly surprising complex of rooms, with ornate crown mouldings brushed in Pepto-Bismal pink. These are clean, tiled rooms with TVs and private terraces, overlooking an industrial yard. Incongruous? Yes, but good value. You'll find it 700m beyond Benteng Kalamata.

Losmen Kita HOTEL $
(Map p408; ☎312 1950; Jl Stadion 2/5; r/superior 200,000/250,000Rp; ❄) Tucked among the huddled tin-roof masses, this friendly garden hotel isn't great, but it is homey with bamboo and wood furnishings, two-tone paint jobs, and built-in desks.

Losmen Gamalama HOTEL $
(Map p408; ☎312 5943; Jl Merdeka 13; r 200,000Rp, superior r 250,000-275,000Rp; ❄) A smart choice for good-value, pale-yellow rooms, set around a bright inner courtyard, with high ceilings, crown mouldings, air-con and decent baths. It has a scruffy side, but is very doable.

Hotel Indah HOTEL $
(Map p408; ☎312 1334; Jl Bosoiri 3; economy/standard/superior r from 60,000/85,000/125,000Rp; ❄) A decent budget choice. Oh, it's scruffy, but the rooms are sizeable with working air-con and hot water in the most expensive rooms.

Hotel Puri Azzalia HOTEL $$
(Map p408; ☎312 1959; puri.azzalia@yahoo.com; Jl Mononutu 275; standard/deluxe/ste from 240,000/305,000/340,000Rp; ❄) Behind a stylish '50s-retro facade, rooms are decent and clean, if sterile, with low ceilings, flat-screen TVs and air-con. English-speaking staff are fun and warm and there are local artefacts and fresh orchids in the common areas.

Safirna Transito Hotel HOTEL $$
(Map p408; ☎312 1222; Jl Anggrek; r/ste 300,000/500,000Rp; ❄) It appears modern and comfortable at first, what with that rather splashy lobby decorated with orchids and tasteful wallpaper. Then you'll wander into a hallway with carpet as deplorable as the furniture. The rooms are fine, with TVs, crown mouldings and double beds, but ceilings are low and all rooms except suites have cold showers.

Boulevard Hotel HOTEL $$
(Map p408; ☎311 0777; Jatiland BS; standard/business/deluxe 302,000/375,000/475,000Rp; ❄📶) The entry is bright and cheery. The hallways are grubby, but most rooms seem clean enough, if dark. The waterfront location is a handy getaway with Halmahera boats nearby.

Eating

Rumah makan (eating houses) offer cheap eats around the markets. Several shacks north of the bemo terminal serve local specialities such as *ikan gohu* (raw-fish morsels in a tangy peanut-edged marinade) and *popeda* (Malukan sago) as part of 25,000Rp all-you-can-eat spreads, including fish, cassava and a dozen other side dishes.

Self-caterers should head to the Multi Mart supermarket at Jati Mall and **Golden Bakery** (Map p408; Jl Pattimura; ⏲9am-10pm), which bakes a decent selection of fresh bread and pastries.

TOP CHOICE **Floridas** SEAFOOD $$
(☎321 4430; mains 15,000-350,000Rp; ⏲10am-11pm) Floridas – a 10,000Rp *ojek* ride southwest of town – sits high above a steep slope of banana trees. Behind the kitschy dining hall, ledge tables provide splendid bay views across to the superimposed volcanic cones of Tidore and Maitara. Try the delicious *ikan woku kenari* fish steak (not boneless!) marinated in a mildly spicy sauce of *kenari* almonds, sweet chilli and lemongrass, then roasted in a banana leaf. Superb!

Central Kota Ternate

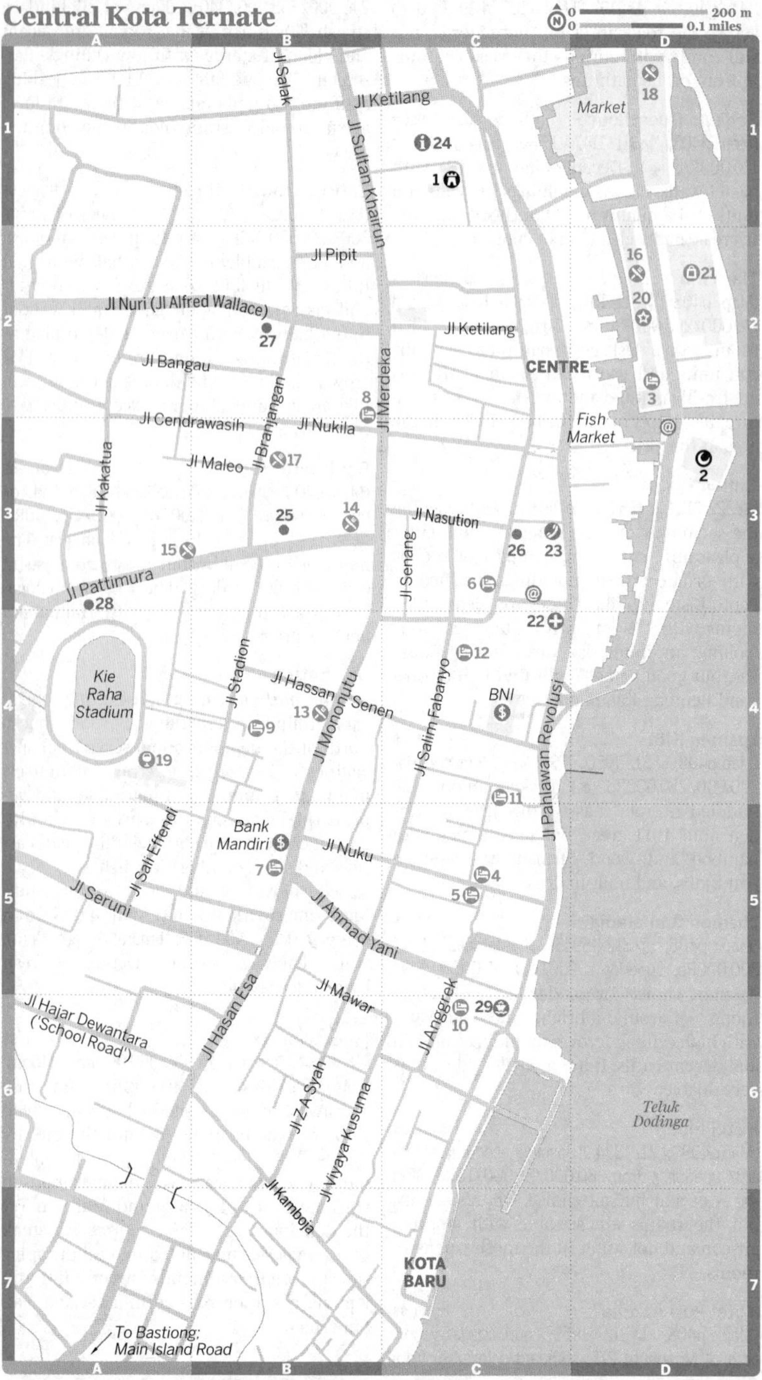

0 200 m
0 0.1 miles

Jl Salak
Jl Ketilang
Jl Sultan Khairun
Market
Jl Pipit
Jl Nuri (Jl Alfred Wallace)
Jl Ketilang
CENTRE
Jl Bangau
Jl Merdeka
Jl Cendrawasih
Jl Nukila
Jl Branjangan
Fish Market
Jl Maleo
Jl Kakatua
Jl Nasution
Jl Senang
Jl Pattimura
Kie Raha Stadium
Jl Stadion
Jl Hassan Senen
Jl Mononutu
Jl Salim Fabanyo
BNI
Jl Pahlawan Revolusi
Jl Sali Effendi
Bank Mandiri
Jl Nuku
Jl Seruni
Jl Ahmad Yani
Jl Mawar
Jl Hajar Dewantara ('School Road')
Jl Hasan Esa
Jl Anggrek
Jl Z A Syah
Jl Viyaya Kusuma
Teluk Dodinga
Jl Kamboja
KOTA BARU
To Bastiong; Main Island Road

1 2 3 4 5 6 7 8 9 10 11 12 13 14 15 16 17 18 19 20 21 22 23 24 25 26 27 28 29

Central Kota Ternate

Sights

1 Benteng Oranye C1
2 Majolica Ulama Indonesia D3

Sleeping

3 Boulevard Hotel D2
4 Hotel Archie C5
5 Hotel Archie 2 .... C5
6 Hotel Indah C3
7 Hotel Puri Azzalia B5
8 Losmen Gamalama B2
9 Losmen Kita B4
10 Safirna Transito Hotel C6
11 Seqavia Guesthouse C4
12 Tiara Inn C4

Eating

13 Bakso Lapangan Tembak Senayan B4
14 Golden Bakery B3
15 Lauk Pauk A3
16 Platinum D2
17 Pondok Katu B3
18 Rumah Makan Popeda Gamalama D1

Drinking

19 Soccer Lounge A4

Entertainment

20 Q Beat D2

Shopping

21 Jati Mall D2

Information

22 Dharma Ibu Rumah Sakit Umum C4
23 Plasa Telkom C3
24 Ternate City Tourist Office C1

Transport

25 Batavia Air B3
26 Eterna Raya Ternate C3
27 Expressair B2
28 Lion Air/Wings Air A3
29 Pelni C6

Rumah Makan Popeda Gamalama POPEDA $
(meals 25,000Rp; ⏲5am-5pm) This wonderful little market shack is the choice spot to try *popeda* in Ternate. The full spread includes plates of different fish (presented with teeth and all), stewed greens and mushrooms, steamed pumpkin, four kinds of *sambal*, and that rich sodium-packed slime that is *popeda*. Leave your culinary inhibitions, textural food fears, and sanitation hang-ups at the door. The locals will be thrilled to have you. And you may even like it.

Lauk Pauk PADANG $
(meals 10,000-20,000Rp; ⏲6am-8pm) If you're hungry for Indo grub you can't do much better than the fervently spiced and curried fish and chicken dishes on display at this pick-and-mix hole in the wall. The devoted local line-up speaks for itself.

Bakso Lapangan Tembak Senayan INDONESIAN $
(Jl Mononutu; mains 18,000-38,000Rp; ⏲10am-10pm) The speciality of this cool, dark, inviting, brick-and-timber house is the *bakso* (meatball) soup, of course. It does *bakso goreng* (fried meatballs) too, along with dozens of classic Indonesian chicken, shrimp, rice and noodle dishes.

Pondok Katu CHINESE, INDONESIAN $$
(☎312 7332; Jl Branjangan 28; mains 30,000-55,000Rp; ⏲10am-10pm; ❄) This long-lasting family favourite serves seafood lunches and good Chinese food in a gently attractive columned dining hall.

Platinum INTERNATIONAL $$
(☎312 2820; Jatiland BS; mains 35,000-110,000Rp; ⏲11am-midnight; ❄📶) Feeding and watering Ternate's upwardly mobile – and there are droves of them – this sleek spot does a handful of Western dishes, such as burgers and pastas, and reams of Indo classics, including a surprisingly excellent *soto ayam* (chicken soup). There's karaoke in the evenings and it does get a bit smoky in here.

Drinking & Entertainment

Ahem, in Ternate, by decree from the sultanate (it's so much fun to write that), alcohol may not be sold in restaurants and beer is fiercely expensive in karaoke bars. Translation: pack a flask.

Soccer Lounge LOUNGE
(Map p408; Hotel Corner Palace, Jl Stadion; ⌚11am-midnight) The Hotel Corner Palace's top-floor bar is looking as run-down as a 40-year-old hooker, but its large windows overlook the Kie Raha Stadium. When Ternate's major-league football team is playing at home, you could watch from here, beer in hand, without risking heatstroke in the ramshackle, overcrowded, exposed stands.

Q Beat KARAOKE
(Map p408; pool tables per hr 44,000Rp; ⌚10am-2am) Across from the new Jati Mall is this thoroughly updated pool hall and family karaoke lounge – yes, the sweet kind of karaoke.

Shopping

The bustling new waterfront **Jati Mall** (Map p408; ⌚10am-10pm) is not going to give Surabaya or Jakarta or even Medan mall envy. However, it's a great place to escape the heat, there's a **Graha Media** bookshop, and you can order an espresso and otherwise hang with Ternate's thriving middle class. Its massive **Multi Mart** outlet has all the groceries and health and beauty supplies a traveller could possibly need.

Information

INTERNET ACCESS **Star Net** (Jl Reklamasi Kelurahen Muhajirin; per hr 7000Rp; ⌚24 hr; @) is a 24-hour warnet with a decent connection, diagonally across the street from the big mosque. **Warnet Game Online** (Jl Christina Martha Tiahahu; per hr 6000Rp; ⌚7am-2am; @) is another reliable choice.

MEDICAL SERVICES **Dharma Ibu Rumah Sakit Umum** (Map p408; Jl Pahlawan Revolusi) is a Dutch-founded holdover from the colonial days and is still set in the original 80-year-old building. The doctor is a nun. Bring a translator.

MONEY There are several banks on Jl Pahlawan Revolusi but only **BNI** (Bank Negara Indonesia; ⌚8am-3pm Mon-Thu, to noon Fri) changes money, and then only US dollars in new, unfolded $100 bills. The shiny new **Bank Mandiri** (Jl Nukila) has a Visa-compatible ATM.

TELEPHONE **Plasa Telkom** (Map p408; cnr Jl Pattimura & Jl Pahlawan Revolusi; ⌚8am-6pm)

TOURIST INFORMATION **Ternate City Tourist Office** (Map p408; ☎311 1211; Benteng Oranye; ⌚8am-2.30pm Mon-Fri) has friendly staff; some speak English, but information is limited.

Getting There & Away

Lion/Wings Air (Almas Mega Travel; Map p408; ☎25566, 021 6379 8000; www.secure2.lionair.co.id; Jl Pattimura 125; ⌚8am-8pm), **Batavia Air** (Map p408; ☎312 4333; Jl Pattimura 10; ⌚8am-6pm & 8-10pm) and **Expressair** (Map p408; ☎312 2846; Jl Pattimura 10; ⌚9am-6pm) have offices in town.

Flight schedule and carriers shift frequently. If you want a current, comprehensive view of exactly who is flying where and when, find **Eterna Raya Ternate** (Map p408; ☎312 1651; Jl Bosoiri 109; ⌚9am-6pm), the best travel agent in Ternate. Departure tax is 16,000Rp.

There's a **Pelni office** (Map p408; ☎312 1434; www.pelni.com; ⌚8am-4pm Mon-Sat) near the port.

Getting Around

Taxis charge an exorbitant 100,000Rp for the 6km from Babullah Airport to central Ternate. However, if you walk 10 minutes south, bemos from outside Hairun University cost only 3000Rp to the central market. From there, bemos run in all directions (3000Rp) but *ojeks* (5000Rp per ride) are generally more convenient.

GUNUNG API GAMALAMA

Ternate's central volcano erupted in 1840, destroying almost every house on the island. Although it has blown its fiery nose as recently as 2003, it is not considered imminently dangerous. However, it isn't necessarily safe, nor was it permissible at research time to bag its peak. There are pleasant, shorter clove-grove hikes from Air Tege Tege village (near the transmitter tower), or from Villa Ma'rasai (p406) in Kampung Gambesi (it arranges day hikes), but even here it gets very steep rapidly. The tourist office can help you find a guide.

OUTSIDE KOTA TERNATE

Head out of Kota Ternate via **Batu Angus**, a gnarled 300-year-old lava flow, and you'll reach **Sulamadaha** (entrance 5000Rp), a popular if somewhat litter-strewn black-sand beach with heavy swells at the top of the island. From a cove some 800m east, public longboats (5000Rp per person) cross to the offshore volcanic cone of **Pulau Hiri** almost hourly from dusk till dawn. Hiri was the last step of the sultan's family's *Sound of Music*-style escape from Ternate during WWII.

Beyond the village of **Takome**, the main road returns to the coast beside the small, muddy **Danau Tolire Kecil**. Less than 1km further, a paved side lane (2000Rp fee) climbs to the rim of **Danau Tolire Besar**. Startlingly sheer cliffs plummet down to the lugubriously green, crocodile-infested waters of this deep crater lake. Local children offer guide services should you want to descend (1½ hours return on foot).

TRANSPORT FROM PULAU TERNATE

Air

DESTINATION	COMPANY	FREQUENCY
Ambon	Expressair	3 weekly
Galela (Halmahera)	Expressair	3 weekly
Makassar	Expressair, Garuda, Sriwijaya	5 weekly
Manado	Lion/Wings Air, Garuda	daily
Surabaya	Batavia Air, Expressair	daily

Boat

DESTINATION	PORT	TYPE	COST (RP)	FREQUENCY
Ambon via Namlea	Ahmad Yani	Pelni	varies	2 monthly
Jailolo (Pulau Halmahera)	Dufa Dufa	*kapal* motor	35,000	3 daily
Jailolo (Pulau Halmahera)	Dufa Dufa	speedboat	50,000	when full
Rum	Bastiong Ferry Port	car ferry	5000	7am, 1pm, 4pm, 6pm
Rum	Bastiong First Port	speedboat	8000 (charters 70,000)	when full
Sidangoli (Pulau Halmahera)	Mesjid Raya	speedboat	50,000 (charters 350,000)	when full
Sofifi (Pulau Halmahera)	Kota Baru	speedboat	30,000-50,000	when full
Sorong	Ahmad Yani	Pelni	varies	2 monthly

A footpath from the southern edge of Dorpedu leads down to **Jouburiki**, the beach where Ternate's very first sultan was supposedly crowned in 1257. **Danau Laguna** is a pleasant, spring-fed bowl lake with a lushly forested perimeter. Across the straits lie the conical islands of Tidore and Maitara, as featured on Indonesia's 1000Rp notes. Those volcanoes align perfectly when viewed from Floridas (p407) restaurant just beyond Ngade. Across the road are the stubby roadside remnants of **Benteng Santo Pedro i Paulo**, once Ternate's main line of defence against a 1606 Spanish attack.

ℹ Getting Around

From Kota Ternate's central terminal, bemos run frequently to Sulamadaha (5000Rp, counterclockwise) and Kastela (5000Rp, clockwise). No single bemo goes right around the island but some north-route vehicles drive as far as Togafo (10,000Rp). From there it's a pleasantly windy 2km walk to Taduma, where the longest south-route bemos start. Consider chartering an *ojek* to loop around the island with photo stops (around 100,000Rp).

Pulau Tidore

☎0921

This is pure village Maluku. A sublime volcanic island dotted with painted wooden homes bordered by flower gardens, shaded by mango trees and coconut palms, and scented by sheets of cloves sun-drying in the street. The island's proud volcanic profile looks especially tempting when viewed from Bastiong on Ternate, and this charming, laid-back island does make a refreshing escape from the bustle of its historical enemy. An independent Islamic sultanate from 1109, Tidore's sultanate was abolished in the Sukarno era, but the 36th sultan was reinstated in 1999. In Tidorean language *sukur dofu* means 'thank you', *saki* means 'delicious' and *sterek* (*lau*) means '(very) good'. Hire an *ojek*, spin all the way around, and you'll come out smiling.

SOASIO

Above the southernmost edge of Tidore's capital, Soasio, lies the sparse, overgrown remnants of **Benteng Tohula**, Tidore's 17th-century Spanish fort. This is exactly what you want from a ruin – overgrown, crumbling fortress walls and spectacular views of Halmahera and Soasio. You'll have to navigate the reasonably sturdy wooden and bamboo ladder to get to the top, but it's well worth it. Around 200m north the **Sonyine Malige Sultan's Memorial Museum** displays the sultan's throne and giant spittoons, plus the royal crown topped with cassowary feathers. The crown is considered as magical as Ternate's *mahkota*. To enter the musem, you'll have to first find the curator, Umar Muhammad, who works at the DIKNAS office in the Dinas Pendidikan dan Kebudayan building, 2km north. Umar has been known to demand rather hefty entry fees of up to 100,000Rp.

A block inland from the museum, sturdy whitewashed base bastions are all that remain of the original *kraton* royal citadel (Istana Sultan) which now contains an unfinished contemporary palace-villa with a garish blue roof. There's a new **BNI** branch with an ATM here too; it's the island's only place to get or change cash.

AROUND TIDORE

Most other Tidorean villages are simply strips of homes on either side of the coast road. None of these are outstanding, though several have small ribbons of beach. **Pantai Akasahu** is underwhelming but popular for its grubby little hot-spring pool. From here the quiet road to Rum is attractive, with fine views over Ternate. A three-minute speedboat hop from Rum, **Pulau Maitara** has clear, blue waters for better snorkelling and swimming. On the southern coast, **Pantai Kajoli** is a slender white-sand beach – the island's best – that kisses turquoise shallows. **Pulau Mare**, just offshore, is famed for its attractive, no-frills pottery. Boat charters (100,000Rp) to and from the island are available from Kajoli.

Sleeping

Tidore is easy to visit as a day trip from Ternate, but Soasio has one rather inviting *penginapan* (simple lodging house).

Penginapan Seroja HOMESTAY $$
(☎316 1456; Jl Sultan Hassanuddin; d 250,000Rp; ❄) Decked out with flowers, this attractive, waterside, family homestay lies 50m south of the museum in Old Soasio. Its air-con twin rooms are decently appointed, but some smell musty. Try to grab one with a sitting area overlooking the water. It's run by a charming *ibu* who can really cook.

Getting Around

Frequent bemos run from Rum to Soasio to Goto (10,000Rp, 30 minutes) using the south-coast road. No bemos use the quiet Rum to Mafututu route, but that pretty road is now asphalted. *Ojeks* cicumnavigate the island for negotiable rates (around 100,000Rp).

BOATS FROM PULAU TIDORE

DESTINATION	PORT	TYPE	COST (RP)	FREQUENCY
Bastiong	Rum	ferry	5000	3 daily
Bastiong	Rum	speedboat	8000	when full
Sofifi (Pulau Halmahera)	Goto	speedboat	50,000	when full 7-9am

Pulau Halmahera

Maluku's biggest island is eccentrically shaped, like a starfish, with four mountainous peninsulas, several volcanic cones and dozens of offshore islands. As it's sparsely populated and hard to get around, the island's potential for diving, birdwatching and beach tourism remains almost entirely untapped. In the riverine interior, the nomadic, seminaked Togutil people still hunt deer with wooden spears, but change is coming with gold mining at Buli and the Weda Bay nickel-mining concession near Kobe. The creation of new regional capitals at Sofifi (North Maluku province), Weda (Central Halmahera) and Jailolo (Western Halmahera) is also stimulating local building booms. The movement of big bureaucracies out of Ternate and Tidore may finally reverse a history throughout which Halmahera has been largely dominated by those tiny islands. Halmahera has a predominantly Muslim population, with Christian villages in several areas of the more developed northern peninsula.

Pulau Halmahera

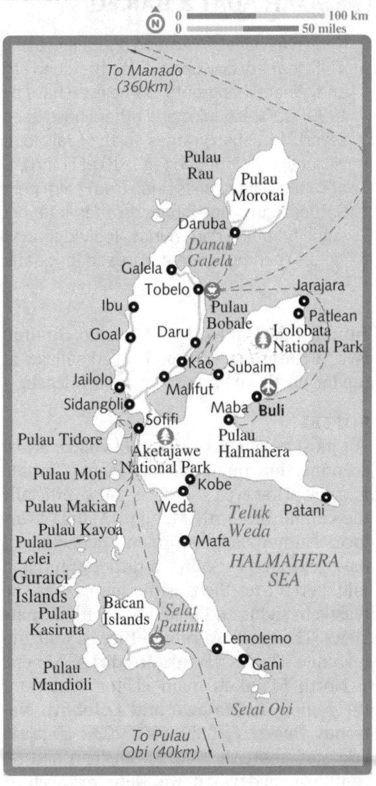

Getting There & Away

Expressair has air links to Galela. Pelni's *Sangiang* loops around Halmahera once or twice a month from Ternate and/or Bitung (Sulawesi). But by far the most popular access is by speedboat from Ternate. For the northwestern coast head for Jailolo. For Tobelo, Galela and the east, cross initially to Sofifi or Sidangoli.

JAILOLO

☎0922

Famed for its fragrant durians, the attractive little port of Jailolo steams gently amid the mangroves at the base of a lush volcanic cone. Before being incorporated by Ternate, Jailolo was an independent sultanate. Today, not even a stone remains of Jailolo's former *kraton* (palace), abandoned in the 1730s. However, the sultan was reinstated in 2003 and now lives in a modest beachfront villa in Marimbati.

Not far from the market and Jailolo's main jetty, you'll find **Penginapan Nusantara** (Jl Gufasa; r with fan/air-con 100,000/165,000Rp; ❄), a deceptively sprawling budget haunt with simple and reasonably clean tiled rooms, though you may have to hunt down reception. Virtually next door, **Penginapan Camar** (☎222 1100; Jl Gufasa; r with fan/air-con 155,000/220,000Rp; ❄) has slightly better, cleaner rooms, the very best of which are a frightening shade of purple. The new, boxy **Hotel d'Hoek** (☎222 1200; Jl Hatebicara; standard/deluxe 286,000/396,000Rp; ❄) has the best rooms in the area, but is inconveniently located 3km out of centre near the Marimbati junction. Nevertheless, if you want air-con and hot water, you'll land here.

Hole-in-the-wall eateries in the market serve superb *nasi ikan* (fish with rice) for about 15,000Rp. Large speedboats to Dufa Dufa (Ternate, 50,000Rp, one hour) leave throughout the day when full. You can also hop a slower, wooden *kapal motor* (35,000Rp, two hours, three times daily).

AROUND JAILOLO

A very pleasant 12km *ojek* excursion takes you to **Marimbati**, set on a long black-sand beach (beware of currents if swimming). En route, the floral villages of **Hoku Hoku**, **Taboso**, **Lolori** and **Gamtala** each maintain their own traditionally thatched *rumah adat* (traditional houses). Reached by an

RUMAH ADAT & BAILEU

Known as *baileu* in Ambon and the Lease Islands (which also have fine examples), *rumah adat* are airy open-sided thatched structures doubling as village meeting places and general hang-outs. Some even have a communal TV. Many were burnt during the 1999–2002 troubles and others have been tastelessly modernised. However, those in several Christian villages north of Jailolo remain original, some dating from the time the villgaes were founded (eg 1910 at Lolori). Several Jailolo-area *rumah adat* display a pair of *sasadu*, hairy balls hung from palm pennants at the end of an elongated apex beam. Rather than crude innuendo, their intended symbolism is as the 'feet' (representing stability) of the community. Tucked away into the palm-woven beams you may spot a *sie-sie* (bamboo pipe-cup), used for quaffing distilled palm wine on special occasions.

entirely different road via Akelamo, **Susupu** is a picturesque volcano-backed village at the far-northern end of Marimbati Beach.

SOFIFI

For most travellers this market village is just a connection point on the Tobelo–Ternate journey. However, Sofifi is now officially the capital of North Maluku (Malut) province. Numerous government departments have relocated to Sofifi – a rather grand and hilly perch over the pristine mangroves (no plastic in sight) and placid bay, with Ternate views. The new governor's office is, well, unmissable. There's a **Bank Mandiri** ATM here.

North Maluku's main visitor centre for the remote **Aketajawe and Lolobata National Parks** (☎0852 4003 7036; aketajawe-lolobata@gmail.com; Jl 40; ⏰9am-4pm) had recently opened when we were researching this book. Don't expect miracles; there was very little in the way of information, just some Indonesian-language brochures and one speaker of basic English on staff when we visited. However, some of the park staff are English-speaking. If you're an ornithologist seeking the exceedingly rare *burung bidadari* (Wallace's standard-wing bird of paradise), you should ask the park staff for a lift to the park, and a letter granting entrance to the conservation area. The **North Maluku Tourist Office** is located on the 4th floor of the **Kantor Bupati Halmahera**, but staff often leave criminally early. Thankfully, the **Kantor Pariwisata Halmahera Utara** (North Halmahera Tourist Office; www.halmaherautara.com; Jl Kawasan Permarintahan 1A, 2nd fl; ⏰8am-noon & 1-4pm Mon-Fri) is fabulous, with drums and handicrafts on display. Here you can expect warm, engaging English-speaking staff who can arrange guides for overland tours to deserted white-sand beaches and spectacular waterfalls (per person 300,000Rp to 350,000Rp), as well as plenty of literature highlighting the best of Halmahera.

There are two hotels in Sofifi, though unless you are organising a tour deep into the interior, there's no reason to sleep here. **Simpang Raya** (Jl Raya Gurapin; meals 20,000-30,000Rp; ⏰8am-10pm) is the only legitimate restaurant in Sofifi – a clean and decent pick-and-mix warung, with Padang food. It's across the road from the sea.

Sofifi–Bastiong speedboats (40 minutes) cost 50,000Rp for fast-filling 12-seaters, and 30,000Rp for bigger versions that might take an hour to fill up. Kijangs bound for Tobelo (100,000Rp, 3½ hours) and Weda (150,000Rp) wait by the dock till early afternoon.

TOBELO

☎0924

Humble Tobelo is northern Halmahera's only real 'town'. Its bay is fronted by a pretty jigsaw of islands, many ringed with golden sandy beaches, though they feel a world apart from this otherwise grotty little backwater. The most accessible isle is Pulau Kakara, where there is now a government-run fishing and diving resort that is Halmahera's only consistent draw.

The main Kao–Galela road (Jl Kemakmuran/Jl H Simange) is bisected just north of the market by Jl Pelabuhan leading 300m to the main port.

Sleeping & Eating

There are a dozen perfectly survivable options, but most are rather lacklustre. Consider sleeping offshore on luscious Kakara Island.

TOP CHOICE **Kakara Island Resort** RESORT $
(☎0852 4084 2579; www.halmaherautara.com; per person incl meals 200,000Rp, 2 dives 650,000Rp,

fishing trips from 1,500,000Rp for up to 4 people; ❄) Two years old at the time of research, this government-run resort offers diving, snorkelling and fishing off the low-lying, mangrove-shrouded Kakara Island, just a short boat ride from Tobelo's shore. This lush isle has a slim band of white sand and is a wonderful alternative to spending sweaty nights in town. Don't get too excited. Rooms are simple concrete-tile jobs, but the setting is special. We didn't dive here, and have heard that much of Halmahera is rather bombed out, but one site did sound interesting: an underwater coral-crusted volcano, with a maximum depth of 27m.

Bianda Hotel HOTEL $$
(☎262 2123; Jl Kemakmuran; standard/superior/deluxe 250,000/300,000/450,000Rp; ❄) The freshest and newest place on the block has spacious rooms with high-end tile floors, flatscreen TVs, recessed lighting, modern wooden furniture, and air-con throughout. Superior and deluxe rooms have hot water.

Hotel President HOTEL $
(☎262 1312; Jl Kemakmuran; standard/superior/VIP 200,000/250,000/302,000Rp; ❄) Decor and wood-panelled ceilings look a little dated, but superior and VIP varietals have hot water. All rooms have air-con and those 2nd-floor sea views make Tobelo almost pretty, in a ramshackle way. Almost.

Penginapan Asean Jaya GUESTHOUSE $
(☎262 1051; Jl Pelabuhan; r 75,000Rp) Super-clean budget rooms with fresh paint, spotless floors and linens, and small shared *mandis*. Anis, the delightful owner, speaks English.

Wisma Slasabila GUESTHOUSE $
(☎262 2389; Jl H Simage 339; standard/deluxe 165,000/220,000Rp; ❄) Lemon-and-lime rooms set around a narrow central strip of water garden. These rooms are cleaner, fresher and more spacious than most in Tobelo. It's easy to miss, two doors north of the better-known Penginapan Regina.

Warung Family INDONESIAN $
(☎21238; Jl Kakmuran; meals 40,000-50,000Rp) It has but two choices, *ikan bakar* (grilled fish) or *ayam goreng* (fried chicken), served in a clean, tiled dining room that's decorated with antique fans, dressed with tablecloths, and smells like a fish market. Well, at least that means the fish is fresh. The food is slathered in chilli sauce and served with steamed cassava and garlic-sautéed water spinach.

Information

BNI (Bank Negara Indonesia; Jl Kemakmuran) has a 24-hour ATM, but no money exchange. The regional tourist office is now in Sofifi.

Getting There & Away

There's a Kijang to Sofifi at 4am daily (100,000Rp) or you can charter one for 350,000Rp. Bemos to Kao and Daru are 25,000Rp and 15,000Rp respectively.

Within town, *ojeks* cost 5000Rp, and *bentor* (motorcycle-rickshaws) cost 5000Rp. The nearest airport is in Galela.

SOUTH OF TOBELO

As unattractive as Tobelo may be, the drive south follows the long languid coastline, alternating between white- and black-sand beaches, with laid-back, but quite poor, villages strung along the road in between. All of this is stitched together with elegant and lush coconut groves, which ramble to the edge of a vast mangrove estuary where black jungle rivers foam into rapids. This is pure, raw, natural living.

Pantai Karlen is a beach of strikingly pure black sand, 1km east of Pitu and 5km south of Tobelo. Around 10km further south, then 2km off the main road, **Kupa Kupa** has a white-sand swimming beach, heavily shaded with mature trees. It's very photogenic when looking north, less so looking south thanks to the Pertamina Oil Terminal next

BOATS FROM PULAU HALMAHERA

DESTINATION	PORT	TYPE	COST (RP)	FREQUENCY
Bitung	Tobelo	Pelni	varies	2 monthly
Morotai	Tobelo	speedboat	100,000Rp	8am, 9am, 10am
Morotai	Tobelo	speedboat	100,000	8am, 9am, 10am
Pulau Ternate	Tobelo	Pelni	varies	2 monthly

door. German-Indo owned **Pantai Kupa Kupa Cottages** (☎0812 4477 6773; r & cottages 150,000-250,000Rp) is reason enough to stay a night or three in the rather lovely shaggy-haired Halmahera-style bungalows, decorated with Papuan handicrafts. There are also rooms in the main house with shared baths and the property is surrounded by a lush garden. There's a fabulous beach cafe where you can sink into a coconut-wood chair, sip superb coffee and enjoy views of the amazing Halmahera peninsula, which wraps around the bay and looks like distant bay islands. However, it's an illusion, as it's all mainland.

There's good snorkelling, just 500m north of the resort. There's also reputedly good snorkelling off the sandy southern tip of **Pulau Bobale**, accessed by a 10,000Rp shared boat from **Daru**. Daru is also the departure point for speedboats to eastern Halmahera. A shipwrecked Japanese freighter lies just off Pantai Sosol at **Malifut**, where it was scuttled at the end of WWII. You'll see it protruding from the water offshore. Keep heading south, past the turn-off towards Sofifi, and you'll reach the port town of Sidangoli where there are public boats (50,000Rp, 30 minutes) to Ternate. These boats are lighter than those that make the Jailolo run and get tossed around by the sea when the swell rises in the afternoon. You'll find smoother rides in the morning. Boats leave when full, or charter for 350,000Rp.

NORTH OF TOBELO

The road north is well surfaced with several very attractive woodland sections, glimpses of coast and a fine brief view (8km) of the active volcano Dukono smoking on the horizon. At **Luari** (13km) there's a beach in a pretty horseshoe-shaped bay. The cream-coloured sandy beach is shaded by *ketapang* trees and gets busy on Sundays. Turning 1.5km inland at **Galela** (aka Soasio, 25km) you come to **Danau Galela** (aka Danau Duma), a sizeable lake lined with villages that suffered particularly in the 1999 troubles. Several burnt-out church ruins remain. Ox carts are common on the lake's 16km 'ring' road. Most folks wind up here to head to or from Halmahera's only airport.

EASTERN HALMAHERA

Way off the tourism radar, eastern Halmahera appeals to travellers who fancy being an area's first foreigner in a generation. One place with potential is **Jarajara**, which has a fine sandy beach, ringed by a protective coral reef with diving possibilities. Deep in the riverine hinterland, at least a two-day trek from Subaim, Jarajara or Patlean, live the nomadic Togutil people, often dressed in nothing but a loin cloth.

Boats from Tobelo run to Patlean (Sunday), Jarajara (some Tuesdays) and Maba (three weekly). If you organise in advance, you can arrange longboat transfers that allow hop-offs at intermediate villages en route.

PULAU AMBON

Maluku's most prominent island is lush and gently mountainous, indented with two great hoops of bay. Around capital Kota Ambon, villages merge into a long, green,

WORTH A TRIP

PULAU MOROTAI

A minor Japanese base during WWII, Morotai leapt to prominence when it was captured by the Allies and used to bomb Manila to bits. That was the sadly destructive fulfilment of General MacArthur's 'I will return' pledge to retake the Philippines. Among the Japanese defenders who retreated to Morotai's crumpled mountain hinterland was the famous Private Nakamura: only in 1973 did he discover that the war was over. A WWII US amphibious tank still lies rusting in a hidden palm grove, a five-minute *ojek* ride behind Morotai's village capital **Daruba**. There are attractive palm-backed fishing beaches along the narrow Nefelves Peninsula, stretching south from Daruba. But for better beaches explore the array of offshore islands in Morotai's sparkling turquoise waters. With a decent longboat (400,000Rp to 750,000Rp) you can make a great day trip combining **Pulau Zum Zum**, **Pulau Kolorai**, and the idyllic and uninhabited **Pulau Dodola**.

Speedboats leave Tobelo (Halmahera) for Morotai (100,000Rp, two hours) at 8am, 9am and 10am, and there's a *kapal motor* at 1pm (50,000Rp, four hours). They return at the same times.

Pulau Ambon

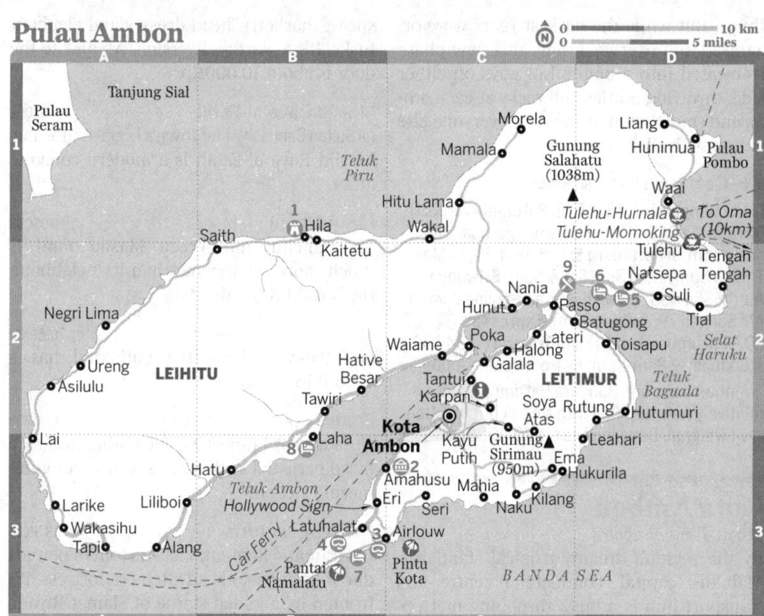

downmarket suburban ribbon. West of the airport, this gives way to a string of charming coastal villages, where light sparkles brilliantly through alluring flower gardens and swaying tropical foliage. If you take the time to explore, you'll find the island to be much more than a vital transport hub to be endured in an effort to reach the lovely Lease, Kei and Banda Islands. In fact, Ambon is a pleasant stop, especially for avid divers.

History

Until 1512 Ambon was ruled by Ternate. The sultans brought the civilising force of Islam to the island's north coast and developed Hitu Lama as a spice-trading port. When the Portuguese displaced the Ternateans, they found Ambon's less developed, non-Islamicised south more receptive to Christianity, and built the fortress around which Kota Ambon would eventually evolve. In 1599, the Dutch renamed this fort Victoria and made Kota Ambon their spice-trading base.

During WWII, Kota Ambon became a Japanese military headquarters, resulting in extensive Allied bombing that destroyed most of its once-attractive colonial architecture. In 1950, Ambon was briefly the centre of the southern Malukan independence movement. This was extinguished within a few months by Indonesian military force.

Pulau Ambon

Sights

1 Benteng Amsterdam B1
2 Museum Siwalima C3

Activities, Courses & Tours

3 Blue Rose Divers B3
4 Maluku Divers B3

Sleeping

5 Aston Natsepa D2
6 Baguala Bay Resort D2
7 Collin Beach Hotel B3
8 Maluku Divers B3
Penginapan Michael .... (see 8)
Pondok Patra .... (see 8)

Eating

9 Pas Van Baguala C2

From 1999 until mid-2002, Ambon was ripped apart by Christian-Muslim intercommunal violence, leaving Kota Ambon looking like 1980s Beirut. After a stable nine years or so, which allowed for a strong economic resurgence that wiped away almost every visible scar of that tragic era, there were once again frayed nerves. In both 2011 and early 2012 sectarian violence flared between reactionary Christian and Muslim thugs. But while the darkest years were organised and overwhelming, this new phase translated into a handful of guys on either side, throwing bottles and rocks at each other, and (mostly) missing, while everyone else got on with their lives.

Getting There & Away

Lion/Wings Air (☎351 532; Pattimura Airport), **Garuda** (☎080 4180 7807; www.garuda-indonesia.com; Jl Pattimura 5; ⏱8am-4.30pm Mon-Thu, to 5pm Fri, to 3pm Sat & Sun), **Sriwijaya Air** (☎354 498; www.sriwijayaair-online.com; Jl AM Sangaji 79; ⏱9am-6pm), **Expressair** (☎323 807; Pattimura Airport) and **Trigana** (☎343 393; Jl Soabali; ⏱8am-8pm) fly from Pulau Ambon.

Ambon's airport, Bandara Pattimura, has a relatively new terminal with a weak but functional wi-fi signal. Departure tax is 30,000Rp.

Kota Ambon

☎0911 / POP 309,000

By the region's dreamy tropical standards, Maluku's capital, commercial centre and transport hub is a busy, throbbing metropolis. Sights are minimal and architecture wins no prizes, but there is a unique cafe culture, some choice sleeps and decent food. Plus, it's well connected to the Banda and Kei Islands, the real reasons you're here.

Sights

TOP CHOICE Commonwealth War Cemetery CEMETERY
(Tantui) Our favourite sight in Ambon city is this trim and neatly manicured cemetery, designed by a British landscape architect in honour of the allied servicemen who died here in WWII. Its greatest feature is the five stunning shade trees, sprouting with bromeliads and orchids.

Museum Siwalima MUSEUM
(☎341 652; admission 3000Rp; ⏱9am-4pm Mon-Fri, from 10am Sat & Sun) In the southern suburbs, the Siwalima has two main buildings separated by 500m of road that snakes beautifully up through steep, lovingly tended gardens. The upper building was under renovation at research time and closed to the public, but views of the mouth of the bay from here are stunning and gratis. The lower annex is already complete, and you'll see everything from stone tools to human skulls to wood carvings. It has an elongated tifa drum crafted from bamboo, ancient bone and brass jewellery, and some astonishing spears, basketry, head dresses and elephant tusks. It's a worthy diversion. An *ojek* to the door is about 10,000Rp.

Masjid Raya al-Fatah MOSQUE
(Jl Sultan Babullah) The town's biggest mosque, Masjid Raya al-Fatah is a modern concrete affair.

Masjid Jami MOSQUE
The fanciful mint-green Masjid Jami is much more photogenic than its neighbour, the Masjid Raya al-Fatah.

Maranatha Cathedral CHURCH
(Jl Pattimura) Maranatha Cathedral has a staid if iconic tower.

Francis Xavier Cathedral CHURCH
(Jl Pattimura) Francis Xavier Cathedral has a facade crusted with saint statues and glimmering steeples.

Benteng Victoria FORTRESS
Undramatic Benteng Victoria (out of bounds due to army use) is a Dutch-era fortress. It's fronted by a gilded statue of Slamet Riyadi, an Indonesian commander who died retaking the place in 1950.

Activities

Aside from wandering around a few churches and mosques and plotting your escape to the Banda or Kei Islands, there's not much to do in the city centre. But you can slip into **Nakamura** (☎345 557; www.nakamura-info.com; Jl Phillips Latumahina SK 5/7; treatments 60,000-215,000Rp), a slice of faux-Shogun heaven. This Japanese-style spa is replete with gurgling fountains and rice-paper massage cubicles, where you can enjoy quality acupressure and shiatsu massage therapy.

Sleeping

There are enticing alternatives around the airport and on beaches at Latuhalat and Natsepa worth considering. While an otherwise manic and relatively charmless town, Ambon has benefited from an influx of choice, affordable rooms.

TOP CHOICE City Hub Hero HOTEL **$$**
(☎342 898; www.cityhubhotels.com; Jl Wim Reawaru 7B; standard/deluxe s 282,000/323,000Rp d 315,000/355,000Rp; ❄@📶) Welcome to the AirAsia of hotels. The look is slick, the service well-priced, and while the policies can be maddening, its value is undeniable. Deluxe rooms are a steal at this new Indo chain,

with floating desks, queen beds and 32-inch wall-mounted LCD flat screens. Standard rooms are slightly smaller and have twin beds. Other perks include free in-room internet and wi-fi in the lobby, and you'll stay even cheaper if you forgo the basic breakfast and shower kit. The hotel can't keep your credit card open so in addition to the room fee, which you'll pay upfront, you'll be asked for a 200,000Rp cash security deposit upon check-in.

Orchid Hotel HOTEL **$$**

(☎346 363; Jl Pattimura 5; standard/superior 330,000/385,000Rp; ❄📶) Another of Ambon's terrific-value modern sleeps. It offers considerably less style than nearby City Hub, but the rooms are bigger, ceilings are higher and it has wood furnishings, queen beds, mini-bar, in-room wi-fi, ample natural light and more hospitality.

Swiss-Belhotel HOTEL **$$**

(☎322 888; www.swiss-belhotel.com; Jl Benteng Kapaha; d from 500,000Rp; ❄📶) Ambon's most fashionable address, if not its very best, offers sizeable rooms with stylish carpeting, floating wooden desks, large flat screens and glass-box showers. Linens are high quality, the breakfast buffet is really good and service is terrific. But you can already see fraying edges. One room we were initially assigned had a massive leak, another had badly stained carpets, and yet another was obviously a smokers' paradise. There should be greater attention to detail for the price. Book online for substantial discounts.

Hotel Mutiara HOTEL **$$**

(☎353 075; www.hotelmutiaraambon.com; Jl Pattimura 12; standard/superior 350,000/400,000Rp; ❄📶) Behind a dainty curtain of tropical foliage, and a bit stodgier and more lived in than the upstart newbies nearby. Rooms have wooden floors, bathtubs, crown mouldings and framed ikat on the walls, as well as ample comfort and grace.

Penginapan The Royal GUESTHOUSE **$**

(☎348 077; Jl Anthony Rhebok 1D; r 175,000-225,000Rp; ❄📶) One of the three newest sleeps in town, rooms have Ikea-chic wardrobes and desks, new air-con units, hot water, flat screens and wi-fi. Some could use a bit more air flow as they can get musty, but at research time it was a steal.

Penginapan Asri GUESTHOUSE **$**

(☎311 217; Jl Baru 33; r 125,000-160,000Rp; ❄) Many rooms lack natural light, but the Asri is very central and much better kept than most other hotels in this price range. More expensive rooms have hot water, and all have air-con and private baths.

Eating

Cheap *rumah makan* abound, especially around Mardika Market, the ports, the Pelni office and Jl Sultan Babullah. Evening warungs appear on Jl Sultan Babullah and Jl Pantai Mardika.

TOP CHOICE **Rumah Makan Nifia** INDONESIAN **$**

(Jl AY Patti 66; meals 20,000-30,000Rp; ⏰9am-9pm Mon-Sat) A wonderful family-run, hole-in-the-wall, pick-and-mix warung with a crazy devoted following – for a good reason. Dishes are fresh, rotate frequently, and include several varieties of roasted and baked fish, fried chicken, fried tempeh, curried and stir-fried vegetables, beef *rendang*, and

THE MALUKAN PALATE

Despite what you'll see in most restaurants, Maluku's traditional staple isn't rice but *kasbi* (boiled cassava) or *papeda* (sago), called *popeda* in Ternate, a thick, colourless, sodium-packed goo that you ladle into plates of *kuah ikan* (fish soup), then suck down as though trying to swallow a live jellyfish. Odd, but surprisingly good when accompanied with *sayur garu* (papaya flower), *kohu-kohu* (a green-bean, coconut and fish mix), *papari* (a unique mixed vegetable), *keladi*-root, cassava-leaf spinach, and extreme hunger. For protein, fish and seafood are king, typically served with a lightly spiced citrus dip called *dabu dabu* or *colo colo*.

Originally unique to the Banda Islands, the spice-yielding kernel of nutmeg *(pala)* grows within a fruit that itself makes deliciously tart jams and distinctive sweet 'wine' (available at Ambon's Sibu-Sibu). Nutmeg grows best in the shade of magnificent *kenari* trees, which themselves yield an almond-like nut used locally in confectionery and sauces. *Kenari*-nut chunks float atop *air goraka*, a distinctive ginger-flavoured coffee hot beverage.

Kota Ambon

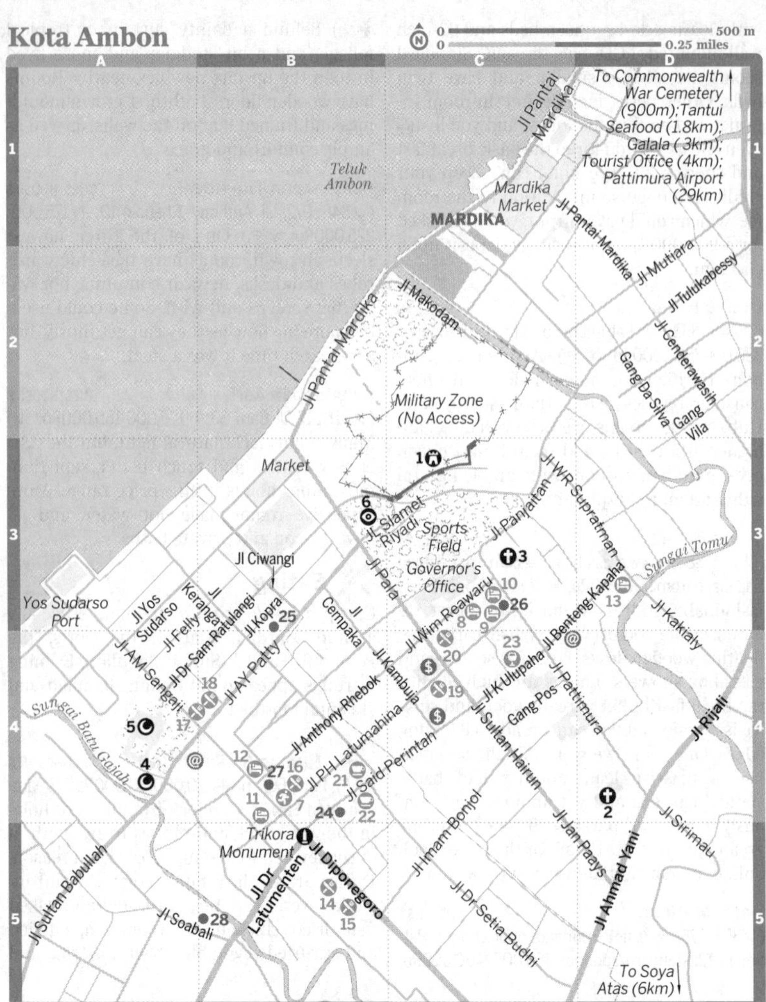

a tasty *soto ayam* (chicken soup), ideal for monsoon season.

Ratu Gurih SEAFOOD $$

(☎0813 4338 8883; Jl Diponegoro 26; meals 50,000-100,000Rp; ⏰10am-10pm) It has fluorescent tiles and the atmosphere is bland, but the fish – perfectly grilled, smothered in chilli and served alongside three tasty sambals – is fall-off-the-bone fresh. Try the *tom yam* (spicy, clear soup) too.

Sari Gurih SEAFOOD $$

(☎341 888; Jl Dana Kopra; mains 40,000-70,000Rp; ⏰9am-11pm) In a converted shingled house with an ever-smoking grill, tubs of fresh catch spill onto the concrete front deck. The well-grilled fish is served with four sambals. The back room, with the laminated macrame tablecloths, becomes a karaoke stage. Be very afraid.

RM Paradise AMBONESE $

(Jl PH Latumahina; dishes 5000Rp, fish market price; ⏰10am-3pm Mon-Sat) Outwardly a typical, cheap, dining barn, the Paradise is considered *the* place for hard-to-find genuine Ambonese food, including *papeda*.

Kota Ambon

Rumah Makan Ayah PADANG $

(meals 25,000-30,000Rp; 6am-11pm) This local chain, disguised as an indie Padang food joint, offers better and fresher food than the usual fried fish and chicken choices you'll find in similar warungs. It's also one of the few places open on Sundays.

Istana Berakat SEAFOOD $$

(Jl Diponegoro; mains 35,000-55,000Rp; 10am-10pm) Decor is entirely lacklustre but this is a hugely popular Chinese-Indo seafood house. It does all the soups, and fish, crab and shrimp dishes you've grown to love. Plus it draws a huge local lunch crowd.

Sarinda BAKERY $

(355 109; Jl Sultan Hairun 11; pastries from 5000Rp; 8am-9.30pm) With its lovely Dutch-colonial windows, ample garden seating and central location, this is a great place to select pastries presented on dozens of oven-warm racks. If only it served coffee.

Drinking

Although proper bars are *instiututa non-grata* in sweaty old Ambon, you must tip your cap to a town that embraces cafe culture. Don't get too titillated, in this town it is mostly sombre dudes sitting around, chain-smoking and drinking coffee. But still, in this age of virtual chat rooms where political discourse is mostly battered and bantered between Facebook avatars, it is refreshing – rehumanising even – to settle into a joint where politics, ideas and, well, other people, are discussed in person (or behind their backs). And all this takes place over good coffee – and a cigarette or 10.

Ud Inti (8am-9pm), a tiny, blink-and-you'll-miss-it mini mart is one of only two places in town where you can buy beer, apart from in a restaurant. It even has Guinness.

TOP CHOICE **Sibu-Sibu** CAFE

(312 525; Jl Said Perintah 47A; juices 8000-14,000Rp, beer 24,000Rp, coffee 5000-10,000Rp, breakfasts from 20,000Rp; 7am-10pm Mon-Sat, 1.30-8pm Sun;) Portraits of Ambon-born stars deck the walls of this sweet little coffee shop, which plays Malukan music and serves local snacks such as the wonderful *koyabu* (cassava cake, 3000Rp) and *lopis pulut* (sticky rice with palm jaggery). It also has good, full breakfasts, fried breadfruit that you'll dip into melted palm sugar, and rocket-fueled ginger coffee.

Kopi Tradisi Joas CAFE

(Jl Said Perintah; coffee 5000-11,000Rp; 6.30am-7.30pm Mon-Sat) Local bigwigs talk politics for hours here over rich mocha-style 'secret-recipe' coffees and slices of deep-fried breadfruit (*sukun goreng*, 1000Rp). This simple but attractive cafe has wood-panelled walls and a central avocado tree.

Shopping

Plaza Ambon is the city's cross between a proper shopping mall and old-school market. In addition to byzantine market stalls, it has the requisite fast-food choices, a Matahari store, and a big Foodmart grocer for self-caterers. The shiny new Ambon City Center is on the outskirts of town, strangely nowhere near the city centre. You can get your blast of polished-up globalisation via any number of its corporate purveyors or stock up on groceries at its enormous Hypermart. Though it may not seem like much to you, proud Ambonese see it as a beacon – a sign of progress in a once-struggling city.

Information

INTERNET ACCESS **Princess Internet** (Jl Benteng Kapaha 25; per hr 4000Rp; ⌚9am-9pm) is centrally located, has several terminals and a passable connection. **Reno.net** (Jl Sultan Babullah; per hr 4000Rp; ⌚10am-midnight), across from the Grand Mosque, is an even better choice. There's also free wi-fi at groovy Sibu-Sibu (p421).

MONEY Change or withdraw enough money in Ambon for trips to outlying islands where there are no exchange facilities. **BCA** (Bank Central Asia; Jl Sultan Hairun 24; ⌚9am-3pm Mon-Fri) exchanges euros and Australian and US dollars, but you can expect a long wait. Its battalion of ATMs allows 2,500,000Rp withdrawals. **BNI** (Bank Negara Indonesia; Jl Said Perintah 12; ⌚9am-3pm Mon-Fri) offers poor exchange rates but relatively swift service and an ATM.

TOURIST INFORMATION **Tourist info desk** (⌚Mon-Sat, timed to meet flights) An unmarked but useful desk, straight ahead once you leave baggage claim. The desk is run by Michael, Ambon's greatest ambassador. He has reams of information for you, a ready smile and an inexpensive nearby homestay (p425). If you're after information, he's a much better resource than the **tourist office** (Dinas Parawisata; ☎312 300; Jl Jenderal Sudirman; ⌚8am-4pm Mon-Fri) in Tantui.

TRAVEL AGENCIES **PT Daya Patal** (☎353 344; spicetr@gmail.com; Jl Said Perintah; ⌚8am-6pm) An ever-obliging agency with several knowledgeable English-speaking staff. They sell airline tickets and can arrange Pelni tickets too. **PT Matrassas Abadi** (☎311 111; mattras_amq@hotmail.com; Jl AY Patty 52; ⌚8am-9pm) is another well-organised English-speaking travel agency for domestic air tickets.

Getting There & Away

Road transport (including buses to Seram via the Hunimua car ferry) starts from various points along Jl Pantai Mardika. For Natsepa (4000Rp), Tulehu-Momoking (5000Rp) and Tulehu-Hurnala (7000Rp) take Waai or Darussalam bemos. Latuhalat (3000Rp) and Amahusu bemos also pick up passengers beside the Trikora monument on Jl Dr Latumenten.

Getting Around

To/From the Airport

Pattimura Airport is 37km round the bay from central Kota Ambon. Hatu- and Liliboi-bound bemos pass the airport gates (6000Rp, 70 minutes from Mardika). There is a ferry (per person/motorbike/car 2000/5000/20,000Rp) across Teluk Ambon to the airport side of the bay. It sails continuously but lingers in port, so it's not always the prudent choice. If you time it right and use the ferry and an *ojek*, it would be comfortable and inexpensive (50,000Rp), so it's worth considering. A taxi costs 150,000Rp to/from the airport. A new bridge is expected to connect the airport directly with the city centre. Construction had just begun at research time and was expected to be completed by 2014.

There is also an **airport bus** (per person 25,000Rp) that leaves from the **Peace Gong** in the city centre three times daily at 5am, 11am and 2pm – timed to feed the Garuda, Batavia and Wings/Lion departures for Jakarta, Surabaya and Makassar. It departs from the airport for the city centre after the inbound flights land at approximately 8am, noon and 4pm.

Bemo

First rule of Ambon bemo travel – green bemos circulate within the city centre and blue bemos head out of town. Get on/off at least 200m away from Mardika Market (the terminus), where vehicles typically jostle interminably through chaotic traffic jams.

Ultrafrequent Lin III bemos *(mobils)* head southwest down Jl Pantai Mardika and either Jl Dr Sam Ratulangi or Jl AY Patty, swinging around the Trikora monument onto Jl Dr Latumenten. After 2km they loop back via Jl Sultan Babullah and Jl Yos Sudarso.

Tantui bemos run northeast from Mardika, passing the Commonwealth War Cemetery and **Tantui Seafood** (☎0852 3223 7888; Tantui; mains from 25,000Rp; ⌚11am-11pm; ❄), then looping back past the tourist office.

Around Pulau Ambon

SOUTHERN LEITIMUR

Latuhalat straddles a low pass culminating in a pair of popular, well-shaded 'Sunday

TRANSPORT FROM PULAU AMBON

Air

DESTINATION	COMPANY	FREQUENCY
Bandaneira	NBA	3 weekly
Jakarta	Batavia Air, Lion/Wings Air, Garuda, Sriwijaya Air	daily
Makassar	Lion/Wings Air, Garuda	daily
Sorong	Lion/Wings Air, Expressair	3 weekly
Ternate	Expressair	3 weekly
Tual	Lion/Wings Air, Trigana	daily

Boat

DESTINATION	PORT	TYPE	COST (RP)	FREQUENCY
Amahai (Pulau Seram)	Tulehu	Bahari Express	economy/VIP 91,000/150,000	9am, 4pm daily
Bandaneira	Kota Ambon	Pelni	varies	2 weekly
Lease Islands	Tulehu	Bahari Express	economy/VIP 50,000/75,000	8 am daily
Lease Islands	Tulehu-Momoking	speedboat	30,000	when full
Papua	Kota Ambon	Pelni	varies	2 weekly
Tual	Kota Ambon	Pelni	varies	2 weekly
Waipirit (Pulau Seram)	Hunimua	car ferry	varies	3 daily

beaches' (admission 2000Rp) – **Santai** and **Namalatu**. Neither offers great swimming but both have hotels, and there's a seasonal dive operation. Walk between the two in 15 minutes or take a becak (bicycle-rickshaw).

The only dive shop in the area is **Blue Rose Divers** (323 883; www.bluerosedivers.com; Jl Hati Ari; 2 dives 1,100,000Rp; Sep-Apr), based at the declining Santai Beach Resort, where the reasonably clean beach is marred by retaining walls buffeted by turquoise surf. Most of its clients sleep at the nearby **Collin Beach Hotel** (323 125; Jl Amalamite I; economy/standard 240,000/360,000Rp;). Its decent spread of rooms is set in three outbuildings perpendicular to the sea, which laps a rocky shore. Rooms are clean with fresh paint, crisp sheets, funny telephone-booth showers, bowl sinks, and wood furnishings, and they open onto a common porch with garden and sea views.

Getting There & Away

Green 'Lt Halat' bemos from Kota Ambon (3000Rp, 40 minutes) run to Namalatu along a pretty waterside road through Eri. Here, an amusing, if fading, Hollywood sign is painted in giant letters on the sea defences.

EASTERN LEIHITU

A handful of bayside retreats offers a striking contrast to the bustle of Ambon 20km away. Family-friendly **Baguala Bay Resort** (362 717; www.bagualabayresort.wordpress.com; Jl Raya Waitatiri; deluxe/cottage 350,000/400,000Rp; @) is set around a swimming pool – relegated to rain collection in the monsoon season – in a lovely waterfront palm garden that can look especially enchanting at night. Rooms are outwardly nice with close proximity to the sea, but are musty with wet patches. Cottages are larger and a bit better than the rooms. The good-value seafront cafe serves Western and local food. It also owns a superb retreat in Seram.

Around 3km further east, **Aston Natsepa** (362 257; www.astonambon.com; Jl Raya Natsepa 36; r/ste 818,000/1,438,000Rp;) is Ambon's first full-blown four-star resort, complete with infinity pool, professional English-

DIVING AMBON

Ambon had become one of Indonesia's hottest new scuba-dive meccas at research time. Given its wide urban bay – as deep as 500m in some places – it's not surprising that Ambon is most celebrated for muck diving. There are as many as 30 dive sites within the bay alone, but there are also 16 reef dives outside the bay along the Ambon coast and around the nearby **Tiga Islands**.

Highlights include coral-crusted volcanic pinnacles off **Mahia**, the blue hole at **Hukurila**, a huge underwater arch at **Pintu Kota**, and the **Duke of Sparta** shipwreck, which was allegedly sunk by the CIA in 1958. Also, during action-packed drift dives between the Tiga Islands you'll meet bumpheads, Napoleons, dogtooth tuna, vast schools of fusiliers, dolphins, sharks and turtles. You can also glimpse the big stuff at **Tanjung Sial Timur** (Bad Corner), where strong currents attract pelagic fish off the southern tip of Seram.

But as special as those sites can be, it's the muck that draws the crowds for such oddities as the psychedelic frogfish (aka Ambon frogfish) discovered here in 2008, with its big lips and bouffant hairdo. You can also find 15 variety of rhinopia, several variety of manta shrimp, zebra crabs, banded pipefish, pygmy squid and seahorses. Basically, there are some Shrek-like creatures down in the muck, and they're worth seeing, though visibility is a challenge during the long monsoon. Plan your trip from October to April.

Maluku Divers (☎336 5307; www.divingmaluku.com; Namalatu; 2/3 tanks from US$95/140, surcharges of US$15-20 for reef dives; ⏲Sep-late May) is the most professionally run operation in Ambon, and is largely responsible for embedding Ambon into the greater scuba zeitgeist. Its local and expat divemasters know the spots intimately, and its brand new resort, geared to serious divers and underwater photographers, is marvelous. It isn't cheap, however it does accept day trippers.

Blue Rose Divers (p423) is less fluent in spoken English, and is a seasonal, if more affordable, operation across the bay.

speaking staff and a soaring Zen-modernist atrium. Fashionably mellow-toned rooms come with fine linen, minibar, safe and sea-facing balconies. This is Ambon's best hotel.

Don't you dare leave the area without stopping into **Pas Van Baguala** (☎0813 4345 8576; Depan Terminal Transit Passo; snacks from 10,000Rp, drinks from 8000Rp; ⏲8am-9pm), an absolutely fabulous cafe strung along the road between Talehu and Ambon. It has an L-shaped patio with ample seating, and is tastefully decorated with framed photography and authentic regional handicrafts. The music is excellent and so are the casaba fries, juices, coffees and teas. It does small meals such as nasi goreng and *mie goreng* (fried noodles).

Waai is famous for its 'lucky' *bulut* (moray eels). For 10,000Rp, a gentleman named Bapak Minggus tempts the eels out of the dark recesses in a concrete-sided carp pond (Jl Air Waysilaka) by feeding them raw eggs. To find the pond (which doubles oddly as the village washing pool), get a Waai bemo and get off one block before the thatched *baileu*, then walk two blocks inland.

Kota Ambon–Natsepa–Waai bemos (4000Rp) run remarkably frequently till around 8pm.

NORTHERN & WESTERN LEIHITU

Western Leihitu is home to some of Ambon's most picturesque and archetypal coastal villages. In **Alang**, at the southern tip of Leihitu, a traditional thatched *baileu,* rebuilt in 2004, sports a carved crocodile. In photogenic **Wakasihu** village, elders while the day away at seaside platforms, with views of an offshore, tree-topped mini-island. A sharper rock shard appears at the roadside beyond **Larike**, where there are 30 to 40 massive eels living under a big boulder in the river. Before you arrive, buy some sardines in the market, so you can lure them to the surface. Compared to the concrete pool and raw-egg feeding in Waai, this is a much more beautiful and natural setting in which to observe them, and you can even walk in the river beside them. The village charges 3000Rp per person for the eel tour. In north **Asilulu** there are multiple boat racks and fine views across to Seram's **Tanjung Sial**. Offshore lies **Tiga Islands**, a trio of islands around which lie several diving and snorkelling spots.

In **Hila**, the 1649 **Benteng Amsterdam** (20,000Rp donation expected; ⏲8am-6pm) is an impressive, old, walled fort. Though the walls are obviously rebuilt with concrete, the inner tower, with its brick floors and thick walls, is fluttering with resident swallows. Gates were open when we visited but you may have to seek out the key master in town. About a block from here you'll find **Gereja Tua Hila**, an ancient, all-wood, thatched Catholic church, built by the Portuguese. It's closed to the public but is still a good photo op. A five-minute walk further inland, and then across a school football field, is Kaitetu's pretty little thatch-roofed **Mesjid Wapaue**. Originally built in 1414 on nearby Gunung Wawane, the mosque was supposedly transferred to the present site in 1664 by 'supernatural powers'.

Laha is a cute, quaint, almost prim little town. It has small concrete houses brushed in pastels, fenced-in front yards blooming with flowers, and a mangrove-shrouded natural harbour right in front of Pondok Patra. It's also the new home of Maluku Divers and a quick 15-minute drive to the airport. Dear readers, this is your blessed Kota Ambon alternative.

Sleeping & Eating

Several simple options cater for travellers taking early flights from Pattimura Airport.

TOP CHOICE Maluku Divers RESORT $$$
(☎336 5307; www.divingmaluku.com; Jl Raya Air Manis, Laha; all-inclusive per person US$250; ❄📶) Here's everything you could possibly want in a dive resort. Notched on a palm-dappled sliver of coastline near the mouth of the bay in Laha, it has 10 spacious, elegant chalets with thatched roofs, beamed ceilings, ceiling fans, air-con, turbo hot-water showers and two desks. Its private deck out front offers capacity for 20 divers, with a maximum of seven per dive boat. In addition, there are professional-grade camera and equipment rooms, excellent dive photography throughout, and lovely lounge and dining areas with dangling lanterns, icy beer, tasty cuisine, and excellent service. Our only criticism is the lack of a jetty means you are often wading or even swimming to the dive boat. Price includes three dives per day.

Penginapan Michael HOMESTAY $
(☎0813 4302 8872; erenst_michael@yahoo.co.id; r 100,000Rp) Opposite the runway, this homestay is run by the welcoming Michael, Ambon's finest tourism ambassador. In addition to his duties at the information desk in baggage claim, he offers three tidy rooms a short *ojek* ride, or longer stroll, to the terminal. Rooms share baths, and include breakfast.

Pondok Patra GUESTHOUSE $
(☎0813 4323 0559; r 180,000-250,000Rp; ❄) Hidden in quaint Laha village, Pondok Patra has a pleasant little rear sitting area on stilts, overlooking a boat-and-mangrove-filled inlet. You can stay here and dive with Maluku Divers.

Getting There & Away

Bemos (5000Rp) leave from Hunut to Hila and from Kota Ambon to Liliboi. To close the loop, charter an *ojek* from near the airport. The road is mostly new asphalt, but landslides are relatively frequent in monsoon season, which means circumnavigation doesn't always pan out.

LEASE ISLANDS

☎0931

Pronounced 'leh-*a*-say', these conveniently accessible yet delightfully laid-back islands have a scattering of old-world villages, lovely bays, and a couple of great-value budget beach retreats. Foreign tourists remain very rare and little English is spoken, but Saparua has some existing tourism inroads.

Pulau Saparua

A sprinkling of offbeat accommodation can be found amid Saparua's shaggy forests and friendly villages. Here, spiny, football-sized durian are piled in the streets right in front of concrete homes brushed in soft pastels. And crystal-clear waters lap or crash the shore depending upon the season. Dugongs reportedly appear in Teluk Saparua and you might spot dolphins en route to uninhabited Pulau Molana, where you don't need Hollywood riches to have a desert island all to yourself. In the wet season it can be torrential; in the dry it's something like paradise.

Getting There & Away

Predawn speedboats run from Itawaka (50,000Rp) to Tulehu-Momoking (Ambon) and from Ihamahu (50,000Rp, one hour) to Namano near Masohi (Seram). Arrive by 4.30am, get your name on the passenger list, and then pay for the ticket when your name is called.

From Haria to Ambon, Bahari Express runs a 7am *kapal motor* (economy/VIP 50,000/75,000Rp, two hours) and during the dry season there are also several speedboats (mostly early morning, 30,000Rp, leave when full). During monsoon months there is just the one daily boat, and waves do crash over the bow, so get that VIP ticket.

Lease Islands

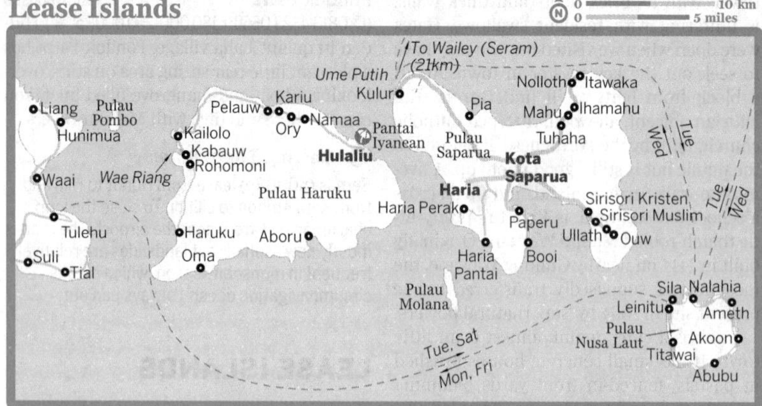

KOTA SAPARUA

Suffused with durian musk, the ramshackle, jungle-island town of Kota Saparua has way-out romance, an extremely friendly countenance, and charm aplenty. The low-walled 1676 **Benteng Duurstede** (admission free), famously besieged by Pattimura in 1817, has been refaced with mouldering grey concrete, but the gateway is original and the cannon-studded ramparts survey a gorgeous sweep of turquoise bay.

A two-minute walk from the fort on one of Kota Saparua's two parallel main streets is the **Penginapan Lease Indah** (☎21069; Jl Muka Pasar; d 100,000-200,000Rp; ❄), a lovely garden guesthouse with two room types to choose from. Opt for a basic, clean and fan-cooled tiled room in the old wing (they have lovely wooden windows), over those in the gaudy, columned new building unless you must have TV, air-con and hot water.

Further along Jl Muka Pasar are a few *rumah makan,* the **market** (⏲Wed & Sat) and a Telkom building, directly behind which is the **bemo terminal** (Jl Belakang). Adjacent to the market, and on the 2nd floor, **Penginapan Mandiri** (☎21063; r with fan 80,000Rp, with air-con 100,000-150,000Rp) is the town's newest choice. Rooms are all cheerily painted and have spotless *mandis* and Disney cabinetry. No, seriously. Its greatest gift is that terrace overlooking the fort and the bay beyond. Simply gorgeous.

Facing the Zeba'ot Church, the innocently ill-named **SS Restaurant** (Jl Belakang; meals 15,000-35,000Rp; ⏲8am-8pm) is a pick-and-mix warung with stately old wooden tables and chairs in the dining room and on the wonderful thatched front porch. It's the most comfortable eatery in town.

Saparua's main port is nearby **Haria**, with two boxy churches, a big thatched *baileu* and a giant white cross above the sapphire-blue bay. A five-minute *ketingting* ride across that bay (or a convoluted 7km *ojek* trip by road and unpaved track) is Haria Perak, from which an 800m trail crosses a scrubby headland.

From Kota Saparua *ojek* fares include Haria (5000Rp), Itawaka (10,000Rp), Ouw (15,000Rp) and Kulur (30,000Rp). If you can manage to find a bemo, it will cost 5000Rp.

PULAU MOLANA

Uninhabited, roadless Pulau Molana has several great snorkelling and diving spots. A beak of soft, dazzlingly white sand at the island's northernmost tip may be rather prone to snag driftwood, but there's great swimming here. The sand slopes down towards the east while directly west a coral wall offers excellent snorkelling. Best of all, you can stay directly behind the beach at the **Molana Bungalows** (☎0852 4343 1818, 0813 4307 7423; www.molanaisland.com; d 350,000Rp, lunch/dinner 30,000/60,000Rp), a *Robinson Crusoe* hideaway that would be ideal for a small group of friends. The site is only staffed when guests are expected, so call well ahead of your planned arrival. Meals (25,000Rp) are somewhat basic. They can help arange your transfer from Haria on their own speedboat (300,000Rp). It's only open in the dry season.

MAHU

Saparua's crystal-clear waters offer richly rewarding diving, and your gateway to these waters also happens to be the island's best sleep. The 15-room **Mahu Lodge** (☎081 197 7232; www.facebook.com/pages/mahu-village-lodge/149115183540; per person half-board 150,000Rp, 2 tanks 700,000-950,000Rp), set in the mangrove fishing village of Mahu, offers basic, very clean rooms. Price includes breakfast and dinner, and its concrete jetty offers easy swimming access in a placid bay. It also has a full-fledged dive operation (September to April) and a dive boat that will get you to the stunning reefs of Nusa Laut, Itawaka and Pulau Molana. The resort is owned by an English speaker born locally, though he lived and worked for much of his life in Jakarta.

Around Pulau Saparua

In the island's northeast, **Nolloth** has Saparua's finest traditional *baileu*, a tin-roofed barn-like church (Gereja Darurat) and a selection of colourfully gaudy Christian statuettes.

On the southeastern flank, Ullath is a traditional-style *baileu,* overshadowed by the tower of the Protestant church. The road deadends at **Ouw**, famous for its simple pottery *(sempe)*. None is obviously on show but any local can lead you to a workshop, where 10,000Rp to 20,000Rp is a reasonable donation to watch sweet *ibu* throw pots in back-porch studios. Their clay comes from Saparua's mountain, it's spun on a wheel, sculpted with a thick chunk of green papaya, and tamped at the rim with a bamboo rod.

PULAU SERAM

☎0914

Some Malukans call Seram 'Nusa Ina' (Mother Island), believing that all life sprang from 'Nunusaku', a mythical peak ambiguously located in the island's western mountains. The best known of Seram's indigenous minority tribes, the Nua-ulu ('upper-river') or Alifuro people, sport red-bandana headgear and were headhunters as recently as the 1940s. The tribe lives in Seram's wild, mountainous interior where thick forests are alive with cockatoos and colourful parrots. Seeing them usually requires a masochistic trek into the remote Manusela National Park, for which you'll need guides and extra permits. Seram's greatest tourist attraction is dramatic Teluk Sawai on the northern coast.

Getting There & Away

The easiest way to get here is to take the twice-daily Amahai-bound Bahari Express (economy/VIP 91,000/150,000Rp, 2½ hours) departing Tulehu-Hurnala (Ambon) at 9am and 4pm, returning at 8am and 2pm (no Sunday service). Grab an *ojek* into Masohi (10,000Rp), then hop a Masohi–Sawai Kijang (per person/vehicle 150,000/700,000Rp, 2½ hours). You can also make the Masohi–Sawai run by *ojek* (around 150,000Rp), with insane jungle views en route. If you're headed to Ora Beach Hotel (p428), get off in Saleman village, and hop on a small motorboat from there to your secluded bay retreat. By prior arrangement management can also arrange private transport in a Kijang from the Amahai harbor to Saleman village, where you'll meet the boat.

Masohi, Namano & Amahai

Neat, if slightly dull, Masohi is the spacious purpose-built capital of central Maluku, a short jaunt from the Amahai harbour. It's only really useful to travellers as a transport interchange. The main street, Jl Soulissa, heads southwest from the terminal, market and Masohi Plaza shopping mall. It becomes

PATTIMURA & TIAHAHU

In 1817, the Dutch faced a small but emotionally charged uprising led by Thomas Matulessy, who briefly managed to gain control of Saparua's Benteng Duurstede. He killed all the fortress defenders but spared a six-year-old Dutch boy. For this minor 'mercy' Matulessy was popularly dubbed Pattimura ('big-hearted'). The rebels were rapidly defeated and dispatched to the gallows but have since been immortalised as symbols of anticolonial resistance. Today their statues dot the whole of Maluku, and Pattimura even features on Indonesia's 1000Rp banknotes.

A much-romanticised heroine of the same saga is Martha Christina Tiahahu, whose father supported Pattimura. After his execution on Nusa Laut, Martha was put on a ship to Java but, grief-stricken, she starved herself to death. Her remains were thrown into the sea but her memory lingers on.

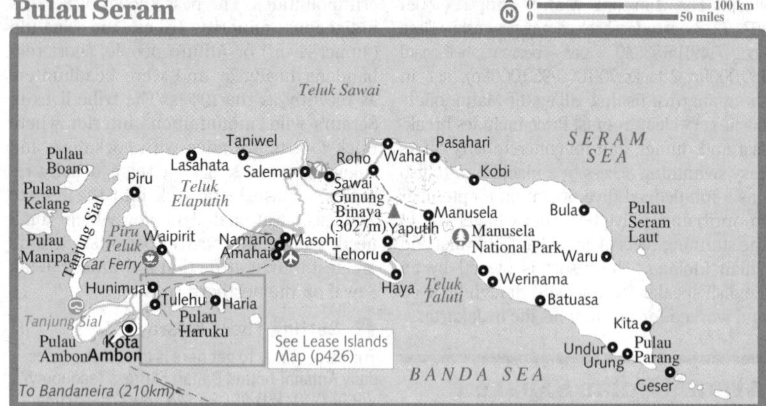

Jl Martha Tiahahu in the Christian suburbs and then continues 6km through Namano to Amahai. Here, just before Amahai's main port, the larger road turns 90 degrees, heading 1km to the airport.

Masohi has a warnet and several ATMs. Friendly, if far from informative, the **Central Maluku Tourist Office** (Dinas Kebudayan & Parawisata; ☎21462; Jl Imam Bonjol; ⌚8am-2pm Mon-Sat) is where you'd start the three-stage application process for Manusela National Park permits. Very few choose to spend more than one night here. If you are stuck in town, grab one of the relatively quiet garden rooms at **Penginapan Irene** (☎21238; Jl MC Tiahahu; r with fan/air-con 85,000/280,000Rp; ❄). It's worth spending the money for one of the nicer rooms. The 'Executive' rooms at **Hotel-Restaurant Isabella** (☎22637; Jl Manusela 17; s with fan 75,000-95,000Rp, d with air-con from 185,000Rp; ❄) may not satisfy your inner Posh Spice, but at least they have windows and hot showers. Grab dinner at **Afsal** (Jl Binaya; meals 13,000-30,000Rp; ⌚7.30am-10.30pm), a clean, ever so slightly upscale, pick-and-mix joint.

Northern Seram

Seram's most accessible scenic highlight is **Teluk Sawai**, a beautiful wide bay backed by soaring cliffs and rugged, forested peaks. Hidden from the best views by a headland, the photogenic stilt-house village of **Sawai** is a great place to unwind and contemplate the moonlit sea. You have two choices here.

In the village, you can nest in the creaky, bamboo-walled **Penginapan Lisar Bahari** (☎0852 3050 5806; per person incl full board 200,000Rp). Perched romantically above the water, rooms at this age-old traveller favourite are predictably somewhat damp (bring a sleeping mat) and showers in the basic en-suite bathrooms are salty. There's no phone, but call the owner's cousin Wati – he speaks good English and can help organise your stay. Cost includes fish dinners, assorted snacks and endless tea. Snorkelling is possible in offshore coral gardens (bring your own gear) though the reefs show signs of bomb-fishing damage. Other possible activities include boat rides to Pulau Raja or to the bay's spectacular western side, where dramatic cliffs rise up above the picturesque village of Saleman. It's famed for flocks of bat-like Lusiala birds, which emerge at dusk, supposedly bearing the souls of human ancestors. En route, tempting little Ora is a handkerchief of marvellously spongy, white-sand beach, where you'll find Seram's very best nest, **Ora Beach Hotel** (☎081 7083 3554; www.bagualabayresort.wordpress.com; beachfront/overwater 400,000/700,000Rp, meals per day 250,000Rp). Grab one of the six beachfront rooms or one of the five brand new romantically rustic overwater bungalows. Activities include snorkelling tours to offshore islands and trips up the Salawai River into the exotic and remote Manusela National Park. Book your room ahead through Baguala Bay Resort (p423) in Ambon.

BANDA ISLANDS

☎0910 / POP 22,000

Combining raw natural beauty, a warm local heart, and a palpable and fascinating history, this remote cluster of 10 picturesque islands isn't just Maluku's choice travel destination, it's one of the very best in all of Indonesia. Particularly impressive undersea drop-offs are vibrantly plastered with multicoloured coral gardens offering superlative snorkelling and tasty diving. The central islands – Pulau Neira (with the capital Bandaneira sprinkled with relics) and Pulau Banda Besar (the great nutmeg island) – curl in picturesque crescents around a pocket-sized tropical Mt Fuji (Gunung Api, 666m). Outlying Hatta, Ai and Neilaka each have utterly undeveloped picture-postcard beaches. And Run, her gnarled limestone sprouting with nutmeg and cloves, is one drop-dead-gorgeous historical footnote. Were they more accessible, the Bandas might be one of Indonesia's top tourist spots. Yet for now you'll have these wonderful islands almost entirely to yourself.

History

Nutmeg, once produced almost exclusively in the Banda Islands, was reputed to ward off bubonic plague, making it one of the medieval world's most expensive commodities. Growing nutmeg takes knowledge but minimal effort, so the drudgery of manual labour was virtually unknown in the Bandas. Food, cloth and all necessities of life could be easily traded for spices with eager Arab, Chinese, Javanese and Bugis merchants, who queued up to do business. Things started to go wrong when the Europeans arrived; the Portuguese in 1512, then the Dutch from 1599. These strange barbarians had no foodstuffs to trade, just knives, impractical woollens and useless trinkets of mere novelty value. So when they started demanding a trade monopoly, the notion was laughable nonsense. However, since the Dutch were dangerously armed, some *orang kaya* (elders) signed a 'contract' to keep them quiet. Nobody took it at all seriously. The Dutch sailed away and were promptly forgotten. But a few years later they were back, furious to find the English merrily trading nutmeg on Pulau Run and Pulau Ai. Entrenching themselves by force, the dominant Dutch played cat and mouse with the deliberately provocative English, while trying unsuccessfully to enforce their mythical monopoly on the locals. In 1621, Jan Pieterszoon Coen, the new governor general of the VOC (Dutch East India Company), ordered the virtual genocide of the Bandanese. Just a few hundred survivors escaped to the Kei Islands.

Coen's VOC thereupon provided slaves and land grants to oddball Dutch applicants in return for a promise that they'd settle permanently in the Bandas and produce fixed-price spices exclusively for the company. These folk, known as *perkeniers* (from the Dutch word *perk*, meaning 'ground' or 'garden'), established nearly 70 plantations, mostly on Banda Besar and Ai.

This system survived for almost 200 years but corruption and mismanagement meant that the monopoly was never as profitable as it might have been. By the 1930s, the Bandas were a place of genteel exile for better-behaved anti-Dutch dissidents, including Mohammed Hatta (future Indonesian vice president) and Sutan Syahrir (later prime minister). The small school they organised while in Bandaneira inspired a whole generation of anticolonial youth.

In the 1998–99 troubles, churches were burnt and at least five people were killed at Walang including the 'last *perkenier*', Wim de Broeke. Most of the Christian minority fled to Seram or Ambon, but the islands rapidly returned to their delightfully torpid calm.

Activities

Crystal-clear seas, shallow-water drop-offs and coral gardens teeming with multicoloured reef life offer magnificently pristine **snorkelling** off Hatta, Banda Besar and Ai. Some Bandaneira homestays rent fins and snorkels to guests (per day 30,000Rp).

German-owned **Blue Motion Dive Center** (☎0812 4714 3922, 0812 8649 4155; www.dive-bluemotion.com; 2 dives 800,000Rp, fuel surcharge 500,000Rp for Run & Hatta), new in 2012 and based in Bandaneira's Hotel Maulana, is the only viable land-based **dive operation** in the Bandas, and it's seasonal. It has new, well-maintained gear, a good speedboat and fair prices, though it does charge a fuel surcharge to dive Run and Hatta. Trips include lunch.

Liveaboards also descend on the Bandas en route from Komodo Island to the Raja Ampat Islands. In addition to all the popular sites around Run, Hatta, Ai and the lava flow off the coast of Pulau Gunung Api, they

Banda Islands

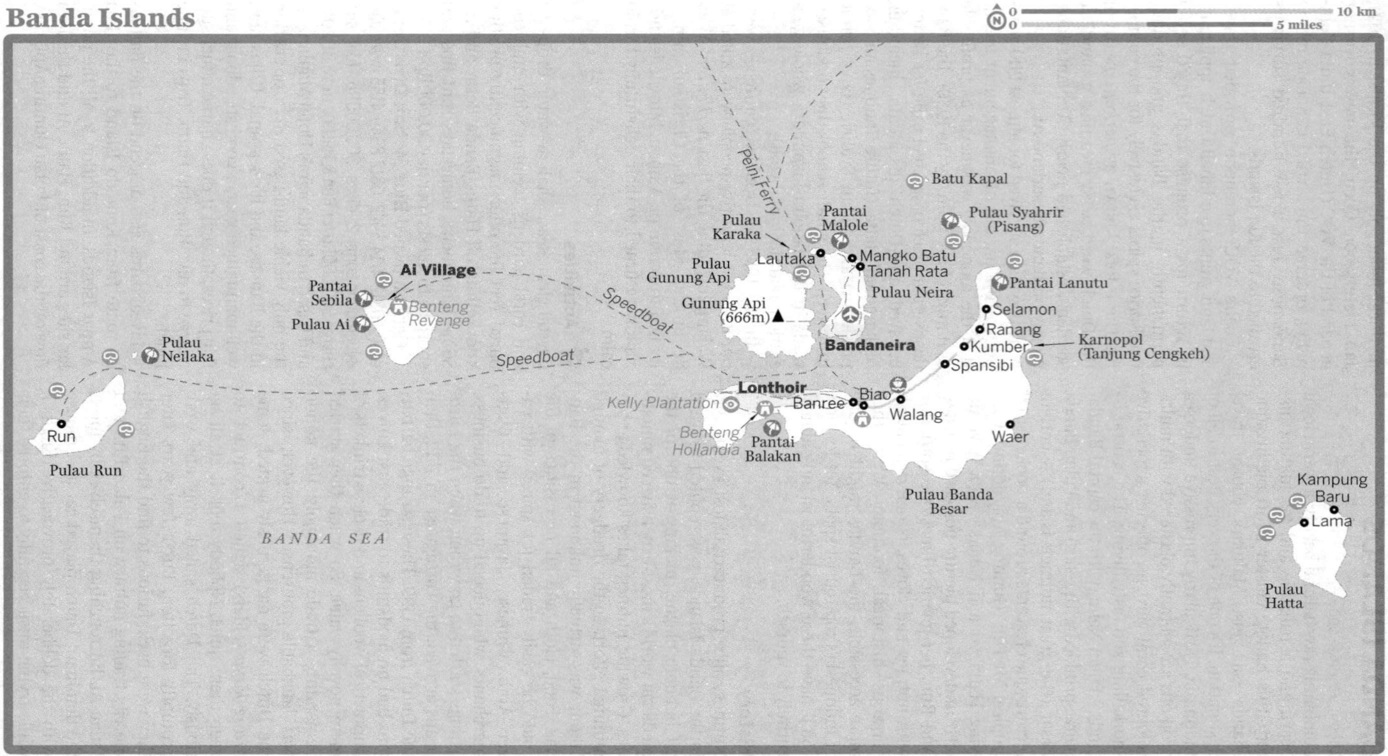

0 10 km
0 5 miles

Batu Kapal
Pulau Syahrir (Pisang)
Pelni Ferry
Pantai Malole
Pulau Karaka
Lautaka
Mangko Batu
Tanah Rata
Pulau Neira
Pantai Lanutu
Pulau Gunung Api
Gunung Api (666m)
Bandaneira
Selamon
Ranang
Kumber
Karnopol (Tanjung Cengkeh)
Spansibi
Ai Village
Pantai Sebila
Benteng Revenge
Pulau Ai
Speedboat
Speedboat
Pulau Neilaka
Lonthoir
Kelly Plantation
Banree
Biao
Walang
Waer
Benteng Hollandia
Pantai Balakan
Run
Pulau Run
Pulau Banda Besar
Kampung Baru
Lama
Pulau Hatta
BANDA SEA

often enjoy muck diving the channel between Bandaneira, Api and Banda Besar.

Bandaneira

POP 9000

Little Bandaneira has always been the Bandas' main port and administrative centre. In the Dutch era the townsfolk virtually bankrupted themselves maintaining a European lifestyle in spacious mansions that needed rebuilding whenever Gunung Api's volcanic huffs burnt them down. Today, Bandaneira's sleepy, flower-filled streets are so quiet that two becak count as a traffic jam. It's a charming place to wander aimlessly, admire late-colonial houses, ponder mouldering ruins, watch glorious cloudscapes over Gunung Api and stumble across the odd historic cannon lying randomly in the grass.

Sights

Several Dutch-era buildings have been restored. If you manage to gain access (knock and hope!), much of the fun is hearing the fascinating life stories of the septuagenarian caretakers, assuming your Bahasa Indonesia is up to the task. Donations (around 10,000Rp per person) are appropriate.

Benteng Belgica FORTRESS

(admission by donation; ⌚sporadic) A classic Vauban-style star fort, the commanding Benteng Belgica was added on the hill above Nassau in 1611. The five massive sharp-pointed bastions were expensively crafted to deflect the cannon fire of a potential English naval bombardment. So in 1796 it caused quite a scandal in Holland when the Brits managed to seize it (albeit briefly) without firing a shot. To reach the upper ramparts (with great views), take the second arch on the left from the central courtyard. Be sure to look for the old jail. That's where local people were imprisoned if they dared sell their spice crops to the English.

Rumah Budaya MUSEUM

(Jl Gereja Tua; admission 20,000Rp; ⌚10am-5pm, by appointment) Bandaneira's main museum is scattered with timeless treasures such as centuries-old Dutch coins, basketry and pottery, an old plantation bell and clay cisterns used on the European ships, a working wind-up gramophone and enough table cannons and muskets to take over the whole archipelago. When closed, the museum's key is available from caretaker Mrs Feni, who lives about 200m further north.

Benteng Nassau FORTRESS

While wandering the old rubble ruins of this gorgeously crumbling yard with real stone arches and incredible views of Gunung Api, it's easy to get lost in the beauty, unless you contemplate its bloody history. In 1608, Dutch Admiral Verhoeven ordered the building of Benteng Nassau on foundations abandoned by the Portuguese in 1529. This was against the most express wishes of local island leaders, who ambushed and executed some 40 Dutch 'negotiators' including Verhoeven himself. The Dutch retaliated in 1621 with the infamous beheading and quartering of 44 *orang kaya* within the fortress, followed by the virtual genocide of the entire Bandanese population.

Hatta's House LANDMARK

(Jl Hatta; admission by donation) Of three early-20th-century 'exile houses', Hatta's House is the most appealing. It's partly furnished and Hatta's distinctive spectacles and neatly folded suit are visible in a display cupboard. In the courtyard, where there are vintage clay cisterns and an old brick well sprouting with bromeliads, you'll also find a schoolhouse that Hatta founded during his exile. It's literally built into the hillside.

Schelling House LANDMARK

(Jl Hatta; ⌚by appoinment) This massive, columned house, owned by the daughter of the last Banda king, has a leafy courtyard, high ceilings and next to no furnishings. It's the kind of place that will inspire 'I could live here' fantasies upon entry. Check out the main bathroom where the stone tub rests against an exposed coral wall. And definitely wander up to that special shuttered loft in the rear courtyard.

Istana Mini LANDMARK

(Jl Kujali) The grand, but eerily empty, 1820s Istana Mini was a later residence for the Bandas' Dutch governors, and a haughty, medal-spangled bust of Dutch King Willem III rusts quietly in the side garden.

Makatita Hall LANDMARK

(Jl Kujali) Makatita Hall occupies the site of the former Harmonie Club (aka 'the Soc') that once boasted seven snooker tables and was the focus of colonial-era social events.

Bandaneira

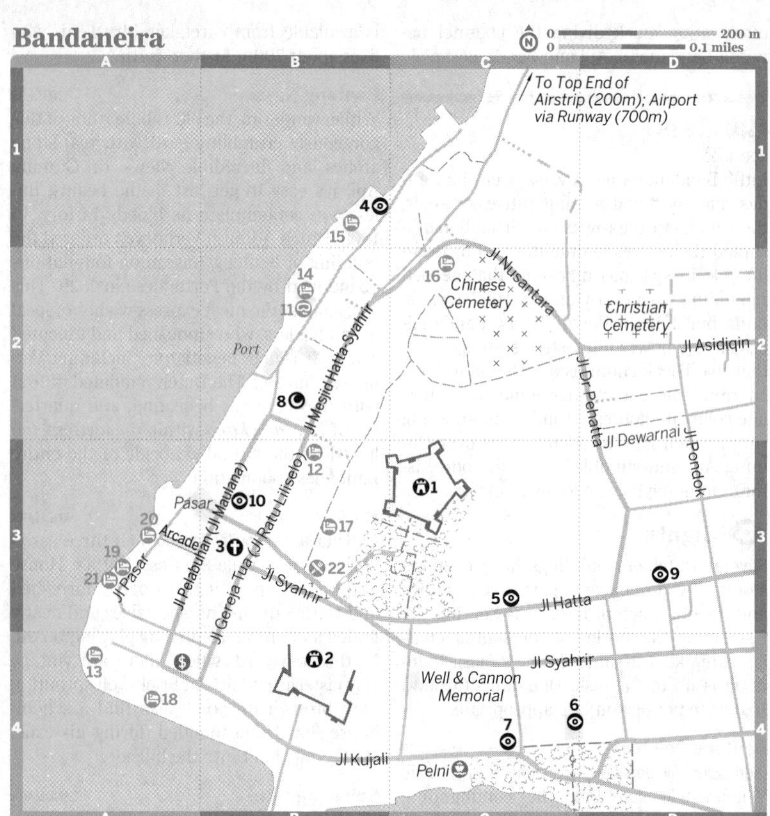

Mesjid Hatta-Syahrir MOSQUE
Behind the main port is the eye-catching Mesjid Hatta-Syahrir. Some locals claim this was converted into a mosque from the mansion that first accommodated Hatta and Syahrir on their arrival in 1936.

Sun Tien Kong Chinese Temple TEMPLE
(Jl Pelabuhan) The 300-year-old Sun Tien Kong Chinese Temple looks intriguing glimpsed through the exterior wall at night.

Church CHURCH
(Jl Gereja Tua) The restored 1852 church has a portico of four chubby columns, a decorative bell-clock and an antique stone floor.

Activities

Though not Banda's best place for **snorkelling**, Bandaneira has pleasant coral gardens at the southern end of Tanah Rata village, off the eastern end of the airstrip and to the northeast off **Pantai Malole**. A notable marine attraction is to spot populations of mandarin fish that emerge at dusk from rubble piles within Neira harbour. Though tiny, these fish are dazzlingly colourful, their whirring fins and lurid blue-orange markings seemingly designed by artistic six-year-olds on acid. Snorkellers can find them near Vita Guesthouse. Divers can find deeper water populations just off the Hotel Maulana – that's where most of the muck diving happens. Bring underwater torches. If you'd rather stay dry, peer from above into a rather crude, 20-year-old stone-and-cement **fish pond** (24hr), where you'll see three black-tip sharks prowling murky waters.

Sleeping

More than a dozen family guesthouses and homestays offer simple but clean rooms, almost all with en-suite *mandi*. Vita, Mutiara and Delfika are best set up for foreign travellers, with spoken English and great free

Bandaneira

breakfasts. Snorkel rentals and help with boat hire is always at hand. Vita, Delfika 2 and a few others offer the major plus of having a waterfront location. Where air-con is available, if you choose not to have it turned on you'll pay only the fan rate.

TOP CHOICE **Mutiara Guesthouse** HOMESTAY $
(☎21344, 0813 3034 3377; www.banda-mutiara.com; r with fan/air-con 140,000/175,000Rp, dinner 70,000Rp; ❄@) A special boutique hotel disguised as a homestay. You are living in a family home decked out with antiques and massive shells with superb-value new rooms and sturdy wood furnishings. The ever-energetic owner, 'Abba', is tirelessly helpful and can arrange trips and tours to the outer islands. Most guests – as well as a few interlopers – meet up for generous, convivial seafood dinners, featuring the best of Banda's natural bounty. Expect grilled fish slathered in almond sauce, rare tuna burgers, slaw dressed in almond-tahini dressing, and much more. The front garden is a wonderful spot for an afternoon snooze, and breakfasts feature home-baked bread or pancakes, and jars of nutmeg jam.

Delfika GUESTHOUSE $
(☎21027; delfika1@yahoo.com; r with fan 100,000-150,000Rp, with air-con 175,000-200,000Rp; ❄@) There are two locations. For great bay views, the spacious upstairs rooms at the **Delfika 2** annex are hard to beat. Meanwhile, the original Delfika has a heart-aching, old-world charm, with an appealing sitting room, atmospheric garden courtyard and a range of rooms, mostly well renovated, on the main village drag. The Delfika Cafe is one of Banda's best, and it has internet (per hour 15,000Rp).

Pantai Nassau Guesthouse GUESTHOUSE $
(☎0878 8557 7833; Jl Kujali; r with fan/air-con 125,000/175,000Rp) A rather nice new building on a black-sand beach with harbour and Gunung Api views. You'll enjoy the antiquated accents including a wide colonnade-like front porch and an old table cannon in the lobby. The four rooms are bright and clean with double beds, but toilets are all Indo squat pots and there are no meals served.

Penginapan Babbu Sallam GUESTHOUSE $
(☎21043; Jl Nairam Bessy; r with fan/air-con 100,000/150,000Rp; ❄) Another romantic waterfront guesthouse with pastel arches on the patio and a deck overlooking the bay. The air-con rooms smell musty. Get one with a fan.

Vita Guesthouse GUESTHOUSE $
(Fita; ☎0812 4706 7099, 21332; allandarman@gmail.com; Jl Pasar; d with fan/air-con from 110,000/135,000Rp; ❄) Though fronted by a new and unfortunate street-side cinder-block construct, it's still rather glorious. It has seven comfortable rooms set in a colonnaded L-shape around a waterfront palm garden. The wonderful wooden jetty area is an ideal perch from which to gaze at Gunung Api while sipping a cold beer. Rooms have original windows and new tiles but can smell musty, so sniff out a good one.

MS Village Inn INN $
(☎0812 4707 8340; Jl Nusantara; r 150,000-200,000Rp; ❄@) Perched on the village hillside, this intimate inn, owned by the niece

of Bandaneira's last king, can be a bit musty. It gets more attention from mop and broom during high season, but the two rooms with air-con and internet overlooking the harbour are certainly worth considering. The smaller and more colourful room smells fresher.

Pondok Wisata Matahari GUESTHOUSE **$**
(☎21050; Jl Pasar; r 150,000Rp; ❄) This antique house with original columns is weather-beaten and ragged, but it has a ramshackle romance about it. Rooms are spacious and have new air-con units, and despite the chipped veneer are reasonably clean. There are special views from the common porch.

Hotel Maulana HOTEL **$$**
(☎21022; lawere@cbn.net.id; r 350,000Rp; ❄) This rebuilt Dutch-colonial hotel has a lovely veranda overlooking the waterfront between palms and shaggy *ketapang* trees. The best views are from the top-floor suites (no elevators). Larger, splashier rooms were under renovation at research time. None of those we saw had character, but they're certainly comfortable. There are rooms of similar standard in the **Laguna Inn** down the block.

Eating

Frequent cups of tea and a light breakfast are generally included in room prices, and almost every place will serve lunch or dinner (35,000Rp to 70,000Rp per person) on advance request. Mutiara's meals are particularly fabulous. Delicious local favourites worth requesting include fish in nutmeg sauce and eggplant with *kenari*-almond sauce. These are available along with seasonal fruit juices and delicious nutmeg-jam pancakes at **Delfika Cafe** (mains 15,000-30,000Rp, no alcohol). Here you can also order *soto ayam*, *nasi ikan* and a variety of other fried noodle and vegetable dishes. One of the few dedicated eateries in town, **Nutmeg Cafe** (mains 15,000-30,000Rp; ⌚8am-9pm) is a charmer. It does fish and rice, a good *soto ayam* and it serves thick pancakes to slather with house-jarred nutmeg jam. **Street vendors** sell presmoked fish on a stick (10,000Rp), sticky rice, dried nutmeg-fruit slices, and pricey but delicious *halua-kenari* almond brittle.

Information

There's no tourist office, but several guesthouses have helpful English-speaking owners. Delfika and Mutiara give guests a free, basic island map and offer slow web access as well (15,000Rp per hour). Bring ample rupiah from Ambon. **BRI Bank** (Bank Rakyat Indonesia; Jl Kujali) has no exchange facilities and no ATM.

Getting There & Away

As you tear your hair over minimalist, ever-changeable transport connections, bear in mind that were it not so infuriatingly awkward to reach, Banda would not be the blissfully unspoilt delight that it is today.

AIR NBA (☎0813 8032 3231; airport) airlines is the latest to win the Ambon–Bandaneira route. Its small, twin-prop plane makes the trip on Wednesday, Thursday and Friday mornings (280,000Rp, 40 minutes). On Wednesdays, the flight continues on to Amahai (Seram). However, flights are frequently cancelled due to weather or lack of passengers, so just because you've bought a ticket, it does not mean you'll be flying that morning. However, if it lands in Bandaneira on any given morning, it will fly back to Ambon for sure. Regardless, it's a wise idea to prebook your return flight.

BOAT If you take the **Pelni** (☎21196; Jl Kujali; ⌚8.30am-1pm & 4-6pm Mon-Sat), hop on the *Ciremai*, which arrives at Bandaneira every Wednesday morning. Twice a month there's

BOATS FROM BANDANEIRA

DESTINATION	TYPE	COST (RP)	FREQUENCY
Amahai (Pulau Seram)	Kapal Malolo (cargo)	40,000	varies
Pulau Ai	public longboat	20,000	noon, 2pm daily
Pulau Ambon	Pelni	Varies	weekly
Pulau Ambon	Kapal Malolo (cargo)	50,000	varies
Pulau Banda Besar	public longboat	5000	when full
Pulau Run	public longboat	25,000	2pm daily
Tehoru (Pulau Seram)	longboat	5,000,000	charter

an extra Ambon–Banda run on the smaller, overcrowded, and reportedly roach-infested (we heard two horror stories) *Kelimutu* (12 hours) continuing to Saumlaki, Tual and Sorong. Beware of pickpockets at any Pelni embarkation.

Getting Around

The island is small and walkable but *ojeks* save sweat at 3000Rp for a short trip, 10,000Rp to the airport or 15,000Rp to Pantai Malole. Mutiara rents mountain bikes (50,000Rp per day). Several guesthouses offer free airport pick-ups. Typical boat-charter rates for full-day trips include snorkelling stops on Ai (350,000Rp), Hatta (600,000Rp), Karnopol and Pisang (400,000Rp), or Run (600,000Rp). Run trips may include a stop on Ai and Neilaka, as well.

Pulau Gunung Api

This devilish little 666m volcano has always been a threat to Bandaneira, Lonthoir and anyone attempting to farm its fertile slopes. Its most recent eruption in 1988 killed three people, destroyed more than 300 houses and filled the sky with ash for days. Historically, Gunung Api's eruptions have often proven to be spookily accurate omens of approaching intruders.

The volcano can be climbed for awesome sunrise views in around three hours, but the unrelenting slope is arduous and the loose scree is scary, especially upon descent. Take more drinking water than you think you'll need. Guides (from 100,000Rp) are prepared to accompany hikers but the path up is fairly obvious. Still, ask a local to point out the direction when you get off your boat. Once you're on the trail it's easy.

The waters around Gunung Api are home to lurid purple-and-orange sea squirts, remarkably fast-growing table corals and concentrations of (mostly harmless) sea snakes. The submerged north-coast lava flows ('New Lava') are especially good for snorkelling and shallow dives.

Pulau Banda Besar

POP 11,000

The largest island of the group, hilly Banda Besar makes a great day trip and offers some interesting woodland walks. Boats shuttle regularly from Bandaneira to several Banda Besar jetties, most frequently to **Walang** (per person/boat 5000/30,000Rp, 15 minutes). *Ojeks* (5000Rp) run via **Biao** village (home of a scraggy pet cassowary) to **Banree** where the asphalt ends.

If you walk 10 minutes west, along the narrow concrete sea-defence wall, you'll emerge at the relatively new but photogenic **Masjid Al Taqwa** mosque in **Lonthoir** (pronounced 'lon-tor'). This is Banda Besar's sleepy, steeply layered 'capital' village. Its main 'street' is actually a long stairway that starts beside **Homestay Leiden** (Jl Warataka; per person 100,000Rp). Leiden offers two neat guest rooms (thin mattresses and shared *mandi*) in the attractive house of earnest, English-speaking Usman Abubakar.

At the top of the stairway turn right – you will find the **Kelly Plantation** where centuries-old, buttressed *kenari* trees tower protectively over a nutmeg grove. Abba at Mutiara Guesthouse (p433) offers wonderful three-hour tours (per person 100,000Rp) to both Kelly Plantation and **Van der Broecke Plantation**, known as the last Dutch-owned plantation on the Bandas. Slain amidst sectarian violence, the long-gone patriarch was helpful in repopulating nutmeg trees throughout the Bandas.

Banree's **Benteng Hollandia** is also not to be missed. Built in 1624, this was once one of the biggest Dutch fortresses in the Indies, until shattered by a devastating 1743 earthquake. The chunky overgrown ruins, high above the village, offer perfect palm-framed views of Gunung Api with a magical foreground of sapphire shallows.

Thanks to a new, smooth road, you can now take an *ojek* from Lonthoir north to **Selamon** (20,000Rp), then walk to the beach at **Timbararu** where there is superb snorkelling off a secluded white-sand beach. You can also take a public boat (5000Rp) directly from Bandaneira to Selamon, and walk from there.

Pulau Hatta

POP 800

A stunning flying-saucer-shaped island of jungle-swathed limestone, trimmed with white sand, Pulau Hatta, once known as Rozengain, had no nutmeg. Thus its only historical relevance was a comical episode where eccentric English Captain Courthope raised a flag merely to enrage the Dutch. The island's two tiny settlements have no facilities, but **Kampung Lama** rests on a lovely white-sand beach connected to Banda's clearest waters and richest reefs. Around

300m west of Lama the beach is empty, raw and gorgeous. Here, a natural underwater 'bridge' creates a beautiful blue hole over part of Hatta's stunning vertical drop-off. Pristine coral, clouds of reef fish and superb visibility make this Banda's top snorkelling spot. We saw three turtles, a 1.5m black-tip reef shark and intact hard and soft corals.

The village is a modest sprouting of concrete paths that branch into various cul-de-sacs, where old cinder-block homes, once brightly painted, fade in the sun. It's a fishing and farming town, and when it's harvest time the whole place is suffused with the sweet, smoked cherry scent of cloves. Locals are warm, very friendly, and are always happy to chat.

From Bandaneira, count on around 600,000Rp to charter a suitably powerful boat, including stops on Hatta, eastern Banda Besar and Pisang.

Pulau Ai

POP 1300

Ai village has a gentle charm, and the beach views of Bandaneira from the jetty are magnificent. But the island's greatest attraction is snorkelling, or diving the remarkably accessible, brilliantly pristine coral drop-offs just a flipper-flap away. There's a lot to see directly in front of the village, especially in October when groups of Napoleon fish appear along with migrating dolphins and whales. Sea life is likewise impressive off **Pantai Sebila**, a 15-minute walk west, where an exceptionally stark wall, crusted with coral and dashed with sea anemone, juts straight down. There's an occasional current, but you'll quite happily drift along with it. Although there is reportedly a cleaning station here that attracts sharks and mantas, we didn't see any mind-blowing species, but the sight of flaring schools of tiny technicolour fish was enough to stir the soul.

Ai blipped on the global map when 17th-century English agents built a fortress here and trained Ai citizen-fighters so well that they managed to resist a 1615 Dutch incursion. Indeed, the islanders then stunned the astonished Dutch with an unexpected counter-attack, inflicting some 200 casualties. A year later the humiliated Dutch were preparing to make a revenge attack when a small British fleet appeared, apparently in the nick of time to defend their Ai comrades. But after a few volleys of cannon fire the English commander ceased hostilities and invited his Dutch opponent for a cup of tea. After a little chat the Dutch offered the Brits nominal trading rights and sovereignty in Pulau Run. Suitably bribed, the duplicitous Brits sloped off to Seram. When they returned, almost the entire Ai population had been massacred or had fled. The Dutch repopulated the island with slaves and prisoners. Ai's four-pointed star fortress, now a sweet community garden with corn, *kankung* (water spinach), chilli, and papaya trees sprouting within the crumbling fort walls, has been poignantly known ever since as **Benteng Revenge**. On a more peaceful note, when the sectarian riots raged in Bandaneira (and Christians were forced to flee for their lives to Ambon), all was peaceful in Ai, where Christians remained without the slightest threat.

Sleeping & Eating

Ai has but a faint cell signal, accessible from the jetty, so phone reservations aren't generally possible, but your Bandaneira guesthouse can send word. Also, virtually none of the homestays have signs, but locals will happily point the way. Be extra careful not to

GO ON, TAKE NEW YORK!

After the 1616 Dutch ravaging of Ai, English forces retreated to their trading post on Run and built an 'impregnable' fort on the tiny, waterless islet of Neilaka. Increasingly besieged, the same eccentric Captain Courthope who had taunted the Dutch on Hatta (formerly Rozengain) put honour above survival in a preposterously futile last stand, refusing even the most reasonable offers to leave. Somehow British sovereignty was maintained, even after the 1621 Dutch atrocities during which all of Run's nutmeg trees were systematically destroyed. That left the English with an economically worthless scrap of land. Eventually, in 1667, Britain agreed to a 'swap'. It gave Run to Holland for a (then equally useless) North American island. That island was Manhattan. Not a bad deal, as it turned out.

waste water: Ai has no springs and all needs are provided by collecting rainwater or by laboriously transporting purchased water from Bandaneira when supplies run dry. There are no restaurants, but accommodation prices include three meals. The island's only power source is the town generator just outside the gates of Benteng Revenge. It's switched on three hours per day.

TOP CHOICE **CDS Bungalow** BUNGALOW $$
(per person 175,000-200,000Rp incl meals) Italian and Indonesian owned, this is the class crash pad on Ai. Two brand new wooden cottages sport wooden floors, genuine spring beds on a raised platform, outdoor baths, and a wide veranda stilted over a secluded beach with commanding views. The slightly older, cheaper bungalow, set back from the bluffs, is a bit bigger and still has those sweet ocean views. It also has its own generator for 24-hour power. Book through Mutiara Guesthouse (p433) in Bandaneira.

Dua Putri Homestay HOMESTAY $
(☎0878 0644 6874; per person 100,000Rp incl meals) Just off the jetty, with gorgeous sea views, you can't miss this new choice. There are just five basic rooms with thin mattresses, two with shared *mandi*, some with sea views, and all the same price.

Ardy HOMESTAY $
(☎0878 4704 2536; per person 100,000Rp incl meals) It has a sign! It also has super-clean garrishly tiled rooms with pink walls and wooden ceilings. It's owned by the former chief of the island who offers a handful of island tours and comes highly recommended by travellers. Beware the rooster-chorus wake-up call.

Revenge 2 HOMESTAY $
(☎0821 9765 1342; per person 100,000Rp) Two really good, clean and spacious rooms in the village. They share a *mandi* in a sparkling-clean house near the fort.

Green Coconut GUESTHOUSE $
(☎0812 4241 0667; ayim_@yahoo.com; Jl Patalima; per person 125,000Rp incl meals) The Green Coconut has the best seafront location, with wonderful sea views from its common balcony and dining room (plus room 4). It has electricity from 6-11pm.

GreenPeace GUESTHOUSE $
(☎21210; mgoderadjaidi@yahoo.co.id; per person 150,000Rp incl meals) Right on the beach and a little ragged around the edges. Rooms are clean enough with double beds, but have plywood ceilings, slimy *mandis* and need a paint job. It does have excellent views of Gunung Api from the front yard, however.

Getting There & Away

Two or three passenger boats (20,000Rp, one hour) leave Ai for Bandaneira when full at around 8am, returning between noon and 2pm. To make day trips from Bandaneira you'll have to charter (350,000Rp).

Pulau Run (Rhun)

The island of Run, for all its historical gravitas, is simply a remote, incredibly picturesque, windswept chunk of limestone, swathed in jungle and surrounded by deep blue sea. The village is an appealing little network of steps and concrete paths backed by vine-draped limestone cliffs, with attractive views between the tamarind trees from the top end of Jl Eldorado. The old English Fort (the one held by Nathanial Courthope) perpetuated the Spice Wars and resulted in the great trade of Run for Manhattan (let's all go play poker in Amsterdam!). It is now just remnant ruins on the northwest point of the island facing Ambon and south to Bandaneira. You can reach it from the cement staircase that peters into a rough track through flowering shrubs, from which it will take another 20 minutes of scrambling to reach the vague ruins. From the pier, walk to the main lower path, turn right, and follow the stairs up, up, and up.

There are two homestays on Run, and both make wonderfully remote retreats worth considering for a spell of simplicity. **Homestay Nailaka** (per person 100,000Rp incl 3 meals) offers two rooms with shared baths in a new concrete home with wooden ceiling and tiled facade. **Homestay Manhattan** (per person 100,000Rp incl meals), another upscale concrete home on the upper tiered path of the village, has three rooms, all with private *mandi*. Neither homestay is signed, but locals can lead you there, and when the owners aren't in they can usually be found on the island within the hour.

Run's main attraction is diving the wall that lies 70m to 150m off the island's northwestern coast (access by boat), known as **Depan Kampung** (next to the village). Visibility is magnificent. Alternatively, beach yourself on the picture-perfect, powdery white sands of **Pulau Neilaka**, an isle so small you can saunter around it in 10 minutes. There are dazzlingly photogenic views towards Gunung Api from the eastern sand spit.

A morning boat (25,000Rp, two hours) leaves Run at 9am for Bandaneira, returning around 2pm. Chartering (600,000Rp return from Bandaneira) makes more sense if you're doing a day trip. You'll need a boat anyway to reach Neilaka and the offshore drop-offs, plus you can stop by Pulau Ai on your way home.

KEI ISLANDS

☎0916

The trump cards for the Kei Islands are kilometres of stunning, yet almost entirely empty, white-sand beaches and a deeply hospitable population. Beneath the mostly Christian facade, Kei culture is fascinatingly distinctive with three castes, holy trees, bride prices paid in *lela* (antique table cannons) and a strong belief in *sasi* (a prohibition spell). In Kei language *bokbok* means 'good', *hanarun* (*li*) means '(very) beautiful' and *enbal* (cassava) is a local food staple. The driest season is September to December, with *Belang* war-canoe races held in November.

Tual & Langgur

POP 65,000

Bridging the two central islands, these twin towns together form the Kei Islands' main commercial centre and transport gateway. Langgur is relaxed with ample space and light. Tual is a jumble of ramshackle humanity which gives it a manic edge and magnifies the 'Hey Mister' quotient a thousand fold. You'll hear a lot of talk about the city's Arabic residents – most of whom live in Tual. Many of these so-called Arabs are (mixed) descendants of an actual migration from the Middle East 250 years ago.

BNI bank (Bank Negara Indonesia; Jl Dr Laimena; ⏱8am-3pm Mon-Fri) has the only official currency exchange (terrible rates) and an ATM. For a decent web connection, find **Kimson Internet** (Jl Jenderal Sudirman; per hr 8000Rp; ⏱8am-midnight), just south of the massive karaoke mall. It has 10 relatively new terminals. The **tourist office** (Dinas Parawisata; ☎24063; Jl Jenderal Sudirman; ⏱8am-2.30pm Mon-Sat, to noon Fri) answers questions and dispenses maps and brochures.

Sleeping

Tual and Langgur have ample, if basic, accommodation, though most wisely head straight for the beachside options.

TOP CHOICE **Hotel Dragon** HOTEL $

(☎21812; Jl Jenderal Sudirman 154; r 175,000-250,000Rp; ❄) Spacious, super-clean, tiled rooms with big beds and crisp sheets. More expensive rooms have hot water; all have air-con, TV and spring mattresses. Second-floor rooms have nice cathedral views from the terrace. Not magical, just solid.

Hotel Vilia HOTEL $

(☎21878; Jl Telaver I; standard/deluxe/VIP 175,000/225,000/275,000Rp; ❄) Clean and airy, professionally run, if somewhat soulless, with mangrove views from the shared 3rd-floor balcony. Standard variety have cold-water baths; deluxe and VIP rooms have hot showers.

Aurelia Hotel HOTEL $$

(☎23748; Jl Jenderal Sudirman; standard/deluxe/VIP 220,000/275,000/440,000Rp; ❄📶) Tucked away and sheltered by a cheesy Roman colonnade, rooms have tasteful elements such as nice wood furnishings, coffee makers, crown mouldings, and free bottled water. But the carpet is threadbare and some smell, well, moist. Oh and it's attached to a massive 'karaoke' club, so there is that.

Eating

TOP CHOICE **Ayah Restaurant** SEAFOOD $

(beside Watdek Bridge; meals 30,000-50,000Rp; ⏱9am-2am) There's no sign, but you can't miss the rickety wooden building before the bridge, stilted over the channel with views of the mangroves. There's no menu either, so just choose your fresh catch or a lobster plucked just for you from the netted farms in the channel.

Lady's Restaurant INDONESIAN $

(Jl Pahalawan Revolusi; meals 40,000-50,000Rp; ⏱8am-10pm) This diner is tucked into the ground floor of a massive nouveau-riche columnar mansion. It does fried noodles, fish, shrimp and squid dishes, and a variety of soups, all with a moderately formal flair.

Getting There & Away

AIR **Wings Air** (☎22186; Jl Jenderal Sudirman; ⏱9am-5pm Mon-Sat, to 2pm Sun) and **Trigana** (☎23743; Jl Pattimura; ⏱8am-4pm Mon-

Sat) have daily flights to/from Ambon (about 1,200,000Rp, 1½ hours), with gorgeous views of Tayando and Bandas en route (south windows). With a new airport in the works for 2013, the hope is that the runway will accommodate large jets, providing a major bump in tourism. Time will tell.

BEMO (MOBIL) & OLEK *Mobil* for Debut (5000Rp), and southern Kei Kecil operate from a station beside Pasar Langgur. From Langgur's Pasar Ohoijang roughly one *mobil* per hour leaves for Ohoililir (for Coaster Cottages, 5000Rp). Or you can take an *ojek* (30,000Rp, 25 minutes) or taxi (150,000Rp).

BOAT **Pelni** (☎22520; Jl Pattimura; ⌚8am-2pm) liner *Ciremai* links Tual to Ambon (18 hours) via Bandaneira (10 hours). Eastbound, it loops through Kaimana and Fak Fak in Papua, returning 36 hours later. The reportedly roach-infested *Kelimutu* and the *Tatamailau* offer similar itineraries.

Getting Around

Bemos (2000Rp per ride) are so common they form a virtual conveyer belt along Langgur's Jl Jenderal Sudirman, mostly continuing to Tual's big Pasar Masrun market. Southbound from Tual, 'Langgur' bemos pass Hotel Vilia and terminate at Pasar Langgur. *Ojeks* cost 5000Rp per ride. Savana Cottages in Ohoidertawun offers motorbike rental (per hour/day 10,000/50,000Rp, plus a hearty fuel surcharge).

Pulau Kei Kecil

OHOIDERTAWUN

The charming village of Ohoidertawun surveys a lovely bay that becomes a vast, white-sand flat at low tide when craftsmen sit in the palm shade carving out canoes. An elfin church and pyramidal mosque coexist harmoniously. A 'holy tree' on the waterfront beside Savana Cottages is believed to enforce peace or bind relationships. And it seems to work an intangible magic on visitors who are frequently mesmerised by this wonderfully peaceful little place. A footpath and stairway leads north to **Ohoider Atas** village. At low tide you can splash across the sand flats past small caves cut in the limestone cliffs (some contain human bones). After around 25 minutes you'll begin to notice red-and-orange **petroglyphs** painted on the cliff faces. Although some designs look new, many are ancient and their origins baffle archaeologists.

Sleeping

The owners of Savana can set you up with village homestays (single/double 100,000/150,000Rp, including three meals) if you wish to go local.

TOP CHOICE **Savana Cottages** BUNGALOW **$**

(☎SMS only 0813 4308 3856; s/d 135,000/150,000Rp, meals 35,000-50,000Rp, beer 17,000Rp) For pure narcotic serenity, few budget guesthouses in Indonesia can beat Savana Cottages. Watch the changing moods of nature, the swooping curlews and the tide retreating in the moonlight, while sipping an ice-cold beer or swinging from the hammock between sighing casuarinas. The colours on this beach, when the tide is out and the blinding white-sand flats stretch to distant ribbons of turquoise sea, are just magnificent. As for the digs, they have four simple, double-bed, bamboo and wood rooms, with rattan chairs on the balcony, and towels for the shared *mandis*. Mosquito nets are available and hearty breakfasts are included at the sweet cafe, which is decorated with gongs, carvings and tinkling wind chimes. Dinners are excellent too. English-

SASI SAVVY

Call it 'magic' or 'earth knowledge', Maluku experiences many hidden undercurrents of almost voodoo-esque beliefs, beautifully described in Lyall Watson's book *Gifts of Unexpected Things*. One such belief still widely prevalent is *sasi*, a kind of 'prohibition spell' used to protect property and prevent trespass. Physically the only barrier is a *janur* palm frond. But few would dare to break a *sasi* for fear of unknown 'effects'. For countless generations *sasi* have prevented the theft of coconuts and ensured that fish aren't caught during the breeding season. However, in 2003 some cunning Kei Islanders put a *sasi* on the Tual-Langgur bridge. All bemo traffic stopped. Nobody dared to walk across. The result was, not unintentionally, a prolonged bonanza for boatmen until the authorities finally stumped up the cash for a *sasi*-removal ceremony. Other jokers made a *sasi* across the access route to Tual's government offices so employees couldn't get to work. The 21st-century *sasi* seems to have become a unique version of the protection racket.

Kei Islands

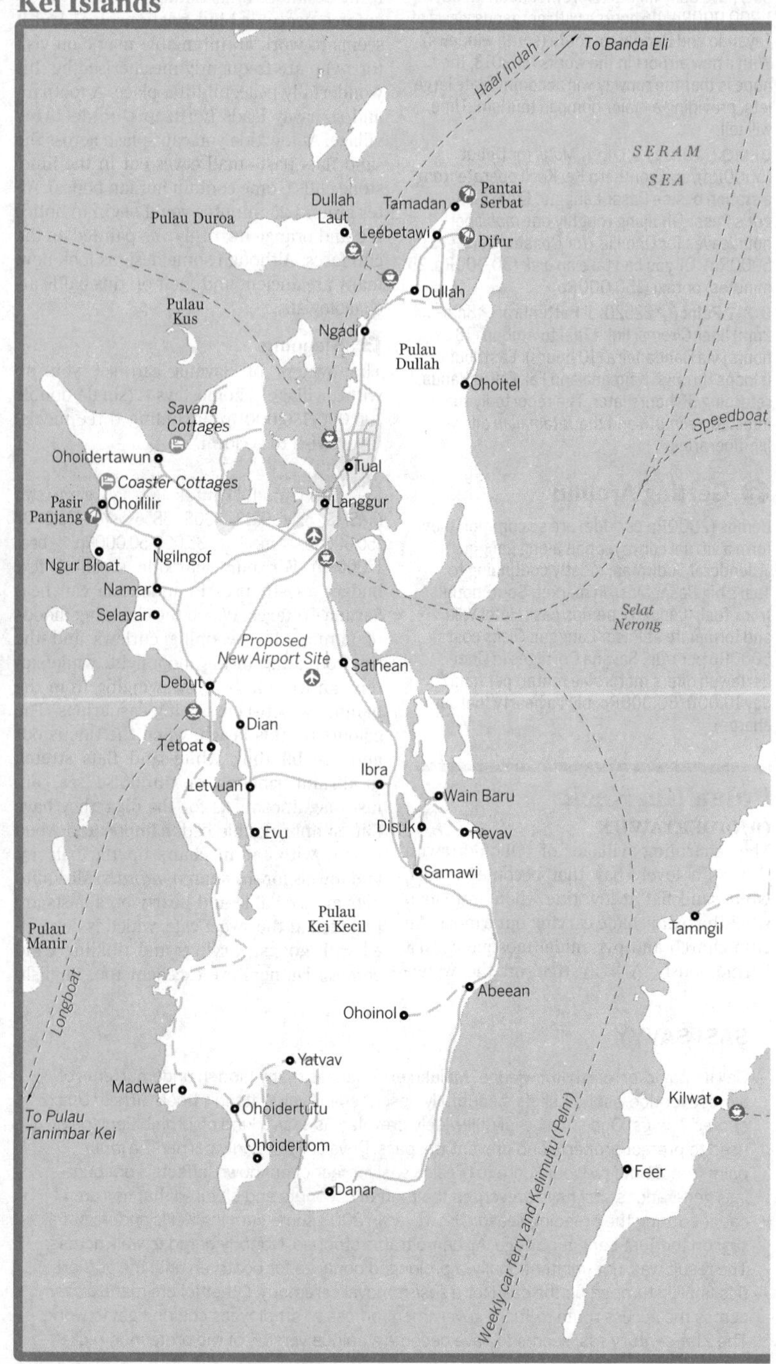
To Banda Eli
Haar Indah
SERAM
SEA
Pantai Serbat
Tamadan
Dullah Laut
Leebetawi
Difur
Pulau Duroa
Dullah
Pulau Kus
Ngadi
Pulau Dullah
Ohoitel
Savana Cottages
Speedboat
Ohoidertawun
Tual
Coaster Cottages
Pasir Panjang
Ohoililir
Langgur
Ngilngof
Ngur Bloat
Namar
Selayar
Selat Nerong
Proposed New Airport Site
Sathean
Debut
Dian
Tetoat
Ibra
Letvuan
Wain Baru
Disuk
Revav
Evu
Samawi
Pulau Kei Kecil
Tamngil
Pulau Manir
Abeean
Ohoinol
Longboat
Yatvav
Madwaer
Kilwat
Ohoidertutu
To Pulau Tanimbar Kei
Ohoidertom
Feer
Danar
Weekly car ferry and Kelimutu (Pelni)

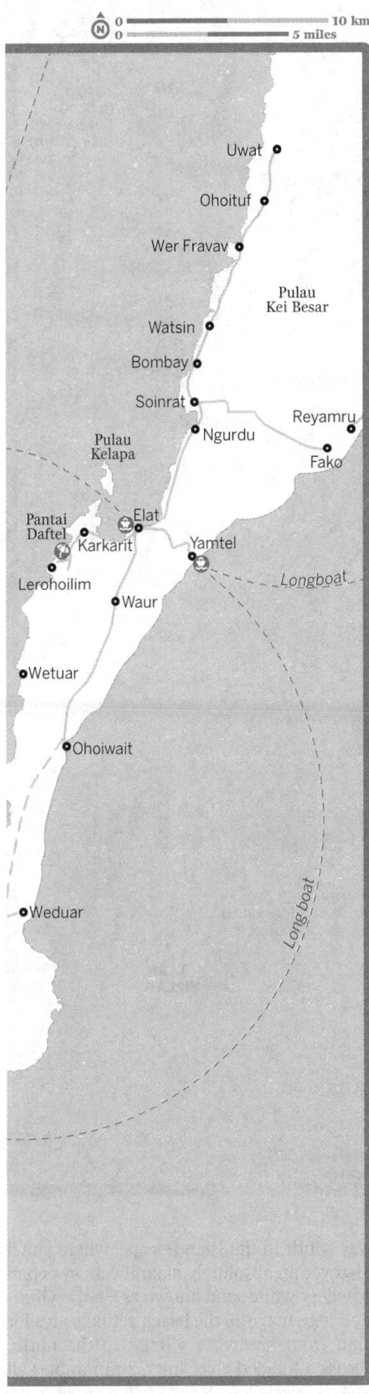

speaking owner Gerson will happily point the way to Kei Kecil's best sights. His wife, Lucy, is a marvellous chef and hilarious in her own right.

Lucy's House BUNGALOW **$**
(☎0813 4308 3856; d 150,000Rp) Gerson and Lucy also rent this wooden house. It's sweetly situated on its own beach, 300m south of the village among the coconut trees. A special spot for honeymooners or marooned writers; there's no kitchen, but they'll bring meals to your door.

PASIR PANJANG

The Kei Islands' most famous tourist draw is Pasir Panjang, 3km of white sand so powdery it feels like flour, fringed with swaying coconut palms. And despite the brochure-cover beauty, the beach is almost entirely deserted – except at weekends when a couple of karaoke outfits crank up the volume near the beach's access points: **Ngur Bloat** (south) and **Ohoililir** (north).

At the beach's reputedly haunted north end, 700m beyond Ohoililir village, **Coaster Cottages** (☎0819 4504 2241, 0819 4502 2818; bob.azyz@yahoo.com; old/new r 150,000/200,000Rp, grand villa 320,000Rp, meals per day 100,000Rp) comprises a range of accommodation. We like the four, spacious new rooms. Think white-tiled concrete constructs with twin beds and mosquito nets, wooden table and chair inside as well as on the shared patio out front, where you'll have audacious beach views. Oh, and those startling clam-shell *mandis* are well worth a photo op. Old rooms are actually closer to the beach, have brick walls and double beds and are a bit cooler, but have older basic *mandis* that are a touch slimy. The **grand villa** has character to spare with vaulted ceilings, an ornate sitting room and two bedrooms with a double bed in each, but it's not necessarily worth the price jump unless you're going family style.

There are also two wooden **government houses** in the shady north end of the village, which you can rent through the *kepala desa* (village head). Other than Coaster Cottages, these are the only accommodation we can wholeheartedly recommend on this beach though there are two bungalow properties on the south end, along with a handful of snack kiosks in Ohoililir proper.

Tual & Langgur

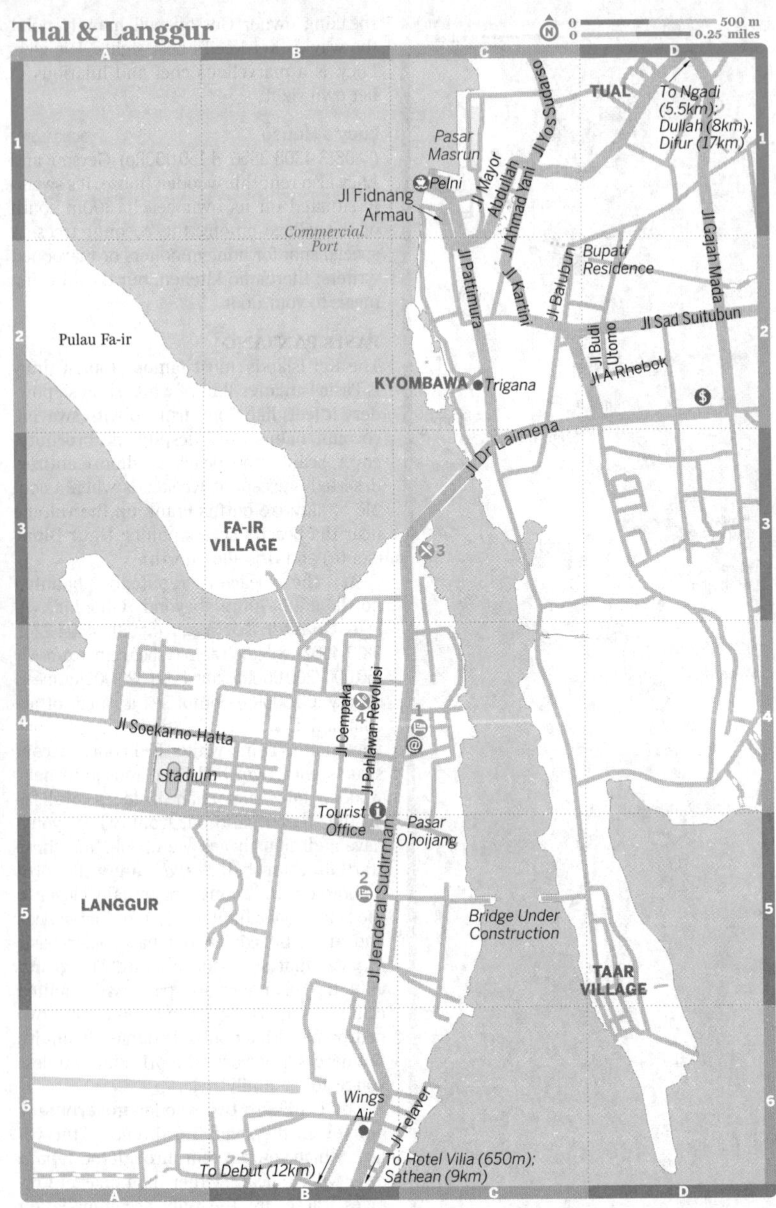

SOUTHERN KEI KECIL

A new bridge, crafted from reclaimed land, links with a rather old and terrifying (yet somehow still stable) suspension bridge. The bridge connects **Debut** with **Tetoat**, from which a rough road continues all the way south to the island's cape, where you'll discover an absolutely magnificent sweep of powdery white sand known as **Pantai Ohoidertutu**. In truth, the beach actually arcs for 5km from **Madwaer village** in the north, across a jungled river inlet, and rambles all

Tual & Langgur

Sleeping
1 Aurelia Hotel.. C4
2 Hotel Dragon B5

Eating
3 Ayah Restaurant C3
4 Lady's Restaurant................................ B4

the way to the cape. No matter where you access it, all you'll see is blinding white sand, coconut palms and the open turquoise sea. Oh, and local children too. So bring a camera and some sweeties for the mob. Madwaer is about 41km from Langgur. Given its daily access to Ambon, you may be surprised just how remote Kei Kecil is, especially the far south. The only way down here is on a horribly rutted road by *ojek* (150,000Rp round trip) or rented motorbike. And if you do make this motorbike-motocross run, bring rain gear and prepare yourself for the 'Hey Mister' brigade. Folks will be joyfully surprised to see you.

Pulau Tanimbar Kei

A series of outlying islands with lovely beaches and turquoise waters surround Kei Kecil, the most intriguing of which is **Pulau Tanimbar Kei**, southwest of Ohoidertutu. Famed for its traditional village, powdery sand and magnificent snorkelling, the only way to get here is by chartering your own speedboat from Langgur or Debut (2,000,000Rp round trip) or with local villagers who come to Langgur to shop aboard their outboard- and wind-powered canoes (they have engines and sails). They only charge 25,000Rp per person, and know the seas much better than the speedboat captains, so this is actually the safer, if much slower, option. However, you will have to find your way back, which could take a few days. There's no formal accommadation on Tanimbar Kei. Upon arrival arrange a **homestay** with the *kepala desa*. You may be able to find housing on the Indonesian **marine base**, as well.

Pulau Kei Besar

Scenic Kei Besar is a long ridge of lush, steep hills edged with remote, traditional villages and several picture-perfect beaches (better for taking photos than for swimming). Expect intense curiosity from locals and take your best *kamus* (dictionary) as nobody speaks English.

Attractively set on a bay featuring three tempting sand-fringed islets, **Elat** is Kei Besar's main village. It has a market and a few rice-and-fish *rumah makan*. All close by dusk, so eat early or snack on biscuits from the few tiny evening shops.

Southwest of Elat, a lane through palm fronds and bougainvillea leads 6km to **Pantai Daftel**, a superb, if shallow-water, white-sand beach that stretches 1.8km to **Lerohoilim**, where there's a scattering of ancient graves atop a rocky outcrop called **Batu Watlus**. Other easy *ojek* excursions from Elat include picturesque **Yamtel** village (20 minutes east), **Waur** (15 minutes south), or the charming west-coast villages of **Ngurdu** (3km), **Soinrat** (4km), **Bombay** (7km) and **Watsin** (8km), all with bay views, stone stairways and rocky terraces.

The **east coast** has attractive, tidal rock pools but no beaches. Villages are comparatively isolated, steeped in superstitious traditions and locals tend to speak the local Kei language rather than Bahasa Indonesia.

Torpedo-shaped 50-seater speedboats shuttle between Watdek (Langgur) and Elat (35,000Rp, 65 to 80 minutes), leaving when full. That's roughly hourly between around 8.30am and 4pm.

Papua

Includes »

Best Places to Eat

» Rumah Makan Ratu Sayang (p451)

» Duta Cafe (p462)

» Yougwa Restaurant (p465)

Best Places to Stay

» Papua Paradise (p455)

» Yenkoranu Homestay (p455)

» Raja4Divers (p455)

» Alberth Elopore's guesthouse (p479)

» Misool Eco Resort (p455)

» Padaido Hotel (p468)

Why Go?

Even a country as full of adventure as Indonesia must have its final frontier. Here it is – Papua, half of the world's second-biggest island, New Guinea. Here, a traditional tribal world still holds its head high amid outside encroachments. This is a place where some people still hunt their food with bows and arrows while others buy it in supermarkets. In this youngest part of Indonesia roads are scarce and to travel any distance you must take to the air or the water. Papua seems like a different country – which is what most Papuans, who are Melanesian and ethnically distinct from other Indonesians, would like it to be.

Travel here is undoubtedly a challenge, and not one that comes cheap. But those who take it on rarely fail to be awed by the charm of Papua's peoples, the resilience of their cultures and the grandeur of both their landscapes and their teeming seascapes.

When to Go

Sorong

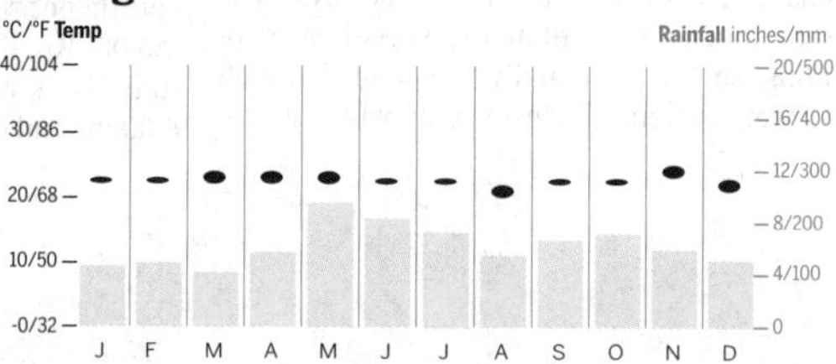

Apr–Dec Generally benign weather in the Baliem Valley; perfect for trekking.

Aug Join in with the feasting and the fun at the Baliem Valley Festival.

Nov–Mar Ideal conditions for marvelling at the aquatic wonders of the Raja Ampat Islands.

History

It's estimated that Papua has been inhabited for 30,000 or 40,000 years, but contact with the outside world was minimal until the mid-20th century. Three colonial powers agreed to divide the island of New Guinea between them in the late 19th century: Holland got the western half, and Britain and Germany got the southeastern and northeastern quarters respectively (these two together now comprise the country of Papua New Guinea). Dutch involvement with Papua was minimal right up to WWII when Japan seized most of New Guinea in 1942. Japan was then driven out in 1944 by Allied forces under US general Douglas MacArthur.

INDONESIA TAKES OVER

When the Netherlands withdrew from the rest of the Dutch East Indies (which became Indonesia) in 1949, it hung on to its half of New Guinea, and then began to prepare it for independence with a target date of 1970. Indonesia's President Sukarno had other ideas and in 1962 Indonesian troops began infiltrating the territory in preparation for an invasion. Under pressure from the USA, which didn't want to risk a damaging defeat for its Dutch ally by the Soviet-backed Sukarno regime, the Netherlands signed the New York Agreement of 15 August 1962. Under this agreement, Papua became an Indonesian province in 1963. The Papuan people were to confirm or reject Indonesian sovereignty in a UN-supervised vote within six years. In 1969, against a background of Papuan revolt and military counter-operations that killed thousands, Indonesia decided that the sovereignty vote would involve just over 1000 selected 'representatives' of the Papuan people. Subjected to threats, the chosen few voted for integration with Indonesia in what was officially named the 'Act of Free Choice'.

The following decades saw a steady influx of Indonesian settlers into Papua – not just officially sponsored transmigrants but also 'spontaneous' migrants in search of economic opportunity. Intermittent revolts and sporadic actions by the small, primitively armed Organisasi Papua Merdeka (Free Papua Organisation; OPM) guerrilla movement were usually followed by drastic Indonesian retaliation, which at times included bombing and strafing of Papuan villages. Indonesia invested little in Papuans' economic or educational development, while the administration, security forces and business interests extracted resources such as oil, minerals and timber.

PAPUA IN THE 21ST CENTURY

Following the fall of the Suharto regime in 1998, the *reformasi* (reform) period in Indonesian politics led many Papuans to hope that Papuan independence might be on the cards. In June 2000 the Papua People's Congress (more than 2500 Papuan delegates meeting in Jayapura) declared that Papua no longer recognised Indonesian rule and delegated a smaller body, the Papua Council Presidium, to seek a UN-sponsored referendum on Papuan independence. But the 'Papuan Spring' was short-lived. The second half of 2000 saw a big security-force build-up in Papua, and attacks on pro-independence demonstrators. In 2001, the Papua Council Presidium's leader Theys Eluay was murdered by Indonesian soldiers.

The year 2001 also saw the passing of a Special Autonomy charter for Papua – Jakarta's response to Papuan grievances. The major provision was to give Papua a bigger share (70% to 80%) of the tax take from its own resources, plus more money to develop education and health. But many Papuans consider that Special Autonomy has not benefited them significantly, complaining that too much of the money disappears into the hands of the bureaucracy. 'Special Autonomy equals more cars and more wives for government,' as one Papuan succinctly put it. They also complain that non-Papuans control Papua's economy and government in their own interests, and are exploiting Papua's natural resources with minimal benefit for the native people. The US-owned Freeport mine, digging the world's biggest recoverable lodes of gold and copper out of the mountains north of Timika, and using the Indonesian police and army as part of its security force, is often considered a classic symbol. Its troubled relationship with local communities has seen violence on numerous occasions, and its installations and workers have been targets of attacks usually attributed to the OPM.

Pro-independence activism and OPM activity have increased in Papua in recent years, and killings, torture, rape and disappearances carried out by the Indonesian security forces have continued to be reported by human rights bodies. Papuans regularly receive jail sentences of 10 years or more for simply raising the Morning Star flag, symbol of Papuan independence. A new meeting of

Papua Highlights

1. Trekking among the thatched-hut villages, unique tribal culture and mountain grandeur of the **Baliem Valley** (p476)
2. Diving and snorkelling in the real-life tropical aquarium of the **Raja Ampat Islands** (p452)
3. Swimming with the whale sharks off **Nabire** (p471)
4. Witnessing spectacular tribal festivities at the **Baliem Valley Festival** (p481) or **Festival Danau Sentani** (p464)
5. Trekking into the mountains around **Manokwari** (p459) in search of birds of paradise and other exotic wildlife
6. Enjoying the island life among the friendly folk of **Pulau Biak** (p467)
7. Searching out the indigenous lowland culture and Australia-like flora and fauna of **Wasur National Park** (p483)

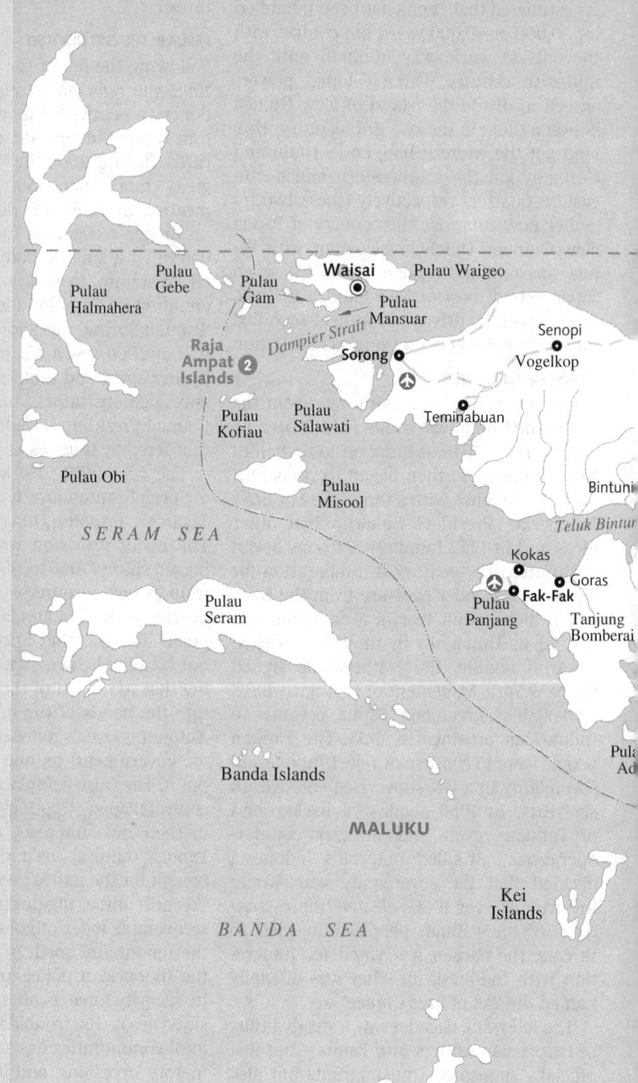

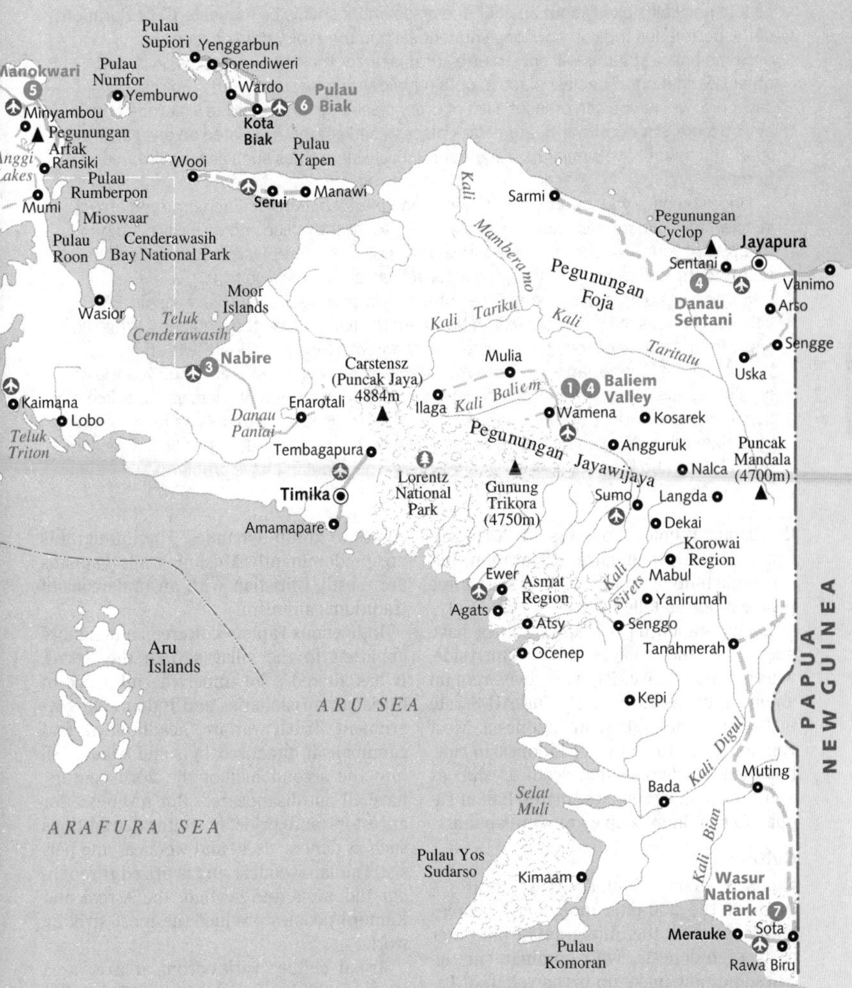

0 250 km
0 150 miles
PACIFIC OCEAN
Equator
Pulau Supiori
Yenggarbun
Sorendiweri
Manokwari
5
Pulau Numfor
Yemburwo
Wardo
Pulau Biak
6
Kota Biak
Minyambou
Pegunungan Arfak
Anggi Lakes
Ransiki
Pulau Rumberpon
Mumi
Mioswaar
Pulau Roon
Cenderawasih Bay National Park
Wooi
Pulau Yapen
Serui
Manawi
Wasior
Moor Islands
Teluk Cenderawasih
Nabire
3
Kali Mamberamo
Sarmi
Pegunungan Cyclop
Jayapura
Sentani
4
Danau Sentani
Pegunungan Foja
Vanimo
Arso
Sengge
Uska
Kali Tariku
Kali Taritatu
Mulia
Carstensz (Puncak Jaya) 4884m
Ilaga
Kali Baliem
1
4
Baliem Valley
Wamena
Kosarek
Kaimana
Lobo
Enarotali
Danau Paniai
Teluk Triton
Tembagapura
Timika
Amamapare
Lorentz National Park
Pegunungan Jayawijaya
Gunung Trikora (4750m)
Angguruk
Nalca
Puncak Mandala (4700m)
Sumo
Langda
Dekai
Korowai Region
Ewer
Asmat Region
Agats
Kali Sirets
Mabul
Yanirumah
Atsy
Senggo
Ocenep
Tanahmerah
Kepi
Aru Islands
ARU SEA
ARAFURA SEA
Kali Digul
Bada
Muting
Selat Muli
Kali Bian
Pulau Yos Sudarso
Kimaam
Wasur National Park
7
Sota
Merauke
Rawa Biru
Pulau Komoran
PAPUA NEW GUINEA

SURAT JALAN & VISA

To visit many places in Papua, foreigners must obtain a travel permit known as a *surat keterangan jalan* (commonly called a *surat jalan*). Rules and procedures for the *surat jalan* change from time to time, and enforcement varies from place to place. At the time of writing, you could visit Jayapura, Sentani, Pulau Biak and Sorong without one. Elsewhere, it's safest to assume you need one, though often you won't need to show it.

A *surat jalan* is usually easily obtained from the police in the capitals of Papua's 30-odd regencies *(kabupaten)*. The relevant police departments are typically open from about 8am to 2pm Monday to Saturday; times and days vary, and some departments can attend you outside their official hours. Take your passport, two passport photos, and photocopies of your passport's personal-details page and your Indonesian visa. The procedure normally takes about an hour and no payment should be requested. The duration of the permit depends on how long you request and the expiry date of your visa.

Some police stations will only issue a *surat jalan* for their own regencies or limited other destinations. The best place to obtain a wide-ranging *surat jalan* is Polresta in Jayapura, where you can present a list of every place that you intend to visit (don't omit any obscure, small, off-the-beaten-track places), and get them all listed on one *surat jalan*. You might have similar luck in other relatively large cities such as Manokwari and Sorong.

Once you have your *surat jalan*, make several photocopies of it. Each time you arrive in a new town, your hotel should report your arrival to the police and they will need photocopies of your passport and/or *surat jalan* to do so. In a few places you may need to report to the police yourself. Carry your *surat jalan* on out-of-town trips.

Some parts of Papua are sometimes off-limits to tourists, usually because of OPM activity. This was the case at research time with the Ilaga area in the highlands. When you apply for a *surat jalan*, the police will tell you if anywhere on your itinerary is off-limits.

Note: some Indonesian embassies may tell you that in order to visit Papua you must obtain a special permit from the Indonesian immigration authorities and/or the police department in Jakarta. Some have even reportedly refused visas to applicants who said they planned to visit Papua. In practice, as long as you have an Indonesian visa when you reach Papua and then get your *surat jalan* there, you shouldn't have problems.

the Papua People's Congress in 2011 reaffirmed its independence declaration but was broken up by troops, with at least three people reported killed.

Living standards in Papua's cities have risen, but the villages and countryside, where most native Papuans live, remain among Indonesia's poorest. The AIDS rate in Papua is the highest in Indonesia. Most Papuans want to be free of Indonesian rule, but their chances of that seem as slim as ever now that, by some estimates, half of Papua's four million people are non-Papuans.

Culture

Papua is a land of hundreds of cultures – those of the 200-plus indigenous peoples and those of all the immigrants from other parts of Indonesia, who dominate in the cities and now make up perhaps half of Papua's population. Relations between native Papuans and immigrants can be good on a person-to-person level but poor when it comes to group dynamics. The immigrants are predominantly Muslim, while Papuans are mostly Christian with an undercoat of traditional animism.

Indigenous Papuan culture is much more apparent in the villages than the towns. It has altered a lot under the influence of Christian missionaries and Indonesian government. Tribal warfare, headhunting and cannibalism, practised by some tribes well into the second half of the 20th century, have all but disappeared. But reverence for ancestors and pride in cultural traditions such as dances, dress and woodcarving persist. Papuan woodcarving is prized throughout Indonesia and beyond: the Asmat and Kamoro peoples produce the most striking work.

Tribal culture varies from area to area starting with languages, of which Papua has approximately 280. Traditional housing varies with the environment – waterside people often live in stilt houses, the Dani of the

Baliem Valley inhabit snug, round, wood-and-thatch huts known as *honai*, and the Korowai of the southern jungles build their homes high in trees. Gender roles remain traditional. Polygamy is still practised by some men, and women do most of the carrying as well as domestic tasks.

Tours

Given the logistical difficulties of Papua travel, it can make sense to take a guided tour, and particular sense for more challenging destinations such as the Asmat or Korowai areas or the little-explored Mamberamo basin in the north. Guided tours are essential (given the bureaucracy involved) for mountaineers wanting to climb Papua's high peaks such as Carstensz Pyramid (Puncak Jaya) or Gunung Trikora.

As well as guides and agencies with local ambits, there are several that offer trips to a range of Papua destinations.

Adventure Indonesia ADVENTURE TOUR
(www.adventureindonesia.com) Top Indonesian adventure-tourism firm that does Asmat, Carstensz and Baliem Valley trips.

Discover Papua Adventure TOUR
(www.discoverpapua.com) An efficient, well-established Biak-based agency that can set up just about any trip you want throughout Papua.

Michael Leitzinger ADVENTURE TOUR
(www.herp-travel.de) With more than two decades of Papua travel under his belt, Michael specialises in intrepid trips far off the beaten path to areas such as the Mamberamo basin, Foja and Bintang mountains, and the Korowai region.

Papua Expeditions BIRDWATCHING
(www.papuaexpeditions.com) This ecotourism-minded, Sorong-based company specialises in birding in all the best Papuan destinations. Its website is a great resource.

Information

Only a handful of banks in Papua will exchange any kind of foreign money, and those that do will usually only accept clean US$100 bills! There are fairly reliable ATMs in all towns, however, with Visa, Visa Electron, MasterCard, Maestro, Cirrus and Plus cards all widely accepted.

Maps of Papua are notoriously unreliable. The best commercially published map of the whole place is Nelles' *Indonesia - Papua, Maluku*.

Getting There & Around

Inter-city roads are still a thing of the future in Papua. Boats are an option for travelling to Papua and between its coastal towns if you have enough time, or along its rivers if you have enough money. Flying is the common way to reach Papua and to travel between its cities and towns.

AIR

To fly to Papua you must first get to Jakarta, Makassar, Denpasar, Manado or Ambon, then take a domestic flight. For the Baliem Valley, fly first to Jayapura and take an onward flight from there. Jayapura is served by six airlines from Jakarta and Makassar, and by Garuda from Denpasar. Jakarta–Jayapura fares start at 1,500,000Rp to 1,800,000Rp with airlines such as Lion Air, Batavia Air and Sriwijaya Air. For the Raja Ampat Islands, direct flights from Manado were expected to start in 2013; otherwise fly to nearby Sorong from Jakarta, Makassar, Ambon or Manado.

A LOT IN A NAME

When the Portuguese first encountered New Guinea and its surrounding islands in the early 16th century, they called them Ilhas dos Papuas, from the Malay word *papuwah* (fuzzy-haired). In 1545, Spanish sailors named the island Nueva Guinea (New Guinea), for its people's supposed resemblance to Africans from the Gulf of Guinea. The Dutch later named the western half of the island Dutch New Guinea, then as this territory prepared for independence in the 1950s and 1960s, local leaders chose West Papua as the name for their future nation. When Indonesia took over in 1962, Sukarno named the territory Irian Barat (West Irian), using a Biak word meaning 'Hot land rising from the sea'. In 1973, Irian Barat was changed to Irian Jaya (Victorious Irian).

To most native Papuans, the name Irian symbolises unwanted Indonesian rule. Papuan nationalists still refer to their land as West Papua. In a nod to their feelings, President Abdurrahman Wahid renamed it Papua in 2000. Its current division into two provinces, rather confusingly named Papua (capital: Jayapura) and Papua Barat (West Papua; capital: Manokwari), dates from 2003.

PAPUA TRAVEL WARNING

Outbreaks of civil unrest and violence do happen in Papua, but they shouldn't deter you from visiting unless some generalised outbreak occurs. Political demonstrations in Abepura, Jayapura and elsewhere sometimes turn violent, and acts of violence between Papuans and non-Papuans, often involving the OPM or the Indonesian army or the police, happen most months. Many of these incidents happen in remote parts of the highlands (where the OPM is strongest), or around the Freeport mine near Timika, although the Baliem Valley and the Jayapura area also see some violence. Foreigners are rarely the targets or victims; tourists are welcomed by the great majority of people in Papua. Stay abreast of current events and ask the police if you have concerns about particular places.

Most Jakarta–Papua flights are overnight, with a small-hours stop in Makassar. Schedules and routes flown by airlines change frequently; Merpati flights are notoriously subject to delays. Of the airlines operating in and to Papua, all except two (Garuda and Batavia Air) are on the European Union's banned list of unsafe airlines at the time of writing.

Most commercial flights within Papua cost around 1,000,000Rp, plus or minus a hundred thousand or two.

Missionary airlines such as the Roman Catholic **Associated Mission Aviation** (AMA; www.ama-papua.com) and Protestant Mission Aviation Fellowship (MAF) do a lot of flying between small, remote airstrips. They will sometimes carry tourists if they have spare seats. Chartering a small plane for seven to 12 people is another option for routes not served by scheduled flights.

Batavia Air (www.batavia-air.com)
Expressair (www.expressair.biz)
Garuda Indonesia (www.garuda-indonesia.com)
Lion Air (www2.lionair.co.id)
Merpati (www.merpati.co.id)
Sriwijaya Air (www.sriwijayaair.co.id)
Susi Air (www.susiair.com) Flies small planes on local routes within Papua.
Trigana Air (www.trigana-air.com)
Wings Air (www2.lionair.co.id)

BOAT

Every two weeks, five Pelni liners sail into Sorong from Maluku, Sulawesi, Kalimantan or Java, continue to Jayapura via various intermediate ports along Papua's north coast, then head back out again. There are also a few sailings connecting Agats and Merauke on Papua's southern coast with Sorong and ports in Maluku.

Various smaller, less comfortable passenger boats serve minor ports, offshore islands and routes on a few rivers such as the Mamberamo and Digul; some have more or less fixed schedules, others don't. On routes without any public service, you can charter a boat, which might be a fast, powerful speedboat, or a *longbot* (large motorised canoe) or a *ketinting* (smaller motorised canoe; long-tail boat). Charter costs are highly negotiable and depend on the boat, its fuel consumption, the distance and the petrol price (which can vary from about 5000Rp/L at main ports to more than 25,000Rp/L in river villages far inland).

WEST PAPUA

The province of West Papua chiefly comprises two large peninsulas – the Vogelkop (Bird's Head/Kepala Burung/Semdoberai) and the more southerly Bomberai Peninsula – and several hundred offshore islands. The attractions here are primarily natural – above all the world-class diving and gorgeous island scenery of the Raja Ampat Islands. Sorong and Manokwari are well-provided urban bases from which to launch your explorations.

Sorong

☎0951 / POP 190,000

Papua's second-biggest city, Sorong sits at the northwestern tip of the Vogelkop. It's a busy port and base for oil and logging operations in the region. Few travellers stay longer than it takes to get on a boat to the Raja Ampat Islands, but Sorong can be quite fun for a day or two, and there are some interesting destinations in the surrounding region.

The city stretches 12km from east to west. Everything you'll need is in the western half of town, between the airport (at the approximate midpoint of the sprawl) and the Tembok Berlin (Berlin Wall) seafront at the west end. One main street runs the whole way; it's called Jl Basuki Rahmat outside the airport, then Jl Yani further west, and then Jl Yos Sudarso after it turns north along Tembok Berlin.

Sleeping

JE Meridien Hotel HOTEL $$

(☎327 999; www.hoteljemeridiensorong.blogspot.com; Jl Basuki Rahmat Km7.5; r incl breakfast 400,000-800,000Rp; ❄@📶) Handily placed opposite the airport, the Meridien offers solid, modern comfort in cool, white, good-sized rooms with tea and coffee makers, plus free rides to the airport or the Raja Ampat ferry. A good coffee shop, an efficient travel agency and the Raja Ampat Tourism Management Office are all in the building.

Hotel Waigo HOTEL $$

(☎333 500; Jl Yos Sudarso; r incl breakfast 445,000-590,000Rp, ste 711,000-917,000Rp; ❄📶) Playfully decked out in pink paint, psychedelic tiles and stylised murals, this hotel facing the Tembok Berlin waterfront has a bright lobby and rooms which, while not quite so sparkling, are good-sized and reasonably appealing. The ocean view 'suites' are massive. The in-house restaurant (mains 20,000Rp to 45,000Rp) is good value.

Hotel Tanjung HOTEL $

(☎323 782; Jl Yos Sudarso; s 201,000-230,000Rp, d 241,000-270,000Rp; ❄📶) At the north end of the Tembok Berlin waterfront, the Tanjung has tired but acceptable rooms, all with air-con.

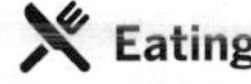

Eating

Sorong restaurants are generally better stocked with alcohol (beer, at least) than those elsewhere in Papua. For cheaper eats, dozens of seafood warungs (food stalls) set up in the evenings along Tembok Berlin (Jl Yos Sudarso).

TOP CHOICE **Rumah Makan Ratu Sayang** SEAFOOD, CHINESE $$

(Jl Yos Sudarso; grilled fish around 50,000Rp; ⏲9am-2.30pm & 5.30-10pm) Pick up the scent of fish on the grill and head inside this two-level eatery for delicious *ikan bakar* (grilled fish). With rice, spinach, three sauces and a drink, this will set you back around 100,000Rp. It's just north of the well-signed turning to Sunshine Beach restaurant.

Sunshine Beach INDONESIAN, CHINESE $$

(Jl Yos Sudarso, beside Hotel Tanjung; mains 25,000-90,000Rp; ⏲9am-midnight Mon-Sat, 4pm-midnight Sun) This spacious, semi-open-air place with sparkling lights is built over the edge of the sea. It offers everything from fried rice or noodles to prawns, crab, fish, squid and beef, prepared in assorted ways. There's an air-conditioned bar too.

Information

ATMs Machines outside Saga supermarket, at about the midpoint of Jl Yani, service Visa, Visa Electron, MasterCard, Maestro, Cirrus and Plus cards.

Polresta Sorong (☎321 929; Jl Yani I) Head to this police station, 1km west of the airport, for a *surat jalan*.

Raja Ampat Tourism Management Office (☎328 358; www.diverajaampat.org; Jl Basuki Rahmat Km7.5, JE Meridien Hotel; ⏲9am-4pm Mon-Fri, to noon Sat) This incredibly helpful office can tell you almost anything you need to know about the Raja Ampat Islands, and it's the

WORTH A TRIP

AROUND SORONG

For information and help with logistics, contact very helpful Rudie Yarangga at **Sorong Regency Tourism Information** (☎0821 9833 0213, 0813 4437 3398; papuarudie75@gmail.com).

Pulau UM, a tiny island in the mouth of **Teluk Dore** inlet, 30km northeast of Sorong, makes a great day trip. Bring a snorkel. Surrounded by a sandy beach and clear waters with coral and dugongs, the island's trees are the roost for thousands of large bats by day and birds by night. Leatherback turtles nest here from October to December. You can take a Kijang from Sorong's Pasar Remu to **Makbon** village (15,000Rp, two hours, about every two hours), then ask for Makbon boatman Maurits Malibela who charges 300,000Rp for a trip to the island.

The lesser bird of paradise lives 1km from **Klasuat** village, some 30km southeast of Sorong. Renting a car and driver to get there and back costs 1,000,000Rp to 1,500,000Rp, and there's a local fee of 100,000Rp per person to pay. Start from Sorong by 5am to see the birds' morning display.

FLIGHTS FROM SORONG

DESTINATION	COMPANY	FREQUENCY
Ambon	Wings Air, Expressair	7 weekly
Jakarta	Batavia Air & Expressair	daily
Jayapura	Expressair, Merpati	daily
Makassar	Sriwijaya Air, Batavia Air, Expressair, Merpati	daily
Manado	Wings Air, Expressair, Merpati	3 weekly
Manokwari	Sriwijaya Air, Expressair, Batavia Air	daily
Nabire	Expressair	3 weekly

best place to buy the tag permitting you to visit the islands.

Getting There & Away

AIR All airlines have airport ticket counters.

BOAT **Pelni** (Jl Yani 13), near the western end of Jl Yani, has five ships sailing every two weeks east to Jayapura (via assorted intermediate ports, including Manokwari, Biak and Nabire) and west to ports in Maluku, Sulawesi and Java. Sample fares (1S/economy class) are 1,178,000/263,000Rp to Biak, 1,346,000/299,000Rp to Jayapura and 749,500/171,000Rp to Ambon. The *Tatamailau* heads down to Agats and Merauke (1st/economy 1,556,500/395,000Rp) on Papua's southern coast, every two weeks.

Getting Around

Official airport taxis charge 100,000Rp to hotels at the west end of town; on the street outside you can charter a public *taksi* for half that or less. Using the yellow public *taksi* (minibuses; 3000Rp), first get one going west outside the airport to Terminal Remu (600m), then change there to another for Jl Yos Sudarso. Short *ojek* (motorcycle) rides of 2km to 3km are 5000Rp; between the west end of town and the airport is 15,000Rp or 20,000Rp.

Raja Ampat Islands

POP 43,000

This group of about 1600 mostly uninhabited islands off Sorong has some of the best diving in the world. Little known until the last few years, Raja Ampat's sheer numbers and diversity of marine life, and its huge, largely pristine coral-reef systems, are a scuba dream come true – and fantastic for snorkellers too. It's like swimming in a tropical aquarium. The sparsely populated islands are also great for birdwatching and just exploring amid sublime scenery of steep, jungle-covered islands, white-sand beaches, hidden lagoons, spooky caves, weird mushroom-shaped islets and pellucid waters. Travel here is not for super-tight budgets, but new homestay accommodation has made Raja Ampat much more accessible than it was.

The four biggest islands are Waigeo (with the small but fast-growing regional capital, Waisai), Batanta, Salawati and Misool. The Dampier Strait between Waigeo and Batanta has many outstanding dive sites, so most accommodation options are on Waigeo, Batanta or three smaller islands between them: Kri, Gam and Mansuar.

Activities

Diving

You can get up close with huge manta rays and giant clams, gape at schools of barracuda, fusiliers or parrotfish, peer at tiny pygmy seahorses or multicoloured nudibranchs ('sea slugs'), and with luck encounter wobbegong and epaulette (walking) sharks. The reefs have hundreds of brilliantly coloured soft and hard corals, and the marine topography varies from vertical walls and pinnacles to reef flats and underwater ridges.

Most dives are drift dives due to the currents washing over the reefs. You can dive year-round, although the usually smooth seas can be rougher in July, August and September (the Raja Ampat/Sorong area gets its heavier rain from May to October). The dive resorts generally offer packages of a week or more and focus on spots within about 10km of their resort. Some will take nonguests diving if they have places available, for €40 to €50 per dive, and €30 to €40 to rent a complete set of equipment, if available.

Homestays on Pulau Kri also offer diving services, but only highly qualified divers should consider this option – the guides are short on professional training and experience and on safety protocols and safety equipment. Ask to see their certifications. The nearest decompression chamber is far away in Manado, Sulawesi.

Here's a very brief selection of top dive areas and spots, in approximate northwest-to-southeast order:

Wayag Islands DIVING

These small, uninhabited and incredibly picturesque islands, 30km beyond Waigeo, feature heavily in Raja Ampat promotional material. It's mainly liveaboards that dive here, but Wayag also attracts nondivers for its scenery, snorkelling and the challenge of scaling its highest peak, Pindito. An all-day speedboat round trip from Waisai for six to 10 people costs around 9,000,000Rp.

Teluk Kabui DIVING

The bay between Waigeo and Gam is packed with picturesque jungle-topped limestone islets. The Batu Lima dive spot in the bay's entrance has a great variety of fish and beautiful soft corals.

The Passage DIVING

This 20m-wide channel between Waigeo and Gam is effectively a saltwater river. It's heaven for advanced macrodivers with its nudibranchs, sponges and tunicates ('sea squirts'). Sharks, archerfish, turtles, rays and schools of bumphead are seen here too.

Fam Islands DIVING

Calm waters, stunning coral and masses of fish, notably at the Melissa's Garden spot.

Manta Sandy DIVING

At this famous site between Mansuar and Arborek islands, numbers of huge manta rays, some with wingspans over 5m, wait above large coral heads to be cleaned by

Raja Ampat Islands

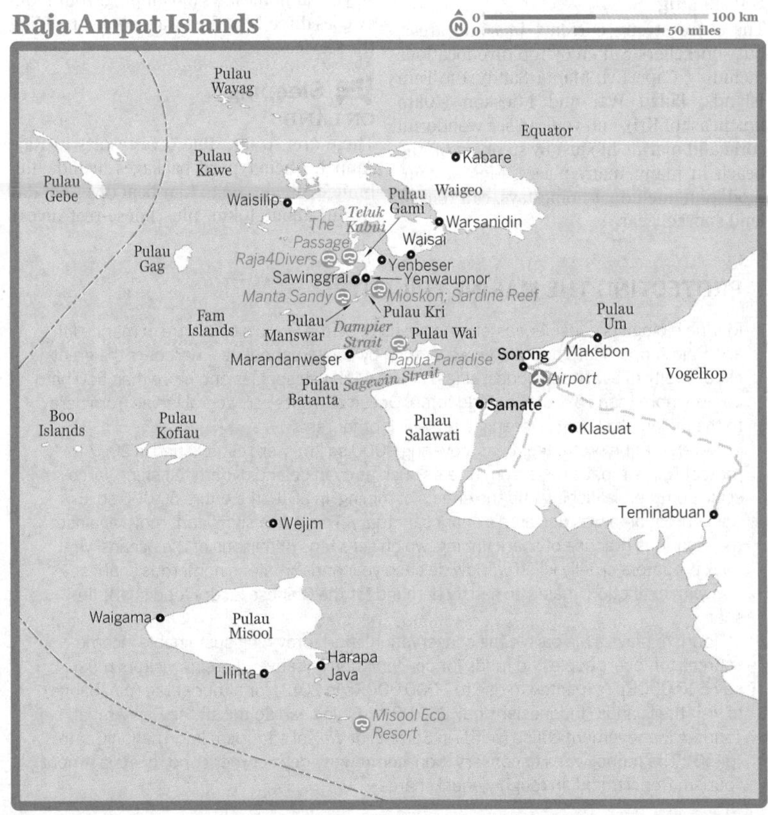

small wrasses. Best from about October to April.

Cape Kri DIVING

The fish numbers and variety at the eastern point of Pulau Kri have to be seen to be believed. A world record of 374 fish species in one dive was counted here in 2012. Schools of barracuda, jacks, batfish and snapper co-exist with small reef fish, rays, sharks, turtles and groupers. Beautiful coral too.

Sardine Reef DIVING

Sardine, 4km northeast of Kri, slopes down to 33m, and has so many fish that it can get quite dark! The fish-and-coral combination is great for photographers. Currents can be strong.

Pulau Misool DIVING

This remote southern island – especially the small islands off its southeastern corner – has stunning coral. The pristine reefs attract pygmy seahorses, epaulette sharks, manta rays and a vast range of other fish.

Snorkelling

There are strong currents in some areas, but snorkellers can enjoy top dive locations including Cape Kri, Manta Sandy, the Fam Islands, Pulau Wai and Mioskon (10km northeast of Kri), and you can see wonderful coral and marine life just by stepping off the beach in many, many places. Most accommodation, including homestays, can rent or lend snorkel gear.

Birdwatching

The many exotic birds on the islands include two fantastically coloured endemic birds of paradise, the red and the Wilson's. The red male has a spectacular courtship dance in which he spreads his wings and shakes like a big butterfly. Village guides in Sawinggrai, Yenwaupnor and Yenbeser on Pulau Gam provide a relatively easy way to see this, charging 100,000Rp to 150,000Rp per person for early-morning walks to nearby display spots. Sorong-based Papua Expeditions (p449) offers specialised Raja Ampat birding trips.

Kayaking

Kayak4Conservation KAYAKING

(www.kayak4conservation.com; kayak/guide per day €35/25, guesthouse per person with/without 3 meals 400,000/300,000Rp) This new venture, based at Sorido Bay Resort on Pulau Kri, provides the exciting chance to tour Raja Ampat by kayak, with or without a guide, staying at homestays or camping. Your money goes directly to the local people providing the services.

Sleeping

ON LAND

There are, so far, nine dive resorts in Raja Ampat. Their typical packages include 'unlimited' diving (up to four boat dives per day within about 10km, plus house-reef dives),

PROTECTING THE MARINE EPICENTRE

Marine biologists consider eastern Indonesia to be the world's epicentre of marine life, and Raja Ampat – dubbed a 'species factory' by conservationists – harbours the greatest diversity of all. This includes, at last count, 1459 fish species and more than 550 hard corals (more than 75% of the world total). Ocean currents carry coral larvae from here to the Indian and Pacific Oceans to replenish other reefs.

Seven marine protected areas, covering 9000 sq km, were established in 2007 to protect Raja Ampat's reefs from threats such as cyanide and dynamite fishing, large-scale commercial fishing and the effects of mining. In 2010, the entire 50,000 sq km Raja Ampat area was declared a shark sanctuary. This was a significant move against the nefarious practice of shark finning, which sees tens of millions of the oceans' vital apex predators cruelly killed worldwide each year and threatens numerous shark species with extinction, mainly to satisfy demand for the Chinese luxury food shark-fin soup.

Tourism plays a big part in the conservation effort, providing sustainable income sources for local people and funds for conservation initiatives. Foreign visitors must pay 500,000Rp (expected to rise to 1,000,000Rp in 2013) for a tourist tag (pin/badge) to visit the islands (Indonesians pay 250,000Rp): you can do this at the Raja Ampat Tourism Management Office (p451) in Sorong, or Waisai's Tourism Information Centre (p456). The money goes to conservation, community development and the Raja Ampat Tourism Department, in roughly equal shares.

accommodation, meals and Sorong transfers on fixed days of the week. Transfers from Waisai should become available when the airport there opens. More distant dives, equipment rental and transfers on non-standard days cost extra.

A growing number of much less expensive 'homestays' are opening up on several islands – the majority on Kri and Gam, but also some in remoter locations such as Sawandarek (south coast of Mansuar), Pulau Wai (off north Batanta), Marandanweser (northwest Batanta) and Harapan Jaya (southeast Misool). Here, local Papuan families provide simple guest quarters with shared Indonesian-style bathrooms and offer snorkelling, birdwatching and other outings. Three (mainly fish-based) meals a day are usually part of the deal. Homestays will normally pick you up in Waisai if you contact them a day or two ahead (best by SMS), typically for 400,000Rp or 500,000Rp per boat one-way to Kri or Gam, and more to more distant places. Boat outings can cost anything from 300,000Rp to 1,500,000Rp or even more, depending how far you go. The Raja Ampat Tourism Management Office in Sorong can help you contact homestays.

The more urban experience of Waisai is not what visiting Raja Ampat is really about, but it has plenty of decent accommodation should you need to stay.

TOP CHOICE Papua Paradise RESORT **$$$**
(www.papuaparadise.com; Pulau Birie; 7-night unlimited diving package €1650;) With large, elegant overwater bungalows on a gorgeous, pristine, small island off northern Batanta, and masses of good diving nearby, this resort also has some of the best prices in Raja Ampat. It's also a good base for birdwatching (including the red and Wilson's paradise birds), and offers PADI courses too.

TOP CHOICE Yenkoranu Homestay HOMESTAY **$$**
(0852 5455 5526, 0821 9849 8519; yenkoranuhomestay@ymail.com; Pulau Kri; full board per person 250,000Rp) On a long, palm-fringed beach with a coral reef offshore, Yenkoranu is a near-perfect getaway. Run with care by a large and lovable family, it has just four simple rooms, an overwater hammock deck where you can watch fabulous sunsets and (with luck) walking sharks, and food that's as good and varied as you'll get in a homestay. They'll take guests snorkelling and diving. Waisai transfers are free if you stay five nights, otherwise 350,000Rp round trip per boat. Nearby alternatives that operate in a similar manner are **Koranu Fyak Bungalows** (0813 4417 4787; robbensauyai@yahoo.com; Pulau Kri; s/d full board 350,000/500,000Rp) and **Mangkur Kodon Homestay** (0853 9904 0888, 0852 4335 9154; enzomo@libero.it; Pulau Kri; s/d full board 400,000/600,000Rp), along the same beach, and **Ransiwor Homestay** (0812 4841 0507; Pulau Ransiwor; r & full board 500,000Rp) on a tiny island in the narrow strait between Kri and Mansuar.

Raja4Divers RESORT **$$$**
(081 1485 7711; www.raja4divers.com; Pulau Pef; 7-night unlimited diving package €2350;) A classy small resort on an idyllic island beach with a reef out front, Raja4Divers sits off western Gam, giving access to some superb dives that are beyond the normal reach of Dampier Strait resorts. There's no extra charge for distant dives here, but you do have to pay (€150 per person each way) for the scheduled Sorong transfers. Large, airy water's-edge bungalows are decked with intriguing artefacts.

Misool Eco Resort RESORT **$$$**
(www.misoolecoresort.com; Pulau Batbitim; 7-night unlimited diving package €2940-3650; closed mid-Jun–mid-Sep;) On a beautiful small island off southeastern Misool (a four- to five-hour trip from Sorong), this comfortable, well-run dive resort has a strong conservation and community ethos and many superb dive sites within a few minutes' boat ride. It maintains a 1220-sq-km no-take zone in the surrounding waters. Most cottages have a veranda over the water; all have open-air bathrooms.

Raja Ampat Biodiversity LODGE **$$**
(0821 8922 2577; www.rajaampatbiodiversity.com; Pantai Yenanas; 7 nights full board incl 12 dives €747-992) Two kilometres east of Yenbeser village on Gam, Spanish-run Biodiversity is a great option for divers on relatively limited budgets. Accommodation is in simple but spacious and comfortable cabins, good Indonesian and Western food is served, the dive operation is of a high standard, and PADI and SSI diving courses are offered too. It also offers short four-night packages, and will pick you up from Waisai, not Sorong, which helps keep costs down.

Kri Eco Resort RESORT $$$
(☎0815 2700 0610; www.papua-diving.com; Pulau Kri; 7-night unlimited diving package €1455-1895) Kri Eco, operating since 1994, is the original Raja Ampat dive lodge, belonging to Papua Diving, whose Dutch founder, Max Ammer, pioneered scuba in Raja Ampat. It's a professional operation with a gorgeous setting. All 13 rooms are on stilts at the edge of the crystal-clear water. Except for one big, beautiful new family room, they share bathrooms (with *mandis*).

Sorido Bay Resort RESORT $$$
(☎0815 2700 0610; www.papua-diving.com; Pulau Kri; 7-night unlimited diving package €2705-2890; ❄@📶) The more luxurious of Papua Diving's two resorts, Sorido offers top diving standards along with Western-style comforts, such as air-con, camera workstations, internet access and hot showers in spacious, well-equipped beachfront bungalows.

Harapan Jaya Homestay HOMESTAY $$
(☎0813 4435 3030; Harapan Jaya village; full board per person 400,000Rp) This superior-standard homestay is currently the only one on large, remote Pulau Misool (actually it's on a small offshore island). A great base, if you have funds, for exploring Misool's islands, beaches, caves and waterfalls.

Kobe Oser Resort GUESTHOUSE $$
(Ibu Maria's; ☎0821 9934 7626; Yenwaupnor, Pulau Gam; full board per person 500,000Rp) Welcoming, relaxed Kobe Oser has two rustic, overwater bungalows at the edge of Yenwaupnor village. They'll take you snorkelling in their boats (250,000Rp for a trip of around three hours, 1,500,000Rp for a full-day circuit of Gam via Teluk Kabui).

Mambefor Homestay HOMESTAY $$
(☎0821 9905 6132; robbensauyai@yahoo.com; Sawinggrai village, Pulau Gam; r & full board 500,000Rp) A neat little overwater homestay and a good base for bird-of-paradise viewing, snorkelling trips and walks to caves and lookouts. Waisai transfers are 1,000,000Rp round trip per boat. Another worthy and welcoming option, in a mangrove-lined cove 500m west, is **Metho's Homestay** (☎0813 5409 1769; methudimara@gmail.com; Sawinggrai village, Pulau Gam; s/d full board 500,000/600,000Rp).

Penginapan Najwa Indah HOTEL $$
(☎0852 4465 3444; Jl Abdul Samad Mayor, Waisai; r incl breakfast 350,000-450,000Rp; ❄@📶) Good clean rooms and free internet.

Acropora Cottage BUNGALOW $$
(☎0812 4885 2777; Jl Badar Dimara, Waisai; 2-bedroom cottages 660,000Rp; ❄) Nice wooden cottages in grassy gardens.

LIVEABOARDS

The ultimate Raja Ampat experience could be cruising around on a Bugis-style schooner specially kitted out for divers. Some 40 Indonesian- and foreign-owned liveaboards do regular one- to two-week dive cruises, usually starting and ending in Sorong. Some itineraries combine Raja Ampat with Maluku, Teluk Cenderawasih, or Teluk Triton (Triton Bay) south of Kaimana. Most boats carry 12 to 16 passengers and some are luxurious, with air-conditioned cabins and en-suite bathrooms. Most cruises run between November and April, when Raja Ampat seas are calmest. Costs typically range between US$300 and US$500 per person per day. **Grand Komodo** (www.komodoalordive.com), a long-running Indonesian operation, has three liveaboards operating year-round and is among the least expensive. The **Seven Seas** (www.thesevenseas.net) is probably the last word in Raja Ampat liveaboard luxury. Other established boats include the **Shakti** (www.shakti-raja-ampat.com), **Pindito** (www.pindito.com) and **Seahorse** (www.indocruises.com). See www.diverajaampat.org for a fuller list.

ℹ Information

Bank BRI (Jl Mohamed Saleh Taesa, Waisai) ATM for MasterCard, Maestro, Cirrus and Link.

Tourism Information Centre (☎0852 5455 0411; Acropora Cottage, Jl Badar Dimara, Waisai; ⌚8am-4pm Mon-Fri)

Warnet (Penginapan Najwa Indah, Jl Abdul Samad Mayor, Waisai; per hr 20,000Rp; ⌚8am-midnight)

ℹ Getting There & Around

Waisai's newly built airport was due to start operating by 2013. Thrice-weekly Wings Air flights to/from Manado, connecting with Silk-Air's Singapore–Manado flights, were expected to be first in the air.

Fast Marina Express passenger boats (economy/VIP 120,000/150,000Rp, two hours) and a larger, slower, boat (100,000Rp, three hours) depart for Waisai from Sorong's **Pelabuhan Feri**

(Pelabuhan Rakyat; Jl Feri, off Jl Sudirman) at 2pm daily. The slower boats have greater open-air deck space. The boats head back from Waisai at 2pm Sunday to Friday, and noon Saturday.

Ojeks to Pelabuhan Feri cost around 15,000Rp from the west end of Sorong or outside the airport; a taxi is around 50,000Rp. *Ojeks* between port and town in Waisai (2km) are 20,000Rp.

An overnight boat to Waigama and Lilinta on Misool leaves Pelabuhan Feri at 10pm every second Friday, but other passenger boats to and around the islands are irregular. To arrange transport around the islands once there, your best bet is to ask at your accommodation or Waisai's Tourism Information Centre. Prices depend on boat, distance and petrol price (9000Rp/L in Waisai at research time), and are usually negotiable.

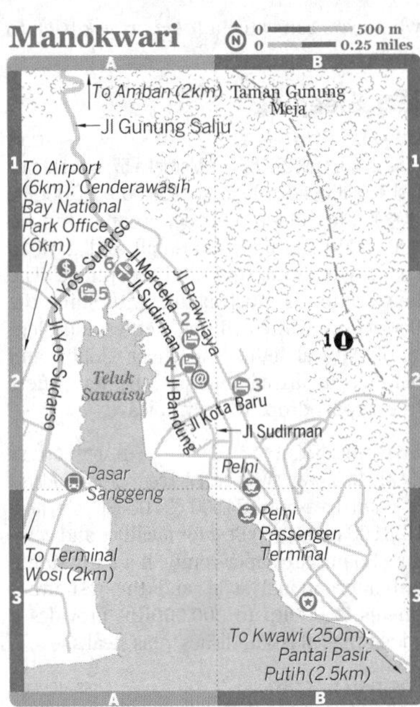

Manokwari

Sights
1 Tugu Jepang B2

Sleeping
2 Billy Jaya Hotel A2
3 Losmen Kagum B2
4 Metro Hotel A2
5 Swiss-belhotel A2

Eating
Billy Cafe & Resto .... (see 2)
6 Hawai Bakery & Coffee Shop A1
Warung Bakso Solo .... (see 4)

Manokwari

☎0986 / POP 60,000

Capital of Papua Barat province, Manokwari sits on Teluk Cenderawasih near the northeastern corner of the Vogelkop. It merits a visit mainly for the natural attractions in the surrounding area, notably the Pegunungan Arfak. Most travellers' facilities are in the area called Kota, on the eastern side of the Teluk Sawaisu inlet. Local transport terminals and the airport (7km) are to the west and southwest.

Sights & Activities

Pulau Mansinam ISLAND

Two German missionaries settled on Mansinam Island off Manokwari in 1855 and became the first to spread Christianity in Papua. The picturesque, rainforest-covered island is home to a small village, a **church**, a **cross memorial** to the missionaries, and a pleasant **beach** along its west and south shores. The coral reef off the south end offers good **snorkelling**. About 150m off the cross memorial, the Cross Wreck is one of several WWII wrecks that attracts dive boats to the waters off Manokwari. It can often be seen from the surface.

Outrigger boats (3000Rp one way) sail to Mansinam from Kwawi, 2.5km southeast of central Manokwari, whenever they have enough passengers.

Pantai Pasir Putih BEACH

About 5km east of town, this 600m curve of clean white sand and clear water is good for swimming, and snorkelling if you have gear. It's generally quiet – except on Sunday when half of Manokwari invades the beach.

Taman Gunung Meja WALKING

(Table Mountain Park) This protected forest makes an enjoyable walk if you start early enough to catch the birdlife and morning cool. A 1km walk up from Jl Brawijaya brings you to the white entrance gate, from which a fairly level 3km track, mostly paved, runs north through the forest. After 800m the **Tugu Jepang**, a Japanese WWII monument, stands 100m to the left along a branch track. From the far end of the forest track, follow the paved road 600m past houses, then go left at a T-junction. This brings you in 400m to the Manokwari–Amban road, where you can catch a *taksi* or *ojek* back to town.

Sleeping

Billy Jaya Hotel HOTEL $$
(☎215 432; fax 215 827; Jl Merdeka 57; r incl breakfast 170,000-400,000Rp, ste 450,000-550,000Rp; ❄📶) The older, cheaper rooms (up to 290,000Rp) range from small and dark to large, windowed, drab and acceptable. The new section is much better, with shiny tile floors, nice white bedding, kettles and plenty of natural light. The cheery lobby and helpful staff are a bonus, and the hotel offers free airport drops when you leave.

Swiss-belhotel LUXURY HOTEL $$
(☎212 999; www.swiss-belhotel.com; Jl Yos Sudarso 8; r incl breakfast 634,500-694,000Rp, ste from 1,013,500Rp; ❄@📶) Best for facilities and comfort. Rooms are super-comfy in a fairly standard international style, and the restaurant (mains 72,000Rp to 300,000Rp) provides a wide range of Asian dishes, plus steaks.

Losmen Kagum GUESTHOUSE $
(☎211 653, 211 618; Jl Brawijaya; s/d incl breakfast & shared bath 100,000/120,000Rp, r incl breakfast & private bath 150,000Rp; ❄) The four rooms (all upstairs) in this appealing house behind Xavier Bookstore are spacious, bright, carpeted, air-conditioned and excellent value. Bathrooms have Western-style facilities.

Metro Hotel HOTEL $$
(☎215 975; Jl Biak; r incl breakfast 275,000-500,000Rp; ❄) Quite clean and modern, with pleasant staff, though cheaper rooms are small.

Eating

Billy Cafe & Resto INDONESIAN, CHINESE $$
(Jl Merdeka 57; mains 30,000-100,000Rp; ⏲7am-noon & 7-11pm) Very clean and bright, the Billy offers a vast range of dishes, and they're tasty, though you might need two plus rice to fill up. Drinks are on the expensive side. You can sit out on the balcony to escape painful live music and karaoke in the evenings.

Hawai Bakery & Coffee Shop CAFE $
(Jl Sudirman 100; cakes & pastries 6000-10,000Rp, drinks 20,000-75,000Rp; ⏲7am-1am) An arm of the Billy empire, this relaxed, air-conditioned spot serves lots of coffees, teas and juices, including espresso and English breakfast, plus tempting banana muffins.

Warung Bakso Solo INDONESIAN $
(Jl Sudirman; mains 20,000-50,000Rp; ⏲closed Sun) A simple place, good for classic Indonesian dishes at decent prices, including *nasi pecel* (rice with a spicy peanut sauce with spinach and bean sprouts) and *nasi ayam panggang lalapan* (grilled chicken with rice and greens).

Information

BNI Bank (Jl Yos Sudarso) The ATMs provide cash for Visa, Visa Electron, MasterCard, Maestro, Plus and Cirrus cards.

Police station (☎211 359; Jl Bhayangkhara; ⏲9am-5pm) A *surat jalan* for surrounding areas is easy to obtain here, 1km southeast of the port.

Toko Biak (Jl Merdeka 46; per hr 8000Rp; ⏲8am-10pm Mon-Sat) Erratic internet connections tempered by soothing air-con.

Getting There & Away

Tickets for the small planes of Susi Air are sold only at the airport.

Every two weeks **Pelni** (☎215 167; Jl Siliwangi 24) has five sailings each to Jayapura (1S/economy class 966,500/222,500Rp) and Sorong (519,500/126,500Rp), four to Makassar, three to Nabire, two each to Biak and Ternate, and one each to Ambon and Banda. ASDP Indonesia Ferry's *Kasuari Pasifik IV* sails to Biak (88,000Rp, 15 hours) at 4pm Thursday.

FLIGHTS FROM MANOKWARI

DESTINATION	COMPANY	FREQUENCY
Ambon	Wings Air	4 weekly
Biak	Susi Air	3 weekly
Jakarta	Batavia Air	daily
Jayapura	Expressair	daily
Makassar	Batavia Air, Sriwijaya Air	daily
Sorong	Sriwijaya Air, Expressair, Batavia Air	daily

Getting Around

Airport taxis to town cost 100,000Rp. Some public *taksi* (3000Rp) pass the airport too, bound for Terminal Wosi, halfway to the centre. At Wosi you might find another *taksi* direct to Kota (6000Rp); otherwise get one to Terminal Sanggeng, then another (or walk) to Kota. Terminal Sanggeng is the starting point for very frequent public *taksi* running through Kota and out to Kwawi and Pantai Pasir Putih.

Around Manokwari

The mountains, jungles, coasts and islands around Manokwari are great for off-the-beaten-track adventures in nature. Best known for their birds of paradise and other exotic species are the mountains of the Pegunungan Arfak. The offshore islands and waters, the lowland forests and the exciting but little-known **Senopi area** 130km west (reachable by a five-hour drive or via Susi Air flights to Kebar) are also ripe for exploring. Senopi village has the good **Senopi Guesthouse** (d 300,000Rp), and **Aiwatar hill**, a few hours' walk way, attracts thousands of birds every morning to its warm saltwater springs and coastal vegetation (40km from the sea).

Activities

Two Manokwari-based guides can help you get the best out of the region:

Arfak Paradigalla Tours BIRDWATCHING, HIKING
(☎0812 4809 2764; yoris_tours@yahoo.com) This effusive, one-man, English- and Dutch-speaking outfit offers city tours as well as Arfak trips. Yoris Wanggai is very knowledgeable about the area's birds, plants and insects. He charges around 800,000Rp per day for overnight trips, not counting transport, accommodation or food.

Charles Roring HIKING, BIRDWATCHING
(☎0813 3224 5180; www.manokwaripapua.blogspot.com) An enthusiastic guide who seeks out exciting natural destinations, Charles offers hiking, camping, birding, nature and snorkelling trips all over the Manokwari region and as far as Teluk Triton south of Kaimana. Browse his websites (gold mines of information) for ideas. His guiding fee is usually between 350,000Rp and 500,000Rp per day; all up, a three-day/two-night Arfak trip for four people might cost around 7,000,000Rp.

TOP PAPUA READS

- *Lost in Shangri-La* by Mitchell Zuckoff (2011)
- *Throwim' Way Leg* by Tim Flannery (2000)
- *Under the Mountain Wall* by Peter Matthiessen (1987)
- *The Lost World of Irian Jaya* by Robert Mitton (1983)
- *Poisoned Arrows* by George Monbiot (1989)
- *Diving Indonesia's Bird's Head Seascape* by Burt Jones & Maurine Shimlock (2011)

PEGUNUNGAN ARFAK

The thickly forested Arfak mountains, rising to more than 2800m south of Manokwari, are a region of beautiful tropical scenery, exotic wildlife (especially birds) and a mostly indigenous Papuan population (the Hatam and other peoples), some of whom still inhabit traditional 'thousand-leg' stilt houses. The first and one of the biggest Papuan revolts against Indonesian rule happened here in 1965–68.

A recently completed road (mostly unpaved) from Manokwari runs through the Arfak via the relatively large village of Minyambou and the Anggi Lakes, and on down to the coastal town of Ransiki. Bring a sleeping bag and food on all trips up here.

The best birdwatching base is **Mokwam**, a collection of small villages a few kilometres down a side road about 50km from Manokwari, before Minyambou. There's accommodation for tourists in two of the villages, Syobri and Kwau. In Syobri ask for **Zeth Wonggor**, a highly experienced guide who has worked here with, among others, Sir David Attenborough. He has forest hides for viewing the magnificent bird of paradise, Western parotia and Arfak astrapia (also birds of paradise), the Vogelkop bowerbird and other exotic feathery species. February and March are best for observing spectacular, iridescent birdwing butterflies with wingspans of up to 25cm. Zeth has tourist **accommodation** (per person 100,000Rp) in a well-built wooden house. He charges about 150,000/300,000Rp per half-day/day for guiding.

You can get a 4WD double-cabin pick up to Mokwam (100,000Rp, 1½ hours) from around 7am, 100m along the street past Manokwari's Terminal Wosi. Talk to drivers the day before, or get to the stop in good time, if you don't want to end up chartering a whole vehicle for 1,000,000Rp. You can also ask here if any public vehicles are making the trip to the Anggi Lakes or Ransiki; otherwise a charter to the lakes (five hours plus stops) is about 2,500,000Rp (or go by *ojek* from Ransiki).

South from Minyambou, the two deep, clear **Anggi Lakes**, 'male' Danau Giji (29 sq km) and 'female' Danau Gita (24.5 sq km), nestle among the hills at 2000m altitude. You could walk here in two days from Mokwam. At the lakes it's possible to sleep in a school teacher's house or local houses for around 80,000Rp per person. From the lakes it's a one-to-two-day walk, or a drive of about two hours, down to the coastal town of **Ransiki**, 80km south of Manokwari. Public *taksi* service links Ransiki with Manokwari's Terminal Wosi (45,000Rp, two to three hours). There's a small **guesthouse** (s/d 50,000/100,000Rp) near Ransiki's post office. An *ojek* from Ransiki to Danau Gita costs 250,000Rp, to Danau Giji 350,000Rp.

CENDERAWASIH BAY NATIONAL PARK

With some 20 islands and 500km of coastline, Cenderawasih Bay National Park is easily the biggest protected area in the waters around the Vogelkop, which harbour a vast diversity of marine life. The potential for diving, snorkelling, hiking and birdwatching is big, but so far there has been very little development. Nearly all visitors are divers on liveaboards, or people visiting the whale sharks from Nabire. The **Cenderawasih Bay National Park office** (Balai Besar Taman Nasional Teluk Cenderawasih; ☎098 621 2303; www.telukcenderawasih-nationalpark.org; Jl Wajib Senyum, off Jl Esau Sesa, Sowi Gunung, Manokwari; ⏲8am-4pm Mon-Fri), on a hillside above Manokwari airport, has information on the park and can usually issue the necessary visitor's permit within an hour (take passport and *surat jalan* photocopies). Charges are 15,000/30,000Rp per person/camera per visit, and 50,000Rp per hour for diving.

The easiest and least expensive island to reach from the Manokwari area is **Pulau Rumberpon**, which offers snorkelling among superb coral and marine life, fine sandy beaches, hiking, and possible boat trips to smaller islands. Chartering a boat from Ransiki to Rumberpon (one to two hours) costs 1,000,000Rp to 2,000,000Rp round trip. On Rumberpon, it's possible to sleep at the national park office at Yembekiri, or homestays in Isenebuai, Yende and Pasir Panjang villages, or Pulau Nusrowi just off the west coast. Bring food.

THE NORTH

Papua province's capital, Jayapura, and its airport town Sentani, are hubs of Papuan travel, and there's a scattering of appealing things to see and do in and around these towns. Further west, Biak is a relaxed offshore island that's good for a spot of beach time, snorkelling or diving, and has evocative WWII sites to investigate. Nabire is the starting point for trips to swim with whale sharks, the world's largest fish.

Jayapura

☎0967 / POP 342,000

Downtown Jayapura is hot, busy with traffic and hard to love, but it has a beautiful setting between steep, forested hills opening on to Teluk Imbi. If you just want to get up to Wamena as soon as possible, you can often make all arrangements in Sentani without coming into Jayapura. But if you want to see Papua's biggest and most important city, this is it.

A small settlement named Hollandia was established here by the Dutch in 1910. In 1944, 80,000 Allied troops landed here to dislodge the Japanese in the largest amphibious operation of WWII in the southwestern Pacific. After WWII, Hollandia became capital of Dutch New Guinea. Following the Indonesian takeover in 1963, it was renamed Jayapura ('Victory City') in 1968. A public consultation exercise in 2010 favoured changing the name to Port Numbay, a name popular with indigenous Papuans, but this has yet to be officially ratified.

The city stretches 6km northeast from its centre, and its conurbation includes the formerly separate towns of Argapura, Hamadi, Entrop, Abepura and Waena, all south of Jayapura proper. Cenderawasih University at Abepura is a particular focus of Papuan nationalism.

Sights

Museum Loka Budaya MUSEUM
(☎571 786; Jl Abepura, Abepura; admission free, donation suggested; ⏲7.30am-4pm Mon-Fri) Cenderawasih University's cultural museum

TRAVELLING BETWEEN PAPUA & PNG

There are no flights between Papua (Indonesia) and Papua New Guinea (PNG), and the only land-border crossing that is open to foreigners is at Skouw (opposite Wutung, PNG), 55km east of Jayapura and 40km west of Vanimo, PNG. This border suffers occasional temporary closures, usually due to political tensions.

To cross the land border in either direction, you need a visa beforehand. It's best to get visas in advance at Indonesian or PNG embassies elsewhere, but if you haven't done this, the **Indonesian consulate in Vanimo** (☎857 1371; www.kemlu.go.id/vanimo; ⊙closed Sat & Sun) issues 30/60-day Indonesian tourist visas for 70/135 kina (about US$35/65), normally within one working day. You might be asked to show a ticket out of Indonesia. The **PNG consulate at Jayapura** (☎096 753 1250; kundujj@jayapura.wasantara.net.id; Blok 6 & 7, Ruko Matoa, Jl Kelapa Dua, Entrop; ⊙9am-noon & 1-2pm Mon-Fri) issues 60-day tourist visas for 225,000Rp, normally in three working days. To apply, you must submit the following in person: an application form completed in blue ink; a letter of request typed in English, addressed to the Papua New Guinea Consulate-General at Jayapura and indicating the purpose of your visit to PNG; a sponsor's or invitation letter from PNG (if this is impossible, explain why in your letter of request); a photocopy of a confirmed onward air ticket out of PNG or Indonesia; a photocopy of your passport; and two colour photos, 4cm by 6cm, with your signature on the back. Regulations and practices at both consulates change from time to time; the information here is the situation at the time of writing. Travellers from Eastern European, Asian or African countries should make advance enquiries at a PNG consulate, as PNG has different regulations for some of these nationalities. The Jayapura consulate is next to Hotel Le Premiere, 600m east of the Entrop *taksi* terminal (p464).

Note that if you are in Indonesia with a visa on arrival (VOA), you must get an exit stamp at Jayapura's immigration office (p463) before travelling to the border to cross to PNG.

Air Niugini links Vanimo with Wewak and Port Moresby three times weekly. Buses and vans (10 to 15 kina, one hour) link Vanimo's market area with the border. Between the border and Jayapura or Sentani you usually need to charter a *taksi* for 250,000Rp to 400,000Rp; the trip takes about two hours.

contains a fascinating range of Papuan artefacts between 80 and 300 years old, including the best collection of Asmat carvings and 'devil-dance' costumes outside Agats, plus fine crafts from several other areas, historical photos and musical instruments. With luck you'll be guided round by an English-speaking staff member and learn a lot about Papuan culture. The museum is next to the large Auditorium Universitas Cenderawasih on the main road in Abepura.

Pantai Base G BEACH
Base G Beach is nearly 3km long, sandy, clean and lined with wooden picnic platforms. The best beach easily accessible from Jayapura, it is usually near empty, except on Sunday when locals come in droves for a bathe and a walk. Beware the many rocks in the water. Base G was the American forces' administrative HQ in 1944. Frequent 'Base G' *taksi* (2000Rp) start from Jl Sam Ratulangi for the 5km trip; the beach is a 10-minute walk downhill from the last stop.

Sleeping

Swiss-belhotel LUXURY HOTEL $$$
(☎551 888; www.swiss-belhotel.com; Jl Pasifik Permai; r incl breakfast 1,208,000-1,970,000Rp, ste from 3,175,000Rp; ❄@📶🏊) There's nothing very Papuan about it, but the Swiss-bel provides high-quality, European-style comfort in a harbourside location, with a good open-air pool and super-comfortable rooms. Check the website for good discounts, especially at weekends.

Hotel Yasmin HOTEL $$
(☎533 222; yasminhotel@yahoo.co.id; Jl Percetakan 8; s 408,375-571,725Rp, d 490,050-653,403Rp; ❄📶) A quite classy place with well-equipped but small rooms, and a 24-hour restaurant. Some of the cheapest rooms lack windows.

Hotel Papua HOTEL $$
(☎531 889; Jl Percetakan 78; s 280,000Rp, d 410,000-450,000Rp; ❄) This place goes the extra decorating mile with colourful, even

Jayapura

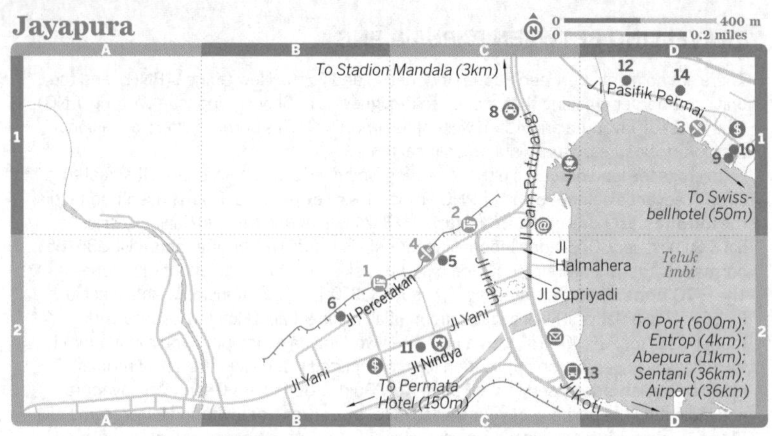

Jayapura

Sleeping
- 1 Hotel Papua ... B2
- 2 Hotel Yasmin ... C1

Eating
- 3 Duta Cafe ... D1
- 4 Excelso Cafe ... C2
- Hotel Yasmin ... (see 2)

Information
- 5 Immigration Office ... C2
- 6 PT Kuwera Jaya ... B2

Transport
- 7 APO Port ... C1
- 8 'Base G' Taksi Stop ... C1
- 9 Expressair ... D1
- 10 Garuda ... D1
- 11 Merpati ... C2
- 12 Sriwijaya Air ... D1
- 13 Terminal Mesran ... C2
- 14 Trigana ... D1

tasteful, murals and photos. It's well kept, and there's a reasonable restaurant.

Amabel Hotel HOTEL $

(☎522 102; Jl Tugu 100; s 198,000Rp, d 242,000-297,000Rp;) Easily the best budget option, the Amabel has neat little rooms with windows and its own inexpensive little restaurant. With 26 rooms, it often has vacancies when other budget places don't. It's signposted from Jl Sam Ratulangi about 100m past the Base G *taksi* stop.

Permata Hotel HOTEL $$

(☎531 333; drsstahwel@yahoo.co.id; Jl Olah Raga 3; s 220,000-480,000Rp, d 295,000-480,000Rp, all incl breakfast;) On the edge of the market zone, the Permata provides modernish rooms with hot showers. Staff are welcoming and the restaurant opens 24 hours.

Eating & Drinking

Jayapura is 'dry' except for the restaurants of the better hotels.

TOP CHOICE **Duta Cafe** SEAFOOD $$

(Duta Dji Cafe; Jl Pasifik Permai; whole fish 40,000-60,000Rp, vegetable dishes 15,000-25,000Rp; 5pm-2am) Long lines of evening warungs open along Jl Pasifik Permai, cooking up all sorts of Indonesian goodies, including seafood galore. At the large, clean Duta Cafe, halfway along the street, an excellent *ikan bakar* comes with five sambals (chilli sauces) lined up on your table, and the juice drinks go down very nicely. Don't confuse with another Duta Cafe further along near the Swiss-belhotel.

Hotel Yasmin INTERNATIONAL $$

(☎533 222; Jl Percetakan 8; mains 42,000-145,000Rp; 24hr) The lobby restaurant here has just about the best prepared and presented food downtown, from good sate prawns to steaks, fish and American breakfasts. It has powerful air-conditioning and will serve you a cold beer – and it never closes.

Excelso Cafe CAFE $$
(☎534 450; Jl Percetakan 38; coffee, cakes & snacks 27,500-66,000Rp; 📶) Recline in large easy chairs while enjoying the air-con, and choose from a range of international coffees (hot or iced), sandwiches and ice-cream concoctions.

☆ Entertainment

Jayapura's soccer team, Persipura (nicknamed Mutiara Hitam – the Black Pearls), were Indonesian champions in 2009 and 2011 – a big source of Papuan pride! Home games are at **Stadion Mandala**, 3km northeast of the centre, reachable by 'Base G' *taksi* from Jl Sam Ratulangi. Check www.ligaindonesia.co.id for fixtures.

ℹ Information

Bank Mandiri (Jl Yani 35; ⊙8am-3pm Mon-Fri) You can exchange US$100 notes here, and there's an ATM.

BCA Bank (Blok C, Ruko, Jl Pasifik Permai; ⊙8am-3pm Mon-Fri) Exchanges cash US dollars, euros and British pounds, with no minimum.

Immigration office (☎533 647; Jl Percetakan 15; ⊙8am-4pm Mon-Fri) This office will issue one 30-day extension to a visa on arrival (VOA), for 250,000Rp: apply at least one week before your visa expires. Travellers with VOAs must come here for a (free) exit stamp before crossing the land border to Vanimo, Papua New Guinea.

Polresta (Polda; Jl Yani 11; ⊙9am-3pm Mon-Fri) Police elsewhere in Papua will often only issue a *surat jalan* for their own regencies, but here you can get one for everywhere you want to go in Papua (that's not off-limits). They do tend to request a donation for 'administrative costs', however. Processing takes about one hour.

Post office (Jl Koti 3; ⊙8am-5pm Mon-Sat)

PT Kuwera Jaya (☎533 333; Jl Percetakan 96; ⊙8am-9pm Mon-Sat, from 10am Sun) This efficient travel agency sells tickets for flights and Pelni boats from Jayapura, and also some flights from other Papuan cities.

Warnet Saka Bahari (Jl Sam Ratulangi; per hr 8000Rp; ⊙9am-11pm) Spacious and air-conditioned.

TRANSPORT FROM JAYAPURA

Air

DESTINATION	COMPANY	FREQUENCY
Biak	Garuda, Merpati, Sriwijaya Air	daily
Denpasar	Garuda	daily
Jakarta	Garuda, Merpati, Batavia Air, Expressair, Lion Air, Sriwijaya Air	daily
Makassar	Merpati, Garuda, Batavia Air, Expressair, Lion Air, Sriwijaya Air	daily
Manado	Merpati	4 weekly
Merauke	Batavia Air, Lion Air, Merpati	daily
Nabire	Merpati, Wings Air, Expressair	daily
Sorong	Expressair, Merpati	daily
Wamena	Trigana, Susi Air	daily

Boat

DESTINATION	COST (RP; 1S/ECONOMY CLASS)	DURATION	FREQUENCY (PER 2 WEEKS)
Ambon	1,745,000/405,000	2½-4 days	3
Banda	1,730,000/395,000	3½ days	1
Biak	693,000/173,500	17-25hr	3
Makassar	3,205,000/720,000	4-5 days	5
Manokwari	990,000/245,000	1-2 days	5
Nabire	930,000/225,000	15-32hr	3
Sorong	1,385,000/325,000	1½-2½ days	6

Getting There & Away

Air

Jayapura airport (☎591 809), actually at Sentani, 36km west, is the hub of Papuan aviation. Most flights arrive and depart between 7am and 1pm. Tickets are available at travel agencies and at the airport and Jayapura offices of the airlines. The airport offices usually close when their flights are finished for the day.

Expressair (☎550 444; Blok G 10, Jl Pasifik Permai)

Garuda (Blok G 11-12, Jl Pasifik Permai)

Merpati (☎533 111; Jl Yani 15)

Sriwijaya Air (Blok A 2, Jl Pasifik Permai)

Trigana (☎535 666; Blok B 12B, Jl Pasifik Permai)

Boat

Six Pelni liners leave here in every two-week period, sailing to some 20 ports in Papua, Maluku, Sulawesi, Kalimantan and Java.

The **port** (Jl Koti) is accessible by any *taksi* going to Hamadi or Entrop. Pelni tickets are sold there and at agencies including PT Kuwera Jaya (p463).

Perintis boats also head along the coast as far as Manokwari, putting in at smaller ports en route and even heading to villages up rivers such as the Mamberamo. They normally leave from the **APO port** (Jl Sam Ratulangi) and typically take a week to get to Manokwari, for around 100,000 Rp. Bring food and drinks!

Getting Around

Official airport taxis from the airport at Sentani to central Jayapura cost a hefty 200,000Rp. Outside the airport gate you can charter a *taksi* for 100,000Rp to 120,000Rp with bargaining. Going by public *taksi* from Sentani to Jayapura involves three changes and takes about 1½ hours. Fortunately, each change is just a hop into another vehicle waiting at the same stop. Start with one from Sentani (outside the airport gate or heading to the right along the main road 400m straight ahead) to Waena (4000Rp, 20 to 30 minutes). Then it's Waena to Abepura (3000Rp, 10 minutes), Abepura to Entrop (3000Rp, 20 minutes) and Entrop to Jayapura (2500Rp, 20 minutes). Heading back from Jayapura, go through the same routine in reverse. You can pick up Entrop-bound *taksi* on Jl Percetakan or at **Terminal Mesran** (Jl Koti).

Sentani

☎0967 / POP 48,000

Sentani, the growing airport town 36km west of Jayapura, sits between the forested Pegunungan Cyclop and beautiful Danau Sentani. It's quieter and cooler than Jayapura and can be used as a base for visiting the bigger city and other interesting spots in the area. The older area, near the airport, has wide, tree-lined streets. West along very busy Jl Raya Kemiri is the much busier part of town where most of the inhabitants and local commerce are found.

Sights

Right by the junction of Jl Airport and the main road in Sentani, where no arriving visitor can miss it, a former football field is now the **Papua Human Rights Abuses Memorial Park** (Jl Raya Kemiri). This contains nothing but the **Grave and Memorial of Theys Eluay**, a Danau Sentani tribal chief and Papuan independence leader who was murdered in November 2001 by members of the Indonesian army's Kopassus special forces. Eluay was chairman of the Papua Council Presidium, which was seeking a UN-sponsored referendum on Papuan independence. He was strangled while travelling in a car with Kopassus soldiers, who later received light sentences for the crime (3½ years' jail for their leader).

Festivals & Events

Festival Danau Sentani PAPUAN CULTURE

(⏲approx 20-30 Jun) The Lake Sentani Festival, inaugurated in 2008, features spectacular traditional dances and chanting as well as boat events, music, crafts and hair braiding. It's very popular with locals and lately has taken place at Kalkhote, on the lakeside 8km east of Sentani town.

Sleeping

Rasen Hotel HOTEL $$

(☎594 455; rasenhotel_papua@yahoo.com; Jl Penerangan; r incl breakfast 230,000-345,000Rp; ❄📶) The best choice near the airport, the Rasen has good-sized, clean rooms with hot showers and large-screen TVs, plus a decent restaurant, free airport drop-offs and even a small fish pond. Unsurprisingly it fills up so try to call ahead. Some staff speak some English.

Travellers Hotel Sentani HOTEL $$$

(☎592 420; www.travellerssentani.com; Jl Raya Kemiri 282; r incl breakfast 1,500,000Rp; ❄@📶) New in 2012, this is almost 2km west of the airport but offers high-quality rooms, facilities and service that you won't find elsewhere in town. Ask about promotions, which can slash published prices.

Hotel Ratna Indah HOTEL $$

(☎591 119; fax 594 449; Jl PLN 1; s/d incl breakfast 250,000/300,000Rp, deluxe 385,000Rp; ❄📶)

Rooms need a spruce-up but they have hot showers and air-con, and airport drops are free.

Hotel Minang Jaya HOTEL $
(☎591 919; Jl Bestour Post 2; r 150,000-230,000Rp; ❄) It's well past its prime, but this budget hotel is kept reasonably clean. Upstairs rooms are brighter. The cheapest rooms share *mandis*; the most expensive have air-con.

Hotel Semeru Anaron HOTEL $
(☎591 447; Jl Yabaso 10; r 220,000Rp; ❄) Rooms are worn and shabby, but it's very convenient for the airport.

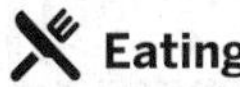

Eating

TOP CHOICE **Yougwa Restaurant** INDONESIAN $$
(☎571 570; Jl Raya Kemiri; mains 20,000-55,000Rp; ⏲10am-8pm Mon-Sat, to 4pm Sun & holidays) Sentani's most charming dining is on the Yougwa's breezy wooden terraces over the lake, 13km east of town. Try *ikan gabus* (snakehead), a tasty lake fish that doesn't fill your mouth with little bones.

Manna House Jaya Restaurant INDONESIAN, CHINESE $$
(Jl Raya Kemiri; mains 20,000-65,000Rp; ⏲9am-3pm & 5-9.30pm) This clean, air-conditioned haven with a Bali-trained chef does New Zealand steaks, as well as excellent Indonesian fare.

Warung Maduratna INDONESIAN $
(Jl PLN; meals 25,000-40,000Rp) An unassuming spot that does excellent chicken sate and gado gado, and they're happy for you to bring in a beer from the shop next door.

Shopping

Aneka Batik TEXTILES
(Jl Hawai; ⏲7.30am-9pm Mon-Sat, 2-9pm Sun) Aneka sells a big range of shirts, T-shirts and cloth in exciting, colourful Papuan-themed designs (albeit made in Java). A 2m sarong length can cost anywhere from 60,000Rp to more than 200,000Rp. Aneka has branches in most main Papuan towns.

Information

ATM Gallery Conveniently placed just outside the airport arrivals hall. If you need to change cash dollars, you must go to Jayapura.

Polres (☎591 110; Jl Yowanibi, Doyo Baru; ⏲8am-2pm Mon-Sat) This police station 5km west of Sentani takes about an hour to issue a *surat jalan* for the Baliem Valley area, but, unlike Polresta in Jayapura, can't issue one for other parts of Papua. An *ojek* from Sentani is 30,000Rp round trip.

Unicom Net (Jl Raya Kemiri 13; internet per hr 7000Rp; ⏲9am-10pm)

Sentani

Sentani

Sights

1 Grave & Memorial of Theys Eluay B1
2 Papua Human Rights Abuses Memorial Park B1

Sleeping

3 Hotel Minang Jaya A1
4 Hotel Ratna Indah A1
5 Hotel Semeru Anaron B2
6 Rasen Hotel A1

Eating

7 Warung Maduratna A1

Getting There & Around

Taxis at the airport ask 50,000Rp to take you the few hundred metres to most hotels, and even *ojeks* want 25,000Rp. Outside the airport gate, *ojeks* are 5000Rp.

Public *taksi* (2000Rp) marked 'Trm Sentani-Hawai' shuttle up and down Jl Raya Kemiri between the *taksi* terminal at the western end of town and the Hawai area in the east.

Around Sentani

Several interesting places around Sentani can be easily visited on day trips.

Around Jayapura & Sentani

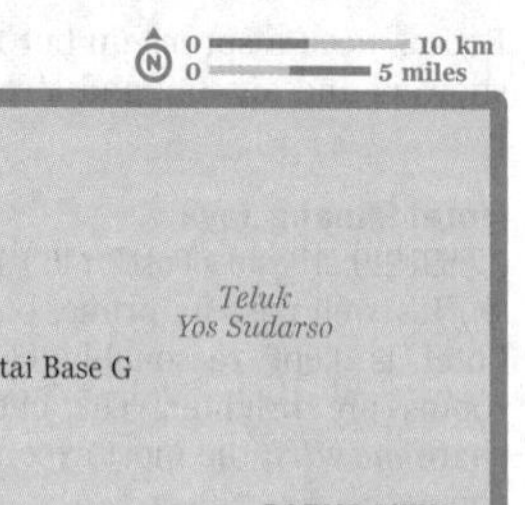

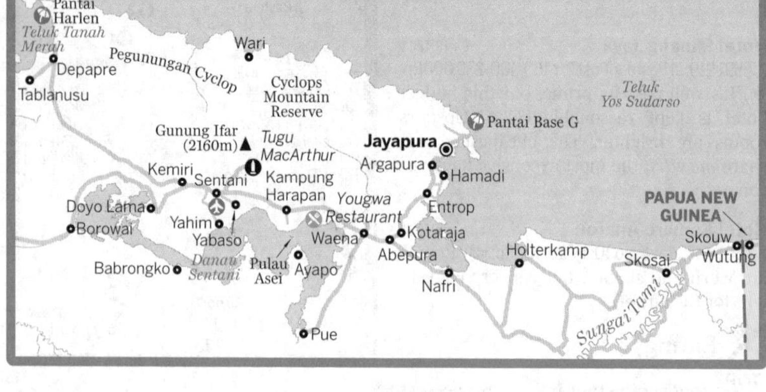

DANAU SENTANI

You get a bird's-eye view of 96.5-sq-km Danau Sentani, snaking its way between picturesque green hills, as you fly in or out of Sentani. This beautiful lake has 19 islands and numerous Papuan fishing villages of wooden stilt houses along its shores. A visit to any of them is a bit like travelling back in time.

Sights

Tugu MacArthur MONUMENT

(admission 5000Rp) For breathtaking views of Danau Sentani, head up to the MacArthur Monument on Gunung Ifar. This was where General Douglas MacArthur set up his headquarters after his US forces took Jayapura (then called Hollandia) in April 1944. Today the site is occupied by a small monument and a room with displays on the American and Japanese participation in the fighting.

The 6km road up to the monument starts 700m east of Jl Airport in Sentani. Charter a *taksi*, or take an *ojek* (40,000Rp round trip) from the bottom of the access road. Halfway up, you must show your *surat jalan* or passport at a military checkpoint.

Situs Megalitik Tutari ARCHAEOLOGICAL SITE

(Tutari Megalithic Site; admission 10,000Rp) On the right, as you enter the village of Doyo Lama, 6km west of Sentani, you'll see the entrance to Situs Megalitik Tutari. This mysterious hillside site comprises various arrangements of rocks and stones, and dozens of rock paintings of fish, turtles, crocodiles and lizards. They are of uncertain age but still considered sacred by the villagers. The stones and paintings are in six different fenced areas, all reached by a 1km concrete path. Try to recruit a local to show you everything and explain some of its significance. If you find the gate closed, no one is likely to mind if you climb over and enter anyway.

Public *taksi* to Doyo Lama (5000Rp) go infrequently from the terminal in Sentani. *Ojeks* charge around 8000Rp one way.

Pulau Asei ISLAND

Asei is the main centre for Sentani bark paintings. Originally done only on bark clothing for women of the chiefs' families, bark paintings are now a Sentani art form. To reach Asei, take a *taksi* to Kampung Harapan, then an *ojek* 2km south to the lake, then a boat to the island.

Yabaso LAKE

An inexpensive way to explore the lake is to stroll 3km southeast along Jl Yabaso from the airport gate. The road (then path) goes through Yabaso village and continues around the lake past several villages.

DEPAPRE

On Teluk Tanah Merah 26km west of Sentani, this fishing village gives access to the area's best beach. **Pantai Harlen**, a 30-minute boat ride out along the east side of the bay, has beautiful white sands and a coral reef good for snorkelling. It gets some visitors at weekends but is never crowded. Boats from Depapre's pier will carry you there for around 300,000Rp return.

The community-run **Suwae Resort** (☎Ibu Popi 0813 4440 3948; cabins/r 400,000/600,000Rp;

❄) at Tablanusu, on a pebbly beach 4km west of Depapre (around 8000Rp by *ojek*), has very nice air-con rooms with terraces and can also take you across to Pantai Harlen for 300,000Rp round trip. Call ahead to ensure meals.

Public *taksi* to Depapre (7000Rp, 45 minutes) leave when full from the *taksi* terminal in western Sentani, or the main road nearby. It's a pretty ride.

Pulau Biak

☎0981

Biak (1898-sq-km) is one of Papua's biggest offshore islands. It's a relaxed place with – even by Papuan standards – exceptionally friendly people, and has good beaches, snorkelling and diving.

Biak saw fierce fighting in WWII, with about 10,000 Japanese and nearly 500 Americans reported killed in the month-long Battle of Biak (1944).

Getting Around

Public *taksi* and a few buses reach most places of interest around the island. You can make things easier by chartering a car or *ojek*, or taking a trip with Janggi Prima (p469) or Discover Papua Adventure (p469). Away from the south coast, most villages are little more than a handful of huts, with no accommodation or food for travellers.

KOTA BIAK

POP 38,000

This main town is your obvious base. The airport is 3km east of the centre, along Jl Yani, which becomes Jl Prof M Yamin.

Activities

Though Biak is not in the same league as the Raja Ampat Islands as a scuba destination, there is still some good **diving** and **snorkelling**. In general you'll see most fish in May, June and July. East of Kota Biak there are wall dives at Marau, Saba and Wadibu, which are also good snorkelling spots, as is Anggaduber. But the best diving and snorkelling is around the offshore Padaido Islands.

Biak Padiving DIVING, SNORKELLING
(☎0853 4412 5415, 0813 4436 6385; biakpadaiving@yahoo.co.id) PADI divemaster Erick Farwas offers two-dive outings to all the better spots. For two people, he asks 1,600,000Rp on the mainland, or 2,500,000Rp to 3,100,000Rp for the Padaido Islands. Equipment rental is 300,000Rp per full set. Farwas also offers all-day snorkelling tours to the islands (1,700,000Rp to 3,400,000Rp for two people), and island stays.

Pulau Biak

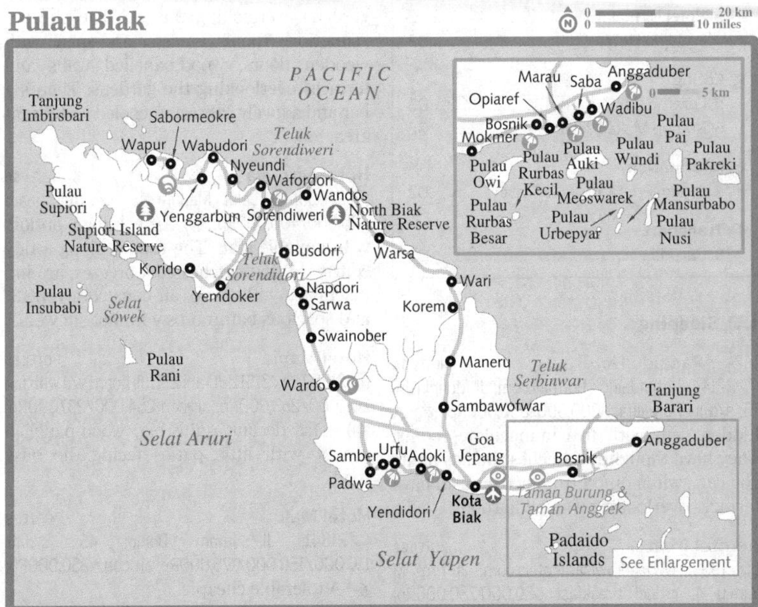

Kota Biak

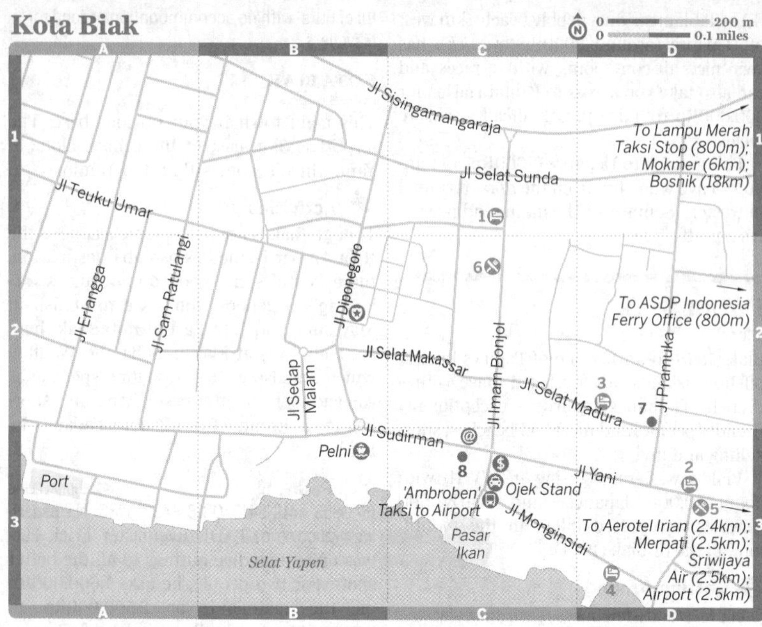

Kota Biak

Sleeping

1 Hotel Maju C1
2 Hotel Mapia D3
3 Hotel Nirmala D2
4 Padaido Hotel D3

Eating

5 Furama Restaurant D3
6 Rumah Makan Jawa Timur C2

Information

7 Janggi Prima Tours & Travel D2

Transport

8 Garuda C3

Sleeping

TOP CHOICE **Padaido Hotel** HOTEL **$$**
(☎22144; hotpadaido@hotmail.com; Jl Monginsidi 16; s/d incl breakfast 300,000/350,000Rp; ✻) A hidden gem with five immaculate rooms. They have thoughtful touches such as lights you can switch on/off from bed, and all have terraces overlooking a small harbour.

Aerotel Irian HOTEL **$$**
(☎21939; www.aerowisatahotels.com; Jl Prof M Yamin 4; r incl breakfast 580,000-780,000Rp; ✻☎✻) Almost opposite the airport terminal, this rambling old hotel recently enjoyed a complete makeover, which managed to maintain some of its 1953 colonial ambience. A semi-infinity pool sits in tropical gardens overlooking the sea. The cheaper ('superior') rooms are spic-and-span, with wooden floors, wood-panelled walls and terraces overlooking the gardens. There's a bar and a lovely, large, fan-cooled restaurant area, too.

Hotel Nirmala HOTEL **$$**
(☎22005; Jl Selat Madura 13; s/d full board 300,000/400,000Rp; ✻) An excellent option, with amiable staff. The rooms, along a tidy courtyard that catches cool breezes, are immaculate, with good air-con, comfy beds, and spacious bathrooms with hot showers.

Hotel Mapia HOTEL **$$**
(☎21383; fax 21511; Jl Yani 23; full board s/d with fan 209,000/253,000Rp, air-con 264,000/297,000Rp; ✻) Has decent, quite big, wood-panelled rooms, with little patios facing the busy road.

Hotel Maju HOTEL **$**
(☎21841; Jl Imam Bonjol 45; s/d/tr 110,000/150,000/175,000Rp, air-con r 250,000Rp; ✻) A tolerable cheapie.

Eating

Rumah Makan Jawa Timur JAVANESE $

(Jl Imam Bonjol 37; mains 15,000-40,000Rp; ❄) It's hard to beat the options that combine *nasi pecel* with fish, chicken or egg. You can dine in the large air-con room for an extra 25% to 30% on prices.

Furama Restaurant INDONESIAN, CHINESE $$

(☎22022; Jl Yani 22; mains 30,000-80,000Rp; ❄) Offers cold Guinness and Bintang as well as plenty of Chinese and Indonesian dishes. Prices are high and service can be slow, but food quality and quantity are above average.

Information

Bank Mandiri (cnr Jl Imam Bonjol & Jl Yani; ⏰8am-3pm Mon-Fri) Exchanges US$100 notes and has Visa and Plus ATMs.

DiBiak.com (Jl Sudirman 4; per hr 12,000Rp; ⏰8am-9pm Mon-Sat) Quite speedy internet connections in air-con comfort.

Discover Papua Adventure (Biak Paradise; ☎0852 4494 0860; www.discoverpapua.com) A well-established agency that can set up just about any trip you want, not only around Biak but throughout Papua and beyond. The experienced, capable manager, Benny Lesomar, speaks excellent English. Call and he'll meet you in town.

Janggi Prima Tours & Travel (☎22973, 0812 4866 8696; cme_pino@yahoo.co.id; Jl Selat Madura 14) This experienced one-man show offers travel advice and help, and can do a range of trips around Biak and nearby islands, including snorkelling and birdwatching.

Police station (☎21294; Jl Diponegoro 3; ⏰8am-4pm Mon-Sat) *Surat jalan* are issued in an hour or so here. For Biak, you normally only need one if you stay on an offshore island or visit neighbouring Pulau Supiori.

Getting There & Away

AIR Tickets for **Garuda** (Jl Sudirman 3), **Merpati** (Jl Prof M Yamin 1) and **Sriwijaya Air** (Jl Prof M Yamin) are sold at travel agencies as well as their offices. Tickets for the small planes of **Susi Air** (☎081 1480 6703; airport; ⏰6am-3pm) are sold only at the airport. Garuda and Merpati (daily) and Sriwijaya Air (three weekly) fly to Jayapura, Makassar and Jakarta. Susi Air heads to Manokwari three times weekly and Nabire daily.

BOAT Every two weeks, **Pelni** (☎23255; Jl Sudirman 37) has three liners heading east to Jayapura (1S/economy class 693,000/173,500Rp, 18 to 27 hours) and west to Sorong (1,187,000/272,000Rp, 19 to 38 hours) and beyond. Some Sorong-bound sailings also call at Nabire and Manokwari. **ASDP Indonesia Ferry** (☎22577; Jl Suci 21) has boats on Tuesday for Manokwari (88,000Rp) and Thursday for Nabire (130,000Rp), sailing from Mokmer, 6km east of Kota Biak.

TAKSI Blue *taksi* to Bosnik (5000Rp, 30 to 40 minutes), passing Mokmer and Taman Burung, run every few minutes; you can catch them at the 'Lampu Merah' (Traffic Lights) stop on Jl Bosnik Raya in the northeast of town. The main terminal for other *taksi* is Terminal Darfuar, about 5km northwest of downtown. On most routes, service winds down in the afternoon. *Taksi* to Anggaduber (9000Rp, one hour) normally go at least hourly.

Getting Around

Yellow public *taksi* (2500Rp) going to the right (west) outside the airport terminal head into town. Returning, take one marked 'Ambroben' from the corner of Jl Imam Bonjol and Jl Mongin-sidi or heading east along Jl Yani.

AROUND KOTA BIAK

Sights

Goa Jepang CAVE

(☎26641; admission 25,000Rp; ⏰7am-5pm) The 'Japanese Cave', 4km northeast of Kota Biak, was used as a base and hideout in WWII by thousands of Japanese soldiers. A tunnel from it is said to lead 3km to the coast at Parai. In 1944, an estimated 3000 Japanese died when US forces bombed a hole in the cave roof, dropped petrol drums into it and then bombarded it from above.

From a concrete walkway, steps lead down into the spooky biggest cavern, with a small tunnel off one chamber that once led to the officer quarters below. In and around the ticket office is a poignant collection of Japanese and US weapons, equipment and photos.

An *ojek* from town costs 10,000Rp. Or take a Bosnik-bound *taksi* and ask to be dropped at the unsigned road that leads 700m up to the cave. After heading uphill for around 300m, when you get to the top a Japanese gun emplacement overlooks the airport. This was the focus of all the fighting.

Taman Burung & Taman Anggrek GARDENS

(Jl Bosnik Raya Km12; admission 10,000Rp; ⏰7am-6pm) At Ibdi, 12km east of Kota Biak on the Bosnik road, the Bird and Orchid Garden contains a sizeable collection of (caged) Papuan birds, including strikingly coloured lories, hornbills, cockatoos and one small female bird of paradise, as well as dozens of types of orchid. A couple of semi-tame cassowaries roam freely.

WILDLIFE

Thanks to Papua's former existence as part of the Australian continent (it was still joined to Australia 10,000 years ago), its wildlife has big differences from the rest of Indonesia. Here dwell marsupials such as tree kangaroos, wallabies, bandicoots and cuscuses, as well as echidnas, which are among the earth's few egg-laying mammals.

Papua is still three-quarters covered in forest. Its diverse ecosystems range from savannahs and mangroves to rainforest, montane forest and the glaciers around 4884m Carstensz Pyramid (Puncak Jaya), the highest peak in Oceania. It's home to more than half the animal and plant species in Indonesia, including more than 190 mammals, 550 breeding birds, 2650 fishes and more than 2000 types of orchid.

The megastars of the feathered tribe are the birds of paradise, whose fantastically coloured males perform weird and wonderful mating dances. Also here are large, ground-dwelling cassowaries, colourful parrots and lorikeets, unique types of kookaburra, crowned pigeons, cockatoos, hornbills, and the curious bowerbirds, whose males decorate large ground-level dens in their efforts to find mates.

Marine life is even more fantastic and varied, especially around the Vogelkop peninsula, where the still-being-explored seas of the Raja Ampat Islands are quickly becoming a mecca for divers.

New species continue to be found in the sea and on land. Two previously unknown types of epaulette shark (also called walking sharks because they use their fins to 'walk' along the seabed) were discovered in Teluk Cenderawasih and Teluk Triton in 2006. A year earlier, a Conservation International expedition in the almost untouched Foja Mountains found types of bird of paradise and bowerbird that had been thought extinct, four new species of butterfly, 20 new frogs, and the golden-mantled tree kangaroo, previously known only on one mountain in Papua New Guinea.

Economic developments threaten Papua's wildlife. Forests are under assault from logging (much of it illegal, with the timber smuggled out to Asia), road construction, mining, transmigration settlements and new oil-palm plantations. Bird-of-paradise feathers have long been used in Papuan traditional dress, and they became so popular as European fashion accessories before WWI that the birds came close to extinction. Trade in the feathers has been illegal in Indonesia since 1990, but birds of paradise continue to be smuggled out of Papua.

Seeing Papua's exotic fauna in the wild requires effort. Birds of paradise, for example, tend to live in remote areas, but with patience, time and a knowledgeable guide, it's quite possible to spot some. The easier locations include the Raja Ampat Islands, Pegunungan Arfak and Wasur National Park. The same areas are excellent for many other birds too.

Most good Papuan tour companies, including birdwatching specialist Papua Expeditions (p449), can arrange birdwatching trips with expert local guides.

BOSNIK & AROUND

Bosnik, 18km from Kota Biak, is a laid-back village strung along the coast for 2km, where you could happily base yourself for a relaxing few days. Its daily morning **market** is busiest on Tuesday, Thursday and Saturday, when Padaido islanders come in biggest numbers. The best section of beach is **Pantai Segara Indah** at the eastern end, with shelters (30,000Rp per day) and some coloured coral offshore. It's virtually empty weekdays.

Guesthouse Beach Bosnik (☎0852 4403 2326; Jl Bosnik Raya; s 150,000Rp, d 175,000-250,000Rp, all incl breakfast; ❄), 500m east of the market, has half a dozen spotless upstairs rooms, four of them air-conditioned and two with private bathroom, in a sturdy brick-and-ironwood house facing the sea. Owner Agustina speaks English and meals are available.

Bosnik-route *taksi* from Kota Biak usually go as far as Opiaref, where the coast road turns inland. You can continue on foot 6km through Opiaref to Marau, Saba and Wadibu, where a road heads 500m inland to join the Anggaduber road. The coral and fish off **Pantai Marau** make for good snorkelling and diving, as do the rocky islets off **Saba**.

Anggaduber, 3km beyond Wadibu, has grass-lawned houses and a fine, palm-lined, sandy beach, with good snorkelling towards its western end.

PADAIDO ISLANDS

This lovely cluster of 36 reefs and islands (only 13 of them inhabited) makes for a great day trip from Kota Biak or Bosnik, and you can stay over on some islands. Virtually all have jungle-backed, white-sand beaches with crystal-clear waters, coral reefs and plenty of marine life. The best **snorkelling** spots include **Pulau Wundi**, which has good coral and many fish near the surface, **Pulau Rurbas Kecil** and **Pulau Meoswarek**. Top diving sites include the western end of Pulau Owi, with good coral and big fish; Pulau Rurbas Besar for coral, sharks, turtles and more big fish; and Pulau Wundi, with a cave, a long wall and good coral.

You can charter a boat from Bosnik to the nearest and most populated islands, Owi and Auki, for 300,000Rp to 500,000Rp round trip, or twice as much for Wundi.

Biak Padiving (p467) offers diving trips, and also sightseeing and snorkelling trips, to the islands. Padiving's Erick Farwas has a basic four-room **guesthouse** (per person with/without meals 250,000/200,000Rp) on Pulau Wundi (meals must be arranged in advance).

The cheapest transport to the islands is from Bosnik on Tuesday, Thursday or Saturday afternoon, when islanders are returning from Bosnik market and you should be able to get a place in a boat for 30,000Rp to 50,000Rp. You can normally find accommodation for 50,000Rp to 100,000Rp per person in an island house or by asking the local church-keeper. Bring food.

Nabire

☎0984 / POP 52,000

For travellers the main attraction of this relatively prosperous town is swimming with whale sharks. The world's biggest fish, whale sharks can grow over 10m long and inhabit warm seas all round the world. They feed mainly on plankton but also on small fish and for this reason they hang around fishing platforms called *bagan* in the southwest of Teluk Cenderawasih, 1½ hours from Nabire by boat. Close encounters with at least a few of these harmless giants are almost guaranteed any day of the year. Don't touch or interfere with the whale sharks, and try to discourage locals from doing so.

Merry Yoweni (☎0821 9830 9115; merrypapua@yahoo.com; AA Hotel, Pantai Yamarel), who runs Nabire's AA Hotel, offers whale-shark trips from Nabire for up to 10 people for 5,000,000Rp, slightly less for just one or two people. Trips can be shared with other hotel guests. **Bram Maruanaya** (☎0813 9211 7215, 081 2489 1651; bram@nabirecyber.com; Warnet F-Tri, Jl Kusuma Bangsa) charges 2,500,000Rp per person; perhaps better value is his three-night package of whale-shark visits, diving, and bird-of-paradise/dugong spotting, with accommodation in local homes, for 8,000,000Rp per person.

Sleeping

Nabire's few hotels can fill up so booking is advantageous.

AA Hotel HOTEL **$$**

(☎0853 4468 4937, 0821 9830 9115; merrypapua@yahoo.com; Pantai Yamarel; r incl breakfast 300,000Rp; ❄📶) Near a grey-sand beach 2.5km from the airport, this new hotel has neat, medium-sized rooms with hot showers and a restaurant. The enthusiastic owners also do whale-shark trips, and offer free airport pick ups and drops if you reserve ahead.

Hotel Nusantara HOTEL **$$**

(☎21180; Jl Pemuda 16; s 275,000-407,000Rp, d 330,000-495,000Rp, all incl breakfast; ❄) Best choice near the airport, with clean rooms, and hot water in most of them.

Ahe Dive Resort RESORT **$$**

(ahepapua@gmail.com; Pulau Ahe; 5-night package per person €817, marine park fee 600,000Rp) This

FLIGHTS FROM NABIRE

DESTINATION	COMPANY	FREQUENCY
Ambon	Wings Air	4 weekly
Biak	Susi Air, Merpati	daily
Jayapura	Wings Air, Merpati, Expressair	6 weekly
Manado	Expressair	3 weekly
Sorong	Expressair	3 weekly

little dive resort on tiny Pulau Ahe, 30km northeast of Nabire, is Dutch-managed but owned and staffed by the welcoming local community. Packages include Nabire transfers, three guided boat dives daily and one whale-shark trip per five days (extra whale-shark trips are available at extra cost). Divers must have advanced-level certification and bring equipment.

Getting There & Away

Pelni sails three times every two weeks to Jayapura (once via Biak), and three times to Manokwari, Sorong and beyond. For anyone wanting to explore the scenic Paniai Lakes region, pick ups to Enarotali (600,000Rp, 13 hours) leave from Pasar Karang at 6am, 7am and a couple of times later each day.

BALIEM VALLEY

The legendary Baliem Valley is the most popular and most accessible destination in Papua's interior. The Dani people who live here were still dependent on tools of stone, bone and wood when a natural-history expedition led by American Richard Archbold chanced upon the valley in 1938. The Dani have since adopted various modern ways and new beliefs, but the valley and surrounding highlands remain one of the world's last fascinatingly traditional areas.

The main valley is about 60km long and 16km wide and bounded by high mountains on all sides. The only sizeable town, Wamena, sits at its centre at an altitude of 1650m. The powerful Kali Baliem (Baliem River), running through the valley, escapes through a narrow gorge at the southern end. Amid this spectacular scenery, the majority of Dani still live close to nature, tending their vegetable plots and pigs around villages composed of circular thatched huts called *honai*. Roads are few, and the raging mountain rivers are crossed on hanging footbridges that may be held together only by natural twine.

Christian missionaries arrived in 1954 and a Dutch government post was established in Wamena in 1956. Since the 1960s, Indonesia has added its own brand of colonialism, bringing immigrants, government schools, police, soldiers, shops, motor vehicles and becaks (bicycle rickshaws) to the valley. Big changes have been wrought in Dani life, but their identity and culture have proved resilient. Tensions between Dani and the security forces and Indonesian immigrants periodically erupt into violence, most notably during a large-scale uprising in 1977 and again in 2000, when clashes led to a temporary exodus of non-Papuans.

It can rain here at any time of year, but from April to December most days are fine and warm and the evenings cool. From January to March, more mud and rain can make trekking hard work.

Information

You must have a *surat jalan* for Wamena and the Baliem Valley, obtainable at Sentani or Jayapura or Wamena itself. If you're going beyond the main Baliem Valley (for example to Danau Habbema or the Yali country) make sure your *surat jalan* covers this. If you are continuing to the Korowai or Asmat regions, get your *surat jalan* for them before you come to Wamena, as Wamena police may be unwilling to issue one.

Carry your *surat jalan* on trips outside Wamena. You normally only have to show it (to police stations or village authorities) if you stay overnight outside Wamena, but you can never be sure.

Some more remote areas in the highlands may be off-limits to foreigners; the Wamena police can tell you about the current situation.

Getting There & Around

Flying into Wamena is the only way to reach the Baliem Valley. Once you're here, trekking is the best way to explore the landscape and local life. It's also possible to get around the main valley and see traditional people and villages, as well as mummies and hanging bridges, by car, bemo (minibus) or *ojek*. Paved roads from Wamena run as far as Bolokme (north), Pyramid (northwest) and Kali Yetni (Yetni River; south). The only vehicle bridge over Kali Baliem in the main valley is at Pikhe, 3km north of Wamena; another is being built at Wesaput.

Wamena

0969 / POP 25,000

Wamena is a sprawling Indonesian creation with nothing traditional about it, but it's the obligatory base for any travels around the valley. The population is a mix of Papuans and non-Papuans and the latter run all the businesses. Penis gourds are no longer banned here, as they were during Indonesia's 'Operasi Koteka' (an attempt to force the Dani to wear clothes) in the 1970s, but rarely will you see one being worn.

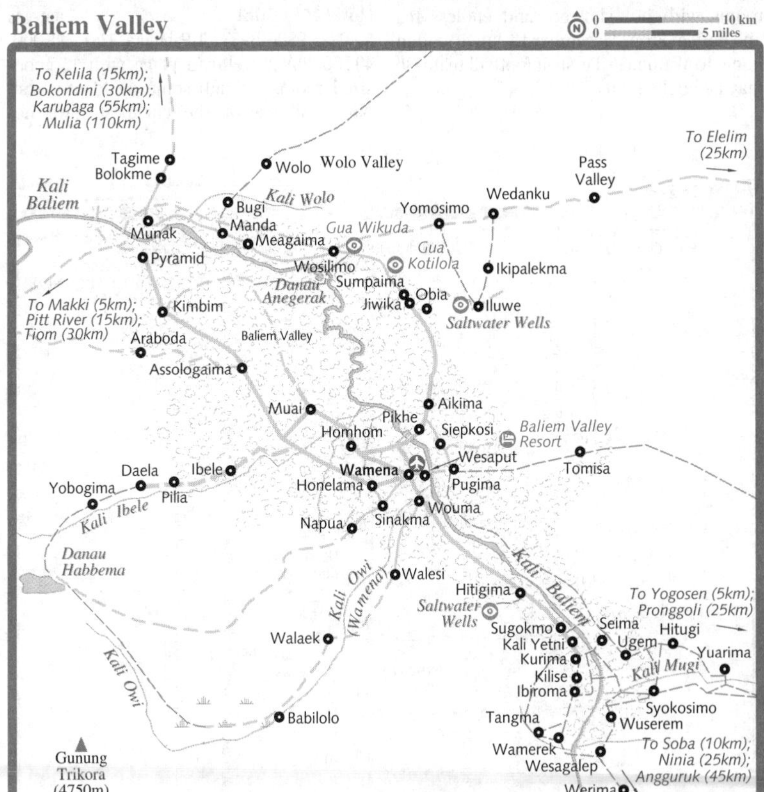

Dangers & Annoyances

Local guides try to latch on to every tourist stepping off a plane at Wamena airport. If someone is meeting you by prior arrangement, well and good. Otherwise, handle any guide who approaches you with caution and firmness. If you accept any help at all, they may try to interpret this as an agreement to hire them, and can be hard to shake off. Don't agree to anything until you have found a guide you're happy with. Guides are useful for many tasks from trekking to arranging pig feasts, but you might not want to choose the one who's trying to choose you, and the best guides (p476) don't usually need to tout for business at the airport.

Sleeping

TOP CHOICE Hotel Rainbow Wamena HOTEL **$$**
(Hotel Pelangi; Jl Irian 26; r incl breakfast 350,000-600,000Rp) This has excellent, clean, well-sized rooms with good hot-water bathrooms and nice touches such as shampoo, tissues, coffee and tea. Staff are friendly and helpful and Restaurant Pelangi is here too.

Baliem Pilamo Hotel HOTEL **$$**
(☎31043; baliempilamohotel@yahoo.co.id; Jl Trikora 114; r incl breakfast 547,000-1,195,000Rp Jul & Aug, 456,000-996,000Rp Sep-Jun; wi-fi) The more expensive rooms are tasteful, contemporary, brown-and-white affairs in the new section at the rear. Of the cheaper ones, the 'standards' are smallish and plain but acceptable, and the 'superiors' have a semi-luxury feel and quirky garden-style bathrooms. The hotel is efficiently run, though most desk staff are surprisingly ignorant about the surrounding area. The included breakfast is an excellent buffet.

Putri Dani Hotel HOTEL **$$**
(☎0812 4825 1889; Jl Irian 40; s/d 440,000/495,000Rp) This small family-run place offers nine spotless, comfortable

rooms with hot showers and endless tea and coffee. From December to July it's often home to Wamena's Persiwa football team, so may be booked out.

Hotel Mas Budi HOTEL $$
(☎0821 9806 3933; Jl Patimura 32; r 348,000-492,000Rp) A well-run place with 12 good-sized rooms, though some could use fresh paint. All except the cheapest have hot

Wamena

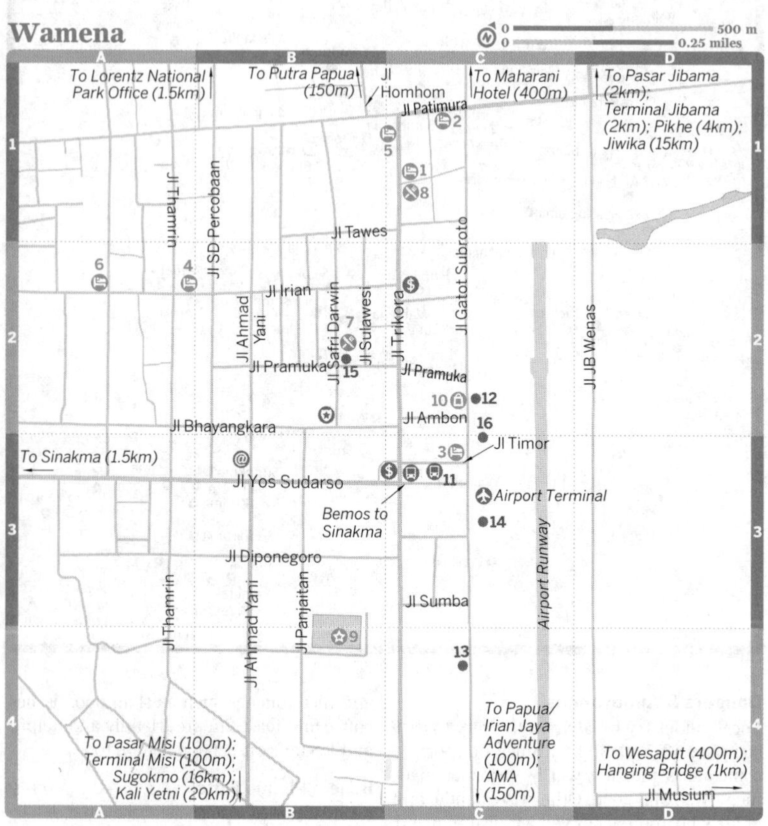

Wamena

Sleeping

1 Baliem Pilamo Hotel ... C1
2 Hotel Mas Budi ... C1
3 Hotel Nayak ... C3
4 Hotel Rainbow Wamena ... A2
5 Hotel Rannu Jaya I ... C1
6 Putri Dani Hotel ... A2

Eating

7 Cafe Pilamo ... B2
Restaurant Pelangi ... (see 4)
8 Rumah Makan Mulyo Agung ... C1

Entertainment

9 Stadion Pendidikan ... B4

Shopping

10 Oi-Tourism ... C2

Transport

11 Bemos to Wesaput ... C3
12 MAF ... C2
13 Qualita ... C4
14 Susi Air ... C3
15 Travel Candra Nusantara Pilamo ... B2
16 Trigana ... C3

showers, and there's a convenient in-house restaurant (mains 30,000Rp to 90,000Rp).

Maharani Hotel HOTEL **$$**
(☎0813 4416 6987, 34418; Jl Gatot Subroto, Senapup; r incl breakfast 300,000Rp) New in 2012, the Maharani is friendly and clean. Its sizeable rooms have cheery colour schemes which offset the shortage of natural light. It offers free airport pick ups and drops.

Hotel Rannu Jaya I HOTEL **$$**
(☎31257; fax 32150; Jl Trikora 109; r incl breakfast 280,000-330,000Rp) A sound option, with hot showers in the more expensive rooms, along with attempts at decor (eg large, kitsch horse prints).

Baliem Valley Resort RESORT **$$$**
(☎0812 4810 0240; www.baliem-valley-resort.de; s/d incl breakfast €115/135) This surprising hotel occupies a gorgeous hillside position 21km east of Wamena, with large, rustic-style but comfortable guest cottages in picturesque grounds. A superb collection of Papuan (especially Asmat) art adorns the semi-open-air dining hall. The German owner has a wealth of Papua expertise, and offers a variety of excursions and expeditions.

Hotel Nayak HOTEL **$$**
(☎31067; Jl Gatot Subroto 63; r incl breakfast 250,000-350,000Rp) This has seen much better days. Rooms are sizeable and reasonably clean, but fixtures and fittings are often in a sad state.

Eating

The expensive local delicacies are large goldfish (*ikan mas* in Bahasa Indonesia), which are farmed in ponds around the valley, and enormous, almost lobster-sized, freshwater prawns *(udang)*. Nowhere in Wamena serves any kind of alcoholic drink.

Restaurant Pelangi INDONESIAN **$$**
(Jl Irian 26; mains 30,000-75,000Rp; ⏲9am-9pm) The Pelangi serves up satisfying dishes, from rice and noodle preparations to fish, seafood and meat with various sauces, in a semi-open-air area with a welcome touch of greenery.

Cafe Pilamo INDONESIAN **$$**
(Jl Safri Darwin 2; mains 25,000-90,000Rp) Cafe Pilamo is clean and pleasant, and even has two pool tables upstairs, but beware the karaoke, which may start up at any time. It does ice cream and passable burgers, as well as many Indonesian dishes. Look for the red-and-white awning.

Rumah Makan Mulyo Agung INDONESIAN **$**
(Jl Trikora; mains 15,000-50,000Rp) A simple, friendly spot doing good gado gado, *nasi pecel* and *lalapan ayam kampung* (fried free-range chicken with greens).

Entertainment

Unbelievably, little Wamena's Persiwa soccer team regularly occupies high placings in the Indonesia Super League. It is almost unbeatable in its home games at **Stadion Pendidikan** (Jl Panjaitan), partly thanks to Wamena's altitude!

Shopping

The Dani are experts in the art of body adornment. Handicrafts include necklaces, pectorals, armbands and nose piercings, made from pig tusks, cowrie shells, bone, carved stone or feathers; as well as grass skirts; carved spears and arrows; *noken* (women's bark-string bags); and assorted head decorations, made of cassowary or bird-of-paradise (or chicken) feathers and topped off with pig tusks. Generally, it's cheaper to buy in the villages, but it's also worth checking out Wamena's main market, **Pasar Jibama** (Pasar Baru; Jl JB Wenas; ⏲daily), 2km north of town, the NGO-run **Oi-Tourism** (Jl Gatot Subroto; ⏲7am-5pm Mon-Sat), or the handful of craft shops on Jl Trikora north of Jl Ambon. Asmat, Korowai and PNG artefacts are also available in the souvenir shops. A Korowai bow with 10 arrows can fetch 500,000Rp.

Of course, the most popular souvenir is the penis gourd. These cost from about 10,000Rp to 100,000Rp depending on size, materials and negotiation.

Stone axe blades (*kapak* in the Dani language), which are still sometimes used by the Dani in preference to metal ones, can cost from 50,000Rp to 500,000Rp or more, depending on the size and the labour involved. Bluestone, the finest material, is more expensive.

Wamena's three main markets, all functioning daily, are colourful places where you can pick up bundles of vegies for your trek. Apart from Pasar Jibama, there's also **Pasar Misi** (Jl Ahmad Yani), in the south of town, and Pasar Sinakma, 2km west.

Information

No banks exchange foreign cash or travellers cheques.

Bank Mandiri (Jl Trikora 92) ATM accepts Visa, Visa Electron and Plus cards.

BRI Bank (Bank Rakyat Indonesia; cnr Jl Yos Sudarso & Jl Trikora) ATM accepts MasterCard and Cirrus.

Papua.com (☎34488; fuj0627@yahoo.co.jp; Jl Ahmad Yani 49; per hr 12,000Rp; ⏰9am-8.30pm Mon-Sat, from 1pm Sun) This efficient internet cafe has fax and scanning services, and also functions as an informal tourist information centre. Its owner is a highly experienced Papua traveller and a willing mine of information.

Police station (☎31972; Jl Safri Darwin; ⏰7am-2pm) Come here to report within 24 hours of arrival, or to obtain a *surat jalan*.

Getting There & Away

Air

Flights are often heavily booked, especially in August. Always allow a couple of days' leeway for possible delays. The carriers between Jayapura (Sentani) and Wamena are **Trigana** (☎31611; airport) and **Susi Air** (☎081 1212 3931; Jl Gatot Subroto). Trigana flies three or more times daily each way, charging 900,000/688,000Rp to/from Wamena. Susi's small planes make one or two flights each way daily, except Sunday and Tuesday (805,000/705,000Rp to/from

HIKING & TREKKING IN THE BALIEM VALLEY

Beyond the reach of roads you come closer to traditional Dani life. In one day, you may climb narrow rainforest trails, stroll well-graded paths past terraces of purple-leafed sweet-potato plants, wend through villages of grass-roofed *honai* (circular thatched huts), cross rivers on wobbly hanging footbridges, and traverse hillsides where the only sounds are birds, wind and water far below.

The classic trekking area, offering up to a week of walking, is in the south of the valley (beyond Kali Yetni), along with branch valleys to the east and west here. Dani life here is still relatively traditional, the scenery gorgeous and the walking varied.

Accommodation is available in nearly all villages. Some have dedicated guesthouses (sometimes in *honai*-style huts); elsewhere you can often stay in a teacher's house, the school or other houses. Either way you'll usually be asked 80,000Rp to 120,000Rp per person. You sleep on the floor, but it may be softened with dried grass and you may get a mat. Make sure you've been invited before entering any compound or hut.

Larger villages have kiosks selling basics such as biscuits, noodles and rice (the final reliable supplies are at Manda and Kimbim in the north and Kurima in the south) and you can obtain sweet potatoes, other vegetables or fruit here and there. But you need to take at least some food with you from Wamena. Villages can normally supply firewood for cooking, for 10,000Rp a load.

Guides & Porters

In the more frequented trekking areas it's possible to head off alone and ask the way as you go, or pick up a local porter-cum-guide for 80,000Rp to 100,000Rp a day if you need one. But for hiking anywhere off the major trails, a guide is an extremely good idea – not only for finding the way but also for smoothing the path with local people.

Finding a good, reliable guide can be a challenge. You should allow at least one day to find a guide you're happy with and make trek preparations. Tricks played by unscrupulous guides may include pocketing some of the money you've given them to get supplies (go with them or get the supplies yourself); sending a junior replacement at the last minute; asking for more money mid-trek and refusing to continue without it; or disappearing and leaving you in the hands of a porter.

A good source of recommendations for reliable guides in Wamena is Papua.com. It's worth seeking out one of the Baliem Valley's 20 or so officially licensed guides. These are not the only good guides around, but they usually speak reasonable English, and have a professional reputation to look after. You can check any guide's credentials with the local coordinator of the Indonesian Tourist Guide Association, Justinus Daby of Papua/Irian Jaya Adventure.

There are no fixed prices in the Baliem trekking world. Hard bargaining is the norm. Don't be put off by glum faces and do insist on clarifying any grey areas. No decent guide

Wamena). Trigana also flies daily, except Sunday, to Dekai (450,000Rp). If Trigana's ticket window tells you a flight is full, ask in the office inside (through the door to the left) where seats for tourists often magically materialise.

You can book onward flights from Jayapura at **Travel Candra Nusantara Pilamo** (cnr Jl Pramuka & Jl Safri Darwin; ⏲9am-5pm Mon-Sat).

Mission airlines **AMA** (Associated Mission Aviation; ☎32400; Jl Gatot Subroto) and **MAF** (Jl Gatot Subroto) fly small planes to many small highland airstrips. They may carry tourists if spare seats are available. There is generally much more chance of seats flying back to Wamena than for outbound flights. A seat from Angguruk to Wamena, for example, costs about 400,000Rp if you are lucky enough to get one. As a rule, MAF doesn't carry tourists outbound at all.

AMA, Susi Air and **Qualita** (☎0821 2555 5725; Jl Gatot Subroto) offer charter flights. Sample rates for eight-passenger planes are 11,000,000Rp to or from Angguruk and 28,000,000Rp to or from Ewer (Agats).

Public Bemo

Overcrowded bemos head out along the main roads from several starting points around Wamena. Most just leave when they are full. The main terminals – **Terminal Jibama** (Jl JB Wenas), **Terminal Misi** and Sinakma – are at Wamena's three markets. Bemos get scarce after 3pm and are less plentiful on Sundays. Few

will agree to anything he's unhappy about. The guides' association requests 400,000Rp to 500,000Rp per day for a guide (and more for harder treks to, for example, the Yali or Korowai areas), but some decent, English-speaking guides will work for less. Dependable Wamena-based agencies and individual guides include these:

Jonas Wenda (☎0852 4422 0825; jonas.wenda@yahoo.com) Highly experienced (your author first trekked with him in 1986) and notably knowledgeable on flora and fauna.

Kosman Kogoya (☎0852 4472 7810) A popular, reliable guide who will quote reasonable prices from the outset and won't waste your time bargaining.

Papua/Irian Jaya Adventure (☎0813 4486 3958; justinusdaby@yahoo.com; Jl Gatot Subroto 15, Wamena) Run by Justinus Daby, a Baliem Valley native who has been guiding here since the year dot. Identify his house/office by the bamboo tree in front of it.

Putra Papua (☎0969 31540; www.putrapapuatours.com; Jl Homhom 5, Wamena) An established agency offering well-organised trekking tours with cooks and good camping gear in the Baliem Valley (around 1,500,000Rp per person per day) and elsewhere. It also offers day trips.

Trek-Papua Tours & Travel (☎0812 4852 7788; www.papuatravels.com) A young but energetic, internet-wise agency, which also offers tours to other parts of Papua.

In addition to a guide, porters are a good idea and cost 70,000Rp to 120,000Rp each per day, depending partly on the toughness of the trek. A cook costs 100,000Rp to 150,000Rp per day, but guides or porters can cook if you're looking to cut costs. You'll have to provide enough food for the whole team (costing around 40,000Rp each per day), and probably cigarettes for them and your village hosts. It's a good idea to have the whole agreement written down and signed by your guide before you start, and it's normal to pay some money up front and the rest at the end. A 10% tip at the end is also expected for each member of the team.

Day Hikes

A number of hikes can be enjoyed using public or private transport on a day out from Wamena:

Wesaput–Pugima–Wesaput (p478) Three hours.

Jiwika–Air Garam–Jiwika (p480) Four hours.

Wosilimo–Danau Anegerak–Gua Kotilola (p480) Three hours.

Sugokmo–Seima–Ugem–Seima–Sugokmo (p478) Seven to eight hours.

BEMOS FROM WAMENA

DESTINATION	DEPARTURE POINT	COST (RP)	DURATION
Aikima	Jibama	5000	15min
Ibele	Sinakma	15,000	1hr (departures until noon)
Jiwika	junction 600m past Jibama	10,000	30min
Kali Yetni	Misi	15,000	1hr
Kimbim	Jibama	15,000	50min
Makki	Sinakma	70,000	3hr (departures 3-5am)
Meagaima	Jibama	20,000	1hr
Sugokmo	Misi	10,000	45min
Tagime	Jibama	25,000	1¾hr
Tiom	Sinakma	150,000	4hr (departures 3-5am)
Wosilimo	Jibama	15,000	40min

villages or attractions are signposted, so ask the conductor to tell you where to get off.

For Pyramid take a bemo to Kimbim then another (10,000Rp, 10 minutes) on to Pyramid. Bemos to Pass Valley (150,000Rp), Bokondini (150,000Rp) and Karubaga (200,000Rp) leave from Bank Mandiri between 5am and 7am.

Chartered Bemo & Car

For more comfort than the public bemos, consider chartering a vehicle for out-of-town trips. A bemo costs 200,000Rp one way to Kali Yetni (a common trek starting point), or 400,000Rp to 500,000Rp for a return trip of about three hours to Jiwika and/or Wosilimo. Cars (parked opposite the airport) cost 800,000Rp to 1,000,000Rp a day (possibly 1,500,000Rp in August).

Ojek

Typical one-way *ojek* prices for out-of-town destinations include 100,000Rp to Jiwika, 150,000Rp to Wosilimo and 200,000Rp to Kimbim.

Getting Around

For trips within town, *ojeks* generally charge 10,000Rp and becaks 5000Rp to 10,000Rp. Bemos marked 'A2' (5000Rp) run from BRI Bank to Jl Irian and up Jl Trikora to Terminal Jibama. An *ojek* to Terminal Jibama is 15,000Rp.

Oi-Tourism (p475) rents mountain bikes for 100,000Rp per day.

Pugima

A walk to Pugima village makes a pleasant introduction to the Baliem Valley countryside. First take an *ojek* (10,000Rp), or a bemo (4000Rp) from Wamena's Jl Timor, to Wesaput on the east side of the airport. At the end of Wesaput's Jl Musium, a 90m-long hanging bridge crosses Kali Baliem, although its glory is diminished by the road bridge that's being built beside it. On the other side of the bridge you are in the countryside; passers-by greet each other and the footpath becomes an unpaved road leading 2.5km across flat country to Pugima, passing Dani compounds, sweet-potato fields and fish ponds. Pugima itself, like many Dani villages, is centred on a large church.

Southern Baliem Valley

South of Wamena, the Baliem Valley narrows and Kali Baliem becomes a ferocious torrent known as the Baliem Falls. Walking times here are based on an average 'tourist pace', including rest stops.

The paved road from Wamena passes through **Sugokmo** village after 16km and ends at the small but fast and turbulent **Kali Yetni**. The only way across the Yetni is on precarious logs for which you need a helping hand from a guide. It's a half-hour walk from the Yetni to **Kurima**, a largish village with a police station (show your *surat jalan* here). If you don't have someone to help you over the Yetni, start walking from Sugokmo, from which it's a 20-minute walk down to a hanging bridge over the Baliem. A path then leads down the east bank to neat **Seima** (1½ hours), from which you can descend to Kurima in 30 minutes, re-crossing the Baliem by another hanging bridge.

From Kurima you can access the network of trails linking villages on the west side of the Baliem, or cross the hanging bridge for the trails and villages on the east side. The following describes a good circular route of four or five days linking both sides.

One hour south (uphill) from Kurima you reach **Kilise**, a *honai* village with glorious views.

Alberth Elopore's guesthouse (per person 120,000Rp) in Kilise is one of the best in the area, with cosy *honai*-style huts and a wonderful grotto-like *kamar mandi*. From Kilise it's about 2¼ hours over the forested ridge southwestward, via Ibiroma and Jibroma, to **Tangma**, in a deep valley with a steep grass airstrip. Tangma has a decent guesthouse, which even boasts a couple of beds.

From Tangma it's one hour downhill to Wamerek, where the knowledgeable Mr Yeki runs the *honai*-style **Kulugima guesthouse**. One hour south from **Wamerek**, an exciting hanging bridge crosses the Baliem and you then have a steep two-hour trek up to **Wesagalep**, where you'll probably sleep in the village hall in the upper part of the village. Six hours of up-and-down walking from Wesagalep leads to **Wuserem**, with great views and a nice grass-floored guesthouse. Halfway between the two villages, take a break beside the lovely Kali Lubuk.

From Wuserem head 1¼ hours northeast up the beautiful **Mugi Valley** to **Syokosimo**, with a couple of guesthouses. You can continue up the valley's south flank to Sesep and Saikama and then descend to a hanging

THE DANI

Dani is an umbrella name for around 30 clans in the main Baliem Valley and its side-valleys and some Mamberamo tributary valleys to the north. They number somewhere over 200,000 people in total.

The Dani are generally friendly to tourists but can be shy. Long handshakes are common. Most Dani speak Bahasa Indonesia but appreciate a greeting in their own language. Around Wamena, the general greeting is *la'uk* to one person, and *la'uk nyak* to more than one – except that men say *nayak* to one other man and *nayak lak* to more than one man. *Wa, wa* is another common greeting expressing respect or offering thanks.

Many Dani men still wear a penis sheath (*horim* in Dani, *koteka* in Bahasa Indonesia) made from a cultivated gourd, and little else apart from a few neck, head or arm adornments. Others now prefer T-shirts and trousers or shorts. Very few women now go bare-breasted, though some still sport grass skirts. Women often still carry string bags called *noken* on their backs, strapped over the head and heavily laden with vegetables, babies or pigs. *Noken* are made from shredded tree bark that's been rolled into thread. Some Dani wear pig fat in their hair and cover their bodies in pig fat and soot for warmth. Many men and some women are enthusiastic smokers.

The Dani often expect money for photos, especially if they are wearing traditional dress (such as it is). Ask beforehand to avoid misunderstandings.

Most Dani are now Christian and one traditional pastime that has gone out of the window is village warfare. Villages used to go to war over land disputes, wife stealing or even pig stealing, with combat happening in brief, semiritualised clashes (with a few woundings and deaths nevertheless). Today such quarrels are settled by other, usually legalistic means.

Villages are mostly composed of extended-family compounds, each containing a few *honai*. The men sleep in a dedicated men's hut, visiting the women's huts only for sex. *Honai* interiors have a lower level with a fire for warmth and sometimes cooking, and an upper platform for sleeping.

After a birth, sex is taboo for the mother for two to five years, apparently to give the child exclusive use of her milk. Some Dani are still polygamous: the standard bride price is four or five pigs, and a man's status is measured partly by how many wives and pigs he has. One of the more unusual (and now prohibited) Dani customs is to amputate one or two joints of a woman's finger when a close relative dies. Many older women have fingers missing up to their second joint.

One thing that hasn't changed and probably never will is the Dani's love for the sweet potato, grown on extensive plots and terraces all over the valley.

bridge at **Yuarima**, which has a guesthouse, in around 3½ hours. A good trail heads back down the north side of the valley to **Hitugi** (1½ hours, with guesthouses) and **Ugem** (1¼ hours from Hitugi, with a trail-side guesthouse above the village), and then turns north up the Baliem Valley to Seima (1¾ hours), with a branch down to the Kurima hanging bridge.

You can lengthen the trek by continuing further up the Mugi Valley from Yuarima, or heading south from Wesagalep to Pukam and Werima. For a shorter trek, on day one you could head from Kurima to Kilise, Ibiroma, Wamerek and Wesagalep (six to seven hours); and on day two from Wesagalep to Wamerek as already described. On day three, diverge from the Wamerek-Syokosimo path to cross Kali Mugi by a hanging bridge, not far upstream from its confluence with Kali Baliem. Then continue up the Baliem to Kurima or Seima (three hours from Wamerek).

Northeastern Baliem Valley

Several interesting places along here are within day-trip reach of Wamena, and some side valleys offer good hiking.

AIKIMA

About 8km from Wamena, nondescript Aikima is famous for its **Werapak Elosak mummy**, the 300-year-old corpse of a great chief, which was preserved (by smoking) to retain some of his power for the village. You'll probably be asked to pay 30,000Rp per person for a viewing. The one at Sumpaima is in better condition.

JIWIKA & AROUND

Jiwika (pronounced Yiwika) is a local administrative centre and home to the celebrated **Wimontok Mabel mummy**. The mummy is kept at the tiny settlement of Sumpaima, 400m north along the main road from the main Jiwika village entrance (look for the faded blue 'Mumi' sign). Wimontok Mabel was a powerful 18th-century chief here and his blackened corpse is the best preserved and most accessible of its kind near Wamena. You may be asked anything from 30,000Rp to 70,000Rp per person for a viewing and possibly more for photos; bargaining is possible!

Anemangi, just behind Sumpaima, and **Obia** (Isinapma) to the south of Jiwika, are among villages where traditional Dani pig feasts and colourful warrior dances based on ritual warfare can be staged for tourists, if requested a day or two ahead. A typical price for both for a couple of tourists (and one smallish pig) is 3,000,000Rp. A warrior dance alone is about 1,000,000Rp.

At Iluwe, 1½ hours up a steep path from Jiwika, is **Air Garam**, a group of saltwater wells. Villagers soak sections of banana trunk in the water, then dry and burn them and use the resulting ashes as salt. Village boys will show you the way for around 25,000Rp, but to see the process at work, try to find a woman who will accompany you from Jiwika (50,000Rp). To avoid climbing in the midday heat, start from Jiwika before 10am.

The road north from Jiwika is flanked by rocky hills with several caves. **Gua Kotilola** (admission 20,000Rp; 8am-4pm) is a sizeable cavern up a short, pretty path behind a Dani compound, about 5km north of Jiwika. It contains the bones of past tribal-war victims – though they don't show these to outsiders.

Opposite the Jiwika village entrance, **Lauk Inn** (per person 100,000Rp) has a few basic, tolerably clean rooms around a small garden, with their own *mandis*. Lunch or dinner costs 50,000Rp. If you're staying overnight at Jiwika, report to the roadside police station 500m south.

WOSILIMO

Wosilimo ('Wosi') is a relatively major village with a couple of kiosks. The cave here, **Gua Wikuda**, is said to be several kilometres long, with an underground river that reaches Danau Anegerak. The visit comprises a decaying wooden walkway that goes about 100m into the cave, and you may or may not find anyone willing to accompany you in. Come equipped with a torch and shoes with good grip. Three small **guest honai** (per person 100,000Rp) near the cave entrance have straw floors, sleeping mats and a shared *mandi* with squat toilet. Bring food and the people there will cook for you.

Two kilometres south from Wosi, along the main road, a path starting in front of a church leads half an hour southwest to a small lake, **Danau Anegerak**, crossing a hanging bridge over Kali Baliem on the way. It's a pleasant walk, though during wet weather it may be impassable.

PASS VALLEY AREA

A rough road heads up over the hills from Wosilimo to Pass Valley, then descends to

BALIEM VALLEY FESTIVAL

To coincide with the busiest tourism season, a two-day festival is held in the Baliem Valley during the second week of August. The highlight is mock tribal fighting, where village men dress up in full regalia and enact an old-fashioned tribal battle and accompanying rituals. The festival also features pig feasts, traditional costumes, and Dani music on instruments such as the *pikon* (a kind of mouth harp). Pig races are fun, too, if not for the pigs, which usually end up roasted on a spit. Other goings-on include tourist-only spear-throwing and archery contests.

In recent years the main events have taken place at Wosilimo. You may be charged an entrance fee of 150,000Rp.

Elelim, about 60km from Wosi. The small **Wedanku valley** between Wosilimo and Pass Valley still retains a traditional Dani culture. Wedanku village's Catholic mission can provide accommodation and from there you can hike one day up through the forest to **Ikipalekma** (where you can find accommodation in local houses), then on the next day to Jiwika, via the Iluwe wells.

Northwestern Baliem Valley

The western side of the valley is less scenic than the eastern. **Kimbim** is a pleasant administrative centre with a few shops and the main market outside Wamena, busiest on Monday and Saturday. An hour's walk away, Araboda houses the 250-year-old Alongga Huby mummy; viewings cost around 20,000Rp. About 7km past Kimbim is **Pyramid**, a graceful mission village named after the shape of a nearby hill, with a theological college and sloping airstrip.

The area further north around Tagime, Bokondini and Karubaga, and the Lani (western Dani) country west of Pyramid and Bolokme, have beautiful scenery and pretty villages, though they're no longer very traditional.

Danau Habbema

This beautiful lake, 30km west of Wamena as the crow flies, sits amid alpine grasslands at 3400m altitude, with dramatic, snow-capped mountains in view (4750m Gunung Trikora rises to the south). The fauna and flora are a big draw for nature lovers. It's possible to visit Habbema in a day trip from Wamena – the drive is around two hours each way. You can rent a 4WD and driver in Wamena for around 3,000,000Rp round trip. The road is paved as far as the military post at Napua, 7km from Wamena.

The ideal way to visit Habbema is to drive there and trek back (three to four days), for which you will need a guide. Much of the route is through rainforest. The usual route starting from the lake is via Yobogima (a forest clearing) and then through a spectacular gorge to Daela village and on to Pilia and Ibele. En route you stand a fairly good chance of seeing cuscus and three birds of paradise (MacGregor's, King of Saxony and superb). Ibele is connected to Wamena by public transport.

Visitors to Habbema officially need a permit from the **Lorentz National Park office** (Balai Taman Nasional Lorentz; ☎0969 34098; Jl SD Percobaan, Potikelek). This costs 20,000Rp plus a 6000Rp official receipt-stamp *(meterai tempel)*, sold at stationery-type shops. The park office may also want to see a *surat jalan* covering Danau Habbema, something the Wamena police are not always willing to grant. In practice, many tourists head to Habbema without a park permit; the Napua military post may request a 'gift' to let them pass. Along the road you might encounter roadblocks at logging centres (offer cigarettes), and locals at the lake may request a (negotiable) fee of perhaps 100,000Rp per person.

Yali Country

Over the eastern walls of the Baliem Valley, amid scenery that is often as stunning, lies the home of the Yali people. They are one of the more traditional highland peoples, although traditional dress is now much less common than it was 15 years ago. The men may wear 'skirts' of rattan hoops, with penis gourds protruding from underneath. Missionaries provide much of the infrastructure here, such as schools and transport. Yali country is a great destination for more adventurous trekkers with enough time. You need about a week to walk there (the Yali themselves can do it, barefoot, in two days) and you should allow at least two or three days to explore once there. You might be able to get on a mission flight back to Wamena, but otherwise you'll have to walk back or charter a plane. Villages with airstrips include **Angguruk**, **Pronggoli**, **Kosarek** and **Welarek**.

The most direct route runs from Sugokmo or Kurima to Ugem, then up the Mugi Valley, over 3500m-plus Gunung Elit with at least one night camping, then down to **Abiyangge**, **Piliam** and **Pronggoli** in Yali country. If you don't have a guide from Wamena, you need to find a local one not later than **Kiroma** village. There are sections of long, steep ascent, and the upper reaches over Gunung Elit involve climbing up and down several rustic wooden ladders. From Pronggoli to Angguruk, the biggest Yali village (with a large market twice a week), takes another one or two days.

An easier but longer option, about eight days from Sugokmo to Angguruk and still with plenty of up and down, is the southern loop via Wesagalep, Werima, Soba and Ninia.

Beyond Yali country it's possible to trek on southeastward into the country of the Mek people, similarly small in stature to the Yali (their main village is Nalca), and even cross Papua's north-south watershed to Langda, main village of the Una people (considered pygmies).

THE SOUTH

Few travellers make it to the low-lying, river-strewn south, but Wasur National Park is one of Papua's best wildlife destinations (for a few months a year), while the Asmat region provides a fascinating taste of life along jungle rivers with a headhunting past and marvellous woodcarving artisanry.

Merauke

☎0971 / POP 59,000

Meraukeis a reasonably prosperous and orderly town of wide, straight streets, renowned as the most southeasterly settlement in Indonesia. The best reason to visit is nearby Wasur National Park, which is like a small slice of Australian bush in Indonesia, wallabies and all.

It's 6km from the airport at the southeast end of town to the port on Sungai Maro at the northwest end. The main street, running almost the whole way, is Jl Raya Mandala.

Sleeping & Eating

A few good hotels are near the midpoint of Jl Raya Mandala.

Swiss-belhotel HOTEL $$$
(☎326 333; www.swiss-belhotel.com; Jl Raya Mandala 53; r incl breakfast from US$91; ❄@🛜) Stylish, luxurious, new in 2012 and by far the best in town.

Hotel Megaria HOTEL $$
(☎321 932; Jl Raya Mandala 166; r incl breakfast 247,000-385,000Rp; ❄) The recently renovated Megaria has a good selection of large, clean, well-furnished rooms. Get one as far away from the motorbike-infested road as possible.

Marina Hotel HOTEL $
(☎326 240; Jl Raya Mandala 23; s/d 165,000/220,000Rp) Acceptable, clean rooms with cold showers.

Rumah Makan Serumpun Indah PADANG $
(☎325 364; Jl TMP Trikora; meals 30,000-40,000Rp; ⏰5.30am-10pm) A five-minute *ojek* ride from mid-Jl Raya Mandala, this big, clean eating hall will help you fill up very satisfactorily on the fish, chicken in coconut sauce, vegetables, prawns and *rendang* (beef cooked in spicy coconut milk) that is set in front of you.

Information

Police station (Jl Brawijaya 27) Come here, opposite the main market, to report your arrival or obtain a *surat jalan*.

Getting There & Around

Batavia Air, Lion Air and Merpati all fly daily to Jayapura, Makassar and Jakarta. Given the competition, fares can be less than 500,000Rp to Jayapura. Merpati also flies to several southern Papua destinations, including Ewer (Agats; three weekly). All airlines have airport ticket offices. Airport taxis cost 50,000Rp into town. Yellow public *taksi* (3000Rp) from the airport parking area, or the road just outside, run along Jl Raya Mandala.

Every two weeks Pelni's *Tatamailau* sails from Merauke to Agats (1st/economy class 706,000/183,000Rp) and Sorong

(1,922,000/484,000Rp). The *Kelimutu* sails to Agats then through southern and central Maluku to Sulawesi, every four weeks. Smaller boats run up and down the coast to Agats and as far inland as Tanahmerah. **PT Bima Suci Irja** (Jl Raya Mandala), on mid-Jl Raya Mandala, sells air and Pelni tickets.

Wasur National Park

The 4130-sq-km Wasur National Park, stretching between Merauke and the PNG border, will fascinate anyone with an interest in wildlife, especially birds and marsupials. But come in the later part of the dry season (mid-July to early November), otherwise most of Wasur's tracks will be impassable. Part of the Trans-Fly biome straddling the Indonesia–PNG border, Wasur is a low-lying area of savannahs, swamps, forests and slow-moving rivers that inundate much of the land during the wet season. Wasur's marsupials includes at least three species of wallaby (locals call them all *kangguru*), and nocturnal cuscuses and sugar gliders. Among the 400 birds are cassowaries, kookaburras, cockatoos, brolgas, magpie geese and three types of bird of paradise.

The southern part of the park is the best for wildlife spotting as it has more open grasslands and coastal areas. At **Rawa Biru**, an indigenous village 45km east of Merauke (300,000Rp one-way by *ojek*, or 2,000,000Rp to 4,000,000Rp round trip in a rented 4WD vehicle with driver), you can stay in local houses for 100,000Rp to 150,000Rp person (bring food and mosquito nets). Local guides cost 150,000Rp per day. From Rawa Biru it's a two-to-three-hour walk to **Prem**, with a small savannah surrounded by water, and a good chance of seeing wallabies and various water birds. Also within reach (20km) is **Yakiu**, where chances are high of seeing the greater, king and red birds of paradise in the early morning and late afternoon. The birds are protected by the villagers, who charge 200,000Rp to 400,000Rp per group to take you to them. To reach Yakiu, get a canoe across Rawa Biru lake (100,000Rp round trip for up to five people), then walk four hours or get an *ojek* (500,000Rp round trip) to Yakiu.

Visiting the park requires a permit (10,000/25,000Rp per person/camera) from the **Wasur National Park Office** (Balai Taman Nasional Wasur; ☎097 132 4532; Jl Garuda Leproseri 3, Merauke; ⏲8am-2.30pm Mon-Thu, to noon Fri), 4km southeast of Merauke airport. Carry your passport, *surat jalan* and photocopies to show to military posts in the villages.

Bony Kondahon (☎0813 4458 3646; bonykondahon@rocketmail.com), an excellent, English-speaking, Merauke-based Papuan guide, can help with arrangements and show you the park. He charges 300,000Rp to 350,000Rp per day for guiding and cooking.

Asmat Region

The Asmat region is a massive, remote, low-lying area of muddy, snaking rivers, mangrove forests and tidal swamps, where many villages, including their streets, are built entirely on stilts. The Asmat people, formerly feared for their headhunting and cannibalism, are now most celebrated for their woodcarvings – the most spectacular of Papuan art. It's a fascinating area to explore but it requires time, money and patience. The one time when more than a handful of visitors appears here is during the annual Asmat Cultural Festival (Festival Budaya Asmat), five or six days of woodcarving exhibits, canoe races and traditional dance, song and dress at Agats in October.

Though Christianity has a strong hold among the Asmat today, many older beliefs and practices survive. All Asmat villages still have their *jeu* (men's house), a long building adorned with carvings where young men sleep from adolescence till marriage, and married men sleep some nights. These are intriguing places to visit if you can get yourself invited.

Asmat woodcarvings were originally made only for ritual use. The famous *bis* poles of interlocked human and animal figures are carved from mangrove trees and can be 6m or more tall. Traditionally they were carved as objects where the spirits of slain warriors could reside until they were liberated by the killing and eating of enemies. Decorated shields, used in funeral ceremonies, also represent and avenge dead relatives. Asmat people still revere their dead ancestors and may keep their skulls as sources of spiritual strength.

AGATS

Capital of the region is the overgrown village of Agats, on the Aswet estuary. Due to the extraordinary tides and location, its streets are raised boardwalks which now support some (thankfully slow-moving) motorbike traffic as well as pedestrians. It's a curious place to wander round, with markets, shops, mosque, churches and hideous monuments, just like any other Papuan town. Report to **Polres Asmat** (Jl Pendidikan) with your *surat jalan* when you arrive. **Bank BRI** (Jl Muyu Kecil) has a MasterCard and Cirrus ATM but you can't guarantee it'll be working.

Don't miss the **Museum Kebudayaan dan Kemajuan Asmat** (Asmat Museum of Culture & Progress; Jl Missi; free but donations accepted; 8am-3pm Mon-Sat), which has a fantastic collection of Asmat art and artefacts, from *bis* poles and skulls to full-body dance outfits. Try to recruit an English-speaking guide as there is little interpretative information.

The government-run **Hotel Assedu** (0813 4425 9244; Jl Pemda 1; s/d incl breakfast 264,000/290,000Rp, deluxe 396,000Rp;) has clean rooms with comfy beds, almost-tasteful plastic flowers and the best restaurant in town (mains 18,000Rp to 30,000Rp).

Getting There & Away

Agats' airfield is at Ewer, a 20-minute, 100,000Rp, speedboat ride north. Flights can be cancelled if the airstrip is waterlogged. Merpati flies three times weekly to Merauke, and Trigana goes twice to Timika (which has flights to Jayapura, Sorong, Bali and Jakarta). Tickets are sold by Pak Udin, who inhabits a small office behind the **Pasar Baru** (New Market; Jl Dolog). Pelni's *Tatamailau* leaves Agats every two weeks for Merauke (1st class/economy 701,000/178,000Rp) southbound, and Timika, Tual and Sorong northbound. The *Kelimutu* comes every four weeks, to Merauke southbound and Timika and Maluku northbound.

The cost of river trips depends on the boat, the petrol price (16,000Rp/L here at research time) and negotiation. A return trip to Atsy, about 45km each way, should cost around 1,000,000Rp in a *longbot* (seven or eight passengers), less in a smaller *ketinting* (longtail boat), and 1,500,000Rp to 2,000,000Rp in a speedboat (three to five passengers). If you can get one, a passage on one of the cargo boats *(kapal)* that head along the coasts and up the rivers, is cheapest of all.

AROUND THE ASMAT REGION

Most visitors who make it here spend time boating along the jungle-lined rivers to different villages, seeing and buying Asmat artefacts, and maybe seeing a traditional dance or ceremony or a demo of the uses of the sago palm (the staple lowland food source). For anything more than a day trip from Agats you'll need a guide (300,000Rp or more per day) and maybe a porter or cook (100,000Rp or more) in addition to boat hire.

Villages to visit for their carving include **Atsy**, **Ambisu** and **Jow**, all south of Agats. **Fos** and **Awok**, east of Agats up Kali Sirets, and **Ocenep**, south of Agats, are places where traditional Asmat celebrations can be laid on for 2,000,000Rp to 3,000,000Rp. A persistent story has it that Ocenep holds the skull of Michael Rockefeller, art collector and son to a former US vice-president, who disappeared nearby in 1961, when headhunting was still a living tradition. Atsy is about the same size as Agats and has some shops and *rumah makan* and the clean, decent **Hotel Marannu** (0868 1213 5019; r 300,000-385,000Rp), but other villages have basic guesthouses at best, and you will need to carry some food and mosquito repellent.

Korowai Region

Far inland from the Asmat, in the region of the Dairam and upper Sirets rivers, live the Korowai people, seminomadic dwellers in tree houses perched 10m to 20m high as refuges against animals, enemies, floods and mosquitoes. The Korowai were not contacted by missionaries until the 1970s and though some have since settled in new villages of ground-level houses, others still live their traditional way of life, wearing few clothes and employing stone and bone tools. Rumour has it that headhunting and cannibalism might persist in some remoter parts of the area.

Recent TV documentaries have helped enthuse some travellers about visiting this unforgiving region. Several agencies, and guides in Wamena and Sentani, can take you on expensive trips which typically fly from Jayapura or Wamena to Dekai, then boat down Kali Brazza and up Kali Pulau to the first Korowai village, **Mabul**. You then spend some days walking along muddy, slippery trails through hot, humid jungles, sleeping in tents, huts or tree houses, and witnessing tribal life, often including some prearranged festivities. You're looking at approximately €2000 to €2500 for a seven- to 10-day trip, with perhaps half that time actually in Korowai territory. It's best to avoid the wettest season, January to March. Michael Leitzinger (p449) is one very experienced Papua guide who offers trips through some of the remoter Korowai areas, where the people have had relatively little contact with outsiders.

Sumatra

POP 50 MILLION

Includes »

Best Places to Eat

- Restauran Bunda (p522)
- One-One (p530)
- Ikan Bakar Pak Agus (p537)
- Jenny's Restaurant (p509)

Best Places to Stay

- On The Rocks (p498)
- Abdi Homestay (p553)
- Casa Nemo (p524)
- Spice Homestay (p537)
- Swiss-Belinn Medan (p492)

Why Go

Few isles tempt the imagination with the lure of adventure quite like the fierce land of Sumatra. An island of extraordinary beauty, it bubbles with life and vibrates under the power of nature. Eruptions, earthquakes and tsunamis are Sumatran headline grabbers. Steaming volcanoes brew and bluster while standing guard over lakes that sleepily lap the edges of craters. Orangutan-filled jungles host not only our red-haired cousins, but also tigers, rhinos and elephants. And down at sea level, idyllic deserted beaches are bombarded by clear barrels of surf.

As varied as the land, the people of Sumatra are a spicy broth of mixed cultures, from the devout Muslims in Aceh to the hedonistic Batak Christians around Danau Toba and the matrilineal Minangkabau of Padang. All are unified by a fear, respect and love of the wild and wondrous land of Sumatra.

When to Go?

Padang

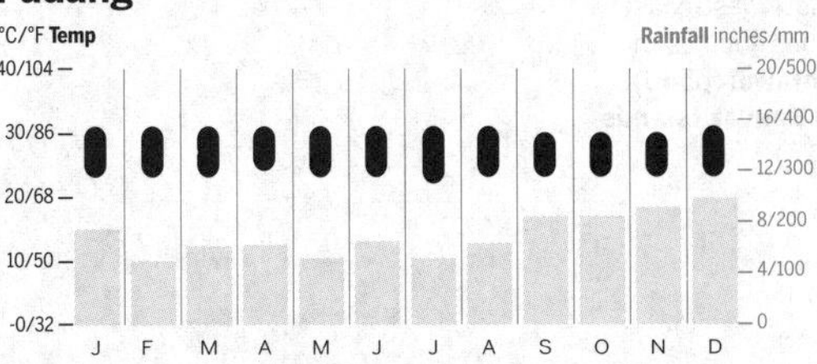

Mid-Jun Take in the chaotic canoe races at the Danau Toba Festival.

Mid-Aug Place your bets at Takwengon's horse racing carnival.

Dec–Jan Most of Sumatra is getting a monsoon soak, but northern Aceh bathes in sun.

Sumatra Highlights

1. Lounging away a few days on the cool shores of **Danau Toba** (p504) and sharing a few drinks with the fun-loving Batak folk
2. Ogling our orangutan cousins in the wild jungles of **Bukit Lawang** (p496)
3. Hiking up beyond the clouds to the steaming peaks of the volcanoes around the hill town of **Berastagi** (p501)
4. Swimming with sharks and turtles in the coral garden off **Pulau Weh** (p523), an underwater paradise
5. Exploring the heartland of the matrilineal Minangkabau people from the sleepy **Harau Valley** (p553) to spectacular **Danau Maninjau** (p553)
6. Getting the real jungle experience in the steamy forests around **Ketambe** (p531), at the heart of the Gunung Leuser National Park
7. Living the surfer dream and searching for barrels around remote west-coast islands such as the **Mentawai** (p540) and **Banyak Islands** (p527)

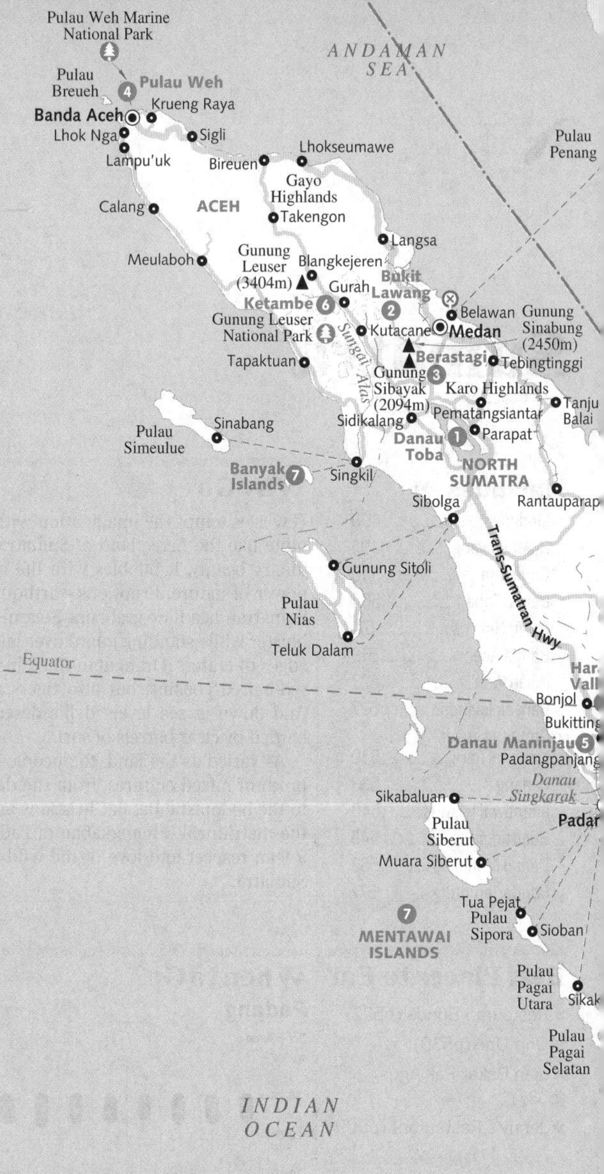

THAILAND
SOUTH CHINA SEA
Ipoh
Lumut
MALAYSIA
KUALA LUMPUR
Pelabuhan (Port) Klang
Strait of Melaka
Melaka
Pulau Rupat
Dumai
Pulau Bengkalis
Pulau Rangsang
Tanjung Buton
SINGAPORE
Pulau Kalimun
Pulau Batam
Pulau Bintan
Selat Panjang
Tanjung Pinang
Sungai Siak
Siak Sri Indrapura
Tanjung Samak
Tanjung Balai
Kijang
Pekanbaru
Pulau Tebingtinggi
Pulau Mendol
Pulau Kundur
ungaipagar
RIAU
Pulau Penuba
Daik
Pulau Lingga
Sungai Buluh
Dabo
Pulau Singkep
LINGGA ISLANDS
Batu Sangkar
Solok
WEST UMATRA
Bukit Tigapuluh National Park
Sungai Batang Hari
JAMBI
Muara Jambi
Tujuh Islands
Selat Berhala
Gunung Kerinci (3805m)
Muarabungo
Jambi
Kerinci Valley
Sungai Penuh
Bangko
Bukit Duabelas National Park
Kerinci Seblat National Park
Mukomuko
Pegunungan Bukit Barisan
Sungai Musi
Ipuh
BENGKULU
Lubuklinggau
Perabumulih
Palembang
Kayuagung
SOUTH SUMATRA
Lais
Curup
Bengkulu
Lahat
Pagaralam
Pasemah Highlands
Baturaja
Manna
LAMPUNG
Danau Ranau
Bintuhan
Kotabumi
Bukit Barisan Selatan National Park
Simpang Sinder
Metro
Way Kanan
Way Kambas National Park
Pulau Enggano
Krui
Jepara
Bandarlampung
Kota Agung
Kalianda
Bakauheni
Pulau Seribu
Gunung Krakatau
Merak
Sunda Strait
JAKARTA
JAVA
Mentok
Belinyu
Sungailiat
Pangkal Pinang
Pulau Bangka
Tanjung Pandan
Pulau Belitung
Pulau Laut
Pulau Matak
Pulau Terempa
Pulau Jemaja
Pulau Natuna Besar
Pulau Midai
Pulau Subi
Pulau Serasan
ANAMBAS ISLANDS
NATUNA SEA
Pulau Mendarik
Pulau Dumdum
TAMBELAN ISLANDS
KALIMANTAN
Equator
Pulau Pejantan

History

Pre-Islamic history is often more myth than fact, but archaeological evidence suggests that Sumatra was the gateway for migrating tribes from mainland Southeast Asia.

The Strait of Melaka, an important trade route between China and India, exposed the east coast of Sumatra to the region's superpowers and cultural influences, such as Islam. The kingdom of Sriwijaya emerged as a local player at the end of the 7th century, with its capital presumably based near the modern city of Palembang. After Sriwijaya's influence waned, Aceh, at the northern tip of Sumatra, assumed control of trade through the strait. The era of Aceh's sultanate prevailed until the beginning of the 17th century, when Dutch traders claimed a piece of the spice trade.

The most influential port of the day, Samudra, near Lhokseumawe, eventually became the name that the traders used to refer to the entire island. It was Marco Polo who corrupted the name to 'Sumatra' in his 1292 report on the area.

Throughout the colonial era, Sumatra saw many foreign powers stake a claim in its resources: the Dutch based themselves in the west Sumatran port of Padang, the British ruled in Bencoolen (now Bengkulu), American traders monopolised pepper exports from Aceh and the Chinese exploited the reserves on the islands of Bangka and Belitung, east of Palembang.

In the early 19th century, the Dutch attempted to assert military control over all of Sumatra, a move met with resistance by its disparate tribes. In 1863 the Dutch finally established authority over Pulau Nias. Treaties and alliances brought other areas of Sumatra under Dutch rule.

The Dutch were never welcomed in Sumatra, which contributed several key figures to the independence struggle. Yet Sumatra was dissatisfied with Jakarta's rule. Between 1958 and 1961, rebel groups based in Bukittinggi and the mountains of south Sumatra resisted centralisation, which led to clashes with the Indonesian military. Fiercely independent Aceh proved to be Jakarta's most troublesome region. Aceh's separatist movement started in the late 1970s and continued until 2006.

No human conflict could compare to the destruction of the 2004 Boxing Day tsunami, in which a 9.0-plus-magnitude earthquake off the northwestern coast of Sumatra triggered a regionwide tsunami. In Aceh province, the land mass closest to the epicentre, waves almost 15m high rose up and swallowed coastal development and dwellers. The Indonesian death count was estimated at more than 170,000 people, mainly in Aceh. Reconstruction is now complete and the one silver lining to the disaster was that it achieved what no amount of peace talks had been able to do – bringing people in Aceh and beyond together – and in the process brought peace to the region.

ℹ Getting There & Away

Once upon a time along the backpacker trail, travellers sailed the high seas to reach the island of Sumatra. But the era of budget airlines has largely made the friendly skies a faster and more affordable option for international arrivals.

Keep in mind that Sumatra is one hour behind Singapore and Malaysia.

AIR

Medan is Sumatra's primary international airport, with frequent flights to mainland Southeast Asian cities such as Singapore, Kuala Lumpur and Penang. In West Sumatra, Padang receives flights from Singapore and Malaysia. Banda Aceh and Pekanbaru also receive international flights from mainland Southeast Asia.

You can hop on a plane from Jakarta to every major Sumatran city aboard **Garuda** (www.garuda-indonesia.com), **Merpati** (www.merpati.co.id), **Lion Air** (www.lionair.co.id) or **Sriwijaya Air** (www.sriwijayaair.co.id), among others. Flights from Sumatra to other parts of Indonesia typically connect through Jakarta.

All Sumatran airports charge a departure tax of 75,000Rp to 150,000Rp for international flights.

BOAT

Many travellers still like the idea of entering Sumatra by sea. Sadly, opportunities to do so are becoming increasingly rare. The once-popular crossing from Penang (Malaysia) to Belawan (close to Medan) has, thanks to cheaper airfares, gone the way of the *Titanic*. Ferries do still travel between Melaka (Malaysia) and Dumai (Indonesia), but Dumai is a long way from anywhere most travellers want to be and few people make this crossing nowadays.

From Singapore, ferries make the quick hop to Pulau Batam and Pulau Bintan, the primary islands in the Riau archipelago. From Batam, boats set sail for Dumai, Palembang and Pekanbaru, but few travellers use these routes.

Ferries swim across the narrow Sunda Strait, which links the southeastern tip of Sumatra at Bakauheni to Java's westernmost point of Merak. The sea crossing is a brief dip in a day-long voyage that requires several hours' worth of bus transport from both ports to Jakarta and, on the Sumatra side, Bandarlampung.

Pelni-operated boats still paddle between Indonesia's islands, carrying freight and families.

Getting Around

Most travellers bus around northern Sumatra and then hop on a plane to Java, largely avoiding Sumatra's highway system. Most of the island is mountainous jungle and the poorly maintained roads form a twisted pile of spaghetti on the undulating landscape. Don't count on getting anywhere very quickly on Sumatra.

AIR

An hour on a plane is an attractive alternative to what may seem like an eternity on a bone-shaking bus. Medan to Banda Aceh and Medan to Padang are two popular air hops. All Sumatran airports charge an airport departure tax (between 20,000Rp and 40,000Rp) that is not included in your ticket.

BOAT

Most boat travel within Sumatra connects the main island with the many satellite islands lining the coast. The most commonly used routes link Banda Aceh with Pulau Weh, Sibolga with Pulau Nias, and Padang with Pulau Siberut (in the Mentawai Islands). Most long-distance ferries have several classes, ranging from filthy and crowded to filthy and less crowded. An upgrade in class might be a necessary luxury.

BUS

Bus is the most common mode of transport around Sumatra, and in many cases it's the only option for intercity travel. But it is far from efficient or comfortable. The primary thoroughfare is the Trans-Sumatran Hwy, which is little more than a jungle-bound track for petrol-eating beasts. It is not uncommon during the rainy season for bridges to wash out and for mudslides to block the road. Buses range from economy sardine cans to modern air-con coaches. At the top of the class structure are super-executive buses with reclining seats, deep-freeze air-con, toilets and an all-night serenade of Scorpions albums. Many passengers come prepared with winter hats, gloves and earplugs.

In some towns, you can go straight to the bus terminal to buy tickets and board buses, while other towns rely on bus-company offices located outside the terminals. Ticket prices vary greatly depending on the quality of the bus and the perceived gullibility of the traveller. It pays to shop around and to ask at your guesthouse about reliable companies; be aware that some accommodation places act as booking agents and charge a commission for their services.

LOCAL TRANSPORT

The usual Indonesian forms of transport – bemo or *opelet* (small minibus), becak (bicycle-rickshaw) and *bendi* (two-person horse-drawn cart) – are available in Sumatran towns and cities. Establish a price for a becak ride before climbing aboard. For an *opelet*, you pay after you disembark.

MINIBUS

For midrange and shorter journeys, many locals and travellers prefer to use minibus services, which can be more convenient than hustling out to the bus terminal. Some minibuses are in superb shape and provide door-to-door service, while others are a little rickety and shovel in more people than a clown car.

TRAIN

The only useful train service in Sumatra runs from Bandarlampung to Palembang, and then on to Lubuklinggau. There are also passenger trains from Medan to Pematangsiantar, Tanjung Balai and Rantauparapat – though these are rarely used by tourists.

NORTH SUMATRA

For most visitors, this is the sole slice of Sumatra they'll taste. And with good reason: ogle the orangutans in Bukit Lawang, veer over the volcanoes of Berastagi and laze away on the shores of Danau Toba. Overall, North Sumatra is a well-trodden and worthy circuit that centres on gateway metropolis Medan.

North Sumatra stretches from the Indian Ocean to the Strait of Melaka. From sea to shining sea, it is anything but homogeneous. The rolling landscape varies from sweaty plains to cool highlands, while the houses of worship switch between the metal domes of mosques to the arrow-straight steeples of Christian churches. The coastal Malays, relatives of peoples from mainland Southeast Asia, live along the Strait of Melaka and are the largest ethnic group. In the highlands around Danau Toba are the delightful Batak, and then there's the megalithic culture of Pulau Nias.

North Sumatra has a population of almost 12 million and is an economically robust province, producing more than 30% of Indonesia's exports. Oil, palm oil, tea and rubber are produced in large quantities, and fine tobacco is grown in the rich soil around Medan.

Medan

☎061 / POP 2 MILLION

Sumatra's major metropolis, and Indonesia's third-largest city, has a bad rep in Southeast Asia backpacker circles and it frequently pops up in 'What's the worst place you've ever visited?' conversations. Question the city's detractors a little further though and you'll find that most have merely rushed straight through without giving the city any time. It's true that physical tourist attractions are somewhat lacking, and that, compared to squeaky-clean Malaysia, the pollution, poverty and persistent catcalls of 'Hello mister!' could be an unnerving jolt of dirt-under-your-fingernails Asia. But it would also be fair to say that this is a city with real Indonesian character, something that can be lacking in many of the more popular North Sumatran tourist towns. So get over the culture shock, give Medan a bit of time and discover an amenity-filled, leafy and modern town with more than a hint of crumbling Dutch-colonial charm.

Sights

Ghosts of Medan's colonial mercantile past are still visible along Jl Ahmad Yani from Jl Palang Merah north to Lapangan Mer-

Medan

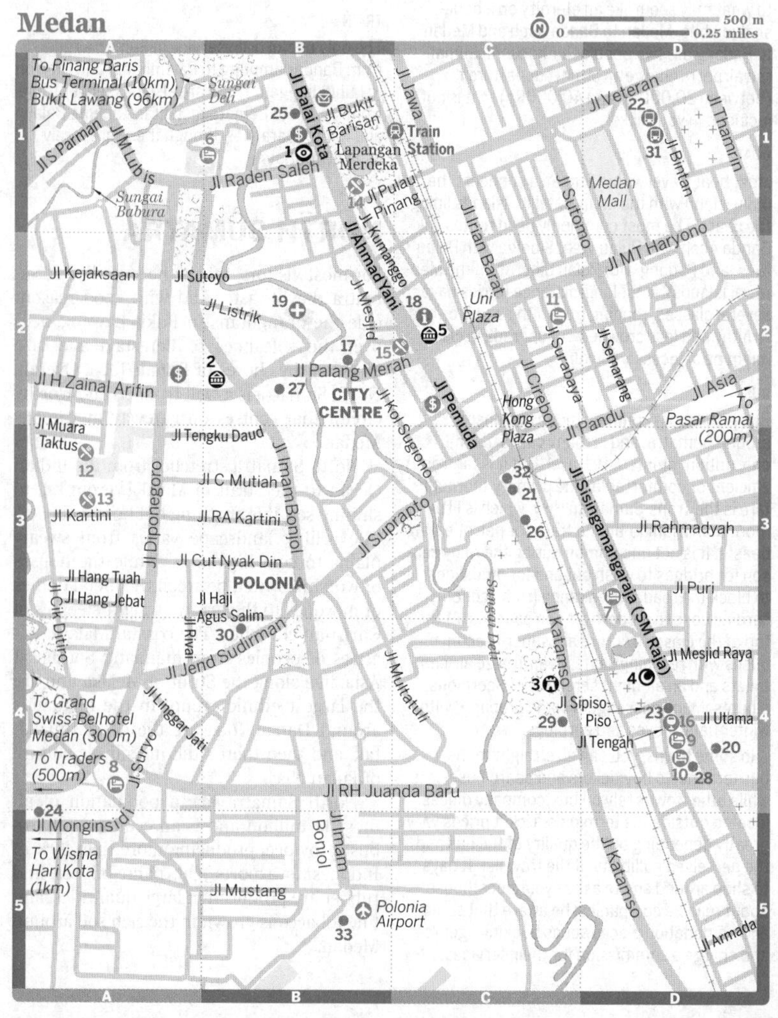

deka, a former parade ground surrounded by handsome colonial buildings, such as the Bank Indonesia, **Balai Kota** (Town Hall; Jl Balai Kota) and the post office. Some are still stately relics, while others have been gutted and turned into parking garages, demonstrating the enduring friendship between Indonesia and its former coloniser.

Istana Maimoon PALACE
(Jl Katamso; admission 5000Rp; ⏲8am-5pm) Standing as grand as ever, the Maimoon Palace was built by the sultan of Deli in 1888. The 30-room palace features Malay, Mogul and Italian influences. Only the main room, which features the lavish inauguration throne, is open to the public. The back wing of the palace is occupied by members of the sultan's family. The current sultan, Aria Mahmud Lamanjiji, was only eight years old when he was installed as the 14th Sultan of Deli in 2005, replacing his father, who died in a plane crash. He is the youngest sultan in Deli history. He currently resides in Sulawesi with his mother, and his role is purely ceremonial.

Traditional music performances take place at 10am and 2pm Monday to Friday and at 2pm on Saturday and Sunday. Note that punctuality isn't the musicians' strong point.

The entry fee is quite steep for what is essentially a poke about just one room.

Mesjid Raya MOSQUE
(cnr Jl Mesjid Raya & SM Raja; admission by donation; ⏲9am-5pm, except prayer times) The impressive Grand Mosque was commissioned by the sultan in 1906. The Moroccan-style building has towering ceilings, ornate carvings, Italian marble and stained glass from China.

Museum of North Sumatra MUSEUM
(☎771 6792; Jl HM Joni 51; admission 1000Rp; ⏲9am-3pm Tue-Sun) The Museum of North Sumatra has a well-presented collection ranging from early North Sumatran civilisations to Hindu, Buddhist and Islamic periods to colonial and military history. Highlights include fine stone carvings from Nias and extravagantly carved wooden coffins. It's a short way east of the centre.

Bukit Barisan Military Museum MUSEUM
(Jl H Zainal Arifin 8; admission by donation; ⏲8am-3pm Mon-Fri) Bukit Barisan Military Museum has a small collection of weapons, photos and memorabilia from WWII, the War of

Medan

Sights
1 Balai Kota B1
2 Bukit Barisan Military Museum B2
3 Istana Maimoon C4
4 Mesjid Raya D4
5 Tjong A Fie Mansion C2

Sleeping
6 Aryaduta Hotel B1
7 Garuda Plaza Hotel D3
8 JJ's Guesthouse A4
9 Ponduk Wisata Angel D4
10 Residence Hotel D4
Sultan Homestay .... (see 9)
11 Swiss-Belinn Medan C2

Eating
12 Bollywood Food Centre A3
13 Medan Club A3
14 Merdeka Walk B1
Ponduk Wisata Angel .... (see 9)
15 Tip Top Restaurant C2

Drinking
16 Corner Café Raya D4
Medan Club .... (see 13)

Information
17 Immigration Office B2
18 North Sumatra Tourist Office C2
19 Rumah Sakit Gleneagles B2
20 Tobali Tour & Travel D4
21 Trophy Tour C3

Transport
Air Asia .... (see 7)
22 Buses to Ketambe D1
23 Fire Fly D4
24 Garuda A5
25 Garuda B1
26 Lion Air/Wings Air C3
27 Malaysian Airlines B2
28 Merpati D4
29 NBA C4
30 Silk Air B4
31 Singkil Raya D1
32 Sriwijaya Air C3
33 Susi Air B5

Independence and the Sumatran rebellion of 1958.

Tjong A Fie Mansion HISTORIC BUILDING
(www.tjongafieinstitute.com; Jl Ahmad Yani 105; admission incl guide 35,000Rp; ⌚9am-5pm) Tjong A Fie Mansion, the former residence of a famous Chinese merchant, mixes Victorian and Chinese style. The exquisite hand-painted ceilings, Tjong's huge bedroom, interesting art pieces, an upstairs ballroom (which now exhibits work by local artists) and Taoist temples help to make it one of the most impressive historic buildings in town.

Tours

Tri Jaya Tour & Travel TOUR
(☎703 2967; www.trijaya-travel.com; Hotel Deli River; two-person tours US$65) Suberb historic city tours. You can also pick up the book *Tours Through Historic Medan and its Surroundings,* written by the owner of this company.

Sleeping

The majority of budget accommodation is on or near Jl SM Raja and, in general, none of it is all that pretty. Expect serious road and Mosque-inspired noise, carbon-monoxide inhalation and grubby rooms with cold-water showers. On the plus side, there are normally plenty of other backpackers hanging around.

If you can push the boat out a little, you'll find Medan has some fabulous-value mid- and top-end places to stay.

TOP CHOICE **Swiss-Belinn Medan** BUSINESS HOTEL $$
(☎452 0505; www.swiss-belhotel.com; Jl Surabaya 88; d incl breakfast from 275,535Rp; ❄@📶) Smart and busy new hotel that almost verges on earning a boutique label. The rooms have lovely cool dark slate floors and bathrooms, rough whitewashed walls, subdued art and deliciously comfortable beds. There's a good range of facilities, including a popular restaurant, and all up it offers the best deal in the city. Note that some rooms have no windows, which can make them dark.

Grand Swiss-Belhotel Medan BUSINESS HOTEL $$$
(☎457 6999; www.swiss-belhotel.com; Jl S Parman 217; d incl breakfast from 608,000Rp; ❄@📶🏊) This huge, modern hotel follows the standard business-class formula of great facilities, an array of different restaurants and a guaranteed good night's sleep, but it also throws in a see-through glass-walled swimming pool and floor-to-ceiling windows that offer breathless city views from the upper floors.

Wisma Hari Kota GUESTHOUSE $
(☎453 3113; Jl Lobak 14; r 77,000-165,000Rp; ❄) We can't begin to tell you how much better value this place – located only 10 minutes from the airport in a quiet and peaceful area – is compared to most cheap options in Medan. Even the cheapest rooms are vast and have been polished until they sparkle; more expensive rooms feature hot-water showers. Breakfast is included (except for the cheaper rooms).

Ponduk Wisata Angel GUESTHOUSE $
(Hotel Angel; ☎732 0702; a_zelsy_travel@yahoo.com; Jl SM Raja 70; s with fan 60,000Rp, d with fan/air-con 100,000/130,000Rp; ❄📶) The best backpacker option in town. Angel's clean rooms are a swirl of vivid blues and yellows, a colour scheme that almost succeeds in offsetting the noisy traffic. It has a sociable street-front cafe.

Hotel Deli River GUESTHOUSE $$
(☎703 2964; Jl Raya Namorambe 129; s/d incl breakfast €55/60; ❄@📶) This family-run hotel, 12km outside the city chaos, is shaded by fruit trees, overlooks the Deli River and provides a peaceful countryside retreat within striking distance of the big smoke. Free transfers from the airport.

Aryaduta Hotel BUSINESS HOTEL $$$
(☎457 2999; www.aryaduta.com; Jl Kapten Maulana Lubis 8; d incl breakfast US$74-176; ❄@📶) One of Medan's finest luxury hotels is international in class, with all the frills you'd expect for the price and sprawling high-rise views across the city. Don't be put off by the above-mall location.

JJ's Guesthouse GUESTHOUSE $
(☎457 8411; www.guesthousemedan.com; Jl Suryo 18; s/d incl breakfast 150,000/180,000Rp; ❄) In an old Dutch villa, JJ's has tidy boarding-house-style rooms run by a mannerly Dutch-speaking Indonesian woman. It's opposite KFC; its lack of signage makes it tricky to find. Ask for the Hotel Pardede and JJ's is right behind it – look for the sticker on the gate reading 'Find us on Facebook'. Said gates are locked, so you'll need to ring the doorbell tucked inside the left-hand side of the gate and be patient – it takes time for the elderly owner to get to you.

Garuda Plaza Hotel BUSINESS HOTEL $$
(☎736 1111; www.garudaplaza.com; Jl SM Raja 18; r incl breakfast 520,000-1,125,000Rp;) Garuda Plaza is Medan's homage to Jakarta, with modern, corporate accents. The lobby is a hive of activity. Discounts of up to 40% are available.

Sultan Homestay HOTEL $
(☎736 3311; Jl SM Raja 66; r 80,000-100,000Rp;) This new guesthouse is in the thick of the backpacker action. It has clean and comfortable rooms that are better than most of the town's other cheapies, but the bathrooms are shared. It was until recently trading under the name of Trav-Fella Homestay and some people may still know it as such.

Residence Hotel HOTEL $
(☎7760 0980; www.residencehotelmedan.com; Jl Tengah 1; r 60,000-150,000Rp;) The lime-green Residence has enough rooms, at a range of different prices, to mean that there's usually something to suit both your mood and your pockets. Warning: the cheaper rooms are windowless prison cells on the top floor and they get hot. The pricier rooms are pleasant.

Eating

Medan has the most varied selection of cuisines in Sumatra, from basic Malay-style *mie* (noodle) and nasi (rice) joints, to top-class hotel restaurants. However, if you've just flown in from Java or Bali, you'll find food much less of a highlight here.

Lots of simple warungs (food stalls) occupy the front courtyards of the houses in the little lanes around Mesjid Raya; the menu is on display with a few pre-made curries, coffee, tea and sometimes juices.

The main fruit market, **Pasar Ramai** (Ramani Market; Jl Thamrin), next to Thamrin Plaza, is a profusion of colours and smells, and has an impressive selection of local and imported tropical fruit.

TOP CHOICE **Merdeka Walk** SOUTHEAST ASIAN $
(Lapangan Merdeka, Jl Balai Kota; dishes 10,000-15,000Rp; 5-11pm;) Inspired by Singapore's al fresco dining, this collection of outdoor cafes in Lapangan Merdeka offers both fast-food and proper restaurants. You can burn off the calories on the bizarre public exercise equipment at the adjoining sports ground or waste some money in the amusement centre that sits at the heart of it all.

Bollywood Food Centre INDIAN $
(☎453 6494; Jl Muara Takus 7; dishes from 12,000Rp) Locals are adamant that this tucked-away little place, which is more like someone's front room and has a family atmosphere to match, serves the most authentic Indian cuisine in the city. There are several Malay-Indian roti shops nearby.

Traders INTERNATIONAL $$$
(Jl Kapten Pattimura 423; mains 60,000-140,000Rp; noon-midnight;) Plush Traders is very much a high-society kind of place and is the perfect spot to blow your dining budget on sushi, snail chowder, lobster dishes or Australian Angus steaks.

Tip Top Restaurant INTERNATIONAL $$
(Jl Ahmad Yani 92; dishes 12,000-25,000Rp;) Only the prices have changed at this old colonial relic, which dates back to 1934 and is great for a drink of bygone imperialism. Though it offers an array of Indonesian, Chinese and Western dishes you certainly don't come here for the quality of the food. Instead, just focus on the setting and atmosphere.

Medan Club INTERNATIONAL $$$
(Jl Kartini 36; dishes 30,000-80,000Rp) Wealthy and well-dressed expats and locals sip cocktails and dine from the broad international menu, which includes Mexican, French and American dishes. The country-park-like complex also contains a cafe, tennis courts and a barbeque area (Friday evening is barbeque night). Note that quoted menu prices don't include a raft of taxes and surcharges, which can easily add 40% to your bill!

Ponduk Wisata Angel INTERNATIONAL $
(Jl SM Raja 70; mains 15,000-20,000Rp) With a laid-back backpacker vibe, this cafe, which serves Indonesian and Western dishes, could almost pass for a beachside shack. That's if it weren't for the insanely busy traffic careering along Jl SM Raja that smothers your banana juice in carbon monoxide. It's a very sociable place to eat, though.

Drinking

Corner Café Raya BAR
(cnr Jl SM Raja & Jl Sipiso-Piso; 24hr) Cold beer and Western sports served to a heady mix of seedy sex-pats and fresh-faced backpackers, which makes its location directly opposite the Mesjid Raya mosque a little puzzling.

Traders COCKTAIL BAR
(Jl Kapten Pattimura 423; ⊙noon-midnight) If you're part of the 'It' crowd then swanky Traders, with its long and glamorous list of cocktails and equally long-legged and glamorous Medan girls, is the place to be seen.

Medan Club BAR
(Jl Kartini 36) A local institution, the Medan Club is still the place for many well-to-do locals to socialise on weekends. A big-screen TV beams out a diet of sporting events.

Information

IMMIGRATION Visa extensions can be processed at the **immigration office** (Jl Mangkubumi; ⊙8am-4pm Mon-Fri). Technically it takes three days, costs US$25 (or equivalent in Rupiah) and can not be processed until a few days before your current visa expires. However, it's likely that they can rush extensions through in urgent cases. They also told us that you must supply a red folder – though why was never made clear! The office you need is on the 2nd floor.

INTERNET ACCESS Internet access is available in every midrange and top-end hotel as well as a growing number of the budget places popular with foreigners. Wireless access can also be found in numerous coffee shops, cafes and posher restaurants. If none of these suit, Medan has speedy warnets (internet stalls) across the city, and internet access is also available at most of the large shopping plazas. Prices range from 3000Rp to 5000Rp per hour.

MEDICAL SERVICES For an ambulance, dial ☎118. **Rumah Sakit Gleneagles** (☎456 6368; Jl Listrik 6) is the best hospital in the city, with a 24-hour walk-in clinic and pharmacy, as well as English-speaking doctors and specialists.

MONEY Medan has branches of just about every bank operating in Indonesia, including **Bank Indonesia** (Jl Balai Kota), **BCA bank** (Bank Central Asia; Jl H Zainal Arifin) and **BNI bank** (Bank Negara Indonesia; Jl Pemuda). Most bank headquarters sit along the junction of Jl Diponegoro and Jl H Zainal Arifin.

POST **Main post office** (Jl Bukit Barisan; ⊙8am-6pm) Located in an old Dutch building on the main square. Internet, fax and photocopying also available.

TOURIST INFORMATION There is a basic tourist-information office immediately to the right as you exit at the international airport terminal. The **North Sumatra Tourist Office** (☎452 8436; Jl Ahmad Yani 107; ⊙8am-3pm Mon-Fri) in the city centre provides excellent information, brochures and maps.

TRAVEL AGENCIES Jl Katamso is packed with travel agencies that handle air tickets. **Tobali Tour & Travel** (☎732 4471; Jl SM Raja 79C) has tourist buses to Danau Toba (100,000Rp, four hours), Bukit Lawang (80,000Rp, 2½ to three hours) and Berastagi (80,000Rp, 2½ hours). **Trophy Tour** (☎415 5777; Jl Katamso 33D) is a ticket agent for most of the airlines (1st floor), and a tour operator (2nd floor).

Getting There & Away

Medan is Sumatra's main international arrival and departure point.

Air

Medan's **Polonia Airport** is 2km south of the city centre. There is an airport tax (p771) for departing flights. The following airlines have offices in Medan:

AirAsia (☎021 2927 0999; www.airasia.com; Jl SM Raja 18)

Fire Fly (☎0415 0077; www.firefly.com.my; Jl Brig Jend Katamso 62D)

Garuda (wwww.garuda-indonesia.com) Jl Monginsidi (☎455 6777; Jl Monginsidi 340); Jl Balai Kota (☎451 6400; Inna Dharma Deli, Jl Balai Kota 2)

Lion Air/Wings Air (☎080 4177 8899; www2.lionair.co.id; Jl Katamso 41)

Malaysian Airlines (☎075 135 888; www.malaysiaairlines.com; Hotel Danau Toba International, Jl Imam Bonjol 17)

Merpati (☎080 4162 1621; www.merpati.co.id/EN; Jl SM Raja 92A)

NBA (Nusantara Buana Air; ☎453 4680; Jl Katamso)

Silk Air (☎453 7744; www.silkair.com; Polonia Hotel, Jl Jend Sudirman 14)

Sriwijaya Air (☎455 2111; www.sriwijayaair.co.id; Jl Katamso 29)

Susi Air (☎785 2169; www.susiair.com; Polonia Airport)

Bus

There are two major bus terminals in Medan: Amplas, which serves southern destinations, and Pinang Baris, which serves northern destinations. For long-distance travel, most people deal directly with the bus ticketing offices located outside of the terminals. **Amplas bus terminal** (Jl SM Raja) is 6.5km south of the city centre. Almost any *opelet* heading south on Jl SM Raja will get you to Amplas (3000Rp). Bus ticket offices line the street nearby at Km 6.

For Bukit Lawang, Berastagi and Banda Aceh (the latter is also served by buses from Amplas), go to **Pinang Baris bus terminal** (Jl Gatot Subroto), 10km west of the city centre. For details of buses around North Sumatra from Medan, see the relevant town's Getting There & Away section.

TRANSPORT FROM MEDAN

Air

DESTINATION	COMPANY	FREQUENCY
Banda Aceh	Garuda, Lion Air, NBA, Sriwijaya Air	several daily
Bandung	AirAsia	4 weekly
Gunung Sitoli	Wings Air (Lion Air), Merpati	5 daily
Jakarta	Garuda, Lion Air, Sriwijaya Air	several daily
Kuala Lumpur	AirAsia, Malaysian Airlines	several daily
Kutacane	NBA, Susi Air	3 weekly
Meulaboh	Susi Air	2 daily
Padang	Lion Air, Sriwijaya Air	2 daily
Panang	AirAsia, Firefly, Lion Air	several daily
Pekanbaru	Lion Air, Sriwijaya Air	3 daily
Pulau Batam	Citi Link	2 daily
Pulau Simeulue	Merpati, NBA, Susi Air	2-3 daily
Sibolga	Wings Air (Lion Air), Merpati, Susi Air	1-3 daily
Silangit	Susi Air	daily
Singapore	Silk Air	2-3 daily
Surabaya	AirAsia	daily

Bus

DESTINATION	COST (RP)	DURATION (HR)	FREQUENCY
Banda Aceh	120,000-200,000	12-14	several daily
Bukittinggi	150,000-245,000	22	2 daily
Jambi	250,000-265,000	30	2 daily
Palembang	280,000-290,000	40	2 daily
Pekanbaru	140,000	13	1 daily

A minibus departs at 8pm daily from **Singkil Raya** (Jl Bintan), past the caged-bird warehouses, for Singkil (75,000Rp-90,000Rp, 10 hours), the departure point for boats to the Banyak Islands. Here you'll also find a **bus** at 7.30pm to Ketambe (120,000Rp, eight hours). Take *opelet* 53 from Jl SM Raja to Medan Mall.

Train

Rail services are very limited, with just two trains a day to Tanjung Balai (economy 10,000Rp). There are four trains daily to Rantauparapat (business/executive 40,000/60,000Rp).

 Getting Around

TO/FROM THE AIRPORT It is cheaper and less of a hassle to sail past the throng of taxi drivers to the becak queue at the airport gate (becak aren't allowed inside the airport). It should cost 50,000Rp to reach the hotel district on Jl SM Raja. If you like to haggle, a taxi ride should cost around 150,000Rp.

PUBLIC TRANSPORT Medan's got more *opelet* than you can shake a spoon player at. The going rate is 3000Rp per ride. Here are a few helpful routes: white Mr X from Jl SM Raja to Kesawan Sq, Lapangan Merdeka and the train station, and yellow 64 from Maimoon Palace to Sun Plaza. For becak, you'll rarely get one across the city centre for less than 15,000Rp unless you're dead keen on haggling for hours.

Bukit Lawang

☎061 / POP 30,000

Lost in the depths of the Sumatran jungle is this sweet little tourist town built around the popularity of its orangutan-viewing centre. But Bukit Lawang has much more to offer beyond our red-haired cousins. It's very easy to while away a few days lounging in the many riverside hammocks, splashing about in the gushing river and watching the jungle life swing and sing around you. The forests surrounding Bukit Lawang are part of the vast Gunung Leuser National Park (p530), which is one of the richest tropical-forest ecosystems in the word. The park as a whole is home to eight species of primate plus tigers, rhinos, elephants and leopards. However, aside from orangutans and various other primates, you are very unlikely to see any other large mammals here (or elsewhere in the park for that matter). The forests immediately surrounding Bukit Lawang are absolutely not pristine jungle – palm-oil plantations extend right up to the edge of the village and at weekends, when foreign tourists are joined by masses of domestic visitors, Bukit Lawang can feel as much like Tarzan country as a busy afternoon in a supermarket.

But don't let this put you off, because when you first come face to face with a tree-swinging gentle giant or spend the night under a tarp in the forest you'll quickly forget the tourist circus that accompanies a visit here.

The village is only 96km northwest of Medan.

Dangers & Annoyances

Not so much a danger as an annoyance: there are over 100 guides and rarely more than a few dozen tourists in town, which means that the guide harangue starts on the bus or at the airport before you've even left Medan. A friendly stranger, full of Bukit Lawang titbits, saddles up beside you and just so happens to be going in the same direction, or, imagine that, they're a guide. If you get cornered at the airport (we once had one latch onto us on the actual aeroplane!) they'll try to grab a bunch of other tourists and load you up into a minibus. Wherever you meet them, on arrival in Bukit Lawang they'll escort you to a guesthouse, sit you down and sign you up for a trek. There's actually nothing wrong with this and it can often be very useful. The trick is to be polite and feel no obligation to book anything unless you want to.

Many budget hotels in Medan also organise cut-price trekking tours. Most people have a good time on these but they're cut-price for a reason – don't expect top-quality guides and don't expect accommodation in any of the better guesthouses (ie those listed here). There's no reason to take one of these tours as everything can be organised within moments of arriving in Bukit Lawang.

Sights

Orangutan Feeding Centre WILDLIFE RESERVE

Bukit Lawang's famous orangutan centre was set up in 1973 to help primates readjust to the wild after captivity or displacement through land clearing. Many of the original duties of the centre have been moved to more remote locations, but twice-daily feedings are still provided to semidependent orangutans. These events are open to the public (no guide required) and provide one of the closest views of the forest ape outside the confines of a zoo.

During the centre's decades-long operation, it has introduced 200 orangutans into the jungle. Many of them had been kept as caged pets; the centre taught them how to forage for food in the wild, build nests, climb trees and other essentials for survival after release. The orangutans are also treated for diseases that they contracted during contact with humans. Today around 16 orangutang live in the vicinity of Bukit Lawang.

Once the apes are on their own in the wild, the centre still provides supplementary feedings in case of awkward transitions or demanding circumstances. These feedings consist of milk and bananas and are considered a fairly bland diet compared to the diversity of food found in the forest. The semiwild apes who appear at the centre's 'welfare' platform are typically nursing or pregnant females in need of an extra source of nutrition.

There are two feeding times a day: 8.30am to 9.30am and 3pm to 4pm. These are the only times visitors are allowed to enter the national park without a guide.

The feeding platform is located on the west bank of Sungai Bohorok within the park boundaries, about a 20-minute walk from the village. The river crossing to the park office is made by dugout canoe. Permits are required to enter the park (20,000Rp). Technically these are only available from the Bukit Lawang Visitors Centre in the village proper, not the office at the foot of the trail to the platform. In reality it's often possible to buy a ticket from the park office and either way you'll need to show a ticket here in order to be allowed to continue to the feeding platform. If you're heading out on a

THE NOTORIOUS MINA

The most well-known inhabitant of Bukit Lawang's jungle is a fiery female orangutan named Mina, who's earned a reputation among locals as the most feared, yet most loved, of the orangutans. She's known for her aggression towards humans – it seems every guide has a tale of a violent encounter with Mina at some point or another. She's attacked numerous guides as well as a few hapless tourists! Yet from the guides you'll hear nothing but love for this bad girl of the jungle, as nearly all run-ins are a result of tourists not heeding guides' advice and getting too close. Now estimated to be in her late 30s, Mina was once held captive as a pet and was one of the first orangutans released into the wild here. Her aggression is largely a result of her expectation of being fed by humans. She is the perfect case study as to why tourists should ensure that they take the proper precautions by never feeding or coming too close to these magnificent apes.

trek afterwards, your guide will normally get you a ticket beforehand, which you can use to visit the feeding platform as well. If you have a camera/video camera you'll have to pay an additional 50,000/150,000Rp at the office, with no refunds if orangutans don't come to the feeding platform – during peak fruit season they often don't. Get to the river crossing around 30 minutes before the scheduled feeding time as it can take a while to ferry everyone across.

Since 1996 the centre has been closed to new arrivals, as the park is considered to be saturated with orangutans. A replacement quarantine centre, just outside Medan, opened in 2002 to carry on the rehabilitation efforts, but it is not open to the public.

Activities

Trekking

Treks into the Gunung Leuser National Park require a guide and can last anywhere from three hours to several days. Most people opt for two days so that they can spend the night in the jungle, which increases their likelihood of seeing orangutans and other wildlife. It is best to hike in the smallest group possible and to set off as early as you can.

There are many guides and the choice can be intimidating. Despite the pressure, take your time in choosing a guide. Talk to returning trekkers and decide how much jungle time you really need.

If you just want a few souvenir pictures and stories, find a guide you like. People who trekked with guides from the village have mainly positive feedback, with the greatest kudos going to the nightly meals and campfire socials. Common complaints include guides who don't know enough about the flora and fauna, the bunching together of treks and the feeding of orangutans.

'Rafting' (an extra 120,000Rp per person) back to town, which actually involves rubber tubes tied together, is a popular option that allows you to trek deeper into the jungle and makes for a fun and relaxing way to finish your trek. Prices include a visit to the feeding centre, basic meals, guide fees, camping equipment and the park permit. Camping involves a tarpaulin sheet thrown over bamboo poles, with everyone sleeping in the same tent.

A word of warning: trekking in the jungle is no stroll in the park. You'll encounter steep, slippery ascents and precipitous drops amid intense humidity, so a good level of fitness is essential. The trails can be well-worn paths or barely visible breaks in the underbrush. Pack at least two bottles of water per day. If you don't have hiking boots, and have small feet, you may be able to buy a pair of cheap but reliable shoes with studded soles, the same as most guides wear, in town.

Short Walks

There are a number of short walks around Bukit Lawang that don't require guides or permits.

The **canal** that runs alongside the river is an easy stroll through the village. In the evening everything gets washed in the rushing waters: frolicking kids, soiled bums, dirty laundry. Activities usually considered private are social in the communal waters.

The most interesting walk, to a **bat cave**, takes 25 minutes and is signposted from the Ecolodge Bukit Lawang. This 2km walk passes through rubber plantations and patches of forest, and by a children's foster home. A lot of the trees are durian, so take

JUNGLE TREKKING FEES

Guide rates are fixed by the Sumatra Guide Association.

TREK DURATION	PRICE PER PERSON (3 OR MORE PEOPLE)	PRICE PER PERSON (1-2 PEOPLE)
½ day	180,000Rp	200,000Rp
1 day	300,000Rp	360,000Rp
2 days	600,000Rp	720,000Rp
3 days	900,000Rp	1,200,000Rp

care in late June and July when the spiked fruits crash to the ground (there are signs warning people not to linger). You'll need a torch (flashlight) to explore the cave. A further 2km will take you to the **ship cave**, so named because it looks like a ship – well, sort of.

Tubing

A shed along the river en route to the orangutan centre rents inflated truck inner tubes (16,000Rp per day), which can be used to ride the Sungai Bohorok rapids. On weekends, the river near the bridge resembles a water theme park, with Indonesian tourists having the time of their lives. But don't underestimate the river. Currents are extremely strong and when the water is high, tubing is officially off limits, though few will tell you this. Avoid the very last section as you approach the village centre.

Sleeping

The further upriver you go, the more likely you are to ogle the swinging monkeys and apes from your porch hammock. You won't find hot water or air-con at any of the guesthouses. The following are listed in geographic order from south to north.

TOP CHOICE **On The Rocks** BUNGALOW $
(☎0812 6303 1119; www.ontherocksbl.com; r 120,000-220,000Rp) More on the hill than on the rocks, the handful of 'tribal' huts here verge on being luxurious in a rustic kind of way. Each hut has a veranda and sunken bathroom, and all are shrouded in peace and beautiful views. The downside to all this tranquillity is that it's a fair old hike from all the action, so it's good it serves decent meals!

Jungle Inn GUESTHOUSE $
(☎0813 6550 5005; superdjoe@yahoo.com; d 50,000-300,000Rp) The last guesthouse along the strip near the park entrance, Jungle Inn is an old favourite of many a reader. One room overlooks a waterfall, while another incorporates the hill's rock face, and the bathroom sprouts a shower from living ferns.

Sam's Bungalows GUESTHOUSE $
(☎0813 7009 3597; samsbungalow@yahoo.com; r 100,000-300,000Rp) There's an excellent range of wooden tree houses here as well as more solidly built rooms painted in sunny Mediterranean colours with huge bathrooms and Italian rain showers.

Back to Nature GUESTHOUSE $
(☎0813 7565 7004; r 100,000-150,000Rp) A world away from the hustle of Bukit Lawang village, this new place has been causing some waves of excitement among travellers. The comfortable wooden rooms, raised off the ground on stilts, are a half-hour walk from the river crossing for the feeding centre and are set on a giant patch of private jungle. In fact, the owner feels so strongly about preserving the jungle that he has purchased a slab of forest that was otherwise destined to have become a palm-oil plantation. It offers its own jungle treks and can organise pick ups from Bukit Lawang.

Rain Forest GUESTHOUSE $
(Nora's Homestay; ☎0813 6207 0656; d 40,000-150,000Rp) Nora's cluster of wooden rooms set close to the gurgling river equals backpacker bliss. Cheaper rooms consist of just a mattress chucked on the floor and some share bathrooms, but pricier rooms are simple and comfortable. There's a friendly dining area (with Western meals like pasta, burgers and all the rest) and it's a super place to hook up with other travellers.

Green Hill GUESTHOUSE $
(☎0813 7034 9124; www.greenhill-bukitlawang.com; r incl breakfast 60,000-250,000Rp) Run by

an English conservation scientist and her Sumatran husband, Green Hill has two lovely stilt-high rooms ideal for couples, with en-suite bamboo-shoot showers that afford stunning jungle views while you wash. The food in the restaurant is good but service can be surly and woefully slow (we've waited two hours for a meal).

Garden Inn GUESTHOUSE **$**
(☎0813 9600 0571; www.bukitlawang-garden-inn.com; r 100,000-150,000Rp) A popular backpacker choice, the ever-growing Garden Inn empire spreads over several buildings, which house a wide array of accommodation, from cosy, wooden jungle shacks to pristine, modern white rooms. There's a sweet little cafe for swapping ape-spotting tales.

Ecolodge Bukit Lawang RESORT **$$**
(☎081 2607 9983; http://ecolodge.yelweb.org; s incl breakfast 155,000-325,000Rp, d incl breakfast 180,000-350,000Rp) Popular with package tourists, the village's most expensive lodging has a range of hotel-style rooms. There are many commendable attempts at ecofriendly business: an organic garden provides produce for the restaurant, a medicinal-plant garden preserves the pharmaceutical aspects of the jungle, and there's recycling. Children under 10 stay free. It's handy for those who just want a place to crash for the night but for more atmosphere head upriver. Note that every tout will try to get you to take a room here.

Eating & Drinking

All the guesthouses along the river en route to the park entrance serve Western food, barbecued fish, nasi goreng (fried rice), fruit salads and a laid-back ambience. This is also where the guides camp out for new arrivals.

If you can't survive without a Thai-style full-moon party, (very) tamed-down parties are held most Saturday nights at **Farina 53**, a guesthouse about halfway along the strip.

J@J INTERNATIONAL **$**
(mains 25,000-50,000Rp) This brand new, foreign-run restaurant and bar is a bit more upmarket than most of the jungle shacks around here. It offers the standard mix of Western and toned-down Indonesian fare.

Information

The nearby village of Gotong Royong, 2km southeast of Sungai Bohorok, is where most of the non-tourist-related facilities can be found. If you arrive by public bus it's about a 1km walk north to where the accommodation begins. There are no banks in these parts, but you'll find moneychangers along the strip and if you need a post office you can buy stamps from the shops and use a local postbox. There is a market on Fridays and Sundays in Bohorok town, 15km away, where you will also find the nearest police station and medical clinic.

Bukit Lawang Guide Association (⏰8am-2pm) This place distributes a rate sheet for hikes and can arrange guides.

Bukit Lawang Visitors Centre (⏰7am-3pm) Displays of flora and fauna found in Gunung Leuser National Park, plus a book of medicinal plants and their uses. Past visitors often record reviews of guides in the sign-in book. This is where you should come to get a park ticket. It's located down in the heart of the village.

Harmony Net (per hr 4000Rp; ⏰8am-midnight) Close to the Bukit Lawang Visitors Centre and with a dozen or so computers with fair connection speeds.

PHKA Permit Office (park entrance; ⏰8-10am & 3-4pm) Timed with the orangutan feedings, the rangers open up this office to check permits. If they're feeling kind they'll also sell you a permit here if you didn't have a chance to get one from the visitors centre.

Getting There & Away

There are direct buses to Medan's Pinang Baris bus terminal every half-hour between 5.30am and 5pm. There's also a tourist minibus (75,000Rp, three hours). Travel information for buses from Butik Lawang is shown below. For details on travelling between Bukit Lawang and Tangkahan, see p500.

DESTINATION	COST (RP)	DURATION (HR)
Berastagi	100,000	5
Parapat	150,000	7
Medan	10,000	4

Tangkahan

This is the place for a truly wild and off-the-map adventure. Having ticked off seeing the orangutans in Bukit Lawang, in-the-know ecotourists are now trickling north to experience the jungle aboard elephants in this undiscovered retreat.

Towards the end of the 1990s a few foreign ecologists and conscientious locals decided to take a stand against the palm-oil loggers working in this wild part of northern Sumatra. Armed with a few rifles and machetes, and using elephants to patrol the jungle against loggers and poachers, the locals have gradually lobbied the government into declaring the region a protected area. Fast forward 15 years and the once-doomed region is still home to all manner of apes, monkeys and, of course, elephants. Not so much a village as a bus stop, a park entrance and a handful of basic riverside bungalows on the wild banks of the Kualsa Buluh River, Tangkahan has a tiny community of amiable loggers-turned-guides selling an experience as close as you'll get to Tarzan living on this untamed isle.

Sights & Activities

For many, the **elephants** are the main draw here: you can give them their daily bath (100,000Rp). It's expensive but great fun; you get to scrub them down, tickle them behind the ears and, as a way of saying thank you, they'll shower you down afterwards with a squirt from their trunks. More elephant antics can be enjoyed on a one-hour elephant trek (650,000Rp). Remember that elephants need holidays too and so on Mondays and Thursdays there are no elephant-based activities.

It's worth bearing in mind that **elephants** (even domesticated ones) kill hundreds of people every year and you should exercise extreme caution in the vicinity of the elephants.

Tubing is also a popular activity (200,000Rp for half-a-day, including lunch).

For something a little cheaper (free) and more relaxing, there are some **hot springs** close to the Jungle Lodge.

Sleeping

Accommodation, which is concentrated on the opposite side of the river from where transport drops you off, is fairly limited. All of the guesthouses serve simple meals. The following are in the order you pass them from the river crossing.

Mega Inn GUESTHOUSE $

(☎0813 7021 1009; www.megainn.com; r 100,000Rp) The first place you come to after the river crossing has pretty bungalows made of twisted wood and some of the bathrooms contain such a mass of foliage they could almost be classed as jungles themselves.

Jungle Lodge GUESTHOUSE $

(☎0813 7633 4787; www.junglelodge.net; r 80,000-150,000Rp) The cottages at this popular place are scattered across the attractive gardens like fallen forest leaves. Some have fab river views. There's a large, thatched restaurant overlooking the bubbling river, and friendly staff.

Linnea Resort GUESTHOUSE $

(☎0812 6046 3071; s/d 150,000/160,000Rp) This new place has cottages scattered about a rock garden a little way back from the river. Although the rooms are arguably the best in the village it needs a little time for the gardens to really mature.

Getting There & Away

There are two direct buses that depart daily to Medan's Pinang Baris terminal (20,000Rp, four hours). Going the other way, you'll be pleased to hear that buses leave at 5.30am and 7.15am. To get to Tangkahan from Bukit Lawang you have a couple of options. You can take one of the many buses to Binjai (10,000Rp to 12,000Rp, 2½ hours). If you time it well you'll be able to get on one of the twice-daily buses from here direct to Tangkahan (25,000Rp, 2½ hours), otherwise take one to Tittamangga (20,000Rp, two hours) and from there hop on the back of a motorbike to Tangkahan (50,000Rp). Alternatively, any of the local guides will take you direct from Bukit Lawang on a moped (200,000Rp, three hours) – be warned that the road is treacherous and this is a very bouncy ride. Or you can do as most people do and team up with other travellers to hire a 4WD (500,000Rp to 600,00Rp, three hours). Most Medan-based travel agents can also arrange 4WD transport (600,000Rp, three to four hours depending on traffic).

Berastagi

☎0628 / POP 46,686

To escape from the infernal heat of sea-level Medan, the colonial Dutch traders climbed high into the lush, cool, volcanic hills. They took one look at the stunningly verdant, undulating landscape and decided to build a rural retreat where Berastagi (also called Brastagi) now stands.

Today weekending Medan folk and foreign visitors alike sigh a crisp, clear breath of relief when they arrive in this quaint agricultural escape situated high among Sumatra's steaming volcanoes. The town itself, a concrete jungle set amid beautiful surrounds, is not overly pretty, but it's an agricultural trade centre and its markets are always humming with activity. On Sundays, the largely Christian community takes the babies and Bibles out for worship.

Beyond the town are the green fields of the Karo Highlands, dominated by two volcanoes: Gunung Sinabung to the west and the smoking Gunung Sibayak to the north. You won't find lava in either Sibayak or Sinabung, but each still has the feel of everything you hoped to experience from an active volcano, with steamy gases gushing from the fumaroles like a mad scientist's laboratory. These volcanoes are a day hike apiece, making them two of Sumatra's most accessible volcanoes, and the primary reason why tourists get off the bus here.

Berastagi is at an altitude of 1300m, and the climate is deliciously cool, sometimes even cold.

Sights & Activities

Berastagi is underused as an escape from Indonesia's intensity. Most people spend a couple of days hiking here and then trek south to Danau Toba. But you can do a lot of unhindered wandering on foot and motorbike, and the town's slow vibe and cool temperatures invite you to stay a little longer.

There are some fine examples of traditional Karo Batak architecture in the villages around Berastagi. Most of the houses are no more than 60 years old – or possibly 100, but certainly not 400, as claimed by some guides.

Trails on both volcanoes are neither clearly marked nor well maintained, and it is easy to get lost or lose your footing. During the wet season, paths can be extremely slippery or even washed out. The weather is variable and views from either mountain are far from guaranteed. Be prepared for abrupt weather changes (fog, cold temperatures and rain can sneak up during a clear day). Bring supplies such as food, drink, rain gear and a torch, in case you get caught out after dark.

People have died on both mountains. A guide is a good idea.

Gunung Sibayak VOLCANO

(hot springs admission 3000-5000Rp) At 2094m, Gunung Sibayak is probably the most accessible of Indonesia's volcanoes. A guide is only essential if taking the route through the jungle, but if you're trekking alone it may be a good idea. Rates for guides are 150,000Rp for the easy way along the road and 250,000Rp through the jungle. The hike can be done in five hours return, and you should set out as early as possible.

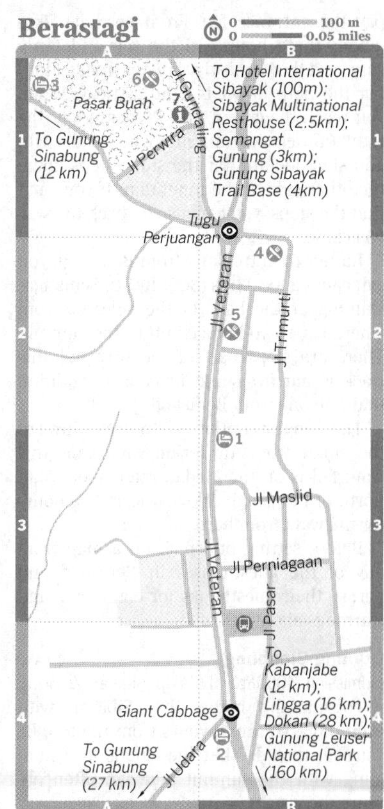

Berastagi

Sleeping

1 Losmen Sibayak Guesthouse B3
2 Wisma Sibayak B4
3 Wisma Sunrise View A1

Eating

4 Café Raymond B2
5 Family Baru B2
6 Fruit & Produce Market A1

Information

Sibayak Trans Tour &Travel ....(see 1)
7 Tourist Information Centre A1

There are three ways to tackle the climb, depending on your energy level. The easiest way is to take the track that starts to the northwest of Berstagi, a 10-minute walk past the Sibayak Multinational Resthouse. Take the left-hand path beside the hut where you pay the entrance fee. From here, it's 7km (about three hours) to the top and fairly easy to follow, mostly along a road. Finding the path down is a little tricky. When you reach the crater, turn 90 degrees to the right (anticlockwise), climb up to the rim and start looking for the stone steps down the other side of the mountain. If you can't find the steps, you can also go back the way you came.

Rather than trekking from Berastagi, you can catch a local bus (3000Rp) to Semangat Gunung at the base of the volcano, from where it's a two-hour climb to the summit. There are steps part of the way, but this track is narrower and in poorer condition than the one from Berastagi.

The longest option is to trek through the jungle from Air Terjun Panorama; this waterfall is on the Medan road, about 5km north of Berastagi. Allow at least five hours for the walk from here.

Before setting out, pick up a map from any of the guesthouses in Berastagi and peruse their guestbooks for comments and warnings about the hike.

Gunung Sinabung VOLCANO

(admission 4000Rp) This peak, at 2450m, is considerably higher than Sibayak, with even more stunning views from the top. Be warned, though, that the clouds love mingling with the summit and can often obscure the vista.

This mountain is much more bad tempered than Sibayak and you should take an experienced guide (350,000Rp), as hikers have gotten lost and died. The path up the mountain from Danau Kawar is fairly well-trodden by locals, but relying on a guide takes the guesswork out of timing your return to town or reading changing weather conditions. The climb takes seven to eight hours, depending on your skill and the descent route.

To reach the trailhead, take an *opelet* to Danau Kawar (8000Rp, 1½ hours). There is a scenic camp site surrounding Danau Kawar for those travelling with gear.

Lingga VILLAGE

(admission 4000Rp) The best-known and most visited of the villages around Berastagi is Lingga, a few kilometres northwest of Kabanjahe. There are about half-a-dozen traditional houses with characteristic horned roofs. Some, such as the *rumah rajah* (king's house), are occupied (by several families) and in good condition. Others, including the *sapo ganjang* (house for young unmarried men), are unused and in various stages of decay. You might be able to talk the ticket man into showing you the interior of one of the houses.

There are regular *opelet* to Lingga from Kabanjahe (2500Rp).

Dokan VILLAGE

The charming little village of Dokan is approximately 16km south of Kabanjahe. Around half-a-dozen traditional houses can be found here and they are all occupied, which immediately gives the place more interest than any of the sanitised museum-like traditional buildings you might have seen elsewhere. However, as they remain family homes you're unlikely to be invited inside to look around. You can get here by the occasional direct *opelet* from Kabanjahe (5000Rp).

Rumah Bolon PALACE

(admission 3000Rp; ⏲8am-6pm) This impressive palace complex on the edge of the village of Pematang Purba was the home of the Simalungan Batak chiefs until 1947 when the last one died. The well-tended site consists of a large main building that functioned as the king's quarters and a harem – today only bats flit through the room. The buffalo skulls inside the main building symbolise the power of the chief. The remainder of the complex consists of meeting halls, assistants' houses and rice-storage areas. There's little in the way of public transport to the site but it's easy to slot a visit into a journey between Berastagi and Danau Toba by private car.

Air Terjun Sipiso-Piso WATERFALL

These narrow but impressive falls cascade 120m down to the north end of Danau Toba, 24km from Kabanjahe and about 300m from the main road. It is fairly easy to get here by yourself; take a bus from Kabanjahe to Merek (10,000Rp) and then walk or hitch a ride on a motorbike.

Hot Springs HOT SPRINGS

(admission 3000-5000Rp) On the descent from Gunung Sibayak, you can stop off at the various hot springs in Semangat Gunung on the road back to Berastagi. You'll be disappointed if you're expecting natural springs; instead you'll find a complex of small concrete pools. As soon as you soak your aching muscles in the delightfully warm waters,

IN THE KNOW ON VOLCANOES

There's nothing like an exhausting hike up a volcano and a nervous peek into the pit to ignite an interest in earth science.

Inside both Sibayak and Sinabung are fumaroles, vents through which gases escape. Sulphur is the most pungent of the steaming vapours and causes difficulty in breathing if you get too close. Sulphur also lends its brilliant yellow colour to some of the surrounding rocks.

Volcanic rocks are classified by how much silica they contain. The easiest types to identify within a volcanic crater are the subsets of rhyolite: pumice and obsidian. The black, glassy obsidian is formed when lava cools quickly, typically a result of effusive lava flows. The white porous material that gives way when you walk on it is pumice, which is the solidified version of a frothy, gas-filled lava eruption.

you won't mind one bit. If you want privacy away from excitable children, it's a good idea to look at a few different places scattered along the road, most of which are empty.

Sleeping

Jl Veteran sees heavy traffic and many rooms in the centre of town are very noisy. Most provide detailed maps of Berastagi and the Karo Highlands.

TOP CHOICE **Sibayak Multinational Resthouse** GUESTHOUSE $

(☎91031; Jl Pendidikan 93; r with/without bathroom 250,000/150,000Rp) Set in immaculate gardens, surrounded by nothing but peace and quiet, and with the perfect hill-country vibe, the vast, modern rooms here virtually sparkle. There's hot water in the bathrooms of the pricier rooms and breakfast is included. The hotel is a short *opelet* ride north of town on the road to Gunung Sibayak.

Wisma Sibayak GUESTHOUSE $

(☎91104; Jl Udara 1; r without bathroom 50,000-60,000Rp, r with bathroom 100,000-200,000Rp; @📶) This is a real travellers' institution. It has tidy and spacious rooms, which are quiet and comfortable. Cheaper rooms have cold showers, pricier ones have hot-water showers. There's lots of excellent travel information, a friendly family feel, a decent restaurant and a big smile from the owner. Book ahead in high season.

Losmen Sibayak Guesthouse GUESTHOUSE $

(☎91122; dicksonpelawi@yahoo.com; Jl Veteran 119; r with bathroom 75,000Rp, r without bathroom 40,000-50,000Rp; @📶) Nice cheapies with a lot of Indonesian personality make this place feel more like a homestay. However, the cheapest rooms directly overlook the main road and are very noisy. Wi-fi in the lobby.

Wisma Sunrise View GUESTHOUSE $

(☎081 9740 6784; Jl Kaliaga; r 65,000-100,000Rp) Here you'll find very basic wood-lined rooms perched on the little hill that earns Sunrise its namesake view. More expensive rooms come with hot-water bathrooms. It's just far enough outside of town to be a convenient stroll, but it doesn't serve food.

Hotel Internasional Sibayak RESORT $$$

(☎20152; www.hotelsibayak.com; Jl Merdeka; d incl breakfast 750,000-1,900,000Rp, ste incl breakfast 2,400,000-4,000,000Rp; 📶) Wooden floors, generous beds, read-the-newspaper toilets: there's a lot right about the Internasional, except the price. Offers up to 40% discount – if you can eke out one of these, you'll earn a shiny frugal star.

Eating & Drinking

The rich volcanic soils of the surrounding countryside supply much of North Sumatra's produce, which passes through Berastagi's colourful **fruit and produce markets**. Passionfruit is a local speciality, as is *marquisa Bandung,* a large, sweet, yellow-skinned fruit. The *marquisa asam manis,* a purple-skinned fruit, makes delicious drinks.

Most of the budget hotels have restaurants, but head into town for more diversity. Along Jl Veteran, there's a variety of evening food stalls, as well as simple restaurants specialising in *tionghoa* (Chinese food). Because this is a Christian community, you'll see a lot of *babi* (pork) on the menu. Another local favourite is *pisang goreng* (fried banana).

Café Raymond INTERNATIONAL $

(Jl Trimurti 49; mains 8000-20,000Rp; ⏰7am-midnight) Berastagi's local bohemians hang out at Café Raymond, which serves fruit juices, beer and Western food.

Family Baru INDONESIAN $
(Jl Veteran; mains 10,000-20,000Rp; ⌚9am-10pm) Popular with local students, this place is half traditional warung and half Western-style cafe. The food is solidly local.

Information

There are several ATMs and banks.

Sibayak Trans Tour &Travel (☎91122; dicksonpelawi@yahoo.com; Jl Veteran 119) Your first and only port of call for almost any onward travel advice as well as local tours.

Tourist information centre (☎91084; Jl Gundaling 1; ⌚8am-5pm Mon-Sat) Has maps and can arrange guides. Opening hours are rather flexible.

Getting There & Away

The **bus terminal** (Jl Veteran) is conveniently located near the centre of town. You can also catch buses to Medan (10,000Rp, 2½ hours) anywhere along the main street; buses run to and from Padang Bulan in Medan between 6am and 8pm. Note that touts will add a few thousand to your ticket price. To reach Danau Toba without backtracking through Medan, catch an *opelet* to Kabanjahe (3000Rp, 15 minutes) and change to a bus for Pematangsiantar (20,000Rp, three hours), then connect with a Parapat-bound bus (10,000Rp, 1½ hours). It's a little bit of a pain, but it gets you there eventually. Berastagi is the southern approach for visits to Gunung Leuser National Park. To reach the park, catch a bus to Kutacane (50,000Rp, five hours).

Getting Around

Opelet to the surrounding villages leave from the bus terminal. They run every few minutes between Berastagi and Kabanjahe (3000Rp), the major population and transport centre of the highlands. Local *opelet* are most easily waved down from the clock tower in town.

Parapat

☎0625

The mainland departure point for Danau Toba, Parapat has everything a transiting tourist needs: transport, lodging and supplies.

The commercial sector of the town is clumped along the Trans-Sumatran Hwy (Jl SM Raja) and has banks, ATMs and other services. The bus terminal is 2km east of town, but most buses pick up and drop off passengers at ticket agents along the highway or at the pier.

Sleeping & Eating

You'll have to crash for the night if your bus gets in after the last boat to Samosir. The highway strip (Jl SM Raja) is well equipped to feed the passing traveller, with every variety of Indonesian cuisine.

Charlie's Guesthouse GUESTHOUSE $
(☎0821 6622 3027; Jl Tiga Raya 7; r 70,000Rp) Located beside the ferry dock, Charlie's is cheap and handy for a quick getaway. It's run by a local Toba music legend.

Hotel Sedayu HOTEL $
(☎41260; Jl SM Raja 171A; r 79,000-199,000; wi-fi) Not far from the bus station, this relatively new place has cheap and clean economy rooms with shared bathrooms and somewhat fancier standard rooms.

Getting There & Away

The **bus terminal** (Jl SM Raja) is about 2km east of town on the way to Bukittinggi, but it is not frequently used (so say the travel agents). There are plenty of tourist minibuses and cars heading off to the most popular destinations. The main operator is **Bagus Taxis** (☎41747) next to the ferry pier. For details of ferries to Pulau Samosir, see p511

Getting Around

Opelet shuttle constantly between the ferry dock and the bus terminal (2000Rp).

Danau Toba

☎0625 / POP 517, 000

Danau Toba has been part of traveller folklore for decades. This grand ocean-blue lake, found high up among Sumatra's volcanic peaks, is where the amiable Christian Batak people reside. The secret of this almost mythical place was opened up to travellers by the intrepid, and Tuk Tuk – the village on the lake's inner island – became as much a highlight for Southeast Asian shoestringers as Haad Rin and Kuta. It was almost overrun with tourism: wild full-moon parties would kick off, and travellers in beach-bum mode would get 'stuck' on the island for months on end. Whilst the travelling world has hardly forgotten about Toba, those heady party days are certainly a thing of the past. Nowadays the Batak people continue

TRANSPORT FROM PARAPAT

DESTINATION	BUS	TOURIST MINIBUS
Berastagi	100,000Rp/4hr	n/a
Bukittinggi	170,000-180,000Rp/15hr	250,000Rp/15hr
Medan	22,000Rp/5hr	65,000Rp/4hr
Padang	190,000Rp/18hr	280,000/18hr
Sibolga	60,000-75,000Rp/6hr	100,000-150,000Rp/6hr

to warmly open their arms to travellers after a lazy, low-key lakeside sojourn.

Expect a chorus of '*horas*' ('welcome') to greet you at every turn, as the locals quietly strum away the afternoon on their guitars while passing around a flagon of jungle juice.

Danau Toba is the largest lake in Southeast Asia, covering a massive 1707 sq km. In the middle of this huge expanse is Pulau Samosir, a wedge-shaped island almost as big as Singapore that was created by an eruption between 30,000 and 75,000 years ago. Well, Bahasa Indonesia calls it an island, but those visiting the west of Toba will discover that Samosir isn't actually an island at all. It's linked to the mainland by a narrow isthmus at the town of Pangururan – and then cut again by a canal.

Directly facing Parapat is another peninsula occupied by the village of Tuk Tuk, which has Samosir's greatest concentration of tourist facilities. Tomok, a few kilometres south of Tuk Tuk, is the main village on the east coast of the island. Pangururan is the largest town on the west coast.

Sights

The following sights and activities are located around Danau Toba.

King Sidabutar Grave HISTORIC SITE
(admission by donation; dawn-dusk) The Batak king who adopted Christianity is buried in Tomok, a village 5km southeast of Tuk Tuk. The king's image is carved on his tombstone, along with those of his bodyguard and Anteng Melila Senega, the woman the king is said to have loved for many years without fulfilment. The tomb is also decorated with carvings of *singa*, mythical creatures with grotesque three-horned heads and bulging eyes. Next to the king's tomb is the tomb of the missionary who converted the tribe and an older Batak royal tomb, which souvenir vendors say is used as a multilingual fertility shrine for childless couples.

The tombs are 500m up a narrow lane lined with souvenir stalls. Very close by are some well-preserved traditional Batak houses, which some might find more interesting.

Stone Chairs HISTORIC SITE
(admission by donation, guides 20,000Rp; 8am-6pm) Ambarita, about 5km north of the Tuk Tuk Peninsula, has a group of 300-year-old stone chairs where important matters were discussed among village elders and wrongdoers were tried – then apparently led to a further group of stone furnishings where the accused were bound, blindfolded, sliced and rubbed with garlic and chilli before being beheaded.

Guides love to play up the story and ask for volunteers to demonstrate the process. It is customary to pay a small fee for the tale, or risk being turned into a garlic-and-chilli-flavoured dinner!

Museum Huta Bolon Simanindo MUSEUM
(admission 30,000Rp; 10am-5pm) At the northern tip of Pulau Samosir, in the village of Simanindo, there's a fine old traditional house that has been restored and now functions as a museum. It was formerly the home of Rajah Simalungun, a Batak king, and his 14 wives. Originally, the roof was decorated with 10 buffalo horns, which represented the 10 generations of the dynasty.

The museum has a small, interesting collection of brass cooking utensils, weapons, Dutch and Chinese crockery, sculptures and Batak carvings.

Displays of traditional **Batak dancing** are performed at 10.30am from Monday to Saturday if enough tourists show up. Put your dancing shoes on if you attend because they love to make foreigners get up and dance around like fools.

The village of Simanindo is 15km from Tuk Tuk and is accessible with a hired motorbike.

Batak Graves HISTORIC SITE

The road that follows the northern rind of Samosir between Simanindo and the town of Pangururan is a scenic ride through the Bataks' embrace of life and death. In the midst of the fertile rice fields are large multistorey graves decorated with the distinctive Batak-style house and a simple white cross. Reminiscent of Thai spirit houses, Batak graves reflect much of the animistic attitudes of sheltering the dead.

Cigarettes and cakes are offered to the deceased as memorials or as petitions for favours. Typical Christian holidays, such as Christmas, dictate special attention to the graves.

Activities

Cycling & Motorcycling

Pulau Samosir's sleepy roads make the island perfect for exploring by motorbike or bicycle. Zipping through the scenic countryside enclosed by lush volcanic mountains and the stunning lake is the highlight of many who visit here. The rice paddies and friendly villages are cultivated around sober Protestant-style churches and tombs merging traditional Batak architecture and Christian crosses. Motorbikes (70,000Rp per day) and bicycles (25,000Rp) can be hired all over Tuk Tuk.

Swimming

Danau Toba reaches a depth of 450m in places and is refreshingly cool. The best swimming on the south coast is said to be at Carolina Cottages, and many cottages on the north coast maintain weed-free swimming.

Across the isthmus, just before Pangururan, there are some *mata air panas* (hot springs) that the locals are extremely proud of. Most foreigners look around at the litter and decide that the waters are too hot.

Trekking

If you don't fully succumb to Samosir's anaesthetising atmosphere, there are a couple of interesting treks across the island. The

THE BATAKS

British traveller William Marsden astonished the 'civilised' world in 1783 when he returned to London with an account of a cannibalistic kingdom in the interior of Sumatra that, nevertheless, had a highly developed culture and a system of writing. The Bataks have been a subject of fascination ever since.

The Bataks are a Proto-Malay people descended from Neolithic mountain tribes from northern Thailand and Myanmar (Burma) who were driven out by migrating Mongolian and Siamese tribes. When the Bataks arrived in Sumatra they trekked inland, making their first settlements around Danau Toba, where the surrounding mountains provided a natural protective barrier. They lived in virtual isolation for centuries.

The Bataks were among the most warlike peoples in Sumatra and villages were constantly feuding. They were so mistrustful that they did not build or maintain natural paths between villages, or construct bridges. The practice of ritual cannibalism, which involved eating the flesh of a slain enemy or a person found guilty of a serious breach of *adat* (traditional law), survived among the Toba Bataks until 1816.

Today there are more than six million Bataks, divided into six main linguistic groups, and their lands extend 200km north and 300km south of Danau Toba.

The Bataks have long been squeezed between the Islamic strongholds of Aceh and West Sumatra and, despite several Acehnese attempts to conquer and convert, it was the European missionaries who finally quelled the waters with Christianity.

The majority of today's Bataks are Protestant Christians, although many still practise elements of traditional animist belief and ritual. The Bataks believe the banyan to be the tree of life; they tell a legend of their omnipotent god Ompung, who created all living creatures by dislodging decayed branches of a huge banyan into the sea.

Music is a great part of Batak culture and a Batak man is never far from his guitar. The Bataks are also famous for their powerful and emotive hymn singing. Most of their musical instruments are similar to those found elsewhere in Indonesia – cloth-covered copper gongs in varying sizes struck with wooden hammers; a small two-stringed violin, which makes a pure but harsh sound; and a kind of reedy clarinet.

BATAK PUPPET DANCE

A purely Batak tradition is the *sigalegale* puppet dance, once performed at funerals but now more often a part of wedding ceremonies. The life-sized puppet, carved from the wood of a banyan tree, is dressed in the traditional costume of red turban, loose shirt and blue sarong. The *sigalegale* stand up on long, wooden boxes where the operator makes them dance to gamelan (percussion orchestra) music accompanied by flute and drums.

One story of the origin of the *sigalegale* puppet concerns a widow who lived on Samosir. Bereft and lonely after the death of her husband, she made a wooden image of him and whenever she felt lonely hired a *dalang* (puppeteer and storyteller) to make the puppet dance and a *dukun* (mystic) to communicate with the soul of her husband.

Whatever its origins, the *sigalegale* soon became part of Batak culture and were used at funeral ceremonies to revive the souls of the dead and to communicate with them. Personal possessions of the deceased were used to decorate the puppet, and the *dukun* would invite the deceased's soul to enter the wooden puppet as it danced on top of the grave.

trails aren't well marked and can be difficult to find, but ask at any of the guesthouses for a map. In the wet season (December to March) the steep inclines are very muddy and slippery and can be quite dangerous.

The central highlands of Samosir are about 700m above the lake and on a clear day afford stunning views of mist-cloaked mountains. The top of the escarpment forms a large plateau and at its heart is a small lake, Danau Sidihoni. Samosir's vast tracts of jungle have long since vanished and the only forest you will pass through on either walk is pine – even this is only in small areas. However, there are many interesting cinnamon, clove and coffee plantations and some beautiful waterfalls.

Most people opt for the short trek from Ambarita to Pangururan. It can be done in a day if you're fit, start very early and catch the bus back from Pangururan (the last one is at 5pm), though it's best to stay overnight in one of the villages. The path starts opposite the bank in Ambarita. Keep walking straight at the escarpment and take the path to the right of the graveyard. The three-hour climb to the top is hard and steep. The path then leads to Partungkaon village (also called Dolok); here you can stay at **Jenny's Guest House** (r 25,000-30,000Rp) or **John's Losmen** (r 25,000-30,000Rp). From Partungkaon, it's about five hours' walk to Pangururan via Danau Sidihoni.

Another enjoyable walk is the three-hour hike between the village of Partungkaon and the Forest House 1, a guesthouse close to Danau Sidihoni.

Bring along wet-weather gear and some snacks. There are no warung along the way but you should be able to buy cups of coffee or even arrange accommodation at villages en route.

Guides aren't essential but they are a good idea if you're alone. The going rate is 150,000Rp and Liberta Homestay (p508) can arrange one.

Festivals & Events

Danau Toba Festival CULTURAL

The week-long Danau Toba Festival is held every year in mid-June. Canoe races are a highlight of the festival, but there are also Batak cultural performances.

Sleeping

The best sleeping options are along the north and south coasts, where little guesthouses are tucked in between village chores: washing the laundry on the rocks and collecting the news from neighbours.

Samosir Cottages HOTEL $

(☎451 170; www.samosircottages.com; Tuk Tuk; r 70,000-500,000Rp; @) A good choice for travellers who want to hang out with young like-minded folk and boisterous young staff. The rooms span a wide variety of prices and styles and range from dark, cell-like cheapies to quite plush rich-boy rooms. It has every traveller service you can imagine – travel agency, tour guides, internet, sunloungers, children's playground and a busy restaurant. The swimming is pretty good too.

Bagus Bay Homestay GUESTHOUSE $
(☎451 287; www.bagus-bay.page.tl; Tuk Tuk; r without/with bathroom from 30,000/75,000Rp; @☜) Rooms in traditional Batak houses overlook avocado trees, a children's playground and a volleyball court. The cheaper rooms are fairly uninspiring, but the more expensive ones come with great bathrooms (complete with hot water – a rarity for a cheap hotel in these parts) and the pot plants add a nice green touch. At night its restaurant, which has frequent film evenings, is a lively spot for travellers to congregate.

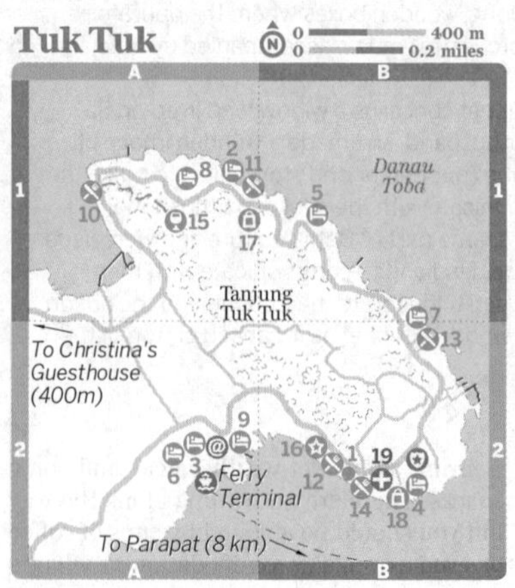

Tuk Tuk

Activities, Courses & Tours
1 Heddy's Cooking Class B2

Sleeping
2 Anju Cottages A1
3 Bagus Bay Homestay A2
4 Carolina Cottages B2
5 Harriara Guesthouse B1
6 Liberta Homestay A2
7 Merlyn Guesthouse B1
8 Samosir Cottages A1
9 Tabo Cottages A2

Eating
10 Bamboo Restaurant & Bar A1
11 Jenny's Restaurant A1
12 Juwita Café B2
13 Rumba Pizzeria & Homestay B2
14 Today's Cafe B2

Drinking
15 Brando's Blues Bar A1

Entertainment
16 Roy's Pub B2

Shopping
17 Gokhan Library A1
18 Penny's Books B2

Information
19 Health Centre B2

Tabo Cottages BUNGALOW $$
(☎451 318; www.tabocottages.com; Tuk Tuk; r 235,000-275,000, cottage 350,000-450,000Rp; @☜) The swankiest accommodation on the island. This German-run lakeside place has beautiful traditional-style Batak houses that come with huge bathrooms and hammocks swinging lazily on the terrace. The homemade cakes are worthy of mention as well.

Liberta Homestay GUESTHOUSE $
(☎451 035; liberta_homestay@yahoo.com.co.id; Tuk Tuk; r with bathroom 40,000-70,000Rp, r without bathroom 25,000Rp; ☜) This place may have only limited lake views, but a chill universe is created here by a lazy-day garden and arty versions of traditional Batak houses. Crawling around the balconies and shortened doors of the rooms feels like being a deck hand on a Chinese junk. The popular Mr Moon is a great source of travel information.

Harriara Guesthouse GUESTHOUSE $
(☎451 183; Tuk Tuk; r 100,000Rp) This guesthouse has a top-notch lakeside setting, riotous tropical flower gardens and rooms that are so sparkling clean you'd never guess they were nearly 25 years old! If there's nobody at the reception enquire in the nearby restaurants.

Merlyn Guesthouse GUESTHOUSE $
(☎0813 6116 9130; Tuk Tuk; r 60,000-70,000Rp) Situated right on the lake shore, this place has been given a much-needed makeover that's really succeeded in breathing new life into it. Choose between sleeping in a traditional wooden Batak house with dwarf-sized doors or a modern room in sunny colours with a hot-water bathroom.

Christina's Guesthouse GUESTHOUSE $
(☎0812 6340 1142; Tuk Tuk; r 60,000, batak house 120,000Rp) Cheap and laid-back, Christina's is out of the way of the main backpacker scene and has a couple of rooms as well as a large, traditional Batak house overlooking the lake. It can organise trekking guides.

Carolina Cottages RESORT $
(☎415 210; www.carolina-cottages.com; Tuk Tuk; r 45,000-180,000Rp; @📶) More popular with holidaying Indonesians than foreigners, this resort-like place is quite faded but the rooms are a good size and it has plenty of facilities, including good lake swimming and a diving board.

Anju Cottages GUESTHOUSE $
(☎451 265; Tuk Tuk; r 60,000-100,000Rp) Anju is a peaceful option right on the waterfront. It has plain rooms, some of which have giant pitched roofs.

Eating

The guesthouses tend to mix eating and entertainment in the evening. Most restaurants serve the Batak speciality of barbecued carp (most from fish farms), sometimes accompanied by traditional dance performances.

Magic or 'special' omelettes are commonly seen on restaurant menus. We probably don't need to tell you that the mushrooms contained in these are not of the sort that you can buy at your local supermarket.

TOP CHOICE **Jenny's Restaurant** INTERNATIONAL $
(Tuk Tuk; mains 20,000-50,000Rp) Although there are lots of different options on the menu at Jenny's, there's only really one thing to eat – grilled or fried lake fish with chips and salad. Follow it up with the fruit pancake, which is almost embarrassingly well proportioned. We enjoyed few meals in Sumatra more than this one. With 24 hours notice they can prepare the Batak wedding-day dish – an entire spit-roasted pig – but do bring friends to share it or you really will be a pig!

Today's Cafe INTERNATIONAL $
(Tuk Tuk; mains 20,000-40,000Rp) This little wooden shack has a laid-back vibe just in keeping with Tuk Tuk life. It's run by a couple of friendly ladies who whip up some fabulous Batak dishes such as *sak sang* (chopped pork with brown coconut sauce and cream and a wealth of spices). It also does some mighty fine pasta dishes, juices and breakfasts. Everything comes served with a dollop of easy chit-chat.

Bamboo Restaurant & Bar INTERNATIONAL $
(Tuk Tuk; mains 20,000-50,000Rp) With incredible lake views, Bamboo is a stylish place to watch the sun slink away, with cosy cushion seating, a down-tempo mood and a reliable menu. Mixes some good cocktails, too.

Rumba Pizzeria & Homestay INTERNATIONAL $
(Tuk Tuk; mains 20,000-70,000Rp) On Saturdays Rumba will stay open late to show English Premiership football, served with delicious pizza where you pick your own ingredients.

COOKING COURSES

Sign up for **Heddy's Cooking Class** (☎451217; 300,000Rp; ⏰1-4pm) at **Juwita Café** (mains 20,000-40,000Rp) and you can learn to cook an Indonesian banquet to impress the folks back home. The three-hour course covers a vegetarian, a chicken and a fish dish, as well as a dessert of your choice. You need to reserve in person the day before. If making your dinner just sounds like too much effort, at least come and eat at the Juwita Café, which has a menu stuffed with decent Indonesian and Batak specials.

Drinking & Entertainment

On most nights, music and spirits fill the night air with the kind of camaraderie that only grows in small villages. The Toba Bataks are extremely musical, and passionate choruses erupt from invisible corners.

Today the parties are all local – celebrating a wedding, a new addition on a house or the return of a Toba expat. Invitations are gladly given and should be cordially accepted.

Bagus Bay Homestay and Samosir Cottages (p507) both have traditional Batak music and dance performances on Wednesday and Saturday evenings at 8.15pm.

Brando's Blues Bar BAR
(☎451 084; Tuk Tuk) There are a handful of foreigner-oriented bars, such as this one, in between the local jungle-juice cafes. Happy 'hour' is a civilised 6pm to 10pm.

Roy's Pub LIVE MUSIC
(Tuk Tuk; ⏰9pm-1am) Has live music (normally local rock bands) several nights a week (Tuesday, Thursday and Saturday) in a graffiti-splattered building. Provides free transport back to your hotel if you're out late.

Shopping

Samosir's souvenir shops carry a huge range of cheap and tacky cotton T-shirts. For something slightly more original, local Gayo embroidery is made into a range of bags, cushion covers and place mats.

Around Tuk Tuk there are numerous woodcarvers selling a variety of figures, masks, boxes and *porhalaan* (traditional Batak calendars), as well as some traditional musical instruments.

Better load up on reading material here, because the rest of Sumatra is a desert for the printed word. **Penny's Books** (Tuk Tuk) and **Gokhan Library** (Tuk Tuk) have used and rental books, plus DVD hire for rainy days.

Information

The following facilities are all located in Tuk Tuk. There is a small **police station** at the top of the road leading to the Carolina Cottages.

INTERNET ACCESS Internet and wi-fi access is available at many of the guesthouses and some restaurants. Cheaper places might charge 10,000Rp per hour for this; more expensive places provide it for free. If you're staying in an unwired guesthouse then **Toba Internet Café** (per hr 8000Rp; ⏲8am-9.30pm) can put you in contact with the world beyond Samosir.

MEDICAL SERVICES There's a small 24-hour **health centre** (☎451 075) close to the turn-off to Carolina Cottages, at the southern end of the peninsula. It's equipped to cope with cuts, bruises and other minor problems.

MONEY Be sure to change your money before you get to Samosir. Exchange rates at the island's hotels and moneychangers are pretty awful.

POST Samosir's only **post office** is in Ambarita, but several shops in Tuk Tuk sell stamps and have postboxes.

Getting There & Away

BOAT Ferries between Parapat and Tuk Tuk (7000Rp) operate about every hour from 8.30am to 6pm. Ferries stop at Bagus Bay (35 minutes); other stops are by request. The first and last ferries from Tuk Tuk leave at about 7am and 4pm respectively; check exact times with your hotel. When leaving for Parapat, stand on your hotel jetty and wave a ferry down. Five ferries a day shuttle vehicles and people between Ajibata, just south of Parapat, and Tomok. There are five departures per day between 7am and 9pm. The passenger fare is 5000Rp. Cars cost 95,000Rp, and places can be booked in advance at the **Ajibata office** (☎41194) or the **Tomok office** (☎451185).

BUS To get a public bus (rather than the more expensive tourist taxis from Parapat) to Berastagi from Samosir, you'll have to catch a bus from Tomok to Pangururan (12,000Rp, 45 minutes), from where you take another bus to Berastagi (35,000Rp, three hours). This bus goes via Sidikalang, which is also a transfer point to Kutacane and Tapaktuan (on the west coast). Most guesthouses and travel agencies can pre-book bus tickets from Parapat for you. See p505 for information on bus travel to/from Danau Toba.

Getting Around

Local buses serve the whole of Samosir except Tuk Tuk, which is an inconvenience for those wanting to explore the island. The peaceful, well-maintained roads are perfect for travelling by motorbike or bicycle. You can rent motorcycles in Tuk Tuk for 70,000Rp a day, which includes petrol and a helmet. Bicycle hire costs from 25,000Rp per day. Minibuses run between Tomok and Ambarita (3000Rp), continuing to Simanindo (6000Rp) and Pangururan (12,000Rp). The road through the neck of the peninsula is a good spot to flag down these minibuses. Services dry up after 5pm.

Sibolga

☎0631 / POP 79,000

The departure point for boats to Nias, Sibolga is a west-coast port town renowned for its touts. As tourist numbers decline, the hassles have diminished to a fish boil of touts when you step off the bus or boat.

Most boats like to get in and out of Sibolga as soon as possible, so it's best to arrive as early in the day as possible to ensure a place on a boat departing that day.

Dangers & Annoyances

Dragging around surf gear can invite inflated prices: either be willing to bargain hard or accept a degree of extra 'service'.

A more serious scam involves being detained on suspicion of carrying drugs. Some travellers have reported being searched and intimidated by groups of uniformed officials demanding bribes before releasing them.

Don't leave your bags unattended or with a 'helpful' guide.

Sights

Most people, in their haste to get to offshore isles, seem to forget that Sibolga sits on the shores of the Indian Ocean and therefore is no sloucher in the sea-and-sand department. **Pantai Pandan** is a popular white-sand beach at the village of Pandan, 11km north of Sibolga. A few hundred metres further on is **Pantai Kalangan**. Both beaches get very crowded at weekends, but are good places to pass the time while you're waiting to catch a boat from Sibolga. *Opelet* run to the beaches all day (3000Rp).

Sleeping & Eating

Decent accommodation isn't a Sibolga strong point. There is a handful of skanky losmen (a kind of budget accommodation) near the ferry terminal, which charge about 50,000Rp a room.

There are plenty of Padang restaurants and coffee shops directly across the street from the harbour.

Hotel Wisata Indah RESORT **$$**
(☎23688; Jl Katamso 51; r incl breakfast from 380,000Rp; ❄🏊) The only upmarket hotel in town, but well past its prime. The Wisata Indah has a pool, comfortable rooms and sea views. Nonguests can use the pool and showers for a day-use fee.

Hotel Pasar Baru HOTEL **$**
(☎22167; cnr Jl Imam Bonjol & Raja Junjungan; d with fan 120,000Rp, d with air-con 180,000-360,000Rp; ❄) A decent enough place to sleep in a pinch, but many rooms suffer from road noise.

Sibolga Square INDONESIAN **$**
(Sibolga Sq; mains 10,000-20,000Rp) At night this semi-pedestrianised street fills with food hawkers and the tempting aromas from dozens of different stalls fills the air.

Information

BNI Bank (Jl Katamso) It is advisable to change money here or to use the ATM as options on Pulau Nias are limited.

Getting There & Away

BOAT Ferries to Pulau Nias leave from the harbour at the end of Jl Horas. There are two port options for Nias: the capital city of Gunung Sitoli, which is at the north of the island and a three-hour bus ride from the surf break; and Teluk Dalam, which is in the south and a 15-minute ride away. Boats to Teluk Dalam are the obvious choice but they don't run every day. **ASDP** (☎25076), in front of the harbour, runs a modern passenger and car ferry (economy/air-con/cabin 70,000/105,000/180,000Rp). The air-con class is the best value: seats recline, and the room is fairly cool and generally quiet. Ferries generally leave one to two hours late. If you arrive in Sibolga and are told you have just missed the boat it is often worth going to the harbour yourself to verify this. Theoretically you don't have to pay extra to carry surfboards on either service but this is not always the case. Boats leave at 8pm for Gunung Sitoli on Tuesday, Thursday and Saturday, and for Teluk Dalam on Monday, Wednesday and Friday. There are no services on Sunday.

BUS The bus terminal is on Jl SM Raja, 2km from the harbour. You can ask the bus driver to drop you off at the harbour. A becak between the two should be 5000Rp.

PULAU NIAS

The Indian Ocean roars onto Indonesia, arriving in one of the world's most spectacular surf breaks here on lonely Pulau Nias: a sizeable but solitary rock off the northern Sumatran coast. Surfers have been coming here for decades for the waves on superb Teluk Sorake, which has deservedly kept this far-flung island on the international surfing circuit. Away from the waves, the ancient megalithic monuments and traditional architecture will satisfy the hunger of any culture vulture.

The locals have a reputation for being somewhat unfriendly and there can be some bad vibes in the water. However, if you come with a relaxed vibe then chances are you'll get along just fine.

The tragic 2004 tsunami and the following aftershock, four months later, resulted in

TRANSPORT FROM SIBOLGA

DESTINATION	BUS	TOURIST MINIBUS
Bukittinggi	90,000Rp/12hr	120,000Rp/12hr
Medan	75,000-85,000Rp/11hr	120,000Rp/10hr
Padang	100,000Rp/14hr	135,000Rp/14hr
Parapat	60,000-75,000Rp/6hr	100,000-150,000Rp/6hr

the deaths of over 600 people and the flattening of the capital city.

History

Local legend tells it that Niassans are the descendants of six gods who came to earth and settled in the central highlands. Anthropologists link them to just about everyone: the Bataks of Sumatra, the Naga of Assam in India, the aborigines of Taiwan and various Dayak groups in Kalimantan.

Nias history is the stuff of campfire tales in which locals practised headhunting and human sacrifice long after the rest of the world started fainting at the sight of blood.

Traditionally, Niassan villages were presided over by a village chief, who headed a council of elders. Beneath the aristocratic upper caste were the common people, and below them the slaves, who were often traded. Until the first years of the 19th century, Nias' only connection with the outside world was through the slave trade.

Sometimes villages would band together to form federations, which often fought each other. Prior to the Dutch conquest and the arrival of missionaries, intervillage warfare was fast and furious, spurred on by the desire for revenge, slaves or human heads. Heads were needed for stately burials, wedding dowries and the construction of new villages.

When the people weren't warring, they were farming, a tradition that continues today. They cultivated yams, rice, maize and taro, despite the thick jungle, and raised pigs as a source of food and a symbol of wealth and prestige; the more pigs you had, the higher your status in the village. Gold and copper work, as well as woodcarving, were important industries.

The indigenous religion was thought to have been a combination of animism and ancestor worship, with some Hindu influences. Today the dominant religions on Nias

Pulau Nias

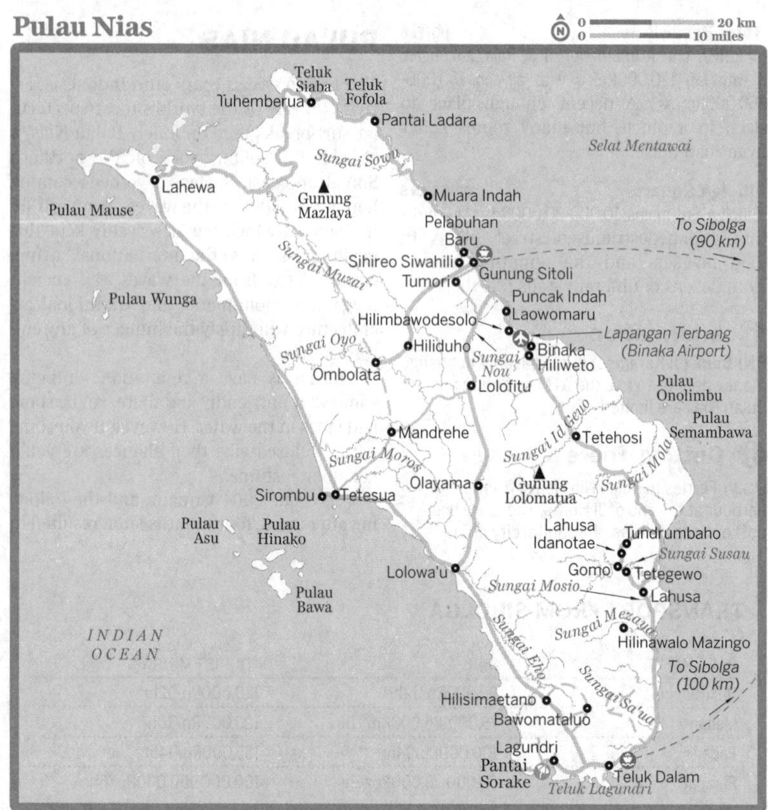

WORTH A TRIP

SURFING'S NEW FRONTIERS

If Nias was the original surfer paradise and the Mentawai Islands are today's flavour of the month, then tomorrow's slice of surf paradise could be the **Telo Islands**, also known as the Batu Islands. This group of islands sits to the north of the main Mentawain island of Siberut and, until recently, it was almost completely unknown to the outside world. Today liveaboard surf-charter boats have started scouting out the reefs here and a couple of surf camps have sprung up. The two best-known surf camps here, **Telo Island Lodge** (www.teloislandlodge.com) and **Resort Latitude Zero** (www.resortlatitudezero.com), have luxury beachside cottages, swimming pools, trained chefs and private plane and speedboat transfers. For a more affordable, but still very comfortable, option, try **Surfing Village** (www.surfing-village.com), which is run by the ever-helpful Mario Fernandes, a Brazilian transplant who guarantees you a good time. Non-surfing travellers are very rare visitors to the Telo Islands, but if you have patience and a sense of adventure, they offer enormous potential for beach lounging, village living and snorkelling. Ferries travel from Nias every other day to the Telo Islands and irregular boats sail between the Telo Islands and Padang. You can fly the same routes once or twice a week with NBA. Cheap and basic losmen (budget accommodation) can be found in the small towns and hiring a boat to check out the islands shouldn't prove difficult.

But if surfing the Telo Islands sounds a bit tame, you don't even have to stick to the coast for maybe the most adventurous, and certainly the most novel, surf destination in all of Indonesia. **Bono** (also known as Seven Ghosts) is a tidal bore wave that breaks on spring tides halfway up a slug-brown river somewhere in the jungles north of Pekenbaru in the remotest reaches of Riau state. When video and photos appeared in 2010 of ex-world-surf champion Tom Curren surfing phenomenal river-borne waves that put many ocean-borne waves to shame, many surfers wondered if they were the butt of an elaborate April Fool's joke. But no, Bono is indeed a real wave and a surf camp has recently opened here allowing anyone the opportunity to surf one of the planet's most perfectly unlikely waves. For more, see www.bonosurf.com.

are Christianity and Islam, overlaid with traditional beliefs.

The island did not come under full Dutch control until 1914. Today's population of about 756,000 is spread through more than 650 villages, most inaccessible by road.

Dangers & Annoyances

Chloroquine-resistant malaria has been reported on Nias, so be sure to take appropriate precautions.

Nias is one of the few places in Sumatra where visitors can expect a bit of hassle, in the form of financial requests (sometimes veiled, sometimes not) and some aggression in the water. After the earthquakes and tsunamis of a few years ago, many generous people who had a relationship with Nias have sponsored the rebuilding of local houses and bungalows destroyed by the tsunami, ostensibly in exchange for free accommodation, but more importantly as true grass-roots giving. The downside is that some locals view every new arrival here as a possible donor and the sales pitch can come from your losmen or from a stranger you meet on the beach, blurring the line between charity and con game. Unless you have a relationship with a family, it is not advisable to expect that your donation will be spent as promised.

Renting surf gear on the island is still a source of unexpected headaches. Be sure you pay a fair price; if it is too cheap, you'll probably pay for it at the end with inflated damage costs.

ℹ Getting There & Away

AIR Binaka airport is 17km south of Gunung Sitoli. In all cases extra fees apply for surfboards.

BOAT Ferries link Nias with the mainland town of Sibolga. **ASDP** (Jl Yos Sudarso) has ticket offices at the ferry ports in both Gunung Sitoli and Teluk Dalam. Boats to Sibolga leave Gunung Sitoli on Mondays, Wednesdays and Fridays at 8pm and Teluk Dalam on Tuesdays, Thursdays and Saturdays at 8pm. An irregular ferry service also connects Teluk Dalam with the Telo Islands to the south. **Pelni** (Jl Chengkeh) has an irregular monthly boat to and from Padang. For fares, see p511.

Getting Around

Getting around Nias can be slow. In Gunung Sitoli, the bus terminal is 1.5km south of the centre of town; an *opelet* from the pier costs 2000Rp. From Gunung Sitoli, there are minibuses to the southern market town of Teluk Dalam (65,000Rp, three hours), which has transport to Lagundri, 13km away. You can also arrange transport directly to Sorake (80,000Rp). You will probably be charged extra to take a surfboard but always whittle down the initial quote as low as a smile can get. Services dry up in the afternoon, so aim to leave before noon. To get to Sorake or Lagundri from Teluk Dalam, catch a local bus from the town centre (5000Rp). Losmen will also hunt the town looking for new arrivals and usually charge 10,000Rp for motorbike transfer.

Gunung Sitoli

☎0639

Gunung Sitoli, on the northeastern coast of Nias, is the island's main town. It was badly damaged by the 28 March 2005 earthquake, but reconstruction is now largely complete.

Sights

Museum Pusaka Nias MUSEUM

(☎21920; Jl Yos Sudarso 134A; admission 2000Rp; ⏲8-11.30am & 1.30-4.30pm Tue-Sat, 2-4.30pm Sun) Museum Pusaka Nias has a good collection of woodcarvings, stone sculptures and ceremonial objects. The garden has an interesting display of local plants and herbs as well as some models of traditional Niassan architecture.

Sleeping & Eating

If you need to stay on the north coast to catch a departing flight, try these options outside the town centre.

Wisma Soliga Resort Hotel RESORT $

(☎21815; d from 100,000Rp; ❄📶) Located about 4km south of town, this is a friendly and well-managed place with rooms that are clean and spacious. Wisma Soliga is set in large grounds – large enough to contain a mini 'zoo', a badminton court and, if you are not already sweaty enough, a running track!

Miga Beach Bungalows RESORT $$

(☎21460; d incl breakfast 300,000-700,000Rp; ❄) About 1.5km out of town, Miga sits right on a small beach with comfortable rooms that are given a sense of place with their driftwood furnishings and earthy tones.

Information

Bank Sumut (Jl Hatta) MasterCard-accessible ATM.

BRI Bank (Jl Imam Bonjol) ATM available.

Post Office (cnr Jl Gomo & Hatta)

Public Hospital (☎21271; Jl Cipto M Kusomo) For dealing with minor emergencies.

EARTHQUAKES

Hardly at the centre of international events, remote Sumatra isn't exactly renowned for its influence on the rest of the world. That is, until you tally up the times that violent natural disasters on the island have literally shaken the planet.

Take for instance the 1883 eruption of Krakatau, 40km off the southern Sumatra coast. This volcanic explosion was equivalent to that from 200 megatonnes of TNT, more powerful than the A-bomb dropped on Hiroshima. So much ash was hurled into the atmosphere that the sky was darkened for days and global temperatures were reduced by an average of 1.2°C for several years.

It is said that the blast that created Danau Toba some 100,000 years ago – before scientists were around to measure such rumblings – would have made Krakatau look like an after-dinner belch.

Then there was the 2004 Boxing Day earthquake, the world's second-largest recorded earthquake (magnitude 9.3). The resulting tsunami hit more than a dozen countries around the Indian Ocean, leaving more than 300,000 people dead or missing and millions displaced. The force of the event is said to have caused the earth to wobble on its axis and shifted surrounding land masses southwest by up to 36m.

Few land masses can claim to have literally moved the planet in the same way as Sumatra.

FLIGHTS FROM GUNUNG SITOLI

DESTINATION	COMPANY	FREQUENCY
Medan	Wings Air (Lion Air), Merpati	5 daily
Sibolga	NBA	3 weekly
Telo Islands	NBA	3 weekly

Teluk Dalam

☎0631

This squat little port town is as loud and chaotic as much larger cities. You'll need to pass through Teluk Dalam for transit connections to the beach or to pick up provisions.

Pantai Sorake & Teluk Lagundri

☎0630

A fish-hook piece of land creates the perfect horseshoe bay of Teluk Lagundri and the surf break at Pantai Sorake, which is generally regarded as one of the best right-handers in the world. The main surfing season is June to October, with a peak in July and August when the waves can be very solid. Folks refer to this area interchangeably as Sorake or Lagundri.

The Boxing Day tsunami destroyed many of the family-run guesthouses and restaurants on the beach. The businesses that could afford to rebuild are all located on Pantai Sorake, which is considered to be more protected from future disasters.

Activities

Surfing

Surfing is to Nias what honeymooning is to the Maldives. It's the island's tourism raison d'être. Sorake's famous right consistently unrolls between June and October. Access to the wave is a quick paddle from the Keyhole, a break in the coral reef that lies between the beach and the bay.

The fortunes of Nias surfing have waxed and waned over the years. In the '80's and '90's it was a very popular surf destination, but at the turn of the millennium the number of visiting surfers dropped dramatically after tales of overly aggressive locals and inconsistent waves combined with the opening up of the wave gardens of the nearby Mentawai Islands. Today that's all changed – the earthquake of 2005 actually lifted up the reef at Sorake Bay by about 1m and in doing so dramatically increased the consistency of the surf here (though on the flipside it also destroyed a lot of other nearby waves). When word of this filtered out, surfers once again descended on the place and today the line-up crawls with wave-hungry surfers at the merest hint of a wave.

Although swells are often much smaller between November and March and the winds less favourable, you can still get some good days with far fewer surfers. Whatever time of year, Nias is not a good place to learn how to surf – it's just not a beginners' wave.

Surfers will arrive with their own gear, but if you need to it's possible to rent equipment from Key Hole Surf Camp, in front of the Keyhole.

Sleeping & Eating

The western part of the bay, known as Pantai Sorake, is the primary location for lodging since the tsunami destroyed much of the infrastructure elsewhere on the bay. Most surfers stay on the northern end so that they can watch the waves.

It is expected that you eat your meals, especially dinner, at your losmen, and enquiries of where you've eaten can range from curiosity to accusation. In general, the more expensive the lodging, the less likely your hosts will care where you spend your money. Food is quite expensive on the island, with dinner prices averaging between 35,000Rp to 50,000Rp for a plate of fish or chicken.

Many of the better places prefer you to take a multiday package, which includes airport transfers and all meals, but they'll always rent a room by the night. Rates at these places are officially quoted in US dollars but payment is always in rupiah.

Key Hole Surf Camp GUESTHOUSE **$$**
(☎0813 7469 2530; per person full board US$55; wi-fi) Key Hole Surf Camp, right in the thick of things, has comfortable rooms and good food.

OFFSHORE SURFING

Popular surfing destinations off Nias include the islands of Asu and Bawa. More exposed than Nias itself, the islands see bigger and more consistent waves. With a left-hander at Asu and a strong right-hander at Bawa, good surf is, or perhaps was, almost guaranteed regardless of wind direction. Surfers on Nias are saying that the earthquake adversely affected the waves on Asu and the end section is now dangerously shallow.

The risk of malaria is high on these islands, particularly Bawa, which has a large swamp in its interior. Visitors should take proper precautions.

Sirombu on Nias' west coast is the jumping-off point for the islands. Ask around to see if any public buses will be heading there; otherwise you can charter transport for about 500,000Rp. From Sirombu there are cargo boats (80,000Rp). You can also charter boats (500,000Rp, maximum of 10 people) from local fishermen at Teluk Dalam and save yourself the hassle of getting to Sirombu.

Bawa has several simple losmen (budget accommodation).

Arico Losmen GUESTHOUSE **$$**
(☎0614 526802; per person full board US$30) Arico's is one of the better places to stay with art-enhanced rooms and a guest lounge with kitchen, DVD player, big-screen TV and views over the surf for live sporting action that beats anything on the box.

Sanali Losmen GUESTHOUSE **$**
(☎0812 6516 0312; per person 175,000Rp) Simple rooms and no real pressure to book a longer stay package. Like many places it can organise boat trips to surf spots that are further afield.

Other recommended places include **Morris Losmen**, **Eddy's Losmen**, **Lisa's Losmen**, **Lili's Losmen** and **JJ Losmen**. All of these are basic beach bungalows run by local families and cost between 80,000Rp and 150,000Rp depending on length of stay, time of year and what kind of room you opt for.

Traditional Villages

For hundreds of years, Nias residents built elaborate villages around cobblestone streets lined with rows of shiplike wooden houses. The traditional homes were balanced on tall wooden pylons and topped by a steep, thatched roof. Some say the boat motif was inspired by Dutch spice ships. Constructed from local teak and held together with hand-hewn wooden pegs, the houses are adorned with symbolic wooden carvings. The technology of traditional architecture proved quite absorbent and these structures fared better in the 2005 earthquake than modern concrete buildings.

Reflecting the island's defensive strategies, villages were typically built on high ground reached by dozens of stone steps. A protective stone wall usually encircled the village. Stone was also used for carved bathing pools, staircases, benches, chairs and memorials.

The island has geographic diversity when it comes to traditional houses. In northern Nias, homes are free-standing, oblong structures on stilts, while in the south they are built shoulder to shoulder on either side of a long, paved courtyard. Emphasising the roof as the primary feature, southern Niassan houses are constructed using pylons and cross-beams slotted together without the use of bindings or nails.

GOMO & AROUND

The villages around Gomo, in the central highlands, contain some of the island's best examples of stone carvings and *menhirs* (single standing stones), some thought to be 3000 years old. Such examples can be found in the village of **Tundrumbaho**, 5km from Gomo, **Lahusa Idanotae**, halfway between Gomo and Tundrumbaho, and at **Tetegewo**, 7km south of Gomo.

HILINAWALO MAZINGO

One of only five such surviving buildings on the island, the **Omo Hada** (Chieftain's House) is situated in the prestigious 'upstream' direction of the remote village, garnering the first rays of morning light. It still serves its traditional purpose as a meeting hall for seven neighbouring villages. In order to repair damages from age and climate, villagers have been trained in traditional carpentry skills, in turn preserving crafts that were nearing extinction.

BAWOMATALUO

Bawomataluo (Sun Hill) is the most famous, and the most accessible, of the southern villages. It is also the setting for *lompat batu* (stone jumping), featured on Indonesia's 1000Rp note.

Bawomataluo is perched on a hill about 400m above sea level. The final approach is up 88 steep stone steps. Houses are arranged along two main stone-paved avenues that meet opposite the impressive **chief's house**, which is thought to be both the oldest and the largest on Nias. Outside are stone tables where dead bodies were once left to decay.

Although Bawomataluo is worth exploring, tourism is in full swing here, with lots of eager knick-knack sellers.

There are also cultural displays of **war dances**, traditionally performed by young, single males, and **stone jumping**. The latter was once a form of war training; the jumpers had to leap over a 1.8m-high stone wall, traditionally topped with pointed sticks. These days the sticks are left off – and the motivation is financial.

From Bawomataluo, you can see the rooftops of nearby **Orihili**. A stone staircase and a trail lead downhill to the village.

Bawomataluo is 15km from Teluk Dalam and is accessible by public bus (5000Rp).

HILISIMAETANO

There are more than 100 **traditional houses** in this large village, 16km northwest of Teluk Dalam. **Stone jumping** and **traditional dancing** are performed here during special events. Hilisimaetano can be reached by public transport from Teluk Dalam (5000Rp).

BOTOHILI & HILIMAETA

Botohili is a small village on the hillside above the peninsula of Pantai Lagundri. It has two rows of **traditional houses**, with a number of new houses breaking up the skyline. The remains of the original entrance, **stone chairs** and paving can still be seen.

Hilimaeta is similar to Botohili and is also within easy walking distance of Lagundri. The *lompat batu* pylon can still be seen here and there are a number of **stone monuments**, including a 2m-high stone penis. A long pathway of stone steps leads uphill to the village.

ACEH

Over the years, this far-flung corner of the Indonesian archipelago has grabbed headlines for all the wrong reasons. Earthquakes, tsunamis, civil war and sharia law are the main associations people have with Sumatra's most northern state. The reconstruction from the Boxing Day tsunami that put this place on television screens around the world is now virtually complete. However, the social wounds incurred by the natural disaster and previous civil war will take much longer to heal. Post-tsunami Aceh is still tender, guns have been laid down, a degree of autonomy has been granted and there is now an air of new beginnings across the province.

For the visitor, politics and disasters are somewhat of a smokescreen. Intrepid travellers to the region are unearthing one of the few remaining undiscovered gems of Southeast Asia. Rich, animal-filled jungle, misty mountain peaks and endless swaths of empty beach lick the coastline, not to mention the rainbow of pristine coral beneath the sea. The tourist infrastructure isn't great, with bungalows and guesthouses making it up as they go along. Western comforts aren't exactly the norm. But this is *the* 'I was there before it was discovered' destination of the moment, and a few sacrificed luxuries are worth the trade-off.

Through all the disagreements and turmoil from recent events, the locals have largely ignored the goldmine of tourism on which the state stands, and very little is being done to encourage tourists to come… leaving it ripe and ready for unbridled discovery.

History

In the days of sailing ships, Aceh competed with Melaka on the Malay Peninsula for control of the important spice-trade route. Aceh was also Islam's entry to the archipelago. The capital, Banda Aceh, was an important centre of Islamic learning and a gateway for Muslims making the pilgrimage to Mecca.

The influx of traders and immigrants and the province's strategic position contributed to Aceh's wealth and importance. The main exports were pepper and gold; others included ivory, tin, tortoiseshell, camphor, aloe wood, sandalwood and spices. Though Aceh's power began to decline towards the end of the 17th century, the province remained independent of the Dutch until

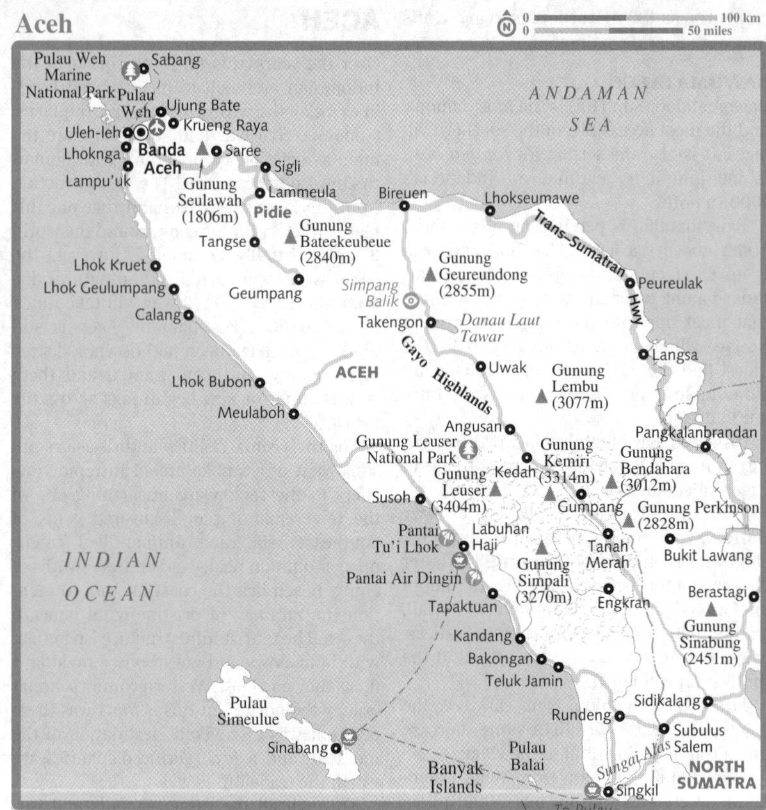

war was declared in 1871. It was 35 years before the fighting stopped and the last of the sultans, Tuanku Muhamat Dawot, surrendered.

In 1951 the Indonesian government incorporated Aceh's territory into the province of North Sumatra. The prominent Islamic Party was angered at being lumped together with the Christian Bataks, and proclaimed Aceh an independent Islamic Republic in September 1953. Prolonged conflict ensued, and in 1959 the government was forced to give Aceh 'special district' status, granting a high degree of autonomy in religious, cultural and educational matters. Despite this special status the government strengthened its grip on Aceh's huge natural-gas reserves.

In December 1976 Gerakan Aceh Merdeka (GAM; Free Aceh Movement) was formed and began fighting for independence. Fighting was limited in the early years of the struggle, but by 1989 GAM had gathered strength and launched a renewed attack on the Indonesian government.

By 1990 the area had been designated a 'special combat zone' and eight years of near-military rule followed. Amnesty International has reported years of human rights abuses perpetrated during this time. In the following years the army launched further attacks, while GAM intimidated whole villages into giving support to the rebel forces. Deaths, tortures, disappearances and arbitrary arrests occurred on a daily basis, with each side blaming the other. The ordinary people of Aceh were the real losers: tens of thousands were displaced and lived in fear of both sides.

At the turn of the millennium, several steps towards peace were made: a brief ceasefire was declared in 2000, and in 2002 Jakarta granted a 'special autonomy' law allowing the province to keep up to 70% of oil and gas revenues and, controversially, implement sharia law. Peace talks were also initiated for the first time since the conflict began, and progressed for a year and a half before crumbling. For two years afterwards, all of the progress toward normality was quickly reversed. Martial law was declared in 2003, paving the way for a full-scale military assault on the separatists – the biggest military operation in Indonesia since the 1975 invasion of East Timor.

The 2004 tsunami provided the necessary counterpoint to open up the sealed province to relief organisations and to renew peace talks between Jakarta and the rebels. On 15 August 2005, a peace accord was signed in Helsinki and many of the important steps of the agreement have been met: GAM rebels successfully surrendered their weapons and the Indonesian troops have withdrawn from the province. Today peace prevails throughout the region.

Banda Aceh

☎0651 / POP 224,000

Indonesian cities are rarely coupled with pleasant descriptions, but Banda Aceh breaks the mould. The sleepy provincial capital is an extremely pleasant spot to spend a few days. The village-like atmosphere and dusty, unobtrusive streets make for a laid-back, easily explored town filled with cheery faces. The proud folk rarely betray the tragedy that they must have experienced during the Boxing Day tsunami; looking at the reconstructed city today it's impossible to reconcile it with the distraught images of 2004. In Banda Aceh alone, 61,000 people were killed and development outside of the city centre was reduced to a wasteland in a matter of a few hours. Today you'd hardly guess that anything had happened.

For a few years the city was awash with aid workers, who not only helped rebuild the town you'll find today but also kick-started the economy to catering to nongovernmental organisations (NGOs). Prices soared and the local economy boomed as foreign expense accounts paid for taxis, steak dinners and overpriced hotel rooms. Now that the NGOs have pretty much gone and the reconstruction is complete, the miniboom is over. However, Aceh has greater control over its resources, in particular oil, so the town is relatively affluent and the streets, the homes and especially the mosques are well maintained and looked after.

Banda Aceh is a fiercely religious city and the ornate mosques are at the centre of daily life. In this devoutly Muslim city, religion and respect are everything. The hassles are few and the people are easy going and extremely hospitable to visitors.

Sights & Activities

Mesjid Raya Baiturrahman MOSQUE

(admission by donation; ⏲7-11am & 1.30-4pm) With its brilliant white walls and liquorice-black domes, the Mesjid Raya Baiturrahman is a dazzling sight on a sunny day. The first section of the mosque was built by the Dutch in 1879 as a conciliatory gesture towards the Acehnese after the original one burnt down. Two more domes – one on either side of the first – were added by the Dutch in 1936 and another two by the Indonesian government in 1957. The mosque survived intact after the 2004 earthquake and tsunami, a sign interpreted by many residents as direct intervention by the Divine. During this time the mosque served as an unofficial crisis centre for survivors, and bodies awaiting identification were laid on the public square in front of the mosque. The best time to visit the mosque is during Friday afternoon prayers, when the entire building and yard are filled with people. A headscarf is required for women.

FREE **Tsunami Museum** MUSEUM

(Jl Iskandar Muda; ⏲9am-midday & 2-4.30pm Sat-Thu) It cost a whopping US$5.6 million to build and today Banda Aceh's impressive Tsunami Museum is the highlight (in a very sad and depressing kind of way) of a trip to Banda Aceh. A visit opens with the sound of muffled and terrified voices and a walk between giant walls of water that simulate the waves of the tsunami. This is followed by a powerful set of images from the aftermath of the waves and another wall engraved in the names of just a few of the dead. Upstairs a very graphic short film is aired, followed by more pictures and models re-creating the scenes of destruction. In between you'll find information on how earthquakes and tsunamis are created and how Aceh's landscapes were altered by this one.

Gunongan HISTORIC BUILDING

(Jl Teuku Umar; ⏲8am-6pm) All that remains today of Aceh's powerful sultanates are on view at Gunongan. Built by Sultan Iskandar Muda (r 1607–36) as a gift for his Malay princess wife, it was intended as a private playground and bathing place. The building consists of a series of frosty peaks with narrow stairways and a walkway leading to ridges, which represent the hills of the princess' native land. Ask around for someone to unlock the gate for you.

Directly across from the Gunongan is a low vaulted gate, in the traditional Pintu Aceh style, which gave access to the sultan's palace – supposedly for the use of royalty only.

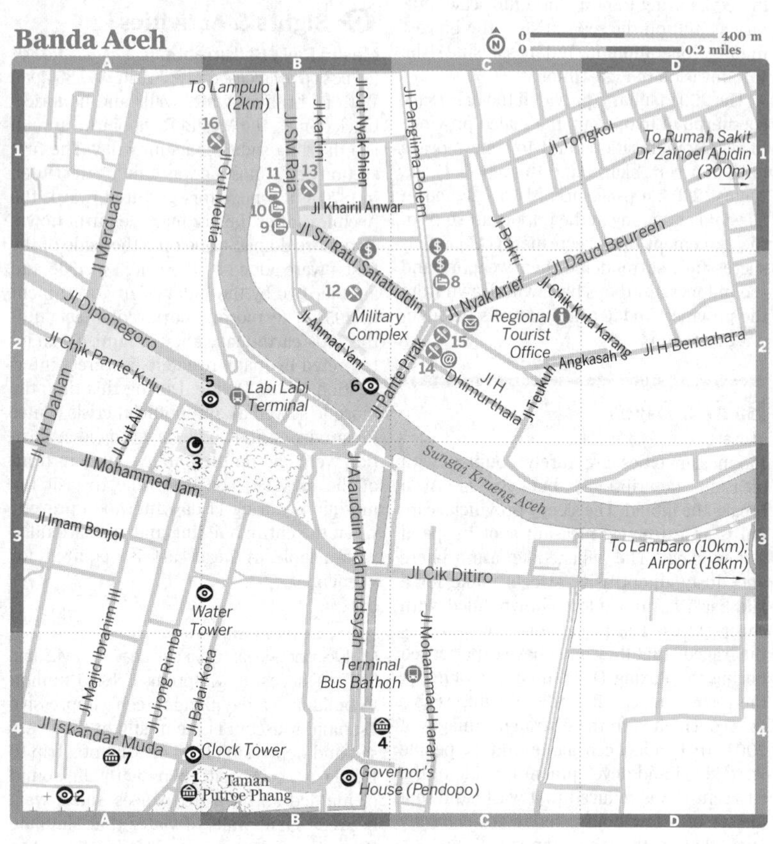

Banda Aceh

Sights

1 Gunongan A4
2 Kherkhof A4
3 Mesjid Raya Baiturrahman A3
4 Museum Negeri Banda Aceh B4
5 Pasar Aceh Central B2
6 Pasar Ikan B2
Rumah Aceh .... (see 4)
7 Tsunami Museum A4

Sleeping

8 Hotel 61 .... C2
9 Hotel Medan B1
10 Hotel Prapat B1
11 Hotel Wisata B1

Eating

12 Country Steakhouse B2
13 Pasar Malam Rek B1
14 PP Cafe & Restaurant C2
15 Restauran Bunda C2
16 Rumah Makan Asia B1

Drinking

Tower Coffee .... (see 14)

To reach Gunongan, take a *labi labi* (*opelet*) bound for Jl Kota Alam (3000Rp).

Kherkhof CEMETERY
(Dutch Cemetery; Jl Teuku Umar; ⏲8am-6pm) Not far from the Gunongan and the Tsunami Museum is the Kherkhof, the last resting place of more than 2000 Dutch and Indonesian soldiers who died fighting the Acehnese. The entrance is about 250m from the clock tower on the road to Uleh-leh. Tablets set into the walls beside the entrance gate are inscribed with the names of the dead soldiers.

To reach the Kherkhof take *labi labi* 9 or 10.

Museum Negeri Banda Aceh MUSEUM
(☎23144; Jl Alauddin Mahmudsyah 12; admission 7500Rp; ⏲8.00am-noon & 2-5pm Tue-Sun) The Museum Negeri Banda Aceh has displays of Acehnese weaponry, household furnishings, ceremonial costumes, everyday clothing, gold jewellery, calligraphy and some magnificently carved *recong* (Acehnese daggers) and swords. It also has a display of a baby two-headed buffalo.

In the same compound as the museum is the **Rumah Aceh** (Jl Alauddin Mahmudsyah 12) – a fine example of traditional Acehnese architecture, built without nails and held together with cord and pegs. It contains more Acehnese artefacts and war memorabilia.

On weekends it's sometimes possible to see traditional dance and music sessions here.

Pasar Aceh Central MARKET
(btwn Jl Chik Pante Kulu & Jl Diponegoro) Market lovers will enjoy the bustle at this colourful-market, just north of the Mesjid Raya.

Pasar Ikan MARKET
(Fish Market; Jl Ahmad Yani) Pasar Ikan defines freshness. Boats ease into the river and unload their cargoes of shark, tuna and prawns onto the vendor carts.

Tsunami Landmarks LANDMARK
It doesn't make for sunny postcard fodder, but seeing the place with your own eyes allows for personal and sacred memorials, and helps feeble imaginations understand the scale of the disaster.

The most famous of the tsunami sights are the **boat in the house** in Lampulo, and the 2500-tonne power-generator vessel that was carried 4km inland by a wave.

There are four **mass graves** in and around Banda Aceh where the dead in the province were buried. The largest site is Lambaro, located on the road to the airport, where 46,000 unidentified bodies were buried. Other grave sites include Meuraxa, Lhok Nga and Darusalam, where another 54,000 bodies were interred. Families who wish to mourn the loss of unlocated relatives choose one of the mass graves based on possible geographic proximity; they have no other evidence of where to lay their prayers.

Sleeping

The influx of international aid workers jacked up the prices but not the standards of the few hotels left in town since the tsunami. Even today there's very little for budget travellers. There are a bunch of cheapies on Jl Khairil Anwar that might be worth a try, but our experience of them is that they permanently seem to be 'full' – a way of saying they don't accept foreigners. Many backpackers, more concerned with saving money than experiencing one of Sumatra's more interesting urban centres, race straight through Banda Aceh and out to the mellower prices of Pulau Weh.

Hotel Medan HOTEL **$$**
(☎21501; Jl Ahmad Yani 17; r with breakfast 185,000-350,000Rp; ❄@📶) This business-class hotel has comfortable and spotless rooms. It's probably the most popular hotel in town with both foreign and Indonesian visitors, and is certainly the best value.

Hotel 61 HOTEL **$$**
(☎638 866; www.hotel61.co.id; Jl Panglima Polem 28; r incl breakfast 600,000-800,000Rp, ste incl breakfast 930,000Rp; ❄📶) Despite its bizarre location inside an amusement centre and fast-food restaurant, this is the best-value top-end hotel in the city centre – that is assuming you get a room away from the noise of the fairground rides and beeping computer games and that they offer you a discount (which they will!). Rooms are comfortable and there's excellent internet reception, which is a real rarity.

Hotel Prapat HOTEL **$**
(☎22159; Jl Ahmad Yani 19; d with fan/air-con 100,000/200,000Rp; ❄) One of the more affordable spots. From the outside Prapat has the feel of a cheap run-down motel, though rooms are good value with Western toilets and clean sheets.

Hotel Wisata HOTEL $
(☎21834; Jl Ahmad Yani 19-20; r 125,000-225,000Rp; @) With a streamlined art-deco facade, the Wisata isn't a bad option but the cheapest rooms are fan only and overall it's quite faded.

Eating

The square at the junction of Jl Ahmad Yani and Jl Khairil Anwar is usually the setting for the **Pasar Malam Rex** (cnr Jl Ahmad Yani & Jl Khairil Anwar), Banda Aceh's lively night food market. Many night food stalls are found on Jl SM Raja.

TOP CHOICE **Restauran Bunda** INDONESIAN $
(☎0813 9680 8482; Jl Pante Pirak 7-9; mains 5000-22,000Rp; ❄) Think bright lights, modern furnishings, a shiny canteen and uniformed waiters piling endless plates of sublime *masakan minang* (basically the same as Padang food) dishes onto your table and you get this fantastic 'posh warung' style restaurant. It also offers a takeaway service – ideal if you have a long bus ride ahead of you.

Rumah Makan Asia INDONESIAN $
(Jl Cut Meutia 37/39; mains 10,000Rp) Aceh's version of *masakan Padang* (Padang dish) has an array of zesty seafood dishes that waiters plonk on to your table, such as *ikan panggang* (baked fish).

Country Steakhouse STEAKHOUSE $$
(☎24213; off Jl Sri Ratu Safiatuddin 45B; mains 15,000-100,000Rp; ⏲noon-10pm; ❄📶) Well hidden down an alley, this wood-panelled restaurant was set up to cater to the international aid workers; now it's often empty. Serves New Zealand steaks, snapper and chips and other Western dishes. Also has beer and Australian red wine, and a TV showing BBC.

PP Cafe & Restaurant INTERNATIONAL $
(Jl H Dhimurthala 31; mains 12,000Rp; ❄📶) Popular with local teenagers, PP's is a great place to escape the heat for a cold drink, a good selection of Indonesian food and some European dishes.

Drinking

Because of sharia law, alcohol is not available as openly here as elsewhere in Indonesia, but a few of the more expensive restaurants and hotels discreetly serve beer. As long as it's kept quiet, most of the locals don't mind.

Tower Coffee CAFE
(Jl Pante Pirak; ⏲to 10pm) One of the most popular coffee shops in town and a good place to fall into conversation with Banda Aceh's young middle class. But if you're a Starbucks executive you may want to avoid passing by for fear of seeing your logo being used and abused!

Information

There are lots of ATMs around town, mainly on Jl Panglima Polem and on Jl Sri Ratu Safiatuddin.

Bank Danamon (Jl Sri Ratu Safiatuddin)

BCA Bank (Jl Panglima Polem)

BII Bank (Jl Panglima Polem)

Pante Pirak Net (Jl Dhimurthala 19; per hr 8000Rp; ⏲9am-10pm) Good connections.

Post office (☎29487; Jl H Bendahara 33; ⏲8am-4pm Mon-Fri) A short walk from the centre; also has internet.

Regional tourist office (Dinas Parawisata; ☎852 020; www.bandaacehtourism.com; Jl Chik Kuta Karang 3) On the 1st level of a government building; the staff are exceptionally friendly and have free copies of an excellent guidebook to the province.

Rumah Sakit Dr Zainoel Abidin (☎34565; Jl Daud Beureuch 108) One of the best hospitals in town.

Getting There & Away

After the tsunami, the port moved to Uleh-leh, 10km northwest of Banda Aceh's city centre. The road to the port goes straight through the tsunami's path – once a two-car-garage suburb, now an eerie, empty landscape. See p524 for boat schedules and fare info.

South of the city centre, you'll find the **Terminal Bus Bathoh** (Jl Mohammed Hasan), which has numerous buses to Medan (economy/air-con 140,000/180,000Rp, 14 hours). Buses depart every hour or so throughout the day until about 11pm. The west-coast road from Banda Aceh to Meulaboh has been rebuilt since the tsunami. A minibus to Meulaboh is 90,000Rp.

For a reliable English-speaking driver for the city and anywhere in Aceh or beyond, give **Mr Firdau** (☎0821 6125 3231) a call.

Getting Around

Airport taxis charge a set rate of 70,000Rp for the 16km ride into town. A taxi from the airport to Uleh-leh port will cost 100,000Rp. *Labi labi* are the main form of transport around town and cost 1500Rp. The **labi labi terminal** (Jl Diponegoro) is that special breed of Indonesian mayhem. For Uleh-leh (5000Rp, 30 minutes), take the blue *labi labi* signed 'Uleh-leh'. You can

FLIGHTS FROM BANDA ACEH

DESTINATION	COMPANY	FREQUENCY
Kuala Lumpur	AirAsia	1 daily
Kutacane	NBA	2 weekly
Medan	Garuda, Lion Air, NBA, Sriwijaya	several daily
Panang	Firefly	3 weekly
Pulau Simeulue	NBA	2 weekly

also reach Lhok Nga and Lampu'uk (10,000Rp). From the bus station, a becak into town will cost around 15,000Rp. A becak around town should cost between 5000Rp and 10,000Rp, depending on your destination. A becak to Uleh-leh from the city centre is 25,000Rp and a taxi 50,000Rp.

Pulau Weh

☎0652 / POP 25,000

A tiny tropical rock off the tip of Sumatra, Pulau Weh is a small slice of peaceful living that rewards travellers who've journeyed up through the turbulent greater mainland below. After you've hiked around the mainland's jungles, volcanoes and lakes, it's time to jump into the languid waters of the Indian Ocean. Snorkellers and divers bubble through the great walls of swaying sea fans, deep canyons and rock pinnacles, while marvelling at the prehistorically gargantuan fish. This is one of the finest underwater hikes you'll find. Both figuratively and geographically, Pulau Weh is the cherry on top for many visitors to Sumatra.

Don't come expecting lazy days on sprawling beaches with swaying palms, though; the stretches of sand are generally short, rocky strips met by the ocean's emerald-green coral garden. Most visitors spend their days underwater, ogling the dazzling kaleidoscope of marine life. Along the twisting island road are little villages with underwear-only kids playing in the yard, lazy cows tied up to a green patch of grass and scrappy goats looking for garden victims.

Pulau Weh is shaped roughly like a horseshoe. On the northeastern leg is the port town of Sabang, where most of Weh's population lives. The primary tourist beaches are Gapang and Iboih, which are about 20km away heading towards the northwestern leg. In the bendy-palms and sandy-toes stakes Iboih probably just outclasses Gapang, but for the best beaches of all, pack a towel and saunter down to Pantai Sumur Tiga. Near Sabang, the beach here is fabulous. Accommodation prices are often too painful for backpackers, but it suits mid-range cruisers looking for a few blissed-out days.

Note that malaria has been reported on the island, so take the proper precautions.

It's always a little rainy on Weh, which has two monsoon seasons. But that shouldn't matter, as you'll be underwater most of the time anyway. Plus the rain keeps the island green and lush, and the water full of plankton, which draws in underwater giants such as manta rays and whale sharks.

A word of warning: Pulau Weh's allure is such that many a traveller's itinerary has been blown out by weeks or even months by what is regarded by many as the best diving in Southeast Asia.

Activities

People don't come to Weh for the nightlife or the bikinis. They come for the diving and snorkelling, which is considered some of the best in the Indian Ocean. On an average day, you're likely to spot morays, lionfish and stingrays. During plankton blooms, whale sharks come to graze. Unlike at other dive sites, the coral fields take a back seat to the sea life and landscapes. There are close to 20 dive sites around the island, most in and around Iboih and Gapang.

There are several dive operators on the island. The two main ones are listed here, both of which offer PADI diving courses. At Iboih, **Rubiah Tirta Divers** (☎332 4555; www.rubiahdivers.com; intro dive/open-water course all inclusive €45/280) is the oldest dive operation on the island. At Gapang, **Lumba Lumba Diving Centre** (☎081 1682 787, 332 4133; www.lumbalumba.com; intro dive/open-water course all inclusive €45/290) is the centre of activity, with the comings and goings of wetsuited creatures. The owners, Ton and Marjan Egbers, maintain a helpful website with detailed descriptions of dives and other need-to-know information.

Snorkelling gear can be hired almost anywhere for around 30,000Rp per day.

Getting There & Away

Sabang is the port town on Pulau Weh. Fast ferries to Sabang leave the mainland from Uleh-leh, situated 5km northwest of Banda Aceh, at 9.30am and 4pm (economy/business/VIP 55,000/65,000/85,000Rp, 45 minutes to one hour). Slow ferries (economy/air-con 18,500/36,500Rp, two hours) leave at 2pm on Mondays, Tuesdays, Thursdays and Fridays. On Wednesdays, Saturdays and Sundays there are two ferries, departing at 11am and 4pm. In the opposite direction, the slow ferry leaves at 8am daily, with an afternoon ferry on Wednesdays, Saturdays and Sundays at 2pm. The fast ferry leaves at 8.30am and 4pm daily. You should get to the port at least 45 minutes before departure to get a ticket. Ferry service is weather pending.

Getting Around

From the port, there are regular minibuses to Sabang (20,000Rp, 15 minutes), and Gapang and Iboih (50,000Rp, 40 minutes).You can catch a minibus from Jl Perdagangan in Sabang to Gapang and Iboih (35,000Rp).

SABANG

The island's main township is an interesting mix of traditional fishing village and old colonial villas. During Dutch rule, Sabang was a major coal and water depot for steamships, but with the arrival of diesel power after WWII it went into decline.

During the 1970s it was a duty-free port, but this status was eliminated in 1986 and Sabang once again became a sleepy fishing town. Today the only industry – other than fishing – is rattan furniture.

Most people see no more of Sabang than a fleeting glimpse of the outskirts from a speeding bus.

Sights

Sabang is surrounded by beautiful beaches. Just 10 minutes' walk away is **Pantai Paradiso**, a white-sand beach shaded by coconut palms. **Pantai Kasih** (Lover's Beach) is a bit further away, and about 30 minutes from town is **Pantai Sumur Tiga**, a popular picnic spot.

Other attractions around Sabang include **Danau Anak Laut**, a serene freshwater lake that supplies the island's water, and **Gunung Merapi**, a semi-active volcano, which holds boiling water in its caldera and occasionally puffs smoke.

Sleeping & Eating

Few people choose to stay in town unless they get stuck, though it's hard to see how you could get stuck here. The following are out on beautiful Pantai Sumur Tiga, 5km east of town.

TOP CHOICE Casa Nemo LODGE $$

(☎0812 1735 4141; www.casanemo.com; Pantai Sumur Tiga; r 150,000Rp, cottage weekday 275,000-300,000Rp, cottage weekend 300,000-350,000Rp) Sitting on the balcony of your luxurious beach hut (which in some cases comes complete with a stone bath) and looking down on a day-glow blue ocean, you'll probably find it impossible to wipe the smile off your face.

Freddies LODGE $$

(☎081 3602 5501; www.santai-sabang.com; Pantai Sumur Tiga; cottage weekday 240,000-265,000Rp, weekend 290,000-305,000Rp) This delightful option (although with slightly disappointing bathrooms) overlooks a pretty stretch of white-sand beach with a coral reef, perfect for those content with snorkelling and lolling under a palm tree. The list of alcohol is impressive and all food is cooked by Freddie, the South African owner.

Information

The **BRI bank** (Jl Perdagangan) has an ATM, as do a couple of other banks.

GAPANG

Occupying a sandy cove, Gapang is a lazy stretch of beach lined with shack restaurants and simple guesthouses. The locals are friendly and the atmosphere is low-key and quiet, with dive chat dominating the evenings.

Sleeping & Eating

Gapang is much less lively than nearby Iboih and by and large the accommodation is, except for one notable exception, pretty down at heel. There are a number of mediocre beach huts available for rent at the far end of the beach. All cost around 50,000Rp per night and there's virtually nothing to distinguish one from the other – in fact it's hard to tell where one set begins and another ends or what any of them are called.

Beachside cafes serving very standard Western and Indonesian food absorb the evening breezes and postdive appetites. **Mama Donut** is a local institution, walking the sand selling delicious vegetable samosas, doughnuts and fried bananas.

Lumba Lumba RESORT $$
(☎332 4133; www.lumbalumba.com/staying.html; r without bathroom €12, r with bathroom €18-30; @📶) Dutch-owned Lumba Lumba has wood-decked cottages with tiled rooms and Western toilets, and offers easily the best-quality accommodation in Gapang. Accommodation is for the exclusive use of those diving with this outfit, but it will happily rent out any spare rooms.

IBOIH

More spread out than Gapang, Iboih (*ee-boh*) follows a rocky headland with a string of simple bungalows along a woodsy footpath. A small path leads through a stone gateway past the village well, and up and over a small hill to the bungalow strip.

Opposite Iboih, 100m offshore, is **Pulau Rubiah**, a densely forested island surrounded by spectacular coral reefs known as the **Sea Garden**. It is a favourite snorkelling and diving spot. The coral has been destroyed in places but there is still plenty to see, including turtles, manta ray, lionfish, tigerfish and occasional sharks.

If you are a strong swimmer it is possible to make your own way there. Beware of strong currents, especially at the southern tip of the island.

Adjacent to the Sea Garden is the **Iboih Forest nature reserve**. It has some good walks, and coastal caves that can be explored by boat.

Sleeping & Eating

Iboih, with its simple palm-thatch bungalows, many built on stilts and overhanging crystal-clear water, is Pulau Weh's backpacker hang-out par excellence. There are dozens of different places to stay with almost nothing differentiating them. Wherever you choose to hang your flip-flops, if you stay for several days you can normally negotiate a discount on the daily rates that can see prices falling as low as 50,000Rp.

Just off the main road are a few shops selling sundries, Indonesian lunches and coffee in front of a small beach.

The following bungalows are listed in geographic order as you'll approach them.

Green House HUT $
(☎0852 7748 3299; r 100,000Rp) One of the first places you come to and no different to any of the others except that you needn't carry your bags far.

Olala HUT $
(r 50,000-150,000Rp) Of the many places offering cheap and cheerful beach huts, Olala is the current flavour of the month. And talking of flavours, its restaurant (open to all) receives an equal amount of praise.

OONG's Bunglalows HUT $
(☎0813 6070 0150; r 50,000-120,000Rp) Good value rooms although the tin roof gets things hot. Cheaper options share bathrooms.

Iboih Inn HUT $$
(☎0812 6904 8397; www.iboihinn.com; r with breakfast 150,000-350,000Rp; ❄📶) The top-dog rooms here come with hot-water showers, air-con and fab sea views and are aimed very much at backpackers who are now too old and tiered to backpack. Room price and quality then drops downward until you get to simple wooden shacks with thin partitioning walls ideal for backpackers filled with youthful zeal.

Yulia's HUT $
(☎0821 6856 4383; r with/without bathroom 200,000/100,000Rp; 📶) A 500m trudge over the cliffs rewards you with the best of Iboih's huts, some excellent front-door snorkelling and a good restaurant with shakes and light fare.

Mama's INTERNATIONAL $
(mains 25,000Rp) Located on the little beach in front of Rubiah Tirta Divers, Mama's serves what many would consider the best food in the village and no matter the time of day there's always a crowd of travellers hanging out here.

Norma's INTERNATIONAL $
(mains 25,000Rp) The restaurant portion of OONG's Bungalows does a nightly seafood dinner around a communal table and serves beer amid scuba chat.

LONG ANGEN

This secluded beach on the western side of the island is ideally located for spectacular sunsets. The beach itself only exists for six months of the year – the sand is swept away by the sea from November to May.

Aceh's West Coast

Rounding the northwestern tip of Sumatra's finger of land is a string of little villages and endless beaches backed by densely forested hills, home to some interesting wildlife, including tigers and bears. This is the perfect recipe for paradise, but several factors have conspired to keep the sands free of beach blankets: the sheer remoteness of the region, the unstable safety situation during the war in Aceh and the Boxing Day tsunami. Most of the houses along the coast are identical in design, having been rebuilt after villages were destroyed in 2004. For the moment, the attractive west coast attracts only the more intrepid travellers and surfers in search of waves.

LHOK NGA & LAMPU'UK

☎0656

Before the tsunami this area was a favourite spot of intrepid surfers and weekending locals from Banda Aceh. These coastal weekend spots, only 17km from Banda Aceh, were levelled by the tsunami. In Lampu'uk (population 1000) the wave travelled some 7km inland, killing four in five people.

There's still not much in the way of accommodation here, although some of the bungalows along the beach in Lampu'uk are rented out by surfers. **Joel's Bungalows** (☎0813 7528 7765; Lampu'uk; r 100,000-300,000Rp) is the area's legendary surfer hang-out. Its huts have been built into and around the cliff face and overlook a drop-dead-gorgeous beach (though dumping shore break can make swimming dangerous). Rooms come in an array of sizes and styles, some of which have bathrooms that basically meld into the cliff face. Its in-house restaurant is known far and wide as the place to come for a wood-fire pizza, beer and a spot of surf chat; it also rents surfboards.

Lhok Nga (population 400) has decent waves too, but its beach is not as nice, particularly with the huge concrete factory and the nearby port.

Take *labi labi* 04 (20,000Rp, 20 minutes) from the *opelet* terminal in Banda Aceh for both Lhok Nga and Lampu'uk. A becak is 50,000Rp.

PULAU SIMEULUE

☎0650 / POP 80,200

The isolated island of Simeulue, about 150km west of Tapaktuan, is a rocky volcanic outcrop blanketed in rainforest and fringed with clove and coconut plantations. An increasing number of surfers make it out here (although wave quality is generally not considered to be as high as on some other offshore Sumatran islands) but non-surfing travellers are a rare breed indeed. This is a pity because the island holds immense potential for genuine, off-the-beaten-track adventure.

You'll find simple **losmen** (r 50,000-100,000Rp) in Sinabang and Sibigo, or if you have a tent you can camp on the beach. The most comfortable sleeping option is the new **Aura Surf Resort** (☎0813 6241 7692; www.simeulue.com; packages per night Oct-Mar US$115, Apr-Sep US$140). Packages include meals and transfers to the waves, but like many such Sumatran surf camps it's hard to see how it can justify such high rates.

Susi Air (☎061 785 2169; www.susiair.com) has one or two flights daily from Medan, while **NBA** (☎453 4680) has three flights a week from Medan.

Ferries run from the mainland ports of Singkil and Labuhan Haji to Pulau Simeuleu's port town of Sinabang.

TAPAKTUAN

☎0656 / POP 15,000

The sleepy seaside town of Tapaktuan, 200km south of Meulaboh, is the main town in south Aceh. It's very laid-back by Sumatran standards and, although it has few specific sights, it can be a pleasant place to hang out for a couple of days. The setting, between forest-draped mountain hills and sapphire-blue sea, couldn't be nicer. Although its location would suggest otherwise, Tapaktuan was not noticeably affected by the tsunami.

The town can be used as a base to explore the lowland **Kluet region** of Gunung Leuser National Park, about 45km south. Kluet's unspoilt swamp forests support the densest population of primates in Southeast Asia and are also good sites for **birdwatching**. It may be possible to hire guides through the national park office in Kandang, 38km south of Tapaktuan.

Pantai Tu'i Lhok and **Pantai Air Dingin**, about 18km north of Tapaktuan, are the best of several good beaches in the area. Opposite both beaches are waterfalls with natural plunge pools where you can cool off.

Most of the cheaper places to stay are located along Jl Merdeka. Otherwise try the gaudy but comfortable **Metro Hotel** (☎065 632 2567; Jl Ben Mahmud 17; r incl breakfast 250,000Rp), a friendly guesthouse with some rooms looking out over the waves.

Buses connect Tapaktuan with Banda Aceh and Medan, and **NBA** (☎061 453 4680) has two flights a week from Medan.

SINGKIL

☎0658 / POP 20,000

Singkil is a remote port at the mouth of Sungai Alas. It's a sleepy town with welcoming locals, although it merits a mention only as the departure point for boats to the Banyak Islands and Pulau Simeulue. Unusually for Indonesia, Singkil is very spread out and has no real centre. Facilities are extremely limited; there is a BRI Bank with an ATM but it only accepts Mastercard – come prepared!

Catching a boat will probably mean spending a night in Singkil, with **Hotel Dina Amalia** (☎0821 6164 2013; elviandi_rs@yahoo.com; Jl Bahari; r 140,000-250,000Rp; ❄) the best option. The manager speaks a little English. You can also find basic **losmen** (r 30,000-70,000Rp). Your first point of contact in Singkil should be Mr Darmawan of **Louser Group** (☎0813 6017 0808, 0813 7721 9667; Jl Perdagangan 84), who can organise any and all forms of onward transport, including speed boats to the Banyaks and minibuses and private cars to almost anywhere. In fact we give him the Stranded Traveller Guardian Angel award for saving our skin!

NBA (☎061 453 4680) has two flights a week from Medan.

There are daily minibuses from Medan to Singkil (1100,000Rp, nine hours), from Sibolga (100,000Rp, six hours) and from Banda Aceh (225,000Rp, 15 hours). If you're travelling from Berastagi or Danau Toba take the Medan bus, and for Tapaktuan jump on the Banda Aceh bus.

There's one overnight ferry per week (Wednesday) to Gunung Sitoli on Pulau Nias (tickets from 50,000Rp, five hours) at 10pm. Ferries also head to Sinabang on Pulau Simeulue (28,000Rp to 68,000Rp, 11 hours) at 8pm on Fridays and Sundays, returning on Saturdays and Mondays. For transport to the Banyak Islands, see p528.

Banyak Islands

POP 5000

If you've ever dreamt about having a tropical island entirely to yourself, complete with palm trees, powdery white beaches and gin-clear waters, the Banyak Islands are a great place to fulfil your Robinson Crusoe fantasy. A cluster of 99 mostly uninhabited islands, the Banyak (Many) Islands are situated about 30km west of Singkil. Remote they might be, but they are now very much on the radar of surfers and, slowly, slowly an increasing number of paradise-seeking travellers. As well as having arguably the finest beaches in Sumatra and a handful of quality surf spots, the Banyaks has some great opportunities for snorkelling (and maybe one day the dive operators will move in).

The 2004 Boxing Day earthquake and tsunami, followed by the 2005 Nias quake, destroyed many coastal dwellings and contaminated freshwater wells. The main town on the island of Pulau Balai was permanently see-sawed by the quake, causing the west coast to rise by about 70cm and the east coast to drop below sea level. The once-beautiful beaches that surrounded the town were permanently washed away, hence most visitors only hang around to arrange transport to one of the other islands not so lacking in the sand department.

Haloban on Pulau Tuangku is the other main village on the islands, which many visitors actually prefer over Balai.

Sights & Activities

The reefs here bubble with colourful fish and corals and there are some fabulous **snorkelling** possibilities off almost any island. **Kayaking** or **boating** between islands is a great way to explore and some of these islands truly look like they were the basis of every tropical-beach postcard cliché. Multiday kayaking excursions can be organised through Yayasan Pulau Banyak.

Most visitors are surfers and there are some world-class **surf spots** here as well as some more average waves. However, don't believe the surf-camp hype about the waves being empty. Fifteen years ago, this was truly a solo surfing adventure, but on our last trip we were shocked to discover dozens of charter boats and up to 30 surfers fighting over one peak!

Yayasan Pulau Banyak Wildlife Watching WILDLIFE RESERVE

(YPB; www.acehturtleconservation.org; Jl Makmur, Balai) Your first port of call on Balai should be Yayasan Pulau Banyak, an NGO that is trying to develop ecotourism as an alternative livelihood for local communities. YPB can provide information on places to stay and transport, as well as guides and tents. It was set up to promote sea-turtle conservation in the region, and continues to do excellent work. If you're keen to see turtles lay their eggs on the beach at Pulau Bangkaru, you'll need to obtain a permit first from YPB. It's also possible to do volunteer work, with duties including nightly beach patrols collecting data on the nesting turtle population and teaching English in local schools.

Sleeping & Eating

Sleeping options on the Banyaks are limited and basic, with only a few islands having bungalows. Camping is another option, and will allow you to stay exclusively on one of the many uninhabited idyllic islands. Tents can be arranged through Yayasan Pulau Banyak.

If staying at one of the bungalows, or if you have a guide, you can arrange food on the islands. Otherwise you'll have to bring provisions with you – or catch your own dinner! It's a good idea to stock up on food and drinking water in Singkil.

BALAI

Balai, which oozes a hot, lazy-day ambience, is a pretty village of quiet streets lined with wood-panelled houses inhabited by disarmingly friendly locals.

Losmen Putri GUESTHOUSE **$**
(☎0812 6313 5099; r 100,000-150,000Rp; ❄) If you get stuck at Balai, arguably the best accommodation is found at Losmen Putri. Most of the simple rooms share bathrooms, which we think makes it a little overpriced, but hey the gardens are nice. It's next to the mobile-phone towers.

Homestay Lae Kombih GUESTHOUSE **$**
(☎0852 9689 5929; Jl Iskandar Muda; r 40,000Rp) This guesthouse overlooks the water and has hot and stuffy rooms. But for this price, what do you expect? The owner is very friendly and speaks good English.

PULAU PALAMBAK BASAR

On Pulau Palambak Basar, you'll find basic bungalows with shared bathrooms at **Lyla's Bungalows** (☎0852 6100 8699; r 80,000Rp). The owner, Erwin, can organise boat transfers and rents snorkelling gear. He also runs the Floating Surf Villas on Ujung Lolok. There used to be a couple of other options but at the time of research they were both closed.

PULAU TAILANA

The small island of Palau Tailana is renowned for reefs that are waves of colour. Dugongs are sometimes sighted in the vicinity and there are plenty of nearby island-hopping possibilities. You'll find three basic bungalows with shared bathrooms at **Pondok Tailana** (☎0852 9671 8219; www.tailana.webs.com; r 80,000Rp). Three square meals a day cost an extra 100,000Rp. Staff can arrange boats to visit the surrounding islands, snorkelling gear, jungle trekking and transfers to/from Balai.

UJUNG LOLOK

The largest island in the Banyaks, Ujung Lolok is draped in dense jungle and retains a wild, end-of-the-earth feeling quite unlike that of the picture-perfect smaller islands to the east.

It's mainly surfers who come out here. Many come on liveaboard surf-charter boats, most of which are very comfortable but offer no real chance to experience Indonesia. Otherwise they do it the way surf trips are supposed to be done, by renting a local fishing boat and living on it.

Banyak Island Lodge LODGE **$$$**
(☎0813 6126 3491; www.banyakislandlodge.com; 7/9/12-night package all-inclusive with flights AU$2500/2750/3000) The only land-based accommodation is the Banyak Island Lodge situated in the so-called 'Bay of Plenty'. Rates include internal flights, transfers and full-board accommodation. However, accommodation is in dorms, the food nonetoo special and the whole place is looking rather shabby. At the time of research they were in the process of constructing a more upmarket lodge on the opposite side of the bay. Rates drop a little outside the May-to-August high season.

Floating Surf Villas LODGE **$$$**
(☎0852 6100 8699; www.floatingsurfvillas.com; per person 7-day package (min 2 people) US$1199) This novel new surf camp should actually be called a surf raft as it sits, floating, out in the waters of the Bay of Plenty. The accommodation is simple but clean and there's easy surf access but we found the attitude of the Indonesian owner varied between bizarre and downright rude and therefore we're reluctant to fully recommend it.

Getting There & Around

There is one ferry a week (Tuesday 10am) between the mainland port of Singkil and Balai (16,000Rp-25,000Rp, three hours). It returns from Balai to Singkil on Friday at 10am. Local boats depart Singkil (30,000Rp, 4½ hours) at around 8am to 9am on Mondays, Thursdays and Saturdays. They return from Balai on Sundays, Wednesdays and Fridays.

By far the most convenient – but expensive – way to reach the islands is to charter a speedboat from Singkil (one way/return around 800,000/1,400,000Rp, two hours).

To travel between islands it's best to ask around at the port on Balai or enquire at Yayasan Pulau Banyak. Small, local fishing boats (you sleep out on deck) can be rented for roughly 800,000Rp per day and the price includes food (which generally consists of rice and fish or fish and rice). This is the perfect way to search out your own slice of paradise.

Gayo Highlands

The beautiful Gayo Highlands deep in the interior of Aceh are ripe for off-the-path picking. This is coffee country, cool and mountainous with spectacular vistas drifting in and out of focus between cool morning mists. The road between Takengon and Blangkejeran, the main towns of the Gayo Highlands, is astoundingly picturesque (and yeah, OK, astoundingly slow!) and can be used as an alternative route to or from Berastagi.

The Gayo people, who number about 250,000, lived an isolated existence until the advent of modern roads and transport. Like the neighbouring Acehnese, the Gayo are strict Muslims and were renowned for their fierce resistance to Dutch rule.

All up, if you're looking to break away from the well-trodden Sumatran banana-pancake backpacker trail, this is the place to do it.

TAKENGON

☎0643 / ELEV 1120M

Takengon is the largest town in the highlands, and while it is not particularly attractive it retains a relaxed charm, with a spectacular setting and a refreshing climate. The town is built on the shores of Danau Laut Tawar, a 26km-long stretch of water, surrounded by steep hills rising to volcanic peaks. Gunung Geureundong, to the north, rises 2855m.

Sights & Activities

Takengon's main attractions are all natural. Admire the views, cruise around the lake in a *perahu* (dugout canoe) or explore caves, waterfalls and hot springs. At weekends locals flock to the cafes and paddling areas on the northern side of the lake (roughly 6km from town). Entrance to these averages 40,000Rp. If you prefer more human contact, the central market is a fascinating place to explore.

Loyang Koro CAVE

(Buffalo Caves; admission by donation) The best cave is Loyang Koro, 6km from town on the lake's southern side. Ask in the house next door for them to turn on the lights and then scramble and crawl through chambers where bats and swifts dart in and out between the stalactites that drip down off the cave roof. Boats can be hired from beside the cave. The road out to the caves passes numerous little fish farms and rural hamlets. A becak from town will cost around 30,000Rp return with waiting time.

Wih Pesame HOT SPRINGS

(entry by donation) At Simpang Balik, about 15km north of Takengon, this sulphurous hot spring is set in a large concrete pool and is said to cure skin diseases.

Festivals & Events

In the week following Independence Day (17 August), Takengon hosts a regional **horse-racing carnival**, held at the track to the west of town. It's a highly spirited affair, with 12-year-old jockeys from all over the highlands riding bareback in the hope of glory.

Sleeping

Hotel Bagu Hill HOTEL $$

(☎22884; Jl Lebe Kader 398B; d incl breakfast 242,000-484,000Rp; 📶) Dare we say it, but this brand new place, just beyond the centre, almost verges on being pop-art cool – with just a hint of Arabic style and over-the-top tack to add some spice to the mix. Beds are a pleasure to crawl into and the water spurting out of the showers is hot. Sadly, some of the front rooms suffer from road noise.

Hotel Mahara HOTEL $$

(☎21728; Jl Sengeda 568; r incl breakfast 225,000-350,000Rp; 📶) One of the more popular town-centre hotels, and certainly one of the better-value ones. This place has aging rooms set around an indoor Indonesian-style pond with bonsai trees. It's comfortable and the staff are helpful.

Arizona Guest House GUESTHOUSE $

(☎0852 6273 0033; Jl Gempar Alam; r from 80,000Rp) No English is spoken here but if you speak Bahasa Indonesia (or enjoy charades) you'll find this guesthouse, which from the outside resembles some kind of US soap-opera palace, has good-value rooms – sadly they're not as palace-like as the exterior leads you to hope. It's on a quiet side street.

Hotel Renggali RESORT **$$**
(☎21144; Jl Bintang; d 200,000-550,000Rp) A wonderful location with rooms perched above the lake and relaxing gardens could easily make this Takengon's best accommodation option but sadly it's very run down and normally utterly empty, which gives it a spooky atmosphere. There's no restaurant and it's a 2km hike into town.

Eating & Drinking

TOP CHOICE **One-One** FISH **$**
(fish around 20,000Rp) Four kilometres out of town on the road to Loyang Karo, this tiny lakeside hamlet consists almost entirely of wooden shacks selling freshly barbequed fish. How fresh, we hear you ask? Well, they'll give you a net and let you fish your lunch straight out of the water. Almost before it's stopped flapping about it's thrown onto hot coals and dished up with rice and spice. Price depends on size of fish. It's worth chartering a becak out here and back at night time because there's little other transport. The name is pronounced 'on-ee on-ee'.

Idola Resto INDONESIAN **$**
(Jl Terminal; mains 10,000-15,000Rp) Technicolour park-style restaurant up from the bus terminal that's as much funfair as place to eat. Serves a wide array of Indonesian dishes and a few Western tastes such as burgers.

TOP CHOICE **Horas Kopi Gayo** CAFE
(☎0813 6169 6234; Jl Sengeda 566; coffee 5,000-20,000Rp) At this simply superb hole-in-the-wall coffee shop, the scent of freshly crushed, roasting beans entices you in. There's always a crowd of locals getting their caffeine fix. Don't miss trying the local speciality, *kopi telor kocok*, a raw egg and sugar creamed together in a glass and topped with coffee.

Getting Around

Labi labi leave from the southern end of Jl Baleatu. Fares around town are 5000Rp. *Perahu* for lake cruising can be hired at the pier at the end of Jl Laut Tawar.

Gunung Leuser National Park

☎0629

The Aceh section of Gunung Leuser National Park has slipped under the tourist radar for years, seeing only a trickle of visitors as the masses head to the more-hyped Bukit Lawang. Its jungle is basically the same minus the well-worn paths and tourists clambering about trying to spot semiwild orangutans. Here is the place for the *real* jungle experience. In the past it's been largely off limits due to the conflict, but now that there's peace in the region it's starting to receive the recognition it deserves.

The World Heritage–listed Gunung Leuser National Park is one of the world's most important and biologically diverse conservation areas. It is often described as a complete ecosystem laboratory because of the range of forest and species types.

Within the park's boundaries live some of the planet's most endangered and exotic species: tigers, rhinoceros, elephants and orangutans. Although your chances of seeing these celebrity animals are remote, you've got a reasonable chance of seeing orangutans, and you can be sure of encountering plenty of other primates. The most common is the white-breasted Thomas leaf monkey, which sports a brilliant, crested punk hairdo.

Habitats range from the swamp forests of the west coast to the dense lowland rainforests of the interior. Much of the area around Ketambe is virgin forest. Above 1500m, the permanent mist has created moss forests rich in epiphytes and orchids. Rare flora includes two members of the rafflesia family,

BUSES FROM TAKENGON

DESTINATION	COST (RP)	DURATION (HR)
Banda Aceh	80,000	8
Blangkejeran	80,000-100,000	7
Ketambe	90,000-140,000	9
Medan	130,000	10

Rafflesia acehensis and *Rafflesia zippelnii,* which are found along Sungai Alas.

More than 300 bird species have been recorded in the park, including the bizarre rhinoceros hornbill, the helmeted hornbill and woodpeckers.

The park faces a great number of challenges. Poachers have virtually wiped out the crocodile population and have severely reduced the number of tigers and rhinoceros. According to the Indonesian Forum for the Environment, a fifth of the park has been adversely affected by illegal logging and road construction. A highly controversial road project called Ladia Galaska runs through the park, linking the eastern and western coasts of the province. Furthermore, during the conflict in Aceh, the jungle was a stronghold of GAM militants, and the national park saw fighting between GAM and Indonesian troops.

This park receives a lot of rain throughout the year, but rain showers tend to lessen in frequency and duration between December and March.

KEDAH

Located 15km west of the scrappy town of Blangkejeran, the small village of Kedah has seen very few visitors since the conflict in Aceh, making it ripe for off-the-beaten-track travel. At the northern edge of Gunung Leuser National Park, Kedah is a magnificent starting point for treks into the jungle, which is home to orangutans, gibbons and other exotic wildlife, birds and plants.

Rainforest Lodge (☎0813 6229 1844; www.gunung-leuser-trek.net; r without bathroom 80,000Rp) is run by the popular Mr Jali, with simple but pleasant bungalows in beautiful jungle surrounds. The lack of electricity adds greatly to its charm. Getting to the lodge is quite the rollicking adventure. Firstly, get to Kedah village and ask around for Mr Jali who lives in a house halfway up the village street; everybody knows him and can point out his house. The Rainforest Lodge is a good hour's walk from here (motorbikes can just about make it along the track but not cars) and is literally in the middle of nowhere. It's a very good idea to let him know in advance that you're coming. He can organise jungle treks for around 350,000Rp per day, including food, guide and park permit.

To get here catch a bus to Blangkejeran, from where you can take a motorbike taxi (50,000Rp, 20 minutes) to Kedah.

KETAMBE

The main tourist centre of the national park, Ketambe (also called Gurah) is a bus stop, a handful of guesthouses and, well, that's about the lot really. Despite, or perhaps because of this, it's one of the most chilled-out places in North Sumatra and a few lazy days relaxing beside the bubbling river and partaking in some jungle hikes is likely to be a highlight of your Sumatran adventures.

Activities

Rafting (half/full day 250,000/500,000Rp) is a fun way to see the forest and keep cool at the same time. Most guesthouses can help organise this.

For serious trekkers and jungle enthusiasts, the trekking (half-day/full-day/overnight 250,000/350,000/700,000Rp) around Ketambe offers a much more authentic experience than that near Bukit Lawang. Be prepared for extreme terrain, hordes of leeches and swarms of stinging insects. Bring plenty of water.

Guides can tailor a trip to specific requests, but here are a few options:

Gurah Recreation Forest TREKKING

The *hutan wisata* (recreation forest) at Gurah is a small, riverside picnic area, but guides lead half- and full-day hikes in the forest that surrounds this and the village. There's a pretty good chance of seeing gibbons, Thomas leaf monkeys and orangutan here.

Hot Springs TREKKING

One of the more popular hikes (but hardly overrun) is this three-day walk to some hot springs deep in the forest.

Bukit Lawang TREKKING

Starting one hour south of Kutacane, this six-day trek through tough terrain passes over 20 river crossings. You have a good chance of seeing orangutans and gibbons, and the trek passes through areas that elephants are known to inhabit. You can arrange to have your luggage delivered to Bukit Lawang separately.

Gunung Kemiri TREKKING

At 3314m, this is the second-highest peak in Gunung Leuser National Park. The return trek takes five to six days, starting from the village of Gumpang, north of Ketambe. It takes in some of the park's richest primate habitat, with orangutans, macaques, siamangs and gibbons.

Gunung Simpali TREKKING

The trek to Gunung Simpali (3270m) is a one-week round trip starting from the village of Engkran and following the valley of Sungai Lawe Mamas. Serious deforestation in the latter part of the trek means this route isn't popular nowadays.

Gunung Leuser TREKKING

The park's highest peak is, of course, Gunung Leuser (3404m). Only the fit should attempt the 14-day return trek to the summit. The walk starts from the village of Angusan, northwest of Blangkejeran.

Sleeping & Eating

Accommodation is scattered along the only road through Ketambe; guesthouses are listed in geographical order as you arrive into town. Each has its own small restaurant.

Wisma Cinta Alam GUESTHOUSE $

(☎0852 7086 4580; www.gunung-leuser-trek.net; r 50,000-150,000Rp) The cheaper rooms here are the same sort of standard huts you'll find everywhere else in the village with just a mattress plonked onto the floor, but the pricier ones come with proper showers and real beds. It can supply excellent, knowledgeable guides. It's also a good choice for those keen on rafting.

Pak Mus Guesthouse GUESTHOUSE $

(☎0813 8020 4305; r 50,000-80,000Rp) It's all about the beautiful garden setting at this charming family-run place with bungalows set beneath a forest backdrop. Thomas leaf monkeys are often sighted feeding on the fruit trees and even the odd orangutan has been known to drop by for breakfast.

Friendship Guesthouse GUESTHOUSE $

(☎0852 9688 3624; www.ketambe.com; r 50,000Rp) This spot has a beautiful riverside location with charming wooden bungalows and Western toilets. Staff are very friendly, and there are plenty of characters lurking about.

Wisma Sadar Wisata GUESTHOUSE $

(☎0852 7615 5741; r 40,000-50,000Rp) Here you'll find a range of good-value bungalows, including some overlooking the river. The friendly owner and her daughter are great for a laugh and they make a decent veggie curry.

Pondok Wisata Ketambe GUESTHOUSE $

(☎0853 5831 3380; r 50,000-70,000Rp) Well-established guesthouse with dark, but spacious wooden rooms set at the end of a forested driveway.

Information

Ketambe, in the heart of the Alas Valley, is one of the main access points to Gunung Leuser National Park. Directly across the river is Ketambe Research Station, a world-renowned conservation research station, which is off limits to tourists. Kutacane, 43km from Ketambe, is the closest town of any note and is the place to go for transport, ATMs and internet. Permits to the park (20,000Rp per day) can be arranged at guesthouses in Ketambe. In theory you will need three photocopies of your passport but this is rarely required. Guides can be hired from any guesthouse in Ketambe. Quality varies, so ask other travellers for recommendations first.

Getting There & Around

NBA (☎061 453 4680) flies from Kutacane to Medan and to Banda Aceh twice weekly. From Kutacane there are countless *labi labi* to Ketambe (10,000Rp, one hour).

KETAMBE RESEARCH STATION

The Ketambe Research Station has been conducting extensive studies of the flora and fauna of Gunung Leuser National Park for almost 30 years.

In the early 1970s, Ketambe was home to Sumatra's orangutan rehabilitation programme, but the project was relocated to Bukit Lawang to allow researchers to study the Ketambe region without the disruption of tourists. Nowadays the station's primary concern is hard-core conservation, research and species cataloguing. Both the centre and the surrounding forest are off limits to almost everyone but the Indonesian and international researchers.

The 450-hectare protected area consists mainly of primary lowland tropical forest and is home to a large number of primates, as well as Sumatran tigers, rhinoceros, sun bears, hornbills and snakes. Despite its protected status, a third of the area has been lost to illegal logging since 1999.

BUSES FROM KUTACANE & KETAMBE

DESTINATION	DEPARTURE TOWN	COST (RP)	DURATION (HR)
Banda Aceh	Kutacane/Ketambe	200,000	20
Blangkejeran	Ketambe	35,000	3
Medan	Kutacane	50,000	7
Takengon	Kutacane/Ketambe	120,000	8

WEST SUMATRA

From the air, Sumatra Barat (West Sumatra) looks as though a giant has plunged their hands into the equator, thrown it high into the air, and let it rain back down to earth. Fertile uplands ring jungle-clad volcanoes, waterfalls cascade into deep ravines and nature takes a breath in deep, silent lakes. Rainforest still clings to the steepest slopes, while rice, tapioca, cinnamon and coffee bring in the wealth.

This is the heartland of the matriarchal Minangkabau, an intelligent, culturally rich and politically savvy people who have successfully exported their culture, language, cuisine and beliefs throughout Indonesia. Their unique buffalo-horned architecture dominates the cities and villages.

Hot, bustling Padang on the Indian Ocean is the gateway and provincial capital, though most tourists head straight for scenic Bukittinggi in the highlands. Surfers and trekkers flock to the perfect breaks and tribal culture of the Mentawai Islands, while nature lovers explore Sumatra's largest national park in Kerinci, just across the border in Jambi province. Danau Maninjau remains the stunning, forgotten jewel in the crown, and the beautiful Harau Valley is definitely worth a Sumatran detour.

History

Little is known about the area's history before the arrival of Islam in the 14th century. However, the abundance of megalithic remains around the towns of Batu Sangkar and Payakumbuh, near Bukittinggi, suggest that the central highlands supported a sizeable community some 2000 years ago.

After the arrival of Islam, the region was split into small Muslim states ruled by sultans. It remained this way until the beginning of the 19th century, when war erupted between followers of the Islamic fundamentalist Padri movement and supporters of the local chiefs, adherents to the Minangkabau *adat* (traditional laws and regulations). The Padris were so named because their leaders were haji, pilgrims who had made their way to Mecca via the Acehnese port of Pedir. They returned from the haj determined to establish a true Islamic society and stamp out the pre-Islamic ways that dominated the ruling houses.

The Padris had won control of much of the highlands by 1821 when the Dutch decided to join the fray in support of the Minangkabau traditional leaders. The fighting dragged on until 1837, when the Dutch overcame the equator town of Bonjol, the stronghold of the Padri leader Imam Bonjol, whose name adorns street signs all over Indonesia. In today's Minangkabau society, a curious fusion of traditional beliefs and Islam is practised.

Padang

0751 / POP 833,000

Most visitors don't give Sumatra's third-largest city a second glance, convinced that it's just another simmering urbo-Indonesian sprawl of traffic, smog and chaos. It's also a city astride one of the planet's most powerful seismic zones, centrally located on the tectonic hotspot where the Indo-Australian plate plunges under the Eurasian plate.

A devastating 7.6-magnitude earthquake did hit the city in 2009, killing more than 1000 people, and destroying hotels and public buildings. Some remote villages in the nearby Kerinci region were wiped out completely from landslides, while the Mentawai Islands, Pantai Bungus, Bukittinggi and Danau Maninjau escaped relatively unscathed. Other significant tremors without major damage followed in 2010 and 2012, and the Sumatran seismic battleground that triggered the 2004 Boxing Day tsunami continues to be active.

West Sumatra

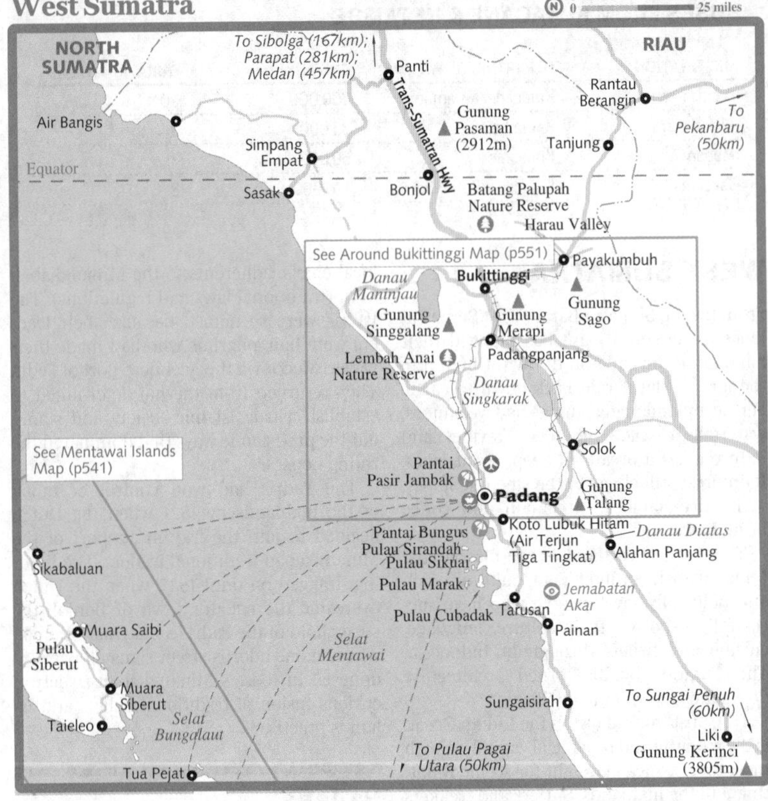

But sandwiched between the mountains and the sea, this once-humble fishing village is also reinventing itself, aided by cheap airfares and its proximity to the region's power centres of Malaysia and Singapore. There's a strong sense of cultural identity among the youthful, well-educated population, and Padang is the modern face of Minangkabau culture and the cuisine the region gave to the world.

Sights & Activities

Colonial Quarter NEIGHBOURHOOD

Although damaged in the 2009 earthquake, Padang's colonial quarter around Jl Batang Arau is still worth a lazy stroll. Old Dutch and Chinese warehouses back onto a river brimming with fishing boats. The beach along Jl Samudera is the best place to watch the sunset.

Adityawarman Museum MUSEUM

(Jl Diponegoro; admission 1500Rp; 8am-4pm Tue-Sun) Adityawarman Museum, built in the Minangkabau tradition, has pleasant grounds, though non-Bahasa Indonesia speakers may find the dusty collections detailing everyday Minangkabau life rather dry. The entrance is on Jl Gereja.

Taman Budaya Cultural Centre ARTS CENTRE

(Jl Diponegoro 31) Taman Budaya Cultural Centre stages sporadic dance performances, poetry readings, plays and art exhibitions. The events schedule is posted outside the building.

Tours

Padang is the launching point for tours of the Mentawai Islands, famous for their hunter-gatherer culture, endemic flora and fauna, and world-class surfing. Local travel agencies can also arrange tours around the surrounding Minangkabau heartland of West Sumatra.

East West Tour & Travel SURFING
(☎36370; Jl Nipah Berok) Indonesian-run charter-boat company offering Mentawai surf trips.

Nando Sumatera Tours TOUR
(☎0852 6335 7645; www.nandosumatratour.com) Friendly owner Nando is a safe and knowledgeable driver and can also arrange tours across north and west Sumatra.

Regina Adventures TOUR, SURFING
(☎0812 6774 5464; www.reginaadventures.com) Trekking on the Mentawai Islands, trips to Danau Maninjau and Bukittinggi, and ascents of Gunung Merapi and Gunung Kerinci. Check the website for good-value surf trips to Mentawai and Krui further south.

Sumatran Surfariis SURFING
(Bevys Sumatra; ☎34878; www.sumatransurfariis.com; Komplek Pondok Indah B 12, Parak Gadang) Long-established Mentawai surf-boat charter company. It's also an excellent contact if you're keen to partake of West Sumatra's surprising golfing scene. The area's three spectacular courses – one designed by a dual winner of the British Open – are virtually empty on weekdays, and local animal spectators may include monkeys and wild pigs.

Festivals & Events

Don't miss the colourful dragon-boat festival held annually in mid-July to commemorate the city's founding.

Pesta Budaya Tabuik CULTURAL
The highlight of the West Sumatran cultural calendar is Pesta Budaya Tabuik (derived from the Islamic festival of Tabut), held at the seaside town of Pariaman, 36km north of Padang. It takes place at the beginning of the month of Muharam (based on the Islamic lunar calendar, usually January or February) to honour the martyrdom of Muhammed's grandchildren, Hassan and Hussein, at the battle of Kerbala.

Central to the festival is the *bouraq,* a winged horse-like creature with the head of a woman, which is believed to have descended to earth to collect the souls of dead heroes and take them to heaven.

Sleeping

Some of Padang's older hotels were demolished following the 2009 earthquake, but a new crop of more modern hotels are now on

THE MINANGKABAU

Legend has it that the Minangkabau are descended from the wandering Macedonian tyrant Alexander the Great. According to the story, the ancestors of the Minangkabau arrived in Sumatra under the leadership of King Maharjo Dirajo, the youngest son of Alexander.

Anthropologists, however, suggest that the Minangkabau arrived in West Sumatra from the Malay Peninsula some time between 1000 and 2000 BC, probably by following Sungai Batang Hari upstream from the Strait of Melaka to the highlands of the Bukit Barisan mountains.

Even if they don't have Alexander's bloodline, the Minangkabau reflect his wanderlust and love of battle, albeit in the milder form of buffalo fighting. Their success in buffalo fighting is believed to have bestowed the people with their tribal name, and the horns of the beast are the focus of their architecture and traditional costumes.

The legend of how the Minangkabau named themselves begins with an imminent attack by a Javanese king. Rather than pit two armies against each other, the Minangkabau proposed a fight between two bulls. When the time came, the West Sumatrans dispatched a tiny calf to fight the enormous Javanese bull, but the half-starved calf was outfitted with sharp metal spears to its horns. Believing the Javanese bull to be its mother, the calf rushed to suckle and ripped the bull's belly to shreds. When the bull finally dropped dead, the people of West Sumatra shouted '*Minangkabau, minangkabau!*', which literally means 'The buffalo wins, the buffalo wins!'.

Linguistic sticklers, though, prefer the far more prosaic explanation that Minangkabau is a combination of two words: *minanga,* which means 'a river', and *kerbau,* which means 'buffalo'. A third theory suggests that it comes from the archaic expression *pinang kabhu,* which means 'original home' – Minangkabau being the cradle of Malay civilisation.

Padang

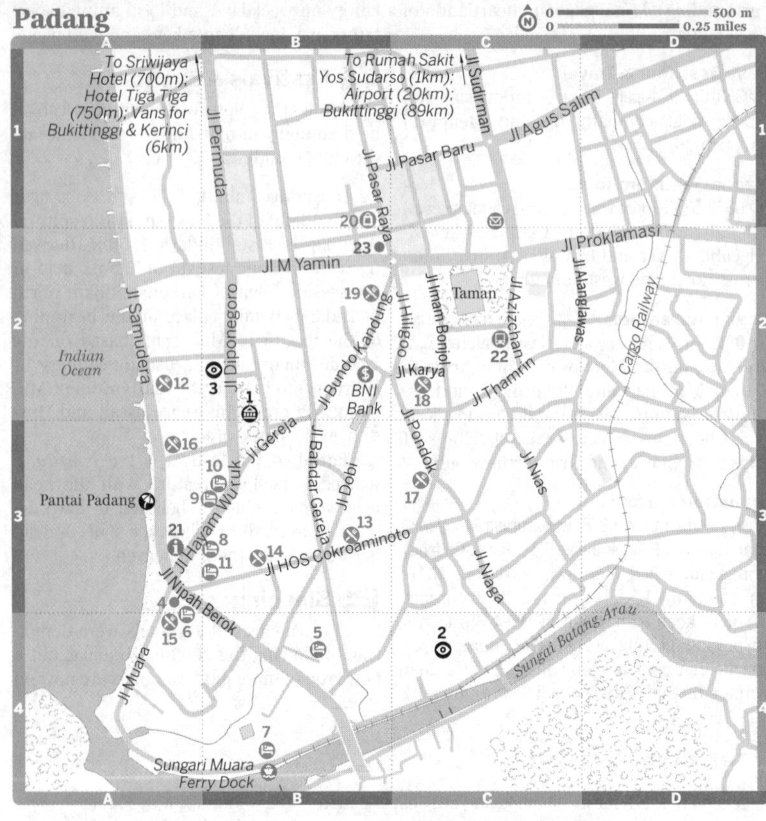

Padang

Sights
1 Adityawarman Museum B2
2 Colonial Quarter C4
3 Taman Budaya Cultural Centre B2

Activities, Courses & Tours
4 East West Tour & Travel A3

Sleeping
5 Brigitte's House B4
6 Golden Homestay A4
7 Grace House B4
8 HW Hotel B3
9 Immanuel Hotel B3
10 Savali Hotel B3
11 Spice Homestay B3

Eating
12 Beach Safari A2
13 Hoya Bakery B3
14 Ikan Bakar Pak Agus B3
15 Metta Padma A4
16 Nelayan Restaurant A3
17 Pagi Sore C3
18 Sari Raso C2
19 Simpang Raya B2

Shopping
20 Pasar Raya B1

Information
21 Tourism Padang A3

Transport
22 Damri C2
23 Opelet Terminal B2

offer. Homestays catering mainly to Mentawai-bound surfers are the best options for budget travellers.

TOP CHOICE **Spice Homestay** HOMESTAY **$$**
(☎25982; spicehomey@yahoo.com; Jl HOS Cokroaminoto 104; r incl breakfast 310,000-355,000Rp; ❄📶) Relocated after the 2009 earthquake, this friendly and relaxed guesthouse is perfect for families and surfers. A compact Zen garden combines with colourful rooms and artwork, and the lovely Balinese owner Sri is the perfect contact for information on onward travel to the islands or Bukittinggi.

Brigitte's House HOMESTAY **$**
(☎36099; http://brigittehouse.blogspot.com.au; Jl Kampung Sebalah 1/14; dm 85,000Rp, s 95,000Rp, d 180,000-220,000Rp; ❄📶) Brigitte's has a relaxed and homely ambience, with options ranging from dorms to double rooms with private bathrooms. The surrounding residential neighbourhood is quiet and leafy, and Brigitte has plenty of information on buses, ferries and Mentawai adventures. A short walk away is a self-contained apartment for families and groups.

Savali Hotel HOTEL **$$**
(☎27660; www.savalihotel.com; Jl Hayam Wuruk 31; r incl breakfast 700,000-900,000Rp; ❄📶🏊) The centrally located Savali is just a short stroll from the beach and good restaurants. The hotel's 23 rooms are arrayed around a Zen-style garden, good English is spoken at reception and there's definitely an open mind to negotiation on room rates. The compact swimming pool is welcome on sultry equatorial afternoons.

Sriwijaya Hotel HOTEL **$$**
(☎21942; www.thesriwijayahotel.com; Jl Veteran 26; r incl breakfast 325,000-425,000Rp; ❄📶) Located just north of central Padang and a short stroll from the beach, the Sriwijaya features modern rooms arrayed around a leafy garden courtyard. Free bicycles are available if you're keen on exploring the nearby beach promenade.

Golden Homestay HOMESTAY **$**
(☎32616; Jl Nipah Berok 1B; dm 125,000Rp, r 200,000-325,000Rp; ❄📶) Spotless dorms and private rooms named after classic Sydney surf breaks. Grab a bed in the shared Bronte room, or splash out on the Bondi or Manly rooms with private bathrooms.

HW Hotel HOTEL **$$**
(☎893 500; www.hwhotelpadang.com; Jl Hayam Wuruk 16; r incl breakfast 700,000Rp; ❄📶) Modern and spacious rooms in a new hotel built after the 2009 earthquake. There's room for negotiation on the rates, especially on weekends.

Grace House HOMESTAY **$**
(☎081 2670 3597; gracehousepadang@yahoo.com; Jl Batang Arau 88B; r 60,000-250,000Rp; ❄📶) New and colourful rooms located just across the road from the departure point for the wooden ferries to the Mentawai Islands. Bathroom and kitchen facilities are shared.

Immanuel Hotel HOTEL **$**
(☎28560; Jl Hayam Wuruk 43; r incl breakfast 150,000-350,000Rp; ❄📶) Another travellers' standby, Immanuel is centrally located with simple rooms, helpful cheery staff and a welcome garden.

Hotel Tiga Tiga HOTEL **$**
(☎22173; Jl Veteran 33; r incl breakfast 140,000-210,000Rp; ❄📶) This old travellers' dosser north of the centre has cheap, simple rooms only five minutes' walk from the sea. Grab any white *opelet* heading up Jl Permuda.

Eating & Drinking

Padang is the birth mother of the cuisine that migrated across Indonesia. Even though everyone swears that Padang cuisine tastes better outside of Padang, pay homage to the native cooks with a visit to one of these famous franchises: **Pagi Sore** (Jl Pondok 143; dishes 9000Rp), **Sari Raso** (Jl Karya 3; dishes 10,000Rp) and **Simpang Raya** (Jl Bundo Kandung; dishes 8000Rp).

Jl Batang Arau is full of cheap warungs that spring to life at night, while discerning foodies head for Jl Pondok and Jl HOS Cokroaminoto. Juice wagons loiter near the end of Jl Hayam Wuruk. For cheap sate, grilled seafood, and a few cold Bintangs (Indonesian beer), head to the beachfront shacks lining Jl Sumadera at sunset.

TOP CHOICE **Ikan Bakar Pak Agus** SEAFOOD **$$**
(Jl HOS Cokroaminoto 91; meals around 50,000Rp) Pak Agus flame-grills his dead sea creatures to perfection with a smoky sambal sauce. The fresh-every-afternoon marine selection includes shoals of different fish, squid, and huge king prawns (around 110,000Rp for three). Fish is definitely more affordable, so

grab a spot at the shared tables and tuck in for a quintessential Padang experience.

Nelayan Restaurant SEAFOOD $$

(Jl Samudera; mains 30,000-50,000Rp) Great seafood the Chinese way, cold beers and one of the best views in town of a Padang sunset. Treat yourself to grilled prawns or crab, but definitely ask the price before you dig in. We're pretty partial to a chilled Bintang with the *cumi asam manis* (squid in a sweet and sour sauce).

Beach Safari CAFE $$

(Jl Samudera 16; mains 30,000-40,000Rp; ⏲from 5pm) Smoothies, juices, good coffee and cold beers all feature at this combination cafe/bakery just across the road from the beach. Padang's bright young things park their scooters in tidy rows and tuck into Western-style meals including pizza, steak and fish and chips.

Hoya Bakery BAKERY $

(Jl HOS Cokroaminoto 48; snacks/meals around 5000/15,000Rp) Padang's go-to spot for freshly baked sweet and savoury goodies. Friendly shop assistants will guide you around the selection before steering you to a colourful table. There are also good burgers, sandwiches and pasta if you're still getting to grips with the spicy local tucker, and the juices and smoothies are soothing antidotes to Padang's tropical buzz.

Metta Padma VEGETARIAN $

(Jl Muara 34-38, Komplek Vihara Buddha; snacks 5000-15,000Rp; 📝) Opening hours are decidedly haphazard, but it's worth dropping by to see if this warung attached to a Buddhist temple and community centre is open. Good-value vegetarian snacks include *popiah* (spring rolls).

Shopping

Pasar Raya MARKET

(Jl Pasar Raya) Pasar Raya – literally 'big market' – is the centre of Padang's shopping universe. The city's biggest shopping malls were demolished following the 2009 earthquake, but at the time of writing a modern replacement was being constructed near the Pasar Raya.

Information

There are ATMs all over town.

BNI Bank (Jl Bundo Kandung) The ATM dispenses up to 2,000,000Rp.

Imigrasi office (☎444 511; Jl Khatib Sulaiman) Visa extensions from 30 days to two months can be made at the Padang Imigrasi

PADANG CUISINE

With *nasi Padang* (Padang cuisine), you sit down and the whole kit and caboodle gets laid out in front of you. You decide which ones look tasty and push the others aside. You pay for what you eat – nibbling, sniffing and fondling included.

The drawback is that you never really know what you're eating, since there's no menu. If the dish contains liquid, it is usually a coconut-milk curry, a major component of Padang cuisine. The meaty dishes are most likely beef or buffalo, occasionally offal or (less likely) even dog.

The most famous Padang dish is *rendang*, in which chunks of beef or buffalo are simmered slowly in coconut milk until the sauce is reduced to a rich paste and the meat becomes dark and dried. Other popular dishes include *telor balado* (egg dusted with red chilli), *ikan panggang* (fish baked in coconut and chilli) and *gulai merah kambing* (red mutton curry).

Most couples pick one or two meat dishes and a vegetable, usually *kangkung* (water spinach), and load up with a plate or two of rice. Carbs are manna in Padang cuisine. Vegetarians should ask for tempeh or *tahu* (tofu), which comes doctored up in a spicy sambal.

Before digging into the meal with your right hand, wash up in the provided bowl of water. Food and sauces should be spooned onto your plate of rice, then mixed together with the fingers. The rice will be easier to handle if it is a little wet. Use your fingers to scoop up the food, and your thumb to push it into your mouth. It's messy even for the locals.

Padang cuisine has an earthy spiciness that might need a little sweet tea or water as a chaser. There is usually a tumbler of lukewarm water (a sign that it has been boiled for sterilisation) on the table.

TRANSPORT FROM PADANG

Air

DESTINATION	COMPANY	FREQUENCY
Kuala Lumpur	AirAsia	daily
Jakarta	Lion Air, Batavia Air, Sriwijaya Air, Garuda	daily
Medan	Sriwijaya Air	daily
Pulau Batam	Batavia Air	daily
Rokot (Pulau Sipora, Mentawai Islands)	NBA	Monday, Thursday

Bus

DESTINATION	COST (RP)	DURATION (HOURS)	FREQUENCY
Bukittinggi	16,000	2	hourly until 6pm
Sungai Penuh	80,000	7	8am, 9am, 7pm, 8pm

office. It's about 5km out of town by *ojek* or taxi.

Post Office (Jl Azizchan 7; per hr 6000Rp) Near the corner of Jl M Yamin and Jl Azizchan. Has internet access.

Rumah Sakit Yos Sudarso (☎33230; Jl Situjuh 1) Privately owned hospital.

Selasih Hospital (☎51405; Jl Khatib Sulaiman 72)

Tourism Padang (☎34186; www.tourism.padang.go.id; Dinas Kebudayaan Dan Pariwisata, Jl Samudera 1; ⏲7.30am-4pm Mon-Fri, 8am-4pm Sat & Sun) Maps and a range of English-language regional brochures.

Getting There & Away

Air

Padang's airport, **Bandara Internasional Minangkabau** (BIM; Jl Adinegoro), is located 20km north of town. There is a 100,000Rp departure tax on international flights.

Boat

For journeys to the Mentawai Islands, Padang has two commonly used ports. The *Sumber Rezeky* and *Pulau Simasin* wooden ferries usually depart from the river mouth (Sungai Muara) on Sungai Batang Arau, just south of Padang's city centre. The more comfortable *Ambu Ambu* steel ferry departs from Teluk Kabung port at Bungus, around 20km (45 minutes) away.

Bus

The days of heading 12km out of town to the Bengkuang terminal at Aie Pacah are over. Most locals prefer to take minibuses directly from Padang.

Tranex (☎705 8577) buses depart for Bukittinggi from the city's northern fringes outside the Wisma Indah building. Catch any white *opelet* (2000Rp) heading north on Jl Permuda and ask for 'Tranex' or 'Wisma Indah.'

Minibuses for other destinations depart from a variety of offices scattered around the city. Ask your hotel to call in advance to arrange a pick up.

The following minibuses, both of which depart from Jl Jhoni Anwar, are the most relevant to travellers. Catch an *opelet* (2000Rp) north along Jl Permuda and Jl S Parman, get off at the white mosque around 5km north of central Padang, and turn right into Jl Jhoni Anwar.

P O Sinar Kerinci (☎783 1299; Jl Jhni Anwar Q4) Regular departures to Sungai Penuh (for Kerinci Seblat National Park).

Putra Mandau (☎782 2218; Jl Jhoni Anwar) Links Padang to Dumai and Pekanbaru if you're travelling to Sumatra by sea from Malaysia or Singapore.

Getting Around

Airport taxis start from 120,000Rp. White **Damri** (☎780 6335) buses (25,000Rp) are a cheaper alternative and loop through Padang. Tell the conductor your accommodation and street and they'll drop you at the right stop. Heading to the airport, they also loop through the city, but have a depot near the *taman* (park). If you're coming from Bukittinggi, alight at the motorway overpass and take an *ojek* to the terminal. There are numerous *opelet* (2000Rp) around town, operating out of the **Pasar Raya terminal** off Jl M Yamin.

Around Padang

If Padang's traffic is frying your brains, or you're waiting for a boat, kick back on one of the nearby beaches. **Pantai Bungus**, 23km south of Padang, is conveniently close to the ferry port of Teluk Kabung, but still sufficiently relaxed to unkink the most frazzled. There's a host of nearby islands to explore, plus the odd gem in the hinterland.

Losmen Carlos (☎0813 6397 3411, 751 153; losemen_carlos.bymaicheil@yahoo.co.id; r 100,000-300,000Rp, tents 50,000Rp; ❄@) has great beachside rooms and a cruisy reggae-fuelled vibe. The eponymous Carlos runs tours to Pulau Pagang and Pulau Sironjong, and can organise Siberut guides for Mentawai visits, and trips to the hinterland. Beach bonfires and fish barbecues are often featured – BYO guitar and laid-back attitude. When we dropped by, Carlos was putting the finishing touches to a few new rooms, and was planning on running Padang food cookery classes (per person 100,000Rp).

Tin Tin Homestay (☎0812 6683 6668; losmentintin@yahoo.com; r 100,000Rp) is a small, quiet family-run losmen with basic, netted rooms, situated 400m south of Losmen Carlos. It also offers island tours with overnight stays (per person 250,000Rp). You'll need to bring your own food for island stays.

The best eating at Pantai Bungus is at **Yangi Beach Cafe** (snacks & meals 5000-20,000Rp). Island trips and boat excursions can be booked, and the airy timber and bamboo pavilion is a great spot for Indonesian and Western food and a few sunset drinks.

Pulau Pagang is a beautiful small island, 90 minutes offshore, with white sandy beaches and a handful of basic bungalows. It's possible to rent a boat from Bungus and stay the night. Ask at Losmen Carlos or Tin Tin Homestay, or among the local fishermen.

Pulau Sikuai and **Pulau Cubadak** both have expensive resorts. **Cubadak Paradiso Village** (☎0812660 3766; www.cubadak-paradisovillage.com) is the better of the two; it also has a **dive school** (☎081 2663 7609).

Further south is **Pulau Marak**, which has a simiang (black gibbon) rehabilitation centre and kilometres of undisturbed coastline. While not officially open to the public, it's worth asking around.

Back on the mainland, and close to Teluk Kabung, the spectacular three-storey waterfall **Air Terjun Tiga Tingkat** (Three Tier Waterfall) is found in the village of Koto Lubuk Hitam.

Jembatan Akar (Bridge of Roots) is a living bridge over the Bayang River made from the entwined roots of weeping fig trees. Follow the highway south through Tarusan towards Painan, and turn left after Pasar Baru onto the Muara Air road, heading for Kampong Pulut-Pulut. The narrow road follows a scenic valley for another 23km.

To reach Pantai Bungus from Padang, take a blue *opelet* labelled 'Kabung Bungus' (10,000Rp, 1 hour) or a taxi (120,000Rp).

Mentawai Islands

Though not a great distance from the mainland, the Mentawai Islands and its people were kept isolated until the 19th century by strong winds, unpredictable currents and razor-sharp corals.

It's thought that the archipelago separated from Sumatra some 500,000 years ago, resulting in unique flora and fauna that sees Mentawai ranked alongside Madagascar in terms of endemic primate population. Of particular interest is *siamang kerdil*, a rare species of black-and-yellow monkey, named *simpai Mentawai* by the locals.

The largest island, Siberut, is home to the majority of the Mentawai population and is the most studied and protected island in the archipelago. About 60% of Siberut is still covered with tropical rainforest, which shelters a rich biological community that has earned it a designation as a Unesco biosphere reserve. The western half of the island is protected as the Siberut National Park.

Pulau Sipora is home to Tua Pejat, the seat of regional government and a surfer drop-off point. The archipelago's airport is located at Rokot. With only 10% original rainforest remaining, it's also the most developed of the Mentawai Islands.

Further south are the Pulau Pagai islands – Utara (North) and Selatan (South) – which rarely see independent travellers.

Change has come quickly to the Mentawai Islands. Tourism, logging, *transmigrasi* (a government-sponsored scheme enabling settlers to move from overcrowded regions to sparsely populated ones) and other government-backed attempts to mainstream the culture have separated the people from the jungle and whittled the jungle into profit. It isn't what it used to be, but it is a long way from being like everywhere else.

Surfers comprise the other island-bound pilgrims, many of whom rank the Mentawais as the ride of their life.

A magnitude 7.7 earthquake hit the islands in October 2010, with a resulting tsunami killing more than 500 people and making more than 8000 homeless in the archipelago's southern islands.

Activities

Trekking

The river scene from *Apocalypse Now* flashes into your mind as you head upstream in a longboat and watch the people and villages growing wilder by the minute. Soon you're out of the canoe and following some shaman-eyed tribesman with crazy tattoos and a loincloth through the mud for the next few hours, passing waterfalls, balancing on slippery tree branches and swimming across rivers, to his humble abode on poles in the middle of nowhere.

There's been fervent discussion about the authenticity of these trips, and what actually constitutes a traditional lifestyle. The mud is real and so are the tattoos – decide for yourself.

In the past, mainland tour agencies had a stranglehold on the tourist dollar, but it's more flexible and sustainable to turn up at Muara Siberut independently than be locked into a 10-day mainland-organised tour. Ask around at the jetty cafes in Maileppet and Muara Siberut. Prices start around 150,000Rp per day, but don't include transport, food, accommodation or tips. Clarify exactly what is and isn't included.

If you prefer a mainland-organised trek, prices in Bukittinggi start at around US$300 for six days and normally include a guide, accommodation, food and transport. However, always check for any additional costs. Most hotels in Padang also offer tours.

Dress for mud wrestling. Most of your gear will get trashed, so bring as little as possible, and bear in mind you may need to swim the odd river. Leave the smartphone somewhere safe.

Double-bag everything in plastic bags and try to keep one set of clothes dry for evening use. Don't walk in beach sandals – one foot into deep bog and you'll never see them again. However, if you dislike having pig excrement between your toes, you might find

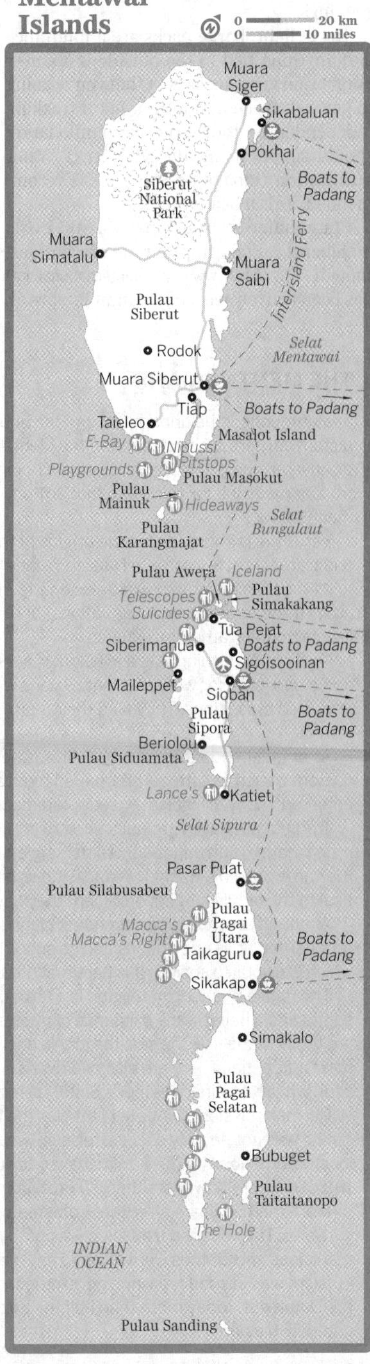

them useful around the communities in the evenings.

Travel light. Large packs are a hindrance and anything tied to the outside is a goner. Forget rain gear, just accept that you're going to get wet. Bring a mosquito net if trekking independently; tour-group accommodation should supply them (though check). Water purification (tablets or Steripen) is recommended, as is a head torch.

Chloroquine-resistant malaria still exists on Siberut, so take appropriate precautions, though **SurfAid** (www.surfaidinternational.org) has been actively working to limit its spread. DDT-strength insect repellent is advisable. Sanitation is poor, with the local river serving all purposes, so bring as much bottled water as you can.

May is generally the driest month, while October and November are the wettest – but it can rain any time.

You can buy most supplies in Muara Siberut, but they are much cheaper in Padang. You'll also need items for barter and gifts.

Surfing

Surfing is big business in Mentawai as the islands have consistent surf year-round at

THE MENTAWAIANS

The untouched, the unbaptised and the unphotographed have long drawn Westerners to distant corners of the globe. And the Mentawaians have seen every sort of self-anointed discoverer: the colonial entrepreneurs hoping to harness the land for profit, missionaries trading medicine for souls and modern-day tourists eager to experience life before the machine.

Very little is known about the origins of the Mentawaians, but it is assumed that they emigrated from Sumatra to Nias and made their way to Siberut from there.

At the time of contact with missionaries, the Mentawaians had their own language, *adat* (traditional laws and regulations) and religion, and were skilled boat builders. They lived a hunter-gatherer existence.

Traditional clothing was a loincloth made from the bark of the breadfruit tree for men and a bark skirt for women. Mentawaians wore bands of red-coloured rattan, beads and imported brass rings. They filed their teeth into points and decorated their bodies with tattoos.

After independence, the Indonesian government banned many of the Mentawaians' customs, such as tattoos, sharpened teeth and long hair. Although the ban has not been enforced, many villagers have adopted modern fashions.

Traditional villages are built along riverbanks and consist of one or more *uma* (communal house) surrounded by *lalep* (single-storey family houses). Several families live in the same building. Bachelors and widows have their own quarters, known as *rusuk*, identical to the family longhouse except they have no altar.

Although essentially patriarchal, society is organised on egalitarian principles. There are no inherited titles or positions and no subordinate roles. It is the *uma*, not the village itself, which is pivotal to society. It is here that discussions affecting the community take place.

The native Sibulungan religion is a form of animism, involving the worship of nature spirits and a belief in the existence of ghosts, as well as the soul. The chief nature spirits are those of the sky, the sea, the jungle and the earth. The sky spirits are considered the most influential. There are also two river spirits: Ina Oinan (Mother of Rivers) is beneficent, while Kameinan (Father's Sister) is regarded as evil.

German missionary August Lett was the first to attempt to convert the local people, but he was not entirely successful: eight years after his arrival Lett was murdered by the locals. Somehow the mission managed to survive and 11 baptisms had been recorded by 1916. There are now more than 80 Protestant churches throughout the islands.

More than 50 years after the Protestants, Catholic missionaries moved in to vie for converts. They opened a mission – a combined church, school and clinic – and free medicines and clothes were given to any islander who converted.

Islam was introduced when government officials were appointed from Padang during the Dutch era. Today more than half the population claims to be Protestant, 16% Catholic and 13% Muslim.

FIXING A SURFING SAFARI

A good fixer is worth their weight in gold. They will meet you at the airport, show you where you can procure various supplies, then get the whole lot to the port and safely stowed on the ferry. They will have already arranged your arrival day to coincide with the ferry schedule, and secured you a cabin. On your return, they'll meet the ferry and get you and all your gear back to the airport.

You then need a second fixer out in the islands, who will meet your ferry, tee up a longboat, ship your gear, and drop you at a cheap losmen or basic hut somewhere close to your favourite break. They'll even arrange a cook if you want one. Of course, all this costs money, and rest assured, your fixer is taking a cut from everybody. But with careful planning and bargaining it's still going to be a whole lot cheaper than two weeks in a resort.

How do you find a fixer? Without any recommendations, your first trip will always be a learning curve. Experienced surfers come back year after year and use the same fixers, boat drivers and hut owners. All business is conducted by mobile phone, and good fixers will also have email addresses. Watch closely what other groups are doing – maybe you can share a taxi to the port, or bum a lift in a speedboat – all the time filling your mobile phone with contact numbers.

There's nothing stopping you doing all this organising yourself, but it's time and energy you'd most likely rather leave for the waves.

If you're looking to set something up before you arrive, contact **Harris Smile** (☎0821 2241 0133; harrissmile@yahoo.com), a friendly Tua Pejat local.

hundreds of legendary breaks. The season peaks between April and October.

In the past, charter boats were the primary means of reaching the top spots, but now land-based resorts are growing in popularity.

With patience, attitude and a handful of contacts, however, it's possible to put together your own independent surfing safari for a fraction of the cost of a package tour. Losmen are blossoming throughout the Mentawais, and chartering a longboat is relatively easy. Check some of the more popular surfing blogs, such as GlobalSurfers (www.globalsurfers.com) and WannaSurf (www.wannasurf.com), or Lonely Planet's own Thorn Tree forum (www.lonelyplanet.com/thorntree), for the latest hotspots.

Tours

Padang-based East West Tour & Travel (p535), Regina Adventures (p535) and Sumatran Surfariis (p535) can arrange tours and surf charters.

Sleeping

Along with transport, accommodation will be your primary expense in the Mentawais. Trekking guides will organise family homestays.

If you want wi-fi, three meals a day and hot showers, then bite the resort or surf-camp bullet. Check if transport is included from mainland Sumatra because this can vary by accommodation. Most operate on a package basis for around 10 days, and pre-booking from overseas is required.

TOP CHOICE **Togat Nusa** RESORT **$$$**
(www.togatnusaretreat.com; d incl meals US$250; ❄📶) The only resort on the private 12-hectare island of Pitojat, Togat Nusa's scattering of bungalows caters to only eight guests at a time. The funky and stylish accommodation is crafted using recycled driftwod, and good snorkelling, yoga and romantic beach dinners make it a good option for surfing/non-surfing couples. The best bar in the Mentawai Islands is the island's social hub.

Wavepark Resort RESORT **$$$**
(☎081 2663 5551; www.wavepark.com; 10-night package incl meals US$3600; ❄@📶) Wavepark has a front-row view of Hideaways and very comfortable private bungalows on an equally private island. The most comfortable speedboat in the islands – the *Koraibi* – is used for transfers from the mainland, and there's yet another great Mentawai bar and restaurant area.

Pitstop Hill Resort RESORT **$$$**
(www.pitstophill.com; Pulau Masokut (Pulau Nyang Nyang); per day from A$180; ❄📶) High on a hill

overlooking Pitstops and close to E-Bay, this Aussie-run resort has accommodation in a main house, and a recently constructed luxury villa for couples and families. It's wildly popular with return visitors, so email for availability and pricing.

Botik Resort RESORT **$$$**
(☎0812 8824 6151; www.botikresort.com; 10-day packages incl meals US$2100; ❄☜) Botik Resort is on a private beach on the compact 72-hectare Pulau Botik. Bank Vaults and Kandui Left are nearby breaks, and a handful of stylish bungalows are almost concealed amid lush gardens and coconut palms. With yoga and massage also available, Botik's chic and laid-back vibe is a good choice for families or couples.

Aloita Resort & Spa RESORT **$$$**
(☎34878; www.aloitaresort.com; per day surfer/nonsurfer US$240/180; ❄☜) Eight bungalows in a breezy garden setting occupy a private beach within easy reach of Telescopes and Iceland. Aloita offers scuba diving and certification, and a spa and yoga terrace make it a good option for surfers planning on bringing partners or family.

Awera Island GUESTHOUSE **$$$**
(Pulau Awera; www.aweraisland.com; per day US$120; ☜) This small, low-key guesthouse has a cruisy beach-house vibe and is just a short hop from Iceland and seven other decent breaks. Accommodation is in airy two-bed bunkrooms, and decent off-peak discounts are available. Ask Aussie owner Fergus how the plans for his microbrewery are going.

Mentawai Surf Camp SURF CAMP **$$$**
(Pei Pei Surf Camp; ☎0852 6304 2032; www.mentawai-surfcamp.com; 10-day package incl meals AU$1699; ❄☜) Run by an affable globetrotting Colombian, Mentawai Surf Camp enjoys a private, beachfront location just a short speedboat spin from Pitstops, Nipussi and E-Bay. Accommodation is either in the rustic main lodge or in a two-storey beachfront cottage. It's just a short walk to the local village of Pei Pei, and post-surfing attractions include massage and table tennis.

Oinan Surf Lodge GUESTHOUSE **$$**
(☎0821 2241 0133; harrissmile@yahoo.com; Jl Mappadejat Km4, Tua Pejat; r incl meals 500,000Rp; ❄☜) Just out of the village of Mappadejat, around 4km from Tua Pejat, the Oinan Surf Lodge has amazing terrace views of the iconic Telescopes wave. Rooms are stylish and chic, and the lodge has its own boat for easy transport to other good breaks. It's also a good alternative to staying in dusty Tua Pejat if you're waiting for a ferry.

Nyang Nyang Surf Camp SURF CAMP **$**
(www.reginaadventures.com; Pulau Masokut (Pulau Nyang Nyang); per night accommodation only 150,000Rp) Shared dorms and walking access to Pitstops and E-Bay feature at this well-run surf camp that's a step up from the other losmen nearby. It's a favourite with groups of surfers who return on a regular basis, often from Brazil, South Africa and the United States. Bookings can be made through Regina Adventures (p535) in Padang.

Wisma Bintang Mentawai HOTEL **$**
(☎0813 7423 6956; Jl Raya Tua Pejat Km0; r incl breakfast 75,000-150,000Rp) If you get stranded in Tua Pejat waiting for a ferry – trust us, it happens – the best place to stay in town is this family-owned hotel a short walk from the port.

Sirruhuudin Hotel HOTEL **$**
(Muara Siberut; r 75,000Rp) If you're stuck in Muara Siberut without a guide, there is very basic accommodation at the Sirruhuudin Hotel on the waterfront (next to the pink Telkom shop).

There are basic losmen around most of the Mentawai ports, and simple beach huts (with/without meals from 200,000/100,000Rp) are available around Pulau Nyang Nyang and E-Bay, to the south of Siberut. Bring all your supplies, drinking water and mosquito nets. To get there, either bum a lift off another group, or charter a longboat from Muara Siberut.

Katiet, at the bottom of Pulau Sipora and home of the classic Lance's breaks, also has a few simple losmen, especially in front of the iconic HT's break. Catch a ferry from Bungus to Sioban, then try to find a speedboat (seat/whole boat 50,000/400,000Rp) heading south. Saturday (market day) is your best bet.

ℹ Information

The islands are very undeveloped. Bring all necessities and plenty of cash.

The **Siberut National Park office** (TNS; ☎0759 21109; ⊙8am-noon & 2-5pm Mon-Fri, 8am-noon Sat), a 10-minute *ojek* ride from the ferry jetty, is only useful if you speak Bahasa Indonesia.

There's an internet cafe in Tua Pejat, and most surf camps and resorts offer wi-fi access. Mobile coverage is limited to main towns, such as Tua Pejat.

Getting There & Away

Air

NBA links Padang to Rokot airport on Pulau Sipora, but the flight is unreliable, with overbooking, weather delays and last-minute cancellations. Book with Regina Adventures (p535) in Padang, but be prepared to be flexible. Tickets are 350,000Rp, and surfboards are charged a whopping 1,500,000Rp.Flights leave Padang Mondays at 7am and Thursdays at 1pm, and Rokot Mondays at 8am and Thursdays at 2pm.

Boat

Three ferries travel from the Sumatran mainland to the Mentawai Islands. All take around 10 to 12 hours, but it can take longer due to weather and sea conditions. It can be a rough crossing; consider taking seasickness medication. In Padang, ferries can be booked through most surfer-friendly homestays, as well as tour agencies such as Regina Adventures (p535), East West Tour & Travel (p535) and Sumatran Surfariis (p535).

Departures are usually in late afternoon or early evening – depending on the tides – and boats depart either from the river mouth (Sungai Muara) on Sungai Batang Arau just south of central Padang, or from the Teluk Kabang port at Bungus, around 20km south.

The more comfortable ferry is the *Ambu Ambu*, a steel ship with options including air-conditioned VIP seats (150,000Rp) and more basic economy seats (70,000Rp). Three air-conditioned cabins (800,000Rp) are rented out by the crew, but these are almost always prebooked by tour operators or surf-camp and resort owners. The *Ambu Ambu* usually leaves from Teluk Kabang.

DAY	FROM	TO
Monday	Tua Pejat	Padang
Tuesday	Padang	Sikakap
Wednesday	Sikakap	Padang
Thursday	Padang	Muara Siberut
Friday	Muara Siberut	Padang
Sunday	Padang	Tua Pegat

Less reliable is the smaller, wooden *Sumber Rezeky*, which leaves from Muara. Options include basic bunks in shared cabins (125,000Rp) and the crowded deck class (105,000). Definitely don't count on the *Sumber Rezeky* getting you back to Padang for an urgent international flight, as the boat is often delayed, and you may be forced to spend a few extra nights on the islands or fork out for a costly speedboat transfer.

DAY	FROM	TO
Monday	Padang	Muara Siberut
Tuesday	Muara Siberut	Padang
Friday	Padang	Sioban–Tua Pejat
Saturday	Sioban–Tua Pejat	Padang

The *Pulau Simasin* is another wooden ferry with similar prices. It usually leaves from Sungai Muara.

DAY	FROM	TO
Wednesday	Padang	Tua Pejat
Friday	Tua Pejat	Padang

Many tour agencies, resorts and surf camps use speedboats to transport guests from Padang. The crossing takes three to four hours and is around 8,000,000Rp to 12,000,000Rp.

Getting Around

Boats to Pulau Siberut arrive at the jetty in Maileppet. It's a 10-minute *ojek* ride (25,000Rp) to the main village of Muara Siberut, where longboats can be hired. Sample charter routes (up to five passengers) include Muara Siberut to E-Bay (800,000Rp, 1½ hours), E-Bay to Playgrounds (600,000Rp, 30 minutes), Playgrounds to Tua Paget (2,500,000Rp, 2½ hours) and Sioban to Katiet (1,500,000Rp, two hours). At the time of writing, the islands were experiencing a petrol shortage and these prices may vary.

In theory it's possible to island hop from Siberut all the way to Tua Pejat on Sipora via E-Bay and Playgrounds, but in reality it would work out cheaper (because you would have to keep the same boat or risk getting stranded) to return to Muara Siberut and take the inter-island ferry. The *KM Nade* winds its way through the islands, but the schedule is extremely flexible and this local ferry is prone to delays. Check the latest timings with your fixer.

Bukittinggi

☎0752 / POP 111,000

Early on a bright, clear morning, the market town of Bukittinggi sits high above the valley mists as three sentinels – fire-breathing Merapi, benign Singgalang and distant Sago – all look on impassively. Sun-ripened crops grow fat in the rich volcanic soil, as frogs call in the paddies, *bendis* (two-person

Bukittinggi

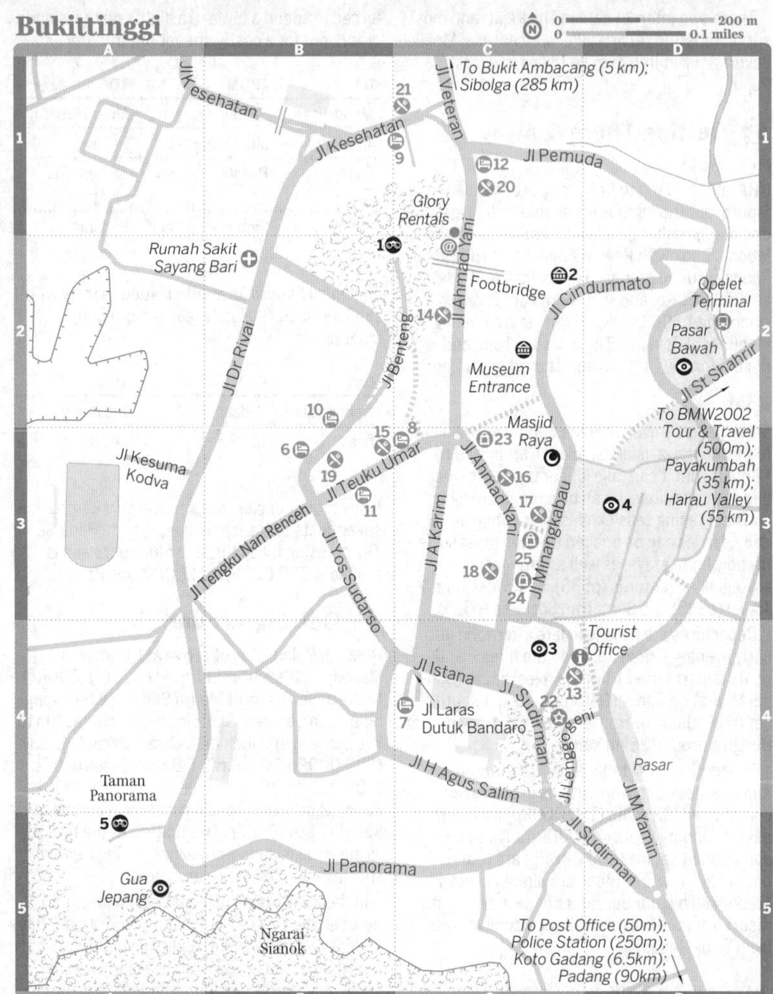

horse-drawn carts) haul goods to the *pasa* (market), and the muezzin's call sits lightly on the town. Modern life seems far removed.

Until 9am. Then the traffic starts up, and soon there's a mile-long jam around the bus terminal and the air turns the colour of diesel. The mosques counter the traffic by cranking their amps to 11, while hotel staff try to pass off cold bread and jam as breakfast.

Such is the incongruity of modern Bukittinggi, blessed by nature, choked by mortals. Lush. Fertile. Busy. And at 930m above sea level, deliciously temperate all year round.

The town (alternatively named Tri Arga, which refers to the triumvirate of peaks) has had a chequered history, playing host at various times to Islamic reformists, Dutch colonials, Japanese invaders and Sumatran separatists.

Bukittinggi was once a mainstay of the banana-pancake trail, but regional instability, shorter visas and the rise of low-cost air carriers have seen the traveller tide reduced to a lower ebb. The town's still definitely worth a visit though, and is a good base for setting out to the Harau Valley and Danau Maninjau.

Bukittinggi

Sights
1 Benteng de Kock........B2
2 Bukittinggi Museum........C2
3 Jam Gadang........C4
4 Pasar Atas........D3
5 Taman Panorama........A5

Activities, Courses & Tours
Lite 'n' Easy Tours........(see 14)
Roni's Tour & Travel........(see 11)

Sleeping
6 Grand Rocky Hotel........B3
7 Hills........C4
8 Hotel Khartini........C3
9 Lima's Hotel........C1
10 Mountain View Hotel........B2
11 Orchid Hotel........B3
12 Rajawali Homestay........C1

Eating
13 @rt Cafe........C4
14 Bedudal Café........C2
15 Canyon Café........B3
16 Mona Lisa........C3
17 Sederhang........C3
18 Selamat........C3
19 Serba Cokelet........B3
20 Turret Café........C1
21 Waroeng Spesifik Sambal........C1

Entertainment
22 Medan Nan Balinduang........C4

Shopping
23 Barhola Adventure........C3
24 Makmur Arts........C3
25 Markas Outdoor........C3

Sights

Pasar Atas MARKET
(east of Jl Minangkabau) Pasar Atas is a large, colourful market crammed with stalls selling fruit and vegetables, second-hand clothing and crafts. It's open daily, but the serious action is on Wednesday and Saturday.

Jam Gadang LANDMARK
(Big Clock Tower; btwn Jl Istana & Jl Sudirman) Jam Gadang is the town's focal point, built in the 1920s to house the clock, a gift from the Dutch queen. Independence in 1945 saw the retrofit of a Minangkabau roof.

Taman Panorama LOOKOUT
(Panorama Park; Jl Panorama; admission 5000Rp) Taman Panorama, on the southern edge of town, overlooks the deep **Ngarai Sianok** (Sianok Canyon), where fruit bats swoop at sunset. Friendly guides will approach visitors – settle on a price (around 25,000Rp) before continuing – to lead you through **Gua Jepang** (Japanese Caves), wartime defensive tunnels built by Japanese slave labour.

Benteng de Kock LOOKOUT
(Benteng Fort; Jl Benteng; admission 5000Rp) Benteng de Kock was built by the Dutch during the Padri Wars, and offers fine views over the town.

Bukittinggi Museum MUSEUM
(Taman Bundo Kandung; admission 1000Rp) A footbridge crosses over Jl Ahmad Yani from Benteng de Kock to Taman Bundo Kandung. Within the leafy park is the Bukittinggi Museum, constructed in 1934 in Minangkabau style. The adjacent zoo is just depressing.

Tours

Local tours fall into two categories – culture and nature – and can range from a half-day meander through neighbouring villages to a three-day jungle trek to Danau Maninjau, or an overnight assault on Gunung Merapi.

Full-day tours start at around 200,000Rp. Some tours have a minimum quota, though Roni's Tour & Travel (p548) and Lite 'n' Easy also run solo tours by motorbike. For DIY motorbike rental, see **Glory Rentals** (Jl Ahmad Yani; per day 60,000Rp) at the Tilal Bookshop.

Apart from the companies listed here, other freelance guides also frequent town. Be clear about what you want, and what is and isn't included. If going solo, make sure somebody knows who you're going with.

There's also a healthy climbing scene here and a day on the cliffs is around US$40. For climbing in the nearby Harau Valley, contact Ikbal at the Abdi Homestay (p553).

Lite 'n' Easy Tours ADVENTURE TOUR
(☎0813 7453 7413; www.liteeasy.nl; Jl Ahmad Yani) The friendly Lite 'n' Easy team are based at the Bedudal Cafe (p549) and offer West Sumatra options including Gunung Merapi, the Harau Valley, Danau Maninjau and

MIXING BUSINESS WITH FRIENDSHIP

In Indonesia, the line between business and socialising isn't as distinct as it is in the West. We expect printed prices and obvious sales tactics. Without a price tag, we assume that it is free or done out of friendship. On the other side of the cultural divide Sumatrans prefer business to resemble friendship: a little chit-chat, a steady sales pitch and a sort of telepathic understanding that payment is expected. They'd rather be helpful than entrepreneurial, but necessity dictates an income. The sluggish state of the Sumatran economy means that unemployment is high, with an overload of young resourceful men supporting themselves by guiding too few tourists.

Once you realise that nothing is gratis, ask about prices. Don't assume that the quoted price is all-inclusive. You are expected to buy lunch and drinking water for your guide. If transport isn't included in the initial price, you should pay for this as well. A tip at the end is also welcome. Most guides are smokers and a pack costs about 10,000Rp. If all this seems steep, keep in mind that the guides have a couple of crumpled rupiah to their name and not a lot of other opportunities.

trekking on the Mentawai island of Siberut. Head honcho Fikar is a good contact for local information.

Roni's Tour & Travel ADVENTURE TOUR
(☎32634, 081 2675 0688; www.ronistours.com; Jl Teuku Umar) Based at the Orchid Hotel, Roni's can arrange everything from local tours to Danau Maninjau and the Harau Valley, to trips to further-afield locations, such as the Mentawai Islands and the Kerinci Seblat National Park.

Festivals & Events

Bukittinggi holds an annual horse race at Bukit Ambacang in early March. Horses are ridden bareback and jockeys wear regional costumes, vying to win kudos for their village, and something else for the onlookers' wallets. Solok and Sawahlunto also hold annual races.

Sleeping

Most hotels include a simple breakfast. Hotel tax is only applied to top-end options and can be negotiated. On weekends and holidays, rooms can fill quickly with Indonesian visitors, but good weekday discounts can usually be negotiated. In Bukittinggi's temperate climate, hot water is more desirable than air-con.

Grand Rocky Hotel HOTEL $$$
(☎627 000; www.rockyhotelsgroup.com; Jl Yos Sudarso; r incl breakfast 830,000Rp; ❄📶) Bukittinggi's newest hotel is also its most comfortable with the multi-level Grand Rocky standing sentinel above town. Rooms are spacious and modern, views stretch to the Sianok Canyon, and it's just a short downhill stroll to the brightish lights of central Bukittinggi. Check online for good discounts if you're keen for a mini-splurge.

Rajawali Homestay HOMESTAY $
(☎26113; ulrich.rudolph@web.de; Jl Ahmad Yani 152; r 70,000Rp) The rooms are basic but cosy in this tiny homestay right in the centre. The irrepressible Ulrich is a fount of local knowledge and has lots of information and advice on the area's attractions. If you're a keen motorcyclist, ask him about his excellent GPS maps. The roof terrace is perfect for a few sunset beers as you watch the twilight squadrons of bats flying past.

Orchid Hotel HOTEL $
(☎32634; roni_orchid@hotmail.com; Jl Teuku Umar 11; r with cold/hot water 110,000/150,000Rp) Roni runs this popular backpacker inn that features clean rooms and a friendly atmosphere. There's a good-value cafe and bar downstairs, and it's also ground zero for arranging tours and activities with Roni's Tour & Travel.

Mountain View Hotel HOTEL $
(☎21621; Jl Yos Sodarso 31; r 150,000Rp) In a stunning location with a huge garden and plenty of room for vehicles. The simple rooms are great value and the hotel is owned by a friendly family.

Hills HOTEL $$
(☎35000; www.thehillshotel.com; Jl Laras Dutuk Bandaro; s/d from 400,000/650,000Rp; ❄📶) Commanding the heights like a Moorish citadel, Hills is usually full of VIPs and their security squads. Sports buffs can get active

with swimming, volleyball, basketball or table tennis, while more passive travellers should drop by the hotel's Anai Bar for great views and relatively pricey drinks.

Lima's Hotel HOTEL $$
(☎22641; www.limashotelbukittinggi.com; Jl Kesehatan 34; r incl breakfast 250,000-400,000Rp; ❄📶) Great views down the valley from the side of the hill. Rooms are showing their age, but there's a friendly ambience, and you can usually get a good discount on published rates. Just across the road there's great eating for fans of spicy sambal dishes.

Hotel Khartini HOTEL $
(☎22885; Jl Teuku Umar 6; r incl breakfast 150,000-250,000Rp) Clean, light-filled rooms, but it's very close to a mosque – it gets noisy with the call to prayer early each morning.

Eating

Bukittinggi has always been the one place in Sumatra where weary road bums can give their poor chilli-nuked organs a chance to recover with lashings of lovingly bland Western food.

TOP CHOICE **Waroeng Spesifik Sambal** INDONESIAN $
(Jl Kesehatan; dishes around 10,000-15,000Rp; 📶) Fans of spicy dishes will love this shady garden warung specialising only in sambal dishes. Squid, prawns, chicken and eel are all cooked in a rich chilli sauce, and the 15 different dishes also include vegetarian spins on eggplant, tempeh and tofu. Grab a few friends and graze on lots of different flavours. There's free wi-fi, and the beer may well be Bukittinggi's coldest.

Bedudal Café CAFE $
(Jl Ahmad Yani; mains 20,000-40,000Rp; 📶) All your old backpacker favourites in a cosy, intimate atmosphere. The waiters break out the bongos and guitars for occasional jam sessions, and it's also the home base for organising activities and excursions with Lite 'n' Easy Tours (p547). Rustle up a few dining companions and order the roast chicken meal with all the fixings (150,000Rp). You'll need to pop in in the morning to order a shared roast.

Mona Lisa CHINESE $
(Jl Ahmad Yani 58; mains 15,000-30,000Rp; 🖉) Grab a respite from *nasi Padang* (Padang cuisine) and tuck into Chinese eats at this classic old-school restaurant in a wonderfully weathered wooden shophouse on the upper reaches of Jl Ahmad Yani. There's a good mix of vegetarian dishes if you need a break from Padang food's meaty focus.

@rt Cafe CAFE $
(adjacent to Jam Gadang; snacks & juices 10,000-20,000Rp; 📶) Black and white pictures of Hollywood stars and 1960s rockers attract a mixed crowd of Indonesian tourists and Bukittinggi's bright young things. Other drawcards include an Indo rock soundtrack, fresh juices, snacks, cold beer and a spacious al fresco deck with misty mountain views.

Canyon Café CAFE $
(Jl Teuku Umar 8; mains 20,000-35,000Rp) Still playing 1970s rock and waiting for the world to change maaan, but the food's always good. Service can be a tad slow, so count on ordering a second juice or Bintang.

Turret Café CAFE $
(Jl Ahmad Yani 140-142; mains 20,000-35,000Rp; @) Good food, cold beer, relaxed outdoor lounges, internet access and the best guacamole in town. Sorted in Sumatra.

Serba Cokelet CAFE $
(Jl Yos Sudarso 6A; snacks around 5000Rp; ⏲8am-4pm) Need a chocolate muffin fix? Try the sublime offerings at Serba Cokelet. The iced coffee is pretty good, too.

NASI PADANG

If you've just arrived in Sumatra via Dumai from Malaysia, Bukittinggi could be your first chance to try the region's spicy Padang cuisine. Dive into the mouth-watering choices at tiny **Sederhang** (Jl Minangkabau 63), or visit **Selamat** (Jl Ahmad Yani), located towards the clock tower. Dishes start at around 8000Rp. Count on spending around 30,000Rp per person.

For more familiar on-the-road options, Jl Ahmad Yani comes alive at night with food stalls doing excellent sate, nasi goreng and *mie goreng*. Locals rave about the sweet *lontong* (a soupy concoction of coconut milk, rice, egg and whatever else is handy) served in a no-name tent opposite the Singgalang Hotel on Jl Ahmad Yani.

Entertainment

Medan Nan Balinduang DANCE

(Jl Lenggogeni; tickets 40,000Rp; 8.30pm) Medan Nan Balinduang presents Minangkabau dance performances. Check with the tourist office for the latest schedule.

Shopping

Bukittinggi is a good place for woven bags, batik shirts, antiques and curios. Box collectors can look out for a couple of Minangkabau versions. Brass *salapah panjang* (long boxes) are used for storing lime and tobacco, and silver *salapah padusi* for betel nut and lime.

Souvenir shops line Jl Minangkabau, while upper Jl Ahmad Yani has traditional crafts and antiques. Try **Makmur Arts** (22208; Jl Ahmad Yani 10) for the best selection.

For outdoor gear, check out **Barhola Adventure** (Jl Ahmad Yani) and **Markas Outdoor** (Jl Ahmad Yani).

Beautiful red and gold Minangkabau embroidery can be found in the *pasar*. Pillowcases, slippers and ceremonial wedding sashes all make easy-to-carry souvenirs.

Information

Banks and ATMs are scattered along Jl Ahmad Yani. The ATM opposite the Mona Lisa restaurant dispenses up to 2,000,000Rp.

For wi-fi, head to @rt Cafe (p549) or Bedudal Café (p549).

One Stop Internet Place (Jl Ahmad Yani; per hr 5000Rp)

Post office (Jl Sudirman; internet access per hr 6000Rp) South of town near the bus terminal. Has internet facilities.

Rumah Sakit Sayang Bari (Jl Dr Rivai) This hospital is just west of central Bukittinggi.

Tourist office (Jl Sudirman; 7am-4pm) Opposite the clock tower. Offers maps, tours and tickets to cultural events. Travel agencies line Jl Ahmad Yani for flight and bus bookings.

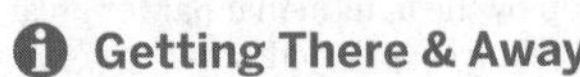

Getting There & Away

The chaos of the Aur Kuning bus terminal 2km south of town is easily reached by *opelet* (2500Rp). Ask for 'terminal'. Heading to town on arrival ask for 'Kampung China'. Other direct destinations include Jambi and Pekanbaru.

Another more comfortable way to get to Dumai – for ferries to Melaka in Malaysia – is with **BMW2002 Tours & Travel** (0812 6775 2002, 626 085; Trad Centre Blok C 11-12, Jl Permuda Banto), a travel agency located on the edge of the town's market area. Minibuses (per person 100,000Rp) leave Bukittinggi nightly at 8pm, and departures are timed to link with the ferry from Dumai to Melaka. Prebooking is required. BMW2002 can also book the ferry for you; you'll need to drop in the day before departure with your passport.

Getting Around

Opelet around town cost 2000Rp. *Bendi* start from 20,000Rp. An *ojek* from the bus terminal to the hotels costs 10,000Rp and a taxi costs 25,000Rp. Transfers to Padang airport can be arranged from any travel agent for around 40,000Rp. A private taxi to Padang airport is around 200,000Rp.

Around Bukittinggi

While Bukittinggi is an interesting market town, visitors come to explore the Minangkabau countryside, hike up an active volcano, or hunt for the fabled rafflesia (a gigantic flower with blooms spreading up to a metre).

HANDICRAFT VILLAGES

Silversmiths occupy the old Dutch houses of **Koto Gadang**, 5km from Bukittinggi (*opelet*

BUSES FROM BUKITTINGGI

DESTINATION	COST (RP)	DURATION (HR)	FREQUENCY
Bengkulu (for Krui)	145,000	18	daily
Danau Maninjau	15,000	1½	frequent
Dumai	75,000	10	nightly
Medan	120,000-140,000	20	daily
Padang	16,000	2	frequent
Parapat (for Danau Toba)	170,000	16	daily
Sibolga (for Pulau Nias)	80,000-110,000	12	daily

Around Bukittinggi

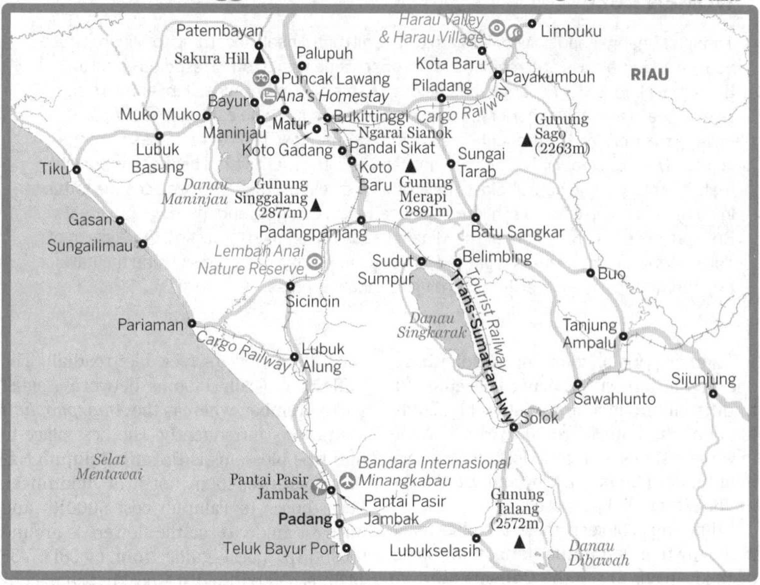

2000Rp). Alternatively, it's an hour's walk from Taman Panorama.

Pandai Sikat (Clever Craftsmen) is famous for *songket* (silver- or gold-threaded cloth) weaving and woodcarving. The village is 13km from Bukittinggi. Take an *opelet* (5000Rp) from Aur Kuning.

Handicrafts fans should also visit **Studio Songket ErikaRianti** (☎783 4253; www.songketminang.com) near Simpang Bukit Batabuah southeast of Bukittinggi. Established in 2005, the studio is dedicated to conserving the traditional Minangkabau art of *songket* weaving. Replicas of heritage *songkets* based on antique cloths in museums and contemporary updates are both woven here. You can purchase a range of *songkets* and visit the studio. Studio Songket ErikaRianti is also dedicated to training young local weavers in the exacting art. From the Aur Kuning bus terminal, catch a yellow *opelet* to Batu Taba (2500Rp), getting off at the SMKN1 (high school). Phone ahead to check the studio is open.

SOUTH OF BUKITTINGGI

The rich volcanic soil of the hilly countryside around Bukittinggi oozes fertility. Stop by the roadside and you can spot cinnamon, betel nut, avocado, coffee, mango and papaya trees. Rice, tapioca and potatoes grow in terraces, while bamboo waterwheels feed irrigation ditches and drive wooden grinding mills.

Hopefully, you'll see a wedding parade. The bride and groom, dressed in full traditional regalia, are accompanied by musicians, family members and half the village. The Minangkabau tribal flags (red, black and yellow) typically mark the site of the festivities.

Rumah Gadang Pagaruyung (King's Palace) is a scaled-down replica of the former home of the rulers of the ancient Minangkabau kingdom of Payaruyung. A fire razed it to the ground in 2007, but it has been reconstructed. Most tours also include the nearby **Istano Silinduang Bulan** (Queen's Palace; donation 2000Rp), damaged by lightning in 2011, but also rebuilt. This building is still used for important clan meetings, and a small donation is expected. Both palaces are located in the village of **Silinduang Bulan**, 5km north of Batu Sangkar, the heartland of the red Tanah Datar clan of Minangkabau.

Batu Sangkar can be reached via public bus (18,000Rp), where you can continue an by *ojek* (5,000Rp) to Silinduang Bulan.

WOMEN RULE

Though Minangkabau society is Islamic, it's still matrilineal. According to Minangkabau *adat* (traditional laws and regulations), property and wealth are passed down through the female line. Every Minangkabau belongs to his or her mother's clan. At the basic level of the clan is the *sapariouk,* those matri-related kin, who eat together. These include the mother, the grandchildren and the son-in-law. The name comes from the word *periouk* (rice pot). The eldest living female is the matriarch. The most important male member of the household is the mother's eldest brother, who replaces the father in being responsible for the children's education, upbringing and marriage prospects. But consensus is at the core of the Minangkabau ruling philosophy and the division of power between the sexes is regarded as complementary – like the skin and the nail act together to form the fingertip, according to a local expression.

Another popular tour stop is **Belimbing**, one of the largest surviving collections of traditional architecture in the highlands. Many of the homes are 300 years old and in various states of decay. Most owners have built modern homes nearby and use the relics for ceremonial purposes.

Ethno-musicologists make the pilgrimage to the town of **Padangpanjang**, 19km south of Bukittinggi, to see the **Conservatorium of Traditional Music** (STSI, ASKI; Jl Bundo Kanduang 35; 8am-3pm Mon-Thu, to noon Fri). Minangkabau dance and music are preserved and performed here. Regular buses run between Bukittinggi and Padangpanjang (10,000Rp).

Train lovers should head to Padangpanjang for Sunday's **Museum Train** trip to the old coal-mining town of **Sawahlunto**. Scenically stunning, this restored service runs alongside **Danau Singkarak**. The trip takes three hours (one way 60,000Rp, departs 7.30am) and there's a two-hour stop in Sawahlunto, where you can ride a steam train, visit the rail museum or head down a coal mine.

On the highway between Padang and Bukittinggi is the **Lembah Anai Nature Reserve**, renowned for waterfalls, wild orchids and giant rafflesia. Any Bukittinggi–Padang bus can drop you nearby.

BATANG PALUPUH NATURE RESERVE & AROUND

West Sumatra is famous for its many orchid species, as well as the massive *Rafflesia arnoldii* and *Amorphophallus titanium,* the largest flowers on the planet. The blossom of the parasitic rafflesia measures nearly a metre across and can weigh up to 11kg, while the inflorescence of *Amorphophallus* can extend to over 3m in circumference. Both flowers reek like roadkill. The rafflesia typically blooms between August and November, whereas the *Amorphophallus* flowers infrequently. The best place to find ripe blossoms is **Batang Palupuh Nature Reserve**, 16km north of Bukittinggi. Local buses to Palupuh cost 5000Rp and hiring a guide to see the flowers is around 80,000Rp. Local guide **Joni** (0813 7436 4439) is a good English-speaking contact. A morning departure from Bukittinggi is recommended to avoid the occasional influx of tour buses.

Also worth visiting in Palupuh is the **House of Rafflesia Luwak Coffee** (0813 7417 8971; www.rafflesialuwakcoffee.org). *Kopi luwak* – praised as the planet's finest coffee – is produced from organic coffee beans ingested and excreted by wild civet cats from the surrounding jungle. You can taste (20,000Rp) and purchase (from 200,000Rp) the caffeine-rich delicacy, and the friendly owner Umul Khair also runs Minangkabau **cooking classes** (per person 350,000Rp). The multi-course menu includes beef rendang and chicken curry, and Umul will even undertake the course for solo travellers. Book via the website or phone to confirm at least one day before you visit.

GUNUNG MERAPI & GUNUNG SINGGALANG

The smouldering summit of **Gunung Merapi** (2891m) looms large over Bukittinggi to the east. Occasionally deemed too dangerous to climb, Merapi is Sumatra's most active volcano.

If Merapi's benign, then visitors typically hike overnight to view sunrise from the summit. The climb begins at the village of Koto Baru and it's normally a 12-hour round trip. You'll need good walking boots, warm clothing, a torch, food and drink.

It's unwise to attempt the climb alone, and people are advised to take a guide or join a group. Travel agencies in Bukittinggi do guided trips to Merapi for around US$30 per person (minimum three people).

Gunung Singgalang (2877m) is a more adventurous undertaking than Merapi, and is rarely climbed by tourists. There are campsites by the beautiful crater lake, Telago Dewi.

Danau Maninjau

☎0752

The first glimpse of this perfectly formed volcanic lake sucks your breath away as your dilapidated bus lurches over the caldera lip and hurtles towards the first of the 44 (yep, they're numbered) hairpin bends down to the lakeshore. Monkeys watch your progress from the crash barriers as the lush rainforest of the heights retreats from the ever-expanding farms and paddies of the lowlands.

When the traveller tide receded from Bukittinggi, Danau Maninjau was left high and dry. The locals looked to more sustainable sources of income and aquaculture to fill the void. Fish farms now dot the lake foreshore.

Ground zero is the intersection where the Bukittinggi highway meets the lake road in the middle of Maninjau village. Turn left or right and drive 60km and you'll end up back here. The lake is 17km long, 8km wide and 460m above sea level. Most places of interest spread out north along the road to Bayur (3.5km) and beyond. Tell the conductor where you're staying and you'll be dropped off at the right spot.

Sights & Activities

Swimming and canoeing in the lake (warmed by subterranean springs) are still

WORTH A TRIP

HARAU VALLEY

Heading east from Bukittinggi takes you through the tapioca-growing area of **Piladang**, famous for *keropok* (tapioca crackers), and the sprawling agricultural centre of **Payakumbuh**. Of Minangkabau's three clans, this is the territory of the 50 Kota (50 Villages) yellow branch. Paddies and daydreaming buffaloes flank the narrow road that leads to the tiny village of Harau. Venture another 3km and spectacular 100m cliffs rise up to enclose the claustrophobic Harau Valley, 15km northeast of Payakumbuh and 55km from Bukittinggi.

Most tourists just pass through on a tour to **Lemba Harau** (admission 5000Rp), a set of waterfalls that either trickles or plummets, depending on the weather. However, the Harau Valley is also the best-developed rock-climbing area in Sumatra. An excellent local contact is Ikbal at the Abdi Homestay, who offers guided climbing excursions for US$20. Check out www.climbing.com and www.rockclimbing.com for blogs and more information.

The recently opened **Abdi Homestay** (☎0852 6378 1842; ikbalharau@yahoo.com; Kab 50 Kota; per person 60,000-100,000Rp) is also a lovely place to stay. Rustic but spotless bungalows sit on the edge of verdant rice paddies and lotus ponds, and meals include one of the best chicken rendangs you'll ever have. Owners Ikbal and Noni are energetic young hosts, and can arrange walks to nearby valleys and waterfalls. Lessons in cooking Minangkabau-style food are also available.

Right under the cliffs in the narrowest part of the valley is **Echo Homestay** (☎775 0306; www.echohomestay.blogspot.com; Taratang Lb Limpato; r with shared bathroom 90,000Rp, r incl breakfast 160,000-540,000Rp), a beautiful place teeming with butterflies and surrounded by forests full of gibbons. Slum it in the basic thatched bungalows or splash out for the Minangkabau-style cottages.

Take a local bus from Bukittinggi to Sarilamak (13,000Rp), then a minivan to Harau village (3000Rp), and finally an *ojek* the rest of the way (3000Rp). Alternatively, take an *ojek* all the way from Sarilamak (12,000Rp). Harau can also be reached on a motorbike tour from Bukittinggi for 200,000Rp.

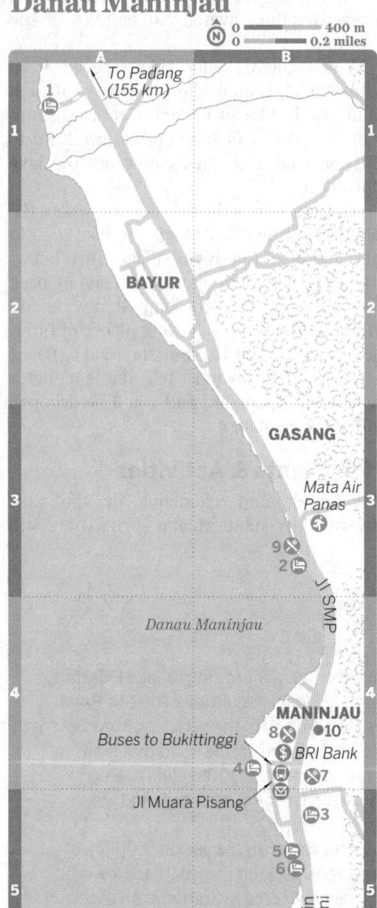

Danau Maninjau

Sleeping

1 'Arlen' Nova's Paradise A1
2 Hotel Tan Dirih B3
3 House of Annisa B5
4 Muaro Beach Bungalows B4
5 Mutiara B5
6 Pillie Homestay B5

Eating

7 Bagoes Café B4
8 Rama Café B4
9 Waterfront Zalino B3

Information

10 PT Kesuma Tour & Travel B4

the main drawcards but there are plenty of other options.

The caldera is a hiker's dream, covered in rainforest that hides waterfalls and traditional villages. Hike to the rim from Bayur, or cheat by catching the bus up the hill to Matur, then walking back down via the lookout at **Puncak Lawang**. Check out the map at Rama Café for more good trekking information.

If this all sounds a bit athletic, try unwinding in a hot spring. Failing all else, grab a moped and zoom off to Sinar Pagi, the point on Ujung Tanjung poking out from the far shore.

Hiking, rafting and paragliding can all be booked through Lawang Adventure Park.

Festivals & Events

Rakik Rakik CULTURAL

Rakik Rakik is celebrated on the night before Idul Fitri (the end of Ramadan) by building a platform to hold a replica Minangkabau house and mosque. The offering is then floated out onto the lake on canoes, accompanied by fireworks and revelry.

Sleeping

Aquaculture has transformed the Maninjau foreshore. Losmen that once overlooked pristine beaches now have views of fish ponds and jetties.

The majority of Maninjau options front onto aquaculture. There is a sprinkling of hotels, cheap losmen and restaurants between Maninjau and Bayur. Outside of Maninjau village, most losmen are reached by walking along rice-paddy paths, so look for the sign by the roadside.

TOP CHOICE **House of Annisa** HISTORIC HOTEL **$$**

(☎0857 6604 1558; Jl H Udin Rahmani, Maninjau; r 250,000Rp) Located around 150m south of Maninjau's main intersection, this wonderful heritage Dutch villa has been lovingly restored by the great-grandchildren of the original owners. There are only three romantic rooms – one with a brass four-poster bed festooned with mirrors – and it's shared bathrooms only. There's a gorgeous balcony filled with antique benches and chairs.

Muaro Beach Bungalows BUNGALOW $
(☎0813 3924 0042, 61189; neni967@yahoo.com; Jl Muaro Pisang 53, Maninjau; r 70,000-100,000Rp) Down a maze of footpaths (about 300m northwest of the main intersection), these beachfront bungalows are the best value in Maninjau. The beach is (almost) free of aquaculture and fish farming, and there's a good restaurant that's also open to outside guests. Local tours and activities are on offer.

Lawang Adventure Park LODGE $$
(☎0812 6737 9777; www.lawangpark.com; Nagari Lawang; r incl breakfast 250,000Rp) Perched high above the lake on the road from Bukittinggi – before the beginning of the 44 hairpin corners – the Lawang Adventure Park has comfortable lodge accommodation, a good restaurant with sunset views to Sumatra's southern coast and on-tap opportunities for paragliding (US$100), caving and hiking (US$20), and river rafting (US$40). Other accommodation options include village homestays incorporating traditional music and dance, and the opportunity to cook Minangkabau cuisine (per person including meals $US40 per night).

'Arlen' Nova's Paradise BUNGALOW $
(☎0815 3520 4714; www.nova-maninjau.id.or.id; Sungai-Rangeh; r 150,000Rp) Walk through rice paddies (5.5km north of Maninjau) to these bungalows on a private beach, with nary a fish pond in sight. It's easily the nicest place on the lake, and there's a breezy restaurant on site.

Hotel Tan Dirih HOTEL $$
(☎61474; Desa Air Angek Km1, Gasang; r 250,000Rp; ❄) Good-value rooms, but the deck looks at fish ponds; 950m north of the crossroads in Maninjau.

Pillie Homestay HOMESTAY $
(☎61048; Maninjau; r 60,000Rp) Simple and cheap rooms 250m south of the main village intersection, with a lovely family and nice veranda.

Mutiara HOMESTAY $
(☎61049; ricojayamozart@yahoo.com; Maninjau; r with fan/air-con 80,000/150,000Rp; ❄) The rooms here are clean and cool with great views from the deck.

Eating

Most of the guesthouses serve standards such as nasi goreng and *mie goreng*, some Western favourites and freshly caught fish.

TOP CHOICE **Rama Café** INDONESIAN $
(Maninjau; mains 25,000-35,000Rp; @) Share a *martabak* (a meat, egg and vegetable pancake-like dish) before hooking into a plate of *ikan panggang* (baked fish) while lazing on cushions amid kites and drums. The lovely owner/chef Anita is an excellent cook, and also a poignant and heartfelt singer who is always keen to pick up her guitar. Look out for the excellent map showing where to go and what to do around Maninjau. Rama is around 300m north of the main intersection.

Waterfront Zalino INDONESIAN $$
(☎0815 3541 1074; Gasang; mains 20,000-70,000Rp) A great lakeside location showcases all your Indonesian foodie favourites, plus a few exotic local specialities like *dendeng kijang balado* (fried deer with chilli and red pepper), freshwater lake shrimp (*udang*) and grilled catfish. If you're keen to go trekking or pig hunting, ask if Zal – AKA 'Mr Porcupine' – is around. You'll find Waterfront Zalino in the village of Gasang around 1km north of the main intersection in Maninjau.

Bagoes Café CAFE $
(Maninjau; mains 15,000-25,000Rp; @) This traveller-friendly place near the main intersection in Maninjau combines backpacker staples with a few local dishes. It also runs movie nights, and is your best option for a few cold beers.

Information

The **post office** sits right at the main intersection. Internet access is available at the Rama Café and Bagoes Café, but at the time of writing there was no wi-fi access in town.

There is one **ATM** in Maninjau, but it only dispenses small amounts. Stock up on rupiah in Bukittinggi before arriving.

PT Kesuma Tour & Travel (☎081 2669 9661, 61422; www.sumatratravelling.com; Jl Panurunan Air Hangat) Arranges transfers to Bukittinggii and jungle treks, and rents outdoor equipment.

Getting There & Around

Buses run hourly between Maninjau and Bukittinggi (15,000Rp, 1½ hours). Taxis from Bukittinggi start from 160,000Rp.

Rent mountain bikes (per day 35,000Rp), motorcycles (per day 80,000Rp) and canoes (per day 25,000Rp) from PT Kesuma Tour & Travel or Waterfront Zalino.

Minibuses (2500Rp) travel the lake road during daylight hours. An *ojek* from the intersection to Bayur will cost around 8000Rp.

Kerinci Valley

0748 / POP 300,000

Kerinci is a stunning mountain valley tucked away high in the Bukit Barisan on Jambi's western border. Many of the cool, lush forests are protected as the Kerinci Seblat National Park. To the south is picturesque Danau Kerinci and a patchwork of rich farmland. Tea and cinnamon account for much of the valley's wealth, with the former ringing the higher villages and the latter forming a buffer between farmland and rainforest.

Minangkabau and native Kerincinese make up most of the population, with a sprinkling of Batak and Javanese who are drawn by the rich soil. Kerinci is in Jambi province but has a close geographic proximity to Padang.

Getting There & Away

The best option for onward travel in buses and shared minibuses is **PO CW Safa Marwa** (22376; Jl Yos Sudarso (Jl Baru) 20) in Sungai Penuh. If you're leaving Kersik Tua for Padang or Bukittinggi, buses can usually pick up en route from Sungai Penuh.

Getting Around

Most places in the valley are accessible by the white minibuses that leave the terminal and surrounding area near the market. Sample destinations and fares are Danau Kerinci (10,000Rp, 1½ hours), Kersik Tua (5000Rp, one hour) and Pelompek (8000Rp, 80 minutes). Watch your pronunciation – Semurup and Semerap are in opposite directions.

SUNGAI PENUH

Sungai Penuh (Full River) is the regional administrative centre and transport hub for the valley. There is a lively market and reliable internet, but most people get in and get out, heading for the more scenic climes of Kersik Tua.

Sights

Mesjid Agung Pondok Tinggi MOSQUE

(admission by donation) Head west up Jl Sudirman (past the post office) and turn left, where you'll find this old wooden mosque with its pagoda-style roof. Built in 1874 without a single nail, the interior contains elaborately carved beams and old, Dutch tiles. Ask the caretaker for permission and dress demurely.

Sleeping

Accommodation options in Sungai Penuh are fairly average. Unless you're planning adventures in the southern end of the park, try to head to Kersik Tua for access to Gunung Kerinci.

Hotel Jaya Wisata HOTEL $$

(21221; Jl Martadinata 7; r incl breakfast 150,000-630,000Rp;) Rooms range from OK-value cold-water cheapies – perfectly fine if you're in Sungai Penuh between buses – to more spacious and stylish rooms. The hotel's had a colourful makeover since our last visit. The location is great – near the cheap eats of the night market – and the funky Mr Ridho Cafe is a new addition in front of the hotel.

Aroma Hotel HOTEL $

(21142; Jl Imam Bonjol 14; d 120,000-262,000Rp) Conveniently located at the top corner of the square, the Aroma's budget rooms are better value than its expensive ones.

Eating & Drinking

Kerinci is known for the local speciality of *dendeng batokok*, charcoal-grilled strips of pounded beef. Street stalls pop up in the evening along Jl Teuku Umar, a block from the square.

After dark along Jl Muradi, other warungs and stalls pop up selling sate and fresh juices. Just look for the wafting clouds of enticing smoke.

BUSES FROM KERINCI VALLEY

DESTINATION	COST (RP)	DURATION (HR)	DEPART
Bukittinggi	90,000	8	10am
Dumai	200,000	24	10am
Jambi	100,000-110,000	12	10am, 7pm
Padang	70,000-90,000	8	10am, 8pm

Minang Soto PADANG $
(Jl Muradi; dishes from 8000Rp) Busy Padang-style eatery, but watch that you get what you ordered. The *tahu* (tofu) arrives with *ayam* (chicken). Eat the *tahu*, pay for the *ayam*.

Cafe Mini INDONESIAN $
(Jl Muradi; mains 10,000-20,000Rp) One of Sungai Penuh's only non-Padang eateries.

Mr Ridho Cafe CAFE
(Hotel Jaya Wisata, Jl Martadinata 7; juices & cocktails 15,000-20,000Rp; wi-fi) Decked out in bright colours – and featuring Sungai Penuh's only espresso machine – this is definitely the coolest spot for many kilometres. Other attractions include free wi-fi and freshly squeezed juices and alcohol-free cocktails. It also does a mean grilled chicken steak if you're getting weary of *nasi Padang*.

Information

For wi-fi, head to the Mr Ridho Cafe.

BNI Bank (Jl Ahmad Yani) The ATM at the centrally located BNI Bank dispenses up to 2,000,000Rp.

Kerinci Seblat National Park Office (Taman Nasional Kerinci Seblat; ☎323701; Jl Basuki Rahmat 11) The park headquarters sells permits but ring first to check it's open. If it's closed, you can get permits from losmen in Kersik Tua.

Luke Mackin (☎0812 6017 3651; www.wildsumatra.com) Based in Sungai Penuh, expat Luke Mackin is a passionate and knowledgeable local contact for information on the surrounding area, especially the Kerinci Seblat National Park. At the time of writing, he was forming alliances with local trekking guides and villages, and keen to grown awareness of the area with travellers.

Post office (Jl Sudirman 1) Decent internet and international phone access.

KERSIK TUA

Darjeeling it's not, but at 1500m, surrounded by tea plantations and dominated by the massive cone of Gunung Kerinci (3805m), Kersik Tua makes a pleasant base for exploring the northern end of Kerinci Seblat.

The town sprawls along one side of the main road, with tea plantations and the mountain on the other. The national park turn-off is indicated by a *harimau* (Sumatran tiger) statue.

Trekking gear, supplies, guides and transport can all be arranged here. There's a market on Saturday and a BNI ATM. The village is 52km north of Sungai Penuh on the road to Padang and can be reached by any Padang–Kerinci bus. Minibuses (5000Rp, one hour) trundle from Sungai Penuh to Kersik Tua between 8am and 5pm.

There are several basic homestays. **Subandi Homestay** (☎0812 7411 4273, 357 009; subandi.home stay@gmail.com; r 90,000Rp), just south of the statue, is the best base camp in the village. Subandi is a trove of local knowledge and can organise mountain, jungle and wildlife treks of varying difficulty and duration.

Other homestays include **Home Stay Paiman** (☎357 030; r 75,000Rp), 200m south of Subandi (near the ATM), and **Home Stay B Darmin** (☎357 070; r 75,000Rp), 300m north of the statue.

Kerinci Seblat National Park

The largest national park in Sumatra, Kerinci Seblat National Park (Taman Nasional Kerinci Seblat; TNKS) covers a 350km swath of the Bukit Barisan range and protects close to 15,000 sq km of prime equatorial rainforest spread over four provinces, with almost 40% of the park falling within Jambi's boundaries.

Most of the protected area is dense rainforest, and its inaccessibility is the very reason the park is one of the last strongholds of the endangered *harimau* (Sumatran tiger). Kerinci Seblat National Park is known as having the highest population and occurrence of tigers anywhere in Sumatra, with 80% of the park showing signs of the species.

Because of the great elevation range within the park, Kerinci has a unique diversity of flora and fauna. Edelweiss and other high-altitude flowers grow in the forest. Lower altitudes bring pitcher plants, orchids, rafflesia and the giant *Amorphophallus*.

As with many of Sumatra's protected areas, encroachment by farmers, illegal logging and poaching are all serious issues for Kerinci. According to a July 2012 report, around 42,000 hectares (420 sq km) of the park's total forests of 1.3 million hectares (13,000 sq km) have been lost.

Kerinci Seblat National Park sees relatively few visitors, and the park's minimal tourist infrastructure is limited to the north around the dual attractions of Gunung Kerinci and Gunung Tujuh. While the park's northern region is more visited, the southern area features elephants – absent in the north – and also has interesting forest-edge communities

ORANG PENDEK

Every culture that has lived among trees tells stories about elusive creatures that straddle myth and reality. Tales about leprechauns, fairies and even Sasquatch have existed for so long that it is impossible to determine which came first: the spotting or the story. The Indonesian version of these myth makers is the *orang pendek*, which has been occasionally spotted but more frequently talked about in the Kerinci forests for generations.

Villagers who claim to have seen *orang pendek* describe the creature as being about 1m tall, more ape than human, but walking upright on the ground. The creature's reclusive habits made it a celebrity in local mythology. Common folk stories say that the *orang pendek* has feet that face backwards so that it can't be tracked through the forest, or that it belongs to the supernatural, not the world of flesh and blood. Others say that the first-hand accounts were only spottings of sun bears.

Scientists have joined the conversation by tramping through the forest hoping to document the existence of *orang pendek*. British researchers succeeded in making a plaster cast of an animal footprint that fits the *orang pendek* description and doesn't match any other known primate. Hair samples with no other documented matches have also led researchers to believe that there is merit to the local lore. Two members of Fauna & Flora International, a British-based research team, even reported separate sightings, but were unable to collect conclusive evidence. Researchers sponsored by the National Geographic Society have resumed the search by placing motion-sensitive cameras in strategic spots in the jungle. So little is known about this region and so many areas are so remote that researchers are hopeful that the *orang pendek* will eventually wander into the frame.

If nothing else, the *orang pendek* helps illuminate aspects of Sumatrans' linguistic and cultural relationship with the jungle. Bahasa Indonesia makes little distinction between man and ape; for example 'orang-utan' (forest man) or 'orang rimba' ('people of the forest', the preferred term for the Kubu tribe) may reflect a perceived blood tie between forest dwellers. This imprecision is often used for comic effect. A common joke is that the *orang pendek* (which means 'short man') does indeed exist, followed by the punch line that the shortest person in the room is the missing link.

living within the park's boundaries, and excellent trekking through pristine forests. Contact Luke Mackin (p557) in Sungai Penuh if you're keen to explore the park's southern reaches. There are buffer areas for local cultivation and agriculture at the northern and southern edges of the park.

Permits and guides are required to enter the park. Both can be arranged at the park office (p557) in Sungai Penuh or through your losmen. There is a park office at the entrance to Danau Gunung Tujuh, but it's rarely staffed.

Permits cost 20,000Rp and guide rates are around 200,000Rp per day for an English-speaking guide. Be sure to clarify exactly what the rate entails, as camping gear, food and transport may be considered additional costs. A good contact for organising a guide is Luke Mackin (p557) in Sungai Penuh.

Kerinci's climate is temperate, and downright cold as you gain altitude. Bring warm clothes and rain gear.

Sights & Activities

Gunung Kerinci VOLCANO

Dominating the northern end of the park is the 3805m Gunung Kerinci, one of Sumatra's most active volcanoes (it last erupted in 2009) and Indonesia's highest non-Papuan peak. On clear days the summit of Southeast Asia's tallest volcano offers fantastic views of Danau Gunung Tujuh, the surrounding valleys and mountains, and sometimes the Indian Ocean to the south.

Summit treks usually start from the national park entrance, 5km from Kersik Tua, and tackle the mountain in two stages. The highest campsite, at 3400m, is normally reached after six hours. The following morning, allow an hour in the predawn to reach the summit by sunrise.

Botanists and twitchers from around the world come for the rare flora and fauna, such as Javanese edelweiss, Schneider's pitta and the crested wood partridge. Nepthenes (pitcher plants), squirrels, geckos and long-tailed macaques can be found in the lower forest, and troops of yellow-handed mitered langurs are also seen.

While the park does have a significant tiger population, spying one in the wild is very rare, and sightings are usually restricted to paw prints and droppings. In previous centuries, local Kerinci people were thought to be weretigers (a shape-shifting synthesis of man and beast), and the tiger is still important in local mysticism and mythology.

The path is very steep and eroded, and above the treeline the scree is extremely slippery. A guide is mandatory and you'll need full camping gear and warm clothes, including a windproof jacket and head torch (all of which can be hired in Kersik Tua). Nights are freezing. Do not attempt the climb in wet weather.

Expect to pay around 800,000Rp for a fully guided trip with food, permits, transport and all gear thrown in. Fully self-sufficient parties needing a guide will only pay around 400,000Rp.

Danau Gunung Tujuh LAKE

(Seven Mountain Lake) At 1996m, the beautiful caldera of Danau Gunung Tujuh is the highest in Southeast Asia and makes for a pleasant day walk or multiday trek.

It takes 3½ hours to climb to the lake from the park entrance, 2km from the village of Pelompek. It's possible to camp near the lake. Subandi Homestay (p557) in Kersik Tua can organise two- or three-day treks, including a canoe crossing. Ask about camping on the opposite side of the lake for the best experience away from other campers. Wildlife in this area includes tapirs and Siamang gibbons, and one of the signature sounds of the forests of Kerinci is the howling call of the gibbon.

Pelompek is 8km beyond Kersik Tua (bus 5000Rp) and 60km from Sungai Penuh (7000Rp). Hire an *ojek* (6000Rp) from Pelompek for the final trip to the park entrance. You'll need a park permit, and if the park office is closed, ask next door at the tiny **Losmen Pak Edes** (r 70,000Rp), which also has two very basic rooms and can arrange guides.

Ladeh Panjang FOREST

This region of rainforest, sulphur lakes and hot springs located on Gunung Kerinci's western flank is seldom visited, and is home to *harimau*, *badak* (rhinoceros), tapir and *beruang* (bear). A five-day, 120km trek traverses the range and exits onto the highway north of Kerinci.

Danau Kerinci LAKE

Danau Kerinci, 20km south of Sungai Penuh, is a small lake nestled beneath Gunung Raya (2535m). There is a popular recreational park and an annual festival, held in July, which displays traditional Kerinci dance and music. **Stone carvings** in the villages around the lake suggest that the area supported a sizeable population in megalithic times. **Batu Gong** (Gong Stone), in the village of Muak, 25km from Sungai Penuh, is thought to have been carved 2000 years ago.

To reach the lake, catch a public bus from Sungai Penuh to Sanggaran Agung (10,000Rp). The last return bus leaves around 4pm.

Air Terjun WATERFALL

Impressive waterfalls dot the whole valley. The easiest to find are the **Air Terjun Telun Berasap** ('Letter W' Waterfalls; admission 3000Rp) in 'Letter W' village 4km north of Pelompek. Look for the 'Air Terjun Telun Berasap' sign then walk 300m to a deep, fern-lined ravine where a thunderous torrent of water crashes onto rocks below.

Other falls include **Air Terjun 13 Tingkat** near Sungai Medang, and Air Terjun Pauh Sago near Batang Merangin on the Bangko Rd.

Gua CAVE

Locals believe that caves act as mediums for communicating with the supernatural, and that entry into these sacred spaces requires a modest ritual. Hiring a guide helps in the exploration of both the physical and esoteric landscapes.

The most extensive network of caves is situated outside the village of Sengering, including the celebrated **Gua Tiangko**. Obsidian-flake tools found in the cave indicate that it was occupied some 9000 years ago. The caves also contain some impressive natural formations.

Sengering is 9km from Sungai Manau, on the Bangko road. Buses leave Sungai Penuh for Bangko in the mornings at 10am.

There are cave paintings in **Gua Kasah**, 5km southeast from Kersik Tua. There are also two cave systems, **Gua Kelelawar** and **Gua Belang**, at Ting Kemulun near Sanggaran Agung.

Air Panas HOT SPRINGS

If you fancy a dip in some hot springs, make your way to **Dusan Buru Air Panas** near Semurup (11km north of Sungai Penuh) or **Sungai Medang Air Panas** across the valley.

BENGKULU

Cut off from its neighbours by the Bukit Barisan range, Bengkulu remains Sumatra's most isolated province. Few tourists make it this far, but those who do are rewarded with the simple pleasures of ordinary Indonesian life. There's also the opportunity to fast track your understanding of Bahasa Indonesia without the support of bilingualism. Good luck.

History

Little is known of Bengkulu before it came under the influence of the Majapahits from Java at the end of the 13th century. Until then it appears to have existed in almost total isolation, divided between a number of small kingdoms such as Sungai Lebong in the Curup area. It even developed its own cuneiform script, *ka-ga-nga*.

In 1685, after having been kicked out of Banten in Java, the British moved into Bengkulu (Bencoolen, as they called it) in search of pepper. The venture was not exactly a roaring success. Isolation, boredom and constant rain sapped the British will, and malaria ravaged their numbers.

The colony was still not a likely prospect in 1818 when Sir Stamford Raffles arrived as its British-appointed ruler. In the short time he was there, Raffles made the pepper market profitable and planted cash crops of coffee, nutmeg and sugar cane. In 1824 Bengkulu was traded for the Dutch outpost of Melaka as a guarantee not to interfere with British interests in Singapore.

From 1938 to 1941 Bengkulu was a home-in-domestic-exile for Indonesia's first president, Sukarno.

A series of earthquakes struck the province in 2007, killing 13 people.

Bengkulu

☎0736 / POP 380,000

A quiet provincial capital, Bengkulu has a few interesting reminders of the colonial era, an expansive beach and good transport links north to Padang and Bukittinggi, and south to Krui and Bandarlampung.

Sights

Benteng Marlborough FORTESS

(admission 5000Rp; ⏱8am-7pm) Set on a hill overlooking the Indian Ocean, Benteng Marlborough, a former British fort, was restored and opened to the public in 1984 after a long period of use by the Indonesian army. It became the seat of British power in Bengkulu after 1719, when it replaced nearby Fort York, of which nothing but the foundations remain. Despite its sturdy defences the fort was attacked and overrun twice – once by a local rebellion just after its completion in 1719, and then by the French in 1760. The old British gravestones at the entrance make poignant reading. There are a few interesting old engravings and copies of official correspondence from the time of British rule, and you can also see where the Dutch incarcerated Sukarno during his internal exile.

Thomas Parr Monument MONUMENT

(Jl Ahmad Yani) This monument is located in front of the Pasar Barukota and was erected in memory of a British governor beheaded by locals in 1807.

Rumah Bung Karno MUSEUM

(Jl Soekarno-Hatta; admission 2500Rp; ⏱8am-4.30pm Mon-Thu, to noon Sat & Sun) Former president Sukarno was exiled to Bengkulu by the Dutch between 1938 and 1941. The small villa in which he lived is maintained as a museum. Exhibits include a few faded photos, a wardrobe and even his trusty bicycle. Around the museum are shops selling local crafts and snacks.

Monumen Inggris MONUMENT

(Jl M Hasan) The Monumen Inggris, near the beach, is dedicated to Captain Robert Hamilton, who died in 1793 'in command of the troops'.

Mesjid Jamik MOSQUE

(Bung Karno Mosque; cnr Jl Sudirman & Jl Suprapto) During his stay in Bengkulu, Sukarno, who was an architect, designed the Mesjid Jamik.

European Cemetery CEMETERY

(Jl Ditra) The poignant graves in the European cemetery behind the small church are testament to the colonialists' vulnerability to malaria.

Pantai Panjang BEACH

Bengkulu's main beach, Pantai Panjang, although not the best in Indonesia, is clean, generally deserted and a good place for a walk. Strong surf and currents make it unsafe for swimming.

Sleeping

Splash Hotel BOUTIQUE HOTEL $$

(☎23333; www.hotel-splash.com; Jl Sudirman 48; r incl breakfast 390,000-490,000Rp; ❄📶)

Bengkulu's first stab at a designer hotel is a goodie and features a colourful designer lobby and well-appointed rooms with modern bathrooms. There's an on site cafe and restaurant. You can also venture across the road for seafood at Kwetiau Sapi Jambi or the most popular of the city's warungs.

Nala 54 Guesthouse GUESTHOUSE **$$**
(☎26398; nala54bkl@gmail.com; Jl Nala 54; r incl breakfast 500,000Rp) Located in a quiet lane a short walk from the beach, Nala 54 has sparkling and spacious rooms with quite possibly Sumatra's most effective air-conditioning. Brrrrr… It's only got a handful of rooms, so staying here is more like staying in a private apartment.

Vista Hotel HOTEL **$**
(☎20820; Jl MT Haryono 67; r with fan/air-con 60,000/150,000Rp; ❄) Located near the bus agents, Vista is excellent value. You might have forgotten what clean means in Sumatra, but Vista can remind you with a good range of clean rooms.

Hotel Samudera Dwinka HOTEL **$**
(☎21604; samuderawinka_hotel@yahoo.co.id; Jl Sudirman 246; r incl breakfast with fan/air-con 190,000/325,000Rp; ❄@📶) Located in the centre of town, Hotel Samudera has rooms that are inexpensive without being depressing. There's a handy on-site travel agent if you need to book flights or buses.

Hotel Bumi Endah HOTEL **$$**
(☎21665; Jl Fatmawati 29; r incl breakfast 225,000-375,000Rp; ❄) A friendly rambling hotel with quiet rooms and airy common spaces in a residential neighbourhood.

Wisma Kendi HOMESTAY **$**
(☎21369; Jl Soekarno Hatta 17; s/d from 40,000/50,000Rp) Simple fan-cooled rooms in a family-owned homestay in a leafy, quiet neighbourhood. Don't expect hot water for this price, though.

Eating

In the evening, several warungs cause a traffic jam along Jl Sudirman, serving freshly grilled seafood. Be sure to try the local favourites, *tempoyak* (durian and fish) and *martabak* (stuffed savoury pancake).

Kwetiau Sapi Jambi SEAFOOD **$**
(Jl Sudirman Pintu Batu 7; mains 20,000-30,000Rp; ⏰11am-11pm) Multiple local recommendations add up to one of Bengkulu's favourite seafood restaurants. Most dishes come with a Chinese flavour and the fried noodles with seafood are especially hearty after a long bus ride down Sumatra's southwest coast.

Warung Makanan Flora INDONESIAN **$**
(Jl Nala; dishes 10,000-15,000Rp; ⏰11am-10pm) Owned by a friendly Chinese family and serving up cheap and cheerful seafood and excellent sate. Look forward to watching Indonesian game shows with the kids.

Roti Holland Bakery BAKERY **$**
(Jl Suprapto 124; pastries 2500Rp) Chocolate doughnuts are wrapped thoughtfully in a cardboard box for those with self-control. Other freshly baked on-the-road snacks are delivered with a friendly welcome.

Sate Solo INDONESIAN **$**
(Jl Suprapto 159; mains 10,000Rp; ⏰10am-10pm) Sate Solo serves plates of *ayam baker* (grilled chicken) and tasty fruit juices to local families, gangs of school kids and courting couples.

Information

BNI Bank (Jl S Parman) BNI ATMs allow for the largest withdrawals, up to 2,000,000Rp.

Post office (Jl RA Hadi 3) Opposite the Thomas Parr monument.

Sanindo Wisata (☎27522; Jl Mt Haryono 73) City tours, as well as excursions to the Curup tea plantations and offshore islands.

Satelit Internet (Jl S Parman 9; per hr 8000Rp)

BUSES FROM BENGKULU

DESTINATION	COST (RP)	DURATION (HR)	DEPART
Bandarlampung	200,000	14	10am & 2pm
Bukittinggi	150,000	15	10am & 11.30am
Jakarta	250,000	24	8.30am
Krui	80,000	10	8am
Padang	150,000	15	10am & 11.30am

Getting There & Away

AIR There are regular *opelet* to town (6000Rp) from the airport, around 10km southeast. Airport taxis charge a standard 60,000Rp to town. Book air tickets at the travel agency in the Hotel Samudera Dwinka (p561) or at Sanindo Wisata (p561).

Lion Air (www2.lionair.co.id), **Batavia Air** (www.batavia-air.com), **Merpati** (www.merpati.co.id) and **Sriwijaya Air** (www.srijijayair.co.id) all fly daily to Jakarta.

BUS Bengkulu has two bus terminals. The **Air Sebakul** terminal, 12km east of town, serves long-distance destinations, while **Panorama** terminal, 7km east, is used by local buses. However, it is much easier to go to the bus company offices on Jl MT Haryono. Ask around and you'll quickly be steered to the most appropriate company for your destination. Options include buses and more comfortable minibuses.

Getting Around

Opelet fares to almost anywhere in town are 3000Rp and *ojek* are 6000Rp. There are no fixed routes for *opelet;* tell the driver where you want to stay or simply ask for the *benteng* (fort). *Opelet* and *ojek* also greet buses when they arrive at Jl MT Haryono or Jl Bali.

RIAU

The landscape and character of Riau province is distinct from the northern and western rind of Sumatra. Rather than mountains and volcanoes, Riau's character was carved by rivers and narrow ocean passages. Trading towns sprang up along the important navigation route of the Strait of Melaka, across which Riau claims cultural cousins.

For the port towns, such as Pekanbaru, and the Riau Islands, proximity to Singapore and Kuala Lumpur has ensured greater access to the outside world than the towns of the interior Sumatran jungle. The discovery of oil and gas reserves has also built an educated and middle-class population within a relatively impoverished island.

The interior of the province more closely resembles Sumatra as a whole: sparse population, dense jungle, surviving pockets of nomadic peoples (including the Sakai, Kubu and Jambisal) and endangered species, such as the Sumatran rhinoceros and tiger.

The Riau Islands are scattered like confetti across the South China Sea. The locals say there are as many islands as there are grains in a cup of pepper. That would be about 3214 islands in all, more than 700 of them uninhabited and many of them unnamed.

Pulau Batam and Pulau Bintam are practically suburbs of Singapore, with the attendant industry and recreation. In fact, the islands prefer to think of themselves as distinct from mainland Sumatra. Further away in the archipelago are the remote islands of Anambas, Natuna and Tambelan.

History

Riau's position at the southern entrance to the Strait of Melaka, the gateway for trade between India and China, was strategically significant.

From the 16th century, the Riau Islands were ruled by a variety of Malay kingdoms, which had to fight off constant attacks by pirates and the Portuguese, Dutch and English. The Dutch eventually won control over the Strait of Melaka, and mainland Riau (then known as Siak) became their colony when the Sultan of Johor surrendered in 1745. However, Dutch interest lay in ridding the seas of pirates, so they could get on with the serious business of trade, and they made little effort to develop the province.

Oil was discovered around Pekanbaru by US engineers before WWII, but it was the Japanese who drilled the first well at Rumbai, 10km north of the city. The country around Pekanbaru is criss-crossed by pipelines that connect the oil wells to refineries at Dumai, as ocean-going tankers cannot enter the heavily silted Sungai Siak.

Pekanbaru

☎0761 / POP 750,000

Before the Americans struck oil, Pekanbaru was little more than a sleepy river port on Sungai Siak. Today it's Indonesia's oil capital, with all the hustle and bustle of modern cities.

Pekanbaru's primary purpose for tourists used to be as a transit point for ferry passengers from Singapore, but the increased affordability of air travel has curtailed the sea passage. If you've still got your heart set on an old-school journey by boat from Singapore to Sumatra, it is still possible – just – and if you do wash up in this oil boomtown, expect a warm welcome from the friendly locals.

The best place to base yourself is around the intersection of Jl Sudirman and Jl Teuku Umar with ATMs, good food and accommodation options.

Sights

Riau Cultural Park PARK
(Jl Sudirman; ⏲8am-2pm Mon-Thu & Sat, 8am-noon Fri) The Riau Cultural Park hosts occasional performances. Ask at the tourist office for details. The neighbouring **Museum Negeri Riau** has rather standard displays.

Soeman HS County Library NOTABLE BUILDING
(Jl Sudirman) Oil money is transforming Pekanbaru's cityscape with some of Indonesia's most interesting modern architecture. This audacious library on Jl Sudirman is Sumatra's biggest library. Nearby is the spectacular **Idrus Tintin building**, which blends modern design with traditional Malay architecture.

Balai Adat Daerah Riau MUSEUM
(Jl Diponegoro; ⏲8am-2pm Mon-Thu & Sat, 8am-noon Fri) Balai Adat Daerah Riau in the town centre contains a few modest exhibits about traditional Malay culture.

Mesjid Raya MOSQUE
(Jl Mesjid Raya) Mesjid Raya, near the river, dates back to the 18th century, when Pekanbaru was the capital of the Siak sultanate. The courtyard holds the graves of the fourth and fifth sultans.

Sleeping

The best location for good-value midrange hotels is around the intersection of Jl Sudirman and Jl Teuku Umar. In this oil boomtown, budget accommodation is thin on the ground.

Hotel Bintang Lima HOTEL $$
(☎24115; hotel.bintanglima@yahoo.co.id; Jl Teuku Umar 18; r 250,000-350,000Rp; ❄📶) This sleek designer hotel features classy red-and-black decor, a cool downstairs coffee shop, and an on site spa and massage centre. Rooms are relatively compact, but the flat-screen TVs and modern bathrooms make it a definite cut above other more tired midrange hotels nearby.

Paramita Hotel HOTEL $$
(☎28333; info@discoveryhotelpekanbaru.com; Jl Teuku Umar 20A; r incl breakfast from 370,000Rp) The Paramita's unique combination of Zen-influenced decor, an on site vegetarian restaurant and a sunny al fresco cafe make it one of Pekanbaru's best places to stay. Rooms are crisp and modern with top-notch bathrooms, and Western visitors are welcomed like long-lost relatives by the friendly staff.

Poppie's Homestay HOMESTAY $
(☎45762; Jl Taskurun 69, Jl Cempedak III; r 80,000Rp) Basic budget rooms in a converted family home within a quiet residential neighbourhood. It is tricky to find, but locals will be able to point you in the right direction once you turn off Jl Nangka.

Eating

Pekanbaru's best street for eating is Jl Gatot Subrato, two blocks south (from the river) of Jl Teuku Umar. There's a good food court on the top floor of the Pekanbaru Mall on the corner of Jl Teuku Umar and Jl Sudirman.

Restoran Seafood Citra SEAFOOD $$
(Jl Gatot Subrato 14; mains 30,000-60,000Rp; ⏲8am-10pm) Cold Tiger beer, grilled seafood and a lengthy menu of Indonesian and Chinese favourites feature at this friendly neighbourhood eatery. The family's kids are usually up and about at night, and will no doubt be exceptionally interested in your visit. Push the boat out with chilli crab if you want something special.

Curry House NYONYA $
(Jl Gatot Subrato 28; dishes 10,000-15,000Rp) With a good selection of Nyonya (Straits Chinese) dishes, this cosy family-owned restaurant reinforces how close Pekanbaru is to Singapore. The curry dishes are light and fragrant, and provide a tasty contrast to the occasional chilli overkill of Padang food found elsewhere across Sumatra.

Information

ATMs are spread along Jl Sudirman.

Post office (Jl Sudirman) Between Jl Hangtuah and Jl Kartini.

Riau Provincial Tourist Office (☎31562; Jl Gajah Mada 200; ⏲8am-4pm Mon-Thu, to 11am Fri) About 1km north of the post office.

Getting There & Away

Air

Pekanbaru's airport is 10km south of the city. Note there's a 60,000Rp international departure tax if you're flying to Singapore or Kuala Lumpur.

Boat

Pekanbaru's Sungai Duku port is at the end of Jl Sultan Syarif Qasyim. From the intersection of Jl Sudirman and Jl Teuku Umarit it's a short *ojek* ride. With the growth in budget airlines, the only ocean link to Pulau Batam is with **Dumai Express** (Indo Kencana; ☎61955; Jl Nangka 24) via Tanjun Buton. A minibus leaves Pekanbaru at 7.30am daily – it does hotel pick ups – and travels three hours to the port of Tanjung Buton. From Tanjung Buton, a ferry (four to five hours) continues to the port of Sekupang on Batam. The whole trip is 290,000Rp. From Sekupang, there are frequent boats to Singapore, but you'll probably need to overnight on Batam. Dumai Express has an infrequently staffed office at Pekanbaru's Sungai Duku port, and a main office on Jl Nangka around 4km southwest of Pekanbaru's intersection.

Bus

Pekanbaru's Terminal Nangka is 5km west of the town centre. Note that buses to Bukittinggi (40,000Rp, eight hours) depart between 2pm and 6pm from the southwestern outskirts of town. A taxi to the Bukittinggi bus departure point is around 60,000Rp.

Getting Around

Airport taxis and taxis from the bus station charge 70,000Rp. The city's new Tranzemetro bus service runs along Jl Sudirman to the bus station (3000Rp).

Pulau Batam

☎0778 / POP 440,000

With the island's proximity to Singapore, Batam is the labour-intensive production leg of the Singapore–Johor Baru–Batam industrial triangle. Many electronics companies have established production plants in the industrial park of Mukakuning. Factory workers are predominantly young women from impoverished areas of Indonesia.

Higher up the economic food chain are the executives who oversee the factories and the engineers who work on the offshore oil rigs and pipelines. More recent investment is flowing in from China with the establishment of steel manufacturing plants and shipbuilding.

Other initiatives across recent years have included developing golf resorts and casinos targetting Asian tourists, and gated retirement communities for East Asians, Singaporeans and Jakarta-based Chinese.

Information

Most travellers to Batam arrive at the northern port of Sekupang by boat from Singapore. The island is also linked to Pekanbaru on the Sumatran mainland by boat and plane. Sekupang has an international and domestic terminal next door to each other and all the short-term necessities that new arrivals need: immigration desk and money changers. There are no ATMs at Sekupang, so arrive with cash to avoid a taxi to Nagoya. The main town on the island is Nagoya, with hotels, banks and other necessities. To the south is the island's administrative centre, Batam Centre, which also has ferry arrivals from Singapore. Waterfront City and Nongsa are resort areas that attract Asian package tourists on weekends. On Batam, Singapore dollars are as easy to spend as Indonesian rupiah.

Batam Tourist Promotion Board (☎322 871; next door to Sekupang domestic terminal) can help with local information and hotel bookings but keeps erratic hours.

TRANSPORT FROM PEKANBARU

Air

DESTINATION	COMPANY	FREQUENCY
Jakarta	Lion Air, Sriwijaya Air, Batavia Air	daily
Kuala Lumpur	Firefly	daily
Medan	Sriwijaya Air	daily
Singapore	Silk Air	daily
Surabaya	Lion Air	daily

Bus

DESTINATION	COST (RP)	DURATION (HR)	FREQUENCY
Bengkulu	170,000	15	5pm
Dumai	50,000	5	hourly from 7am
Jambi	170,000	12	10am & 5pm

DUMAI TO MELAKA BY SEA

Like most of Pekanbaru's oil, travellers enter and exit Dumai through its busy port. Airfares between Malaysia and Sumatra are usually more competitive, but a ferry also links Dumai to Melaka. Buses also link Bukittinggi to Dumai if you're hell-bent on transiting between Sumatra and Malaysia without flying.

Dumai has loads of accommodation, but if you time it right, it's relatively straighforward to link to or from Bukittinggi without overnighting in Dumai.

The Dumai Express ferry from Melaka (around two to three hours) arrives in Dumai around 8am. The port area is a bit of a scrum, so keep an eye out for BMW2002 Tours & Travel (p550), which runs shared minibuses (per person 100,000Rp) direct to Bukittinggi. There are also frequent buses from Dumai to Padang (100,000Rp, 12 hours) if you're visiting the Mentawai Islands.

From Dumai the ferry to Melaka (per person 240,000Rp, around two to three hours) departs at 11am daily. If you're travelling from Bukittinggi, BMW2002 has a nightly minibus (around 10 hours) linking with the ferry's morning departure.

Getting There & Away

AIR

Hang Nadim airport is on the eastern side of the Pulau Batam.

BOAT

TO PULAU BINTAN The ferry dock at Telaga Punggur, 30km southeast of Nagoya, is the main port for frequent speedboats to Bintan's Tanjung Pinang harbour (40,000Rp, 45 minutes). There are also regular boats to Bintan's Lagoi resort area (110,000Rp, 1½ hours).

TO PEKANBARU From Batam's Sekupang port, **Dumai Express** (PT Lestari Indoma Bahari; ☎325 173; Sekupang domestic terminal) runs a daily ferry (four to five hours) to the port of Tanjung Buton on mainland Sumatra. From there a minibus (around three hours) links to Pekanbaru. The cost is 290,000Rp. You'll need to overnight in Pekanbaru before an onward bus to Bukittinggi.

TO SINGAPORE Frequent services (S$17 to S$22) shuttle between Singapore and Batam, taking around 40 minutes. Boats depart Harbourfront Centre in Singapore and go to Sekupang and Batam Centre on Pulau Batam. There is a S$7 harbour-departure tax upon leaving Batam and an hour time difference between Indonesia and Singapore.

Getting Around

Taxis are the primary way to get around Pulau Batam. They cost around 120,000Rp to Sekupang and 80,000Rp to Nagoya. There's also a public bus from the Telaga Punggur dock to Nagoya (15,000Rp). A taxi on the same route is 85,000Rp.

NAGOYA

This is the original boom town, showing a lot more skin than you'll find in the rest of Sumatra. The heart of town is the Nagoya Entertainment District, dotted with beer bars and massage parlours. Other attractions include Nagoya's shopping centres – Nagoya Hill Mall is the most popular – which are often packed with Malaysian and Singaporean weekend visitors.

Like Singapore, Nagoya is divided up into main avenues and tributary blocks and exhibits a certain Chinese industriousness similar to the city-state.

It ain't pretty, but Nagoya is ultimately functional, and an interesting enough overnight stay it you're hell-bent on arriving in Sumatra by boat via Singapore and Pulau Bintan.

Sleeping

Goodway Hotel HOTEL **$$**
(☎426 888; www.goodwayhotel.com; Jl Imam Bonjol; r incl breakfast 450,000-850,000Rp; ❄) This recently refurbished, classic hotel channels a colonial Raffles-like vibe. There are spacious rooms with wooden furniture and massive beds, several restaurant options, including a Japanese teppanyaki bar, and a good downstairs pub. Check online for good discounts.

Hotel Grand Palace HOTEL **$**
(☎432 529; Komplek Nagoya Business Centre, Block 1, No 37-40; d from 150,000Rp; ❄) OK value for those on a tight budget. The tiled-floor rooms come with air-con, hot water, cable TV and clean, sleepable beds. It's a short walk to the good eats at the Nagoya Hill Mall. After dark it can get a tad noisy from nearby bars.

FLIGHTS FROM PULAU BATAM

DESTINATION	COMPANY	FREQUENCY
Bandarlampung	Batavia Air	daily
Jakarta	Lion Air, Batavia Air, Garuda	daily
Kuala Lumpur	Firefly	daily
Medan	Sriwijaya Air	daily
Padang	Batavia Air	daily
Pekanbaru	Lion Air	daily

Eating & Drinking

Nagoya has a tasty mix of Indonesian and Chinese restaurants. For local warungs, head to the night market or the big and raucous Pujasera Nagoya. The Nagoya Hill Mall has a specialist 'Food Street', which offers many different cuisines.

Golden Prawn SEAFOOD **$$**
(mains from 60,000Rp) This famous *kelong* (open-air seafood restaurant on a Malay-style fishing platform) is considered one of the best on the island. Everything is charged by the kilogram.

Goodway Wine Bar PUB
(Goodway Hotel, Jl Imam Bonjol) Through the Wild West saloon doors is a comfortable tap room for unwinding expats. Live TV sport, cold beer and bar snacks provide an escape if you've been on the road in Asia just a little too long.

Pulau Bintan

0771 / POP 200,000

Just across the water from Batam, Pulau Bintan is trying to market itself as a high-end playground for well-heeled visitors from East Asia. Top-end resorts huddle around the Lagoi area on the island's northern coast – in close proximity to Singapore – and the east coast around Pantai Trikora is a more affordable and laid-back option for Bintan beach bums.

Check out www.welcometobintan.com and www.bintan-resorts.com.

Getting There & Away

AIR

Kijang airport is located in the southeast of the island. A taxi to Tanjung Pinang should be around 100,000Rp. There are daily flights to/from Jakarta on Lion Air, Batavia Air and Sriwijaya Air.

BOAT

Bintan has three ports and services to Palau Batam, Singapore and other islands in the Riau archipelago.

Tanjung Pinang is the busiest harbour and the best option for folks planning to stay in Tanjung Pinang or Pantai Trikora. If you're bound for the resort area of Lagoi, the port at Kota Sebung is more convenient. Tanjung Uban is the third option. At the time of writing a fourth port on the east coast was rumoured, potentially providing easier access to the beach scene around Pantai Trikora.

TO PULAU BATAM Regular speedboats depart from the main pier in Tanjung Pinang for Telaga Punggur on Batam (40,000Rp, 45 minutes) from 8am to 5.45pm daily. There are also boats that go from Lagoi to Batam's Telaga Punggur (110,000Rp, 1½ hours).

TO ELSEWHERE IN INDONESIA Daily ferries depart from Tanjung Pinang's main pier to other islands in the Riau chain, such as Pulau Karimum, Pulau Lingga and Pulau Penuba.

TO MALAYSIA There are boats to Johor Bahru in Malaysia (280,000Rp, five departures daily) from Tanjung Pinang. Tickets can be bought from agents on Jl Merdeka in Tanjung Pinang, just outside of the harbour entrance.

TO SINGAPORE Boats from Tanjung Pinang go to Singapore's Tanah Merah (one way 160,000Rp, two hours) around six times between 7am and 4.30pm. There are more frequent services on the weekend.

Bintan Resort Ferries (www.brf.com.sg) is the only company that handles transport between Lagoi and Singapore; ticket prices range from S$25 to S$50, depending on the day and time of travel.

TANJUNG PINANG

The main port town on the island is a bustling mercantile centre with more ethnic diversity than most Sumatran towns. There is a lot of provincial-style shopping and nibbling on Chinese and Indonesian specialities. Located nearby are several traditional-style villages and temple attractions.

Sights & Activities

The older part of town is found around the narrow piers near Jl Plantar II. The harbour hosts a constant stream of vessels, from tiny sampans to large freighters.

Pulau Penyenget ISLAND

Across the harbour from Tanjung Pinang, tiny Penyenget was once the capital of the Riau rajahs. The island is believed to have been given to Rajah Riau-Lingga VI in 1805 by his brother-in-law, Sultan Mahmud, as a wedding present. Another historical footnote is that the Penyenget-based sultanate cooperated with Sir Stamford Raffles to hand over Singapore in exchange for British military protection in 1819.

The island is littered with interesting relics and can be walked in a couple of hours. The coastline is dotted with traditional Malay stilted houses, while the ruins of the **old palace** of Rajah Ali and the **tombs** and **graveyards** of Rajah Jaafar and Rajah Ali are clearly signposted inland. The most impressive site is the sulphur-coloured **mosque**, with its many domes and minarets. Dress appropriately or you won't be allowed in.

There are frequent boats to Pulau Penyenget from Bintan's main pier (5000Rp, between 7am and 5pm). There's a 3000Rp entry charge at weekends.

Senggarang VILLAGE

The star attraction in this village, just across the harbour from Tanjung Pinang, is an old **Chinese temple**, now suspended in the roots of a huge banyan tree.

The temple is to the left of the pier, where boats from Tanjung Pinang dock. Half a kilometre along the waterfront, **Vihara Darma Sasana**, a complex of three temples said to be more than a century old, occupies a large courtyard facing the sea.

Boats to Senggarang (15,000Rp) leave from Pejantan II wharf, around 1km northwest of the town's main pier. Boats are more frequent on weekends.

Jodoh Temple TEMPLE

Sungai Ulur (Snake River) swims through mangrove forests to Jodoh temple, the oldest Chinese temple in Riau Islands. The temple is decorated with gory murals depicting the trials and tortures of hell. Charter a sampan (flat-bottomed wooden boat; five people 100,000Rp) from Tanjung Pinang harbour.

Sleeping & Eating

Most of the accommodation closest to the harbour is overpriced and lacklustre, so you're better off grabbing an *ojek* and staying slightly out of central Tanjung Pinang. Many hotels also price their rooms in Singaporean dollars.

The best place to eat near the harbour is at the Hotel Melia. In front of the volleyball stadium on Jl Teuku Umar, an open-air food court showcases tasty meals and fresh juices.

The colourful *pasar buah* (fruit market) is at the northern end of Jl Merdeka. In the evening there are several food stalls scattered around town serving *mie bangka,* a Hakka-style dumpling soup.

Hotel Panorama HOTEL $

(☎22920; www.bintanpanorama.com; Jl Haji Agus Salim 12; r incl breakfast S$25-30; ❄@📶) Friendly staff and clean and spacious rooms feature at this recent opening around a 10-minute walk from the ferry terminal. Cane furniture adds a touch of the tropics, and the attached Bamboo cafe and karaoke room is popular with Singaporean visitors on weekends. Ask about its free shuttle transfer from the ferry terminal when you book.

Hotel Melia HOTEL $$

(☎21898; Jl Pos 25; d incl breakfast from S$48; ❄📶) Bright and airy rooms and enormous suites with harbour views feature at this long-established place. Downstairs a huge deck extends out into the harbour; it's a top spot for cold beer and freshly grilled seafood. Hotel rates are cheaper between Sunday and Friday.

Wisma Bintan Harmoni HOTEL $

(☎28742; Jl Ir H Juanda; r 100,000-130,000Rp) Simply furnished but spacious rooms feature at this good-value place around 1km from the ferry terminal. All you need for an overnight stay if you're kicking on to Singapore or Pulau Batam.

Information

There are plenty of ATMs, mainly on Jl Teuku Umar. For internet access head to the **Bintan Internet Centre** (Jl Pos; per hr 10,000Rp; ⏰9am-10pm).

Post office (Jl Merdeka) Near the harbour, on Tanjung Pinang's main street.

Tourist information centre (☎31822; Jl Merdeka 5; ⏰8am-5pm) Behind the police station. The helpful English-speaking staff organise city tours.

Getting Around

Bintan has a fledgling public transport system with three *opelet* services – A, B and C – leaving from just north of the Bintan Indah mall. Destinations are listed on the *opelets* (3000Rp).

A taxi from Tanjung Pinang to Pantai Trikora is a long ride and will cost 250,000Rp. An *ojek* to Trikora should be around 125,000Rp. Another option is to rent a car, which gives you flexibility in exploring the beaches around the island. Renting a car in Tanjung Pinang (per day around 300,000Rp) is cheaper than relying on the resorts in Lagoi.

PANTAI TRIKORA & AROUND

Bintan's east coast is lined with rustic beaches that are becoming increasingly popular with Singaporean weekend visitors. Accommodation is laid-back and simple, and the area is an easygoing contrast to the flasher resorts on Bintan's northern coast. If you've been doing some hard travelling through Sumatra, here's your chance to regroup and recharge.

The main beach is **Pantai Trikora**, which is pretty enough at high tide but turns into kilometres of mud flats at low tide. The beaches to the north around Malangrupai have more consistent water. The small islands off Pantai Trikora are well worth visiting and there is good **snorkelling** outside the monsoon season (November to March).

Accommodation owners can organise snorkelling trips to the offshore islands and also fishing excursions on the *kelongs* (Malay-style fishing platforms) that dot the seascape.

Sleeping & Eating

Marjoly Beach RESORT **$$**
(☎0813 2743 0039; www.marjolybeach.com; Pantai Trikora Km33; d incl breakfast weekday/weekend S$65/75; ❄) Trikora's newest opening features spacious bungalows cooled by ocean breezes. Relax on the private decks or commandeer one of the simple beachside gazebos. Marjoly Beach is popular with kitesurfers from Singapore, and there's a good restaurant (mains 25,000Rp to 40,000Rp) that sometimes hosts live music on weekends.

Shady Shack HOMESTAY **$**
(☎0813 6451 5223; www.lobo.kinemotion.de; Pantai Trikora Km41; dm/d S$12/30) Run by a friendly local family, this easygoing place features a handful of rustic weather-beaten shacks facing directly to the sea. There's excellent snorkelling in a variety of locations nearby, but you'll need to bring your own snorkelling gear to maximise your underwater viewing opportunities. Quad rooms (S$50) are good value for families. Lobo the owner can arrange fishing trips and excursions to nearby islands.

LAGOI

Bintan's resort area stretches along the northern coastline of the island along Pasir Lagoi, with hectares of wilderness buffering the hotels from commoners to the south. Security is in full effect, with checkpoints at access roads and at hotel entrances. The beaches are sandy and swimmable, the resorts have polished four- and five-star service and there are water-sports activities and entertainment for all ages.

There are also three golf courses in Lagoi designed by champion golfers. See www.bintan-resorts.com/discover/golf for more information.

Sleeping

There are three resort compounds comprising several hotel clusters, private beaches and golf courses. Check with travel agents about weekday discounts, which can be as generous as 50%. See www.bintan-resorts.com.

Angsana Resort & Spa Bintan RESORT **$$$**
(☎0770 693 111; www.angsana.com; r incl breakfast from US$210; ❄📶) The dressed-down Angsana is best suited to young professionals. The breezy common spaces are decorated in zesty citrus colours, with private rooms sporting a contemporary colonial style. The superior rooms are nice but the suites are super.

Banyan Tree Bintan RESORT **$$$**
(☎0770 693 100; www.banyantree.com; r incl breakfast from US$330; ❄📶) The private and privileged Banyan Tree has famed spa facilities and a high-powered retreat deep in the jungle. The hotel shares the 900m-long beach with Angsana Resort & Spa Bintan.

Getting Around

Most resorts organise shuttle service between the harbour at Kota Sebong and the Lagoi hotels as part of the package price.

JAMBI

For such a centrally located province, Jambi is not easy to reach and sees few foreign visitors. The province occupies a 53,435-sq-km slice of central Sumatra, stretching from the highest peaks of the Bukit Barisan range in the west to the coastal swamps facing the Strait of Melaka in the east.

The eastern lowlands are mainly rubber and palm-oil plantations. Timber is also big business, as is oil; Jambi's main field is southeast of the capital (Jambi) on the South Sumatran border.

In the western portion of the province is the Kerinci Seblat National Park (p557), home to Sumatra's highest peak, Gunung Kerinci (3805m), Sumatran tigers (Jambi's faunal mascot) and rhinos. The park is best reached from Padang.

Most of the province is sparsely populated, and many locals are migrants from Java and Bali. In the province's fast disappearing forests, the Orang Rimba are an endangered hunter-gatherer tribe.

History

The province of Jambi was the heartland of the ancient kingdom of Malayu, which first rose to prominence in the 7th century. Much of Malayu's history is closely and confusingly entwined with that of its main regional rival, the Palembang-based kingdom of Sriwijaya. The little that is known about Malayu has mostly been gleaned from the precise records maintained by the Chinese court of the time.

It is assumed that the temple ruins at Muara Jambi mark the site of Malayu's former capital, the ancient city of Jambi – known to the Chinese as Chan Pi. The Malayu sent their first delegation to China in 644 and the Chinese scholar I Tsing spent a month in Malayu in 672. When he returned 20 years later he found that Malayu had been conquered by Sriwijaya. The Sriwijayans appear to have remained in control until the sudden collapse of their empire at the beginning of the 11th century.

Following Sriwijaya's demise, Malayu re-emerged as an independent kingdom and stayed that way until it became a dependency of Java's Majapahit empire, which ruled from 1278 until 1520. It then came under the sway of the Minangkabau people of West Sumatra.

In 1616 the Dutch East India Company opened an office in Jambi and quickly formed a successful alliance with Sultan Muhammed Nakhruddin to protect its ships and cargoes from pirates. It also negotiated a trade monopoly with Nakhruddin and his successors. The major export was pepper, which was grown in great abundance. In 1901 the Dutch East India Company moved its headquarters to Palembang and effectively gave up its grip on Jambi.

Jambi

☎0741 / POP 490,000

The capital of Jambi province is a busy river port about 155km from the mouth of the Sungai Batang Hari. It's not known as a tourist destination, but has a pleasantly low-key and friendly vibe, especially around the riverfront food stalls that kick off at dusk.

Sights & Activities

Jambi is the starting point for excursions to the archaeological site of Muara Jambi.

Museum Negeri Propinsi Jambi MUSEUM

(cnr Jl Urip Sumoharjo & Jl Prof Dr Sri Sudewi; admission 2500Rp; 8.30am-3pm Mon-Fri) Museum Negeri Propinsi Jambi, one of the city's few attractions, is out in Telanaipura. It has a selection of costumes and handicrafts, as well as a small historical display. Take an *ojek* (4000Rp).

Batik Centre MARKET

(Telanaipura) Out in Telanaipura is a batik centre selling traditional Jambi textiles featuring striking floral motifs. The centre also has a range of handicrafts from all over the province, including *songket* weaving and finely woven split-rattan baskets. The centre provides employment for local women.

Sleeping

Traditionally accommodation in Jambi hasn't been much of a bargain, but a few new openings make the city worthy of a stopover.

Hotel Duta BOUTIQUE HOTEL $$

(☎755 919; hotelduta@yahoo.com; Jl Sam Ratulangi 65-68; r incl breakfast 350,000-525,000Rp; ❄) Opened just days before we dropped by, the Duta features compact rooms with modern decor and snazzy bathrooms. Flat-screen TVs – with plenty of English-language content – and a wildly ostentatious reception area are other cosmopolitan surprises in sleepy Jambi. It's a short stroll to al fresco street-food treats down on the riverbank.

Hotel Fortuna HOTEL $

(Jl Jendral Gatot Subrato; r 150,000-250,000Rp; ❄) With modern bathrooms and flat-screen TVs, your travel budget goes a long way at the Fortuna. Rooms are simple and sparsely furnished, but all you need after a long day on

ORANG RIMBA

Jambi's nomadic hunter-gatherers are known by many names: outsiders refer to the diverse tribes collectively as Kubu, an unflattering term, while they refer to themselves as Orang Rimba (People of the Forest) or Anak Dalam (Children of the Forest). Descended from the first wave of Malays to migrate to Sumatra, they once lived in highly mobile groups throughout Jambi's lowland forests.

As fixed communities began to dominate the province, the Orang Rimba retained their nomadic lifestyle and animistic beliefs, regarding their neighbours' adoption of Islam and agriculture as disrespectful towards the forest. Traditionally the Orang Rimba avoided contact with the outsiders, preferring to barter and trade by leaving goods on the fringes of the forest or relying on trusted intermediaries.

In the 1960s, the Indonesian government's social affairs and religion departments campaigned to assimilate the Orang Rimba into permanent camps and convert them to a monotheistic religion. Meanwhile the jungles were being transformed into palm-oil and rubber plantations during large-scale *transmigrasi* (government-sponsored scheme to encourage settlers to move from overcrowded regions to sparsely populated ones) from Java and Bali.

Some Orang Rimba assimilated and are now economically marginalised within the plantations, while others live off government funds and then return to the forests. About 2500 Orang Rimba retain their traditional lifestyles within the shrinking forest. The groups were given special settlement rights within Bukit Duabelas and Bukit Tigapuluh National Parks, but the protected forests are as vulnerable to illegal logging and poaching as other Sumatran parks.

In the opinions of the NGO groups that work with the Orang Rimba, it isn't a question of *if* the tribes will lose their jungle traditions but *when*. In the spirit of practical idealism, the organisation WARSI (www.warsi.or.id) established its alternative educational outreach. Rather than forcing educational institutions on the Orang Rimba, teachers join those that will accept an outsider and teach the children how to read, write and count – the equivalent of knowing how to hunt and forage in the settled communities.

Sumatran roads. The Fortuna is concealed in a quiet retail plaza near the Abadi Hotel – a local landmark – and there are Chinese noodle shops nearby for a quick breakfast.

Hotel Da'lia HOTEL $
(☎755 2309; Jl Camar 100; d with shared bathroom 80,000Rp, d with air-con 160,000Rp; ❄) Basic and clean, this is the best you'll get in the super-cheap range. You'll find the Da'lia tucked away near Jambi's market area.

Eating

Taman Tanggo Rajo INDONESIAN $
(near Wiltop Trade Centre; snacks from 5000Rp) This is Jambi's essential evening destination for riverside promenading. Stalls sell local favourites, such as *nanas goreng* (fried pineapples) and *jagung bakar* (roasted corn slathered with coconut milk and chillis). The sate Padang is also good. Nearby is the **Wiltop Trade Centre**, a modern shopping mall with Western restaurants and a multiplex cinema.

Pasar Makanan INDONESIAN $
(Jl Sultan Iskandar Muda; dishes from 8000Rp) Lots of regional Palembang specialities, which Jambi also claims as its own, get top billing at this busy market.

Munri Food Centre INDONESIAN $
(Jl Sultan Agung; mains 10,000Rp) More nighttime eats set the night ablaze at this al fresco dining area. Look for the *mie pangsit Jambi* and *mie pokk*, two local noodle dishes.

Saimen Perancis BAKERY $
(Jl Raden Mattaher; pastries 2000Rp) An excellent bakery that also serves Indonesian and European meals.

Information

Jambi's ATMs cluster around Jl Dr Sutomo. Several of the international fast-food restaurants in the Wiltop Trade Centre offer wi-fi access.

Culture & Tourism Office (☎445 056; Jl H Agus Salim) The English-speaking staff can organise city tours.

Post office (Jl Sultan Thaha 9) Near the port.
Thamrin Internet (Jl Gatot Subroto 6; per hr 5000Rp; ⏲10am-10pm) Internet access near Gloria Bookshop.

Getting There & Away

AIR The Sultan Thaka Airport is 6km east of the centre.

BUS Bus-ticketing offices occupy two areas of town: Simpang Rimbo, 8km west of town, and Simpang Kawat, 3.5km southwest of town on Jl M Yamin.

There are frequent economy buses to Palembang (60,000Rp, seven hours). **Ratu Intan Permata** (☎20784; Simpang Kawat, Jl M Yamin) has comfortable door-to-door minibus services to Pekanbaru (190,000Rp, 10 hours), Bengkulu (180,000Rp, 10 hours), Palembang (110,000Rp, six hours) and Padang (180,000Rp, 13 hours). **Safa Marwa** (☎65756; Jl Pattimura 7) runs a similar service to Sungai Penuh in the Kerinci Valley (1000,000Rp, 10 hours). Buses depart from the companies' offices.

Getting Around

Airport taxis charge a standard 70,000Rp. Rawasari *opelet* terminal is off Jl Raden Mattaher in the centre of town. The standard fare around town is 2000Rp. An *ojek* to the bus offices in Simpang Rimbo is around 15,000Rp. For Simpang Kawat, count on 10,000Rp.

Muara Jambi

The large temple complex at Muara Jambi, 26km downstream from Jambi, is the most important Hindu-Buddhist site in Sumatra. It is assumed that the temples mark the location of the ancient city of Jambi, capital of the kingdom of Malayu 1000 years ago. Most of the temples, known as *candi,* date from the 9th to the 13th centuries, when Jambi's power was at its peak. However, the best artefacts have been taken to Jakarta.

For centuries the site lay abandoned and overgrown in the jungle on the banks of the Batang Hari. It was 'rediscovered' in 1920 by a British army expedition sent to explore the region.

Sights

Muara Jambi RUINS
(admission by donation; ⏲8am-4pm) It's easy to spend all day at Muara Jambi. The forested site covers 12 sq km along the north bank of the Batang Hari. The entrance is through an ornate archway in the village of Muara Jambi and most places of interest are within a few minutes' walk.

Eight temples have been identified so far, each at the centre of its own low-walled compound. Some are accompanied by *perwara candi* (smaller side temples) and three have been restored to something close to their original form. The site is dotted with numerous *menapo* (smaller brick mounds), thought to be the ruins of other buildings – possibly dwellings for priests and other high officials.

The restored temple **Candi Gumpung**, straight ahead of the donation office, has a fiendish *makara* (demon head) guarding its steps. Excavation work here has yielded some important finds, including a *peripih* (stone box) containing sheets of gold inscribed with old Javanese characters, dating the temple back to the 9th century. A statue of Prajnyaparamita found here is now the star attraction at the small **site museum** nearby.

Candi Tinggi, 200m southeast of Candi Gumpung, is the finest of the temples uncovered so far. It dates from the 9th century but is built around another, older temple. A path leads east from Candi Tinggi to **Candi Astano**, 1.5km away, passing **Candi Kembar Batu** and lots of *menapo* along the way.

The temples on the western side of the site are yet to be restored. They remain pretty much as they were found – minus the jungle, which was cleared in the 1980s. The western sites are signposted from Candi Gumpung. First stop, after 900m, is **Candi Gedong Satu**, followed 150m further on by **Candi Gedong Dua**. They are independent temples despite what their names may suggest. The path continues west for another 1.5km to **Candi Kedaton**, the largest of the

FLIGHTS FROM JAMBI

DESTINATION	COMPANY	FREQUENCY
Jakarta	Lion Air, Batavia Air, Garuda, Sriwijaya Air	daily
Pulau Batam	Sriwijaya Air	daily

temples, then a further 900m northwest to **Candi Koto Mahligai**.

The dwellings of the ordinary Malayu people have long since disappeared. According to Chinese records, they lived along the river in stilted houses or in raft huts moored to the bank.

 Getting There & Away

There is no public transport to the park. You can charter a speedboat (400,000Rp) from Jambi's river pier to the site. You can also hire an *ojek* (40,000Rp).

SOUTH SUMATRA

The eastern portion of South Sumatra shares a common Malay ancestry and influence with Riau and Jambi provinces from its proximity to the shipping lane of the Strait of Melaka. Rivers define the character of the eastern lowlands, while the western high peaks of the Bukit Barisan form the province's rugged underbelly. The provincial capital of Palembang was once the central seat of the Buddhist Sriwijaya empire, whose control once reached all the way up the Malay Peninsula.

Despite the province's illustrious past, there aren't very many surviving attractions, except for the hospitality that occurs in places where bilingual Indonesians don't get a lot of opportunity to practise their English.

Palembang

0711 / POP 1.67 MILLION

Sumatra's second-largest city is a major port and prospers on the core industries of oil refining, fertiliser production and cement manufacturing.

The city's spicy fare is subject of much debate (positive and negative) in Sumatra, and it's worth establishing your own opinion for cuisine chats around the rest of the island.

Palembang sits astride Sungai Musi, the two halves of the city linked by the giant Jembatan Ampera (Ampera Bridge). The river is flanked by a hodgepodge of wooden houses on stilts.

History

A thousand years ago Palembang was the centre of the highly developed Sriwijaya civilisation. The Chinese scholar I Tsing spent six months in Palembang in 672 and reported that 1000 monks, scholars and pilgrims were studying and translating Sanskrit there. At its peak in the 11th century, Sriwijaya ruled a huge slab of Southeast Asia, covering most of Sumatra, the Malay Peninsula, southern Thailand and Cambodia. Sriwijayan influence collapsed after the kingdom was conquered by the south Indian king Ravendra Choladewa in 1025. For the next 200 years, the void was partly filled by Sriwijaya's main regional rival, the Jambi-based kingdom of Malayu.

Few relics from this period remain – no sculptures, monuments or architecture of note – nor is there much of interest from the early 18th century, when Palembang was an Islamic kingdom. Most of the buildings of the latter era were destroyed in battles with the Dutch.

The city's name comes from two words: *pa* (place) and *limbang* (to pan for gold). The prosperity of the Sriwijayan city is said to have been based on gold found in local rivers.

 Sights

Museum Sumatera Selatan MUSEUM
(Jl Sriwijaya 1, Km5.5; admission 2000Rp; 8am-4pm Sun-Thu, to 11am Fri) Museum Sumatera Selatan houses finds from Sriwijayan times, as well as megalithic carvings from the Pasemah Highlands, including the famous *batu gajah* (elephant stone). There is a magnificent *rumah limas* (traditional house) behind the museum. The museum is about 5km from the town centre off the road to the airport.

Mesjid Agung MOSQUE
(Jl Sudirman) The imposing Mesjid Agung was built by Sultan Machmud Badaruddin at the beginning of the 19th century.

Dutch Fort RUINS
The remains of a late-18th-century Dutch fort, occupied today by the Indonesian army, can be seen to the north of Jl Merdeka. Only sections of the fort's outside walls still stand.

Festivals & Events

Bidar Race RACE
Palembang's annual tourist event is the *bidar* race held on Sungai Musi in the middle of town every 16 June (the city's birthday) and 17 August (Independence Day). A *bidar* (canoe) is about 25m long, 1m wide and is powered by up to 60 rowers.

Sleeping

A few recent openings are good value, but budget digs remain thin on the ground.

Zuri Express BOUTIQUE HOTEL **$$**
(☎0711 710 800; reservation.plm@zuriexpress-hotels.com; Jl Dr Mohammed Isa 988; d incl breakfast from 350,000Rp; ❄📶) Located just north of Palembang's market area, Zuri Express fills a colourful and modern building with equally colourful and modern accommodation. Rooms are relatively compact, but filled with all mod cons, including designer bathrooms, flat-screen TVs and wi-fi access. Downstairs is a well-priced cafe with good snacks and espresso coffee.

Rio City Hotel BOUTIQUE HOTEL **$$**
(☎379 696; www.riocityhotel.com; Jl Lingkaran; d incl breakfast 330,00-780,000Rp; ❄📶) Opened in mid-2012, the centrally located Rio City brings a stylish elegance to sometimes-gritty Palembang. The downstairs lobby is a confection in white and marble, and the rooms are spacious and modern. Look forward to Palembang's best breakfast buffet, and a location near good seafood restaurants and the city's markets.

Hotel Al Fath Melia HOTEL **$**
(☎370 488; Jl KS Tuban 19; d incl breakfast 200,000-350,000Rp; ❄) The best you'll get for under 250,000Rp. Hotel Al Fath Melia is set on a quiet street and has a grand old staircase that winds around to the lobby, generating a sleepy post-colonial ambience. Note that not all rooms have windows.

Wisma Bari HOTEL **$**
(☎315 666; Jl Letnan Sayuti 55; d incl breakfast 160,000-230,00Rp; ❄) Well positioned in a quiet lane, with modest but tolerable rooms.

Eating

Palembang fare takes a while to get used to. The area's southern Indian influences are found in the spicy vegetable and fish dishes favoured here. But it's the heavy use of the funky durian that sends many Westerners running.

The best-known dishes are *ikan brengkes* (fish served with a spicy durian-based sauce) and *pindang* (a spicy, clear fish soup). Another Palembang speciality is *pempek,* also known as *empek-empek,* a mixture of sago, fish and seasoning that is formed into balls and deep-fried or grilled. Served with a spicy sauce, *pempek* is widely available from street stalls and warungs; you typically pay for what you eat.

Palembang food is normally served with a range of accompaniments. The main one is *tempoyak,* a combination of fermented durian, *terasi* (shrimp paste), lime juice and chilli that is mixed up with the fingers and added to the rice. *Sambal buah* (fruit sambals), made with pineapple or sliced green mangoes, are also popular.

The main **night market** (Jl Sayangan), to the east of Jl Sudirman, has dozens of noodle and sate stalls.

Selatan Indah INDONESIAN **$**
(Jl Letkol Iskandar 434; dishes from 7000Rp) A recommended joint for trying Palembang food where the English menu removes the lottery factor found in other places.

Floating Restaurant INDONESIAN **$**
(mains 10,000-20,000Rp; ⏲noon-10pm) Palembang's favourite restaurant, which serves local specialities, is directly on Sungai Musi.

Rumah Makan Sri Melayu INDONESIAN **$$**
(Jl Demang Lebar Daun; mains 25,000-35,000Rp) To be fully immersed in Palembang food and culture, visit this showpiece restaurant with wooden seating around a stylish pond.

Shopping

Tanjung Tunpung, 2km from the town centre, is the handicraft village where Palembang's local *songket* industry is based. Ground-floor showrooms display sarongs used in marriage ceremonies and traditional costumes, as well as more functional scarves and textiles.

Makmur Jaya ARTS & CRAFTS
(Jl Beringin Janggut II 33) Beyond tourist-market selections of fine silk and batiks.

Pasar 16 Ilir MARKET
(Jl Mesjid Lama) Near the river just off Jl Pangeran Ratu, this market sells batik and other textiles from Sumatra and Java, as well as homewares.

Information

ATMs dot central Palembang.

Palembang City tourist office (☎358 450; Museum Sultan Machmud Badaruddin II, Jl Pasar Hilir 3) A useful office at the Museum Sultan Machmud Badaruddin II, off Jl Sudirman. The staff can arrange trips down the Sungai Musi and handicraft tours.

Post office (Jl Merdeka) Close to the river, next to the Garuda monument. Internet facilities available.

Provincial tourist office (☎357 348; Jl Demang Lebar Daun) A useful office outside of the town centre.

PT Novia Wisata (☎512 584; Jl Jend A Yani 3) City and river tours and trips to Bangka and Danau Ranau.

Getting There & Away

AIR Sultan Badaruddin II airport is 12km north of town. PT Novia Wisata can book flights.

Domestic airlines serving Palembang include Merpati, Garuda, Wings Air, Lion Air, Batavia Air and Sriwijaya, with destinations including Jakarta, Yogakarta, Medan, Surabaya and Jambi. The city also has two international connections, with AirAsia flying to Kuala Lumpur and Silk Air to Singapore.

BUS The **Karyajaya Bus Terminal** is 12km from the town centre, but most companies have ticket offices on Jl Kol Atmo. For door-to-door minibus services, check out the agents' offices along Jl Veteran.

TRAIN Kertapati train station is 8km from the city centre on the south side of the river. Trains northwest to Lubuklinggau also stop at Lahat (for the Pasemah Highlands). It's four hours to Lahat and seven to Lubuklinggau, but the fares are the same.

Getting Around

Opelet around town cost a standard 2500Rp. They leave from around the huge roundabout at the junction of Jl Sudirman and Jl Merdeka. Any *opelet* marked 'Karyajaya' (4000Rp) will get you to the bus terminal. Any *opelet* marked 'Kertapati' (4000Rp) will get you to the train station. Taxis to the airport cost around 80,000Rp. A taxi from the station to the town centre should cost around 50,000Rp.

Krui

Sweeping slithers of white sand lick the coast north and south of Krui, and the meandering coastline is dotted with surf breaks that draw an increasing number of intrepid boardriders.

Most of the action is focused on the village of Tanjung Setia, 30km south of Krui and right in front of the world-renowned Karang Nyimbor surf break. Depending on weather and tides, other excellent breaks up and the down the coast are also options, all easily reached by motorbike.

While surfers still make up most of the tourist traffic, the area's laconic and laid-back buzz is also perfect if you're overlanding to Java down Sumatra's southern coast. Around midway between Bengkulu and Bandarlampung, it's a good spot to relax and recharge after one too many long Sumatran bus journeys. If you're a surfing newbie, Albert at Hello Mister offers surf lessons (per person 20,000Rp) on longboards on more-forgiving beach breaks.

Arrive fully stocked with rupiah – the nearest ATM is an hour's bus ride away in Liwa.

Sleeping

TOP CHOICE **Lovina Krui Surf** BUNGALOW **$**
(☎0853 7780 2212; www.lovinakruisurf.com; Jl Pantai Wisata, Tanjung Setia; d 200,000Rp; ❄@) Opened just weeks before we checked it out, Lovina Krui Surf has three lovely A-frame cottages set back from the beach. Decor and design are a big step up from Tanjung Setia's traditional focus on simple bungalows, and the attached cafe and lounge is cool and cosmopolitan. Each cottage sleeps up to four,

TRANSPORT FROM PALEMBANG

Bus

DESTINATION	COST (RP)	DURATION (HR)	FREQUENCY
Bandarlampung	188,000	10	2 daily
Bengkulu	150,000	12	3 daily
Jambi	110,000	8	3 daily
Lahat	60,000	4	hourly

Train

DESTINATION	COST (RP)	DURATION (HR)	FREQUENCY
Bandarlampung	64,000-130,000	10	2 daily
Lubuklinggau	20,000-75,000	7	2 daily

BUSES FROM KRUI

DESTINATION	COST (RP)	DURATION (HR)	DEPART
Bandarlampung	40,000	8	6am, 7am, 8am, 10am
Bengkulu	80,000	10	8am

making them a good option for families and groups.

Damai Bungalows BUNGALOW **$$**
(☎0813 6930 7475; www.damaibungalows.com; Jl Pantai Wisata, Tanjung Setia; 7 days incl meals per person A$350; ❄) Leafy gardens, comfortable bungalows with private bathrooms, and great food make Damai one of the best places to stay in Tanjung Setia. There's excellent service from the Aussie-Indonesian owners, and the bar – with quite possibly Sumatra's coldest beer – provides front-row views of the iconic Karang Nyimbor left-hander. Damai is often booked by groups, but individual guests are also welcome.

Family Losmen BUNGALOW **$**
(☎0813 8043 1486; www.familylosmen.com; Jl Pantai Wisata, Tanjung Setia; per person incl all meals 175,000Rp) One of Tanjung Setia's longest-established losmen is still one of the area's best, with stylish concrete bungalows with private verandas, and a terrific rooftop viewing platform that's perfect for wave spotting and a few end-of-day Bintangs.

Paradise Surf Camp BUNGALOW **$**
(☎0813 7928 8750; www.paradisesurfcampsumatra.com; Jl Pantai Wisata, Tanjung Setia; per night incl all meals 195,000Rp) Owned by a couple of friendly sisters, Paradise has rustic, private bungalows and a laid-back, ramshackle vibe. Table tennis, billiards and a big-screen TV provide social diversions if the surf's not up to scratch.

ℹ Information

Internet access (per hour 5000Rp) is available at Lovina Krui Surf, but at the time of writing there was no one offering wi-fi.

Hello Mister (☎081 5389 3911; kruimotorent@gmail.com; Jl Pantai Wisata, Tanjung Setia) Stop by and see the wisecracking Albert at Hello Mister for everything from bus transport to Bandarlampung, jungle tours (half-day per person 50,000Rp), motorbike rental (per day 50,000Rp) and surf lessons. He can also arrange longer day trips south to the Bukit Barisan Selatan National Park.

ℹ Getting There & Away

Buses from Bengkulu to Bandarlampung will stop on request at Tanjung Setia. Most accommodation can also arrange transport from Bandarlampung airport if you're visiting Krui on a dedicated surfing trip. A private transfer to Bandarlampung airport is around 800,000Rp.

LAMPUNG

At the very tip of this bow-shaped landmass is Sumatra's southernmost province, which was not given provincial status by Jakarta until 1964. Although the Lampungese have had a long history as a distinct culture, the most recent tug of Jakarta's gravitational force is altering Lampung's independent streak. Big-city TV news and fashions have crept across the Sunda Strait, as did Javanese settlers under the *transmigrasi* policies, designed to offload excess population and turn a profit in the wilds of Sumatra.

Outside the provincial capital of Bandarlampung, the province's robust coffee plantations dominate the economy and the unclaimed forests, closely followed by timber and pepper. There are also large areas of rubber and palm-oil plantation.

Today many Jakarta weekenders hop over to tour the Krakatau volcano or visit the elephants of Way Kambas National Park. The rugged western seaboard is ostensibly protected as the Bukit Barisan Selatan National Park.

History

Long before Jakarta became the helm of this island chain, there's evidence that Lampung was part of the Palembang-based Sriwijayan empire until the 11th century, when the Jambi-based Malayu kingdom became the dominant regional power.

Megalithic remains at Pugungraharjo, on the plains to the east of Bandarlampung, are thought to date back more than 1000 years and point to a combination of Hindu and Buddhist influences. The site is believed to have been occupied until the 16th century.

WORTH A TRIP

PASEMAH HIGHLANDS

The Pasemah Highlands, tucked away in the Bukit Barisan west of Lahat, are famous for the mysterious megalithic monuments that dot the landscape. The stones have been dated back about 3000 years, but little else is known about them or the civilisation that carved them. While the museums of Palembang and Jakarta now house the pick of the stones, there are still plenty left in situ. The main town of the highlands is Pagaralam, 68km (two hours by bus) southwest of the Trans-Sumatran Hwy town of Lahat.

Considered to be the best examples of prehistoric stone sculpture in Indonesia, the Pasemah carvings fall into two distinct styles. The early style dates from around 3000 years ago and features fairly crude figures squatting with hands on knees or arms folded over chests. The best examples of this type are at a site called **Tinggi Hari**, 20km from Lahat, west of the small river town of Pulau Pinang.

The later style, incorporating expressive facial features, dates from about 2000 years ago and is far more elaborate. Examples include carvings of men riding, battling with snakes and struggling with elephants. There are also a couple of tigers – one guarding a representation of a human head between its paws. The natural curve of the rocks was used to create a three-dimensional effect, though all the sculptures are in bas-relief. Sculptures of this style are found throughout the villages around Pagaralam, although some take a bit of seeking out.

Tegurwangi, about 8km from Pagaralam on the road to Tanjung Sakti, is the home of the famous **Batu Beribu**, a cluster of four squat statues that sit under a small shelter by a stream. The site guardian will wander over and lead you to some nearby dolmen-style stone tombs. You can still make out a painting of three women and a dragon in one of them.

The village of **Berlubai**, 3km from Pagaralam, has its own **Batu Gajah** (Elephant Stone) sitting out among the rice paddies, as well as tombs and statues. There is a remarkable collection of stone carvings among the paddies near Tanjung Aru. Look out for the one of a man fighting a giant serpent.

The dormant volcano of **Gunung Dempo** is the highest (3159m) of the peaks surrounding the Pasemah Highlands and dominates Pagaralam. Allow two full days to complete the climb. A guide is strongly recommended as trails can be difficult to find. The lower slopes are used as a tea-growing area, and there are *opelet* from Pagaralam to the tea factory.

The best source of information about the highlands is the **Hotel Mirasa** (☎073 062 1484; Jl Mayor Ruslan; d 80,000-200,000Rp), around 2km out of Pagaralam. It can also arrange transport to the carvings, and trekking guides if you're keen to tackle Gunung Dempo. There are a couple of ATMs in the town's dusty main street, and the nightly market features a lot of food stalls guaranteed to maximise your travel budget.

Every bus travelling along the Trans-Sumatran Hwy calls in at Lahat, nine hours northwest of Bandarlampung and 12 hours southeast of Padang. There are regular buses to Lahat from Palembang (60,000Rp, five hours), and the town is a stop on the train line from Palembang to Lubuklinggau. There are frequent small buses from Pagaralam to Lahat (15,000Rp, two hours) and Bengkulu (20,000Rp, six hours). There are *opelet* to the villages near Pagaralam from the town centre's *stasiun taksi* (taxi station). All local *opelet* services cost 2000Rp.

Lampung has long been famous for its prized pepper crop, which attracted the West Javanese sultanate of Banten to the area at the beginning of the 16th century and the Dutch East India Company in the late 17th century.

The Dutch finally took control of Lampung in 1856 and launched the first of the *transmigrasi* schemes that sought to ease the chronic overcrowding in Java and Bali. Most migrants came to farm the fertile plains of eastern Lampung and today the area is something of a cultural melting pot.

Bandarlampung

☎0721 / POP 850,000

Bandarlampung was once a major backpacker thoroughfare connecting Java and Sumatra, and you'll immediately notice the jump in 'Hello Mister's and toothy smiles as the locals welcome Western faces like long-lost relatives.

Perched on the hills overlooking Teluk Lampung, Bandarlampung is the region's largest city and its administrative capital. The fourth-largest city in Sumatra, it is the product of an amalgamation of the old towns of Telukbetung (coastal) and Tanjungkarang (inland).

Most places of relevance to travellers are in Tanjungkarang, including the train station and the bulk of the hotels. The Rajabasa bus terminal is 10km north of the town centre; the airport is 24km away.

Krakatau and the Way Kambas National Park are the main spots to check out in the area when passing through.

Sights

Krakatau Monument MONUMENT

(Jl Veteran) The Krakatau monument is a lasting memorial to the force of the 1883 eruption and resulting tidal wave. Almost half of the 36,000 victims died in the 40m-high tidal wave that funnelled up Teluk Lampung and devastated Telukbetung. The huge steel maritime buoy that comprises the monument was washed out of Teluk Lampung and deposited on this hillside.

Lampung Provincial Museum MUSEUM

(Jl Teuku Umar; admission 2500Rp; ⏲9am-4.30pm Tue-Sun) Lampung Provincial Museum, 5km north of central Tanjungkarang, houses a dusty collection of bits and pieces – everything from Neolithic relics to stuffed animals. To reach the museum, catch a grey *opelet* (2500Rp).

Sleeping

Bandarlampung has a competitive selection of hotels lining centrally located Jl Raden Intan.

Hotel Andalas HOTEL $

(☎263 432; hotelandalas1@yahoo.co.id; Jl Raden Intan 89; s/d incl breakfast from 175,000/200,000Rp) Cosy rooms with a quirky sense of colour are concealed behind this hotel's heritage facade on Bandarlampung's main street. We're not sure about the blue carpet, but the friendly team at reception and good rates are two big ticks. Welcome to Bandarlampung's best-value hotel.

Amalia Hotel HOTEL $$

(☎250 555; www.amaliahotellampung.com; Jl Raden Intan 55; r incl breakfast 460,000-708,000Rp; ❄📶) Here's your chance for a splurge-worthy farewell to Sumatra if you've been roughing it on the highways and byways of the planet's sixth-largest island. Spacious, centrally located rooms and the option of a non-smoking floor – hooray – add up to one of the city's best hotels. Spa services are on tap, and downstairs are two well-priced restaurants serving up Indonesian and Western food.

Hotel Grande HOTEL $$

(☎261 448; Jl Raden Intan 77; r 230,000-410,000Rp; ❄📶🏊) With big comfortable rooms, a swimming pool and lots of nearby eating spots, this well-managed and well-maintained main-drag hotel is just the ticket if you're kicking on north or south on a Sumatran overland odyssey.

Hotel Arinas HOTEL $$

(☎266 778; www.arinashotel.com; Jl Raden Intan 35; d incl breakfast 260,000-330,000Rp; ❄📶) Handily located in a quiet spot just off the main street, the Arinas features clean, comfortable and modern rooms, all with TV and hot water. There's an on site coffee shop if you've done your dash with *nasi Padang*.

Kurnia Perdana Hotel HOTEL $

(☎262 030; Jl Raden Intan 114; r incl breakfast 200,000-290,000Rp; ❄📶) Clean, comfortable rooms with TV and hot water, all located on a central intersection with excellent sate just a short stroll away.

Eating

The **market stalls** around the **Bambu Kuning Plaza** offer a wide range of snacks, and food stands punctuate Jl Raden Intan after dark.

Rumah Putih CAFE $

(Jl Amir Hamzah 5/66; snacks & meals 15,000-25,000Rp; 📶) Rumah Putih's sleek combination of a cool cafe and leafy garden seating is a real surprise in dusty, noisy Bandarlampung. It's definitely worth seeking out in a quiet neighbourhood just south of the centre of town, and there's occasional live music and DJ gigs on weekends. This is your best chance to meet a few younger, English-speaking locals.

Bandarlampung

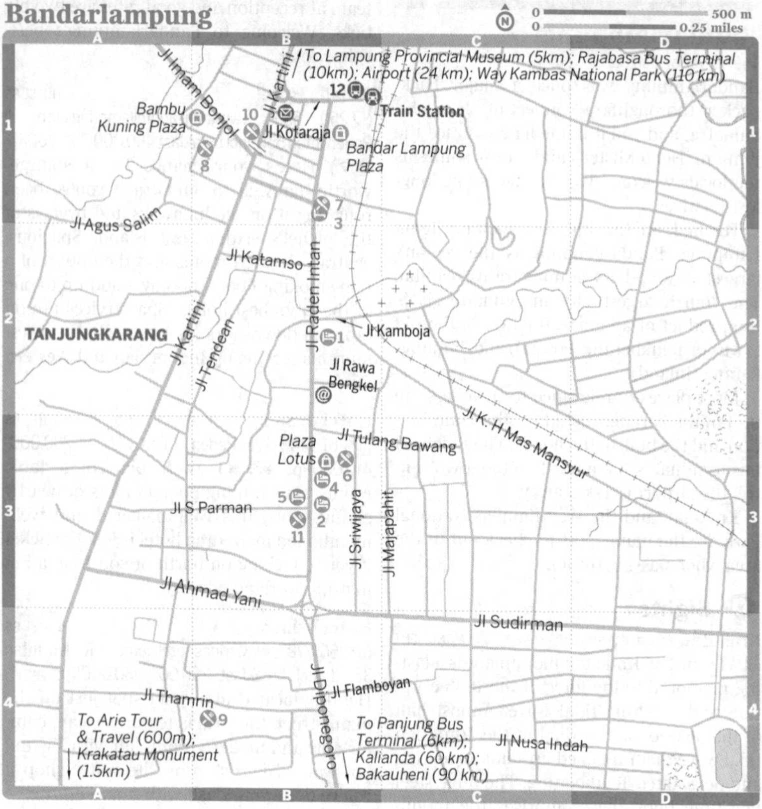

Sate Cak Umar INDONESIAN $
(Jl Raden Intan 118; sate 10,000-15,000Rp) Take your pick from eight different variations on sate at this popular, centrally located spot. Try the *ayam spesial* sate or push the boat out with a hearty meal of grilled chicken. Head inside if you're not partial to a heady side order of traffic fumes.

Cito Cafe CAFE $
(Plaza Lotus, Jl Raden Intan; snacks 10,000-15,000Rp; wi-fi) Head to the rear of the **Plaza Lotus** shopping centre for Cito Cafe's surprisingly cosmopolitan mix of espresso coffee, *sheesha* (water pipes) and a cross-section of Bandarlampung's student crowd tucking into well-priced snacks. There's free wi-fi, and occasional live music after dark.

Sari Bundo PADANG $
(dishes 8000Rp) Located near the markets on Jl Imam Bonjol, Sari Bundo is a good introduction to Padang-style food if you've just arrived in Sumatra.

European Bakery & Restaurant BAKERY $
(Jl Raden Intan 35; pastries 2500Rp) For those in need of a sugar fix. Also handy if you're setting out on a day trip to Gunung Krakatau.

Shopping

Lampung produces weavings known as ship cloths (most feature ships), which use rich reds and blues to create primitive-looking geometric designs. Another type is *kain tapis*, a ceremonial cloth elaborately embroidered with gold thread.

Mulya Sari Artshop HANDICRAFTS
(Jl Thamrin 85) A good collection of both ship cloths and *kain tapis* can be found here.

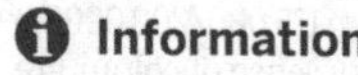

Information

ATMS dot central Bandarlampung with BNI machines dispensing up to 2,000,000Rp. For wi-fi access, head to Cito Cafe.

Bandarlampung

Sleeping

1	Amalia Hotel	B2
2	Hotel Andalas	B3
3	Hotel Arinas	B1
4	Hotel Grande	B3
5	Kurnia Perdana Hotel	B3

Eating

6	Cito Cafe	B3
7	European Bakery & Restaurant	B1
8	Market Stalls	B1
9	Rumah Putih	B4
10	Sari Bundo	B1
11	Sate Cak Umar	B3

Transport

12	Damri	B1

Arie Tour & Travel (☎474 675; www.arietour.com; Jl W Monginsidi 143) A helpful travel agent located outside the city centre. Trips taking in Gunung Krakatau and Way Kambas National Park can be booked here.

E-Net (Jl Raden Intan; per hr 6000Rp) Internet access.

Post office (Jl Kotaraja) The city's most central branch.

Getting There & Away

AIR The airport is 24km north of the city. Arie Tour & Travel is a good booking agent.

BUS There are two bus terminals in Bandarlampung. The city's sprawling Rajabasa bus terminal is 10km north of town and serves long-distance destinations. Panjang bus terminal is 6km southeast of town along the Lampung Bay road and serves local and provincial destinations.

The most convenient option for heading to Java is the **Damri** bus-boat combination ticket (business/executive 120,000/160,000Rp, eight to 10 hours). Damri buses leave from outside Bandarlampung's train station at 10am, 9pm and 10pm, shuttling passengers to the Bakahueni pier, and then picking them up at Java's Merak pier for the final transfer to Jakarta's train station.

TRAIN The train station is in the town centre at the northern mouth of Jl Raden Intan.

Getting Around

For the airport, taxis charge around 100,000Rp for the ride to/from town. All *opelet* pass through the basement of the **Bandar Lampung Plaza** on Jl Raden Intan and the standard fare around town is 2500Rp. To reach the Rajabasa bus terminal, take a green *opelet* (3000Rp). To reach the Panjang bus terminal, take a green *opelet* to Sukaraja and then transfer to a red *opelet* (3000Rp).

Way Kambas National Park

This national park is one of the oldest reserves in Indonesia. It occupies 1300 sq km of coastal lowland forest around Sungai Way Kambas on the east coast of Lampung. What little remains of the heavily logged forests is home to endangered species of elephants, rhinos and tigers.

It is believed that close to 200 wild Sumatran elephants *(Elephas maximus sumatrensis)* live in the park, but reliable estimates are uncertain and poaching and development pressures are constant. The Sumatran elephant is a subspecies of the Asian elephant and is found only in Sumatra and Kalimantan. Another rare but endemic creature in Way Kambas is the Sumatran rhino, the only two-horned rhino of the Asian species. Its hide is red in colour with a hairy coat.

The area around Way Kanan, a subdistrict of the park, is frequently visited by birdwatchers. Of the most remarkable species, the white-winged duck and Storm's stork get the binoculars fogged up.

Also in the park is the Sumatra Rhino Sanctuary, where four rhinos formerly held in captivity are introduced to wild surroundings in the hope of successful breeding. The Sumatran rhino is a solitary animal and its habitat in the wild is so fractured that conservationists fear the species will die out without intervention. Breeding centres for rhinos are a controversial component of species-protection campaigns as they are expensive to maintain and have reported few successful births. For more information, visit the website of the International Rhino Foundation (www.rhinos-irf.org), one of the lead organisations involved with the centre and antipoaching patrols in the park. It's estimated around 25 to 35 wild Sumatran rhinos still live within the park.

For the average visitor not engaged in wildlife conservation, a visit to the park is a nice break from the concrete confines of Jakarta, but it's not a true wild safari. Most visitors are led through the forest on elephants or by canoes on the Sungai Way Kanan and surrounding waterways. The most commonly spotted animals on the tour include

TRANSPORT FROM BANDARLAMPUNG

Air

DESTINATION	COMPANY	FREQUENCY
Bengkulu	Merpati	daily
Jakarta	Batavia Air, Garuda, Lion Air, Merpati, Sriwijaya Air	daily
Palembang	Merpati	daily
Pulau Batam	Batavia Air	daily

Bus

DESTINATION	COST (RP)	DURATION (HR)	FREQUENCY
Bukittinggi	200,000-310,000	22	daily
Palembang	130,000	10	daily

Train

DESTINATION	COST (RP)	DURATION (HR)	FREQUENCY
Lubklinggau	70,000-145,000	17	2 daily
Palembang	64,000-130,000	10	2 daily

primates and birds. Herds of elephants are seen here from time to time but sightings of the Sumatran tiger are extremely rare.

A day trip to Way Kambas costs around US$120 per person for a minimum of two people and can be arranged through tour operators in Jakarta. Bandarlampung-based tour agents include Arie Tour & Travel (p579).

You could visit the park independently, but transport is limited and expensive. To strike out on your own, hire an *ojek* from Rajabasalama to Way Kanan, where you can hire a guide (around 100,000Rp) and arrange transport.

Sleeping & Eating

Tourist facilities within the park are limited. About 13km from the entrance to the park is Way Kanan, where there is a collection of simple **guesthouses** (100,000Rp) on the banks of Sungai Way Kanan. **Food stalls** nearby cater to day trippers and close after dark, so you'll need to bring food if you're staying the night.

Another option is to stay at the **Satwa Elephant Ecolodge** (764 5290; www.ecolodgesindonesia.com; Jl Taman Nasional Way Kambas; r incl breakfast from US$65; ❄), around 500m from the park entrance. Four spacious cottages are scattered through the lodge's leafy orchard of tropical fruit trees, and activities include elephant rides, river trips and mountain-bike rides through the forest. The lodge is also popular with keen birdwatchers. Four-day packages departing from Jakarta – including all meals and transport – are US$595 per person.

Getting There & Away

The entrance to Way Kambas is 110km from Bandarlampung. There are buses from Bandarlampung's Rajabasa bus terminal to Jepara (30,000Rp, 2½ hours). They pass the entrance to Way Kambas, an arched gateway guarded by a stone elephant, in the village of Rajabasalama, 10km north of Jepara. Alternatively, you can catch a bus to Metro (15,000Rp, one hour) and then another to Rajabasalama (15,000Rp, 1½ hours). From the park entrance, you can also hire a motorcycle to take you to and from the park.

Kalianda

0727

Kalianda is a quiet little town overlooking Teluk Lampung 30km north of the Bakauheni ferry terminal. The main reason for passing through is to visit Krakatau, but the town can also be used as an alternative base to Bandarlampung. Nearby are pretty white-sand beaches, simple fishing villages and a dedicated resort area that's becoming a weekend retreat for Jakarta residents.

To reach Krakatau, stop in at Hotel Beringin and ask about organised tours, or head down to the Canti harbour on weekends to pair up with local groups chartering boats.

Sights & Activities

Gunung Rajabasa VOLCANO
Overlooking the town is Gunung Rajabasa (1281m), an easily scaleable volcano.

Pulau Sebuku & Pulau Sebesi ISLANDS
Situated off the coast, Pulau Sebuku and Pulau Sebesi have snorkelling and swimming. Cargo boats leave from Canti to these islands, or you can charter a tour from the local fisherfolk.

Hot Springs HOT SPRINGS
Soak in the hot springs at Wartawan Beach, just beyond Canti. Beaches around Canti have relaxing sea breezes. An *opelet* to the beach costs 7000Rp.

Sleeping & Eating

The **food stalls** that appear in Kalianda's town centre at night are the best places to eat.

Hotel Beringin HOTEL $
(☎322 008; Jl Kesuma Bangsa 75; d incl breakfast 70,000-80,000Rp) Close to the centre of town, this is an old Dutch villa with high ceilings and languid fans. The hotel has lots of local information, and can arrange trips to nearby attractions including Gunung Krakatau.

Getting There & Around

There are regular buses between Kalianda and Bandarlampung's Rajabasa bus terminal (25,000Rp, 1½ hours). Most buses don't run right into Kalianda, but drop you on the highway at the turn-off to town. From there, simply cross the road and wait for an *opelet* into town (3000Rp). There are a few direct buses from the Bakauheni ferry terminal to Kalianda (25,000Rp), but it's usually quicker to catch any north-bound bus and get off at the junction for town.

Gunung Krakatau

Krakatau may have come closer to destroying the planet than any other volcano in recent history, when it erupted in 1883. Tens of thousands were killed either by the resulting tidal wave or by the pyroclastic flows that crossed 40km of ocean to incinerate Sumatran coastal villages. Afterwards all that was left was a smouldering caldera where a cluster of uninhabited islands had once been. Perhaps peace had come, thought local villagers. But Krakatau, like all scrappy villains, re-awoke in 1927 and resulting eruptions built a new volcanic cone since christened Anak Krakatau (Child of Krakatau). It's estimated that Anak Krakatau is growing by around 5m every year.

Tours to the island launch from West Java or from Kalianda on the Sumatran coast. Organised day trips with Arie Tour & Travel (p579) in Bandarlampung cost US$242 per person (based on two people). Hotel Beringin in Kalianda can also organise tours for 690,000Rp.

You can also join up with weekenders chartering boats from Canti, a fishing village outside of Kalianda, or from Pulau Sebesi. Charters usually cost around 1,000,000Rp for up to 15 people. There are regular *opelet* from Kalianda to Canti (7000Rp), and an *ojek* from Kalianda to Canti is around 20,000Rp.

Bakauheni

Bakauheni is the major ferry terminal between Java and southern Sumatra.

The journey between the two islands sounds like a snap until you factor in land transport between the ferry terminals and the major towns on either side. Bakauheni is 90km from Bandarlampung, a bus journey of about two hours. In Java, the bus transfer from the port of Merak to Jakarta is another two-hour journey. Damri (p579) runs bus-boat-bus combinations linking Sumatra and Java.

Bukit Barisan Selatan National Park

At the southern tip of Sumatra, this national park comprises one of the island's last stands of lowland forests. For this reason the World Wildlife Fund has ranked it as one of the planet's most biologically outstanding habitats and is working to conserve the park's remaining Sumatran rhinos and tigers. The park is also famous for many endemic bird species that prefer foothill climates, and several species of sea turtle that nest along the park's coastal zone.

Of the 365,000 hectares originally designated as protected, only 324,000 hectares remain untampered. The usual suspects are responsible: illegal logging and plantation conversion, and poachers are also at work.

Tourist infrastructure in the park is limited and most people visit on organised tours. The easiest access point into the park is through the town of Kota Agung, 80km west of Bandarlampung.

Kantor Taman Nasional Bukit Barisan Selatan (☎072 221 095; Jl Raya Terbaya; ⏰8am-4.30pm Mon-Thu, to noon Fri) sells permits into the park (5000Rp) and can arrange guides and trekking information.

Less-accessible access points are Sukaraja, 20km west of Kota Agung, and Liwa, the northernmost entry way.

Kota Agung has several basic hotels and there is a camping ground near Sukaraja.

There are frequent buses from Bandarlampung to Kota Agung (12,000Rp).

Kalimantan

POP 13,800,000

Includes »

Best Jungle River Journeys

- » Sungai Bungan (p618)
- » Sungai Mahakam (p596)
- » Sungai Sekonyer (p619)

Best Places to Stay

- » Nunukan Island Resort (p609)
- » Wisma Alya (p632)
- » Wehea Forest Lodge (p605)
- » Hotel Gran Senyiur (p590)

Why Go?

If jungle rivers get your blood running, then be prepared for rapids. Occupying three-quarters of Borneo, the world's third-largest island Kalimantan harbours a vast and legendary jungle cut by countless rivers, including two around 1000km in length. Within this primordial puzzle something extraordinary always lies around the next bend. You'll encounter exotic wildlife, such as the unforgettable orangutan, mysterious Dayak villages with only one foot in the modern world, and pure boating thrills. Adventure travellers of all levels can participate, from novices enjoying the romantic *klotok* (canoes) of Tanjung Puting to hardened trekkers shooting rapids on the landmark Cross-Borneo Trek. Divers will revel in the Derawan Archipelago, a world-class underwater destination. Cities here are mostly transit points, and foreigners exceedingly rare, but locals everywhere will greet you with a cheerful 'Hey Mistah!', making travel a tropical breeze.

When to Go

Pontianak

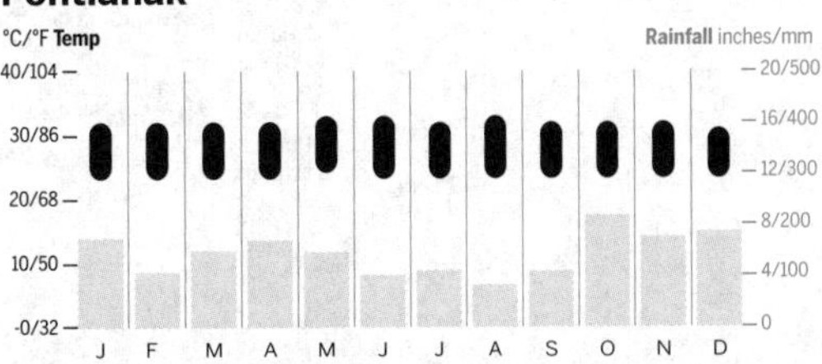

Jan–Feb Rough weather limits diving trips in the Derawan Archipelago.

Feb–Apr Blooming fruit brings orangutans into view.

Aug–Sep Dry season makes roads better, skies clearer.

Kalimantan Highlights

1. Completing the landmark **Cross-Borneo Trek** (p587) – if you can
2. Meeting the orangutans of **Tanjung Puting National Park** (p619)
3. Travelling up **Sungai Mahakam** (p596)– and into the past
4. Living the (inexpensive) high life in **Balikpapan** (p588)
5. Exploring the **Derawan Archipelago** (p607), both under water and above
6. Settling into village life in lovely **Loksado** (p631)
7. Cruising **Sungai Kahayan** aboard the luxurious *Rahai'i Pangun* (p626)
8. Ascending the tower of the extraordinary **Islamic Centre of Samarinda** (p593)
9. Hiking unspoiled **Wehea Forest** (p605): the Earth as it used to be

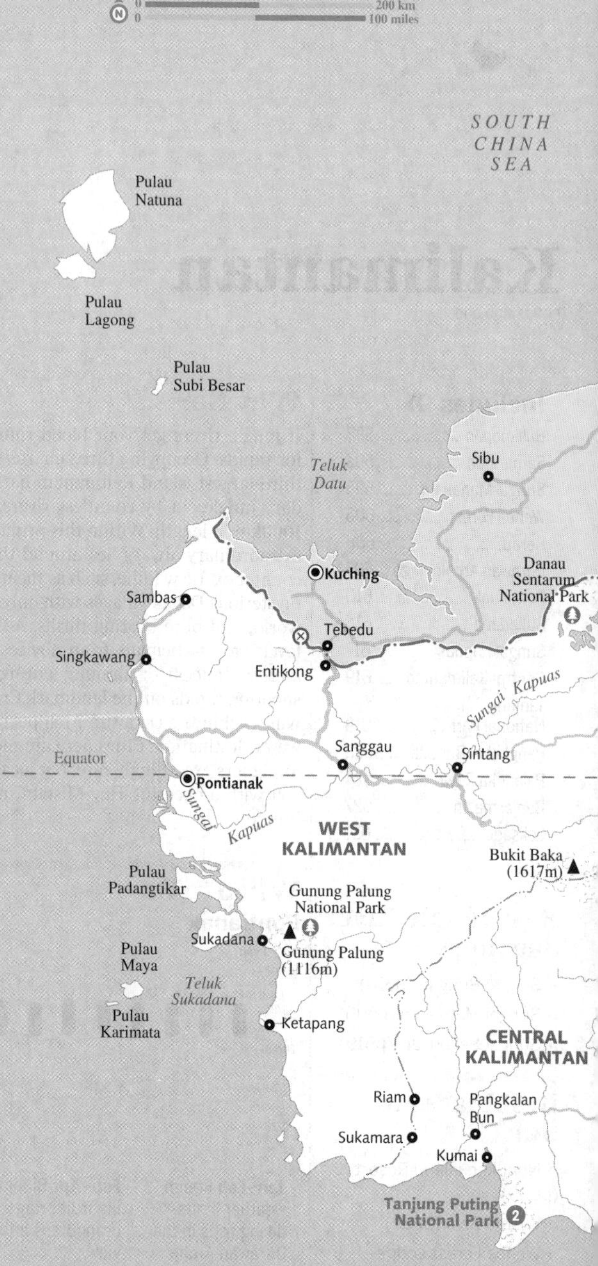

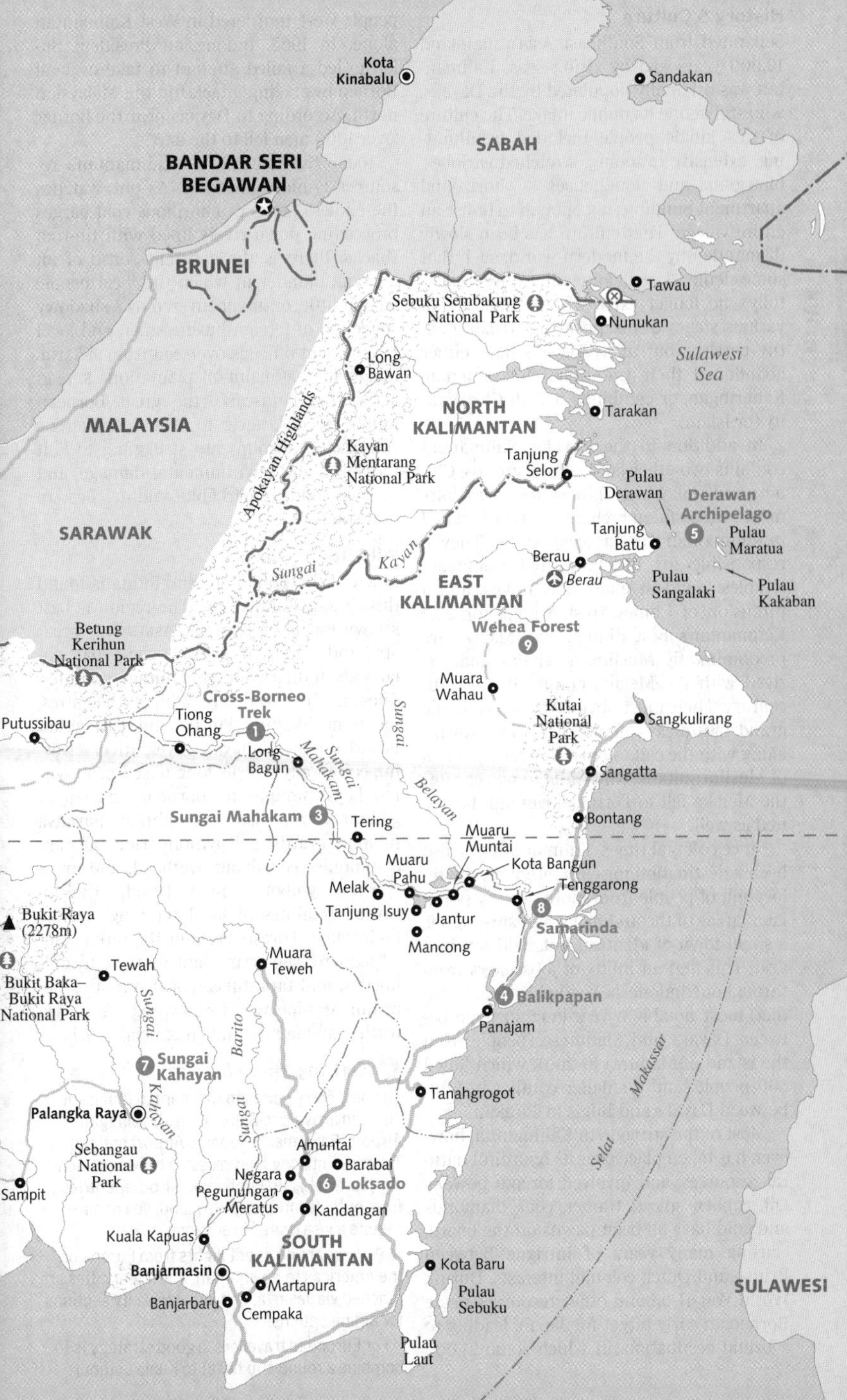

Kota Kinabalu
Sandakan
SABAH
BANDAR SERI BEGAWAN
BRUNEI
Tawau
Sebuku Sembakung National Park
Nunukan
Sulawesi Sea
Long Bawan
MALAYSIA
Apokayan Highlands
NORTH KALIMANTAN
Tarakan
Kayan Mentarang National Park
Tanjung Selor
Pulau Derawan
Derawan Archipelago
5
SARAWAK
Tanjung Batu
Pulau Maratua
Berau
Berau
Sungai
Kayan
EAST KALIMANTAN
Pulau Sangalaki
Pulau Kakaban
Wehea Forest
9
Betung Kerihun National Park
Muara Wahau
Cross-Borneo Trek
1
Sungai
Kutai National Park
Putussibau
Tiong Ohang
Sangkulirang
Long Bagun
Sungai Mahakam
Sangatta
Belayan
Sungai Mahakam
3
Bontang
Tering
Muaru Muntai
Kota Bangun
Muaru Pahu
Tenggarong
Melak
Tanjung Isuy
Jantur
8
Samarinda
Bukit Raya (2278m)
Mancong
Muara Teweh
Tewah
Bukit Baka–Bukit Raya National Park
4
Balikpapan
Panajam
Sungai
Barito
Makassar
7
Sungai Kahayan
Kahayan
Tanahgrogot
Palangka Raya
Sungai
Selat
Amuntai
Sebangau National Park
Barabai
Negara
6
Loksado
Sampit
Pegunungan Meratus
Kandangan
Kuala Kapuas
SOUTH KALIMANTAN
Kota Baru
Banjarmasin
Martapura
SULAWESI
Pulau Sebuku
Banjarbaru
Cempaka
Pulau Laut

History & Culture

Separated from Southeast Asia's mainland 10,000 years ago by rising seas, Kalimantan was originally populated by the Dayaks, who still define its public image. The culture of this jungle people included headhunting, extensive tattooing, stretched earlobes, blowguns and longhouses – horizontal apartment buildings big enough to house an entire village. That culture has been slowly dismantled by the modern world, such that some elements, such as headhunting (thankfully), no longer exist, while others are in various stages of disappearing. Tribal identity persists, but many Dayaks have either abandoned their traditional folk religion, Kaharingan, or combined it with Christianity (or Islam).

In addition to the Dayaks, Kalimantan contains two other large ethnic groups, Chinese and Malay. The Chinese are the region's most successful merchants, having traded in Kalimantan since at least 300BC. They're responsible for the bright-red Confucian temples found in many port towns, and a profusion of Chinese restaurants, some of Kalimantan's best dining. The Malays are predominantly Muslim, a religion that arrived with the Melaka empire in the 15th century. Their most obvious presence is the grand mosques in major cities and towns, along with the call to prayer. Several palaces of Muslim sultans, who came to power after the Melaka fell to Portugal, can still be visited as well.

Since colonial times, Kalimantan has also been a destination for *transmigrasi*, the relocation of people from more densely populated areas of the archipelago. A sure sign is a small town of identical huts laid out in a grid. This and an influx of jobseekers from throughout Indonesia has led to some conflict, most notably a year-long struggle between Dayaks and Madurese (people from the island of Madura) in 2001, which killed 500 people, and a smaller conflict in 2010 between Dayaks and Bugis in Tarakan.

Most of the struggle in Kalimantan, however, has taken place over its bountiful natural resources, and involved foreign powers. Oil, rubber, spices, timber, coal, diamonds and gold have all been pawns on the board, causing many years of intrigue between British and Dutch colonial interests. During World War II oil and other resources made Borneo an early target for Japan, leading to a brutal occupation, in which some 21,000 people were murdered in West Kalimantan alone. In 1963, Indonesian President Sukarno led a failed attempt to take over all Borneo by staging attacks on the Malaysian north. According to Dayaks near the border 'over 1000 men fell to the dart'.

Today the struggle for Kalimantan's resources is more insidious. As one watches the endless series of enormous coal barges proceeding down rivers lined with tin-roof shacks, there is the constant sense of an ongoing plunder in which the local people benefit little, outmanoeuvered by a shadowy collection of foreign businessmen and local government officials overseen from Jakarta. Meanwhile, as palm-oil plantations spread across the landscape, the great Bornean jungle recedes, never to return. Numerous conservation groups are struggling to halt the social and environmental damage, and to save some remarkable wildlife. Best to visit soon.

Wildlife

Much of the same flora and fauna is found throughout Kalimantan. The region is best known for its orangutans, Asia's only great ape, and a most impressive sight, particularly given their endearing human qualities. These are best seen at rehabilitation centres, including Tanjung Puting and Orangutan Island on the Kahayan River. River cruising commonly reveals long-nosed proboscis monkeys (unique to Borneo), macaques, gibbons, crocodiles (including gharials), monitor lizards and pythons. Hornbills are commonly seen flying overhead, and are a spiritual symbol for many Dayaks; the upturned rooflines of local buildings mimic their wings. Forests harbour the rare clouded leopard, sun bear, giant moths and millipedes, and tarantulas. For divers, the Derawan Archipelago is renowned for its sea turtles, manta rays and large pelagic fish.

Getting There & Away

The only entry points to Kalimantan that issue visas on arrival are Balikpapan's Sepinggan Airport, Pontianak's Supadio Airport and the Tebedu–Entikong land crossing between Kuching (Sarawak) and Pontianak. All other entries from outside Indonesia – by land, sea or air – require a visa issued in advance.

AIR There are no direct flights from Europe or the Americas to Kalimantan. The major cities are reached via Jakarta. See individual city sections for airline options.

For European travellers, a good strategy is to combine a round-trip ticket to Kuala Lumpur

THE CROSS-BORNEO TREK: A WORLD-CLASS ADVENTURE

Borneo offers one of the world's greatest, and most overlooked, adventure-travel routes. East and West Kalimantan are divided by the Muller mountain range, which also serves as the headwaters for Indonesia's two longest rivers *(sungai)*. Sungai Mahakam flows 930km to the east coast, by Samarinda, while Sungai Kapuas, the world's longest island river, snakes 1143km to the west coast, by Pontianak. Thus, by travelling up the Mahakam, hiking over the Muller Range, and travelling down the Kapuas (or vice versa) it is possible to cross the world's third-largest island from one side to the other, forming a single Cross-Borneo Trek. This three-part jungle-river extravaganza takes you into the very heart of Borneo, and out again, stitching together virtually everything Kalimantan has to offer, from wildlife to culture to pure adventure, including some absolutely thrilling boat rides. There are even international airports near either end, with visas availabile on arrival, making getting there and away a simple matter. Be forewarned, however: while the two river journeys are easily managed, the central trek of five days or more across the Muller Range is a significant undertaking, for serious jungle trekkers only. On the other hand, if you can't do the entire Cross-Borneo Trek, the first stage is great by itself.

Stage One: Sungai Mahakam (p596) The preferred cross-Borneo route begins in Balikpapan, the one cosmopolitan city in Kalimantan, where you can collect your visa and prepare yourself for what's ahead with an inexpensive five-star hotel room, a day at the beach, and some lively nightlife. From there you travel overland to Samarinda, whose great mosque stands like an exotic sentinel at the start of your upriver journey. After several days in a succession of boats, making side trips into lakes and marshes, spotting wildlife, and visiting small river towns, you'll finally arrive at Tiong Ohang, near the trailhead for stage two. Allow a full week.

Stage Two: The Muller Mountains (p603) You do this jungle trek for the same reason you climb Mt Everest: because it's there. Noted for its river fordings, hordes of leeches, and treacherous slopes, it requires the assistance of a professional guiding company, a critical decision. We recommend only two: De'Gigant Tours (p593) in Samarinda for east-west itineraries, and Kompakh (p617) in Putussibau for west-east crossings. If you walk steadily eight hours a day, you can make it across in five days, but seven is more comfortable and safer.

Stage Three: Sungai Kapuas (p618) This leg begins with a single day-long boat ride along the upper Kapuas and its tributary, Sungai Bungan, the latter being the most thrilling part of the entire journey. After reaching Putussibau, it's best to fly or drive to Pontianak the next morning, as boat travel down the lower Kapuas is unscheduled, meaning it can take several days to weeks. This makes the last stage only two days long.

The east-to-west itinerary above is preferable, as the Mahakam gets progressively wilder the further up you go – the perfect beginning – whereas the day-long boat trip downriver to Putussibau, from boiling rapids to a placid sunset arrival, is a fine ending. In contrast, the lack of public transport from Pontianak to Putussibau cuts the Kapuas journey in half, you miss the downriver sleigh ride on the Bungan, and the Muller trek is steeper and thus more difficult from the west.

In local terms, the Cross-Borneo Trek is a bit pricey due to transport costs, which increase the further you go into the interior. The total is around 22,000,000Rp per person for two people, 20,000,000Rp for three, and 17,000,000Rp for four. But the overall experience, while by no means easy, is a noteworthy achievement, something you'll remember for the rest of your life.

If you haven't had enough of Kalimantan, you can continue from Pontianak along the southern coast all the way back to Balikpapan, via Sukadana, Ketapang, Tanjung Puting, Pangkalan Bun, Palangka Raya, Banjarmasin and Loksado, forming a great circle. Once you've done this, you've done Kalimantan and will know it far better than the locals, who sadly cannot afford this luxury.

TRANSPORT SAFETY

Road washouts, river rapids, flash floods, weaving scooters, speeding Kijangs, overweight canoes, questionable airlines and a general lack of maintenance and safety equipment require an extra dose of caution when travelling in Kalimantan.

with a discount ticket from KL to Balikpapan on **AirAsia** (www.airasia.com), which also reaches KL from London. **Silk Air** (www.silkair.net) flies between Singapore and Balikpapan, but not inexpensively. **Batavia Air** (www.batavia-air.co.id) flies between Kuching (in Sarawak) and Pontianak.

BOAT Major ferry ports in Kalimantan include Balikpapan, Samarinda, Banjarmasin and Pontianak. **Pelni** (www.pelni.co.id) and other carriers connect to Jakarta, Semarang and Surabaya on Java, and Makassar, Pare Pare, and others on Sulawesi. At time of research the ferry from Tawau (Sabah) to Nunukan and Tarakan wasn't operational, but there was an alternative speedboat service.

BUS Air-con buses link Pontianak with Kuching (140,000Rp to 200,000Rp, nine hours), cities along Sarawak's central coast, and even Brunei (600,000Rp, 25 hours).

Getting Around

Kalimantan is both immense and undeveloped. River travel is as common as road travel, and transport options can form a complex picture. To assess your options locally it is often easiest to visit a travel agent, as the situation is ever-changing and many fares are unpublished.

Highways between major cities range from excellent to pockmarked, with the region from Muara Wahau to Berau being the worst. Many connections feature basic buses or air-con for a bit extra. A Kijang (4WD minivan) taxi can be chartered between cities; the front seat is best. Intracity journeys can be taken in a Colt, a small minibus, usually blue, green and orange, which operates on given routes. An *ojek* (motorcycle that takes passengers) means you are really going native – just wear a helmet.

River travel is done by a variety of craft, including *kapal biasa* (river ferry with second-storey accommodation), *klotok* (river boat with covered passenger cabins), longboats (a speedboat with passenger seats) and motorised canoes, including *ces*, the local longtail. *Tok-toks* are narrow open fishing boats that sound just like their name, and are used to reach offshore islands. Bring your earplugs.

Kalimantan's five regional provinces – East, North, West, Central and South – are political entities, but serve the traveller mainly as geographical coordinates.

EAST KALIMANTAN

Balikpapan

☎0542 / POP 459,000

Kalimantan's only cosmopolitan city, Balikpapan is also the only one worthy of being considered a destination unto itself, particularly with children. The influx of oil money has had a tremendous impact here in recent years. At once both Western (with its heavy expat influence) and Asian, the city is clean and vibrant, with several enormous shopping areas and (for Kalimantan) some rare beaches. High-end hotels abound, at very reasonable prices, including some fabulous ones. And the nightlife surprises, from the heights of the world-class Skybar to the smoky depths of waterfront clubs. The city sprawls in all directions, but most of the action takes place in the centre, off Jl Sudirman: the place to stay. This main drag comes alive at night, flush with scooters and clothed in advertising. Overall the city makes a fine weekend break, and a great place to begin or end more adventurous travels.

Sights

TOP CHOICE Ruko Bandar NEIGHBOURHOOD

(Jl Sudirman) This excellent waterfront development offers everything you need for a night out and more, including above-par restaurants, hot nightclubs, and a dozen fun but easy-to-miss cafes (at the rear, facing the sea). Make this your first stop.

Kemala Beach BEACH

(Jl Sudirman) A beach in Kalimantan! Yes, and it's clean, with good sand, plenty of adjacent bars and a laid-back vibe. If you need a break from the jungle, urban or natural, this is your best local option, although it gets hot at midday.

Masjid Agung At-Taqwa MOSQUE

(Jl Sudirman) An impressive sight, this mosque is adorned with a complex sheath of Islamic geometrical patterns and lit up in multicoloured splendour at night.

Tours

Indra GUIDE
(☎081 2585 9800; indrahadi91@yahoo.com) The first choice for Japanese tourists; his English is serviceable too.

Ahmad GUIDE
(☎0821 5180 8818; ahmad_tour74@yahoo.com) An experienced city and jungle guide with excellent English and organisational skills.

Balikpapan

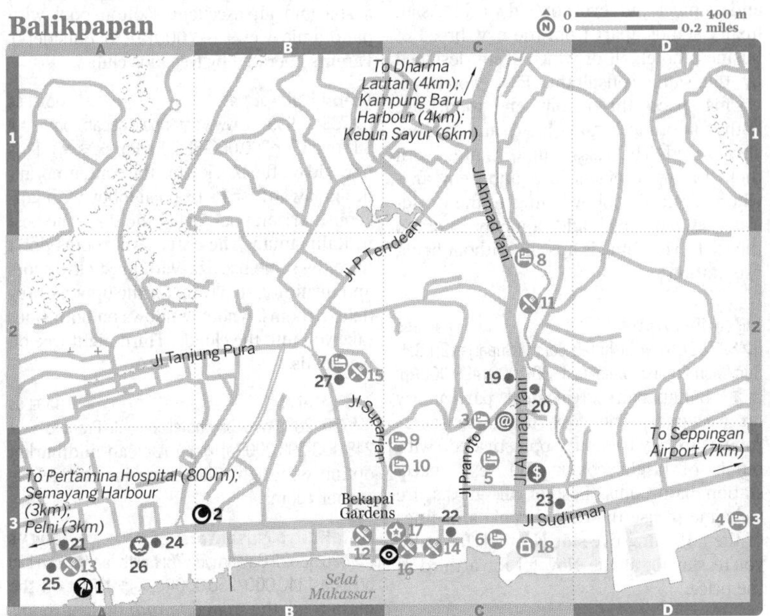

Balikpapan

Top Sights
Ruko Bandar ... C3

Sights
1 Kemala Beach ... A3
2 Masjid Agung At-Taqwa ... B3

Sleeping
3 Aiqo Hotel ... C2
4 Aston Balikpapan ... D3
5 Hotel Citra Nusantara ... C3
6 Hotel Gajah Mada ... C3
7 Hotel Gran Senyiur ... B2
8 Hotel Pacific ... C2
9 Ibis Hotel ... C3
10 Novotel Balikpapan ... C3

Eating
11 Bondy ... C2
12 De Cafe ... B3
13 Kemala Beach & Resto ... A3
14 Ocean's Resto ... C3
15 Sky Bar/Sky Grill ... B2
16 Zeus ... C3

Entertainment
17 Connexion ... C3

Shopping
18 Balikpapan Plaza ... C3

Information
19 Aero Travel ... C2
20 Bayu Buana Travel ... C2
21 Kantorimigrasi Kelas ... A3

Transport
22 Batavia Air ... C3
23 Garuda ... C3
24 Merpati ... A3
25 New Agung Sedayu ... A3
26 Prima Vista ... A3
27 SilkAir ... B2

Sleeping

TOP CHOICE Hotel Gran Senyiur HOTEL $$$
(☎080 0122 6677; http://gran.senyiurhotels.com; Jl ARS Muhammad 7; r incl breakfast from 780,000Rp; ❄📶) Unique in Kalimantan, this expansive and genteel purveyor of old-world Asian luxury stands apart from the new breed of business hotel, all of which seem designed by the same consultant. Fine woodwork warms spaces throughout, and rooms are both sumptuously appointed and reasonably priced. The classy junior suites, with their Dayak artefacts, are unbeaten anywhere. From the lobby lounge to the world-class Sky Bar, which adds a modern note to the roof, everything is upscale without being ostentatious.

TOP CHOICE Ibis Hotel HOTEL $$
(☎820 821; www.ibishotels.com; Jl Suparjan 2; r Sat-Sun/Mon-Fri incl breakfast 300,000/499,000Rp; ❄📶) Balikpapan's great steal, particularly on weekends. The cosy, design-conscious rooms are stylish and sophisticated, with bursts of bright colour and sexy space-station bathrooms. Best of all, guests are welcome to use the considerable amenities of the adjoining five-star Novotel. Basically, you're staying at the Novotel for a third of the price.

Hotel Pacific HOTEL $$
(☎750 888; www.hotelpacificbalikpapan.com; Jl A Yani 33; d incl breakfast 435,000Rp; ❄📶) An excellent midrange boutique hotel, dated in style but not in quality. The staff is friendly, the rooms comfy and the public spaces worth an extra star. Discounts on weekends.

Le Grandeur Balikpapan HOTEL $$$
(☎420 155; www.legrandeurbalikpapan.com; Jl Sudirman; r 1,100,000Rp; ❄📶🏊) If you're in town for a weekend getaway, you can't do much better than this luxury hotel, which offers a great beachfront location with all associated amenities (such as waterfront dining) and some classy touches (eg live jazz). When you're done with the sea, there's an elegant pool, too. Babysitting available. On Jl Sudirman about 2km east of Ruko Bandar.

Hotel Gajah Mada HOTEL $$
(☎734 634; info@gajahmada-hotel.com; Jl Sudirman 328; s 206,000-400,000Rp, d 261,000-415,000Rp; ❄🏊) Rooms are concrete boxes, but freshly painted and spotless, with either en suite Western bathroom or *mandi*.

Novotel Balikpapan HOTEL $$$
(☎820 820; www.novotel.com/asia; Jl Suparjan 2; r incl breakfast 990,000-1,200,000Rp; ❄📶🏊) A world-class, family-friendly hotel, with an ubermodern interior and all amenities, including a patisserie, gym, numerous cafes, a spa and an excellent rooftop pool with panoramic views (45,000Rp to outsiders). Parents liberated by free kids club.

Aston Balikpapan HOTEL $$
(☎733 999; www.astonbalikpapan.com; Jl Sudirman 7; r 700,000-888,000Rp; ❄📶🏊) This new kid on the block wins the contemporary design award for its tropical lobby with gorgeous horizon pool facing the sea – the best in Kalimantan. The entry-level rooms don't have the same pizzazz, with plastick-y doors and furniture, so pay up for the upper-storey deluxe rooms, where windows on both sides take you into the clouds. Third night free on weekends.

Aiqo Hotel HOTEL $$
(☎750 288; www.aiqohotel.com; Jl Pranoto 9; r 248,000-298,000Rp; ❄📶) A clean midmarket option with light-filled superior and deluxe corner rooms.

Hotel Citra Nusantara LOSMEN $
(☎425 366; Jl Gajahmada 76; r with fan/air-con incl breakfast 140,000/250,000Rp; ❄📶) Just off the main road, the shared *mandi* budget rooms in this losmen (budget guesthouse) are basic, though the higher ranks are surprisingly modern. Couples need proof of marriage.

Eating & Drinking

TOP CHOICE Ocean's Resto SEAFOOD $
(☎739 439; Ruko Bandar; mains from 18,000Rp; ⊙noon-3pm, 6-10pm) The anchor restaurant on the Ruko Bandar, this oceanside seafood classic, with a reef's worth of iced fish to choose from, is always popular, both inside and out (so think about reserving). The tiny open-air curry house, upstairs and to the right before you enter, is a good place for appetisers.

TOP CHOICE Sky Bar/Sky Grill SEAFOOD $$
(Jl ARS Muhammad, Hotel Gran Senyiur; mains from 55,000Rp; ⊙3-11pm) The Gran Senyiur Hotel has an awesome rooftop, combining glass-walled al fresco dining (mains 55,000Rp) and a sophisticated piano bar with panoramic city views. You pay for it, with the signature Cosmopolitan drink at 95,000Rp, but this is a world-class spot not to be missed.

WORTH A TRIP

AROUND BALIKPAPAN

There's a potpourri of sights around Balikpapan that make for an interesting full-day trip, but given transport, navigation, and reservation requirements, it is best to use a local tour guide. Indra (p589) will take two to three people to the following for 1,500,000Rp, including car, lunch, boat and admission fees:

KWPLH Sun Bear Sanctuary (http://en.beruangmadu.org) Home to several sun bears in their natural habitat. Catch the morning feeding at 9am (another is at 3pm).

Hanging Bridge (Bukit Bankirai) Walk a rope bridge through the forest canopy, around 50m above ground, and enjoy great views.

Black River Canoe the mangrove forest of Balikpapan Bay in search of proboscis monkeys and bird life.

Samboja Lestari (☎0542-702 3600; www.orangutan.ord.id) Research centre focused on orangutan reintroduction, sun-bear protection, and reforestation.

Penangkaran Buaya Crocodile Farm This commercial venture won't win any ecotourism awards, but harbours some real brutes. There's a nice longhouse next door.

Beach House Restaurant The perfect end to the day.

Beach House Restaurant INTERNATIONAL $
(Jl Mulawarman Km19; mains from 20,000Rp; ⏲lunch & dinner) These rattan tables by the sea, set in a tropical park 6km past the airport, are a little slice of Bali. The diverse menu offers great sandwiches, steaks, burgers, pasta and pizza alongside Eastern specialities. The plush waterfront cabanas go fast.

Bondy WESTERN $
(Jl Ahmad Yani; mains 30,000-50,000Rp; ⏲10.30am-10pm) An expat oasis offering steaks, homemade ice cream, and choose-your-own seafood on ice, with al fresco dining.

Kemala Beach & Resto INDONESIAN $
(Jl Sudirman, Pantai Polda; mains from 25,000Rp; ⏲10am-10pm) Billowing white curtains beckon you to this unique open-air pavilion at the end of Kemala Beach, where a long line of food stalls covers the gamut of culinary options, and a large Balinese restaurant surrounds a freshwater pond. Choose your own fresh seafood here (the crab is excellent) and enjoy live music Saturday and Monday.

Zeus ASIAN $
(Ruko Bandar; mains from 18,000Rp; ⏲11am-3am) An excellent Asian dim sum restaurant with plenty of outdoor seating. Upstairs is a cool new lounge (beer 45,000Rp) that is easily missed: take the door to the right as you enter. A great place to hang out and talk if there's no live music.

De Cafe FUSION $$
(Jl Sudirman; mains from 45,000Rp; ⏲11am-2pm, 6-11pm; wi-fi) This cosy bakery-cafe offering a wide assortment of irresistible desserts is a welcome anomaly. Comfy sofas and wi-fi create a homey atmosphere, while the Asian fusion menu nods to Western tastes.

☆ Entertainment

TOP CHOICE **Connexion** LIVE MUSIC
(Ruko Bandar) Don't let the cover charge (100,000Rp for bands) hold you back: this small club is an absolute blast, with the best bands brought in from around Indonesia and walkway dancers who keep the whole house shaking until the early hours. Whew!

Shopping

Shopping is concentrated at City Balcony and **Balikpapan Plaza** (cnr Jl Sudirman & Jln Ahmad Yani), two huge malls separated by a Hypermart (for groceries).

Pesar Kebun Sayur SOUVENIRS
(⏲9am-6pm) Market for local handicrafts, gemstones and souvenirs. Ten minutes by taxi west of the city centre.

Information

Aero Travel (☎443 350; jony_satriavi@yahoo.com; Jl Ahmad Yani 19) Organises specialist river trips up Sungai Mahakam. Also books flights and can help you get to Derawan Archipelago. Ask for English-speaking Jony.

Bayu Buana Travel (☎422 751; www.bayubuanatravel.com; Jl Ahmad Yani) Very helpful English-speaking staff for flights, Sungai Mahakam tours.

Haji La Tanrung Star Group (Jl Ahmad Yani 51; ⏰7.30am-9pm) Moneychanger with several branches.

Kantorimigrasi Kelas (☎421 175; Jl Sudirman 23) Immigration office.

Pertamina Hospital (☎734 020; www.rspb.co.id; Jl Sudirman 1)

Speedy Internet (Jl Ahmad Yani 7; per hr 7000Rp) Air-con, moderately speedy and no smoking.

ℹ Getting There & Away

Air

Batavia Air (☎739 225; Jl Sudirman 15C)

Citilink (☎080 4108 0808; airport)

Garuda (☎422 301; Jl Sudirman 2, Adika Hotel Bahtera)

Kalstar (☎737 473; Jl Marsaiswahyudi 12)

Lion Air (☎707 3761; airport)

Merpati (☎424 452; Jl Sudirman 32)

SilkAir (☎730 800; Jl ARS Muhammad 7, Hotel Gran Senyiur)

Boat

Balikpapan has several ports along its gulf coast. If arriving from Banjarmasin by bus you'll take the ferry from Penajam to Kariangau Harbour. Further south lies Kampung Baru Harbour, which serves Sulawesi. Semayang Harbour, at the entrance to the gulf, is the main cargo and passenger port.

Dharma Lautan (☎422 194; Kampung Baru dock)

New Agung Sedayu (☎420 601; Jl Sudirman 28) Best source for all boat tickets.

Pelni (☎424 171; Jl Yos Sudarso 76)

Prima Vista (☎732 607; Jl Sudirman 138)

Bus

Buses to Samarinda leave from Batu Ampar bus terminal at the north end of town. Buses to Banjarmasin leave from the terminal across the harbour. To get there take *angkot* (city minibus) 6 to Jl Monginsidi and hop on a speedboat (10,000Rp to 20,000Rp, 10 minutes) to the other side. If ar-

TRANSPORT FROM BALIKPAPAN

Air

DESTINATION	COMPANY	COST (RP)	DURATION	FREQUENCY
Banjarmasin	Batavia Air, Sriwijaya Air	375,000	45min	daily
Berau	Batavia Air, Sriwijaya Air	550,000	1hr	daily
Jakarta	Lion Air, Sriwijaya Air, Batavia Air, Garuda, Citilink	625,000	2hr	daily
Jogjakarta	Garuda, Lion Air, Batavia Air, Sriwijaya Air	800,000	2hr	daily
Kuala Lumpur	AirAsia	440,000	2½hr	3-4 weekly
Makassar	Lion Air, Sriwijaya Air, Garuda, Merpati	550,000	1½hr	daily
Singapore	Silk Air	4,300,000	2½hr	Mon-Sat
Surabaya	Batavia Air, Sriwijaya Air, Lion Air, Garuda, Citilink	575,000	1hr	daily
Tarakan	Lion Air, Sriwijaya Air, Batavia Air	400,000	1hr	daily

Boat

DESTINATION	COMPANY	COST (RP)	DURATION (HR)	FREQUENCY
Makassar	Dharma Lautan, Prima Vista, Pelni	175,000	19-24	5 weekly
Pare Pare	Prima Vista	162,000	19	Mon, Tue
Surabaya	Dharma Lautan, Prima Vista	275,000	36	almost daily
Tarakan-Nunukan	Pelni	294,000	3	Sun, Mon, Wed

riving, your bus ticket will automatically include a ferry across the harbour. However, since this can mean an hour wait, it may be better to get off at the ferry landing and take a speedboat.

Getting Around

Taxis from the city centre cost 50,000Rp to Sepinggan Airport (30 minutes) and 15,000Rp to Batu Ampar bus terminal. Balikpapan Plaza is a focal point for *angkot* (3000Rp) and *ojeks* (from 10,000Rp).

Samarinda

0541 / POP 726,000

Samarinda! The very name oozes exoticism, like some capital in the *Arabian Nights*. And happily, you will find some of that here in this sprawling riverfront city. The enormous mosque of the new Islamic Centre stands like a sentinel at the gates of the mighty Mahakam River, a most impressive sight, giving the city a welcome dash of Istanbul. But like many fairy-tale settings, there is also a jarring profusion of highs and lows, from a few quality hotels to the thousands of rusting tin-roofed shacks spread over the surrounding hills. Unlike Balikpapan, anything goes here, for better or worse, so take a taxi after 9pm.

Sights

TOP CHOICE Samarinda Islamic Centre MOSQUE
(Jl Slamet Riyadi; tower admission 10,000Rp; mosque 8-10am & 4-6pm, tower 7am-6pm) The skyline of Samarinda is dominated by this new must-see complex containing an awe-inspiring mosque and adjacent tower. The latter is the highest point in the city, offering panoramic views up and down a great bend in the Mahakam. The muezzin's call at sunset is a captivating moment here.

Mesjid Siratal Mustaqim MOSQUE
(Samarinda Seberang) A 400-year-old wooden mosque designed by a Dutchman, in colonial architectural style, with a unique wooden minaret. On the south side of the river near the boat landing.

Mesjid Raya Darussalam MOSQUE
(Jl Niaga Selatan) A striking mosque with missile-like minarets.

Tours

TOP CHOICE De'Gigant Tours ADVENTURE
(0812 584 6578, 700 0774; www.borneotourgigant.com; Jl Martadinata 21) De'Gigant is the best tour company to deal with in Kalimantan, offering strong and trustworthy management, experienced guides and island-wide contacts. Its sharp Dutch owner, Lucas Zwaal, speaks English, German, Indonesian, Dayak, Kutai, Banjarese and Javanese. This is one of only two tour companies we recommend for the Cross-Borneo Trek (p587), and the best for an east-to-west itinerary, with expertise all the way up the Mahakam. For a memorable jungle trek or river cruise, start here.

MOSQUE ATTIRE

You don't need to be Muslim or Confucian to admire the architecture of Samarinda's great buildings. Visitors are welcome. But when it comes to mosques, both men and women should wear plain, loose-fitting clothing, and remove hats and sunglasses upon entrance. Men can wear short-sleeve shirts, but women should be covered to the wrists and wear a headscarf. Men and women occupy different rooms in a mosque, so if you are in mixed company you will be separated during your visit; sometimes there are also separate entrances.

Sleeping

Don't skimp here: budget digs are gloomy and upgrading to midrange options only adds a Western toilet to your concrete cube. However, top-end hotels can be good value, particularly on weekends, when many offer steep discounts. Rooms fill up accordingly, so reserve ahead on weekends.

TOP CHOICE Hotel Mesra HOTEL $$
(732 772; www.mesra.com/hotel; Jl Pahlawan 1; s/d incl breakfast 350,000/400,000Rp, d cottage 820,000Rp;) The Mesra is a welcome surprise, a true resort privately located on a hilltop in town and very reasonably priced, attracting families from near and far on weekends. Rooms have balconies overlooking the expansive grounds, which include two pools open to the public (30,000Rp), gardens, tennis courts, a spa and an excellent restaurant. The latter offers Western, Asian and Indonesian cuisine in an atmospheric traditional wooden building, if you don't mind the enormous *garuda* (mythical

Samarinda

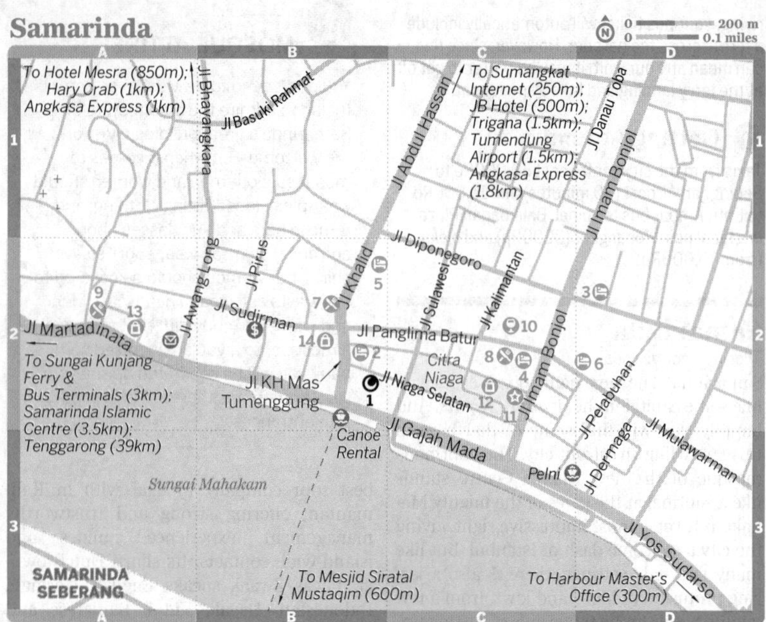

Samarinda

Sights
1 Mesjid Raya Darussalam B2

Sleeping
2 Aida B2
3 Aston Samarinda D2
4 Hotel Grand Jamrud 2 .... C2
5 Hotel MJ B2
6 Swiss-Belhotel D2

Eating
7 Hero Supermarket B2
8 Sari Pacific Restaurant C2
9 Teluk Lerong Restaurant & Café A2

Drinking
10 Déjà Vu Bar C2

Entertainment
11 Maximum C2

Shopping
12 Citra Niaga C2
13 Hendra Art Shop A2
14 Pasar Pagi B2

bird) staring down at you. Worth coming just for the breakfast (90,000Rp).

Aston Samarinda HOTEL **$$**
(☎732 600; www.astonsamarinda.com; Jl Pangeran Hidayatullah; r 760,000;) A bargain at this price, this brand-new, attractively designed hotel and convention centre sports a collonaded pool, comfy rooms that cross over from business to leisure, and if you can pull your eyes away from the huge flat-screen TVs, some grand views of the river. Fine dining and an in-house spa round out the luxury. Promo rate on Sunday and 10% online discount.

Swiss-Belhotel HOTEL **$$$**
(☎200 888; www.swissbelhotel.com; Jl Mulawarman 6; s 995,000-1,055,000Rp, d 1,055,000-1,710,000Rp;) This nicely decorated business hotel with its large glass lobby, pool and extensive buffet is new, and much cheaper than the published rates quoted here when you factor in the walk-in discount. All rooms numbered 18– face the river. Credit cards accepted.

Hotel MJ HOTEL $$
(☎747 689; www.mjhotel.com; Jl Khalid 1; r incl breakfast 275,000-495,000Rp, ste incl breakfast 465,000-575,000Rp; ❄📶) Part of this hotel has been renovated to great effect, although the new rooms had not yet been priced at time of research. The cafe is bright and cheery and there is an excellent buffet. All rooms have air-con, en suites, TVs, comfortable beds, hot water and Dayak artwork. Ask about discounts.

Hotel Grand Jamrud 2 HOTEL $$
(☎731 233; Jl Panglima Batur 45; r incl breakfast 300,000-470,000Rp; ❄📶) Centrally located, with clean concrete cubes as rooms, this is a better choice than its sibling the Jamrud 1, but check rooms to avoid mould and view issues. The breakfast is OK, but the cafe looks out on a wall.

JB Hotel HOTEL $$
(☎737 688; jbhotel_samarinda@yahoo.com; Jl Agus Salim 16; r 228,000-333,000Rp; ❄📶) A bit out of the way, JB is seemingly undecided whether it's art deco or Moorish kitsch. Air-con rooms are large and clean, but only deluxe rooms have hot water.

Aida HOTEL $
(☎742 572; Jl KH Mas Tumenggung; d incl breakfast 180,000-240,000Rp, tr 255,000Rp; ❄) The nondescript rooms here are cheap, but that's about it. The cheapest rooms have a fan and cold water; the rest air-con and hot water. They could all be cleaner.

Eating

Night cafes proliferate opposite Mesra Indah Mall, with tasty warungs (food stalls) and unpretentious seafood restaurants further up Jl Abdul Hassan.

TOP CHOICE **Teluk Lerong Restaurant & Café** INTERNATIONAL $
(Jl Martadinata; mains 20,000Rp; ⏰8am-1am Mon-Thu, to 2am Fri-Sun; 📶) Perched above the busy riverside drive, this new and stylish cafe is a breath of fresh air in a city that sorely needs more like it. The open-air dining is atmospheric, if a bit loud, and the menu offers something for everyone, be it Chinese, pasta or steak.

TOP CHOICE **Lipan Hill Resto & Cafe** INTERNATIONAL $
(Jl Kusumo, Samarinda Sebarang; mains from 30,000Rp; ⏰breakfast, lunch & dinner) With a commanding location overlooking the Mahakam from its southern bank, about 2km south of the bridge, this is a refreshing spot, as it takes advantage of the city's greatest asset: its river views. The excellent food brings in the locals. Live music 10am to 11pm.

Hary Crab SEAFOOD $$
(Jl Pahlawan 41; crab 75,000Rp; ⏰6-10pm) A unique local institution, these streetside outdoor benches are generally packed with people digging into some delicious crab. Wear your bib.

Sari Pacific Restaurant INTERNATIONAL $
(Jl Panglima Batur; mains 33,000Rp; ⏰9am-10pm) Plush dining, with a menu featuring tenderloin and T-bone steaks as well as beef burgers. Perfect for a carb injection before the basic fare up the Mahakam, although portions are small. Live music daily.

Hero Supermarket SUPERMARKET $
(Mesra Indah Mall) Good place to stock up on snacks before heading upriver.

Drinking

Déjà Vu Bar BAR
(Jl Panglima Batur; ⏰10pm-2am) This complex contains a booming nightclub (admission 75,000Rp) with cocktail tables and lots of security and a separate, very classy dinner restaurant frequented by a hip and dressy crowd. The menu includes international cuisine plus a spectrum of cocktails. Yikes: a bottle of tequila is $150.

Entertainment

Maximum DISCO
(Jl Niaga Timur 21; ⏰8pm-close) In the Citra Niaga, this ear-splitter is the most popular dance club in the city. Go after midnight. Cover (50,000Rp) buys a free drink.

WORTH A TRIP

PAMPANG DAYAK CEREMONIES

Every Sunday at 2pm, Pampang, 25km west of Samarinda, has authentic Kenyah Dayak ceremonies at its longhouse, one of the last places to see traditional long ears. Offer a donation for taking photographs. Take a public minibus from Segiri terminal (10,000Rp, one hour), or charter a taxi or Kijang with other travellers (100,000Rp).

PROSTITUTION

Prostitution is integrated into Kalimantan society to a degree perhaps unmatched anywhere else in the world, and for reasons that have nothing to do with foreign tourists. Most hotel spas, massage centres, karaoke bars (with private rooms), nightclubs and pubs offer 'the extras'. In some cases the scale of these operations is truly audacious, with bars, karaoke and dance clubs united in huge multi-level entertainment complexes attached to five-star hotels. Apart from a growing focus on HIV, Kalimantan society as a whole turns a huge blind eye on this booming enterprise. Indeed, many Muslim-run hotels still demand that couples produce a marriage licence.

Shopping

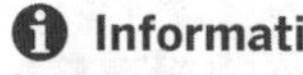

Hendra Art Shop ANTIQUES
(734 949; hendra.art@gmail.com; 9am-5pm) Carved bison skull, anyone? For curios, antiques, and other Borneo exotica, the two packed floors of this rare shop can't be beat. Before testing your haggling skills, ensure that what you are buying is authentic and can be removed from the country.

Citra Niaga MARKET
(@) Contains several souvenir shops offering beautiful batik sarongs and Dayak carvings. There's also a food court (mains 25,000Rp to 35,000Rp).

Pasar Pagi MARKET
(Morning Market; Jl Sudirman) A wonderfully chaotic morning market.

Information

Angkasa Express (200 281; aexsri@telkom.net; Plaza Lembuswana) Air tickets.

Bank Central Asia (BCA; Jl Sudirman) For foreign exchange.

Main post office (cnr Jl Gajah Mada & Jl Awang Long)

Prima Tour & Travel (737 777; prima_sriol@yahoo.co.id; Jl Khalid 1, Hotel MJ) Air tickets and cars.

Rumah Sakit Haji Darjad (732 698; Jl Dahlia) Modern, massive hospital. Off Jl Basuki Rahmat.

Sumangkat Internet (Jl Agus Salim 35; per hr 7000Rp; 8am-midnight) Plus postal services and wartel (telephone office).

Getting There & Away

Air

Kalstar (747 972; Jl Subroto 80, en route to airport) The only airline serving Samarinda. Most flights connect through Balikpapan.

Boat

Pelni (741 402; Jl Yos Sudarso 76)

Mahakam ferries (*kapal biasa*) leave at 7am from Sungai Kunjang terminal (3km via *angkot*)

Pelni ferries leave from the main harbour on Jl Yos Sudarso. See the harbour master (Jl Yos Sudarso 2) for service to Pare Pare aboard *Queen Soya*.

Bus

Samarinda has multiple bus terminals:

Sungai Kunjang terminal For Kota Bangun (23,000Rp, three hours) and Balikpapan (27,000Rp, two hours).

Lempake terminal (north end of town) For Bontang (25,000Rp, three hours), Sangatta (20,000Rp, four hours) and Berau (150,000Rp, 16 hours).

Harapan Baru terminal (south bank of Sungai Makaham, *angkot* route G) For minibuses to Tenggarong (10,000Rp, one hour).

Segiri terminal (north end of Jl Pahlawan) For minibuses to Pampang (7000Rp, one hour).

A direct bus to Balikpapan Airport (50,000Rp) departs from the office of Prima Tour & Travel six times per day.

Car & Kijang

A Kijang seat is 300,000Rp to Kota Bangun, and 250,000Rp to Berau. Hiring a car and driver is 500,000Rp per day. A 4WD doubles the price. You can organise a car through Prima Tour & Travel.

Getting Around

Minibuses, called *angkot* or taxis (3000Rp), converge at Pasar Pagi. Taxis from Tumendung Airport (3km) cost 35,000Rp. Alternatively, walk 100m to Jl Gatot Subroto, turn left and catch *angkot* B into town.

Cross-Mahakam ferries to Samarinda Seberang (5000Rp) leave from the end of Jl Tumenggung.

Sungai Mahakam

The second-largest river in Indonesia, the mighty Mahakam is at once a major highway, a cultural tour and a wildlife-spotting expedition. It is also the only major river with public transport all the way into the heart of Borneo, making its 930km length entirely accessible.

Activites

Travelling up this jungle river is a journey in the fullest sense of the word. One heads away from the industrial centre of Samarinda and slips deeper and deeper into the jungle, and into Borneo's past. A week later it is either time to start the difficult next stage of the Cross-Borneo Trek, or turn back. Along the way there is great variety, including the many boats that ply the river and local wildlife. Between Tanjung Isuy and Mancong our research trip encountered river otter, gold-ringed snake, python, proboscis monkey, macaque, kingfisher, monitor lizard, hornbill, stork, and an unidentified condor. There are many opportunities for exploration, from towns and longhouses to huge lakes, wetlands and other rivers. This is a place that rewards travellers with time on their hands and hence the ability to jump off the boat and wait for the next one, even if it means staying overnight.

As you continue upriver, tourist facilities recede – and what there is ain't great. On the other hand, the Mahakam is one of those places where you shouldn't worry too much about the details. Homestays materialise, 'my brother's boat' appears, closed stores open. Westerners in particular will be greeted with legendary hospitality. Transport gets increasingly expensive the further upriver you go, due to the cost of lugging fuel that far, but everything else is dirt cheap, so a little money goes a long way.

In summary, this is off-the-beaten-track travel of the highest order. Outside the summer season, you'll probably not see another foreigner your entire trip. There are few creature comforts, making health precautions particularly wise, but you also have the flexibility to turn back whenever you think you've seen enough (and the current downriver cuts the return journey in half). If you are comparing this with rivers elsewhere in Borneo, it is the defining experience.

STAGES OF TRAVEL

The Mahakam is ascended from Samarinda in different stages, each requiring its own form of transport, although there are also some personal choices to be made. Here is an ideal itinerary:

Stage One: Samarinda to Kota Bangun By Land While Samarinda is where Mahakam journeys are arranged, it is not where they typically begin. Travellers usually go overland to Kota Bangun via Tenggarong, either by bus (20,000Rp, three hours) or by hiring a car (450,000Rp), as this stretch of river is highly developed. Otherwise it is an eight-hour journey from Samarinda by *kapal biasa*, which depart every morning at 7am.

TRANSPORT FROM SAMARINDA

Air

DESTINATION	COMPANY	COST (RP)	DURATION	FREQUENCY
Balikpapan	Kalstar	316,000	30min	2 daily
Berau	Kalstar	720,000	45min	3 daily
Nunukan	Kalstar	1,274,000	3hr	1 daily
Tarakan	Kalstar	983,000	2hr	1 daily

Boat

DESTINATION	COMPANY	COST (RP)	DURATION	FREQUENCY
Long Bagun (seasonal)		350,000	36hr	daily
Long Iram		120,000	18hr	daily
Melak		100,000	16hr	daily
Pare Pare	Pelni	250,000	22hr	2 weekly
Surabaya	Pelni	381,000	3 days	monthly
Tenggarong		20,000	2hr	daily

Stage Two: Kota Bagun to Muara Pahu by Ces This wonderful section of rivers, lakes and marshes, which is full of wildlife, requires a *ces* to explore. Otherwise you can stay on the main river and take the *kapal biasa*, but you are really missing out. *Kapal biasa* head upriver every morning at 9am.

Stage Three: Muara Pahu to Long Bagun by Kapal Biasa A fulfilling stretch of riverboat travel, with an overnight stay on the boat.

Stage Four: Long Bagun to Tiong Ohang by Longboat The most exhilirating part of the entire journey. Ever shot rapids upstream in a 400 horsepower speedboat?

Note that *kapal biasa* reach Long Bagun, 523km from Samarinda (350,000Rp, 36 hours), when water levels permit. Otherwise they stop in Tering, 409km upstream (155,000Rp, 18 hours). From here on, transport gets expensive, with charter rates of 100,000Rp per hour for a *ces* and 1,000,000Rp per hour for a speedboat. Be prepared to haggle, and remember that the larger the group, the cheaper the individual cost to charter a boat.

GUIDES

If you do not speak Bahasa, you will need a guide, as English becomes harder to find the further upriver you go. You can get by on the *kapal biasa* without it, but step ashore and you're lost. If you buy a tour package a guide will be provided, and costs defined ahead of time. If not, you'll have to hire a guide yourself. Some travellers do so as they move along the lower river, but it is better to take the time to find a suitable guide in Samarinda, where they are relatively plentiful, rather than having this requirement hanging over your head. A short interview is essential to confirm any guide's language skills.

Guide fees generally range from 150,000Rp to 200,000Rp per day, with the best getting 250,000Rp. The client is responsible for a guide's expenses as well, but be clear about what this entails ahead of time. Usually the client picks up the guide's meals, which are inexpensive. Guides can generally arrange their own local accommodation, too, which is relatively cheap or even free. Transport can be very expensive, especially beyond Long Bagun, but guides can often get the price of their own ticket reduced. In general, the best guides will look out for their client's financial interests, leading to savings that actually defray their fee. But be aware that, while you are with them for one journey, they deal with the same locals all the time.

The following recommended guides speak English:

Ahmad GUIDE
(☎0821 5180 8818; ahmad_tour74@yahoo.com) An experienced cross-Borneo guide with excellent organisational skills.

Abdullah GUIDE
(☎0813 4727-2817; doe21@yahoo.com) Friendly and resourceful.

Suriyadi GUIDE
(☎081 6450 8263) Speaks German.

Rustam GUIDE
(☎081 2585 4915, 735 641)

Jaelani GUIDE
(☎0813-4633 8343)

THE HOT ROD OF THE MAHAKAM

Need a *ces* (motorised canoe with long propellor shaft) to explore the waters beyond Kota Bangun? Cheerful **Udin** (☎0812 5311 1357) has the perfect ride. Powerful, gaily painted and comfortable, with a cushion seat below and a canopy overhead, this colourful canoe is as cool as river travel gets. Udin also knows how to slow down for wildlife, navigate the narrowest paths and keep you dry. A full day's itinerary – Kota Bangun, Muara Muntai, Jantur, Tanjung Isuy, Mancong, and back to Tanjung Isuy – is 1,500,000Rp for the entire boat, drinks included. Seats six comfortably.

TENGGARONG

☎0541 / POP 75,000

Tenggarong is an important destination, but also a heartbreaker. Once the capital of the mighty Kutai sultanate, it made a recent attempt to recreate that past grandeur, and failed mightily. Several years ago the local regent and his cohorts, flush with mining profits, made a massive investment in the city's infrastructure. The development focused on turning Pulau Kumala, the city's river island, into a huge tourist attraction,

CHARIOTS OF THE MAHAKAM

You'll need several different types of boat to go the length of the Mahakam. Here are the principal varieties:

Kapal Biasa These bi-level riverboats ply the lower Mahakam, from Samarinda to Long Bagun. The open lower deck holds cargo, the kitchen (meals 20,000Rp) and basic bathrooms (visualise a hole in the deck). The closed upper deck is the sleeping area, a floating hostel where 60 people or so bed down, side by side, on simple mattresses (provided). If you're making an overnight journey, head directly upstairs to stake a claim. The atmosphere is very congenial; everyone else is used to this madness. The secret treasure is the balcony at the front, directly over the captain, which provides an awesome elevated viewing platform. As the boat chugs upstream and kilometres of jungle pass by, you can sit there serenely for hours on end in shaded comfort, munching on strange fruit from the last stop. There is only room for five people or so, though, so let one be you, as it truly makes the voyage.

Longboats Long speedboats with a canvas top and rows of seating for passengers, these powerful craft, with 400 horsepower behind them, are necessary for handling the rapids in the upper river. If you sit up front, you'll bounce around a lot but it's worth it, as visibility is better. While sitting in the middle is smoother, you'll end up in a blue haze, as everyone smokes like a chimney. Expensive, but a hell of a ride.

Ces What else can we say? This is one romantic way to travel. These narrow wooden canoes are powered by a lawnmower engine, attached to a propeller via a long stalk – the same longtails seen elsewhere in Asia. They are also surprisingly stylish, with upturned snouts, raked sterns, occasional cabanas and colourful paint jobs. Best of all, they provide access to the narrowest and shallowest stretches on the river, including some vast marshes. All things considered, there is nothing, *nothing* like exploring the jungle on a beautiful day in one of these, a private journey fit for a sultan. Sit on the cushioned hull in shaded comfort, eagerly awaiting the next source of amazement. Just bring your earplugs.

River travel! The joy of Kalimantan.

with a hotel, restaurants, amusement park and sky tower. It also included the construction of a large suspension bridge across the Mahakam, dubbed 'Indonesia's Golden Gate'. Today Pulau Kumala lies unfinished and bankrupt, its history plagued by a massive corruption scandal. Far worse, in 2011 the bridge suddenly collapsed into the river, killing 36 people. The result is a setting worthy of Greek drama. The waterfront is framed by a massive statue of a *lembuswana*, a mythical winged horse with an elephant's trunk, which perches at the end of Pulau Kumala; and by the enormous, twisted remains of the collapsed bridge, its fallen roadway spearing the Mahakam.

Sights

TOP CHOICE Keraton/Mulawarman Museum MUSEUM

(Jl Diponegoro; admission 5000Rp; ⌚9am-4pm, closed Mon & Fri) The former sultan's palace *(keraton)* is known for its excellent museum, which ranges widely across culture, natural history and industry, and has English signage. However, it is the building itself that is the star attraction. The sparkling white exterior, with its strong parallel lines, is a futurist vision worthy of Shangri-La, and reminiscent of Frank Lloyd Wright. Built by the Dutch in 1937, this is a significant work of architecture that has fallen off the world's radar screen; further information is difficult to come by. Nearby you'll find the sultan's cemetery, a souvenir market and an ATM.

Pulau Kumala ISLAND

While the future of this island amusement park is uncertain, a boat trip and stroll to the huge *lembuswana* at the tip is a worthwhile outing. Boats (per person 20,000Rp) leave 100m from Keraton.

Festivals & Events

Erau Festival CULTURAL

In July thousands of Dayaks hold a vast intertribal party punctuated by traditional dances, ceremonies and other events that is not to be missed. Ask at hotels for schedule.

Sleeping & Eating

Grand Elty Singgasana Hotel HOTEL $$
(☎664 703; Jl Pahlawan 1; r 589,000-697,000Rp; ❄) The only comfortable hotel anywhere nearby, this one ultimately maddens, as its beautiful hillside location, attractive villa courtyard and quality rooms are consistently marred by peeling paint, broken walkways, a malfunctioning website and clueless staff. The silver lining: a prime candidate for price negotiation.

Hotel Anda Dua HOTEL $
(☎0821 5684 9766; Jl Sudirman 65; r 120,000-170,000Rp; ❄) This wooden lodge has fan-cooled rooms with shared *mandi* and, out the back, comfortable air-con rooms with private bathroom and breakfast.

Rumah Makan Tepian Pandan INDONESIAN $
(Jl Diponegoro 23; mains 15,000Rp; ⏲breakfast, lunch & dinner) A relaxed, open-air restaurant serving Indonesian cuisine, with superb river views.

Getting There & Away

The *kapal biasa* dock is 2km north of town, with *angkot* (2500Rp) service to the centre. *Ojeks* cost 10,000Rp. Boats depart for Samarinda at 7am daily (20,000Rp, two hours) and Kota Bangun at 9am daily (50,000Rp, six hours).

Petugas bus terminal is 5km south of town, also with *angkot* service to the centre (5000Rp). Buses depart hourly from 9am to 4pm for both Samarinda (10,000Rp) and Kota Bangun (23,000Rp).

There is no regular car service from Tenggarong. Kijang can be chartered for 150,000Rp for the first hour, 100,000Rp thereafter.

KOTA BANGUN

This busy town and transport hub is where upriver journeys generally begin. You can hire a *ces* from here to take you through a complex of rivers, lakes and marshes interspersed with villages. You'll cross lakes with wide-open skies, twist and turn through wetland channels, pass through forests of silver-barked trees, lunch at riverside warungs, and generally breeze along, pausing for the odd monkey or some of the last few Irrawaddy dolphins. Don't miss it.

Sleeping

Losmen Muzirat LOSMEN $
(☎081 2553 2287; Jl Mesjid Raya 46; r 40,000Rp) Colourfully painted, with simple, fan-cooled rooms and shared *mandi*. Pay up for light. There's a decent veranda to watch spectacular sunsets, nearby warungs and, further down the road, an internet cafe and ATM.

Getting There & Around

A *ces* from Kota Bangun takes 1½ hours to Muara Muntai (250,000Rp), just over two hours to Jantur (325,000Rp), three hours to Tanjung Isuy (500,000Rp) and 6½ hours to Mancong (900,000Rp).

MUARA MUNTAI

This riverside town is remarkable for its massive boardwalk, more than 2km long, which serves as the main street. After sitting in a *ces* for hours, it's the perfect spot to stretch your legs and hunt for a snack.

Sleeping

Penginapan Srimuntai LOSMEN $
(☎0853 4963 0030; s/d 50,000/100,000Rp) Nice wide hallways and cleaner rooms elevate this one above the competition.

Penginapan Adi Guna LOSMEN $
(☎0853 4963 0030; r 50,000Rp) Basic fan-cooled rooms and large, shared *mandi*. There's free coffee and tea and a welcome breeze on the balcony.

MAHAKAM BY HOUSEBOAT

There is no better way to cruise the rivers of Kalimantan than by houseboat. The *Budi Sejati* is a rare opportunity to do this on the Mahakam. The 18m, two-storey craft, a larger version of the *klotok* seen in Tanjung Puting, has a kitchen, toilet and shower, a crew of two, an air-conditioned stateroom and, best of all, your own private shaded balcony at the front of the upper deck, the perfect viewing platform. Add an English-speaking guide, a cook and all provisions, and you are off on your own private river expedition – in first class. The highly varied itinerary includes river villages, wildlife, culture and more. For a four-day trip, the cost per person is 7,676,000Rp for two or three people; 6,144,000Rp for four or five; 5,268,000Rp for six to eight people; and 4,428,000Rp for nine to 12, all expenses included. For more information contact De'Gigant Tours (p593).

Getting There & Away

Get here from Samarinda by *kapal biasa* (70,000Rp, 10 hours) or bus to Kota Bangun (23,000Rp, three hours) and *ces* from there (250,000Rp, two hours).

JANTUR

Jantur is the most interesting river town on the Mahakam, partly because of its location, where the river enters a huge lake (Lake Jempang) bordered by wetlands; partly because it is built on stilts, with two huge boardwalks connecting each side of the river; and partly because it is missing from every map. The latter is particularly surprising, as this is no small village. As you enter, it just keeps on going.

The town was founded by Banjarese from Negara, which has a similar topography, and the brightly painted houses reflect this. A big, commanding yellow mosque, with its bright aluminum dome, sits proudly upon the river, an impressive sight as you emerge from the forest. Unfortunately there's no accommodation, but if you can arrange a homestay, do so. The friendly people hardly ever see tourists, making for some great exchanges, while the surrounding area is unique on the river, a vast wetlands savannah with a huge sky, like the Everglades. In any case, be sure to get out and stroll the boardwalk, which is also a stroll through village life; your camera will be clicking every few seconds. One example is the storks at the end of people's docks, which are used as guard animals. If they start squawking, someone is pinching your dried fish!

TANJUNG ISUY

Tanjung Isuy is the first Dayak village as you head upriver. You're equally likely to hear a shaman chanting as a mobile phone chirruping, as modern culture is only skin deep.

Sleeping

Louu Taman Jamrout LONGHOUSE **$**
(Jl Indonesia Australia; r per person 60,000Rp) This longhouse is part craft centre, part hostel and part stage. Travellers can commission a Dayak dance for 500,000Rp. Weavings are available at reasonable prices. Rooms are boxlike and clean, with warm showers in shared bathrooms, and share a lively communal dinner table.

Losmen Wisata LOSMEN **$**
(Jl Indonesia Australia; s/d 35,000/50,000Rp) About 500m from the jetty, offers rooms with double beds and mosquito nets off a central dining area. The airy common space has wall-to-wall windows for superior views.

Getting There & Away

Tanjung Isuy is not on the *kapal biasa* route from Samarinda. Chartering a *ces* from Muara Muntai (250,000Rp, 1½ to two hours) is the easiest way to get here. A public *ces* to Muara Muntai leaves daily in the early morning (from 75,000Rp, depending on number of passengers). You can charter a *ces* direct to Kota Bangun (500,000Rp, three hours), then catch a bus and be in Samarinda or Balikpapan that night. In dry season, Tanjung Isuy is 30 minutes by *kijang* or *ojek* from Mancong.

MANCONG

For optimum jungle drama Mancong is best reached by boat on the Ohong river, meandering past monitor lizards, sapphire-hued kingfishers, bulb-nosed proboscis monkeys and marauding macaques. The journey beneath towering banyan trees, their roots foraging like witches' fingers in the dark river, is as much a part of the experience as your arrival.

Sleeping

Mancong Longhouse LONGHOUSE **$**
(Mancong; per person 50,000Rp) This exquisitely restored 1930s longhouse (no bedding, food or electricity), surrounded by woodcarved sentinels, is the centrepiece of the village. As in Tanjung Isuy, the locals oblige with welcome dances, available on request for 500,000Rp, and there's an interesting souvenir shop.

Getting There & Away

To visit Mancong charter a *ces* from Tanjung Isuy (500,000Rp return, about three to four hours each way) early in the morning. In the dry season, it's possible to travel to/from Tanjung Isuy by *ojek* (100,000Rp, 30 minutes).

THE LAST IRRAWADDY DOLPHINS

The freshwater Irrawaddy dolphin (*pesut*) was common all along Sungai Mahakam until the 1980s. Today there are around 90 left. They can generally be seen near Muara Pahu and, more frequently, en route to Muara Muntai from Muara Kaman. If you have a particular interest in seeing them, contact Budiono or Danielle Kreb at yk.rasi@gmail.com.

MUARA PAHU

Lining one side of a big curve in the Mahakam, this town is known mainly for its proximity to the Irrawaddy dolphin. There's an extensive boardwalk, a good place for a stroll where you can also find warungs.

Sleeping

Pension Anna LOSMEN $
(s/d 50,000/100,000Rp) Two identical well-lit rooms in the front of a private home, near the bridge.

Getting There & Around

You can charter *ces* around Muara Pahu for from one hour to all day (150,000Rp to 600,000Rp). It's also possible to combine dolphin-watching with transport to Maura Muntai or Tanjung Isuy (400,000Rp) via Sungai Baroh, an area rich with birds and monkeys, and to Melak (500,000Rp). Trained boatmen go slow for wildlife viewing, so travel times vary. *Kapal biasa* to/from Samarinda (80,000Rp, 12 hours) pass by in the early evening.

MELAK

Unlike other towns on the river, Melak is not defined by its waterfront. As you walk up the landing into town, and keep going, you could be anywhere in roadside Kalimantan, meaning generally unpleasant sprawl. This is primarily a coal-mining town, with a rough-and-ready aspect. From Dayak funeral rights to cockfights, you never know what you might run into. But there are a few souvenir shops, an ATM on Jl Tendean, and an internet cafe.

Sights around Melak include an orchid garden and some longhouses, but they require renting a car, the road is terrible and the sights themselves underwhelming. Best to continue on when transport allows.

Sleeping & Eating

You can find some decent seafood here, but the hotels are particularly unpleasant and very much alike – musty concrete boxes without a drop of character that we might not otherwise list. They are all near one another so, if you must, walk around and choose the least painful option. A much better idea: take this opportunity for a homestay on the river. It's roughing it in a different way, but it's cooler, prettier, cheaper, and far more educational.

Hotel Monita HOTEL $
(☎081 154 7316; Jl Dr Sutomo 76; r incl breakfast 150,000-330,000Rp; ❄) The best concrete box in town, but about 2km from the port. Often full with mining clients so book ahead.

Hotel Flamboyan HOTEL $
(☎0812 5323 1994; Jl A Yani; r with fan/air-con 80,000/130,000Rp; ❄) Offers private *mandi* with Western toilets, but definitely not flamboyant.

Penginapan Rahmat Abadi LOSMEN $
(☎0813 5023 2282; Jl Tendean; r 50,000Rp) Close to the pier, with fan-only rooms and shared bathrooms.

Ketapang INDONESIAN $
(Jl A Yani; mains 30,000Rp; ⏰6-9pm) The town's most popular restaurant, with sizzling fried prawns, chicken and fish dishes. Opposite the boat landing.

Rumah Makan Jawah Indah SEAFOOD $
(Jl A Yani; mains 25,000-35,000Rp; ⏰7am-9pm; 📶) Clean and cool seafood joint by the river.

FLOATING HOMESTAY

Mahakam river towns often contain floating houses, and the bank opposite Melak is lined with them. These are very basic homemade huts constructed on logs pulled from the river, logs which must be replaced every five years or so. In this unique environment, people go about living lives that are as recognisable as they are different. Children jump into the river to bathe before putting on their school uniforms. Their school bus is a canoe. Satellite dishes sit on top of roofs made from cast-off lumber. A homestay in this environment is very basic, as it involves sleeping on a mat and using the river outhouse, like everyone else. But at the same time it is a window on life that only opens this way. Sitting outside your floating house with a cup of coffee, watching river traffic at sunset, is a lasting memory.

Murni (☎no English 0813 5042 8447; Melak; r incl dinner & breakfast per person 50,000Rp), a *ces* taxi driver, offers a homestay in his floating house directly across from the harbour, with free pick up and return. Additional sightseeing trips are 200,000Rp.

Information

Ruma Pelangi (per hr 5000Rp; ⌚8am-10pm) To find this internet cafe, from the harbour turn left at intersection and go another 50m.

Getting There & Away

Boats leave for Samarinda daily between 11am and 2pm (120,000Rp, 15 hours, 325km). To/from Tanjung Isuy, charter a *ces* (600,000Rp, four hours). The *kapal biasa* to Tering departs at 2am (150,000Rp, five hours). A *ces* will cost 500,000Rp to 800,000Rp, depending on your negotiating skills. The daily bus to Samarinda (100,000Rp, nine hours) is a very uncomfortable ride.

TERING

A planned community deep in gold-mining country, Tering (140,000Rp, 24 hours from Samarinda) is sometimes the last stop for *kapal biasa*, depending on the water level. It's really two settlements straddling the river: **Tering Lama**, a Bahau Dayak village on the northern bank, and **Tering Baru**, a Malay village where the *kapal biasa* docks. The latter is an ordered grid of cottages that can be circumnavigated on foot in 15 minutes, but you'll want to pause at the highlight, a magnificent wooden **church** with intricate painted pillars and a bell tower supported by totem poles. A speedboat to Long Bagun is 300,000Rp per person.

LONG BAGUN

Sleeping

TOP CHOICE **Penginapan Polewali** LOSMEN $

(☎081 350 538 997; r 50,000Rp) This mountain lodge with traditional furnishings is a breath of fresh air after the concrete boxes downriver. In fact, it is the best hotel on the Upper Mahakam. Rooms are small, and bathrooms shared, but a nice breeze on the porch keeps you outside, and there are warungs nearby. Turn right after you get off the boat.

TIONG OHANG

Divided by the Mahakam, Tiong Ohang is united by its creaking pedestrian suspension bridge, offering scenic views of the surrounding hills. This is the last stop before starting the second stage in the Cross-Borneo Trek, the hike across the Muller Range. Guides/porters are assembled here, although this should be done by a tour company. The trailhead is two hours upriver by *ces* (1,000,000Rp). In the past the Muller trek began another three hours further on, at scenic **Long Apari**, but the added expense, which is considerable this far upriver, now makes this impractical.

DON'T MISS

THE HEART OF BORNEO

From Long Bagun you embark upon the most thrilling ride on the Mahakam, the longboat to **Tiong Ohang** (800,000Rp, four hours). You'll need to wait until the boat has enough passengers, or pay more. This serpentine adventure takes you through some spectacular gorges, with scenic waterfalls, ancient volcanic peaks and plenty of rapids to keep you bouncing around as the powerful boat strains against the current. Somewhere along this ride, surrounded by lush and dense primary growth forest, comes the uncanny realisation that you've entered the heart of Borneo.

Around four hours into the trip you'll pass **Data Dawai**, which has the only airport upriver from Samarinda. **Susi Air** (☎0542 764 416; www.susiair.com; Jl Pupuk Raya 33) flies charters here from Samarinda on Sunday, Wednesday and Friday (800,000Rp), although this unpublished schedule is undoubtedly dynamic.

Sleeping

Putra Apari LOSMEN $

(r 60,000Rp) The only accommodation in town, and surprisingly hospitable. Typical losmen rooms have no fan and shared *mandi*, but a nice porch with a cross-breeze overlooks the main street. Small shops and warungs nearby.

The Muller Mountains

The second stage of the larger Cross-Borneo Trek (p587), the journey from Tiong Ohang across the Muller Mountains to Tanjung Lokan (or vice versa) is a very different experience from what precedes it. This is neither a cultural tour nor a wildlife-spotting expedition. In fact, views of any kind are scarce. This is a jungle trek, and a very difficult one, whose primary purpose is to get to the other side. It can also be dangerous if you are not prepared. The trailside grave of a Dutchman who died in 2011 after hitting his head in a fall reinforces this fact.

The trek requires five days of walking steadily eight hours a day. Most people do it in seven days or more. There are several bare campsites along the way, but otherwise you're following a narrow path – if that – through a green maze, with the occasional need for the *mandau* (machete). You are also constantly crossing the same river switchbacks. In the beginning the fords are ankle deep, but as you get further downstream they become chest high. The mountains themselves are an anticlimax, as a pass makes crossing over them far easier than you'd expect. The leeches are not to be underestimated, however. Even with the proper protection, it is difficult to keep them out. The walk from breakfast to lunch will typically yield 20-or so small travellers on your shoes. They pose no danger, apart from slightly itchy bites, but they are high on the disgusting index, particularly after they have gorged themselves on your blood, at which point they are the length of a thumb.

The journey should be organised by a tour company such as De' Gigant Tours (p593) in Samarinda or Kompakh (p617) in Putussibau, who will send a guide with you upriver. In turn, this guide will arrange for local porters and guides near the trailhead (eg Tiong Ohang). One of the more interesting parts of the journey is watching these forest people trek, sometimes walking barefoot. Armed with *sumpit* (blowgun) and spear, and carrying homemade rattan packs, they move through difficult undergrowth as if on a footpath, hopping from wet stone to mossy rock with the sure-footedness of a mountain goat. Campsites are put up with the clever use of sticks and machete, without any modern gear except for a tarp. Cooking is done over an open fire.

All things considered, the experience hasn't changed much since George Muller first crossed his namesake range in 1825. While that first trek ended with the locals cutting off Muller's head, the primary risk today is breaking a leg or merely twisting an ankle so far from outside help. To that end, heed all the precautions, and ensure that your tour company will as well, prior to departure.

The Muller Trek is a horizontal Everest. You tackle it for the same reasons you climb. And when you succeed, it is both a lifetime memory and a noteworthy achievement. Very few Westerners have crossed from one side of Borneo to the other. But with the proper precautions in place, it is now entirely possible to do so.

Kutai National Park

This park is a disappointment. The only reason to come here is if you want to see a wild orangutan and have no chance to do so anywhere else. The park's once-vast acreage, long the target of natural-resource exploitation, has now dwindled to 10km of trails,

MULLER TREK SAFETY REQUIREMENTS

» Choose a professional local tour company. Do not even think of organising this yourself.

» Wear proper shoes. When it rains in the forest, the trail changes dramatically. What was a walk across leaves on solid ground becomes a slog across leaves on mud. In these conditions the locals wear a rubber version of a football cleat, with six spikes. Real football cleats would do fine, although you will have to wear them wet, as you cannot afford to take your shoes off and put them on again at every ford.

» Wear gloves to protect your hands from thorns.

» Wear proper leech protection. The only full solution here is a pair of spandex pants, such as cyclists wear. Otherwise expect many leech bites.

» Be firm about setting the pace at which you walk. Local guides and porters are not always aware of the difference between their skill level and your own. It is also in their interest to get across and back as soon as possible. Be sure to spread walking hours evenly among the days of the journey.

» Do not trek at night. Locals have no problem with this, but it greatly magnifies the risk, particularly if it is raining.

» Ensure that someone in your party has first-aid training and a first-aid kit.

» Bring 10 days' worth of food. If there is a problem midway, you'll need enough to last until someone walks to the nearest village and returns with help.

helping to concentrate its wildlife, so sightings are nearly assured (particularly if you call ahead, so the ranger can find one). The best time is April to August, when fruit is on the trees.

Access is gained by entering a foul river next to a sewage treatment facility, with a huge pipe pumping wastewater directly into it. You then follow this upstream in a canoe for half an hour until you reach Camp Kakap, the park's lodge, located on an otherwise attractive bend. Do not attempt this at night, even if asked to do so: the combination of an overloaded canoe with gunwales inches from the waterline, large logs hurtling downstream and no flotation devices, is a recipe for disaster. The lodge is rundown and basic, with bare rooms and a communal squat toilet. The trails need maintenance too. The picture is completed by the local gas exploration crews cutting through the forest in their grey jumpsuits.

To get here, take a bus from Samarinda to Sangatta (30,000Rp, three hours) and a taxi to Kantordesa Kabo Jaya (Kabo) where one of the rangers, **Udin** (☎081 3464 17675) or **Mr Supliani** (☎081 3463 48803), will meet you. Be sure to call ahead so they can organise your permit. The boat ride is 300,000Rp return. Park permits are 15,000Rp. Half-day treks cost 100,000Rp, full-day treks 200,000Rp.

Wehea Forest

Compared to Kutai, Wehea is an extraordinary breath of fresh air. This is the rainforest as you imagined it to be, in all its primordial glory. From atop its lone watchtower, you look over misty mountains that take you back to another Earth. The forest is home to many of Borneo's most interesting species, including the clouded leopard, sun bear, Storm's stork, grizzled langur, Bornean gibbon and orangutan. To date, 82 mammal species have been documented, of which 22 are vulnerable or endangered. Having said that, this is raw rainforest with few trails, making wildlife spotting difficult, and a good local guide essential.

Surprisingly, there is an excellent wooden lodge built by WWF, beautifully situated on a rushing river bend, with a generator, space for 20 people in private rooms, and a waterfall. The sounds of the forest and the river are priceless here. It takes some doing to arrange a stay, however, as the lodge is not permanently staffed. On the other hand, that's why the forest exists in such a pristine state and why it is such a great opportunity to visit now, as an incongruous helicopter pad attests: the US embassy flies in VIPs from Jakarta.

Wehea is not a national park, but a 38,000-hectare forest protected by *adat* (traditional law), a different conservation model spearheaded by Ledjie Taq, leader of the Wehea Dayak. The forest is patrolled by *petkuq mehuey* (forest guardians), a cadre of 35 to 40 rangers who keep it free from illegal activities such as poaching and logging. Their cause is assisted by Integrated Conservation (www.integratedconservation.org), a small and highly dedicated NGO run by Brent Loken and Sheryl Gruber, who have placed 75 photo traps on various wildlife trails to document the forest's biodiversity. See the results on the website.

So how do you visit? There are two ways. At time of research Integrated Conservation was nearing completion of a new conservation centre in the small village of Nehas Liah Bing, which will serve as the gateway to the forest. It is the first new longhouse to be built in many years, with modern facilities such as solar power and internet access, and three guest rooms. The centre will provide information on the forest, register visitors and arrange visits, including transport, food, lodging and guides drawn from the *petkuq mehuey*. Prices are still being established, but advance enquires may be made by email (info@integratedconservation.org).

Getting to Nehas Liah Bing is no small feat, however. First you must get to Muara Wahau, either by driving up from Sangatta by 4WD, or taking the bus (150,000Rp, three times daily). Either way it is six or seven hours on a notoriously bad road, one of the worst in Kalimantan. However, this *Top Gear* adventure has its rewards, at least in a 4WD, and the last two hours are very scenic. In Muara Wahau you can overnight in basic **Hotel Aldi** (☎0819 9915 7970; Muara Wahau; r 50,000rP-150,000Rp), which offers clean rooms with en suite *mandi*. To get to Nehas Liah Bing, take the main road from here to Berau, but keep straight when it curves to the right. Turn right on a small dirt road exactly 2km later, just past a post office (*kantor pos*). Continue on for 200m and follow the road as it curves to the left. After another 300m you'll see the Wehea Conservation Center (also referred to locally as the 'kantor

PM') on your left. At least one day's advance notice of your arrival is key to avoid delays. Centre staff can also arrange a day trip to two interesting limestone caves at Kombeng and Gua Maria (250,000Rp-400,000Rp).

Once your visit is arranged, you must still get to the forest. This requires a 2½-hour drive from Nehas Liah Bing down remote logging roads, which may be impassable during the rainy season (during our research trip a flash flood came in the car doors). This last leg creates a welcome sense of separation from the world, heightening your anticipation. You are really heading into the wild.

The other way to access Wehea Forest is to purchase a package tour from De'Gigant Tours (p593), the only regular provider of this itinerary. A four-day all-inclusive trip for two or three people, including round-trip transport from Balikpapan, is 6,372,000Rp. Compare rates, access and expertise with the above alternative. De'Gigant frequently bundles Wehea with a trip to the Derawan Archipelago, combining jungle and reef in one itinerary. This involves coming down to Wehea from Berau, avoiding the drive from Sangatta.

Berau

☎0554 / POP 52,000

Berau's new international airport has made this flat riverside town the first stop en route to the Derawan Archipelago. Another reason to come here is not readily apparent.

Sights

Museum Batiwakkal MUSEUM
(Gunung Tabur Kraton; admission by donation; ⏲8am-5.30pm Tue-Thu, 8am-1pm Sat & Sun) An eclectic collection of sultan-obilia.

Sleeping & Eating

Berau is saturated with overpriced concrete-box hotel rooms. There is little escape. Even worse, the rooms are often full, taken by mining workers. Best to move on if possible.

Hotel Sederhana HOTEL $$
(☎21353; Jl P Antasari 471; r incl breakfast 280,000-365,000Rp; ❄📶) The deluxe rooms here are the best in town, but nothing to write home about. Some renovations were under way at time of research.

Hotel Berau Plaza HOTEL $$
(☎23111; Jl P Antasari; r incl breakfast 297,000-440,000Rp; ❄) Rooms here are clean and have high ceilings, Western en suites, TV and air-con, but are crippled by lack of light. VIP1 rooms are best.

Hotel Kartika HOTEL $
(☎21379; Jl P Antasari; r 140,000-200,000Rp; ❄) Cheap but rough: these concrete cubes are dark and badly need paint.

De Bunda Cafe BAKERY $
(☎21305; Jl Antasari 5; dessert 5000Rp; ⏲7am-8pm) Chocolate and sponge cakes, iced coffees, fruit shakes and fresh spring rolls. Watch the morning rush hour al fresco from under an umbrella.

Sari Ponti Restaurant CHINESE $
(Jl Durian II 35; mains from 20,000Rp; ⏲8am-9pm) The local Chinese favourite: clean, well-lit, attentive staff, reliable food.

Warung Asri INDONESIAN $
(Jl A Yani; mains 15,000-20,000Rp; ⏲7am-9pm) Overlooking the riverfront, this friendly nook does classic warung fare well. Good choice for lunch.

Entertainment

BP Club CLUB
(Jl Isa; ⏲7pm-2am) The most popular night-club in the city.

Information

Arabic Net (Jl Niaga I; per hr 5000Rp; ⏲6am-5pm) Private cubicles.

BNI Bank (Jl Maulana) Foreign exchange.

THM Travel (☎21238; Jl Niaga II) English-speaking staff help with flights and transport in the Derawan Archipelago.

Getting There & Away

See Getting There & Around in the Derawan Archipelago section for information on reaching Berau from there.

Air

Batavia Air (☎26777; Hotel Derawan Indah, Jl Panglima Batur 396)

Kalstar (☎21007; Jl Maulana 45)

Sriwijaya Air (☎202 8777; Jl Pemuda 50)

Trigana (☎202 7885; Jl Tendean 572)

Bus & Kijang

The **bus terminal** (Jln H Isa) is just south of the market on *angkot* routes. Buses to Tanjung Batu (50,000Rp, two hours) drop you off at the dock,

Berau

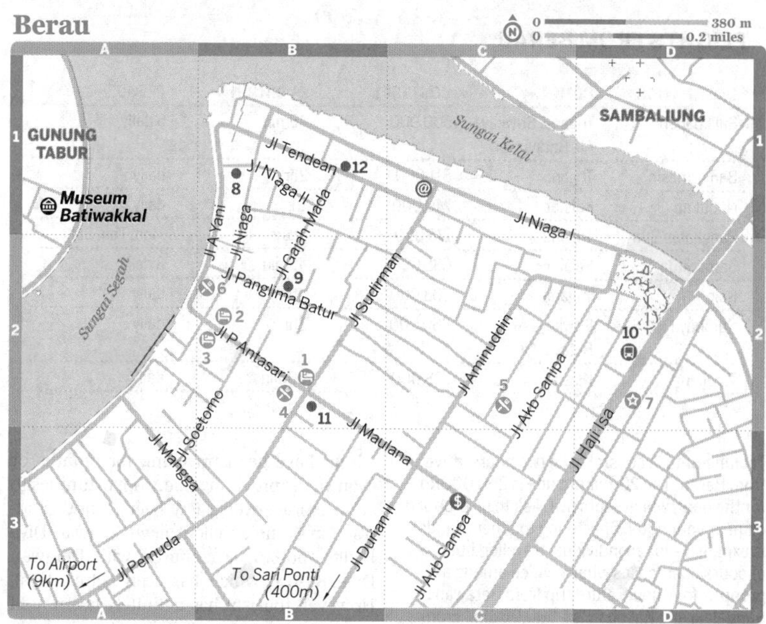

from where you pick up a speedboat to Derawan Island.

Kijang gather across from the terminal and demand a minimum of four passengers. Buy multiple seats to leave faster. Destinations include Tanjung Batu (60,000Rp, two hours), Tanjung Selor (70,000Rp, 2½ hours) and Samarinda (250,000Rp, 14 to 18 hours).

Getting Around

Taxis to the airport (9km) cost 50,000Rp. *Angkot* cost 3000Rp. River crossings by canoe cost 3000Rp; charters cost 50,000Rp per hour.

Derawan Archipelago

Occupying a large area of ocean east of Berau, the Derawan Archipelago consists of 31 named islands, of which the most significant to travellers are Derawan, Maratua, Sangalaki, Kakaban, Nabucco and Nunukan. This archipelago is unique in Kalimantan. It offers the chance to explore some classic tropical isles, including a huge atoll, and enjoy some of the best scuba diving there is. It's also very hard to get around (although it can be done), so it pays to think through your itinerary very carefully and give yourself plenty of time. Seas are rough in January and February, limiting diving.

Berau

Top Sights

Museum Batiwakkal ... A1

Sleeping

1 Hotel Berau Plaza ... B2
2 Hotel Kartika ... B2
3 Hotel Sederhana ... B2

Eating

4 De Bunda Cafe ... B2
5 Sari Ponti Restaurant ... C2
6 Warung Asri ... B2

Entertainment

7 BP Club ... D2

Information

8 THM Travel ... B1

Transport

9 Batavia Air ... B2
10 Bus Terminal ... D2
11 Kalstar ... B2
12 Trigana ... B1

Getting There & Around

There is no regularly scheduled public transport in the Derawan Archipelago. Chartered speedboats for Pulau Derawan leave from the dock at

FLIGHTS FROM BERAU

DESTINATION	COMPANY	COST (RP)	DURATION	FREQUENCY
Balikpapan	Trigana, Sriwijaya Air, Batavia Air	500,000	45min	5 daily
Banjarmasin	Trigana	811,000	2hr	daily
Nunukan	Kalstar	740,000	1hr	daily
Pangkalan Bun	Trigana	175,000	5½hr	Mon, Thu, Sat
Samarinda	Kalstar	635,000	45min	3 daily
Solo	Trigana	203,000	4hr	daily
Surabaya	Sriwijaya Air, Batavia Air	860,000	3hr	daily
Tarakan	Kalstar	378,000	30min	daily

Tanjung Batu, a coastal town two hours' drive from Berau. The 20-minute ride is 250,000Rp for the boat, which seats five. Ask to be dropped off near your hotel. Chartering to other islands is expensive for an individual traveller, but of course decreases when divided among a group. A four-hour return trip from Derawan to Sangalaki and Kakaban is 1,500,000Rp. From Tanjung Batu to Nabucco costs 3,250,000Rp return. Enquire about specifics at the speedboat dock, and take your driver's mobile phone number for future reference.

Nabucco Island Resort operates a fast shuttle from the centre of Berau to Nabucco (1,450,000Rp return, three hours), departing on Wednesdays and Saturdays, returning Tuesdays and Fridays. Depending on the tide, this boat can also drop off passengers at Derawan, midway to the mainland. This is the quickest way to get to the outer islands. Call for reservations.

The cheapest, and slowest, way to get between islands is by *tok-tok*, a local open fishing boat with a noisy little engine. You can arrange this in any village, just be aware of the time involved, as you may be bobbing around in the sun for hours (eg Berau to Maratua is eight hours). Having said that, it is a fun way to get between nearby islands, like Nabucco and Maratua (50,000Rp).

At time of research an airport was under construction on Maratua, projected to open in 2014. This will make the outer islands much more accessible. So go now.

PULAU DERAWAN

The closest and best known of the islands, Derawan is also overbuilt and increasingly dirty. With a sandy main street lined with budget restaurants and hotels, it has long been a backpacker magnet, and this is part of its attraction. There are fascinating, amiable people wandering the streets, many of whom have been travelling for months or even years, providing many opportunities to swap stories over a few beers. Another attraction is the excellent new Derawan Dive Lodge (not to be confused with Derawan Dive Resort, which has seen better days). However, tourism has definitely taken hold and the local reef is degraded; if you're looking for more idyllic surroundings, consider Maratua. Beware of stingrays when walking at low tide.

Activities

Derawan Dive Lodge DIVING

(☎0878 4646 2413; www.derawandivelodge.com; ❄) The best dive centre on the island is clearly this brand-new operation, with two fast dive boats reaching Maratua, Sangalaki and Kakaban. A full day diving Derawan (up to three dives) is US$115; a dive trip to Maratua, Kakaban and Sangalaki is US$165. Lodging packages available.

Sleeping & Eating

TOP CHOICE **Derawan Dive Lodge** HOTEL $$$

(☎0878 4646 2413; www.derawandivelodge.com; s/d incl breakfast US$80/95) This is the only upscale place to stay on Pulau Derawan, and very well done. Located on the edge of town, it has its own private beach and 10 comfortable, individually designed rooms, with a cosy outdoor cafe. If you want to combine a dive holiday with some island life, this is your top choice in the archipelago. Full board US$20, airport transfer US$50.

TOP CHOICE **Pelangi Guesthouse** LOSMEN $$

(☎0813 4780 7078; r 200,000-300,000Rp; ❄) Derawan has many losmen built out on docks, but this is the best one, offering colourful en suite rooms with private verandas over the sea, a basic cafe/restaurant, and sea turtles for free.

Lestari I LOSMEN $
(☎0813 4722 9636; Pulau Derawan; r 75,000-150,000Rp; ❄) Imagine a longhouse on a pier and you have this pleasant losmen, with colourful verandas, some with air-con. The owner will take you to neighbouring islands for 700,000Rp.

April's Restaurant INDONESIAN $
(☎0813 5058 2483; mains 25,000Rp; ⏰7am-8pm) Wedged between Danakan and Lestari 1, guacamole-green April's dishes up reliable Indonesian favourites.

If Pelangi is full, there are three similar waterfront losmen nearby: **Sari** (☎0813 4653 8448; r incl breakfast with fan/air-con 175,000/225,000Rp) has sizeable adjoining rooms and nice end units; **Dira** (☎0813 4795 5950; r with fan/air-con 150,000/200,000Rp) has a restaurant overlooking the water; **Danakan** (☎086 8121 6143; r with fan/air-con 150,000/250,000Rp; ❄) has large baths but suffers from a rough entrance.

PULAU MARATUA

Maratua is an enormous U-shaped atoll almost completely untouched by tourism. There are two fishing villages at opposite ends with a pleasant surprise in between: a nicely paved path through the jungle some 15km in length. The tidy village of **Bohesilian**, directly across from Nabucco Island, is the best base, with tightly packed cottages on the edge of the jungle, pleasant sea views, a little market, cheerful residents and several homestays. **Senterbung**, near the pier, offers a front room with double bed for 200,000Rp, including three meals, but look at a few and decide. **Bohebekut**, the village at the other end of the trail, is poorer and the beach is dirty.

For backpackers with time on their hands, Maratua is a slice of heaven. Hire a scooter for a day (150,000Rp) and explore to your heart's content, passing over bridges between islets, heading down long jetties and swimming in the lagoon. Like Kakaban, there is a stingless freshwater jellyfish pond, although it's difficult to reach. The island's striking dorsal ridge is also begging for exploration. Add a special someone and a visit here could easily stretch into days...

NABUCCO & NUNUKAN ISLAND RESORTS

These two small islets in the mouth of the Maratua atoll are owned by Extra Divers, a German dive resort operator with eight properties worldwide. As such, the upscale clientele is about 80% German and Austrian, although the managers speak English. Both islands are run by the same professional couple, Rainer and Evelyne, each well schooled in hospitality. Some visitors split their time between islands: an excellent idea.

Sleeping

TOP CHOICE **Nunukan Island Resort** RESORT $$$
(☎0542 594 655; www.nunukanislandresort.com; r per person incl full board s/d €127/190) This island is surprisingly different from its sister. The resort is built on the blackened remains of a reef that resembles a razor-sharp lava field. All common areas are up on stilts, with boardwalks between them, a design that is uniquely attractive. The private beachfront bungalows are very luxurious, with four-poster platform beds and inventive showers with one-way windows on the sea. The reclining sofa on the large porch will hold you for hours, particularly when the stars are out. There is also a small spa with a dipping pool perfectly situated at the base of a long walkway leading to another islet, yet to be developed. A dive is €32.

TOP CHOICE **Nabucco Island Resort** RESORT $$$
(☎0542 593 635; www.nabuccoislandresort.com; r per person incl full board s/d €127/190; ❄)

DERAWAN DIVING HIGHLIGHTS

Pulau Sangalaki Famous for its manta rays, which are present throughout the year. Sea turtles also abound.

Pulau Kakaban Big pelagic fish and a cave dive offshore; a rare lake full of non-stinging jellyfish inland.

Pulau Maratua Known for 'the channel' frequented by big pelagic fish, eagle rays and huge schools of barracuda. Occasional thresher sharks.

Pulau Derawan Small creatures draw photographers: ghostpipe fish, frogfish, harlequin shrimp, jawfish, blue-ring octopus.

When you get off the dock at Nabucco, the sign says 'Welcome to Paradise' and this charming little island really does fit the bill. Located in the Maratua lagoon, it has interesting views in all directions and well-kept parklike grounds with swaying palms, boardwalks and white beaches, all of which can be circumnavigated in 10 minutes. The large, varnished duplex bungalows come with mosquito nets and each one faces the sea, with shared porches. The Asian fusion food is outstanding. Almost everyone is here for the diving, but a snorkeller would fit right in. Dives are €41 each, and courses are available.

PULAU KAKABAN & PULAU SANGALAKI

These two undeveloped islands beyond Maratua are begging for exploration. Pulau Sangalaki is pretty and unspoiled, all forest and deserted beaches, with a sea-turtle nursery (www.turtle-foundation.org) open to visitors. Pulau Kakaban is known for its freshwater lake full of non-stinging jellyfish. Travellers speak highly of the eerie experience of swimming among them.

NORTH KALIMANTAN

☎0551

North Kalimantan is a brand-new province carved out of the top of East Kalimantan. It includes the island of Nunukan (not to be confused with the one in the Derawan Archipelago), Sembakung, Bulungan, Tanjung Selor, Tarakan, Krayan, Kayan Mentarang and the Apokayan. This area includes some of the most pristine forests on Borneo, making it one of the last frontiers for hardcore jungle trekking. Only a handful of people have crossed the vast jungle of Kayan Mentarang.

The most common reason for travellers to pass through North Kalimantan is on their way to or from Malaysian Borneo. At time of research the direct ferry from Tawau (Sabah) to Tarakan wasn't operating, but there is a speedboat service from Tawau to Tarakan (140,000Rp, four hours) via Nunukan (two hours) where you switch boats. The boat leaves Tawau at noon, but show up an hour early to clear immigration and ensure a seat. Save five ringgits for the terminal fee. The quicker but more expensive route is the daily MASwings flight from Tawau to Tarakan (550,000Rp-800,000Rp).

To get from Tarakan to Berau/Derawan Archipelago, take an early morning boat to Tanjung Selor (80,000Rp) and then a car from the harbour (55,000Rp to 75,000Rp). For air tickets see **Angkasa Express** (☎30288; fax 24848; Jln Yos Sudarso, Hotel Tarakan Plaza) or **Derawan Travel** (☎35599; fax 35799; Jln Mulawarman 21, Hotel Paradise). The **immigration office** (☎21242; Jln Sumatra) has information on visas. If you need to stay over, **Hotel Bungamuda** (☎21349; Jl Yos Sudarso 7, Tarakan; r 55,000-132,000Rp; ❄📶) is a good budget option, while **Swiss-Belhotel Tarakan** (☎21133; www.swiss-belhotel.com; Jln Mulawarman 15; r incl breakfast 440,000-594,000Rp; ❄) is an upscale bargain.

WEST KALIMANTAN

Pontianak

☎0561 / POP 550,000

Standing astride the equator, Pontianak is a gateway to all points of the compass: Putussibau (east), Singkawang (north), Sukadana (south) and Natuna (west). Commerce keeps things buzzing, but the city is otherwise a grey jumble, brightened only by some inexpensive luxury hotels and lukewarm sights.

Sights

Taman Alun Kapuas PARK
(Jl Rahadi Usman) This riverside park swells with families, hawkers and food stalls at night.

Istana Kadriyah MUSEUM
(admission by donation; ⌚8.30am-4pm) If you're up for an outing that will show you a bit of the town, the leaking palace of Pontianak's first sultan, now a half-hearted museum, lies on the east bank of Sungai Kapuas next to his mosque, **Mesjid Abdurrahman**. Get there by canoe taxi (2500Rp) from the foot of Jl Mahakam.

Vihara Bodhisatva Karaniya Metta TEMPLE
(Jl Sultan Muhammad) KalBar's oldest Chinese temple (1679) is a sensory feast.

Museum Provinsi Kalimantan Barat MUSEUM
(West Kalimantan Provincial Museum; Jl A Yani; admission 1000Rp; ⌚8am-2.30pm Tue-Thu, 8-11am & 1-2.30pm Fri, 8am-2pm Sat-Sun, closed Mon) A nice succinct overview of local culture, with English placards, including a longhouse,

WORTH A TRIP

NATUNA ARCHIPELAGO

If you're up for some real off-the-beaten-track exploration, you'd be hard-pressed to find a better opportunity than this. Located northwest of Kalimantan, the Natuna Archipelago contains 272 islands, of which Pulau Natuna is the largest. They include some spectacular landscapes of towering volcanic domes, white sandy beaches and colourful coral reefs. **Orion Expeditions** (www.orionexpeditions.com), a high-end specialty cruise line, has visited the islands several times in recent years: a very good sign. The archipelago is not part of West Kalimantan but in the newly formed Riau Islands province, which includes the Anambas Archipelago and Batam.

Trigana has recently begun air service from Pontianak to Pulau Natuna. Flights leave twice weekly (754,000Rp). Start with a room in Natuna's **Central Hotel** (0819 9120 1133; r 200,000-350,000Rp) where owner Yuli speaks English. Simple fishing boats can be hired to move between islands. The rest is up to you.

shop and restaurant (mains 15,000Rp to 35,000Rp). Take a red or pink *opelet* (intracity minibus) south along Jl Yani.

Patung Khatulistiwa MONUMENT
(Equator Monument; Jl Khatulistiwa; 8.30am-4.30pm, closed Mon) If you desire to stand astride the equator, here's your formal chance. You may even get a certificate signed by the governor. Cross the river by ferry or bus and take Jl Khatulistiwa 1.6km northwest. The monument is roadside.

Tours

Times Tours & Travel TRAVEL AGENCY
(770 259; Jl Komyos Sudarso 6) Organises tours to Kapuas Hulu and beyond. Owner Iwan speaks excellent English and is super-responsive and very efficient. Call before visiting.

Borneo Access Adventurer TRAVEL AGENCY
(081 2576 8066; www.borneoaccessadventurer.com; Jl Tanjung Harapan Gang HD Usman 46) West Borneo Tour Guide Association chairman Alex Afdhal knows the landscape and means well. Clarify your tour expectations with him.

Sleeping

TOP CHOICE **Hotel Santika** HOTEL $$
(733 777; www.santika.com; Jl Diponegoro 46; r incl breakfast 360,000Rp;) If you can wangle one of its steep discounts (around 40% – included in price quoted here), this contemporary business-leisure hotel is the best value in Kalimantan. The spacious rooms are very comfy, staff is as friendly as can be, the breakfast buffet excellent, and the public spaces top-notch, including a winning spa. The nearby rooftop terrace, with pool and running water, offers an attractive setting for relatively inexpensive meals (if it's not raining). Tight budget? Splurge.

TOP CHOICE **Aston Pontianak** HOTEL $$
(761 118; Jl Gajah Mada 21; r incl breakfast 518,000-658,000Rp) This island of luxury has all the amenities one needs to recover from a jungle trek, although the prices are higher than the competition's (ask for discounts). In the rooms, wood, leather and glass combine to form a sophisticated decor; the executive rooms are particularly superb. Beyond lies a big open lobby with glass elevator, and a swanky bar. The breakfast buffet with Western menu is enough to last you through the day. And the enormous RiverX entertainment complex will definitely perk you up at night.

Hosanna Inn HOTEL $
(735 052; www.hosannainn.com; Jl Pahlawan 224/2; s/d incl breakfast 98,000/138,000Rp;) The city has no standout budget rooms, but the best are here, particularly room 205, which has windows and access to a public balcony. Room 307 is similar but has no balcony. The spiral staircase will test your tolerance for Bintang (an Indonesian beer).

Kartika Hotel HOTEL $$
(734 401; fax 738 457; Jl Rahadi Usman 2; r incl breakfast 288,000-432,000Rp;) The quiet riverside location sets this hotel apart. The standard doubles are the best, particularly those on the river, as the more expensive the room, the worse value they are. The Panorama Restaurant is a plus; the fish farm in front is a question mark.

Pontianak

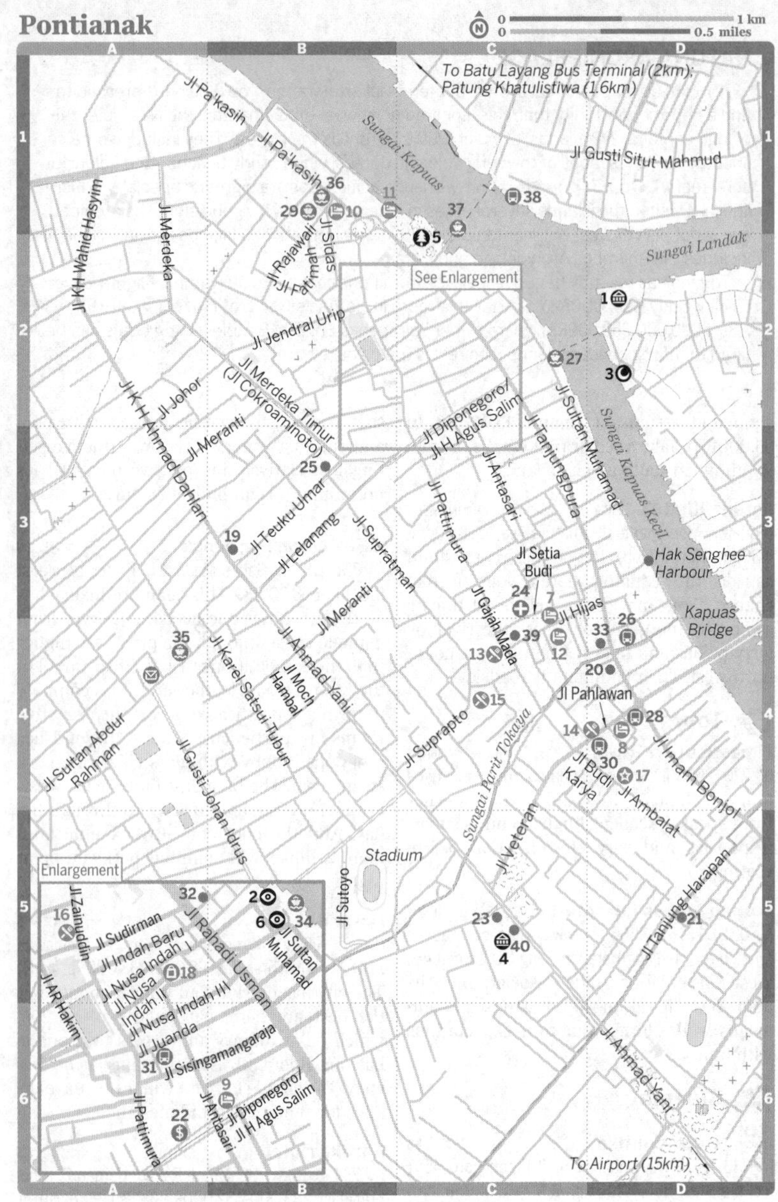

Mess Hijas HOTEL $

(☎081 256 960 03; Jl Hijas 106; s & d 75,000-150,000Rp; ❄) Hidden behind a scooter dealer, this hotel surprises with attractive wooden design elements (in some rooms), hot water and air-con. Find one with a window.

Hotel Surya HOTEL $

(☎734 337; Jl Sidas 11A; r incl breakfast 150,000Rp; ❄@) Clean, basic concrete boxes with air-con and private bathroom (squat toilet and *mandi*).

Pontianak

Sights
1 Istana Kadriyah D2
2 Kapuas Indah Building B5
3 Mesjid Abdurrahman D2
4 Museum Provinsi Kalimantan Barat C5
5 Taman Alun Kapuas C2
6 Vihara Bodhisatva Karaniya Metta B5

Sleeping
7 Aston Pontianak C3
8 Hosanna Inn D4
9 Hotel Santika B6
10 Hotel Surya B1
11 Kartika Hotel B1
12 Mess Hijas C4

Eating
13 Café Corner C4
14 General Chef D4
Panorama Restaurant ..... (see 11)
15 Restoran Hawaii C4
16 Somay Bandung A5

Entertainment
17 Café Tisya D4

Shopping
18 Borneo Art Shop A5

Information
19 Antya Tour B3
20 Aria Tour D4
21 Borneo Access Adventurer D5
22 Haji Tunrung Star A6
23 Immigration Office C5
24 Klinik Kharitas Bhakti C3

Transport
25 Batavia Air B3
26 Bintang Jaya D4
27 Canoe Taxis to Istana Kadriyah C2
28 Damri D4
29 Dharma Lautan Utama B1
30 Executive Buses to Kuching D4
31 Executive Buses to Kuching A6
32 Garuda A5
33 Kalstar D4
34 Longboats to Sukadana B5
35 Pelni A4
36 Prima Vista B1
37 River Ferries to Siantan C1
38 Siantan Bus & Ferry Terminal C1
39 Sriwijaya C4
40 Trigana C5

Eating

Warungs and stalls abound along Jl Diponegoro/H Agus Salim, Jl Pattimura, Jl Hijas and Jl Setia Budi. At night, new stalls sprout, particularly along Jl Gajah Mada.

TOP CHOICE **General Chef** CHINESE $
(cnr Jl Gajah Mada & Jl Pahlawan; mains from 20,000Rp; 10am-10pm) Conveniently located at the intersection of Gajah Mada and Pahlawan, this newcomer has raised the bar on local cuisine. Service is quick and efficient, the food creative and sophisticated, and the overall presentation excellent. Ever tried jellyfish?

TOP CHOICE **Somay Bandung** INDONESIAN $
(Jl Zainuddin 15; mains 9000-16,000Rp; lunch & dinner) Mobbed at lunch for the national version of *siomay* (steamed dough, potatoes, tofu, and cabbage drowned in peanut sauce), this restaurant has a great dose of local atmosphere, with benches arrayed beneath a large awning.

Café Corner CAFE $
(Jl Gajah Mada; mains 20,000Rp; 7am-1am) This popular cafe on the corner of a city block is an excellent place to hang out, with coffee flowing from morning to night and, after jungle adventures, a refreshing dose of beer and European football. It's 150m north of Jl Suprapto intersection.

Restoran Hawaii CHINESE $
(Jl Suprapto 16; mains 20,000-60,000Rp; 9.30am-9.30pm) Local Chinese-cuisine legend in a large banquet hall.

Panorama Restaurant SEAFOOD $
(Jl Rahadi Usman; mains from 25,000Rp; 7am-11pm) Unique for its riverfront setting, this chicken and seafood spot in the Kartika Hotel is popular with local families.

Entertainment

TOP CHOICE **Café Tisya** LIVE MUSIC
(Jl Budi Karya; 7pm-2am) A fun and gentle nightspot occupying the open corner of a

city block, this is where you go to have a few Bintangs, enjoy some live music and meet the locals, from university students to an entire ship's crew.

Shopping

For general souvenirs, visit the crafts shops lining Jl Pattimura.

TOP CHOICE **Borneo Art Shop** ANTIQUES
(☎0813 5227 7796; Jl Nusa Indah I; ⏰9am-5pm) The name is misleading: come here to enter the world of exotic curios from around Borneo.

Information

Antya Tour (☎733 688; Jl Teuku Umar 62) Kijang and car-rental specialist.

Aria Tour (☎577 868; Jl Imam Bonjol, near Hotel Garuda) Good for airline tickets.

Haji Tunrung Star (Jl Diponegoro 155) Foreign-exchange broker.

Immigration Office (☎765 576)

Klinik Kharitas Bhakti (☎734 373; Jl Siam 153; ⏰7.30am-9pm) Medical centre.

Main post office (Jl Sultan Abdur Rahman 49; ⏰7.30am-9.30pm Mon-Sat, 8am-2pm Sun) Poste restante.

Getting There & Away

Air

Batavia Air (☎734 488; Jl Cokroaminoto 278A)

Garuda (☎734 986; Jl Rahadi Usman No 8A)

IAT (Indonesia Air Transport; ☎ext 212 Jakarta 021 8087 0668; airport)

Kalstar (☎739 090; Jl Tanjungpura 429)

Lion Air (☎706 661 11; airport)

MASwings (☎603 7843 3000 Malaysia; airport)

Sriwijaya Air (☎768 777; Jl Gajah Mada 70)

Trigana (☎749 090; Megamall, Jl Ahmad Yani)

Boat

Boats to Java leave from the main harbour on Jl Pak Kasih, north of the Kartika Hotel. Ferry companies:

Dharma Lautan Utama (☎765 021; Jl Pak Kasih 42F)

Pelni (☎748 124; www.pelni.co.id; Jl Sultan Abdur Rahman 12)

Prima Vista (☎761 145; Jl Pak Kasih 90B)

The jetboat to Ketapang leaves from Hak Senghee Harbour on Jl Barito; air-con class is worth the extra fare. If no one is present, call **Bahari Express** (☎760 820) or **Poly Express** (☎741 536).

Longboats (☎Dedek for reservations 9.30am boat 0856 5440 9299, Jony for reservations 8.30am boat 0813 4598 2328, Surya for reservations 9.30am boat 0813 5213 4440) to Sukadana leave from behind the **Kapuas Indah Building** at 8.30am and 9.30am.

There are no scheduled passenger boats upriver to Putussibau, but travel agents may be able to find a speedboat going to Sanggau. If time is not an issue, try finding passage by *bandung*, a combination freighter and general store that can take several days to a month for the 800km journey. Price negotiable.

Bus

It is wise to consult a travel agent regarding the complex landscape of bus and Kijang options.

WORTH A TRIP

VILLA BUKIT MAS, SINGKAWANG

The **Villa Bukit Mas** (☎0562 333 5666; Singkawang; s/d 560,000/600,000Rp) is a sophisticated hotel and restaurant complex that sits on top of a hill overlooking the city of Singkawang, three hours north of Pontianak. With excellent rooms, fine dining, swimming and panoramic views, this establishment reaches surprising heights of quality as well as altitude. The rooms at the very top are the best in the city, with wooden floors, private porches and a refined seclusion. The restaurant has grand open-air seating and specialises in *shabu shabu* (59,000Rp for four), a Japanese fondue. Reserve ahead for weekends.

Meanwhile, the largely Chinese city below feels at times like Shanghai circa 1930. There are some classic shophouses, a vibrant street market (Jl Diponegoro), rickshaws and Chinese temples. A new fairy-tale mosque – Mesjid Raya –has arisen, too, dressed in green. The people hardly ever see tourists, so Western visitors will encounter many new friends, none of whom speak any English at all. This is travel at its most authentic, with the past in the valley below and the future growing atop the surrounding hills. Buses leave for Singkawang daily from Pontianak (35,000Rp). A **taxi** (☎0821 4876 9999) direct from Pontianak Airport is 120,000Rp.

TRANSPORT FROM PONTIANAK

Air

DESTINATION	COMPANY	COST (RP)	DURATION	FREQUENCY
Jakarta	Sriwijaya Air, Garuda, Lion Air, Batavia Air	650,000	1½hr	daily
Ketapang	Kalstar, IAT	365,000-509,000		
Kuching	MASwings	765,000	45min	daily
Kuching	Batavia Air	765,000-980,000	45min	Tue, Thu, Sun
Natuna	Trigana	754,000	1½hr	Wed, Fri
Pangkalan Bun	Kalstar	450,000-720,000	1½hr	daily
Putussibau	Kalstar	814,000	1hr	daily
Singapore	Batavia Air	1,500,000	1½hr	Mon, Fri
Sintang	Kalstar, IAT	476,000-700,000	45min	3 weekly
Yogyakarta	Batavia Air	1,100,000	1½hr	daily

Boat

DESTINATION	COMPANY	COST (RP)	DURATION (HR)	FREQUENCY
Jakarta	Pelni, Prima Vista	170,000	36	weekly
Ketapang (jetboat)	Bahari Express, Poly Express	170,000	8	daily
Natuna	Pelni	140,000	28	weekly
Semarang	Pelni, Prima Vista, Dharma Lautan	216,000	40	weekly
Sukadana (longboat)		175,000	4	daily 8am/9am
Surabaya	Pelni	259,000	44	weekly

Bus

DESTINATION	COST (RP)	DURATION (HR)	FREQUENCY
Brunei	600,000	25	daily 7am, 9pm
Entikong	60,000	9	daily
Kuching	170,000-240,000	9	daily 7am, 9pm
Puttussibau	200,000-300,000	16-18	daily
Sambas	45,000	5	daily
Sanggau	53,000	6	daily
Singkawang	35,000	3	daily

For Singkawang, Sambas, Sanggau and the Entikong border crossing use the Batu Layang bus terminal north of town. For air-con express buses to Kuching see **Bintang Jaya** (☎659 7402; Jl Tanjungpura 310A) and the companies on Jl Sisingamangaraja. **Damri** (☎744 859; Jl Pahlawan 226/3) also serves Brunei. Buses to Putussibau via Sintang leave from the Kapuas Indah Building.

Car

Travel agencies can arrange a car with driver for 450,000Rp per day.

Getting Around

Airport taxis cost 90,000Rp to town (15km). *Opelet* (2500Rp) routes converge around Jl Sisingamangaraja. Becaks (bicycle rickshaws) are available, but a dying breed. Taxis are unmetered and scarce. Some hotels have Kijangs standing by; fares for these 'hotel taxis' start at 40,000Rp.

Sukadana

☎0534 / POP 15,000

After Pontianak, Sukadana is a most welcome surprise, all the more so because few people seem to know about it. Half the fun is just getting there, via a wonderful four-hour river trip by longboat from Pontianak. After travelling down the Kapuas, all bets are off as to what the route actually is, as no published map reflects it. You enter a tributary which eventually broadens into a lake, **Warah Kubu**, full of attractive jungle-covered hills and various islands. Along the way you stop for lunch at a scenic riverside warung serving world-class fried chicken. Then you're back in the region known as **Teluk Air**, which contains a vast and largely uninhabited mangrove swamp. Finally you reach a broad bay on the South China Sea and skirt the coastline, passing **Batu Daya**, where a vertical wall of rock soars in the distance. Sukadana is hidden in a fold of this coastline. As you round a corner, its major landmark, the Makhota Kayong, appears suddenly, making you wonder how a huge hotel built on pilings over the water can exist this far from anywhere. You then enter a horseshoe-shaped bay with an attractive beach surrounded by rolling hills of green jungle. Add nearby Gunung Palung National Park and some offshore islands to explore, and you have the makings for an excellent getaway. The new BNI ATM adds the final essential element (accessible 8am to 3pm Monday to Friday, but knock and, reportedly, the 24-hour guard will let you in any time).

Sights

TOP CHOICE **Pulau Datok Beach** BEACH

This is a well-kept town beach that feels far more exotic, as it is encircled by jungle hills and looks out on some alluring islands. There are two basic restaurants and a cart that sells fresh sugar cane (10am to 5pm Saturday and Sunday). More private beaches lie further along the coast; ask locally.

Juanta Island ISLAND

There are several islands near Sukadana to explore, some with attractive beaches, of which Juanta is the most popular. A round trip costs around 350,000Rp for a slow boat, 600,000Rp for a speedboat; enquire at Sukadana Harbour.

Sleeping & Eating

Sukadana has one very interesting hotel and several budget digs of the concrete-box variety. For meals, the Mahkota and Anugrah

GUNUNG PALUNG: A PARK THAT'S HARD TO LOVE

With a large population of resident orangutans and diverse other wildlife, Gunung Palung National Park has a lot of potential that is sadly being squandered by poor management and rampant illegal logging (you may even hear chainsaws). The three tour companies that once provided entry have been whittled down to one, **Nasalis Tour and Travel** (☎0534 772 2701; http://gunungpalung.net; Jl Gajah Mada 24, Ketapang), which now controls the park for its own economic benefit, including some expensive tour packages that require at least one overnight stay. The company is a for-profit enterprise run by park administrators; outside guides are charged the tourist rate. The prices of these packages further include a transfer from Ketapang. Travellers who enter from Sukadana, which is much closer, report that a second price list appears when this important distinction is raised. Note Sukadana is vastly preferable to Ketapang as a gateway to the park. The latter adds to transport costs, has no tourism value of its own, and cuts out the wonderful longboat trip from Pontianak.

The easiest and least expensive package is a two-day, one-night return trip to Lubuk Baji. The posted price from Ketapang – 1,910,000Rp for two people, including a guide, meals and accomodation in a basic jungle lodge – drops to 1,350,000Rp from Sukadana. The trip entails a fairly gentle two-hour hike in and out. Once they get past park management, travellers enjoy this experience. Other options include homestays, canoeing and visiting the small **Cabang Panti** (http://people.bu.edu/orang) orangutan research station. For more information visit the **park office** (Jl Tangjungpura 41, ⊙8am-4pm Mon-Fri) in Sukadana or consult the Nasalis website; there is no separate park website, as there is no separate park...

(Jl Bhayangkara) hotels have decent restaurants, but **Satay** (Jl. Sungai Mengkuang), across from the ASRI clinic, is the local favourite.

TOP CHOICE **Mahkota Kayong Hotel** HOTEL $$
(☎772 2777; www.mahkotakayonghotel.com; Jl Irama Laut; r/ste 350,000/700,000Rp; ❄) This grand anomaly has an amusing personality all its own. Built on piles over the water, in a lovely if remote situation, it dwarfs the rest of the town's accommodation, but empties when its convention market dries up, leaving the staff in a situation comedy. The rooms are a bit pricey and beaten up by the sea air – do negotiate – but you come here for an interesting story, not an ironed duvet. Or hot water.

Penginapan Family LOSMEN $
(Jl Tanjungpura Sukadana; r with fan 50,000Rp, d/tw 175,000/200,000Rp) Definitely the nicest people you could ever rent a room from, this family provides free bikes to guests, solving your local transport problem and proving the name is no exaggeration.

Getting There & Around

Longboats (☎Darwin for reservations 9.30am boat 0852 5207 6070, Indira for reservations 9.30am boat 0813 5207 0117, Untung for reservations 8.30am boat 0812 5613 3570) to Pontianak depart Sukadana harbour twice each morning (one-way 175,000Rp; ⏰departs 8.30am & 9.30am). The journey takes four hours. Sukadana can also be reached by bus or car from Ketapang, which has an airport, but the longboat trip is not to be missed. Tanjung Puting is reached by flying from Ketapang to Pangkalan Bun.

Sukadana is spread out, requiring transport. If you can't wangle a bike from Penginapan Family, the ASRI clinic can help you find a scooter. Otherwise don't be afraid to stick out your thumb.

Sungai Kapuas

Indonesia's longest river, Sungai Kapuas begins in the foothills of the Muller Range and snakes 1143km to the sea. Unlike the Mahakam, however, there is no *kapal biasa* to make your way upstream from Pontianak, nor are the views as good, as the forests of the lower Kapuas have been heavily logged and developed. Buses have replaced boats as the primary means of transport all the way to Putussibau, via unremarkable Sintang. Thus, for the traveller the primary area of interest lies upriver, in the area known as **Kapuas Hulu** (upper Kapuas), half of which is now a protected area.

PUTUSSIBAU

This lively river port town is the last stop for airlines and long-distance buses, the last ATMs and the launch point for excursions into the forests of Kapuas Hulu. There's a lively morning market along Jl Yani.

Tours

TOP CHOICE **Kompakh** ADVENTURE
(☎085 6500 2101; www.kompakh.org; Jl Kenanga Komp. Ruko Pemda 3D) This unique organisation should be your first stop upon entering Putussibau. A WWF ecotourism initiative, the folks here know everything about Kapuas Hulu and can arrange all sorts of tours, including Danau Sentarum National Park, longhouse visits, river cruising and jungle treks. This is one of two organisations in Kalimantan qualified to offer the Cross-Borneo Trek. Manager Hermas (hrmaring@yahoo.com) speaks fluent English – unique among guides in Putussibau.

Sleeping

TOP CHOICE **Mess Pemda** HOTEL $
(☎21010; Jl Merdeka 11; r 137,000-165,000Rp; ❄) Called 'Wisma Uncak Kapuas' by its sign outside, this government hostel offers surprisingly nice rooms, each with air-con, TV, Western toilet and *mandi*, arrayed around the central living area of a large single-level house. The well-lit rooms in front are best. Like it or not, there is no better value in

ASRI TO THE RESCUE

Admirable **ASRI** (Alam Sehat Lestari; ☎0813 5246 6704; www.alamsehatlestari.org; Jl Sungai Mengkuang), an NGO based in Sukadana, is applying a unique lever against the logging in Gunung Palung: those communities who opt to conserve the forest are given access to affordable health and dental care. Patients are offered long-term payment options and allowed to use compost, handicrafts and organic vegetables to barter. Interested in participating? Six-week volunteer opportunities are available for medical and dental professionals, conservationists, engineers and other skilled tradespeople.

Putussibau. From Jl A Yani, turn left on Jl Dahar and make two rights to Jl Merdeka.

Sanjaya Hotel HOTEL $$
(☎21653; Jl Yos Sudarso 129; r incl breakfast 100,000-375,000Rp; ❄) The few deluxe rooms here, which line a refreshing hallway of contemporary design, are the only somewhat upmarket accommodation in town. However, the economy rooms are unlit tombs.

Aman Sentosa Hotel HOTEL $
(☎21691; Jl Diponegoro 14; r 70,000-200,000Rp; ❄) It was once Putussibau's best hotel but now Aman Sentosa's rooms are battered from years of neglect and its car park has turned into a scrapyard.

Eating & Drinking

Pandung Meranti INDONESIAN $
(Jl Yos Sudarso; mains 12,000-15,000Rp) A big, blue, open warehouse full of polished wooden tables, this restaurant has both personality and excellent food, including barbecued chicken. Half the menu is given over to imaginative drinks, including killer milkshakes from tasty cappuccino to wacky avocado flavour. On a hot day, you could easily polish off several. In fact...

Pondok Fajar PADANG $
(Jl Yos Sudarso; mains 5000-30,000Rp; ⏰6am-11pm) This Padang place packs 'em in for its buffet.

TOP CHOICE **Cafetenda** CAFE
(milkshake 3000Rp; ⏰8am-3am) This new cafe near the bridge, located next to a ruined temple, has large, simple tables spread around a riverside park, making it a uniquely popular place to hang out, at all hours.

Information

For internet access try popular Rifki Cafe on Jl Komyos Sudarso.

Getting There & Around

Putussibau Airport is only served by **Kalstar** (☎0821 5202 2213), which has a daily flight to Pontianak at 1.15pm. Taxis from the airport (10km) cost 35,000Rp, if you can find one; *ojeks* cost 20,000Rp.

The local bus terminal is on Jl Diponegoro, near the market. Buses leave daily for Sintang at 6.30am (120,000Rp, 10 hours), from where you can connect to the Entikong border, and for Pontianak at 10am, noon and 2pm (economy/air-con 175,000/200,000Rp, 16 hours).

River boats use the pier on Sungai Kapuas east of the bridge. From Jl Merdeka, take any street south to the waterfront.

The only way to get around Putussibau is to hire a scooter (100,000Rp per day), as *angot* have gone away.

TANJUNG LOKAN & SUNGAI BUNGAN

For those coming across the Muller Range on the Cross-Borneo Trek, the first stop in Kapuas Hulu is the village of Tanjung Lokan, a small group of huts with a basic lodge (50,000Rp) located on Sungai Bungan, a tributary of the Kapuas. From here it is possible to travel all the way to Putussibau in one extraordinary seven-hour journey. But beware: while undoubtedly a welcome sight after several days walking in the jungle, this village is infamous for its fickle memory. Promises to numerous trekking companies have been made and never kept, sometimes within a half-hour period, and trekkers have been charged exorbitant rates for downriver passage. During our visit in May 2012 the local chief and his advisors agreed to price the trip to Putussibau at 1,000,000Rp per seat, up to 4,000,000Rp per fully chartered boat, with guides travelling free. This was set out in writing in the chief's logbook with all his advisors present. Travellers should reference this agreement if necessary.

WORTH A TRIP

DANAU SENTARUM NATIONAL PARK

If you have two days or more, this 132,000-hectare seasonal wetland area, which resembles the lakes area of the Mahakam, is begging for exploration. Surrounded by attractive mountains, it offers numerous islands, some intriguing villages, wildlife (including the red arowana, a trophy aquarium fish) and interesting boat journeys. Reach the park via minibus from Putussibau to **Lanjak** (85,000Rp, 3½ hours), where you can rent a boat and see the islands. Don't miss the newly renovated field station on **Pulau Tekaneng**, which has six rooms with shared baths (100,000Rp with meals), or the village of **Meliau**, at the southern end of the lake, where you can find a basic homestay in a longhouse. For more information contact Kompakh (p617).

The canoe trip downriver is one you will never forget. It begins by tackling Sungai Bungan, the most thrilling stretch of water in Kalimantan. As the river picks up pace, you pass through roaring gorges knifing through the jungle – a beautiful setting. The canoe is crewed bow and stern with amazing skill, with the stern operator using the engine and steering at the bow done with a paddle. In this way you hurtle downstream, twisting and turning to avoid the rocks in your path. At one point the canoe must be slowly lowered downstream by rope. When Sungai Bungan meets the Kapuas the rapids die off and the rest of the journey is a pleasant cruise through the jungle until Putussibau. If you make this journey in the opposite direction, it takes twice as long due to the current, and costs twice as much.

WORTH A TRIP

BOBO

About three hours walk from Tanjung Lokan is an astonishing vertical shaft of rock thrusting skyward out of the jungle for hundreds of metres. Known as Bobo, it has never been climbed, locals say. A recent *National Geographic* expedition, the first to investigate the area, discovered the remains of a 5000-year-old settlement strewn with artefacts nearby. A good circuit and investigation would probably require a day, and can be combined with the Muller trek, which passes nearby. This is raw exploration, of a kind increasingly difficult to find.

CENTRAL KALIMANTAN

Tanjung Puting National Park

Tanjung Puting offers a safe and comfortable jungle river cruise, open to anyone, that brings you up close and personal with Borneo's great ape, the orangutan. This winning combination, part *African Queen* and part *National Geographic*, has made it the most popular tourist destination in Kalimantan, with many people flying in and out on their way to Bali or Borobodur. Cruises go up Sungai Sekonyer, in one corner of the huge 4150-sq-km park, and past three orangutan feeding stations, where you come ashore and watch the 'people of the forest' emerge from hiding – an amazing moment.

Just as amazing, the park is largely the result of a single remarkable woman. Dr Biruté Galdikas is a member of Leakey's Angels, a trio of young women trained by famous naturalist Louis Leakey to study the world's great primates in the wild. For Diane Fossey it was the gorilla, for Jane Goodall the chimpanzee, and for Galdikas the orangutan. In 1971 the young primatologist arrived at Tanjung Puting by canoe and soon established Camp Leakey, where she still lives at certain times of year. Here she made such seminal discoveries as the orangutan's eight-year birth cycle, which makes the species highly vulnerable to extinction. A very personal approach to 'her' orangutans has lost her some supporters in the academic establishment, but the fact remains that the 6000 wild orangutans living in Tanjung Puting today form the single largest population in the world.

The park serves as an orangutan rehabilitation centre, where orphaned or formerly captive individuals are trained to live in the wild. Part of that process is daily hour-long feedings at jungle platforms, open to visitors. Females arrive with their clinging young to feed on a pile of bananas, which they peel with their lips. If you're lucky, they'll scatter before a large male, with his enormous cheek pads and powerful body – a most impressive sight. The highlight is spotting the current alpha male, Tom, but since males range widely, this is hit or miss. Wild orangutans can also be seen along the river, particularly at low tide, when they come to eat palm fruit, and around Camp Leakey, where they like to sit on the boardwalk. While some may appear deceptively tame, do not attempt to touch or feed them, or to get between a mother and child, as certain apes are prone to bag-snatching and occasionally biting visitors.

The other significant reason for Tanjung Puting's popularity, which should not be underestimated, is the *klotok*. The Sekonyer is navigated on your own private riverboat, a romantic form of travel that leaves you feeling like a rajah. These two-storey, 8m to 10m wooden craft come with captain, mate and cook, and serve as both home and viewing platform. During the day you sit up top on an open deck, surveying the jungle with binoculars in one hand and a drink in the other, as the boat chugs along its narrow channel. Come twilight you moor on the edge of the jungle, listening to its primordial sounds as the cook makes a fine dinner. Later you retire to your own mattress and mosquito net, with stars twinkling overhead. Believe us when we say that you could get used to this life, particularly when its price is so reasonable. And that is why you won't be alone, especially in July and August, when feeding stations get very crowded. But, apart from seeing other rajahs passing by, this is still an authentic experience, as our own research trip confirmed, when a rare clouded leopard swam right in front of the boat in broad daylight. More common sights include macaques, pot-bellied proboscis monkeys, darting kingfishers, majestic hornbills and – if you're lucky – toothy gharials, a remarkable crocodile best seen at low tide, and the reason why you should avoid swimming (a visitor was eaten at Camp Leakey a decade ago).

Tanjung Puting is best visited during the dry season (May to September). The park's 200 varieties of wild orchid bloom mainly from January to March, but the abundance of March fruit may lure orangutans away from feeding platforms. At any time, bring rain protection and insect repellent. For an even more luxurious jungle cruise, consider the *Rahai'i Pangun* (p626) in Palangka Raya.

Sights & Activities

The Sekonyer River is opposite the port of Kumai, where you meet your *klotok*. It is largely muddy due to upstream mining operations, although it eventually forks into a more natural, tea-coloured tributary that leads to Camp Leakey. The upriver journey contains several noteworthy stops (listed here in order):

Tanjung Harapan WILDLIFE

(Tanjung Harapan; ⏲feeding 3pm daily) Feeding station with small interpretation centre.

Sekonyer Village VILLAGE

A small village that arose around Tanjung Harapan but has since been relocated across the river. There's a small shop and lodging.

Pasalat FOREST

(Pasalat camp) A reforestation camp where native saplings are being reintroduced after fire damage. Popular for birding. The 800m forest boardwalk will be excellent once repairs are made; otherwise be careful.

Pondok Tanggui WILDLIFE

(Pondok Tangui; ⏲feeding 9am daily) Feeding station.

Camp Leakey WILDLIFE

(Camp Leakey; ⏲feeding 2pm daily) Feeding station. Good for birds.

You won't necessarily see everything in this order, as you may choose to see some of these on the return trip.

The ideal journey is three days and two nights, giving you ample time to see everything. If you only have one day, you should take a speedboat from Kumai. A *klotok* can reach Camp Leakey in 4½ hours, making a return trip possible in one day if you leave at 6am, but this is not recommended.

During the dry season, there is an overnight trek from Pondok Tanggui to Pasalat (1,500,000Rp all inclusive). This is a unique chance to see nocturnal wildlife and can be combined with a boat trip. Your guide can arrange this, or enquire at Flora Homestay (p622) in Sekonyer Village.

ORANGUTANS

Adult male orangutans are said to be eight times stronger than a human. Semi-solitary in nature, they undergo vicious battles to ascend to alpha status, often losing teeth and fingers in the process. Tom, the present alpha at Camp Leakey, deposed his predecessor after a long reign, exiling him to the jungle. A male's cheek pads grow with his accession to dominance and wither after he is demoted. Mothers rear their young for seven years – the longest nursery time in the animal kingdom. During this intimate period they teach them everything they need to know to thrive in the jungle, from how to climb through the canopy by brachiation (travelling from branch to branch) to the medicinal qualities of plants, which nuts are poisonous, which critters they should avoid and how to mentally map the forest. Rehabilitation of orphans involves as close an approximation to this as possible.

Tours

You have the choice of hiring a *klotok* (and guide) yourself, or having a tour operator do it for you. The former is cheaper, the latter easier.

Tour Companies

TOP CHOICE Borneo Wisata Permai Tours ADVENTURE
(081 2500 0508; www.borneowisata.com) The best tour company in the area. Diligent owner Harry Purwanto knows every *klotok*, captain and guide and can help you organise the best trip from all available choices.

Borneo Orangutan Adventure Tour ADVENTURE
(0062-852 745 600; www.orangutantravel.com) Run by the excellent Ahmad Yani, the first official guide in the area.

Klotok Hire

The cost of hiring a klotok varies. The sizes range from small (two to four passengers, 400,000Rp to 450,000Rp per day) to large (eight to 10 passengers, 650,000Rp to 700,000Rp per day), including captain, mate and fuel. Cooks and food are an additional 100,000Rp per person per day. If you stay overnight you'll be charged for two full days so bargain if you want to come back early.

When you factor in permits and fees, the total cost for a three-day, two-night guided trip for two people is about 3,295,000Rp, a very reasonable price with seasonal fluctuations (expect a premium in summer). Note that not all boats have generators, necessary for showers. Some recommended boats:

Kingfisher BOAT TOUR
(Harry 081 2500 0508; harnavia@yahoo.com; Tanjung Puting) For small parties of two to four people, you can't do better than *Kingfisher*, the first *klotok* at Tanjung Puting. The attentive crew know exactly what they are doing, the food is excellent and the boat spotless.

Harapan Mina BOAT TOUR
(Muslian 0813 4961 7210) Freshly painted, clean, with a good crew and a quiet engine, this is a larger boat handling six to eight people.

Queen Ratu BOAT TOUR
(Yatno 081 2507 8490; garudaratu@yahoo.com) The best *klotok* choice for large parties (sleeps 10).

KLOTOK RENTAL COSTS

The cost of renting a *klotok* can be confusing, given the number of factors that go into it. Here is the breakdown for a typical three-day, two-night trip:

» Boat 425,000Rp per day x 3 days = 1,275,000Rp

» Cook & Food 100,000Rp per person x 2 people x 3 days = 600,000Rp

» Guide 200,000Rp per day x 3 days = 600,000Rp

» Registration 120,000Rp per person per day x 2 people x 3 days = 720,000Rp

» Camera (one-time fee) = 50,000Rp

» Boat Parking (one-time fee) = 50,000Rp

» TOTAL: 3,295,000Rp

Guides

It is not mandatory to hire a guide, but recommended, as it facilitates a smooth trip. Guides purchase food, set your itinerary, communicate with your *klotok* driver, take you trekking, spot animals and tell you about the park. They can also help you find a boat. To acquire a licence each guide has to speak basic English and undergo survival training and wildlife knowledge. Fees range from 150,000Rp to 250,000Rp per day.

Some recommended guides:

Erwin GUIDE
(0858 6666 0159; erwinvanjava@gmail.com) Intelligent, well-read and good company, Erwin knows the park inside out, and shows interesting photos of local wildlife on his cell phone.

Andy Arysad GUIDE
(0813 5295 0891; andijaka01@gmail.com) The park's most experienced guide.

Ancis Banderas GUIDE
(0813 4920 5251; ecotourism.820@gmail.com) Excellent English, passionate about nature, points out much along the way.

Sleeping & Eating

If you're looking to stay outside the park (typically before or after your cruise), see Kumai or Pangkalan Bun reviews; the latter offers the only upscale accommodation in the area. If you wish to stay on terra firma inside the park, you can do that in two locations:

Rimba Lodge HOTEL $$$
(☎0532 671 0589; www.ecolodgesindonesia.com; r incl breakfast 585,000-1,485,000Rp; ❄) This riverside lodge set in the jungle has the right ambience, with comfortable en suite cabanas, warm showers and traditional decor. Its restaurant (mains 50,000Rp, set menus 150,000Rp; open 7am to 9pm) serves Chinese and Indonesian food. Book via an agent and get 20% off.

Flora Homestay HOMESTAY $$
(☎0812 516 4727; r 450,000Rp) Offers three basic en suite rooms with fans. Located at the entrance to Tanjung Harapan village. A speedboat here from Kumai is 150,000Rp.

Information

Contact the following organisations for additional information about the region's orangutans, conservation efforts and volunteer opportunities:

Friends of the National Parks Foundation (FNPF; www.fnpf.org) Rescue and relocation of orangutans.

Orangutan Foundation International (OFI; www.orangutan.org; 4201 Wilshire Blvd, ste 407, Los Angeles, CA, USA 90010) Founded by Biruté Galdikas, runs the park's feeding stations.

Orangutan Foundation UK (www.orangutan.org.uk; 7 Kent Tce, London, NW1 4RP) Major UK organisation with focus on saving orangutan habitat.

Getting There & Around

Tanjung Puting is typically reached via a flight to nearby Pangkalan Bun and a taxi to Kumai (120,000Rp, 20 minutes). Visitors should register at Pangkalan Bun police station upon arrival. Bring photocopies of your passport and visa (airport taxi drivers know the steps). This can also be organised by your guide. Once in Kumai, the next stop is the **PHKA office** (National Parks Office; fax 23832; Jln HM Rafi'I Km 1.5; ⏲8am-2pm Mon-Thu, 8am-11am Fri, 8am-1pm Sat) located portside. Registration costs 120,000Rp per day per person, 50,000Rp per trip for a *klotok* parking permit (30,000Rp per speedboat) and 50,000Rp per trip for a camera licence. Provide a copy of your police letter from Pangkalan Bun and another photocopy of your passport. When the park office is closed, it may be possible to arrange entry at the first feeding station, Tanjung Harapan. Ask your boat captain or guide.

Speedboats from Kumai cost 500,000Rp per day, and take about two hours to reach Camp Leakey, but this is pure transport, not wildlife spotting. Canoes are a quieter alternative for exploring Sungai Sekonyer's shallow tributaries, and can be rented at Sekonyer Village store for 50,000Rp per day.

Kumai

☎0532 / POP 23,000

The port of departure for Tanjung Puting National Park, Kumai is also known for its bird-nest business, which fills the town with screeching warehouses. A handful of guesthouses and warungs line the main street, Jl Idris. Backpackers sometimes meet here to share the price of a *klotok*. There's an ATM near the harbour.

Sleeping & Eating

TOP CHOICE **Losmen Aloha** LOSMEN $
(☎61210; Jl HM Idris 465; s/d 40,000/60,000Rp) Across from the harbour, Caribbean-hued Aloha has a restaurant with chequered tables and local fare downstairs, and rooms above with shared bathrooms and a nice porch for hanging out. The street-facing rooms with windows are best.

Losmen Permata Hijau LOSMEN $
(☎61325; Jl HM Idris; r with fan/air-con 70,000/100,000Rp; ❄) These budget rooms are good value for the price, with clean shared bathrooms, if you don't mind a lack of windows.

Mentari Hotel HOTEL $
(☎no phone; Jl Gerliya 98; r incl breakfast 125,000Rp; ❄) Basic concrete boxes, although they do have windows and air-con. Only one has hot water.

Getting There & Away

Reach Kumai by minibus from Pangkalan Bun (1000Rp, 20 minutes). Taxis from Pangkalan Bun airport to Kumai cost 150,000Rp.

Ferries run by **Pelni** (☎24420; Jln HM Idris), opposite the market, and **Dharma Lautan Utama** (☎081 3483 33444, 61008; Jln Gerilya 265) connect Kumai with Semarang (155,000Rp, 28 hours) once or twice weekly, and Surabaya (160,000Rp, 26 hours) almost daily. Tickets available at Aloha Travel, part of Losmen Aloha.

Aloha also sells bus tickets to Banjarmasin (economy/air-con 125,000/165,000Rp, 14 hours) via Sampit (economy/air-con 60,000/75,000Rp, six hours) and Palangka

Raya (economy/air-con 80,000/120,000Rp, 10 hours). The bus departs daily at 4pm.

Pangkalan Bun

☎0532 / POP 250,000

Pangkalan Bun is another transit city, with an airport, some hotels and very few ways to spend your time. But if you want something better than backpacker digs before or after visiting Tanjung Puting, you'll find it here.

Sights & Activities

Pangkalan Bun Park PARK

The town's tidy park, visible from the riverfront along JL Antasari, is crowned by the former sultan's home, **Istana Kuning** (Yellow Palace; 8am-2pm Mon-Thu, 8am-1pm Fri, 8-11am Sat, closed Sun). This large and mostly empty wooden building was built in 1806 and rebuilt in 1990 after a deranged woman burned it to the ground. It's not yellow, but was originally draped in yellow fabric.

TOP CHOICE **Hotel Avila Pool** SWIMMING

(Jl Diponegoro 81; admission 25,000Rp) Blink blink – can it be? This fabulous Mediterranean-style hotel pool with adjoining restaurant is a lifesaver on a scorching hot day. It's 1km east of town.

Sungai Arot BOAT TOUR

You can wave to almost any boat on the river and take an educational circuit around the ramshackle waterfront for 50,000Rp.

Sleeping & Eating

TOP CHOICE **Yayorin Homestay** HOMESTAY $$

(☎29057; www.yayorin.org; Jl Bhayangkara, Km 1; r incl breakfast 300,000Rp; ❄) A unique woodland setting with a working fishpond sets these charming cottage rooms apart. Yayorin is a local NGO working to preserve Kalimantan's forests. About 4km east of town.

TOP CHOICE **Swiss-Belinn** HOTEL $$

(☎27888; www.swiss-belhotel.com; Jl Ahmad Yani Km2; r incl breakfast 650,000-850,000Rp; ❄) Easily the top business hotel in the city, this new three-star is also your only upscale choice. It's a bit austere, but there's a pool and in-house spa to warm things up, plus a decent restaurant. Follow Jl Yani east 2km from town.

Hotel Bahagia HOTEL $

(☎21226; Jl P Antasari 100; r 85,000-245,000Rp; ❄📶) A great option for Tanjung Puting backpackers if you can't find a closer room in Kumai. Upper-floor economy rooms 201, 206, and 210 have streetside windows and a

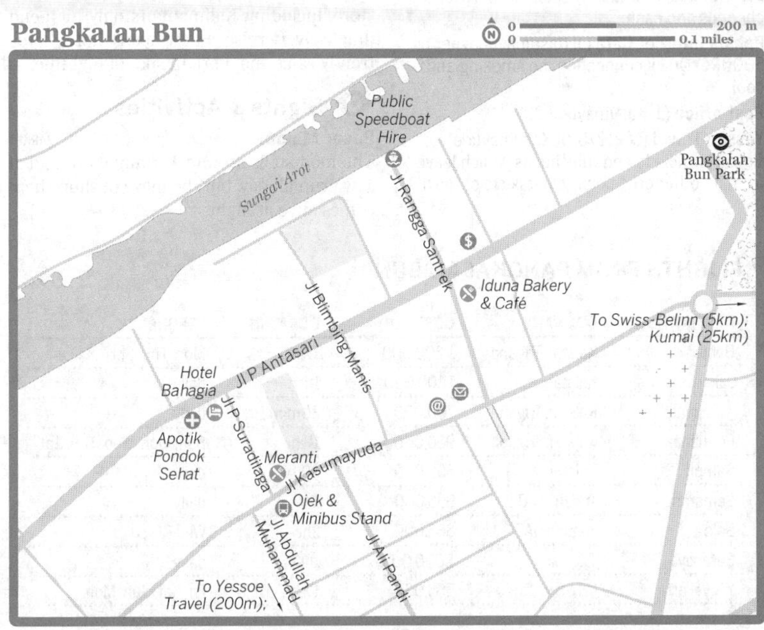

common porch; other rooms are more upscale.

Hotel Andika HOTEL $
(☎21218; Jl Hasanudin 20A; r incl breakfast 70,000-110,000Rp; ❄) Rooms here are more interesting than the usual concrete box – all have windows facing a verdant courtyard. A new addition nearing completion promises even better options. Midway down Jl Hasanudin.

TOP CHOICE **Iduna Bakery & Café** WESTERN $
(☎24007; Jl Rangga Santrek 5; mains 15,000-32,000Rp; ⏰9am-9pm) A sophisticated surprise, uniting a warm and trendy cafe with a tasty bakery (closes at 5pm).

Pranaban Fish Restaurant SEAFOOD $
(Jl Hasanudin; mains from 40,000Rp; ⏰8am-10pm) Down the road from Kalstar this semi-al fresco resto is a real gem renowned by locals and expats for its grilled and fried *bakar* (fish), chicken and duck. Low-key, friendly vibe.

Information

Many businesses close late in the afternoon and reopen after dark.

Apotik Pondok Sehat (☎21276; Jl P Antasari 86) Well-stocked pharmacy with doctor's offices.

BNI Bank (Jl P Antasari) Exchanges travellers cheques and cash.

Pahala Internet Café (Jl Kasumayuda; per hr 5000Rp) Quick connection, no smoking and cool.

Post office (Jl Kasumayuda 29)

Yessoe Travel (☎21276; Jl Kasumayuda) Books air tickets and runs buses, which leave from its other office on the outskirts of town.

Getting There & Away

There are no longer any flights connecting Pangkalan Bun and Palangka Raya. The best option is to fly from Pangkalan Bun to Sampit, then take a Kijang (75,000Rp, buy two front seats if possible) to Palangka Raya. Reserve a **car** (☎0852 4920 5991, English shaky) ahead. Otherwise it is a brutal 15-hour bus trip, although you could get off in Sampit if you can't take any more.

Buses are run by Yessoe Travel, departing from its office for Sampit (60,000Rp to 85,000Rp, six hours) and Banjarmasin (125,000Rp to 195,000Rp, 16 to 18 hours).

Getting Around

Taxis to/from the airport (5km) cost 50,000Rp. *Opelet* around town cost 10,000Rp. Minibuses to Kumai (20,000Rp, 20 minutes) and *ojeks* leave from the roundabout at the end of Jl Kasumayuda. Taxis to Kumai cost 150,000Rp.

Palangka Raya

☎0536 / POP 213,000

Originally envisioned by President Sukarno as a new capital city for Indonesia – and even for a pan-Asian state – Palangka Raya was built from scratch beginning in 1957. It shows in the streets, which are clearly laid out to plan, giving the city wide boulevards and a refreshing orderliness. While Sukarno's dream died, the city has a few surprises in store, including Kalimantan's only high-end jungle river cruise, a new luxury hotel, some trendy cafes and a bright spot of nightlife.

Sights & Activities

Pasar Malam MARKET
The food stalls around Jl Halmahera and Jl Jawa run all day, but the maze of shops here comes alive at night.

FLIGHTS FROM PANGKALAN BUN

DESTINATION	COMPANY	COST (RP)	DURATION	FREQUENCY
Banjar	Kalstar, Trigana	1,200,000	1½hr	Mon, Thu, Sat
Jakarta	Kalstar	1,100,000	1hr	daily
Ketapang	Kalstar, Trigana	700,000	30min	daily
Pontianak	Kalstar, Trigana	920,000	1½hr	Sun, Mon, Wed, Thu, Sat
Sampit	Kalstar	550,000	30min	daily
Semarang	Trigana/IAT	955,000	1hr	daily
Solo	Trigana/IAT	665,000	2hr	Wed & Sun
Surabaya	Trigana	1,000,000	1hr	daily
Yogyakarta	IAT	665,000	1½hr	Fri, Sat, Sun, Mon

Palangka Raya

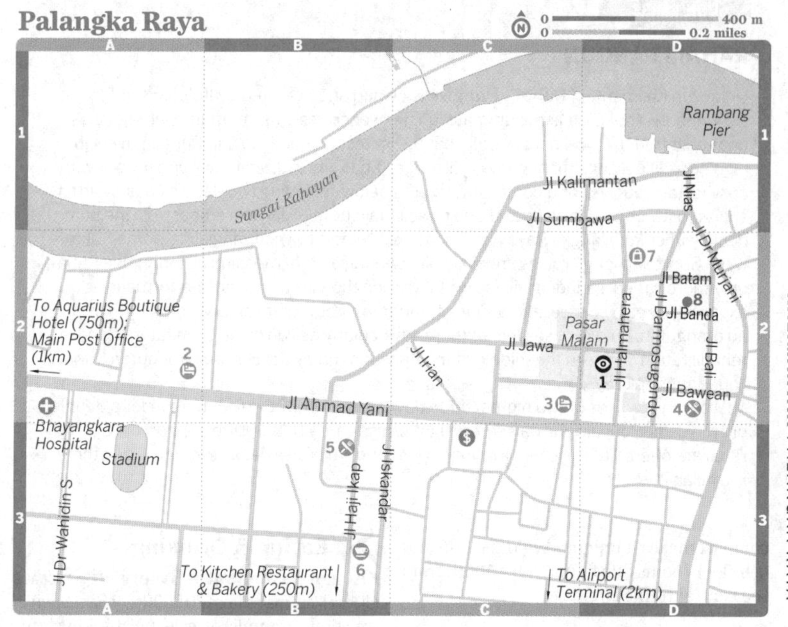

Borneo Orangutan Survival Foundation ZOO

(330 8414; www.orangutan.or.id; Jl Tjinik Riwut Km29; admission by donation; 9am-3pm Sat & Sun) This is one of several conservation efforts run by the Borneo Orangutan Survival Foundation. Normally a dozen or so orangutans (and some sun bears) are visible through floor-to-ceiling windows in this sophisticated facility simulating the forest floor. Hire an *ojek*, or use taxi route A to Jl Tjinik Riwut Km8 station and take a minibus.

Tours

TOP CHOICE **Kalimantan Tour Destinations** BOAT TOUR

(322 2099; www.wowborneo.com; Jl Milono Km 1; 9am-5pm Mon-Fri, 9am-3pm Sat) This eco-award-winning business, run by savvy Australian entrepreneur Gaye Thavisin, operates deluxe river cruises aboard the romantic *Rahai'i Pangun* (p626). A second boat, the *Spirit of Borneo*, is being refurbished. Homestays and local tours can also be arranged. Head south on Jl Milono (taxi route E) to the office.

Palangka Raya

Sights

1 Pasar Malam D2

Sleeping

2 Hotel Dian Wisata A2
3 Hotel Sakura C2

Eating

4 Family D2
5 Warung Makan Bu Leman B3

Drinking

6 Bistro de Garage B3

Shopping

7 Souvenir Shops D2

Information

8 Yessoe Travel D2

Sleeping

TOP CHOICE **Aquarius Boutique Hotel** HOTEL $$

(324 2121; www.aquariusboutiquehotel.com; Jl Imam Bonjol 5; d 600,000-850,000Rp;) Rooms here are some of the best in the city (be sure to ask for discounts) and the facilities excellent, including a rooftop pool and fitness centre. The superb entertainment

DON'T MISS

RAHAI'I PANGUN

Unique in Kalimantan, **Rahai'i Pangun** is owned and operated by Kalimantan Tour Destinations (p625). It is the ultimate jungle river cruiser, a 19m traditional wooden boat built from tropical hardwoods, that navigates the Kahayan and Rungan rivers in high style, like a huge mahogany royal barge. It has a broad, split-level upper deck with cosy rattan couches, and comfy staterooms below, including two double cabins with shared bathroom, two twins and one triple. A favourite of Jakarta embassies, the boat docks either in Palangka Raya or the ramshackle port town of Tangkiling, some 30km west. Short and long cruises are available, offering an itinerary similar to Tanjung Puting only more varied, including village visits with longhouses and dance performances, exploring lakes by canoe, and a rubber plantation. You won't get an arm's length from an orangutan, but you'll see lots of them, particularly as you circle Orangutan Island, a rehabilitation centre in the middle of the Kahayan run by the Borneo Orangutan Survival Foundation (p625).

Weekend cruises of two nights/three days cost 5,181,000Rp per person for a double or twin cabin; longer four-day, three-night cruises are 7,058,000Rp per person. Special rates are offered to travellers turning up just prior to cruise departures, provided there is availability.

complex makes it unique. Avoid the 5th- and 6th-floor rooms due to noise. It's 500m from the central traffic circle.

TOP CHOICE Swiss-Belhotel HOTEL $$
(☎081 1528 433; www.swiss-belhotel.com; Jl Tjilik Km5; s 555,000-685,000Rp, d 620,000-750,000Rp; ❄📶) This extensive new luxury property, a successful combination of business and resort hotel, raises the local bar, although not without minor growing pains. There is a vast marble lobby, an excellent buffet breakfast with Western choices, and comfy rooms with glass showers, ranging from entry-level standards to the 5,000,000Rp Presidential Suite. It feels a bit like an architect's model, but management is wise and the price is right (ask about discounts). Located 5km from the central traffic circle on Jl Tjilik.

Hotel Dian Wisata HOTEL $
(☎322 1241; Jl A Yani 68; r incl breakfast 120,000-220,000Rp; ❄) The interesting design of this hotel, with its central well-lit atrium and colourful stairwell, leading down into subterranean rooms, separates it from the boring concrete boxes that define its competition. Easy access to buses.

Hotel Sakura HOTEL $$
(☎322 1680; Jl A Yani 87; r incl breakfast 250,000-425,000Rp; ❄) This hotel's tranquil courtyard offers a welcome respite from the city. The best rooms have courtyard windows; some come with rare two-person tubs. Overall good value.

Eating & Drinking

Kitchen Restaurant & Bakery INTERNATIONAL $
(Jl Haji Ikap; mains from 20,000Rp; ⏲6am-9pm) A welcome example of eclectic thinking, this two-storey restaurant with its own waterfall is known for having the only pizza in town, part of a broad Western-Asian menu featuring Thai, Chinese and Indonesian dishes in big portions. Live music at night.

Family CHINESE $
(☎322 9560; Jl Bawean 16; mains 20,000-25,000Rp; ⏲8am-9.30pm) The best Chinese food in the city, with a standard menu. Known for its *ikan jelawat* (90,000Rp), a river fish cooked many ways. Serves beer (35,000Rp).

Warung Makan Bu Leman INDONESIAN $
(Jl Haji Ikap; mains from 20,000Rp; ⏲7am-4pm) Open-air dining around small communal tables makes this convivial local favourite very popular; the chicken soup does the rest.

TOP CHOICE Bistro de Garage CAFE
(Jl Haji Ikap 22; coffee 7500Rp; ⏲10am-midnight; 📶) A rare find, this trendy cafe is located in a colourfully painted house, garage included. It offers free wi-fi, basic food (spaghetti, desserts), outdoor seating and live music.

Entertainment

If you're looking for night life in Palangka Raya, the entertainment complex at the Aquarius Boutique Hotel (p625) is the only game in town, and no slacker. **Blu Music Hall** (⌚8pm-1am) is a small but atmospheric blues bar that surprises with its sophistication. The adjacent **Vino Club** (⌚10pm-2am) is a cosy state-of-the-art DJ club that doubles as the city's major performance venue. **Luna Karaoke** (⌚2pm-3am) is the third, more local leg in the stool. A tall Bintang will run you 75,000Rp at any of these places. Overall this complex is where the city's style-conscious young professionals come to hang out, representing a new wave of urban life. Find it 500m along Jl Bonjol from central traffic circle.

Shopping

Souvenir shops are located along Jl Batam.

Information

Bank Mandiri (Jl A Yani; ⌚8am-3pm Mon-Fri) Currency exchange.

Bhayangkara Hospital (☎322 1520; Jl A Yani)

Kevin Maulana Tours (☎323 4735; ptkevin_maulana@yahoo.com; Jl Milono Km1.5) Friendly KM can sort out air tickets, taxi charters and Kijang. Head south on Jl Milono (taxi route E).

Main post office (Jl Imam Bonjol; ⌚7.30am-2.15pm) On taxi route D. West side of town, 500m south of main traffic circle.

Sumerta Sari Travel (☎322 1033; Jalan Cilik Riwut Km1)

Yessoe Travel (☎322 1436; Jl Banda 7)

Getting There & Away

AIR Garuda, Lion Air, Sriwijaya Air, and Batavia Air fly daily to Jakarta (400,000Rp, 1½ hours) and Surabaya (425,000Rp, one hour). You'll find all the airline offices at the airport, which is only 2km from the eastern end of Jl Yani.

BUS Morning and evening buses depart from **Milono bus terminal** (☎3227 7765; Bundaran Burung, Jl Milono Km4.5) 5km on taxi route E. Yessoe Travel also runs buses at comparable fares from its in-town terminal just north of the market area. It is not clear when the new bus terminal, 10km south of the city centre, will be operational, if ever.

KIJANG Yessoe Travel serves Banjarmasin (90,000Rp, five hours). Sumerta Sari Travel serves Sampit (70,000Rp, five hours) and Pangkalan Bun (145,000, 10 hours).

Getting Around

Yellow minibuses ('taxis', 3000Rp) ply major thoroughfares. Airport service (6km, 15 minutes) costs 60,000Rp. Becak congregate on Jl A Yani around the petrol station near Jl Halmahera.

SOUTH KALIMANTAN

Banjarmasin

☎0511 / POP 611,000

Banjarmasin has been called the Venice of the East, a jaw-dropping exaggeration. Sadly, this enormous city, which lies at the confluence of several rivers, sprawls in all directions but offers very little for its size. It is best known for the boat trip to its floating markets, an experience both interesting and discomfiting, as it passes through great poverty. You may benefit from moving outside your comfort zone, but don't come expecting St Mark's Sq.

Sights

Mesjid Raya Sabilal Muhtadin MOSQUE

(Jl Sudirman) This massive mosque resembles a landed spaceship. During Ramadan, the famous **Pasar Wadai** (Cake Fair) runs along the adjacent riverfront.

Tours

Floating Market & Canal Tour CULTURAL TOUR

(tour incl guide 200,000Rp; ⌚5.30am-9.30am) You can see most of what Banjarmasin has to offer in a single journey. This begins by catching a dawn boat under Jembatan Dewi (Dewi Bridge) to the floating markets, where canoes full of wares mill about in search of a buyer. It takes an hour or so to get there via canals lined with ramshackle homes (many of which are collapsing into the water), each with its own outhouse. Along the way hordes of children will wave at you

BUSES FROM PALANGKA RAYA

DESTINATION	COST (RP)	DURATION (HR)	FREQUENCY
Banjarmasin	45,000	5	2am daily
Pangkalan Bun	80,000-150,000	10	7am & 4pm daily
Sampit	50,000-75,000	5	7am & 4pm daily

and try to swim out to your boat through the fetid water. While their smiles are the enduring image, passing through them in a sightseeing boat elevates the foreign tourist to a privileged status that can be profoundly discomfiting. Having said that, a floating market is interesting to see – there are two to choose from and either will do. Here you can sample a variety of exotic fruits as the river world comes to life.

A worthwhile stop on the return trip is **Pulau Kembang** (tour from 100,000Rp), where macaques walk the boardwalk. Another is gaily painted **Masjid Sultan Suriansyah**, one of the first mosques in Kalimantan, now beautifully restored.

Guides

You'll need a guide (who will secure a boat as well) to explain what you're seeing on the floating markets tour. Tour guides in Banjarmasin typically range up into the Meratus Mountains, too (see Loksado section for more trekking guides), although this interesting area demands more than a day trip.

Joe Yas GUIDE
(☎0812 5182 8311; joyas64@gmail.com) A trekking expert who also gives city tours.

Sarkani Gambi GUIDE
(☎0813 5187 7858; kani286@yahoo.com) Friendly Sarkani runs tours for large foreign groups as well as customised trips for individuals.

Muhammad Yusuf GUIDE
(☎0813 4732 5958; yusuf_guidekalimantan@yahoo.co.id) Yusuf is friendly, energetic and professional.

Mulyadi Yasin GUIDE
(☎0813 5193 6200; yadi_yasin@yahoo.co.id) Professional guide with extensive experience in Banjarmasin and the Meratus.

Sleeping

Book ahead on weekends.

TOP CHOICE **Swiss-Belhotel Borneo** HOTEL $$
(☎327 1111; www.swiss-belhotel.com; Jl Pangeran Antasari 86A; s/d incl breakfast 650,000/700,000Rp; ❄📶) Unlike other Swiss-Bels, this one eschews modern business decor in favour of a traditional boutique feel, to include a Banjar roof and the warm use of wood throughout. Prices quoted are after the standard discount. Junior suite 201 (1,590,000Rp) is exceptionally nice, a corner room with both city and river views. The hotel restaurant is also a top-choice listing, and there's live jazz from 8pm to 11pm.

Hotel Victoria Riverview HOTEL $$
(☎336 0255; hotel_victoria48@yahoo.com; Jl Lambung Mangkurat 48; r incl breakfast 425,000-750,000Rp; ❄📶) The riverside location makes this hotel stand out. Interestingly, certain 'classic' rooms (eg 323) have a better view than more expensive ones. The show-stealer is the Victoria Suite (1,200,000Rp), one of the most stylish rooms in Kalimantan, with such touches as a flat-screen TV embedded in a glass wall, and a waterfront veranda. The coffee shop is nicely situated too, although the breakfast doesn't equal the view. Ask about discounts.

Hotel Perdana HOTEL $
(☎335 2376; hotelperdana@plasa.com; Jl Katamso 8; r 100,000-160,000Rp; ❄) Popular with tourists, this excellent budget choice features 40 Caribbean-hued rooms around an inner atrium, many of them with air-con and en suites. There's no hot water, but staff speak English so at least they will understand your complaint.

Hotel SAS HOTEL $
(☎335 3054; Jl Kacapiring Besar 2; r incl breakfast 204,000-259,000Rp; ❄) Standard double rooms here have attractive rattan floors and bamboo beds. Good value for the price.

Eating & Drinking

TOP CHOICE **Jukung** INTERNATIONAL $
(Swiss-Belhotel Borneo, Jl Pangeran Antasari 86A; mains from 25,000Rp; ⏲breakfast, lunch & dinner) Real burgers! Plus a nice setting in the Swiss-Belhotel, a great variety of Asian and Western dishes and live music makes this a very pleasant dinner spot.

Cendrawasih SEAFOOD $
(Jl Pangeran Samudera; mains from 20,000Rp; ⏲9am-10pm) Delve deeper into Banjar cuisine at this renowned spot. Pick fish, seafood or chicken to cook on the outside grill and enjoy it inside with a cornucopia of sauces.

Rumah Makan Abdullah INDONESIAN $
(Jl Ahmad Yani Km1; mains 18,000-25,000Rp; ⏲10am-midnight) Locals say the *nasi kuning* (saffron rice) at this unassuming place is Banjarmasin's best.

Rumah Makan Jayakarta CHINESE $$
(Jl Haryono MT 7; mains 50,000-65,000Rp; ⏲11am-1.30pm & 5-11pm) All-day Chinese cafe selling

Central Banjarmasin

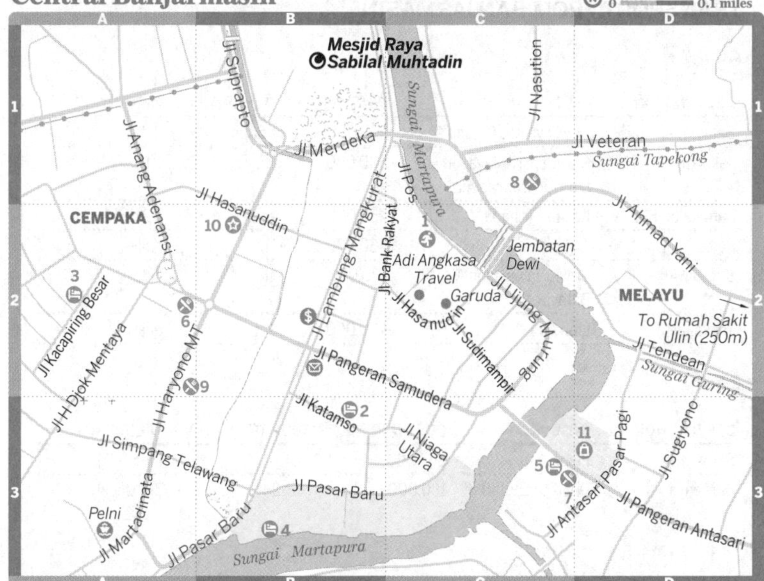

kepitang (crab), *ikan* (fish), *kodok* (frogs) and excellent *ayam* (chicken). Food is cooked on the outside range and beer is sold.

TOP CHOICE **Sante** BAR
(Mercure Hotel, Jl Ahmad Yani 98; noon-11pm) This colourful pool bar at the Mercure Hotel is a great place for happy hour (4pm to 5pm) and beyond.

Entertainment

TOP CHOICE **Dynasty** DJ, KARAOKE
(Hotel Aria Barito, Jl Haryono; admission male/female 50,000/25,000Rp) This vast new entertainment complex with disco, bar, and karaoke packs them in.

Shopping

Mitra Plaza has ATMs, fast-food outlets and Western-style shops in an air-con environment. Interesting Dayak handicrafts are sold opposite, along Jl Pangeran Antasari.

Information

Adi Angkasa Travel (436 6100; Jl Hasanudin 27) Flight bookings via a few members of staff who speak English.

BNI Bank (Bank Negara Indonesia; Jl Lambung Mangkurat)

Central Banjarmasin

Top Sights
Mesjid Raya Sabilal Muhtadin B1

Activities, Courses & Tours
1 Joe Yas C2

Sleeping
2 Hotel Perdana B3
3 Hotel SAS A2
4 Hotel Victoria Riverview B3
5 Swiss-Belhotel Borneo C3

Eating
6 Cendrawasih A2
7 Jukung C3
8 Rumah Makan Abdullah C1
9 Rumah Makan Jayakarta A2

Entertainment
10 Dynasty B2

Shopping
11 Mitra Plaza D3

Family Tour & Travel (326 8923; familytourtravel@yahoo.com; Jl A Yani Km4.5, Komp Aspol Bina Brata 1E; closed Sun) Books flights and buses to Pangkalan Bun as well as Balikpapan. Speak to owner Sam.

TRANSPORT FROM BANJARMASIN

Air

DESTINATION	COMPANY	COST (RP)	DURATION	FREQUENCY
Balikpapan	Sriwijaya Air, Trigana	325,000	45min	2 daily
Jakarta	Garuda, Sriwijaya Air, Lion Air, Batavia Air	500,000	1hr	10 daily
Pangkalan Bun	Kalstar, Trigana	450,000	1hr	1-2 daily
Solo	Trigana	450,000	1hr	daily
Surabaya	Sriwijaya Air, Lion Air, Batavia Air	270,000	1hr	7 daily
Yogyakarta	Lion Air	480,000	1hr	daily

Boat

DESTINATION	COMPANY	COST (RP)	DURATION (HR)	FREQUENCY
Semarang	Pelni	395,000	24	Mon & Fri
Surabaya	Dharma Lautan	160,000	18-24	3-5 weekly

Bus

DESTINATION	COST (RP)	DURATION (HR)	FREQUENCY
Balikpapan	115,000-170,000	1	several daily
Kandangan	45,000	3	several daily
Negara	50,000	4	several daily
Palangka Raya	40,000	6	several daily
Pangkalan Bun	110,000	20	several daily
Samarinda	140,000-195,000	13	several daily

Main post office (cnr Jl Pangeran Samudera & Jl Lambung Mangkurat)

Rumah Sakit Ulin (Jl A Yani Km2) Medical centre.

Getting There & Away

Air

Batavia Air (☎327 4110; Jl A Yani Km4 221B)

Garuda (☎335 9065; Jl Hasanudin 31)

Lion Air (☎470 5277; airport)

Sriwijaya Air (☎327 2377; Jl A Yani Km2.5)

Boat

Ferries depart from Trisakti Pinisi Harbour (3km).

Dharma Lautan Utama (☎441 4833; Jl Yos Sudarso 8)

Pelni (☎335 3077; Jl Martadinata 10)

Bus

The main bus terminal is at Jl A Yani Km6, southeast of the city centre.

Getting Around

Angkot routes (3000Rp) fan out from terminals at Jl Pangeran Samudera circle in the city core and Antasari Centre to the east. Becak and *ojeks* for hire gather around market areas. Taxis to/from Syamsuddin Noor Airport (26km) cost 100,000Rp.

Kandangan

☎0517 / POP 45,000

While almost completely untouristed, Kandangan is one of the more attractive towns in Kalimantan: tidy and well planned, with two interesting budget hotels, a bustling market (with a huge new building under construction) and numerous restaurants. It is also the gateway to lovely Loksado. This is a perfect place to chill out and meet locals, particularly for budget travellers, but reserve ahead as rooms are few.

Sleeping & Eating

TOP CHOICE Wisma Duta HOTEL $
(☎21073; Jl Permuda 9; r fan/air-con 90,000/100,000Rp; ❄) Charm at last: a converted country home with the feel of a Chinese temple makes this unassuming hotel a rare and welcome find. Rattan walls are a nice touch.

Hotel Mutia HOTEL $
(☎21270; Jl Suprapto; r incl breakfast 175,000-250,000Rp; ❄📶) Formerly a private home, this interesting wooden building has large public spaces and basic box rooms.

The Kandangan bus terminal doubles as a food court, and is lined with enough warungs to keep you well fed for days. ATM nearby.

Getting There and Around

Colts run frequently to/from Banjarmasin's Km6 terminal (40,000Rp, 4½ hours) until midafternoon. Buses for Balikpapan and Samarinda (125,000Rp to 165,000Rp, 14 hours) leave 10 times per day from Kandangan terminal. Pick-up trucks located on Muara Bilui will take you to Loksado (50,000Rp, 1½ hours). Becak will run you around town for 20,000Rp per half hour.

Negara

Northwest of Kandangan, the riverside town of Negara is the gateway to a vast wetland ranch where water buffalo swim from their elevated corrals at sunrise in search of grazing areas and are herded back at dusk by cowboys in canoes – an interesting sight if you're there in late afternoon. The town is a memorable sight too, with its huge mosque and brilliant dome rising across the bridge as you enter. Surprisingly, there is no hotel. Rent a boat across the street to see the swimming cattle (200,000Rp).

To get here from Kandangan take a public minibus (7000Rp, one hour), shared Japanese sedan with four people (15,000Rp per person, charter 60,000Rp), or *ojek* (40,000Rp).

Loksado

Loksado is an absolutely charming hamlet of gingerbread cottages flanking a rushing stream, Sungai Amandit, with a pedestrian suspension bridge. Set amidst beautiful mountain scenery, it stands apart from the rest of Kalimantan's tropical jungle, a feeling reinforced by the wonderful drive in, which curves through green hills until you reach the end of the road, 40km from Kandangan (great by motorcycle!). You'll find the best backpacker pad in Kalimantan here, as well as a vibrant Wednesday market, and numerous hiking trails for exploring Pegunungan Meratus, a 2500-sq-km mountain range spotted with Dayak villages. If you're looking for a place to hang out indefinitely, you can't beat this combination.

Activities

Mountain Trekking HIKING
There are innumerable hiking trails in the Meratus combining forest, villages, rivers, suspension bridges and longhouse visits. However, deforestation has taken its toll: it's a good five hours' walk to get to primary

FROM BANJARMASIN TO KANDANGAN

The road from Banjarmasin to Kandangan isn't pretty, but contains three interesting stops accessible by Colt minibus:

Cempaka Diamond Fields (⏱Sat-Thu) Twenty wooden prospecting rigs spread over a large field of sand reveal diamond mining in its most basic form. At the huge roundabout just past Banjarbaru, switch to a green taxi to Alur (2000Rp) and walk 1km from the main road.

Museum Lambung Mangkurat (☎0511 477 2453; Jl A Yani 36; admission 5000Rp; ⏱8.30am-3pm Sun-Thu, 8.30-11am Fri, 8.30am-2pm Sat) An above-average museum of local arts – textiles, ceramics, sculpture – both contemporary and antique, housed in several interlinked buildings in Banjarbaru (Km30).

Penggosokkan Intan (Diamond Polishing; ⏱9am-4pm Sat-Thu) Watch diamonds from the nearby mines being polished. You can also shop for precious stones if you know what you are doing. Ask the Colt driver to let you off here (1km from Banjarbaru roundabout).

forest these days. The best one-day trek is from Loksado to Bali Haritai (four to six hours, depending on the route), which includes some waterfalls. For first timers, this is an excellent introduction to jungle trekking, with a moderate change in altitude, areas of dense foliage, and a few leeches for company. Multiday itineraries top out (literally) at the summit of Mt Besar (1901m), the tallest peak in the Meratus range (seven days). Be sure to be prepared for your particular route, and don't be afraid to rein in your guide if the pace or terrain is beyond your skill level. For advice on advanced jungle trekking, see p604.

Bamboo Rafting RAFTING
It's fun to be poled downriver on a narrow bamboo raft, particularly when negotiating mild rapids. Ask your guide or hotelier for local providers; 90 minutes (250,000Rp) should suffice.

Muara Tanuhi Hot Springs HOT SPRINGS
(admission 3000Rp) These hot springs located in the Tanuhi resort, 2km west of Loksado, are the perfect ending to a long trek, although the resort itself is in disrepair.

Tours

To trek safely, hire an English-speaking guide. Some recommended English-speakers (see also p621):

Shady GUIDE
(☎0813 4954 5994; borneowanderer@yahoo.com) A young and enthusiastic guide from Kandangan with extensive trekking experience and a great sense of humour.

Amat GUIDE
(☎0813 4876 6573) A personable Dayak and long-standing Loksado resident with complete knowledge of the area.

Sleeping

TOP CHOICE **Wisma Alya** LOSMEN $
(☎0821 5330 8276; r 150,000Rp) Backpacker heaven! This two-storey cabin with rough-hewn wooden walls (the green house as you enter town) has five identical rooms, four upstairs accessed via a steep ladder and one down. They're bare as can be, with a floor mattress and small window, but the entire building is perched on rushing Sungai Amandit, with an overhanging balcony affording great views of the mountains. The shared *mandi* is large, clean and powered by mountain water. Laundry and *ojeks* are on offer, and the market is across the street. A sense of serenity sinks deeply into you here, ensuring a great night's sleep.

Amandit River Lodge LODGE $
(☎0813 4826 3467; r 200,000Rp) It's too bad this lodge lies 3km from town, because it has a stunning location, with the river winding in front and a dramatic piton rising behind. If you have your own transport, though, the simple en suite rooms with Western toilets are good value. Open by appointment, so call ahead and speak with the resident caretaker.

Wisma Loksado HOTEL $
(☎0852 5154 4398; r 220,000Rp) If you want an en suite room in Loksado, you can come here, but you will end up in a concrete box, missing the point of Loksado entirely. At the end of the suspension bridge.

Getting There & Around

Pick-up trucks leave Kandangan terminal for Loksado (50,000Rp, 1½ hours) in the afternoon and leave Loksado for Kandangan early in the morning.

Sulawesi

POP 17.5 MILLION

Includes »

Best Places to Eat

» Lae Lae (p640)

» Rumah Makan Kawana (p667)

» Raja Sate (p681)

» Gazebo (p654)

Best Places to Stay

» Living Colours (p684)

» Sunshine Guesthouse (p645)

» Poya Lisa Cottages (p674)

Why Go?

If you think Sulawesi looks crazy on the map, just wait until you see it for real. The massive island's multilimbed coastline is drawn with sandy beaches, fringing coral reefs and a mind-boggling variety of fish. Meanwhile, the interior is shaded by impenetrable mountains and jungles thick with wildlife such as the rare nocturnal tarsiers and flamboyantly colourful maleo birds. Cultures have been able to independently evolve here, cut off from the rest of the world by the dramatic topography. Meet the Tana Toraja with their elaborate funeral ceremonies in which buffaloes are sacrificed and *balok* (palm wine) flows freely; nearby in Mamasa life revolves around the Christian church, and in the far north the Minahasans offer you spicy dishes of everything from stewed forest rat to grilled fish; the coastal regions are mainly inhabited by the Bugis, Indonesia's most famous seafarers.

When to Go

Makassar

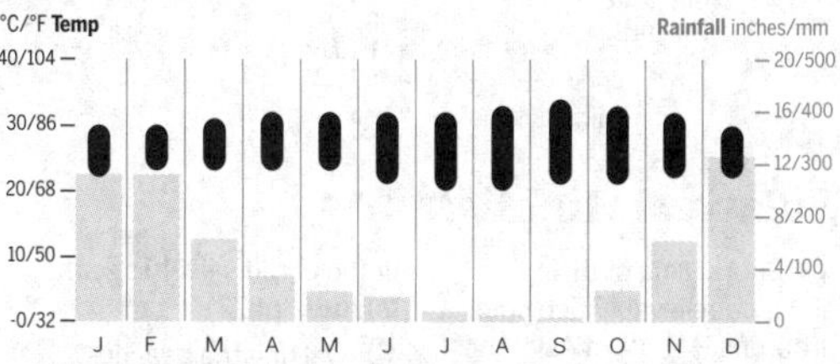

Apr–Oct Dry season: roads are in more passable shape and seas are more calm

Nov–Mar Lembeh Strait critters tend to come out of the muck more in the wet season

Jun–Aug The best months to experience Tana Toraja's biggest funeral ceremonies

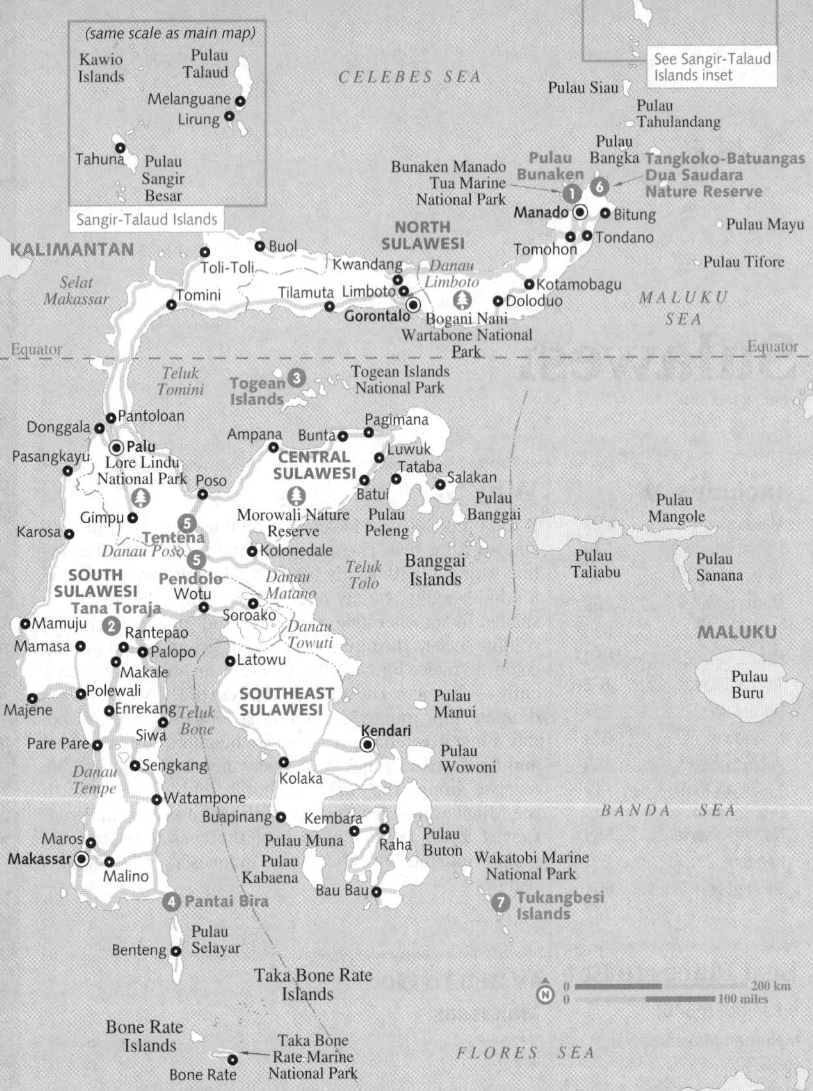

Sulawesi Highlights

1 Snorkelling or diving along unbelievably rich coral drop-offs – some of Asia's best – around chilled-out **Pulau Bunaken** (p683)

2 Attending an elaborate funeral ceremony in **Tana Toraja** (p649)

3 Island-hopping from one outrageous beach to the next in the paradisaical **Togean Islands** (p672)

4 Walking the beaches, diving the waters and exploring the diverse countryside around **Pantai Bira** (p644)

5 Feeling the cool air off glistening Danau Poso at the quiet lakeside towns of **Pendolo** (p666) and **Tentena** (p666)

6 Spotting sprightly tarsiers, ornery black macaques and a bevy of birds at **Tangkoko-Batuangas Dua Saudara Nature Reserve** (p689)

7 Exploring one of Jacques Cousteau's favourite diving haunts: the remote and rarely visited **Tukangbesi Islands** (p694)

History

The interior of the island provided a refuge for some of Indonesia's earliest inhabitants, some of whom preserved elements of their rich cultures well into the 20th century. The Makassarese and Bugis of the southwestern peninsula and the Christian Minahasans of the far north are the dominant groups of Sulawesi. The unique traditions, architecture and ceremonies of the Toraja people make the interior of South Sulawesi a deservedly popular destination.

Other minorities, particularly Bajau Sea nomads, have played an integral role in the island's history. The rise of the kingdom of Gowa – Sulawesi's first major power – from the mid-16th century was partly due to its trading alliance with the Bajau. The Bajau supplied valuable sea produce, especially the Chinese delicacy trepang (sea cucumber), tortoiseshell, birds' nests and pearls, attracting international traders to Gowa's capital, Makassar.

Makassar quickly became known as a cosmopolitan, tolerant and secure entrepôt that allowed traders to bypass the Dutch monopoly over the spice trade in the east – a considerable concern to the Dutch. In 1660 the Dutch sunk six Portuguese ships in Makassar harbour, captured the fort and forced Gowa's ruler, Sultan Hasanuddin, into an alliance in 1667. Eventually, the Dutch managed to exclude all other foreign traders from Makassar, effectively shutting down the port.

Even after Indonesia won its independence, ongoing civil strife hampered Sulawesi's attempts at postwar reconstruction until well into the 1960s. A period of uninterrupted peace delivered unprecedented and accelerating development, particularly evident in the ever-growing Makassar metropolis.

Tragically, the Poso region in Central Sulawesi fell into a cycle of intercommunal violence in 1998.

Getting There & Away

AIR

DOMESTIC The three transport hubs are Makassar and Manado, which are well connected with the rest of Indonesia, and Palu, which offers connections to Balikpapan in Kalimantan. There are direct flights to Java, Bali, Kalimantan, Maluku and Papua. Merpati Nusantara Airlines, Garuda Indonesia and Lion Air are the main carriers, but Batavia Air, Sriwijaya Air and Wings Air also service a handful of destinations.

INTERNATIONAL Silk Air flies between Manado and Singapore four days per week for S$567 (one way). AirAsia has daily flights from Makassar to Kuala Lumpur for around 1,400,000Rp each way.

BOAT

Sulawesi is well connected, with around half the Pelni fleet calling at Makassar, Bitung (the seaport for Manado), Pare Pare and/or Toli-Toli, as well as a few other minor towns. Some of the more important boats that stop at Makassar and/or Bitung (Manado) include the following:

BOAT	DESTINATION(S)
Bukit Siguntang	East Kalimantan, Nusa Tenggara
Ciremai	Maluku, Papua, Java
Kelimutu	Java, Bali, Nusa Tenggara, Maluku
Kerinci	East Kalimantan
Labobar	Java, Papua
Lambelu	Java, Maluku, Northern Maluku
Sirimau	Nusa Tenggara, Java, East Kalimantan
Tilongkabila	Nusa Tenggara, Bali

Getting Around

AIR

Merpati, Lion Air, Batavia Air and Sriwijaya are the main carriers to get around Sulawesi.

BOAT

The few Pelni ships that link towns within Sulawesi are a comfortable alternative to long and rough bus trips. At least six ships depart regularly from Makassar for Bau Bau and onto various destinations including Ambon and Bitung (for Manado).

The most useful service is the *Tilongkabila*, which sails every two weeks from Makassar to Bau Bau, Raha and Kendari; up to Kolonedale, Luwuk, Gorontalo and Bitung; across to Tahuna and Lirung in the Sangir-Talaud Islands; and returns the same way to Makassar.

Elsewhere along the coast, and to remote islands such as the Togean and Banggai, creaky old passenger ships, or *kapal kayu* (wooden boats), are the normal mode of transport, although speedboats are also occasionally available for charter. Around the southeastern peninsula, the *kapal cepat* (fast boat) or 'super-jet' are the ways to go.

BUS, BEMO & KIJANG

Regions around Makassar and the southwestern peninsula, and around Manado and the northeastern peninsula, have good roads and frequent, comfortable buses (as well as less

THE WALLACE LINE

Detailed surveys of Borneo and Sulawesi in the 1850s by English naturalist Alfred Russel Wallace resulted in some inspired correspondence with Charles Darwin. Wallace was struck by the marked differences in wildlife, despite the two islands' proximity and similarities in climate and geography. His letters to Darwin, detailing evidence of his theory that the Indonesian archipelago was inhabited by one distinct fauna in the east and one in the west, prompted Darwin to publish similar observations from his own travels. The subsequent debate on species distribution and evolution transformed modern thought.

Wallace refined his theory in 1859, drawing a boundary between the two regions of fauna. The Wallace Line, as it became known, divided Sulawesi and Lombok to the east, and Borneo and Bali to the west. He believed that islands to the west of the line had once been part of Asia, and those to the east had been linked to a Pacific-Australian continent. Sulawesi's wildlife was so unusual that Wallace suspected it was once part of both, a fact that geologists have since proven to be true.

Other analyses of where Australian-type fauna begin to outnumber Asian fauna have placed the line further east. Lydekker's Line, which lies east of Maluku and Timor, is generally accepted as the western boundary of strictly Australian fauna, while Wallace Line marks the eastern boundary of Asian fauna.

comfortable bemos or minibuses, known in Sulawesi as *mikrolet* or *pete-pete*). Elsewhere, roads are often rough, distances are long, and public transport can be crowded and uncomfortable. Allow plenty of time to travel overland in Central Sulawesi, especially in the wet season. On the southeastern and southwestern peninsulas, sharing a Kijang (a type of 4WD taxi) is a quick, but not necessarily more comfortable, way of getting around.

SOUTH SULAWESI

South Sulawesi (Sulawesi Selatan; often shortened to Sul-sel) is huge, and in Sulawesi big equals diverse. Makassar in the far south is the capital of the island and is fittingly tumultuous yet friendly. Stop here for a day or two to get your last chance for nightlife, plus feast on some of the best seafood on the island. From here you could head further south to Bira, which has the sleepy feel of a Greek isle with its dry climate and goats aplenty, or do what most people do and go directly to Tana Toraja to experience a dizzying blend of mountains carved with rice paddies, outlandish funeral ceremonies involving animal sacrifices and some of the craziest local-style architecture in Asia. In between these places there are plenty of buzzing towns and ports not used to seeing visitors, where you could stop awhile and soak in the culture. On the long bus rides in between you'll pass coastal salt farms and coffee, sugarcane and cotton plantations inland.

The estimated nine-million-plus inhabitants include the Bugis (who make up two-thirds of the population), the Makassarese (a quarter) and the Toraja. The Makassarese are concentrated in the southern tip, mainly around Makassar. The Bugis (centred around Watampone) and Makassarese have similar cultures; both are seafaring people who for centuries were active in trade, sailing to Flores, Timor and Sumba, and even as far afield as the northern coast of Australia. Islam is the dominant religion, but both people retain vestiges of traditional beliefs.

History

The leading powers of the south were long the Makassarese kingdom of Gowa (around the port of Makassar) and the Bugis kingdom of Bone. By the mid-16th century, Gowa had established itself at the head of a major trading bloc in eastern Indonesia. The king of Gowa adopted Islam in 1605 and Bone was soon subdued, spreading Islam to the whole Bugis-Makassarese area.

The Dutch United East India Company found Gowa a considerable hindrance to its plans to monopolise the spice trade. It found an anti-Gowa ally in the exiled Bugis prince Arung Palakka. The Dutch sponsored Palakka's return to Bone in 1666, prompting Bone to rise against the Makassarese. A year of fighting ensued and Sultan Hasanuddin of Gowa was forced to sign the Treaty of Bungaya in 1667, which severely reduced Gowa's power. Bone, under Palakka, then became the supreme state of South Sulawesi.

Rivalry between Bone and the other Bugis states continually reshaped the political landscape. After their brief absence during the Napoleonic Wars, the Dutch returned to a Bugis revolt led by the queen of Bone. This was suppressed, but rebellions continued until Makassarese and Bugis resistance was finally broken in the early years of the 20th century. Unrest lingered on until the early 1930s.

The Makassarese and Bugis are staunchly Islamic and independent-minded – revolts against the central Indonesian government again occurred in the 1950s. Makassar and Pare Pare are still the first to protest when the political or economic situation is uncertain.

Makassar

☎0411 / POP 1.6 MILLION

The metropolis of Makassar is thick with honking horns, strong smells and general pandemonium, but it maintains a nearly backwater charm thanks to its friendly people and delicious, down-home seafood warungs (food stalls). The city's seething mass is expanding in every direction, with new suburbs everywhere and maybe even a light rail system in the near future. Tanjung Bunga looms to the southwest of the city and may become the centre one day, while Panukkukang to the east is chock-a-block with mighty, modern shopping malls.

As the gateway to eastern Indonesia for centuries, it was from Makassar that the Dutch controlled much of the shipping that passed between the west and the east. Today it's still a thriving port and important transport hub. Fort Rotterdam, once the site of a Gowanese fort, is Makassar's main tourist attraction and stands as a reminder of the Dutch occupation.

In the area surrounding Makassar are the palace of the Gowanese kings, waterfalls where the naturalist Alfred Wallace collected butterflies and cave paintings left by the first inhabitants of Sulawesi.

Sights

Fort Rotterdam ARCHITECTURE

(Jl Pasar Ikan; admission 10,000Rp; 8am-5pm) One of the best-preserved examples of Dutch architecture in Indonesia, Fort Rotterdam continues to guard the harbour of Makassar. A Gowanese fort dating back to 1545 once stood here, but failed to keep out the Dutch. The original fort was rebuilt in Dutch style after the Treaty of Bungaya in 1667. Parts of the crumbling wall have been left untouched and provide a comparison with the restored buildings, but really the fort isn't anything spectacular.

Inside the fort are two museums, the better one being the **Museum Negeri La Galigo** (Jl Pasar Ikan, Fort Rotterdam; admission 1700Rp; 8am-12:30pm Tue-Sun) to the right when you come through the gate. There's an assortment of exhibits, including Tana Toraja rice bowls, kitchen tools, musical instruments and various costumes. It's hardly riveting, but at this price who can complain? The museums seem to keep the same hours as the fort. One ticket covers both museums, so hold onto it.

Avoid visiting on Sunday when school children and English students swarm the place.

FREE **Old Gowa** HISTORIC SITE

Remnants of the former kingdom of Gowa, 7km from town on the southeastern outskirts of Makassar, include **Makam Sultan Hasanuddin** (Jl Pallantiang, off Jl Sultan Hasanuddin), which memorialises the ruler of Gowa from the mid-17th century. Outside the tomb compound is the **Pelantikan Stone**, on which the kings of Gowa were crowned.

Benteng Sungguminasa (Jl Kh Wahid Hasyim; admission free; 8am-4pm), a fort that was once the seat of the sultan of Gowa, is 5km further south at Sungguminasa. The former royal residence, now known as **Museum Balla Lompoa**, houses a collection of artefacts, including gifts from the indigenous Australians of Elcho Island, who have a history of trade with the Bugis. Although the royal regalia can be seen only on request, the wooden Bugis-style palace itself is the real attraction.

To go to Old Gowa and Sungguminasa, take a *pete-pete* marked 'S Minasa' from

WHAT'S IN A NAME?

From the early 1970s until 1999 the official name of Makassar was Ujung Pandang. During his final days as president, BJ Habibie made the popular decision to change the name back to Makassar. In reality both names are still used, as they have been for centuries, and neither title is politically charged.

Makassar

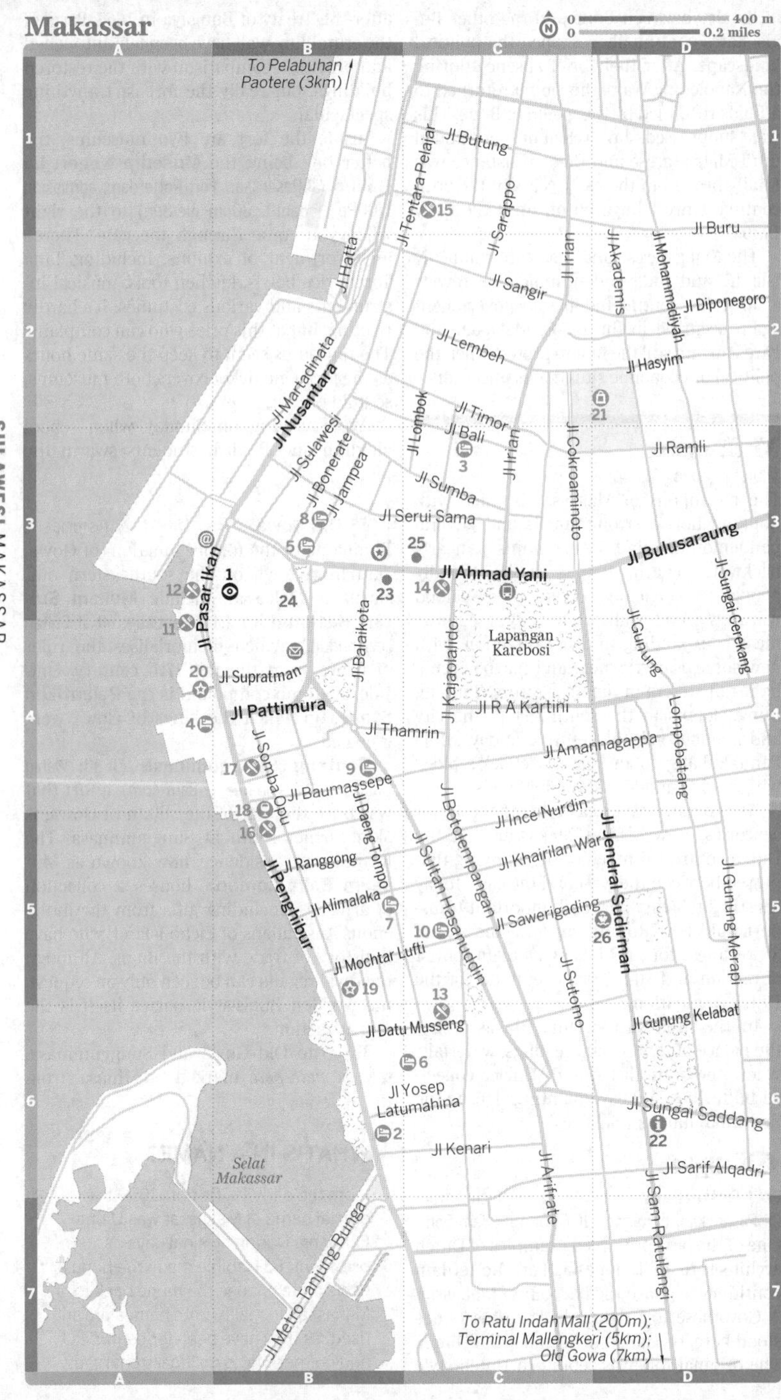

0 400 m
0 0.2 miles
To Pelabuhan Paotere (3km)
Jl Butung
Jl Tentara Pelajar
Jl Sarappo
Jl Buru
Jl Irian
Jl Akademis
Jl Mohammadiyah
Jl Hatta
Jl Sangir
Jl Diponegoro
Jl Lembeh
Jl Hasyim
Jl Martadinata
Jl Nusantara
Jl Lombok
Jl Timor
Jl Bali
Jl Ramli
Jl Sulawesi
Jl Bonerate
Jl Jampea
Jl Cokroaminoto
Jl Sumba
Jl Serui Sama
Jl Bulusaraung
Jl Pasar Ikan
Jl Ahmad Yani
Jl Sungai Cerekang
Lapangan Karebosi
Jl Gunung
Jl Balaikota
Jl Supratman
Jl Kajaolalido
Jl Pattimura
Jl R A Kartini
Jl Thamrin
Lompobatang
Jl Somba Opu
Jl Amannagappa
Jl Baumassepe
Jl Daeng Tompo
Jl Botolempangan
Jl Ince Nurdin
Jl Sultan Hasanuddin
Jl Ranggong
Jl Khairilan War
Jl Jendral Sudirman
Jl Gunung Merapi
Jl Penghibur
Jl Alimalaka
Jl Sawerigading
Jl Mochtar Lufti
Jl Sutomo
Jl Gunung Kelabat
Jl Datu Musseng
Jl Yosep Latumahina
Jl Sungai Saddang
Jl Kenari
Jl Sarif Alqadri
Selat Makassar
Jl Arifrate
Jl Sam Ratulangi
Jl Metro Tanjung Bunga
To Ratu Indah Mall (200m); Terminal Mallengkeri (5km); Old Gowa (7km)

Makassar

Sights

1	Fort Rotterdam	B3
	Museum Negeri La Galigo	(see 1)

Sleeping

2	Asoka Homestay	B6
3	Hotel Lestari	C3
4	Hotel Pantai Gapura	A4
5	Hotel Yasmin	B3
6	Imperial Aryaduta Hotel	C6
7	Mercure Royal Regency Hotel	B5
8	New Legends Hostel	B3
9	Pondok Suada Indah	B4
10	Santika Hotel	C5

Eating

11	Fish Warungs	A4
12	Kampoeng Popsa	A3
	Kios Semarang	(see 18)
13	Lae Lae	C6
14	Pizza Ria	C3
15	Rumah Makan Malabar	C1
16	Sentosa	B5
17	Shogun	B4

Drinking

	Ballairate Sunset Bar	(see 4)
18	Kafe Kareba	B4

Entertainment

19	Botol Café	B5
20	Zona Cafe	A4

Shopping

21	Makassar Mall	D2

Information

22	Sulawesi Tourism Information Centre	D6

Transport

23	Batavia Air	B3
24	Garuda	B3
25	Lion Air	C3
26	Pelni	D5

Makassar Mall to the turn-off for the 1km walk to the tomb. A becak (bicycle-rickshaw) from there to the fort should cost around 12,000Rp. Another becak will take you to Mallengkeri Terminal, from where *pete-pete* return to central Makassar; the *pete-pete* should cost about 6000Rp.

Pelabuhan Paotere HARBOUR
(Paotere Harbour; admission 500Rp) Pelabuhan Paotere, a 15-minute becak ride north of the city centre, is where the Bugis sailing ships berth and is arguably the most atmospheric part of the city. There is usually lots of activity on the dock and in the busy **fish market** a few streets south.

Sleeping

Makassar's sleeping options are expensive and disappointing. The most pleasant area to stay is along the waterfront south of the port (which also has the best nightlife), while choices a few blocks away from the sea or around Jl Ahmad Yani are central and a short walk to the action. All places listed here have Western-style bathrooms. Unless noted otherwise, all of the following prices include breakfast.

Imperial Aryaduta Hotel HOTEL $$$
(☎870 555; www.aryaduta.com; Jl Somba Opu 297; r from 790,000Rp; ❄@📶) This is *the* place to see and be seen with the ritzy Asian business elite. Huge rooms with amazing sea views would be better if the carpets weren't stained, but you can easily forget about this at the spa, the seaside pool or at any of the several smoky bars and chic cafes.

Hotel Yasmin HOTEL $$
(☎328 329; yasminmakassar@yahoo.co.id; Jl Jampea 5; r from 336,000Rp; ❄@📶) Victorian patterned wallpaper and upholstered chairs add a little decadence to this bustling, great-value business hotel. Rooms are small but in good shape and the staff are professional. There's a cafe-restaurant and karaoke-dance bar on site.

Santika Hotel HOTEL $$
(☎332 233; www.santika.com; Jl Sultan Hasanuddin 40; r from 570,000Rp; ❄@📶) The modern, slightly edgily-designed Santika isn't well located for views, but the rooms are luxurious and have a calming beige-and-white decor. Rates for walk-ins can be cheaper than booking online if you happen to get there when it's slow.

Hotel Pantai Gapura HOTEL **$$$**
(325 791; www.pantaigapura.com; Jl Pasar Ikan 10; r from 600,000Rp, cottages from 1,000,000Rp;) The closest thing you'll find to a resort in the city centre, Hotel Pantai Gapura is a bit kitsch but the ocean views, pool, palm trees and water gardens do make it feel like a holiday destination. Rooms are poor value but the giant Bugis-style over-the-water cottages are truly special. There is also a sunset bar-restaurant in a funny old cargo boat. Rates double over weekends and holidays.

Pondok Suada Indah HOTEL **$**
(317 179; Jl Sultan Hasanuddin 12; r from 200,000Rp;) One of Makassar's more interesting options, this place is set in a spacious, old colonial-era house that feels far from the city's hubbub just out the front door. Rooms are huge and are decorated with a tatty mix of heavy antiques and cheap modern furniture; some have age-worn bathtubs and all have little TVs with local channels. It's not pristine but it's a great deal in this price range.

Mercure Royal Regency Hotel HOTEL **$$**
(365 0099; www.mercure.com; Jl Daeng Tompo 8; r from 375,000Rp;) This is another bland but relatively comfortable business-oriented place that stands out for its excellent and copious buffet breakfasts.

Hotel Lestari HOTEL **$**
(327 337; Jl Savu 16; r 190,000-260,000Rp;) Rooms have satellite TV, minibar, hot water and air-con – angle for one with a window. There's not much character but with all the amenities it's a good deal.

Asoka Homestay HOMESTAY **$$**
(873 476; Jl Yosep Latumahina; r 250,000-350,000Rp;) Just steps from the waterfront, this charming family-run place has five rooms surrounding an immaculate flowery courtyard. The little breakfast tables are draped in pink lace and the rooms are large and airy. The breakfasts are small, however, and travellers have reported problems with the air-conditioning.

New Legends Hostel HOSTEL **$**
(313 777; Jl Jampea 5G; dm 65,000Rp, r 90,000-125,000Rp;) Catering to backpackers, this clean and very helpful place has a tiny upstairs cafe where you can meet other travellers over breakfast or movies at night. Rooms and dorms are small, windowless and box-like. Cheaper rooms are fan-only and have shared bathrooms.

Darma Nusantra II HOTEL **$$**
(481 3377; Jl Banda Baru; r 280,000-300,000Rp;) Makassar's only 'airport hotel' is a few kilometres away and is passably clean and comfortable. You can book this place at its airport desk and there's a free shuttle.

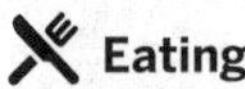

Eating

For many, it's the food that makes Makassar a great destination. There's an abundance of seafood, Chinese dishes, local specialities such as *coto Makassar* (a hearty, well-seasoned soup made from buffalo innards), *mie titi* (also called *mie kering* – crispy noodles with gravy, chicken and shrimp), *pisang epe* (grilled flattened bananas covered with cane syrup and/or chocolate – found all around the city at small stalls at night) and a few international surprises.

Try the string of makeshift **fish warungs** (Jl Pasar Ikan) set up every night on the foreshore opposite Fort Rotterdam and south along the waterfront, that serve some of the tastiest, cheapest seafood in town (about 15,000Rp per fish, baked, grilled or fried). Roaming buskers provide tableside entertainment.

Jl Timor, in the heart of the Chinese quarter, is where you'll find restaurants serving delicious *mie pangsit* (wonton soup).

TOP CHOICE **Lae Lae** SEAFOOD **$**
(334 326; Jl Datu Musseng 8; fish from 20,000Rp; lunch & dinner) A very basic dining hall jam-packed with food-frenzied locals, this place is as social as the seafood is good. Servers lead you to the ice box where you choose your fish (or squid, crab or just about any other sort of sea critter) that gets grilled while you make friends at your table. Wash up, roll up your sleeves and dive into the flaky fish, sambal (chilli sauce) and other sauces hands-first.

Kampoeng Popsa FOOD COURT **$**
(Jl Pasar Ikan; meals around 25,000Rp; breakfast, lunch & dinner) Clean, modern food court right on the water with some plush seating, breezes, plenty of hip clientele and lots of choices from *mei titi* to Japanese food, pizza and ice cream. There's often live music at night. Find it right across the street from Fort Rotterdam.

Kios Semarang SEAFOOD **$$**
(Jl Penghibur; mains 15,000-40,000Rp; lunch & dinner) The closest thing to a Makassar institution. Climb the stairs to the 3rd floor

where you will be rewarded with a rowdy expat crowd, good seafood and cheap beer. Start with a sunset and a Bintang or two before trying the fresh squid or shrimp.

Shogun JAPANESE $$
(☎324 102; Jl Penghibur 2; sushi & sashimi platters from 95,000Rp; ⏰lunch & dinner) The only authentic Japanese restaurant in town. The sushi is excellent, but portions are small in comparison to the hefty price tag. There are also teppanyaki sets, yakitori, sate and steaks.

Rumah Makan Malabar INDIAN $
(☎319 776; Jl Sulawesi 264; curry 22,000Rp; ⏰lunch & dinner) Run by a second-generation Keralan, Malabar is a little slice of the Indian subcontinent, serving up flaky naan and tender *kare kambing* (goat curry).

Sentosa INDONESIAN $
(☎326 062; Jl Penghibur 26; soup 8000Rp) Locals flock to this basic cafe with sea views across the street and delicious wonton soup.

Pizza Ria PIZZA $
(cnr Jl Kajaolalido & Jl Ahmad Yani; pizza from 22,000Rp; ⏰lunch & dinner) The atmosphere here is a little 'cheesy' but the pizzas are surprisingly good and a few have a spicy Indonesian twist.

Drinking

A lot of the bars around the port area are little more than brothels disguised as karaoke bars and are best avoided by all but the proverbial drunken sailor. You really want to know how bad it is? Locals call it Vagina St.

Further south on Jl Penghibur, there are several lively places. Kios Semarang (p640) is definitely *the* watering hole in town.

Ballairate Sunset Bar BAR
(Hotel Pantai Gapura; Jl Pasar Ikan 10) Built on stilts over the sea, this is the best-located bar in town. Walk right through the hotel to discover draft Bintang by the pitcher and a perfect view of the sunset. Sundays are a bad idea as the Makassar jet-ski crowd strut their stuff on the water here.

Kafe Kareba BEER GARDEN
(Jl Penghibur) This outdoor beer garden features live bands and the drinks flow. It also has a pretty extensive menu of food for those wanting entertainment while they eat.

☆ Entertainment

Drinking at nightclubs can be prohibitively expensive, as this is how they rake in the cash. It's best to warm up at a bar before delving into the dance zone. Most of the clubs rumble on until about 3am.

Many of the top-end hotels house nightclubs with pricey drinks and bands playing MTV hits. Entry costs 35,000Rp to 60,000Rp, which usually includes a soft drink or beer.

Zona Cafe CLUB
(www.zonacafe.info; Jl Pasar Ikan; admission varies) Housed in the old Benteng Theatre, this is the 'in' club in town. DJs and bands from Jakarta and expensive drinks all round, this is where the hipsters hang out.

Botol Café CLUB
(Jl Somba Opu 235, Quality Hotel) By far the most popular of the hotel nightclubs, this one is tucked away rather uninvitingly in the basement car park.

Studio 21 CINEMA
(Jl Sam Ratulangi) Showing current Western films in their original language (with Bahasa Indonesia subtitles). On the top floor of the Ratu Indah Mall complex.

Shopping

Jl Somba Opu has plenty of shops with great collections of jewellery, 'antiques' and souvenirs, including crafts from all over Indonesia, such as Kendari filigree silver jewellery, Torajan handicrafts, Chinese pottery, Makassarese brasswork, and silk cloth from Sengkang. Shopping centres are the place to be for most Makassarese.

Makassar Mall MALL
(cnr Jl Kyai Kaji Ramli & Jl Agus Salim) A sprawling mess and more like a market than a mall – go here to experience Makassar at its craziest.

Ratu Indah Mall MALL
(Jl Sam Ratulangi) The best of the more central malls, this one could be anywhere in the world.

ℹ Information

Emergency

Police Station (☎110; Jl Ahmad Yani)

Immigration

Immigration office (☎584 559; Jl Perintis Kemerdekaan) On the road to the airport, 13km from the city centre.

Internet Access & Post

Internet centres are found across the city, most charging 7000Rp per hour.

Expresso Cafe Net (cnr Jl Pasar Ikan & Jl Ahmad Yani; ⏲8am-12am) Clean private booths and fast connections.

Main Post Office (Jl Slamet Riyadi; ⏲8am-9pm) Has a poste restante service, a Telkom office and an internet centre.

Medical Services

RS Awal Bros Hospital (☎452 725; http://makassar.awalbros.com; Jl Jendral Urip Sumoharjo 43) The most convenient and well-equipped hospital. It's out near the toll road.

Money

The streets surrounding Lapangan Karebosi are loaded with banks and ATMs that accept all major credit cards. Most are on Jl Ahmad Yani and can also change cash and travellers cheques. At the airport several moneychangers offer slightly lower rates than in the city, and some of the ATMs there accept credit cards.

Telephone

The most convenient option is to buy a SIM card (5000Rp). Telkomsel is the carrier with the best coverage in Sulawesi. You shouldn't need more than 5000Rp credit to get you through a one-month stay.

Tourist Information

Sulawesi Tourism Information Centre (☎872 336; cnr Jl Sam Ratulangi & Jl Sungai Saddang; ⏲8am-4pm) There is not much on offer here, but the staff are helpful and friendly. Take any red *pete-pete* (a type of *mikrolet* or bemo) travelling south along Jl Jendral Sudirman to get here.

Travel Agencies

There are travel agencies all around Makassar and at many hotels through which you can book flights and Pelni ship voyages. Just about everyone in Makassar wants to take you on a tour of Tana Toraja but you'll get the same (or better) services at lower prices if you find a guide in Rantepao. Be careful of commiting to a tour and making a hefty payment upfront. While these tours are often OK, some travellers have reported being ripped off by seemingly professional 'tour organisers' whose tours never materialise.

Getting There & Away

Air

Makassar is well connected to the rest of Indonesia, as many flights between Java, Maluku and the easternmost islands call here en route.

Batavia Air (☎365 5255; Jl Ahmad Yani 35) Offers flights three to four days a week to and from Gorontalo, Luwuk, Manokwari, Palu, Ambon and Balikpapan and daily flights to Kendari.

Garuda (Garuda Indonesia; ☎365 4747; Jl Slamet Riyadi 6) Flies directly to and from Manado, Denpasar, Jakarta, Jayapura and Yogyakarta among many other destinations.

Lion Air (☎327 038; Jl Ahmad Yani 22) Flies daily to and from Manado, Kendari, Gorontal, Palu, Yogyakarta, Surabaya, Balikapapan, Ternate and Sorong.

Merpati (☎442 892; Jl Bawakaraeng) Connects Makassar to Jakarta, Balikpapan, Kendari, Surabaya, Palu, Yogyakarta, Toli-Toli, Bau Bau and more.

Sriwijaya Air (☎424 800; Jl Lanto Daeng Pasewang) Flies to Biak, Balikpapan, Jayapura, Manado, Ternate, Surabaya, Palu, Gorontalo, Kendari and Ambon.

Boat

Around half the Pelni fleet stops in Makassar, mostly on the way to Surabaya and Jakarta, East Kalimantan, Ambon and Papua. Useful services include the *Tidar* to Balikpapan, the *Sirimau* to Larantuka in Flores, and the *Tilongkabila* to Bau Bau and then up along the east coast to Kendari (economy/ 1st class 181,000/465,000Rp), Kolonedale, Luwuk, Gorontalo and Manado.

The **Pelni office** (☎331 401; Jl Jendral Surdiman 38; ⏲8am-2pm Mon-Sat) is efficient and computerised. Tickets are also available at any Pelni agency around town. The chaotic Pelabuhan Makassar port, which is used by Pelni boats, is only a short becak ride from most hotels.

Bus & Kijang

Buses run all day but are most frequent in the morning, so it's good to get to the terminals no later than 8am.

Makassar has numerous terminals but three are most useful.

Terminal Daya In the eastern suburbs on the road to the airport, where there are buses and Kijangs to all points north, including Sengkang (43,000Rp, four hours) and Rantepao (from 80,000Rp, eight hours). Kijangs often take shorter routes than the buses and are worth the slightly more expensive tickets. To get to Terminal Daya, catch any *pete-pete* (3000Rp, 30 minutes) marked 'Daya' from Makassar Mall or from along Jl Bulusaraung.

Terminal Mallengkeri About 10km southeast of the city centre. From here, buses and Kijangs go to places southeast of Makassar, including Bulukumba (32,000Rp, three hours) and Pantai Bira (55,000Rp, four hours). For Pantai Bira, you may have to change in Bulukumba.

Terminal Sungguminasa Has regular *pete-pete* services to Malino (16,000Rp, 1½ hours).

To get to Mallengkeri or Sungguminasa Terminals, take a *pete-pete* marked 'S Minasa' from Makassar Mall or from along Jl Jendral Sudirman. Ask to be dropped at Mallengkeri, or continue on to Terminal Sungguminasa.

Getting Around

To/From the Airport

Hasanuddin Airport is 22km from the centre of Makassar.

BUS Taxi drivers will tell you there's no bus but there is. A Damri bus (35,000Rp) runs regularly between 8am and 9pm daily from the basement level of the airport to Lapangan Karebosi in central Makassar.

OJEK It's possible to get an *ojek* (motorcycle taxi) to the airport from downtown Makassar for around 75,000Rp.

PETE-PETE These can be convenient (although time consuming) if you want to skip Makassar all together. Free shuttles run from the basement level of the airport to the main road (about 500m from the terminal) about every 15 minutes; that's where you can flag down a *pete-pete* to Terminal Daya. From Terminal Daya you can transfer to *pete-pete* going to the other bus terminals or get buses to points north, including Rantepao.

TAXI Prepaid taxis are easy to arrange at the arrivals area. There are three fares from 85,000Rp to 100,000Rp, depending on the destination, but most hotels are in the centre, which costs 100,000Rp. To the airport, a metered taxi is about 85,000Rp.

Public Transport

Makassar is hot, so using a becak, *pete-pete* or taxi can be a relief.

BECAK The friendly old crooks that are the becak drivers like to kerb-crawl, hoping you'll succumb to their badgering and/or the heat. The going rate is 10,000Rp around town, but you inevitably have to bargain for this.

PETE-PETE The main *pete-pete* terminal is at the Makassar Mall, and the standard fare around town is 4000Rp.

TAXI Air-conditioned taxis have meters and are worth using; flagfall is 5000Rp and each kilometre is 700Rp.

Around Makassar

PULAU SAMALONA

A tiny speck just off Makassar, Pulau Samalona is popular for fishing and snorkelling, particularly on Sundays. Otherwise, there's nothing much to do – it takes a full two minutes to walk around the island. If you ask around, you can buy cold drinks and fresh fish meals. Snorkelling gear is also available. Compared to Makassar harbour, the water's pretty clear!

To get here you will have to charter a boat for about 350,000Rp one way from the special jetty in Makassar and prearrange to be picked up later. On Sunday you can probably share a boat with some day-trippers.

PULAU KAYANGAN

This tiny island is cluttered with strange tourist attractions and is not great for swimming (although plenty of locals do it). It's very busy on Sundays, but almost completely empty for the rest of the week. Some of the restaurants around the island are positioned over the water, and many are perfect for sunsets.

Charter a boat from the special jetty in Makassar for around 300,000Rp return.

BANTIMURUNG

Air Terjun Bantimurung (admission 10,000Rp), 42km from Makassar, are waterfalls set amid lushly vegetated limestone cliffs. Looking up, it's straight out of Jurassic Park, but then you scan the ground level and it's a classic *objek wisata* (tourist object). That translates as crowded with day-trippers on weekends, and peppered with litter and creative concrete, but it remains a wonderful and picturesque retreat from the heat of Makassar. Upstream from the main waterfall there's another smaller waterfall and a pretty but treacherous pool (you will need a torch to make it through the cave en route). Bantimurung is also famous for its beautiful butterflies. The naturalist Alfred Wallace collected specimens here in the mid-1800s; however, numbers are plummeting as locals trap them to sell to visitors, so try not to encourage the trade.

Catch a Damri bus or *pete-pete* (10,000Rp, one hour) to Maros from Makassar Mall in Makassar, and a *pete-pete* to Bantimurung (6000Rp, 30 minutes).

GUA LEANG LEANG

A few kilometres before Bantimurung is the road to these caves, noted for their ancient paintings. The exact age of the paintings is unknown, but relics from nearby caves have provided glimpses of life from 8000 to 30,000 years ago. There are 60 or so known caves in the Maros district, as the limestone karsts here have more holes than Swiss cheese.

Catch a *pete-pete* from Maros to the 'Taman Purbakala Leang-Leang' turn-off on the road to Bantimurung, and then walk the last couple of kilometres. Alternatively, charter a *pete-pete* from Maros and combine it with a trip to Bantimurung.

MALINO

0417

Malino is a hill resort, once famous as the meeting place of Kalimantan and East Indonesian leaders who endorsed the Netherlands' ill-fated plans for a federation. More recently, peace agreements have been struck for Maluku and Poso in the Resort Celebes. There are many scenic walks, and **Air Terjun Takapala** is a spectacular waterfall set amid rice fields 4km east of town. Look for the 'Wisata Alam Lombasang Malino' sign as you come into town for the waterfall turn-off.

Hotel Pinang Mas (21173; Jl Karaeng Pado; r from 200,000Rp) is the place for huge views, but the prices are equally huge given the standard of the rooms. It's on the main road, about 150m above the muddy market.

Resort Celebes (21300; Jl Hasanuddin 1; r from 300,000Rp) is a must for those with a sense of history, as many an important political agreement has been hammered out here. All rooms include satellite TV and hot water. It's a very peaceful place.

Both hotels have popular restaurants; otherwise you can eat at hole-in-the-wall warungs.

Terminal Sungguminasa has regular *pete-pete* services to Malino (16,000Rp, 2½ hours). Make sure you leave early before Malino's infamous rain sets in.

Pantai Bira

0413

Goats outnumber vehicles in the charmingly lethargic beach village of Bira, and it's a particularly inexpensive spot for backpackers to stop for a while and chill out. The powdery white-sand beach gets spacious at low tide and there's great snorkelling a short swim from the shore. There are several more remote beaches, hiking and a few caves with freshwater pools to explore in the surrounding area. The diving here is very good, with more fish than you'll find at Bunaken or in the Togeans, but strong currents make it suitable only for experienced divers.

Sights

Boat builders use age-old techniques to craft **traditional ships** at Marumasa near Bira village and at Tanah Beru on the road to Bulukumba. Boats of various sizes can be seen at different stages of construction.

There is a small market, **Pasar Bira** held in the village every two days.

A short hike from the road near Pantai Timur takes you to the top of **Pua Janggo**, a small hill with great views. Staff of all the hotels and guesthouses can tell you how to get to caves and deserted beaches nearby by public transport.

If you want to visit the beach, bear in mind that the locals are fairly conservative around here, so topless bathing for women is a major no-no. Wearing a bikini is fine (on beaches only) but you will get stared at and Makassar day-trippers will probably ask to get their photo taken with you. Besides the central Bira beaches we've listed here, there are also several more remote beaches and swimming areas several kilometres out of town that are worth exploring by motorbike.

The tides can be severe, but **Pantai Barat** (West Beach) is a perfect stretch of beach, about 100m northwest of Bira Beach Hotel. You can hire huge inflatable rubber tyres, and enjoy the serenity – except on Sunday, when the place is usually crawling with daytrippers from Makassar.

Pantai Bara, about a 20-minute walk along the beach north from Pantai Bira (low tide only) is the most beautiful beach in the area and it stays very quiet even on weekends. At high tide you can get here via a 45-minute walk from Pantai Bira's main drag along a shady dirt road.

Pantai Timur (East Beach) is a coconut-fringed affair near the boat dock in Bira Village but it's often covered in rubbish.

Activities

The waters off Bira are particularly popular with sharks, rays and huge groupers, and there is superb coral at several drop-offs. May to June is whale-shark season although you'd be lucky to see one. The best spots are around Pulau Selayar, Marumasa, northern Pulau Lihukan, and southern and eastern Pulau Betang.

Snorkelling is also impressive off Bira and it's worth chartering a boat to get to the best spots. A trip around Pulau Lihukan and Pulau Betang will cost about 300,000Rp per day for a boat for up to 10 people. The beach in front

Around Pantai Bira

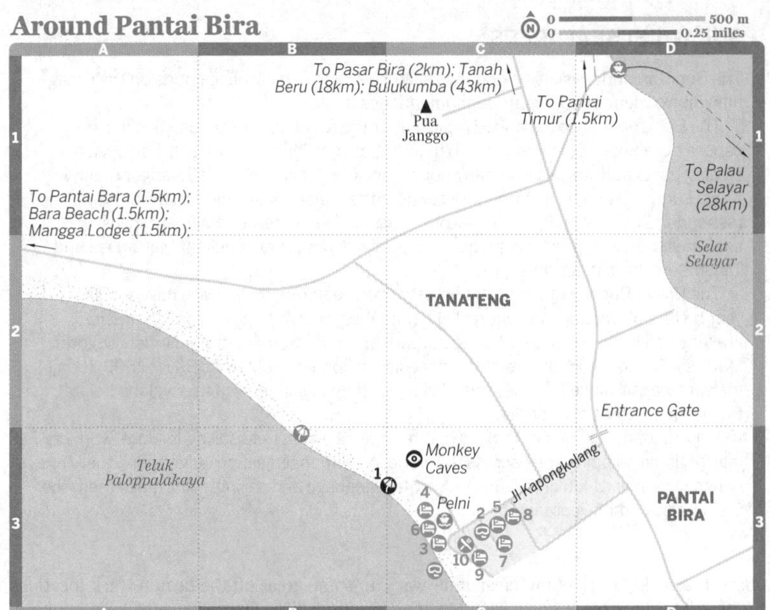

of Bira View Inn is good, but don't venture too far out – the currents can be surprisingly strong and people have drowned. Equipment can be rented for about 50,000Rp per day from several hotels, including Riswan Guest House, Bira View Inn and Bira Beach Hotel.

Bira Divers DIVING
(biradivers@hotmail.com; dives €35) Opened in 2012, this centre is the collaboration between a local who's been diving the area most of his life and a friendly English dive instructor. They have great new equipment and a convenient location near where the main road hits the beach.

South Sulawesi Diver DIVING
(☎082 1244 436626; www.south-sulawesi-diver.com; dives €30) Elvis, the German dive instructor here has been leading dives around Bira longer than anyone. Find him at Mangga Lodge (p646).

Sleeping

Places are close together so you can shop around before deciding where to stay – a good idea since most are not very well kept.

TOP CHOICE **Sunshine Guesthouse** GUESTHOUSE $
(Nini's Place; ☎082 1909 31175; ninibone@hotmail.com; r with breakfast 120,000Rp) Perched up on

Around Pantai Bira

Sights
1 Pantai Barat.......C3

Activities
2 South Sulawesi Diver.......C3

Sleeping
3 Amatoa Beach Resort.......C3
4 Anda Beach Resort.......C3
5 Anda Bungalows.......C3
6 Bira Beach Hotel.......C3
7 Riswan Guest House.......C3
8 Salassa Guest House.......C3
9 Sunshine Guesthouse.......C3

Eating
10 Food & Drink Stalls.......C3

a hill with ocean views, British-Indonesian-run Sunshine has a fresh coat of paint, a wonderful communal terrace with sea breezes, a convivial atmosphere and is easily the best-tended place in Bira. Comfy rooms in a big wooden house have spotless shared bathrooms.

Amatoa Beach Resort RESORT $$$
(☎081 3533 76865; www.amatoaresort.com; 6 Jl Pasir Putih; bungalows €150;) Perched

SULAWESI SEAFARERS

The Bugis are Indonesia's best-known sailors, trading and carrying goods on their magnificent wooden schooners throughout Indonesia.

The Bugis' influence expanded rapidly after the fall of Makassar, resulting in a diaspora from South Sulawesi in the 17th and 18th centuries. They established strategic trading posts at Kutai (Kalimantan), Johor (north of Singapore) and Selangor (near Kuala Lumpur), and traded freely throughout the region. Bugis and Makassarese *pinisi* (schooners) are still built along the south coasts of Sulawesi and Kalimantan, using centuries-old designs and techniques. You can see boats being built at Marumasa and Tanah Beru, both near Bira.

The Bajau, Bugis, Butonese and Makassarese seafarers of Sulawesi have a 500-year history of trading and cultural links with Aboriginal Australians, and their ships are featured in pre-European Aboriginal cave art in northern Australia. British explorer Matthew Flinders encountered 60 Indonesian schooners at Melville Bay in 1803; today many more still make the risky (and illegal) journey to fish reefs in the cyclone belt off the northern coast of Australia.

Many Minahasans of North Sulawesi, relative newcomers to sailing folklore, work on international shipping lines across the world. As with their Filipino neighbours, the Minahasans outward-looking culture, plus their language and sailing skills, make them the first choice of many captains.

above the rocks overlooking clear blue water, this luxurious place has a Mediterranean feel to it. Think stone work, naturalistic wood features, cactus and breezy neutral-toned drapes. Don't forget the infinity pool, cushioned day beds and gourmet food. Bliss.

Mangga Lodge HOTEL **$$**
(☎270 0756; www.mangga-lodge.com; Jl Poros Bara; r from €45; ❄@) This lovely arched building reminiscent of a winery has comfortable stylish rooms a stone's throw from Bara Beach. This is a good choice for divers as South Sulawesi Divers is located here and there are lots of other organised outings on offer to the surrounding area. German-run.

Bara Beach BUNGALOWS **$$**
(☎0813 42906750; www.bara-beach.com; Jl Poros Bara; bungalows 700,000-950,000Rp) Overlooking dreamy Pantai Bara, the several new, very tidy bungalows here are super-sized with plush bathrooms and terraces. All are in a flowery garden and are priced according to their distance from the beach. The friendly sea-view restaurant is a fabulous place for a sunset Bintang or a meal whether you're staying here or not.

Salassa Guest House GUESTHOUSE **$**
(☎081 2426 5672; r 80,000Rp) A family-run place, Salassa has basic rooms with an Indonesian-style shared bathroom in a wooden house on stilts. The owners are very helpful, speak English and can direct you to some great off-the-beaten-track locations around Bira. The restaurant here is one of the best in town.

Anda Beach Resort HOTEL **$$$**
(r850,000-950,000Rp; ❄) Relatively new and occupying a plumb part of Pantai Bira, this is one of the area's plusher options, although the comfortable, tiled rooms are already starting to look older than they actually are. Bintang and meals (Indonesian and Western) at the stylish restaurant – built like a giant ship – go down well with the sunset.

Riswan Guest House GUESTHOUSE **$**
(☎0812 4265627; s/d 75,000/95,000Rp; @) Rooms here are simple but very clean and have attached bathrooms. Host Riswan is friendly and knowledgeable and the family atmosphere is simply charming.

Anda Bungalows BUNGALOWS **$$**
(☎82125; bungalows 400,000-650,000Rp; ❄) All the bungalows here have air-con and are set around a lovely landscaped garden away from the sea; the newer cement ones are quite comfy. Cheaper wooden bungalows aren't as posh but are still OK value and the big restaurant here has lots of choices.

Eating

Most guesthouses serve family-style meals while the hotels have more expensive restaurants. The **Bira Beach Hotel** (☎83522; bungalows 150,000-250,000Rp; ❄) right where the main road hits the beach is a good place for a sunset Bintang followed by a meal (about 20,000Rp), as are a few of the other guesthouses mentioned under Sleeping.

There are also a couple of local Indonesian restaurants and **food and drink stalls** serving Indonesian fare and freshly grilled fish along the main drag and beachfront.

Information

Almost everything is located along a small section of the road into Pantai Bira, Jl Kapongkolang. Foreign tourists must pay 5000Rp per person at the toll booth when they first enter 'town'. There's a BNI Bank ATM at the harbour entrance and many guesthouses offer internet access via a GSM-enabled data stick.

Getting There & Away

BOAT The harbour at Pantai Timur has daily services to Pulau Selayar (two hours, 75,000Rp). Every Sunday night, there is a direct boat to Labuanbajo in Flores (111,000Rp), but it's a slow ride, taking almost two days.

BUS, BEMO & KIJANG From Makassar (Terminal Mallengkeri), a few Kijangs go directly to Pantai Bira for 55,000Rp; the trip takes between five and seven hours. Alternatively, catch a Kijang or bemo to Bulukumba, and another to Pantai Bira (transport from Bulukumba to Pantai Bira stops at around 3pm). Direct Kijangs from Pantai Bira to Makassar (55,000Rp) can sometimes be booked through your hotel the day before; otherwise get a *pete-pete* from Pantai Bira to Bulukumba and take a Kijang to Makassar from there; the price also works out to 55,000Rp.

Pulau Lihukan & Pulau Betang

Weavers at **Ta'Buntuleng** make heavy, colourful cloth on hand looms under their houses. On the pretty beach west of the village there is an interesting old **graveyard**, and off the beach there are acres of sea grass and coral, but mind the currents and sea snakes. To see the best coral, which is further out, you'll need a boat. In fact, you'll need to charter a boat to visit Lihukan and the nearby, uninhabited Pulau Betang, also known as Pulau Kambing.

Sleeping & Eating

Wisma & Restaurant Leukang Loe GUESTHOUSE **$**
(☎081 3425 78515; Pulau Lihukan; 200,000Rp per person incl 3 meals) Right on the white beach overlooking the mainland and in front of good snorkelling, no English is spoken here but the polished wood bungalows are surprisingly modern. If you just want to eat, fresh fish with veg and rice costs 35,000Rp.

Pulau Selayar

☎0414

This long, narrow island lies off the southwestern peninsula of Sulawesi and is inhabited by the Bugis, the Makassarese and the Konjo. Most reside along the infertile west coast and in **Benteng**, the main town. Like at Pantai Bira, Selayar's long coastline is a repository of flotsam from nearby shipping lines, perhaps accounting for the presence of a 2000-year-old Vietnamese Dongson drum, kept in an annexe near the former **Benteng Bontobangun** (Bontobangun Fort), a few kilometres south of Benteng.

Selayar's main attractions are its sandy **beaches** and picturesque scenery. The snorkelling near small **Pulau Pasi**, opposite Benteng, is good, but you will have to charter a boat.

Stay at **Selayar Island Resort** (☎217 590; www.selayarislandresort.com; cottages per person €90-190; ❄📶), a posh place perched on a rocky outcrop next to its own beach. There's a range of comfortable rooms as well as a dive centre that leads dives to some extraordinary, little-visited sites.

There is a daily ferry (two hours, 75,000Rp) from Pantai Timur harbour near Pantai Bira to/from Pamatata on Selayar. The hotel should know the current schedule (it was 10am at the time of research) or can arrange private transport. Buses leave Terminal Mallengkeri in Makassar each morning to link with the ferry from Pantai Bira.

Taka Bone Rate

Southeast of Pulau Selayar and north of Pulau Bone Rate, is the 2220-sq-km Taka Bone Rate, the world's third-largest coral atoll. The largest, Kwajalein in the Marshall Islands, is just 20% bigger. Some of the islands and extensive reefs in the region are now part of **Taka Bone Rate Marine National Park** (Taman Laut Taka Bone Rate), a marine reserve with a rich variety of sea and bird life.

There is no official accommodation on the islands, but if you manage to get here you can stay with villagers if you ask the *kepala desa* (village head) at Bone Rate on Pulau Bone Rate. Boats leave irregularly from Selayar. Most visitors are divers on liveaboard trips.

Watampone

☎0481 / POP 84,000

Known more simply as Bone (bone-eh) by locals, Watampone is a small town with a good range of hotels. The only reason most foreigners come here is to go to/from Kolaka in Southeast Sulawesi from the nearby port of Bajoe or to break up a trip to Tana Toraja.

While in town, visit **Museum Lapawawoi** (Jl Thamrin; admission free; ⏰7am-4pm), a former palace housing one of Indonesia's most interesting regional collections, including an odd array of court memorabilia and dozens of photographs of state occasions.

If you do end up staying overnight, try **Wisma Bulo Gading** (☎24750; 38 Jl Ahmad Yani; r fan/air-con 85,000/150,000Rp), which is clean and excellent value although little English is spoken.

Pantai Kering near the bus station is the best place to eat with lots of warungs, market stalls and music at night.

Getting There & Away

BOAT Bajoe is the major regional port, 8km from Watampone, for connections to Kolaka. Ferries (eight hours) leave every evening from Bajoe for Kolaka, the gateway to the southeastern peninsula. Tickets are 62,000/90,000Rp for deck/business class. From Watampone, bemos go to Bajoe every few minutes from a special stop behind the market. From the bus terminal at the end of the incredibly long causeway in Bajoe, buses head off to most places, including Makassar and Rantepao, just after the ferry arrives. Get off the ferry and jump on an *ojek*, bus or bemo to Watampone.

BUS & BEMO Several Kijangs and buses travel to Bulukumba (65,000Rp, three hours) for connections to Bira and Makassar (60,000Rp, five hours). Buses also run to Palopo and Pare Pare. The terminal is 2km west of town, so take an *ojek* or bemo from Jl Sulawesi. Kijangs to Sengkang (35,000Rp, two hours) leave from Jl Mangga in the centre of Watampone. If you're heading to Rantepao (65,000Rp), get a connection in Palopo. Several bus agencies along Jl Besse Kajuara, on either side of the bus terminal, sell tickets for the through trip to Kendari (150,000Rp).

Sengkang

☎0485

Sengkang is a small yet traffic-clogged town with a nearby scenic lake and a traditional hand-woven silk industry. **BNI bank** (Bank Negara Indonesia; Jl Ahmad Yani) has an ATM and can change money.

Sights & Activities

Danau Tempe LAKE

(100,000Rp with a guide) Danau Tempe is a large, shallow lake fringed by wetlands, with floating houses and magnificent birdlife. Geologists believe the lake was once a gulf between southern Toraja and the rest of South Sulawesi. As they merged, the gulf disappeared and geologists believe the lake will eventually disappear too. Silt from deforestation is speeding up the process.

There are no organised boat tours, but the guesthouses can help you arrange a charter boat for about 100,000Rp for two hours, in which time you can speed along **Sungai Walanae**, visit **Salotangah village** in the middle of the lake, go across to **Batu Batu village** on the other side, and come back. A boat trip is particularly charming at dusk.

You could try to haggle for a cheaper rate on your own at the longboat terminal opposite the sports field on Jl Sudirman.

Silk Weaving CRAFT

Sengkang's other attraction is its *sutera* (silk) weaving industry. Silk-weaving workshops are found around 5km out of town, while the nearest silkworm farms are about 15km from Sengkang. Ask the staff at your hotel to recommend some workshops, and charter a *pete-pete* from the terminal. Alternatively, just walk around the market in Sengkang, where silk scarves and sarongs are on sale.

Sleeping & Eating

All room prices include breakfast.

Pondok Eka GUESTHOUSE $$

(☎21296; Jl Maluku 12; r 175,000-280,000Rp; ❄📶) If you want clean, head here. Rooms, surrounding a sparkling courtyard with a murky pool, are huge and all have air-con and HBO. It's family-run, well located and helpful.

Hotel Al Salam II HOTEL $

(☎21278; fax 21893; Jl Emmi Saelan 8; r 70,000-250,000Rp) Service is friendly and there's a range of large rooms with attached bathrooms. Unfortunately, mattresses are musty and there is plenty of dust in the room corners. There's also a little restaurant and bar on the premises.

Getting There & Away

To/from Rantepao (six hours), take a bemo to Lawawoi (25,000Rp) and catch a bus from there (50,000Rp); alternatively you can go through Palopo. There are regular buses to/from Terminal Daya in Makassar (43,000Rp, six hours), but Kijangs and bemos (60,000Rp, four hours) take a shorter route. Bemos to local destinations leave from the bus terminal behind the market on Jl Kartini. Agencies for long-distance buses, Kijangs and Pelni boats are a few metres south of the terminal.

Pare Pare

☎0421 / POP 114,000

Pare Pare is a bright, hilly town with plenty of greenery, and it's a quiet stopover between Tana Toraja or Mamasa and Makassar. It's also the second-largest port in the region, with many Pelni services and boats to Kalimantan.

Sleeping & Eating

Hotel Gandaria I HOTEL $

(☎21093; Jl Bau Massepe 395; s/d with fan 65,000/100,000Rp) A friendly, family-run spot which has good-value rooms. There's a second location, with the same prices, on Jl Samporaja.

Hotel Kenari Bukit Indah HOTEL $$

(☎21886; Jl Jendral Sudirman 65; s/d from 250,000/350,000Rp; ❄) This hotel is a little way out of town, but for those with transport it is worth it for the superb sea views and well-regarded restaurant. The rooms are some of the most comfortable in Pare Pare, with air-con, TV and hot water, although they are a bit age-worn.

There are several small *rumah makan* (eating houses) along Jl Baso Daeng Patompo, in the vicinity of Hotel Siswa. At night, warungs line the esplanade, each with exactly the same choice of rice and noodle dishes.

Information

The town is stretched out along the waterfront. At night, the esplanade turns into a lively pedestrian mall with warungs. Most of what you might need is on the streets running parallel to the harbour. The major banks change money and internet can be found at the main post office on Jl Karaeng Burane.

Getting There & Away

BOAT The main reason to come to Pare Pare is to catch a ship to East Kalimantan. Every two weeks **Pelni** (☎21017; Jl Andicammi) runs the *Tidar* to Nunukan in Kalimantan and the *Siguntang* to Balikpapan (tickets from 145,000Rp). Every one or two days, several passenger boats travel from Pare Pare to Samarinda (22 hours) and Balikpapan (two nights), but these boats have a poorer safety record than the Pelni ships (in January 2009 one of these passenger boats sank, killing 180 people). Details and bookings are available from agencies near the port and just north of Restaurant Asia.

BUS Plenty of buses and Kijangs go to Makassar (27,800Rp, three hours) and Rantepao (40,000Rp, five hours). Most buses travel through Terminal Induk, several kilometres south of the city, but it's often easier to hail a bus as it flies through town. Kijangs to Polewali (26,000Rp, two hours) leave from Terminal Soreang, 3km northeast of town.

TANA TORAJA

A trip to Tana Toraja is like a cultural documentary brought to life. Sweeping and elaborately painted houses with boat-shaped roofs dot terraced rice paddies where farmers work the fields alongside their doe-eyed buffalo. It's an island hemmed in by mountains on all sides and rich with traditional culture. Life for the Toraja revolves around death, and their days are spent earning the money to send away their dead properly. Funeral ceremonies bring together families who may have dispersed as far as Papua or even Australia. Buffalo and pigs are sacrificed, there is a slew of traditional dances and enough food and drink for everyone who can make it to the party. High-class Toraja are entombed in cave graves or hanging graves in the steep cliffs, which are guarded over by *tau tau* (life-sized wooden effigies) carved in their image – you'll find these eerie yet beautiful cliff cemeteries scattered throughout the region.

The biggest funerals are usually held in the dry-season months of July and August, but there are funerals (even big ones) year-round. During July and August the tourist numbers swell to uncomfortable proportions and prices soar. Outside these months, you'll share this cool countryside with the locals and only a handful of foreign travellers. While most people consider attending a funeral a highlight, Tana Toraja also offers some great do-it-yourself trekking opportunities where you can explore the fresh and clean outdoors and meet some of the most hospitable people you'll ever encounter.

Tana Toraja

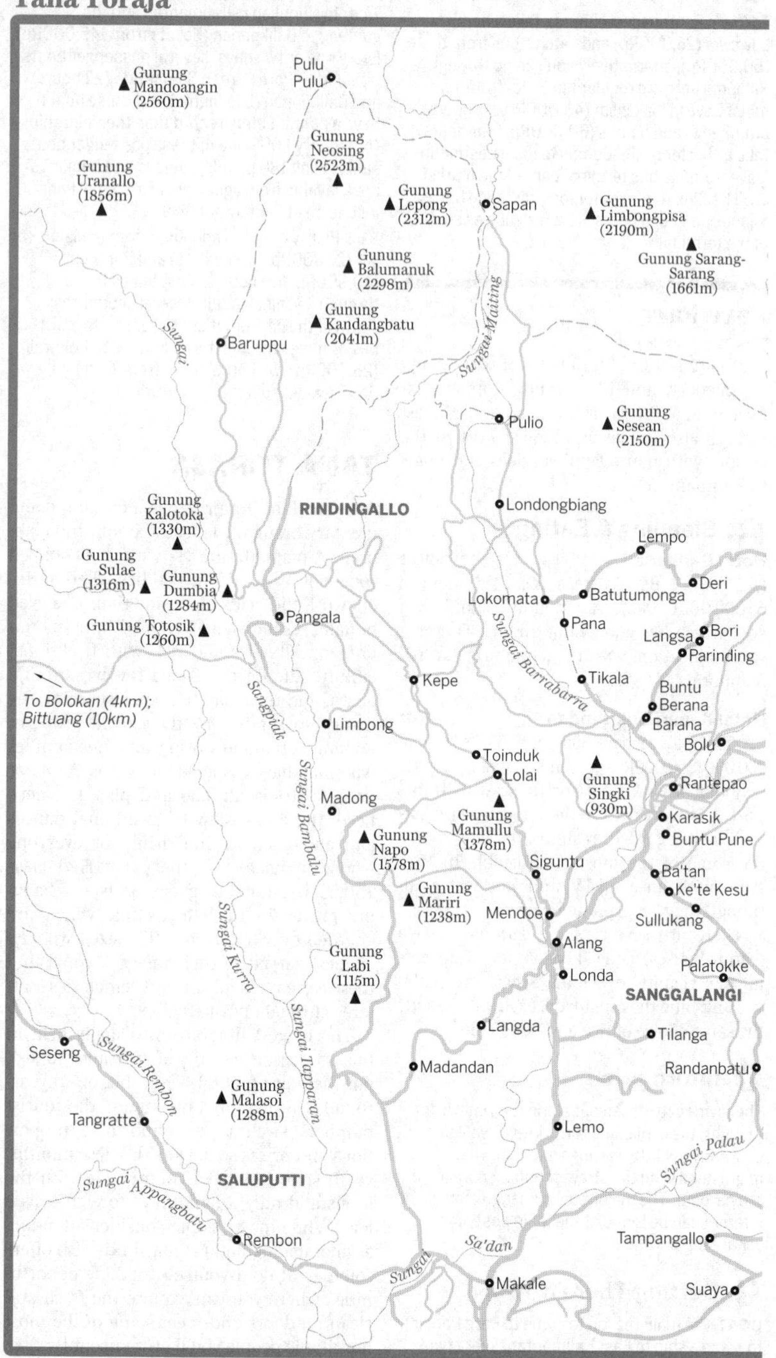
Gunung Mandoangin (2560m)
Pulu Pulu
Gunung Neosing (2523m)
Gunung Uranallo (1856m)
Gunung Lepong (2312m)
Sapan
Gunung Limbongpisa (2190m)
Gunung Sarang-Sarang (1661m)
Gunung Balumanuk (2298m)
Gunung Kandangbatu (2041m)
Baruppu
Sungai
Sungai Maiting
Pulio
Gunung Sesean (2150m)
Londongbiang
RINDINGALLO
Gunung Kalotoka (1330m)
Gunung Sulae (1316m)
Gunung Dumbia (1284m)
Gunung Totosik (1260m)
Pangala
Lempo
Deri
Lokomata
Batutumonga
Pana
Sungai Barrabarra
Langsa
Bori
Paringding
Tikala
Kepe
To Bolokan (4km); Bittuang (10km)
Sangpiak
Limbong
Buntu Berana
Barana
Bolu
Toinduk
Lolai
Gunung Singki (930m)
Rantepao
Sungai Bambalu
Madong
Gunung Mamullu (1378m)
Gunung Napo (1578m)
Karasik
Buntu Pune
Siguntu
Ba'tan
Ke'te Kesu
Gunung Mariri (1238m)
Mendoe
Sullukang
Sungai Kurra
Alang
Gunung Labi (1115m)
Londa
Palatokke
SANGGALANGI
Sungai Tapparan
Langda
Tilanga
Seseng
Sungai Rembon
Madandan
Randanbatu
Gunung Malasoi (1288m)
Tangratte
Lemo
Sungai Palau
SALUPUTTI
Sungai Appangbatu
Rembon
Sa'dan
Tampangallo
Sungai
Makale
Suaya

Rantepao

☎0423 / POP 45,000

Rantepao is an easy-to-manage place that's in striking distance of most of the major sites and has a good range of accommodation and restaurants. It's the largest town and commercial centre of Tana Toraja, but traffic isn't too heavy and the streets are fringed by greenery. It's the obvious place to base a trip to the region. Nights can be cool and there is rain throughout the year.

Sights

Pasar Bolu MARKET

Rantepao's main market is held every six days (but operates in a reduced capacity daily). The main market is a very big, social occasion that draws crowds from all over Tana Toraja. Ask around Rantepao for the exact day, or seek out other markets in the area. There is a 10,000Rp charge to enter the livestock market, where the leading lights from the buffalo community are on parade. Many cost more than a small car. Pasar Bolu is 2km northeast of town and easily accessible by bemo.

Activities

Most of the activities lie in the hills beyond. However, most of the hotels that have **swimming pools** allow nonguests to swim for a fee of about 15,000Rp.

Tours

There are independent guides to the countryside around Rantepao. There are also agencies in Rantepao, which can arrange more luxurious tours (including trekking and cultural tours), vehicles and guides.

Indosella TREKKING, RAFTING

(☎25210; www.sellatours.com; Jl Andi Mappanyukki 111) The only tour company in Rantapao that has stood the test of time. It's not cheap but it is reliably good.

Sleeping

Prices in Rantepao usually rise in the tourist season (June–August), when some private homes also accept guests. Most budget and midrange places include breakfast in their prices, but they don't offer air-conditioning or a fan, as the nights are cool.

Location and views are often the selling points for midrange places, which are mostly located along the roads from Rantepao to Makale or Palopo. They cater almost exclusively for tour groups with their own transport, but individuals are welcome, and rates are pretty negotiable during the long, quiet low season.

Pia's Poppies Hotel GUESTHOUSE **$**
(☎21121; s/d 99,000/120,000Rp; 📶) Rooms here have some quirky details such as stone bathrooms and each terrace overlooks a languorous garden. Sheets are changed daily, everything is spotless, there's hot water and you're even served a welcome fruit juice on arrival. Plus the charming cafe serves the best food in the region – don't miss the Torajan specialties ordered a few hours in advance.

Rantepao

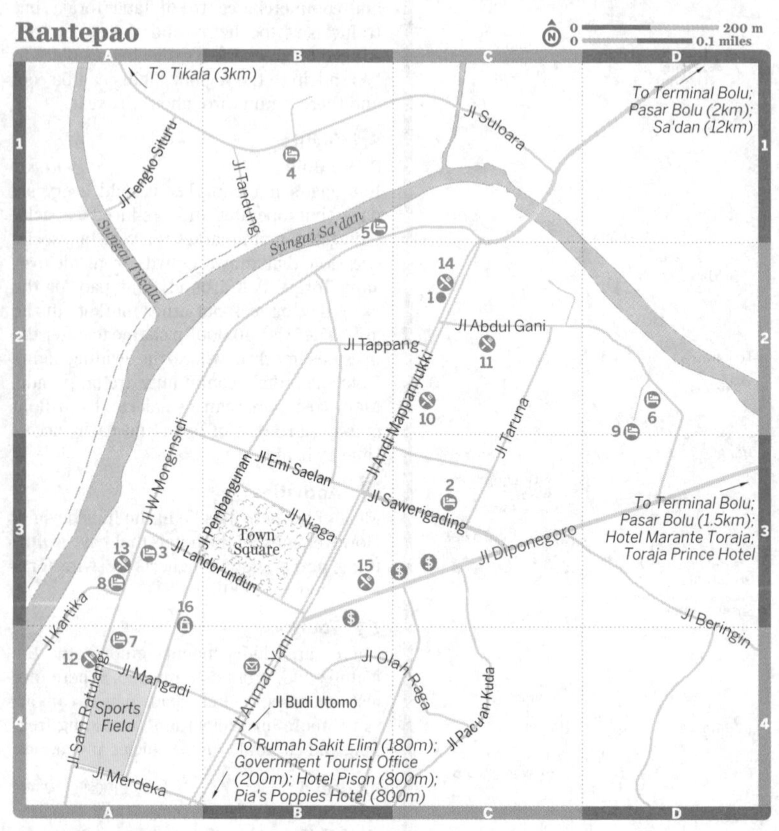

Rantepao

Activities
1 Indosella ... C2

Sleeping
2 Duta 88 Cottages ... C3
3 Hotel Indra Toraja ... A3
4 Madaranda ... B1
5 Wisma Imanuel ... B1
6 Wisma Irama ... D2
7 Wisma Maria I ... A4
8 Wisma Monika ... A3
9 Wisma Monton ... D2

Eating
10 Cafe Aras ... C2
11 Gazebo ... C2
12 Mart's Café ... A4
13 Restoran Mambo ... A3
14 Rimiko Restoran ... C2
15 Rumah Makan Saruran ... B3

Shopping
16 Todi ... A3

Breakfast is not included in the price and it's about a five- to 10-minute walk (or short becak ride) to the town centre.

Luta Resort Toraja HOTEL $$$
(☎21060; www.torajalutaresort.com; 26 Jl Dr Ratulangi; r 575,000-1,010,000Rp incl breakfast; ❄📶) The only luxury hotel in the centre of town is also Tana Toraja's most stylish place to stay. The very comfortable rooms are all tiled and decorated with modern, muted colours. It's worth upgrading to a Superior room which have balconies overlooking the lush central garden, or a Deluxe which have river views. There's a pool and lovely open-air restaurant right at the river's edge.

Hotel Indra Toraja HOTEL $$
(☎21163; www.indratorajahotel.com; Jl Landorundun 63; standard/deluxe r 240,000/700,000Rp; ❄📶) Right in the centre of Rantepao, rooms here are in good shape and have terraces overlooking a common courtyard area. All are clean, have hot water and HBO, breakfasts are good and the service is stellar. It's a busy, happy place.

Wisma Maria I GUESTHOUSE $
(☎21165; adespasaka1@yahoo.com; Jl Sam Ratulangi 23; s/d 60,000/90,000Rp, d with hot water 120,000Rp) At our favourite rock-bottom cheapie in the town centre, rooms are plain but good-sized, bright and very clean. This place also rents out scooters and bicycles and they can suggest itineraries. It's all set around a large garden.

Heritage Toraja RESORT $$$
(☎21192; www.torajaheritage.com; r US$100-175; ❄📶) The Heritage is by far the swankiest resort, with many of the elegant rooms set in huge *tongkonan*-style (traditional Torajan) houses. Standards are high (with some odd details like a fresh flower in the toilet bowls) and there are lush gardens and a lagoon-like pool. Rooms in the more ordinary block are just as nice as the ones inside the Torajan-style houses but are less expensive. Ask for a top-floor room with a view. It's about 3km from town towards Ke'te Kesu.

Madaranda HOTEL $$
(☎23777; Jl Sadan 21; d 350,000Rp) The huge, modern and clean rooms inside Torajan-style houses are great value for the money. In low season you can easily bargain for better rates. Staff are friendly and the grounds are pleasant, central to town and shady.

BALOK

Rantepao and Makale markets have whole sections devoted to the sale of the alcoholic *balok* (palm wine, also known as *tuak* and toddy). *Balok* is sold in huge jugs around town and comes in a variety of strengths, colours (from clear to dark red, achieved by adding bark) and flavours (sweet to bitter).

Coffee is Toraja's other famous brew, an excellent antidote to a night of *balok* tasting.

Hotel Pison HOTEL $
(☎21344; s/d 120,000/150,000Rp; 📶) The bland but good-value Pison has 32 rooms, each with a clean bathroom and minibalcony with mountain views. All rooms come with hot water.

Hotel Marante Toraja HOTEL $$$
(☎21616; www.marantetoraja.com; Jl Poros Rantepao; deluxe r US$80, cottages US$90) Cement cottages with Torajan-style roofs look great from the outside but are far more bland on the inside. Rooms have the same interiors as the cottages and could use a coat of paint. Fortunately, the staff are exuberant and helpful.

Wisma Monton HOTEL $
(☎21675; Jl Abdul Gani 14A; r 200,000Rp) Hidden away down a side lane, this three-storey establishment has clean and comfortable rooms with hot water. The building is speckled with Toraja decoration and there's a rooftop restaurant with fine views.

Wisma Monika GUESTHOUSE $
(☎21216; 36 Jl Sam Ratulangi; r 100,000-200,000Rp) A very friendly family-run central spot with 20 rooms in a newish cement building. Inspect a few to find a bright one.

Toraja Torsina Hotel HOTEL $$
(☎21293; s/d from US$45/60) Set in the rice fields near the turn-off to Ke'te Kesu, the rooms here are clean and comfortable and worth the rupiah considering the swimming pool. It's dated and a bit tacky but service is good.

Toraja Prince Hotel HOTEL $$
(☎21430; r 430,000-600,000Rp; ❄) Inconveniently located a few kilometres from town on the road to Palopo, the colonial-style rooms here are in good shape. There's an old

THE TORAJA

Inhabiting the vast, rugged landscape of the South Sulawesi highlands are the Toraja, a name derived from the Bugis word *toriaja* that had negative connotations similar to 'hillbilly' or 'bumpkin'.

For centuries Torajan life and culture had survived the constant threat from the Bugis from the southwest, but in 1905 the Dutch began a bloody campaign to bring Central Sulawesi under their control. The missionaries moved in on the heels of the troops, and by WWII many of the great Torajan ceremonies (with the exception of funeral celebrations) were rapidly disappearing from their culture.

Beliefs

Prior to the arrival of Christianity, the Toraja believed in many gods but worshipped Puang Matua as the special god of their family, clan or tribe. Christianity undermined some traditional Torajan beliefs, but the ceremonies are still a vital part of life.

Torajan mythology suggests that their ancestors came by boat from the south, sailed up Sungai Sa'dan (Sa'dan River) and dwelled in the Enrekang region before being pushed into the mountains by the arrival of other groups.

Buffalo are a status symbol for the Toraja and are of paramount importance in various religious ceremonies. The buffalo has traditionally been a symbol of wealth and power – even land could be bought with buffalo. Sought-after albino buffalo can change hands for more than US$8000.

Despite the strength of traditional beliefs, Christianity in Toraja is a very active force. One of the first questions asked of you will be your religion, and Protestants are given immediate approval.

Traditional Houses

One of the most noticeable aspects about Tana Toraja is the size and grandeur of the *tongkonan* (traditional house). It is the place for family gatherings and may not be bought or sold.

The towering roof, rearing up at either end, is the most striking aspect of a *tongkonan*. Some believe the roof represents the horns of a buffalo; others suggest it represents the bow and stern of a boat. The more buffalo horns visible, the higher the household's status.

1970s-style swimming pool and lots of lush garden space, so this isn't a bad choice for families with transport. The staff we met spoke no English.

Wisma Irama GUESTHOUSE $
(☎21371; Jl Abdul Gani 16; r from 90,000Rp) On a quiet road, the pleasant but ageing rooms here surround a grassy courtyard with a traditional rice barn in the centre.

Wisma Imanuel GUESTHOUSE $
(☎21416; Jl W Monginsidi 16; r 90,000-130,000Rp) Set in a large house backed by the river (but there's no access), the rooms here are a generous size and the more expensive include hot-water showers. Big balconies out front offer views over the garden and street-action beyond.

Duta 88 Cottages GUESTHOUSE $
(☎23477; Jl Sawerigading 12; r 200,000Rp) A slight step up in rupiah from the rest of the budget choices gets you a lovely *tongkonan*-style (traditional Torajan) cottage, set around a verdant little garden. All come with hot water and satellite TV. Rates include breakfast but service can be hit or miss.

Eating

Going to ceremonies or local restaurants offers a great opportunity to sample Torajan food. The best-known dish is *pa'piong* (meat stuffed into bamboo tubes along with vegetables and coconut). If you want to try it in a restaurant, order several hours in advance because it takes time to cook.

Gazebo TORAJAN $
(Jl Abdul Gani; meals 15,000-40,000Rp; ⏲breakfast, lunch & dinner) The nicest setting for a meal in town is at this carved rice barn-style place with a front garden and a semi-outdoor eating area. The menu is mostly

Funerals

Of all Torajan ceremonies, the most important is the *tomate* (funeral; literally 'deceased'). Without proper funeral rites the soul of the deceased will cause misfortune to its family.

The Toraja generally have two funeral ceremonies, one immediately after death and an elaborate second funeral after preparations have been made. The bigger ones are usually scheduled during the dry months of July and August, but there are funerals year-round.

Before the second funeral, the deceased remains in the family house. An invitation to visit the deceased is an honour. If you accept, remember to thank the deceased and ask permission of the deceased when you wish to leave – as you would of a living host.

The second funeral can be spread over several days and involve hundreds of guests. The Toraja believe that the souls of animals should follow their masters to the next life, hence the importance of animal sacrifices. Festivities often start with bullfights where lots of lively betting takes place and some famous fighting bulls may be imported for the event from the distant reaches of the country. The bullfights will be disturbing for animal lovers while the sacrifices will be very traumatic – these two kinds of events are best avoided if you cringe at the sight of blood..

Visitors attending a funeral should wear black or dark-coloured clothing and bring gifts of sugar or cigarettes for the family of the deceased.

Graves & Tau Tau

The Toraja believe that you can take possessions with you in the afterlife, and the dead generally go well equipped to their graves. As this led to grave plundering, the Toraja started to hide their dead in caves.

These caves are hollowed out by specialist cave builders. Coffins go deep inside the caves, and sitting on balconies in the rock face in front of the caves are *tau tau* – wooden effigies of the dead.

You can see *tau tau* carvers at work at Londa. There are many *tau tau* at Lemo and a few elsewhere, but it's becoming increasingly difficult to see them in Tana Toraja. So many have been stolen that the Toraja now keep them in their homes.

Indonesian with plenty of Torajan specialties that need to be ordered a few hours in advance. There's also another location out of town on the road towards Ke'te Kesu.

Mart's Café INDONESIAN, WESTERN **$**
(Jl Sam Ratulangi 44; dishes 15,000-45,000Rp; ⏲breakfast, lunch & dinner) The best tourist trap in town, Mart's gets lively in the evenings when the resident guides start crooning and strumming their guitars. The food is bland but OK and includes Western fare, Indonesian staples and Torajan specialties (order in advance). The Bintang flows and it's almost like a real night out. There were rumours this place was going to close when we passed but we're leaving it in the guidebook in the hope it doesn't!

Cafe Aras INDONESIAN, STEAK **$$**
(Jl Andi Mappanyukki; dishes 20,000-80,000; ⏲breakfast, lunch & dinner) A sign that Rantepao might be getting hip, this new place has an urban-cafe-meets-tribal-art decor and mellow music is pumped throughout. Besides Indonesian food and a good selection of steaks, you'll find the best pizza in town here.

Rumah Makan Saruran INDONESIAN, CHINESE **$**
(Jl Diponegoro 19; mains around 15,000Rp; ⏲breakfast, lunch & dinner) Indonesian-style Chinese food is served at this hopping restaurant that's popular with young travelling Indonesians. The atmosphere is basic but the food is good and cheap.

Rimiko Restoran WESTERN, INDONESIAN **$**
(Jl Andi Mappanyukki; dishes from 15,000Rp; ⏲breakfast, lunch & dinner) This place serves the best food of the tourist-oriented restaurants and has a few Torajan specialties on the menu that don't require ordering in advance. It's two doors down from the Indosella office.

Restoran Mambo WESTERN $
(Jl Sam Ratulangi; dishes from 15,000Rp; ⌚breakfast, lunch & dinner; 📶) Geared towards tourists, this place has a long menu including everything from an interesting interpretation of a burrito to buffalo meat.

Shopping

Woodcarving, weaving and basketry are the main crafts of Tana Toraja – some villages are noted for particular specialities, such as Mamasan boxes (used to store 'magic', salt and betel nuts), huge horn necklaces and wooden figurines. Woodcarvings include trays, panels and clocks. The carvers at Ke'te Kesu and Londa are renowned for the quality of their work.

Artefacts sold in souvenir shops, especially around the market building in town, include small replicas of Torajan houses with exaggerated overhanging roofs; Torajan weaving (especially good in Sa'dan); and the longer cloths of the Mamasa Valley. Necklaces made of seeds, chunky silver, and amber or wooden beads festoon the gift shops, but the orange-bead necklaces are authentic Torajan. Black-and-red velvet drawstring bags are popular with tourists, to the amusement of locals who use them for carrying betel nut to funerals.

Todi CRAFTS
(www.todi.co.id; 19 Jl Pembangunan) The leading *ikat* (cloth in which the pattern is produced by dyeing the individual threads before weaving) gallery in Tana Toraja has a stunning showroom and there are some fine pieces available. Prices are high and you are expected to bargain a little – although hard haggling falls flat.

Information

If you're doing some serious hiking, pick up a copy of the detailed *Tana Toraja* (1:85,000) map, published by Periplus.

There are internet cafes all over town and the cheaper ones charge 5000Rp per hour.

The best exchange rates are available from moneychangers.

Bank Danamon (Jl Diponegoro) Has an ATM; also offers heftier cash advances.

BNI Bank (Bank Negara Indonesia; Jl Diponegoro) Another ATM.

Government Tourist Office (☎21277; Jl Ahmad Yani 62A) The friendly staff here can provide accurate, independent information about local ceremonies, festivals and other activities as well as arrange guides.

Marazavalas (Jl Diponegoro) Moneychanger with reasonable rates.

Post Office (Jl Ahmad Yani; ⌚8am-4pm Mon-Sat)

Rumah Sakit Elim (☎21258; Jl Ahmad Yani) The main hospital in town. If anything serious should befall you in Toraja, make for Makassar, as facilities here are basic.

Getting There & Away

AIR Rantepao has an airstrip, but at the time of writing no airlines were servicing the town.

BUS & BEMO Most long-distance buses leave from the bus company offices along Jl Andi Mappanyukki. Buses often run at night, and prices vary according to speed and the level of comfort and space.

The most comfortable buses to/from Makassar (with slightly higher prices to match) are Charisma (which has wi-fi), Bintang Prima and Litha. Try to book tickets a day or so in advance. Various companies also have services to Mamuju via Polewali, from where there are connections to Mamasa. From Terminal Bolu, 2km north of Rantepao, there are regular vehicles to Palopo. From the corner of Jl Landorundun and Jl Andi Mappanyukki, Kijangs leave every few minutes to Makale (5000Rp, 20 minutes) and other places in Tana Toraja including Terminal Bolu.

BUSES FROM RANTEPAO

DESTINATION	COST (RP)	DURATION (HR)
Makassar (Terminal Daya)	80,000-100,000	8
Mamasa (from Makale)	100,000	12
Palu	150,000	20
Pare Pare	40,000	5
Pendelo	100,000	8
Poso	120,000	12
Tentena	110,000	10

GETTING TO THE TOGEAN ISLANDS

Many visitors want to get from Tana Toraja to the Togean Islands, and fast. Unfortunately, this is Sulawesi and fast doesn't translate well along the winding, potholed mountain roads. Until something changes (there has been talk of an airport in Ampana although this is unlikely to happen soon) here are your options:

Longest but easiest Bus to Tentena, overnight or longer in Tentena, bus to Ampana, overnight in Ampana, ferry to Togean Islands. Total time: about three days.

Quicker but expensive Bus to Poso, private car (for up to four people) from Poso to Ampana (500,000Rp; arrange from Rantepao and haggle hard) at around 2am to catch the morning ferry to the Togeans. Total time: 1½ days.

Most comfortable Bus to Makassar, plane to Poso, Luwuk or Gorontolo, ferry to Togeans. Total time: two to three days.

Of course you can also mix and match these routes like staying over in Tentena then getting a private car to Ampana (700,000Rp), or getting a private car direct from Rantepao to Amapana (2,000,000Rp) but any method is tiring and will ultimately leave you happy to have a beach to lie on for a few days.

Getting Around

Rantepao is small and easy to walk around. A becak should cost around 5000Rp in town.

Makale

☎0423

Makale is the administrative capital of Tana Toraja, but has very few of the amenities of Rantepao. It's a small town built around an artificial lake and set amid whitewashed churches sitting atop cloud-shrouded hills. The market, however, is a blur of noise and colour. On the main market day, held every six days, you'll see pigs strapped down with bamboo strips for buyers' close inspection, buckets of live eels, piles of fresh and dried fish, and a corner of the market is reserved just for *balok* sales.

Though well connected to most of Tana Toraja by bemo, other than to switch buses or visit the market there's not much reason to stick around.

Getting There & Away

From dawn to dusk, Kijangs race between Rantepao and Makale (5000Rp, 20 minutes) – just flag one down. Most of the bus companies based in Rantepao also have offices near the corner of Jl Merdeka and Jl Ihwan Rombe in Makale. Buses will pick up prebooked passengers in Makale for any destination from Rantepao. The only direct bus connection between Tana Toraja and Mamasa is with Disco Indah every morning at around 8.30am (100,000Rp, 12 hours).

Around Tana Toraja

To really experience all that Tana Toraja has to offer, you'll need to spend a few days – or, even better, a few nights – in this tantalising countryside. Stunning scenery, cascading rice fields, precipitous cliff graves, other-worldly *tau tau,* hanging graves, soaring *tongkonan* and colourful ceremonies – this is the wild world of Tana Toraja and it lies just a short walk or ride away from Rantepao.

There are many places that can be reached via day trips from Rantepao, but longer trips are possible, staying overnight in villages or camping out. Public transport, organised tours, motorbike or mountain-bike rental, vehicle rental with a driver-cum-guide or, best of all, walking – anything is possible.

The roads to major towns, such as Makale, Palopo, Sa'dan, Batutumonga, Madandan and Bittuang, are paved, but many other roads around Tana Toraja are constructed out of compacted boulders – vehicles don't get stuck, but your joints get rattled loose. Walking is often the only way to reach the remote villages.

A few areas such as Londa, Lemo, Tampangallo, Ke'te Kesu and, to a lesser extent, Palawa have become a bit like tourist traps with lots of stalls selling trinkets and a jaded welcome, but it happened because these places are exceptionally beautiful. There are still plenty of lesser-visited gems to get to, especially if you take off on foot far from the tour-bus circuit.

Activities

TREKKING

This is the best way to reach isolated areas and to get a feel for the countryside and the people. You should always take good footwear; a water bottle and food; a strong torch (flashlight) and spare batteries in case you walk at night, stay in villages without electricity or want to explore caves; and an umbrella or raincoat – even in the dry season, it's more likely than not to rain. If you're taking advantage of Torajan hospitality, bring gifts for your hosts (1kg sacks of sugar and cigarettes are favourites) or pay your way.

If you prefer a professional trekking company, contact Indosella. Shorter hikes are available, but a few of the popular longer treks include the following routes:

Batutumonga–Lokomata–Pangala–Baruppu–Pulu Pulu–Sapan Three days of superb scenery. The Batutumonga to Pangala stretch is on a motorbike-accessible road, while the rest is more serious uphill-trail hiking.

Bittuang–Mamasa Three days.

Pangala–Bolokan–Bittuang Two days on a well-marked trail through pristine villages.

Sa'dan–Sapan–Pulu Pulu–Baruppu–Pangala Three days; tough and mountainous – a real mountain trek.

RAFTING

Indosella (☎25210; www.sellatours.com; Jl Andi Mappanyukki 111) is the most professional and reliable outfit offering rafting trips on Sungai Sa'dan's 20 rapids, including a few that are Class IV (read: pretty wild). Rafting trips, including transport to/from your hotel (anywhere in Tana Toraja), equipment, guide, insurance and food, cost 700,000Rp per person (minimum two people) for one day on Class II to III rapids, or US$285 per person for three days on Class III to IV rapids, with overnight stays in local rest huts. Trips get cheaper per person as the tour group gets bigger.

A cheaper and more minimalist approach is to hire an independent guide (however, they usually do not have insurance or good equipment – ask first) for around 500,000Rp per day per person without an overnight stay.

Getting Around

MOTORBIKE & BICYCLE Motorbikes and mountain bikes are available through hotels and some agencies. Remember that roads out of Rantepao and Makale are good but often windy, steep and narrow, so they are more suitable for experienced motorbike riders. Bikes can be used along some walking trails, but the trails are often too rocky.

CHOOSING A GUIDE

In this region, many guides hold a government-approved licence, obtained by undertaking a course in culture, language and etiquette, and being fluent in the local language. Nevertheless, there are competent guides with no certificate (and incompetent licensed guides). The best way to choose a guide is to sit down and talk through a trip before committing. If you feel the guide is pressuring you (or hitting on you), this is probably a good sign to go and find a different guide. There is often a lively discussion about Toraja's better guides on the Thorn Tree forum at lonelyplanet.com/thorntree.

Guides will approach you everywhere and charge 300,000Rp for an all-day circuit by motorbike, including a funeral if there's one on. You can also hire a guide with a car (for up to four people) for 450,000Rp per day, but much of the Toraja region is only accessible on foot or by motorbike so this is a limiting option. For trekking, guides charge 500,000Rp per day. All these rates are slightly negotiable but the 100 or so guides in the area try to keep their rates equal and fixed – you'll have a hard time bargaining with the better and busier guides in high season.

Hiring a guide can be useful to help you get your bearings, learn about the culture and cover a lot of ground quickly, but if you have a sense of direction, a decent map, know a few relevant phrases of Bahasa Indonesia and are not going too far off the beaten track, you won't go too wrong travelling without one. Many people hire a guide for a day or two, then set out on their own.

BEMO & KIJANG Local public transport leaves from central Rantepao and Makale, as well as from the scruffy and muddy Terminal Bolu north of Rantepao; there are regular bemos and Kijangs to all main villages, but the vehicles are poorly signed so you may have to ask around the terminal. See the Rantepao map (p652) for where to catch bemos in central Rantepao that are heading to La'bo, Madandan, Sa'dan and Tikala.

Some of the more useful services head to the following destinations from Rantepao and Makale:

Bittuang For treks to Mamasa, only leaves from Makale
La'bo Via Ke'te Kesu
Lempo Useful for hiking up to Batutumonga
Pangala Via Batutumonga
Sa'dan Usually via Tikala
Sangalla Only leaves from Makale

BATUTUMONGA

One of the easiest places to stay overnight and also one of the most beautiful, Batutumonga occupies a dramatic ridge on the slopes of Gunung Sesean, with panoramic views of Rantepao and the Sa'dan Valley, and stunning sunrises. It's located about 20km north of Rantepao via Deri, so you could also day-trip here for some hiking and a local lunch.

Sleeping & Eating

All these sleeping options are right on the roadside before Batutumonga.

Mentirotiku GUESTHOUSE $$
(☎081 342 579588; tongkonan 100,000Rp per person, d 300,000Rp) With commanding views across the valley below, this place has very authentic traditional *tongkonan* crash pads – as in, there are three mattresses squashed together in a space that's about the size of a small elevator – but they do have terraces and if you snag one with a view, you're laughing. There are also less interesting large modern rooms with bathroom. The rather classy restaurant serves basics from 15,000Rp and traditional Toraja dishes for around 27,000Rp. It's all clean and the grounds are charming. Accomodation prices include breakfast.

Mama Yos GUESTHOUSE $
(100,000Rp per person incl breakfast & dinner) This simple house has a row of small, clean guest rooms with matresses on the floor and a basic Indonesian-style shared bathroom. No English spoken.

ENTRANCE FEES

Most of the tourist sites around Tana Toraja have an entry fee of 20,000Rp. There is usually a ticket booth at each place, complete with the odd souvenir stall…or 10 or more in the case of Lemo and Londa.

Mama Rina's Homestay GUESTHOUSE $
(☎081 343 896754; r incl breakfast & dinner per person 100,000Rp) Another very rustic family affair, Mama Rina's Homestay has rooms in a *tongkonan* with saggy mattresses and grotty bamboo walls, but it has a warm, friendly ambience and the views are stunning.

Coffee Shop Tinimbayo INDONESIAN $
(mains 10,000Rp) Located a few kilometres east of Batutumonga, this little cafe has a killer location, perched on a hairpin bend with infinite views over the cascading rice fields. Get tea, coffee, sodas, cold Bintang or *mie rebus* (noodle soup).

Getting There & Away

Simply take a bemo (12,000Rp) to Batutumonga from Terminal Bolu in Rantepao. Sometimes the bemo only goes as far as Lempo (2km downhill), but the walk from Lempo to Batutumonga is pleasant.

North of Rantepao

The north is the most scenic region of Tana Toraja, with dramatic bowls of cascading rice terraces, small villages of *tongkonan* and lots of interesting, harder-to-reach sights that don't make it on every tour bus itinerary.

For good shopping, go to the weaving centre of **Sa'dan** (12km north of Rantepao; take a bemo from Terminal Bolu for 6000Rp), where local women set up a market to sell their woven cloth. It's all handmade on simple looms, but not all is produced in the village.

Activities

The following are some good options for day walks but many of the towns and sights listed here are also popular stops on motorbike and car day-tours with guides.

Batutumonga to Tikala TREKKING

From Batutumonga, a beautiful walk west takes you to **Lokomata**, a village with cave graves hewn into a rocky outcrop, and outstanding scenery. Backtrack and take a small, unmarked trail down the slopes to **Pana**, with its ancient hanging graves, and some baby graves in nearby trees. You can see tiny villages with towering *tongkonan*, women pounding rice, men scrubbing their buffalo and children splashing in pools. The path ends at **Tikala** and, from there, regular bemos return to Rantepao. Alternatively, backtrack through Lempo to **Deri**, the site of rock graves, walk down to the Rantepao–Sa'dan road and catch a bemo back to Rantepao. This is a very pleasant downhill walk (five hours on a paved road) through some of the finest scenery in Tana Toraja.

Gunung Sesean TREKKING

At 2150m above sea level, Gunung Sesean is not the highest peak on Sulawesi, but it's one of the most popular for trekking. The summit is accessible via a trail from Batutumonga. The return trip to the summit takes five hours. A guide is a good idea if you're inexperienced or speak little Bahasa Indonesia.

Pangalla to Baruppu TREKKING

Beyond Gunung Sesean is **Pangala**, 35km from Rantepao (20,000Rp by bemo), one of the biggest villages in the region – it has a few streets and a little ayam goreng (fried chicken) stall. The village is famous for being the hometown of Pongtiku, a fearless warrior who fought against the Dutch. Pongtiku's tomb and a statue of the warrior can be seen at the edge of the village. From here it's a lovely 10km trek to Baruppu.

Palawa to Parinding TREKKING

The traditional village of **Palawa**, east of Batutumonga, is similarly attractive but less popular than Ke'te Kesu, and has *tongkonan* houses and rice barns. There are possibilities of staying here overnight in one of the traditional houses but this can only be organised with a guide as part of a trek. In the dry season you can walk southwest, fording a river and walking through rice fields to **Pangli**, with its *tau tau* and house graves, and then to **Bori**, the site of an impressive *rante* (ceremonial ground) and some towering megaliths. About 1km south of Bori, **Parinding** has *tongkonan* houses and rice barns. From here you can walk back to Rantepao or on to Tikala.

Sleeping & Eating

Losmen Sando GUESTHOUSE $

(r per person 110,000Rp) Pangala's accommodation looks abandoned from the outside but has surprisingly comfortable rooms, and a spacious restaurant overlooking a coffee plantation. It offers good advice about local trekking.

West of Rantepao

About 2km west across the river from Rantepao, **Gunung Singki** (930m) is a steep hill. There's a slippery, overgrown hiking trail to the summit, which has panoramic views across Rantepao and the surrounding countryside. Return to the road to **Siguntu** (7km from Rantepao), which offers more superb views of the valleys and Rantepao.

The 3km walk from Siguntu to the Rantepao–Makale road at Alang Alang is also pleasant. Stop on the way at the traditional village of **Mendoe**. From Alang Alang, where a covered bridge crosses the river, head to Londa, back to Rantepao, or remain on the western side of the river and continue walking south to the villages of **Langda** and **Madandan**.

South of Rantepao

Many popular cultural sights are in this region and most are accessible by car, so it's not a great region for walking – but it is suitable for a motorbike day tour.

Sights

Tour buses love this area for the easy access but also because the sights are simply stunning. We've listed these by distance heading south from Rantepao.

Karasik MEGALITHS

On the outskirts of Rantepao, just off the road to Makale, is Karasik, with traditional-style houses arranged around a cluster of megaliths on a hill.

Buntu Pune VILLAGE

Just off the road towards Ke'te Kesu is Buntu Pune, where there are two *tongkonan* houses and six rice barns. According to local legend, one of the two houses was built by a nobleman named Pong Marambaq at the beginning of the 20th century. During Dutch rule he was appointed head of the local district, but planned to rebel and was subsequently exiled to Ambon (Maluku), where he died. His body was returned to Tana Toraja and buried at the hill to the north of Buntu Pune.

Ke'te Kesu VILLAGE

About 1km from Buntu Pune is Ke'te Kesu (5km from Rantepao), renowned for its woodcarving and traditional *tongkonan* and rice barns. On the cliff face behind the village are some cave graves and very old hanging graves. The rotting coffins are suspended on wooden beams under an overhang. Others, full of bones and skulls, lie rotting in strategic piles. This is one of the most popular sights in Tana Toraja and it can get quite crowded.

Sullukang & Palatokke CAVE, CEMETERY

From Ke'te Kesu you can walk on a paved road to Sullukang, which has a *rante* (ceremonial ground) marked by a number of large, rough-hewn megaliths, and on to Palatokke. In this beautiful area of lush rice paddies and traditional houses, there is an enormous cliff face containing several cave graves and hanging graves. Access to the caves is difficult, but the scenery makes it worthwhile. From Palatokke there are roads to La'bo and Randanbatu, where there are more graves, and on to Sangalla, Suaya and Makale.

Londa CAVE, CEMETERY

Londa (6km south of Rantepao) is a very extensive burial cave at the base of a massive cliff face. The entrance to the cave is guarded by a balcony of *tau tau*. Inside the cave is a collection of coffins, many of them rotted away, with the bones either scattered or heaped in piles. A local myth says that the people buried in the Londa caves are the descendants of Tangdilinoq, chief of the Toraja when they were pushed out of the Enrekang region and forced to move into the highlands. Many visitors site this as one of their favorite places in Tana Toraja.

It's mandatory to take a guide (who will be a family member of the deceased) to take you through the cave with an oil lamp (20,000Rp). The guides speak excellent English (and a few other languages) and are happy to answer all your questions. If you're thin, and don't suffer from claustrophobia, squeeze through the tunnel connecting the two main caves, past some interesting stalactites and stalagmites. A bemo between Rantepao and Makale will drop you off at the turn-off, about 2km from the cave. Visit in the morning for the best photos.

Tilanga SWIMMING

Two kilometres south, and east off the Rantepao–Makale road, is Tilanga (10km from Rantepao), where during the rainy season you'll find a lovely, natural cool-water swimming pool. You can swim here, but don't be surprised if some friendly eels come to say hello.

Lemo CEMETERY

Lemo (10km south of Rantepao) is the best-known burial area in Tana Toraja. The sheer rock face has a whole series of balconies for *tau tau*. According to local legend, these graves are for descendants of a Toraja chief who reigned over the surrounding district hundreds of years ago and built his house on top of the cliff into which the graves are now cut. Because the mountain was part of his property, only his descendants could use it. The chief himself was buried elsewhere because the art of cutting grave caves had not yet been developed. The biggest balcony has a dozen figures with white eyes and black pupils, and outstretched arms like spectators at a sports event. It's a good idea to go before 9am for the best photos. A Rantepao–Makale bemo will drop you off at the turn-off to the burial site, from where it's a 15-minute walk to the *tau tau*.

East of Rantepao

This region is often visited on day tours between the north and the south. It's flatter than the north but almost as beautiful with plenty of rice fields, sleepy traditional villages and grazing buffalo.

Sights

Marante VILLAGE

Marante is a fine traditional village, just north of the road to Palopo. Near Marante there are stone and hanging graves with several *tau tau*, skulls on the coffins and a cave with scattered bones. From Marante you can cross the river on the suspension bridge and walk to pretty villages set in rice fields.

Nangalla VILLAGE

This village has a particularly grandiose traditional house and an impressive fleet of 14 rice barns. The rice barns have a bizarre array of motifs carved into them, including soldiers with guns, Western women and cars.

Keep an eye out for a colony of huge black bats hanging from trees at the end of the village. Nangalla is about 7km off the Palopo road to the south, 16km from Rantepao; take a bemo from Terminal Bolu for 5000Rp, but you may have to walk from the Palopo road.

Activities

From Nanggala you can walk south to **Paniki**, a tough hike (five hours) along a dirt track up and down the hills. The trail starts next to the rice barns, and along the way are coffee-plantation machines grinding away. From Paniki walk (two hours) to **Ledo** and **Buntao** (15km from Rantepao), which have some house graves and *tau tau*. Alternatively, catch a bemo from Paniki to Rantepao. About 2km from Buntao is **Tembamba**, which has more graves and is noted for its fine scenery.

East of Makale

This area is pretty far away from everything except a few sights but if you want to stay the night, **Hotel Sangalla** (☎0423 24112; r from 110,000-165,000Rp) has quiet gardens and is a great bargain; you'll probably have the whole place to yourself.

Sights

Tampangallo CEMETERY

The *tau tau* here are one of the most stunning sights in Tana Toraja. The graves belong to the chiefs of Sangalla, descendants of the mythical divine being Tamborolangiq, who is believed to have introduced the caste system, death rituals and agricultural techniques into Torajan society. The former royal families of Makale, Sangalla and Menkendek all claimed descent from Tamborolangiq, who is said to have descended from heaven on a stone staircase. Take a Kijang from Makale to Sangalla, get off about 1km after the turn-off to Suaya, and walk a short distance (less than a kilometre) through the rice fields to Tampangallo.

Kambira Baby Graves CEMETERY

Torajans traditionally bury babies in a tree and this is one of the biggest in the region, holding around 20 deceased infants (by Torajan definition a baby is a child who hasn't yet grown teeth). It's a shady, tranquil spot. The babies' bodies are buried upright and the belief is that they will continue to grow with the tree.

WEST SULAWESI

Mamasa Valley

Another area of outstanding natural beauty in Sulawesi, the Mamasa Valley is often referred to as West Tana Toraja, but this overplays the connection between Mamasa and Tana Toraja. Mamasan *tongkonan* have heavy wooden roofs, which are quite different from the exaggerated boat-shaped bamboo roofs to the east. Torajan ceremonies and funerals survive in the Mamasa Valley, but on the whole these are far less ostentatious affairs than those around Tana Toraja.

Mamasans have embraced Christianity with unfettered enthusiasm: choir groups regularly meet up and down the valley, flexing their vocal cords in praise of God. *Sambu* weaving is a craft that still thrives in the hills around Mamasa village. These long strips of heavy woven material are stitched together to make blankets, which are ideal insulation for the cold mountain nights.

Like in Tana Toraja, the best way to explore the valley is on foot. The paths tend to follow the ridges, giving hikers stunning views of the mountainous countryside. There are few roads, and many paths to choose from, so you'll need to constantly ask directions or hire a guide. The other source of confusion is that village districts, such as Balla, cover broad areas and there are few villages within them. Even centres within the village area, such as Rante Balla, Balla Kalua and Buntu Balla, are very spread out.

MAMASA

Mamasa is the only real town in the valley. The air is cool and clean, and the folk are hospitable. The rhythm of life has a surreal, fairytale quality for those used to the hustle of Indonesia's big cities. The highlight of the week is the market every Monday, where hill people trade their produce. Look for locally made woven blankets, a must for those cold mountain nights. While walking through hill villages, trekkers will also be offered plenty of fine-looking blankets direct from weavers, so take money or goods, such as condensed milk, chocolate, sugar or *kretek* (Indonesian clove cigarettes), to barter with.

Sleeping & Eating

Mamasa Cottages GUESTHOUSE $$

(Kole; s/d US$40/46) Built over hot springs at Kole, 3km north of Mamasa. It offers lovely rooms for a negotiable price. Hot-spring water flows to every bathroom.

Wisma Tongkonan Mamasa GUESTHOUSE $
(☎0813 5543 6663, 0813 1919 5535; Jl Demmajannang; r 150,000-200,000Rp) This is one of the more more posh places in town set in a distinctly Indonesian homey style with heavy wooden carved furniture, china cups on the table waiting for tea, and crystal in the cabinets. Rooms are big, with attached bathrooms, but simple, and the owner is nice, helpful and speaks enough English to get by.

Dian Satria GUESTHOUSE $
(☎0428 2481 066; Jl Poros Polowi; r 120,000Rp incl breakfast) Clean, new, homey place conveniently located across the street from a very good restaurant of the same name.

Mantana Lodge 2 CABINS $$
(☎0852 4261 1875; Jl Poros Polowi; cabins 300,000Rp incl breakfast) Up on a little hill above the main road, these big, double-occupancy polished pine cabins have hot-water bathrooms and pleasant terraces. They are clean and relatively comfy but you may get local kids climbing on your roof in the morning to get a look at you, and the breakfasts consist of coffee and a small bun.

Guest House Gereja Toraja GUESTHOUSE $
(Church Guesthouse; ☎081 355 819752; Jl Demmatande 182; r 85,000-100,000Rp) There are five basic rooms in this simple wooden house surrounded by a wild garden. The more expensive ones have terraces. Little English spoken.

Mantana Lodge 1 GUESTHOUSE $
(☎0852 4261 1875; Jl Emmy Saelan 1; r 100,000Rp) Close to town, there are big but basic old rooms here with attached cold water bathrooms.

Losmen Mini GUESTHOUSE $
(Jl Ahmad Yani; r from 85,000Rp) A sort of creaky old mountain lodge in the heart of town. The rooms upstairs are a lot brighter than the dark offerings down below.

Dian Satria Restaurant INDONESIAN $
(Jl Poros Polowi; meals 20,000-30,000Rp; ⊙breakfast, lunch & dinner) There are a few basic warung and restaurants around town but this place is one of the cleaner and more spacious. Get your basic Indonesian noodle and rice dishes in heaped servings and wash it down with a cold Bintang. At night you may get serenaded by the local lady boys singing (very pro) karaoke.

Mamasa

Sleeping

1 Guest House Gereja Toraja B2
2 Losmen Mini A2
3 Mantana Lodge 1..................................A2
4 Wisma Tongkonan Mamasa...............A2

Getting There & Away

FROM MAKASSAR

Two big buses leave for Mamasa (125,000Rp, 12 hours) from Makassar's Terminal Daya every day at 8.30am while around four minibuses (100,000Rp) depart at 7am. These fill fast so it's best to get your hotel or guesthouse to help you reserve a ticket the day before. Another option is to take a bus to Polewali then catch a Kijang (50,000Rp, six hours) to Mamasa from there – these Kijangs depart about every three hours from early morning through the early afternoon.

FROM RANTEPAO

On a map, Mamasa looks tantalisingly close to Rantepao, but there's no direct transport because the road is so bad.

BUS Every day, one bus leaves Rantepao for Mamasa at 8.30am while another leaves Mamasa for Rantepao at the same time.The fare is 100,000Rp and it takes around 12 long, bumpy hours.

KIJANG It's rough going with lots of transfers and you'll probably have to stay overnight at least once along the way, but it is possible to take local transport between Mamasa and Rantepao via Bittuang – at least during the dry season. Kijangs leave Mamasa for Ponding daily at 9am (50,000Rp, two to three hours) and then from Ponding to Bittuang the following day at 9am (50,000Rp, two to three hours). From

MAMASA TO RANTEPAO TREKKING PRACTICALITIES

Be prepared to seriously rough it on this trek that takes you through remote villages, coffee plantations and plenty of big mountain scenery. There's not much in the way of boat-roofed architecture until Ponding, when you're officially on Tana Toraja land. Toilets can be little more than a plank over a stream, a bed means a quilt on a hard floor and you'll have absolutely no privacy (bring sarongs for showering). Half the village children will follow you with laughter and good-natured converstaion. Losmen (often unmarked so you'll have to ask around) along the way charge 100,000Rp to 125,000Rp per person including a simple breakfast and dinner. For lunch you'll also have to ask around but someone will surely offer to make you a meal for around 25,000Rp. Expect to eat plenty of rice, packet noodles and goldfish that are raised in the rice fields, but not much fruit or vegetables. Bring plenty of water and/or a water filter (some boiled water is available at losmen), warm clothes, sweets for the kids and gifts like sugar and cigarettes for the families who take you in at night. Guides (an excellent idea if you don't speak Indonesian or have a poor sense of direction) cost 500,000Rp per day and can be easily found in Mamasa. You can ship your big pack to Rantepao by bus but if you still need help carrying your stuff, a horse with a horseman costs 300,000Rp to 400,000Rp per day. Note that the tiny Mamasan horses don't usually carry people, so don't count on getting a lift.

Bittuang there are Kijangs to Makale (30,000Rp, one hour) where you can catch a bemo on to Rantepao (5,000Rp). In the other direction, Kijang leave from Bittuang to Ponding daily at 9am and from Ponding to Mamasa the following day at 9am. There are sometimes other vehicles tackling this road at other hours and you can often flag them down and get a ride for the same price as public transport – if you can do this you could theoretically do the whole trip in a single day.

TREKKING The walk between Mamasa and Bittuang is a classic trek and there are a few ways to do it – the first two options described here take three days if you walk the whole way. The easiest route to find is to take the Kijang road described above, stopping in Timbaan the first night (23km from Mamasa, about eight hours walking), to Paku the next (20km, about six hours), then onto Bittuang the following morning (16km, about three hours). Otherwise you can take a more quiet footpath though the jungle from Tandiallo a few kilometres north of Mamasa via Sóbok and Minanga to stay overnight the first night in Kelama (about eight hours walking). The following night you can make it to Ponding via Buka, Mawai and Tandung (eight hours) then continue on the main Kijang road to Bittuang the next day (about four hours). A third option takes in Salurea and Bulo Sandana, but takes four days to complete.

AROUND MAMASA

The countryside surrounding Mamasa is strikingly beautiful. You can hire motorbikes around town for a negotiable 120,000Rp per day. You can charter a bemo or Kijang along the valley's couple of main roads, but footpaths and very slender suspension bridges are the only access to most villages.

Many places are easy to reach from Mamasa, but take warm clothes and gifts for your hosts if you plan to stay overnight. As most people grow their own coffee here, in return for any hospitality bring condensed milk, chocolate, sugar, *kretek* and other goods from town.

NORTH OF MAMASA

Rante Buda (4km) has an impressive 25m-long *tongkonan* building known as Banua Layuk (High House), an old chief's place with colourful motifs. This *tongkonan* is one of the oldest and best preserved in the valley, built about 300 years ago for one of five local leaders, the chief of Rambusaratu. A donation of about 5000Rp is expected.

Kole (3km) has hot springs, tapped for the guests at Mamasa Cottages. **Loko** (4km) is a traditional village with old houses, set in the jungle. The only way there is to hike via Kole or Tondok Bakaru. Hardy hikers can continue from Loko up the steep hill to **Mambulilin Sarambu** (a waterfall), and on to the peak of **Gunung Mambulilin** (9km). **Taupe** (5km) is a traditional village with jungle walks and panoramic views.

SOUTH OF MAMASA

Rante Sopang (12km) is a busy centre for weaving and retailing crafts. The path up the hill from the roadside craft shop leads to a few workshops, where women weave long strips of heavy cloth for Mamasa's distinctive, colourful blankets.

Osango (3km) is the site of *tedong-tedong* (burial houses), which are supposedly up to 200 years old. There are lots of paths and the village is *very* spread out, so you may find that you'll need to ask for directions along the way. **Mesa Kada** (2km) are hot springs that are suitable for a swim.

Tanete (8km) has mountain graves under a cave. Tanete and nearby **Taibassi** are also centres for traditional weaving and carving. **Rante Balla** (12km) has big, beautiful *tongkonan* and blanket- and basket-weaving.

Buntu Balla (15km) has beautiful views, traditional weaving and *tedong-tedong* burial sites. Close to Buntu Balla there's a waterfall at **Allodio**, a traditional village at **Balla Peu**, megalithic remains at **Manta** and views along the whole valley from **Mussa**. Further south, **Malabo** (18km) has *tedong-tedong* burial sites.

Southeast of Mamasa, **Orobua** (9km) has a fine old *tongkonan,* one of the best in the area. There are more sweeping views from **Paladan** further south.

CENTRAL SULAWESI

Nearly abandoned by tourism during and after a period of religious violence spanning from 1998 to 2006, Central Sulawesi is back on the itinerary for travellers who are moving up or down between the Togean Islands and Tana Toraja. The towns on the vast Danau Poso are an ideal place to stop awhile or break up a long bus ride, but there's much, much more to this province and it's simply begging to be explored. Tranquil Tentena is the easiest place to arrange treks into the Lore Lindu National Park, which is filled with mysterious megaliths and has a wildlife-rich jungle; those with lots of time and a nose for anthropology should head to the adventurous Morowali Nature Reserve to seek out the Wana people; divers and beach bums can laze around on the white sands of Tanjung Karang near Palu.

It's a vibrant and extremely varied region scarred by its recent history and still a little shaky, but the people here want their foreign visitors back. While it's unlikely tensions will flare again soon, it is still wise to check the current situation before visiting this area.

History

Undated remains from a cave near Kolonedale indicate a long history of human settlement. The most spectacular prehistoric remains are the Bronze Age megaliths found throughout Central Sulawesi, but no one knows who was responsible for their creation. The highest concentration is along Sungai Lariang in the Bada Valley, and there are others throughout the region, down to Tana Toraja in South Sulawesi.

CENTRAL SULAWESI'S TROUBLED PAST

It's been pretty quiet around Central Sulawesi since late 2006, but for eight years prior the region was torn apart by Christian versus Muslim violence. The big trouble began in 1998 when a drunken brawl between Christian and Muslim youths sparked clan fighting in Poso. By 2000 paramilitary groups called the Red Force (backing the Christians) and the Laskar Jihad (backing the Muslims) were engaged in full warfare against each other, armed with machetes and bows and arrows as well as homemade bombs and heavy artillery. Christians grouped in predominantly Christian Tentena, while Muslims stood their ground in Poso and Palu. The Indonesian government stepped in in 2001 by organising the Malino Peace Treaty, signed in 2002 by both sides, which produced a decline in the violence but did not stop it. By the end of 2006, more than 1000 people had been killed, houses had been burned, markets bombed and children beheaded. Tourists were never targets but the region was, for obvious reasons, best avoided.

It's still debated what caused these communities to start fighting each other after generations of living peacefully together. Some analysts believe this was just another arm in the fighting that had been going on between Muslim and Christian communities in Maluku. The more common belief is that the influx of Muslim immigrants from Java under President Suharto's transmigration program abruptly shifted the Christian majority and power in the region.

Today locals chat easily about this dark time and about how happy they are it's over. As one Poso Muslim told us, 'Nowadays I go on vacation to Tentena but before I was afraid I'd get killed if I even went near there.'

DANAU POSO

Indonesia's third-largest lake, Danau Poso, covers an area of 32,300 hectares and reaches an average depth of 450m. The lake is 600m above sea level – so the evenings are pleasantly cool without being too cold. With mountains on all sides and mist hovering over the calm waters in the early morning, it's a breathtaking spot.

Pendolo

Pendolo is a dusty, sparse strip of a village right on the southern shore of Danau Poso. There's not much going on here beyond swimming at some of the area's surprisingly lovely white-sand beaches – it's this calm environment as well as the connection with the charming locals that draws in the few visitors that stop here.

There's a strip of decent and cheap *rumah makan* along the main road that cater to stopping long-distance buses. You can stay at **Pendolo Cottages** (Jl Ahmad Yani 441; r 60,000Rp, bungalow s/d 55,000/80,000Rp), right next to the boat landing, about 1km east of the village centre, which is a rustic place that gets good traveller reviews on service and ambience.

More upmarket is **Mulia Poso Lake Hotel** (Jl Pelabuhan Wisata 1; r from 100,000Rp, cottages from 150,000Rp), the smartest place in Pendolo which also has an elegant restaurant.

Getting There & Away

Pendolo is on the main Palopo–Poso highway, but there is no bus terminal. To go north, the best option is to catch a bemo to Tentena (45,000Rp), then transfer there. If you're going south, see if your hotel can help you reserve a seat on one of the many long-distance buses that blaze through town. You could also try your luck flagging one down from the main road (heading to destinations such as Poso, Palu and Rantepao) – but many are full.

Tentena

0458

Tentena is a town of white picket fences and churches, cool breezes from the lake and lots of wonderfully strange things to eat. Surrounded by clove-covered hills, it's a peaceful and very easy-to-manage town with several good places to stay, an interesting market and some natural treasures to explore nearby. There are no beaches in the town itself, but it's easy to hire a motorbike or an *ojek* to get to some.

Tentena is the host of the annual **Festival Danau Poso**, the undisputed highlight of Central Sulawesi's social calendar, in late August. Villagers from far afield gather for a colourful celebration of culture, with dancing, songs and traditional sports.

Sights & Activities

Most of the things to do and see are around Tentena. The best way to spend a day is to either rent a motorbike (full/half-day 70,000/60,000Rp – ask at your hotel) or hire an *ojek*.

With wheels you can visit **Air Terjun Salopa** (entrance fee 10,000Rp), a waterfall about 15km from Tentena, from where you can hike through the forest and up alongside the falls for a few kilometres. The forest is clean and shady and the falls are a spectacular place for a swim.

From here drive another 5km to Siuri Cottages, where you can swim in the lake at the white-sand **beach** and have lunch. An *ojek* to get to these two spots for a half-day should cost about 80,000Rp.

In town, Tentena's pretty, 210m covered bridge marks where the lake ends and Sungai Poso begins its journey to the coast. V-shaped **eel traps** north of the bridge snare the 2m monsters for which Tentena is famous. Live specimens are available for inspection and sale at warungs in the centre of town.

Chartering a boat to explore the lake can be surprisingly difficult – the asking rate is 100,000Rp for two hours.

Sleeping

All prices include breakfast.

TOP CHOICE **Siuri Cottages** BUNGALOWS $$
(0813 4116 7345; bungalows from 225,000Rp)
Twenty kilometres from Tentena on the road to Pendolo, these big, well-kept but simple bungalows are lined up along a sparkling white lakeside beach with views that take in all the size and splendour of Danau Poso. The owner speaks English and there's a basic restaurant for meals, but note that this place is completely isolated. To get here

from Tentena, you can catch an afternoon bemo for 17,000Rp; from Pendelo a bemo should cost 35,000Rp. The owner can help you rent a canoe to explore the lake, but you'll have to haggle for the price.

Hotel Victory GUESTHOUSE **$**
(☎21392; Jl Diponegoro 18; s 80,000Rp, d 100,000-200,000Rp; ❄) Most travelers happily end up here. The rooms are big, clean and surround a little garden, it's centrally located in Tentena and the helpful owners will come and get you at the bus stop if you call in advance. Only the higher-end rooms have hot water. Just hope you're not there when the karaoke is on next door.

Hotel Pamona Indah Permai HOTEL **$**
(Jl Yos Sudarso 53; r with shared bathroom 80,000Rp, r with bathroom 100,000-300,000Rp; meals from 15,000Rp) This place doesn't take advantage of its lakeside location but the rooms are bright and tidy and the restaurant is the best in town.

Eating

Rumah Makan Kawana INDONESIAN **$**
(meals around 10,000Rp) The local speciality is *sugili* (eel) and *ikan mas* (goldfish). For these specialties as well as spicy bat dishes, pull up a chair at one of the riverside *rumah makan* at the market near the bridge – the best is Rumah Makan Kawana. After dinner don't miss trying the tasty *pisang molen* (banana fried in a sweet pastry) at stalls in front of the eastern part of the town bridge.

Hotel Pamona Indah Permai Restaurant INDONESIAN **$**
(meals from 15,000Rp; ⏰breakfast, lunch & dinner) Pick from the extensive menu that includes everything from nasi goreng to both *sugili* (eel) and *ikan mas* (goldfish) in a variety of sauces.

Information

There are only a handful of guides in Tentena but they all organise treks to Lore Lindu National Park and Morowali Nature Reserve. All guides speak English and know the area well. Ask at your hotel or at the tourist office by the market that's run by friendly Anton who was once a guide himself. There are a few internet cafes around town charging 3,000Rp per hour and there's a Mandiri Bank ATM across the street from the bus terminal.

Getting There & Away

BUS & BEMO You'll need to catch an *ojek* (5000Rp) or organise pick up by your hotel to/from Tentena's bus and bemo terminal, 3km from the town centre.

Note that there's only one afternoon bus to Poso from Tentena on Sundays, which gets you to Poso too late to catch onward transport to Ampana. There's also no bus to Bomba and only a few afternoon bemos to Pendelo on Sundays.

JEEP The availability and price of jeeps to Gintu in Lore Lindu National Park depends on the condition of the road. The price should be around 1,500,000Rp to charter one for a return day trip for up to four people.

Poso

☎0452 / POP 47,000

Poso is the main town, port and terminal for road transport on the northern coast of Central Sulawesi. It's a spread-out, noisy place and there's little reason to stop other than to stay overnight to break up a trip to/from Ampana and the Togean Islands, use an ATM or change buses.

The northern part of Poso, around Jl Haji Agus Salim, is more like a small village but it has limited shops and restaurants. Most facilities are along or near busy Jl Sumatera.

Poso is the last sure chance for Togean- and Tentena-bound travellers to change money; the best option is BNI bank, with

BUSES & BEMOS FROM TENTENA

DESTINATION	PRICE (RP)	DURATION (HR)	FREQUENCY
Bomba (for Lore Lindu)	60,000	4	once per day
Palu	80,000	10	night buses
Pendelo	50,000	2	frequent
Poso	25,000	2	3 per day
Rantepao	110,000	10	morning buses

BUSES FROM POSO

DESTINATION	PRICE (RP)	DURATION (HR)	FREQUENCY
Ampana	75,000	5	3 daily
Kolonodale	100,000	8	8am daily
Manado	250,000	30	1 daily
Palu	80,000	6	3 daily
Tentena	20,000	2	3 daily

an ATM, near the port about 2km from the town centre – take an *ojek*.

Sleeping

Kartika Beach Hotel HOTEL $$
(☎325276; Jl Pulau Sabanang Kayamanya; r 180,000-245,000Rp) About 2km out of town on the Palu road, go here if you want a little more comfort – although it's still far from posh. Only the most expensive rooms have hot water but all have air-con, TVs and bathrooms. It's on the water and an open lounging area was being built overlooking the sea when we passed through.

Losmen Alugoro GUESTHOUSE $
(☎324735; Jl P Sumatra 20; s/d 65,000/90,000Rp, d with air-con 130,000-200,000Rp; ❄) A reliably decent but characterless place that's central for the bus offices and restaurants on Jl Sumatera.

Rumah Makan & Losmen Lalang Jaya GUESTHOUSE $
(☎22326; Jl Yos Sudarso; r 90,000Rp) Very rustic but definitely interesting, this rickety place is perched over the sea (right next to the port and the BNI bank) and looks like somewhere Popeye would have lived had he been Indonesian. There's also a basic seafood restaurant here.

Getting There & Away

AIR Merpati flies infrequently to Poso's Kasiguncu airport about 20km west of town. Destinations include Balikpapan, Jakarta and Makassar.

BUS & MINIBUS The bus terminal is about 5km out of town. There are plenty of *ojek* and bemos that will take you into central Poso for 5000Rp.

For Palu and Ampana, you can also catch minibuses from offices along Jl Sumatera. Bemos to nearby villages and beaches leave from a terminal next to the market.

Around Poso

There are plenty of good places for swimming and snorkelling around Poso. **Pantai Madale** is a snorkelling spot 5km east of Poso; **Pantai Matako** is a white-sand beach about 20km further east; and **Pantai Toini**, 7km west, has a few *rumah makan* with great seafood. All three can be reached by bemo from the terminal near the market in Poso.

Lembomawo, 4km south of Poso near the bus terminal, is renowned for its ebony carving and you can see carvers sawing and sanding in their workshops. Take a bemo from the terminal at the Poso market or it's a five-minute *ojek* ride (5000Rp or less) from the bus terminal, which makes for a nice little trip if you have a long wait for your bus.

Lore Lindu National Park

As if the lush jungle filled with impressive hornbills and shy tarsiers wasn't enough, Lore Lindu is also famous for its megalithic remains – giant freestanding stones. Covering an area of 250,000 hectares, this remote national park (a Unesco Biosphere Reserve) has been barely touched by tourism. It's a perfect place to seek out an off-the-beaten-path adventure but take note that it's rough going. Trips are best organised from Palu or Tentena and it's highly recommended that you hire a guide.

Sights

Attractions in the park include ancient megalithic relics, mostly in the **Bada**, **Besoa** and **Napu Valleys**; remote peaks, some more than 2500m high; birdwatching around **Danau Tambing**, including the opportunity to spot hornbills, the 3150-hectare lake **Danau Lindu**; the village of **Wuasa**; and heading along the **Anaso Track** that leads to the top of 2000m-high **Gunung Rore Kitimbu**.

Activities

Hikes (with a guide) include Rachmat to Danau Lindu (six hours one way) and Sadaunta to Danau Lindu (four hours one way).

The roads around Lore Lindu have improved in recent years and now many of the old trekking routes are used by buzzing motorbikes although even these can get muddy and impassable in the rainy season. The best place to get into the jungle, free of motor noise but rich in wildlife, is the trail between Doda and Gimpu (a two-day walk), but there aren't any megaliths on this route. Megalithic remains are found mostly along the motorbike road between Tonusu and Gimpu, via Tuare and Moa, or Doda and Hangirah. There are also megaliths to see along the road between Doda and Wuasa that is accessible by car.

Food is readily available in the villages and there are several basic losmen, but it's wise to bring other necessities, such as mosquito repellent and sunblock lotion, plus gifts to repay any hospitality and warm clothes since it can get cold at night. Conversely, during the day it can get very hot, so you'll want to have plenty of water.

Guides

For long-distance trekking a guide is compulsory, and also necessary if you're intent on finding the megaliths. An organised one-day visit from Tentena with a guide and vehicle (for up to four people) costs 1,500,000Rp and prices go up from there. The guides from Tentena speak English.

If travelling independently, arrange a guide at Kulawi, Wuasa, Bomba, Badu or the tourist office or national park office in Palu. Guides start at 400,000Rp per day but rarely speak English so be sure to bring a good phrasebook if you don't have a good grasp of Bahasa Indonesia.

Information

You can buy permits (20,000Rp) at the small field offices (which have no accommodation) at Kulawi and Wuasa, and at the **Balai Taman Nasional Lore Lindu office** (☎0451-457 623; Jl Prof Mohammad Yamin SH). Good information online can be found at the birding website **Burung Nusantara** (www.burung-nusantara.org).

Getting There & Away

There are three main approaches to the park, one from Tentena and two from Palu. From Palu buses run all the way to Gimpu and Doda twice a day from Terminal Petobu. From Tentena there is a daily bus to Bomba or charter a jeep; they run according to demand and road conditions to Bomba or Gintu. From Gimpu, Doda and Bomba you should be able to hire *ojeks* that can tackle the tracks between Gintu and Gimpu via Moa and from Gintu to Doda. You can also hike this scenic route, but you will have motorbikes buzzing by you. The track between Doda and Gimpu can only be done on foot.

Palu

☎0451 / POP 282,000

Palu, the capital of Central Sulawesi, is characterless but loaded with banks and ATMs, cheap internet cafes, travel agencies, supermarkets and, oddly, pharmacies (all along Jl Emmi Saelan). It's a good place to do errands when arriving from or heading out by ship to Kalimantan or treks to Lore Lindu National Park. Nearby is the rarely visited yet wonderfully quaint village of Donggala and the beach area of Tanjung Karang. Situated in a rain shadow for most of the year, Palu is one of the driest places in Indonesia.

The best part of town to wander around is the busy Jl Hasanuddin II area.

Sleeping & Eating

All rates include breakfast.

Rama Garden Hotel HOTEL **$$**
(☎429 500; www.hotelramagarden.com; Jl Monginsidi 81; r 190,000-600,000Rp; ❄☜) This place is a garden of tranquillity inside, with winding paths, lots of plants and mini-lawn areas, plus a pool and a terrace dining area. Take a swim, order room service and watch a movie on HBO.

Hotel Sentral HOTEL **$$**
(☎422 789; Jl Kartini 6; r 175,000-600,000Rp; ❄@) Even the cheapest rooms here have satellite TV and air-con, and it's a smiling, friendly place. There's a travel agent and internet cafe here as well.

Purnama Raya Hotel GUESTHOUSE **$**
(☎423 646; Jl Wahidin 4; s/d 60,000/75,000Rp) This is a family-run place that has a village feel even though it's in the heart of Palu. Rooms with attached Indonesian-style

Palu

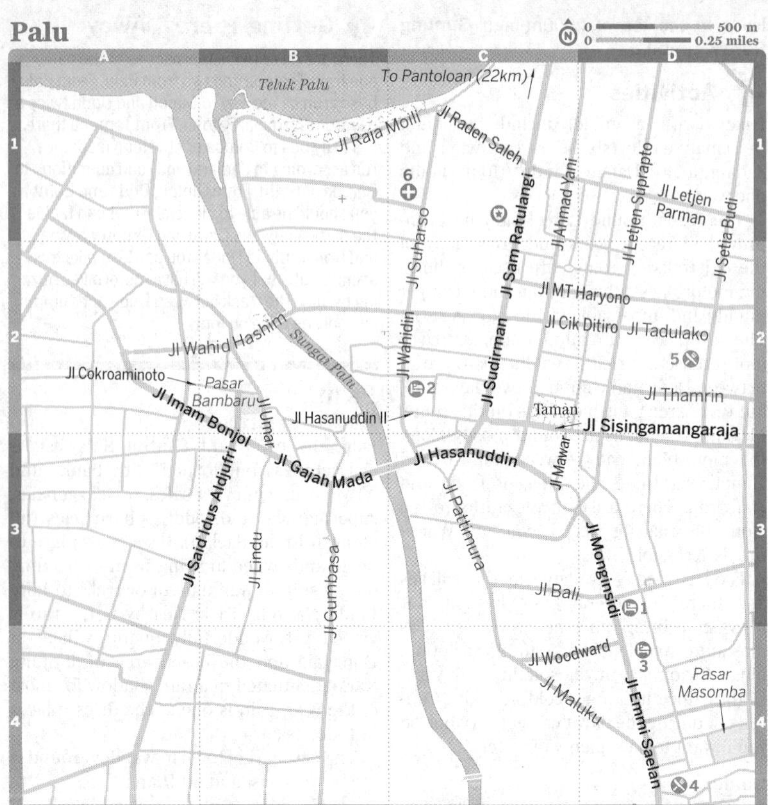

Palu

Sleeping

1 Hotel Sentral D3
2 Purnama Raya Hotel C2
3 Rama Garden Hotel D4

Eating

4 Mall Tatura Palu D4
5 Restoran Marannu D2

Information

6 Rumah Sakit Umum Propinsi Undata C1

bathrooms are clean but worn and they can be a little noisy from the traffic outside.

Mall Tatura Palu FOOD COURT $
(Jl Emmi Saelan) Mall Tatura Palu has a good food court on the top level, as well as a few more upmarket restaurants and cafes and a supermarket.

Restoran Marannu CHINESE $
(Jl Setia Budi; mains 20,000-40,000Rp; ⏲breakfast, lunch & dinner) At one of the smarter spots in town, the menu includes tasty seafood and Chinese cuisine.

There are plenty of night warungs along the breezy seafront esplanade, Jl Raja Moili.

Information

Balai Taman Nasional Lore Lindu office (☎457 623; Jl Prof Mohammad Yamin SH) No English is spoken but they do their best to help and can set you up with Bahasa Indonesian-speaking guides.

Police station (☎421 015; Jl Sam Ratulangi)

Rumah Sakit Umum Propinsi Undata (☎421 270; Jl Suharso) Large and reasonably well-equipped hospital.

Tourist Office (☎455 260; Jl Dewi Sartika 91) Inconveniently located and hard to find; has some information about Lore Lindu National Park.

Getting There & Away

AIR There are flights to Makassar with Merpati, Batavia Air and Lion Air. Merpati also flies from Palu to Kendari, Luwuk, Manado and Yogyakarta, while Batavia Air flies to Pontianak, Balikpapan, Surabaya and Pulau Batam.

BOAT Travelling by boat is one way to avoid long and uncomfortable bus rides through Central Sulawesi. Palu is also well connected to East Kalimantan. Every two weeks, the Pelni liner Doro sails to Balikpapan and the *Dorolonda* goes to Bitung. These boats dock at Pantoloan, 22km north of Palu, which is accessible by shared taxi from Terminal Manonda in Palu, or by metered taxi (about 50,000Rp). The **Pelni office** (☎421 696; Jl Kartini) in Palu is efficient; there's another one at Pantoloan.

BUS & SHARE TAXI Buses and minibuses to Poso (80,000Rp, six hours), Ampana (140,000Rp, 11 hours) and Rantepao (180,000Rp, 19 hours) all leave from bus-company offices inconveniently dotted around the suburbs of Palu. Kijangs to Donggala (for Tanjung Karang) leave from Terminal Tipo, about 5km northwest of Palu, but it's easier to take an *ojek*. There are buses to Gimpu and Doda (for Lore Lindu National Park) that leave twice a day from Terminal Petobu, about 2km east of Palu.

Getting Around

Mutiara Airport is 7km east of town. Public transport is difficult to find, so take a metered taxi for about 55,000Rp from the city centre. Transport around Palu is by bemo. Routes are not signed and are flexible, so flag down one that looks like it's going your way. Taxis are air-conditioned and cheap and drivers generally use the meters.

Donggala & Tanjung Karang

☎0457

Donggala is an old-fashioned country town that's full of colourful houses, small flower gardens, a few dirt roads and lots of interesting local characters. From here it's a short *ojek* ride to Tanjung Karang's slice of white sand studded with rickety beach bungalows, roaming buffalo and a decent dive centre.

Although it's hard to believe, Donggala was once the administrative centre under the Dutch and was briefly the most important town and port in Central Sulawesi. When the harbour silted up, ships used the harbours on the other side of the bay, and Palu became the regional capital.

Activities

The main attractions are sun, sand and water at Tanjung Karang (Coral Peninsula), about 5km north of Donggala. The reef off Prince John Dive Resort is good for **snorkelling** and beginner-level **diving**. Individual dives cost around €35 and PADI courses are also run here. Diving and snorkelling equipment is available.

Sleeping & Eating

There are lots of budget shacks along Tanjung Karang that are geared towards local tourists – it's easy to shop around and you'll probably be the only foreigner. There's nowhere to eat out at Tanjung Karang, so you'll be relying on what's served at your homestay or resort.

Prince John Dive Resort RESORT **$$**
(☎71104; www.prince-john-diveresort.com; bungalows for 2 people incl meals from 380,000Rp) The newly renovated, comfortable varnished-wood bungalows with large bathrooms have shady sea views. The only dive resort in the Palu area, its bungalows are spread out on a well-planted hillside and there's a small beach with a few umbrellas for rent for non-guests, as well as a restaurant.

Getting There & Away

Kijangs to Donggala (17,000Rp) leave when full from Terminal Tipo, about 5km outside Palu – you'll have to flag down a bemo from anywhere in Palu to take you to the terminal (3500Rp). From Donggala you can catch an *ojek* to Tanjung Karang (6000Rp). It works out to be only a bit more expensive (and takes half the time) to take an *ojek* directly from Palu to Tanjung Karang (35,000Rp).

Luwuk

☎0461 / POP 48,000

Luwuk, the biggest town on Sulawesi's isolated eastern peninsula, is a possible stepping stone to the Togean Islands and the Banggai Islands. Nearby attractions include **Air Terjun Hengahenga**, the 75m-high waterfall 3km west of Luwuk; and the **Bangkiriang Nature Reserve**, which is 80km southwest of Luwuk and home to Central Sulawesi's largest maleo bird population.

Maleo Cottages (☎tel/fax 324 068; www.maleo-cottages.com; Jl Lompobattang; s/d incl breakfast 180,000/200,000Rp) is by far the best place to stay in the area, about 16km from town. There are rooms in the main house and simple but atmospheric cottages. Meals are available, as are private car transfers to Ampana for 750,000Rp. This is the base for **Wallacea Dive Cruise** (www.wallacea-divecruise.com), so it's a good place to arrange diving in the Banggai Islands or liveaboards to the Togean Islands. The hotel can also help arrange independent trips to the remote, beautiful Banggai Islands and offers treks to some remote forest regions nearby.

Batavia Air, Lion Air and Wings Air all fly regularly to/from Makassar.

Every week the Pelni liner *Tilongkabila* links Luwuk with Bau Bau and Bitung and many stops between; it is an excellent way to travel to this remote part of Sulawesi. There's a **Pelni office** (☎21888; Jl Sungai Musi 3) in town.

There are also buses to Pagimana (two hours), Poso (12 hours) and Ampana (seven hours).

Ampana

☎0464

The main reason for travellers to come to Ampana is to catch a boat to/from the Togean Islands, but it's a laid-back, pleasant town with a vibrant market, and a good stopover while you recover from, or prepare for an assault on the Togeans.

Note that the sole ATM in town only takes MasterCard and maximum withdrawals are 500,000Rp per day. There are plenty of internet cafes around town charging 5000Rp per hour.

Sleeping & Eating

Oasis Hotel HOTEL $

(☎21058; Jl Kartini; r with fan/air-con from 100,000/185,000Rp; ❄) Run in conjunction with the Kadidiri Paradise Resort in the Togeans, this place has clean rooms and great service, but don't expect to sleep till the karaoke shuts down at 11pm. The most expensive rooms include air-con and hot water. Prices include a decent breakfast.

Marina Cottages COTTAGES $

(☎21280; cottages 120,000Rp) Perched on a rocky beach, the rustic cottages boast a seafront setting and friendly service, and are in a perfect location for boats to Bomba. They are in Labuhan village, a 10-minute *bendi* (horse-drawn cart) ride from Ampana. The restaurant is worth visiting for the sunsets alone.

Getting There & Away

Several minibuses travel each day to Luwuk (120,000Rp, seven hours), Poso (75,000Rp, five hours) and Palu (150,000Rp, 11 hours). Boats to Poso, Wakai in the Togean Islands and beyond leave from the main boat terminal at the end of Jl Yos Sudarso, in the middle of Ampana. Boats to Bomba in the Togeans leave from a jetty in Labuhan village, next to Marina Cottages.

WORTH A TRIP

TANJUNG API NATIONAL PARK

The 4246-hectare Tanjung Api (Cape Fire National Park) is home to *anoa* (pygmy buffalo), *babi rusa (wild pigs)*, crocodiles, snakes and maleo birds, but most people come to see the burning coral cliff fuelled by a leak of natural gas. To get here you need to charter a boat around the rocky peninsula from Ampana (from there it's 24km east). It's more interesting at dusk.

Togean Islands

Yes, it takes determination to get to the Togean Islands, but believe us, it takes much more determination to leave. Island-hop from one forested golden-beach beauty to the next, where hammocks are plentiful, the fish is fresh and the welcome is homey. Most islands have only one or two family-run guesthouses that can accommodate just a few people, while popular Kadidiri has a small but lively beach scene with night-time bonfires and cold beers all around. The surrounding sea of Teluk Tomini is still recovering from its past brushes with cyanide and dynamite fishing, but the corals are coming back and most divers and snorkellers are thrilled with the rich diversity of marine life they find.

When you decide to get out of the water, there's a surprising variety of wildlife to look for in the undisturbed and wild jungles, as well as other remote beaches to find and even an active volcano to climb on Pulau Una Una (by day trip). Seven or so ethnic groups share this region, but all are happy see visitors and are exceptionally hospitable.

Most of the rooms are in wooden cottages and right on the beach. Most have a mosquito net but no fan because the sea breezes keep everything cool. Bathroom facilities range from communal and rustic to private and porcelain. Prices are usually per person and rates include three local meals. It's a good idea to bring along some snacks and treats. Beer, soft drinks and mineral water are available from shops and homestays. Bring plenty of cash as there are no banks on the islands.

Activities

The Togeans are the only place in Indonesia where you can find all three major reef environments – atoll, barrier and fringing reefs – in one location. Two atolls and their deep lagoons lie to the northwest of Pulau Batu Daka. Barrier reefs surround many islands at the 200m-depth contour (5km to 15km offshore), and fringing reefs surround all of the coasts, merging with sea grass and mangroves. There is also a sunken WWII B-24 bomber plane, which is a 30-minute trip by speedboat (or one hour by regular boat) from Kadidiri.

The mix of coral and marine life is spectacular and unusually diverse, although many reefs are recovering from dynamite and cyanide fishing. The more conspicuous residents include brightly marked coral lobsters, a colony of dugong, schools of a hundred or more dolphins, the occasional whale, commercially important species of trepang (sea cucumber), and natural pearls.

Check sleeping listings for dive-centre locations. Prices start from €25 per dive and PADI courses are also available.

A range of activities are on offer throughout the Togeans although the easiest place to organise them is Kadidiri. Apart from diving, snorkelling gear can be rented at many guesthouses for about 25,000Rp per day and you can hike island trails (bring something along to mark your path as some visitors have gotten *very* lost).

Prices for excursions depend on the distances from your island of choice. There are treks around volcanic Pulau Una Una (from 500,000Rp for up to eight people), excursions to 'jellyfish lake' where you can swim with stinger-free jellyfish (one of the few places in the world where this is possible; from 50,000Rp per person) and visits to other nearby islands for snorkelling (from around 150,000Rp).

Getting There & Away

Yes, it's complicated. The quickest way to get to the Togeans is to fly from Manado to Luwuk and travel by road from there to Ampana (six hours) – you'll have to stay overnight, then catch the ferry the next morning. Alternatively, if you can get the boat schedule right, you can fly to Gorontalo from Manado, then catch the overnight ferry to the Togeans. Overland travellers often make their way up from Tana Toraja to Ampana, while plenty of people also take the bus from Manado to the port in Gorontalo.

Representatives from resorts and hotels will usually meet the ferries at each stop and shuttle you to their accommodation free of charge, or for a small fee if you don't end up staying with them.

GETTING IN TOUCH WITH THE TOGEANS

There's no internet in the Togean Islands and mobile phone reception is patchy at best. While many guesthouses have an email address and phone number, you may have to give it a few days or more before anyone writes back or returns your call. In most cases you won't need a reservation anyway and can just turn up.

FROM AMPANA

The *Puspita* ferry departs Ampana for the Togean Islands on Monday, Tuesday, Wednesday and Saturday.

DESTINATION	DEPARTURE TIME	COST (RP)
Ampana	10am	n/a
Wakai	2pm	40,000
Katupat	4.30pm	45,000
Malenge	6pm	50,000

In the reverse direction the ferry leaves Malenge at 6am on Sunday, Tuesday, Thursday and Saturday. Do note that the ferry schedule changes frequently, so don't plan flight connections around it. The best way to find out current schedules is to call one of the guesthouses in Ampana.

To go direct to Bomba it's better to take small local boats (25,000Rp, three hours) that leave every other day from a jetty in Labuhan village, next to Marina Cottages.

FROM GORONTALO

You have two choices from Gorontalo: the KM *Tuna Tomini* leaves from the port at Gorontalo directly to Wakai (one-way from 75,000Rp) and is the easiest option from this direction if you want to go to Katupat, Kadidiri or Bomba. The KM *Tanjung Api* is the best option if you're going to Malenege or Walea Kodi. It leaves from Marisa (about a three-hour taxi or a four-hour bus ride from Gorontalo) and goes to the village of Dolong on Pulau Walea Kodi (one-way from 21,000Rp) – from here small boats run to Malenge (10,000Rp, five hours).

The KM *Tuna Tomini* departs Gorontalo on Tuesday and Friday at 8pm, arriving in Wakai on Wednesay and Saturday at 7am. On the way back, it departs Wakai on Thursday and Sunday at 5pm, arriving on Friday and Monday at 6am.

The KM *Tanung Api* departs Marisa on Saturday at 12am, arriving in Dolong on Sunday at 6am, and departs Dolong on Tuesday at 10.30am, arriving in Marisa on Tuesday at 5pm.

CHARTERS

Marisa Speedboats between Marisa (about 150km west of Gorontalo) and Wakai or Kadidiri cost about 3,000,000Rp for up to five people. Both Black Marlin Dive and Kadidiri Paradise Resort (both based on Pulau Kadidiri) can arrange boat charters.

Bunta Few people go this way, but it's a fast route. Take a morning flight from Manado to Luwuk, charter a car to Bunta (800,000Rp, four hours) and then charter a boat to Kadidiri (1,200,000Rp).

Getting Around

You can jump on the ferries to/from Ampana to island hop or charter small, local boats. Finding a charter is relatively easy in Wakai, Bomba and Kadidiri, but it's more difficult to arrange in smaller settlements because there are simply not many boats around. The rates are fairly standard among the cartel of local operators (300,000Rp from Wakai or Kadidiri to Bomba on a speedboat). Ask at your homestay.

PULAU BATU DAKA

The largest and most accessible island is Pulau Batu Daka, which is home to the two main villages, Bomba and Wakai.

Bomba is a tiny outpost at the southwestern end of the island, which most travellers sail past on the way to and from Wakai (for Pulau Kadidiri). Bomba is an appealing alternative to Kadidiri; it has some of the Togean's best beaches, good snorkelling and it's social in a very mellow way.

It's a pleasant walk to the **bat caves** in the hills behind Bomba village, but you'll need a guide and a torch (flashlight).

The largest settlement in the Togeans, Wakai is mainly used as the departure point for boats to Pulau Kadidiri, but there are several well-stocked general stores and a lively market. A small **waterfall** a few kilometres inland from Wakai is a pleasant hike – ask for directions in the village.

Sleeping

Poya Lisa Cottages GUESTHOUSE $
(Bomba; cottages without/with bathroom 125,000/150,000Rp) On its own private island, swimming distance from Island Retreat, this little paradise has two perfect beaches and a dozen or so big, clean but simple wooden cottages. The meals here are among the best in the Togeans and the family that runs the place is as sweet as can be. Rustic Togean perfection with no internet or mobile phone connections.

Island Retreat RESORT $$
(☎0852 4115 8853, 0868 1101 7582; www.togian-island-retreat.com; Bomba; r per person US$15-28) Run by an expat Californian woman and her band of friendly dogs, the 20 or so well-cared-for cottages here sit serenely on the beautiful beach at Pasir Putih. While simple, it's relatively luxurious for the Togeans and the internationally inspired food alone is

Togean Islands

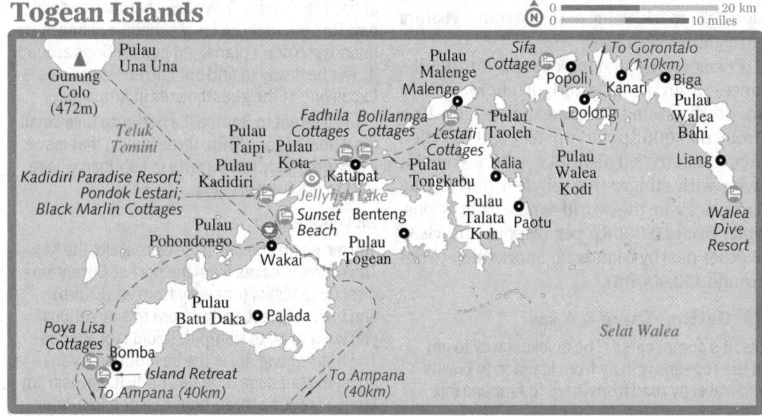

CONSERVATION OF THE TOGEANS

Home to over 500 types of coral, 600 reef fish species and an estimated 500 mollusc species, Teluk Tomini around the Togean Islands is one of the richest reef areas in all of Indonesia. In 2004 the Indonesian Ministry of Forestry signed a bill that turned 362,000 hectares of this fragile area into a national park – great news to conservation groups – but some local NGOs claim national-park status restricts local livelihoods and leaves the region open to other types of exploitation. It will take time to find out the real impact.

The Togeans' shaky ecological record really started when cyanide and dynamite fishing was introduced to the islands in the early 1990s. While this boosted the local catch, it also caused untold damage to fragile reef ecosystems. By the early 2000s locals (often with help from local NGOs and the dive centres) began to understand the destructiveness of these practices and many went back to traditional fishing techniques. Some villages even began creating their own protected areas, and a guardhouse was completed in 2006 to patrol certain regions against illegal fishing practices. Today, islanders are hailing larger fishing yields closer to home and healthy coral beds – proof that reef protection works.

But the Togeans are relatively poor islands and the fishing ain't what it used to be. The fishing of valuable Napoleon fish (for foreign Chinese restaurants) has all but wiped this fish out of these waters and resulted in a catastrophic increase in the number of crown-of-thorns starfish, which destroy coral at an alarming rate.

Luckily, as the water quality has improved, some families are starting seaweed farms. Seaweed farming's potential twice-yearly harvest and a stable market price offer another lucrative option for locals.

worth staying here for. There's a dive centre here, plus snorkelling gear.

Sunset Beach GUESTHOUSE $
(☎0856 5670 8146; Wakai; 125,000-150,000Rp) Highlights at this new place include the bubbly owner, lovely dining area over the pretty beach, good food and the location on a private island between Wakai and Pulau Kadidiri.

PULAU KADIDIRI

This is definitely the island to go to if you're feeling social, but during the low season you could still potentially wind up on your own here. Just a short boat trip from Wakai, the three lodging options (all right next to each other) are on a perfect strip of sand with good snorkelling and swimming only metres from the door and superb diving beyond.

Sleeping

Kadidiri Paradise Resort RESORT $$
(☎0464-21058; www.kadidiriparadise.com; r from €18) This resort on stunning landscaped grounds nearly surrounded by water is Kadidiri's poshest option. Rooms are huge and all have generous decks and big stone bathrooms. The dive centre is particularly well run. The pontoon here is an excellent place for a sunset Bintang whether you're staying here or not.

Pondok Lestari GUESTHOUSE $
(www.lestari.ladz.de; bungalows 100,000Rp) Stay with a charming Bajau family who take their guests on free daily snorkelling trips and fishing excursions where you can catch your own dinner. Both the older bamboo bungalows and newer wooden ones are pretty rustic but the setting is dreamy. All bungalows share a rudimentary *mandi* bathroom.

Black Marlin Cottages GUESTHOUSE $$
(☎0435-831 869; www.blackmarlindiving.com; cottages €16-55) Home to British-run Black Marlin Dive, the cottages here are large, well decorated and have particularly good bathrooms. It's a fun spot and if Ali is around be prepared for a night of drinking *arak*, the local fermented beverage.

KATUPAT

These two small, private islands are a five-minute boat ride from Katupat village on Pulau Togean.

Sleeping

Fadhila Cottages GUESTHOUSE $
(☎0813 4117 9990; fadhilacottage@gmail.com; cottages 125,000-200,000Rp) Clean wooden bungalows with terraces line a palm-shaded beach that faces Katupat village. There's a good dive centre here and a breezy, classy

WORTH A TRIP

PULAU UNA UNA

The Togeans are part of an active volcanic belt. Pulau Una Una, which consists mostly of **Gunung Colo** (472m), was torn apart in 1983 when the volcano exploded for the first time in almost 100 years. Ash covered 90% of the island, destroying all houses, animals and most of the crops. Thankfully, Una Una's population had been safely evacuated. These days you can trek to the top of the volcano (three hours) and admire the awesome lava landscapes all around the island.

There is nowhere to stay on Una Una. The bigger homestays and resorts on Kadidiri and at Bomba can organise dive trips or guided treks up the volcano.

restaurant area. Take a free canoe to find snorkelling spots around the island.

Bolilangga Cottages GUESTHOUSE $
(☎0852 4100 3685; bolilanggaisland@gmail.com; cottages from 125,000Rp) On a white-sand isle facing Katupat village, this basic, friendly place is a slice of true tranquillity.

PULAU MALENGE

Malenge is remote and secluded, with wonderful **snorkelling** just offshore from the village. Some locals, with the aid of NGOs, have established excellent **walking trails** around the mangroves and jungles to help spot the particularly diverse fauna, including macaques, tarsiers, hornbills, cuscuses and salamanders.

Sleeping

Lestari Cottages GUESTHOUSE $
(☎0852 4100 3685; malengeisland@gmail.com; cottages 125,000-150,000Rp) There's a spectacular setting here with jungle behind and a view in front of Malenge village, one of the prettiest stilt fishermen's villages in the archipelago. A winding wood bridge links the guesthouse's island with the village. The big wooden bungalows grace an alabaster beach.

PULAU WALEA KODI

Dolong is a busy fishing village, and the only settlement on the island. You'll find peace and paradise once you get to your resort.

Sleeping

Walea Dive Resort RESORT $$$
(☎0411 402101; www.waleadiveresort.com; 7-night packages for non-divers/divers €786/996) Italian-run, which means the food is sublime, this place is very much geared towards divers and is very popular with (you guessed it) Italians. Packages include a cute, spotless cottage, three meals, transport from Luwuk, spa access and three dives a day if you're on the dive deal.

Sifa Cottage GUESTHOUSE $
(www.waleakodi.com; cottage without/with bathroom 125,000/150,000Rp) One of the newest places, the big, rustic wood cottages here grace a flat, coconut palm-covered white beach that extends to aqua blue. There's a dive centre with rates slightly cheaper than other places.

NORTH SULAWESI

Northern Sulawesi has lots to offer in a relatively condensed space. You can dive over some of the world's best coral reefs at Bunaken one day, climb a volcano near Tomohon the next and visit the lowland Tangkoko-Batuangas Dua Saudara Nature Reserve and its wildlife the next. Economic prosperity from tourism and agriculture (mostly cloves and coconuts) means that North Sulawesi is the most developed province on Sulawesi and prices are higher here than elsewhere on the island.

THE BAJAU

Nomadic Bajau 'sea gypsies' still dive for trepang, pearls and other commercially important marine produce, as they have done for hundreds, perhaps thousands, of years. The Bajau are hunter-gatherers who spend much of their lives on boats, travelling as families wherever they go.

There are several permanent Bajau settlements around the Togean Islands, and even some stilt villages on offshore reefs, but the itinerant character of Bajau culture still survives. Newlyweds are put in a canoe and pushed out to sea to make their place in the world. When they have children, the fathers dive with their three-day-old babies to introduce them to life on the sea.

The two largest distinct groups in the region are the Minahasans and the Sangirese, but there are many more subgroups and dialects. The kingdoms of Bolaang Mongondow, sandwiched between Minahasa and Gorontalo, were also important political players. The Dutch have had a more enduring influence on this peninsula than anywhere else in the archipelago: Dutch is still spoken among the older generation, and well-to-do families often send their children to study in the Netherlands.

The Sangir-Talaud island group forms a bridge to the Philippines, providing a causeway for the movement of peoples and cultures. As a result, the language and physical features of Filipino peoples can be found among the local Minahasans.

History

A group of independent states was established at a meeting of the linguistically diverse Minahasan peoples around AD 670 at a stone now known as Watu Pinabetengan (near Kawangkoan).

In 1677 the Dutch occupied Pulau Sangir and, two years later, a treaty with the Minahasan chiefs saw the start of Dutch domination for the next 300 years. Although relations with the Dutch were often less than cordial, and the region did not actually come under direct Dutch rule until 1870, the Dutch and Minahasans eventually became so close that the north was often referred to as the '12th province of the Netherlands'.

Christianity became a force in the early 1820s, and the wholesale conversion of the Minahasans was almost complete by 1860. Because the school curriculum was taught in Dutch, the Minahasans had an early advantage in the competition for government jobs and positions in the colonial army.

The Minahasan sense of identity became an issue for the Indonesian government after independence. The Minahasan leaders declared their own autonomous state of North Sulawesi in June 1957. The Indonesian government then bombed Manado in February 1958 and, by June, Indonesian troops had landed in North Sulawesi. Rebel leaders retreated into the mountains, and the rebellion was finally put down in mid-1961.

Gorontalo

☎0435 / POP 153,000

The port of Gorontalo has the feel of an overgrown country town, where all the locals seem to know each other and everyone is superfriendly. The town features some of the best-preserved Dutch houses in Sulawesi and still retains a languid colonial feel.

Gorontalo's local hero is Nani Wartabone, an anti-Dutch guerrilla, and there is a large statue of him in the square, Lapangan Nani Wartabone, adjacent to the Melati Hotel.

There are a few banks with ATMs along Jl Jend Ahmad Yani.

Activities

Diving is available in the Gorontalo area with **Tomini Diving Center** (☎0811 431421; www.tominidivingcenter.com; Jl Samratulangi 11) – you can get in touch with them at the Melati Hotel (p678).

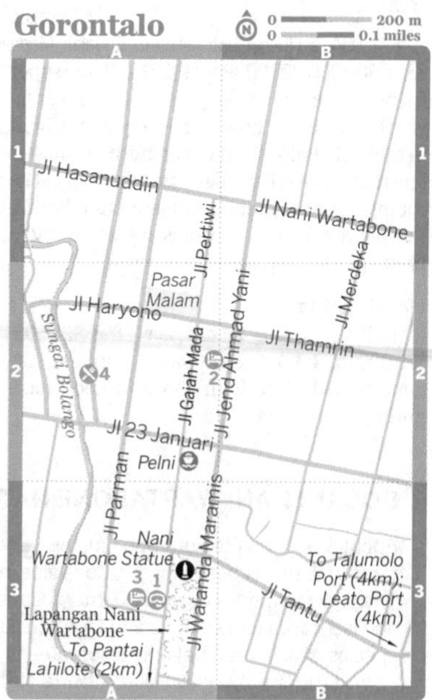

Gorontalo

Activities, Courses & Tours
1 Tomini Diving Center A3

Sleeping
2 Hotel Karina A2
3 Melati Hotel A3

Eating
4 Rumah Makan Sabar A2

If you decide to stay, there are several sights around Gorontalo that are all accessible by local transport – ask for directions at your hotel. On the outskirts of Gorontalo, an old Portugese fort, **Benteng Otanaha**, is on a hill at Lekobalo overlooking Danau Limboto. It was probably built by the Portuguese. Today there are the remains of just three towers.

Pantai Lahilote is a white-sand beach 2km south of Gorontalo, and **Lombongo hot springs**, 17km east of Gorontalo, at the western edge of Bogani Nani Wartabone National Park, has a swimming pool filled with hot-spring water. A nicer spot is the swimming hole at the foot of a 30m waterfall, which is a 3km walk past the springs.

Sleeping

TOP CHOICE **Melati Hotel** HOTEL $
(☎822 934; avelberg@hotmail.com; Jl Gajah Mada 33; r 100,000-220,000Rp; ❄@☜) The super friendly Melati is the long-time backpacker favourite. It's based around a lovely home, built in the early 1900s for the then harbour master (current owner Pak Alex's grandfather). The rooms in the original house are basic but atmospheric; the newer rooms are set around a pretty garden and are well furnished.

Hotel Karina HOTEL $
(☎828 411; Jl Jend Ahmad Yani 28; r 126,500-198,000Rp; ❄☜) A great-value, spotless, air-conditioned place with TVs and good nasi goreng breakfasts.

Eating & Drinking

The local delicacy is *milu siram,* which is a corn soup with grated coconut, fish, salt, chilli and lime. You'll find it at the stalls around the market at night. The night market has a vast number of warungs selling cheap and tasty food.

Rumah Makan Sabar INDONESIAN $
(Jl Sutoyo 31; meals from 15,000Rp; ⏰breakfast, lunch & dinner) The colonial-style terrace draws you in and the food makes you come back for seconds. Try the *nasi campur Makassar* with rice, crispy noodles, tender beef, shredded vegetables and a boiled egg.

Getting There & Away

AIR You can travel to/from Manado daily with **Lion Air** (☎830 035; Jl Rachmat 15). From Makassar and Jakarta there are daily flights divided between the carriers Lion Air, **Sriwijaya** (☎827 878; Jl Agus Salim18) and **Batavia Air** (☎823 388; Jl DI Panjaitan 233). All airlines have offices at the airport, or tickets can be bought at agencies around town.

BOAT Gorontalo has two ports, both about 4km from the town centre: Talumolo port for the Togeans and Leato port for Pelni ferries. Both are easily accessible by *mikrolet* (small taxi) along Jl Tantu. Tell the driver your boat's destination and he'll drop you off at the right place.

Every two weeks the Pelni liner *Tilongkabila* links Gorontalo with Bitung (for Manado) while the *Sangiang* tackles the same route about once a week. The **Pelni office** (☎821 089; cnr Jl 23 Januari & Jl Gajah Mada) is efficient and conven-

BOGANI NANI WARTABONE NATIONAL PARK

About 50km west of Kotamobagu, this very rarely visited national park (193,600 hectares) has the highest conservation value in North Sulawesi, but it's mostly inaccessible. The park (formerly known as Dumoga-Bone) is at the headwaters of Sungai Dumoga and is a haven for rare flora and fauna, including black-crested macaque *(yaki)* and a species of giant fruit bat only discovered in 1992.

Visit the **Bogani Nani Wartabone National Park office** (☎0434-22548; Jl AKD), on the road to Doloduo, about 5km from central Kotamobagu, the nearest town. At this office you can buy permits (30,000Rp per visit), pick up useful tips, look at decent trekking maps and ask lots of questions.

The area around the park entrance at Kosinggolan village has several trails, lasting from one to nine hours, and there are various options for overnight jaunts through the jungle if you have camping equipment. Take a regular *mikrolet* to Doloduo from the Serasi terminal in Kotamobagu. Then walk about 2km west (or ask the *mikrolet* driver to continue) to the ranger station at Kosinggolan, just inside the park, where you must register and pick up a compulsory guide for 80,000Rp per short hike (more for longer trips).

In Kotamobagu there are ATMs and a supermarket – stay at the **Hotel Ramayana** (☎21188; Jl Adampe Dolot 50; s/d 50,000/85,000Rp).

ient. See p673 for more information about boats to the Togean Islands.

BUS The main bus terminal is 3km north of town and accessible by bemo, *bendi* or *ojek*. There are direct buses to Palu (120,000Rp, 17 hours) and Manado (regular/air-con 85,000/100,000Rp, 10 hours), departing every hour. Most people make the Manado trip by minibus or in Kijangs. Seats are priced by how close they are to the front: 100,000Rp to 150,000Rp. From the terminal next to the market, *mikrolet* go in all directions to regional villages.

Getting Around

The airport is 32km north of Gorontalo. For 50,000Rp a shared car can be booked at the taxi desk inside the terminal, and you'll be taken to your requested address. To get to the airport, book the same service through the airline, travel agency or your hotel.

Manado

☎0431 / POP 451,893

With an overabundance of shopping malls and cavernous holes in the footpaths, Manado doesn't usually register as one of North Sulawesi's highlights. It's a well-serviced and friendly place, though, with more than its share of comfortable hotels and some good places to eat. Around the city are nearby adventures at Bunaken, Tomohon, the Lembeh Strait and Tangkoko-Batuangas Dua Saudara Nature Reserve, and to get to these places most travellers will have to spend one night or more in Manado.

A recommended tour company based in Manado is **Bunaken Tour & Travel** (☎084 2958; www.bunakentourtravel.com; Jl Yos Sudarso Paal Dua, Komp Pasar Segar Blok KG 11) in partnership with Michael Lietzinger, who has been specialising in tours around Sulawesi, Papua and Maluku since 1993.

History

In 1844 Manado was levelled by earthquakes, so the Dutch redesigned it from scratch. Fourteen years later the famous naturalist Alfred Wallace visited and described the city as 'one of the prettiest in the East'. That was 150 years ago and time hasn't been kind to the place.

Rice surpluses from Minahasa's volcanic hinterland made Manado a strategic port for European traders sailing to and from the 'Spice Islands' (Maluku). The Dutch helped unite the diverse Minahasan confederacy. By the mid-1800s, compulsory cultivation schemes were producing huge crops of cheap coffee for a Dutch-run monopoly. Minahasans suffered from this 'progress', yet economic, religious and social ties with the colonists continued to intensify. Elsewhere, Minahasan mercenaries put down anti-Dutch rebellions in Java and beyond, earning them the name *anjing Belanda* (Dutch dogs).

The Japanese occupation of 1942–45 was a period of deprivation, and the Allies bombed Manado heavily in 1945. During the war of independence that followed, there was bitter division between the nationalists and those favouring Dutch-sponsored federalism, and the city was bombed by Indonesian military in 1958.

Today, the development of Bitung's deep-sea port, and direct air links with the Philippines, Malaysia and Singapore, have helped to promote Manado's trade and tourism.

Along Jl Sam Ratulangi, the main road running north-south, there are upmarket restaurants, hotels and supermarkets. The 'boulevard', Jl Piere Tendean, is a monstrous thoroughfare with hotels and shopping malls; it has limited coastal access.

Sights

Most of the main sights lie beyond the city.

Public Museum of North Sulawesi MUSEUM
(Museum Negeri Propinsi Sulawesi Utara; ☎870 308; Jl Supratman 72; admission 5000Rp; ⏲8am-4pm Mon-Thu, 8-11.30am Fri, 9am-2pm Sat) Features a large display of traditional costumes and housing implements, with captions in English.

Kienteng Ban Hian Kong TEMPLE
(Jl Panjaitan) The 19th-century Kienteng Ban Hian Kong is the oldest Buddhist temple in eastern Indonesia and has been beautifully restored. The temple hosts a spectacular festival in February (dates vary according to the lunar calendar).

Festivals & Events

Minahasans love an excuse to party. Watch out for these main festivals:

Tai Pei Kong CULTURAL
Held at Kienteng Ban Hian Kong in February.

Pengucapan Syukur CULTURAL
A harvest festival that can take place any time from June to August.

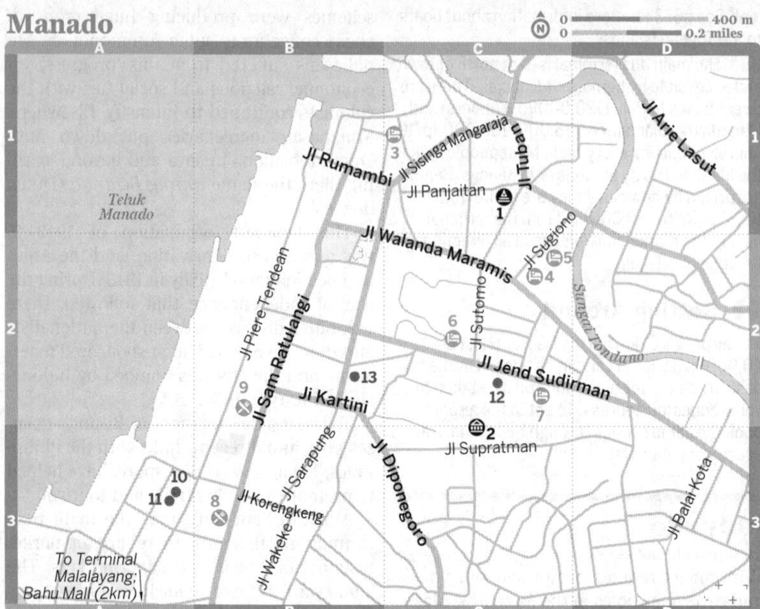

Manado

Sights

1 Kienteng Ban Hian Kong C1
2 Public Museum of North Sulawesi C3

Sleeping

3 Celebes Hotel C1
4 Hotel Regina C2
5 Rex Hotel C2
6 Sintesa Peninsula Hotel C2
7 Swiss Belhotel Maleosan C2

Eating

8 Rumah Makan Green Garden B3
9 Singapura Bakery B2

Transport

10 Batavia Air A3
11 Lion Air A3
12 Merpati C2
13 Silk Air B2

Manado Beach Festival CULTURAL
The city's anniversary party lasts a week in mid-July.

Traditional Horse & Bull Races EVENT
Late September.

Sleeping

Hotels near and on Jl Sam Ratulangi are an easy walk to food and shopping but can be noisy due to the traffic. Places a little further from the city centre are more peaceful and you can easily hop on one of the ubiquitous *mikrolet* to get wherever you need to go. The dive lodges are about a 40-minute drive from town in peaceful settings and you'll be relying on your hosts for tours and activities.

The better budget places fill quickly with Indonesian businesspeople, so reserve in advance.

Hot water and included breakfasts are standard at all the midrange and top end places.

IN TOWN

TOP CHOICE **Hotel Minahasa** HOTEL **$$**
(☎874 871; www.hotelminahasa.com; Jl Sam Ratulangi 199; r with fan/air-con from 260,000/450,000Rp; ❄📶) Manado's answer to a boutique hotel has flower-filled grounds stretching up the hill to a luxurious pool and fitness centre with city views. Fan rooms are basic and you may be tempted to upgrade to a much more elegant, superior room with a terrace and a view. All options are overpriced but it's the most pleasant place in town.

Hotel Regina HOTEL $
(☎850 090; Jl Sugiono 1; r from 200,000 incl breakfast; ❄📶) Bland but big rooms here are spotless and very plush for the price. The hearty Indonesian breakfasts make this the area's best deal but because of this it's often full.

Swiss Belhotel Maleosan HOTEL $$
(☎021 560 6040; www.swiss-belhotel.com/manado; Jl Jenderal Sudirman 85-87; r from 650,000Rp; ❄@📶) This is the classiest place in town with very comfortable, large, bright, well-furnished rooms with half marble and half carpeted floors. The pool is busy with kids but the spa is serene. Popular with the Indonesian jet set.

Sintesa Peninsula Hotel HOTEL $$$
(☎855 008; www.sintesapeninsulahotel.com; Jl Jend Sudirman; r from US$95; ❄@📶) A gleaming white fortress on a hill in the middle of town, the Sintesa has all bases covered from the marble-clad lobby to its fitness centre, free internet and big swimming pool.

Rex Hotel HOTEL $
(☎851 136; Jl Sugiono 3; s/d with fan 44,000/93,500Rp, r with air-con 115,500Rp; ❄) These are the best budget rooms in town: all are clean but there is lots of noise via the road, other guests and thin walls. Shared-bathroom economy rooms are microscopic, but air-con standards with private bathrooms are quite comfortable.

Celebes Hotel HOTEL $
(☎870425; hotelcelebesmdo@yahoo.com; Jl Rumambi 8A; s/d with fan and shared bathroom from 110,000/120,000Rp, r with air-con & bathroom 165,000-385,000Rp) A rambling cheapy with gritty charm, this massive place sits between the port and a bustling market area. Rooms are small but clean. Angle for one on an upper floor with a view of the sea.

COASTAL DIVE RESORTS

TOP CHOICE **Lumbalumba Diving** DIVE RESORT $$
(☎838 440; www.lumbalumbadiving.com; bungalows per person from €30) A serene, intimate resort on the sea and surounded by gorgeous gardens, about a 20-minute drive from town. Divers will love the small groups and knowlegable staff while non-divers can melt the days away at the pool with a marine park view. Fantastic value.

Bahowo Lodge DIVE RESORT $$$
(☎0819 404 5261; www.bahowolodge.com; Bahowo Village; r US$60-160 incl breakfast & dinner; ❄@) A clean, modern, freindly, place in Bahowo village on a mangrove-laden coast (no beach). Rooms have tiled floors and some have sea views. The British owners are very involved in local village life and there's always lots going on. It's about 15km north of Manado on the coast.

Hotel Santika Manado DIVE RESORT $$
(☎858 222; www.santika-manado.com; Tongkaina Bunaken; r from 500,000Rp; ❄@📶) This is a world away from Manado (it's 13km to the north on the coast), with a large swimming pool and walkway access through mangroves to the sea. The dive centre gets rave reviews, but the rooms are definitely past their prime.

Eating

Adventurous Minahasan cuisine can be found around Manado. Get a taste for *rica-rica,* a spicy stir-fry made with *ayam* (chicken), *babi* (pork) or even *r.w.* (pronounced 'air weh' – dog!). *Bubur tinotuan* (corn porridge) and fresh seafood are local specialities worth looking out for.

Most of the malls have extensive food courts on their upper floors. The best ones are those at Mega Mall and Bahu Mall, but even the smaller shopping centres have cheap eats. Choose from Indonesian, Chinese, Italian and more.

TOP CHOICE **Raja Sate** INDONESIAN, INTERNATIONAL $$
(Jl Pierre Tendean 39; sate from 16,000RP; ⏱2.30-11pm Mon-Sat; 📶) Chose from a tasty array of sate, curries and even New Zealand steaks – everything is excellent. The atmosphere is lively and a touch posh.

Singapura Bakery INDONESIAN $
(Jl Sam Ratulangi 22; pastries from 5000Rp) Has a mind-boggling array of baked goods, fresh juices and shakes, plus a popular cheap cafe next door serving yummy Javanese fare.

Rumah Makan Green Garden INDONESIAN $
(Jl Sam Ratulangi; meals 20,000Rp) Looks like another hole in the wall but the food here is really good. Try the tofu dishes and fresh juices.

Information

ATMs and banks are clustered along Jl Sam Ratulangi, plus out at the airport.

Immigration Office (☎841 688; Jl 17 Agustus)

Main Police Station (☎emergencies 110, inquiries 852 162; Jl 17 Agustus) Main police station.

North Sulawesi Tourism Office (☎852 723; Jl Diponegoro 111; ⏰8am-2pm Mon-Sat) You can get a map and sign the guest book, but that's about it.

Rumah Sakit Umum (☎853191; Jl Monginsidi) The general hospital is about 4.5km from town and includes a decompression chamber.

Tourist Information (☎0812 4403 7100) At the airport and only open for international arrivals, this glass booth has very helpful service.

Getting There & Away

Air

Tickets for domestic flights often cost about the same at travel agencies as they do online. The domestic departure tax is 30,000Rp and international departure tax is 100,000Rp.

Batavia Air (☎386 4338; Mega Mall)

Garuda (☎877 737; Jl Sam Ratulangi)

Lion Air (☎847 000; Mega Mall)

Merpati (☎842 000; Jl Jend Sudirman 111)

Silk Air (☎863 744; Jl Sarapung)

Boat

All Pelni boats use the deep-water port of Bitung, 55km from Manado. There's no Pelni office in Manado – the nearest one is in Bitung – but you can get information and purchase tickets from numerous travel agents around town.

Small, slow and uncomfortable boats leave Manado every day or two for Tahuna and Lirung, also in the Sangir-Talaud Islands; and to Mangole, Sanana, Tobelo and Ambon in Maluku. Tickets are available from the stalls outside the port. From Bitung, four overnight ferries a week also travel to Ternate in North Maluku.

For Bunaken boats, see p686.

Bus

There are three reasonably orderly terminals for long-distance buses and the local *mikrolet*.

Terminal Karombasan (5km south of the city) Services Tomohon (6500Rp) and other places south of Manado.

Terminal Malalayang (far south) Services Kotamobagu (30,000Rp) and Gorontalo (85,000Rp, eight hours).

Terminal Paal 2 (eastern end of Jl Martadinata) Varied public transport runs to Bitung (8000Rp) and the airport (400Rp).

Getting Around

TO/FROM THE AIRPORT *Mikrolet* from Sam Ratulangi International Airport go to Terminal Paal 2 (3500Rp), where you can change to a *mikrolet* heading to Pasar 45 or elsewhere in the city, for a flat fee of 2200Rp. Fixed-price taxis cost 85,000Rp from the airport to the city (13km).

TRANSPORT FROM MANADO

Air

DESTINATION	COMPANY	FREQUENCY
Ambon	Lion Air	daily
Balikpapan	Lion Air, Batavia Air	daily
Denpasar	Lion Air, Garuda	daily
Gorontolo	Lion Air	daily
Jakarta	Batavia Air, Merpati, Garuda, Lion Air	daily
Makassar	Lion Air, Sriwijaya	daily
Sorong	Lion Air, Sriwijaya	1 weekly
Singapore	Silk Air	3 weekly
Ternate	Garuda, Sriwijaya, Lion Air	1 weekly

Boat

DESTINATION	BOAT	COST (RP; ECONOMY/1ST CLASS)
Banggai	Sinabung	899,000/3,383,500
Luwuk	Tilongkabila	159,500/603,500Rp
Pantoloan	Dorolonda	233,500/902,500
Sorong	Tatamailau	287,500/1,200,000
Ternate	Sangiang, Lambelu	138,500/518,500

PUBLIC TRANSPORT Manado's *mikrolet* literally clog up Manado's streets, so finding one with a spare seat is a matter of waiting a second or two. *Mikrolet* heading south on Jl Sam Ratulangi with 'Wanea' on the window sign will go to Terminal Karombasan. Most *mikrolet* heading north go through Pasar 45 and past the Pasar Jengki fish market, but some go directly to Terminal Paal 2 along Jl Jend Sudirman. *Mikrolet* heading to Terminal Malalayang go down Jl Pierre Tendean. The fare for any destination around town is 2200Rp. Private taxis circle the city but very few drivers are willing to use the meter, so negotiate before setting off.

Pulau Bunaken

☎0431

This tiny, coral-fringed isle is North Sulawesi's top tourist destination but (so far) it's managed to avoid becoming resort-land and maintains a rootsy island soul. Tourist accommodation is spread out along two beaches – other than that, the island belongs to the islanders; these friendly folk have a seemingly endless reserve of authentically warm smiles. There are no hassles here, just laid-back beachy bliss.

However, most people come to Bunaken for the diving. The marine biodiversity is extraordinary, with more than 300 types of coral and 3000 species of fish, so when you first get your head in the water and see the abundant corals, sponges and phenomenally colourful life all around you, it's a life-shaking experience. The 808-hectare island is part of the 75,265-hectare **Bunaken Manado Tua Marine National Park** (Taman Laut Bunaken Manado Tua), which includes Manado Tua (Old Manado), the dormant volcano that can be seen from Manado and climbed in about four hours; Nain and Mantehage islands; and Pulau Siladen, which has some more accommodation options.

With the developing and expanding city of Manado right next door, Bunaken is becoming more and more accessible. Within two hours of arriving in Manado from Singapore, Kuala Lumpur or most parts of Indonesia, you can be in a bamboo beach shack on Bunaken watching the sunset. Unfortunately, this proximity also means that the huge amounts of garbage generated by the city can sweep onto Pantai Liang, turning the picturesque tropical beach into a refuse heap. The scarcity of fresh water has limited the island's development, and villagers must import their drinking water from Manado.

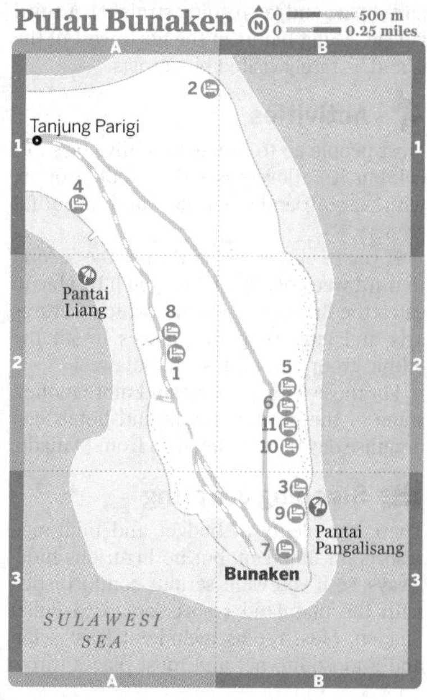

Pulau Bunaken

Sleeping

1 Bunaken Island Resort A2
2 Cha Cha A1
3 Daniel's Homestay B3
4 Froggies A1
5 Living Colours B2
6 Lorenso's Beach Garden B2
7 Novita Homestay B3
8 Panorama A2
9 Seabreeze Resort B3
10 The Village Bunaken B2
11 Two Fish B2

Washing water is drawn from small, brackish wells.

Prices from accomodation to a Bintang are much higher than in mainland Sulawesi and some resorts discriminate against non-divers, either by charging higher accommodation prices or turning them away.

There is a concrete and dirt path connecting Pangalisang and Liang, about a 30-minute walk. Pangalisang is connected to Bunaken village by a new paved road used by scooters, while Liang has a complicated network of forest footpaths towards the main village (hint: stay on the overgrown paved part and keep going straight). A third village, Alung Banua at the northwest of the island, is rarely visited by tourists.

Activities

Most people go to Bunaken to dive or snorkel, but it's a lovely island to walk around, with very friendly villages and beautiful scenery.

If you're on the island during the second to third week of September, you'll be able to catch the **Bunaken Festival**, which features arts and cultural performances by all the ethnic groups around North Sulawesi.

For those with less time and more money, some of the dive operators and hotels can organise day trips to Bunaken from Manado.

Sleeping & Eating

There are plenty of budget and midrange resorts on Bunaken, but no luxurious hideaways, so if you want serious comfort, stick with the mainland resorts or go to Pulau Siladen. Most rooms include at least a fan and a mosquito net and most places throw in transfers to and from the jetty in Bunaken village, in some cases to the mainland. Consider bringing some snacks and treats from the mainland, as there is not much available on the island beyond the set meals. All prices are per person and include three meals per day.

Note also that for budget places the rates are much cheaper when you book in person than what you'll see quoted online.

PANTAI PANGALISANG

Pantai Pangalisang is a stretch of white sand tucked behind the mangroves with some outrageous snorkelling just beyond. The beach all but disappears at high tide. There are plenty of other good choices beyond the more established places we've listed here, so you can easily just turn up on the boat and shop around.

TOP CHOICE **Living Colours** DIVE RESORT **$$**
(☎081 2430 6063; www.livingcoloursdiving.fi; bungalows from €50; @ 📶) By far the most comfortable choice on this main strip of beach, this Finnish-run place has wooden

DIVING & SNORKELLING AROUND PULAU BUNAKEN

Bunaken's unique situation of being surrounded by deep water with strong, nutrient-laden currents, plus having a mangrove ecosystem that protects much of the beaches and subsequently the corals from erosion, makes it one of the best diving and snorkelling spots in the world. Beyond drop-offs you'll find caves and valleys full of brightly coloured sponges, thriving corals and fish – it is also common to see turtles, rays, dolphins and sharks. The most accessible (and one of the most spectacular) diving and snorkelling site is the coral drop-off by Pantai Liang, which plummets from 1m to 2m depths into dark oblivion. For DIY snorkellers, the easiest place to get in is in front of Lorenso's Beach Cottages.

Most guesthouses, resorts and dive centres have maps of all the sites around Bunaken and where you go will most likely depend on the current conditions. If you're staying somewhere without a dive centre it's easy to shop around for outings with a nearby place.

Well-worn snorkelling equipment can be rented from most homestays for about 50,000Rp per day, but it is often worth paying a little more to rent some quality equipment from one of the dive centres.

Trips around Bunaken and nearby islands will cost from €55 for two dives (there's nearly always a two-dive per trip minimum – for one dive you'll have to wait out the second dive on the boat) and around €390 for PADI courses. Equipment rental is extra and costs around €15 per day for scuba gear, fins, mask and snorkel. Snorkellers can go along with the dive boats for around €5 per person.

It is worth checking whether companies are members of the **North Sulawesi Watersports Association** (NSWA; www.divenorthsulawesi.com), which promotes conservation activities and local community initiatives. This organisation has about 15 members and keeps on growing.

The places that charge more per dive usually do so because they invest in better equipment. Check out the state of what's on offer and ask about the centre's safety procedures before you commit.

WORTH A TRIP

THE BANGKA ISLANDS: MINING VERSUS THE ENVIRONMENT

Strategically located off the northern tip of Sulawesi between Pulau Bunaken and the Lembeh Strait, the Banggka Islands complete this region's dive haven trifecta. This is where to go for pinnacle diving and it's also a prime spot for big fauna: dolphins, manta rays and at least nine species of whale all migrate through these waters around March and April and again in August and September. At all times you're likely to see tuna, batfish, jacks and barracuda. There is often a fairly strong current but these make the plentiful soft corals bloom. Away from the pinnacles, you'll find pygmy seahorses, nudibranches and leaf fishes in the coral gardens.

At the time of writing a Chinese company, Mikgro Metal Perdana, had started 'iron exploration' on Bangka Island and local groups have stated this is only a front for a massive mining operation. Large-scale mining could damage not only the island's ecology but also stir up underwater sediment and potentially threaten the coral life of the entire region, including around Bunaken Island. Technically it's illegal for mining to take place on Bangka, which is zoned solely for tourism, so it's been questioned if the company will be able to side-step these regulations. Bangka Islanders have strongly opposed mining on their island.

For now at least, it's still a phenomenal place to visit. Dive centres from Bunaken and Lembeh often dive the Bangka Islands but you can also choose to stay at one of the increasing number of dive resorts. We recommend the following:

Blue Bay Divers (www.blue-bay-divers.de; dive packages per day from €100) On the beautiful tiny island of Sahuang across from Pulau Bangka, Blue Bay Divers has beachfront bungalows and offers small dive groups. Prices include three meals and two dives per day. The also offer liveaboard dive cruises – check the website.

Gangga Island Resort & Spa (0413-889 4009; www.ganggaisland.com; r per person incl meals US$165-225;) Still intimate but more upscale with a spa, satellite TV and excellent dining. Prices are per person not including diving and there's a three-day minimum stay.

bungalows with enormous terraces, stylish furniture clad in drapy white fabrics and spacious hot-water bathrooms. It's perched up on a little hill and both the food and service are fantastic.

Cha Cha RESORT $$$

(081 3560 03736; www.bunakenchacha.com; bungalows from US$85;) In splendid isolation on the northeastern tip of the island, 'The Last Resort' (as it is sometimes nicknamed) has an intimate atmosphere. Of all Bunaken's options, this is the place where you will get pampered the most, which makes it great if you're not a hardcore diver. Expect Italian and Japanese flavours to complement the local meals.

Seabreeze Resort RESORT $$

(081 143 9558; www.bunakendivers.com; room/bungalows €25/35;) Rooms and bungalows grace a garden slope to the sea. Rooms have bamboo floors and woven bamboo walls, while bungalows are much more spacious and have great verandas. There's not much beach here but the waterfront restaurant is sublime and the beers are very cold thanks to the Aussie owner.

The Village Bunaken RESORT $$

(081 3407 57268; www.bunakenvillage.com; bungalows from €35;) With a chic dipping pool, a fabulously friendly welcome and a refreshing Javanese–Balinese style, this is one of Bunaken's swankier options and is a good choice for families.

Daniel's Homestay GUESTHOUSE $

(0852 4086 1716; www.immanueldivers.com; bungalows from 165,000Rp;) This is a busy but relaxing place with plenty of mingling with locals and dive-tired backpackers. Wood bungalows in a mature flower-filled garden are very basic but spacious. Pay a little more for a seafront bungalow.

Lorenso's Beach Garden GUESTHOUSE $

(0852 5697 3345; www.lorensobunaken.com; r & bungalows 150,000-250,000Rp) Lorenso's has simple wood rooms and flashier, more private bungalows. Meals invariably involve lots of fresh fish, some of the island's best snorkelling is just through the mangroves and if Lorenso and his tin-can band decide to play, be prepared for a rockin' night.

Two Fish DIVE RESORT **$$**
(☎081 143 2805; www.twofishdivers.com; three-day two-night packages from €176 per person; @📶) Budget rooms are dark and basic so it's worth upgrading to pleasant cottages that have terraces looking out to the beach. But more importantly, this place has one of the most professional and eco-aware dive centres on the island. A pool was being built when we passed through.

Novita Homestay GUESTHOUSE **$**
(r 150,000) Right in Bunaken village (at the northern end), these spotless rooms with shared bathrooms in a charming family home are the place to stay for an authentic local experience.

PANTAI LIANG

The beach at Pantai Liang has suffered from considerable erosion and rising sea levels, and has thus become a svelte though pleasant strip of white sand. Bungalows are closer together and there's more beachside action here (such as seaside food and trinket vendors). However, it's a sorry sight when the rubbish washes in from Manado.

The beach just south of Pantai Liang is a protected turtle nesting ground, so keep off of it even though it looks inviting.

Bunaken Island Resort RESORT **$$$**
(☎0813 4021 7027; www.bunaken.nl; bungalow €55-79; ❄📶) A gorgeous hillside resort overlooking the sea with huge polished wood bungalows with hardwood furniture, shady terraces and rain showers in the bathrooms. The restaurant serves fresh food and has fantastic views; service is tip top.

Panorama GUESTHOUSE **$**
(☎0813 4021 7306, 0813 4021 7027; enjypitcha@yahoo.com; bungalows from 150,000Rp) Tucked in corner up on a hillside, the basic wood bungalows with terraces and commanding views are one of the best budget deals on the island. It's a friendly, family-style place with their own small dive shop.

Froggies RESORT **$$**
(☎081 2430 1356; www.divefroggies.com; cottages €30-40; 📶) Very professionally run, this was one of the first dive centres on the island and it's still going strong under the friendly touch of the Belgian manager/dive guru. It has a good beachfront location and good renovated, tiled rooms with terraces overlooking the water.

PULAU SILADEN

Three kilometres north of Bunaken and the smallest island of the archipelago, beach-laden Siladen boasts a wall of gorgeous corals (especially good for nudibranches) and mostly upmarket resorts.

Tanta Moon RESORT **$$$**
(www.tantamoon.ru; bungalow €175 for 2 people incl meals & transfers; ❄) Step out of your elegant polished wood villa and into a dreamy underwater world of flourishing corals. Dine on international cuisine against a tropical sunset. There's no dive centre here but the friendly staff can arrange diving elsewhere.

Tante Martha Homestay GUESTHOUSE **$**
(☎0852 4009 7488; bungalows 200,000Rp) Basic bungalows on a simply sublime beach with great snorkelling steps away.

Siladen Resort & Spa RESORT **$$$**
(www.siladen.com; r from €175; ❄) A beautiful resort with sumptuously furnished villas. Facilities include a lagoon pool, an indulgent spa, and a dive centre.

ℹ Information

In an attempt to finance conservation activities, rubbish disposal, mangrove rehabilitation, local education programs and the policing of any illegal fishing practices, the Bunaken Manado Tua Marine National Park charges an entry fee of 50,000Rp (for a day pass) to 150,000Rp (if you stay any longer; good for one year). Pay at your hotel or dive centre. If no one asks you to pay, go to the national park headquarters on Pantai Liang to pay yourself since the money goes to a good cause. There's an informative diorama-style museum about the flora and fauna of Bunaken at the helpful and informative national park headquarters.

ℹ Getting There & Away

Every day (except Sunday) at about 3pm, a public boat (50,000Rp, one hour) leaves the harbour, near Pasar Jengki fish market in Manado, for Bunaken village and Pulau Siladen. You'll have to walk from the boat landing in Bunaken village to your homestay. The boat leaves Bunaken between 7am and 8am daily (except Sunday), so it's not possible to day-trip from Manado using the public boat.

The more upmarket options on Bunaken offer on-demand boat shuttles to/from Manado for their clients. Otherwise, most guest houses can help you charter a boat (often small and rickety) for around 250,000Rp each way for the whole boat.

When conditions are rough the public boat stops running, but private boats will usually make the shorter, half-hour crossing between Bunaken and either the Hotel Santika (about one hour from Manado) or the town of Wori (two hours from Manado). Bear in mind that conditions are sometimes too choppy for any boats to make the crossing.

Tomohon

0431 / POP 30,000

Tomohon is a pleasant, cool respite from Manado, with a stunning setting below the volcano, Gunung Lokon. It's popular with city folk on weekends; for travellers, it's a possible (though spread-out) alternative to Manado, and an ideal base from which to explore the many nearby attractions.

Sleeping

If you plan on climbing Gunung Lokon stay at Volcano Resort which is right at the base. To get there, get out at 'Gereja Pniel', about 3km before Tomohon from Manado. From there you'll have to walk or catch an *ojek* the remaining 500m towards the mountain.

To get to Onong's Palace or Highland Resort, get off the *mikrolet* from Manado at 'Kinilow', about 5km before Tomohon, and walk the 300m signposted from the main road.

All of the following places have restaurants, and breakfast is included in the price.

Onong's Palace GUESTHOUSE $$

(315 7090; www.tomohon-onong.com; r from €20 incl breakfast; @) The chic bungalows here are perched along an exceptionally lush and shady hillside. All have big decks, massive windows, artistic bamboo Bali-style details and hot water. There's a reasonably good on-site restaurant.

Highland Resort RESORT $$

(353 333; www.highlandresort.info; r €30-60; wi-fi) A tidy place with all the staff in matching red T-shirts, Highland Resort has a huge collection of plain but clean wooden rooms of varying sizes. Lots of tours and tour information are on offer, and there are nice views over the jungle. There's also a full spa.

Volcano Resort GUESTHOUSE $

(352 988; cottages 120,000-200,000Rp) Spread out around a grassy garden, these clean, wooden bungalows are a great deal, plus the staff are helpful and speak English.

TOMOHON'S MACABRE MARKET

It's said that the Minahasan people will eat anything on four legs, apart from the table and chairs, and nowhere is this more evident than at Tomohon's daily market. Visiting the market (which is right next to the *mikrolet* terminal) is a slaughterhouse-like experience, with dead and alive dogs, pigs, rats and bats all on display. The most radical moments are when yelping dogs are pulled out of their cages and killed by a bludgeon on the back of the head. The market is at its 'best' on Saturday morning when the snake butchers come to town.

Eating

Adventurous Minahasan cuisine is served in a string of restaurants on a cliff overlooking Manado, just a few kilometres before Tomohon. The bus from Manado to Tomohon will drop you off at any restaurant, but buses back to Manado are often full.

Getting There & Around

Mikrolet regularly travel to Tomohon (7000Rp, 40 minutes) from Terminal Karombasan in Manado. From the terminal in Tomohon, *mikrolet* go to Manado, and *mikrolet* and buses go to Tondano and various other towns. There are a few *bendi* around town, but a good way to see local sights in little time is to charter a *mikrolet* or a more comfortable but expensive taxi. The taxis line up opposite the *mikrolet* terminal.

Around Tomohon

Gunung Lokon (1580m) contains a simmering crater lake of varying hues, which takes about three hours to reach (and another hour to the peak) from Tomohon. Before climbing any volcano in the area, report to the **volcanology centre** (Kantor Dinas Gunung Berapi; 351 076; Jl Kakashashen Tiga). The centre can provide advice about the hike. Volcano Resort in Tomohon can help to arrange this and other hikes in the area for guests.

You can drive almost all the way to the top of **Gunung Mahawu**, where you'll be rewarded with views over the whole region and into a 180m-wide, 140m-deep sulphuric crater lake. There's no public transport but lots of tours go here. This place gets swarmed by locals on the weekends.

There are numerous other places to explore from Tomohon, and all are accessible by *mikrolet*. **Danau Linow**, a small, highly sulphurous lake that changes colours with the light, is home to extensive birdlife. Take a *mikrolet* to Sonder, get off at Lahendong and walk 1.5km to the lake. From Danau Linow you can hike 8km to **Danau Tondano**, but you'll need to ask directions.

Bitung

☎0438 / POP 137,000

Bitung is the chief regional port and home to many factories. Despite its spectacular setting, the town is unattractive, so most travellers make for Manado or beyond as soon as possible.

Regardless of what time you arrive by boat in Bitung, there will be buses going to Manado, but if you need to leave Bitung by boat early in the morning, it may be prudent to stay overnight. Be vigilant around the docks, as plenty of pickpockets turn up to greet the Pelni liners.

Wisma Pelaut (☎083 6078; Jl Pakadoodan; r 200,000Rp) is the best place to stay if you get stuck here and there are plenty of basic *rumah makan* in the town centre and near the port.

Its proximity to the Philippines makes the port at Bitung an unfortunate hot spot for wildlife smuggling. **Tasikoki** (☎0857 5747 1090; www.tasikoki.org; per person including three vegetarian meals per day from US$70) is an entirely volunteer-run organisation that rescues and cares for animals confiscated from smugglers. Its goals are to rehabilitate the animals and release them back into the wild. You can make a day visit to the centre (free but donations are very appreciated), stay in their very comfortable ecolodge or sign on longer as a volunteer but note that if you turn up unannounced you will be curtly sent on your way (we speak from experience). The centre is about a 45-minute taxi ride from Bitung.

There are currenly over 200 animals of 40 different species at the centre and during your visit you'll learn about the illegal animal trade and the animals themselves.

Getting There & Away

All sorts of vehicles leave regularly from Terminal Paal 2 in Manado (8000Rp, one hour). The driver stops at Terminal Mapalus, just outside Bitung, from where you have to catch another *mikrolet* (10 minutes) to town or the port. The port is in the middle of Bitung, and the **Pelni office** (☎35818) is in the port complex.

Pulau Lembeh & the Lembeh Strait

Lembeh is known almost exclusively for its diving and has emerged as the critter capital of Indonesia. There are dives available for all levels from searching the muddy shallows for the bizarre stuff, more classic coral dives, five wrecks, and fantastic night dives lit by

THE WEIRD & WILD CRITTERS OF THE LEMBEH STRAIT

For the uninitiated, welcome to an alien world on our very own planet. Critters are the wonderful creatures that inhabit murky depths, are much admired by underwater photographers and have probably inspired more than a few movie monsters. Here's just a sample of what you may find:

Hairy frogfish (*Antennarius striatus*) Camoulflaged to look like a rock, covered in whispy-coral-like hairs and with a frown only the keenest diver could love, these guys are most known for the built-in appendage on their forehead that they dangle like a worm to draw in prey. They don't swim like normal fish, but walk on their fins.

Mimic octopus (*Thaumoctopus mimicus*) This recently discovered underwater thespian can convincingly imitate over 15 other animals including sea snakes, crabs, sting rays and jellyfish. It does this by contorting its body into a new shape, changing colours then mimicing the behavior of said species.

Pygmy seahorse (*Hippocampus bargibanti*) Under 2cm tall, these hard-to-spot cuties have the same texture and colour as the fan corals on which they live.

phosphorescence. The corals, beaches and above water activities are arguably better at Bunaken but Lembeh has amazing underwater variety and less visitors.

Two tank dives cost around €60 and PADI Open Water Diving courses are usually about €350.

Sleeping & Eating

As Lembeh's fame grows, so does the number of dive resorts, and most have a sister operation on Bunaken or around Manado. All are set in secluded bays, but without transport it is near-impossible to travel between them and there's little to do besides dive.

Better-value packages that include diving are usually available, but the following prices are for room and board only per person unless otherwise specified.

Two Fish DIVE RESORT **$$**
(☎0821 9480 6676; www.twofishdivers.com; r €20-30, cottages €40; 📶) Lovely wooden cottages, a good dive-central location, friendly management and small dive groups make this English-run place an excellent choice. Reserve in advance especially for one of the four budget rooms – these fill quickly. The food is just OK but the laid-back ambience can't be beat.

Black Sand Dive Retreat DIVE RESORT **$$$**
(www.blacksanddive.com; bungalows €70; 📶) The serene, dark sand beach location on the mainland may be remote above water but it's smack in the middle of everything as far as diving is concerned. With only 12 guests at a time, you'll get plenty of personalised attention and the owner is particularly passionate about local wildlife.

NAD DIVE RESORT **$$**
(☎0813 4026 2850; www.nad-lembeh.com; three-night packages with five dives from US$310 per person; ❄📶) English-Malaysian run, this place faces the mainland and offers big, clean rooms and fantastic food (everything from Western to Thai and Indian). There's a small black sand beach out front.

Lembeh Resort RESORT **$$$**
(☎0438-30667; www.lembehresort.com; cottages US$159; ❄@📶) This is a lovely Balinese-style, formally run resort that gets many returning customers, particularly from the US. With a spa, pool and plenty of non-dive tours on offer, it's probably the best choice if you've got landlubbers in your group.

Tangkoko-Batuangas Dua Saudara Nature Reserve

With 8800 hectares of forest bordered by a sandy coastline and offshore coral gardens, Tangkoko is one of the most impressive and accessible nature reserves in Indonesia. The park is home to black macaques, cuscuses and tarsiers, maleo birds and endemic red-knobbed hornbills, among other fauna, and rare types of rainforest flora. Tangkoko is also home to a plethora of midges, called *gonones,* which bite and leave victims furiously scratching for days afterwards. Always wear long trousers, tucked into thick socks, and take covered shoes and plenty of insect repellent. Sadly, parts of the park are falling victim to encroachment by local communities, but money generated from visitors might help stave that off.

Bring plenty of cash as the nearest ATM, in Girian, often runs dry.

Sights & Activities

Most people arrive at the park entrance at Batuputih in the afternoon, take a three-hour guided night walk (starting at 4.30pm; 85,000Rp per person) into the park to see the

DON'T MISS

TARSIERS

If you're visiting Sulawesi's Tangkoko-Batuangas Dua Saudara Nature Reserve or Lore Lindu National Park, keep your eyes peeled for something looking back at you: a tiny nocturnal primate known as a tarsier. These creatures are recognisable by their eyes, which are literally larger than their stomachs, so big in fact that they cannot rotate them within their sockets. Luckily, their heads can be rotated nearly 360 degrees, so their range of vision isn't compromised. Tarsiers also have huge, sensitive ears, which can be retracted and unfurled, and disproportionately long legs, which they use to jump distances 10 times their body length. They use their anatomical anomalies and impressive speed to catch small insects. Tarsiers live in groups of up to eight, and communicate with what sounds like high-pitched singing. They are found only in some rainforests of Indonesia and the Philippines.

SANGIR-TALAUD ISLANDS

Strewn across the sea between Indonesia and the southern Philippines are the volcanic island groups of Sangir and Talaud. There are 77 islands, of which 56 are inhabited. The capital of the group is Tahuna on Sangir Besar; the other major settlement is Lirung on Pulau Salibabu.

The islands offer dozens of unspoilt sandy beaches, a few crumbling Portuguese forts, several volcanoes to climb, many caves and waterfalls to explore, and some superb diving and snorkelling (bring your own gear). But like most wonderfully pristine places, the islands are not easy to reach and only a few intrepid foreigners ever make it here. There are a few rustic places to stay on Tahuna and if you turn up, chances are they will find you.

Once a week, Lion Air flies from Manado to Naha, which is about 20km from Tahuna, and twice a week it flies from Manado to Melanguane, which is near Lirung in the Talaud group.

From Bitung, the Pelni liner *Sangiang* stops at Tahuna and Lirung once every two weeks. The seas can get quite rough during the high wind from October to April.

tarsiers (when sightings are nearly guaranteed), and then another guided walk the next morning (200,000Rp per person, five hours) to see lively troupes of black macaques. It's worth staying longer to enjoy the gorgeous beach setting and friendly folk at Batuputih and to take a variety of other **tours** including **dolphin-spotting and snorkelling tours** (full day up to 4 people 750,000Rp), and **birdwatching** (full-day 350,000Rp) or **fishing tours** (5 hours for up to 4 people 750,000Rp). All tours and walks can be arranged at your guesthouse, which will invariably be swarming with guides.

Sleeping & Eating

If you need any luxury you're best off staying in Manado and taking a day trip to the park (offered through every travel agent and big hotel in town for around US$85 per person). But to really get a feel for the place, enjoy it at a more leisurely pace and save a whole lot of money on tour prices, stay in one of the several basic losmen in Batuputih village.

Dove Villas GUESTHOUSE **$$**
(☎0813 5624 5160; www.tangkokodovevillas.com; d 300,000Rp incl breakfast) This place is a step up in comfort and organisation from the rest, but 8km from the park entrance and in the middle of nowhere. You get your own wood villa with fan, mosquito net and cold water bathroom. It's very friendly and serves good food.

Tarsius Homestay GUESTHOUSE **$**
(☎0813 5622 5545; r without/with bathroom 100,000-200,000Rp per person incl three meals) This place has the cleanest and most pleasant rooms in town, some with attached bathrooms. It's family-run and super friendly.

Mama Roos GUESTHOUSE **$**
(☎0813 4042 1454; mamaroos@ymail.com; r 250,000-300,000Rp per person incl three meals) Batuputih's most popular option is bright, friendly and serves big but basic Indonesian meals.

Getting There & Away

To get to Batuputih from Manado, take a bus to Bitung (8000Rp), get off at Girian and catch a *mikrolet* or pick-up truck (10,000Rp) to Batuputih. If you get let off at Tongkoko bus terminal (the main bus terminal for the town, not to be confused with the park itself) instead of downtown Girian you'll need to take one of the frequent *mikrolet* between the two for 2000Rp.

SOUTHEAST SULAWESI

Few visitors make it to Southeast Sulawesi, but the handful of travellers that are prepared to venture a little off the beaten track will find themselves rewarded with some striking scenery and hospitable cultures, as well as surprisingly good transport links. The top attraction here is Wakatobi Marine National Park, located in the remote Tukangbesi Islands off the southern tip, offering some of Indonesia's best snorkelling and diving.

History

Some of the earliest records of life in Southeast Sulawesi are depicted in prehistoric paintings on the walls of caves near Raha. The red ochre paintings include hunting scenes, boats and warriors on horseback.

The region's most powerful pre-colonial kingdom was Buton, based at Wolio, near Bau Bau. Its control and influence over other regional states was supported by the Dutch colonialists. Buton came under direct Dutch rule after the fall of Makassar in 1669, and was granted limited autonomy in 1906.

Other local trading centres maintained a low profile, probably for reasons of self-preservation. Kendari was one of the busiest, but the island of Bungkutoko at the mouth of Kendari harbour hid the town so well it was not really 'discovered' by the Dutch until 1830.

The civil strife of the 1950s and 1960s was a time of extreme hardship for the people of the province. Farms and villages were plundered by rebel and government forces alike, decimating the region's agricultural sector. Today Southeast Sulawesi is supported by mining, agriculture and timber plantations and is a centre for transmigration, which has boosted its population to almost two million.

Kolaka

☎0405

Kolaka is readily accessible by boat from Bajoe, and is the major boat gateway to Southeast Sulawesi province from South Sulawesi. The centre of town is the bus terminal, about 500m north of the ferry terminal. There are ATMs but not many other facilities.

Getting There & Away

All day and night, plenty of buses, bemos and Kijangs travel between Kolaka and Kendari (75,000Rp, six hours). While you are on the ferry you may be able to find a spare seat on a bus going directly to Kendari or Makassar – just check with the bus drivers. Three ferries travel overnight from Kolaka to Bajoe (62,000/90,000Rp deck/business class, eight hours), the main port on the eastern coast of the southwest peninsula. Up-to-date information on the ferries (in Bahasa Indonesia only) is available at www.indonesiaferry.co.id.

Kendari

☎0401 / POP 235,000

The capital of Southeast Sulawesi province has long been the key port for trade between the inland Tolaki people and seafaring Bugis and Bajau traders. The town's isolation continues to cushion it from dramatic developments elsewhere. Kendari is a bustling town with little to recommend it except the range of decent accommodation.

Kendari begins in a tangle of lanes in the old *kota* (city) precinct adjacent to the original port in the east, and becomes progressively more modern as each era has added another suburb to the west. The one very, very long main road has most of the facilities, except the bus terminals.

Festival Teluk Kendari (Kendari Bay Festival) is held each April and is the highlight of the social calendar. Expect dragon-boat races, traditional music and plenty of partying.

Sleeping

Swiss-Belhotel Kendari HOTEL $$
(☎312 8777; www.swiss-belhotel.com; Jl Edi Sabara 88; r from 650,000Rp; ❄📶) The swankiest place in town. It's new and with good service but many of the rooms smell like an ashtray.

Hotel Cendrawasih GUESTHOUSE $
(☎312 1932; Jl Diponegoro 42; r with fan/air-con 88,000/150,000Rp; ❄) A long-running place, just off the main road, with friendly staff. The fan rooms are ageing these days, but have balconies. The air-con rooms are in better shape.

Getting There & Away

AIR Connections to Kendari and Makassar include **Merpati** (☎322 242; Jl Sudirman) and **Lion Air** (☎329 911; Jl Parman 84). Ask the staff about transport to the remote airport.

BOAT Adjacent to a church on top of a hill, the **Pelni office** (☎321 915) is just up from a roundabout, and not far from the Pelni dock. Kendari is not well serviced by Pelni, but is relatively close to the major port of Bau Bau. Every two weeks the slow boat *Tilongkabila* heads up the coast to Kolonedale (12 hours), and then goes on to Luwuk, Gorontalo and Bitung for Manado. Going the other direction the same boat goes to Raha, Bau Bau and Makassar (22 hours).

The Super-jet *kapal cepat* (fast boat) leaves the Pelni dock at Kendari at about 9am daily for Raha (130,000Rp, 3½ hours) and Bau Bau (180,000Rp, five hours). You can buy your ticket directly from the **Super-jet** (☎329 257; Jl Sukowati 8) office near the Pelni dock.

BUS, BEMO & KIJANG The main terminal is at Puwatu, about 10km west of town. From there, plenty of buses, Kijangs and bemos go to Kolaka (50,000Rp, six hours). It's more convenient to book a ticket (and board the bus) at one of the

Kendari

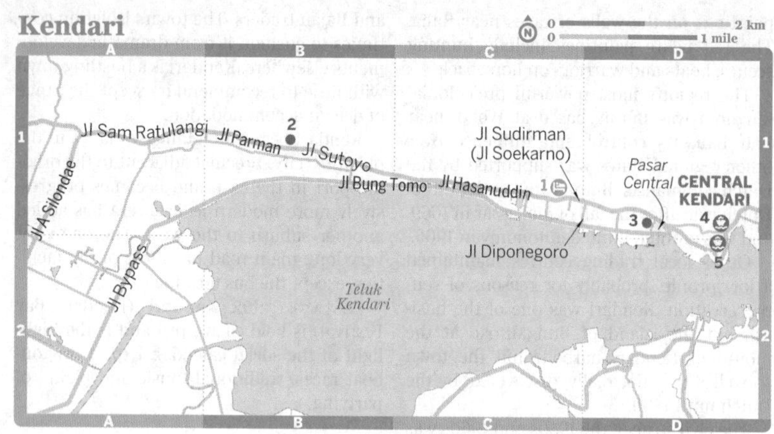

Kendari

Sleeping

1 Hotel Cendrawasih C1

Transport

2 Lion Air B1
3 Merpati D1
4 Pelni D1
5 Super-jet D2

agencies in town. Most buses leave Kendari at about 1pm to link with the 8pm ferry (which means arriving in Bajoe at about 4am).

Getting Around

Contact the airline offices about transport to the airport, which is 30km southwest of Kendari – both airlines usually run a bus with certain pick-up points in town. From the airport, you can jump in a shared vehicle or if you don't mind the extra cost, charter one. Kendari is *very* spread out. For short distances, take a becak; for anything along the main road, take a *pete-pete;* to anywhere else, catch an air-conditioned taxi.

Raha

0403

Raha, the main settlement on Pulau Muna, is a quiet backwater about halfway between Kendari and Bau Bau. Raha is famous for its horse fighting, cave paintings and lagoons.

Raha's main attraction is Napabale, a pretty lagoon at the foot of a hill about 15km out of town. The lagoon is linked to the sea via a natural tunnel, so you can paddle through when the tide is low. It is a great area for hiking and swimming, and you can hire canoes (50,000Rp) to explore the lake. You can reach it by *ojek*, or by regular *pete-pete* to Lohia village, from where the lagoon is another 1.5km walk, at the end of the road; alternatively small boats run from Port Raha. There is usually a couple of food stalls, and often a few more on Sunday, when it's generally crowded.

Festival Danau Napabale is held each June at the village of Latugho, 30km inland from Raha. The festival features horse combat, as well as the more gentle spectacle of kite flying. Horse fighting is a Muna tradition with a robust following – it's not for the tender-hearted.

Sleeping

Hotel Ilham HOTEL $

(21070; Jl Jati 15; r with fan 80,000Rp, with air-con 200,000Rp;) One of the few places in town to offer an air-con escape during the hot season, this is a friendly operation.

Getting There & Away

Raha is the only stop between Kendari and Bau Bau on the fast Super-jet. Purchase tickets the day before departure from the Super-jet (p691) office in Kendari. These boats are scheduled to leave for Kendari (130,000Rp, 3½ hours) at 8.30am and 1.30pm; and for Bau Bau (80,000Rp, 1½ hours) at about 1pm. Be ready for the onboard scramble to claim a seat.

Every two weeks the Pelni liner *Tilongkabila* stops at Raha on its way up (via Kendari) and down (via Bau Bau) the east coast of Sulawesi. The Pelni office is at the end of the causeway.

Bau Bau

☎0402 / POP 83,000

With comfortable accommodation, great views from the well-preserved citadel walls and some decent beaches within easy *ojek* range, Pulau Buton's prosperous main town of Bau Bau is a great place to await a boat connection to Maluku, North Sulawesi, or the diving paradise of Tukangbesi.

The terminal, main mosque and market are about 500m west of the main Pelni port, along Jl Kartini, which diverges from the seafront esplanade, Jl Yos Sudarso. Jl Kartini crosses a bridge then curves south past the post office towards the *kraton* (walled city palace).

Sights

The area around Bau Bau is blessed with beaches, waterfalls and caves. Ask around for more off-the-beaten-path spots.

Kraton HISTORIC SITE

Banking steeply behind the town centre is the *kraton*, the Wolio royal citadel with impressively long and well-preserved 16th-century walls that offer great views over the town and its north-facing bay. Amid trees and flowers within the walls are timeless semi-traditional homes and the old royal mosque.

Pusat Kebudayaan Wolio MUSEUM

Some 500m beyond the citadel's south gate is Pusat Kebudayaan Wolio, a cultural centre and museum in a restored old mansion-palace, which is the focal point of Bau Bau's **Festival Kraton** each September.

Pantai Nirwana BEACH

Eleven kilometres southwest of Bau Bau, the nearest white-sand beach is the attractively palm-lined Pantai Nirwana, though there is a certain amount of rubbish. Locals believe the waters here can cure a variety of skin disorders. For swimming it's better to continue on another 10km to the local favourite beach, **Pantai Batuaga**.

Pantai Lakeba BEACH

About 7km from central Bau Bau, find white sand, shady coconut palms, lightly rolling waves and a fantastic beach restaurant serving local specialties.

Sleeping & Eating

You'll find restaurants and warungs (many set up at night) along the esplanade, a few hundred metres west of the port.

Hillhouse Resort RESORT $

(☎21189; r from 100,000Rp) This little place has one of the most spectacular settings in Sulawesi. It's about half a click above Pusat Kebudayaan Wolio, set amid a hilltop flower garden with outstanding panoramic views of the bay. The rooms are simple, with mosquito nets and shared bathroom. It's recommended to call ahead, although the phone isn't always answered. Add 20,000Rp for breakfast.

Hotel Ratu Rajawali HOTEL $$

(☎22162; www.raturajawalihotel.com; Jl Sultan Hasanuddin 69; r from 360,000Rp; ❄📶) Right opposite the Pelni office, 2km east of the port, the comfortable rooms here include air-con and TV, plus small balconies that overlook the gardens and swimming pool towards the sea beyond.

Penginipan Wolio GUESTHOUSE $

(☎040 226 999; 20 Jl Mayjen Sutoyo; r 35,000Rp) The eight fan-cooled rooms here (shared bathroom) are set about 200m from the harbour. The owner here speaks English and the price includes breakfast. It's often full.

Getting There & Away

Air

Lion Air and Merpati run daily flights (45 min) to/from Makassar that connect through Bau Bau to Wanci (20 minutes) in the Tukangbesi Islands. Bau Bau airport is a few kilometres out of town.

Boat

FROM RAHA & KENDARI The fast Super-jet boat takes 1½ hours to Raha (80,000Rp) and five hours to Kendari (180,000Rp).

FROM TUKANGBESI ISLANDS An overnight boat from Bau Bau to Wanci (104,000Rp, 9½ hours) leaves at 8.30pm nightly. From Wanci, there are boats onward to Kaledupa (around two hours) from where you can catch a boat to Hoga (50,000Rp per boat). Another option is to take a smaller wooden ship that leaves a few times per week from Bau Bau to Buranga harbour on Kaledupa Island (120,000Rp). Take a motorbike taxi (10,000Rp per person) from Buranga Harbour to Ambeua village where there are boats to Hoga (50,000Rp per boat, 20 minutes).

FROM ELSEWHERE IN SULAWESI Every two weeks the Pelni liners *Ciremai*, *Lambelu*, *Sinabung*, *Tilongkabila* and *Kelimutu* link Bau Bau with Makassar and most also go to Ambon, southern Maluku and/or Papua. Every two weeks the *Tilongkabila* goes up and down the east coast of Sulawesi, stopping off at Kendari and Bitung (for Manado), among other places.

Tukangbesi Islands

According to Jacques Cousteau, the Tukangbesi Islands offered 'possibly the finest diving in the world' when he surveyed the area in the 1980s. Most of the islands are now part of **Wakatobi Marine National Park** (Taman Laut Wakatobi) and although the corals aren't in the same shape as when Cousteau visited, few divers leave disappointed. Positioned remotely off the far southeast coast, the islands are difficult to reach, but they do offer superb snorkelling and diving, a blaze of corals and marine life, isolated beaches and stunning landscapes.

Getting There & Away

The easiest way to get to the Tukangbesi Islands is by taking a daily flight on Lion Air, Merpati or Express Air to Wanci from Makassar. There's no public transport at the airport so you'll have to take a taxi into town (100,000Rp, 30 minutes). Also note that there's a 20,000Rp departure tax when you fly out of Wanci.

Public speedboats leave from Pelabuhan Mola to Hoga and Tomia at around 9.30am. See p693 for details on transport to/from Bau Bau.

Public boats to Pulau Kaledupa (50,000Rp) leave Mola Utara (the 'northern jetty'), about one kilometre north of the main harbour, daily at 9am.

Once every four weeks the Pelni liner *Kelimutu* travels from Makassar to Bau Bau then on to Ambon via Wanci.

WANCI (PULAU WANGI WANGI)

Wanci is the main, wooden-boat-clogged settlement on Pulau Wangi Wangi, which lies outside of the Wakatobi Marine National Park boundary. Cycling is a great way to get around this petite island since it's relatively flat and has decent roads with plenty of good beaches and interesting caves to stop at. Central Wanci is a colourful place with a lively harbour and tasty night market.

Wanci has a surprising amount of hotels and guesthouses, several of which are found along the busy road that leads south from the harbour to the market. For a splurge, stay at **Patuno Resort** (0811 400 2221; www.patunoresortwakatobi.com; bungalows from US$72 incl breakfast & airport transfers;), a luxury dive resort on the white-beach northern tip of the island.

PULAU KALEDUPA

Much bigger than Pulau Wangi Wangi and wilder too, there's essentially no tourist infrastructure on beautiful, forested and beach-laden Pulau Kaledupa. The island is a part of the Wakatobi Marine National Park and the main village, Ambeua, is pleasant and lively. In general the island is just a stopover for many travellers, albeit a rather stunning one. If you want to stay overnight or longer it's rumoured that homestays are easy to arrange if you ask around.

PULAU HOGA & PULAU TOMIA

For most travellers, the Tukangbesi Islands mean Pulau Hoga. This small island is only 2km over relatively shallow water from Kaledupa and there are no services at all besides a few guesthouses. Fresh water is scarce and all drinking water is brought over from Kaledupa, so do your part by taking short showers and keeping usage to a minimum. The best times to visit Pulau Hoga are October and February – during the rest of the year Operation Wallacea is often full with up to 200 students and the island can feel quite crowded. When not diving or snorkelling you can walk around parts of the island (best at low tide; some areas are only accessible by boat) and visit the fishing village at the northern end.

Pulau Tomia is another small island about 8km south of Pulau Kaledupa and is known to the outside world mostly for its ultra-exclusive Wakatobi Dive Resort.

Sleeping

All accommodation except Wakatobi Dive Resort are on Pulau Hoga. It is also possible to arrange informal homestays on this island for about 50,000Rp including meals. Some basic snorkelling equipment is available, but bring your own if you want to be sure.

Wakatobi Dive Resort DIVE RESORT **$$$**
(www.wakatobi.com; five-night packages from US$1950;) On Pulau Onemobaa just off Pulau Tomia, this ultra-exclusive hideaway offers beautiful bungalow accommodation and one of the most celebrated house reefs in Indonesia. Packages include diving, full board and charter flights from Bali. It is also the base for the elegant liveaboard **Pelagian** (www.pelagian.wakatobi.com). Private charter flights direct to/from Bali are available.

Operation Wallacea LODGE **$**
(www.opwall.com; huts 100,000Rp) With 200 beds, this is the main place to stay on Pulau

Hoga and most visitors end up here. This British-based NGO organises pre-booked 'volunteer' programs in marine conservation from March to September. They may be able to hook people up with a homestay during busy periods. Meals cost 40,000Rp, snorkelling gear is 60,000Rp per day and dives cost 400,000Rp including equipment rental.

Hoga Island Dive Resort DIVE RESORT **$$**
(0852 4162 8287; www.hogaislanddiveresort.com; nightly packages including accomodation, two dives & three meals from 1,000,000Rp per person) Has eight big wooden bungalows right on the beach. The resort supports the community by providing a boat for the local children to go to school on Pulau Kaledupa each day.

Understand Indonesia

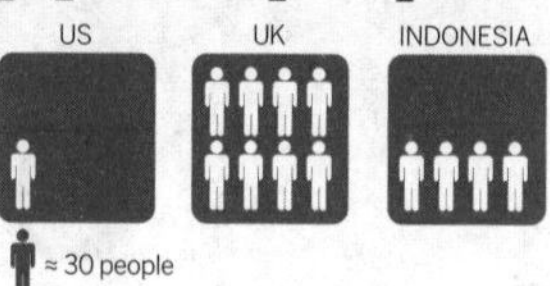

Indonesia Today

Stability

As diverse as Indonesia is, perhaps what's so remarkable about the place is how often it is the same. Sure there may be those 300 spoken languages (or was it 400?) but virtually everybody can speak one language: Bahasa Indonesia, a tongue that helps unify this sprawling, chaotic collection of peoples with a past that's had more drama than a picnic on Krakatau in say, 1883. Destructive colonialism, revolution, mass slaughter, ethnic warfare, dictatorship and more have been part of daily life in Indonesia in just the past 100 years. That's one of the reasons why recent elections are so remarkable: they were unremarkable.

The 2009 national elections were a watershed. More than a dozen parties waged high-energy campaigns. Rallies throughout the myriad islands were passionate and vibrant. Yet what happened in the end? President Susilo Bambang Yudhoyono's incumbent Democratic Party won; Indonesians chose to go with the status quo. This is a remarkable development for a nation where the looting of a single KFC by protestors with a, er, beef is portrayed in the West as a complete breakdown of civil order.

Regional elections since have mostly gone well and Indonesia's democracy is showing a vibrant and youthful spunk. There are dozens of parties, with new ones continually forming and allegiances in constant flux.

» Population: 245 million

» Area: 1,904,600 sq km

» GDP per capita: US$4944

» Number of islands: 17,000-20,000

» Percentage of teens with mobile phones: 75%

» Population density Java: 1064 per sq km

» Population density Papua: under nine per sq km

Tolerance or Intolerance?

It wasn't that long ago, at the Millennium, when there was blood in the streets from Lombok to the Malukus as religious and political factions settled scores and simply ran amok. The calm of late is balm for anyone worried that the world's largest Muslim nation (numerous large religious minorities aside) could somehow come under the influence of radical

Do

» Be respectful in places of worship

» Remove shoes in mosques

» Dress modestly in mosques

» Wear a sash and sarong at sacred Bali temples

» Use both hands when handing somebody something

Don't

» Show public displays of affection

» Go topless if you're a woman (even in Bali); you'll incite trouble in conservative areas and simply offend in others

» Show a lot of skin, although many local men wear shorts

» Talk with your hands on your hips; it's a sign of aggression

» Ignore guestbooks in remote villages and requests for donations

» Take photos of someone without asking – or miming – for approval

belief systems
(% of population)

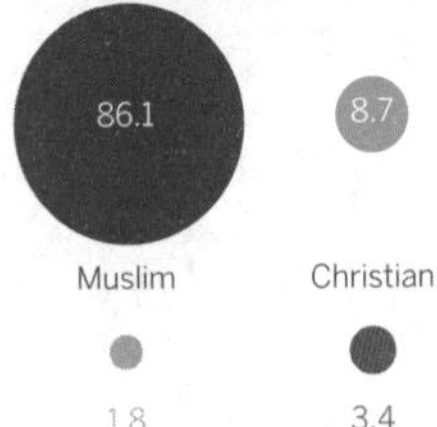

if Indonesia were 100 people

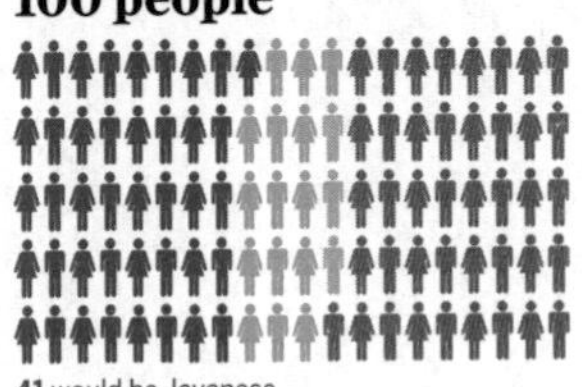

41 would be Javanese
15 would be Sundanese
3 would be Maderanese
41 would be other

groups dedicated to reversing the so far relatively successful Indonesian experiment in modest secularism.

Although memories of bombings earlier in the decade in Bali and Jakarta have faded significantly, there are regular reminders of security concerns. There were hotel bombings in Jakarta in 2009, and in 2012 police in Bali shot dead five suspected terrorists.

There was also justice as Umar Patek was convicted in 2012 of helping to assemble the 2002 Bali bombs and sentenced to 20 years in jail. A year earlier, Muslim cleric Abu Bakar Bashir was sentenced to 15 years in prison for supporting a jihadi training camp in Aceh. He'd previously been accused of various links to terror groups and is renowned for his hardline anti-Western rhetoric.

Indonesia has a reputation for corruption at all levels of society, indeed in 2012 it placed at 100 on Transparency International's corruption perceptions index (an improvement from 2009's 125). Neighbours Malaysia and Singapore are at 60 and five respectively.

What is Porn?

The passing of a so-called antipornography law (p728) in 2008 potentially made many traditional forms of behaviour across the archipelago illegal – from wearing penis gourds on Papua, to the modest gyrations of traditional Javanese dancers (to say nothing of the brazenly topless on Bali's beaches).

Exactly what the antiporn law means is still not known. After it was singled out by a quasi-governmental group for being 'immoral' in 2009, yoga on Bali is being taught and practised by more people than ever. And there have been assurances from the government that Balinese dance and other cultural forms of expression across the archipelago are safe from the law's ill-defined strictures. Still, many internet providers now block a wide range of sites deemed immoral and there has been a general chilling of freedom of expression. In 2011, the pop singer Ariel (aka Nazril Irham) was sentenced to more than three years in prison

Top Reads

Rimbaud in Java (Jamie James) Recreates poet Arthur Rimbaud's Java escape in 1876

Four Corners (Kira Salak) The author ventures to the remotest parts of Papua and New Guinea

Stranger in the Forest (Eric Hansen) Possibly the first non-local to walk across Borneo

Krakatoa – The Day the World Exploded (Simon Winchester) History, geology and politics, centred on the 1883 eruption

The Year of Living Dangerously (Christopher J Koch) A tale of a journalist in Sukarno's Indonesia of 1965

Top Writers

» Pramoedya Ananta Toer (1925–2006) stands above other Indonesian writers for his quartet of novels, *This Earth of Mankind*. Toer paints a canvas of Indonesia under Dutch rule and the emergence of nationalist feeling among Indonesians.

when a sex tape he made ended up on the internet, after his laptop was stolen.

While the law is being fiercely debated there is general agreement that conservative Islam is a rising tide in many parts of Indonesia, yet how this will play out remains to be seen. In the 2009 elections, the optimistically named Prosperous Justice Party (Partai Keadilan Sejahtera; PKS), which campaigned with a goal of bringing Islamic shariah law to Indonesia, received 8% of the vote, although both the party and poll-watchers had predicted a share of as much as 15%.

Boom Times

Indonesia is on track to receive 8 million visitors a year. These visitors are most likely to hail from Singapore, followed in descending order from Malaysia, Australia, China and Japan.

While large parts of the world have struggled with bad economies, the Indonesian economy is booming with economic growth topping 6% annually in recent years. Exports of raw materials such as coal and palm oil are up and for the first time more than half of workers do service-industry jobs rather than agriculture. Wages have risen and the World Bank says that half the population qualifies as middle class. Certainly this can be seen at places such as Bali, where domestic tourists now greatly outnumber Australians in Kuta.

With wealth has come associated problems. The nation's infrastructure is sagging under a surge of car and motorbike ownership and there are increasing demands by workers for improved wages. Meanwhile, development has caused extreme pressure on the environment, and the government is seemingly bewildered by the need for more roads, water treatment and the like. Exploitation of the countryside continues; Greenpeace says that the rampant destruction of forests has made the country the world's third-largest net emitter of greenhouse gases.

Top Downloads

Gamelan music is hypnotic and addictive. The following are top-sellers on iTunes:

» 'Gamelan Salunding'

» 'Gamelan Suling'

» 'Sekaha Ganda Sari'

Pack

» An emergency stash of cash for remote areas or when ATMs are down

» Sunscreen and insect repellent; both are hard to find outside tourist areas

» A set of earplugs for the mosque and traffic wake-up calls

» A torch (flashlight)

» Photos of loved ones – they're amazing ice-breakers

» A mental note to purchase a sarong – it's a fashion statement, blanket, beach mat, sheet, mattress cover, towel and shade from the pounding sun

History

Indonesia is a young country and even the idea of a single nation encompassing all of its territory is barely a century old. The word Indonesia itself was little known until the 1920s, when colonial subjects of the Dutch East Indies seized on it as the name for the independent nation they dreamed of. Their dream was realised in 1949 after a long, hard battle to throw off colonial rule. Since then independent Indonesia's growing pains have encompassed rebellions, religious strife, three decades of military dictatorship, much bloodshed, extremes of wealth and poverty, and expansionist adventures into neighbouring territories. Today, economic development has come a long way and Indonesia is maturing as a multiparty democracy, though not without its problem areas.

Before Indonesia, there was the Dutch East Indies – itself an idea that mutated repeatedly over three centuries as hundreds of disparate island states came one by one under the umbrella of a colonial administration. And before that, there were thousands of islands with connections of commerce and culture, some of which were grouped together under the same ruler, while others were often not even united within themselves.

The story of how Indonesia became what it is today is a colourful dance of migrants and invaders, rebels and religions, kingdoms and empires, choreographed by Indonesia's island nature and its location on millennia-old Asian trade routes. It's a story full of heroes and villains, victors and victims, but the strangest part is how these 17,000-plus islands with their 739 languages and diverse cultures ever came to be a nation at all.

Simple iron tools, such as axes and plough tips, arrived from China around 200 BC, spurring Indonesians to find their own metal deposits and make their own knives, arrowheads, urns and jewellery.

The Trading Archipelago

Indonesians inhabit a diverse island world where a short sea voyage or journey inland can take a traveller into a whole new ecosystem providing a different set of useful commodities. Long ago forest dwellers were collecting colourful bird feathers and tree resins and exchanging them

TIMELINE

60,000–40,000 BC

Indonesia's western islands are still connected to the Asian mainland. The first Homo sapiens arrive, probably ancestors of the Melanesians in today's population, who are now found mainly in Papua.

About 8000 BC

Sea levels rise after the end of the last glacial period, separating Sumatra, Borneo, Java and Bali from the Asian mainland, and the island of New Guinea from Australia.

About 2000 BC

Austronesian people originating from Taiwan start to arrive in Indonesia, probably by sea routes. They absorb or displace Melanesians. The earliest evidence of settlements dates from the 6th century for turtle shells or salt from people who lived by the sea. Some of these goods would find their way to nearby islands, from which they then reached more distant islands. By about 500 BC, routes sailed by Indonesian islanders began to overlap with those of sailors from mainland Asia. Thus, 2000 years ago, bird-of-paradise feathers from Papua could be depicted on beautiful bronze drums cast by the Dong Son people of Vietnam, and some of the drums then ended up in Java, Sumatra and Bali.

Indonesia's main western islands – Sumatra, Kalimantan and Java – lie in the middle of the sea routes linking Arabia, India, China and Japan. Indonesia was destined to become a crossroads of Asia, and trade has been its lifeblood for at least 2000 years. It has brought with it nearly all the biggest changes the archipelago has seen through the centuries – new people, new ideas, new crops, new technologies, new religions, new wars, new rulers.

Indian Influence & Sriwijaya

Contact between Indonesia and India goes back a long way. Pepper plants, originally from India, were spicing up western Indonesian food as early as 600 BC. Indonesian clothing got a lot smarter when boats from Indonesia reached India by the 2nd century BC and brought back cotton plants. In the early centuries AD, Hindu traders from southern India started to settle along the coast of mainland Southeast Asia. From there they found their way to early coastal trading settlements in Java, Sumatra and Kalimantan. The Indians brought jewellery, fine cloth, pottery, as well as Hindu and Buddhist culture.

Central Java's unmissable Borobudar and Prambanan complexes are the best ancient monuments in Indonesia, dating to the 8th century. The former is an iconic Buddhist monument built from two million stones while the latter has elaborate Hindu decoration.

From the 4th century AD, Chinese travellers also arrived in Indonesian ports, and in the 7th century Chinese reports started mentioning the port state of Sriwijaya. Buddhist Sriwijaya, in the Palembang-Jambi area of southeast Sumatra, may have been a grouping of ports or a single kingdom whose capital sometimes changed location. It was a powerful state, and its sailors were able to collect pepper, ivory, resins, feathers, turtle shells, mother of pearl and much more from Sumatra and ports around the Java Sea, and carry them to China, from which they brought back silk, ceramics and iron. An entrepôt for Indian, Indonesian, Arab, Southeast Asian and, eventually, Chinese traders, Sriwijaya remained important until the 14th century.

Traders From Arabia

The first Muslim traders from Arabia appeared in Indonesian ports within a few decades of the death of the Prophet Mohammed in AD 632. Arabian ships bound for China, carrying spices and rare woods or Indian cloth, would call in at Sumatra or other Indonesian islands to add local

500–1 BC
Local trade routes mesh with mainland Asia's. Chinese iron tools, large Vietnamese bronze drums and Indian glass beads reach Indonesia. Local products such as spices reach India and China.

5th century AD
Under influence from India, some Indonesian trading ports have turned from animism to Hinduism or Buddhism. Indonesia's earliest known inscriptions are carved in west Java and near Kutai, Kalimantan.

6th century
Muslim traders begin arriving in Indonesian ports bringing their religion as well as goods for trade. Over the next few centuries, thriving Muslim communities are established.

7th century
Farmers flourish by growing rice on lush islands across the archipelago. Terraces and complex irrigation systems are developed, allowing wealth to be accumulated.

products such as aromatic woods, resins and camphor to their cargoes. By the 13th century, Arabs had established settlements in major Indonesian ports. Sulaiman bin Abdullah bin al-Basir, ruler of the small north Sumatran port of Lamreh in the early 13th century, was the first Indonesian ruler known to have adopted Islam and taken the title Sultan.

Majapahit

The first Indonesian sultanates came into being while the greatest of Indonesia's Hindu-Buddhist states, Majapahit, was flourishing in eastern Java. Like the earlier Sriwijaya, Majapahit's success was trade-based. Its powerful fleets exacted tribute from ports spread from Sumatra to Papua (disobedient states were 'wiped out completely' by the Majapahit navies, according to court poet Prapanca), and enabled its traders to dominate the lucrative commerce between Sumatran ports and China. Prapanca reported that traders in Majapahit ports came from Cambodia, Vietnam and Thailand. He also claimed, less credibly, that Majapahit ruled a hundred foreign countries. Majapahit was eventually conquered by one of the newly Islamic north Java ports, Demak, in 1478.

The Majapahit kingdom reached its zenith during the reign of King Hayam Wuruk (1350–89) who was ably assisted by his prime minister and brilliant military commander Gajah Mada. Their names mean, respectively, Rotting Chicken and Rutting Elephant.

Spices & the Portuguese

As Islam continued to spread around the archipelago, another new breed of trader arrived – Europeans. With advanced ship design and navigation technology, European sailors could now cross oceans in search of wealth. Portuguese ships crossed the Indian Ocean from southern Africa to India and then pushed on eastward. In 1511 they conquered Melaka, key to the vital Strait of Melaka between Sumatra and Malaya, and set up bases strung across Indonesia. They also established settlements in mainland ports from India to China and Japan.

The prize that drew the Portuguese to Indonesia was three little plant products long valued in Europe, China, the Islamic world and Indonesia itself: cloves, nutmeg and mace. All three, in high demand because they made food taste more interesting, were native to Maluku, the Spice Islands of eastern Indonesia. Cloves (the sun-dried flower buds of a type of myrtle tree) were produced on a few small islands off the west coast of Halmahera. Nutmeg and mace, both from the nut of the nutmeg tree, came from the Banda Islands. The sultans of the small Maluku islands of Ternate and Tidore controlled most of the already valuable trade in these spices.

Portuguese traders joined western Indonesians in buying spices in Maluku. They brought exotic new things to the islands such as clocks, firearms, sweet potatoes and Christianity. Clove and nutmeg cultivation was stepped up to meet their demand. After they fell out with the

7th–13th centuries

Buddhist Sriwijaya in southeast Sumatra dominates in western Indonesia. It may have been a collection of ports or a single state; its trade routes reached China and India.

8th–9th centuries

The Buddhist Sailendra and Hindu Sanjaya (or Mataram) kingdoms flourish on Java's central plains, creating the huge – and still standing – Borobudur and Prambanan temple complexes respectively.

ANDRAS JANCSIK/GETTY IMAGES ©

» Prambanan Temples (p132)

Ternate sultan Babullah and were expelled in 1575, they set up on the nearby island of Pulau Ambon instead.

The Portuguese also traded at Aceh (north Sumatra) and Banten (northwest Java), where the principal product was pepper, which had also been used for many centuries to liven up taste buds in Europe, China and elsewhere.

In the 17th century the Portuguese were pushed out of the Indonesian condiment business by a more determined, better armed and better financed rival. The Dutch newcomers didn't just want to buy spices, they wanted to drive other Europeans out of Asian trade altogether.

From Animism to Islam

The earliest Indonesians were animists – they believed animate and inanimate objects had their own life force or spirit, and that events could be influenced by offerings, rituals or forms of magic. Indonesia's scattered prehistoric sites, and animist societies that have survived into modern times, provide evidence that there was often a belief in an afterlife and supernatural controlling powers, and that the spirits of the dead were believed to influence events. Megaliths, found from Pulau Nias to Sumba and Sulawesi's Lore Lindu National Park, are one manifestation of ancestor cults. Some megaliths may be 5000 years old, but in Sumba animist religion is still alive and well, and concrete versions of megalithic tombs are still being erected.

The British, keen to profit from the spice trade, kept control of the Maluku island of Run until 1667. Then they swapped it for a Dutch-controlled island, Manhattan.

Hinduism & Buddhism

It was contact with the comparatively wealthy cultures of India in the first few centuries AD that first led Indonesians to adopt new belief systems. Indian traders who settled in Indonesia continued to practise Hinduism, or its offshoot Buddhism. Some built their own temples and brought in priests, monks, teachers or scribes. Impressed local Indonesian rulers

THE CHINESE IN INDONESIA

As Indonesian trading states grew richer and more complex they came increasingly to rely on their growing numbers of Chinese settlers to oil the wheels of their economies. Indonesia's first recorded Chinese settlement was located at Pasai, Sumatra in the 11th century. By the 17th century, Chinese were filling a whole spectrum of roles as middlemen, artisans, labourers, tax-collectors, businessmen, financiers, farmers and keepers of shops, brothels and opium dens. Today ethnic-Chinese Indonesians own many of the country's biggest and most profitable businesses. For centuries they have also been the subject of jealousy and hatred, and the victims of repeated outbreaks of violence, including during the shocking 1998 Jakarta riots.

1294–1478

The Hindu-Buddhist Majapahit kingdom monopolises trade between Sumatra and China and exacts tribute from across Indonesia. The splendid Majapahit court is imitated by many later Indonesian states.

13th–15th centuries

Influenced by Arab merchants, two north Sumatran towns adopt Islam, followed by Melaka on the Malay peninsula, the eastern island of Ternate and northern Java ports including Demak, which conquers Majapahit.

1505

Portuguese ships reach Indonesian waters. Interested in spices, the Portuguese go on to establish trading settlements across the archipelago, joining Indians, Arabs, Chinese, Malays and islanders in the sea trade.

1520

Java's complete conversion to Islam means that Bali is isolated as a Hindu island. Religious and artistic refugees from Java greatly strengthen Bali's culture which flourishes.

started to use the Indian titles Raja or Maharaja or add the royal suffix *varman* to their names. It was a short step for them to cement their ties with the Indian world by adopting the Indians' religion or philosophy too. The earliest records of Indianised local rulers are 5th-century stone inscriptions in Sanskrit, found in west Java and near Kutai (now Tenggarong), Kalimantan. These record decrees and tales of the glorious deeds of the kings Purnavarman and Mulavarman, respectively.

The major Indonesian states from then until the 15th century were all Hindu or Buddhist. Sriwijaya, based in southern Sumatra, was predominantly Buddhist. In central Java in the 8th and 9th centuries, the Buddhist Sailendra kingdom and the predominantly Hindu Sanjaya (or Mataram) kingdom constructed the great temple complexes of Borobudur and Prambanan respectively. They sought to recreate Indian civilisation in a Javanese landscape, and Indian gods such as Shiva and Vishnu were believed to inhabit the Javanese heavens, though this did not obliterate traditional beliefs in magical forces or nature spirits. In the 10th century, wealth and power on Java shifted to the east of the island, where a series of Hindu-Buddhist kingdoms dominated till the late 15th century. The greatest of these was Majapahit (1294–1478), based at Trowulan. Javanese Indian culture also spread to Bali (which remains Hindu to this day) and parts of Sumatra.

Islam

Majapahit was eventually undone by the next major religion to reach Indonesia – Islam. Muslim Arab traders had appeared in Indonesia as early as the 7th century. By the 13th century Arabs had established settlements in major Indonesian ports, and it was then that the first local rulers, at Lamreh and Pasai in north Sumatra, adopted Islam. Gradually over the next two centuries, then more rapidly, other Indonesian ports with Muslim communities switched to Islam. Their rulers would become persuaded by Islamic teachings and, keen to join a successful international network, would usually take the title Sultan to proclaim their conversion. Melaka on the Malay Peninsula, controlling the strategic Strait of Melaka, switched to Islam in 1436 and became a model for other Muslim states to emulate.

In 1292, Marco Polo on one of his forays east visited Aceh and noted that local inhabitants had already converted to Islam.

In Java, Sumatra and Sulawesi, some Muslim states spread Islam by military conquest. The conversion of several north Java ports in the late 15th century meant that Hindu-Buddhist Majapahit was hemmed in by hostile states. One of these, Demak, conquered Majapahit in 1478.

Indonesian Islam has always had a 'folk religion' aspect in that legends of Islamic saints, holy men and feats of magic, and pilgrimages to sites associated with them, have played an important part in Muslim

16th–17th centuries

Islam continues to spread around Indonesian ports. The Islamic Mataram kingdom is founded (1581) in the lands of the old Hindu Sanjaya kingdom in central Java.

1595

Four small Dutch ships reach the pepper port Banten in northwest Java. Despite setbacks, the expedition returns home with enough spices to make a small profit.

1602

Holland merges competing merchant companies into the VOC (United East Indian Company). It aims to drive other European nations out of Asian trade, especially in spices.

1611–1700

From its headquarters at Batavia (now Jakarta), the VOC expands its control through deals, alliances and battles. A chain of Dutch-controlled ports leads to the Spice Islands.

life. Tradition has it that Islam was brought to Java by nine *wali* (saints) who converted local populations through war or feats of magic.

The greatest of the Indonesian Muslim kingdoms, Mataram, was founded in 1581 in the area of Java where the Sailendra and Sanjaya kingdoms had flourished centuries earlier. Its second ruler, Senopati, was a descendant of Hindu princes and helped to incorporate some of the Hindu past, and older animist beliefs, into the new Muslim world.

Christianity

The last major religion to reach Indonesia was Christianity. The Catholic Portuguese made some conversions among Islamic communities in Maluku and Sulawesi in the 16th century, but most reverted to Islam. The Protestant Dutch, who gradually took control over the whole archipelago between the 17th and 20th centuries, made little effort to spread Christianity. Missionaries active in the 19th and 20th centuries were steered to regions where Islam was weak or nonexistent, such as the Minahasa and Toraja areas of Sulawesi, the Batak area of Sumatra, and Dutch New Guinea (now Papua).

Rajas & Sultans

The Hindu, Buddhist and Muslim states of Indonesia were not charitable organisations dedicated to their subjects' welfare. The great majority were absolute monarchies or sultanates, whose rulers claimed to be at least partly divine. Their subjects were there to produce food or goods which they could pay as tribute to the ruler, or to do business from which they could pay taxes, or to fight in armies or navies, or to fill roles in the royal entourage from astrologer to poet to tax collector to concubine. Land was generally considered to belong to the ruler, who permitted subjects to use it in exchange for taxes and tribute. Slaves were an integral part of the scene well into the 19th century.

Other states could pay tribute too and the largest kingdoms or sultanates, such as the Java-based Hindu-Buddhist Majapahit (1294–1478) and Muslim Mataram (1581–1755), built trading empires based on tribute from other peoples whom they kept in line through the threat of a military bashing. Majapahit lived on in the memory of later Indonesian states for the fine manners, ceremony and arts of its court, and because some of its princes and princesses had married into the ruling families of Muslim sultanates. Many later rulers would assert their credentials by reference to family connections with the Majapahit kingdom.

Shared religion was no bar to belligerence. Sultan Agung of Mataram had no qualms about conquering neighbouring Muslim states in the 1620s when he wanted to tighten control over the export routes for Mataram's rice, sugar and teak. Nor did past loyalty or even blood ties

1670–1755
VOC exploits Mataram's internal turmoils to win control of the kingdom. In 1755 it splits Mataram into two kingdoms, with capitals at Yogyakarta and Surakarta (Solo) and now controls Java.

1795–1824
In the Napoleonic Wars, Britain takes the possessions of the Dutch East Indies. An 1824 agreement divides the region between the Dutch and British; the borders are similar to modern Indonesia and Malaysia.

1800
The now overstretched, corrupt and bankrupt VOC is wound up. Its territories pass to the Netherlands crown, converting a trading empire into a colonial one, the Netherlands East Indies.

1825–30
Prince Diponegoro, supported by many Muslims, the poor and some fellow Javanese aristocrats, rebels against the Dutch and their vassals. Some 200,000 Javanese die, most from famine and disease.

guarantee personal favour. In the first year of his reign, Agung's successor Amangkurat I massacred at least 6000 subjects, including his father's advisers and his own half-brothers and their families, to remove any possible challenges to his authority.

European Influence

The coming of Europeans in the 16th and 17th centuries introduced new ways for Indonesian states and contenders to get one over on their rivals. They could use the Europeans as trading partners or mercenaries or allies, and if the Europeans became too powerful or demanding, they expected they could get rid of them. In Maluku the Muslim sultanate of Ternate, a small but wealthy clove-growing island, drove out its former trading partners, the Portuguese, in 1575. It later awarded the Dutch a monopoly on the sale of its spices and used the revenue to build up its war fleet and extract tribute from other statelets. Ternate eventually controlled 72 tax-paying tributaries around Maluku and Sulawesi.

Such agreements, alliances and conquests, eventually gave the Dutch a hold over much Indonesian trade and territory. Their involvements in the endless internal feuds of the powerful Javanese Mataram kingdom won them such a stranglehold over the region that in 1749 the dying king Pakubuwono II willed them control over his kingdom. In 1755 the Dutch resolved yet another Mataram succession dispute by splitting it into two kingdoms, with capitals at Surakarta (Solo) and Yogyakarta. Both royal families later split again, so that by the early 19th century there were four rival royal houses in this tiny part of central Java.

So long as local rulers and aristocrats cooperated, the Dutch were content to leave them in place, and these traditional rulers eventually became the top rank of the 'Native' branch of the colonial civil service, continuing to run their kingdoms under the supervision of a sprinkling of Dutch administrators.

Dutch Domination

When the Dutch first arrived at Banten in 1595 and set up the United East India Company (Vereenigde Oost-Indische Compagnie; VOC) to conduct all their business in the East Indies in 1602, they did not plan to end up running the whole of what came to be Indonesia. They just wanted to drive other European powers out of the lucrative spice trade in Indonesia. Their strategy was to sign exclusive trade agreements with local rulers where possible, and to impose their will by military force where necessary. Their powerful fleets and effective soldiers made them a potent ally for local strongmen, and in return the Dutch could extract valuable trading rights.

The name Indonesia was coined in the 1850s by a Scot, James Logan (editor of the Singapore-published *Journal of the Indian Archipelago and Eastern Asia*) as a shorter equivalent for the term Indian Archipelago.

1820s–1910
Holland takes control of nearly all the archipelago through economic expansion, agreements with local aristocrats and warfare. Many aristocrats become representatives of the Dutch administration.

1830–70
The Cultivation System: two million Javanese peasants have to grow and pay tax in export crops (coffee, tea, tobacco, indigo, sugar). Holland is saved from bankruptcy, but most peasants suffer.

1830
Slavery, which had flourished among various kingdoms and sultanates, goes into final decline when the Balinese royalty renounce the practice. Proceeds had been used to finance wars and palaces.

1845–1900
Private (European) enterprise is encouraged, forced cultivation is slowly wound down. Transportation infrastructure is greatly improved. Notoriously brutal rubber and tobacco plantations develop on Sumatra.

Moving In

In the beginning the Dutch concentrated primarily on the spice trade. In 1605 they drove the Portuguese out of Ambon. They then set up their own chain of settlements in Muslim ports along the route to the Spice Islands, with their headquarters at Jayakarta, a small vassal port of Banten in northwest Java. When Banten, with English help, tried to expel them in 1619, the Dutch beat off the attack, rebuilt the town and renamed it Batavia. Today it's called Jakarta.

In the 1650s and 1660s Banten's Sultan Ageng Tirtajasa decreed that all men aged 16 or over must tend 500 pepper plants.

By varied means the Dutch took control of Banda in 1621, Melaka in 1641, Tidore in 1657, Makassar in 1669, and then several Javanese ports. In Banda they exterminated or expelled almost the whole population in the 1620s and replaced them with slave-worked nutmeg plantations.

The Javanese Mataram kingdom tried unsuccessfully to drive the Dutch out of Batavia in 1628 and again in 1629. In the 1640s, Mataram's King Amangkurat I, facing a host of internal challenges, decided it was wiser to make peace with the VOC. He went further and gave it the sole licence to carry Mataram goods.

While Chinese, Arabs and Indians continued to trade in Indonesia in the 17th and 18th centuries, the VOC ended up with all the best business. Asian traders carried rice, fruit and coconuts from one part of the archipelago to another; Dutch ships carried spices, timber, textiles and metals to other Asian ports and Europe.

The VOC's trading successes brought it an ever larger and costlier web of commitments around the archipelago. By 1800 it controlled most of Java and parts of Maluku, Sulawesi, Sumatra and Timor. It was overstretched, corrupt – and bankrupt. The Dutch crown took over the company's possessions but then lost them (first to France, then to Britain) during the Napoleonic Wars. Control was restored to the Dutch in 1816 following the Anglo-Dutch Treaty of 1814.

Nathaniel's Nutmeg by Giles Milton offers a fascinating account of the battle to control trade from the Spice Islands. Now known as the Banda Islands, they still have many colonial-era sites and are well worth visiting.

Commerce Rules

As the 19th century progressed, European private enterprise was encouraged to take over export agriculture. Privately owned rubber and tobacco plantations, both of which featured brutal working conditions, helped to extend Dutch control into eastern Sumatra. The colonial administration concentrated on creating a favourable investment climate by the construction of railways, improving roads and shipping services, and quashing unrest. They also waged military campaigns to subjugate the last non-compliant local statelets.

The Banjarmasin sultanate in Kalimantan came under direct Dutch rule in 1863 after a four-year war; resource-rich Aceh in northern Sumatra was finally subdued in 1903 after 30 years of vicious warfare; southwest

1901

The Ethical Policy is introduced to raise Indonesian welfare through better irrigation, education and health, but Europeans benefit most. The growth of cities spawns a new Indonesian middle class.

1912

Sarekat Islam (Islamic Union) emerges as a Javanese Muslim economic assistance group, with anti-Christian and anti-Chinese tendencies. It grows into a million-member anticolonial movement.

1920

The Indonesian Communist Party (PKI) is founded. A pro-independence party with support from urbanites, it is sidelined when uprisings in Java (1926) and Sumatra (1927) are suppressed by the Dutch.

1927

The Indonesian National Party (PNI) emerges led by a young engineer, Sukarno. It grows quickly into the most powerful pro-independence organisation. In 1930 its leaders are jailed.

Sulawesi was occupied from 1900 to 1910; and Bali was brought to heel, after several attempts, in 1906. Some Balinese aristocrats killed their families and retainers and committed suicide rather than submit to the Dutch. In the late 19th century Holland, Britain and Germany all agreed to divide up the unexplored island of New Guinea.

The Ethical Policy

The end of the 19th century saw the rise of a new Dutch awareness of the problems and needs of the Indonesian people. The result was the Ethical Policy, launched in 1901, which aimed to raise Indonesians' welfare and purchasing power through better irrigation, education, health and credit, and with a decentralised government. The Ethical Policy's immediate effects were mixed, and its benefits often accrued to Europeans rather than Indonesians. An increase in private land ownership increased the number of locals without land. Local revolts and strikes were fairly frequent. But the colony's trade continued to grow. By the 1930s the Dutch East Indies was providing most of the world's quinine and pepper, over one-third of its rubber and almost one-fifth of its tea, sugar, coffee and oil.

The Dutch introduced coffee to Indonesia in 1696. United East India Company (VOC) officials got west Java nobles to instruct their farmers to grow coffee bushes, paying with cash and textiles for the harvested beans.

Breaking Free

The longer-term effects of the Ethical Policy were truly revolutionary. Wider education spawned a new class of Indonesians aware of colonial injustices, international political developments and the value of their own cultures. These people were soon starting up diverse new political

THE CULTIVATION SYSTEM

The seemingly intractable problems the Dutch had with their colony were made much worse by the devastating Diponegoro War in Java (1825–30). This conflict started when Prince Diponegro got angry after the Dutch built a new road across land that contained his parents memorial. Hostilities began and the prince received widespread support by others in Java who had grievances with the Dutch. To quell the conflict, the Dutch eventually needed to bring in troops from Sulawesi, Holland and even Dutch African colonies at huge expense.

After the war, Holland desperately needed to make the East Indies profitable. Its answer was the new Cultivation (or Culture) System. Up to two million Javanese peasants were obliged to grow the export crops of coffee, tea, tobacco, indigo or sugar, and pay a proportion of their crop in tax, and sell the rest to the government at fixed prices. This saved Holland from bankruptcy, and while some villagers prospered, the cultivation system also resulted in famines, loss of rice-growing lands, poverty and corruption.

1928

Nationalism is given a boost when the All Indonesia Youth Congress proclaims its historic Youth Pledge, establishing goals of one national identity and one language (Bahasa Indonesia).

1930s

The Dutch East Indies provides most of the quinine used in the world's tonic water, to the delight of gin lovers everywhere. Pepper, rubber and oil are also major exports.

1936

Americans Robert and Louise Koke build simple bamboo bungalows on Bali's otherwise deserted Kuta Beach. They also introduce a sport called surfing they had learned in Hawaii.

» Kuta Beach (p207), Bali

and religious groups and publications, some of which were expressly dedicated to ending Dutch colonial rule.

The First Nationalists

Clove-impregnated *kretek* cigarettes, popular throughout Indonesia today, were first marketed by Nitisemito, a man from Kudus, Java, in 1906. His Bal Tiga (Three Balls) brand grew into one of the biggest Indonesian-owned businesses in the Dutch East Indies.

Today Indonesians look back to 1908 as the year their independence movement began. This was when Budi Utomo (Glorious Endeavour) was founded. Led by upper-class, Dutch-educated, Indonesian men, Budi Utomo wanted to revive monarchy and modernise Javanese culture for the 20th century. It was soon followed by more radical groups. Sarekat Islam (Islamic Union), which emerged in 1912, began as a Javanese Muslim economic mutual-help group, with a strong anti-Christian and anti-Chinese streak. Linking with other groups, it grew steadily into a million-member anticolonial movement trying to connect villagers throughout the colony with the educated elite.

In 1920 the Indonesian Communist Party (PKI), which had operated within Sarekat Islam, split off on its own. A pro-independence party with support from urban workers, it launched uprisings in Java (1926) and Sumatra (1927) but was neutralised when these were quashed by the Dutch, who imprisoned and exiled thousands of communists.

A key moment in the growth of nationalist consciousness came in 1928 when the All Indonesia Youth Congress proclaimed its historic Youth Pledge, establishing goals of one national identity (Indonesian), one country (Indonesia) and one language (the version of Malay called Bahasa Indonesia). Meanwhile the Indonesian National Party (PNI), which emerged in 1927 from the Bandung Study Group led by a young engineer, Sukarno, was rapidly becoming the most powerful Indonesian nationalist organisation – with the result that in 1930 the Dutch jailed its leaders.

Anyone interested in the WWII campaigns in Indonesia, and the sites and relics that can be found there today, should check out the fascinating Pacific Wrecks (www.pacificwrecks.com).

Nationalist sentiment remained high through the 1930s, but even when Germany invaded the Netherlands in 1940, the Dutch colonial government was determined to hold fast.

WWII

Everything changed when Japan invaded the Dutch East Indies in 1942 and swept aside Dutch and Allied resistance. Almost 200,000 Dutch and Chinese civilians and Allied military were put into prison camps, in some of which 30% of the inmates would die. Many Indonesians at first welcomed the Japanese as liberators, but feelings changed as they were subjected to slave labour and starvation. The 3½ year Japanese occupation did however strengthen the Indonesian nationalist movement, as the Japanese used anti-Dutch nationalists to help them run things and allowed them limited political activity. Sukarno was permitted to travel

1942

Japan invades Indonesia. Europeans are sent to prison camps. Indonesians initially welcome the Japanese as liberators, but sentiment changes as the harshness of the occupation becomes apparent.

1942–45

The Japanese collaborate with nationalist leaders because of their anti-Dutch sentiments, and establish an Indonesian militia that later forms the backbone of the anti-Dutch resistance after WWII.

Aug 1945

Japan surrenders. Indonesian nationalist students kidnap Sukarno and Hatta and pressure them to declare independence, which they do on 17 August. Sukarno becomes president and Hatta vice-president.

Sep–Nov 1945

Allied troops take over and suppress the nationalists. Sukarno wants independence through diplomacy, but other nationalists want to fight. The Battle of Surabaya leaves thousands dead.

around giving nationalist speeches. The Japanese also set up Indonesian home-defence militias, whose training proved useful in the Indonesians' later military struggle against the Dutch.

As defeat for Japan loomed in May 1945, the Investigating Agency for Preparation of Independence met in Jakarta. This Japanese-established committee of Indonesian nationalists proposed a constitution, philosophy (Pancasila) and extents (the whole Dutch East Indies) for a future Indonesian republic.

The Revolution

When Japan announced its surrender on 15 August 1945, a group of *pemuda* (radical young nationalists) kidnapped Sukarno and his colleague Mohammed Hatta and pressured them to declare immediate Indonesian independence, which they did at Sukarno's Jakarta home on 17 August (you can see the text of their proclamation on the 100,000Rp banknote). A government was formed, with Sukarno president and Hatta the vice-president.

British and Australian forces arrived to disarm the Japanese and hold the Indonesian nationalists until the Dutch could send their own forces. But Indonesians wanted independence. Some, like Sukarno and Hatta,

PANCASILA - THE FIVE PRINCIPLES

In government buildings and TV broadcasts, on highway markers and school uniforms you'll see the *garuda*, Indonesia's mythical bird and national symbol. On its breast are the five symbols of the philosophical doctrine of Indonesia's unitary state, Pancasila (which means Five Principles in Sanskrit and Pali, the sacred languages of Hinduism and Buddhism). Pancasila was first expounded by Sukarno in 1945 as a synthesis of Western democracy, Islam, Marxism and indigenous village traditions. Enshrined in the 1945 constitution, it was raised to the level of a mantra by Suharto's New Order regime. Suharto's successor BJ Habibie annulled the requirement that Pancasila must form the basic principle of all organisations, but it remains an important national creed. The five symbols:

Star Represents faith in God, through Islam, Christianity, Buddhism, Hinduism or any other religion.

Chain Represents humanitarianism within Indonesia and in relations with humankind as a whole.

Banyan Tree Represents nationalism and unity between Indonesia's many ethnic groups.

Buffalo Symbolises representative government.

Rice & Cotton Represent social justice.

1946–49

Dutch troops arrive to regain control; the nationalists form a Republican Army. Despite Dutch offensives and rifts between Sukarno's government, Muslim movements and the communists, resistance continues.

1949

Faced with an unwinnable war and hostile international opinion, the Netherlands transfers sovereignty over the Dutch East Indies (apart from Netherlands New Guinea) to the Indonesian republic.

1950–62

Armed movements challenge the republic. Darul Islam (House of Islam) wages guerrilla war in several islands, continuing until 1962 in western Java. Regionalist rebellions break out in Sumatra and Sulawesi.

1955

The PNI, regarded as Sukarno's party, tops the polls in parliamentary elections, but no clear winner emerges. Short-lived coalition governments continue. The economy struggles after commodity prices drop.

favoured a negotiated path to freedom; others wanted to fight to get it as fast as possible. The early months of the revolution were a particularly chaotic period: with massacres of Chinese, Dutch and Eurasian civilians and Indonesian aristocrats; attempted communist revolutions in some areas; and clashes between Indonesian struggle groups and the British and Japanese. In the bloody Battle of Surabaya in November 1945, thousands died: not just from British bombing and street fighting with the British, but also in nationalist atrocities against local civilians. In December the nationalists managed to pull diverse struggle groups together into a republican army.

By 1946, 55,000 Dutch troops had arrived. They soon re-captured major cities on Java and Sumatra. Ruthless tactics by Captain Raymond Westerling in southern Sulawesi saw at least 6000 Indonesians executed (40,000 by some accounts). The first of two big Dutch offensives – called 'police actions' – reduced republican territory to limited areas of Java and Sumatra in August 1947, with its capital at Yogyakarta.

Differences among the Indonesian forces erupted viciously. In Madiun, Java, the republican army and Muslim militias fought procommunist forces in August 1948, leaving 8000 dead. The second Dutch 'police action' in December 1948 won the Dutch more territory, and they captured Sukarno, Hatta and their prime minister Sutan Syahrir. But the independence forces kept up a guerrilla struggle, and international (especially US) opinion turned against the Dutch. Realising that its cause was unwinnable, the Netherlands finally transferred sovereignty over the Dutch East Indies (apart from Dutch New Guinea) to the Indonesian republic on 27 December 1949. At least 70,000, possibly as many as 200,000, Indonesians had lost their lives in the revolution, along with 700 Dutch and British troops and some thousands of Japanese troops and European, Chinese and Eurasian civilians.

At the entrance to a neighbourhood or village you may see an arch with the words 'Dirgahayu RI' painted across it. This translates as 'Long live the Republic of Indonesia' – the arch has been built to celebrate Independence Day, 17 August.

'Bung' Karno

Independent Indonesia had a troubled infancy. Tensions between Muslims and communists persisted, with the secular nationalists like Sukarno and Hatta trying to hold everything together. The economy was in a sorry state after almost a decade of conflict, and a drop in commodity prices in the early 1950s made things worse.

Early Divisions

There were some who wanted Indonesia to be an Islamic republic, and there were some who didn't want their home territories to be part of Indonesia at all. The western-Java-based Darul Islam (House of Islam) wanted a society under Islamic law. It linked up with similar organisations in Kalimantan, Aceh and south Sulawesi to wage guerrilla war against the

1957

Sukarno proclaims 'Guided Democracy'. A military-Muslim-communist coalition replaces Western-style democracy. The army becomes the bedrock of national unity.

1961–63

With the economy in the doldrums, Sukarno is aggressive towards Netherlands New Guinea. Indonesia takes control there in 1963. Subsequent opposition from the local Papuan people is brutally put down.

1963–66

Sukarno stages *konfrontasi* (confrontation) with the newly formed Malaysia. Fighting takes place along the Indonesia–Malaysia border in Borneo. The communist party (PKI) organises land seizures by hungry peasants.

1964–65

Worried by the military's power, Sukarno decides to arm the communist party by creating a new militia, heightening tensions with the regular forces. Rumours of a planned communist coup circulate.

republic, which lasted until 1962 in western Java. In Maluku, Ambonese former soldiers of the Dutch colonial army declared an independent South Moluccas Republic in 1950. They were defeated within a few months.

Guided Democracy

Coalition governments drawn from diverse parties and factions never lasted long, and when the much-postponed parliamentary elections were finally held in 1955, no party won more than a quarter of the vote. Sukarno responded with 'Guided Democracy', effectively an uneasy coalition between the military, religious groups and communists, with increasing power concentrated in the hands of the president (ie himself). In 1959 Sukarno also took on the job of prime minister for good measure. The elected legislature was dissolved in 1960, and of the political parties only the PKI continued to have any clout.

Sukarno's growing accumulation of power was one factor behind regional rebellions in Sumatra and Sulawesi in 1958, led by senior military and civilian figures. The rebels, who had backing from the CIA, were also opposed to the increasing influence of the communists, the corruption and inefficiency in central government, and the use of export earnings from the outer islands to import rice and consumer goods for Java. The rebellions were smashed within a few months and in response Sukarno forged a new alliance with Indonesia's army.

The Asia-Africa Conference staged at Bandung in 1955 launched the Non-Aligned Movement, comprising countries that wanted to align with neither the USA nor the USSR. It also gave birth to the term Third World, originally meaning countries that belonged to neither Cold War bloc.

Monuments & Confrontations

Unable to lift the economy from the doldrums, Sukarno built a series of ostentatious nationalist monuments as substitutes for real development – such as Jakarta's National Monument (Monas, also dubbed 'Sukarno's last erection') and Mesjid Istiqlal. He diverted Indonesians' attention outward with a lot of bluster and aggression towards the supposedly threatening remnants of Western imperialism around Indonesia, Dutch New Guinea and Malaysia.

The New Guinea issue had already led Indonesia to seize all Dutch assets in the country and expel 50,000 Dutch people in 1957–58 after the UN rejected Indonesian claims to Dutch New Guinea. Bolstered by Soviet military backing, Indonesia finally took control of the territory in 1963 after a few military sorties and, more importantly, US pressure on the Netherlands to hand over. Subsequent opposition from the local Papuan population was brutally put down.

Breaking the Silence is a collective memoir of 15 people who survived the anti-communist purges of 1965–66 when over 500,000 were killed. It was published in 2012 to great acclaim.

Coup & Anti-Communist Purge

Meanwhile back in the heartland, the PKI was encouraging peasants to seize land without waiting for official redistribution, leading to violent

1965

On October 1, military rebels shoot dead six top generals in and near Jakarta. General Suharto mobilises forces against the rebels and the coup fails after only a day of fighting.

1965–66

The armed forces and armed anti-communist civilians take the attempted coup as a cue to slaughter communists and supposed communists. About 500,000 are killed, chiefly in Java, Bali and Sumatra.

1966–68

When Suharto's troops surround his palace, Sukarno signs the 11 March Order (1966), permitting Suharto to act independently. After anti-Sukarno purges, the MPR names Suharto president (March 1968).

1967

Suharto's 'New Order', supported by the West, holds Indonesia together under military dictatorship for the next 30 years. The economy develops, dissent is crushed and corruption rages.

clashes in eastern Java and Bali. By 1965 the PKI claimed three million members, controlled the biggest trade union organisation and the biggest peasant grouping, and had penetrated the government apparatus extensively. Sukarno saw it as a potential counterweight to the army, whose increasing power now had him worried, and decided to arm the PKI by creating a new militia. This led to heightened tensions with the regular armed forces, and rumours started to circulate of a planned communist coup.

On 1 October 1965, military rebels shot dead six top generals in and near Jakarta. General Suharto, head of the army's Strategic Reserve, quickly mobilised forces against the rebels and by the next day it was clear the putsch had failed. Just who was behind it still remains a mystery, but there's no mystery about its consequences. The armed forces under Suharto, and armed anti-communist civilians, took it as a cue to ruthlessly target both communists and supposed communists. By March 1966, 500,000 or more people were killed, chiefly in Java, Bali and Sumatra. The anti-communist purge provided cover for settling all sorts of old scores.

The film and novel title *The Year of Living Dangerously* is that of a major 1964 speech by Sukarno, which was drawn from Italian leader Mussolini's slogan 'Live Dangerously', which itself was originally penned by 19th-century German philosopher Friedrich Nietzsche!

Sukarno Pushed Aside

Sukarno remained president but Suharto set about manoeuvring himself into supreme power. On 11 March 1966, Suharto's troops surrounded Sukarno's presidential palace, and Sukarno signed the 11 March Order, permitting Suharto to act on his own initiative to restore order. Sukarno loyalists in the forces and cabinet were soon arrested, and a new six-man inner cabinet including Suharto was established. After further anti-Sukarno purges and demonstrations, the People's Consultative Assembly (MPR) named Suharto acting president in March 1967. A year later, with Sukarno now under house arrest, the MPR appointed Suharto president.

Sukarno died of natural causes in 1970. An inspirational orator and charismatic leader, he is still held in great affection and esteem by many older Indonesians, who often refer to him as Bung Karno – *bung* meaning 'buddy' or 'brother'. He was a flamboyant, complicated and highly intelligent character with a Javanese father and Balinese mother, and was fluent in several languages. His influences, apart from Islam, included Marxism, Javanese and Balinese mysticism, a mainly Dutch education and the theosophy movement. He had at least eight wives (up to four at once) at a time when polygamy was no longer very common in Indonesia. Throughout his political career he strove to unite Indonesians and, more than anyone else, he was the architect and creator of Indonesia.

Peter Weir's gripping *The Year of Living Dangerously* (1982), based on the eponymous novel by Australian Christopher Koch (1978), stars Mel Gibson as a young Australian journalist caught up in Indonesia's 1965 upheavals. Mel's best movie?

'Pak' Harto

Once the dust had settled on the killing of communists and supposed communists, and a million or so political prisoners had been put behind bars, the 31 years of Suharto's rule were really one of the duller periods

1971

The army party Golkar wins 236 of the 360 elective seats in the MPR, which now also includes 276 military and 207 Suharto appointees. Few believe this veneer of pseudo-democracy.

1973

Opposition parties are compulsorily merged – the Muslim parties into the Development Unity Party (PPP) and others into the Indonesian Democratic Party (PDI). Political activity in villages is banned.

1975

Indonesia invades and annexes former Portuguese colony East Timor, where left-wing party Fretilin has won a power struggle. A 20-year guerrilla war begins; over 125,000 die in fighting, famines and repression.

1979–84

The government's transmigration program reaches its peak with almost 2.5 million people moving to outer islands from overpopulated Java, Bali and Madura before the program ends in 2000.

WHOSE COUP?

Some things about the 1965 attempted coup have never quite added up. Six of the country's top generals were killed by a group of officers who included members of Sukarno's palace guard and who said they were acting to save Sukarno's leadership – presumably from the threat of a plot. If that was really what they were doing, it was a very botched job.

These rebels appear to have made no effort to organise support elsewhere in the armed forces or the country. Both Sukarno and the communist leader DN Aidit visited the rebels at Halim air base near Jakarta but kept their distance from events – Sukarno leaving for the mountains in a helicopter and Aidit instructing his party to take no action and remain calm. If the officers expected the armed forces simply to fall into line under Sukarno's leadership, or the communists to rise up and take over, they miscalculated fatally.

The biggest question mark hangs over why they didn't also eliminate General Suharto, who was at least as senior as several of the generals they did kill. There is even a theory that Suharto himself might have been behind the attempted coup. Given his manipulatory talent and inscrutability, this can't be ruled out, though no evidence to confirm it has ever come to light.

of Indonesian history. Such a tight lid was kept on opposition, protest and freedom of speech that there was almost no public debate. Under the New Order, as Suharto's regime was known, everybody just had to do what he and his generals told them to, if they weren't already dead or imprisoned.

Career Soldier

Whereas Sukarno had led with charisma, Suharto's speeches seemed designed to stifle discussion rather than inspire. 'Enigmatic' was one of the kinder epithets used in his obituaries when he died in 2008. The normally restrained *Economist* magazine called him a 'kleptocrat' and 'a cold-war monster', behind whose 'pudgily smooth, benign-looking face lay ruthless cruelty'. Suharto wielded a supreme talent for manipulating events in his own interests and outwitting opponents of all kinds.

Born in Java in 1921, he was always a soldier, from the day he joined the Dutch colonial army in his late teens. He rose quickly up the ranks of the Indonesian army in the 1950s, and was involved in putting down the South Moluccas and Darul Islam rebellions. He was transferred to a staff college after being implicated in opium and sugar smuggling in 1959, but in 1962 Sukarno appointed him to lead the military campaign against Dutch New Guinea.

1989

The Free Aceh Movement (GAM), founded in 1976, reemerges as a guerrilla force, fighting for independence for the conservatively Islamic Sumatran region. An estimated 15,000 people die through 2005.

1990s

NGOs, many of them started by middle-class Indonesians, emerge as a focus of dissent, campaigning on issues from peasant dispossessions to destructive logging and restrictions on Islamic organisations.

1997–98

The Asian currency crisis savages Indonesia's economy. After troops kill four at a Jakarta demonstration in May 1998, rioting and looting cause an estimated 1200 deaths. Suharto quits on 21 May.

1998

Vice President BJ Habibie becomes president. He releases political prisoners and relaxes censorship, but the army kills at least 12 in a Jakarta student protest. Christian/Muslim violence erupts in Jakarta and Maluku.

TROUBLED EXTREMITIES

Two regions at opposite ends of Indonesia, Sumatra's Aceh and Papua resisted efforts to create a unified state over the last several decades, although Aceh now seems to have found a way to coexist.

Aceh

The conservatively Islamic, resource-rich region of Aceh was only brought under Dutch rule by a 35-year war ending in 1908. After the Dutch departed, Aceh wasn't happy about Indonesian rule either. The Free Aceh Movement (Gerakan Aceh Merdeka; GAM), founded in 1976, gathered steam after 1989, waging a guerrilla struggle for Acehnese independence. The 1990s saw Aceh under something close to military rule, with the population suffering from abuses by both sides. Peace talks collapsed in 2003 and Aceh was placed under martial law.

Everything changed with the tsunami on 26 December 2004, which wrought its biggest devastation on Aceh, killing some 170,000 people. The government was forced to allow foreign aid organisations into Aceh and to restart negotiations with GAM. A deal in 2005 formally ended three decades of armed struggle which had cost an estimated 15,000 lives. The peace has held remarkably well since.

Papua

Like Aceh, Papua wasn't brought into the Dutch East Indies until late in the colonial period. Papuan people are culturally distinct from other Indonesians, being of dark-skinned Melanesian stock and having had very limited contact with the outside world until the 20th century. Today most of them are Christian. Resistance to Indonesian rule has continued ever since Sukarno's takeover in 1963, in the form of sporadic guerrilla attacks by the Organisasi Papua Merdeka (Free Papua Organisation; OPM). The Indonesian army keeps a large number of troops in the province and there are sporadic skirmishes with rebels and regular reports of human rights abuses by international groups such as Human Rights Watch.

Papua is a resource-rich region seen by many Indonesians as ripe for exploitation. About half the population is Indonesian – primarily migrants – and this adds to Jakarta's reasons for keeping Papua close. That the economy and administration are dominated by non-Papuans, fuels indigenous people's grievances and makes an Aceh-type autonomy solution impossible. Pro-independence sentiment among Papuans is high.

The New Order

The New Order did give Indonesia stability of a sort, and a longish period of pretty steady economic development. Whereas Indonesians had thought of Sukarno as Bung Karno, Suharto was never more than the more formal Pak (father) Harto, but he liked to be thought of as Bapak

1999

Some 78% vote for independence in East Timor. Militias backed by Indonesian military conduct a terror campaign before and after the vote. East Timor finally achieves independence in 2002.

Jun–Oct 1999

Following Indonesia's first free election since 1955, Abdurrahman Wahid of the country's largest Islamic organisation, Nahdatul Ulama (Rise of the Scholars), becomes president as leader of a multi-party coalition.

1999–2001

Wahid tries to reform government, tackle corruption, reduce military power, bring Suharto to justice and address the grievances of Aceh and Papua. But his efforts are hamstrung by opponents.

2001

Violence erupts in Kalimantan between indigenous Dayaks and Madurese migrants. Over a million people are displaced by conflicts in East Timor, Maluku, Kalimantan and elsewhere. Wahid is deposed.

Pembangunan – the Father of Development. Authoritarianism was considered the necessary price for economic progress.

Suharto and his generals believed Indonesia had to be kept together at all costs, which meant minimising political activity and squashing any potentially divisive movements – be they Islamic radicals, communists or the separatist rebels of Aceh, Papua (former Dutch New Guinea) and East Timor.

Suharto Inc

Near absolute power allowed the forces and Suharto's family and business associates to get away with almost anything. The army was not just a security force, it ran hundreds of businesses, legal and illegal, supposedly to supplement its inadequate funding from government. Corruption went hand-in-hand with secrecy and most notorious was the Suharto family. Suharto's wife Ibu Tien controlled the state monopoly on the import and milling of wheat; his daughter Tutut won the 1987 contract to build the Jakarta toll road; his son Tommy gained a monopoly on the cloves used in Indonesia's ultra-popular *kretek* cigarettes in 1989.

In 1995 Indonesia was ranked the most corrupt of all the 41 countries assessed in the first-ever Corruption Index published by Transparency International (TI). In 2004 TI placed Suharto at the top of its all-time world corruption table, with an alleged embezzlement figure of between US$15 billion and US$35 billion from his 32 years in power.

Extending Indonesia

Suharto's regime saw to it that the former Dutch New Guinea stayed in Indonesia by staging a travesty of a confirmatory vote in 1969. Just over 1000 selected Papuan 'representatives' were pressured into voting unanimously for continued integration with Indonesia, in what was named the Act of Free Choice.

In 1975 the left-wing party Fretilin won a power struggle within the newly independent former Portuguese colony East Timor. The western part of Timor island, a former Dutch possession, was Indonesian. Horrified at the prospect of a left-wing government in a neighbouring state, Indonesia invaded and annexed East Timor. Fretilin kept up a guerrilla struggle and at least 125,000 Timorese died in fighting, famines and repression over the next 2½ decades.

The End Of The New Order

The end of the New Order was finally precipitated by the Asian currency crisis of 1997, which savaged Indonesia's economy. Millions lost their jobs and rising prices sparked riots. Suharto faced unprecedented widespread

2001–04

Vice-president Megawati Sukarnoputri, Sukarno's daughter, leading the PDI-P (Indonesian Democratic Party – Struggle) and supported by conservative elements, succeeds Wahid.

2002

Terrorist bombs in Kuta, Bali, kill 202 people, mainly foreign tourists. The Islamic militant group Jemaah Islamiah is blamed. Several of its members are jailed and three are executed in 2008.

SYLVAIN GRANDADAM/GETTY IMAGES ©

» 2002 Bali bombings memorial wall (p209)

2004

Anticorruption group Transparency International puts Suharto at the top of its all-time world corruption table, with an alleged embezzlement figure of between US$15 and US$35 billion.

calls for his resignation. Antigovernment rallies spread from universities to city streets, and when four students at Jakarta's Trisakti University were shot dead by troops in May 1998, the city erupted in rioting and looting, killing an estimated 1200. Even Suharto's own ministers called for his resignation, and he finally resigned shortly thereafter.

The Road to Democracy

Suharto's fall ushered in a period known as *reformasi* (reform), three tumultuous years in which elective democracy, free expression and human rights all advanced, and attempts were made to deal with the grievances of East Timor, Aceh and Papua. It was an era with many positives and some disasters. Since 2004, President Susilo Bambang Yudhoyono (known as SBY), a retired general with moderately liberal leanings, has pursued a cautious, undramatic style of governing which has steered Indonesia free of serious troubles, produced some reforms and kept the economy growing robustly. SBY was re-elected for a second presidential term with an increased share of the vote in 2009. Though survivors from the Suharto era still dominate politics, the 2009 elections, peaceful and without major corruption scandals, showed that Indonesian democracy has put down roots.

Of 18 people tried by an Indonesian human-rights court for abuses in East Timor in 1999, only militia leader Eurico Guterres was convicted. His conviction for a massacre of 12 people was quashed by the Indonesian Supreme Court in 2008.

The Habibie Presidency

Suharto's vice-president BJ Habibie stepped up as president when Suharto resigned. Habibie released political prisoners, relaxed censorship and promised elections, but he still tried to ban demonstrations and reaffirmed the political role of the unpopular army. Tensions between Christians and Muslims in some parts of Indonesia also erupted into violence – especially Maluku, where thousands died in incidents between early 1999 and 2002.

The Wahid & Megawati Presidencies

Indonesia's first free parliamentary elections for 44 years took place in 1999. No party received a clear mandate, but the MPR elected Muslim preacher Abdurrahman Wahid president as leader of a coalition. The eccentric Wahid, from the country's largest Islamic organisation, Nahdatul Ulama (Rise of the Scholars), was blind, had suffered two strokes and disliked formal dress and hierarchies. He embarked on an ambitious program to rein in the military, reform the legal and financial systems, promote religious tolerance, tackle corruption, and resolve the problems of Aceh and Papua. Unsurprisingly, all this upset everybody who was anybody, and in July 2001 the MPR dismissed Wahid over alleged incompetence and corruption.

Vice President Megawati of the Indonesian Democratic Party – Struggle (PDI-P) took over as president in Wahid's place. Supported by many

Oct 2004

In Indonesia's first direct presidential elections, Susilo Bambang Yudhoyono (SBY) of the new Democratic Party, a former general regarded as a liberal, wins a run-off vote against Megawati.

Dec 2004

Over 200,000 Indonesians die in the 26 December tsunami that devastates large areas of Sumatra, especially Aceh. SBY restarts peace talks there, leading to a peace deal in 2005.

2004

SBY's presidency sees progress against B-list corruption. The army is edged away from politics and most of its business enterprises.

2006

Bantul, near Yogyakarta, is hit by an earthquake on 27 May – 5800 die and 200,000 are left homeless across central Java. Another 700 die in a 17 July earthquake.

EAST TIMOR TROUBLES

Indonesia under President Habibie agreed to a UN-organised independence referendum in East Timor, where human rights abuses, reported by Amnesty International among others, had blackened Indonesia's name internationally. In the 1999 vote, 78% of East Timorese chose independence. But the event was accompanied by a terror campaign by pro-Indonesia militia groups and Indonesian security forces, which according to Amnesty International killed an estimated 1300 people, and left much of East Timor's infrastructure ruined. East Timor finally gained full independence in 2002.

conservative, old-guard elements, Megawati – daughter of the legendary Sukarno – had none of her father's flair or vision and did little for reform in her three years in office.

SBY In Charge

The year 2004 saw Indonesia's first-ever direct popular vote for president. Susilo Bambang Yudhoyono (SBY), leading the new Democratic Party (formed as his personal political vehicle), won in a run-off vote against Megawati. A popular and pragmatic politician, SBY quickly won favour by making sure foreign aid could get to tsunami-devastated Aceh and sealing a peace deal with Aceh's GAM rebels.

SBY's unspectacular but stable presidency saw the military forced to divest most of their business enterprises and edged away from politics (they lost their reserved seats in parliament in 2004). There was also progress against corruption. A former head of Indonesia's central bank, an MP, a governor of Aceh province and a mayor of Medan were all among those jailed thanks to the Corruption Eradication Commission, established in 2002, although no really big names were ensnared.

Fears of an upsurge in Islamic radicalism, especially after the Bali and Jakarta terrorist bombings of 2002 to 2005, proved largely unfounded. The great majority of Indonesian Muslims are moderate and while Islamic parties receive a sizeable share of the vote in elections, they can only do so by remaining in the political mainstream.

Indonesians clearly appreciated the stability and non-confrontational style of SBY's presidency, and his successful handling of the economy, for they re-elected him in 2009 with over 60% of the vote. Interestingly neither religion nor ethnicity played a major part in determining how people voted, suggesting that many Indonesians valued democracy, peace and economic progress above sectarian or regional issues. Predictions that hardline Islamist parties would make huge gains proved false when they received only 8% of the vote.

The word *sembako* refers to Indonesia's nine essential culinary ingredients: rice, sugar, eggs, meat, flour, corn, fuel, cooking oil and salt. When any of these become unavailable or more costly, repercussions can be felt right through to the presidency.

2007

SBY orders a review of Indonesia's transport system after a series of air, ferry and rail disasters. The EU bans Indonesian airlines from Europe. Transport disasters continue.

2009

SBY is re-elected president with over 60% of the vote.

2009

Terrorist leader Nordin M Top is killed by police near Solo, Java. Top was alleged to be the mastermind behind terrorist attacks in Indonesia from 2002 to 2009.

Sep 2009

An earthquake kills over 1100 around Padang in West Sumatra. Thirteen months later, an earthquake off the nearby coast kills 435 and spawns a tsunami that hits the Mentawi islands.

Culture

National Identity

Indonesia comprises a massively diverse range of societies and cultures; the differences between, say, the Sumbanese and Sundanese are as marked as those between the Swedes and Sicilians. Even so, a strong national Indonesian identity has emerged, originally through the struggle for independence and, following that, through education programs and the promotion of Bahasa Indonesia as the national language. This is despite the fact that Indonesia continues to be stretched by opposing forces: 'strict' Islam versus 'moderate' Islam, Islam versus Christianity versus Hinduism, outer islands versus Java, country versus city, modern versus traditional, rich versus poor, the 21st century versus the past.

The annual Ubud Writers & Readers Festival (www.ubudwritersfestival.com) in Bali, held around October, showcases both local and international writers and has an annual theme.

One Culture or Many?

The differences within Indonesian culture may challenge social cohesion and have at times been used as an excuse to incite conflict, but the nation still prevails. And, with notable exceptions such as Papua, the bonds have grown stronger, with the notion of an Indonesian identity overlapping rather than supplanting the nation's many pre-existing regional cultures. The national slogan, *Bhinneka Tunggal Ika* (Unity in Diversity) – even though its words are old Javanese – has been adopted by Indonesians across widely varying ethnic and social standpoints.

Religion as Culture

A cultural element that bridges both the regional and the national is religion - the Pancasila principle of belief in a god (p711) holds firm. Though Indonesia is predominantly Islamic, in many places Islam is interwoven with traditional customs, giving it unique qualities and characteristics. Some areas are Christian or animist and, to leaven the mix, Bali has its own unique brand of Hinduism. Religion plays a role in the everyday: mosques and musholla (prayer rooms) are in constant use, and the vibrant Hindu ceremonies of Bali are a daily occurrence, to the delight of visitors.

Nationalism and Ethnic Conflict in Indonesia by Jacques Bertrand investigates the reasons behind the violence in areas such as Maluku and Kalimantan.

Trends & Traditions

Mobile phones, huge malls, techno-driven nightclubs and other facets of international modernity are common in Indonesia. But while the main cities and tourist resorts can appear technologically rich, other areas remain untouched. And even where modernisation has taken hold, it's clear that Indonesians have a very traditionalist heart. As well as adhering to religious and ethnic traditions, Indonesians also maintain social customs. Politeness to strangers is a deeply ingrained habit throughout most of the archipelago. Elders are still accorded great respect. When visiting someone's home, elders are always greeted first, and often

SMALL TALK

One thing that takes many visitors by surprise in Indonesia is what may seem like over-inquisitiveness from complete strangers. Questions from them might include the following:

- *Dari mana?* (Where do you come from?)
- *Mau kemana?* (Where are you going?)
- *Tinggal dimana?* (Where are you staying?)
- *Jalan sendiri?* (Are you travelling alone?)
- *Sudah kawin?* (Are you married?)
- *Anak-anak ada?* (Do you have children?)

Visitors can find these questions intrusive or irritating, and in tourist areas they may just be a prelude to a sales pitch, but more often they are simply polite greetings and an expression of interest in a foreigner. A short answer or a Bahasa Indonesia greeting, with a smile, is a polite and adequate response. Try the following:

- *Jalan-jalan* (Walking around)
- *Makan angin* (literally 'Eating wind', ie 'Walking')

If you get into a slightly longer conversation, it's proper to ask some of the same questions in return. When you've had enough chatter, you can answer the question 'Where are you going?' even if it hasn't been asked.

customary permission to depart is also offered. This can occur whether in a high-rise in Medan or a hut in the Baliem Valley.

Lifestyle

Daily life for Indonesians has changed rapidly in the last decade or two. These days, many people live away from their home region and the role of women has extended well beyond domestic duties to include career and study.

Family Life

The importance of the family remains high. This is evident during such festivals as Idul Fitri (Lebaran, the end of the Islamic fasting month), when highways become gridlocked with those returning home to loved ones. Even at weekends, many travel for hours to spend a day with their relatives. In many ways, the notions of family and regional identity have become more pronounced: as people move away from small-scale communities and enter the milieu of the cities, the sense of belonging becomes more valued.

Village Life

Beyond family, the main social unit is the village. Almost half the population still lives in rural areas (it was 80% in 1975) where labour in the fields, the home or the market is the basis of daily life. So, for younger Indonesians, is school – though not for as many as might be hoped. Nine out of 10 children complete the five years of primary schooling, but only six out of 10 get through secondary school. Kids from poorer families have to start supplementing the family income at an early age.

The village spirit isn't restricted to rural areas: the backstreets of Jakarta are home to tightknit neighbourhoods where kids run from house to house and everyone knows who owns which chicken. A sense of community may also evolve in a *kos* (apartment with shared facilities), where tenants, far from their families, come together for meals and companionship.

Traditional Life

For the many Indonesians who still live in their home regions, customs and traditions remain a part of the everyday: the Toraja of Sulawesi (p654) continue to build traditional houses due to their social importance; the focus of a Sumbanese village (p389) remains the gravestones of their ancestors due to the influence they are believed to have in daily happenings. These aren't customs offered attention once a year – they are a part of life. And even where modernity has found purchase, age-old traditions can still underpin life: Bali, for example, still scrupulously observes its annual day of silence, Nyepi (Balinese Lunar New Year), when literally all activity stops and everyone stays at home (or in their hotels) so that evil spirits will think the island uninhabited and leave it alone.

Life for women in Indonesian society is, like so many other things, full of contradictions. While many are well educated and well employed, and women in cities can enjoy bars and clubbing just like men, traditional family roles are still strong. The pressures of conservative Islam make many women wary that recently gained freedoms may be eroded.

Gay Life

Contradictions also run through the status of gays in Indonesian society. Plenty of Indonesians of both sexes are actively gay, and except in some very conservative areas such as Aceh, active repression is absent. But so is positive recognition of gay identity or gay rights. *Waria* (transgender or transvestite) performers and prostitutes have quite a high profile. Otherwise gay behaviour is, by and large, accepted without being particularly approved of. Bali, with its big international scene, and some Javanese cities have the most open gay life.

COWBOYS IN PARADISE

Cowboys in Paradise, directed by Amit Virmani, has made headlines for its unflinching portrait of real-life gigolos in Bali. Fixtures of Kuta Beach, these men are popular with some female tourists.

Multiculturalism

Indonesia is a country of literally hundreds of cultures. Every one of its 700-plus languages denotes, at least to some extent, a different culture. They range from the matrilineal Minangkabau of Sumatra and the artistic Hindu Balinese, to the seafaring Bugis and buffalo-sacrificing Toraja of Sulawesi and Papua's penis-gourd-wearing Dani, to name but a few. Indonesia's island nature and rugged, mountainous terrain have meant that groups of people have often developed in near isolation from each other, resulting in an extraordinary differentiation of culture and language across the archipelago. Even in densely populated Java there are distinct groups, such as the Badui, who withdrew to the western highlands as Islam spread through the island and have had little contact with outsiders.

One Nation, Many Cultures

The notion that all these peoples could form one nation is a relatively young one, originating in the later part of the Dutch colonial era. Indonesia's 20th-century founding fathers knew that if a country of such diverse culture and religion was to hold together, it needed special handling.

MIGRATION & HOMOGENISATION

Ethnic and cultural tensions in Indonesia have often been fuelled by transmigrasi (transmigration), the government-sponsored program of migration from more overcrowded islands (Java, Bali and Madura) to less crowded ones such as Kalimantan, Sumatra, Sulawesi and Papua. Over eight million people were relocated between 1950 and 2000. Local residents have often resented their marginalisation due to a sudden influx of people with little regard or use for local cultures and traditions. That the newcomers have the full sponsorship of the government adds to the resentment.

They fostered Indonesian nationalism and a national language (Bahasa Indonesia, spoken today by almost all Indonesians but the mother tongue for only about 20% of them). They rejected ideas that Indonesia should be a federal republic (potentially centrifugal), or a state subject to the law of Islam, even though this is the religion of the great majority. Today most Indonesian citizens (with the chief exceptions of many Papuans and some Acehnese) are firmly committed to the idea of Indonesia, even if there is a lingering feeling that in some ways the country is a 'Javanese empire'.

Riri Reza's *Gie*, the story of Soe Hok Gie, an ethnic Chinese antidictatorship activist, was submitted for consideration in the Best Foreign Film category of the 2006 Academy Awards.

Religion

Indonesia's constitution affirms that the state is based on a belief in 'the One and Only God'; yet it also, rather contradictorily, guarantees 'freedom of worship, each according to his/her own religion or belief'. In practice, this translates into a requirement to follow one of the officially accepted 'religions', of which there are now six: Islam, Catholicism, Protestantism, Hinduism, Buddhism and Confucianism.

Islam is the predominant religion, with followers making up about 86% of the population. In Java pilgrims still visit hundreds of holy places where spiritual energy is believed to be concentrated. Christians make up about 9% of the population, in scattered areas spread across the archipelago. Bali's Hindus comprise nearly 3% of the population.

Nevertheless, old beliefs persist. The earliest Indonesians were animists who practised ancestor and spirit worship. When Hinduism and Buddhism and, later, Islam and Christianity spread into the archipelago, they were layered onto this spiritual base.

In the Shadow of Swords by Sally Neighbour investigates the rise of terrorism in Indonesia and beyond, from an Australian perspective.

Islam

Islam arrived in Indonesia with Muslim traders from the Arabian Peninsula and India as early as the 7th century AD, within decades of the Prophet Muhammed receiving the word of Allah (God) in Mecca. The first Indonesian rulers to convert to Islam were in the small North Sumatran ports of Lamreh and Pasai in the 13th century. Gradually over the following two centuries, then more rapidly, other Indonesian states adopted Islam. The religion initially spread along sea-trade routes, and the conversion of Demak, Tuban, Gresik and Cirebon, on Java's north coast, in the late 15th century was an important step in its progress.

The first Indonesian rulers to adopt Islam chose to do so from contact with foreign Muslim communities. Some other states were converted by conquest. Java's first Islamic leaders have long been venerated and mythologised as the nine *walis* (saints). Many legends are told about their feats of magic or war, and pilgrims visit their graves despite the official proscription of saint worship by Islam.

CUSTOMS

Today Indonesia has the largest Muslim population of any country in the world and the role Islam should play in its national life is constantly debated. Mainstream Indonesian Islam is moderate. Muslim women are not segregated nor, in most of the country, do they have to wear the *jilbab* (head covering), although this has recently become more common. Muslim men are allowed to marry two women but must have the consent of their first wife. Even so, polygamy in Indonesia is very rare. Many pre-Islamic traditions and customs remain in place. The Minangkabau society of Sumatra, for example, is strongly Islamic but remains matrilineal according to tradition.

Islam requires that all boys be circumcised, and in Indonesia this is usually done between the ages of six and 11. Muslims observe the fasting

RAMADAN

One of the most important months of the Muslim calendar is the fasting month of Ramadan. As a profession of faith and spiritual discipline, Muslims abstain from food, drink, cigarettes and other worldly desires (including sex) from sunrise to sunset. However, many of the casually devout will find loopholes in the strictures.

Ramadan is often preceded by a cleansing ceremony, Padusan, to prepare for the coming fast (*puasa*). Traditionally, during Ramadan people get up at 3am or 4am to eat (this meal is called *sahur*) and then fast until sunset. Special prayers are said at mosques and at home.

The first day of the 10th month of the Muslim calendar is the end of Ramadan, called Idul Fitri or Lebaran. Mass prayers are held in the early morning, followed by two days of feasting. Extracts from the Koran are read and religious processions take place. During this time of mutual forgiveness, gifts are exchanged and pardon is asked for past wrongdoing.

During Ramadan, many restaurants and warungs are closed in Muslim regions of Indonesia. Those owned by non-Muslims will be open, but in deference to those fasting, they may have covered overhangs or will otherwise appear shut. In the big cities, many businesses are open and fasting is less strictly observed. Street stalls, mall food courts and warungs all come alive for the evening meal.

Though not all Muslims can keep to the privations of fasting, the overwhelming majority do and you should respect their values. Do not eat, drink or smoke in public unless you see others doing so.

Note that for a week before and a week after the official two-day Idul Fitri holiday, transport is chaotic; don't even consider travelling during this time as roads and buses are jammed, flights full and ferries bursting. You will be better off in non-Muslim areas – such as Bali, east Nusa Tenggara, Maluku or Papua – but even these areas have significant Muslim populations. Plan well, find yourself an idyllic spot and stay put.

Ramadan and Idul Fitri move back 10 days or so every year, according to the Muslim calendar.

month of Ramadan. Friday afternoons are officially set aside for believers to worship, and all government offices and many businesses are closed as a result. In accordance with Islamic teaching, millions of Indonesians have made the pilgrimage to Mecca.

ISLAMIC LAWS

An attempt by some Islamic parties to make sharia (Islamic religious law) a constitutional obligation for all Indonesian Muslims was rejected by the national parliament in 2002. Sharia was firmly outlawed under the Suharto dictatorship, but elements of it have since been introduced in some cities and regions. Aceh was permitted to introduce strict sharia under its 2005 peace deal with the government. In Aceh gambling, alcohol and public affection between the sexes are all now banned, some criminals receive corporal punishment, and the *jilbab* is compulsory for women. Public displays of intimacy, alcohol and 'prostitute-like appearance' are outlawed in the factory town of Tangerang on Jakarta's outskirts, and the *jilbab* is obligatory in Padang on Sumatra.

If you've ever wondered why some hotel rooms have a small arrow pointing in a seemingly random direction on the ceiling, it's actually indicating the direction of Mecca for Muslims who want to pray but can't get to a mosque.

The result of recent elections is that the great majority of Muslims are moderates and do not want an Islamic state. Neither of Indonesia's two biggest Muslim organisations (each has about 30 millions members, but are not political parties) – the traditionalist Nahdatul Ulama (Rise of the Scholars) and the modernist Muhammadiyah – now seeks an Islamic state.

MILITANT ISLAM

Militant Islamist groups that have made headlines with violent actions speak for only small minorities. Jemaah Islamiah was responsible for the

2002 Bali bombings and other acts of terror. The Indonesian government has captured or killed many of its principals, including cleric Abu Bakar Bashir who was jailed for 15 years in 2011.

Christianity

The Portuguese introduced Roman Catholicism to Indonesia in the 16th century. Although they dabbled in religious conversion in Maluku and sent Dominican friars to Timor and Flores, their influence was never strong. The Dutch introduced Protestantism but made little effort to spread it. Missionary efforts came only after the Dutch set about establishing direct colonial rule throughout Indonesia in the 19th century. Animist areas were up for grabs and missionaries set about their work with zeal in parts of Nusa Tenggara, Maluku, Kalimantan, Papua, Sumatra and Sulawesi. A significant number of Chinese Indonesians converted to Christianity during the Suharto era.

Protestants (about 6% of the population) outnumber Catholics, largely because of the work of Dutch Calvinist and Lutheran missions and more recent Evangelical movements. The main Protestant populations are in the Batak area of Sumatra, the Minahasa and Toraja areas of Sulawesi, Timor and Sumba in Nusa Tenggara, Papua, parts of Maluku and Dayak areas of Kalimantan. Catholics comprise 3% of the population and are most numerous in Papua and Flores.

Ayat-Ayat Cinta (Verses of Love), is a Hanung Bramantyo–directed romantic melodrama with an Islamic theme that attracted more Muslim viewers than ever before to Indonesian cinemas.

Hinduism & Buddhism

These belief systems of Indian origin have a key place in Indonesian history but are now practised by relatively small numbers. Arriving with Indian traders by the 5th century AD, Hinduism and Buddhism came to be adopted by many kingdoms, especially in the western half of Indonesia. All of the most powerful states in the archipelago until the 15th century – such as Sriwijaya, based in southeast Sumatra, and Majapahit, in eastern Java – were Hindu, Buddhist or a combination of the two, usually in fusion with earlier animist beliefs. Indonesian Hinduism tended to emphasise worship of the god Shiva, the destroyer, perhaps because this was closer to existing fertility worship and the appeasement of malevolent spirits. Buddhism, more a philosophy than a religion, shunned the Hindu pantheon of gods in its goal of escaping from suffering by overcoming desire.

Though Islam later replaced them almost everywhere in Indonesia, Hinduism and Buddhism left a powerful imprint on local culture and

Outside India, Hindus predominate only in Nepal and Bali. The Hinduism of Bali is literally far removed from that of India.

BELIEFS OUTSIDE THE OFFICIAL BOX

Fascinating elements of animism, mostly concerned with the spirits of the dead or fertility rituals, survive alongside the major religions all over Indonesia today – especially among peoples in fairly remote places. These often colourful belief systems are the basis for tourism and include the following:

» Nusa Tenggara's Sumbanese (p389)

» Kalimantan's Dayaks (p586)

» Sumatra's Bataks (p506)

» Sumatra's Mentawaians (p542)

» Sumatra's Minangkabau (p535)

» Sumatra's Niassans (p512)

» Sulawesi's Toraja (p654)

» Papua's Dani (p479)

» Papua's Asmat (p483)

spirituality. This is most obvious today in the continued use of stories from the Hindu Ramayana and Mahabharata epics in Javanese and Balinese dance and theatre – as well as in major monuments like the great Javanese temple complexes of Borobudur (Buddhist) and Prambanan (Hindu). Bali survived as a stronghold of Hinduism because nobles and intelligentsia of the Majapahit kingdom congregated there after the rest of their realm fell to Islam in the 15th century.

Most Buddhists in Indonesia today are Chinese. Their numbers have been estimated at more than two million, although this may come down at the next count following the reinstatement of Confucianism as an official religion in 2006. Confucianism, the creed of many Chinese Indonesians, was delisted in the Suharto era, forcing many Chinese to convert to Buddhism or Christianity.

Women in Indonesia

For Indonesian women, the challenges of balancing traditional roles and the opportunities and responsibilities of the modern era are most pronounced. Many are well educated and well employed; women are widely represented in the bureaucracy and business, and a record 100 women were elected to 18% of the seats in parliament in 2009. Yet many of the same women still see roles such as housekeeping and child rearing as their domain. Two-income households are increasingly common and often a necessity.

Bali: Island of Dogs, a film by Lawrence Blair and Dean Allan Tolhurst, shows the complicated lives of the island's misunderstood dogs. Many are being slaughtered in a misguided effort to eradicate rabies.

As a predominantly Islamic society Indonesia remains male-oriented, though women are not cloistered or required to observe *purdah* (the practise of screening women from strangers by means of a curtain or all-enveloping clothes). The *jilbab* has become more common, but it does not necessarily mean that women who wear it have a subservient personality or even deep Islamic faith. It can also be a means of deflecting unwanted male attention.

Tenuous Gains?

Despite the social liberation of women visible in urban areas, there are those who see the advances made by conservative Islam in the past decade as a threat to women. Pressure on women to dress and behave conservatively comes from elements of sharia law that have been introduced in areas such as Aceh.

An attempt to reform family law in 2005 and give greater rights to women never even got to be debated in parliament after Islamic fundamentalists threatened those who were drafting it. Women still cannot legally be heads of households, which presents particular problems for Indonesia's estimated six million single mothers.

Author Djenar Maesa Ayu rocked Indonesia's literary scene with her candid portrayal of the injustices tackled by women. Her books include *They Say I'm a Monkey* and *Nyala*.

Arts

Indonesians are very artistic people. This is most obvious in Bali, where the creation of beauty is part of the fabric of daily life, but it's apparent throughout the archipelago in music, dance, theatre, painting and in the handmade artisanry, of which every different island or area seems to have its own original form.

Theatre & Dance

Drama and dance in Indonesia are intimately connected in the hybrid form that is best known internationally – Balinese dancing. The colourful Balinese performances, at times supremely graceful, at others almost slapstick, are dances that tell stories, sometimes from the Indian Ramayana or Mahabharata epics. Balinese dance is performed both as enter-

GRIN & ENJOY IT

A smile goes a very long way in Indonesia. It's said Indonesians have a smile for every emotion, and keeping one on your face even in a difficult situation helps to avoid giving offence. Indonesians generally seek consensus rather than disagreement, so maintaining a sense of accord, however tenuous, is a good idea in all dealings. Anger or aggressive behaviour is considered poor form.

tainment and as a religious ritual, playing an important part in temple festivals.

Java's famed *wayang* (puppet) theatre also tells Ramayana and Mahabharata stories, through the use of shadow puppets, three-dimensional wooden puppets, or real people dancing the *wayang* roles. It too can still have ritual significance. Yogyakarta and Solo are centres of traditional Javanese culture where you can see a *wayang* performance.

Yogyakarta and Solo are also the centres of classical Javanese dance, a more refined, stylised manner of acting out the Hindu epics, performed most spectacularly in the Ramayana Ballet at Prambanan.

Many other colourful dance and drama traditions are alive and well around the archipelago. The Minangkabau people of West Sumatra have a strong tradition of Randai dance-drama at festivals and ceremonies, which incorporates *pencak silat* (a form of martial arts). The Batak Sigalegale puppet dance sees life-sized puppets dancing for weddings and funerals. Western Java's Jaipongan is a dynamic style that features swift movements to rhythms complicated enough to dumbfound an audience of musicologists. It was developed out of local dance and music traditions after Sukarno banned rock 'n' roll in 1961.

The best bet for traditional dance? Ubud on Bali where you can see several performances by talented troupes every night of the week.

Central Kalimantan is home to the Manasai, a friendly dance in which tourists are welcome to participate. Kalimantan also has the Mandau, a dance performed with knives and shields. Papua is best known for its warrior dances, easiest seen at annual festivals at Danau Sentani and in the Baliem Valley and Asmat region.

Music

TRADITIONAL

Gamelan orchestras dominate traditional music in Java and Bali. Composed mainly of percussion instruments such as xylophones, gongs, drums and *angklung* (bamboo tubes shaken to produce a note), but also flutes, gamelan orchestras may have as many as 100 members. The sound produced by a gamelan can range from harmonious to eerie, with the tempo and intensity of sound undulating on a regular basis. Expect to hear powerful waves of music one minute and a single instrument holding court the next.

Indonesia's conservative Muslim clerics successfully got a Lady Gaga concert cancelled in Jakarta in 2012. Although the shows were already sold out, promoters pulled the plug after numerous threats were made to the performer and potential audience members.

Balinese gamelan is more dramatic and varied than the refined Javanese forms, but all gamelan music has a hypnotic and haunting effect. It always accompanies Balinese and Javanese dance, and can also be heard in dedicated gamelan concerts, particularly in Solo and Yogyakarta in Java. Similar types of ensemble are also found elsewhere, such as the *telempong* of West Sumatra.

Another ethereal traditional music is West Java's serene *kacapi suling*, which features the *kacapi* (a harplike instrument) and *suling* (a bamboo flute).

CONTEMPORARY

Indonesia has a massive contemporary music scene that spans all genres. The popular *dangdut* is a melange of traditional and modern, Indonesian

THE PORN LAW

One of the issues that has aroused most emotion in Indonesia in recent years is the 'anti-pornography' law finally passed by parliament and signed into law by President Susilo Bambang Yudhoyono in 2008. Promoted by Islamic parties, the law has a very wide definition of pornography that can potentially be applied to every kind of visual, textual or sound communication or performance, and even conversations and gestures. It also allows for a public role in preventing the production, distribution and use of pornography.

Opponents of the law include some secular political parties as well as women's, human-rights, regional, Christian, artists' and performers' groups and tourism industry interests. They argue that the law could be used by Islamic militants against many types of artistic and cultural expression (including for example Balinese dancing and the representation of naked figures) and forms of dress. (The wearing of bikinis on tourist beaches was, however, exempted from the law.)

So far enforcement of the law has been patchy but its mere presence on the books has led some to fear that it is having a chilling effect on free expression.

IWAN FALS

Rock legend Iwan Fals has been around for decades but still packs stadiums. His anti-establishment bent has caused him to be arrested several times.

and foreign musical styles that features instruments such as electric guitars and Indian tablas, and rhythms ranging from Middle Eastern pop to reggae or salsa. The result is sexy, love-drunk songs sung by heartbroken women or cheesy men, accompanied by straight-faced musicians in matching suits. The beats are gutsy, the emotion high, the singing evocative and the dancing often provocative.

The writhings of *dangdut* star Inul Daratista (whose adopted stage name means 'the girl with breasts') were one reason behind the passage of Indonesia's controversial 'antipornography' legislation. Yet her popularity continues to grow and she regularly sells out 10,000-seat venues around the archipelago.

Painting

Galleries in the wealthier neighbourhoods of Jakarta are the epicentre of Indonesia's contemporary art scene, which has flourished with a full panoply of installations, sculptures, performance art and more, and which can be either extremely original, eye-catching and thought-provoking, or the opposite. Jakarta (www.jakartabiennale.org) and Yogyakarta (www.biennalejogja.org) both hold big biennale art events.

Traditionally, painting was an art for decorating palaces and places of worship, typically with religious or legendary subject matter. Foreign artists in Bali in the 1930s inspired a revolution in painting: artists began to depict everyday scenes in new, more realistic, less crowded canvases. Others developed an attractive 'primitivist' style. Much Balinese art today is mass-produced tourist-market stuff, though there are also talented and original artists, especially in and around Ubud. Indonesia's most celebrated 20th-century painter was the Javanese expressionist Affandi (1907–90), who liked to paint by squeezing the paint straight out of the tube.

Architecture

Indonesia is home to a vast and spectacular variety of architecture, from religious and royal buildings to traditional styles of home-building, which can differ hugely from one part of the archipelago to another. Indian, Chinese, Arabic and European influences have all added their mark to locally developed styles.

The great 8th- and 9th-century temples of Borobudur, Prambanan and the Dieng Plateau, in Central Java, all show the Indian influence that predominated in the Hindu-Buddhist period. Indian style, albeit with a distinctive local flavour, persists today in the Hindu temples of Bali, where the leaders of the Hindu-Buddhist Majapahit kingdom took refuge after being driven from Java in the 16th century.

Bali Style, by Barbara Walker and Rio Helmi, is a lavishly photographed look at Balinese design, architecture and interior decoration. *Java Style* is part of the same series.

TRADITIONAL HOUSES

For their own homes Indonesians developed a range of eye-catching structures whose grandeur depended on the family that built them. Timber construction, often with stilts, and elaborate thatched roofs of palm leaves or grass are common to many traditional housing forms around the archipelago. The use of stilts helps to reduce heat and humidity and avoid mud, floods and pests. Tana Toraja in Sulawesi, Pulau Nias off Sumatra, and the Batak and Minangkabau areas of Sumatra exhibit some of the most spectacular vernacular architecture, with high, curved roofs.

ROYAL PALACES

Royal palaces around Indonesia are often developments of basic local housing styles, even if far more elaborate as in the case of Javanese *kraton* (walled palaces). Yogyakarta's *kraton* is effectively a city within a city inhabited by over 25,000 people. On Bali, where royal families still exist – even if they often lack power – the 'palaces' are much more humble.

COLONIAL BUILDINGS

The Dutch colonists initially built poorly ventilated houses in European style but eventually a hybrid Indo-European style emerged, using elements such as the Javanese *pendopo* (open-sided pavilion) and *joglo* (a high-pitched roof). International styles such as art deco started to arrive in the late 19th century as large numbers of factories, train stations, hotels, hospitals and other public buildings went up in the later colonial period. Bandung in Java has one of the world's largest collections of 1920s art deco buildings.

The Banda Islands in Maluku are a virtual theme park of Dutch colonial architecture with old forts and streets lined with old columned buildings sporting shady verandas.

The glossy monthly English-language magazine *Jakarta Java Kini* (www.jakartajavakini.com) contains interesting articles on what's hot in the arts and entertainment, with a Jakarta focus.

MODERN ARCHITECTURE

Early independent Indonesia had little money to spare for major building projects, though President Sukarno did find the funds for a few prestige projects such as Jakarta's huge and resplendent Mesjid Istiqlal. The economic progress of the Suharto years saw Indonesia's cities spawn their quota of standard international high-rise office blocks and uninspired government buildings, though tourism helped to foster original, even spectacular, hybrids of local and international styles in hotels and resorts. Bali in particular has some properties renowned for their architecture around the coast and overlooking the river valleys around Ubud.

BALINESE ARCHITECTURE

The basic feature of Balinese architecture is the *bale* (pronounced 'balay'), a rectangular, open-sided pavilion with a steeply pitched roof of palm thatch. A family compound will have a number of *bale* for eating, sleeping and working. The focus of a community is the *bale banjar*, a large pavilion for meeting, debate, gamelan practise and so on. Buildings such as restaurants and the lobby areas of hotels are often modelled on the *bale* – they are airy, spacious and handsomely proportioned.

Like the other arts, architecture has traditionally served the religious life of Bali. Balinese houses, although attractive, have never been lavished with the architectural attention that is given to temples. Even Balinese palaces are modest compared with the more important temples. Temples are designed to fixed rules and formulas, with sculpture serving as an adjunct, a finishing touch to these design guidelines.

MOSQUES

Mosque interiors are normally empty except for five main features: the *mihrab* (a wall niche marking the direction of Mecca); the *mimbar* (a raised pulpit, often canopied, with a staircase); a stand to hold the Koran; a screen to provide privacy for important worshippers; and a water source for ablutions. There are no seats and if there is any ornamentation at all, it will be verses from the Koran.

All mosques are primarily places of prayer, but their specific functions vary: the *jami mesjid* is used for Friday prayer meetings; a *musalla* is used Sunday to Thursday; and the *mashad* is found in a tomb compound.

It's generally no problem for travellers to visit mosques, as long as appropriately modest clothing is worn – there is usually a place to leave shoes, and headscarves are often available for hire.

Crafts

History, religion, custom and modern styles are all reflected in Indonesia's vastly diverse range of crafts, which fills many an extra bag when visitors return home. Broadly speaking, there are three major influences.

The first major influence is the traditions of animism and ancestor worship, which forms the basis of many Indonesian crafts, particularly in Sumatra, Kalimantan, Sulawesi, Nusa Tenggara, Maluku and Papua. The second influence is the wave of Indian – and to a lesser extent Indo-Chinese – culture brought by extensive trading contacts, which created the Hindu-Buddhist techniques and styles reflected in Javanese and Balinese temple carvings, art forms and crafts. The third major influence, Islam, only modified existing traditions. In fact Islam actively employed arts and crafts for dissemination of the religion. The highly stylised floral motifs on Jepara woodcarvings, for example, reflect Islam's ban on human and animal representation.

Though the religious significance or practical function of many traditional objects is disappearing, the level of craftsmanship remains high. The sophistication and innovation of the craft industry is growing throughout the archipelago, driven by more discerning tourist tastes and by a booming export market. Javanese woodcarvers are turning out magnificent traditional panels and innovative furniture commissioned by large hotels, and Balinese jewellers influenced by Western designs are producing works of stunning quality.

JAVA'S TOP 5 CLASSICAL MOSQUES

Indonesia's most revered mosques tend to be those built in the 15th and 16th centuries in Javanese towns that were among the first to convert to Islam. The 'classical' architectural style of these mosques includes tiered roofs clearly influenced by the Hindu culture that Islam had then only recently supplanted. They are curiously reminiscent of the Hindu temples still seen on Bali today. During the Suharto era in the late 20th century, hundreds of standardised, prefabricated mosques were shipped and erected all around Indonesia in pale imitation of this classical Javanese style.

» Mesjid Agung, Demak (p152)

» Mesjid Al-Manar, Kudus (p153)

» Mesjid Agung, Solo (p138)

» Mesjid Agung, Banten (p71)

» Masjid Kuno Bayan Beleq, Lombok (p326)

Tourist centres are fostering an increasing cross-fertilisation of craft styles: the 'primitive' Kalimantan statues, so in vogue in Balinese art shops, may well have been carved behind the shop or – more likely – in the vast crafts factories of Java.

Made in Indonesia: A Tribute to the Country's Craftspeople, by Warwick Purser, provides great photos and background information on the crafts of the country.

Woodcarving

Though the forests are vanishing, woodcarving traditions are flourishing. Often woodcarving is practised in conjunction with more practical activities such as house building. All traditional Indonesian dwellings have some provision for repelling unwanted spirits. The horned lion heads of Batak houses, the water buffalo representations on Toraja houses and the serpent carvings on Dayak houses all serve to protect inhabitants from evil influences.

On the outer islands, woodcarvings and statues are crafted to represent the spirit world and the ancestors who live there. Woodcarving is an intrinsic part of the Toraja's famed funerals: the deceased is represented by a *tau tau* (a life-sized wooden statue), and the coffin is adorned with carved animal heads. In the Ngaju and Dusun Dayak villages in Kalimantan, *temadu* (giant carved ancestor totems) also depict the dead.

The most favoured and durable wood in Indonesia is *jati* (teak), though this is getting increasingly expensive. Sandalwood is occasionally seen in Balinese carvings, as is mahogany and ebony (imported from Sulawesi and Kalimantan). Jackfruit is a common, cheap wood, though it tends to warp and split. Generally, local carvers use woods at hand: heavy ironwood and meranti (a hard wood) in Kalimantan, and belalu (a light wood) in Bali.

REGIONAL CARVING

Perhaps Indonesia's most famous woodcarvers are the Asmat of southwestern Papua. Shields, canoes, spears and drums are carved, but the most distinctive Asmat woodcarvings are *mbis* (ancestor poles). These poles show the dead, one above the other, and the open carved 'wing' at the top of the pole is a phallic symbol representing fertility and power. The poles are also an expression of revenge, and were traditionally carved to accompany a feast following a head-hunting raid.

In many regions, everyday objects are intricately carved. These include baby carriers and stools from Kalimantan, lacquered bowls from South Sumatra, bamboo containers from Sulawesi, doors from West Timor and horse effigies from Sumba.

Balinese woodcarving is the most ornamental and elaborate in Indonesia. The gods and demons of Balinese cosmology populate statues, temple doors and relief panels throughout the island. Western influence and demand for art and souvenirs has encouraged Balinese woodcarvers to reinvent their craft, echoing the 1930s revolution in Balinese painting by producing simpler, elongated statues of purely ornamental design with a natural finish.

In Java, the centre for woodcarving, especially carved furniture, is Jepara. The intricate crafts share Bali's Hindu-Buddhist tradition, adjusted to reflect Islam's prohibition on human representation. Another Javanese woodcarving centre is Kudus, where elaborate panels for traditional houses are produced.

Ikat

The Indonesian word 'ikat', meaning 'to tie' or 'to bind', signifies the intricately patterned cloth of threads that are painstakingly tie-dyed before being woven together. Ikat is produced in many regions, most notably in Nusa Tenggara.

GIFTS: HIGH

Amidst the endless piles of tourist tat, Indonesia has truly extraordinary items that make perfect gifts. The secret is finding them. Here are a few ideas:

» West Timor, Alor and Sumba have some spectacular naturally dyed ikat for sale. The best of the best can be found in Waingapu.

» Maubesi in Nusa Tenggara is home to a fab textile market. Look for shops selling local ikat, antique masks, statues, and carved beams, reliefs and doors from old Timorese homes.

» On South Sumatra, look for ceremonial *songket* sarongs that are used for marriages and other ceremonies near Palembang. They can take a month to make.

» Dayak rattan, *doyo* (bark beaten into cloth), carvings and other souvenirs from Kalimantan can be world-class.

» Street vendors in Bandaneira sell scrumptious kenari-nut brittle, a treat found only on the Banda Islands.

» Intricate and beautiful rattan items made in an ancient village in Bali are sold by Ashitaba, which has shops across the island and where you can shop for exquisite and artful goods for days on end.

Ikat garments come in an incredible diversity of colours and patterns: the spectacular ikat of Sumba and the elaborately patterned work of Flores (including *kapita,* used to wrap the dead) are the best known.

IKAT SEASONS

There are traditional times for the production of ikat. On Sumba the thread is spun between July and October, and the patterns bound between September and December. After the rains end in April, the dyeing is carried out. In August the weaving starts– more than a year after work on the thread began.

MAKING IKAT

Traditionally, ikat is made of hand-spun cotton. The whole process of ikat production – from planting the cotton to folding the finished product – is performed by women. Once the cotton is harvested, it is spun with a spindle. The thread is strengthened by immersing it in baths of crushed cassava, rice or maize, then threaded onto a winder.

In Tenganan (Bali), a cloth called *gringsing* is woven using a rare method of double ikat in which both warp and weft threads are pre=dyed.

Traditional dyes are made from natural sources. The most complex processes result in a rusty colour known as *kombu* (produced from the bark and roots of the *kombu* tree). Blue dyes come from the indigo plant, and purple or brown can be produced by dyeing the cloth deep blue and then dyeing it again with *kombu.*

Any sections that are not coloured are bound together with dye-resistant fibre. Each colour requires a separate tying-and-dyeing process. The sequence of colouring takes into consideration the effect of each application of dye. This requires great skill, as the dyer has to work out – before the threads are woven – exactly which parts of the thread are to receive which colour in order to create the pattern of the final cloth. After the thread has been dyed, the cloth is woven on a simple hand loom.

ORIGINS & MEANING OF IKAT

Ikat technique was most likely introduced 2000 years ago by Dongson migrants from southern China and Vietnam.

Ikat styles vary according to the village and the gender of the wearer, and some styles are reserved for special purposes. In parts of Nusa Tenggara, high-quality ikat is part of a bride's dowry. Until recently on Sumba, only members of the highest clans could make and wear ikat textiles. Certain motifs were traditionally reserved for noble families (as on Sumba and Rote) or members of a specific tribe or clan (as on Sabu or among the Atoni of West Timor). The function of ikat as an indicator of social status has since declined.

MOTIFS & PATTERNS

Some experts believe that motifs found on Sumba, such as front views of people, animals and birds, stem from an artistic tradition even older than Dongson, whose influence was geometric motifs like diamond and key shapes (which often go together), meanders and spirals.

One strong influence was *patola* cloth from Gujarat in India. In the 16th and 17th centuries these became highly prized in Indonesia, and one characteristic motif – a hexagon framing a four-pronged star – was copied by local ikat weavers. On the best *patola* and geometric ikat, repeated small patterns combine to form larger patterns, like a mandala. Over the past century, European styles have influenced the motifs used in ikat.

Batik painting, an odd blend of craft and art that all-too-often is neither, remains popular in Yogyakarta, where it was invented as a pastime for unemployed youth. Though most batik painting is tourist schlock, there are some talented artists working in the medium.

Songket

Songket is silk cloth interwoven with gold or silver threads, although imitation silver or gold is often used in modern pieces. *Songket* is most commonly found in heavily Islamic regions, such as Aceh, and among the coastal Malays, but Bali also has a strong *songket* tradition.

Batik

The technique of applying wax or other dye-resistant substances (like rice paste) to cloth to produce a design is found in many parts of the world, but none is as famous as the batik of Java. Javanese batik dates from the 12th century, and opinion is divided as to whether batik is an indigenous craft or imported from India along with Hindu religious and cultural traditions.

The word 'batik' is an old Javanese word meaning 'to dot'. Javanese batik was a major weapon in the competition for social status in the royal courts. The ability to devote extensive resources to the painstaking

CHOOSING IKAT

Unless you are looking for inexpensive machine-made ikat, shopping is best left to the experts. Even trekking out to an 'ikat village' may be in vain: the photogenic woman sitting at a wooden loom may be only for show. But if you insist, here are some tips on recognising the traditional product:

Thread Hand-spun cotton has a less perfect 'twist' to it than factory cloth.

Weave Hand-woven cloth, whether made from hand-spun or factory thread, feels rougher and, when new, stiffer than machine-woven cloth. It will probably have minor imperfections in the weave.

Dyes Until you've seen enough ikat to get a feel for whether colours are natural or chemical, you often have to rely on your instincts as to whether they are 'earthy' enough. Some cloths contain both natural and artificial dyes.

Dyeing method The patterns on cloths which have been individually tie-dyed using the traditional method are rarely perfectly defined, but they're unlikely to have the detached specks of colour that often appear on mass-dyed cloth.

Age No matter what anybody tells you, there are very few antique cloths around. There are several processes to make cloth look old.

creation of fine batik demonstrated wealth and power. Certain designs indicated courtly rank, and a courtier risked public humiliation, or worse, by daring to wear the wrong sarong.

In 2009 Unesco added Indonesian batik to its Intangible Cultural Heritage list.

MAKING BATIK

The finest batik is *batik tulis* (hand-painted or literally 'written' batik). Designs are first traced out onto cloth, then patterns are drawn in hot wax with a *canting*, a pen-like instrument. The wax-covered areas resist colour change when immersed in a dye bath. The waxing and dyeing, with increasingly darker shades, continues until the final colours are achieved. Wax is added to protect previously dyed areas or scraped off to expose new areas to the dye. Finally, all the wax is scraped off and the cloth boiled to remove all traces of wax.

Basketwork & Beadwork

Some of the finest basketwork in Indonesia comes from Lombok. The spiral woven rattan work is very fine and large baskets are woven using this method; smaller receptacles topped with wooden carvings are also popular.

In Java, Tasikmalaya is a major cane-weaving centre, often adapting baskets and vessels to modern uses with the introduction of zips and plastic linings. The Minangkabau people, centred around Bukittinggi, also produce interesting palm-leaf bags and purses, while the *lontar* palm is used extensively in weaving on West Timor, Rote and other outer eastern islands. The Dayak of Kalimantan produce some superb woven baskets and string bags.

Some of the most colourful and attractive beadwork is made by the Toraja of Sulawesi. Beadwork can be found all over Nusa Tenggara and in the Dayak region of Kalimantan. Small, highly prized cowrie shells are used like beads and are found on Dayak and Lombok works, though the best application of these shells is as intricate beading in Sumbanese tapestries.

Kris

No ordinary knife, the wavy-bladed traditional dagger known as a kris is a mandatory possession of a Javanese gentleman; it's said to be endowed

GIFTS: LOW

Looking to show close friends and relatives just how deep you plunged into Indonesian culture? Then give them a penis gourd.

Papua is the sweet spot for Indonesian penis gourds; in one stroke you can come up with a gift that will literally keep giving. Traditionally used by indigenous men in the province's highlands, they are attached to the testicles by a small loop of fibre. Sizes, shapes and colours vary across cultural groups but you can pick one up for around 5000Rp to 60,000Rp. A good place to check out the merchandise is Wamena. Remember: bargain hard as competition is stiff.

If you'd rather not give something as intimate as a penis gourd, then perhaps you should do just the opposite and give the prized possession of head-hunters everywhere: a *mandau* from Kalimantan. Once the Dayak weapon of choice, this indigenous machete is still slung from the hips of most men in the Kalimantan interior. You can purchase traditional pieces for around 100,000Rp to 250,000Rp. A good place to shop is in the longhouse village of Tanjung Isuy.

Obviously, you'll need to check a bag to get a *mandau* home, but you can probably simply wear your new gourd. And if your visit doesn't take you near these places, you can always buy the top-selling souvenir on Bali: a bottle opener shaped like a penis.

with supernatural powers and to be treated with the utmost respect. A kris owner ritually bathes and polishes his weapon, stores it in an auspicious location, and pays close attention to every rattle and scrape emanating from the blade and sheath in the dead of the night.

Some think the Javanese kris (from *iris,* meaning 'to cut') is derived from the bronze daggers produced by the Dongson around the 1st century AD. Bas-reliefs of a kris appear in the 14th-century Panataran temple complex in East Java, and the carrying of the kris as a custom in Java was noted in 15th-century Chinese records. The kris remains an integral part of men's ceremonial dress.

Distinctive features, the number of curves in the blade and the damascene design on the blade are read to indicate good or bad fortune for its owner. The number of curves in the blade has symbolic meaning: five curves symbolise the five Pandava brothers of the Mahabharata epic; three represents fire, ardour and passion. Although the blade is the most important part of the kris, the hilt and scabbard are also beautifully decorated.

Although the kris is mostly associated with Java and Bali, larger and less ornate variations are found in Sumatra, Kalimantan and Sulawesi.

Puppets

The most famous puppets of Indonesia are the carved leather *wayang kulit* puppets. These intricate lace figures are cut from buffalo hide with a sharp, chisel-like stylus, and then painted. They are produced in Bali and Java, particularly in Central Java. The leaf-shaped *kayon* representing the 'tree' or 'mountain of life' is also made of leather and is used to end scenes during a performance.

Wayang golek are three-dimensional wooden puppets found in Central and West Java. The *wayang klitik* puppets are the rarer flat wooden puppets of East Java.

A carefully selected list of books about art, culture and Indonesian writers, dancers and musicians can be found at www.ganeshabooksbali.com.

Jewellery

The ubiquitous *toko mas* (gold shop) found in every Indonesian city is mostly an investment house selling gold jewellery by weight – design and workmanship take a back seat. However, gold and silverwork does have a long history in Indonesia. Some of the best gold jewellery comes from Aceh, where fine filigree work is produced, while chunky bracelets and earrings are produced in the Batak region.

Balinese jewellery is nearly always handworked and rarely involves casting techniques. Balinese work is innovative, employing both traditional designs and those adapted from jewellery presented by Western buyers.

Kota Gede in Yogyakarta is famous for its fine filigree work. Silverware from here tends to be more traditional, but new designs are also being adapted. As well as jewellery, Kota Gede produces a wide range of silver tableware.

Sport

Soccer and badminton are the national sporting obsessions. Indonesian badminton players had a good record at the Olympics (three medals in 2008) until London in 2012. Disaster struck when two key players on the women's doubles team were booted off the team after they admitted to throwing matches in an effort to manipulate the quarter-final draw.

Although international success has eluded Indonesian soccer (football) teams, it is played with fervour on grassy verges across the archipelago.

Many regions, particularly those with a history of tribal warfare, stage traditional contests of various kinds to accompany weddings, harvest

MASKS

Although carved masks exist throughout the archipelago, the most readily identifiable form of mask is the *topeng*, used in *wayang topeng*, the masked dance-dramas of Java and Bali. Dancers perform local tales or adaptations of Hindu epics such as the Mahabharata, with the masks used to represent different characters. Masks vary from the stylised but plain masks of Central and West Java to the heavily carved masks of East Java.

Balinese masks are less stylised and more naturalistic than in Java – the Balinese save their love of colour and detail for the masks of the Barong dance, starring a mythical lion-dog creature who fights tirelessly against evil. Look for masks in shops in and around Ubud.

festivals and other ceremonial events. Mock battles are sometimes staged in Papua, caci whip fights are a speciality in Flores and men fight with sticks and shields in Lombok, but the most spectacular ceremonial fight is seen during Sumba's Pasola Festival (p399), where every February and March horse riders in traditional dress hurl spears at each other.

In Bali and on other islands, the real sporting passion is reserved for cockfighting, which means the spectators (virtually all men) watch and bet while birds brawl. Although nominally illegal, restrictions were recently eased so that many matches can be held openly.

Environment

The Land

It makes sense that Indonesians call their country Tanah Air Kita (literally, 'Our Land and Water'), as it's the world's most expansive archipelago. Of the 17,000-plus islands, about 6000 are inhabited. These diverse lands and surrounding waters have an astonishing collection of plant and animal life. Yet this very bounty of life is its own worst enemy, as resource development threatens virtually every corner of Indonesia.

Volcanoes

If you're keen to ascend spectacular peaks, watch the sun rise through the haze of steaming craters and peer into the earth's bubbling core, you've come to the right place. Indonesia is the destination for volcano enthusiasts.

On most of the main islands, the landscape is dominated by volcanic cones, most long dormant, others very much active. Some of these volcanoes have erupted with such force that they have literally made history. The ash clouds from the cataclysmic 1815 eruption of Gunung Tambora in Sumbawa modified the global climate for a year, causing massive crop failures in Europe. The 1883 eruption of Krakatau between Java and Sumatra generated tsunamis that killed tens of thousands. It became the first global media event, thanks to the newly completed global telegraph network.

The archipelago's ubiquitous volcanoes play a pivotal role in most Indonesian cultures. In Bali and Java, major places of worship grace the slopes of prominent volcanic cones, and eruptions are taken as demonstrations of divine disappointment or anger.

Wild Indonesia

From tiny tarsiers to massive stinking flowers, the range of natural attractions in Indonesia is phenomenal. In 2006, the discovery of several new species of wildlife in Pegunungan Foja, a Papuan mountain range, highlighted the archipelago's astounding biodiversity. Unfortunately,

RING OF FIRE

Indonesia lies on a significant segment of the Pacific 'Ring of Fire', where two large crustal plates (the Indian Ocean and western Pacific) are forced under the massive Eurasian plate, where they melt at approximately 100km beneath the surface. Some of the magma rises and erupts to form the string of volcanic islands across Indonesia. Its volcanoes do erupt, sometimes with shocking consequences. With tectonic activity comes devastating earthquakes and tsunamis, such as those of Boxing Day 2004, off Java in July 2006 and Sumatra in 2009.

discoveries are lagging far behind destruction of natural habitats, meaning that much of Indonesia's rich biological heritage will pass unrecorded into extinction.

Papua is home to more than half the animal and plant species in Indonesia, including more than 190 mammals, 550 breeding birds, and more than 2000 types of orchid.

Animals

Indonesia's wildlife is as diverse as everything else about the archipelago. Great apes, tigers, elephants and monkeys – lots of monkeys – plus one mean lizard are just some of the more notable critters you may encounter. And then there are the thousands of species that you've never seen on a nature special or in a zoo, such as the one-horned Javan rhinoceros. This is one of the world's most critically endangered mammals whose last refuge in Indonesia is the Ujung Kulon National Park. Consider underwater life as well and the biodiversity here is astonishing.

ORANGUTANS

Exemplifying a placid lifestyle that appeals to many a human slacker, Indonesia's orangutans are an iconic part of the nation's image. The world's largest arboreal mammal, they once swung through the forest canopy throughout all of Southeast Asia, but are now found only in Sumatra and Borneo. Researchers fear that the few that do remain will not survive the continued loss of habitat to logging and agriculture.

Deeply fascinating to view, orangutans (literally, 'people of the forest') have an important role in drawing people into the Indonesian wild. Travellers exposed to the exotic beauty of these lands often return home ready to fight for its salvation.

At the other end of the scale, the Sangkulirang Mountains in East Kalimantan are home to what must be the least disturbed orangutans on the planet: the 2000 here were only discovered in 2008.

For more info on orangutans, see p620.

KOMODO DRAGONS

Tales of beasts with huge claws, menacing teeth and evil yellow forked tongues floated around the islands of Nusa Tenggara for centuries. This continued until around 100 years ago, when the first Westerners brought one out of its namesake island home near Flores.

As menacing as these 2.5m-long lizards look, their disposition is worse. Scores of humans have perished after being attacked, and the Komodos regularly stalk and eat small deer. One researcher compared the sound of a Komodo pounding across the ground in pursuit to that of a machine gun. Only in 2009 was one of the lizard's deadly secrets revealed: venom in its bite sends its victim into shock and prevents blood from clotting. Yikes!

BEST PLACES TO SEE ORANGUTANS

Although Sumatra is famous for orangutans, don't underestimate Kalimantan.

Sumatra – Bukit Lawang Home to around 5000 orangutans, this rehabilitation centre allows you to get up close and personal with Asia's great ape.

Kalimantan – Tanjung Puting National Park Offers several feeding stations like Bukit Lawang, but strings them together in an authentic jungle river cruise, making this our top choice.

Kalimantan – Palangka Raya Circumnavigate the Sungai Kahayan's Orangutan Island in high style (p626) and visit the nearby Nyaru Menteng rehabilitation facility.

Kalimantan – Wehea Forest This virgin rainforest offers the purest experience of them all, but you'll need an excellent guide, patience, and trekking shoes.

ENDANGERED SPECIES

The Greater Sunda Islands, comprising Sumatra, Java, Kalimantan and Bali, were once highland regions of a land mass – now called the Sunda Shelf – that extended from the Asian mainland. Some large Asian land animals still survive in this area, including tigers, rhinoceroses, leopards and sun bears, but their existence is tenuous at best.

Despite frequent claims of sightings, the Javan tiger is probably extinct. The Sumatran tiger is literally fighting for survival, as there have been several incidents of tigers killing loggers trespassing in protected habitats. Leopards (the black leopard, or panther, is more common in Southeast Asia) are rare but still live in Sumatra and in Java's Ujung Kulon National Park. This park is also home to the rare, almost extinct, one-horned Javan rhinoceros. Rhinos have not fared well in Indonesia and the two-horned variety, found in Sumatra, is also on the endangered list.

Perhaps the most famous, and most endangered Indonesian animal is the orangutan, which is under constant threat from logging. Incidents of animals being killed are ongoing. One especially tragic tale reported by the Indonesian news agency Antara in 2012 was about an adult orangutan which wandered onto a palm oil plantation and died after locals set the tree it was sheltering in on fire to drive it off.

Sumatran elephants are another celebrity endangered species, being driven into overcrowded, underfunded refuges as their forest habitats are cleared for plantations and farming. Kalimantan also has a few wild elephants in the northeast at Sebuku Sembakung, but they are very rare and the species is most probably introduced.

In 2011 the International Rhino Foundation declared the Javan rhino extinct in Vietnam, leaving the estimated 50 critters living on Java's Ujung Kulon Peninsula the only examples left in the wild.

Birds

Astrapias, sicklebills, rifle birds and manucodes are just some of the exotic and beautifully feathered creatures you'll see in the skies of Indonesia. On Papua alone, there isn't just one type of bird called 'bird of paradise', but 30. For many birdwatchers, the dream of a lifetime is to witness a pair of these birds perform their spectacular mating dance.

Birdwatching is popular in many of the national parks; guides will always be ready to point out birds, although they may not know much more about them than you. Periplus's illustrated guidebook *Birding Indonesia* makes a good companion. On Kalimantan, Tangkoko-Batuangas Dua Saudara Nature Reserve has regular birdwatching tours. In Bali, you can go on guided walks looking for birds in and around Ubud.

Papua easily wins the birdwatching crown, however. Its range of birds includes migrating species from Australia and as far as Siberia.

Life Underwater

Indonesia's incredible range of life on land is easily matched beneath the waves. The waters around Komodo, Sulawesi, the east coast of Papua, and even some spots in Java and Bali are home to a kaleidoscopic array of corals, reef dwellers and pelagic marine life.

Huge sunfish, up to 2.5m long and twice as high, are a much-treasured sight for divers. These enigmatic fish can usually be found feeding on jellyfish and plankton in the balmy waters around many of Indonesia's islands, large and small. Manta rays are also found in abundance. Even above the waves you're likely to see porpoises or other sea mammals.

One hawksbill sea turtle that visited Bali was tracked for the following year. His destinations: Java, Kalimantan, Australia (Perth and much of Queensland) and then back to Bali.

Plants

Simply wandering a deserted back lane in Bali, a cathedral of bamboo arching over the road, will be enough to convince you of Indonesia's botanical magic.

BEAUTY SPOTS

Jaw-dropping beauty can be found across Indonesia, often when you least expect it. Here are five of our favourites (culled from a long list).

Gunung Bromo It may not be Java's tallest volcano, but it's easily its most magnificent. From its summit you can see two other volcanoes (one in various stages of activity), all set in the vast caldera of yet another volcano.

Pulau Weh An idyllic tropical island off Sumatra with superb diving in its azure waters.

Togean Islands An adventure to reach, but the effort is more than repaid with rings of perfect beaches, dense jade-green forests and a perfect low-key vibe.

Banda Islands On the verge of being descended upon by the tourist mobs, but like cookies in a jar to a kid, the Banda Islands remain tantalisingly out of reach. The 10 islands spiral and twist around each other, agleam with white, deserted sands.

Danau Sentani A lake near the coast of Papua, dotted along the shore with timeless fishing villages built on stilts over the reflecting waters. At sunset and sunrise the water glows with every colour in the rainbow.

Whether cultivated or wild, frangipani trees are alive with fragrant blooms, many ready to drop into your hand. Head off on a trek and be prepared for a profusion of orchids (2500 different species at last count), flowers, vines and magnificent brooding banyan trees. You can expect a riot of bougainvillea, lotus blossoms, hibiscus and a kaleidoscope of other blooms across the archipelago. Impossibly complex heliconias hang from vines in all their multifaceted crimson, orange and golden glory. In forested areas, teak, clove, rattan and a plethora of palms are among the trees providing welcome shade from the equatorial sun.

Amid all of the luxuriant flora are many edible plants. Passionfruit is common, as are bananas. Look for coffee plantations, especially in the hills of Bali near Munduk. On Maluku – the original Spice Islands – you can still catch the scent of vanilla. Throughout Indonesia, markets abound with oodles of tropical fruits and citrus.

But it wouldn't be Indonesia without some real characters. Consider *Rafflesia arnoldii*, the world's largest flower, and the *Amorphophallus titanum*, the world's tallest flower. Both can be found on Sumatra and parts of Kalimantan and Java. In fact, the former may well be the world's stinkiest flower.

National Parks & Protected Areas

Despite a constant nipping at the edges by illegal loggers and settlers, Indonesia still has large tracts of protected forest and national parks, and many new national parks have been proclaimed in recent years. The parks are managed by the Directorate General of Forest Protection and Nature Conservation (PHKA or KSDA). National parks receive greater international recognition and funding than nature, wildlife and marine reserves, of which there are also many in Indonesia.

Most of Indonesia's national parks are very isolated, but the extra effort required to get to them is more than rewarded by the country's magnificent wilderness. Visitor facilities are minimal at best, but at many of the parks you'll find locals who are enthusiastic about their park and ready to guide you to its hidden gems.

Environmental Issues

Indonesian forests continue to be cleared at a horrific rate, both through illegal logging and conversion to palm-oil plantations. Greenpeace estimates that 50% of Indonesia's 150 million hectares of forests have been cleared, and the government allows an average 1.8 million hectares a year in additional clearance. Furthermore, upwards of 70% of Indonesia's mangrove forests have been damaged according to the US-based Mangrove Action Project. It's a double tragedy given the important role mangroves play in filtering the country's ever-more-polluted waters.

The side effects of deforestation are felt across the nation and beyond: floods and landslides wash away valuable topsoil, rivers become sluggish and fetid, and haze from clearing fires blankets Malaysia and Singapore every dry season. The problems flow right through to Indonesia's coastline and seas, where more than 80% of reef habitat is considered to be at risk by the UN.

TOP 10 NATIONAL PARKS & RESERVES

PARK	LOCATION	FEATURES	ACTIVITIES	BEST TIME TO VISIT
Gunung Leuser	Sumatra	biologically diverse conservation area, rivers, rainforest, mountains; tigers, rhinoceroses, elephants, primates such as orangutans and white-breasted Thomas' leaf monkeys	orangutan viewing, wildlife spotting, birdwatching; trekking, rafting	Dec-Mar
Tanjung Puting	Kalimantan	tropical rainforest, mangrove forest, wetlands; orangutans, macaques, proboscis monkeys, diverse wildlife	orangutan viewing, birdwatching	May-Sep
Kelimutu	Nusa Tenggara	coloured lakes	vulcanology, short walks	Apr-Sep
Gunung Rinjani	Nusa Tenggara	volcano	trekking, volcano climbing	Apr-Sep
Ujung Kulon	Java	lowland rainforest, scrub, grassy plains, swamps, sandy beaches; one-horned rhinoceroses, otters, squirrels, white-breasted Thomas' leaf monkeys, gibbons	jungle walks; wildlife spotting	Apr-Oct
Gunung Bromo	Java	volcanic landscape	crater climbing	Apr-Oct
Pulau Bunaken	Sulawesi	coral fringed islands	snorkelling, diving, island lazing	Jun-Jan
Kerinci Seblat	Sumatra	mountainous rainforest, one of Sumatra's highest peaks	trekking; wildlife spotting, birdwatching	Dec-Mar
Komodo	Nusa Tenggara	Komodo dragon	snorkelling, diving	Apr-Sep
Bali Barat	Bali	low hills, grasslands, coral-fringed coasts	snorkelling, diving; wildlife spotting	year round

Of course the people most affected are those who live closest to, or within, the forested areas. Evictions, restricted access and loss of land has seen many local communities lose their lifeline and spill into spreading urban areas, with ever-increasing populations living below the poverty line.

Norway has pledged to contribute $1 billion to a fund designed to slow the loss of Indonesia's forests and reduce its carbon emissions. In an effort to combat past abuses, the money carries significant safeguards against corruption.

The rampant consumerism of the burgeoning middle class is straining the nation's wholly inadequate infrastructure. Private vehicles clog urban streets, creating massive air pollution; waste-removal services have difficulty coping with household and industrial garbage; and a total lack of sewerage disposal systems makes water from most sources undrinkable without boiling, putting further pressure on kerosene and firewood supplies.

Local Action

Many Indonesians are not just idly standing by while there are environmental threats to their nation. There is a burgeoning environmental movement across the nation. One example is the work being done by Yayasan Orangutan Indonesia (Yayorin; Indonesia Orangutan Foundation; www.yayorin.org) in Kalimantan, which aims to teach people to protect orangutans and their environment.

Another group which wins plaudits is the SOS Sea Turtles campaign (www.sos-seaturtles.ch), which spotlights turtle abuse. Its successes include spotlighting the illegal poaching of turtles at Wakatobi National Park in Sulawesi for sale in Bali. Together with groups such as Profauna (www.profauna.or.id), concerned locals have made real progress in the conservation of sea turtles in Indonesia.

Local Issues

There is much to be done to try to protect Indonesia's magnificence, a matter important to all the world. There are many pressing issues across the archipelago.

JAVA

Deforestation and rampant development causes massive flooding in Jakarta and other cities, including Semarang, every rainy season. This

ENVIRONMENTAL CONCERNS

Environmental issues often seem to be alien in Indonesia, and Indonesians are wont to say to Westerners: 'We are a poor country that needs to exploit our natural resources. How can you tell us not to cut down our forests when you have already cut down all your own?' That said, Indonesia has a growing environmental awareness and environmental laws, even if they are poorly enforced.

There are laws to protect endangered species, but you still see such creatures for sale in local bird markets. Many souvenirs are made from threatened species: turtle-shell products, sea shells, snakeskin, stuffed birds and framed butterflies are readily available in Indonesia. Not only does buying them encourage ecological damage, but import into most countries is banned and they will be confiscated by customs. See the Convention on International Trade in Endangered Species (CITES; www.cites.org) for more information.

There are plenty of ways you can help protect Indonesia's environment during your visit, including trekking and diving responsibly. There are also groups you can contact that are active in preserving Indonesia's environment.

See p17 for a list of ways you can help protect Indonesia's environment during your visit. Also see p37 for ways to responsibly trek on land and p30 for ways to responsibly dive underwater. See p766 for groups active in preserving Indonesia's environment.

results in mass social upheaval and chokes surviving coastal mangroves. In 2011, Jakarta's environmental agency found that 71% of the city's rivers were 'heavily polluted'.

BALI

This beautiful island is its own worst enemy: it can't help being popular. Walhi, the Indonesian Forum for Environment (www.walhi.or.id), estimates that the average hotel room accounts for 3000L of water used by and for guests. The typical golf course needs three million litres a day. Hence, a place fabled for its water is now running short. In addition, rice fields are being converted to commercial land at a rate of about 600 to 1000 hectares a year.

Traffic jams and clogged roads are a blight on the southern part of the island.

World surfing champion Kelly Slater caused a stir with his 2012 tweet: 'If Bali doesn't Do Something serious about this pollution it'll be impossible to surf here in a few years. Worst I've ever seen'.

NUSA TENGGARA

On southern Lombok, there is constant rumour and talk about huge developments to the so-far mostly untouched beautiful beach area of Kuta. There is little existing infrastructure now to support major projects.

Environmental concerns over a huge new mining operation in Bima caused crowds of locals to protest in early 2012. This turned deadly when police opened fire on the crowd, killing three. Shortly thereafter a mob burned local government offices and the mine's permits were temporarily revoked.

Elsewhere, dynamite fishing and poaching by locals is an ongoing concern in Komodo National Park, a Unesco-recognised site. A joint-venture to protect the site, partially funded by the Nature Conservancy, collapsed in 2010 and reported incidents of reef and fish destruction have soared according to reports in the *Jakarta Globe*.

MALUKU

Maluku has a major rubbish disposal problem. Although taking ferries rather than planes is considered ecologically preferable, boats regularly dump enormous amounts of rubbish into the once-pristine waters of these isolated islands.

The *Jakarta Globe* has reported on the arrest and harassment of activists who have been critical of mining companies.

PAPUA

Papua is a target for rogue loggers. The government has supposedly clamped down on this but a WWF report said: 'As commercial stands of timber in Sumatra and Kalimantan (Indonesian Borneo) are increasingly exhausted, the logging industry has shifted eastwards to New Guinea... In Papua Province, vulnerable tree species such as merbau are cut illegally and exported to China, Japan, Korea and Vietnam, despite a logging ban imposed in 2001'.

Meanwhile, even as efforts were being made to reduce logging, land clearances for palm-oil production are up, the *Guardian* reports.

WALHI

Walhi, the Indonesian Forum for Environment, is working to protect Indonesia's environment. Find out more and offer your support at www.walhi.or.id.

SUMATRA

Deforestation is a massive problem, threatening the jungle and all its inhabitants.

According to a report released by World Wildlife Fund (WWF) in 2008: 'The resulting average annual CO_2 from forest loss, degradation, peat decomposition and fires between 1990–2007 in Riau province alone was 0.22 gigatons – higher than that of the Netherlands, or equivalent to 58% of Australia's total annual emissions or 39% of the UK's annual emissions'. Sumatran tigers and elephants are being hardest hit. The elephant population in Riau has decreased by 84% from an estimated 1067 to 1617 in 1984 to possibly as few as 210, and tiger numbers have decreased by 70% in 25 years, from 640 to 192.

Every year, smoke and haze from fires used to clear farmland and plantations choke the skies over the island and its neighbours. At times Singapore seems to be under a permanent haze.

KALIMANTAN

In Gunung Palung National Park you can hear chainsaws at work every day. And this is but one example of the threats to the environment across Borneo. On the positive side, the World Wildlife Fund has set up a series of large protected areas with the goal of protecting 220,000 sq km of the island – almost one third – by 2020. Meanwhile in the Wehea Forest, a community-run protected area is experiencing some success by tying the health of the forest to the health of the Wehea Dayak culture, and using a large group of local rangers to patrol it. This is an important test case of a new conservation model.

Recent bad decisions have had a huge impact. In 2002, for example, the East Kalimantan administration built a 60km road through Kutai National Park. New villages were soon built in very sensitive orangutan habitat and the number of orangutans collapsed. Today, it barely qualifies as a national park.

Its proximity to the Philippines makes the port at Bitung on Sulawesi an unfortunate hot spot for wildlife smuggling. Tasikoki (www.tasikoki.org) is an entirely volunteer-run organisation that rescues and cares for animals confiscated from smugglers.

SULAWESI

There are concerns over reports of a new Chinese-financed mining operation near the beautiful dive areas of Bangka Islands. This would be but one more mine in an area riddled with illegal tin mines, as Bloomberg Business Week reported. Soaring demand for tin – vital for gadgets such as cell phones – has destroyed large swaths of the island and caused a huge increase in toxic tailings running off into the water.

Food & Drink

When you eat in Indonesia you savour the essence of the country. The abundance of rice reflects Indonesia's fertile landscape, the spices are reminiscent of a time of trade and invasion, and the fiery chilli echoes the passion of the people. Indonesian cuisine is really one big food swap. Chinese, Portuguese, colonists and traders have all influenced the ingredients that appear at the Indonesian table, and the cuisine has been further shaped over time by the archipelago's diverse landscape, people and culture.

Indonesian cooking is not complex, and its ingredients maintain their distinct flavours. Coriander, cumin, chilli, lemon grass, coconut, soy sauce and palm sugar are all important flavourings; sambal is a crucial condiment and comes in myriad variations.

Fish is a favourite and the seafood restaurants are often of a good standard. Indonesians traditionally eat with their fingers, hence the stickiness of the rice. Sate (skewered meat), nasi goreng (fried rice) and gado gado (vegetables with peanut sauce) are some of Indonesia's most famous dishes.

In the Banda Islands you'll find nutmeg jam served on bread and pancakes, fitting as these were the original Spice Islands, where nutmeg was first cultivated.

Regional Flavours

Java

The cuisine of the Betawi (original inhabitants of the Jakarta region) is known for its richness. Gado gado is a Betawi original, as is *ketoprak* (noodles, bean sprouts and tofu with soy and peanut sauce; named after a musical style, as it resembles the sound of ingredients being chopped). *Soto Betawi* (beef soup) is made creamy with coconut milk. There's also

SURPRISING TASTES

Everyday eating in Indonesia can challenge your palette. Here are a few favorites:

» In Nusa Tenggara Timor (Alor and Flores in particular), there is a scintillatingly spicy, oily and mildly astringent dish called *ikan kuah assam* (tamarind fish soup). It is absolutely sensational. It's basically a fish steak or half a fish (bones often included) steamed and swimming in spicy tamarind broth. It's simple, life affirming, bliss inducing and could easily be your favourite dish of the trip.

» The durian has a serious public-image problem. This fruit's spiky skin looks like a Spanish Inquisition torture tool; opening it releases the fruit's odorous power. Most people form a lifelong passion – or aversion – on their first taste of this sulphury, custardy fruit.

» Balinese specialities are readily available; look for warungs advertising *siobak* (minced pig's head, stomach, tongue and skin cooked with spices).

» For avocado juice, take an avocado, blend with ice and condensed milk (or chocolate syrup) and serve. Indonesians don't consider this strange, as the avocado is just another sweet fruit.

nasi uduk (rice cooked in coconut milk, served with meat, tofu and/or vegetables).

In West Java, the Sundanese love their greens. Their specialities include *karedok* (salad of long beans, bean sprouts and cucumber with spicy sauce), *soto Bandung* (beef-and-vegetable soup with lemon grass) and *ketupat tahu* (pressed rice, bean sprouts and tofu with soy and peanut sauce). Sundanese sweet specialities include *colenak* (roasted cassava with coconut sauce) and *ulen* (roasted sticky rice with peanut sauce); both best eaten warm. Bandung's cooler hills are the place for *bandrek* (ginger tea with coconut and pepper) and *bajigur* (spiced coffee with coconut milk).

Central Javan food is sweet, even the curries like *gudeg* (jackfruit curry). Yogyakarta specialities include *ayam goreng* (fried chicken) and *kelepon* (green rice-flour balls with a palm-sugar filling). In Solo, specialities include *nasi liwet* (rice with coconut milk, unripe papaya, garlic and shallots, served with chicken or egg) and *serabi* (coconut-milk pancakes topped with chocolate, banana or jackfruit).

SWEET & SPICY

Java's Cianjur region is famous for its sweet, spicy cuisine. Dishes include: *lontong* (sticky rice with tofu in a delicious, sweet coconut sauce); the best beef sate in Java, locally known as *marangi*; and *pandan wangi* rice, fragrantly flavoured rice that's often cooked with lemon grass and spices.

There's a lot of crossover between Central and East Javan cuisine. Fish is popular, especially *pecel lele* (deep-fried catfish served with rice and *pecel*). The best *pecel* (peanut sauce) comes from the town of Madiun.

Two very popular Madurese dishes are *soto Madura* (beef soup with lime, pepper, peanuts, chilli and ginger) and *sate Madura* (skewered meat with sweet soy sauce).

Bali

Balinese specialities are easy to find, as visitor-friendly warungs offer high-quality Balinese dishes, with several options of spiciness. Many restaurants offer the hugely popular Balinese dish, *babi guling* (spit-roast pig stuffed with chilli, turmeric, garlic and ginger) on a day's notice, although you're best off getting it from any of many warungs that specialise in it. Look for the pigs head drawn on the sign or a real one in a display case. Also popular is *bebek betutu* (duck stuffed with spices, wrapped in banana leaves and coconut husks, and cooked in embers).

The local sate, *sate lilit*, is made with minced, spiced meat pressed onto skewers. Look for spicy dishes like *lawar* (salad of chopped coconut, garlic and chilli with pork or chicken meat and blood).

Nusa Tenggara

In dry east Nusa Tenggara you'll eat less rice (although much is imported) and more sago, corn, cassava and taro. Fish remains popular and one local dish is Sumbawa's *sepat* (shredded fish in coconut and mango sauce).

The Sasak people of Lombok like spicy *ayam Taliwang* (roasted chicken served with a peanut, tomato, chilli and lime dip) and *pelecing* sauce (made with chilli, shrimp paste and tomato). Also recommended is *sate*

COOKING COURSES

If you want to carry on enjoying the tastes of Indonesia after you go home, Bali has several cooking schools where you can learn everything from how to shop in the markets and the basics of Indonesian cuisine to advanced cooking techniques. Best of all though is that you get to eat what you make! The following are two of the best:

Bumbu Bali Cooking School (p232) Long-time resident and cookbook author Heinz von Holzen runs a cooking school from his excellent South Bali restaurant.

Casa Luna Cooking School (p252) Half-day courses cover cooking techniques, ingredients and the cultural background of the Balinese kitchen.

pusut (minced meat or fish sate, mixed with coconut and grilled on sugar-cane skewers). Nonmeat dishes include *kelor* (soup with vegetables) and *timun urap* (cucumber with coconut, onion and garlic).

Maluku

A typical Maluku meal is tuna and *dabu-dabu* (raw vegetables with a chilli and fish-paste sauce). Sometimes fish is made into *kohu-kohu* (fish salad with citrus fruit and chilli). Sago pith is used to make porridge, bread and *mutiara* (small, jelly-like 'beans' that are added to desserts and sweet drinks). Boiled cassava (*kasbi*) is a kitchen staple as it's cheaper than rice.

Papua

Little rice is grown here: indigenous Papuans get their carbs from other sources and the rice eaten by migrants from elsewhere in Indonesia is mostly imported. In the highlands of Papua the sweet potato is king. The Dani people grow around 60 varieties, some of which can only be eaten by the elders.

In the lowlands the sago palm provides the starchy staple food: its pulped-up pith is turned into hard, moist sago cakes, to which water is added to make *papeda*, a kind of gluey paste usually eaten with fish in a yellow turmeric-and-lime sauce. You may find the fish tastier than the *papeda*. Some lowlanders also eat the sago beetle grubs found in rotting sago palms.

Rice in the field is called *padi;* rice grain at the market is called *beras;* cooked rice on your plate is called *nasi.*

Sumatra

In West Sumatra, beef is used in *rendang* (beef coconut curry). The region is the home of Padang cuisine, and the market in Bukittinggi is a great place to sample *nasi Kapau* (cuisine from the village of Kapau). It's similar to Padang food but uses more vegetables. There's also *ampiang dadiah* (buffalo yoghurt with palm-sugar syrup, coconut and rice) and *bubur kampiun* (mung-bean porridge with banana and rice yoghurt).

In North Sumatra, the Acehnese love their *kare* or *gulai* (curry). The Bataks have a taste for pig and, to a lesser extent, dog. Pork features in *babi panggang* (pork boiled in vinegar and pig blood, and then roasted).

The culinary capital of South Sumatra is Palembang, famous for *pempek* (deep-fried fish and sago dumpling; also called *empek-empek*). South Sumatra is also home to *pindang* (spicy fish soup with soy and tamarind) and *ikan brengkes* (fish in a spicy, durian-based sauce). Palembang's sweetie is *srikaya* (green custard made from sticky rice, sugar, coconut milk and egg).

At Banjarmasin's floating produce market in Kalimantan, you can sample exotic fruit to your heart's content. The range will include all manner of alien-looking treats.

Kalimantan

Dayak food varies, but you may sample *rembang*, a sour fruit that's made into *sayur asem rembang* (sour vegetable soup). In Banjarmasin, there's *pepes ikan* (spiced fish cooked in banana leaves with tamarind and lemon grass). Kandangan town is famous for *ketupat Kandangan* (fish and pressed rice with lime-infused coconut sauce). The regional soup, *soto Banjar*, is a chicken broth made creamy by mashing boiled eggs into the stock. Chicken also goes into *ayam masak habang*, cooked with large red chillies.

There is a large Chinese population and restaurants usually have specialities such as birds nest soup and jellyfish on the menus.

Sulawesi

South Sulawesi locals love seafood, especially *ikan bakar* (grilled fish). Another local dish is *coto Makassar* (soup of beef innards, pepper, cumin

NO WIMPY SAMBAL!

Sambal, the spicy condiment, comes in myriad forms and can be the best part of a meal, but all too often, servers will assume you are a timid tourist who wants the tame ketchup-like stuff from a bottle. Insist on the real stuff, which will have been prepared fresh in the kitchen from some combination of ingredients that can include garlic, shallots, chilli peppers in many forms, fish sauce, tomatoes and more.

and lemon grass). For sugar cravers, there's *es pallubutun* (coconut custard and banana in coconut milk and syrup).

The Toraja people have their own distinct cuisine with a heavy emphasis on tastes of indigenous ingredients, many of them odd to Western palettes.

If a North Sulawesi dish has the name *rica-rica,* it's prepared with a paste of chilli, shallots, ginger and lime. Fish and chicken are two versions (also look out for dog). Things get very fishy with *bakasang* (flavouring paste made with fermented fish), sometimes used in *bubur tinotuan* (porridge made with corn, cassava, rice, pumpkin, fish paste and chilli).

Jajanan (snacks) are sold everywhere – there are thousands of varieties of sweet and savoury snacks made from almost anything and everything: peanuts, coconuts, bananas, sweet potato etc. They are cheap so sample at will.

Drinks

Tea

Indonesia's most popular brew is black tea with sugar. If you don't want sugar ask for *teh pahit* (bitter tea), and if you want milk buy yourself a cow. Various forms of ginger tea are popular, including *bandrek* (ginger tea with coconut and pepper) and *wedang jahe* (ginger tea with peanuts and agar cubes slurped from a bowl).

Coffee

Indonesian coffee, especially from Sulawesi, is of exceptional quality, though most of the best stuff is exported. Warungs serve a chewy concoction called *kopi tubruk* (ground coffee with sugar and boiling water). Most urban cafes and restaurants offer quality coffee; beans from Sumatra and Bali are especially prized.

Ice & Fruit Drinks

Indonesia's *es* (ice drinks) are not only refreshing, they are visually stimulating, made with syrups, fruit and jellies. There are plenty of places serving *es jus* (iced fruit juice) or cordial-spiked *kelapa muda* (young coconut juice). But beware of ice outside of urban areas (ice in cities is made with filtered water).

A popular – and protein-filled – drink in Aceh is *kopi telor kocok*, one raw egg and sugar creamed together in a glass and topped up with coffee. Look for it in Takengon.

Alcoholic Drinks

Islam may be the predominant religion in Indonesia, but there's a range of alcohol available, including *tuak* (palm-sap wine), *arak* (rice or palm-sap wine) and Balinese *brem* (rice wine). Be careful when buying *arak*. In recent times, there have been cases where it has been adulterated with chemicals that have proved deadly.

Of the domestic breweries, iconic Bintang, a clean, slightly sweet lager, is the preferred choice of beer for many. Bali's Storm brewery has some excellent ales.

Note that rapacious duties are added to imported alcohol sold in stores and restaurants, which means you'll be hard-pressed to find affordable Australian wine or British gin in Bali. That bottle of Bombay Sapphire which is US$25 at duty-free shops before your flight is US$100 in Bali, so buy your allowed litre.

In conservative areas and rural places, such as Papua, you'll be hard-pressed to find any alcoholic beverages for sale.

Celebrations

Whether a marriage, funeral or party with friends, food – and lots of it – is essential. Celebratory meals can include any combination of dishes, but for special occasions a *tumpeng* is the centrepiece: a pyramid of yellow rice, the tip of which is cut off and offered to the VIP.

Muslims

For Muslims, the largest celebrations are Ramadan and Idul Adha. Each day of Ramadan (p724), Muslims rise before sunrise to eat the only meal before sunset. It might sound like a bad time to be in Indonesia – you may have to plan meals and go without lunch – but when sunset comes, the locals' appreciation of a good meal is contagious.

The first thing Indonesians eat after fasting is *kolak* (fruit in coconut milk) as a gentle way to reacquaint the body with food. Then, after prayers, the evening meal begins with aplomb. In some areas, such as in Bukittinggi, cooks set out food on the street. People gather to savour and enjoy their food as a community. Foreign guests are always made welcome.

After Ramadan, much of the nation seems to hit the road to go home to their families and celebrate Idul Firi (Lebaran) with their families. During this time, *ketupat* (rice steamed in packets of woven coconut fronds) are hung everywhere, like seasonal ornaments.

Seventy days after Lebaran is Idul Adha, marked by the sight of goats tethered to posts on both city streets and rural pathways throughout the archipelago. Individuals or community groups buy these unfortunate animals to sacrifice in commemoration of Abraham's willingness to sacrifice his son at divine command. This is one of Indonesia's most anticipated festivals, as the sacrificial meat is distributed to the poor in each community.

MSG is widely used in Indonesia. In warungs, you can try asking the cook to hold off on the *ajinomoto*. If you get a look of blank incomprehension, well, the headache only lasts for a couple of hours.

Balinese

The Balinese calendar is peppered with festivals and such celebrations are always observed with a communal meal, sometimes eaten together from one massive banana leaf piled with dishes.

DINING WITH LOCALS

In Indonesia hospitality is highly regarded. If you're invited to someone's home for a meal, you'll be treated warmly and social hiccups will be ignored. Nevertheless, here are some tips to make the experience more enjoyable for everyone:

» When food or drink is presented, wait until your host invites you to eat.

» Indonesians rarely eat at the table, preferring to sit on a mat or around the lounge room.

» Don't be surprised if, when invited to a home, you're the only one eating. This is your host's way of showing you're special, and you should have choice pickings. But don't eat huge amounts, as these dishes will feed others later. Fill up on rice and take a spoonful from each dish served.

» While chopsticks are available at Chinese-Indonesian eateries, and a fork and spoon in restaurants, most Indonesians prefer to eat with their hands. In a warung, it is acceptable to rinse your fingers with drinking water, letting the drops fall to the ground. Use only your right hand. If left-handed, ask for a spoon.

» In Islamic areas, be sure not to eat and drink in public during Ramadan. Restaurants do stay open, though they usually cover the door so as not to cause offence.

» Though antismoking regulations are becoming common, smoking remains acceptable almost anywhere, anytime.

Festivals aside, every day in Bali you'll see food used to symbolise devotion: rice in woven banana-leaf pockets are placed in doorways, beside rice fields, at bus terminals – wherever a god or spirit may reside. Larger offerings studded with whole chickens and produce are made to mark special occasions such as *odalan* (temple anniversary). You'll see processions of women gracefully balancing offerings on their heads as they make their way to the temple.

NATIONAL DISH

Indonesia's national dish is *nasi campur*, which is essentially the plate of the day. Served in stalls, warungs and restaurants it is always a combination of many dishes and flavours. At warungs you often choose your own combination from dozens of tasty items on offer.

Eating Out

Outside of larger cities and tourist areas, there are limited choices for dining out in Indonesia. Warungs are simple open-air eateries that provide a small range of dishes. Often their success comes from cooking one dish better than anyone else. *Rumah makan* (eating house) or *restoran* refers to anything that is a step above a warung. Offerings may be as simple as those from a warung but usually include more choices of meat and vegetable dishes, and spicy accompaniments.

As Indonesia's middle class grows, the warung is also going upmarket. In urban areas, a restaurant by any other name advertises itself as a 'warung', and serves good local dishes to customers that become more demanding by the year.

Indonesia's markets are wonderful examples of how food feeds both the soul and the stomach. There's no refrigeration, so freshness is dependent on quick turnover. You'll also find a huge range of sweet and savoury snacks. Supermarkets and convenience stores are common in cities and tourist areas like Bali.

For information on business hours, see p758 and for the price bands used in this book, see p760.

Quick Eats

As many Indonesians can't afford fine service and surrounds, the most authentic food is found at street level. Even high rollers know this, so everyone dines at stalls or gets their noodle fix from roving vendors who carry their victuals in two bundles connected by a stick over their shoulders: a stove and wok on one side, and ready-to-fry ingredients on the other.

Then there's *kaki lima* (roving vendors) whose carts hold a work bench, stove and cabinet. '*Kaki lima*' means 'five legs': two for the wheels

FRUITY DELIGHTS

It's worth making a trip to Indonesia just to sample the tropical fruits:

» *Belimbing* (star fruit) is cool and crisp; slice one to see how it gets its name.

» Durian is the spiky fruit people either love or hate.

» *Jambu air* (water apple) is a pink bell-shaped fruit with crisp and refreshing flesh.

» *Manggis* (mangosteen) is a small purple fruit with white fleshy segments and fantastic flavour.

» *Nangka* (jackfruit) is an enormous, spiky fruit that can weigh over 20kg. Inside are segments of yellow, moist, sweet flesh with a slightly rubbery texture. The flesh can be eaten fresh or cooked in a curry.

» *Rambutan* is a bright-red fruit covered in soft spines; the name means 'hairy'. Break it open to reveal a delicious white fruit similar to lychee.

» *Salak* is recognisable by its brown 'snakeskin' covering. Peel it off to reveal segments that resemble something between an apple and a walnut.

» *Sirsak* (soursop or zurzak) is a warty, green-skinned fruit with a white, pulpy interior that has a slightly lemonish taste.

of the cart, one for the stand and two for the legs of the vendor. You'll find any and every type of dish, drink and snack sold from a *kaki lima*. Some have a permanent spot, others roam the streets, calling out what they are selling or making a signature sound, such as the 'tock' of a wooden *bakso* bell. In some places, sate sellers operate from a boat-shaped cart, with bells jingling to attract the hungry.

Cradle of Flavor by James Oseland (the editor of *Saveur* magazine) is a beautiful tome covering the foods of Indonesia and its neighbours.

Vegetarian Fare

Vegetarians will be pleased to know that tempeh and *tahu* (tofu) are in abundance, sold as chunky slabs of *tempe penyet* (deep-fried tempe), *tempe kering* (diced tempeh stir-fried with sweet soy sauce) and *tahu isi* (deep-fried stuffed tofu). Finding fresh vegies requires more effort. Look for Chinese establishments; they can whip up *cap cai* (mixed vegetables). Vegetarian fried rice or noodles can be found at many other eateries. And there's always the iconic gado gado.

A huge number of places, including Padang restaurants, offer what's essentially the national dish: *nasi campur* (rice with a variety of side dishes). Here you can skip meat options and go for things like tofu, tempeh, jackfruit dishes, egg dishes and leafy vegies.

And there's always fantastic fruit available at the local market.

Eating with Kids

There's always the fear that a hidden chilli is going to make your child explode. But most Indonesian children dread chilli attacks, so a proprietor will often warn you if a dish is spicy. In any case, you can always ask '*Pedas tidak?*' ('Is it spicy?') or '*Makanan tidak pedas ada?*' ('Are there nonspicy dishes?').

Children may enjoy nasi goreng, *mie goreng* (fried noodles), *bakso* (meatball soup), *mie rebus* (noodle soup), *perkedel* (fritters), *pisang goreng* (banana fritters), sate, *bubur* (rice porridge), fruit and fruit drinks. Indonesia's sugar-rich iced drinks are useful secret weapons for when energy levels are low. All of these are available at street stalls and restaurants. Not available, however, are highchairs and kiddy menus. That's not to say children aren't welcome; in fact, they'll probably get more attention than they can handle.

In touristy areas and cities you'll find plenty of familiar fast-food joints and convenience stores selling Western snacks. A Magnum bar can quell the worst tantrum.

FOOD GLOSSARY

acar	pickle; cucumber or other vegetables in a mixture of vinegar, salt, sugar and water
air	water
arak	spirits distilled from palm sap or rice
ayam	chicken
ayam goreng	fried chicken
babi	pork; since most Indonesians are Muslim, pork is generally only found in market stalls and restaurants run by the Chinese, and in areas where there are non-Muslim populations, such as Bali, Papua and Tana Toraja on Sulawesi
bakar	barbecued, roasted
bakso/ba'so	meatball soup

bandrek	ginger tea with coconut and pepper
brem	rice wine
bubur	rice porridge
cassava	known as tapioca in English; a long, thin, dark brown root which looks something like a shrivelled turnip
colenak	roasted cassava with coconut sauce
daging kambing	goat
daging sapi	beef
es buah	combination of crushed ice, condensed milk, shaved coconut, syrup, jelly and fruit
gado gado	very popular dish of steamed bean sprouts and various vegetables, served with a spicy peanut sauce
gudeg	jackfruit curry
ikan	fish
jajanan	snacks
karedok	salad of long beans, bean sprouts and cucumber with spicy sauce
kelepon	green rice-flour balls with a palm-sugar filling
ketoprak	noodles, bean sprouts and tofu with soy and peanut sauce
ketupat tahu	pressed rice, bean sprouts and tofu with soy and peanut sauce
kopi	coffee
krupuk	shrimp with cassava flour, or fish flakes with rice dough, cut into slices and fried to a crisp
lombok	chilli
lontong	rice steamed in a banana leaf
martabak	a pancake-like dish stuffed with meat, egg and vegetables
mie goreng	fried wheat-flour noodles, served with vegetables or meat
nasi	rice
nasi campur	steamed rice topped with a little bit of everything (some vegetables, some meat, a bit of fish, a krupuk or two; usually a tasty and filling meal)
nasi goreng	fried rice
nasi liwet	rice with coconut milk, unripe papaya, garlic and shallots, served with chicken or egg
nasi uduk	rice cooked in coconut milk, served with meat, tofu and/or vegetables
nasi putih	white (*putih*) rice, usually steamed
pecel	peanut sauce
pecel lele	deep-fried catfish served with rice and *pecel*
pempek (empek-empek)	deep-fried/grilled fish and sago balls (from Palembang)
pisang goreng	fried banana fritters
roti	bread; nearly always white and sweet
sambal	a hot, spicy chilli sauce served as an accompaniment with most meals

sate	small pieces of various types of meat grilled on a skewer and served with peanut sauce
sayur	vegetables
serabi	coconut-milk pancakes topped with chocolate, banana or jackfruit
soto	meat and vegetable broth; soup
soto Bandung	beef-and-vegetable soup with lemon grass
soto Betawi	beef soup
soto Madura	beef soup with lime, pepper, peanuts, chilli and ginger
tahu	tofu or soybean curd
teh	tea
teh pahit	tea without sugar
telur	egg
tuak	palm-sap wine
udang	prawns or shrimps
ulen	roasted sticky rice with peanut sauce

Survival Guide

Directory A–Z

Accommodation

Accommodation in Indonesia ranges from a basic box with a mattress to the finest five-star luxury resorts. Costs vary considerably across the archipelago, but in general Indonesia is one of the better bargains in Southeast Asia.

Travellers' centres have plenty of reasonably priced food and accommodation; Bali has the highest standards and whether you want to spend US$5, US$50 or US$500 per night you will get excellent value. Accommodation prices don't necessarily increase in outer and more remote provinces, but less competition often means lower standards.

Some hotels have fixed prices and display them, but prices are often flexible, especially during quiet periods. This applies particularly to midrange and top-end hotels, where discounts of 10% to 50% are readily available both in person and online.

Budget rooms often consist of a fan-cooled room in a losmen (simple, family-run hotel) or basic hotel, with a bed and shared *mandi* (Indonesian-type bath), although in the main cities such as Jakarta and Yogyakarta rooms often come with a private *mandi*. Midrange accommodation is usually in a hotel and you can expect a private *mandi* or Western bathroom, more comfortable beds with a modicum of furniture, air-con and TV. Of course standards vary greatly depending on where you are (budget places on Bali often include a pool etc). Top end is generally a more comfortable version of midrange, with newer interiors and satellite TV. Luxury resorts in Bali rival those anywhere in the world.

All hotels charge a 10% government tax, although many cheap hotels either ignore the tax or absorb it into their room rates. Midrange and top-end hotels have a 21% tax-and-service charge (called 'plus plus'), but not all include it in their advertised tariffs, so ask when checking in to avoid a headache on your way out.

Budget hotel chains with modern amenities (air-con, wi-fi etc) are proliferating in cities and Bali. Brands include Citihub, Fave, Grandmas, Ibis Style, Tune, Whiz etc. With bold colours and Ikea-like interiors, they replace individuality with reliability.

Online Booking

For hotels, especially midrange and top-end places, you can often find the best deal by shopping around online. Some hotels offer internet deals on their websites; many more work with agents and brokers to sell their rooms at discounts off the published rates.

Besides the main internet travel websites, the following sites often have good rates on rooms in Java, Bali and other touristed areas:

Asia Rooms (www.asiarooms.com)

Agoda (www.agoda.com)

Bali Discovery (www.balidiscovery.com)

PRACTICALITIES

» English-language press includes the *Jakarta Post* and the *Jakarta Globe*. Tempo magazine has an English-language edition and website (www.tempointeractive.com).

» Pirated DVDs are abundant and most can be played on all-region software, although you usually get what you pay for in terms of viewability. Legitimate copies are uncommon.

» Tap water is never safe to drink.

» Indonesia uses the international metric system for weights and measures.

» Anti-smoking rules prohibit smoking in many public places but enforcement is uncommon.

Lonely Planet (www.lonelyplanet.com/indonesia/bali)

Camping

Camping in national parks is popular among Indonesian youth, though formal camping grounds with power and other facilities are rare. Outside of the parks, camping is unknown and villagers will regard campers as a source of entertainment. Some Kalimantan and Papua treks may include camping.

A sleeping sleeve or just a sarong will be sufficient for the lowlands, but you must be properly equipped to camp at higher elevations. Late-afternoon or night rain is common in mountain areas all year round, which can pose a danger of exposure to the inexperienced or unprepared. You'll also want a mosquito net to guard against insects and other things that crawl and slither in the night.

Hostels

Indonesia doesn't have many hostels, mainly because there are so many inexpensive hotels. One exception is Jakarta. There are a handful of hostels in a few other places, but it's easy to travel through Indonesia on a tight budget without ever staying in one.

Staying in Villages

In many places in Indonesia you'll often be welcome to stay in the villages. If the town has no hotel, ask for the *kepala desa* (village head), who is generally very hospitable and friendly, offering you not only a roof over your head in a homestay, but also meals. You may not get a room of your own, just a bed.

Payment is usually expected: about the same price as a cheap losmen (50,000Rp in Java) as a rule of thumb. The *kepala desa* may suggest an amount, but often it is *terserah* (up to you), and you should always offer to pay. While the village head's house sometimes acts as an unofficial hotel, you are a guest and often an honoured one. Elaborate meals may be prepared just for you. It's also a good idea to have a gift or two to offer your host – cigarettes, photographs or small souvenirs from your country are popular. Homestays and village stays are a great way to socialise with families and neighbours, contribute to the local economy and experience life at a much closer level.

Villages on Baliem Valley trekking routes often have basic guesthouses for tourists. Otherwise you stay in a teacher's house, or a school, or a room in the village government building (80,000Rp to 120,000Rp without food). Raja Ampat Islands have recently opened 'homestays' in several villages – typically 300,000Rp to 500,000Rp per person including meals.

In towns where no accommodation is available, ask at the local police station or any vaguely official-looking office. Oil-palm plantations generally have accommodation for visiting employees. Act friendly and don't mention rainforest conservation.

ACCOMMODATION PRICE RANGES

Accommodation rates are for high season (May to September and Christmas/New Year) and may drop by 20% or more during low season.

The following price ranges refer to a double room with bathroom. Unless otherwise stated relevant taxes are included in the price.

Bali & Lombok

$ less than 450,000Rp

$$ 450,000–1,400,000Rp

$$$ more than 1,400,000Rp

Rest of Indonesia

$ less than 250,000Rp

$$ 250,000–800,000Rp

$$$ more than 800,000Rp

Villas & Long-Term Accommodation

Luxury villas are popular accommodation in Bali, although they are not without their environmental costs in terms of water usage and placement amidst once pristine rice fields. Many come with pools, views, beaches and more. Often the houses are staffed and you have the services of a cook, driver etc.

Rates range from under US$200 per night for a modest villa to US$1200 per night and beyond for your own tropical estate. There are often deals, especially in the low season, and several couples sharing can make something grand affordable.

For longer stays, you can find deals easily for US$800 a month. Look in the *Bali Advertiser* (www.baliadvertiser.biz). If your tastes are simple, you can find basic bungalows among the rice fields in Ubud for US$300 a month.

Agents include:

Bali Discovery (www.balidiscovery.com)

Bali Private Villas (☎0361-316 6455; www.baliprivatevillas.com)

Bali Tropical Villas (☎0361-732 083; www.bali-tropical-villas.com)

Bali Ultimate Villas (☎0361-857 1658; www.baliultimatevillas.com)

Some things to keep in mind and ask about when renting a villa:

» How far is the villa from the beach and stores?

» Is a driver or car service included?

» If there is a cook, is food included?

» Is laundry included?

Business Hours

The following are typical opening hours found across Indonesia. Unless a place's hours differ greatly from these, hours are not included in listings.

Banks 8am to 2pm Monday to Thursday, 8am to noon Friday, and 8am to 11am Saturday.

Government office hours generally 8am to 3pm Monday to Thursday, 8am to noon Friday.

Post offices 8am to 2pm Monday to Friday. (Note: in tourist centres, the main post offices are often open longer and/or on weekends.)

Private business offices 8am to 4pm or 9am to 5pm Monday to Friday. Many open until noon on Saturday.

Restaurants 8am to 10pm or 11pm.

Shopping 9am or 10am to 5pm; larger shops and tourist areas to 9pm. Many closed Sunday.

Children

Travelling anywhere with children requires energy and organisation. Most Indonesians adore children, especially cute Western kids; however, children may find the constant attention overwhelming.

Health standards are low in Indonesia compared to the developed world, but with proper precautions, children can travel safely. As with adults, contaminated food and water present the most risks, and children are more at risk from sunstroke and dehydration. It depends where and how you travel. Indonesians may have to take their toddlers on gruelling eight-hour journeys in hot, stuffy buses, but you'd be well advised to take an air-con bus or rent a car. And many adults can comfortably sample warung (food stall) food, but parents with kids will want to be more careful.

If you're travelling only to the main cities and tourist areas, like the resorts of southern Bali, the malaria risk is minuscule, but it's probably not worth the risk to travel to known malarial areas like Papua or Pulau Nias in Sumatra.

Practicalities

Kid-friendly facilities such as high chairs in restaurants and cots in hotels are generally limited to Bali, which caters well to holidaying families. Bali has a ready supply of babysitters and plenty for kids to do. Java doesn't have Bali's mega-tourism industry, so it caters less to children, but it's well developed with a range of amenities, transport, hotel and food options. Travel outside cities requires patience, hardiness and experience – for both parents and kids.

Nappy-changing facilities usually consist of the nearest discreet flat surface. Baby wipes, disposable nappies and baby formula are all readily available in cities and big towns but seldom elsewhere.

Breastfeeding in public is acceptable in areas such as Papua and Sumatra but virtually unseen in Maluku, Sulawesi and Kalimantan. In some parts of Java it's simply inappropriate. The rule of thumb of course is always to take your cue from local mothers.

Customs Regulations

Indonesia has the usual list of prohibited imports, including drugs, weapons, fresh fruit and anything remotely pornographic. Items allowed include the following:

» 200 cigarettes (or 50 cigars or 100g of tobacco)

» a 'reasonable amount' of perfume

» 1L of alcohol

Surfers with more than two or three boards may be charged a 'fee', and this could apply to other items if the officials suspect that you aim to sell them in Indonesia. If you have nothing to declare, customs clearance is usually quick.

Discount Cards

The International Student Identity Card (ISIC) is useful for discounts on some domestic flights, although maximum age limits (usually 26) often apply. A very few attractions such as Borobudur offer student discounts. Check out www.istc.org for information and details on the application process.

Electricity

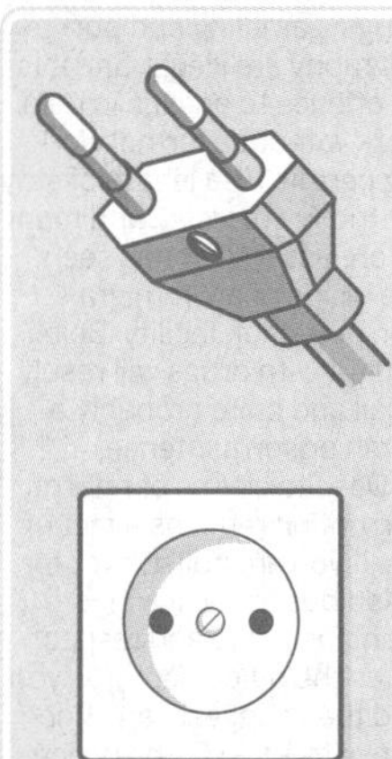

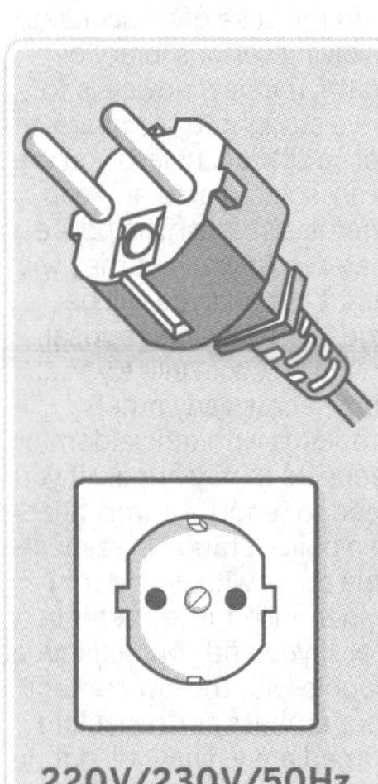

Embassies & Consulates

It's important to realise what your own embassy can and can't do to help you if you get into trouble. Generally speaking, it won't be much help if whatever trouble you're in is remotely your own fault. Remember that you are bound by the laws of the country you are in. In genuine emergencies you might get some assistance, but only if other channels have been exhausted. If you have all your money and documents stolen, your embassy might assist with getting a new passport, but that's about it.

Foreign embassies are located in Jakarta; Bali and Medan have a few consulates. There are also some in towns close to foreign borders.

Bali

Australian Consulate (Map p238; ☎0361-241 118; www.bali.indonesia.embassy.gov.au; Jl Tantular 32, Denpasar; ⏰8am-4pm Mon-Fri) The Australian consulate has a consular sharing agreement with Canada.

US Consulate (off Map p238; ☎0361-233 605; amcobali@indosat.net.id; Jl Hayam Wuruk 310, Renon, Denpasar; ⏰9am-3.30pm Mon-Fri)

Jakarta

Australian Embassy (Map p56; ☎021-2550 5555; www.indonesia.embassy.gov.au; Jl HR Rasuna Said Kav C 15-16, Jakarta Selatan)

Brunei Darussalam Embassy (Map p54; ☎021-3190 6080; www.mofat.gov.bn; Jl Teuku Umar 9, Menteng)

Canadian Embassy (Map p56; ☎021-2550 7800; www.jakarta.gc.ca; 6th fl, World Trade Centre, Jl Jenderal Sudirman Kav 29-31)

French Embassy (Map p54; ☎021-2355 7600; www.ambafrance-id.org; 40th fl, Menara BCA, Jl MH Thamrin No 1)

German Embassy (Map p54; ☎021-3985 5000; www.jakarta.diplo.de; Jl MH Thamrin 1)

Malaysian Embassy (Map p56; ☎021-522 4974; www.kln.gov.my/web/idn_jakarta; Jl HR Rasuna Said Kav X/6, 1-3, Kuningan)

Dutch Embassy (Map p56; ☎021-524 8200; http://indonesia.nlembassy.org; Jl HR Rasuna Said Kav S-3)

New Zealand Embassy (Map p56; ☎021-2995 5800; www.nzembassy.com; Jl Asia Afrika 8, 10th fl, Sentral Senayan 2)

Papua New Guinea Embassy (Map p56; ☎021-725 1218; Jl Jenderal Sudirman 1, 6th fl, Panin Bank Centre)

Singaporean Embassy (Map p56; ☎021-2995 0400; www.mfa.gov.sg/jkt; Jl HR Rasuna Said, Block X/4 Kav 2)

Thai Embassy (Map p54; ☎021-390 4052; www.thaiembassy.org/jakarta; Jl Imam Bonjol 74)

UK Embassy (Map p54; ☎021-2356 5200; http://ukinindonesia.fco.gov.uk; Jl MH Thamrin 75)

US Embassy (Map p54; ☎021-3435 9000; http://jakarta.usembassy.gov; Jl Medan Merdeka Selatan 3-5)

Kupang

Timor Leste Consulate (☎8133-9367 558; Jl El Tari)

Medan

Malaysian Consulate (☎061-453 1342; Jl Diponegoro 43)

Food

Indonesia has a vast array of culinary delights and regional specialities. For the tasty details, see p745.

Gay & Lesbian Travellers

Gay travellers in Indonesia (especially in Bali) will experience few problems. Physical contact between same-sex couples is acceptable, even though a boy and a girl holding hands may be seen as improper. Homosexual behaviour is not illegal. Gay men in Indonesia are referred to as *homo* or *gay;* lesbians are *lesbi*.

Indonesia's community of transvestite/transsexual *waria* – from the words

EATING PRICE RANGES

The following ranges represent meals.

Bali & Lombok

$ less than 60,000Rp

$$ 60,000–250,000Rp

$$$ more than 250,000Rp

Rest of Indonesia

$ less than 50,000Rp

$$ 50,000–200,000Rp

$$$ more than 200,000Rp

wanita (woman) and *pria* (man) – has always had a very public profile. Also known by the less polite term *banci,* they are often extroverted performers or stage entertainers.

Islamic groups proscribe homosexuality, but such views are not dominant and there is no queer-bashing or campaigns against gays. It pays to be less overt in some orthodox areas, though.

Indonesia has a number of gay and lesbian organisations. The coordinating body is **GAYa Nusantara** (www.gayanusantara.or.id), which publishes the monthly magazine *GAYa Nusantara*. In Bali, **Hanafi** (Map p212; ☎0818 568 364; www.hanafi.net; Jl Pantai Kuta 1E) is a gay-friendly tour operator.

Insurance

A travel-insurance policy to cover theft, loss and medical problems is essential. There is a wide variety of policies, most sold online; if you're planning to travel outside cities and tourist areas it's wise to take a policy that will facilitate a speedy evacuation in the event of a medical emergency.

Theft is a potential problem in Indonesia, so make sure that your policy covers expensive items adequately. Many policies have restrictions on laptops and expensive camera gear, and refunds are often for depreciated value, not replacement value.

Worldwide travel insurance is available at www.lonelyplanet.com/travel_services. You can buy, extend and claim online anytime – even if you're already on the road.

Internet Access

Indonesia is somewhat wired, but speed varies from fast to painfully slow. All sizeable population centres have at least one warnet (public internet centre) or internet centre charging 5000Rp to 10,000Rp an hour.

Wi-fi is increasingly available in hotels and cafes. It is often free but watch out for hotels that may charge ridiculous rates by the hour or by data use.

In urban areas and Bali, 3G networks enable you to get a USB modem for your laptop and a cheap pay-as-you-go data plan from any of the mobile companies.

Language Courses

Bahasa Indonesia language courses for English-speakers are offered in Yogyakarta in Java, plus Seminyak and Ubud in Bali.

Legal Matters

Drugs, gambling and pornography are illegal, and it is an offence to engage in paid work without a formal working permit. Visa length of stay is strictly enforced, and many a careless tourist has seen the inside of an immigration detention facility. Being caught with drugs will result in jail and quite probably a harsh prison sentence.

Despite claims of reform, corruption remains a fact of life. If you are pulled over for a dubious traffic infringement, be polite and respectful as the officer lectures you and then suggests an alternative to a trip to the police station and a courthouse date. Generally, 50,000Rp is plenty, but 100,000Rp is more the norm on Bali.

In the case of an accident involving serious injury or death, the best advice is to drive straight to the nearest police station, unless you are in an isolated area and can offer assistance. The police may detain you, but they will sort it out and you will be safe from possible reprisal.

Tourists are unlikely to come across any other problems with officialdom or requests to pay bribes. If you need to report a crime, head to a police station in respectable dress with an Indonesian friend or interpreter in tow. If you find yourself in real trouble with the law contact your embassy or consulate immediately. They will not be able to arrange bail but will be able to provide you with an interpreter and may be able to suggest legal counsel.

Maps

Locally produced maps are often inaccurate. Periplus produces useful maps of most of the archipelago and the major cities. The Nelles Verlag map series covers Indonesia in a number of separate sheets, and they're usually reliable although they can be dated for places such as Bali. Both series are available in Indonesia and overseas.

Free tourist maps of major Javanese, Sumatran and Balinese cities can be found in hotels but are of highly variable quality and usefulness.

Hikers will have little chance of finding accurate maps of remote areas. It's far more useful (and wise) to employ the services of a local guide, who will be able to navigate seemingly uncharted territory.

Money

The unit of currency used in Indonesia is the rupiah (Rp). Coins of 50Rp, 100Rp, 200Rp, 500Rp and 1000Rp are in circulation. Notes come in 2000Rp, 5000Rp, 10,000Rp, 20,000Rp, 50,000Rp and 100,000Rp denominations. For change in amounts below 50Rp, expect to receive a few sweets.

Try to carry a fair amount of money in bills 20,000Rp and under as getting change for larger bills is often a problem.

ATMs

» ATMs are increasingly common across Indonesia; most now accept cards affiliated with the major international networks.

» ATMs in Indonesia have a maximum limit for withdrawals; sometimes it is 2,000,000Rp, but it can be as low as 500,000Rp – not much in foreign-currency terms, especially if you want to get large amounts to limit service charges.

» Many ATMs have a sticker that specifies whether the machine dispenses 50,000Rp or 100,000Rp notes. When possible go with the former as the latter are always hard to break.

» Always carry a sizeable amount of rupiah when you are travelling outside of cities and tourist areas as ATM networks go down and/or you can be on an island where the only ATM is broken.

Cash & Travellers Cheques

» Generally, having a large amount of cash in the form of rupiahs is the one sure way to avoid money woes in Indonesia.

» Travellers cheques are nearly impossible to exchange or use.

Credit Cards

» In cities and touristed areas (eg Bali), credit cards will be accepted at midrange and better hotels and restaurants. More expensive shops as well as airline offices will also accept them.

» MasterCard and Visa are the most widely accepted credit cards. Amex is a distant third. Cash advances are possible at many ATMs or banks. If you'll be off the main track, check with your card issuer to find out where you can get cash. Remember, however, that outside of urban areas and resorts your credit card may not be useful at all.

» Before leaving home, inform your credit card issuer that you will be travelling in Indonesia, otherwise your account may be frozen for suspected fraud the first time you try to use it.

Moneychangers

» The US dollar is the most widely accepted foreign currency in Indonesia. Australian, British, euros and Japanese currencies are exchangeable only in the most touristed areas of Bali and Java.

» Outside of cities and tourist areas, banks may only be willing to exchange crisp, new US$100 bills. And in many rural areas they won't offer any exchange.

» Moneychangers range from the honest to dishonest. Signs bearing the phrases such as 'official' and licensed are meaningless.

Follow these steps to avoid getting ripped off when exchanging money:

» Find out the going exchange rate online. Know

THE ART OF BARGAINING

Many everyday purchases in Indonesia require bargaining. Accommodation has a set price, but this is usually negotiable in the low season, or if you are staying at the hotel for several days. Bargaining can be an enjoyable part of shopping, so maintain your sense of humour and keep things in perspective. Try following these steps:

» Have some idea of what the item is worth.

» Establish a starting price – ask the seller for their price rather than making an initial offer.

» Your first price can be from one-third to two-thirds of the asking price – assuming that the asking price is not outrageous.

» With offers and counter-offers, move closer to an acceptable price.

» If you don't get to an acceptable price, you're entitled to walk away – though the vendor may call you back with a lower price.

» Note that when you name a price, you're committed – you must buy if your offer is accepted.

that anyone offering a better rate will need to make a profit through other means.

» Stick to banks, exchange counters in airports or large and reputable storefront operations.

» Skip any place offering too-good exchange rates and claiming to charge no fees or commissions.

» Avoid exchange stalls down alleys or in otherwise dubious locations (that sounds obvious but scores of tourists are taken in daily).

» Common exchange scams include rigged calculators, sleight of hand schemes, 'mistakes' on the posted rates and demands that you hand over your money before *you* have counted the money on offer.

» Use an ATM to obtain rupiah. Check with your bank about fees, but if they are not outrageous, this will save you from carrying large amounts of cash and get you a decent exchange rate.

Tipping

A set percentage is not expected in Indonesia, but if the service is good, it's appropriate to leave a tip of 5000Rp or 10% or more.

» Most midrange hotels and restaurants and all top-end hotels and restaurants add 21% to the bill for tax and service (known as 'plus plus'). This service component is distributed among hotel staff (one hopes).

» Hand cash directly to individuals if you think they deserve recognition for their service.

» Tip good taxi drivers, guides, people giving you a massage or fetching you a beer on the beach etc; 5000Rp to 10,000Rp is generous.

Photography

Indonesia and Indonesians can be very photogenic, but whatever you do, photograph with discretion and manners. It's always polite to ask first, and if the person says no, don't take the photo. A gesture, a smile and a nod are all that is usually necessary. Few subjects expect payment, but all will appreciate a copy of the photo or at least a glimpse of its digital form.

Post

Sending postcards and normal-sized letters (ie under 20g) by airmail is cheap but not really fast. For anything over 20g, the charge is based on weight. You can send parcels up to 20kg and have them properly wrapped and sealed at any post office.

Every substantial town has a *kantor pos* (post office). In tourist centres, there are also postal agencies. They are often open long hours and provide postal services. Many will also wrap and pack parcels.

Have poste restante mail sent to you at major post offices. It should be addressed to you with your surname underlined and in capital letters, then 'Kantor Pos', the name of the town, and then the name of the island and 'Indonesia'. It may or may not arrive. You can also have mail sent to a hotel.

Express companies such as FedEx and UPS can be found in Bali and cities and offer reliable, fast and expensive service.

Public Holidays

Following are the national public holidays in Indonesia. Unless stated, they vary from year to year. Also, there are many regional holidays. See p20 for additional festive days that are holidays for many.

New Year's Day 1 January.

Imlek (Chinese New Year) National holiday in late January to early February.

Good Friday Late March or early April.

Paskah (Easter) Late March or early April.

Nyepi (Balinese New Year) The island of Bali closes down for one day, usually in March, sometimes in April; it's a cultural marvel, albeit a quiet one.

Waisak Day Marks the Buddha's birth, enlightenment and death. Falls in May.

Ascension of Christ May.

Hari Proklamasi Kemerdekaan (Independence Day) 17 August.

Hari Natal (Christmas Day) 25 December.

The following Islamic holidays have dates that change each year.

Muharram (Islamic New Year) Usually late January.

Maulud Nabi Muhammed The birthday of the Prophet Muhammed. Varies each year.

Isra Miraj Nabi Muhammed Celebration of the ascension of the Prophet Muhammed.

Idul Fitri Also known as Lebaran, this two-day national public holiday marks the end of Ramadan and is a time to avoid travel.

Idul Adha Islamic feast of the sacrifice.

Safe Travel

It's important to note that, compared with many places in the world, Indonesia is fairly safe. There are some hassles from the avaricious, but most visitors face many more dangers at home. Petty theft occurs, but it is not prevalent.

It's best to avoid buying *arak*, the locally produced fermented booze made from rice or palm. Deaths and injuries happen – especially in Bali – when unscrupulous vendors stretch stocks with poisonous chemicals.

Drugs

Indonesia has demonstrated its zero-tolerance policy

towards drugs with a spate of high-profile arrests and convictions. Australian Schapelle Corby captured news headlines around the world when she received a 20-year prison sentence for smuggling marijuana. In the same year five Australians were caught with several kilograms of heroin strapped to their bodies at Denpasar Airport. Along with their accomplices they became known (sensationally) as the 'Bali Nine'. Seven received life sentences (later reduced to 20 years) and two were sentenced to death by firing squad.

Random raids of nightclubs in Jakarta and Bali and mandatory urine tests for anyone found with drugs occur regularly (entrapment schemes are not unknown – that friendly dealer may be a cop).

Private parties in Bali have also been raided, and hotel owners are required by law to report offenders. The law does not provide for differentiation of substance types or amounts. Whether found with a full bag of heroin or a few specks of marijuana dust in your pocket, you will be in very serious trouble.

GOVERNMENT TRAVEL ADVICE

It is always worthwhile to check with official government sources before visiting Indonesia in order to check current travel conditions and the overall safety situation. But bear in mind that government sources generally take a conservative and over-cautious view. Follow news sources in order to get a more realistic picture.

Government travel advisories:

Australia (www.smartraveller.gov.au)

Canada (www.voyage.gc.ca)

New Zealand (www.mfat.govt.nz)

UK (www.fco.gov.uk/travel)

US (www.travel.state.gov)

Safety

Security in touristed areas increased after the 2002 and 2005 Bali bombings but has since tended to fade. The odds you will be caught up in such a tragedy are low. Large luxury hotels that are part of international chains tend to have the best security, though they also make the most tempting targets, as shown in Jakarta in 2003 and 2009.

Security issues in Indonesia are often exaggerated by the foreign media, who portray rambunctious protest rallies and minor incidents of civil unrest as nationwide pandemonium. Foreign governments add to the hype with heavy-handed, blanket travel warnings. While it's true that small sections of Indonesia experience flashes of conflict, overall the archipelago is safe. Although there are regular reports of suspected terror cells being broken up, so it pays to follow the news.

Scams

As in most poor countries, plenty of people are out to relieve you of your money in one way or another. It's really hard to say when an 'accepted' practice like overcharging becomes an unacceptable rip-off, but plenty of instances of practised deceit occur.

Con artists are always to be found. Usually those smooth talkers are fairly harmless guides seeking to lead you to a shop where they receive a commission. Just beware of instant friends and watch out for excessive commissions.

As the main tourist destination, Bali is the home of many scams. And there are continuing reports of shortchanging moneychangers. But you should always be aware of any local who appears out of nowhere the instant you get a flat tyre. As always, trust your common sense, as most Indonesians you meet in such situations are genuinely trying to help.

Hard-luck stories are common in tourist areas and are a recognised way to make money. But most Indonesians suffer in silence and would never ask for money; consider giving to aid programs if you want to help.

Theft

Theft can be a problem. However, if you are mindful of your valuables and take precautions, the chances of being ripped off are small.

Most thefts are the result of carelessness or naivety. The chances of theft are highest in crowded places and when travelling on public bemos, buses and trains. Unattended items on beaches and unsecured hotel rooms are literally ripe for the picking.

Note however that bag snatching from thieves on motor-scooters is on the rise in cities and Bali. There have been reported smash-and-grabs of items left exposed in parked cars.

Report any theft to the police, but without witnesses don't expect action. Bus companies and hotels will automatically deny any responsibility. Reported theft is usually termed *kehilangan*, or 'loss' – you lost it and it is your responsibility to prove theft. Police will provide a report, which is necessary for replacement passports and travellers cheques, and for insurance claims.

Telephone

Cheap SIM cards and internet calling have made it easier to stay in touch with home from Indonesia at reasonable prices.

Wired phone service is provided by a government monopoly, Telekomsel (Telekom). The usual warning about using phones in hotel rooms apply: rates may be obscene.

Internet Calling

Internet connections fast enough to support services like Skype and Apple's FaceTime are now common in the larger cities and the touristed parts of Bali. But realise that speeds elsewhere may be so slow as to make this impossible. Many internet centres allow you to use Skype or other forms of internet calling for a fee.

Mobile Phones

There are several local mobile/cell phone service providers, including Indosat, Telkomsel and XL.

SIM cards for your unlocked GSM mobile phone in Indonesia cost only 50,000Rp. They come with cheap rates for calling other countries, starting at US$0.20 per minute. You can buy them everywhere, just ask. You can buy a cheap phone for about US$20.

As usual, if you try to use you phone from home – especially the US – you may be hit with outrageous roaming fees. There are 3G data networks in cities and in Bali.

In more remote areas such as parts of Kalimantan, Papua, Sulawesi, Sumatra and myriad smaller islands, there may be no service at all, although this is changing quickly.

Phone Codes

Directory assistance ☎108

Indonesia country code ☎62

International call prefix ☎001/017

International operator ☎102

Telephone Offices

A *kantor telekomunikasi* (telecommunications office) is a main telephone office operated by Telkom where you can make calls. You can also make calls from most internet centres. Rates on landline phones at these places may average about US$1 per minute to other countries. It is difficult to make reverse-charge or collect calls.

BALI PHONE CONFUSION

Bali's landline phone numbers (those with area codes that include 0361 across the south and Ubud) are being changed on an ongoing basis through 2014.

To accommodate increased demand for lines, a digit is being added to the start of the existing six- or seven-digit phone number. So 0361-761 xxxx might become 0361-4761 xxxx. The schedule and plans for the new numbers change regularly, but *usually* you'll hear a recording first in Bahasa Indonesia and then in English telling you what digit to add to the changed number.

Time

There are three time zones in Indonesia. Java, Sumatra, and West and Central Kalimantan are on Western Indonesian Time, which is seven hours ahead of GMT/UTC. Bali, Nusa Tenggara, South and East Kalimantan, and Sulawesi are on Central Indonesian Time, which is eight hours ahead of GMT/UTC. Papua and Maluku are on Eastern Indonesian Time, nine hours ahead of GMT/UTC. In a country straddling the equator, there is of course no daylight-saving time.

Allowing for variations due to summer or daylight-saving time, when it is noon in Jakarta it is 9pm the previous day in San Francisco, midnight in New York, 5am in London, 1pm in Singapore and Makassar, 2pm in Jayapura and 3pm in Melbourne and Sydney.

Strung out along the equator, Indonesia has days and nights that are approximately equal in length, and sunrises and sunsets occur very rapidly with almost no twilight. Sunrise is around 6am and sunset is around 6pm, varying slightly depending on distance from the equator.

Note that there have been proposals by the Indonesian government to place the far-flung nation under one time zone.

Toilets

In most of Indonesia, the bathroom features a large water tank and a plastic scooper. *Kamar mandi* means bathroom and *mandi* means to bathe or wash.

Climbing into the tank is very bad form indeed – it's your water supply and it's also the supply for every other guest that comes after you, so the idea is to keep the water clean. Scoop water out of the tank and pour it over yourself.

Most tourist hotels have showers, and the more expensive ones have hot water, especially in Bali and cities.

Indonesian toilets are basically holes in the ground with footrests on either side, although Western-style toilets are common in tourist areas. To flush the toilet, reach for the plastic scooper, take water from the tank and pour. Public toilets are rare – find a cafe and smile.

As for toilet paper, it is seldom supplied in public places, though you can easily buy your own. Many Indonesians instead use their left hand and copious quantities of water – again, keep that scooper handy. If you need to use toilet paper, see if there is a wastebasket next to the toilet (that's where the paper should go, not down the toilet). If you plug up a hotel's plumbing with toilet paper, the management will be annoyed.

Kamar kecil is Bahasa Indonesia for toilet, but people usually understand 'way-say' (WC). *Wanita* means women and *pria* means men.

Tourist Information

Indonesia's national tourist organisation, the **Ministry of Culture and Tourism** (☎021-383 8167; www.budpar.go.id; Jl Merdeka Barat 17), maintains a head office in Jakarta as well as offices in each province. Its website is a good source of links; otherwise, you won't find it overly useful.

Most tourist offices in Indonesia offer little of value. Three notable exceptions are the tourist offices in Ubud, Bali; Yogyakarta; and the Raja Ampat Tourism Management Office in Sorong, Papua.

Travellers with Disabilities

Indonesia has very little supportive legislation or special programs for people with disabilities, and it's a difficult destination for those with limited mobility.

Building regulations in Indonesia do not specify disabled access, and even international chain hotels often don't have facilities.

Pavements (sidewalks) are a minefield of potholes, loose manholes, parked motorcycles and all sorts of street life, and are very rarely level for long until the next set of steps. Even the able bodied walk on roads rather than negotiate the hassle of the pavement.

Public transport is also difficult, but cars with driver can be hired readily at cheap rates and are much more common than self-drive rentals. Minibuses are easily hired, but none have wheelchair access. Guides are found readily in the tourist areas and, though not usual, they could be hired as helpers if needed.

Bali, with its wide range of tourist services and facilities, is the most favourable destination for travellers with disabilities although this does not mean it is easy.

Visas

Visas are the biggest headache many travellers face in their Indonesian trip. They are not hard to obtain, but the most common – 30 days – is awfully short for such a big place. Many travellers find even the 60-day visa restrictive.

Indonesian visa requirements are prone to fluctuations so you need to contact the Indonesian embassy in your home country before you plan your trip.

The Ministry of Foreign Affairs website (www.kemlu.go.id) has links to Indonesian embassies and consulates worldwide and has current visa information. This is useful as embassies and consulates often have out-of-date info.

Study & Work Visas

You can arrange visas for study, short-term research, visiting family and similar purposes if you have a sponsor, such as an educational institution. These social/cultural *(sosial/budaya)* visas must be applied for at an Indonesian embassy or consulate overseas. Normally valid for three months on arrival, they can be extended every month after that for up to six months without leaving the country. Fees apply.

People wishing to study in Indonesia must apply directly to the Central Immigration Office in Jakarta for a Limited-Stay Visa (*Kartu Izin Tinggal Terbatas*, or *Kitas*). First, though, contact your nearest embassy for the most direct avenue and to find out what qualifies as 'study'. Those granted limited stay are issued a Kitas card, which is much-prized among travellers.

If you're planning to work in Indonesia your employer will need to organise your visa – it's a long and complicated process.

Tourist Visas

Most visitors obtain a 30-day visa on arrival (VOA) at recognised entry points in Indonesia, which comprise 20 airports, 23 sea ports and the land crossing at Etikong in Kalimantan.

The ferry ports to/from Sumatra–Penang–Belawan, Melaka–Dumai and Singapore–Batam/Bintan – issue VOAs as do all major international airports. For most land border crossings you'll need to arrange a visa in advance.

At the time of writing, citizens of over 64 countries were eligible for a VOA, including those from Australia, Canada, much – but not all – of the EU including Germany, Ireland, the Netherlands and the UK, plus New Zealand and the USA. The cost is US$25 and it is best to have exact change in US currency.

You can renew a VOA for another 30 days for US$25. To do so you must go to a local immigration office at least one week before your VOA expires and be prepared to spend at least a day jumping through hoops. One way to avoid this in Jakarta and Bali is to pay a visa agency to jump through the hoops for you. Rates vary.

Other important considerations:

Passport Validity Your passport must be valid for

six months following your date of arrival.

60-Day Visa To get a much-prized 60-day tourist visa, you have to go through an embassy or consulate outside Indonesia. Some travellers have reported being able to extend a 60-day tourist visa if they can find an Indonesian willing to act as their sponsor. This can be done 30 days at a time for up to six months. However, there's a fair amount of paperwork involved, so first check with an immigration office to find out the latest details.

Onward Ticket/Funds Although seldom enforced, immigration officers can ask to see that you have an onward ticket from Indonesia and/or sufficient funds for your stay. This is one more reason to be polite and smile a lot.

Restricted Visas Citizens of Israel and several other countries will need special visas that are difficult to obtain. However, it's an urban myth that a stamp from Israel in your passport will cause problems.

Overstaying Your Visa Even staying one day beyond your visa expiration date can result in fines and hassles.

Travel Permits

Special permits are required for travel in Papua (p448).

Volunteering

There are excellent opportunities for aspiring volunteers in Indonesia.

Borneo Orangutan Survival Foundation (www.orangutan.or.id) Accepts volunteers for its orangutan and sun bear rehabilitation and reforestation programs at Samboja Lestari between Balikpapan and Samarinda.

East Bali Poverty Project (☎0361-410 071; www.eastbalipovertyproject.org) Works to help children in the impoverished mountain villages of east Bali.

Friends of the National Parks Foundation (☎0361-977 978; www.fnpf.org; Jl Bisma, Ubud) Main office in Bali. Has volunteer programs in and around Tanjung Puting National Park in central Kalimantan as well as programs on Nusa Penida in Bali.

IDEP (Indonesian Development of Education & Permaculture; ☎0361-294 993; www.idepfoundation.org) Has projects across Indonesia; works on environmental projects, disaster planning and community improvement.

ProFauna (☎081-7970 6066; www.profauna.or.id) A large nonprofit animal-protection organisation operating across Indonesia; the Bali office has been aggressive in protecting sea turtles. Volunteers needed to help with hatchery releases and editing publications.

Smile Foundation of Bali (Yayasan Senyum; ☎0361-233 758; www.senyumbali.org) Organises surgery to correct facial deformities; operates the **Smile Shop** (☎233 758; www.senyumbali.org; Jl Sriwedari) in Ubud to raise money.

SOS (Sumatran Orangutan Society; www.orangutans-sos.org) An Ubud-based group that works to save endangered species throughout Indonesia.

Volunteer in Java (www.volunteerinjava.com) Organises volunteers to teach English in the schools of West Java.

STOPPING CHILD SEX-TOURISM

Indonesia has become a destination for foreigners seeking to sexually exploit local children. A range of socio-economic factors render many children and young people vulnerable to such abuse and some individuals prey upon this vulnerability. The sexual abuse and exploitation of children has serious, life-long and even life-threatening consequences for the victims. Strong laws exist in Indonesia to prosecute offenders and many countries also have extraterritorial legislation which allows nationals to be prosecuted in their own country for these crimes.

Travellers can help stop child-sex tourism by reporting suspicious behaviour. Reports can be made to the **Anti-Human Trafficking Unit** (☎021-721 8098) of the Indonesian police. If you know the nationality of the individual, you can contact their embassy directly.

For more information, contact the following organisations:

ECPAT (End Child Prostitution & Trafficking; www.ecpat.org) A global network working on these issues, with over 70 affiliate organisations around the world. **Child Wise** (www.childwise.net) is the Australian member of ECPAT.

Humantrafficking.org (www.humantrafficking.org) International group has numerous links to groups working to prevent human exploitation in Indonesia.

PKPA (Center for Study & Child Protection; www.pkpa-indonesia.org) An organisation committed to the protection of Indonesia's children and the prevention of child-sex tourism.

Yakkum Bali (Yayasan Rama Sesana; ☎0361-247 363; www.yrsbali.org) Dedicated to improving reproductive health for women across Bali.

Yayasan Bumi Sehat (☎0361-970 002; www.bumisehatbali.org) Operates an internationally recognised clinic and gives reproductive services to disadvantaged women in Ubud; accepts donated time from medical professionals.

International Organisations

Another possible source for long-term paid or volunteer work in Bali or Lombok are the following agencies:

Australian Volunteers International (www.australianvolunteers.com) Organises professional contracts for Australians.

Global Vision International (www.gviusa.com) Organises short-term volunteer opportunities doing things like primate research in Sumatra (you pay costs); has offices in Australia, the UK and the US.

Global Volunteers (www.globalvolunteers.org) Arranges professional and paid volunteer work for US citizens.

Voluntary Service Overseas Canada (www.voyage.gc.ca); Netherlands (www.vso.nl); UK (www.vso.org.uk) British overseas volunteer program that accepts qualified volunteers from other countries.

Volunteer Service Abroad (www.vsa.org.nz) Organises professional contracts for New Zealanders.

Women Travellers

Plenty of Western women travel in Indonesia either solo or in pairs, and most seem to travel through the country without major problems. Women travelling alone in Bali are common, especially in Ubud. However, women travelling solo will receive extra attention, and some of it will be unwanted. To avoid this, some women invent a boyfriend or, even better, a husband, whom they are 'meeting soon'. A wedding ring can also be a good idea, while a photo of you and your 'partner' also works well. Sunglasses and a hat are a good way to avoid eye contact and to stop you feeling so exposed.

While Indonesian men are generally very courteous, there is a macho element that indulges in puerile behaviour – horn honking, lewd comments etc. Ignore them totally, as Indonesian women do; they are unsavoury but generally harmless.

There are some things you can do to minimise harassment – the most important is dressing appropriately. Dressing modestly won't stop the attention, but it will lessen its severity. In fundamentalist regions such as Aceh in northern Sumatra, it is essential that women cover up as much as possible (including the arms, although a loose-fitting T-shirt which covers the tops of your arms will do). Walk around in shorts and a singlet and you'll be touched, grabbed and leered at by men in the street; cover up and they'll call out as you walk past.

Transport

GETTING THERE & AWAY

There are many ways into Indonesia: by boat from Malaysia and Singapore, and overland to Kalimantan, Papua and West Timor. But most people will fly, landing at – or transiting through – Jakarta or Bali.

Flights, tours and rail tickets can be booked online at lonelyplanet.com/bookings.

Entering the Country

Entering Indonesia by air is relatively simple and straightforward, particularly if you use a visa on arrival (VOA). Numerous sea ports are similarly easy; if you're arriving by land you'll have no problems as long as you have a valid visa in advance.

Passport

Your passport *must* be valid for six months after your date of arrival in Indonesia. Before passing through immigration you will fill out a disembarkation card, half of which you must keep to give to immigration when you leave the country. For visa information, see p765.

Air

Indonesia is well connected to the rest of the world by numerous airlines. Many international flights, especially those to Bali, stop first in Singapore due to runway restrictions at Bali airport.

Airports & Airlines

The principal gateways for entry to Indonesia are Jakarta's **Soekarno-Hatta International Airport** (www.jakartaairportonline.com) and Bali's **Ngurah Rai International Airport** (www.baliairport.com). Both are in the midst of massive expansion and rebuilding projects. Other airports with international links – albeit limited – include Balikpapan, Medan, Surabaya, Lombok and Manado.

Airlines serving Indonesia include:

AirAsia (www.airasia.com) Serves a wide range of Indonesian destinations from Kuala Lumpur, Bangkok and Singapore.

Cathay Pacific Airways (www.cathaypacific.com) Serves Bali and Jakarta from Hong Kong.

China Airlines (www.china-airlines.com) Serves Bali and Jakarta from Taipei.

Emirates (www.emirates.com) Serves Jakarta from Dubai.

Eva Air (www.evaair.com) Serves Bali and Jakarta from Taipei.

Firefly (www.fireflyz.com.my) Serves major cities on Sumatra from Kuala Lumpur and Penang in Malaysia.

Garuda (www.garuda-indonesia.com) Indonesia's main national airline serves Bali and Jakarta from Australia, Asia and Amsterdam.

Japan Airlines (www.jal.co.jp) Serves Jakarta from Tokyo.

KLM (www.klm.com) Serves Jakarta and Bali from Amsterdam.

Korean Air (www.koreanair.com) Serves Bali and Jakarta from Seoul.

Lion Air (www.lionair.co.id) Rapidly expanding carrier with a web of services across Indonesia and the region. Wings Air is its regional subsidiary.

Lufthansa (www.lufthansa.com) Serves Jakarta from Frankfurt.

Malaysia Airlines (www.mas.com.my) Serves Bali and Jakarta from Kuala Lumpur.

Merpati Nusantara Airlines (www.merpati.co.id) Serves East Timor from Bali.

Qantas/Jetstar Airways (www.qantas.com.au) Serves Bali and Jakarta from Australia.

> **DEPARTURE TAX**
>
> Indonesian airports typically charge a departure tax to passengers flying out. This charge varies by airport (typically 150,000Rp) and is payable in cash.

INDONESIAN AIRLINE SAFETY

There's no way around it: Indonesia's airlines do not have a good safety record. Flying conditions are often challenging (monsoons, volcanic eruptions etc), safety standards can be lax and the airlines themselves run in a less-than-professional manner.

Although the major carriers have made improvements, many Indonesian airlines remain banned by the EU (www.ec.europa.eu/transport/air-ban/list_en.htm) from its airspace because of safety concerns. Notable exceptions are Garuda Indonesia, Mandala, Batavia and Indonesia AirAsia.

Should you be worried? The odds of a fatal flight in Indonesia are very small, even if they are higher than elsewhere. When possible, pick a major airline over a smaller one and in really remote locations, feel free to do your own inspection of the plane and crew before you fly.

Qatar Airways (www.qatarairways.com) Serves Bali from Doha.

Silk Air (www.silkair.com) Serves numerous Indonesian destinations from Singapore including Bandung, Balikpapan, Lombok, Manado, Medan, Palembang, Pekanbaru, Solo and Surabaya.

Singapore Airlines (www.singaporeair.com) Runs numerous flights to Bali and Jakarta daily.

Thai Airways International (www.thaiair.com) Serves Bali and Jakarta from Bangkok.

Tiger Airways (www.tigerairways.com) Singapore-based budget carrier serving Jakarta.

Virgin Australia (www.virginaustralia.com) Serves Bali from several Australian cities.

Tickets

Check websites to get an idea of airfares to Indonesia. Don't limit yourself to major sites either; search for 'Indonesian airfares' and you may well find sites belonging to small travel agents who specialise in Indonesian travel. This can be particularly helpful when you are trying to book a complex itinerary to remote locations.

Asia Indonesia is closely linked to most of Asia. A plethora of airlines serves Bali and Jakarta, but carriers like AirAsia and Lion Air serve a huge range of Indonesian cities from major Asian cities.

Australia Numerous direct flights to Bali and Jakarta are available from all major Australian cities on multiple carriers.

Canada From Canada you'll change planes at an Asian hub for Bali and Jakarta.

Continental Europe KLM and Lufthansa link Amsterdam and Frankfurt respectively with one-stop, same-plane service to Jakarta (and Bali for KLM). But a huge number of airlines such as Emirates, Qatar Airways and major Asian carriers, offer connections between major European cities and Jakarta, and often Bali as well.

New Zealand From New Zealand you will have to connect through Australia or an Asian hub.

UK Options to fly to Jakarta and Bali from London (or Manchester) involve connecting through a major hub somewhere in Asia.

USA The best connections are through any of the major Asian hubs with nonstop service to Bali and Jakarta, although residents of the East Coast may find shorter routings via Europe or the Middle East. No US airline serves Indonesia.

Land

Border Crossings

There are three possible land crossings into Indonesia.

Regular buses between Pontianak (Kalimantan) and Kuching (Sarawak, eastern Malaysia) pass through the border post at Entikong. They take around 10 hours and if travelling from Pontianak, buses stop at the border in the wee hours until it opens at 9am. You need to get off the bus and clear immigration on either side.You can get a visa on arrival on this route.

The border crossing between West and East Timor at Motoain is now open; a visa is required when travelling from East to West Timor.

The road from Jayapura or Sentani in Indonesia to Vanimo in Papua New Guinea can be crossed, depending on the current political situation. A visa is required if travelling into Indonesia.

Sea

There is currently no sea travel between the Philippines, Papua New Guinea and Indonesia.

Australia

Classic Cruises (www.classicintcruises.com) runs cruises to Bali from Western Australia.

East Timor

There is a regular ferry service between Dili in East Timor and Oecussi which borders West Timor. If crossing into Indonesia from here you will have to have organised your visa already in Dili.

Malaysia

Regular and comfortable high-speed ferries run the two-hour journey between Melaka (Malaysia) and Dumai (Sumatra). Similar ferries travel between Penang (Malaysia) and Belawan (Sumatra), taking about five hours.

From Johor Bahru in southern Malaysia, daily ferries run to Pulau Bintan in Sumatra's Riau Islands.

Ferries connect Tarakan and Nunukan in East Kalimantan with Tawau in Sabah daily except Sunday. Speedboats run daily between Nunukan and Tawau.

Singapore

From Batam speedboats travel to Tanjung Buton with minibus connections to Pekanbaru on the Sumatran mainland. Otherwise, Pelni ships pass through Batam to and from Belawan (the port for Medan) and Jakarta.

Boats also travel between Pulau Bintan and Singapore. Services include **Bintan Resort Ferries** (www.brf.com.sg).

GETTING AROUND

Air

Airlines in Indonesia

The domestic flight network in Indonesia continues to grow extensively; schedules and rates are in a constant state of flux. Local carriers servicing small routes often operate cramped and dated aircraft, whereas flights to Jakarta, Bali and other major destinations are usually on larger, newer craft.

Depending on the size of the airline and where they fly, timetables will vary from accurate, national schedules to hand-adjusted printouts of localised areas or provinces on specific islands. Website information is useful for the bigger carriers but nonexistent for the smaller ones. The best option is to check with local airline offices and travel agents, and local hotel and tour operators to see what's available.

With tiny regional airlines it helps to reconfirm your ticket and to hang around the check-in desk if the flight is full. Sometimes reservations are 'lost' when another passenger with better connections shows up.

Major airlines flying domestically include the following:

AirAsia (www.airasia.com) Fast-growing Malaysian-based budget carrier with a web of Indonesian domestic flights.

Batavia Air (www.batavia-air.com) Serves numerous destinations; has the enigmatic slogan: 'Trust us to fly'. Has been bought by AirAsia.

Garuda (www.garuda-indonesia.com) Serves major destinations across the archipelago with a young fleet.

Lion Air (www.lionair.co.id)

Merpati (www.merpati.co.id) Flies to some of the more obscure destinations in Indonesia.

Sriwijaya Air (www.sriwijayaair.co.id) Serves Java, Kalimantan, Sumatra and Sulawesi.

Transnusa (www.transnusa.co.id) Good for flights within Nusa Tenggara and for flights from Denpasar to places like Labuanbajo.

Tickets

The larger Indonesian-based carriers have websites listing fares, however it may be hard, if not impossible, to purchase tickets over the internet from outside Indonesia because of restrictive laws that limit sales to local credit cards.

Try these methods:

Website Some carriers, notably Garuda and AirAsia, have websites that typically accept cards from customers worldwide.

Booking Sites Major websites such as expedia.com may be a means to buy tickets on Indonesian airlines from outside the country.

Travel Agents A good way to buy domestic tickets once in Indonesia.

Friends Get an Indonesian friend or guesthouse owner to buy you a ticket on a website using their credit card, then pay them back.

Airport Sometimes the best way to get a domestic ticket

CLIMATE CHANGE & TRAVEL

Every form of transport that relies on carbon-based fuel generates CO_2, the main cause of human-induced climate change. Modern travel is dependent on aeroplanes, which might use less fuel per kilometre per person than most cars but travel much greater distances. The altitude at which aircraft emit gases (including CO_2) and particles also contributes to their climate change impact. Many websites offer 'carbon calculators' that allow people to estimate the carbon emissions generated by their journey and, for those who wish to do so, to offset the impact of the greenhouse gases emitted with contributions to portfolios of climate-friendly initiatives throughout the world. Lonely Planet offsets the carbon footprint of all staff and author travel.

DOMESTIC DEPARTURE TAX

The domestic departure tax in Indonesia varies by airport and costs from 10,000Rp to 50,000Rp. It's payable in cash at the airport.

for travel is to simply go to the airport and compare prices. Many airlines are strictly cash-based, and offer last-minute deals if there are empty seats.

Bicycle

If reasonably fit, and with a bit of preparation and a ton of common sense, a cyclist will enjoy an incomparable travel experience almost anywhere in the archipelago. The well-maintained roads of Bali, Lombok, East Java and South Sulawesi are suitable for cyclists of all ability levels, while the pros can head for the hills along the length of Sumatra or Nusa Tenggara.

The two primary difficulties are the heat and traffic. Resting during the hottest hours of the day remedies the first, and you can avoid most traffic problems by keeping to back roads or even jumping on a truck or bus to cover really dangerous sections. The third annoyance is being a constant focus of attention but you just have to get used to it.

You can rent bikes fairly easily on Bali and other tourist centres such as Yogyakarta, just ask at your accommodation. Rates range from 15,000Rp to 50,000Rp per day. However in places like Papua, bikes for hire are as common as snowballs.

Bicycling is gaining popularity among Indonesians and bicycle clubs will be delighted to aid a foreign guest. **Bike to Work** (www.b2w-indonesia.or.id) has an extensive national network. Many tourist areas, particularly Bali, Lombok and Yogyakarta offer organised, vehicle-supported bicycle tours.

At major sights you can usually find a parking attendant to keep an eye on your bicycle for 2000Rp.

Boat

Sumatra, Java, Bali, Nusa Tenggara and Sulawesi are all connected by regular ferries, and you can use them to island-hop all the way from Sumatra to Timor. These ferries run either daily or several times a week, so there's no need to spend days in sleepy little port towns. Check with shipping companies, the harbour office or travel agents for current schedules and fares.

Going to and between Kalimantan, Maluku and Papua, the main connections are provided by Pelni, the government- run passenger line. The increase in competitive airline prices has had a significant impact on many of Pelni's routes with frequencies down. Furthermore, Pelni ships generally only operate every two or four weeks, so you will have to plan carefully.

All of Indonesia's major ports and the majority of the archipelago's outlying areas are linked by the **Pelni** (www.pelni.co.id) fleet of large vessels. Pelni's website is a good resource, showing arrivals and departures about a month in advance.

Its ships operate set routes around the islands, either on a fortnightly or monthly schedule. The ships – most rather modern – usually stop for a few hours in each port, so there's time for a quick look around. Note that sailing times can be in flux until the last moment.

It's best to book at least a few days in advance. Pelni is not a tourist operation, so don't expect any special service, although there is usually somebody hidden away in the ticket offices who can help foreigners.

Fares can be quite cheap if you go for the cheaper classes but at higher levels of accommodation, budget airlines are competitive if not cheaper.

Pelni ships range from the modern, clean and well-run to less-modern, less-well-run and less-clean. Details include the following.

Classes Pelni ships have two to six classes. Economy class, which is the modern version of deck class, is a bare-bones experience. As you move up the price ladder, you exchange a seat on the deck for small accommodations until you reach a level that may give you your own private cabin with two beds (this is some variation of first class). Note that these are functional at best and far from lavish.

Security There are no locker facilities, so you have to keep an eye on your gear if you are in any kind of group class.

Crowding At busy times such as Idul Fitri boats seem to have passengers crammed into every available space including decks, passages and stairwells. Conditions can get grim.

Food Bring your own food and drink. Where there are food facilities, the conditions are basic and if the boat is crowded you may have a hard time stepping over other passengers to reach the restaurant.

Boarding Getting aboard a Pelni ship can leave you bruised as it is truly every man, woman and child for him or herself as people try to get to scarce space first.

Other Vessels

There's a whole range of boats you can use to hop between islands, down rivers and across lakes. Just about any sort of vessel can be rented in Indonesia.

Boat options include:

Fishing boats Small boats

TRAVELLING SAFELY BY BOAT

Boat safety is an important consideration across Indonesia, where boats that barely seem seaworthy may be your only option to visit that idyllic little island. In many cases these services are accidents waiting to happen, as safety regulation is not even spotty. This is especially true on the busy routes linking Bali, Nusa Lembongan, Lombok and the Gilis. In 2010 a boat between Lombok and Gili T capsized, killing three. Fast boats between Gili T and Bali have had accidents, and in each case, the tourists and crew aboard were lucky to survive by swimming to shore or being rescued by other boats that happened to be passing by. Also, conditions are often rough in Indonesia's waters. Although the islands are in close proximity and are easily seen, the ocean between can get more turbulent than is safe for small speedboats zipping across the heavy seas. With these facts in mind, it is essential that you take responsibility for your own safety, as no one else will.

Consider the following points for any boat travel in Indonesia:

Bigger is better It may take you 30 minutes or longer in travel time, but a larger boat will simply deal with the open ocean better than the over-powered small speedboats.

Check for safety equipment Make certain your boat has life preservers and that you know how to locate and use them. In an emergency, don't expect a panicked crew to hand them out. Also, check for life rafts.

Avoid over-crowding Travellers report boats leaving with more people than seats and with aisles jammed with stacked luggage.

Look for exits Cabins may only have one narrow entrance making them death traps in an accident.

Avoid fly-by-nighters Taking a fishing boat and jamming too many engines on the rear in order to cash in on booming tourism is a recipe for disaster.

can be chartered to take you to small offshore islands.

Longboat The *longbot* is a long, narrow boat powered by a couple of outboard motors, with bench seats on either side of the hull for passengers to sit on. They are mainly used in Kalimantan.

Outrigger canoes Used for some short inter-island hops, such as the trip out from Manado in North Sulawesi to the coral reefs surrounding nearby Pulau Bunaken. On Lombok these motorised boats are used for the short hop from Bangsal harbour to the Gilis.

River ferries Commonly found on Kalimantan, where the rivers *are* the roads. They're large, bulky vessels that carry passengers and cargo up and down the water network.

Tourist boats Often very fast speedboats outfitted to carry 40 or more passengers, most commonly used to buzz between Bali, Nusa Lembongan, Lombok and the Gilis.

Bus

Buses are the mainstay of Indonesian transport (excepting Papua). At any time of the day, thousands of buses in all shapes and sizes move thousands of people throughout Indonesia. The 'leave-when-full' school of scheduling applies to almost every service, and 'full' sometimes means the aisles are occupied too.

On major runs across Indonesia you will find air-con buses that are at least somewhat tolerable. The ever-more crowded roads mean that buses are often stuck in traffic. And on major routes, say the 24-hour run from Bali to Jakarta, budget airlines are competitive price-wise.

Still, in most cases buses are hot, bumpy, banged-up affairs with a lack of suspension. The going is generally slow. But they are undoubtedly the best way to meet and socialise with locals.

Bring as little luggage as possible – there is rarely any room to store anything on buses. A large pack with a frame will be difficult to find space for (and often ends up on your lap).

Take precautions with your personal belongings and keep your passport, money and any other valuables close at hand, preferably in a concealed money belt.

Classes

The main classes of bus are:

» Economy-class *(ekonomi)* buses that run set routes between towns. They can be hot, slow and crowded, but they're also ridiculously cheap and provide a never-ending parade of Indonesian life.

» Express *(patas)* buses look much the same as the economy buses, but stop only at selected bus terminals en route and (officially) don't pick up from the side of the road. Air-con *patas* buses are more comfortable and seating is often guaranteed.

» Air-con buses (or 'executive' buses) come in a variety of price categories, depending on whether facilities include reclining seats, toilets, TV, karaoke (usually very bad) or snacks. These buses should be booked in advance; ticket agents often have pictures of the buses and seating plans, so check to see what you are paying for when you choose your seat.

Costs

Economy-class bus prices vary from region to region and with the condition of the road. The daytime buses that depart early in the morning – carrying chickens, pigs and goats – are usually the cheapest. An eight-hour journey will cost 50,000Rp to 60,000Rp. By way of comparison, an eight-hour journey on an air-con overnight bus will cost 80,000Rp to 120,000Rp.

Reservations

Vehicles usually depart throughout the day for shorter routes over good roads; for longer routes, get down to the bus terminal early in order to get a vehicle. On bad roads, there'll be fewer vehicles, so buying a ticket beforehand can be a good idea. Air-con buses should be booked in advance.

Often, hotels will act as agents or buy a ticket for you and will arrange for the bus to pick you up at the hotel – they sometimes charge a few thousand rupiah for this service but it's worth it.

Car & Motorcycle

Driving Licence

To drive in Indonesia, you officially need an International Driving Permit (IDP) from your local automobile association. This permit is rarely required as identification when hiring/driving a car in Indonesia, but police may ask to see it. Bring your home licence as well – it's supposed to be carried in conjunction with the IDP. If you also have a motorcycle licence at home, get your IDP endorsed for motorcycles too.

Fuel

After decades of subsidies, fuel prices are now adjusted to reflect international oil prices. Only recently, premium petrol cost 5500Rp per litre (still cheap by Western standards). The opening of the domestic fuel market to foreign operators has spurred national oil company Pertamina to build full-service outlets *(pompa bensin)* throughout the archipelago.

Hire

CAR HIRE

Self-drive 4WDs can be hired for as little as 80,000Rp to 150,000Rp a day with limited insurance in Bali, but become increasingly expensive and hard to come by the further you get from tourist areas.

It is very common for tourists to hire a car with a driver and this can usually be arranged for 400,000Rp to 1,000,000Rp per day (500,000Rp per day is average in popular places like Bali, while remote areas like Papua and Kalimantan are the most expensive).

With a small group, a van and driver is not only economical but also allows maximum travel and touring freedom. Hotels can always arrange drivers.

MOTORCYCLE HIRE

Motorcycles and motorbikes are readily available for hire throughout Indonesia.

Motorcycles and scooters can be hired across Indonesia for 25,000Rp to 50,000Rp per day. Be sure to get a crash helmet, as wearing one is supposed to be compulsory. On Bali, many motorbike rentals come with a rack for your surfboard.

You need to have a licence, especially to satisfy travel insurance in case of an accident, though you'll rarely need to show it.

Some travel insurance policies do not cover you if you are involved in an accident while on a motorcycle. Check the small print.

Insurance

Rental agencies and owners usually insist that the vehicle itself is insured, and minimal insurance should be included in the basic rental deal – often with an excess of as much as US$100 for a motorcycle and US$500 for a car (ie the customer pays the first US$100/500 of any claim).

Your travel insurance may provide some additional protection, although liability for motor accidents is specifically excluded from many policies.

A private owner renting out a motorcycle may not offer any insurance at all. Ensure that your personal travel insurance covers injuries incurred while motorcycling.

Road Conditions

The relentless traffic congesting every Indonesian city makes driving an exhausting activity. On the open road, expect delays due to potholes and congestion. Finding your way around the main tourist sites on any island can be a challenge, as roads are only sometimes signposted and maps are often out of date.

In much of the country count on averaging only 35km per hour.

Road Rules

Indonesians drive on the left side of the road (sometimes the right, sometimes the pavement), as in Australia, Japan, the UK and most of Southeast Asia.

Considering the relatively small cost of a driver in relation to the total rental, it makes little sense to take the wheel yourself. Driving requires enormous amounts of concentration and the legal implications of accidents can be a nightmare as a foreigner – it's *your* fault.

Hitching

Hitching is not part of the culture but if you put out your thumb, someone may give you a lift. On the back roads where no public transport exists, hitching may be the only alternative to walking, and passing motorists or trucks are often willing to help.

Bear in mind, however, that hitching is never entirely safe in any country, and we do not recommend it. Travellers who decide to hitch should understand that they are taking a small but potentially serious risk. People who do choose to hitch will be safer if they travel in pairs and let someone know where they are planning to go.

Local Transport

Becak

These are three-wheeled bicycle-rickshaws. Unlike the version found in India where the driver sits in front of you, or the Filipino version with the driver at the side, in Indonesia the driver sits at the rear, with you riding point.

Many drivers rent their vehicles, but those who own them add personal touches: brightly painted pictures, bells or whirring metal discs strung across the undercarriage.

The becak is now banned from the main streets of some large cities, but you'll still see them swarming the back streets, moving anyone and anything.

Negotiate your fare *before* you get in; and if there are two passengers, make sure that it covers both people, otherwise you'll be in for an argument when you get to your destination. Becak drivers are hard bargainers but they will usually settle on a reasonable fare, around 2000Rp to 4000Rp per kilometre.

Hiring a becak for a period of time or for a round trip often makes good sense if you're planning to cover a lot of ground in one day, particularly in large places like Yogyakarta or Solo.

Bus

Large buses aren't used much as a means of city transport except on Java (although there is a nascent system on Bali). There's an extensive system of buses in Jakarta and these are universally cheap, but beware of pickpockets.

Dokar

A dokar is the jingling, horse-drawn cart found throughout the archipelago. The two-wheeled carts are brightly coloured with decorative motifs and bells, and the small horses or ponies often have long tassels attached to their bridle. A typical *dokar* has bench seating on either side, which can comfortably fit three or four people.

Foreigners may have to charter; 10,000Rp to 15,000Rp should get you just about anywhere around town.

Minibus

Public minibuses are used for local transport around cities and towns, short intercity runs and the furthest reaches of the transport network.

Minibuses are known as *bemos* or *angkot*, although they are called *taksi* in many parts of Papua, Kalimantan and East Java. Other names include *opelet*, *mikrolet*, *angkudes* and *pete-pete*.

Most minibuses operate a standard route, picking up and dropping off people and goods anywhere along the way. On longer routes between cities you may have to bargain a bit. Minibus drivers often try to overcharge foreigners and ask you for triple the amount they just accepted from a local. It's best to ask somebody, such as your hotel staff, about the *harga biasa* (normal price) before you get on; otherwise, see what the other passengers are paying and offer the correct fare.

Drivers wait until their vehicles are crammed to capacity before moving, or they may go *keliling* – driving endlessly around town looking for a full complement of passengers.

Conditions can be extremely cramped, especially if you have luggage.

Note also that on Bali, as much of the population have bought motorbikes, the *bemo* system is in decline.

Ojek

Ojeks (or *ojegs*) are motorcycle riders who take pillion passengers for a bargainable price. They are found at bus terminals and markets, or just hanging around at crossroads. They will take you around town and go where no other public transport exists, or along roads that are impassable in any other vehicle. They are the preferred method for navigating Jakarta traffic. They can also be rented by the hour for sightseeing (starting at around 20,000Rp to 30,000Rp).

Taxi

Metered taxis are readily available in major cities. If a taxi has a meter *(argo)*, make sure it is used. Most drivers will use them without fuss but like anywhere there are a few sharks. Where meters don't exist, you will have to bargain for the fare in advance. If available, always opt for licensed taxis that use metres, offers of 'transport' are almost always more costly than using a metered taxi.

In Jakarta and south Bali, Bluebird taxis are the best way to get around.

At airports, taxis usually operate on a prepaid system, payable at the relevant booth.

Tours

A wide range of trips can be booked from tour companies within Indonesia. But some of the best tours are with local guides, such as the ecotrips to Halimun National Park in Java with local guides in Bogor. We recommend dozens of local options.

There are also specialist tour companies that utilise their in-depth knowledge of local dialects, culture and experience to create experiences you'd have a hard time equaling independently.

Finally there are operators that can transport you around the archipelago in high style, say in a classic sailing ship.

A few to consider:

Adventure Indonesia (www.adventureindonesia.com) Top Indonesian adventure-tourism firm with offices in Jakarta, Bali, Papua, Kalimantan and Sulawesi.

Dewi Nusantara (www.dewi-nusantara.com) A 57m, three-masted traditional-style sailing ship that makes luxurious live-aboard diving journeys around the Malukus and Raja Ampat.

Discover Papua Adventure (☎0981 23196, 0852 4494 0860; www.discoverpapua.com; Hotel Arumbai, Jl Selat Makassar 3) A well-established Biak-based agency that can set up just about any trip you want, not only around Biak but throughout Papua and beyond.

Expedition Jungle (☎0813 7060 7035; www.expedition-jungle.com) North Sumatra travel, tours and jungle treks.

Laszlo Wagner (www.east-indonesia.info) Tailor-made trips around Maluku and Papua by a Hungarian-born writer.

SeaTrek Sailing Adventures (www.seatrekbali.com) Runs itineraries on sailing ships from Bali to Flores, as well as Banda Islands and Papua trips.

Silolona Sojurns (www.silolona.com) This luxury yacht built in the style of classic Spice Islands trading vessels sails through Nusa Tenggara, Maluku and Papua.

Train

Train travel in Indonesia is restricted to Java and Sumatra.

In Java, trains are one of the most comfortable, fastest and easiest ways to travel. In the east, the railway service connects with the ferry to Bali, and in the west with the ferry to Sumatra. Sumatra's limited rail network runs in the south from Bandarlampung to Lubuklinggau, and in the north from Medan to Tanjung Balai and Rantauparapat.

There are three classes, smoking is not allowed in any.

» Executive (*Eksecutif*) – air-con with mandatory reservations.

» Business (*bisnis*) – no air-con but mandatory seat reservations.

» Economy (*ekonomi*) – no air-con, crowded and unreserved.

The **railway's website** (☎0361-227 131; www.kereta-api.co.id) has more information; use the drop-down menus on the right, or '*Jadwal*' (schedule) can point you to schedules.

Health

Treatment for minor injuries and common traveller's health problems is easily accessed in larger cities and in Bali but standards decline the more remote you get in Indonesia. For serious conditions, you will need to leave Indonesia.

Travellers tend to worry about contracting infectious diseases when in the tropics, but infections are a rare cause of serious illness or death in travellers. Pre-existing medical conditions, such as heart disease, and accidental injury (especially traffic accidents) account for most life-threatening problems. Becoming ill in some way, however, is relatively common; ailments you may suffer include gastro, overexposure to the sun and other typical traveller woes.

It's important to note what precautions you should take in Indonesia. In Bali your major concerns are rabies, mosquito bites and the tropical sun. But elsewhere in the country there are numerous important considerations.

The following advice is a general guide only and does not replace the advice of a doctor trained in travel medicine.

BEFORE YOU GO

Make sure all medications are packed in their original, clearly labelled containers. A signed and dated letter from your physician describing your medical conditions and medications (including generic names) is also a good idea. If you are carrying syringes or needles, be sure to have a physician's letter documenting their medical necessity. If you have a heart condition ensure you bring a copy of your electrocardiogram taken just prior to travelling.

If you happen to take any regular medication bring double your needs in case of loss or theft. You can buy many medications over the counter without a doctor's prescription, but it can be difficult to find some of the newer drugs, particularly the latest antidepressant drugs, blood-pressure medications and contraceptive pills.

Insurance

Even if you are fit and healthy, don't travel without sufficient health insurance – accidents do happen. If you're uninsured, emergency evacuation is expensive – bills of more than US$100,000 are not uncommon.

Find out in advance if your insurance plan will make payments directly to providers or reimburse you later for overseas health expenditures. (In many countries doctors expect payment in cash at the time of treatment.) Some policies ask you to call back (reverse charges) to a centre in your home country where an immediate assessment of your problem is made.

Recommended Vaccinations

Specialised travel-medicine clinics are your best source of information; they stock all available vaccines and will be able to give specific recommendations for you and your trip.

Most vaccines don't produce immunity until at least two weeks after they're given. Ask your doctor for an International Certificate of Vaccination (otherwise known as the yellow booklet), which will list all the vaccinations you've received.

The World Health Organization's vaccination recommendations for Southeast Asia include the following:

Adult diphtheria and tetanus Single booster recommended if none in the previous 10 years. Side effects include sore arm and fever.

Hepatitis A Provides almost 100% protection for up to a year; a booster after 12 months provides at least another 20 years' protection. Mild side effects such as headache and sore arm occur in 5% to 10% of people.

Hepatitis B Now considered routine for most travellers. Given as three shots over six months. Life-time protection occurs in 95% of people.

Measles, Mumps & Rubella (MMR) Two doses of MMR are required unless you have had the diseases. Many young adults require a booster.

Polio Only one booster required as an adult for lifetime protection. Inactivated polio vaccine is safe during pregnancy.

Typhoid Recommended unless your trip is less than a week and only to developed cities. The vaccine offers around 70% protection, lasts for two to three years and comes as a single shot.

Varicella If you haven't had chickenpox, discuss this vaccination with your doctor.

These immunisations are recommended for long-term travellers (more than one month) or those at special risk.

Japanese B Encephalitis Three injections in all. Booster recommended after two years. Sore arm and headache are the most common side effects.

Meningitis Single injection. Recommended for long-term backpackers aged under 25.

Rabies Three injections in all. A booster after one year will then provide 10 years' protection. Side effects are rare – occasionally headache and sore arm.

Tuberculosis (TB) Adult long-term travellers are usually recommended to have a TB skin test before and after travel, rather than vaccination. Only one vaccine given in a lifetime.

Required Vaccinations

The only vaccine required by international regulations is yellow fever. Proof of vaccination will only be required if you have visited a country in the yellow-fever zone (primarily some parts of Africa and South America) within the six days prior to entering Southeast Asia.

Medical Checklist

Recommended items for a convenient personal medical kit (more specific items can be easily obtained in Indonesia if needed):

» antibacterial cream (eg muciprocin)

» antihistamine – there are many options (eg cetirizine for daytime and promethazine for night)

» antiseptic (eg Betadine)

» contraceptives

» DEET-based insect repellent

» first-aid items such as scissors, bandages, thermometer (but not a mercury one) and tweezers

» ibuprofen or another anti-inflammatory

» steroid cream for allergic/itchy rashes (eg 1% to 2% hydrocortisone)

» sunscreen and hat

» throat lozenges

» thrush (vaginal yeast infection) treatment (eg clotrimazole pessaries or diflucan tablet)

Websites

There is a wealth of travel health advice on the internet.

World Health Organization (WHO; www.who.int/ith/) Publishes a superb book called *International Travel & Health*, which is revised annually and is available online at no cost.

MD Travel Health (www.mdtravelhealth.com) Provides travel health recommendations for every country.

Centers for Disease Control & Prevention (CDC; www.cdc.gov) This website also has good general information.

Further Reading

Lonely Planet's *Asia & India: Healthy Travel* is a handy pocket-sized book that is packed with useful information, including pre-trip planning, emergency first aid, immunisation and disease information and what to do if you get sick on the road.

HEALTH ADVISORIES

It's usually a good idea to consult your government's travel health website before departure, if one is available:

Australia (www.smartraveller.gov.au)

UK (www.nhs.uk/nhsengland/healthcareabroad)

US (www.cdc.gov/travel)

IN INDONESIA

Availability & Cost of Health Care

It is difficult to find reliable medical care in rural areas, but most capital cities now have clinics catering specifically to travellers and expats. These clinics are usually more expensive than local medical facilities, but are worth utilising, as they will offer a superior standard of care. Additionally, they understand the local system and are aware of the safest local hospitals and best specialists. They can also liaise with insurance companies should you require evacuation.

If you think you may have a serious disease, especially malaria, do not waste time – travel immediately to the nearest quality facility to receive attention.

Local medical care in general is not yet up to international standards. Foreign doctors are not allowed to work in Indonesia, but some clinics (such as those in Bali and Jakarta) catering to foreigners have 'international advisors'. Almost all Indonesian doctors work at government hospitals during the day and in private practices at night. This means that private hospitals often don't have their best staff available during the day. Serious cases are evacuated to Australia or Singapore.

PHARMACIES

In Jakarta, other large cities and Bali, pharmacies are usually reliable. The Kimia Farma chain is good and has many locations. Singapore's Guardian chain of pharmacies is also found in tourist areas. Elsewhere be careful, as fake medications and poorly stored or out-of-date drugs are common.

Infectious Diseases

BIRD FLU

Otherwise known as avian influenza, the H5N1 virus has claimed more than 100 victims in Indonesia. Most cases have been in Java, west of Bali, although two people died in rural areas of Bali in 2007. Treatment is difficult, although the drug Tamiflu has some effect.

DENGUE FEVER

This mosquito-borne disease is a major problem. As there is no vaccine available it can only be prevented by avoiding mosquito bites. The mosquito that carries dengue bites day and night, so use insect avoidance measures at all times. Symptoms include high fever, severe headache and body ache. Some people develop a rash and experience diarrhoea. There is no specific treatment, just rest and paracetamol – do not take aspirin as it increases the likelihood of haemorrhaging. See a doctor to be diagnosed and monitored.

FILARIASIS

A mosquito-borne disease that is very common in the local population, yet very rare in travellers. Mosquito-avoidance measures are the best way to prevent this disease.

HEPATITIS A

A problem throughout the region, this food- and water-borne virus infects the liver, causing jaundice (yellow skin and eyes), nausea and lethargy. There is no specific treatment; you just need to allow time for the liver to heal. All travellers to Southeast Asia should be vaccinated against hepatitis A.

HEPATITIS B

The only sexually transmitted disease that can be prevented by vaccination, hepatitis B is spread by body fluids, including sexual contact. In some parts of Southeast Asia up to 20% of the population are carriers of hepatitis B.

HIV

HIV is a major problem in many Asian countries, and Bali has one of the highest rates of HIV infection in Indonesia. The main risk for most travellers is sexual contact with locals, prostitutes and other travellers.

The risk of sexual transmission of the HIV virus can be dramatically reduced by the use of a *kondom* (condom). These are available from supermarkets, street stalls and drugstores in tourist areas, and from the *apotik* in almost any town (from about 1500Rp to 3000Rp each – it's worth getting the more expensive brands).

JAPANESE B ENCEPHALITIS

While this is a rare disease in travellers, many locals are infected each year. This viral disease is transmitted by mosquitoes. Most cases occur in rural areas and vaccination is recommended for travellers spending more than one month outside of cities. There is no treatment, and a third of infected people will die while another third will suffer permanent brain damage.

MALARIA

The risk of contracting malaria is greatest in rural areas of Indonesia.

Two strategies should be combined to prevent malaria: mosquito avoidance and antimalarial medications.

Most people who catch malaria are taking either inadequate or no antimalarial medication.

Travellers are advised to prevent mosquito bites by taking these steps:

» Use a DEET-containing insect repellent on exposed skin. Wash this off at night, as long as you are sleeping under a mosquito net. Natural repellents such as citronella can be effective, but must be applied more frequently than products containing DEET.

» Sleep under a mosquito net impregnated with permethrin.

» Choose accommodation with screens and fans (if not air-conditioned).

» Impregnate clothing with permethrin in high-risk areas.

» Wear long sleeves and trousers in light colours.

» Use mosquito coils.

» Spray your room with insect repellent before going out for your evening meal.

There are a variety of medications available:

Artesunate Derivatives of Artesunate are not suitable as a preventive medication.

Chloroquine & Paludrine The effectiveness of this combination is now limited in most of Southeast Asia. Generally not recommended.

Doxycycline This daily tablet is a broad-spectrum antibiotic that has the added benefit of helping to prevent a variety of tropical diseases, including leptospirosis, tick-borne disease, typhus and melioidosis. Potential side effects include a tendency to sunburn, thrush in women, indigestion, heartburn, nausea and interference with the contraceptive pill.

Lariam (Mefloquine) Lariam has received much bad press, some of it justified, some not. This weekly tablet suits many people. Serious side effects are rare but include depression, anxiety, psychosis and having fits.

Malarone A combination of Atovaquone and Proguanil. Side effects, most commonly nausea and headache, are uncommon and mild. It is the best tablet for scuba divers and for those on short trips to high-risk areas. It must be taken for one week after leaving the risk area.

RABIES

Rabies is a disease spread by the bite or lick of an infected animal, most commonly a dog or monkey. Once you are exposed, it is uniformly fatal if you don't get the vaccine very promptly. Bali has had a major outbreak dating to 2008. Other cases have been reported in Nias and other islands off Sumatra.

To minimise your risk, consider getting the rabies vaccine, which consists of three injections in all. A booster after one year will then provide 10 years' protection. The vaccines are often unavailable on Bali, so get them before you go.

Also, be careful to avoid animal bites. Especially watch children closely.

Having the pre-travel vaccination means the post-bite treatment is greatly simplified. If you are bitten or scratched, gently wash the wound with soap and water, and apply an iodine-based antiseptic. It would be a good idea to also consult a doctor.

Those not vaccinated will need to receive rabies immunoglobulin as soon as possible. Clean the wound immediately and do not delay seeking medical attention. Note that Indonesia is known to run out of rabies immunoglobulin, so be prepared to go to Singapore immediately for medical treatment.

TYPHOID

This serious bacterial infection is spread via food and water. Its symptoms are a high and slowly progressive fever, headache and possibly a dry cough and stomach pain. It is diagnosed by blood tests and treated with antibiotics.

TRAVELLER'S DIARRHOEA

Traveller's diarrhoea (aka Bali belly) is by far the most common problem affecting travellers – between 30% and 50% of people will suffer from it within two weeks of starting their trip. In over 80% of cases, traveller's diarrhoea is caused by bacteria (there are numerous potential culprits), and therefore responds promptly to treatment with antibiotics.

Traveller's diarrhoea is defined as the passage of more than three watery bowel actions within 24 hours, plus at least one other symptom such as fever, cramps, nausea, vomiting or feeling generally unwell.

Loperamide is just a 'stopper' and doesn't get to the cause of the problem. However, it can be helpful, for example, if you have to go on a long bus ride. Don't take Loperamide if you have a fever or blood in your stools. Seek medical attention quickly if you do not respond to an appropriate antibiotic. Otherwise follow these guidelines:

- Stay well hydrated; rehydration solutions such as Gastrolyte are the best for this.
- Antibiotics such as Norfloxacin, Ciprofloxacin or Azithromycin will kill the bacteria quickly.

GIARDIASIS

Giardia lamblia is a parasite that is relatively common in travellers. Symptoms include nausea, bloating, excess gas, fatigue and intermittent diarrhoea. The parasite will eventually go away if left untreated but this can take months. The treatment of choice is Tinidazole, with Metronidazole being a second-line option.

Environmental Hazards

DIVING

Divers and surfers should seek specialised advice before they travel to ensure their medical kit contains treatment for coral cuts and tropical ear infections, as well as the standard problems. Divers should ensure their insurance covers them for decompression illness – get specialised dive insurance through an organisation such as **Divers Alert Network** (DAN; www.danseap.org). Have a dive medical before you leave your home country.

HEAT

Most parts of Indonesia are hot and humid throughout the year. For most people it takes at least two weeks to adapt to the hot climate. Swelling of the feet and ankles is common, as are muscle cramps caused by excessive sweating. Prevent these by avoiding dehydration and excessive activity in the heat. Be careful to avoid the following conditions:

Heat Exhaustion Symptoms include feeling weak; headache; irritability; nausea or vomiting; sweaty skin; a fast, weak pulse; and a normal or slightly elevated body temperature. Treatment involves getting out of the heat and/or sun, fanning the victim and applying cool wet cloths to the skin, laying the victim flat with their legs raised, and rehydrating with water containing one-quarter of a teaspoon of salt per litre. Recovery is usually rapid and it is common to feel weak for some days afterwards.

Heatstroke A serious medical emergency. Symptoms

DRINKING WATER

» Never drink tap water in Indonesia.

» Widely available and cheap, bottled water is generally safe, however, check the seal is intact when purchasing. Look for places that allow you to refill containers, thus cutting down on landfill.

» Most ice in restaurants is fine if it is uniform in size and made at a central plant (standard for large cities and tourist areas). Avoid ice that is chipped off larger blocks (more common in rural areas).

» Avoid fresh juices outside of tourist restaurants and cafes.

come on suddenly and include weakness, nausea, a hot dry body with a body temperature of over 41°C, dizziness, confusion, loss of coordination, fits and eventually collapse and loss of consciousness. Seek urgent medical help and commence cooling by getting the person out of the heat, removing their clothes, fanning them and applying cool wet cloths or ice to their body, especially to hot spots such as the groin and armpits.

Prickly Heat A common skin rash in the tropics, caused by sweat being trapped under the skin. The result is an itchy rash of tiny lumps. Treat by moving out of the heat into an air-conditioned area for a few hours and by having cool showers.

BITES & STINGS

During your time in Indonesia, you may make some unwanted friends.

Bedbugs These don't carry disease but their bites are very itchy. They live in the cracks of furniture and walls and then migrate to the bed at night to feed on you as you sleep. You can treat the itch with an antihistamine.

Jellyfish Most are not dangerous, just irritating. Stings can be extremely painful but rarely fatal. First aid for jellyfish stings involves pouring vinegar onto the affected area to neutralise the poison. Do not rub sand or water onto the stings. Take painkillers, and anyone who feels ill in any way after being stung should seek medical advice.

Ticks Contracted after walking in rural areas, ticks are commonly found behind the ears, on the belly and in armpits. If you have had a tick bite and experience symptoms such as a rash at the site of the bite or elsewhere, fever or muscle aches, you should see a doctor.

SKIN PROBLEMS

Fungal Rashes There are two common fungal rashes that affect travellers. The first occurs in moist areas that get less air such as the groin, armpits and between the toes. It starts as a red patch that slowly spreads and is usually itchy. Treatment involves keeping the skin dry, avoiding chafing and using an antifungal cream such as Clotrimazole or Lamisil. Tinea versicolor is also common – this fungus causes small, light-coloured patches, most commonly on the back, chest and shoulders. Consult a doctor.

Cuts & Scratches Easily infected in tropical climates, take meticulous care of any cuts and scratches. Immediately wash all wounds in clean water and apply antiseptic. If you develop signs of infection see a doctor. Divers and surfers should be careful with coral cuts as they become easily infected.

SUNBURN

Even on a cloudy day sunburn can occur rapidly, especially near the equator. Don't end up like the dopey tourists you see roasted pink on Bali's Kuta Beach. Instead follow these guidelines:

» Use a strong sunscreen (at least SPF 30+).

» Reapply sunscreen after a swim.

» Wear a wide-brimmed hat and sunglasses.

» Avoid baking in the sun during the hottest part of the day (10am to 2pm).

Women's Health

In tourist areas and large cities, supplies are easily found. This becomes more difficult the more rural you go.

Birth-control options may be limited so bring adequate supplies of your own form of contraception.

Language

WANT MORE?

For in-depth language information and handy phrases, check out Lonely Planet's *Indonesian Phrasebook*. You'll find it at **shop .lonelyplanet.com**, or you can buy Lonely Planet's iPhone phrasebooks at the Apple App Store.

Indonesian, or Bahasa Indonesia as it's known to the locals, is the official language of Indonesia. It has approximately 220 million speakers, although it's the mother tongue for only about 20 million – most people also speak their own indigenous language. As a traveller you shouldn't worry too much about learning local languages, but it can be fun to learn a few words – we've included the basics for Balinese and Javanese in this chapter. For practical purposes, it probably makes better sense to concentrate your efforts on learning Bahasa Indonesia.

Indonesian pronunciation is easy to master. Each letter always represents the same sound and most letters are pronounced the same as their English counterparts. Just remember that *c* is pronounced as the 'ch' in 'chat' and *sy* as the 'sh' in 'ship'. Note also that *kh* is a throaty sound (like the 'ch' in the Scottish *loch*), and that the *ng* and *ny* combinations, which are also found in English at the end or in the middle of words such as 'ringing' and 'canyon' respectively, can also appear at the beginning of words in Indonesian.

Syllables generally carry equal emphasis – the main exception is the unstressed *e* in words such as *besar* (big) – but the rule of thumb is to stress the second-last syllable.

In written Indonesian there are some inconsistent spellings of place names. Compound names are written as one word or two, eg Airsanih or Air Sanih, Padangbai or Padang Bai. Words starting with 'Ker' sometimes lose the *e*, eg Kerobokan/Krobokan. Some Dutch variant spellings also remain in use, with *tj* instead of the modern *c* (eg Tjampuhan/Campuan), and *oe* instead of *u* (eg Soekarno/Sukarno).

Pronouns, particularly 'you', are rarely used in Indonesian. *Anda* is the egalitarian form used to overcome the plethora of words for 'you'.

BASICS

Hello.	*Salam.*
Goodbye. (if leaving)	*Selamat tinggal.*
Goodbye. (if staying)	*Selamat jalan.*
How are you?	*Apa kabar?*
I'm fine, and you?	*Kabar baik, Anda bagaimana?*
Excuse me.	*Permisi.*
Sorry.	*Maaf.*
Please.	*Silahkan.*
Thank you.	*Terima kasih.*
You're welcome.	*Kembali.*
Yes.	*Ya.*
No.	*Tidak.*
Mr/Sir	*Bapak*
Ms/Mrs/Madam	*Ibu*
Miss	*Nona*
What's your name?	*Siapa nama Anda?*
My name is ...	*Nama saya ...*
Do you speak English?	*Bisa berbicara Bahasa Inggris?*
I don't understand.	*Saya tidak mengerti.*

ACCOMMODATION

Do you have any rooms available?	*Ada kamar kosong?*
How much is it per night/person?	*Berapa satu malam/ orang?*
Is breakfast included?	*Apakah harganya ter masuk makan pagi?*
I'd like to share a dorm.	*Saya mau satu tempat tidur di asrama.*

campsite	*tempat kemah*
guesthouse	*losmen*
hotel	*hotel*
youth hostel	*pemuda*

a ... room	*kamar ...*
single	*untuk satu orang*
double	*untuk dua orang*

air-conditioned	*dengan AC*
bathroom	*kamar mandi*
cot	*velbet*
window	*jendela*

DIRECTIONS

Where is ...?	*Di mana ...?*
What's the address?	*Alamatnya di mana?*
Could you write it down, please?	*Anda bisa tolong tuliskan?*
Can you show me (on the map)?	*Anda bisa tolong tunjukkan pada saya (di peta)?*

at the corner	*di sudut*
at the traffic lights	*di lampu merah*
behind	*di belakang*
in front of	*di depan*
far (from)	*jauh (dari)*
left	*kiri*
near (to)	*dekat (dengan)*
next to	*di samping*
opposite	*di seberang*
right	*kanan*
straight ahead	*lurus*

EATING & DRINKING

What would you recommend?	*Apa yang Anda rekomendasikan?*
What's in that dish?	*Hidangan itu isinya apa?*
That was delicious.	*Ini enak sekali.*
Cheers!	*Bersulang!*
Bring the bill/check, please.	*Tolong bawa kuitansi.*

I don't eat ...	*Saya tidak mau makan ...*
dairy products	*susu dan keju*
fish	*ikan*
(red) meat	*daging (merah)*
peanuts	*kacang tanah*
seafood	*makanan laut*

KEY PATTERNS

To get by in Indonesian, mix and match these simple patterns with words of your choice:

Where's (the station)?	*Di mana (stasiun)?*
When's (the next bus)?	*Jam berapa (bis yang berikutnya)?*
How much is it (per night)?	*Berapa (satu malam)?*
I'm looking for (a hotel).	*Saya cari (hotel).*
Do you have (a local map)?	*Ada (peta daerah)?*
Is there (a toilet)?	*Ada (kamar kecil)?*
Can I (enter)?	*Boleh saya (masuk)?*
Do I need (a visa)?	*Saya harus pakai (visa)?*
I have (a reservation).	*Saya (sudah punya booking).*
I need (assistance).	*Saya perlu (dibantu).*
I'd like (the menu).	*Saya minta (daftar makanan).*
I'd like to (hire a car).	*Saya mau (sewa mobil).*
Could you (help me)?	*Bisa Anda (bantu) saya?*

a table ...	*meja ...*
at (eight) o'clock	*pada jam (delapan)*
for (two) people	*untuk (dua) orang*

Key Words

baby food (formula)	*susu kaleng*
bar	*bar*
bottle	*botol*
bowl	*mangkuk*
breakfast	*sarapan*
cafe	*kafe*
children's menu	*menu untuk anak-anak*
cold	*dingin*
dinner	*makan malam*
dish	*piring*
drink list	*daftar minuman*
food	*makanan*
food stall	*warung*
fork	*garpu*

Question Words

How?	*Bagaimana?*
What?	*Apa?*
When?	*Kapan?*
Where?	*Di mana?*
Which	*Yang mana?*
Who?	*Siapa?*
Why?	*Kenapa?*

glass	*gelas*
highchair	*kursi tinggi*
hot (warm)	*panas*
knife	*pisau*
lunch	*makan siang*
menu	*daftar makanan*
market	*pasar*
napkin	*tisu*
plate	*piring*
restaurant	*rumah makan*
salad	*selada*
soup	*sop*
spicy	*pedas*
spoon	*sendok*
vegetarian food	*makanan tanpa daging*
with	*dengan*
without	*tanpa*

Meat & Fish

beef	*daging sapi*
carp	*ikan mas*
chicken	*ayam*
duck	*bebek*
fish	*ikan*
lamb	*daging anak domba*
mackerel	*tenggiri*
meat	*daging*
pork	*daging babi*
shrimp/prawn	*udang*
tuna	*cakalang*
turkey	*kalkun*

Fruit & Vegetables

apple	*apel*
banana	*pisang*
beans	*kacang*
cabbage	*kol*
carrot	*wortel*
cauliflower	*blumkol*
cucumber	*timun*
dates	*kurma*
eggplant	*terung*
fruit	*buah*
grapes	*buah anggur*
lemon	*jeruk asam*
orange	*jeruk manis*
pineapple	*nenas*
potato	*kentang*
raisins	*kismis*
spinach	*bayam*
vegetable	*sayur-mayur*
watermelon	*semangka*

Other

bread	*roti*
butter	*mentega*
cheese	*keju*
chilli	*cabai*
chilli sauce	*sambal*
egg	*telur*
honey	*madu*
jam	*selai*
noodles	*mie*
oil	*minyak*
pepper	*lada*
rice	*nasi*
salt	*garam*
soy sauce	*kecap*
sugar	*gula*
vinegar	*cuka*

Drinks

beer	*bir*
coconut milk	*santan*

Signs

Buka	Open
Dilarang	Prohibited
Kamar Kecil	Toilets
Keluar	Exit
Masuk	Entrance
Pria	Men
Tutup	Closed
Wanitai	Women

coffee	*kopi*
juice	*jus*
milk	*susu*
palm sap wine	*tuak*
red wine	*anggur merah*
soft drink	*minuman ringan*
tea	*teh*
water	*air*
white wine	*anggur putih*
yogurt	*susu masam kental*

EMERGENCIES

Help!	*Tolong saya!*
I'm lost.	*Saya tersesat.*
Leave me alone!	*Jangan ganggu saya!*
Call a doctor!	*Panggil dokter!*
Call the police!	*Panggil polisi!*
I'm ill.	*Saya sakit.*
It hurts here.	*Sakitnya di sini.*
I'm allergic to (antibiotics).	*Saya alergi (antibiotik).*

SHOPPING & SERVICES

I'd like to buy ...	*Saya mau beli ...*
I'm just looking.	*Saya lihat-lihat saja.*
May I look at it?	*Boleh saya lihat?*
I don't like it.	*Saya tidak suka.*
How much is it?	*Berapa harganya?*
It's too expensive.	*Itu terlalu mahal.*
Can you lower the price?	*Boleh kurang?*
There's a mistake in the bill.	*Ada kesalahan dalam kuitansi ini.*

credit card	*kartu kredit*
foreign exchange office	*kantor penukaran mata uang asing*
internet cafe	*warnet*
mobile/cell phone	*hanpon*
post office	*kantor pos*
signature	*tanda tangan*
tourist office	*kantor pariwisata*

Numbers

1	*satu*
2	*dua*
3	*tiga*
4	*empat*
5	*lima*
6	*enam*
7	*tujuh*
8	*delapan*
9	*sembilan*
10	*sepuluh*
20	*duapuluh*
30	*tigapuluh*
40	*empatpuluh*
50	*limapuluh*
60	*enampuluh*
70	*tujuhpuluh*
80	*delapanpuluh*
90	*sembilanpuluh*
100	*seratus*
1000	*seribu*

TIME & DATES

What time is it?	*Jam berapa sekarang?*
It's (10) o'clock.	*Jam (sepuluh).*
It's half past (six).	*Setengah (tujuh).*
in the morning	*pagi*
in the afternoon	*siang*
in the evening	*malam*
yesterday	*kemarin*
today	*hari ini*
tomorrow	*besok*

Monday	*hari Senin*
Tuesday	*hari Selasa*
Wednesday	*hari Rabu*
Thursday	*hari Kamis*
Friday	*hari Jumat*
Saturday	*hari Sabtu*
Sunday	*hari Minggu*

TRANSPORT

Public Transport

bicycle-rickshaw	*becak*
boat (general)	*kapal*
boat (local)	*perahu*
bus	*bis*
minibus	*bemo*
motorcycle-rickshaw	*bajaj*
motorcycle-taxi	*ojek*
plane	*pesawat*
taxi	*taksi*
train	*kereta api*

LOCAL LANGUAGES

Bahasa Indonesia is a second language for 90% of Indonesians. More than 700 *bahasa daerah* (local languages) rank Indonesia second only to Papua New Guinea in linguistic diversity. As a visitor, you'll never be expected to speak any local languages, but there's no doubt that locals will appreciate your extra effort.

Here are some useful basic phrases in Balinese (which has around four million speakers in Bali) and Javanese (spoken by about 80 million people in Java). Note that these languages don't have specific phrases for greetings like 'hello' or 'goodbye'. Also, there are three distinct language 'levels' – the differences are related to the social status of the speaker. We've provided the 'middle level' understood by all Balinese and Javanese speakers.

Balinese

How are you? *Kenken kabare?*
Thank you. *Matur suksma.*
What's your name? *Sire wastene?*
My name is ... *Adan tiange ...*
I don't understand. *Tiang sing ngerti.*
How much is this? *Ji kude niki?*
Do you speak Balinese? *Bisa ngomong Bali sing?*
What do you call this in Balinese? *Ne ape adane di Bali?*
Which is the way to (Ubud)? *Kije jalan lakar kel (Ubud)?*

Javanese

How are you? *Piye kabare?*
Thank you. *Matur nuwun.*
What's your name? *Nami panjenengan sinten?*
My name is ... *Nami kula ...*
I don't understand. *Kula mboten mangertos.*
How much is this? *Pinten regine?*
Do you speak Javanese? *Sapeyan saged basa Jawi?*
What do you call this in Javanese? *Napa namine ing basa Jawi?*
Which is the way to (Kaliurang)? *Menawi bade dateng (Kaliurang) langkung pundi, nggih?*

I want to go to ... *Saya mau ke ...*
At what time does it leave? *Jam berapa berangkat?*
At what time does it arrive at ...? *Jam berapa sampai di ...?*
Does it stop at ...? *Di ... berhenti?*
What's the next stop? *Apa nama halte berikutnya?*
Please tell me when we get to ... *Tolong, beritahu waktu kita sampai di ...*
Please stop here. *Tolong, berhenti di sini.*

a ... ticket *tiket ...*
1st-class *kelas satu*
2nd-class *kelas dua*
one-way *sekali jalan*
return *pulang pergi*

first/last *pertama/terakhir*
platform *peron*
ticket office *loket tiket*
timetable *jadwal*
train station *stasiun kereta api*

Driving & Cycling

I'd like to hire a ... *Saya mau sewa ...*
4WD *gardan ganda*
bicycle *sepeda*
car *mobil*
motorcycle *sepeda motor*

child seat *kursi anak untuk di mobil*
helmet *helem*
mechanic *montir*
petrol *bensin*
pump (bicycle) *pompa sepeda*
service station *pompa bensin*

Is this the road to ...? *Apakah jalan ini ke ...?*
(How long) Can I park here? *(Berapa lama) Saya boleh parkir di sini?*
The car/motocycle has broken down. *Mobil/Motor mogok.*
I have a flat tyre. *Ban saya kempes.*
I've run out of petrol. *Saya kehabisan bensin.*

GLOSSARY

adat – traditional laws and regulations
air – water
air panas – hot springs
air terjun – waterfall
AMA – Associated Mission Aviation; Catholic missionary air service operating in remote regions of Papua
anak – child
angklung – musical instrument made from different lengths and thicknesses of bamboo suspended in a frame
angkot – or *angkota;* short for *angkutan kota* (city transport); small minibuses covering city routes, like a *bemo*
angkudes – short for *angkutan pedesaan;* minibuses running to nearby villages from cities, or between villages
anjing – dog
arja – refined operatic form of Balinese theatre
Arjuna – hero of the *Mahabharata* epic and a popular temple gate guardian image

babi rusa – wild deer-like pig
bahasa – language; Bahasa Indonesia is the national language
bajaj – motorised three-wheeler taxi found in Jakarta
bale – open-sided Balinese pavilion, house or shelter with steeply pitched roof; meeting place
balok– palm wine
bandar – harbour, port
bandara – airport
banjar – local division; a Balinese village consisting of married adult males
bapak – often shortened to *pak;* father; also a polite form of address to any older man
barat – west
Barong – mythical lion-dog creature
batik – cloth made by coating part of the fabric with wax, then dyeing it and melting the wax out
batik cap – stamped batik
batik tulis – hand-painted or literally 'written' batik
becak – bicycle-rickshaw
bemo – minibus
bendi – two-person horse-drawn cart; used in Sulawesi, Sumatra and Maluku
bensin – petrol
benteng – fort
bentor – motorised *becak*
Betawi – original name of Batavia (now Jakarta); ethnic group indigenous to Jakarta
bis – bus
bouraq – winged horselike creature with the head of a woman
Brahma – the creator; with Shiva and Vishnu part of the trinity of chief Hindu gods
bu – shortened form of *ibu*
bukit – hill
bule – common term for foreigner
bupati – government official in charge of a *kabupaten*

caci – a ceremonial martial art in which participants duel with whips and shields
candi – shrine or temple; usually Hindu or Buddhist of ancient Javanese design
cenderawasih – bird of paradise
colt – minibus

dalang – puppeteer and storyteller of *wayang kulit*
danau – lake
dangdut – popular Indonesian music that is characterised by wailing vocals and a strong beat
desa – village
dinas pariwisata – tourist office
dokar – two-person, horse-drawn cart
dukun – faith healer and herbal doctor; mystic

Gajah Mada – famous Majapahit prime minister
gamelan – traditional Javanese and Balinese orchestra
gang – alley or footpath
Garuda – mythical man-bird, the vehicle of Vishnu and the modern symbol of Indonesia
gereja – church
gili – islet, atoll
Golkar – Golongan Karya (Functional Groupings) political party
gua – or *goa*; cave
gunung – mountain
gunung api – volcano; literally 'fire mountain'

harga touris – tourist price
hutan – forest, jungle

ibu – often shortened to *bu;* mother; also polite form of address to an older woman
ikat – cloth in which the pattern is produced by dyeing the individual threads before weaving

jadwal – schedule or timetable
jalan – abbreviated to Jl; street or road
jalan jalan – to go for a stroll
jalan potong – short cut
jam karet – 'rubber time'; time is flexible
jamu – herbal medicine
jembatan – bridge
jilbab – Muslim head covering worn by women

kabupaten – regency
kain – cloth
kaki lima – mobile food carts; literally 'five feet' (the three feet of the cart and the two of the vendor)
kala – demonic face often seen over temple gateways
kamar kecil – toilet; literally 'small room'; also known as WC (pronounced way-say)
kampung – village, neighbourhood

kantor – office

Kantor Bupati – Governor's Office

karang – coral, coral reef, atoll

kav – lot, parcel of land

kepala desa – village head

kepulauan – archipelago

keraton – see kraton

ketoprak – popular Javanese folk theatre

Ketuktilu – traditional Sundanese (Java) dance in which professional female dancers perform for male spectators

kijang – a type of deer; also a popular Toyota 4WD vehicle, often used for public transport (Kijang)

KKN – Korupsi, Kolusi, Nepotisme; Corruption, Collusion, Nepotism; buzz word of the post-Suharto reform era

kora-kora – canoe (Papua)

kramat – shrine

kraton – walled city palace

kretek – Indonesian clove cigarette

kris – wavy-bladed traditional dagger, often held to have spiritual or magical powers

krismon – monetary crisis

kulit – leather

lapangan – field, square

laut – sea, ocean

Legong – classic Balinese dance performed by young girls; Legong dancer

lontar – type of palm tree; traditional books were written on the dried leaves of the lontar palm

losmen – basic accommodation, usually cheaper than hotels and often family-run

MAF – Mission Aviation Fellowship; Protestant missionary air service that operates in remote regions

Mahabharata – venerated Hindu holy book, telling of the battle between the Pandavas and the Kauravas

Majapahit – last great Javanese Hindu dynasty, pushed out of Java into Bali by the rise of Islamic power

makam – grave

mandau – machete (Kalimantan)

mandi – common Indonesian form of bath, consisting of a large water tank from which water is ladled over the body

marapu – term for all spiritual forces, including gods, spirits and ancestors

mata air panas – hot springs

menara – minaret, tower

meru – multiroofed shrines in Balinese temples; the same roof style also can be seen in ancient Javanese mosques

mesjid – *masjid* in Papua; mosque

mikrolet – small taxi; tiny *opelet*

moko – bronze drum from Pulau Alor (Nusa Tenggara)

muezzin – mosque official who calls the faithful to prayer five times a day

ngadhu – parasol-like thatched roof; ancestor totem of the Ngada people of Flores

nusa – island

Odalan – temple festival held every 210 days (duration of the Balinese year)

ojek – or *ojeg;* motorcycle taxi

oleh-oleh – souvenirs

opelet – small minibus, like a *bemo*

OPM – Organisasi Papua Merdeka; Free Papua Movement; main group that opposes Indonesian rule of Papua

orang putih – white person, foreigner; *bule* is more commonly used

pak – shortened form of *bapak*

PAN – Partai Amanat Nasional; National Mandate Party

pantai – beach

pasar – market

pasar malam – night market

pasar terapung – floating market

pasir – beach, sand

patas – express, express bus

patola – ikat motif of a hexagon framing a type of four-pronged star

PDI – Partai Demokrasi Indonesia; Indonesian Democratic Party

PDI-P – Partai Demokrasi Indonesia-Perjuangan; Indonesian Democratic Party for Struggle

pegunungan – mountain range

pelabuhan – harbour, port, dock

pelan pelan – slowly

pelawangan – gateway

Pelni – Pelayaran Nasional Indonesia; national shipping line with a fleet of passenger ships operating throughout the archipelago

pencak silat – form of martial arts originally from Sumatra, but now popular throughout Indonesia

pendopo – large, open-sided pavilion that serves as an audience hall; located in front of a Javanese palace

penginapan – simple lodging house

perahu – or *prahu;* boat or canoe

pesanggrahan – or *pasanggrahan;* lodge for government officials where travellers can usually stay

pete-pete – a type of *mikrolet* or *bemo* found in Sulawesi

PHKA – Perlindungan Hutan & Konservasi Alam; the Directorate General of Forest Protection & Nature Conservation; manages Indonesia's national parks; formerly PHPA

pinang – betel nut

pinisi – Makassar or Bugis schooner

PKB – Partai Kebangkitan Bangsa; National Awakening Party

pondok – or *pondok wisata;* guesthouse or lodge; hut
PPP – Partai Persatuan Pembangunan; Development Union Party
prahu – boat or canoe
prasada – shrine or temple; usually Hindu or Buddhist of ancient Javanese design
pulau – island
puputan – warrior's fight to the death; honourable, but suicidal, option when faced with an unbeatable enemy
pura – Balinese temple, shrine
pura dalem – Balinese temple of the dead
pura puseh – Balinese temple of origin
puri – palace
pusaka – sacred heirlooms of a royal family
puskesmas – short for *pusat kesehatan masyarakat;* community health centre

rafflesia – gigantic flower found in Sumatra and Kalimantan, with blooms spreading up to a metre
Ramadan – Muslim month of fasting, when devout Muslims refrain from eating, drinking and smoking during daylight hours
Ramayana – one of the great Hindu holy books; many Balinese and Javanese dances and tales are based on stories from the Ramayana
rangda – witch; evil black-magic spirit of Balinese tales and dances
rawa – swamp, marsh, wetlands
rebab – two-stringed bowed lute
reformasi – reform; refers to political reform after the repression of the Suharto years
RMS – Republik Maluku Selatan; South Maluku Republic; main group that opposed Indonesian rule of southern Maluku
rumah adat – traditional house
rumah makan – restaurant or *warung*
rumah sakit – hospital, literally 'sick house'

sarong – or *sarung;* all-purpose cloth, often sewn into a tube, and worn by women, men and children
Sasak – native of Lombok
sawah – an individual rice field; wet-rice method of cultivation
selat – strait
selatan – south
sembako – Indonesia's nine essential culinary ingredients: rice, sugar, eggs, meat, flour, corn, fuel, cooking oil and salt
semenanjung – peninsula
sirih pinang – betel nut, chewed as a mild narcotic
songket – silver- or gold-threaded cloth, hand woven using floating-weft technique
suling – bamboo flute
sungai – river
surat jalan – travel permit

taksi – common term for a public minibus; taxi
taman – ornamental garden, park, reserve
taman laut – marine park, marine reserve
taman nasional – national park
tanjung – peninsula, cape
tarling – musical style of the Cirebon (Java) area, featuring guitar, *suling* and voice
taxi – besides the Western definition which often applies, in some places this can be a small minibus like a *bemo*
taxi sungai – cargo-carrying river ferry with bunks on the upper level
telaga – lake
telepon kartu – telephone card
teluk – bay
timur – east
tirta – water (Bali)
TNI – Tentara Nasional Indonesia; Indonesian armed forces; formerly ABRI
toko mas – gold shop
tomate – Torajan funeral ceremony
tongkonan – traditional Torajan house with towering roof (Sulawesi)
topeng – wooden mask used in dance-dramas and funerary dances
tuak – homemade fermented coconut drink

uang – money
ular – snake
utara – north

wali songo – nine saints of Islam, who spread the religion throughout Java
Wallace Line – hypothetical line dividing Bali and Kalimantan from Lombok and Sulawesi; marks the end of Asian and the beginning of Australasian flora and fauna zones
waringin – banyan tree; large, shady tree with drooping branches that root and can produce new trees
warnet – short for *wartel internet;* internet stall or centre
warpostel – or *warpapostel;* wartel that also handles postal services
wartel – short for *warung telekomunikasi;* private telephone office
warung – simple eatery
wayang kulit – shadow-puppet play
wayang orang – or *wayang wong;* people theatre
wayang topeng – masked dance-drama
Wektu Telu – religion peculiar to Lombok that originated in Bayan and combines many tenets of Islam and aspects of other faiths
wisma – guesthouse or lodge

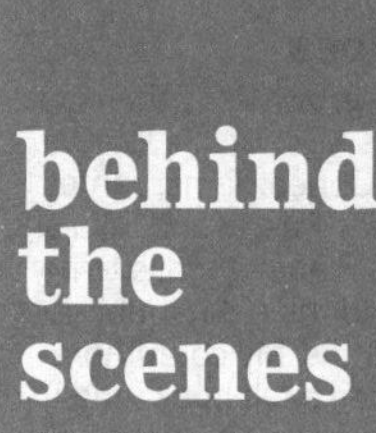

SEND US YOUR FEEDBACK

We love to hear from travellers – your comments keep us on our toes and help make our books better. Our well-travelled team reads every word on what you loved or loathed about this book. Although we cannot reply individually to postal submissions, we always guarantee that your feedback goes straight to the appropriate authors, in time for the next edition. Each person who sends us information is thanked in the next edition – the most useful submissions are rewarded with a selection of digital PDF chapters.

Visit **lonelyplanet.com/contact** to submit your updates and suggestions or to ask for help. Our award-winning website also features inspirational travel stories, news and discussions.

Note: We may edit, reproduce and incorporate your comments in Lonely Planet products such as guidebooks, websites and digital products, so let us know if you don't want your comments reproduced or your name acknowledged. For a copy of our privacy policy visit lonelyplanet.com/privacy.

OUR READERS

Many thanks to the travellers who used the last edition and wrote to us with helpful hints, useful advice and interesting anecdotes:

Alejandro, Brian Aardvaark, Sybrandus Adema, Mauricio Aguilera Linde, John Ahern, Linda Ambrosio, Kenneth Anderson, Luc Anthonis, Bagus Aropasa Yopri Sam, Rebecca Austin, Yuri Awanohara, Marwa Ayadi, Christiaan Baan, Danielle Barkerwood, Alison Barton, Isabella Bauer, Sebastien Beauchamps, Hanna Beckmann, Rutger Bimmel, Amei Binns, Katrin Bock, Anja Bohnsack, Yvonne Bohr, Erwin Bolwidt, Milan Boom, Gary Borgan, Tobias Bothe, Erik Bouwmeester, Sonja Brady, Kim Brandis, Bonnie Brown, Doris Buchholzer, Nikki Buran, Gregory Campbell, John Carey, Celine Carnegie, Kirk Chen, Brendan Cherry, David Christian Berg, Marie Christiansson, Agnieszka Chrzanowska, Aimee Clark, Bruno Clarke, Roxanne Cole, Paul Cooper, Fabrice Coradin, Thomas Coremans, Monique Counihan, Francis Cousin, Daisy Crawford, Martha Crunkleton, Jakub Danilewicz, Geoff De Burca, Herman De Wild, Massimiliano De Reviziis, Sarah De Wulf, Stefanie Decker, Cristina Delgado, Jack Dempsey, Henk Den Toom, Walter Denzel, Toon Dewerchin, Putri Diah Ekowati, Anne Dickson, Gerhard Dieter Ruf, Christopher Dolan, Evelyne Donnadieu, John Donoghue, Kelly Douglas, Carl Downer, Eveline Ebbeling, Edy Edison, Mary Elliiot, Ben Elliott, Steven Engelsman, Sisca Esperanza, Guido Faes, Kees Faling, David Feldman, Nic Fitzgerald, Ollie Forbes, Don Foster, Marjorie Foster, Katrin Frey & Andreas Held, Jan Fribert, Tina Fromme, Jane Fuller, Uschi Gaida, Rex-Marten Gaidies, Laurent Galice, Tatjana Gazibara, Hans Gerber, Crispin Gibbs, Asiya Giniatullina, Gauthier Ginisty, Wouter Glaser, Luke Glenday, Lisa Godden, François Goutorbe, Alice Grejon, Alexandra Griesmeier, Julie Grieve, Peter Groenenberg, Diane Guldemond, Luis Gutiérrez, Rudolf Hahn, Sonja Hampel, Handra Harbi, Juniadi Hasyim, Stephen Hegedus, JW Heijstek, Joliene Heimgartner, Luuk Heling, Martin Hellwagner, Adam Hill, David Hill, Walter Hirschle, Donna Holmes, Kristin Houghton, Annika Hughes, Ferry Husen, James Huxley, Tommy Iskandar, Dany Jacobs, Sarah Jaffe, Magdalena Janowski, Sophie Jenot, Eva Johnson, Claudia Kaefer, Karsiyah Karsiyah, Lars Kastö, Giovanna Katchan, George Kechagioglou, James Keddie, Stephan Kehry, Virginia Keizer, Kristel Kessels, Mike Kessler, Andy King, Magnus Köhler, Maaike Koopman, Wai Kuan Wong, Belinda Kumaat, Dale Kwamsoos, Caroline Landaz, Erik Laridon, Fredrik Larsen, Tim Laslavic, Etienne Le Jeune, Joe Le Merou, Zach Leigh, Ruud Leijtens, Lydia Lemieux, Steffen Lempp, Wilco

Lindenberg, Patrik Lindenthal, Richard Lloyd Parry, Thomas Long, Michael Luethi, Geugje Luik, Martin Lutterjohann, Danny Maas, Mandy Macjames, Linda Madani Grondin, Anna Maehr, Luc Major, Alessandro Mario Fabbri, Tom Mason, Stefan Matser, Dean Mchenry, Jr, Adam Mcinnis, Els Mellink, Anja Mertens, Elisabeth Mihou, Ian Miller, Sheila Miller, Nam Misuk, Braydon Moloney, Paul Morse, Caroline Mozley, Roberta Muccioli, Andreas Mueller, Tessa Nagels & Folkert Veenkamp, John Nally, Michal Nebus, Maëlle Nexer, Doris Nicholson, Olly Niewold, Sri Ningsih, Pae Nope, Bart Nys, Donal O'halloran, Thomas O'keefe, Awa Okon, René Olde Olthof, Danielle Onesto, Ronald Oosting, Diana Oser, Carl Ottow, Margherita Palomba, Verena Papenfuß & Paul Baade, Daniel Paquet, Lewa Pardomuan, Ronald Perkel, Nancy Peterson, Marland Philippe, Jesse Pietilä, Martin Pils, Rosemarie Pippan, Ellie Pot, Simon Pratt, Phil Prescott, Iestyn Prosser, Adriansyah Putera, John Pyle, Vikki Radford, Teemu Rahkola, Oliver Ramseyer, Asher Rapkin, Peter Ras & Bas Vriesema, Timothy Rea, Ian Reed, Ludwig Reinhard, Kai Riedl, Katrin Riegelnegg, Herwig Ronsmans, Freddie Rousseau, Hasyim Rudiansyah, Max Rudolph, Natalie Ryan, Bernard Sambare, Xandra Savelkouls, Jen Schoenau, Wilgis Schoffelmeijer, George Schoneveld, Chiel Schoorl, Sven Schubbe, Yvonne Schuller, Anne Schulze, Johan Segers, Caroline Seymour, Laura Shapiro Kramer, Hera Shinysmile, Linda Sihombing, Ina Silas, Ken Silver, Ray Sinniger, Michael Sipes, Niels Smidt, Jan Smit, Janice Smith, Maja Sontag, Marijn Souren, Delphine Sprüngli, Jaroslav Stedron, Mike Steuri, Peter Stevens, Hans Steyskal, Matt Stovold, Tunya Struzina, Yanev Suissa, Nienke Sweers, Helge Swendrak, Paul Tanis, Janneke Tax, Brian Thompson, Ellenoor Tinselboer & Tim De Putter, Michel Tintin Deslanes, Lidija Tkalcec, Kay Turner, Keith Turner, Anna Van Beek, Astrid Van Wijk, Brenda Van Lier, Carolien Van Zuilekom, Dana Van De Kamp, Gerald Van Der Wijngaart & Deirdre Veen, Ilona Van Breugel, Jeanette Van Oostrum, Oliver Van Straaten, Sanne Van Oosten, Sarah Van Den Bos, Wouter Van Der Meulen, Johan Van't Geloof, Adrien Venot, Rob Verdaasdonk, Wiebe Vijn, Patricia Villalain, Jeff Vize, Nienke Vos, Tanya Ward, Silvia Wasserbacher, Petr Weikert, Jo Weston, Ted Wetselaar, Remy Wetzels, Angela Whitney, Judith Whittle, Lyndsey Whyte, Endro Wicaksana, Wida Widyawati, Erica Wijarnako, Julia Wijnmaalen, Jeanette Willighagen, Paul Wilson, Lennart Wingelaar, Matt Winters, Rg Winters, Brian Worsley, Gabriella Wortmann, Brogan Wray, Katrien Wuyts, Johan Yasin, Natasha Yeend, Tai Yoo, George Young, Andrea Zanchi, Monica Zehnder, Juergen Zemsauer, Volker Zizelmann, Anne Zouridakis

AUTHOR THANKS

Ryan Ver Berkmoes

This list just seems to grow. Many thanks to friends like Pattycakes Miklautsch, Ibu Cat, Hanafi, Nengah, Eliot Cohen, Jamie James, Kerry and Milton Turner, Pascal and Pika and many more. At Lonely Planet, thanks to my buddy Ilaria Walker and the entire publishing and production teams. My co-authors rock and have produced a fab book. And to Frank Sinatra who night and day picked me a (golden) plum.

Brett Atkinson

Terima kasih to Nando for the road trip and for always making time for good Sumatran coffee. Thanks to Elvis, Scuzz and Ulrich, and across on the Mentawai Islands, special thanks to Harris and the boat crew for ensuring I reached the archipelago's hidden nooks and crannies. Thanks to my fellow scribes and the Lonely Planet inhouse team – especially Ilaria Walker for her support – and finally, thanks to Carol for holding the fort back home in Selandia Baru.

Celeste Brash

I had a small army of travellers and locals who helped me. Particular thanks to Emre Sirakaya, excellent travel buddy. Huge thanks to Nini and Gav (Geordie connection!), Pudin at Pondok Lestari, Elda Tato and family, Domingus, Mathee, Elena, Shiela and Glen Ord, Eva Cmorejova, Simon at NAD, Lorenso, Giorgio and Daniele, @lelakibugis, Edy at Oasis and the many other locals and travellers who I met and helped me on the way. As always, endless gratefulness to my ever-patient family.

Stuart Butler

First and foremost I must thank my wife, Heather, for her patience and understanding on this project and to my young son, Jake, for putting up with his daddy going away for so long. Thank you also to Mario Fernandes for his patience, Dave Pentland and Amy Ilic for company on the road and Mr Darmawan for being a saviour!

John Noble

Thanks to all who helped my Papua mission with guidance, facts and fun, especially Andy Keller, Bakau Tiau, Benny Lesomar, Bony Kondahon, Charles Roring, Dinas Pariwisata Asmat, Felix Berlin, 'Fuji' Fujiwara, Justinus Daby, Lipius Kogoya, Marcel Toung, Merry Yoweni and family, Michael Leitzinger, 'Milou Sly', Mono Melemono, Pino Moch, Reynaldo Corral, Rolando Edmond, Rudie Yarangga, Wendius Melemono, the Yenkoranu gang and Yoris Wanggai.

Adam Skolnick

Thanks to Edwin Lerrick, Simion Liddiard, Marcus Stevens, Andy Wheatcroft, Fern Perry, Will Goodman, Paul Landgraver, Astrid and Grace at Karma Kayak, Alina in Senggigi, Barbara at Lombok Guide, Marij in Labuanbajo, Sandrine and Komang at Swasti, Diego and Maria in Rote, Abba in the Bandas, Michael in Ambon. Philip at Sumba Adventure, and the wonderful Pantai Oro family. Thanks as always to Brett and Made in Bali, Ryan and my co-authors, and to sweet and lovely Georgiana Johnson.

Iain Stewart

Java would be impossible to cover without some incredible contacts and friends. Thanks to Simon 'which page is that on' Pitchfork; the Cianjur boys; Enoss in Bandung; Paul in Batu Karas; Jack in Borobudur; Eno (of course!), Atik, Yuono in Yogya; Fitri in Semarang; Tim in Surabaya; Adi in Madura; Agus and Sebastian in Malang. And to all at Lonely Planet, including Ilaria, Ryan and my co-authors.

Paul Stiles

My thanks to the many people who guided me safely from one end of Kalimantan to the other, and back again: Lucas, Rahim, Ahmad, Kaya and family, Alex, Erwin, Gaye, Aini, Shady. To my co-authors, for all their valuable advice and comments along the way. And to Ilaria, for making the Cross-Borneo Trek possible.

ACKNOWLEDGMENTS

Climate map data adapted from Peel MC, Finlayson BL & McMahon TA (2007) 'Updated World Map of the Köppen-Geiger Climate Classification', Hydrology and Earth System Sciences, 11, 163344.

Cover photograph: Borobudur Temple, Java. Antony Giblin/Lonely Planet Images ©

This Book

The 1st edition of Indonesia, way back in 1986, was the collective work of Alan Samalgaski, Ginny Bruce and Mary Covernton. Cramming this immense, sprawling jewel of an archipelago into one action-packed volume has kept us busy ever since. In subsequent editions we've had 23 different authors travelling the country in search of adventure, enlightenment and ferry timetables. The 9th edition was coordinated by Ryan Ver Berkmoes, who lead a crack team of authors including Celeste Brash, Muhammad Cohen, Mark Elliott, Trent Holden, Guyan Mitra, John Noble, Adam Skolnick, Iain Stewart and Steve Waters. This 10th edition was again coordinated by our Indo Guru, Ryan Ver Berkmoes, and expertly researched and written by Brett Atkinson, Celeste Brash, Stuart Butler, John Noble, Adam Skolnick, Iain Stewart and Paul Stiles. This guidebook was commissioned in Lonely Planet's Melbourne office, and produced by the following:

Commissioning Editor Ilaria Walker
Coordinating Editors Elin Berglund, Luna Soo
Coordinating Cartographer Hunor Csutoros
Coordinating Layout Designer Wibowo Rusli
Managing Editors Sasha Baskett, Bruce Evans
Managing Cartographers Anita Banh, Diana von Holdt
Managing Layout Designers Chris Girdler, Jane Hart
Assisting Editors Andrew Bain, Janice Bird, Jessica Crouch, Kate Daly, Carly Hall, Lauren Hunt, Kellie Langdon
Assisting Cartographers Karusha Ganga, Laura Matthewman, Chris Tsismetzis
Assisting Layout Designer Katherine Marsh
Cover Research Naomi Parker
Internal Image Research Aude Vauconsant
Language Content Branislava Vladisavljevic

Thanks to Imogen Bannister, David Carroll, Laura Crawford, Ryan Evans, Justin Flynn, Larissa Frost, Gabrielle Innes, Jouve India, Andi Jones, Kate McDonell, Catherine Naghten, Trent Paton, Raphael Richards, Jessica Rose, Dianne Schallmeiner, Amanda Sierp, Angela Tinson, Tasmin Waby, Gerard Walker, Juan Winata

index

000 Map pages
000 Photo pages

C

000 Map pages
000 Photo pages

I

J

000 Map pages
000 Photo pages

000 Map pages
000 Photo pages

000 Map pages
000 Photo pages

N

O

000 Map pages
000 Photo pages

000 Map pages
000 Photo pages

Y

how to use this book

These symbols will help you find the listings you want:

- Sights
- Beaches
- Activities
- Courses
- Tours
- Festivals & Events
- Sleeping
- Eating
- Drinking
- Entertainment
- Shopping
- Information/ Transport

These symbols give you the vital information for each listing:

- Telephone Numbers
- Opening Hours
- Parking
- Nonsmoking
- Air-Conditioning
- Internet Access
- Wi-Fi Access
- Swimming Pool
- Vegetarian Selection
- English-Language Menu
- Family-Friendly
- Pet-Friendly
- Bus
- Ferry
- Metro
- Tram
- Train

Reviews are organised by author preference.

Look out for these icons:

- TOP CHOICE — Our author's recommendation
- FREE — No payment required
- A green or sustainable option

Our authors have nominated these places as demonstrating a strong commitment to sustainability – for example by supporting local communities and producers, operating in an environmentally friendly way, or supporting conservation projects.

Map Legend

Sights
Beach
Buddhist
Castle
Christian
Hindu
Islamic
Jewish
Monument
Museum/Gallery
Ruin
Winery/Vineyard
Zoo
Other Sight

Activities, Courses & Tours
Diving/Snorkelling
Canoeing/Kayaking
Skiing
Surfing
Swimming/Pool
Walking
Windsurfing
Other Activity/ Course/Tour

Sleeping
Sleeping
Camping

Eating
Eating

Drinking
Drinking
Cafe

Entertainment
Entertainment

Shopping
Shopping

Information
Bank
Embassy/ Consulate
Hospital/Medical
Internet
Police
Post Office
Telephone
Toilet
Tourist Information
Other Information

Transport
Airport
Border Crossing
Bus
Cable Car/ Funicular
Cycling
Ferry
Monorail
Parking
Petrol Station
Taxi
Train/Railway
Tram
Underground Train Station
Other Transport

Routes
Tollway
Freeway
Primary
Secondary
Tertiary
Lane
Unsealed Road
Plaza/Mall
Steps
Tunnel
Pedestrian Overpass
Walking Tour
Walking Tour Detour
Path

Geographic
Hut/Shelter
Lighthouse
Lookout
Mountain/Volcano
Oasis
Park
Pass
Picnic Area
Waterfall

Population
Capital (National)
Capital (State/Province)
City/Large Town
Town/Village

Boundaries
International
State/Province
Disputed
Regional/Suburb
Marine Park
Cliff
Wall

Hydrography
River, Creek
Intermittent River
Swamp/Mangrove
Reef
Canal
Water
Dry/Salt/ Intermittent Lake
Glacier

Areas
Beach/Desert
Cemetery (Christian)
Cemetery (Other)
Park/Forest
Sportsground
Sight (Building)
Top Sight (Building)

John Noble

Papua John has been entranced by Indonesia – its multifarious cultures, translucent seas, jungle-fringed sands, lumbering dragons, exhibitionist birds of paradise, above all the fact that every single island is a different world – ever since his first visit during the Suharto era. He has devoted recent trips to remote, restive, untamed Papua, a piece that doesn't really fit the jigsaw, which despite (or because of) its contradictions is probably the most exciting region of all.

Read more about John at:
lonelyplanet.com/members/ewoodrover

Adam Skolnick

Maluku, Nusa Tenggara Adam Skolnick writes about travel, culture, health and politics for Lonely Planet, *Outside*, *Men's Health* and *Travel & Leisure*. He has coauthored 18 Lonely Planet guidebooks to destinations in Europe, the US, Central America and Asia. His 11-week research trip to Nusa Tenggara and Maluku included stops on 37 islands. He hired, hopped or hitched 21 planes, 45 cars, five bemo, 12 buses, 25 motorbikes, 32 boats, six horse carts, one bicycle and one becak. You can read more of his work at www.adamskolnick.com or find him on Twitter @adamskolnick.

Iain Stewart

Java Iain's been travelling in Indonesia since 1992, journeying between West Sumatra and East Nusa Tenggara in search of wildlife in national parks and the highlife in Jakarta and Bali. He's covered Indonesia seven times for various Lonely Planet guides. He authors books about Vietnam, Central America and Spain and writes for newspapers including the *Independent*, *Guardian*, *Telegraph* and *Times*. He's a keen scuba diver, free diver, hiker and, when circumstances allow, a weekend warrior (or is that hacker?) on the tennis court of Brighton, UK. Highlights of Iain's trip across Java were hanging out with the Cianjur crew, hiking in Baluran, motorbiking around Batu Karas, munching in Semarang and hooking up with co-author Adam in Gili T.

Paul Stiles

Kalimantan Paul specialises in islands, ecotourism, and adventure travel for Lonely Planet, so Kalimantan was a natural. For this book he completed the entire Cross-Borneo Trek, crossing the Muller Range in five days. His only regret is that he did not have his camera when a rare clouded leopard swam right in front of his boat. Guide: 'I don't know, looks like a wild cat…Oh my god, *macan dahan!*'

Read more about Paul at:
lonelyplanet.com/members/paulwstiles

OUR STORY

A beat-up old car, a few dollars in the pocket and a sense of adventure. In 1972 that's all Tony and Maureen Wheeler needed for the trip of a lifetime – across Europe and Asia overland to Australia. It took several months, and at the end – broke but inspired – they sat at their kitchen table writing and stapling together their first travel guide, *Across Asia on the Cheap*. Within a week they'd sold 1500 copies. Lonely Planet was born.

Today, Lonely Planet has offices in Melbourne, London, Oakland and Delhi, with more than 600 staff and writers. We share Tony's belief that 'a great guidebook should do three things: inform, educate and amuse'.

OUR WRITERS

Ryan Ver Berkmoes

Coordinating Author, Bali Ryan Ver Berkmoes first visited Indonesia in 1993. On his visits since, he has criss-crossed the archipelago, trying to make a dent in those 17,000 islands. Recent thrills included finally reaching the amazing Banda Islands after 18 years of trying and finding the perfect flat on Bali. Off-island, Ryan travels the world writing. Read more at ryanverberkmoes.com and on Twitter @ryanvb.

Brett Atkinson

Sumatra After sampling spicy nasi Padang on previous Indonesian journeys from Bali to Flores, finally experiencing the cuisine in its West Sumatran heartland didn't disappoint. Other Sumatran adventures included exploring the remote Mentawai Islands by speedboat, and chilling out in the beautiful Harau Valley. Brett's based in Auckland, New Zealand, and has covered more than 45 countries as a guidebook author and travel and food writer. See www.brett-atkinson.net for what he's been eating recently, and where he's travelling to next.

Celeste Brash

Sulawesi Celeste first visited Indonesia in 1995 after concentrating in Southeast Asian studies at the University of California. Even with the earthquakes, volcanoes and terrible bus rides, the country seduced her and she's since spent many months exploring, from Sumatra to Bali and up through Sulawesi. She currently lives in Portland, Oregon and has contributed to over 40 Lonely Planet titles. Find out more about her at www.celestebrash.com.

Stuart Butler

Sumatra Stuart Butler first hit the shores of Indonesia many years ago at the end of a long trans-Asia surf trip. Not surprisingly it was the highlight of his trip. Today Stuart lives with his wife and son on the beautiful beaches of southwest France. His travels for Lonely Planet and a variety of international surf magazines have taken him across Indonesia and beyond, from the desert beaches of Yemen to the coastal jungles of the Congo. His website is www.stuartbutlerjournalist.com.

OVER PAGE MORE WRITERS

Published by Lonely Planet Publications Pty Ltd
ABN 36 005 607 983
10th edition – May 2013
ISBN 978 1 74179 845 6

10 9 8 7 6 5 4 3 2 1
Printed in Singapore